Microsoft® Project 98 Bible

Microsoft® Project 98 Bible

Nancy Stevenson and Elaine Marmel

IDG Books Worldwide, Inc.
An International Data Group Company

Foster City, CA ✦ Chicago, IL ✦ Indianapolis, IN ✦ Southlake, TX

Microsoft® Project 98 Bible

Published by
IDG Books Worldwide, Inc.
An International Data Group Company
919 E. Hillsdale Blvd., Suite 400
Foster City, CA 94404

http://www.idgbooks.com (IDG Books World Wide Web site)

Library of Congress Catalog Card No.: 97076683

ISBN: 0-7645-3155-7

Printed in the United States of America

10 9 8 7 6 5 4 3 2

1DD/RX/RR/ZX/FC

Distributed in the United States by IDG Books Worldwide, Inc.

Distributed by Macmillan Canada for Canada; by Transworld Publishers Limited in the United Kingdom; by IDG Norge Books for Norway; by IDG Sweden Books for Sweden; by Woodslane Pty. Ltd. for Australia; by Woodslane Enterprises Ltd. for New Zealand; by Longman Singapore Publishers Ltd. for Singapore, Malaysia, Thailand, and Indonesia; by Simron Pty. Ltd. for South Africa; by Toppan Company Ltd. for Japan; by Distribuidora Cuspide for Argentina; by Livraria Cultura for Brazil; by Ediciencia S.A. for Ecuador; by Addison-Wesley Publishing Company for Korea; by Ediciones ZETA S.C.R. Ltda. for Peru; by WS Computer Publishing Corporation, Inc., for the Philippines; by Unalis Corporation for Taiwan; by Contemporanea de Ediciones for Venezuela; by Computer Book & Magazine Store for Puerto Rico; by Express Computer Distributors for the Caribbean and West Indies. Authorized Sales Agent: Anthony Rudkin Associates for the Middle East and North Africa.

For general information on IDG Books Worldwide's books in the U.S., please call our Consumer Customer Service department at 800-762-2974. For reseller information, including discounts and premium sales, please call our Reseller Customer Service department at 800-434-3422.

For information on where to purchase IDG Books Worldwide's books outside the U.S., please contact our International Sales department at 650-655-3200 or fax 650-655-3295.

For information on foreign language translations, please contact our Foreign & Subsidiary Rights department at 650-655-3021 or fax 650-655-3281.

For sales inquiries and special prices for bulk quantities, please contact our Sales department at 650-655-3200 or write to the address above.

For information on using IDG Books Worldwide's books in the classroom or for ordering examination copies, please contact our Educational Sales department at 800-434-2086 or fax 817-251-8174.

For press review copies, author interviews, or other publicity information, please contact our Public Relations department at 650-655-3000 or fax 650-655-3299.

For authorization to photocopy items for corporate, personal, or educational use, please contact Copyright Clearance Center, 222 Rosewood Drive, Danvers, MA 01923, or fax 978-750-4470.

is a trademark under exclusive
license to IDG Books Worldwide, Inc.,
from International Data Group, Inc.

ABOUT IDG BOOKS WORLDWIDE

Welcome to the world of IDG Books Worldwide.

IDG Books Worldwide, Inc., is a subsidiary of International Data Group, the world's largest publisher of computer-related information and the leading global provider of information services on information technology. IDG was founded more than 25 years ago and now employs more than 8,500 people worldwide. IDG publishes more than 275 computer publications in over 75 countries (see listing below). More than 60 million people read one or more IDG publications each month.

Launched in 1990, IDG Books Worldwide is today the #1 publisher of best-selling computer books in the United States. We are proud to have received eight awards from the Computer Press Association in recognition of editorial excellence and three from *Computer Currents'* First Annual Readers' Choice Awards. Our best-selling *...For Dummies®* series has more than 30 million copies in print with translations in 30 languages. IDG Books Worldwide, through a joint venture with IDG's Hi-Tech Beijing, became the first U.S. publisher to publish a computer book in the People's Republic of China. In record time, IDG Books Worldwide has become the first choice for millions of readers around the world who want to learn how to better manage their businesses.

Our mission is simple: Every one of our books is designed to bring extra value and skill-building instructions to the reader. Our books are written by experts who understand and care about our readers. The knowledge base of our editorial staff comes from years of experience in publishing, education, and journalism — experience we use to produce books for the '90s. In short, we care about books, so we attract the best people. We devote special attention to details such as audience, interior design, use of icons, and illustrations. And because we use an efficient process of authoring, editing, and desktop publishing our books electronically, we can spend more time ensuring superior content and spend less time on the technicalities of making books.

You can count on our commitment to deliver high-quality books at competitive prices on topics you want to read about. At IDG Books Worldwide, we continue in the IDG tradition of delivering quality for more than 25 years. You'll find no better book on a subject than one from IDG Books Worldwide.

John Kilcullen
CEO
IDG Books Worldwide, Inc.

Steven Berkowitz
President and Publisher
IDG Books Worldwide, Inc.

Eighth Annual Computer Press Awards ≥1992

Ninth Annual Computer Press Awards ≥1993

Tenth Annual Computer Press Awards ≥1994

Eleventh Annual Computer Press Awards ≥1995

IDG Books Worldwide, Inc., is a subsidiary of International Data Group, the world's largest publisher of computer-related information and the leading global provider of information services on information technology. International Data Group publishes over 275 computer publications in over 75 countries. Sixty million people read one or more International Data Group publications each month. International Data Group's publications include: **ARGENTINA:** Buyer's Guide, Computerworld Argentina, PC World Argentina; **AUSTRALIA:** Australian Macworld, Australian PC World, Australian Reseller News, Computerworld, IT Casebook, Network World, Publish, Webmaster; **AUSTRIA:** Computerwelt Osterreich, Networks Austria, PC Tip Austria; **BANGLADESH:** PC World Bangladesh; **BELARUS:** PC World Belarus; **BELGIUM:** Data News; **BRAZIL:** Annuário de Informática, Computerworld, Connections, Macworld, PC Player, PC World, Publish, Reseller News, Supergamepower; **BULGARIA:** Computerworld Bulgaria, Network World Bulgaria, PC & MacWorld Bulgaria; **CANADA:** CIO Canada, Client/Server World, ComputerWorld Canada, InfoWorld Canada, NetworkWorld Canada, WebWorld; **CHILE:** Computerworld Chile, PC World Chile; **COLOMBIA:** Computerworld Colombia, PC World Colombia; **COSTA RICA:** PC World Centro America; **THE CZECH AND SLOVAK REPUBLICS:** Computerworld Czechoslovakia, Macworld Czech Republic, PC World Czechoslovakia; **DENMARK:** Communications World Danmark, Computerworld Danmark, Macworld Danmark, PC World Danmark, Techworld Denmark; **DOMINICAN REPUBLIC:** PC World Republica Dominicana; **ECUADOR:** PC World Ecuador; **EGYPT:** PC World Middle East, PC World Middle East; **EL SALVADOR:** PC World Centro America; **FINLAND:** MikroPC, Tietoverkko, Tietoviikko; **FRANCE:** Distributique, Hebdo, Info PC, Le Monde Informatique, Macworld, Reseaux & Telecoms, WebMaster France; **GERMANY:** Computer Partner, Computerwoche, Computerwoche Extra, Computerwoche FOCUS, Global Online, Macwelt, PC Welt; **GREECE:** Amiga Computing, GamePro Greece, Multimedia World; **GUATEMALA:** PC World Centro America; **HONDURAS:** PC World Centro America; **HONG KONG:** Computerworld Hong Kong, PC World Hong Kong, Publish in Asia; **HUNGARY:** ABCD CD-ROM, Computerworld Szamitastechnika, Internetto online Magazine, PC World Hungary, PC-X Magazin Hungary; **ICELAND:** Tolvuheimur PC World Island; **INDIA:** Information Communications World, Information Systems Computerworld, PC World India, Publish in Asia; **INDONESIA:** InfoKomputer PC World, Komputek Computerworld, Publish in Asia; **IRELAND:** ComputerScope, PC Live!; **ISRAEL:** Macworld Israel, People & Computers/Computerworld; **ITALY:** Computerworld Italia, Macworld Italia, Networking Italia, PC World Italia; **JAPAN:** DTP World, Macworld Japan, Nikkei Personal Computing, OS/2 World Japan, SunWorld Japan, Windows NT World, Windows World Japan; **KENYA:** PC World East African; **KOREA:** Hi-Tech Information, Macworld Korea, PC World Korea; **MACEDONIA:** PC World Macedonia; **MALAYSIA:** Computerworld Malaysia, PC World Malaysia, Publish in Asia; **MALTA:** PC World Malta; **MEXICO:** Computerworld Mexico, PC World Mexico; **MYANMAR:** PC World Myanmar; **NETHERLANDS:** Computer! Totaal, LAN Internetworking Magazine, LAN World Buyers Guide, Macworld Netherlands, Net, WebWereld; **NEW ZEALAND:** Absolute Beginners Guide and Plain & Simple Series, Computer Buyer, Computer Industry Directory, Computerworld New Zealand, MTB, Network World, PC World New Zealand; **NICARAGUA:** PC World Centro America; **NORWAY:** Computerworld Norge, CW Rapport, Datamagasinet, Financial Rapport, Kursguide Norge, Macworld Norge, Multimediaworld Norge, PC World Ekspress Norge, PC World Nettverk, PC World Norge, PC World ProduktGuide Norge; **PAKISTAN:** Computerworld Pakistan; **PANAMA:** PC World Panama; **PEOPLE'S REPUBLIC OF CHINA:** China Computer Users, China Computerworld, China InfoWorld, China Telecom World Weekly, Computer & Communication, Electronic Design China, Electronics Today, Electronics Weekly, Game Software, PC World China, Popular Computer Week, Software Weekly, Software World, Telecom World; **PERU:** Computerworld Peru, PC World Profesional Peru, PC World SoHo Peru; **PHILIPPINES:** Click!, Computerworld Philippines, PC World Philippines, Publish in Asia; **POLAND:** Computerworld Poland, Computerworld Special Report Poland, Cyber, Macworld Poland, Networld Poland, PC World Komputer; **PORTUGAL:** Cerebro/PC World, Computerworld/Correio Informático, Dealer World Portugal, Mac*In/PC*In Portugal, Multimedia World; **PUERTO RICO:** PC World Puerto Rico; **ROMANIA:** Computerworld Romania, PC World Romania, Telecom Romania; **RUSSIA:** Computerworld Russia, Mir PK, Publish, Seti; **SINGAPORE:** Computerworld Singapore, PC World Singapore, Publish in Asia; **SLOVENIA:** Monitor; **SOUTH AFRICA:** Computing SA, Network World SA, Software World SA; **SPAIN:** Communicaciones World España, Computerworld España, Dealer World España, Macworld España, PC World España; **SRI LANKA:** Infolink PC World; **SWEDEN:** CAP&Design, Computer Sweden, Corporate Computing Sweden, Internetworld Sweden, it.branschen, Macworld Sweden, MaxiData Sweden, MikroDatorn, Nätverk & Kommunikation, PC World Sweden, PCaktiv, Windows World Sweden; **SWITZERLAND:** Computerworld Schweiz, Macworld Schweiz, PCtip; **TAIWAN:** Computerworld Taiwan, Macworld Taiwan, NEW ViSiON/Publish, PC World Taiwan, Windows World Taiwan; **THAILAND:** Publish in Asia, Thai Computerworld; **TURKEY:** Computerworld Turkiye, Macworld Turkiye, Network World Turkiye, PC World Turkiye; **UKRAINE:** Computerworld Kiev, Multimedia World Ukraine, PC World Ukraine; **UNITED KINGDOM:** Acorn User UK, Amiga Action UK, Amiga Computing UK, Apple Talk UK, Computing, Macworld, Parents and Computers UK, PC Advisor, PC Home, PSX Pro, The WEB; **UNITED STATES:** Cable in the Classroom, CIO Magazine, Computerworld, DOS World, Federal Computer Week, GamePro Magazine, InfoWorld, I-Way, Macworld, Network World, PC Games, PC World, Publish, Video Event, THE WEB Magazine, and WebMaster; online webzines: JavaWorld, NetscapeWorld, and SunWorld Online; **URUGUAY:** InfoWorld Uruguay; **VENEZUELA:** Computerworld Venezuela, PC World Venezuela; and **VIETNAM:** PC World Vietnam.   3/24/97

Credits

Acquisitions Editor
Andy Cummings

Development Editors
June Waldman
Susan Pines

Technical Editor
Vickey Quinn

Copy Editors
June Waldman
Anne Friedman

Project Coordinator
Katy German

Graphics & Production Specialists
Vincent F. Burns
Ritchie Durdin
Jude Levinson
Mark Schumann
Deirdre Smith
Ian Smith
Trevor Wilson

Quality Control Specialist
Mick Arellano
Mark Schumann

Proofreader
Arielle Mennelle

Indexer
Elizabeth Cunningham

About the Authors

Nancy Stevenson taught project management seminars to companies in many industries for several years while employed at Symantec Software in Calfornia. In addition, she has managed projects of all sizes in the publishing, video, and graphic design fields. As a freelance author and consultant for the last several years, Nancy has written more than a dozen books on computer topics, as well as consulting with various publishers on new series development and acquisitions. In addition, she has been an instructor in technical writing at the university level.

Elaine Marmel is president of Marmel Enterprises, Inc., an organization that specializes in technical writing and software training. She has employed project management software and skills to manage critical business projects. Elaine spends most of her time writing and has authored or coauthored more than 20 books about software, including Word for Windows, Word for the Mac, Quicken for Windows, Quicken for DOS, 1-2-3 for Windows, Lotus Notes, and Excel. Elaine is a contributing editor to *Inside Peachtree for Windows,* a monthly magazine about the Peachtree for Windows accounting package.

Elaine left her native Chicago for the warmer climes of Florida (by way of Cincinnati, Ohio; Jerusalem, Israel; Ithaca, New York; and Washington, D.C.) where she basks in the sun with her PC and her cats, Cato and Watson. Elaine also sings in the Toast of Tampa, an International Champion Sweet Adeline barbershop chorus.

To Graham for putting up with the late night writing sessions and solitary breakfasts. Hey, honey, it's a book!

— Nancy Stevenson

To my mom with love for all her understanding.

— Elaine Marmel

Preface

Managing projects can be as exciting as scheduling the next space shuttle or as mundane as planning routine production line maintenance. A project can be as rewarding as striking oil or as disastrous as the maiden voyage of the Titanic. Projects can have budgets of $5 or $5 million. But one thing all projects have in common is their potential for success or failure, the promise that if you do it right, you'll accomplish your goal.

Microsoft Project is a tool for implementing project management principles and practices that can help you succeed. That's why this book provides not only the information about which buttons to press and where to type project dates but also the conceptual framework to make computerized project management work for you.

This book strives to offer real-world examples of projects from many industries and disciplines. You'll see yourself and your own projects somewhere in this book. A wealth of tips and advice show you how to address, control, and overcome real-world constraints.

You can use *Microsoft Project 98 Bible* as a linear tool to learn Project. Or you can put it on the shelf and use it as your Project reference book, to be pulled down as needed for advice, information, and step-by-step procedures. Either way, this book will enrich your Microsoft Project experience and make you a better project manager.

Who Is This Book For?

Unlike word processing or spreadsheet software, many of you may have come to project management software never having used anything quite like it before. If that's the case, this book is for you. The early chapters explain the basic concepts of computerized project management and what it can do for you so that you have a context for learning Project.

If you have used earlier versions of Project or other project management software, this book is also for you. It explains what's new in the latest version of Project and shows you techniques for using the software that you many not have considered before.

You will benefit most from this book if you have at least a basic understanding of the Windows 95 environment, have mastered standard Windows software conventions, and are comfortable using a mouse. But beyond that, you need only the desire to succeed as a project manager, which this book will help you do.

Conventions Used in This Book

To help you use this book most efficiently, we have used the following formatting conventions:

✦ Text you are to type into a Project schedule appears in **boldface**.

✦ When using the mouse, *click* indicates a left mouse-button click and *right-click* indicates a right mouse-button click. *Double-click* designates two quick, successive clicks of the left mouse button.

✦ Keystroke combinations look like this: Alt+tab. Hold down the first key and, without letting it go, press the second key.

✦ Menu commands are shown with the command arrow; for example, Choose File⇨Open.

✦ New terms appear in *italic.*

Special Elements

Throughout the book we've included special icons to call your attention to certain types of information, such as added advice or warnings about potentially disastrous courses of action. Here's a rundown of these elements:

The Note icon signals additional information about a point under discussion or background information that might be of interest to you.

A tip is a bit of advice or a hint to save you time and indicate the best way to get things done.

Cautions are warnings about procedures or steps that could cause problems, such as a loss of data or an irrevocable change to your file.

This icon highlights a new feature in Project 98.

The CD-ROM icon flags helpful software and templates that you'll find on the accompanying CD-ROM.

Sidebars

Sidebars are brief departures into background details or interesting information. Sidebar information provides additional context and depth to your understanding of Project's functions.

How the Book Is Organized

This book is organized in the way that you will use Microsoft Project. It begins with some basic concepts and progresses through the features you need to build a typical schedule and then track its progress. The later chapters provide more advanced information for customizing Project, using it in workgroup settings, and taking Project online.

Part I: Project Management Basics

Part I of the book explains the basic project management concepts and terminology that you'll need in order to learn Project. In Chapter 1 you take a look at the nature of projects themselves, how Microsoft Project can help you control them, and the life cycle of a typical project. In Chapter 2 you get your first glimpse of the Project software environment.

Part II: Getting Your Project Going

In this section you learn about the type of information Project needs to do its job. Part II is where you begin to build your first schedule, adding tasks in an outline structure in Chapter 3. In Chapter 4 you assign timing and construct timing relationships among those tasks. Chapter 5 is where you begin assigning people and other resources to your project; this chapter is also where you learn to determine how these resources add costs to a project and how to handle issues such as overtime and shift work.

Part III: Refining Your Project

Before your project is ready for prime time, you need to tweak things, just as you check spelling in a word processed document. Chapter 6 explains how to view that information to gain perspective on your project. Chapter 7 shows you how to make your project schedule look more professional by formatting the text and modifying the appearance of chart elements. The next two chapters delve into the tools Project provides to resolve conflicts in your schedule. Chapter 8 explores resolving conflicts in the timing of your schedule so you can meet your deadlines. Chapter 9 considers the issue of resolving resource conflicts, such as overworked people and underutilized equipment.

Part IV: Tracking Your Progress

Here's where you get the payoff for all your data entry and patient resolution of problems in your schedule. After you set your basic schedule and the project begins, you can track its progress and check data on your status from various perspectives. Chapter 10 gives you an overview of the tracking process. Chapter 11 shows you how to track progress on your individual tasks and view that progress in various ways. Chapter 12 is where you explore the power of generating reports on your projects for everyone from management to individual project team members. Finally, Chapter 13 gives advice and methods for analyzing your progress and making adjustments as needed to stay on schedule and within your budget.

Part V: Working in Groups

Most projects worth the effort of tracking in Project aren't done by a single person: workgroups, teams, and committees often form a day-to-day working project team. Chapter 14 shows you how to keep members of your workgroup in touch and how to keep your project files secure. Learn how to coordinate multiple projects to run concurrently or to consolidate smaller projects into larger schedules in Chapter 15.

Part VI: Advanced Microsoft Project

Part VI provides advice and information to make your use of Microsoft Project easier. Learn about customizing the Project environment in Chapter 16. Chapter 17 provides information on macros, simple programs that enable you to record and automatically play back series of steps that you use frequently , saving you time and effort. Chapter 18 deals with importing information from other software into Project; this procedure eliminates having to reenter existing information. Chapter 19 explores Microsoft Project and its role on the World Wide Web.

Project Management Glossary

The glossary at the end of the book contains many project management–specific terms and concepts that have evolved over time. These terms are defined when they are first used in the book, but you may want to look them up at a later date. Use this handy alphabetical listing to do so.

Appendixes

The Appendixes provide helpful additional material to make your work easier. Appendix C covers the contents and installation for the companion CD-ROM that contains trial software and time-saving templates.

Acknowledgments

Thanks to all my friends at IDG Books for giving me the chance to work with them on this book. Thanks especially to Ellen Camm and Andy Cummings for shepherding me through the ins and outs of acquiring this book and to Sue Pines and June Waldman for editing it so it all makes sense. And my gratitude as well to the technical editor, production staff, and manufacturing people who make it all come together.

Thanks also go to my coauthor, Elaine Marmel, for stepping in to add her expert touch to the book. It's always a pleasure, Elaine!

— Nancy Stevenson

I'd like to thank Nancy Stevenson and the folks at IDG for the opportunity to work on this book. I'd also like to thank my mom, Sue Marmel, and my friend Sue Plumley for their encouragement and support — you two have no idea how much it means to know you're there. A special thanks to Arielle Mennelle for doing her job above and beyond the call.

— Elaine Marmel

Contents at a Glance

Contents

● ●

Chapter 18: Importing and Exporting Project Information 425

Chapter 19: Project on the Web 453

Project Management Basics

The Nature of Projects

Everybody does projects. Building a tree house is a project; so is putting a man on the moon. From the simplest home improvement to the most complex business or scientific venture, projects are a part of most of our lives. But exactly what is a project, and what can you really do to manage all of its facets?

Some projects are defined by their randomness. Missed deadlines, unpleasant surprises, and unexpected problems seem to be as unavoidable as the weekly staff meeting. Other projects have few problems. Nevertheless, the project that goes smoothly from beginning to end is rare. Good planning and communication can go a long way toward avoiding disaster. And although no amount of planning will prevent all possible problems, good project management allows you to deal with those inevitable twists and turns in the most efficient manner possible.

In this chapter you begin exploring tools and acquiring skills that can help you become a more efficient and productive project manager using Microsoft Project 98. The goal here is to provide a survey of what a project is, what project management is, and how Microsoft Project fits in the picture.

Understanding Projects

When you look up the word *project* in the dictionary, you see definitions like "plan" and "concerted effort." A project in the truest sense, then, isn't a simple one-person effort to perform a task. By this definition, getting yourself dressed, difficult though that task may seem on a Monday morning, isn't a project.

A *project* is a series of steps, often performed by more than one person. In addition:

✦ A project has a specific and measurable goal. You know you have finished the project when you have successfully met your project goal.

✦ Projects have a specific time frame. One measurement of the success of a project is often how it relates to the amount of time allotted to it.

✦ Projects use resources. Resources aren't just people; resources can include money, machinery, materials, and more. How well these resources are allocated and orchestrated is another key measure of a project's success or failure.

✦ All projects consist of interdependent, yet individual, steps called *tasks*. No piece of a project exists in a vacuum. If one task runs late or over budget, it typically affects other tasks, the overall schedule, and the total cost.

Another key attribute of projects is that they are dynamic. Projects can last for months or even years. In addition, projects tend to grow, change, and behave in ways that you can't always anticipate. Consequently, you, as a project manager, have to remain alert to the progress and vagaries of your projects, or you will never reach your goals. Documentation and communication are your two key tools for staying on top of a project throughout its life.

Exploring project management

Project management is a discipline that looks at the nature of projects and offers ways to control their progress. Project management attempts to organize and systematize the procedures in a project to minimize the number of surprises you encounter.

Project management and project managers concern themselves with certain key areas:

✦ Scheduling

✦ Budgeting

✦ Managing resources

✦ Tracking and reporting progress

To manage these aspects of projects, certain tools have evolved over the years. Some of these are conceptual, like the critical path; others involve specific formats for charting progress, like a Gantt chart. The following sections introduce some key project management concepts and tools.

Critical path and slack

Critical path is the series of tasks in a project that must be completed on time for the overall project to stay on time. The following example illustrates this concept.

Suppose you are planning a going away party at your office. You have three days to plan the party. Here are some of the tasks involved and their time frames:

Task	Duration
Signing the good-bye card	three days
Ordering food	one day
Reserving a room	one hour
Buying a good-bye gift	one day

The longest task involves getting everyone to sign a greeting card. The shortest task, reserving a room, takes only one hour. Assuming that plenty of rooms are available for holding the party, you could delay reserving the room until the last hour of the third day. Delaying this task won't actually cause any delay in holding the party, as long as you accomplish this task by the end of the longest task, getting the good-bye card signed. Therefore, the task of reserving a room isn't on the critical path. However, you can't delay the task of signing the good-bye card, which is projected to take three days to accomplish, without delaying the party. Therefore, the card-signing task is on the critical path. (Of course, this example is very simple; typically, a whole series of tasks that can't afford delay form an entire critical path.)

Slack is the amount of time available to delay a task before that task moves onto the critical path. Another name for slack is *float*. In the preceding example the one-hour-long task, reserving a room, has slack. This task can slip a few hours, even a couple of days, and the party could still happen on time. However, if you wait until the last half hour of the third day to reserve a room, that task would have used up its slack; it would then move onto the critical path.

The critical path in a project changes as the project progresses. Knowing where your critical path tasks are at any point during the project is crucial to staying on track. A critical path is a way of prioritizing tasks that have no leeway in their timing to make sure they don't run late and affect your overall schedule. Figures 1-1 and 1-2 show the same schedule — first with all tasks displayed and then filtered to show only those tasks on the critical path.

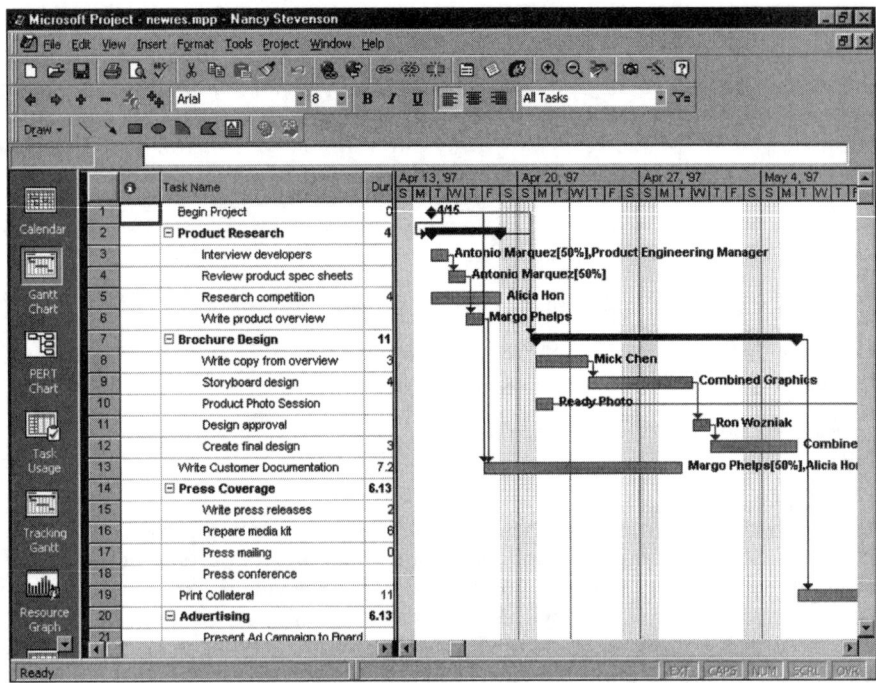

Figure 1-1: Tasks with slack display alongside those on the critical path.

Durations and milestones

Most tasks in a project take a certain amount of time to accomplish. Tasks can take five minutes or five months. The length of time needed to complete a task is called the task's *duration*. You should always try to break long tasks in a project into smaller tasks of shorter duration so that you can track their progress frequently; for example, break a five-month-long task into five, month-long tasks. Checking off the completion of the smaller tasks each month reduces the odds of a serious surprise five months down the road.

Some tasks, called *milestones*, have no (zero) duration. Milestones are merely points in time that mark the start or completion of some phase of a project. For example, if your project involves designing a new brochure, the approval of the initial design might be a milestone. Although you can assign a duration to the process of routing the design to various people for review, assigning a length of time to the actual moment when you have everyone's final approval is probably impossible. Therefore, this task has a duration of zero — that is, approval of the design is a milestone that simply marks a key moment in the project.

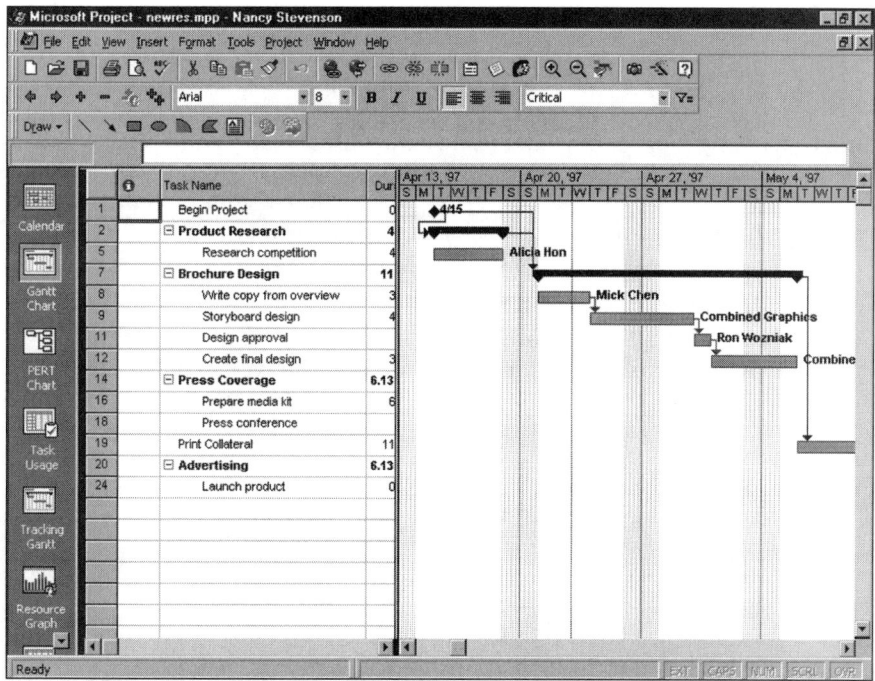

Figure 1-2: With the appropriate filter applied, only tasks that can't afford any delay appear in your schedule.

Resource-driven schedules and fixed-duration tasks

Some tasks take the same amount of time no matter how many people or other resources you throw at them. Flying from San Francisco to New York is likely to take five hours no matter how many pilots or flight attendants you add. You can't speed up a test on a mixture of two solvents that must sit for six hours to react by adding more solvent or hiring more scientists to work in the laboratory. These tasks have a *fixed duration;* they are also called *fixed tasks,* and their timing is set by the nature of the task.

On the other hand, the number of available resources does affect the duration of some tasks. If one person needs two hours to dig a ditch, adding a second person usually cuts the time in half; two people can dig the same ditch in one hour. The project still requires two hours of effort, but two resources can perform the task simultaneously. Tasks whose durations are affected by the addition or subtraction of resources are *resource-driven tasks.*

In real-world projects the calculation is seldom so exact. Because people have different skill levels and perform work at different speeds, two people don't always cut the time of a task exactly in half. In addition, the more people you add to a task, the more you must consider issues of communication, cooperation, and training. Although Microsoft Project handles additional assignments of resources as a strictly mathematical calculation, you can still use your judgment of the resources involved to modify this calculation somewhat (see Chapter 9).

Gantt charts and PERT charts

Gantt charts and PERT charts are two tools of project management that have evolved over many years. They are simply charts that you can use to track different aspects of your project. Figure 1-3 shows a Microsoft Project Gantt chart, and Figure 1-4 shows a PERT chart.

Before people used computers to manage their projects, managers drew these charts by hand. Any self-respecting project war room had a 10-foot PERT or Gantt chart tacked to the wall. By the end of the project, this chart was as marked up and out of date as last year's appointment calendar. Thankfully, project management software makes these charts easier to generate, update, and customize.

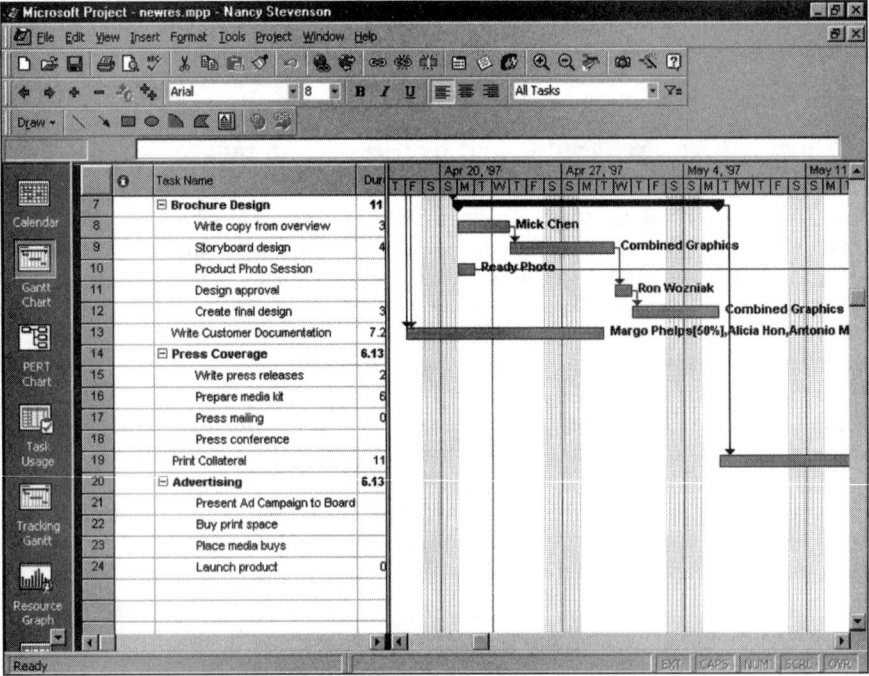

Figure 1-3: The Gantt chart bars represent timing of tasks in a project.

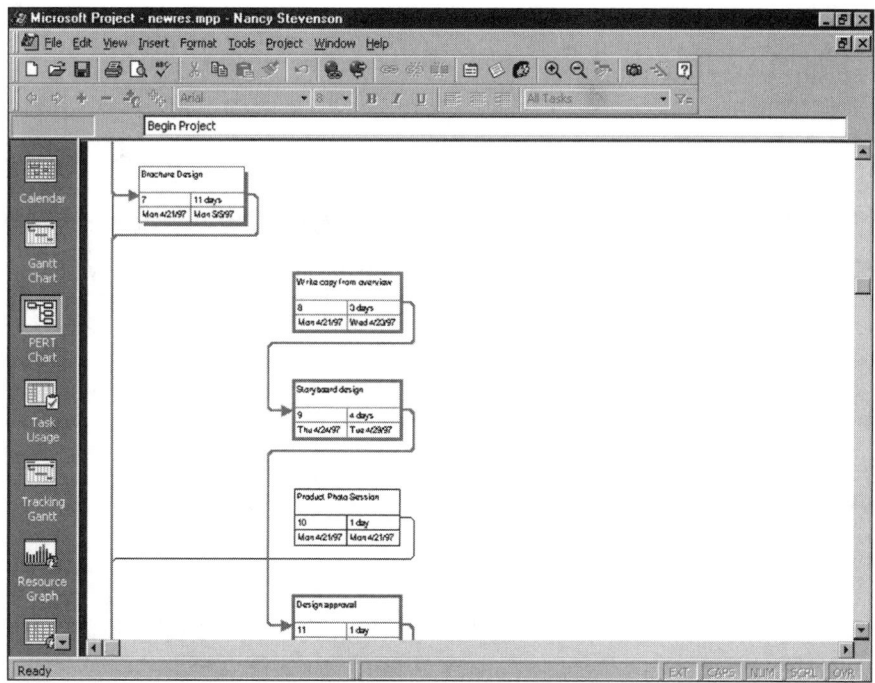

Figure 1-4: The PERT chart resembles a flowchart for work in a project.

A Gantt chart represents the tasks in a project with bars that reflect the duration of individual tasks. Milestones are shown as diamond-shaped objects. You learn more about the various elements of the Gantt chart in Chapter 2. For now, the important point is that Gantt charts enable you to visualize and track the timing of a project.

PERT charts, on the other hand, don't accurately detail the timing of a project. Instead, a PERT chart shows the flow of tasks in a project and the relationships of tasks to each other. Each task is contained in a box called a *node*, and lines that flow among the nodes indicate the flow of tasks.

Note

PERT stands for Program Evaluation and Review Technique. The Special Projects Office of the U.S. Navy devised this method for tracking the flow of tasks in a project when it was designing the Polaris submarine in the late 1950s.

Dependencies

One final project management concept you should understand is *dependencies*. The overall timing of a project isn't simply the sum of the durations of all tasks, because all tasks in a project don't usually happen simultaneously. For example, in a construction project, you have to pour the foundation of a building before you can build the structure. You also have to enclose the building with walls and windows before you lay carpeting. In other words, project managers anticipate and establish relationships among the tasks in a project. These relationships are called dependencies. Only when you have created tasks, assigned durations to them, and established dependencies, can you see the overall timing of your project. (Chapter 4 covers several kinds of dependencies.)

Managing projects with project management software

Many people manage projects with stacks of outdated to-do lists and colorful hand-drawn wall charts. They scribble notes on calendars in pencil, knowing that, more often than not, dates and tasks change over time. They hold meetings, meetings, and more meetings to keep everyone in the project informed. People have developed these simple organizational tools because projects typically have so many bits and pieces that no one can remember them all.

Some set of procedures is necessary to manage any project. Project management software automates many of these procedures. With project management software you can

✦ Plan the various elements of a project up front. Consequently, you can more accurately estimate the time and resources required to complete the project.

✦ View progress on an ongoing basis from various perspectives so you can see whether you are likely to meet your goal.

✦ Recognize conflicts of time and resources early and try out various what-if scenarios to resolve those conflicts.

✦ Make adjustments to task timing and costs and automatically update all other tasks in the project to reflect the impact of your changes.

✦ Generate professional looking reports on the status of your project to help team members prioritize and help management make informed decisions.

With improved workgroup, intranet and e-mail capabilities, Microsoft Project also makes communication and cooperation among workgroup members much easier and more productive.

What's required of you

Many people contemplate using project management software with about as much relish as they do a visit to the dentist. They anticipate hours of data entry time before they can get anything out of the software. To some extent, that vision is true. You have to provide a certain amount of information about your project for any software to estimate schedules and generate reports, just as you have to enter numbers for a spreadsheet to calculate a budget or a loan pay-back schedule.

On the other hand, after you enter your basic project information into Microsoft Project, the ongoing upkeep of that data is far easier than generating handwritten to-do lists that become obsolete in a day. In addition, the accuracy and professionalism of reports that you generate with Project can make the difference between a poorly managed project and a successful one. And, like a quarterly budget you create with spreadsheet software, after you enter the data, Project performs its calculations automatically.

So, exactly what do you have to do to manage your project with Microsoft Project? To create a schedule in Microsoft Project, you must enter the following information about your tasks:

✦ Individual task names

✦ Task durations

✦ Task dependencies

To allocate and track costs on those tasks, you add certain information about resources, including

✦ Resources and their costs for both standard and overtime hours

✦ Resource assignments to specific tasks

To track a project over its lifetime, you need to enter this information:

✦ Progress on tasks

✦ Changes in task timing or dependencies

✦ Changes in resources, that is, resources that are added to or removed from the project

✦ Changes in resource time commitments and costs

What Microsoft Project can do to help

Even though you still must enter a great deal of information into your project schedule, Microsoft Project has various shortcuts that can help you automate this chore.

✦ If you often do similar types of projects, you can create project templates with typical project tasks already in place; you can then modify the templates for individual projects.

✦ If you have tasks that repeat throughout the life of a project, such as weekly meetings or regular reviews, you can create a single repeating task and Project will duplicate it for you.

✦ You can use workgroup features that allow individual team members to enter and track progress on smaller pieces of the project. By tracking in this way, no one person has an overwhelming amount of data entry to do. Also, team members feel more accountable and involved in the project. Chapter 14 covers workgroup features in detail.

✦ You can take advantage of Microsoft's Visual Basic language to build macros that automate repetitive tasks, such as generating weekly reports. See Chapter 17 for more on macros.

On the CD-ROM Finally, you can take advantage of sample project templates on this book's companion CD-ROM. These templates represent a cross section of typical industries and project types.

The Life Cycle of a Project

Projects typically consist of several phases. Understanding the nature of each phase can help you to relate the features of Microsoft Project to your own projects.

Identifying your goal and the project's scope

Before you can even begin to plan a project, you have to identify the *goal*, which isn't always as obvious as it sounds. Various participants may define a project's goal differently. In fact, many projects fail because the team members are really working toward different goals without realizing it. For example, is the goal to perform a productivity study, or to actually improve productivity? Is the outcome for your project to agree on the final building design, or is it to complete the actual construction of the building? As you analyze your goal and factor in the perspectives of other team members, make sure that your project isn't actually just one step in a series of projects to reach a larger, longer-term goal.

To identify your goal, you can use various communication tools, such as meetings, e-mail, and conference calls. The important thing is to conduct a dialog at various levels (management through front-line personnel) that gets ideas on the table and answers questions. Take the time to write a goal statement and circulate it among the team members to make sure that everyone understands the common focus of the project.

Note Be careful not to set a long-range goal that is likely to change before the project ends. Smaller projects or projects broken into various phases are more manageable and more flexible.

After you understand your goal, you should also gather the information you need to define the project's scope. This endeavor may take some research on your part. The *scope* of a project is a statement of more specific parameters or constraints for its completion. Project constraints usually fall within the areas of time, quality, and cost, and they often relate directly to project deliverables.

Here are some sample goal and scope statements:

Project A

Goal: to locate a facility for our warehouse.

Scope: by October 15, to find a modern warehouse facility of approximately 5,200 square feet, with a lease cost of no more than $3,000 a month in a location convenient to our main office.

Project B

Our goal is to launch a new cleaning product.

The scope of this project includes test marketing the product, designing packaging, and creating and launching an advertising campaign. The launch must be completed before the end of the third quarter of 1998 and must cost no more than $750,000.

Notice that the second scope statement designates major phases of the project (test marketing, designing packaging and an ad campaign); the statement provides a starting point for planning the individual tasks. In fact, you might eventually decide to break this project into smaller projects of test marketing, designing packaging, and launching an advertising campaign. Writing out the scope of the project may encourage you to redefine both the goal and scope to make the project more manageable.

Tip

Keep your goal and scope statements short and to the point. If you can't explain your goal or scope in a sentence or two, then your project may be too ambitious and complex — consider breaking it into smaller projects.

Writing a simple goal and scope statement ensures that you've gathered key data, such as deliverables, timing, and budget, and that you and your team agree on the focus of everyone's efforts. These activities are likely to occur before you ever open a Microsoft Project file.

Planning

When you understand the goal and scope of a project, you can begin to work backwards to determine the steps you need to take to reach the goal. Look for major phases first. Then break each phase into a logical sequence of steps.

One aspect of planning is to plan for resources. *Resources* can include equipment of limited availability, materials, individual workers, and groups of workers. Take into account various schedules and issues such as overtime, vacations, and shared resources between projects. Time, money and resources are closely related — you can save time with more resources, but resources typically cost money. You need to understand the order of priority among time, quality, and money.

Note

There's truth to the old joke: Time, budget, or quality — pick two. Throwing resources (which usually become costs) at a schedule can shorten the time but can also cause loss of quality control. Stretching out the time can improve quality but usually causes resource conflicts and added costs. Microsoft Project helps you see the trade-offs among these three important criteria throughout the life of your project.

Planning is the point at which you begin to enter data in Microsoft Project and see your project take shape. Figure 1-5 shows an initial Microsoft Project schedule.

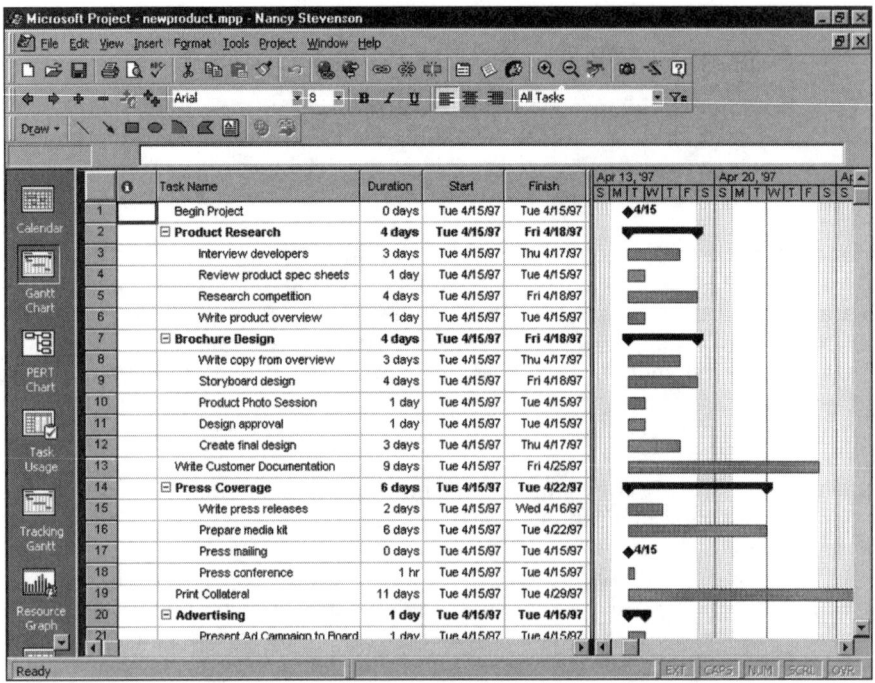

Figure 1-5: The outline format of a Project schedule clearly shows the various phases of your project. Notice that dependencies among tasks have not yet been established.

Revising

Most of the time, you send an initial project schedule to various managers or coworkers for approval or input so that you can refine it based on different factors. You can use the reporting features of Microsoft Project to generate several drafts of your plan.

Be prepared to revise your plan after everyone has a chance to review it. You might want to create and save multiple Project files to generate what-if scenarios based on the input you receive. Being able to see your plans from various perspectives is a great way to take advantage of Project's power.

Another aspect of planning and revising is finding resolutions to conflicts in timing and resource allocation. Project helps you pinpoint these conflicts; for example:

✦ A team member or resource booked on several projects at once

✦ A task beginning before another task that must precede it

✦ Unusually high use of expensive equipment in one phase that is throwing your budget out of whack

Tip

This book contains many tricks and techniques for resolving these types of conflicts. Chapters 8 and 9 especially focus on using Microsoft Project features to resolve scheduling and resource problems.

When your project plan seems solid, you can take a picture of it, called a *baseline*, against which you can track actual progress. Chapter 10 explains how to set a baseline.

Tracking

You should try to determine your tracking methods before your project ever begins:

✦ Do you want to track your progress once a week or once a month?

✦ Do project participants actually track their own work or merely report their progress to you?

✦ Do you want to roll those smaller reports into a single, less-detailed report for management?

Knowing how you will track your project's progress and who needs to know what and when helps your team establish efficient tracking mechanisms from the outset.

Tip

You can save interim baselines of a schedule at various points during your project. This approach helps you see where major shifts occurred and shows how you accommodated those shifts.

The Microsoft Project schedule in Figure 1-6 shows the original baseline tracked against actual progress.

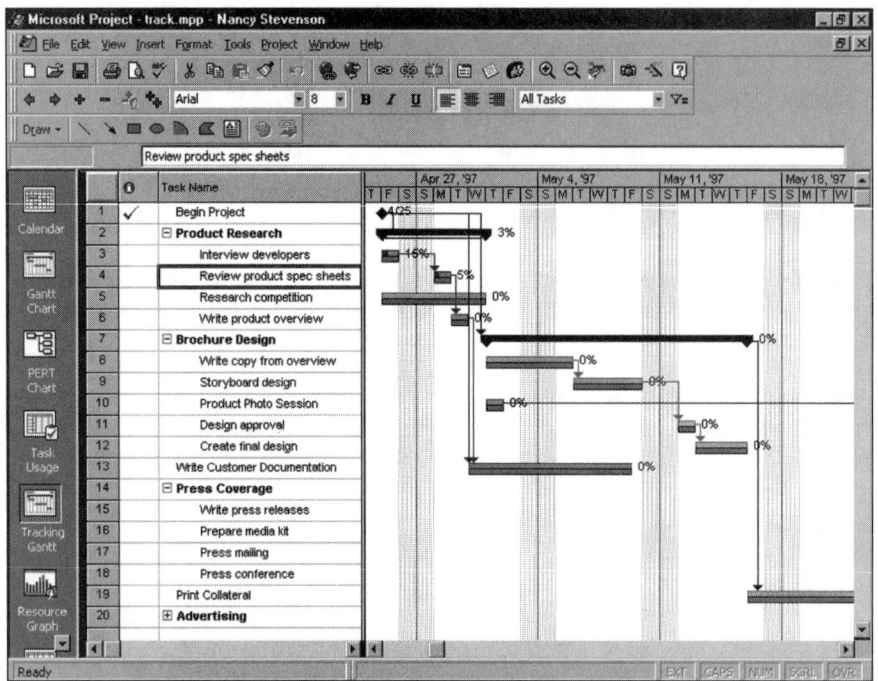

Figure 1-6: The darker portion of each bar and the percentage figure to the right of each bar indicate the percentage of each task that is complete.

Learning from your mistakes

Learning project management software isn't like learning to use a word processor. Project management entails conceptual layers that transcend the tools and features of the software. Having the experience and wisdom to use these features effectively comes from repeated use. You probably won't be a proficient Microsoft Project user right out of the gate. You have to work through one or more projects before you really know the most effective way to enter information about your project. You can expect to develop efficient tracking methods over time. Don't worry. It took you time to learn all you know about managing projects. If you pay attention to what goes on during your projects when you first implement Microsoft Project schedules, you can learn from your mistakes.

Microsoft Project enables you to review your first few projects and see clearly where you estimated incorrectly, made adjustments too slowly, or didn't break phases into manageable chunks. Project keeps your original schedule's baseline in a single file along with your final tracked schedule. When planning future projects, you can use these older baselines to help gauge the duration of tasks, how much things cost, how many resources are too many resources, and how many aren't nearly enough.

In the end, I guarantee you'll be a more successful and efficient project manager. You can easily show your boss the specific actions you've taken to avoid problems and provide solutions. In addition, you'll have the tools you need to help you and your manager understand the issues you face and to get the support you need.

Summary

This chapter presents a survey of the discipline called project management and explains how project management software can help you manage projects.

✦ Projects involve a stated goal, a specific time frame, and multiple resources (which can include people, equipment, and materials).

✦ Project management seeks to control issues of time, quality, and money.

✦ Critical path, slack, task durations, milestones, fixed tasks, resource-driven tasks, and dependencies are project management concepts that help you build and monitor a project.

✦ Project management software can assist you in planning, tracking, and communicating with team members and reporting on projects with tools such as Gantt and PERT charts.

✦ Although using Project takes some effort on your part, this effort pays off in increased productivity and efficiency.

✦ Projects typically go through five phases: setting the goal and defining scope; planning; revising; tracking; and reviewing to learn from your mistakes.

Chapter 2 takes a closer look at the Project environment and describes some of the tools that you can use to manage a project.

✦   ✦   ✦

Exploring the Microsoft Project Environment

Microsoft Project has come a long way in the past few years. It now sports an interface that makes managing a project almost as easy as maintaining your personal calendar. If you're a user of other Microsoft products, such as Word or Excel, the menus and tools in Project will, happily, look like old friends. And although Project's many views can be a bit overwhelming at first, they enable you to choose the perspective you need to monitor the progress of your project at any given time.

This chapter introduces Project's environment as well as the powerful tools Project puts at your disposal. You practice moving among different views and work with some of the tools and onscreen elements that you can use to create schedules.

Taking a First Look at Project

Although Microsoft Project doesn't come with Microsoft Office software, it is a member of the Microsoft Office family. Consequently, Project uses the standard Microsoft Office menu and toolbar structure and contains some of the familiar Microsoft Office tools.

Tip

If you've used Microsoft's organizer and calendar program, Outlook, you'll recognize several features of Project, including the bar on the left of the screen that enables you to switch among views and functions in the software. Project calls this feature the View bar.

Opening a Project file

The first time you choose Microsoft Project from the Programs section of the
Windows Start menu, the Welcome screen in Figure 2-1 appears. This screen offers
some useful choices for the user who is new to Project software or to this version
of Project.

Tip   If Project does not appear on your Windows Start menu, you can use the Run
command on the Start menu. Run the file called Winproj.exe in the Microsoft
Project folder on your hard drive. You can also open Project by double-clicking on
a project file in a directory contained in the My Computer area. Project files are
saved with the extension .mpp.

Figure 2-1: Project offers three options for getting help with
your Project planning.

At this point you have four possible actions:

✦ You can select Learn While You Work to get a series of demonstrations that
help you create your first project.

✦ You can select Watch a Quick Preview to see a demonstration of major
Project features.

✦ You can select Navigate with a Map to display a map of the steps typically
involved in managing a project.

✦ You can choose not to take advantage of any of these options and proceed to
a new, blank Project schedule by clicking on the Close button in the top-right
corner of the window.

Note

If you don't want to see this Welcome screen at startup, click on the Don't display this startup screen again check box in the lower-left corner. You can return to any of these Help options by choosing Help⇨Getting Started from the main Project menu bar.

Chapter 3 covers these three Help options in more detail.

If you wish to begin with a new, blank schedule or to open an existing project, you can close the Welcome window by clicking on the Close button in the top-left corner. When you do, you see a blank project, as shown in Figure 2-2.

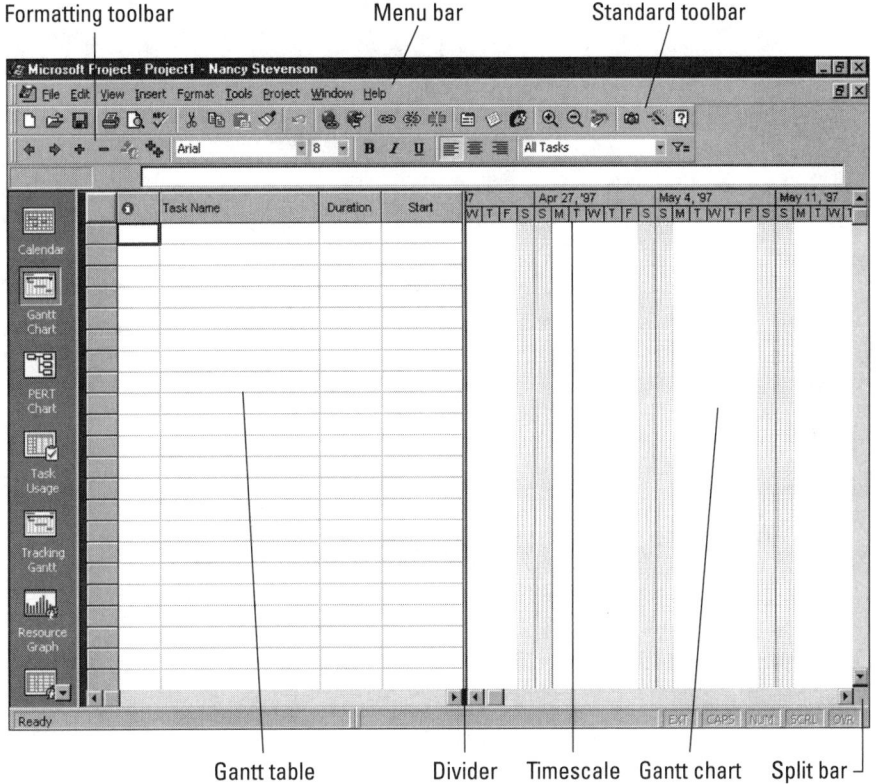

Figure 2-2: A blank project contains no project information; when you enter information, the split pane displays the data both textually and graphically.

Project always opens a new project schedule in the Gantt view. You see other views throughout this book, but you're likely to spend a great deal of your time in the Gantt view. This view offers a wealth of information about your project in a single snapshot.

Examining the Gantt Chart view

The Gantt Chart view has two main sections: the Gantt table and the Gantt chart. After you enter task information, the Gantt table (in the left pane) holds columns of information about your project, such as Task Name, Duration, Start date, and more. The Gantt chart (in the right pane) is a graphic representation that helps you see the timing and relationships among tasks, as shown in Figure 2-3.

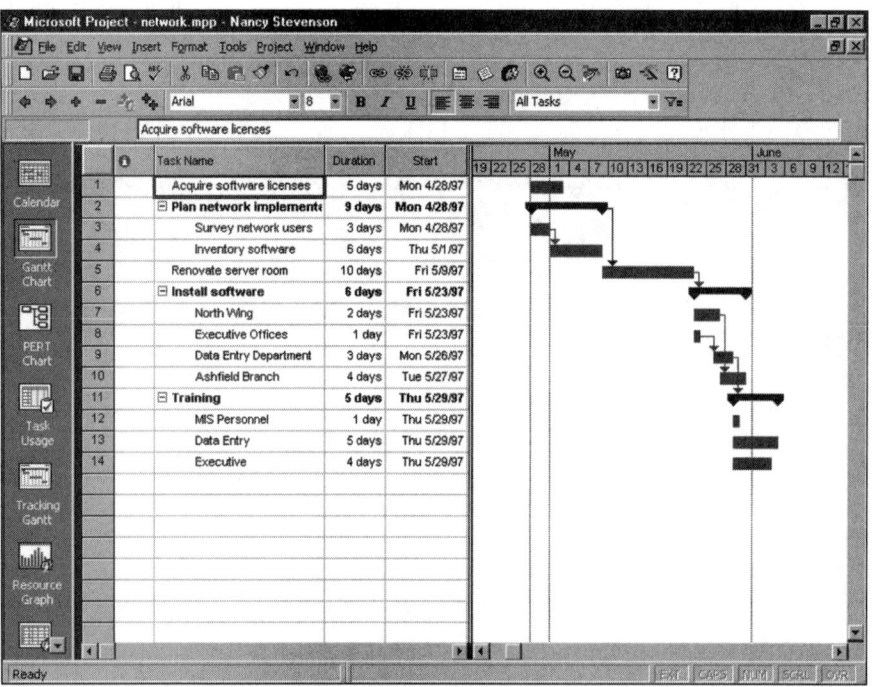

Figure 2-3: A sample project with task details in the Gantt table and bars representing tasks in the Gantt chart.

The timescale along the top of the Gantt chart acts like a vertical calendar. Think of it as a ruler against which you draw the tasks in your project. However, instead of marking off inches, this ruler marks off the hours, days, weeks, and months of your project. Notice that the chart displays two timescales: the major timescale along the top and a minor timescale beneath it. These two timescales help you see two levels of timing at once, such as the day and hour or the week and day.

Note

You can customize your timescale to show unusual time increments, such as thirds of months, or make the timescale display larger on your screen. Double-click on the timescale itself to display the Timescale dialog box. You can adjust these and other settings for the major and minor timescale on the Timescale tab. Also note that Project uses default settings for the number of hours in a workday, days in a week, and so on. To adjust these settings to display or hide nonworking days, you can use the settings on the Nonworking Time tab in the Timescale dialog box. Chapter 3 explains how to modify the calendars that control a project.

One of Project's strengths is that it enables you to modify what you see on screen in this and in other views. After you practice moving among these views, you'll be able to access information about timing, budget, or resource assignments in detail, or look at just the big picture. You can also customize what each view shows you depending on what you need to see. For example, you can use the divider that runs between the Gantt table and Gantt chart to adjust how much of the window each pane occupies. Clicking on this divider and dragging it to the right reveals more columns of data about your project in the Gantt table. Clicking on and dragging this divider to the left displays more of the task bars in your project in the Gantt chart.

In addition to modifying how much of each pane is displayed on screen, you can zoom in or out to larger or smaller time increments to see different perspectives of your project's schedule. You can show smaller time increments in the Gantt chart by clicking on the Zoom In button, or you can show larger increments of time by clicking on the Zoom Out button. A daily perspective on a three-year project enables you to manage day-to-day tasks, whereas a quarterly representation of your project might be of more interest when you're discussing larger issues with your management team.

Notice that the two panes of the Gantt Chart view have their own sets of scroll bars. To perform actions on information, you must use the appropriate scroll bar and select objects in the appropriate pane.

Using Project menus

Several of Project's menus, accessed through the menu bar at the top of the screen, offer commands that are probably quite familiar to you, such as Save, Print, and Copy. Other menus on the menu bar are very specific to the tasks you perform with Project.

Table 2-1 shows the various types of functions you can perform from each menu.

Table 2-1
Microsoft Project Menus

Menu	Types of Functions Available
File	Open and close new and existing files, save and print files, adjust page setup and document properties, and route files to e-mail recipients.
Edit	Cut, copy, and paste text or objects; manipulate data with Fill, Clear, and Delete commands; link and unlink task relationships; and locate information with Find, Replace, and Go To commands.
View	Select various default views of your project, access standard report formats, choose to display or hide various toolbars, use the Zoom feature, or enter header and footer information.
Insert	Insert new tasks, another Project file, or columns in views; also insert various objects into your schedule, including drawings, Excel charts, Word documents, media clips, and even hyperlinks to Web sites.
Format	Adjust the appearance of text, task bars, the Timescale display, or the overall appearance of a view's layout.
Tools	Run or modify Spelling and AutoCorrect functions to proofread your schedule, access workgroup features, establish links between projects, and modify your working calendar or resources. You can also customize standard views and functions with the Organizer, Options, or Customize commands, or record macros and initiate tracking functions.
Project	Display task or project information or notes, or use commands to sort or filter tasks to see specific details. You can also control outlining features of your project tasks from here.

The remaining two menus, Window and Help, contain commands to arrange windows on screen and access Help features, respectively; see Chapter 3 for more on Help.

Note that Microsoft has placed corresponding tool symbols and keyboard shortcuts (such as Ins or Shift+F2) next to the menu commands, as you can see in Figure 2-4. This display helps you learn the various ways to get things done in Project more quickly. Notice also that the main menus sometimes open up *side menus* (also called *submenus* or *cascading menus*). A black arrow to the right of a command indicates the presence of a side menu.

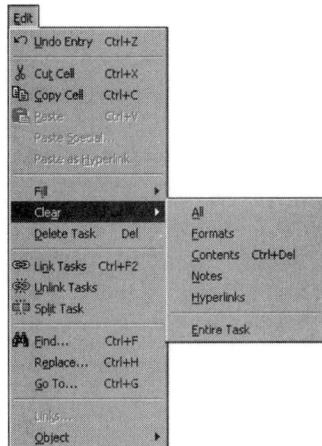

Figure 2-4: Tool symbols appear to the left and keyboard shortcuts to the right of commands on Project menus. Side menus offer more choices.

Examining the toolbars

You're probably already familiar with tools in Windows programs and the way in which they appear by category on toolbars. When you open Project, two default toolbars are visible: the Standard toolbar and Formatting toolbar seen in Figure 2-5.

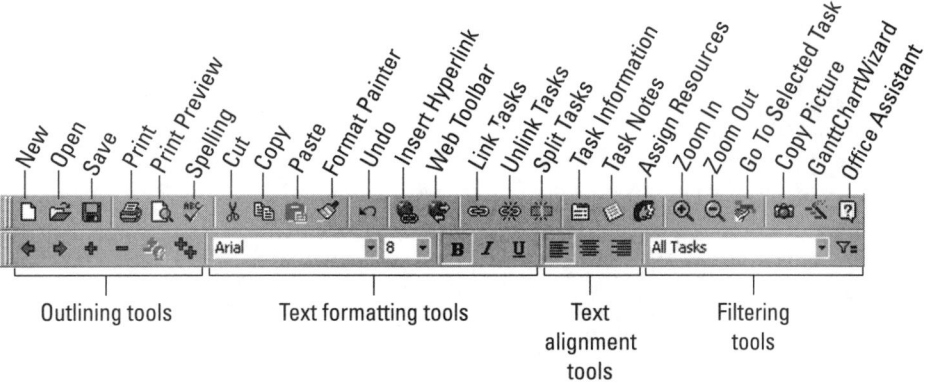

Figure 2-5: The Standard toolbar and the Formatting toolbar are Project's default toolbars.

When you connect two tasks with a dependency relationship, you create a *link*. The Link Tasks and Unlink Tasks tools enable you to manipulate these relationships. You can also use the Edit menu to establish links among tasks. You learn more about establishing dependencies in Chapter 4.

In some software programs the tools available to you are context sensitive; that is, they change according to the function you're performing. In Project the default toolbars are fairly consistent. The major change on these two toolbars when you perform different functions or change views is that some tools become unavailable: They appear grayed out, and nothing happens when you click on them.

If you insert an object from another Microsoft application, such as Excel or PowerPoint, into your Project, the other program's environment replaces Project's toolbars and menus when you select that object. Therefore, you can use the other program's tools to modify the object without having to leave Project. Project toolbars and menus reappear when you click anywhere outside the inserted object.

In addition to the Standard and Formatting toolbars, several other toolbars are available. They sometimes appear automatically when you're performing certain types of activities. However, you can also display any of these toolbars at any time by choosing View⇨Toolbars and choosing from the toolbar side menu (see Figure 2-6).

Figure 2-6: You can use this side menu to display the appropriate tools for your job.

Tip These toolbars appear as floating toolbars when you choose to display them. You can move floating toolbars anywhere on your screen by clicking on their title bars and dragging them. Alternatively, you can anchor any floating toolbar at the top of your screen near the default toolbars; simply click on the toolbar title bar and drag it to the top of the screen. Conversely, you can convert the Standard and Formatting toolbars into floating toolbars; just click anywhere on a toolbar (not directly on a tool, though) and drag it to any position on your screen.

Using the Entry bar

Several views or portions of views in Project, such as the Gantt table, use a familiar spreadsheet-style interface. Information is entered and displayed in columns and rows. The intersection of a column and a row is an individual *cell*. Each task in your project has an ID number, indicated by the numbers that run down the left of the spreadsheet. You can enter information either in dialog boxes (see Chapter 4) or directly into cells. When you select a cell, the Entry bar displays the information in the cell.

If you've ever used Microsoft Excel or other popular spreadsheet programs, you'll understand the function of the Entry bar. It runs along the top of the screen, directly under the Formatting toolbar (see Figure 2-7). When you select a cell, your cursor appears in the Entry bar (to the right of any existing text). You can type new text or edit existing text by clicking anywhere within the text in the Entry bar. Two buttons on the left of the bar enable you to cancel or accept an entry.

Figure 2-7: The Entry bar is where you edit text from individual cells.

Chapter 4 covers entering and editing text in more detail.

Changing views with the View bar

Project offers multiple views in which you can display project information. A single view cannot possibly show all the information you need about timing, relationships among tasks, resource allocations, and project progress; in fact, each type of information requires special kinds of graphical and textual displays for you to interpret them accurately. You learn more about which view you should use to gain a specific perspective on your project a little later in this chapter. For now, take a look at the View bar shown in Figure 2-8; this feature enables you to jump from view to view.

Click here to see more views

Figure 2-8: The View bar offers several predefined views of your project.

The View bar contains icons for eight views; click on the down arrow near the bottom of the bar to see them all. When you move down the View bar, an up arrow appears near the top of the bar so that you can return to the top of the View bar. You can display any of the views listed here by clicking on it in the View bar. At the bottom of the View bar is an item called More Views. Click on More Views to open the More Views dialog box, shown in Figure 2-9.

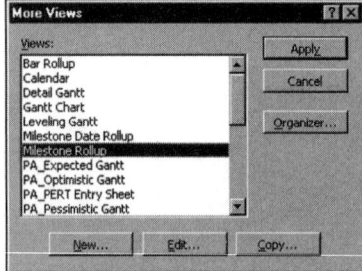

Figure 2-9: Project has 26 built-in views — and you can add your own as well.

You can create custom views by clicking on New in the More Views dialog box (see Chapter 16).

Project Views

Now that you've seen the major elements of the Project environment in the Gantt view, it's time to explore Project's other views in a little more detail. Here's an analogy to help you understand why a project needs multiple views: A project is like a small business. As in any business, different people attend to various aspects of the work. The accounting department thinks mainly of the costs of doing business. The plant supervisor focuses on deadlines and having enough machinery to get the job done. Your human resources department thinks of people: their salaries, hours, benefits, and so on.

As the owner of your project, you are likely to wear all these hats — and more — during the project. Rather than changing caps as you move from one responsibility to another, in Project you simply switch to another view to see your work from a different perspective. Each view helps you focus on a different aspect or aspects of your project.

Manipulating views

You can manipulate views to see either a single or combination configuration. Combination views display the view you've selected from the View bar as well as a second view, for example, the Task Form view that includes information about the selected task. Figure 2-10 shows the PERT view with a combination of visual and textual information.

You can display a combination in any view by moving your pointer to the split bar, shown in Figure 2-10, until the cursor becomes two horizontal lines with arrows; then double-click. You can also click and drag the split bar toward the top of your screen to display the Task Form view, or choose Window⇨Split. You can return to the simple PERT view shown in Figure 2-11 by double-clicking on the split bar again.

If you are displaying a combination view and you switch views, the new view also appears as a combination view. If you want to display a new view and have it occupy the full screen, hold down the Shift key when you click on the view in the View bar. You can always tell which portion of the split view you're in by the active view bar, a dark blue line that appears to the left when you click on the upper or lower view.

PERT view

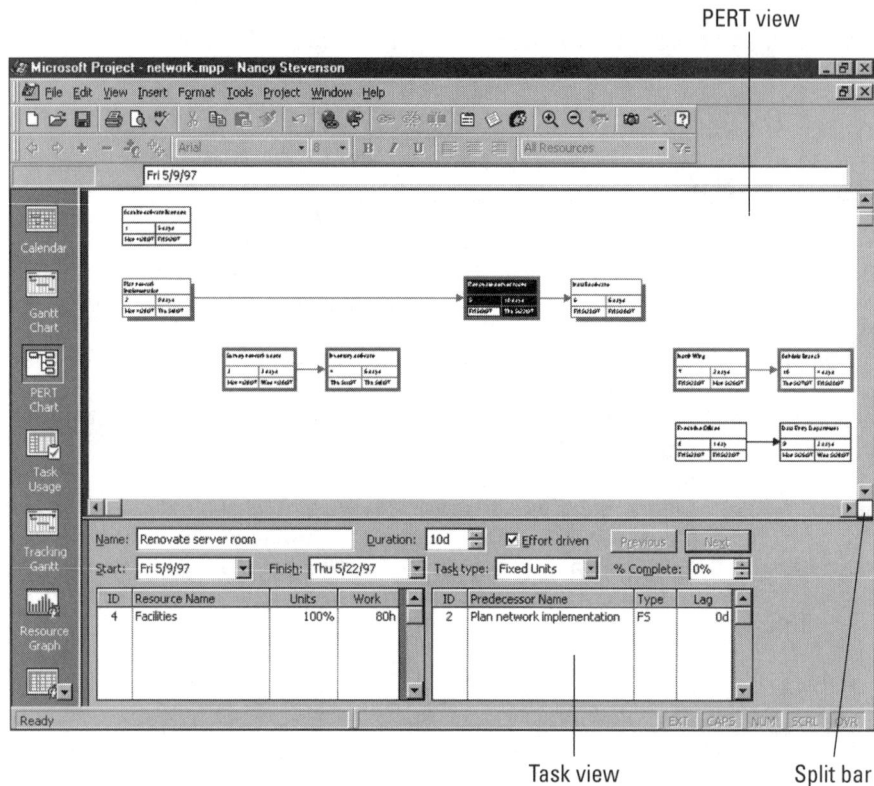

Task view   Split bar

Figure 2-10: A combination view displays information for selected tasks.

Choosing the most appropriate view

Deciding which of Project's 26 built-in views (or any of your custom views) suits a particular purpose can be a little tricky. As you become more familiar with the features of Project and project management concepts and terms, you'll get more comfortable selecting views by name. The View bar lists the eight most frequently used views. The following sections describe how these views enable you to look at different aspects of your project. Notice the wealth of detail available to you about your project.

Chapter 7 covers views in more detail; the discussion of views will be more meaningful to you after you learn more about building a project.

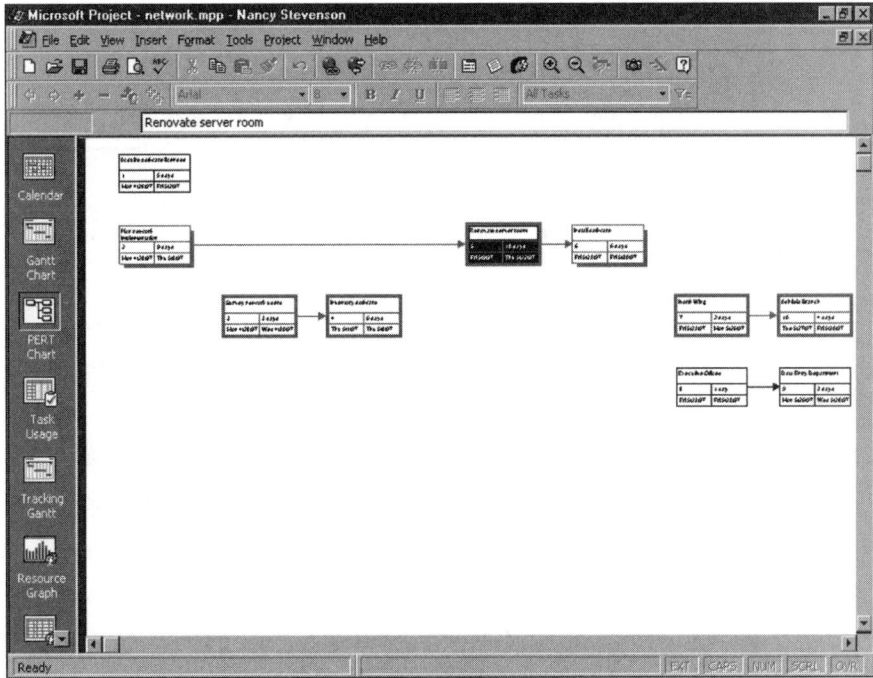

Figure 2-11: Hiding the Task From view shows you an overview of your project without focusing on any single task's details.

The Calendar view

The top selection on the View bar is the Calendar view, shown in Figure 2-12. The strength of this view lies in its familiarity. Using a month-by-month calendar format, the Calendar view indicates the length of a task with a bar running across portions of days, or even weeks. On the Calendar view, nonworking days (which you learn how to define in Chapter 8) are shaded. Although a task bar may extend over nonworking days, such as Saturday and Sunday in this example, the work of the task doesn't actually progress over those days.

You can move from month to month using the large up- and down-arrow keys in the top-right corner of the view. Every project has a *calendar* (not to be confused with the Calendar view) that tells Project how to handle events, such as 24-hour shifts, weekends, and holidays off, over the life of your project.

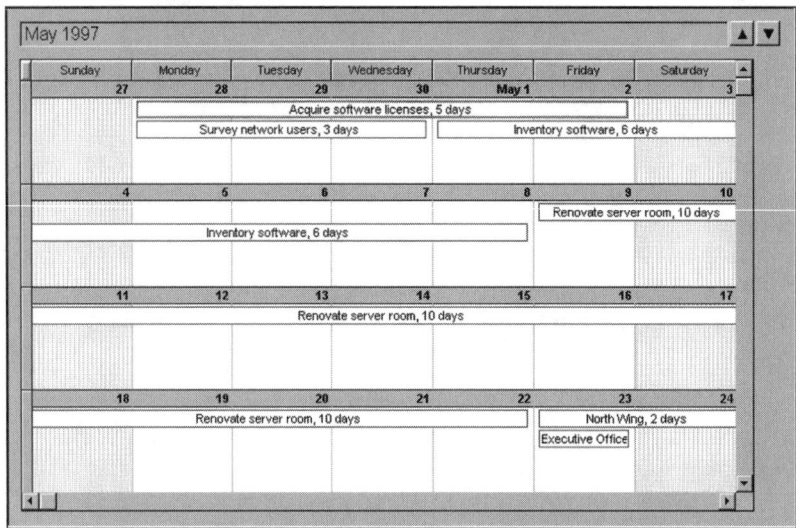

Figure 2-12: The Calendar view features a familiar, easy-to-read format.

To modify the appearance of the Calendar view — for example, to shade working days and leave nonworking days clear — double-click anywhere on the calendar to open the Timescale dialog box and change the corresponding settings. You can also use this dialog box to change settings and to mark individual tasks as working or nonworking.

The Calendar view is useful when you want to see how changes to the working calendar (on which you are basing your project) affect your schedule.

You can see slightly more than a month at a time on screen by using the Zoom Out tool on the Standard toolbar while in Calendar view. Zoom Out shrinks the calendar to accommodate about a month and a half of your schedule.

The PERT Chart view

The PERT Chart view shown in Figure 2-13 has less to do with timing than it has to do with the general flow of work and the relationships between tasks in your project.

The PERT view places each task inside a node. The node, which you can see close up in Figure 2-14, contains the task name, task ID number in the sequence of the project outline, duration, start date, and end date. The lines that flow between the nodes represent *dependencies*. A task that must come after another task is complete, called a *successor* task, appears to the right or sometimes below its *predecessor*.

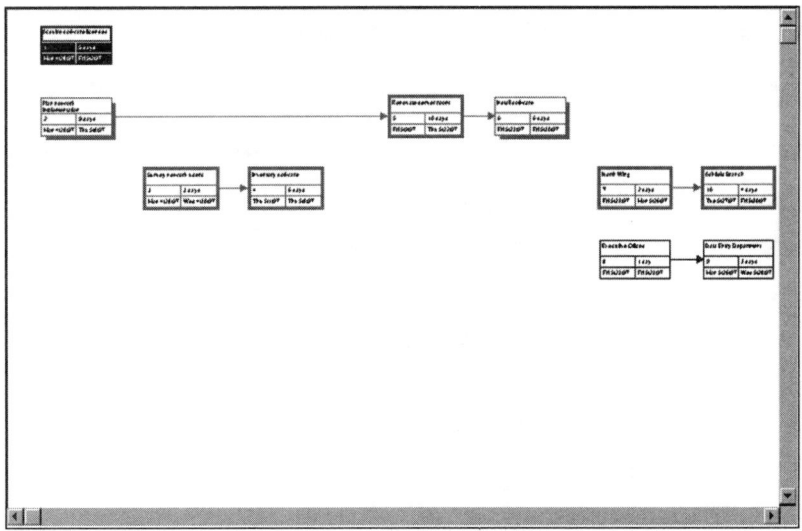

Figure 2-13: These boxes contain information about the individual tasks in your project.

Caution

Although you can enter task information here, you can't use filtering to view tasks that meet certain criteria in the PERT Chart view. You also can't move tasks around in your schedule in this view.

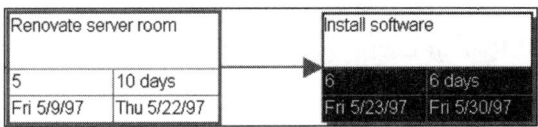

Figure 2-14: Use the Zoom In tool to see the detail of individual nodes in the PERT Chart view.

The Task Usage view

The fourth view choice available on the View bar is called Task Usage. This view, shown in Figure 2-15, allows you to focus on the hours of work that resources have performed on a task. As Chapters 12 and 13 explain, you can measure a project's costs in several ways. For example, a project can include costs relative to the number of person hours spent times the resources' rates per hour or the fixed costs involved in items such as fees for renting equipment or purchasing licenses. You can also look at estimated costs (baseline costs) versus actual costs, at the percentage of work performed, or at monies spent to date.

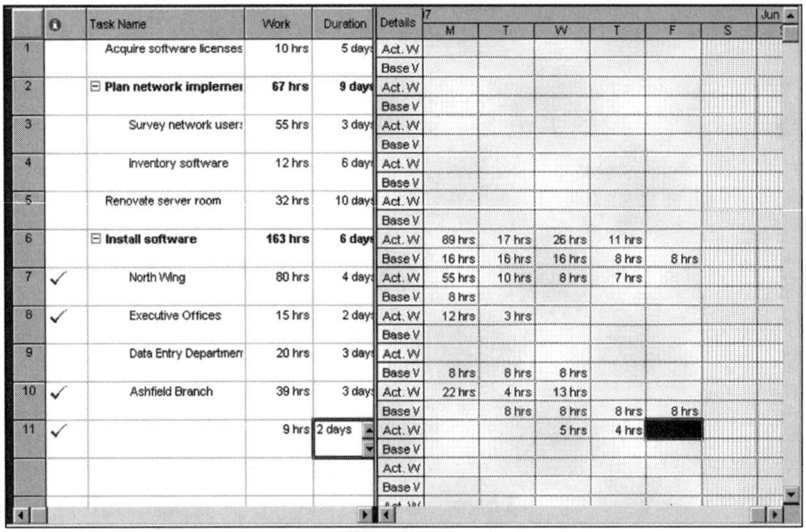

	❶	Task Name	Work	Duration	Details	M	T	W	T	F	S	Jun
1		Acquire software licenses	10 hrs	5 days	Act. W							
					Base V							
2		⊟ Plan network implemei	67 hrs	9 days	Act. W							
					Base V							
3		Survey network users	55 hrs	3 days	Act. W							
					Base V							
4		Inventory software	12 hrs	6 days	Act. W							
					Base V							
5		Renovate server room	32 hrs	10 days	Act. W							
					Base V							
6		⊟ Install software	163 hrs	6 days	Act. W	89 hrs	17 hrs	26 hrs	11 hrs			
					Base V	16 hrs	16 hrs	16 hrs	8 hrs	8 hrs		
7	✓	North Wing	80 hrs	4 days	Act. W	55 hrs	10 hrs	8 hrs	7 hrs			
					Base V	8 hrs						
8	✓	Executive Offices	15 hrs	2 days	Act. W	12 hrs	3 hrs					
					Base V							
9		Data Entry Departmen	20 hrs	3 days	Act. W							
					Base V	8 hrs	8 hrs	8 hrs				
10	✓	Ashfield Branch	39 hrs	3 days	Act. W	22 hrs	4 hrs	13 hrs				
					Base V		8 hrs	8 hrs	8 hrs	8 hrs		
11	✓		9 hrs	2 days	Act. W			5 hrs	4 hrs	██████		
					Base V							
					Act. W							
					Base V							
					Act. W							

Figure 2-15: This Task Usage chart displays the baseline estimates of work hours required above the tracked actual work hours.

You can enter actual work hours by including an Actual Work field in the Details pane on the right.

Note

How can you do 55 hours of work in three 8-hour days, as indicated in the sample project shown in Figure 2-15? Remember, this view shows *total* resource hours — perhaps ten people put in 5.5 hours each, or three very dedicated people may have each worked a slightly extended 18-hour day.

Tracking Gantt view

The Tracking Gantt view differs somewhat from the standard Gantt view, specifically in the way it displays actual work performed that you've tracked on your project. Look at Figures 2-16 and 2-17. Figure 2-16 is a standard Gantt view of a project that has had some activity. Figure 2-17, on the other hand, shows the same schedule displayed in the Tracking Gantt view. This view contains columns that clearly compare planned activity versus what has actually occurred.

The standard Gantt view shows the progress on tasks as a black bar within the baseline task bar. Tasks that depend on the completed tasks have been moved out to reflect any delays in actual work completed. The Tracking Gantt view, on the other hand, shows completed work as a dark bar separate from the baseline task. Baseline task bars stay put, and only actual work bars push out to reflect delays in timing.

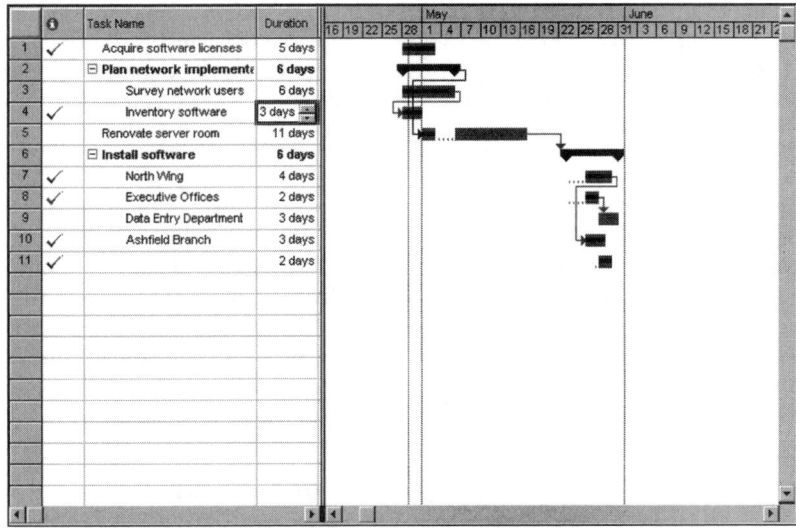

Figure 2-16: The standard Gantt view shows you the reality of your project timing at the moment, based on actual work done.

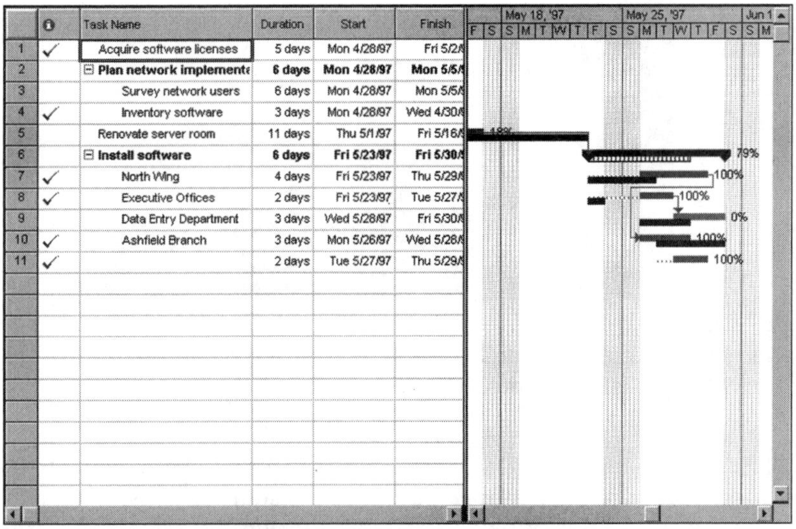

	0	Task Name	Duration	Start	Finish
1	✓	Acquire software licenses	5 days	Mon 4/28/97	Fri 5/2/
2		☐ Plan network implement	6 days	Mon 4/28/97	Mon 5/5/
3		Survey network users	6 days	Mon 4/28/97	Mon 5/5/
4	✓	Inventory software	3 days	Mon 4/28/97	Wed 4/30/
5		Renovate server room	11 days	Thu 5/1/97	Fri 5/16/
6		☐ Install software	6 days	Fri 5/23/97	Fri 5/30/
7	✓	North Wing	4 days	Fri 5/23/97	Thu 5/29/
8	✓	Executive Offices	2 days	Fri 5/23/97	Tue 5/27/
9		Data Entry Department	3 days	Wed 5/28/97	Fri 5/30/
10	✓	Ashfield Branch	3 days	Mon 5/26/97	Wed 5/28/
11	✓		2 days	Tue 5/27/97	Thu 5/29/

Figure 2-17: The Tracking Gantt view shows the discrepancy between your estimates and the real-world activity in your project.

The Tracking Gantt view shows how your project has shifted from your original estimates and helps you decide how to adjust your plans to accommodate any delays. Theoretically, if a project ever goes faster than you've anticipated, you could also see the amount of extra time you've bought yourself through your efficiency. (However, projects so seldom go faster than projected that I won't show that option here!)

The Resource Graph view

The Resource Graph view highlights resource conflicts: people, equipment, or other resources that are being overworked or underutilized. Looking at the Resource Graph view as both a single and combination chart can show you how assignments on individual tasks are affecting a resource's utilization on a project. Figure 2-18 shows the main Resource Graph view; Figure 2-19 shows the combination view with details of the tasks being performed at the bottom of the Project window.

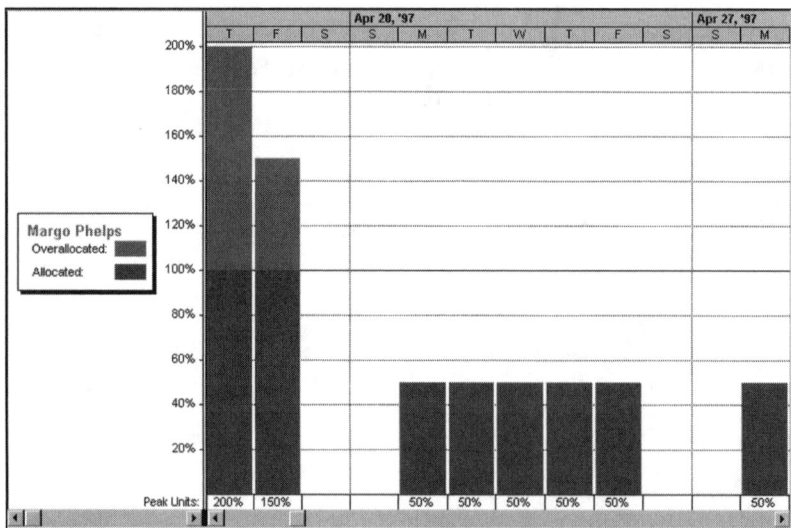

Figure 2-18: Percentage of a person's available work time is tracked and displayed as overallocated and underallocated.

Project displays a resource's total work hours on any particular day as a bar. A bar that falls short of the 100 percent mark indicates a resource that isn't working full time; it may be underutilized. A bar that extends beyond 100 percent shows that somebody is working too many hours in a day. The percentage of the workday that the resource is working appears at the bottom of the usage bars.

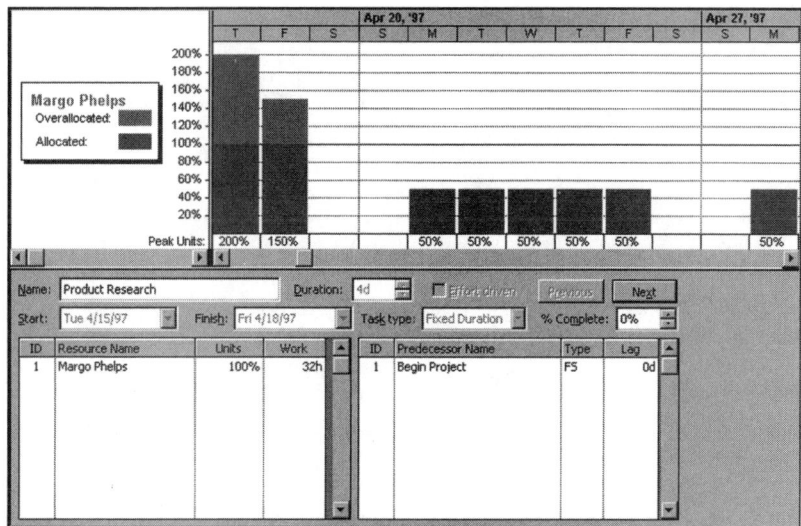

Figure 2-19: Displaying task information beneath a Resource Graph can help you see which work assignments are keeping the resource busy.

Note

Underutilization may indicate that a resource is busy with other projects the rest of that day, and overutilization may signal occasional and acceptable overtime. See Chapter 7 for more information about interpreting these bars and Chapter 9 for more about resolving conflicts in resource time.

You can use the Resource Graph view to spot and correct resources that are inappropriately allocated. Note that the Resource Graph view shows information for one resource at a time.

The Resource Sheet view

The Resource Sheet view shown in Figure 2-20 gives you a wealth of information about the resources assigned to your project, including standard and overtime rates, availability for overtime work, and fixed costs.

Tip

By assigning group designations to resources such as Marketing, Facilities, or Temporary Help, you can use filters to study resource information for just one or two groups at a time.

This columnar interface is a great way to prepare to assign resources if, for example, you want to assign lower-cost people to most tasks and higher-cost people to certain mission-critical tasks. This view clearly shows to which group a resource belongs.

	ⓘ	Resource Name	Initials	Group	Max. Units	Std. Rate	Ovt. Rate	Cost/Use	Accrue At	Base Cale
1	◈	Margo Phelps	M		100%	$50.00/hr	$50.00/hr	$0.00	Prorated	Standard
2		Antonio Marquez	A		100%	$20.00/hr	$25.00/hr	$0.00	Prorated	Standard
3	◈	Alicia Hon	A		100%	$20.00/hr	$30.00/hr	$0.00	Prorated	Standard
4	◈	Ron Wozniak	R		100%	$75.00/hr	$75.00/hr	$0.00	Prorated	Standard
5		Mick Chen	M		100%	$25.00/hr	$35.00/hr	$0.00	Prorated	Standard
6		Combined Graphics	C		100%	$100.00/hr	$100.00/hr	$0.00	Prorated	Standard
7		Ready Photo	R		100%	$125.00/hr	$150.00/hr	$0.00	Prorated	Standard
8	◈	Advertising Agency	A		100%	$0.00/hr	$0.00/hr	$25,000.00	Prorated	Standard
9	◈	Raoul Sanchez	R		100%	$45.00/hr	$45.00/hr	$0.00	Prorated	Standard
10		Arnold Mailing Services	A		100%	$50.00/hr	$75.00/hr	$0.00	Prorated	Standard
11		Arthur Kensington	A		100%	$0.00/hr	$0.00/hr	$0.00	Prorated	Standard
12		Gabrial & Alan Printers	G		100%	$0.00/hr	$0.00/hr	$10,000.00	Prorated	Standard
13	◈	Muriel Tszchorsky	M		100%	$75.00/hr	$75.00/hr	$0.00	Prorated	Standard
14		Liam Allard	L		100%	$35.00/hr	$45.00/hr	$0.00	Prorated	Standard
15		Product Engineering Mar	P		100%	$100.00/hr	$150.00/hr	$0.00	Prorated	Standard

Figure 2-20: You can view both standard and overtime rates in the Resource Sheet.

Tip

Note the warning flags in the Indicators column on the far left of this view. These flags indicate resources with allocation problems. Switch back to the Resource Graph to get details on these problems resource by resource.

The Resource Usage view

Whereas the Resource Graph view displays resource allocations on a resource-by-resource basis, the Resource Usage view shown in Figure 2-21 enables you to see all resources on a project at one time. The Resource Name column on the left displays the resource name and all the tasks to which it is assigned. The Work column displays the estimated number of hours the resource should spend on each task. The right pane of this window shows you those hours on a scrolling calendar, so you can see exactly when the work will be performed.

New Feature

Notice that many of the available views include a column headed with a small *i*. The *i* stands for "indicator field," and it's new to Project 98. This column includes indicators for recurring tasks, tasks that need resource leveling to resolve resource conflicts, and tasks that have missed some constraint you associated with them. The indicator field alerts you to important issues for each task.

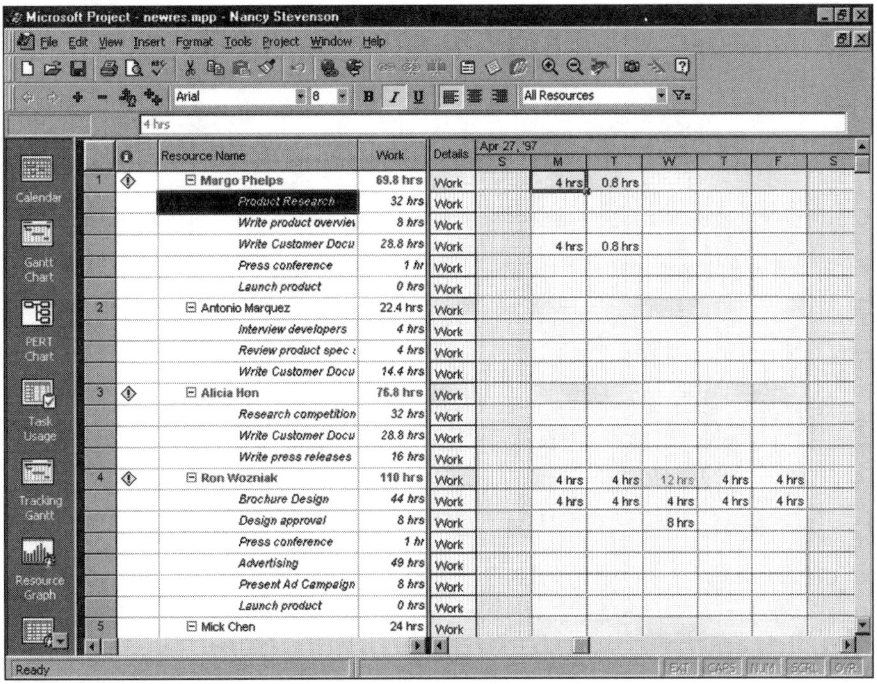

Figure 2-21: You can figure out who's doing what and when in the Resource Usage view.

Summary

This chapter introduces the Project environment and the many ways in which you can display project information. Chapter 2 describes the following techniques:

✦ Opening an existing file or creating a new Project schedule

✦ Using Project menus and toolbars

✦ Using the Entry bar for entering text in your project

✦ Using the timescale to gauge timing in your project in certain views

✦ Using the View bar to move through various views

✦ Using views to focus on various aspects of your project

Chapter 3 explains how to get help in Project and how to save Project files.

✦   ✦   ✦

Getting Your Project Going

Creating a New Project

Now that you have some project management concepts under your belt and you've taken a stroll around Project's environment, you are ready to create your first schedule. The first step, before you ever type a date into a Project schedule, is to assemble the relevant information about your project. Then you can open a new Project file and begin to build your project tasks, using a simple outline structure.

In this chapter you begin to build your first Project schedule and learn how to take advantage of Project's various Help features. At the end of the chapter, you learn how to save your project.

Gathering Information

As you learned in Chapter 1, several elements must be in place before you can begin to build a project schedule. First you need to understand the overall goal and scope of the project so that you can clearly see the steps that lie between you and that goal. A good way to start is by delineating the major steps involved. Don't worry about the order of the tasks at this point — just brainstorm all the major areas of activity. For example, take a project like organizing an annual meeting for your company. Here are some possible steps:

- ◆ Book the meeting space
- ◆ Schedule speakers
- ◆ Arrange for audio/visual equipment
- ◆ Order food
- ◆ Send out invitations
- ◆ Mail out annual reports

Now that last item brings up a question of scope: Is it within the purview of your project to create the annual report or simply to obtain copies from, say, the marketing department, and mail them out to stockholders before the meeting? In some corporations the person responsible for organizing the annual meeting is also responsible for overseeing the production of the annual report. Be sure you answer these questions of scope and responsibility at this stage of your planning.

For this example you can assume that another department is creating the annual report. Your job is to make sure that someone mails copies of the report to all stockholders before the annual meeting.

Determining detail tasks

Now that you have prepared a list of major tasks, the next step is to break them down into more detailed tasks. Take one of the items on the list, *Order food*, for example. How can you break down this task? How detailed should you get? Here's one possible breakdown of the order food task:

Order food

    Create a budget

    Determine menu

    Select a caterer

        Send out requests for bid

        All estimates received

        Review estimates and award contract

    Final headcount to caterer

    Confirm caterer one week ahead

Could you do without the detailed tasks under *Select a caterer*? Do you need more detail under *Create a budget*? That's up to you based on your knowledge of your project and procedures. However, here are some points to keep in mind:

✦ Create tasks that remind you of major action items, but don't overburden yourself with items of such detail that keeping track of your schedule becomes a full-time job. That's the purpose of daily to-do lists.

✦ Include milestones to mark off points in your project. For example, the task *All estimates received* under the summary task *Select a caterer* is a milestone — it marks a point in time by which you want to have made a major decision. If that time comes and goes and you haven't selected the caterer, will missing the deadline affect other subsequent tasks? If so, including that milestone could be vital to your success.

✦ Include tasks that management will want to know about. One of the key uses of a Project schedule is to report progress. If your boss wants to see that you've sent out a purchase order to the caterer per your new accounting department procedures, you might want to include the task, even if you don't think that level of detail is important.

Establishing time limits

After you have an idea of the tasks involved in your project, you need to have some idea of their timing. Should you allow two weeks for caterers to come back with bids? Not if you have only three weeks to organize the meeting. One approach to determining task timing is to build an initial schedule in Project, assign timing to tasks, and see how close you can come to your deadline. If you're way off, you can go back and tweak the timing for individual tasks until your schedule works.

At this point you might be tempted to trim time off your tasks to make them fit a deadline, which can make for an unrealistic schedule. The solution? Use the initial schedule to convince your boss that you need more time, money, or resources to complete this project on time. If he or she wants to trim time from a specific task to meet the deadline, you may have grounds to ask for more help.

At this early planning stage, get any information you need to assign timing to tasks (for example, contact vendors or subcontractors to get their timing estimates, which you need to reflect in your schedule). If your project has a drop-dead completion date, you should be aware of it. However, leave it to Project to show you whether your estimates work in an overall schedule.

Lining up your resources

Before you can build a Project schedule, you have to understand what resources are available to you as well as their costs. You don't necessarily have to know these resources by name, but you should know that your project needs three engineers at a cost of $75 per hour and one piece of earth-moving equipment at a daily rental cost of $450, for example.

You need to identify these resources and assign them to individual tasks early in the project-planning process (see Chapter 5). Find out anything you can about the availability of these resources: Are some resources available only half-time for your project? Will all the engineers be unavailable during the third week of August because of a professional conference? Research the cost and availability of resources as much as possible as you begin to build a project.

Looking at dependencies

The final part of your research before entering project information into a schedule is to be aware of relationships among tasks. Does the CEO have to approve the menu before you book the caterers? Are you required to wait three weeks after applying for a permit before starting construction on a building? If your project faces issues involving the order and relationships of tasks, you will save yourself some headaches down the line and build a more realistic schedule if you can identify these obstacles now.

Opening a Project File

Okay, you've done your homework. You've made some notes about your upcoming project's tasks, timing, resources, and dependencies. You're ready to start building your first schedule; the first step is to use Project to build the task outline. From the Windows Start menu, select Programs➪Microsoft Project.

When you first open Microsoft Project, a Welcome screen offers you three Help options. If you are building your first project, you might want to view the Quick Preview or glance at the Project Map, shown in Figure 3-1. This map shows you the logical order in which you can build a schedule; you can click on various places on this window to get advice about project management and planning.

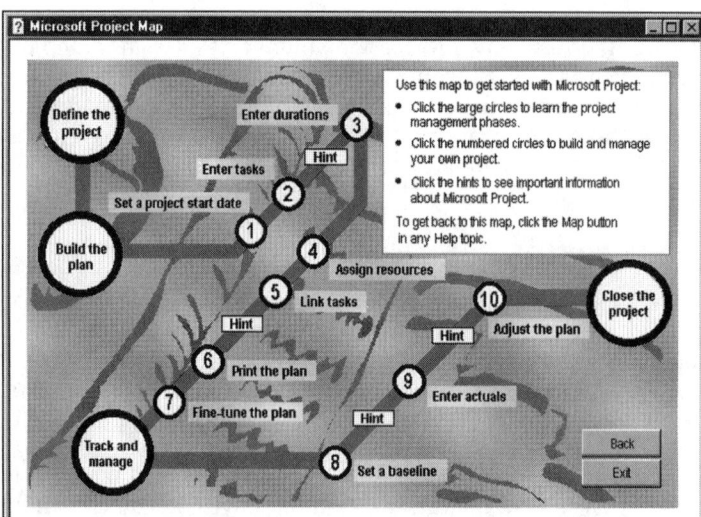

Figure 3-1: Click on the Hints to learn more about Project.

When you close the Welcome window (or any Help window selected from it), your screen displays a blank schedule. When you are in Project and you want to work with a schedule, you have three options:

✦ You can open an existing Project file by choosing File➪Open.

✦ You can start a new Project file while an existing file is open by choosing File⇨New. If you haven't saved the currently opened file, Project asks whether you want to; if you've already saved the currently opened file, Project immediately creates a new file for you and opens the Project Information dialog box.

✦ You can begin your new project using the blank schedule that Project opens for you when you first enter Project.

Entering Project Information

With the blank schedule on screen, choose Project⇨Project Information to start defining your project. The Project Information dialog box shown in Figure 3-2 appears.

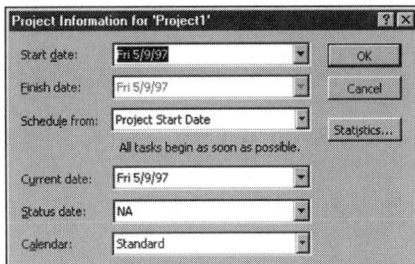

Figure 3-2: The Project Information dialog box is the starting point for every project.

You can enter six pieces of information in the Project Information dialog box:

✦ **Start date:** If you set a start date for the project, all tasks begin on that date until you assign timing or dependencies to them.

✦ **Finish date:** If you know a final deadline, you can enter it here and then work backwards to schedule your project. You must change the setting in the Schedule from field to access this option.

✦ **Schedule from:** You can build schedules from completion to start by setting this field to Project Finish Date. Alternatively, you can build your schedule from the start date forward by accepting the default setting, Project Start Date.

✦ **Current date:** Project uses your computer clock for the default entry in this field. If you want to use a different date, you can change the current date in this field. You can adjust this setting to generate reports that provide information on your project as of a certain date or to go back and track your project's progress from an earlier date.

✦ **Status date:** This field performs earned-value calculations and identifies the complete-through date in the Update Project dialog box; Status date also enables Project to place progress lines. If you leave the status date set at NA, the status date equals the current date set on your computer clock and calendar.

✦ **Calendar:** You can select the calendar on which to base your schedule. The standard calendar is the default — it schedules eight hours of work, five days a week.

You should enter either a Start or Finish date, but not both. Only one will be available to you, depending on the choice you've made in the Schedule from field. To enter one of these dates, click on the down arrow next to the text box. (The arrow is not available if the Schedule from field isn't set for that choice.) Select a date from the pop-up calendar, as shown in Figure 3-3.

Caution

If you decide to schedule backwards from a Finish date, Project cannot use tools like resource leveling to resolve conflicts in your schedule.

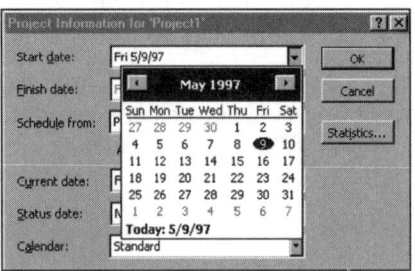

Figure 3-3: Use the arrow keys near the top of this calendar to choose other months.

You can change your start date during the planning phase, trying out alternative what-if scenarios by modifying this field. As you build your tasks going forward, Project indicates the finish date dictated by the length of your tasks and their timing relationships. When you're satisfied with the overall time frame, you can set the start date that works best when you're ready to begin.

Tip

If you have already started the project, you can set the start date to be in the past to accurately reflect the real start date. Tasks on the Gantt chart appear to have occurred before the current date line.

If you know the date by which something must be completed (as with the annual meeting project, for example, or a Christmas party that must happen on December 25), you can schedule tasks moving backwards from the finish date. When you do so, Project builds the tasks going back in time. You might be surprised when Project generates a schedule telling you that you should have started three weeks earlier to finish in time. In that case you can either add resources to get the work done faster or reduce the scope of the project.

When beginning a new schedule, you would typically accept the default settings for Current date and Status date. Changing them has to do with generating project reports and project tracking when your project is underway.

For now, you can leave all the default settings (that is, scheduling from the start of the project, having the current date be today, and starting the project today, as well as basing your schedule on the standard calendar). Click on OK to close the Project Information dialog box.

Looking at Project Calendars

The Project Information dialog box enables you to set the basic parameters of the project's timing. Those parameters and the information you're about to enter for specific tasks are based on the *base calendar*. You can create a base calendar for each group of resources in your project. For example, if the plant workers work a nine-hour day from 6 a.m. to 3 p.m. and the office workers work an eight-hour day from 8 a.m. to 5 p.m., you can create two base calendars. When you assign one day of, say, an office worker's time, Project understands it to be an eight-hour day. In the Project Information dialog box, you designate whether you want your project to use a standard, 24-hour or Night Shift calendar for most of your work assignments.

Project also has *resource calendars* in which you can set exceptions to base calendars for specific resources in your project whose work hours are different from the rest of the group. When you first create a resource for your project, Project uses the standard base calendar as the default (8-hour day, 40-hour week) if you haven't changed that setting in the Project Information dialog box. However, you can assign a new calendar to any resource. You learn more about resource calendars in Chapter 5.

Project makes default assumptions about certain items, such as the number of days in a week that form the basis for the default base calendar (or the *project calendar)*. Project uses this calendar for resources unless you assign another calendar to them. You can see Project's assumptions — and change them if necessary — in the Options dialog box.

Setting calendar options

Project's default calendar for scheduling a resource's time is the project calendar. Project makes certain assumptions about this calendar. Those assumptions answer certain basic questions such as, What do you mean when you say a day or a week? Does a day start at 8 a.m. or at 9 a.m.? How many hours are in your typical work week?

To customize the standard calendar to your own working schedule, choose Tools⇨Options. Select the Calendar tab in the Options dialog box (see Figure 3-4).

Caution

Any changes you make to these options apply to the current schedule only. To save your changes across all schedules, click on the Set as Default button in the Calendar tab.

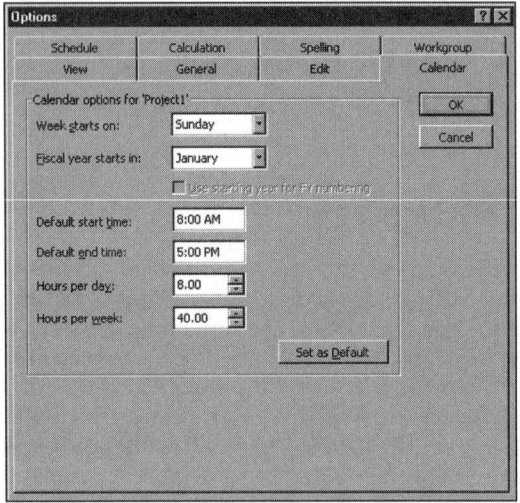

Figure 3-4: Make sure that you and Project are speaking the same language when you enter task durations by first reviewing the settings in the Calendar tab in the Options dialog box.

New Feature

In earlier versions of Project you had two choices for the first day of your work week: Sunday or Monday. In Project 98 you can select any day of the week as your start day. For example, if you run a restaurant that closes on Sundays and Mondays, you might want to designate a work week of Tuesday through Saturday. In that case you would set the Week starts on field to Tuesday.

If your company uses a fiscal year other than the calendar year (January through December), you may want to set the Fiscal year starts in option. This setting is especially useful when you generate reports showing costs per quarter or year.

The final four settings in the Calendar tab of the Options dialog box enable you to designate specific start and end times for each day, as well as the number of hours in a day and the number of days in a week. You could set the workday to start at 9:00 a.m. and end at 6:00 p.m., assign nine hours to your workday (no lunch for you!), and end up with a 45-hour week, for example.

Setting schedule options

You can also modify the way in which Project enters task information. Click on the Schedule tab of the Options dialog box to change the default settings for entering tasks (see Figure 3-5). Here you determine the default unit of time for entering task durations (the default is days), work time (hours), and whether new tasks start on the project start date or the current date. For example, if you are working on a five-year project in which most tasks run months, not days, you may want to change the default setting for the Duration is entered in field. If you prefer to have any new tasks begin no earlier than the current date, you can adjust the setting for New tasks start on. As you gain experience in entering information, you will find ways to customize Project to match your work style. (Chapters 4 and 5 cover the other settings on this sheet.)

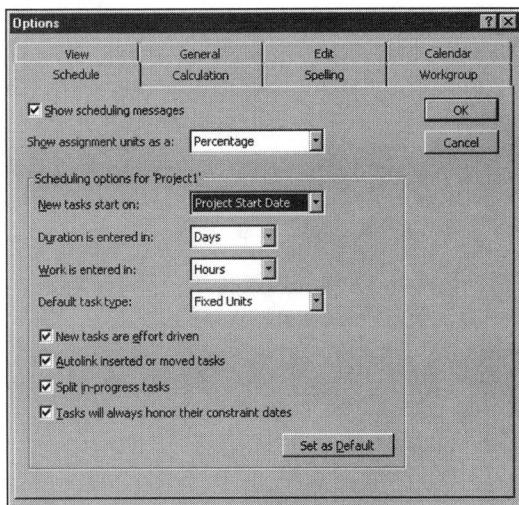

Figure 3-5: The Schedule tab is where you modify the default settings for entering tasks.

When you are satisfied with the settings in the Schedule tab, click on OK to close the Options dialog box.

Entering Tasks

To start building a project, enter the major steps to reach your goal in roughly the order in which you expect them to occur. (Don't worry if you're not quite accurate about the sequence of events; Project makes it easy to reorganize tasks in your schedule at any time.)

For the sample project — organizing a corporate annual meeting — follow these steps to create your first task: booking the meeting space.

1. Click on the Task Name column in the first row of the Gantt table.

2. Type **Book Meeting Space**. The text appears in the entry bar above the Gantt table.

3. Click on the check mark button to the left of the entry bar to accept the text.

Tip

You can also accept an entry in a cell by pressing a directional arrow key on your keyboard to move to another cell, clicking on another cell with your mouse pointer, pressing Enter, or pressing Tab.

Notice that information is starting to appear in your schedule (see Figure 3-6). For example, Project lists the task name in the Task Name column and makes a corresponding entry in the Duration column. (Remember the default setting in the Schedule tab of the Options dialog box? The default length of new tasks is one day.) According to the Start column, the task begins today; in addition, a task bar reflects the one-day duration of the task graphically.

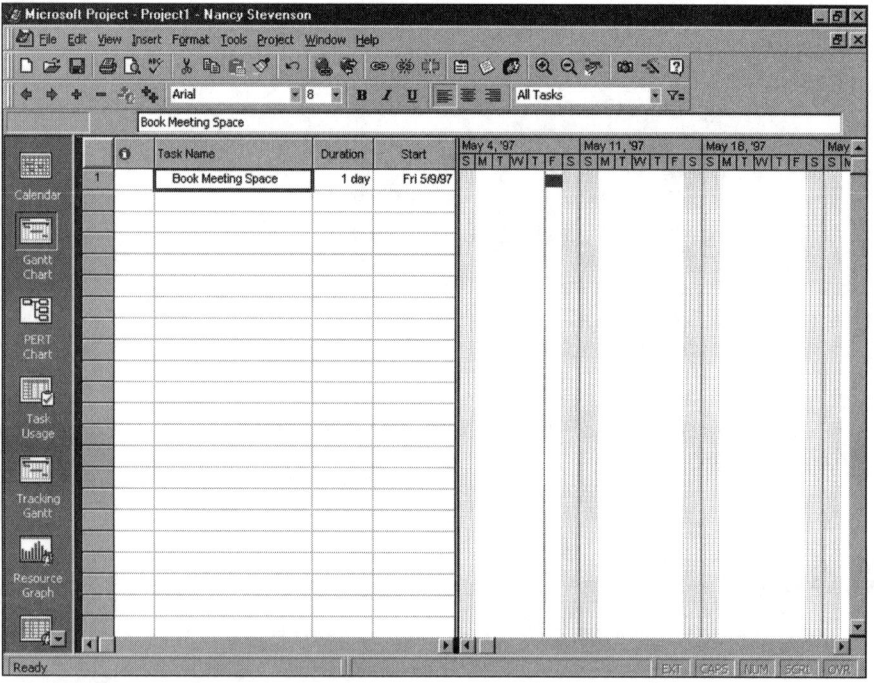

Figure 3-6: The task begins on the project start date automatically, though you could use the Options dialog box to change it to start on the current date.

If you use the scroll bar at the bottom of the Gantt table to move to the right, you see the Finish date entry. Because this task is a one-day task, it will be completed by the end of the day.

Using either your mouse pointer or the down-arrow key on your keyboard, move to the second row in the Task Name column and enter this task: **Schedule Speakers**. Then enter the following tasks in the next four rows: **Arrange for Audio/Visual Equipment**, **Order Food**, **Send Invitations**, and **Mail Annual Reports**. Your schedule should now look like the schedule in Figure 3-7.

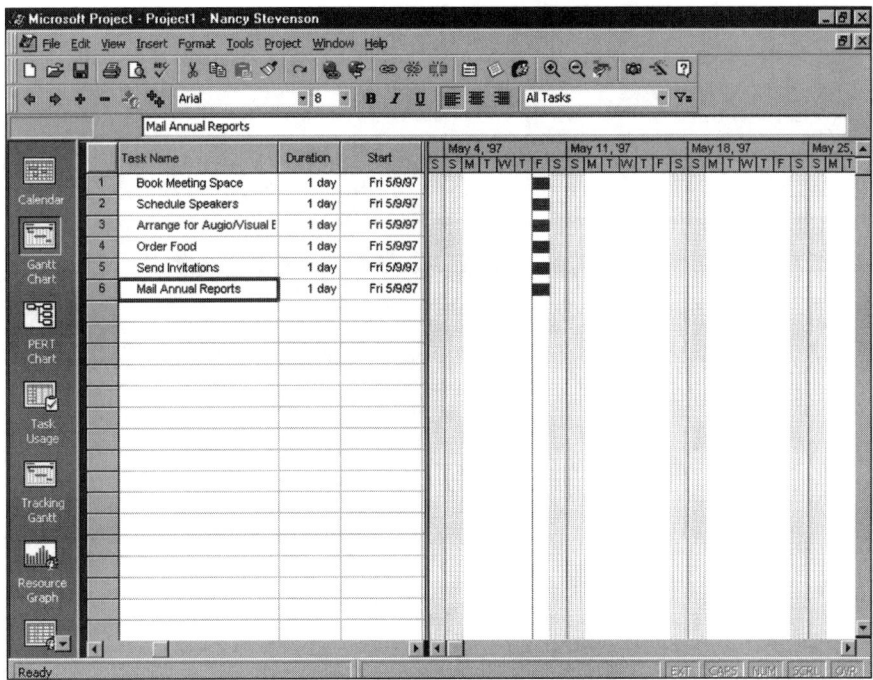

Figure 3-7: Note that each task is the same length by default, and each begins on the project start date.

Adding Subtasks

After you enter the major tasks in your project, you can begin to flesh out the details by adding *subordinate tasks,* also referred to simply as *subtasks.* When you add subtasks, the upper-level task becomes a *summary task.* Summary tasks and subtasks provide an easy-to-apply outline structure to your schedule.

Project's outline approach also enables you to display and print your project information with various levels of detail. For example, with only summary tasks showing, you see a higher-level overview of the project that you might want to present to management. On the other hand, you could reveal the details of only one or two phases of a project so that you can discuss those tasks with the people who will be performing them. The outline structure gives you a lot of flexibility in working with your schedule.

When you insert a new task, it appears above the currently selected task. Begin by adding subtasks under the *Book Meeting Space* task. Follow these steps to insert a new task:

1. Click on the task *Schedule Speakers*.

2. Choose Insert⟿New Task. Row 2 becomes a blank row, and all the other tasks move down one. Your cursor rests in the new task row.

3. Type **Request purchase order** and click on the check mark button to accept the new task.

4. Click on the Indent button on the Formatting toolbar (it looks like a right-facing arrow) to indent the subtask, as shown in Figure 3-8.

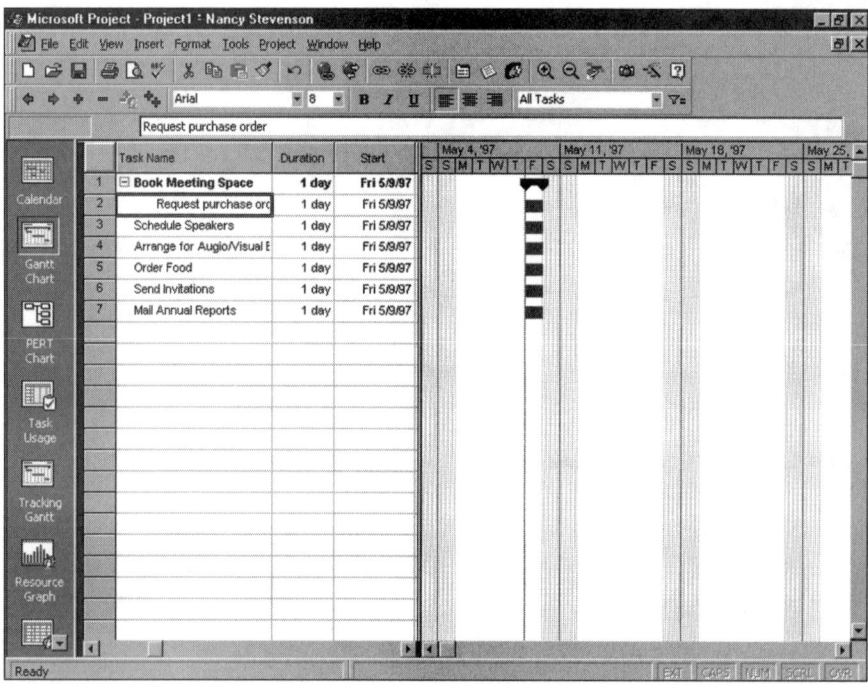

Figure 3-8: The summary task now appears in boldface type.

Note   Summary tasks appear in boldface and subtasks in normal type by default; however, some people like to differentiate these task types even more. In traditional outlining you sometimes vary the capitalization of items depending on their level; for example, you can capitalize the first letters of all the words in the summary tasks (headline style) and capitalize only the first letter of the first word in the subtasks (sentence style), as in this example. The choice is yours; however, if you decide to use some special effect as you enter text, be consistent so others looking at your schedule can recognize your system. And if others will work on your schedule, make sure that they follow the formats you have established.

Notice that the summary task now displays a solid black line on the Gantt chart with a downward arrow shape marking its beginning and end. When a task becomes a summary task — that is, it contains subtasks — the timing of the summary task reflects the total amount of time required to complete the subtasks. If a task has a duration assigned to it and you make it into a summary task, the timing of the subtasks overrides the assigned duration. If you change the timing of a subtask, the summary task duration changes to reflect the change.

You can add other subtasks by following these steps:

1. Click on the task *Schedule Speakers*.

2. Press Insert on your keyboard (which is a shortcut alternative to using Insert⇨New Task). A new blank row appears.

3. Type **Confirm space** and click on the check mark to accept the new task. The new task comes in at the same level of indentation as the task above it.

4. Click on the task Schedule Speakers.

5. Press Insert.

6. Type **Order Flowers** and click on the check mark button to accept the new task.

The second new task has also come in at the subordinate level. To move the task higher in the outline hierarchy, you could simply use the Outdent button on the toolbar, but try using your mouse to move it.

1. Move your mouse over the task Order Flowers until the cursor becomes a two-way pointing arrow.

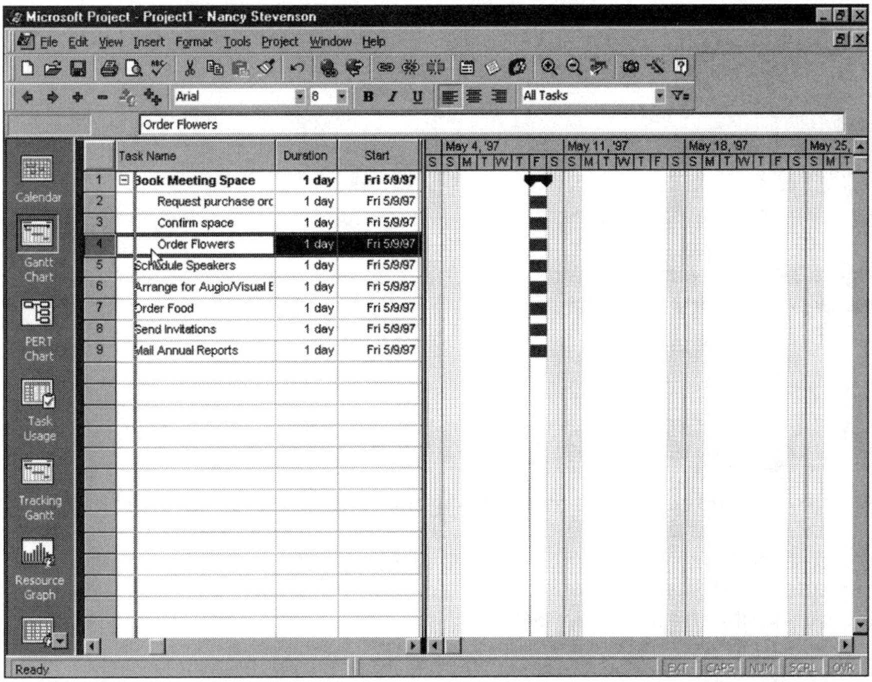

Figure 3-9: You can use your mouse to drag tasks in or out in the outline hierarchy.

2. Click and drag the task to the left until a thick gray line indicates that it is lined up with the upper-level tasks in the outline (see Figure 3-9).

3. Release the mouse button to complete the move.

Your schedule now looks like the schedule in Figure 3-10. Adding details is as simple as inserting new tasks wherever you want them and then moving them in or out in the outline structure.

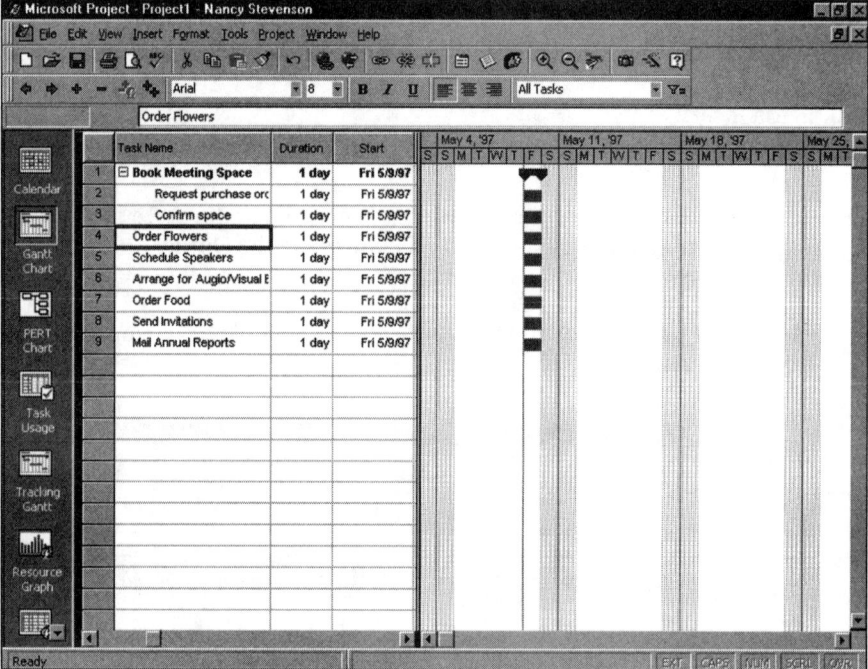

Figure 3-10: The outline structure lets you see summary and subtasks as manageable chunks of work.

Working with the Project Outline

After you build the outline, reorganizing the sequence of individual tasks is easy. You can also manipulate the outline to show more or less detail about your project. Outlining features work the same way in many software products; for example, Word for Windows, PowerPoint, and Project, all Microsoft products, have the same outlining tools and features.

Moving tasks in an outline

To move tasks in an outline, you can either use the cut and paste functions from the keyboard or perform a drag and drop with your mouse.

One important thing to remember is that although you can move tasks wherever you like, when you move a summary task, its subtasks move with it. Also, to move a subtask on its own to another location in the outline, you first have to promote (outdent) it to the highest task level.

Moving subtasks up one level can be a little tricky. For example, to move the task *Request purchase order* under the task *Order Food*, you must first promote *Request purchase order* to the highest level. When you do so, however, the other subtask under *Book Meeting Space* (that is, *Confirm space*) becomes subordinate to *Request purchase order*. Moving the upper task also moves its subordinate. The solution is to promote the *Confirm space* task so that it is no longer subordinate, move the *Request purchase order* task where you wish, and then go back and indent *Confirm space* to be subordinate, once again, to the *Book Meeting Space* task. In the beginning this process is a little confusing, so you should get some practice by trying the steps that follow.

Tip

To move a summary task on its own, you must first promote all its subtasks to a higher level.

Try reorganizing tasks using both the toolbar tools and your mouse by following these steps:

1. Click on the ID number for the task *Order Flowers*. The entire row is highlighted.

2. Click on the Cut tool on the Standard toolbar.

3. Click on the ID number for the task *Send Invitations*. The row is highlighted.

4. Click on the Paste tool on the Standard toolbar. The task *Order Flowers* appears in its new location above the task Send Invitations.

5. Place your cursor over the subtask name, *Request purchase order,* until the pointer becomes a double-arrow.

6. Click and hold down your mouse button while you drag the task to the left, promoting it in the outline hierarchy. Your schedule now looks like the schedule in Figure 3-11.

7. Click on the task *Confirm space*; hold down your mouse button and drag the task to the left to outdent it.

8. Click on the ID number to the left of the task *Request purchase order*.

9. Hold down your mouse button while you drag the task *Request purchase order* to below the task *Order Food*. A gray line indicates the new position as you drag.

10. Click on the Indent button on the Formatting toolbar to make the task subordinate.

11. Click on the task *Confirm space* and click on the Indent button.

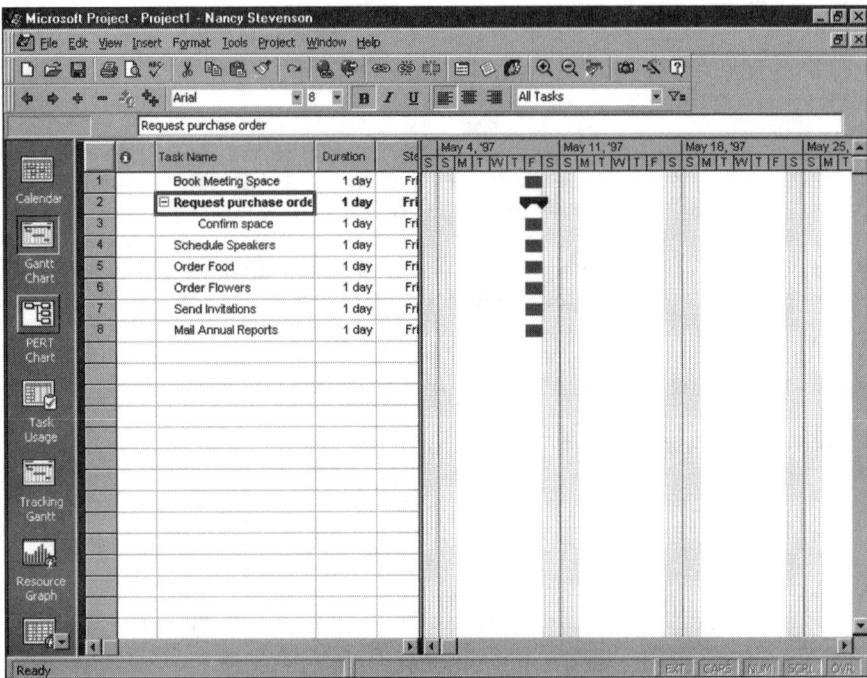

Figure 3-11: When you outdent a task, you may shift the hierarchy structure of subtasks beneath it.

Your schedule now has two tasks with subtasks beneath them (see Figure 3-12). As you can see, moving subtasks around your outline can be a little cumbersome. However, don't despair — in a well-planned outline, you are much more likely to move summary tasks and their subtasks as a unit.

Tip

One other solution to moving a subtask without taking other subtasks with it is to move the designated task to the bottom of the list of subtasks before outdenting it. This approach saves you the step of outdenting subsidiary subtasks.

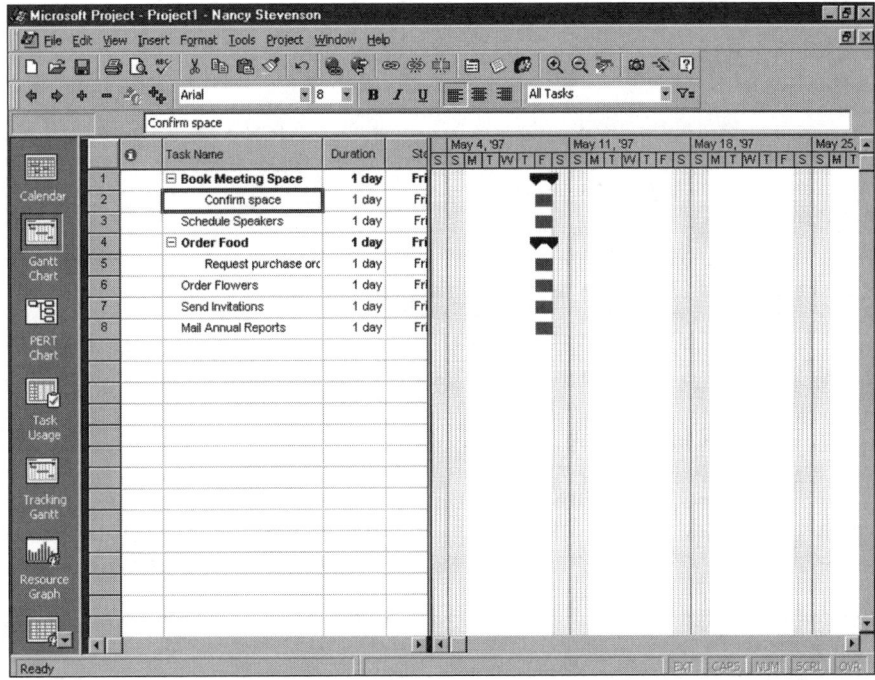

Figure 3-12: *Book Meeting Space* and *Order Food* have subtasks beneath them.

Copying tasks

Copying tasks is also simple to do and can come in very handy while building a project outline. For example, if you were entering tasks in a project to test various versions of a compound to see which works best as a fixative, you might repeat the same series of tasks — Obtain compound sample, Test in various environments, Write up test results, Analyze results, and so on — several times. Instead of typing those tasks 10 or 20 times, you can save time by *copying* them.

You can copy tasks two ways:

✦ Select a task by clicking on its ID number. Then hold down the Shift key while you drag your mouse up or down to select other tasks. With the tasks selected, you can use the Edit⇨Copy and Edit⇨Paste commands (or their corresponding tools on the Standard toolbar) to copy the set of tasks to another location.

Tip

Remember, to copy a summary task and its subtasks, you need only select the summary task and copy it. Project automatically copies the summary's subtasks for you.

✦ Copy a task by clicking on its ID number to select it; then hold down the mouse button and the Ctrl key while you drag the task to another location. Release the mouse button to complete the copy.

If you have several repetitive phases of a project, such as the development and production of several models of a single product, consider creating a macro to copy and paste sets of tasks to build your schedule. Macros are discussed in detail in Chapter 17.

Displaying and hiding tasks

One of the great strengths of the outline structure is that it enables you to view your project at different levels of detail by expanding or collapsing the summary tasks.

In Figure 3-12 a small box with a minus sign appears to the left of each summary task. This symbol indicates that not all subtasks are in view. If you click on the minus sign, any subtasks disappear from view and a plus sign appears next to the summary task name. The plus indicates that the task is associated with some hidden detail tasks. Click on the plus sign to reveal the "hidden" subtasks.

You can also select a task and use the Hide Subtasks or Show Subtasks buttons on the Formatting toolbar to hide or display subtasks. The Show All Subtasks tool is also useful for quickly expanding all the detail tasks in your schedule.

How many levels of detail can an outline have? Just about as many as you need. For example, the schedule shown in Figure 3-13 has several levels of detail regarding the annual meeting example. Any task that has subtasks also has the plus and minus mechanism for displaying or hiding them.

Using too many levels of outline indentation (usually more than three or four) makes it hard to see your entire schedule onscreen. In fact, a very detailed project outline may indicate that you need to rethink the scope of the project and break it into smaller, more manageable projects.

You can use the hide and show features of the outline to focus on just the amount of detail you wish. You can take the same schedule in Figure 3-13, for example, and show just the highest level of detail for a report to management to summarize project activity, as shown in Figure 3-14.

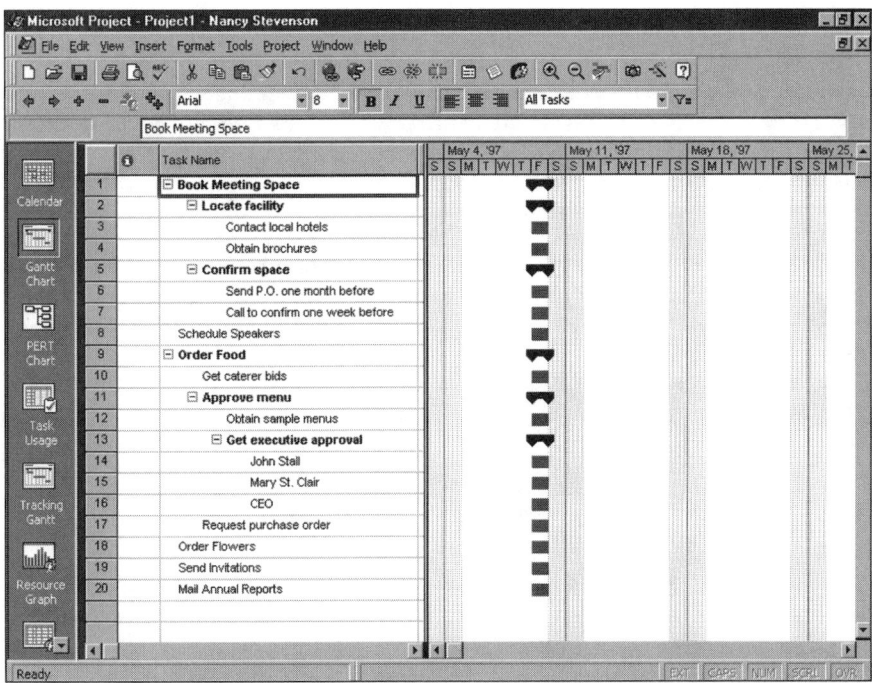

Figure 3-13: You can expand or collapse any task that has a subtask.

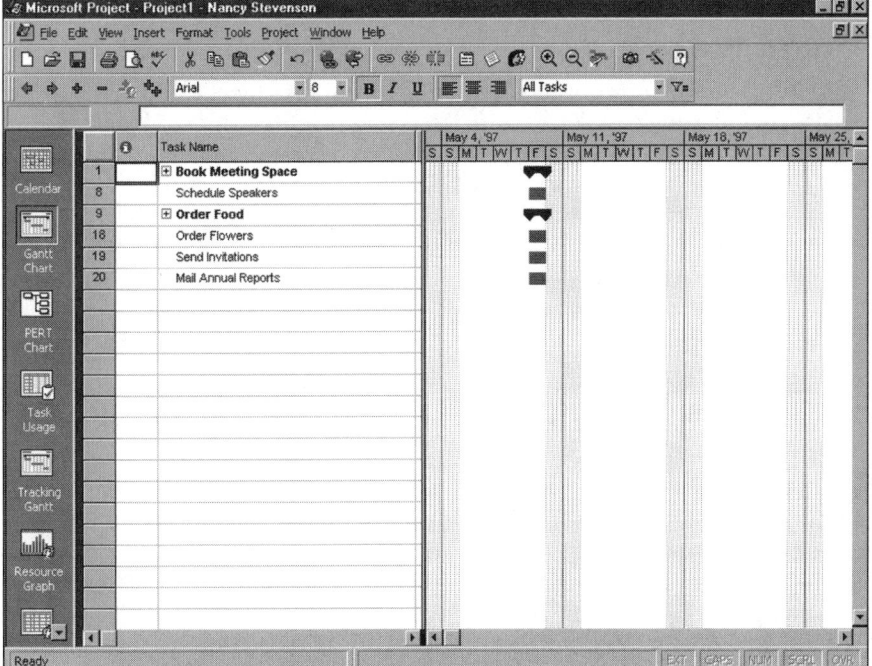

Figure 3-14: The detailed tasks are now hidden. But the plus symbols and the summary-style task bar indicate that more is here than meets the eye.

Getting Help

As you begin to build tasks in a schedule, you're likely to have questions about using Project that Project's Help system can answer. Project's Help is similar to the Help feature in other Windows products. If you've used any Microsoft Office product, the Help environment in Project will be very familiar. Figure 3-15 shows the Help menu.

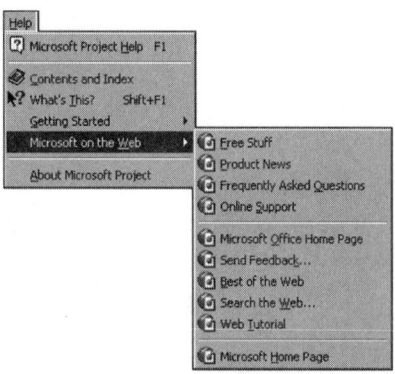

Figure 3-15: Microsoft on the Web is a rich source of additional support and information.

The following sections cover some of the most useful Help features: Contents, Index, and Find.

Using the Help tabs

The Contents and Index option on the Help menu takes you to the familiar Help Topics window shown in Figure 3-16. Descriptions of the three tabs follow.

✦ **The Contents tab:** Lists topic areas that you can open, level by level, until you reach the specific information you require. This feature is similar to working your way through a table of contents in a book to find a particular topic.

✦ **The Index tab:** Provides a searchable index of topics and subtopics. Like a book index, you can look up a specific term or phrase by finding it in an alphabetical listing.

✦ **The Find tab:** Enables you to search for words and phrases used within Help topics. Find uses a search engine and a Help database to conduct its searches.

The Index tab

The Index tab shown in Figure 3-16 enables you to type in a specific topic and then display information about it. Follow these steps to locate information on Project's outlining feature. (If you haven't already opened the Contents and Index area of Help, do so now by choosing Help➪Contents and Index and then selecting the Index tab.)

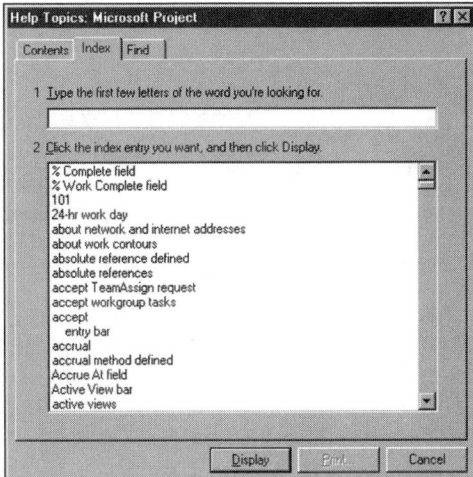

Figure 3-16: The Index tab is the default
selection in the Help Topics dialog box.

1. Type the letters **ou**. Help moves you to the first topic beginning with those letters, which is *outdent inserted projects*.

2. Type the letters **tl**. Project narrows down to the topic, *outline a project*. This "quick pick" functionality enables you to type only as many letters as Project needs to identify the topic. You can also use the scroll bar and mouse to select topics.

3. Click on the topic *outlines*, which is now visible in the Help dialog box, lower down in the list.

4. Click on the Display button at the bottom of the Index tab dialog box. A Topics Found dialog box appears, as shown in Figure 3-17.

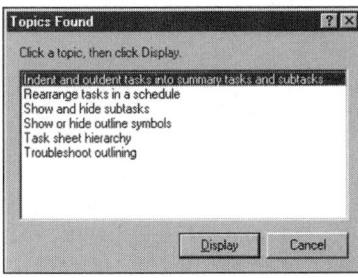

Figure 3-17: Several subtopics might
exist for any topic in the Help Index.

5. Click on Display to read Help information for the first topic in this list. Figure 3-18 displays detailed information about topic selected in Figure 3-17.

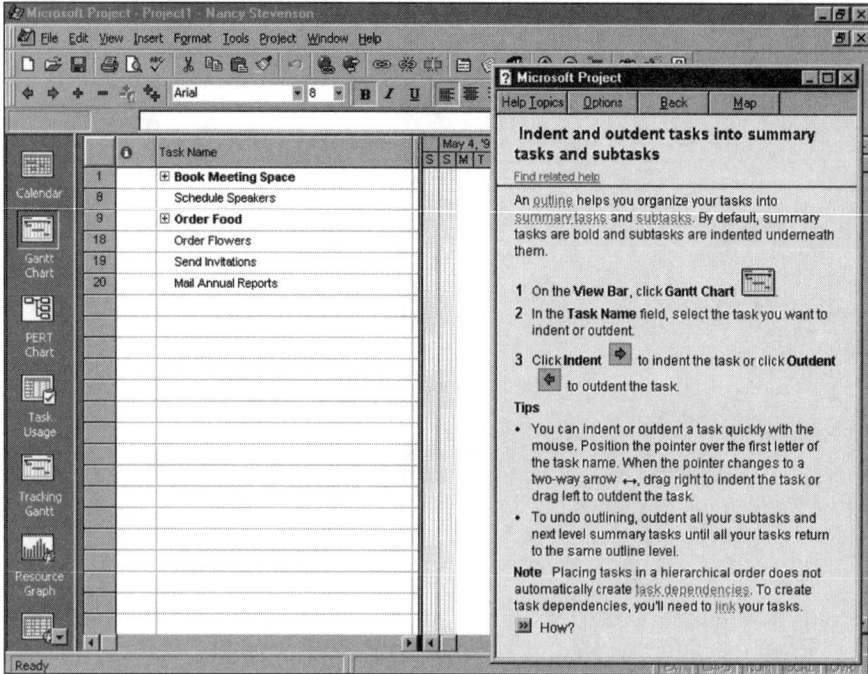

Figure 3-18: You may have to move through two or three layers of subtopics to get to a Help information screen.

Note

Help information often contains steps required to complete a procedure. In addition, a Find related help hyperlink takes you to related topics when you click on that text. Finally, the Help text might contain hyperlink text, a button to show you how to accomplish some task, and even demos.

The Contents tab

Figure 3-19 shows the second tab of the Help Topics dialog box: Contents. You can use this tab to locate information by general topic areas. When you open any of these topics, Help takes you to a list of subtopics. By narrowing down these subtopics, you eventually get to the information you want.

The Contents tab is simply a way to get help if you know the general topic you want to learn about but perhaps aren't familiar enough with the terminology to type a specific phrase or term in the Index. The Contents tab and the Index tab often end up at exactly the same information screen. For example, if you select the topic Creating a Project Hierarchy Using Outlining, double-click to display subtopics, and then select the subtopic Indent and outdent tasks into summary tasks and subtasks, the Contents tab displays the same information as the Index tab displayed in the earlier example.

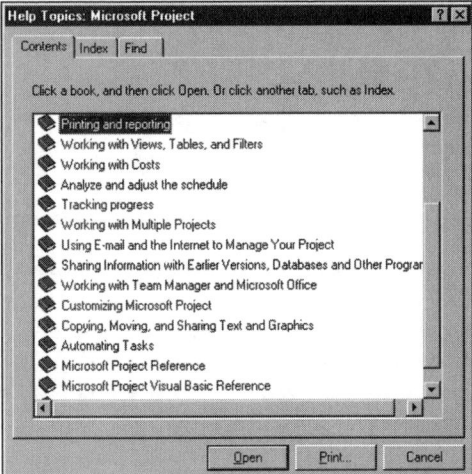

Figure 3-19: The Contents tab provides general topic areas to help you locate what you need.

Tip

Use the buttons across the top of the Help information screen to return to the Help Topics; go Back to the previously displayed screen; display Options for printing the topic, placing a bookmark on it, or keeping the Help window displayed as you work; or display a Map of the project management process.

The Find tab

When you select the Find tab of the Contents and Index portion of Help for the first time, you see the Find Setup Wizard dialog box shown in Figure 3-20. This wizard sets up the Help database based on keywords from the Project Help file.

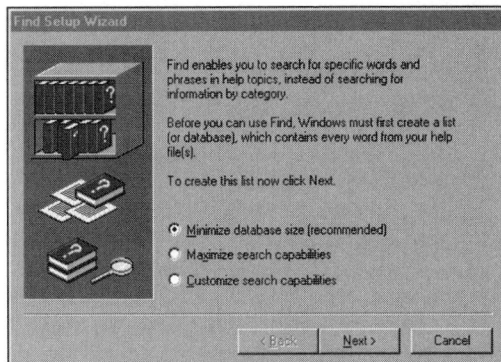

Figure 3-20: The Find Setup Wizard dialog box appears the first time you use the Find feature.

Project offers you three options for setting up the Help database so that you can decide how much memory to devote to this feature. The Minimize database size option creates a database of almost 1,700 entries, more than enough to answer most of your questions. If, however, you're using Project from a network server and memory is of less concern, you might prefer to use the largest Help database. The custom setup enables you to select any of the four Project documentation databases to use for the Find database.

Whichever option you choose, when you finish the setup according to the wizard's instructions, you see topics listed on the Find tab, shown in Figure 3-21. Although the Find tab and the Index tab are similar (you type in a specific term to initiate the process in both tabs), the Find tab also enables you to select by topic. In addition, you can use the Options button on the Find tab to access a slightly more sophisticated search feature in which you can set parameters for matching a term.

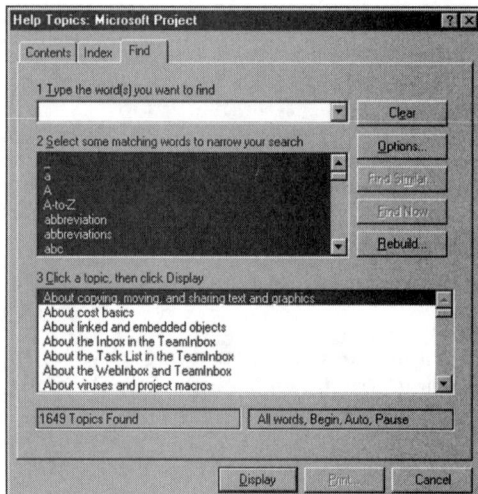

Figure 3-21: The Find tab enables you to set parameters for matching a term.

Tip

If you decide at a future date that you'd like to set up the Find database in a different way, click on the Rebuild button on the Find tab.

Getting started

Two of the three Help options that you see on the Welcome screen when you first open Project — Watch a Quick Preview and Learn While You Work — are also available from a side menu when you choose Help⇨Getting Started. However, the Getting Started menu refers to the latter option as Create Your Project. The third choice on the Getting Started menu (which is not available on the Welcome screen) is Microsoft Project 101: Fundamentals.

Note An additional Help option on the Welcome screen, called Navigate with a Map, is a simple map of the flow of activity in a typical project. This feature, which is helpful to new Project users, is not available in the Getting Started menu.

Quick Preview

Quick Preview, shown in Figure 3-22, is a survey of what you can do with Project. Offering more of a marketing spin on features than hard information, Quick Preview is probably the least useful of the three Getting Started options.

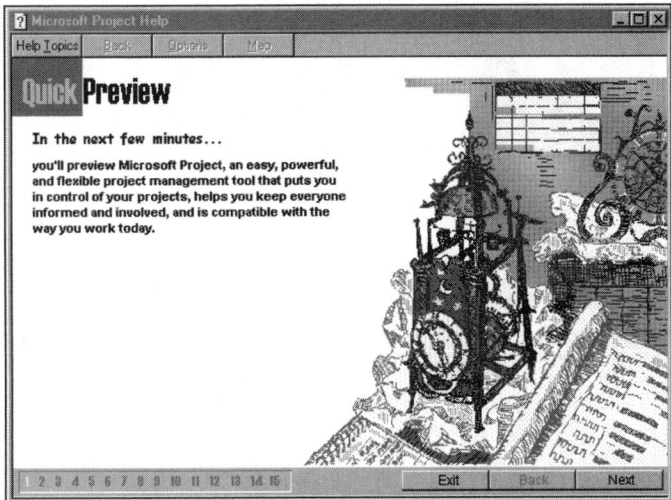

Figure 3-22: Click on the Next button to move through the 15 Preview windows.

Create Your Project

Create Your Project — which is labeled Learn While You Work on the Project Welcome screen — demonstrates Project's key schedule-building procedures. Topics such as those in the Create Your Project index shown in Figure 3-23 serve as a visual guide through the processes you use to add tasks, resources, and dependencies to your project.

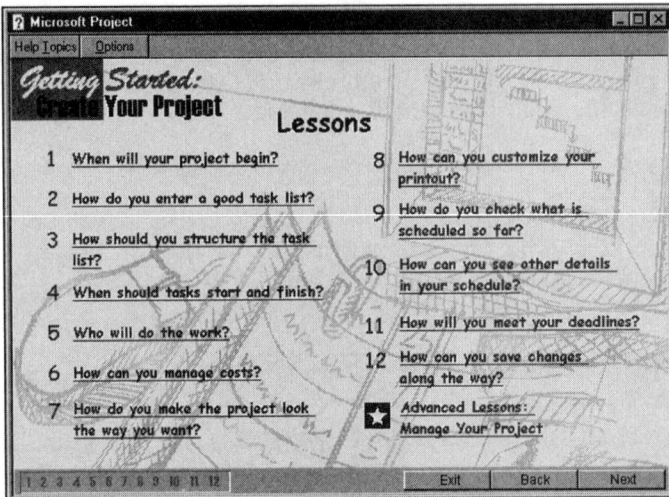

Figure 3-23: Various demonstrations are available through the Create Your Project Help files.

Microsoft Project 101: Fundamentals

Perhaps the most helpful feature in the Getting Started side menu is Microsoft Project 101: Fundamentals. This primer on computerized project management (see Figure 3-24) contains a great deal of useful information.

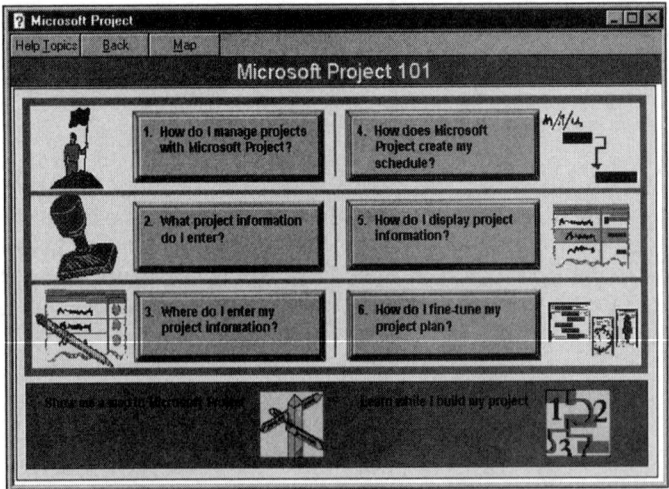

Figure 3-24: Project 101 is a primer on computerized project management procedures.

When you select one of these topics, Project displays a general statement about the topic. Click on the Show me button for a demonstration of how to use the various features (see Figure 3-25).

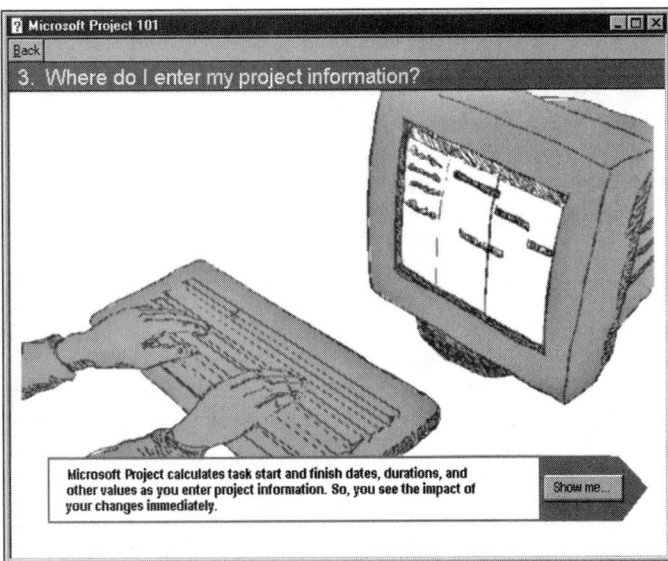

Figure 3-25: Click on the Show me button to see how Project accomplishes various tasks.

Finding online help

In its software with the 97 designation, Microsoft made a significant move to providing direct links to the World Wide Web. If you're connected to the Internet, Microsoft's effort is good news — it opens up a world of support; information; and even freeware, shareware, or products-for-a-price that work along with Project.

On the CD-ROM The companion CD-ROM includes several products from third-party vendors; for more information about these products or to contact their creators, go to

```
http://microsoft.saltmine.com/project/resultsCompany.asp
```

Figure 3-26 shows the Microsoft on the Web side menu, which offers many choices for online help.

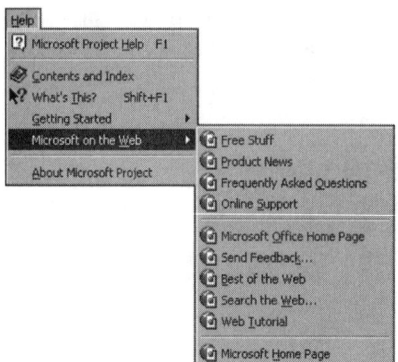

Figure 3-26: Microsoft provides an onramp to the information superhighway with its Microsoft on the Web option.

Check out the Free Stuff item to get things like downloadable graphics, macros, or templates that you can use with Microsoft products. If you have a technical question about Project, you can either access Online Support or go to the Microsoft Office Home Page and look up articles on the various Microsoft products. To go to any Web page, click on its name in the Help menu. Assuming you're set up to access the Internet, the Internet Explorer (built into Windows 95) takes you wherever you need to go.

Note   Another fast way to find an answer to your questions is by looking at Frequently Asked Questions. If your problem has already been discussed here, you won't have to wait a day or two for a response from technical support.

Saving Project Files

Of course, you should always save your work frequently. With the often mission-critical information centralized in a Project file, frequent saving is even more important. When saving Project files, you have the option of setting up protection for them. You can also save your files as *templates*, that is, files on which you can base other schedules.

Saving files

To save any Project file for the first time, choose File⇨Save — or click on the Save tool on the Standard toolbar. You specify where to save a file and the format you want to use in the File Save dialog box (see Figure 3-27).

You can use the arrow next to the Save in field to display a hierarchy of your computer's drive and directory organization. Click on the Up One Level tool to move up one level in that hierarchy. To create a new folder for this file, move to the directory where you want Project to create it and then use the Create New Folder tool.

Up One   Look in   Create New
Level   Favorites   Folder   List   Details   Properties

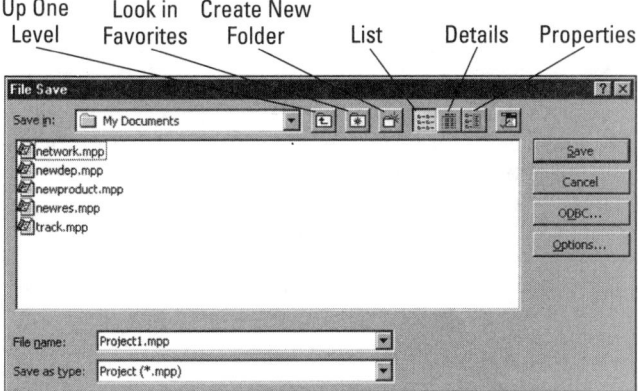

Figure 3-27: Use the familiar buttons and tools of the File Save dialog box to tell Project where to save a file and what format to save it in.

Note

After you save a project for the first time, you can simply click on the Save button to save the file without bringing up this dialog box. If you want to change a setting or save the file with a new name, choose File⇨Save As to display this dialog box again.

By default, Project saves files with the extension .mpp. If you want to save a file in a different format, for example, as a Microsoft Access database (.mdb), you can select that format in the Save as type drop-down list. After you enter a filename and designate its location, click on Save to save the file.

Saving files as templates

One format in the Save as type selection is Template. Template files have an extension of .mpt. The template feature is especially useful in project management because your projects are often similar to ones that precede or follow them. A template file saves all the settings you may have made for a particular project, such as formatting, commonly performed tasks, and calendar choices. Keeping template files on hand can save your coworkers (and yourself) from having to reinvent the wheel each time you want to build a similar project.

You may ask, Can't I just save my previous project's file with a new name and use that for my next project? Yes, you can, but after you track progress on tasks, opening that final project file and stripping it back to its baseline settings is a cumbersome routine.

A much better approach is to save the initial schedule as a template on which you can build new schedules. To create a new schedule, simply open the template and save the file as a standard Project file with a new name.

Protecting files

Some projects are as top secret as an FBI file. In this case some people within the organization, and certainly people from outside the organization, should not have access to the details. If your projects fit this mold, you need a way to keep your Project files secure from prying eyes. You can set a measure of security by clicking on the Options button in the File Save dialog box to display the Save Options dialog box in Figure 3-28.

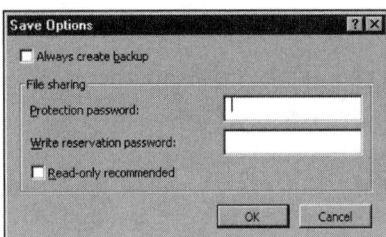

Figure 3-28: Don't use your phone extension, birthday, or spouse's name as a password — such passwords are much too easy to break!

Assigning the Protection password protects the file from being opened. Only someone with the assigned password can open a file protected this way. The Write reservation password, on the other hand, permits anyone to open the file without a password, but as a read-only file (that is, no one else can make any changes to the file). Finally, if you check the Read-only recommended option, Project displays a message recommending that anyone opening the file not make changes to it. This choice doesn't actually prevent someone from making changes, however.

Both the Protection and Write reservation passwords are case sensitive. If you assign a password of JoeS, you cannot open the file if you type in joes.

Closing Project

When you're finished working in Project, you can save and close your files as described previously and then use one of the following methods to close the program:

✦ Click on the Close button in the upper-right corner of the Project window.

✦ Choose File⇨Exit.

If you haven't saved any open files, Project prompts you to do so.

Summary

In this chapter you start to build your first project by creating summary tasks and subtasks. You learned about the following aspects of Project:

✦ Gathering the data you need to begin creating your schedule

✦ Entering Project information and setting up some calendar defaults

✦ Creating summary and subtasks

✦ Working with the outlining hierarchy to move, copy, and display subtasks

✦ Using the Help system to search for information, access demonstrations of basic project management information, and obtain online help

✦ Saving files and closing Project

In Chapter 4 you start to add details about task types, add timing, and establish relationships among your tasks.

✦   ✦   ✦

Building Tasks

Hessiod, that classic Greek project manager, once said, "Observe due measure, for right timing is in all things the most important factor." You could do worse than to use this truism from around 700 B.C. as your personal project management mantra today. When it comes to projects, timing is, indeed, all.

In Chapter 3 you created several tasks and used the outlining feature of Project to organize them. But every task in your schedule has the default length (one day), and they all occur on the very same day. In essence, you have listed the steps to get to your goal, but with no related timing, your schedule might as well be a shopping list.

You have to add *durations* to your tasks; that is, you must establish exactly how long (or how many hours of effort) each task will take. But timing consists of more than determining how many hours, days, or weeks it takes to complete each task. Timing for your project becomes clear only when each task has a set duration and when the relationships among the tasks, called *dependencies*, are established. Only then can you accurately predict how much time you will need to complete the project.

Establishing Timing for Tasks

Your boss asks how long it will take to write that report, and you tell her it'll be about a week. Your coworker calls and asks when you'll finish repairing the computer network, and you tell him it'll take another day. You make estimates about task durations every day. You know your own business, and you're probably pretty good at setting the timing for everyday tasks based on many factors.

Exactly how do you figure out the timing for a task in a project? The method is virtually identical to the seemingly automatic process you go through when someone asks you how long it will take to complete a task, such as placing an order for materials. For example:

1. You estimate that you will spend about 40 minutes to do the research and perform the calculations to determine how many square feet of lumber you'll need for the job.

2. You consider how long the actual task — placing a phone order for materials — will take. This duration could be a matter of only minutes, but if you factor in playing a few rounds of phone tag, you might want to allow half a day.

3. You also think about what's involved in getting a purchase order. With your system, cutting a purchase order can take up to four days. Some of that time requires your presence, but most of it consists of waiting.

So how long is your task? You could say you need exactly four days, four hours, and 40 minutes; but just to be safe, you should probably allow about five days. In addition, Project has some issues specific to task timing that you need to understand to estimate task durations accurately.

To pad or not to pad?

Although most people agree that delays are inevitable and that you should allow for them, people who schedule projects accommodate these delays in various ways.

Some schedulers build in extra time at the task level, adding a day or two to each task's duration — just in case. Unfortunately, padding each task may leave you with an impossibly long schedule, and may suggest to your boss that you're not very efficient. Why should it take two days to run a three-hour test? It doesn't — but because you know that setting up the test parameters properly the first time is an error-prone process, you allow a couple of workdays to complete the testing. Just make sure your boss understands that you're building a worst-case scenario; when you bring the project in early, he or she will be glad to share the praise.

Some project managers add one long task, maybe two weeks or so in duration, at the end of the schedule, and they name it something like Critical Issues Resolution Period. This type of task is a placeholder that covers you if individual tasks run late. This approach can help you see how the overall time left for delays is being used up as the project proceeds. For example, if the final two-week task is running a week late because of earlier delays, you know that you've eaten up half the slack that task represents.

One other approach is to build a schedule with best-case timing. Then you can document any problems and delays that occur, and request additional time as needed. In the case of a project that has little time to begin with, you may have to work this way. However, best-case timing sets you up for potential missed deadlines.

Which approach should you use? Possibly a combination. For example, try building a best-case schedule. If the completion date is one week earlier than your deadline, by all means add a little time to the tasks most likely to encounter problems, such as those performed by outside vendors.

By default, Project creates *resource-driven* tasks. Here's a simple example. You have to plant a tree. One person needs two hours to plant a tree. If you add another person (another resource), together they need only one hour to complete the task. That is, two resources, each putting in an hour of effort, complete the two hours of effort in only one hour. With resource-driven scheduling, when you add resources, the task timing becomes shorter; if you take resources away, the task takes longer. The resource-driven method is Project's default scheduling method. In Project 98 the setting for resource-driven tasks is called *fixed-unit tasks*.

New Feature

Caution

The reduction of time required on a resource-driven task is strictly a mathematical calculation in Project: Ten people get work done in one-tenth the time of one person. However, whenever two or more people work on a task, the time savings are seldom so straightforward. You also need to factor in the time for those people to communicate, miscommunicate, hold meetings, and so on.

Fixed-work and fixed-duration tasks

Another type of task in Project is the *fixed-duration task*. The number of resources does not affect the timing of this type of task. If you want to allow a week for a committee to review the company's new ad campaign, no matter how many people are on the committee, the task has a fixed duration. You cannot shorten the task's duration by adding resources to it. In fact, adding people to the review process might lengthen it. Their effort has no impact on getting the work done more quickly.

New Feature

Fixed-work task is another new setting in Project 98. You set the duration of the task, and Project assigns a percentage of effort sufficient to complete the task in the time allotted for each resource you assign to the task. For example, if you assign three people to work on a one-day task, Project would say that each person should spend 33 percent of his or her time on the task to complete it in one day.

Effort-driven tasks

In addition to knowing how the three task types — fixed work, fixed duration, and fixed unit — relate to resource effort, you should understand the purpose of the Effort driven check box on the Advanced tab of the Task Information dialog box. (See the following section, "Assigning Task Timing.")

Selecting the Effort driven check box tells Project to modify the percentage of total work allocated to each resource based on the number of assigned resources if the number of resources changes. The work required to complete the task remains the same, but Project redistributes the work equally among all assigned resources. This setting is the default when the task type is fixed work. Effort driven is also the default for fixed-unit and fixed-duration tasks, but you can turn off this box if you don't want Project to change the original allocation of work.

In Chapter 5 you'll learn more about how resource assignments modify task timing. For now, the durations you assign to tasks in this chapter are, by default, resource driven. Therefore, a five-day task requires five days of resource effort to complete.

Assigning Task Timing

You now have an idea of how to estimate task timing and you understand the basics of how task timing relates to effort expended on the task by resources. The actual process of assigning durations is quite simple. To assign a duration to a task, you can use one of three methods:

✦ Enter a duration in the Duration column of the Gantt table

✦ Use your mouse to drag a task bar to the required length, or use a dialog box to enter duration information

✦ Use the Task Information dialog box to enter and view information about all aspects of a task, including its timing, constraints, dependencies, resources, and priority in the overall project

Entering task durations

Follow these steps to assign durations from the Task Information dialog box:

1. Display the Gantt Chart view. Double-click on a Task Name to open the Task Information dialog box shown in Figure 4-1.

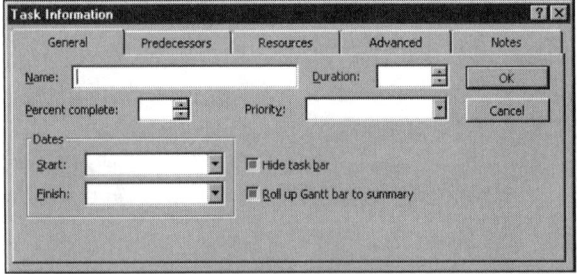

Figure 4-1: If you double-click on an already entered task name, that name appears in the Name field in this dialog box; if you double-click on a blank task name cell, you can fill in the name here.

2. Use the arrows in the Duration field to reduce or increase the duration from the default setting of 1 day. Each click changes the duration by one day.

3. Click on the Duration field and highlight the current entry to enter a duration in increments other than a day.

4. Type a new duration using the following abbreviations: m for minutes, h for hours, and w for weeks.

5. Click on OK to establish the task duration. For example, the Gantt chart task bars in Figure 4-2 reflect the new task lengths.

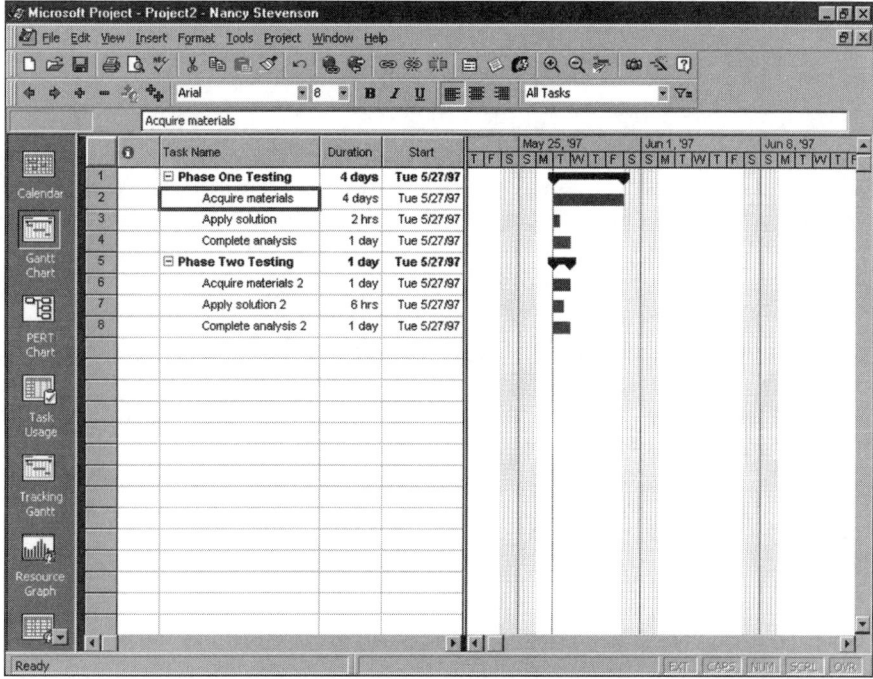

Figure 4-2: Task bars become more meaningful after you assign durations.

To enter a task's duration on the Gantt table, simply click on the Duration column and type in the duration.

New
Feature

You can type in a duration in a few different ways. For example, Project 98 recognizes all three of the following entries as three weeks: 3 w, 3 wks, 3 weeks. Recognition of multiple abbreviations is a new feature in Project 98.

Start and finish versus duration

You could use the Start and Finish fields in the Task Information dialog box to set a start date and finish date for the task, rather than entering a duration. However, if you use the Start and Finish dates, Project uses only working days in that date range. If you enter a duration, Project calculates the beginning and end of the task, taking into account weekends and holidays for you. These two methods could have different results.

For example, suppose you have a four-day task that starts on December 23, 1998. Here's how that week looks on a calendar:

Mon	Tues	Weds	Thurs	Fri	Sat	Sun
22	23	24	25	26	27	28

December 25, 1998, falls on a Thursday. If you entered 12/23/98 as the Start date and 12/26/98 as the Finish date, Project would calculate that as a three-day task (assuming that your company closes for Christmas) with work on December 23, 24, and 26. However, if your Duration field entry is four days, the calculated Start and Finish dates would be 12/23/98 and 12/29/98, respectively, taking into account both the Christmas holiday and a weekend. The work days in this instance would be December 23, 24, 26, and 29.

If a task has immutable timing, for example, a Christmas celebration on Christmas day, use the Start and Finish fields; if you're definite about how many work days a task will require, but not on which days it will occur, use the Duration field to set timing and let Project calculate the actual work dates based on your company's calendar.

Finally, follow these steps to adjust a task's duration using your mouse and the task bar:

1. Place your mouse pointer on the right edge of a task bar until the cursor becomes a vertical line with an arrow extending to the right of it.

2. Click and drag the bar to the right. As you do, Project displays the proposed new task duration and finish date (see Figure 4-3).

3. Release the mouse button when the duration you want appears in the information box.

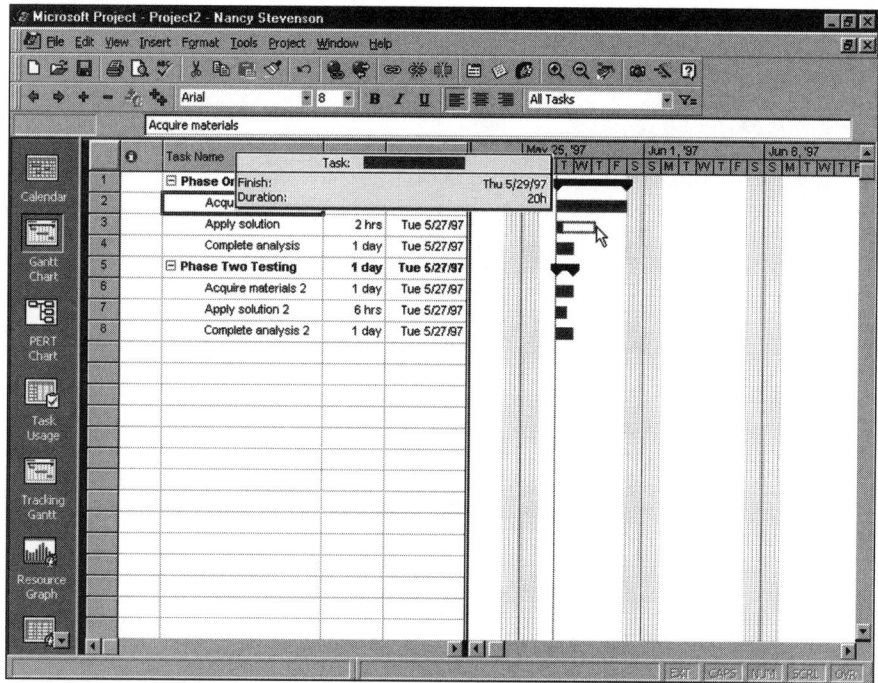

Figure 4-3: If you're a visually oriented person, dragging task bars to change durations might be the best method for you.

Creating milestones

Milestones are tasks of zero duration. Managers often use milestones to mark key moments in a project, such as the completion of a phase or approval of a product or activity. To create a milestone, you simply assign a duration of zero to a task. The symbol for a milestone on the Gantt chart is a diamond shape. For example, the diamond in the Gantt chart in Figure 4-4 indicates that the End of Testing task is a milestone.

You can mark any task as a milestone on the Advanced tab of the Task Information dialog box. If you do, the task duration won't change to zero; however, the element representing it in the Gantt chart changes from a bar, reflecting the task's duration, to a milestone diamond symbol, representing the task as a moment in time.

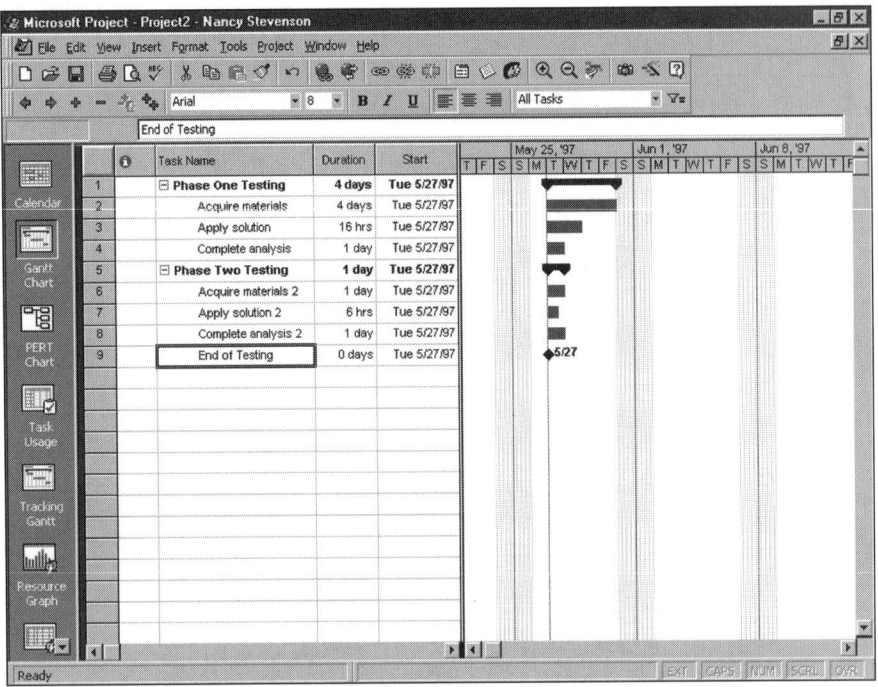

Figure 4-4: A milestone is typically a task of no duration: it simply marks a noteworthy point in your project.

Timing for summary tasks

How do you assign durations for summary tasks? You don't. Remember, summary tasks simply roll up the timing of their subtasks. Therefore, they don't have any timing of their own. If three subtasks occur one right after the other and each is three days long, the summary task above them takes nine days from beginning to end. If you open the Task Information dialog box for a summary task, most timing settings are grayed out, indicating that they're not available.

Using Recurring Tasks

Projects quite often have tasks that occur on a regular basis: weekly staff meetings, quarterly reports, or monthly budget reviews are examples of these *recurring* tasks. Rather than have you create, say, 20 or so, weekly staff-meeting tasks over the life of a five-month project, you can use Project's recurring-task feature. This feature enables you to create the Meeting task once and assign it a frequency and timing. Follow these steps to create a recurring task:

1. Choose Insert⇨Recurring Task to open the Recurring Task Information dialog box shown in Figure 4-5.

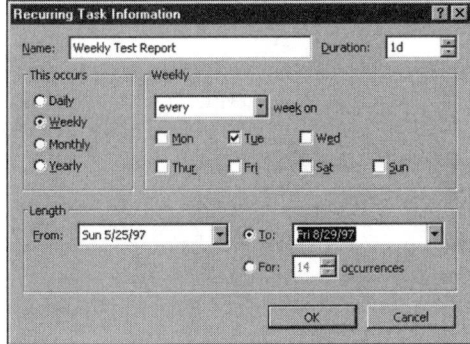

Figure 4-5: If a task occurs at regular intervals during the life of a project, you can save yourself time by creating it as a recurring task.

2. Set the task duration in the Duration field; does the meeting run for two hours, or does a report take a day to write? Enter that here.

3. Set the occurrence of the task by selecting one of the This occurs control buttons: Daily, Weekly, Monthly, or Yearly. Depending on the occurrence you select, the timing settings to the right of the control buttons may change. Figure 4-6 shows the Monthly settings.

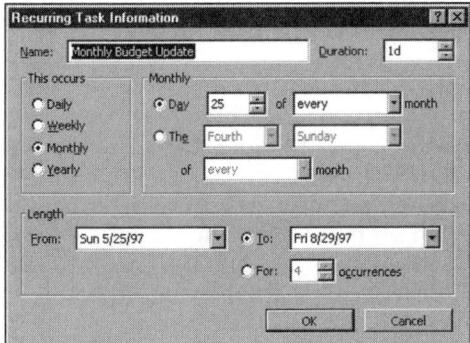

Figure 4-6: Daily, Weekly, Monthly, and Yearly occurrences require you to make slightly different choices.

4. Select the appropriate settings for the occurrence frequency. For a Weekly setting, place a check next to the days of the week on which you want the task to occur; for example, the task in Figure 4-5 occurs every Tuesday. For Monthly or Yearly, set the day of the month on which you want the task to occur; the task in Figure 4-6 occurs of Day 25 of every month.

Note

The only choice for a Daily task is whether you want it to occur every day or only on scheduled workdays. For example, if you want to schedule a computer backup for every day of the week — regardless of whether anyone is at work — you could have the task occur every day. Your MIS department is responsible for automating the process so that it occurs even when nobody is at work.

5. Set the Length of time during which the recurring task should occur by entering From and To dates. If you need to repeat a test weekly for only one month of your ten-month project, you could set From and To dates that designate a month of time; the For field would automatically show four occurrences of the weekly task (or in a longer month, possibly five).

Tip

If you click on the For control button and enter the number of occurrences, Project calculates the date range required to complete that many occurrences of the recurring task. This method can be useful if one of these events falls on a holiday: Project schedules one extra occurrence of the task to compensate. For a weekly staff meeting, you probably don't want to schedule an extra meeting because of a holiday; you can just skip that meeting or schedule it on a different day. On the other hand, if you must repeat a test 16 times during the project cycle, you would want to add one more occurrence of the test task to compensate for the holiday. Therefore, you need to set the number of occurrences, rather than the time range.

6. Click on OK to create the task. Project creates the appropriate number of tasks and displays them as subtasks under the summary task, Meeting; note the recurring task symbol in the Indicators column of the Gantt table in Figure 4-7.

Note

The symbol next to each Weekly Test Report task in the schedule in Figure 4-7 represents a task with a timing constraint applied to it. Project applies this constraint automatically as you enter settings for the recurring task. If you move your mouse pointer over one of these symbols, you can see an explanation of that constraint; for example, the first Weekly Test Report task has a Start No Earlier Than constraint, based on the timing you set in the Recurring Task Information dialog box. The first recurring task can start no earlier than the From date entered there, and each task occurs weekly thereafter. You learn more about how to set timing constraints in the next section.

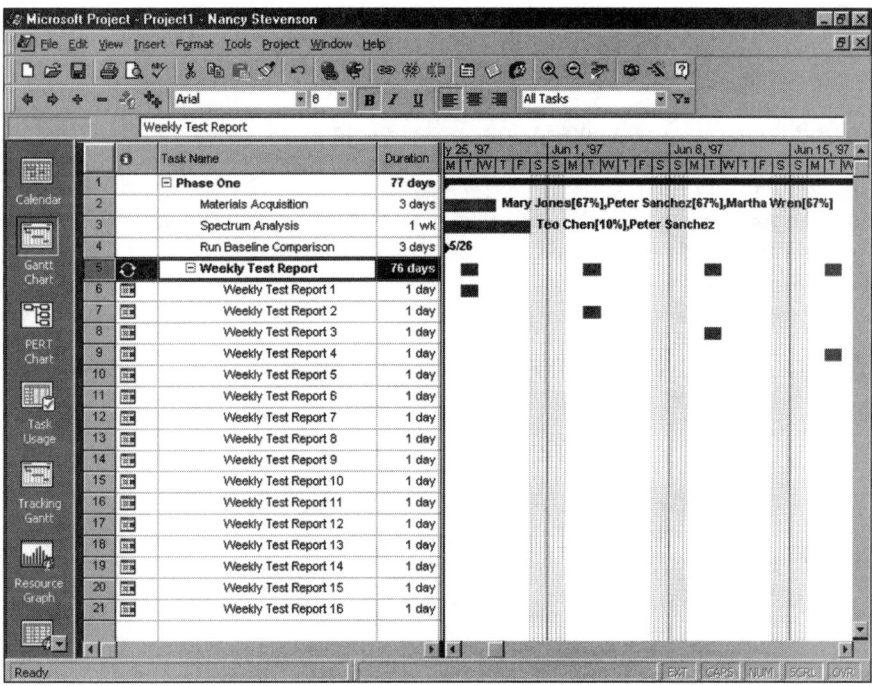

Figure 4-7: Task bars appear for each occurrence of the recurring task in the Gantt chart.

Establishing Constraints

Constraints affect the timing of a task relative to the start or end of your project or to a specific date. By default, all tasks you create are set to start As Soon As Possible. Barring any dependency relationships with other tasks (see "Establishing Dependencies among Tasks" later in this chapter), the task would start on the first day of the project. Other constraints are

✦ **As Late As Possible:** Forces a task to start on a date such that its end occurs no later than the end of the project

✦ **Finish No Earlier Than/Finish No Later Than:** Sets the completion of a task to fall no sooner or later than a specific date

✦ **Must Finish On/Must Start On:** Forces a task to finish or start on a specific date

✦ **Start No Earlier Than/Start No Later Than:** Sets the start of a task to fall no sooner or later than a specific date

Only the Must Finish On/Must Start On settings constrain a task to start or end on a particular date; all the other settings constrain the task to occur within a certain time frame.

You set constraints on tasks in your project using the Advanced tab of the Task Information dialog box, shown in Figure 4-8. Select a constraint type in the Type drop-down list. For all settings in the Type list other than As Late As Possible and As Soon As Possible, you have to designate a date by clicking on the arrow next to the Date field and choosing a date from the drop-down calendar that appears, or by typing in a date.

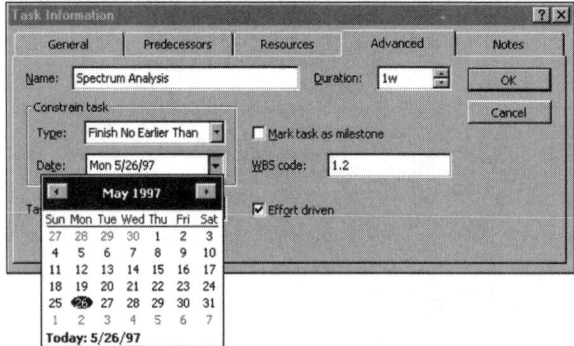

Figure 4-8: Click on the arrow next to the Type field to show the various constraints.

Here are some examples of situations in which constraints would be useful:

✦ In a project that involves preparing a new facility for occupancy, you want the final inspection of that facility to happen *as late as possible*.

✦ The approval of a yearly budget must *finish no later than* the last day of the fiscal year, ready to begin the new year with the budget in place.

✦ Billing of a major account must *start no sooner than* the first day of the next quarter so that the income doesn't accrue on your books this quarter.

✦ Presentation of all severance packages for laid off employees *must finish on* the day a major takeover of the company is announced.

You see how constraints and dependencies interact in establishing the timing of tasks in the section "Establishing Dependencies among Tasks" later in this chapter.

Manipulating the Gantt Chart to View Timing

After you enter several tasks and task durations, you'll probably want to manipulate the timescale in the Gantt chart to view information about these tasks using different increments of time. Here are the methods you can use to modify the appearance of items in your Gantt chart:

✦ You can adjust how much of the window is taken up by the Gantt table and how much is used by the Gantt chart by moving your mouse pointer over the divider line until it turns into two arrows pointing in opposite directions. Click and drag the divider to the right or left to adjust the percentage of the window taken up by the two panes.

✦ You can modify the width of columns in the Gantt table so you can see more columns onscreen by moving your mouse pointer over a column's right edge until you see the two-directional arrow cursor. Click and drag the column edge to the right or left to adjust its width.

You can double-click on the column heading and change the column width in the Column Definition dialog box that appears. This dialog box is also where you change the title and alignment of that title in the column.

✦ You can modify the increments of time displayed in the timescale itself either by double-clicking on the timescale or by choosing Format⇨Timescale. The Timescale dialog box shown in Figure 4-9 appears. You can change the units for both the major timescale (shown on the top) and minor timescale (shown just beneath the major timescale). These adjustments enable you to concentrate on a particular period in your project or to view larger increments with less detail. The Count field controls how many instances of the unit Project marks off on your Gantt chart.

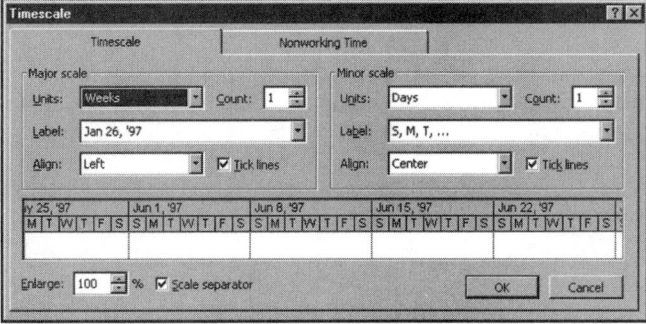

Figure 4-9: Adjust the units to display and how many to include in the Timescale dialog box.

Figure 4-10, for example, shows a major timescale in months and a minor timescale in weeks. The Count for each is 1: one month with each of its four weeks shown. If you change the Count for weeks to 2, the weekly timescale marks display in two-week increments, as shown in Figure 4-11.

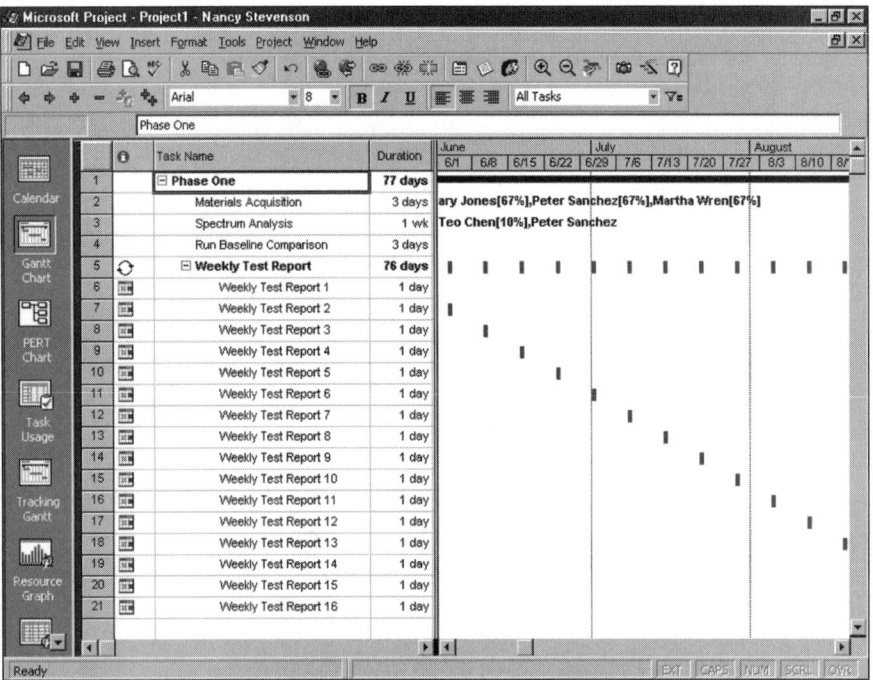

Figure 4-10: When you specify one week in the Count field of the Timescale dialog box, Project marks off every week on the minor timescale.

Tip

To shrink the timescale even more — that is, to see more of your project on screen — use the Enlarge setting in the Timescale dialog box. This setting enables you to view the timescale at a percentage of its full size.

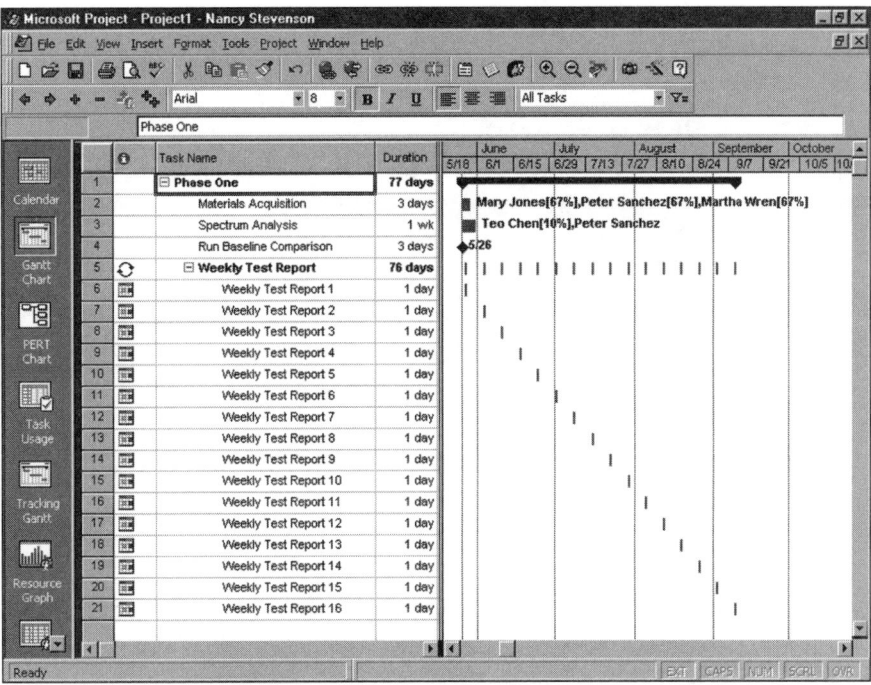

Figure 4-11: Changing the Count field for weeks to 2 causes Project to mark off weeks in two-week chunks.

Entering Task Notes

You can attach notes to individual tasks to remind you of certain parameters or details for the task. For example, if a task involves several subcontractors, you might want to list their contact information here so it's close at hand when you're working on the project schedule. Or use the Notes field to note company regulations relative to that type of procedure. When you add a note to a task, you can display the note onscreen and include the note in a printed report.

You can also attach notes to individual resources and to their assignments, as you learn in Chapter 5.

To enter a note for a task, follow these steps:

1. Double-click on a task to open the Task Information dialog box.

2. Click on the Notes tab to select it (see Figure 4-12).

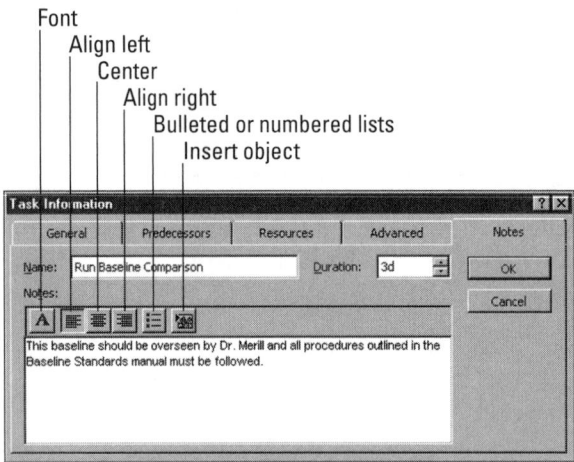

Figure 4-12: The Notes tab provides simple word processing–like tools for formatting your notes.

   3. Type your note in the area provided. You can use the tools identified in Figure 4-12 to format your note text.

   4. Click on OK to attach the note to your task.

A Note icon now appears in the Indicators column of the Gantt table, as shown in Figure 4-13. Move your cursor over this icon to display the note and any constraints applied to the task.

You can also print notes along with your schedule. To do so, follow these steps:

   1. Choose File➪Page Setup.

   2. Click on the View tab to display the settings shown in Figure 4-14.

   3. Click on the Print notes check box to have Project print notes for tasks.

   4. Click on OK.

You learn more about printing schedules in Chapter 6.

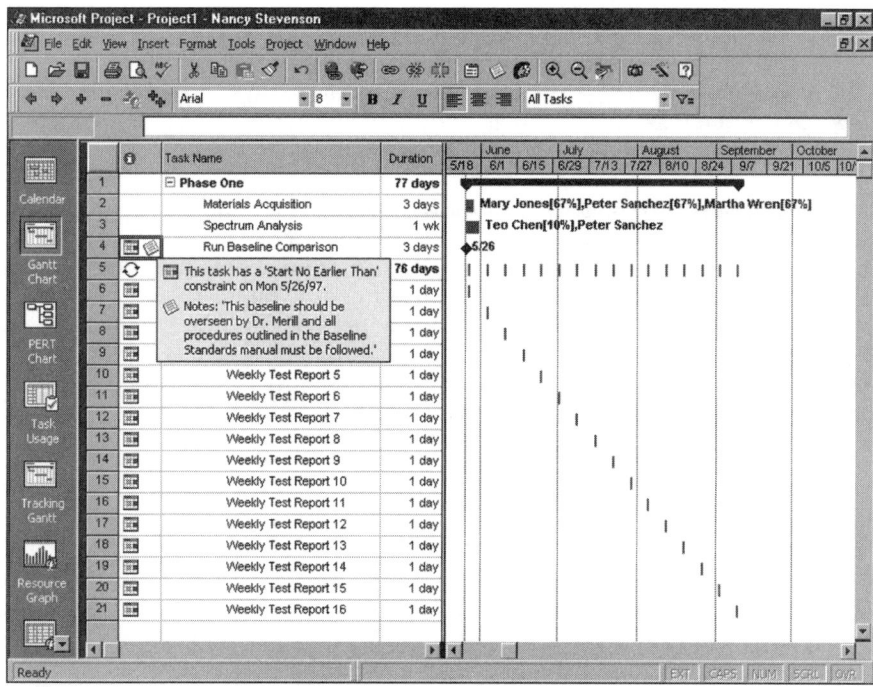

Figure 4-13: Project automatically adds an icon to the Indicators column for the task.

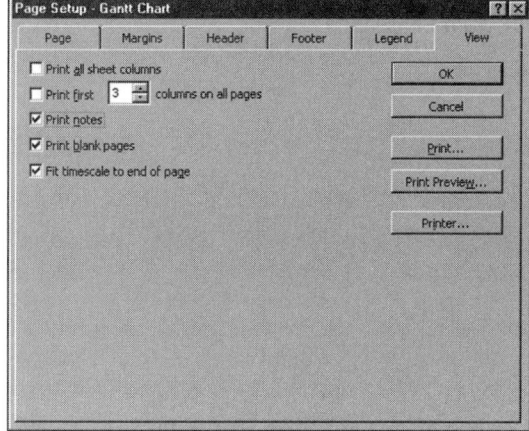

Figure 4-14: Notes appears as the right-most column in your Gantt table when you place a check next to Print notes.

Establishing Dependencies among Tasks

Whereas constraints tie tasks to the project start or end or to particular dates, *dependencies* tie tasks to the timing of other tasks in the project. Dependencies are central to visualizing the true length of a project.

Dependencies exist because all tasks in a project rarely can happen simultaneously; usually, some tasks have to start or finish before others can begin. Tasks overlap for many reasons: the inability of resources to do more than one task at a time, the lack of availability of equipment, or the nature of the tasks themselves (you can't start construction until you receive a construction permit). You can't really know the total time you will need to complete a project until you establish durations and dependencies. For example, a project that comprises five 10-day-long tasks with no dependencies among the tasks takes ten days to complete. But the same project with five 10-day-long tasks happening one after the other requires 50 days.

Understanding dependencies

A task that must occur before another task is a *predecessor* task. The task that occurs later in the relationship is a *successor* task. A task can have multiple predecessors and successors. Tasks with dependency relationships are *linked*. Gantt charts show these links as lines running between task bars; an arrow at one end points to the successor task. Some dependency relationships are as simple as one task ending before another can begin. However, some relationships are much more complex. For example, if you're moving into a new office and the first task is assembling cubicles, you don't have to wait until all the cubicles are assembled to begin moving in furniture. You might work in tandem, using the first morning to set up cubicles on the first floor. Then you can begin to move chairs and bookcases into the first-floor cubicles while the setup task continues on the second floor.

Understanding the interactions between constraints and dependencies

Both constraints and dependencies drive the timing of a task. Consider for a moment how constraints and dependencies might interact when you apply one of each to a task. Say that you have a task — to open a new facility — that has a constraint set so that it must start on June 6. You then set up a dependency that indicates the task should begin after a task — fire inspection — that is scheduled for completion on June 10. When you try to set up such a dependency, Project displays a Planning Wizard dialog box, like the one in Figure 4-15. This dialog box indicates a scheduling conflict. Project displays this dialog box when a conflict exists among dependencies or between constraints and dependencies.

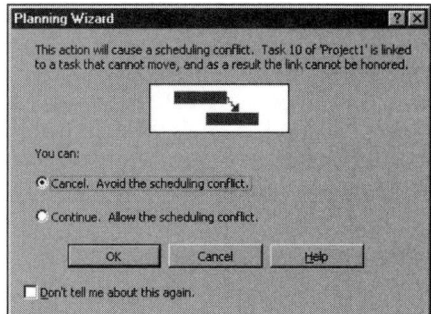

Figure 4-15: Multiple dependencies or a combination of dependencies and constraints can cause conflicts in timing.

If a conflict exists between a constraint and a dependency, the constraint drives the timing of the task; the task bar does not move from the constraint-imposed date. You can modify this functionality by choosing Tools➪Options. On the Schedule tab of the Options dialog box, deselect the Tasks will always honor their constraint dates check box. When you change this option, dependencies, rather than constraints, determine timing. (See Chapter 8 for more about resolving such timing conflicts.)

You can create dependencies in one of three ways:

✦ You can select two tasks and use a Link Tasks command on the Edit menu or Link Tasks button on the Standard toolbar. The first task you select becomes the predecessor in this relationship.

✦ You can open the successor task's Task Information dialog box and enter predecessor information on the Predecessors tab.

✦ You can use your mouse button to click on a predecessor and drag to create a link to a successor task.

Tip If you want to link a whole range of tasks to be consecutive (one finishes, the next begins, and so on down through the list of tasks), select the first task (predecessor), hold down the mouse button, and drag to select a range of predecessor tasks. Then use the Link Tasks button or Link Tasks command in the Edit menu to create a string of such relationships at one time.

Allowing for overlap and delays

Although many dependency relationships are relatively clear cut — Task A can begin only when Task B is complete, or Task C can start only after Task B has started — some are even more finely delineated. These relationships involve *overlap* and *delay,* or *lag* time.

The best way to understand these two concepts is to look at examples. Your project is to test a series of metals. The predecessor task is to apply a solution to the metal, and the successor task is to analyze the results. However, time can be a factor, so you want the analysis to begin only when several days have passed after the application of the solution. You build in delay between the finish of the first task and the start of the second. Figure 4-16 shows a relationship with some lag between two tasks; the line between the two tasks indicates the dependency, and the space between the bars indicates the gap in time between the finish of one and the start of the next.

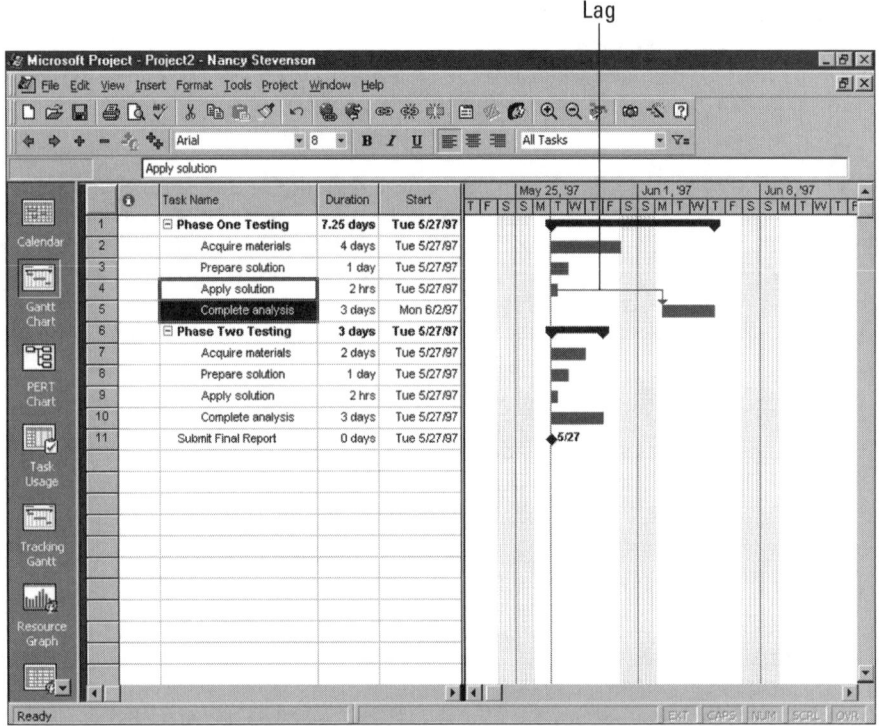

Figure 4-16: After you apply the solution, you must wait four days to analyze the results.

Another test in your project involves applying both a solution and heat. You want to start by applying the solution for three hours and then begin to apply heat as well. Notice the overlap between the tasks: the predecessor — applying the solution — begins at 8 a.m. and runs to 5 p.m.; the successor task — applying heat — begins three hours after the start of the predecessor. The project in Figure 4-17 has some overlap between tasks.

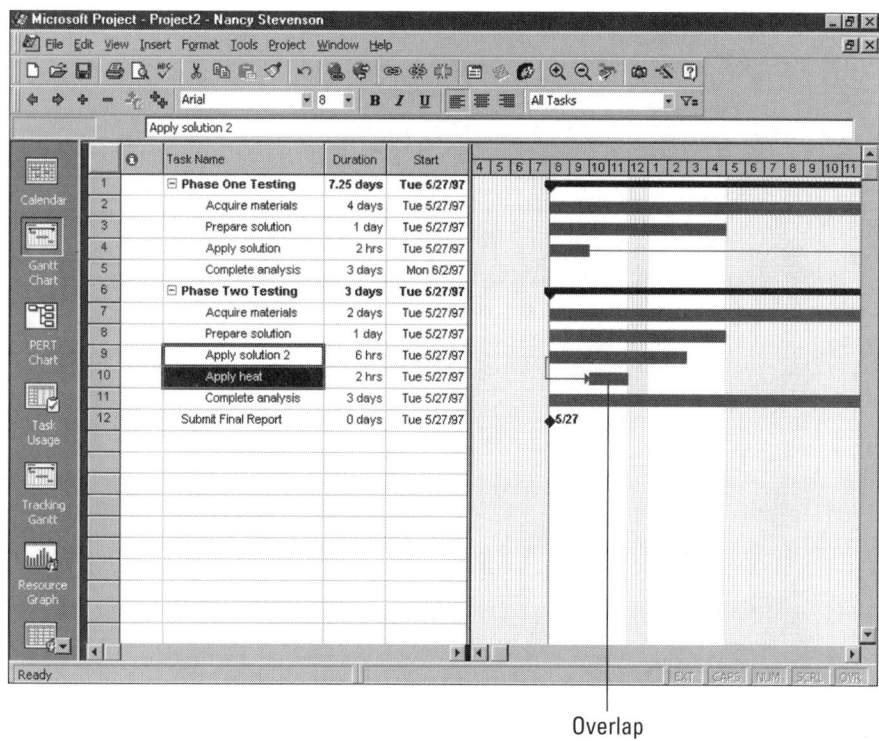

Overlap

Figure 4-17: Some overlap occurs between the application of the solution and the application of the heat in this testing project.

Note

Some people prefer to build a task to represent lag, rather than to establish a dependency relationship. For example, instead of placing a dependency between application of the solution and analysis, you could create a three-day-long task — Solution Reaction Period. Then create a simple dependency relationship between Solution Reaction Period and the analysis so that the analysis task won't begin until Solution Reaction Period is complete. Adding the lag tasks can generate a very long schedule with multiple tasks and relationships to track. But in a simpler schedule, this approach enables you to see relationships as task bars. You can try both methods, and see which works best for you.

Dependency types

Four basic dependency relationships describe the relationship between the start and finish of tasks. These dependency types are start-to-finish, finish-to-start, start-to-start, and finish-to-finish. You set these dependency relationships on the Predecessors tab of the Task Information dialog box, shown in Figure 4-18.

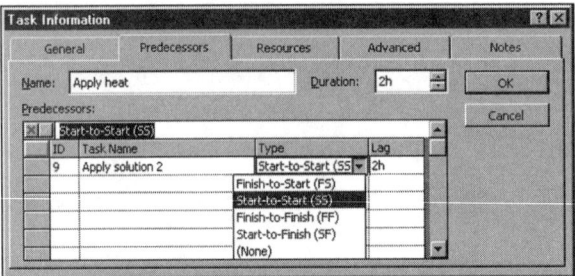

Figure 4-18: Four types of dependencies enable you to deal with every variable of how tasks can relate to each other's timing.

The first timing mentioned in each relationship name relates to the predecessor task and the second to the successor. Therefore, a start-to-finish dependency relates the start of the predecessor to the finish of the successor, and a finish-to-start relationship relates the finish of the predecessor to the start of the successor. Project refers to these relationships by their initials, such as SS for a start-to-start relationship.

Finish-to-start (FS)

A finish-to-start relationship is one of the most common types of dependencies and is, in fact, the only relationship you can create using your mouse or Link Tasks tool or command. The finish-to-start relationship is between the finish of one task and the start of another. Examples of this relationship are

✦ You must write a report before you can edit it.

✦ You must have a computer before you can install your software.

Figure 4-19 shows the FS relationship, where the successor task can start as soon as its predecessor is finished.

Start-to-finish (SF)

With the start-to-finish relationship, the relationship occurs between the start of one task and the finish of another. Here are some examples:

✦ You can finish scheduling production crews only when you start receiving materials.

✦ Employees can start using a new procedure only when they have finished training on it. If the use of the new procedure is delayed, you also want to delay the training so that it occurs as late as possible before the implementation.

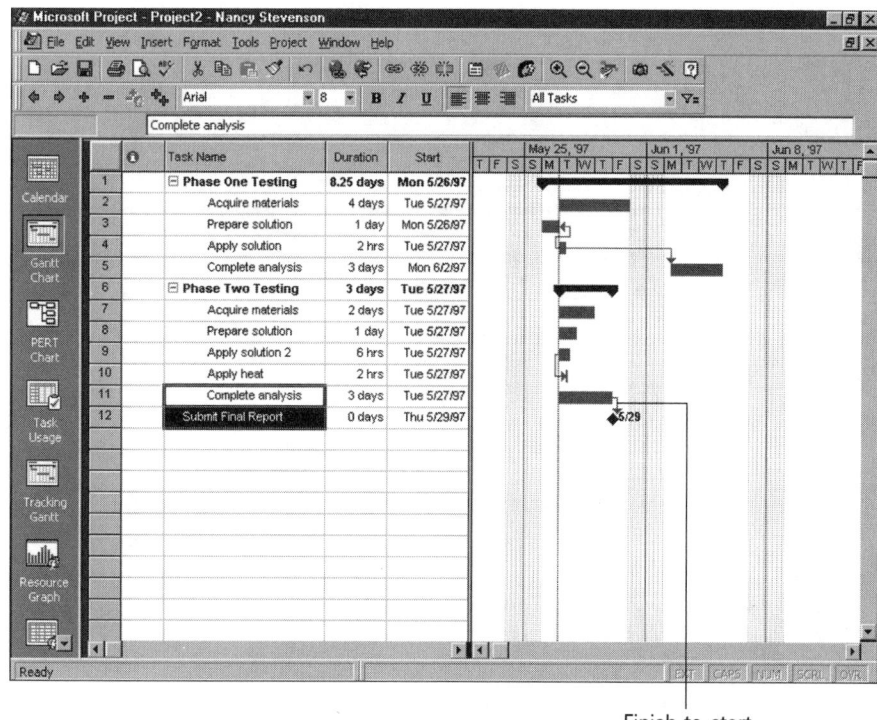

Finish-to-start

Figure 4-19: In the FS relationship, when you have finished the final analysis, you can submit the final report.

Note

Could you set up this start-to-finish example as a finish-to-start relationship? Not really. The idea is to have no delay between training and implementation. If you set the new procedure to start only when the training finishes, the new procedure could start any time after the training ends, depending on how other relationships might delay it. If the training task has to finish just before the other task starts, delays of the later task (implementation) also delay the earlier task. This fine distinction will become clearer when you see projects in action.

Figure 4-20 shows a start-to-finish relationship between preparing a solution and applying it. Assuming that you should apply the solution as soon as it's ready, you want to make sure the preparation finishes just before you start applying it.

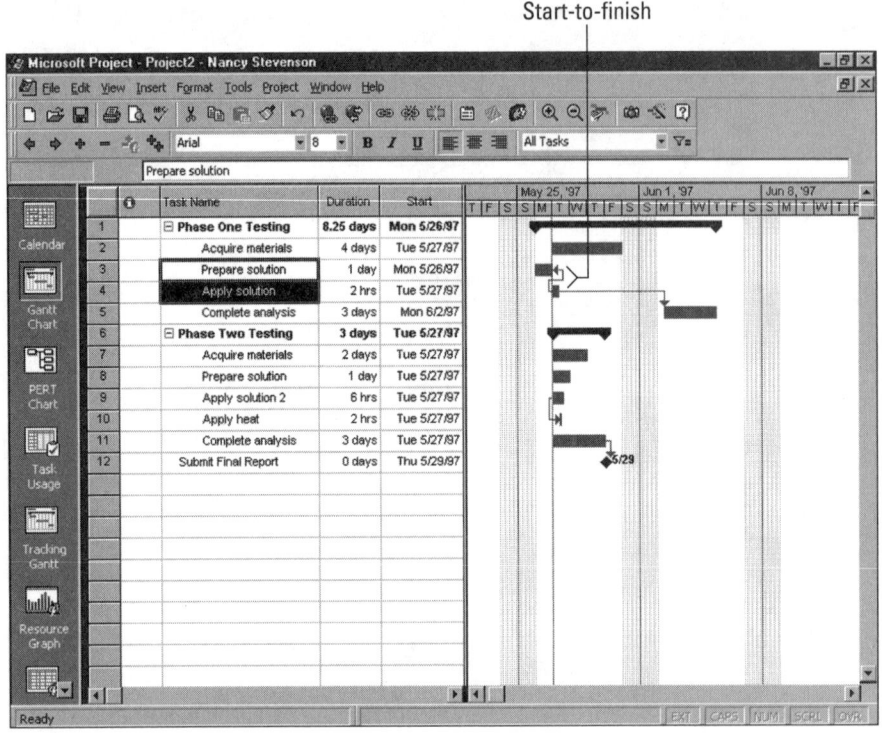

Figure 4-20: You can tell by the arrow on the line between these tasks that the timing of the start of Apply solution is driving the timing of the end of Prepare solution.

Start-to-start (SS)

The start-to-start relationship is between the start of the predecessor and the start of the successor, as with these tasks:

✦ When you start getting results in an election, you can begin to compile them.

✦ When the drivers start their engines, the flagger can start the race.

Figure 4-17 shows a start-to-start relationship with some built-in overlap.

Finish-to-finish (FF)

In the finish-to-finish dependency, the end of one task relates to the end of another. For example:

✦ You finish installing computers at the same time that you finish moving employees into the building so that they can begin using the computers right away.

✦ Two divisions must finish retooling their production lines on the same day so that the CEO can inspect them at the same time.

If the two phases of testing in Figure 4-21 must finish at exactly the same time, a finish-to-finish dependency guarantees that if one is delayed, the other also experiences a delay.

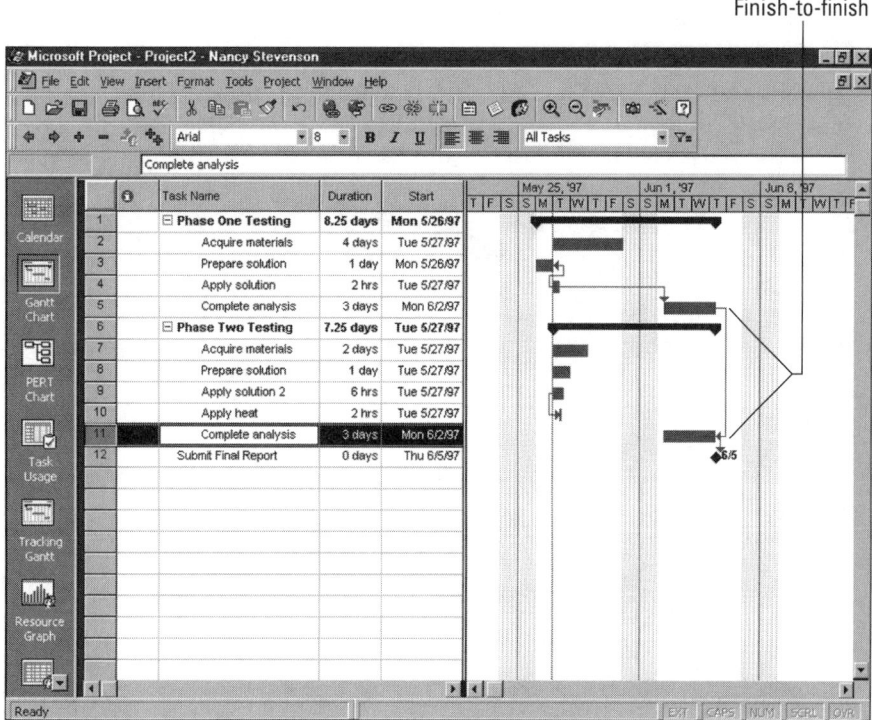

Figure 4-21: Whichever task has the later finish drives the timing of these two analysis tasks.

Establishing dependencies

As mentioned earlier, you can set dependencies in a few different ways. If you use the tasks on the Gantt chart to set dependencies, you must establish finish-to-start relationships. To establish more complex relationships, including delay and overlap, use the Task Information dialog box.

Note

You can set dependencies between two summary tasks or between a summary task and subtask in another task group, but not between a summary task and any of its own subtasks. Remember that if you set, say, a finish-to-start a relationship between a summary task and another task, all subtasks under the summary task must finish before the linked task can begin.

Using task bars to set dependencies

With the Gantt chart displayed, you can use your mouse, the Link Tasks tool, or Link Tasks command from the Edit menu. You can use any of these methods to set a simple finish-to-start relationship.

1. Place your mouse pointer over the predecessor task until the cursor turns into four arrows pointing outward.

2. Click and hold your mouse button and drag the cursor to the second task. An information box describes the relationship you are about to create; for example, in Figure 4-22 Project you are creating a Finish-to-Start Link.

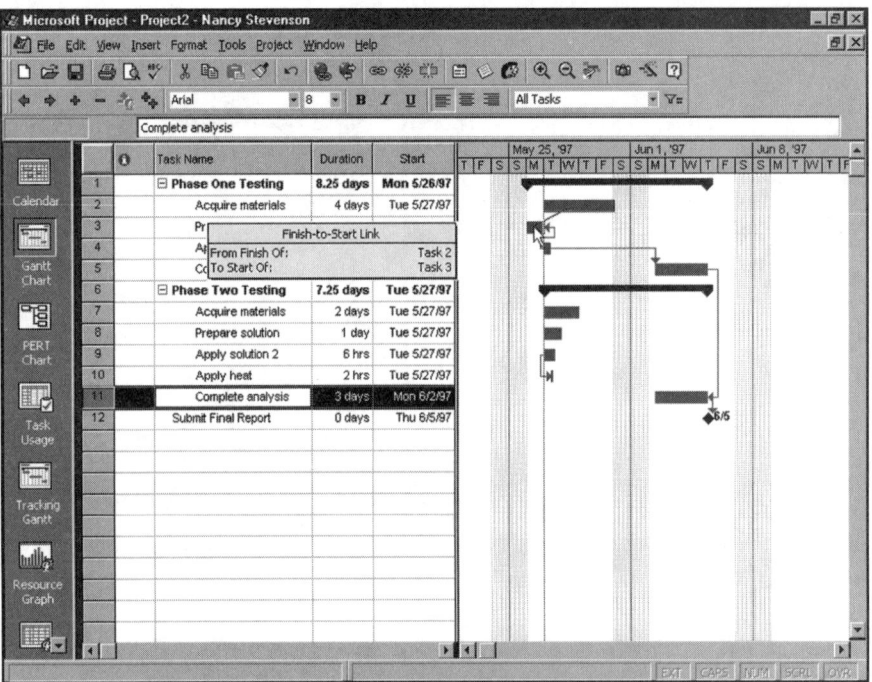

Figure 4-22: The relationship isn't established until you release the mouse button. If you have second thoughts, just drag back to the predecessor task before releasing your mouse.

3. Release your mouse button when you're satisfied with the relationship. The link is established.

To use the Link Tasks tool or command, simply follow these steps:

1. Click on the name of the predecessor task in the Task Name column of the Gantt table.

2. Hold down the left mouse button and drag to select an adjacent task. (If you drag through a series of tasks, or press Shift and click on a later task, you establish the finish-to-start relationship consecutively on all tasks from the first selected task to the last.)

3. Click on the Link Tasks tool, or Choose Edit⇨Link Tasks. The link is established.

Using the Task Information dialog box to set dependencies

Using the Task Information dialog box to set dependencies enables you to set any of the four dependency types and establish lag and overlap relationships. Using this method, you always open the Task Information dialog box for the successor task and build the relationship on the Predecessors tab.

1. Double-click on the task you want to make a successor. When the Task Information dialog box opens, select the Predecessors tab if it's not already displayed.

2. Click on the Task Name column; an arrow appears at its far end.

3. Click on the arrow to display the drop-down list of task names shown in Figure 4-23.

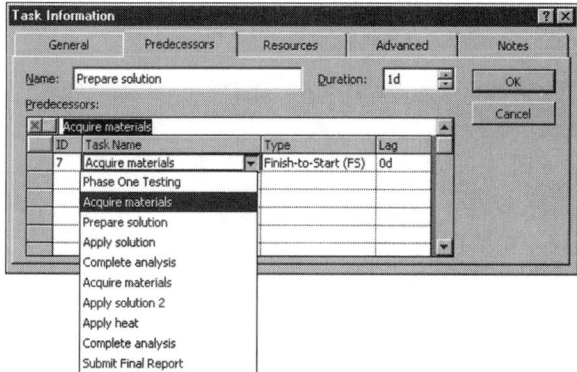

Figure 4-23: Every task you create for your project appears on this list.

Caution

Because of the repetitive nature of this testing project, several tasks have the same name, such as Acquire materials. This situation can cause problems when you try to select the specific task to which you want to create a dependency relationship. The solution is to place a number or other signifier related to the test or procedure you're performing next to the task names under that phase. For example, Apply solution in the second testing segment has a *2* to differentiate it from Apply solution in the first test.

4. Click on the task you want to make the predecessor to this task.

5. Click on the Type field; an arrow appears.

6. Click on the arrow to drop down a list of dependency types.

7. Click on the type of dependency you wish to establish, such as start-to-start or start-to-finish.

To establish a dependency with no delay or overlap, click on OK at this point to create the relationship. If you want to establish any delay, click on the Lag column and either use the arrow keys or type in an amount of time for the delay. If you want to establish overlap, simply enter a negative number in the Lag column. For example, if you want the successor to finish one week before the predecessor finishes, use a finish-to-finish relationship and type – **1 week** in the Lag column.

Viewing Dependencies

When you've established several dependencies in a project, you can study them in several ways. You can, of course, open each task's Task Information dialog box and look at the relationships listed on the Predecessor tab. You can also view the lines drawn between tasks to see dependencies. Finally, you can scroll to the right in the Gantt table to display the Predecessors column, as in Figure 4-24. This column lists any relationships, using the two letter abbreviations for the dependency type and positive and negative numbers to show lag and overlap.

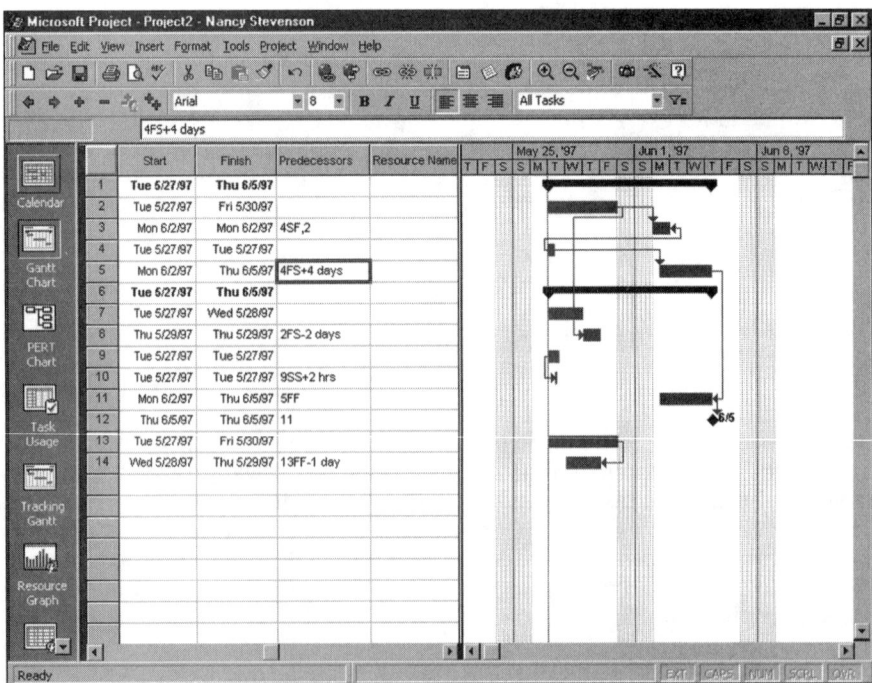

Figure 4-24: Display the Predecessors column to show all the relationships for a task.

You can also view dependency relationships from another perspective in the PERT Chart view, shown in Figure 4-25. Here the lines indicate relationships among tasks, although the exact timing of these relationships isn't as clear as it is in the Gantt Chart view.

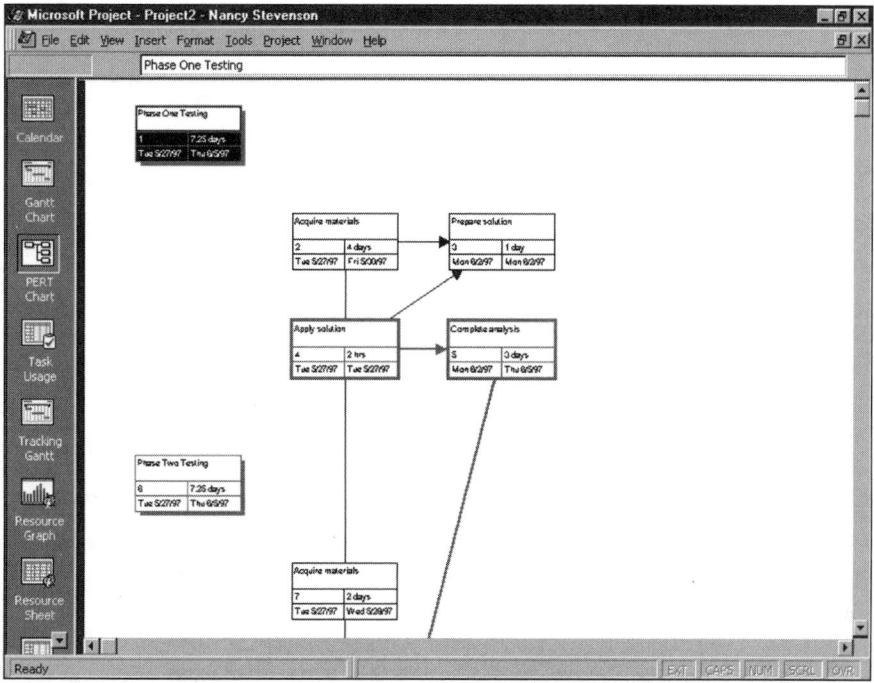

Figure 4-25: The PERT Chart view focuses on work flow, rather than on timing, so exact relationships such as overlap and delay aren't always as clear as they are in the Gantt Chart view.

Note

To create dependencies with the PERT chart view displayed, simply move your mouse over a task node until the cursor becomes a large white cross and then click and drag to the task with which you want to create a finish-to-start dependency. The relationship is established.

Deleting Dependencies

Here are several techniques for deleting dependencies:

✦ Open the Task Information dialog box for the successor task, select the Predecessors tab, click on the task name for the link to be broken, and press Delete on your keyboard.

✦ Display the Predecessors column in the Gantt table, click on that column for the successor task, and either press Delete to delete all relationships or edit the predecessor information in the entry bar.

✦ Click on the first task and then select the second task; click on the Unlink Tasks tool or Choose Edit⇨Unlink Tasks.

If you delete a dependency, the task bars may shift accordingly to reflect any new timing.

Summary

In this chapter you've learned more about the timing of tasks, including how to set task durations and dependencies. You know how to

✦ Establish task durations

✦ View those durations by making adjustments to the timescale

✦ Create recurring tasks

✦ Add and view task notes

✦ Apply constraints to tasks to relate them to the start or finish of a project or to a particular date

✦ Differentiate between resource-driven and fixed scheduling

✦ Set the various types of dependencies

In Chapter 5 you begin to assign resources to tasks and to learn more about the relationship between resource assignment and task timing.

✦   ✦   ✦

Creating Resources and Assigning Costs

The *management* portion of the term *project management* suggests that you are overseeing and, supposedly, controlling what goes on during the project's lifetime. In the last chapter you learned how to build the tasks that make up the project. Now you need to identify the resources for each task. Some tasks require people only; other tasks may require equipment also.

As you learn to create resources, you'll see that various rates are associated with a resource. As you assign the resource to a task in your project, Microsoft Project automatically begins to calculate the cost of your project.

Understanding Resources

Resources are the people, supplies, and equipment that enable you to complete the tasks in your project. Resources cost money and therefore affect the cost of the project. To manage a project effectively, you must define the necessary resources and assign those resources to tasks in the project. Then you need to know how Project uses those resource assignments to change the duration and length of your project.

Note

If you expect to use the same resources for several projects, consider setting up the resources in a special project that contains no tasks. Then you can use Project's *resource pooling* feature and the "resource project" to share resources across multiple projects. This approach enables you to set up resources once — but use them repeatedly on many different projects.

For more information on resource pooling, see Chapter 9. For more information on managing multiple projects, see Chapter 15.

How resources work

By defining and then assigning resources, you accomplish several goals:

✦ You can keep track of the whereabouts of resources — because Project shows you where the resources are assigned.

✦ You can identify potential resource shortages that could force you to miss scheduled deadlines and possibly extend the duration of your project.

✦ You can identify underutilized resources. If you reassign these resources, you may be able to shorten the project's schedule.

The resources you assign to a task affect the duration of the task. For example, if you assign two people to do a job, the job typically gets done in less time than if you assigned only one person to the job. But, you ask, what about the cost? Does the use of additional resources increase the project's cost? Perhaps yes; perhaps no. You may find that completing the project in less time (by using more resources) saves you money because you can accept more projects. Or you may be eligible for a bonus if you complete the project earlier than expected.

How Project uses resource information to affect the schedule

Project uses the resource information you provide to calculate the duration of the task and, therefore, the duration of the project. However, if you set up a task with a fixed duration (refer to Chapter 4), Project ignores the resources assigned to the task for this calculation. Similarly, if you don't assign resources, Project calculates the schedule using only the task duration and task dependency information that you provide.

Assigning a resource to a task can affect the duration of the project because work on the task cannot begin until the resource is available. Project uses a *resource calendar* to define the working days and times for a resource, but the resource's availability also depends on other tasks to which you assigned the resource.

If the work assigned to a resource exceeds the time available, Microsoft Project assigns the resource to the task and indicates that the resource is overallocated. This technique enables you to see the problem and decide how to fix it.

Note

You also have the option of assigning costs to resources when you define them. The section "Creating a Resource List" later in this chapter explains how Project uses the cost information you supply.

How Project gathers cost information?

Assigning costs to resources and then assigning resources to tasks is one way that Project calculates the cost of a project. In addition to resource-associated costs, Project also handles fixed costs, as you learn near the end of this chapter.

Assigning costs enables you to monitor and to control the money you're spending on a project. Project shows you where and how you are spending your money; this information enables you to control when a project's costs accrue, which, in turn, helps you schedule paying your bills. The cost-related information that Project provides helps you verify the following items:

✦ The cost of resources and materials for any task

✦ The cost of any phase of your project as well as the cost of the entire project

Cost information that you gather on one project may help you calculate bids for future projects.

Creating a Resource List

Project gives you the option of creating resources one at a time, as you think of them, or of entering all (or most) resources using the Resource Sheet. To display the Resource Sheet, click on the Resource Sheet button in the View bar (see Figure 5-1) or choose View➪Resource Sheet.

If you use the Resource Sheet to define most of the resources for your project, the actual process of assigning resources goes much faster because you don't have to stop to create the resource first. Also, using the Resource Sheet is a safe way to define resources; the visual presentation helps you avoid accidentally creating the same resource twice. For example, if you define Vickey and Vicki, Project sees two resources, even though you might have simply misspelled the name the second time.

You can create the basics for the resource by filling in the Resource Sheet; press the Tab key to move from field to field. The Resource Sheet in Figure 5-1 does not show all the fields described in this section; scroll to the right to see the rest of the Resource Sheet.

Note

A *field* is the box under a column heading into which you type appropriate information. Any view that is either a table or a form contains fields. You can also add fields to any table or form view to customize.

You can learn more about fields and adding them to views in Chapter 7.

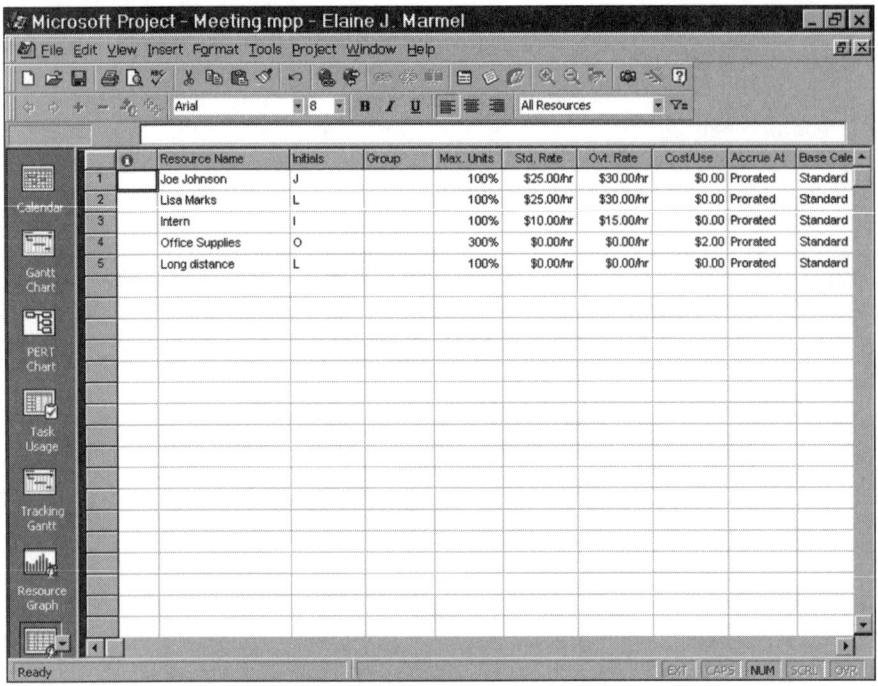

Figure 5-1: The Resource Sheet displays a list of the resources available to your project.

Each field on the Resource Sheet serves a specific purpose.

✦ **Indicators:** Although you can't type in the Indicators field, icons appear here from time to time. Some of the icons appear as Project's response to an action you've taken. For example, you may see an icon in the Indicators field for an overallocated resource. In other cases the icon appears because you entered a note about the resource (see "Adding Notes to a Resource" later in this chapter).

Tip

If you point at an icon in the Indicators field, Project displays the information associated with the icon.

✦ **Resource Name:** Type the name of the resource. For manpower, you might type a person's name or you might type a job description, such as Product Analyst 1 or Product Analyst 2.

✦ **Initials**: Type initials for the resource, or accept the default Project provides, which is the first letter of the resource name. This designation appears on any view to which you add the Initials field. Typically, a resource's name appears, but you can customize the view to display initials if you prefer.

✦ **Group**: Assign resources to groups if they share some common characteristic, such as job function. Then you can use this field as a filtering or sorting mechanism and display information about the group (a particular job function), as opposed to a specific resource. You can just type a name to create a group.

Tip

Be sure to type the name the same way each time you use it if you want to filter or sort by group.

✦ **Max. Units**: Project expresses the amount of the resource you have available for assignment as a percentage. For example, 100 percent equals one unit, or the equivalent of one entire full-time resource; 50 percent equals one-half of a unit, or one-half of a full-time resource's time; and 200 percent equals two entire full-time resources.

✦ **Std. Rate**: The *standard rate* is the rate you charge for regular work for a resource. Project calculates the default rate in hours; you can, however, charge a resource's work in other time increments (minutes, days, weeks, or years). To specify a time increment other than hours, type a slash and then the first letter of the word representing the time increment. For example, to charge a resource's use in days, type **/d** after the rate you specify.

✦ **Ovt. Rate**: The *overtime rate* is the rate you charge for overtime work for a resource. Again, Project calculates the default rate in hours, but you can change the default unit the same way you changed it for the Standard Rate.

✦ **Cost/Use**: The *cost per use rate* is the rate you use to charge a one-time rate for a resource. Use this rate for costs that are charged on a per/unit basis (such as material costs), rather than on some time-related basis.

✦ **Accrue At:** This field specifies how and when resource costs at the standard or overtime rate are charged to a task. The default option is Prorated, but you also can select Start or End.

- If you select Start and assign that resource to a task, Project calculates the cost for a task as soon as the task begins.

- If you select End and assign that resource to a task, Project calculates the cost for the task when the task is completed.

- If you select Prorated and assign that resource to a task, Project accrues the cost of the task as scheduled work is completed.

Tip

If you set a cost per use rate for a resource and assign that resource to a task, Project always charges the cost of the resource at the beginning of a task.

✦ **Base Calendar**: Base calendar identifies the calendar that Project should use when scheduling the resource. The calendar identifies working and nonworking time. The default calendar is called the Standard calendar, but, as you learn later in this chapter, you can create calendars for resource groups — perhaps to handle shift work — or you can modify an individual resource's calendar to reflect vacation or other unavailable time.

✦ **Code:** You can use this field as a catch-all field to assign any information you want to a resource, using an abbreviation of some sort. For example, suppose your company uses cost-center codes; you may want to supply the cost-center code for the resource in the Code field. You can sort and filter information by the abbreviations that you supply in the Code field.

Note After you create a resource, Project displays a number on the very left edge of the Resource Sheet, to the left of the Indicators column. That number is the resource's ID number.

Modifying Resource Information

You just learned a quick way to set up a resource by typing on the Resource Sheet. In addition, you can use the Resource Information dialog box to fine-tune your resource's definition.

Making general modifications

Use the Resource Information dialog box to modify resource information. To display the Resource Information dialog box (see Figure 5-2), double-click on any resource on the Resource Sheet or choose Project⇨Resource Information. Then click on the General tab.

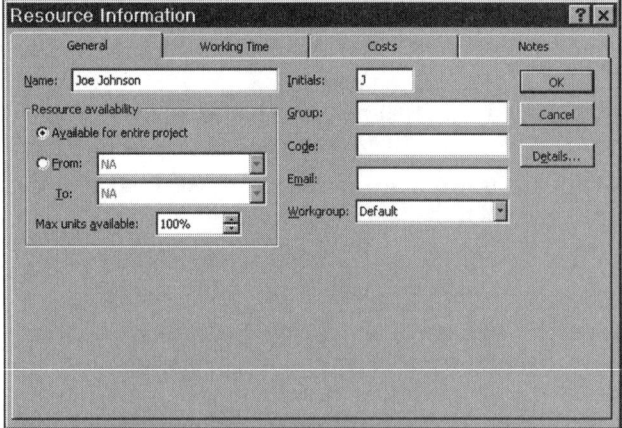

Figure 5-2: As you would expect, you can make general changes to resource information from the General tab of the Resource Information dialog box.

You already provided most of the information on this tab on the Resource Sheet, so this section focuses on the fields in the dialog box that weren't available on the Resource Sheet.

Assigning a communication method

Use the Email field to supply the e-mail address of a resource. You must fill in this field if you want to use Project's workgroup feature, which enables you to assign, accept, or decline work electronically. You can make a selection from the Workgroup drop-down list to specify an electronic communication method. (See Chapter 14 for more about the workgroup feature.)

Adding notes to a resource

Click on the Notes tab of the Resource Information dialog box. The Notes text box in Figure 5-3 is a free-form text box in which you can type any information you want to store about the resource. For example, you might want to store a reminder about a resource's upcoming vacation.

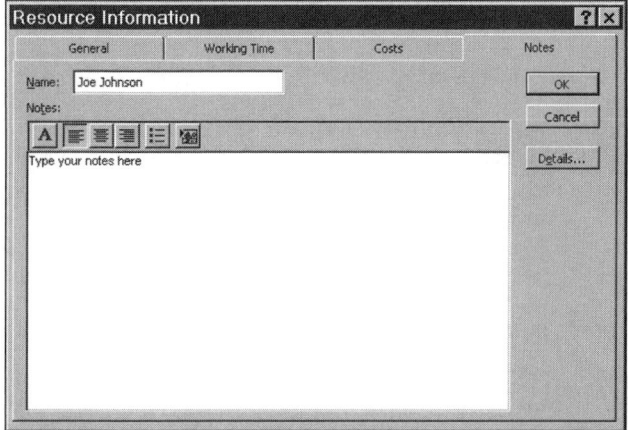

Figure 5-3: Use this text box to store any information about a resource.

After you type text in this box and click on OK, a note-indicator icon appears in the Indicators column on the Resource Sheet (see Figure 5-4).

Tip

You don't need to reopen the Resource Information dialog box to read the note. Point at its icon with the mouse, and Project displays the contents of the note.

Indicates a note exists for this resource

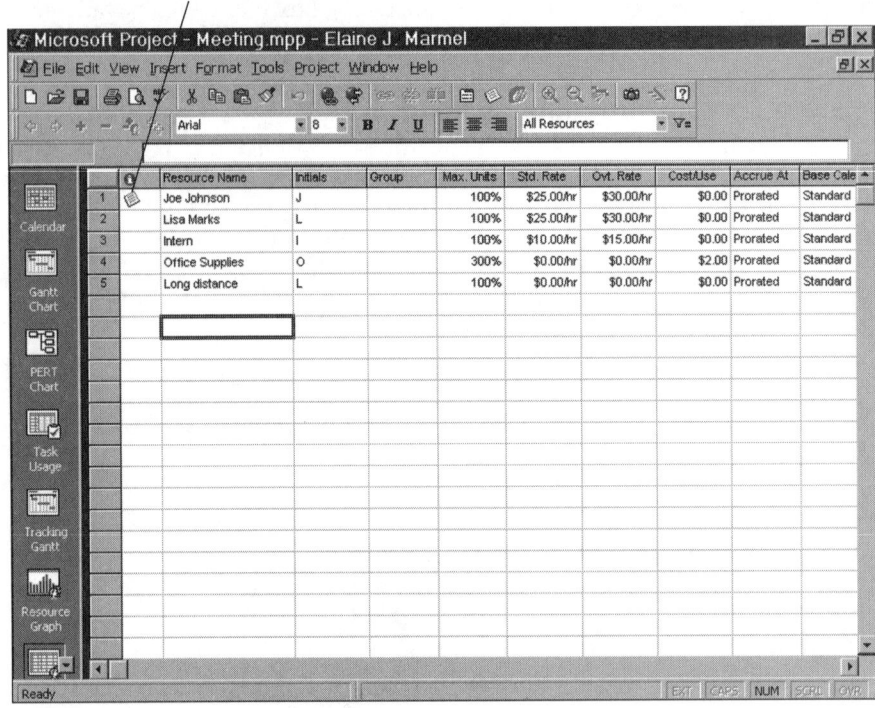

Figure 5-4: After you create a resource note, Project displays the note indicator icon in the Indicators field on the Resource Sheet.

Calendars and resources

As you learned in Chapter 3, Project uses a base calendar called the Standard Calendar to calculate the timing of the project. You also learned in Chapter 3 that you can modify the calendar availability of a resource by creating resource calendars. Or you can modify the Standard Calendar for an individual resource.

Note

The entire project has a Standard Calendar, and each resource also has his or her standard calendar.

Setting up a standard resource calendar

You set up the basic parameters for the Standard Calendar from the Options dialog box, shown in Figure 5-5. Choose Tools⇨Options and then click on the Calendar tab to display this dialog box.

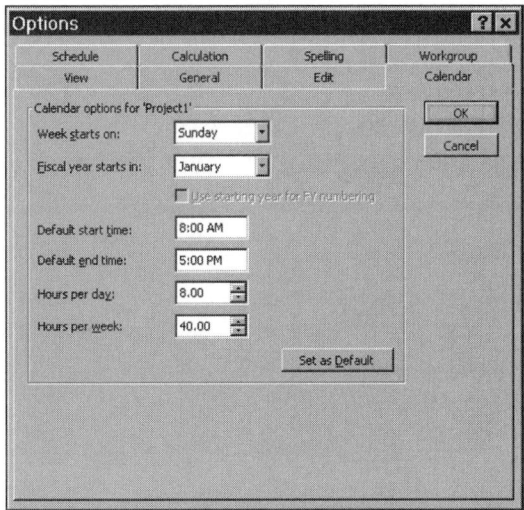

Figure 5-5: Use the Options dialog box to set the information for the Standard Calendar.

Using calendars for specific resource groups

You may find that all members of a specific group of resources work on the same calendar — but their calendar is different from the Standard Calendar. For groups like these, you can use or create a special *resource calendar*. A resource calendar serves the same purpose as the Standard Calendar, but it contains different information. In addition to the Standard calendar, Project comes with two predefined resource calendars — a 24-hour calendar and a Night Shift calendar. To view the available resource calendars, choose Tools➪Change Working Time to display the Change Working Time dialog box shown in Figure 5-6.

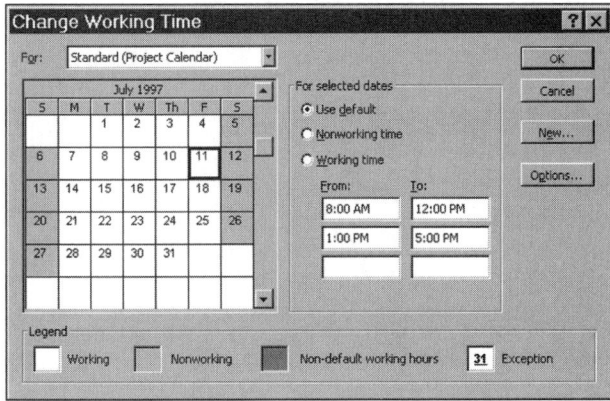

Figure 5-6: By default, Project displays the settings for the Standard (Project Calendar) in the Change Working Time dialog box.

To view the 24-hour calendar, select 24 Hours in the For drop-down list (see Figure 5-7).

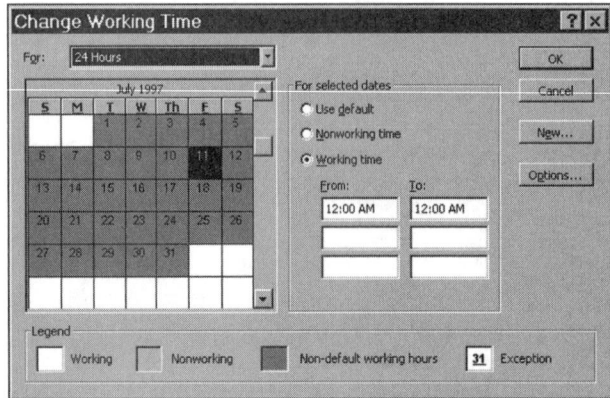

Figure 5-7: The 24-hour calendar defines working time as 12:00 AM to 12:00 AM.

To view the Night Shift calendar, select Night Shift in the For drop-down list (see Figure 5-8).

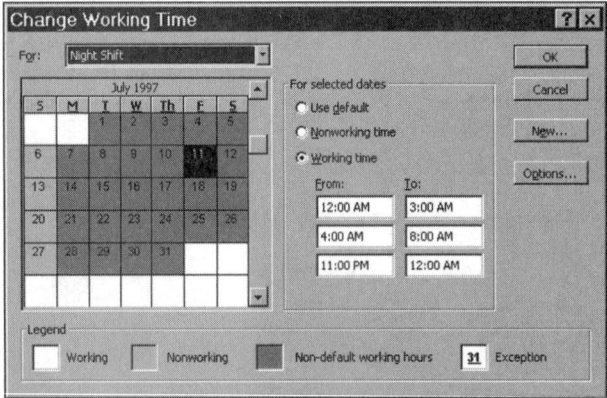

Figure 5-8: The Night Shift calendar defines working time from 11 PM to 8 AM with a lunch break.

If these calendars don't meet your needs, you can create a custom calendar by clicking on the New button. Project displays the Create New Base Calendar dialog box (see Figure 5-9).

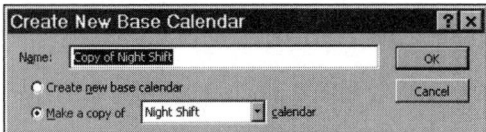

Figure 5-9: From the Create New Base Calendar dialog box, you can create a copy of an existing calendar or you can create a new Standard Calendar.

If you want to model your calendar on an existing calendar, select the existing calendar from the Make a copy of drop-down box.

Tip

By default, Project suggests that you copy the calendar you were viewing when you chose the New button.

After you create a resource calendar, you use the calendar by assigning it to the resources to which it applies. On the Resource Sheet, click on the Base Calendar field for the resource to which you want to assign a calendar. Then use the list box arrow to view your calendar choices and select a calendar for that resource.

Changing the calendar for a single resource

If you have already defined resources, their names appear in the For list box in the Change Working Time dialog box (refer to Figure 5-8). You can modify an individual resource's calendar in a number of ways:

✦ You can change a resource's availability.

✦ You can change a resource's working hours.

✦ You can block off a period of time for a resource, making it unavailable during that period. You might want to use this feature to block off vacation time or perhaps a trip out of town on other business.

Modifying a resource's project availability

Sometimes a resource is not available for the entire duration of a project. By modifying the resource's availability dates, you can use Project to guarantee that you don't accidentally overallocate the resource by assigning it during a period when it won't be available.

From the Resource Sheet, double-click on the resource to display the Resource Information dialog box and click on the General tab. In the Resource Availability box, select the From option. When you open the From list box, Project displays a calendar, as shown in Figure 5-10, from which you can specify the date when a resource will become available. Use the arrows that appear on either side of the month name to change the calendar forward or backward one month at a time. Then click on a date.

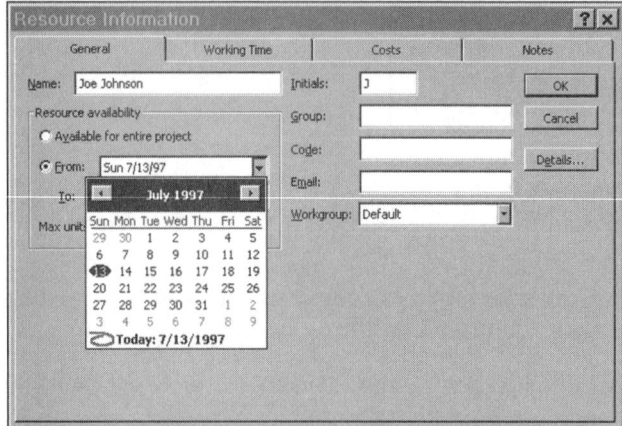

Figure 5-10: Specify the dates a resource will be available to a project.

You can also use the To list box calendar to specify an ending date for the resource's availability.

Modifying a resource's working hours

Another possibility is that a specific resource won't be available all day on a given day, or even on several specified days. To change the working hours of a single resource, use the Working Time tab of the Resource Information dialog box. Double-click on the resource on the Resource Sheet to open the dialog box (see Figure 5-11).

Figure 5-11: Modify an individual resource's calendar using the Resource Information dialog box.

The resource's calendar appears with today's date selected. The Legend at the bottom of the dialog box identifies Working days, Nonworking days, Non-default working hours, and Exceptions.

Using standard Windows selection techniques, select the dates your resource will be on vacation.

Note

To select contiguous days, click on the first day. Then press the Shift key as you click on the last day you want to select. To select noncontiguous days, press Ctrl as you click on each day you want to select.

To change a resource's working hours, click on the Working time option button and then make the necessary changes in the From and To text boxes. Because you set an exception to the regular schedule, the dates you selected appear underscored in the individual's calendar (see Figure 5-12). Even if you don't select the date, you can tell that the exception involves nonstandard working hours by comparing the date to the Legend.

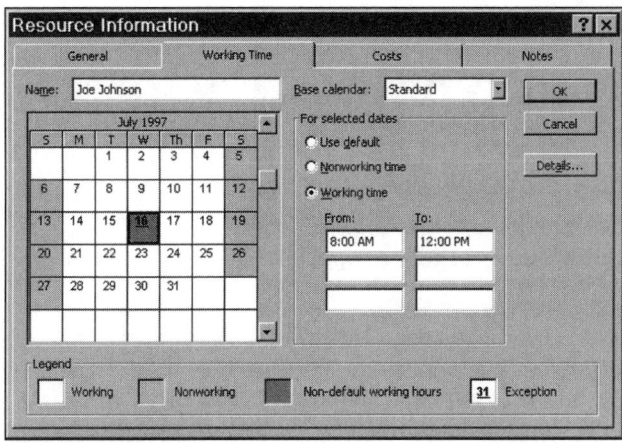

Figure 5-12: Project marks exceptions to the typical schedule with an underscore.

Tip

If you have a resource that works only mornings, you can't simply modify its working time. Instead, you need to create a special calendar for that resource to avoid overallocating it.

Blocking off vacation time

Human resources do take time off from work, and, to avoid overallocating a person by assigning work during a vacation period, you should mark vacation days on the resources calendar.

Double-click on the resource to display the Resource Information dialog box and click on the Working Time tab. Find the date or dates you want to block for vacation time using the scroll bar next to the calendar.

Tip

Scroll up to see an earlier month; scroll down to see a later month.

With the vacation dates selected, select the Nonworking time option, as shown in Figure 5-13. Click on any other date on the calendar to cancel the selection; each date you marked as vacation time appears with an underscore. Again, by comparing the date to the Legend, you can tell the reason for the exception.

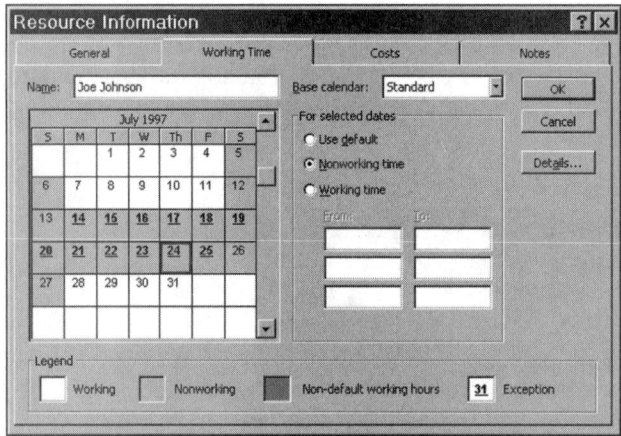

Figure 5-13: Dates marked as Nonworking time appear as exceptions on the calendar.

Tip

If you have a resource that works the regular schedule except, say, for Tuesdays, you can block off Tuesday on that resource's calendar. On the Working Time tab in the Resource Information dialog box, click on the letter of the day the resource doesn't work. Project selects all of those days, in all months. Then select Nonworking time.

Using Resources and Tasks

You've spent a lot of time in this chapter learning to define resources and fine-tune your resource definitions. Now you can finally assign resources to tasks. As noted earlier in this chapter, using resources helps you manage your project more effectively, both in scheduling and in cost.

This section explains not only how to assign resources to tasks but also how to remove a resource assignment or replace one resource with another.

Assigning resources to tasks

The easiest way to assign resources to tasks is to view the tasks in the Gantt Chart view. To assign a resource to a task, use the View bar to switch to the Gantt Chart view and then follow these steps:

1. Select the task from the Task Name column to which you want to assign a resource.

2. Click on the Assign Resources button or choose Tools⇨Resources⇨Assign Resources to open the Assign Resources dialog box (see Figure 5-14).

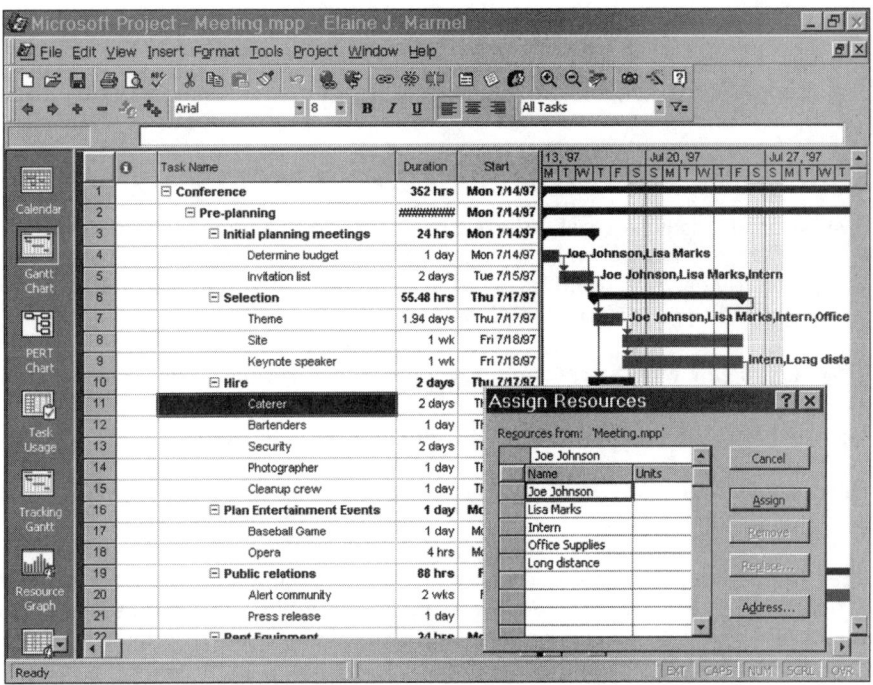

Figure 5-14: Use the Assign Resources dialog box to assign a resource to a task.

3. Select the resource you want to assign from the Name list of the Assign Resources dialog box.

   If you have any other Microsoft Office products installed, the Address button is available. You can click on the Address button to select a resource from your address book.

Tip

Did you forget to define a resource? You don't need to return to the Resource Sheet. Just type the name of the resource in the Name column of the Assign Resources dialog box.

4. Do one of the following to assign the amount of a resource:

- To assign any amount other than 100 percent of a resource, type the quantity of the resource as a percentage in the Units column. (Project defines units as percentages, so 100 percent equals one unit of the resource.)

- To assign 100 percent of a resource, leave the Units column blank. Project assigns 100% by default.

Note

You don't need to type the % sign; Project assumes percentages. Also, if you type **.5**, Project converts your entry to 50%.

5. Click on Assign. Project places a check in the left-most column of the Assign Resources dialog box to indicate the resource is assigned to the selected task.

6. Repeat steps 3, 4, and 5 to assign additional resources or click on Close.

Some tips about resource assignments

First, you can assign several different resources to the same task by simply selecting each resource. You can select a single resource and immediately click on Assign, or you can use standard Windows selection techniques to select several resources and then click on Assign only one time.

Second, you can assign a resource to a task on a part-time basis by assigning less that 100 in the Units column. The number you type represents the percentage of working time you want the resource to spend on the task.

Third, you can assign more than one of a resource by assigning more than 100 in the Units column.

After you assign a resource to a task, the resource name appears next to the task bar on the Gantt Chart by default. Depending on the task type you set, you may be able to use resource assignments to modify individual task lengths and the entire project schedule. For example, if you assign additional resources to an effort-driven fixed-unit task, Project shortens the duration of the task. As you learned in Chapter 4, the amount of work to be done doesn't change, but the extra concurrent effort shortens the time necessary to get the work done. Or if you assign a resource to work part-time on an effort-driven task, you might find that you can complete several tasks at the same time.

Tip

If you overallocate a resource by assigning more than you have available, Project displays the resource in red on the Resource Sheet view. Chapter 9 explains how to handle these problems.

Removing or replacing a resource assignment

To remove a resource assignment, select the task from which you want to remove the resource assignment — use the Gantt Chart view. Then click on the Assign Resources button or choose Tools➪Resources➪Assign Resources to display the Assign Resources dialog box. Highlight the resource you want to remove from the task; you should see a check next to the resource in the left-most column of the dialog box. Click on Remove.

You can be sure that at some point in your project you will want to move resource assignments around. Here's the easy way to switch from one resource to another on a given task:

1. Select the task on which you want to switch resources.

2. Open the Assign Resources dialog box.

3. Highlight the resource you want to remove from the task; a check mark appears next to the assigned resource.

4. Select Replace. Project displays the Replace Resource dialog box on top of the Assign Resources dialog box (if you move the Replace Resource dialog box, you can see them both). The Replace Resource dialog box enables you to easily select replacement resources (see Figure 5-15).

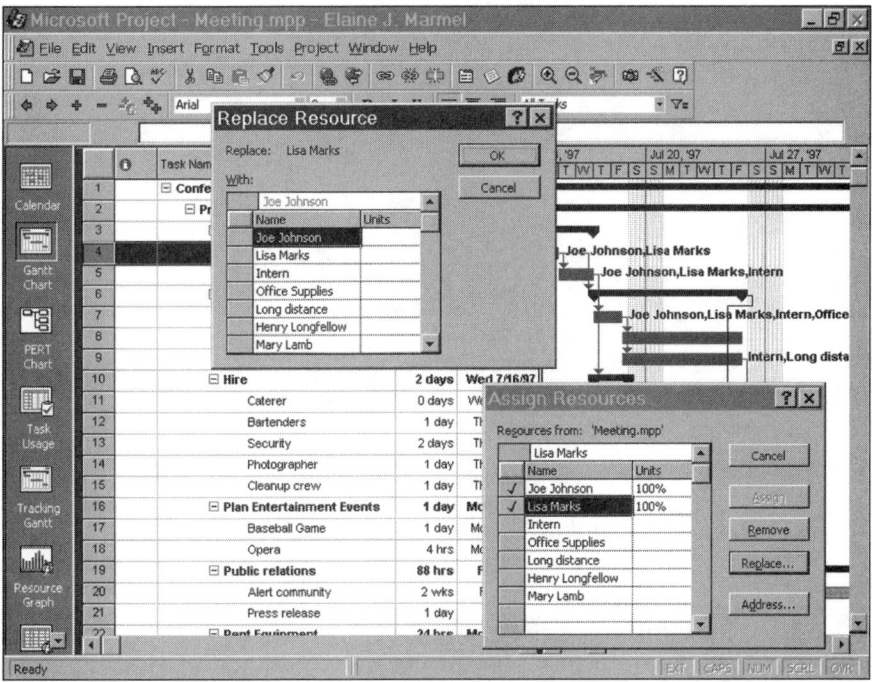

Figure 5-15: The Replace Resource dialog box looks very similar to the Assign Resource dialog box.

5. Highlight each resource you want to assign and supply units.

6. Click on OK.

Handling Unusual Cost Situations

Resources go hand in hand with tasks if you're trying to figure out how long it will take to complete a project. If you assign costs to your resources, those costs also affect the cost of your project. But assigning a cost to a resource is *not* the only way to assign a cost to a project. For example, projects can have fixed costs associated with them. This section starts with a quick look at overall project costs and then focuses on handling unusual cost situations.

Looking at the project's cost

You've seen how to assign costs to resources. You've also seen how to assign resources to tasks — and logic dictates that assigning a resource to which you have assigned a cost will cause your project to have a cost. Are you wondering what that cost is? From either the Gantt Chart view or the Resource Sheet view, choose Project⇨Project Information to open the Project Information dialog box. Select Statistics to open the Project Statistics dialog box (see Figure 5-16).

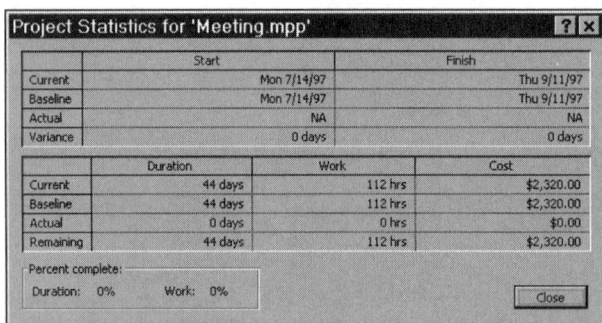

Figure 5-16: Check the cost of your project in the Project Statistics dialog box.

Note   Part IV covers tracking, recording actual work done, and analyzing and reporting on progress. Chapter 12 explains additional ways to view project costs. The following sections consider ways to assign unusual costs to a project.

Assigning fixed costs

This chapter has, so far, focused on resources, and you have learned how to assign costs to a resource. But the costs of some tasks need to be calculated differently.

In Project you can assign a fixed cost to a task or you can assign a fixed resource cost to a task.

Assigning a fixed cost to a task

Some tasks are fixed-cost tasks; that is, you know that the cost of a particular task stays the same regardless of the duration of the task or the work performed by any resources on the task. In cases like these you assign the cost directly to the task. If you assign a cost to a task, Project adds the fixed cost of the task to the cost of any resource work you assign to the task when calculating costs for the project.

To assign a fixed cost to a task, use the Gantt Chart view and apply the Cost table. Follow these steps:

1. Use the View bar to switch to the Gantt Chart view.

2. Choose View⇨Table⇨Cost to switch to the Cost table view of the Gantt Chart (see Figure 5-17).

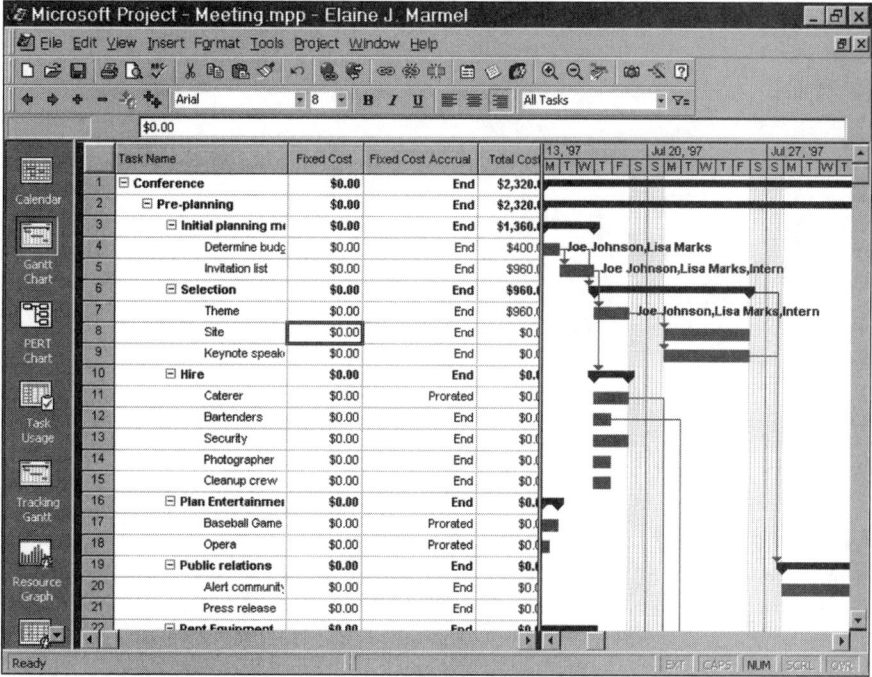

Figure 5-17: Use the Cost table view of the Gantt Chart to assign costs to tasks.

3. Select the task to which you want to assign a fixed cost.

4. Type the cost for that task in the Fixed Cost column and press Enter.

You can control the way Project accrues the fixed cost for a task from the Fixed Cost Accrual column. Your choices are Start, Prorated, and End (see Figure 5-18). These choices have the same meaning as the accrual choices for resources discussed earlier in this chapter.

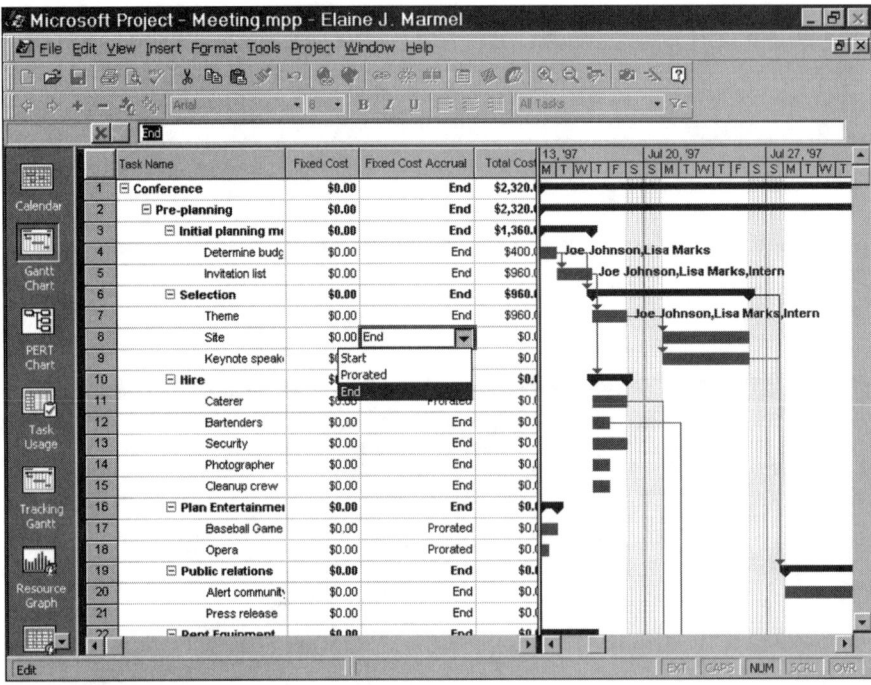

Figure 5-18: Use the Fixed Cost Accrual column to control the way Project accrues fixed costs.

Tip

To control the way Project accrues all fixed costs, use the Calculation tab of the Options dialog box (choose Tools⇨Options).

Assigning a fixed resource cost to a task

When a resource requires a fixed amount of money for a task, such as material or supply costs, you can assign a fixed cost resource to the task.

1. Use the View bar to switch to the Gantt Chart view.

2. Select a task from the Task Name column.

3. Add the resource to the task using the steps explained earlier in this chapter to assign a resource to a task. Don't worry about the number of units you assign.

4. Choose Window⇨Split.

5. Select the resource from the Resource Name column in the bottom pane.

6. Choose Format⇨Details⇨Resource Cost. A pane appears at the bottom of the Gantt Chart.

7. Type **O** in the Units column for the resource.

8. Type the fixed-resource cost in the Cost field. Figure 5-19 shows a fixed-resource cost for Long distance.

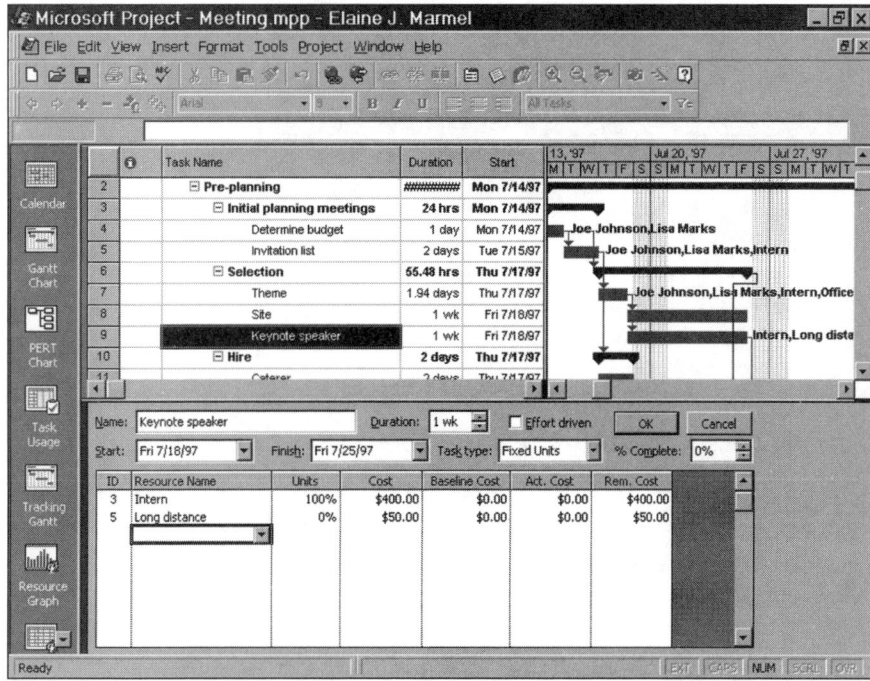

Figure 5-19: Adding a fixed resource cost.

9. Click on OK.

Project adds a fixed resource cost to other resource costs when calculating the total cost of a task, but the cost does not depend on the time a resource spends working on the task.

Tip Choose Window⇨Remove Split to close the bottom pane in the Gantt Chart view or drag the Split Bar.

Accounting for resource rate changes

In some situations you must charge different rates on different tasks for the same resource. Or possibly, you expect a resource's rate to change during the life of your project. Project uses Cost Rate tables to accurately reflect resource costs as they change. On Cost Rate tables you can identify up to 125 rates for a single resource, and you can identify the effective date of each rate. Cost Rate tables help you account for pay increases or decreases to resources during the life of your project and enable you to charge the same resource at different rates, depending on the task.

To assign multiple rates to a resource, use the Costs tab of the Resource Information dialog box. On the Resource Sheet view, double-click on the resource to which you want to assign multiple rates. Click on the Costs tab in the Resource Information dialog box (see Figure 5-20).

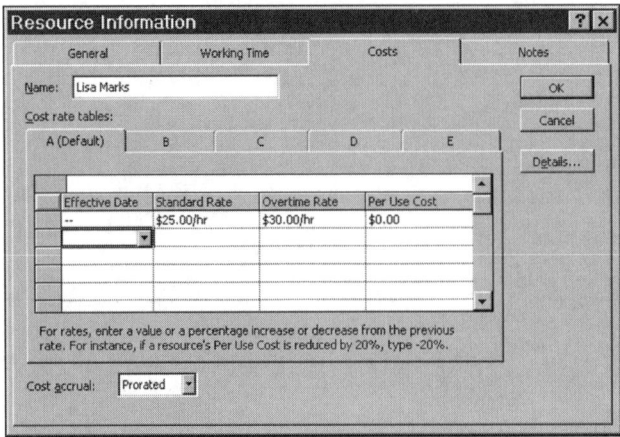

Figure 5-20: Use Cost Rate tables to assign different rates to a resource.

The Costs tab displays five Cost Rate tables (tabs A through E) that you can use to assign different rates to a resource for use on different dates throughout a project's life. On each Cost Rate table, you can enter up to 25 rates for the selected resource and indicate an effective date for each rate. Project uses the effective dates you supply to apply the correct rate to a resource at different times during the project.

Tip

If you are specifying a new rate as an increase or decrease of an existing rate, you can specify the new rate in a percentage (+10% or -10%); Project calculates the value of the rate for you. You must enter the percent sign.

If you charge different amounts for resources depending on the type of work they perform, you might want to use each Cost Rate table tab to represent sets of rates for different kinds of work.

To assign the correct resource rate to a task, follow these steps:

1. Assign the resource to the task using the Assign Resource dialog box, as you learned earlier in this chapter.

2. Use the View bar to switch to the Task Usage view (see Figure 5-21).

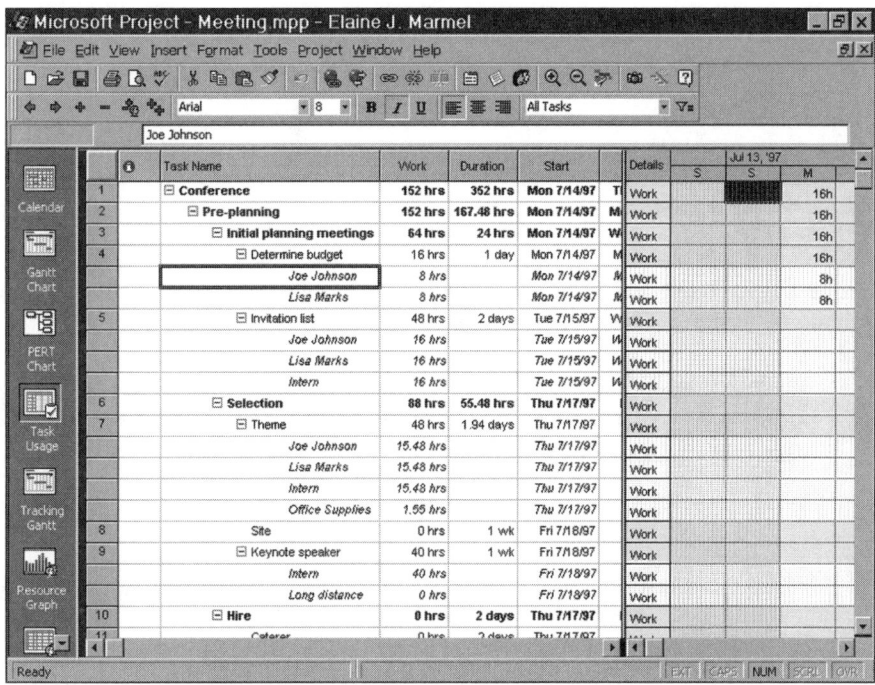

Figure 5-21: The Task Usage view shows you how much time a resource is assigned to a particular task.

3. Select the desired resource under the task to which you assigned it in the Task Name column.

4. Click on the Assignment Information button on the Standard toolbar to display the Assignment Information dialog box. Click on the General tab (see Figure 5-22) to select a Cost rate table.

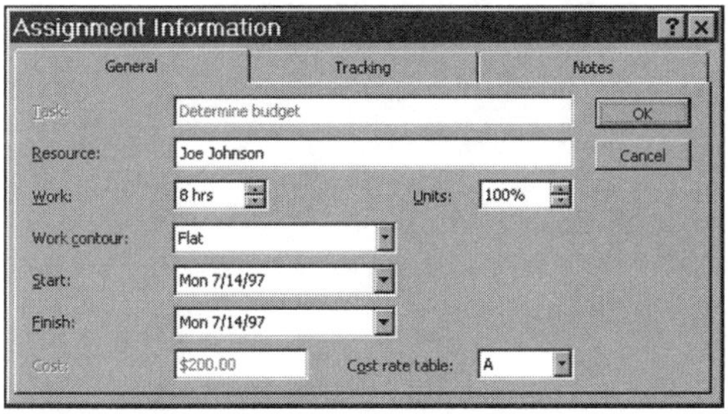

Figure 5-22: Use the General tab of the Assignment Information dialog box to select a Cost rate table.

5. Select the correct Cost Rate table from the Cost Rate Table drop-down list.

6. Click on OK.

Chapter 12 covers the topic of project costs in more detail.

Summary

In this chapter you learn more about using resources in Project, including how to create and assign resources. You've learned how to

✦ Create a resource list

✦ Modify resource information, including using various calendars for individual resources or groups of resources

✦ Assign resources to tasks and remove resource assignments

✦ Handle fixed costs, both for individual tasks and for resources

✦ Set up different rates for resources to account for pay increases or decreases or for charging resources at different rates on different tasks.

In Chapter 6 you learn about using the various views in Project.

✦   ✦   ✦

Refining Your
Project

Using Views to Gain Perspective

Views in Project enable you to enter, organize, and examine information in various ways. Project provides a variety of views, and you have already looked at several of them. This chapter focuses on the views that are not yet familiar.

What Is a View?

A view is a way to examine your project. Different views enable you to focus on different aspects of the project.

Project uses three types of views:

✦ **Chart or graph views:** Present information by using pictures. You've already seen the Gantt Chart view, which is a chart view.

✦ **Sheet views:** Present information in rows and columns, similar to the way a spreadsheet program presents information. The Task Sheet view and the Resource Sheet view are both sheet views, and each row on the sheet contains all the information about an individual task or resource in your project. Each column represents a field that identifies the information you're storing about the task or resource.

✦ **Forms:** Present information in a way that resembles a paper form. You saw the Task Form view in Chapter 4; a form displays information about a single item (task) in your project.

Tip

Shortcut menus are available in many views. Right-click on the view to see a shortcut menu.

What Views Are Available?

Here is a list of the default views available in Project:

- ✦ Bar Rollup
- ✦ Calendar
- ✦ Detail Gantt
- ✦ Gantt Chart
- ✦ Leveling Gantt
- ✦ Milestone Date Rollup
- ✦ Milestone Rollup
- ✦ PA_Expected Gantt
- ✦ PA_Optimistic Gantt
- ✦ PA_PERT Entry Sheet
- ✦ PA_Pessimistic Gantt
- ✦ PERT Chart
- ✦ Resource Allocation
- ✦ Resource Form
- ✦ Resource Graph
- ✦ Resource Name Form
- ✦ Resource Sheet
- ✦ Resource Usage
- ✦ Task Details Form
- ✦ Task Entry
- ✦ Task Form
- ✦ Task Name Form
- ✦ Task PERT
- ✦ Task Sheet
- ✦ Task Usage
- ✦ Tracking Gantt

You can modify the default views by switching what appears onscreen. You can also create custom views (see Chapter 16). The two sections that follow describe some common ways of manipulating views:

- ✦ Switching the table of any view that includes a table

✦ Adding or changing the details that appear in any view that contains a Details section

Note

In Chapter 16 you learn how to create and save a combination view. In a *combination view,* you actually see one format in one pane of the window and another format in another pane. To switch between the panes, press F6 or click on the pane in which you want to work. A dark bar along the side of a pane indicates the active pane.

Changing a table

If a view contains a table, you can use the Select All button to quickly switch to another table. The Select All button appears in the upper left of the table portion of the view. Right-click on the Select All button to open the menu that appears in Figure 6-1.

Select All button

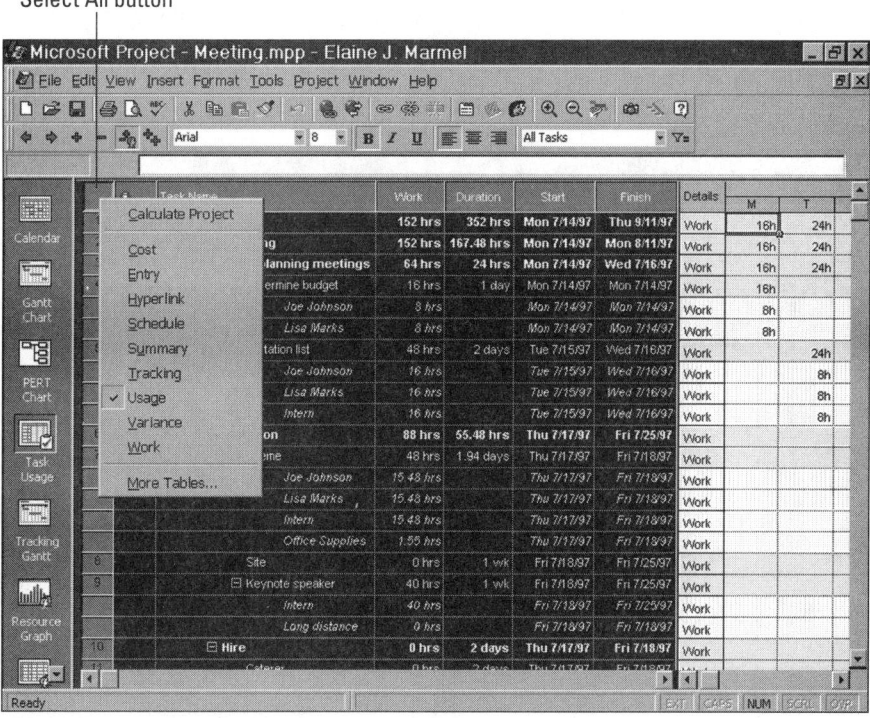

Figure 6-1: Switch tables by choosing from the menu that appears when you right-click on the Select All button.

Choose More Tables to open the More Tables dialog box that displays all the tables available in Project (see Figure 6-2).

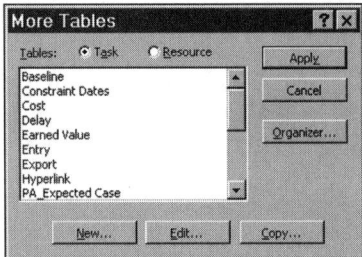

Figure 6-2: The More Tables dialog box shows the tables to which you can switch in the Task Usage view.

Changing a details section

You also can change the information that appears on the Details section of any view that displays a Details section. Choose any item on the Format⇨Details menu (see Figure 6-3).

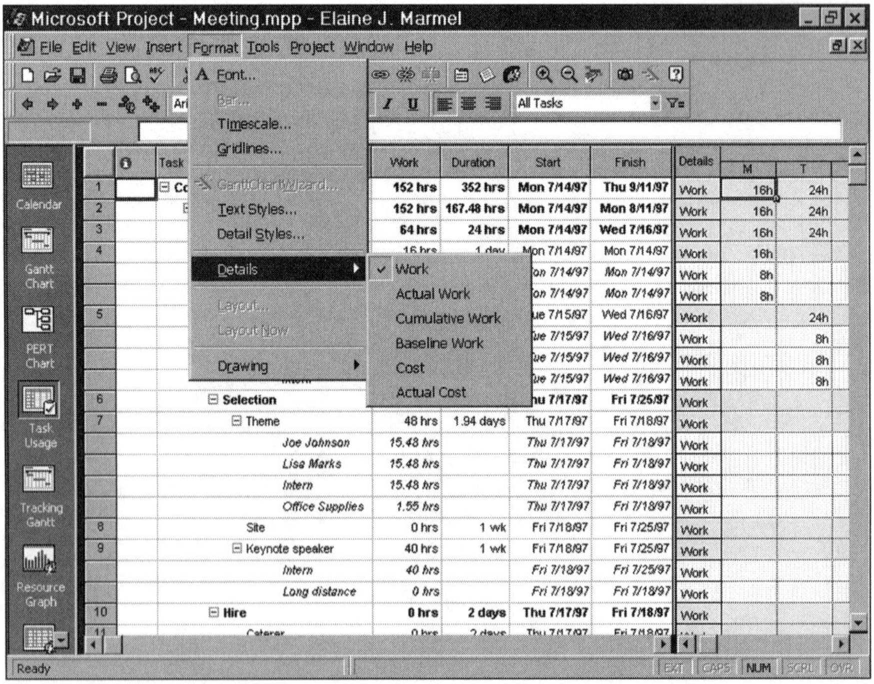

Figure 6-3: Change the information that appears in the Details section of the view by selecting from this list.

Note Project adds rows to the Details section when you make selections from this menu. To remove a row, choose Format➪Details and select the item you want to remove.

You can also use the Detail Styles dialog box (choose Format➪Detail Styles) in Figure 6-4 to add other information to the Details section.

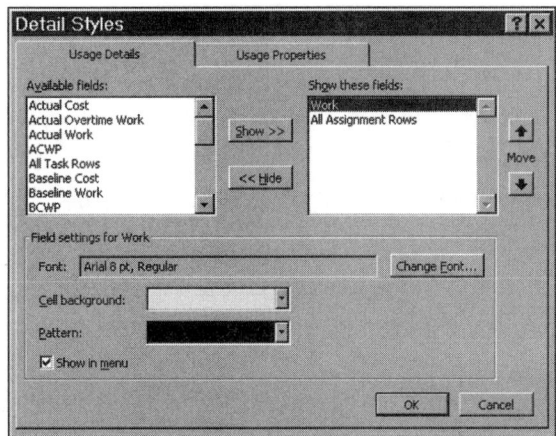

Figure 6-4: The Detail Styles dialog box supplies additional choices you can display on the Details section of a view.

Examining Indicators and New Views in Project 98

Project 98 contains several new views as well as new view-related features. For example, the View bar, which you learned about in Chapter 2, is new. The Indicators field is also new; it appears on various table views and, at times, displays an icon indicating additional information about the row; you saw the Indicators field in Chapter 5 when you learned how to add a note to a resource. *AutoFilters* are new and enable you to limit the information you see onscreen; AutoFilters are available in any sheet view. This topic is covered in more detail near the end of the chapter.

Project 98 contains some views that didn't exist in earlier versions of the product:

- ✦ Task Usage
- ✦ Resource Usage
- ✦ PA_Expected Gantt

✦ PA_Optimistic Gantt

✦ PA_Pessimistic Gantt

✦ PA_PERT Entry Sheet

✦ Bar Rollup

✦ Milestone Date Rollup

✦ Milestone Rollup

Before exploring these views, however, take a more in-depth look at indicators.

Understanding indicators

Indicators are icons that appear in the Indicators field on table views; the Indicators field appears to the right of the ID field. Indicators represent additional information about the row in which they appear. For example, your own notes appear in this field if you assign a note to a resource (refer to Chapter 5). Different icons represent different types of indicators.

Tip To identify the purpose of an indicator, point at it. Project tells you what the indicator means or displays additional information to remind you of important details.

Constraint indicators: These indicators identify the type of constraint assigned to a task. For example, a task can have a flexible constraint, such as Finish No Later Than, for tasks scheduled from the finish date. Or a task can have an inflexible constraint, such as Must Start On, for tasks scheduled from the start date. Constraint indicators also show that the task hasn't been completed within the time frame of the constraint.

Task Type indicators: Task type indicators may identify special conditions about a task, such as whether the task is a recurring task or whether the task has been completed. Task type indicators also identify the status of projects inserted in a task. You can learn more about inserted projects in Chapter 18.

Workgroup indicators: Workgroup indicators provide some information about the task and its resources. For example, a workgroup indicator can tell you that a task has been assigned but that the resource hasn't yet confirmed the assignment.

Contour indicators: Contour indicators identify the type of contouring used to distribute the work assigned to the task. You learn more about contouring in Chapter 9.

Miscellaneous indicators: Miscellaneous indicators identify a note or a hyperlink that you created or a resource that needs leveling.

Task Usage view

This powerful new view (see Figure 6-5) enables you to focus on how resources affect the task by showing resource assignments for each task. Use this view to organize resources by task; evaluate work effort and cost by task; and compare scheduled and actual work and costs.

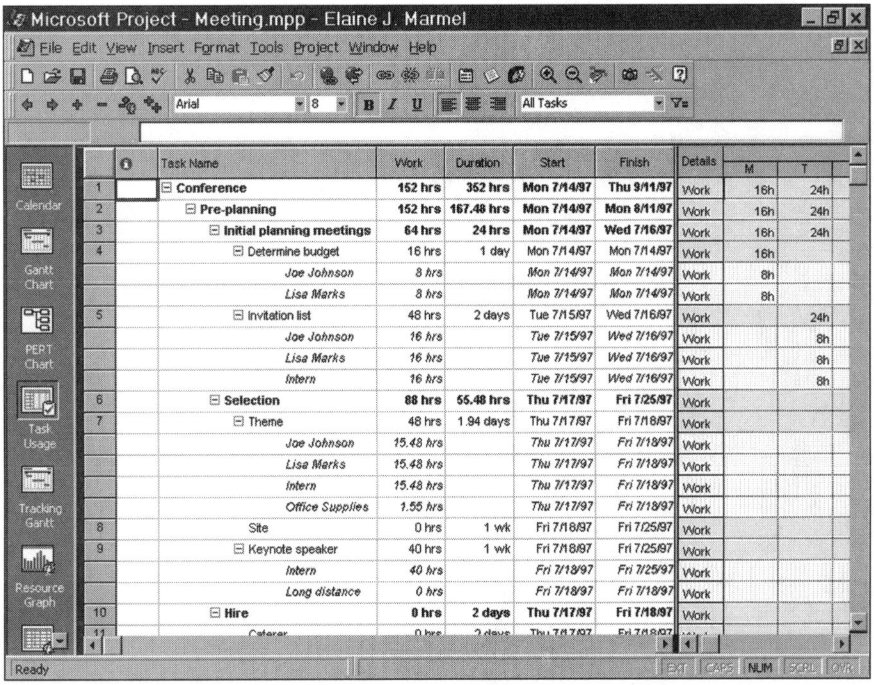

Figure 6-5: The Task Usage view shows resources grouped under the tasks to which they are assigned.

The default table for the left side of the view, is the Usage task table, but you can display other tables by using the Table Selection button, as described earlier in this chapter. Also, by default, Project shows Work in the Details section; again, you can select any item from the Format⇨Details menu or in the Details Styles dialog box (choose Format⇨Detail Styles). For more information on the Task Usage view, see Chapter 2.

Resource Usage view

As you can see from Figure 6-6, the Resource Usage view is the inverse of the Task Usage view; the former shows each resource and the tasks assigned to it. You can use the Resource Usage view to enter and edit resource information, and you can assign or reassign tasks to resources on this view by dragging the tasks between resources. The Resource Usage view is also useful when you want to

✦ Check resource overallocations

✦ Examine the number of hours or the percentage of capacity at which each resource is scheduled to work

✦ View a resource's progress or costs

✦ Determine how much time a particular resource has for additional work assignments

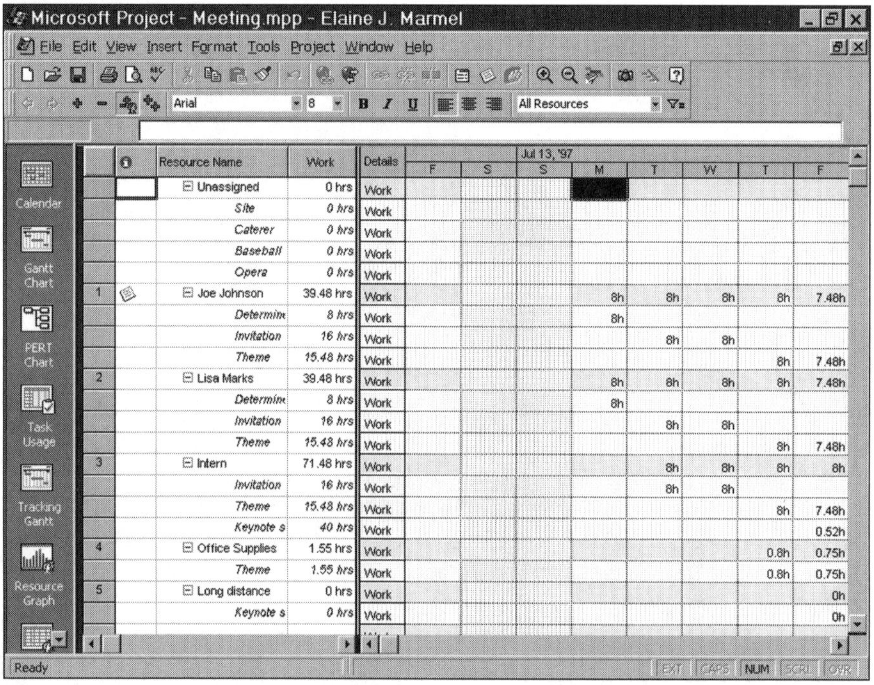

Figure 6-6: The Resource view organizes task assignments by resource.

The default table on the left side of this view is the Usage table. You can use the Table Selection button described earlier to switch to a different table. Similarly, you can use either the Format⇨Details or the Format⇨Detail Styles commands to add to or change the information that appears in the Details section. (Work is the default selection.) For more information on the Resource Usage view, see Chapter 2.

PERT analysis views

PERT analysis is sometimes called what-if analysis, and many project managers use this approach to estimate a probable outcome. The probable outcome you estimate might be the duration of a task, its start date, or its end date. As a function of the estimating process, you specify the optimistic, pessimistic, and expected durations of tasks in your project. Then Microsoft Project calculates a weighted average of the three durations. As you might guess, PERT analysis has little to do with the PERT Chart view. But you can use four PERT analysis views in Project to help you make your estimates:

✦ PA_PERT Entry Sheet

✦ PA_Expected Gantt

✦ PA_Optimistic Gantt

✦ PA_Pessimistic Gantt

You can use the PERT Analysis toolbar (see Figure 6-7) to perform PERT analysis. Choose View⇨Toolbars⇨PERT Analysis to display the toolbar.

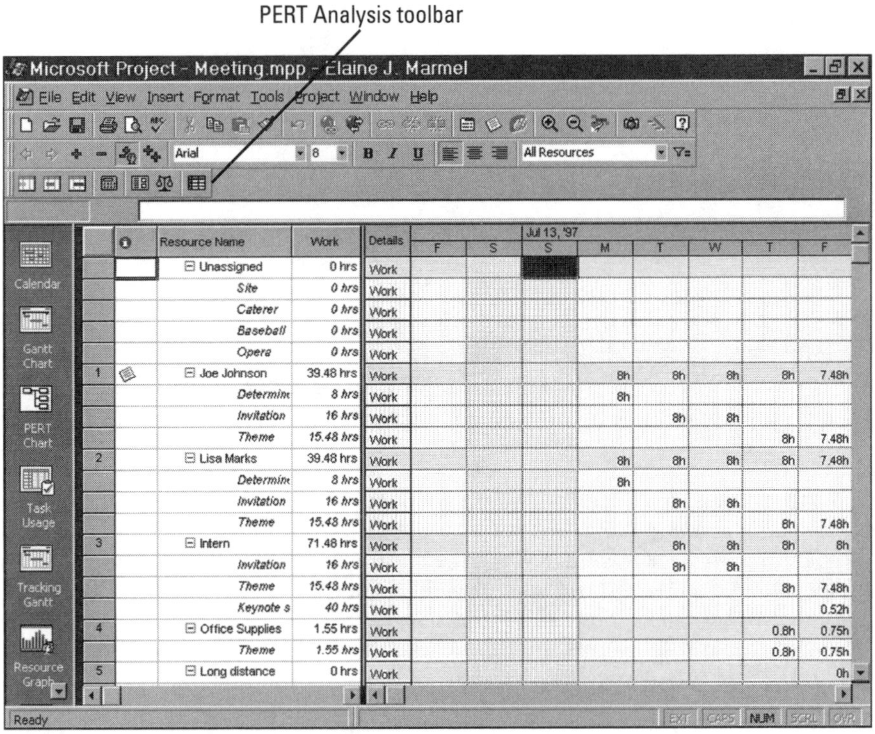

Figure 6-7: Use this toolbar to help you with PERT analysis tasks.

Note   *PERT* stands for "Program Evaluation and Review Technique." The Special Projects Office of the U.S. Navy devised this method of tracking the flow of tasks in the late 1950s.

PA_PERT Entry Sheet view

The PA_PERT Entry Sheet view in Figure 6-8 focuses PERT analysis entirely on durations. Click on the PERT Entry Sheet button on the PERT Analysis toolbar to display this sheet.

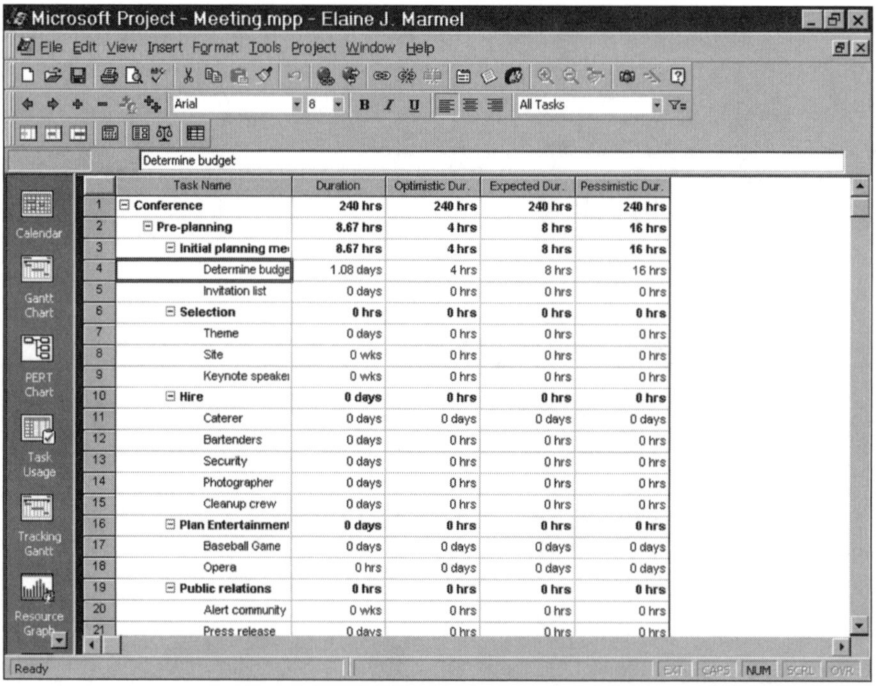

Figure 6-8: Use this view to focus on entering estimated durations for PERT analysis.

Using this sheet, you enter optimistic, expected, and pessimistic durations for each task. When you click on the Calculate PERT button on the PERT Analysis toolbar, Project uses a weighted average of the numbers you supply and calculates the probable duration of the task. Project displays the result in the Duration column for that task. Notice the duration of 1.08 days for the Determine budget task; Project calculated this duration using the weighted average of the numbers in the Optimistic Dur., Expected Dur., and Pessimistic Dur. columns for the task

The default table for this view is the PA_PERT Entry table; you can change the default by using the Select Table button.

PA_Expected Gantt view

After you have entered optimistic, expected, and pessimistic durations on the PA_PERT Entry Sheet and calculated, you can view the expected results for your entire project on the PA_Expected Gantt view. Click on the Expected Gantt button on the PERT Analysis toolbar to display the PA_Expected Gantt view (see Figure 6-9). As its name implies, the PA_Expected Gantt view is a variation of the Gantt Chart view. After you enter information into the left side of the PA_Expected Gantt view, Project displays bars on the right side, like the chart portion of the Gantt Chart view.

If you prefer to estimate with start dates and end dates or to focus entirely on expected durations, you can use this view to enter and evaluate the expected scenarios for task durations, start dates, and end dates. If you use this approach, you also need to supply start and end dates on the PA_Optimistic Gantt view and the PA_Pessimistic Gantt view before you click on the Calculate button.

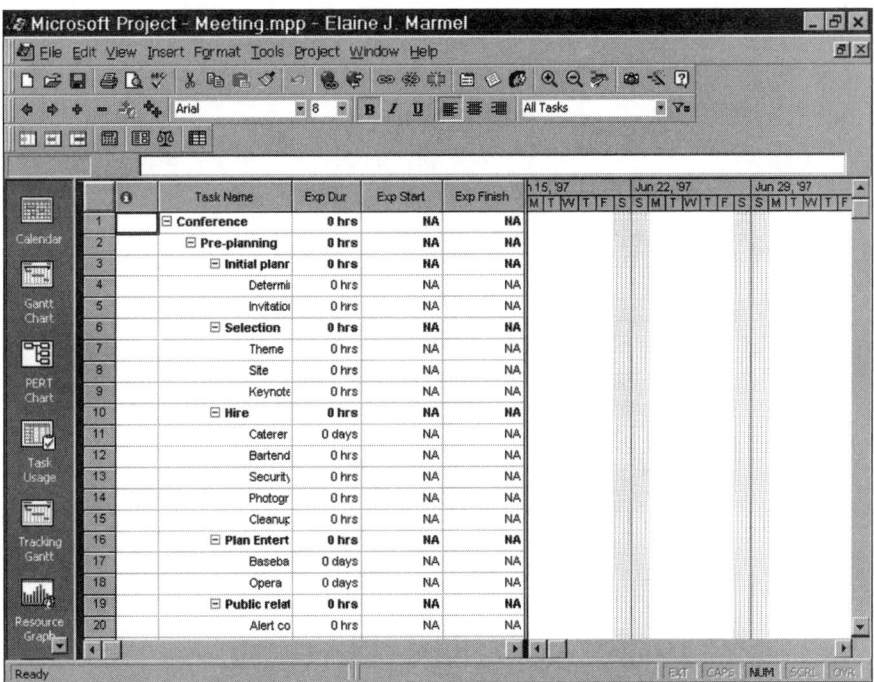

Figure 6-9: Use the PA_Expected Gantt view to help create expected task durations.

Note

Figure 6-9 has optimistic, expected, and pessimistic duration entries for only one task, the Determine Budget task.

The default table for this view is the PA_Expected Case table; use the Select Table button to change the table.

PA_Optimistic Gantt view

After you have entered optimistic, expected, and pessimistic durations in the PA_PERT Entry Sheet view and calculated, you can view the optimistic results for your entire project on the PA_Optimistic Gantt view. Click on the Optimistic Gantt button on the PERT Analysis toolbar to display the PA_Optimistic Gantt view (see Figure 6-10). Like its companion the PA_Expected Gantt, the PA_Optimistic Gantt view is a variation of the Gantt Chart view. After you enter information into the left side of the PA_Optimistic Gantt view, Project displays bars on the right side, like the chart portion of the Gantt Chart view. You can use this view to enter and evaluate the optimistic scenarios for task durations, start dates, and end dates.

If you prefer to work with start dates and end dates or to focus entirely on optimistic durations while estimating, you can use this view to enter and evaluate the optimistic scenarios for task durations, start dates, and end dates. If you use this approach, you also need to supply start and end dates on the PA_Expected Gantt view and the PA_Pessimistic Gantt view before you click on the Calculate button.

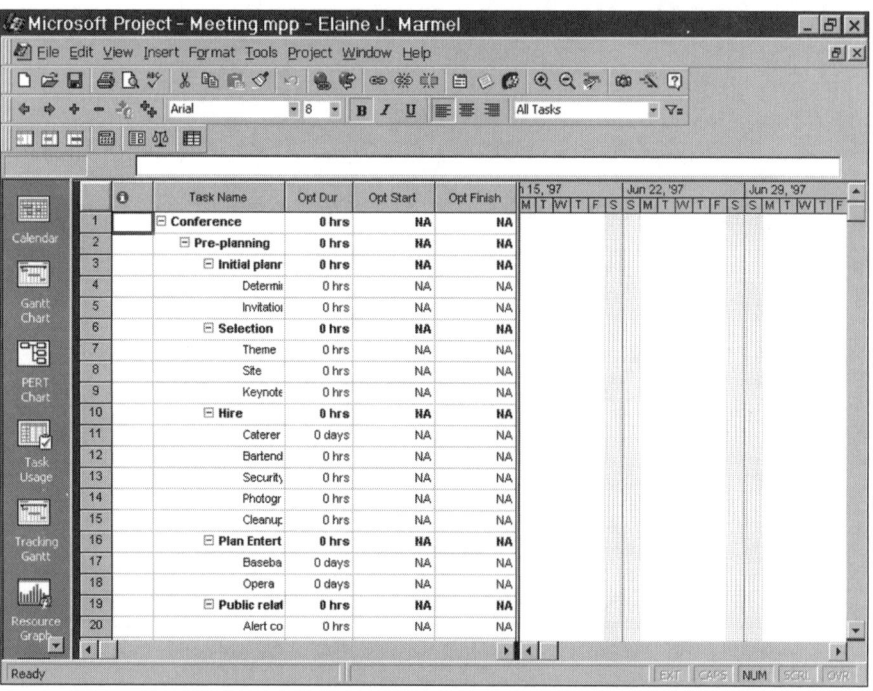

Figure 6-10: Use the PA_Optimistic Gantt view to help create optimistic task durations.

Note

Figure 6-10 shows optimistic, expected, and pessimistic durations for only one task, the Determine Budget task.

The default table for this view is the PA_Optimistic Case table; use the Select Table button to change the table.

PA_Pessimistic Gantt view

After you enter optimistic, expected, and pessimistic durations on the PA_PERT Entry Sheet view and perform the calculations, you can view the pessimistic results for your entire project on the PA_Pessimistic Gantt view. Click on the Pessimistic Gantt button on the PERT Analysis toolbar to display the PA_Pessimistic Gantt view (see Figure 6-11). Like its cousins, the PA_Expected Gantt and the PA_Optimistic views, the PA_Pessimistic Gantt view is also a variation of the Gantt Chart view. Again, after you enter information into the left side of the PA_Pessimistic Gantt view, Project displays bars on the right side, like the chart portion of the Gantt Chart view. You can use this view to enter and evaluate the pessimistic scenarios for task durations, start dates, and end dates.

If you prefer to work with start dates and end dates or to focus entirely on pessimistic durations while estimating, you can use this view to enter and evaluate the pessimistic scenarios for task durations, start dates, and end dates. If you use this approach, you also need to supply start and end dates on the PA_Expected Gantt view and the PA_Optimistic Gantt view before you click on the Calculate button.

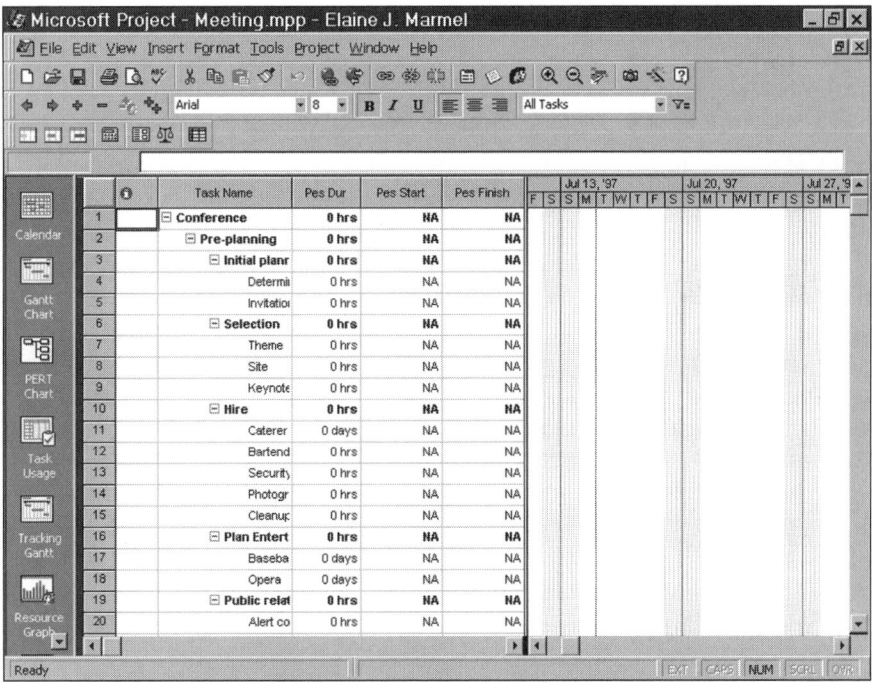

Figure 6-11: Use PA_Pessimistic Gantt view to help create pessimistic task durations.

Note   Figure 6-11 has entries for optimistic, expected, and pessimistic durations for only one task, the Determine Budget task.

The default table for this view is the PA_Pessimistic Case table; use the Select Table button to change the table.

PERT Weights

Project calculates a weighted average when you use PERT analysis. You can control the weights Project applies to each scenario from the Set PERT Weights dialog box (see Figure 6-12). Click on the PERT Weights button on the PERT Analysis toolbar (second button from the *right* edge of the toolbar). Note that the values you enter must sum to 6 using the following formula:

$$(\text{optimistic duration}) + 4(\text{expected duration}) + (\text{pessimistic duration}) \div 6$$

You can use different weights to change the emphasis Project applies to its calculation of each scenario.

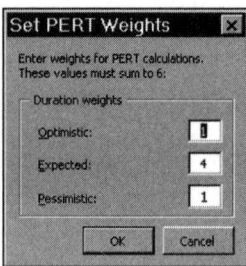

Figure 6-12: Use the Set PERT Weights dialog box to adjust the weights Project applies when making PERT calculations.

Rollup views

Project contains a special macro called the Rollup_Formatting macro. When you run this macro, Project displays, on the Gantt Chart view, a summary bar that contains symbols that represent tasks; you can think of these tasks as rolled up onto the summary bar. This type of view helps you create a summarized version of your project and makes important dates visible. Three new views help you see your focus on your project's summary tasks:

New Feature

✦ Bar Rollup

✦ Milestone Date Rollup

✦ Milestone Rollup

Note

A rollup view displays only the tasks that you format as rollup tasks.

This macro won't work unless you first mark tasks on the project as tasks you want to roll up. Follow these steps to mark tasks and run the Rollup Formatting macro:

1. Select tasks in the Gantt Chart view.

Tip

You can use Windows selection techniques to select several tasks simultaneously. Click on the first task you want to select. Then, to select contiguous tasks, press Shift and click on the last task. Or to select noncontiguous tasks, press Ctrl and click on each task.

>   **2.** Click on the Task Information button on the Standard toolbar to open the General tab of the Task Information dialog box (see Figure 6-13).

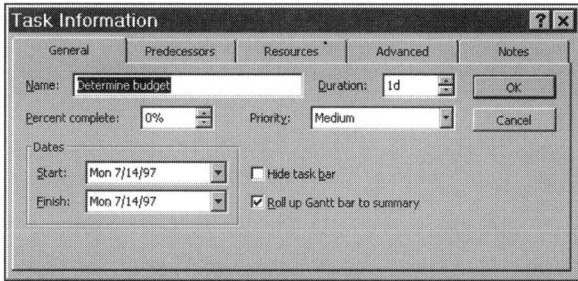

Figure 6-13: Use the General tab of the Task Information dialog box to mark tasks for rollup.

>   **3.** Place a check in the Roll up Gantt bar to summary check box.
>
>   **4.** Click on OK.
>
>   **5.** Choose Tools➪Macros. Then choose Macros from the side menu to open the Macros dialog box (see Figure 6-14).

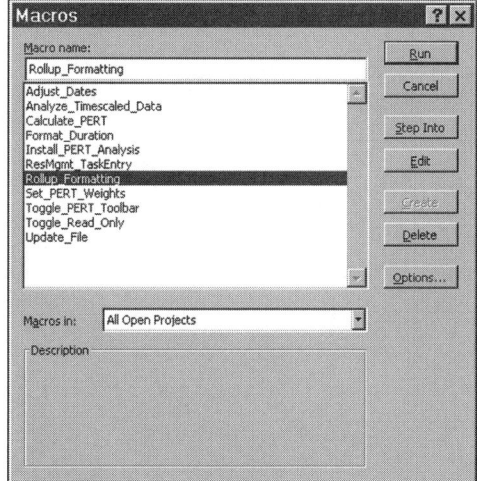

Figure 6-14: Run macros from the Macro dialog box.

6. Select the Rollup Formatting macro and click on Run. Project displays the Rollup Formatting dialog box (see Figure 6-15).

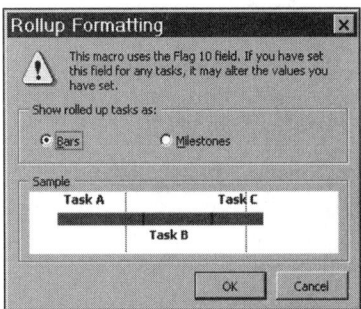

Figure 6-15: Choose the style of formatting you want for your rollup.

7. Select Bars to display rolled up tasks as bars, or select Milestones to display rolled up tasks as milestones.

8. Click on OK.

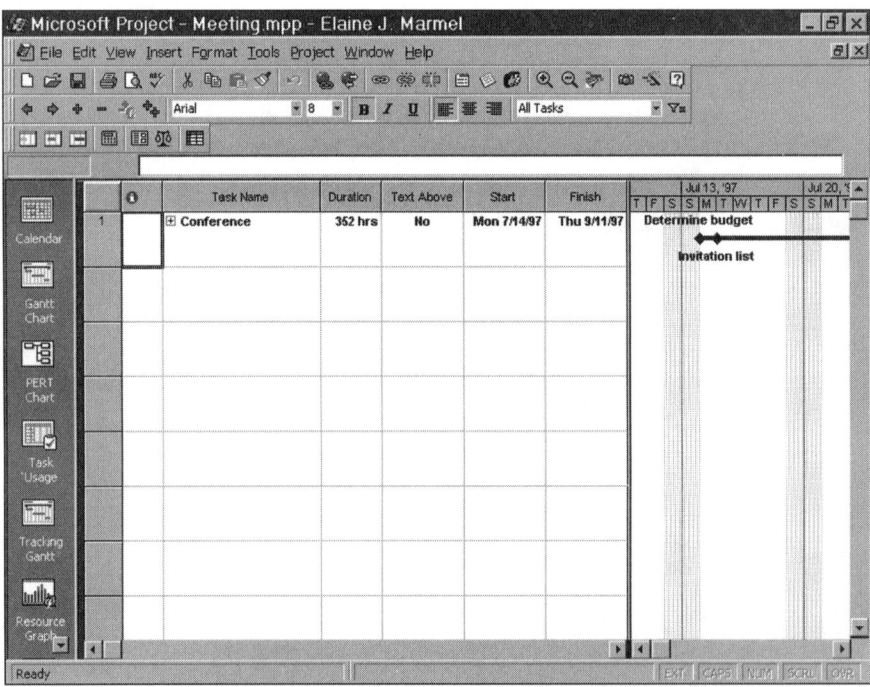

Figure 6-16: When you format rollup tasks as milestones, Project displays your project using the Milestone Rollup view.

When you use the Rollup Formatting macro, Project displays *only* those tasks you formatted for rollup. The table you see in the sheet portion of all of these views is the Rollup table, but you can switch to another table using the techniques explained earlier in the chapter. Figure 6-16 shows the Milestone Rollup view that Project displays if you selected Milestones in step 7.

If you select Bars in step 7, Project displays the Bar Rollup view (see Figure 6-17).

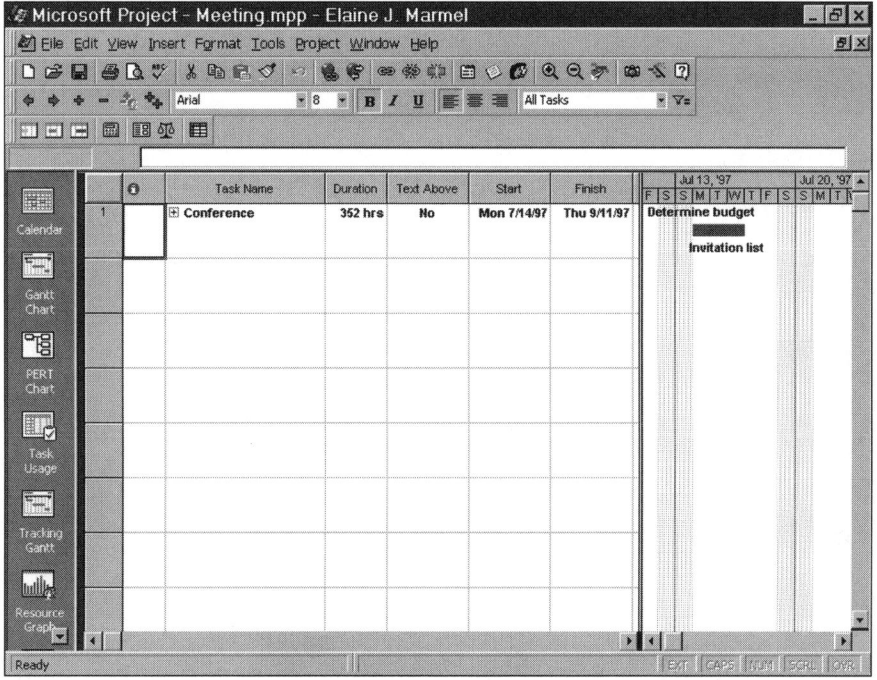

Figure 6-17: When you format rollup tasks as bars, Project displays your project using the Bar Rollup view.

Tip

To redisplay all subtasks in a typical Gantt Chart view, click on the Display All Subtasks button on the Formatting toolbar (the button containing the double plus sign).

Using the More Views dialog box (click on the More Views button on the View Bar), you can display the Milestone Date Rollup view (see Figure 6-18).

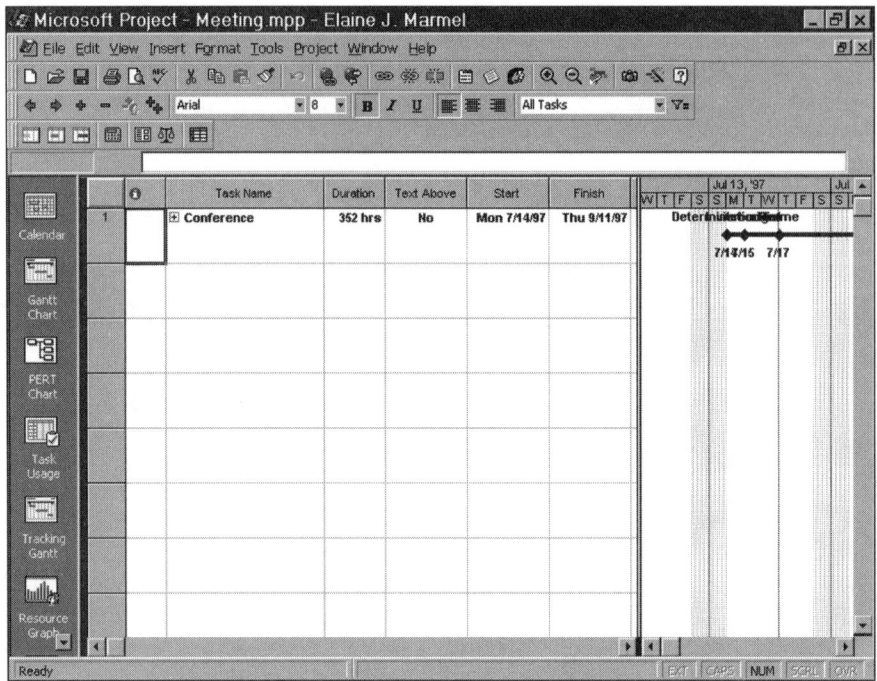

Figure 6-18: Use this view to see rollup tasks along with their start dates.

Note If your start dates are close together, Project overwrites the task names, making them difficult or impossible to read.

Admiring the Other Views...

Project contains 26 standard views; those that appear on the View bar were introduced in previous chapters. This section reviews all the standard views and refers you to the earlier chapters for additional information.

Calendar

You saw this view in Chapter 2. The familiar format of the Calendar view (see Figure 6-19) makes it easy to use.

In the Calendar view your tasks appear as bars that span days or weeks. This view is useful for entering a simple project and for reviewing what needs to be done on a given day.

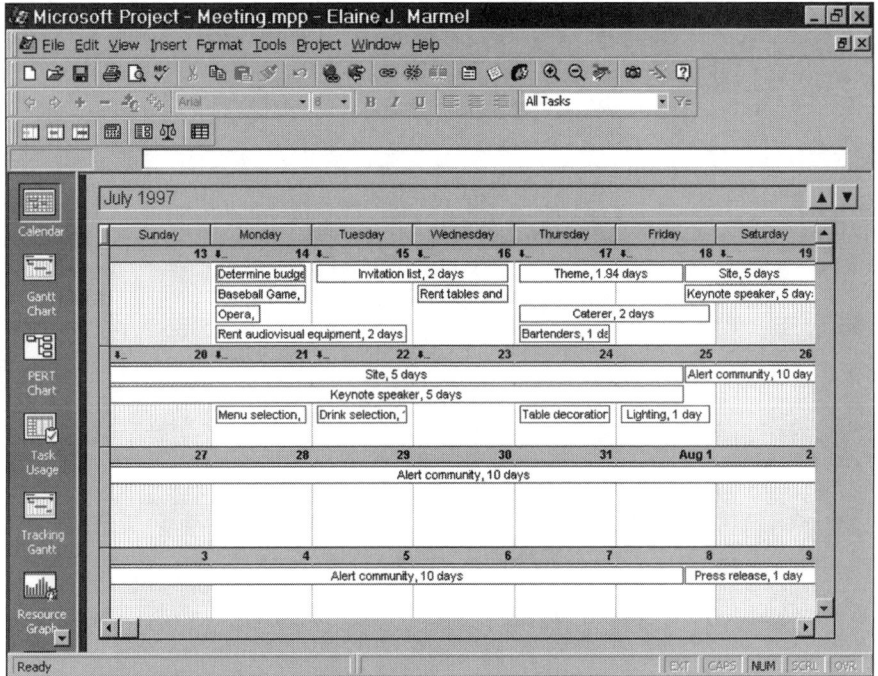

Figure 6-19: The Calendar view.

Detail Gantt

The Detail Gantt view shows a list of tasks and related information as well as a chart that displays slack time and slippage as thin bars between tasks (see Figure 6-20). Choose this view from the More Views dialog box (choose View➪More View).

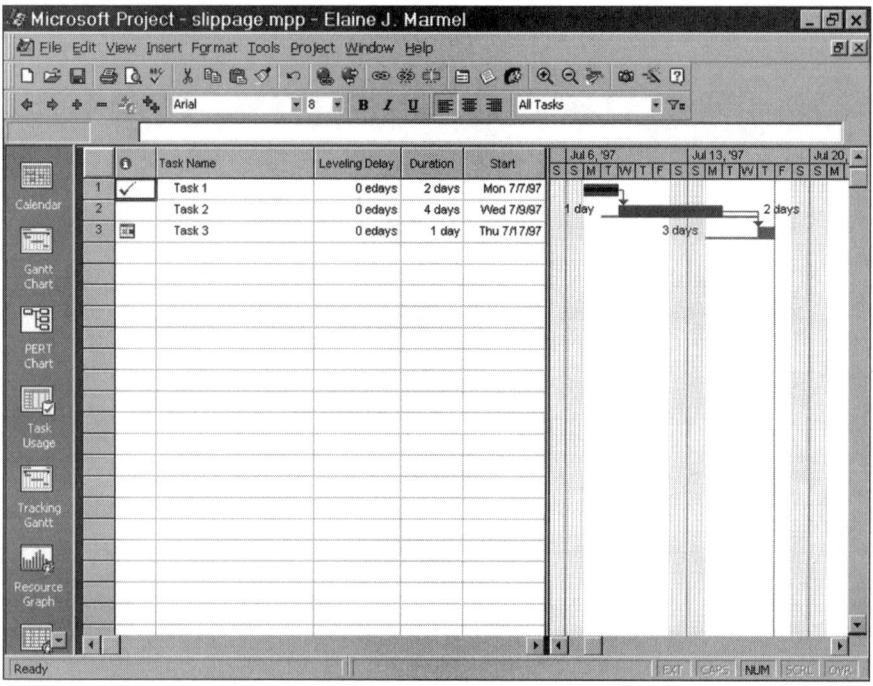

Figure 6-20: The Detail Gantt view.

The thin bar extending from the right edge of the second task shows slack time between the second and third tasks, and the thin bar that appears at the left edge of the second task represents slippage between the first task and the second task. The number of days appears in both cases. You can think of slack time as flexibility in the schedule. Slippage results when you save a baseline on a project initially, you have started a task but not necessarily completed the task, and the finish date for the task is later than the baseline finish date.

This view is most useful for evaluating slack and slippage. The default table in the Detail Gantt view is the Delay table; use the techniques described earlier in this chapter to change the table.

You may want to incorporate the Task Details Form view in the bottom pane of the Detail Gantt view so that you can look more closely at the tasks associated with slippage or slack. Choose Window⇨Split, or use the Split Bar to display the Task Details Form view in the bottom pane.

Note

You can create a combination view with the Detail Gantt view in the top pane and the Task Details Form view in the bottom pane that you can save and use later. See Chapter 16 for details.

Gantt Chart

Chapter 2 covers the Gantt Chart view (see Figure 6-21) in detail. This view makes it easy for you to create a project, link tasks to create sequential dependencies, see how your project is progressing over time, and view tasks graphically while still having access to details.

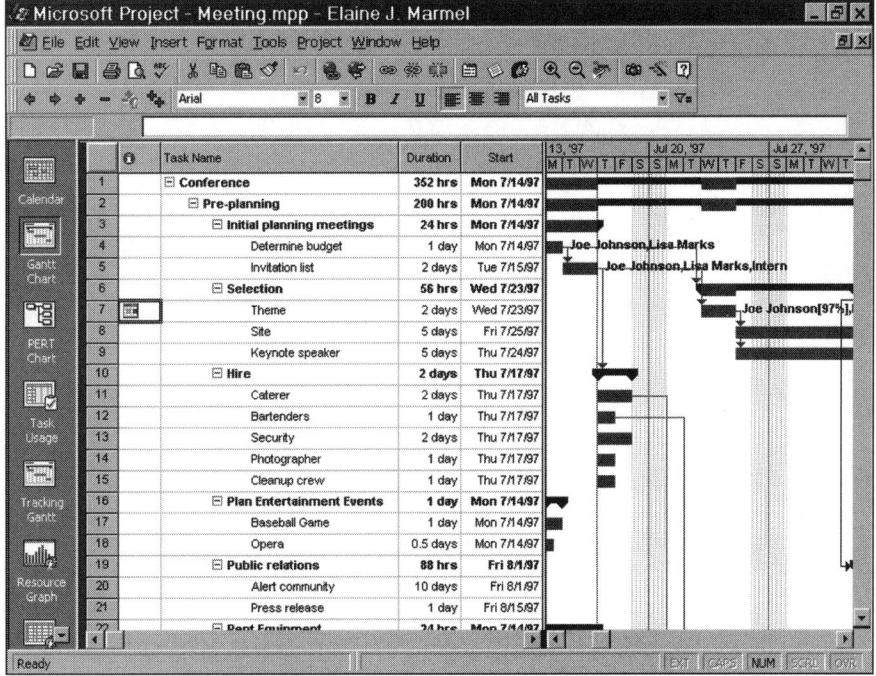

Figure 6-21: The Gantt Chart view.

Leveling Gantt

The Leveling Gantt view (see Figure 6-22) focuses on task delays. This view provides a graphic representation of delayed tasks while still providing task detail information. The chart portion of the view shows the effects before and after leveling. The default table that appears in the Leveling Gantt view is the Delay table, but you can change the table using the techniques described earlier in this chapter. You can use the Delay table to add or remove delay time and see the effects of your changes.

Note

Leveling is the process of resolving resource conflicts or overallocations by delaying or splitting certain tasks. You learn more about resource leveling in Chapter 9.

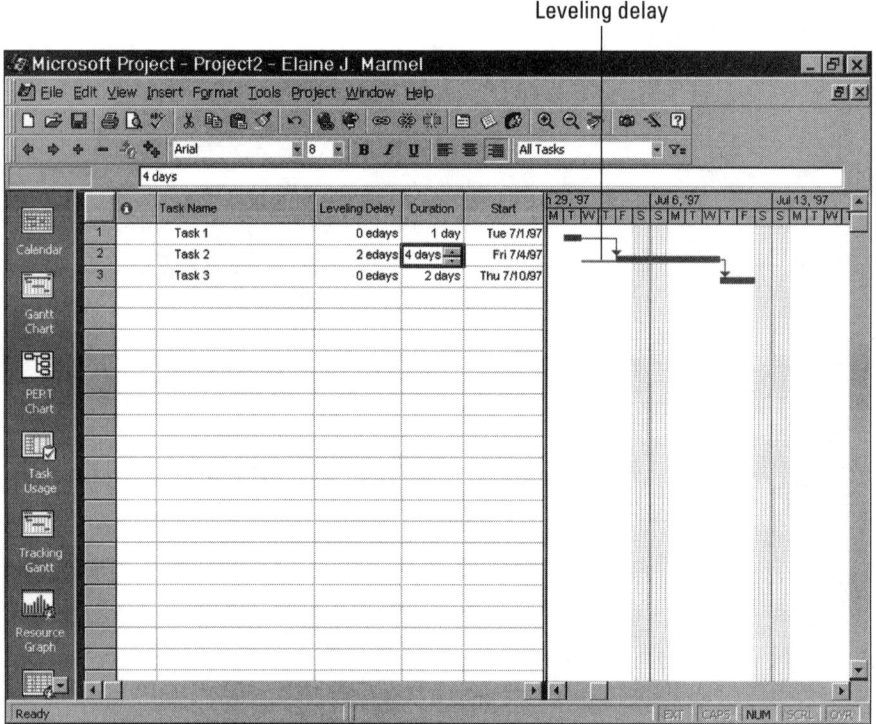

Figure 6-22: The Leveling Gantt view.

On this chart the bar to the left of Task 2 represents delay time of two days, as indicated in the table.

Tracking Gantt

The Tracking Gantt view is also based on the Gantt Chart view. On the chart portion of the view, you see two bars for every task. The bottom bar shows baseline settings. The top bar reflects current scheduled start and finish dates if a task has not yet been started. If a task has been started — that is, you have supplied some amount of work that has been completed — the top bar shows actual start and finish dates. In Figure 6-23 the Determine Budget task has been completed, and the Invitation List task is 75 percent complete, so the top bar for these tasks displays actual start and finish dates. No other tasks have been started, so the top bars on all other tasks represent scheduled start and finish dates.

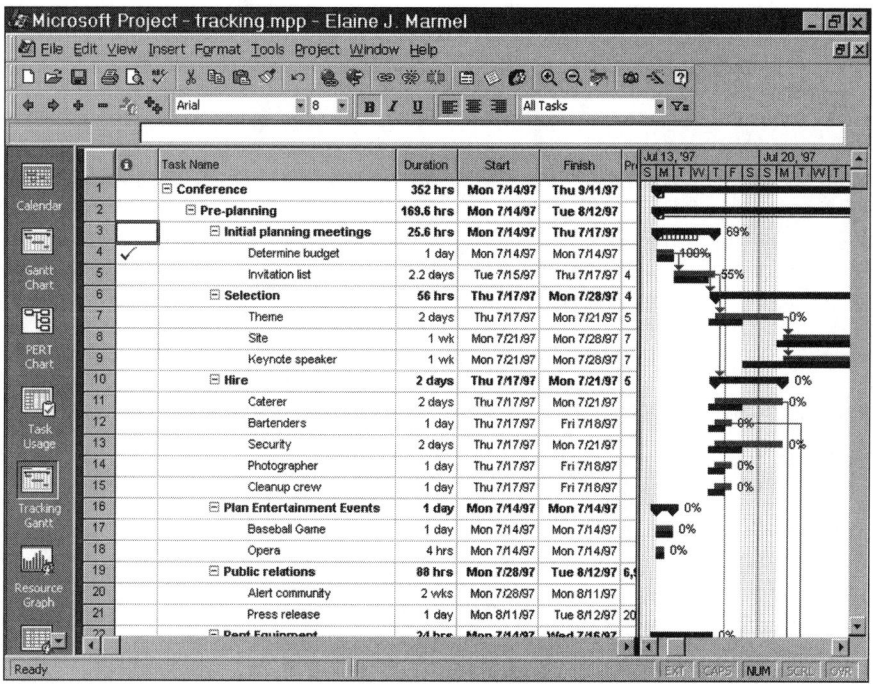

Figure 6-23: You can evaluate the progress of individual tasks and the project as a whole in the Tracking Gantt view.

The Tracking Gantt view provides a great pictorial way to evaluate the progress of individual tasks and the project as a whole. The default table that appears in the Tracking Gantt view is the Entry table, which you can change by using the techniques described earlier in this chapter. The Tracking Gantt view is a great overall view because you can use it to create a project, add resources to tasks, and set task dependencies by linking tasks.

PERT Chart

You also saw the PERT Chart view (see Figure 6-24) in Chapter 2. This view makes it easy for you to evaluate the flow of your project and check tasks dependencies. Each node on the PERT Chart view represents a task in your project.

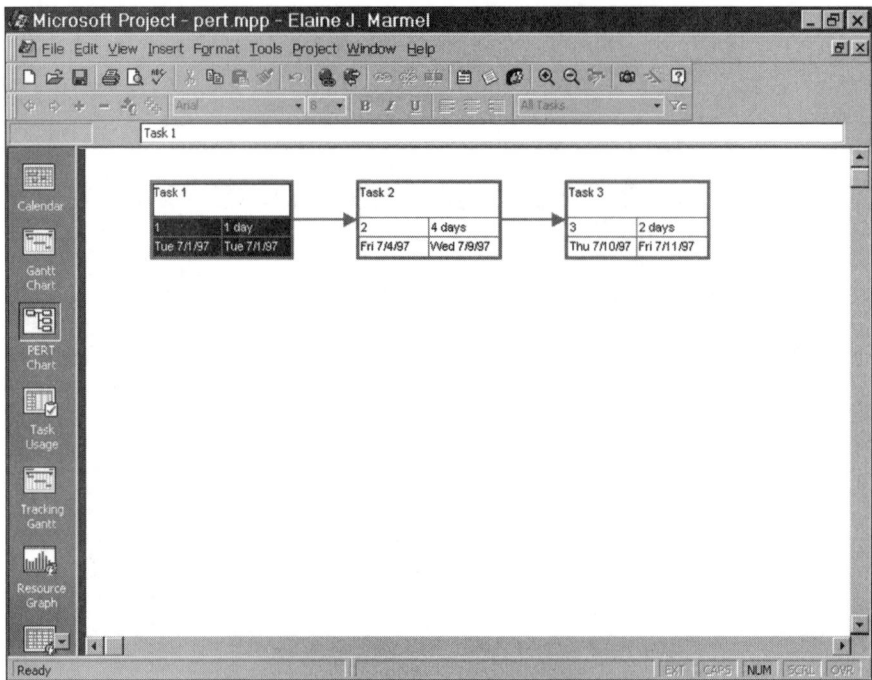

Figure 6-24: The PERT Chart view.

Resource Allocation

The Resource Allocation view is a combination view. For example, in Figure 6-25 the Resource Usage view appears in the top pane, and the Gantt Chart view appears in the bottom pane. (The Resource Usage view is covered earlier in this chapter, and the Gantt Chart view is covered in Chapter 2.)

The default table that appears on the Resource Usage view (the upper pane of the combination view) is the Usage table; the default table that appears on the Gantt Chart view (the lower pane of the combination view) is the Entry table. You can use the techniques described earlier in this chapter to change either table.

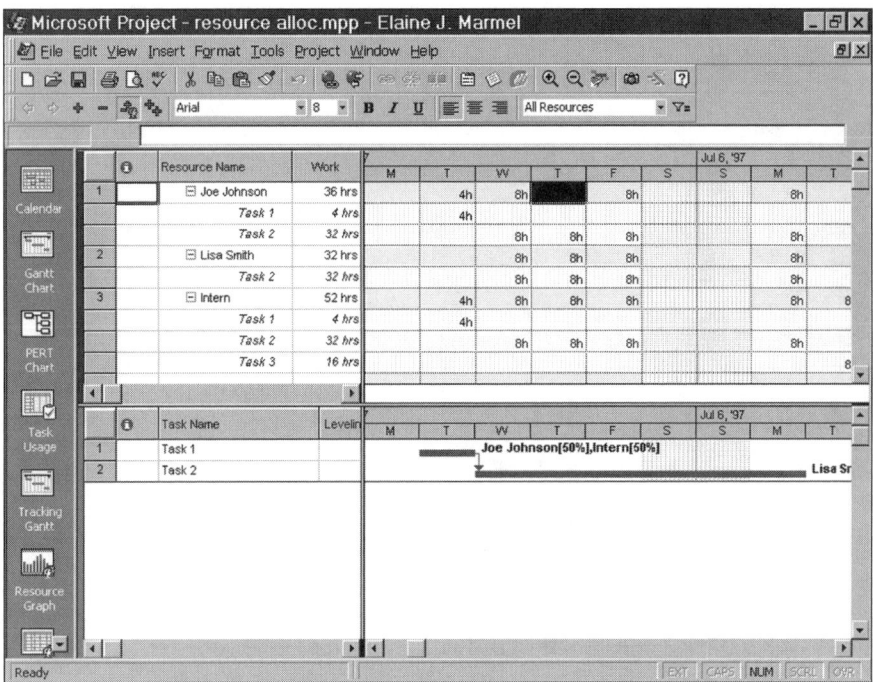

Figure 6-25: The Resource Allocation view displays resource allocation relative to the project timing.

Resource Form

The Resource Form view displays detailed information about one resource at a time (see Figure 6-26).

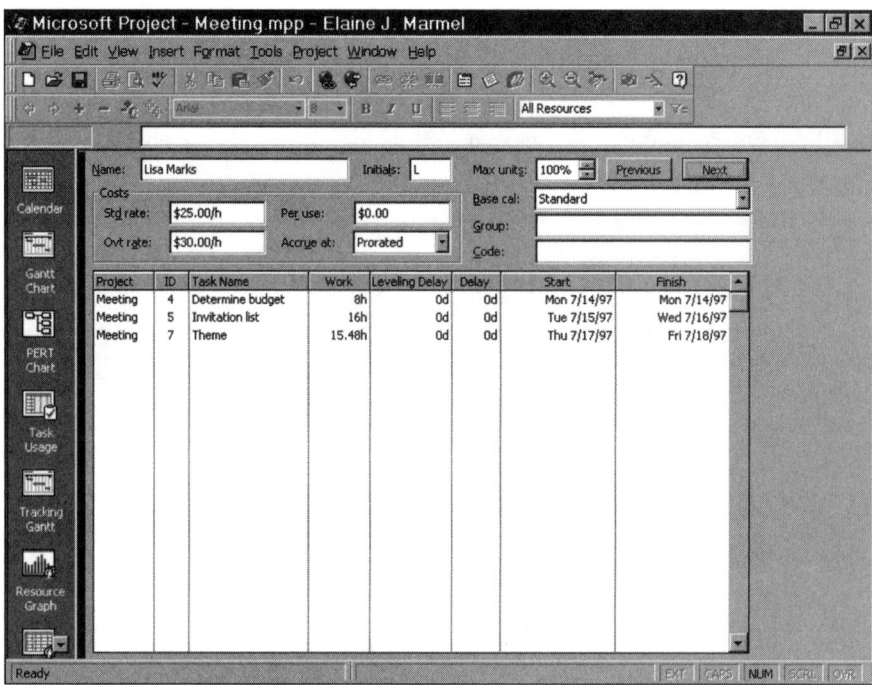

Figure 6-26: The Resource Form view.

Use the Next and Previous buttons in the upper-right corner of the window to display different resources; if you haven't sorted or filtered resources, Project shows them to you in ID number order.

Resource Graph

You saw the Resource Graph view in Chapter 2; it shows resource allocation, work, and cost information in a graph format(see Figure 6-27).

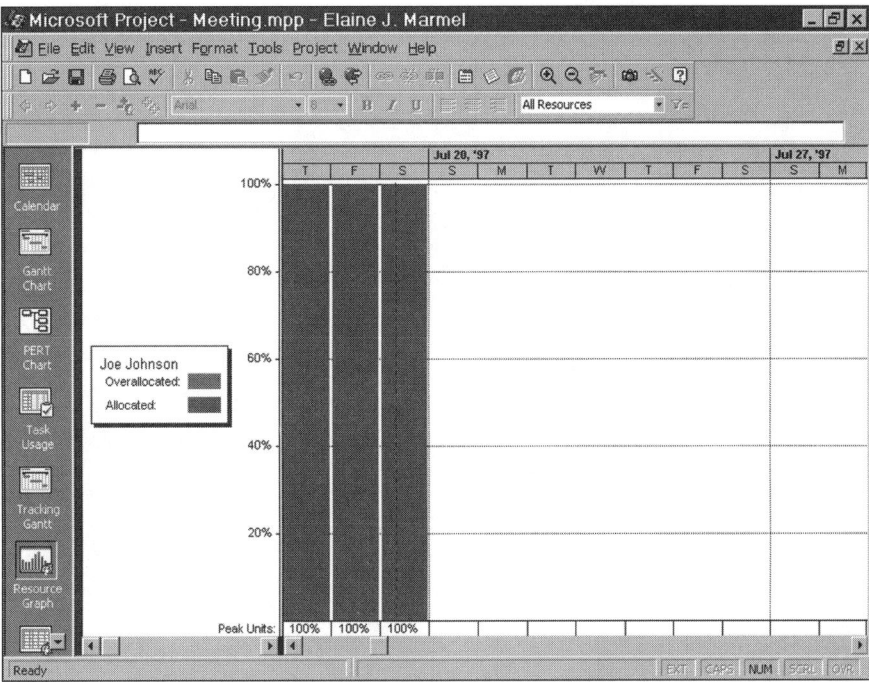

Figure 6-27: The Resource Graph view.

The Resource Graph view shows how a particular resource is being used on a project. To view a different resource, click on the scroll arrows that appear below the left pane in this window. This view works well as part of a combination view.

Resource Name Form

The Resource Name Form view is a simplified version of the Resource Form view. (Compare Figure 6-28 with Figure 6-26.) None of the Cost information appears in this view, nor do you see the resources maximum units, base calendar, group, or code.

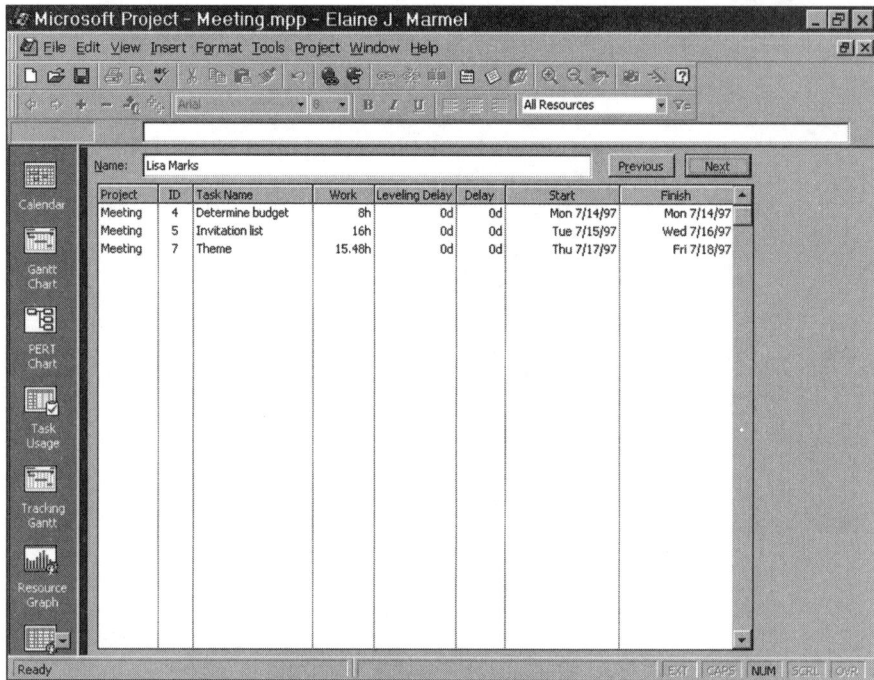

Figure 6-28: The Resource Name Form view.

You can use this view to set up basic information about resources for a project — which can give you a good idea about a resource's workload. Use the Previous and Next buttons to view different resources.

Resource Sheet

You saw the Resource Sheet view in Chapter 2, and you spent a great deal of time with the Resource Sheet view in Chapter 5. As you can see from Figure 6-29, this view displays resource information in a spreadsheet format. You can add, edit, and inspect resource information in this view.

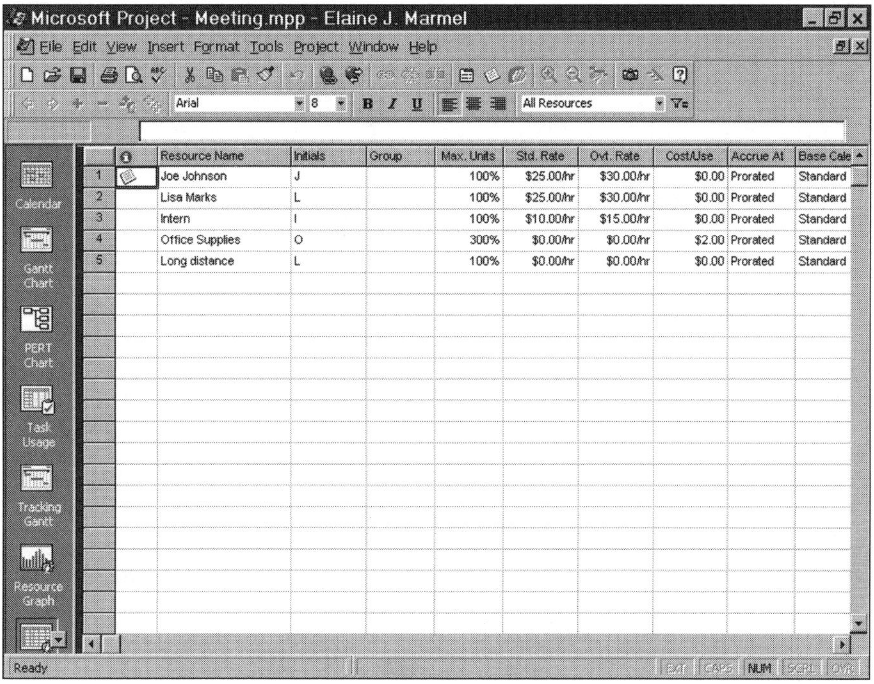

		O	Resource Name	Initials	Group	Max. Units	Std. Rate	Ovt. Rate	Cost/Use	Accrue At	Base Cale
1			Joe Johnson	J		100%	$25.00/hr	$30.00/hr	$0.00	Prorated	Standard
2			Lisa Marks	L		100%	$25.00/hr	$30.00/hr	$0.00	Prorated	Standard
3			Intern	I		100%	$10.00/hr	$15.00/hr	$0.00	Prorated	Standard
4			Office Supplies	O		300%	$0.00/hr	$0.00/hr	$2.00	Prorated	Standard
5			Long distance	L		100%	$0.00/hr	$0.00/hr	$0.00	Prorated	Standard

Figure 6-29: Use the Resource Sheet view to add, edit, or inspect resource information.

The default table that appears on the Resource Sheet view is the Entry table, but you can change the table using the techniques described earlier in this chapter.

Task Details Form

The Task Details Form view in Figure 6-30 enables you to view and edit tracking information about one task at a time.

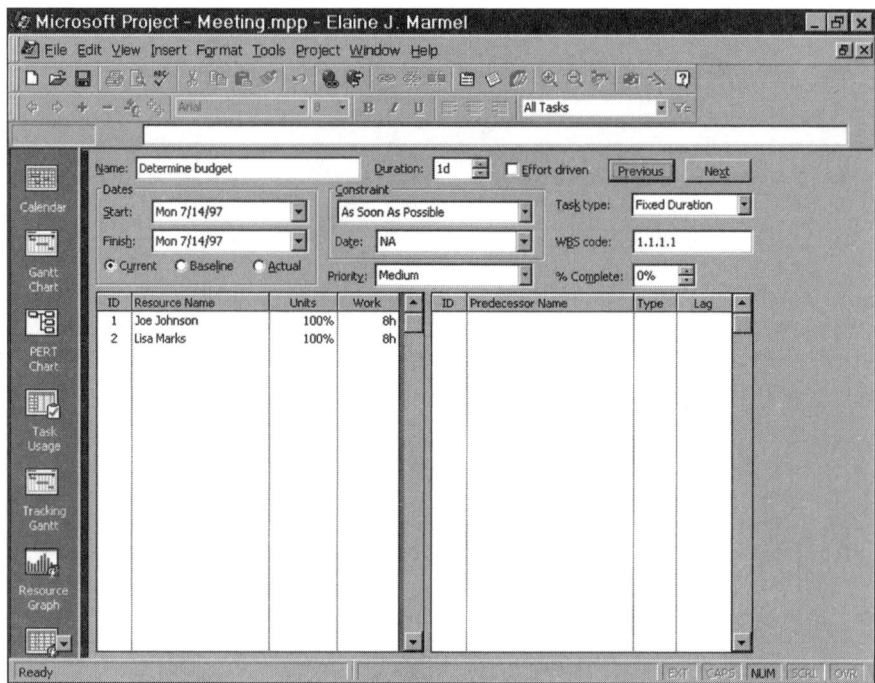

Figure 6-30: The Task Details Form view.

Use the Previous and Next buttons to switch from task to task. If you haven't sorted or filtered tasks, Project displays them in ID number order. The Task Details Form view is a good choice for part of a combination view.

This view is very similar to the Task Form view and the Task Name Form view.

Task Entry

The Task Entry view is a combination view. In Figure 6-31 the Gantt Chart view appears in the top pane, and the Task Form view appears in the bottom pane. To see information about a task in the Task Form view, select the task in the Gantt Chart view.

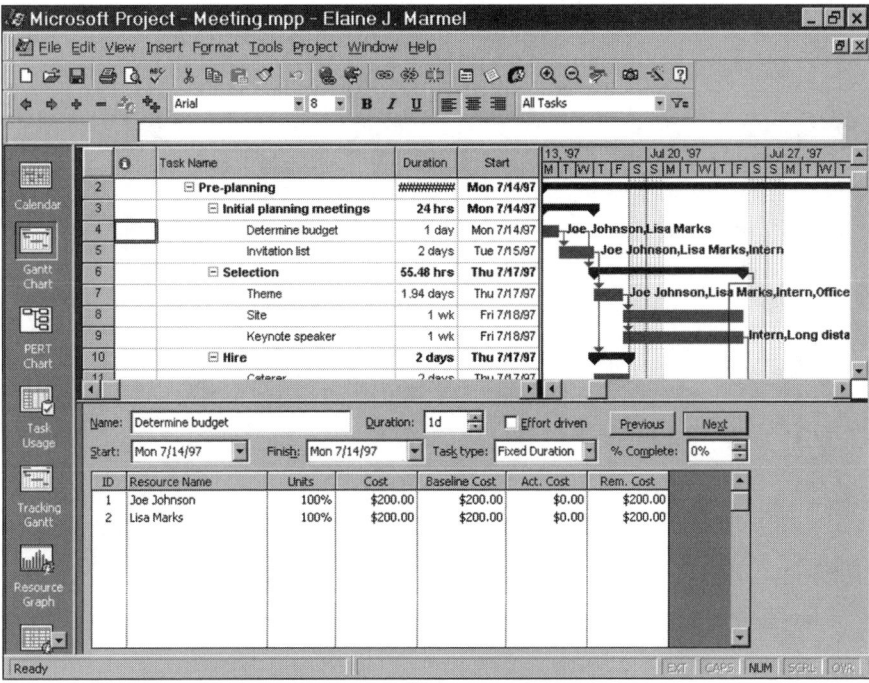

Figure 6-31: The Task Entry view.

Only the Gantt Chart view in the top pane uses a table. The default table is the Entry table, but you use the techniques described earlier in this chapter to change the table.

Task Form

The Task Form view appears on the bottom portion of the Task Entry view, as you saw in Figure 6-31. The Task Form view (see Figure 6-32) closely resembles the Task Details Form view (refer to Figure 6-30).

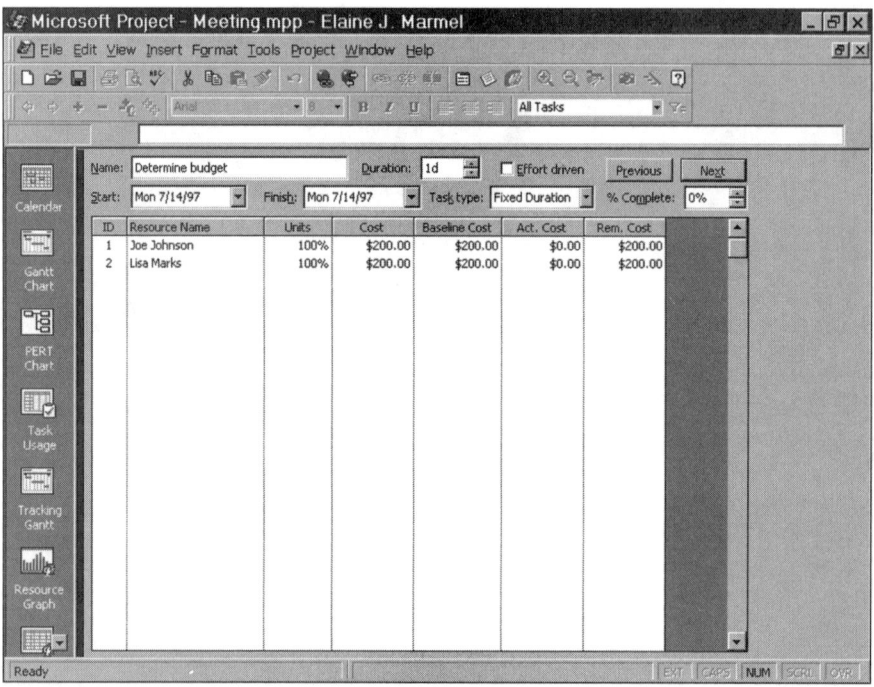

Figure 6-32: The Task Form view.

The Task Form view provides more resource information, such as costs, than the Task Details Form view, and the Task Details Form view provides more task information, such as predecessors, than the Task Form view. Use the Previous and Next buttons to switch tasks. The Task Form view also closely resembles the Task Name Form view (described next).

Task Name Form

The Task Name Form view is a cousin to the Task Details Form view and the Task Form view. This simplified version displays the basic characteristics of tasks, one task at a time (see Figure 6-33).

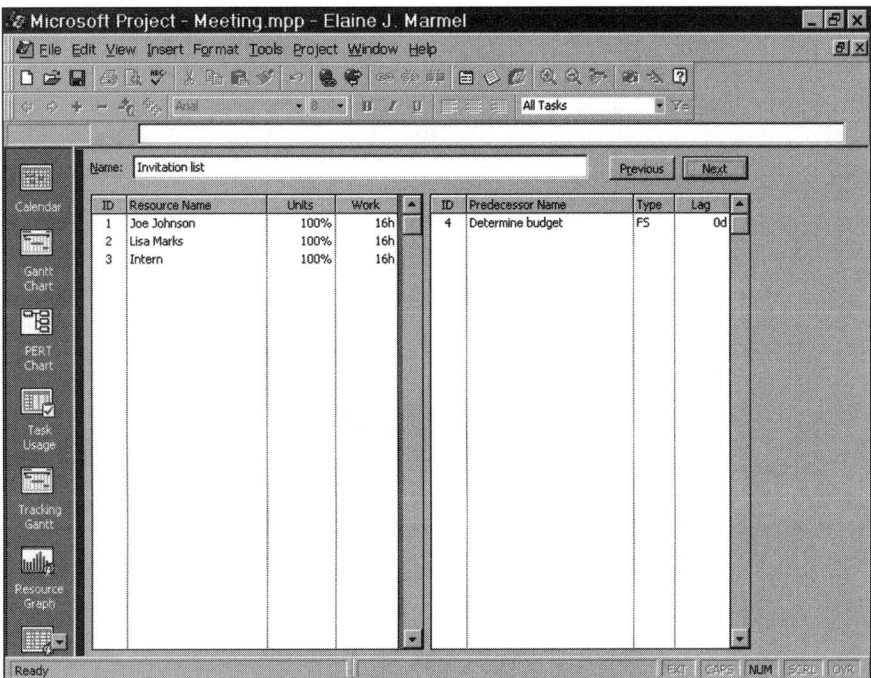

Figure 6-33: The Task Name Form view.

Use the Previous and Next buttons to switch tasks. Again, if you compare Figures 6-30, 6-32, and 6-33, you can see how closely these views resemble each other. The Task Name Form view works well as part of a combination view.

Task PERT

This special version of the PERT Chart view (see Figure 6-34) displays the current task in the center of the pane, with the task's predecessors to the left and successors to the right. When you are working on a large project, this graphic view helps you focus on one task and the tasks linked to it.

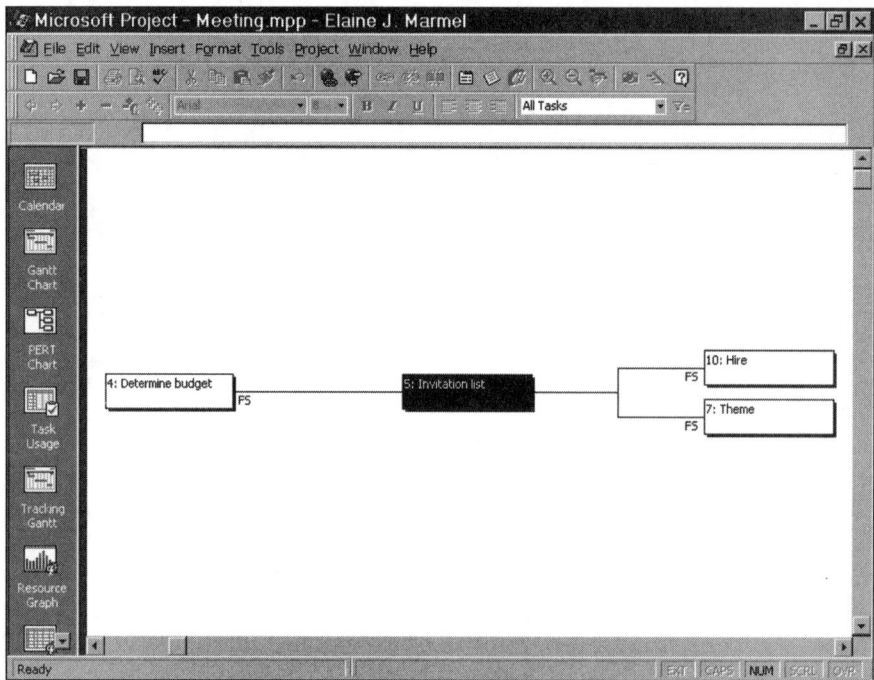

Figure 6-34: The Task PERT view.

Task Sheet

The Task Sheet view is the counterpart of the Resource Sheet view in that the Task Sheet view displays task information in a spreadsheet type of format. In this view you can create tasks, link tasks (establishing dependencies), and even assign resources (see Figure 6-35).

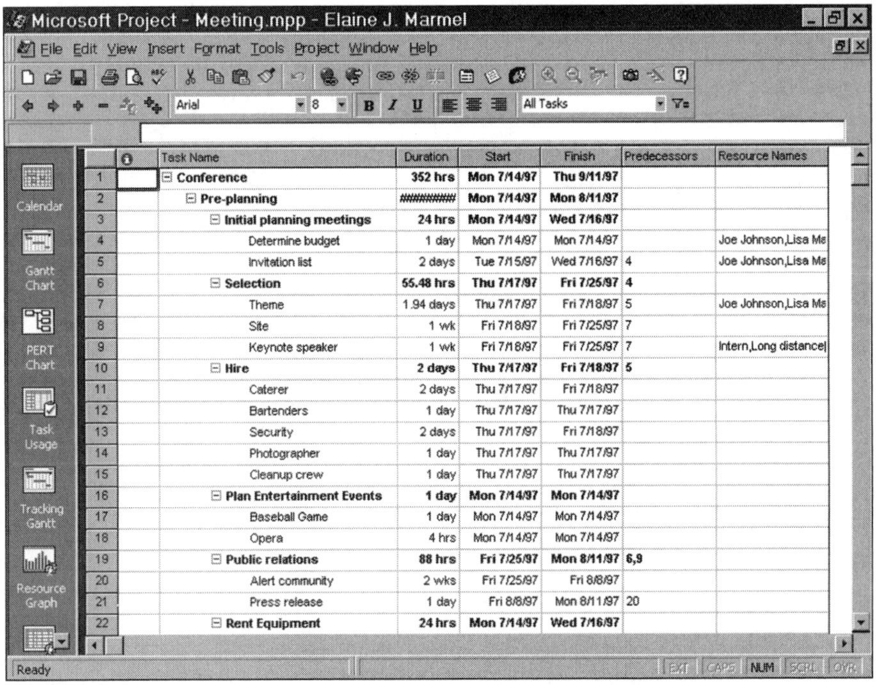

Figure 6-35: The Task Sheet view helps you see tasks in chronological order.

This view closely resembles the left portion of the Gantt Chart view and makes it easy to view tasks in chronological order. The default table that appears on the Task Sheet view is the Entry table, but you can use the techniques described earlier in this chapter to change the table.

Filtering Views

Filters help you to focus on your project. Suppose, for example, that you want to view the tasks assigned to only certain resources. Or suppose you want to display only the tasks on the critical path of your project. You can apply filters to views to limit the information you see and to help you focus on a particular issue.

You can apply a filter to any view except the PERT Chart view. Project filters come in two varieties: task filters, which enable you to view specific aspects of tasks, and resource filters, which enable you to view specific aspects of resources. The next two sections describe the filters available in Project (many of the filters perform similar functions).

Default task filters

Use these filters to help you focus on a particular aspect of the tasks on your project:

✦ **All Tasks:** This filter displays all the tasks in your project.

✦ **Completed Tasks:** This filter displays all finished tasks.

✦ **Confirmed:** This filter displays the tasks on which specified resources have agreed to work.

✦ **Cost Greater Than:** This filter displays the tasks that exceed the cost you specify.

✦ **Cost Overbudget:** This calculated filter displays all tasks with a cost that exceeds the baseline cost.

✦ **Created After:.** This filter displays all tasks that you created in your project on or after the specified date.

✦ **Critical:.** This filter displays all tasks on the critical path.

✦ **Date Range:.** This interactive filter prompts you for two dates and then displays all tasks that start after the earlier date and finish before the later date.

✦ **In Progress Tasks:** This filter displays all tasks that have started but haven't finished.

✦ **Incomplete Tasks:** This filter displays all tasks that haven't finished.

✦ **Late/Overbudget Tasks Assigned To:** This filter prompts you to specify a resource. Then, Project displays tasks that meet either of two conditions: (1) The tasks assigned to that resource that exceed the budget you allocated for them, or (2) the tasks that haven't finished yet and will finish after the baseline finish date. Note that completed tasks *do not* appear when you apply this filter, even if they completed after the baseline finish date.

✦ **Linked Fields:** This filter displays tasks to which you have linked text from other programs.

✦ **Milestones:** This filter displays only milestones.

✦ **Resource Group:** This filter displays the tasks assigned to resources that belong the group you specify.

✦ **Should Start By:** This filter prompts you for a date and then displays all tasks not yet begun that should have started by that date.

✦ **Should Start/Finish By:** This filter prompts you for two dates: a start date and a finish date. Then Project uses the filter to display those tasks that haven't started by the start date and those tasks that haven't finished by the finish date.

✦ **Slipped/Late Progress**: This filter displays two types of tasks: those that have slipped behind their baseline scheduled finish date and those that are not progressing on schedule.

✦ **Slipping Tasks:** This filter displays all tasks that are behind schedule.

✦ **Summary Tasks**: This filter displays all tasks that have subtasks grouped below them.

✦ **Task Range**: This filter shows all tasks that have ID numbers within the range you provide.

✦ **Tasks with Attachments**: This filter displays tasks that have objects attached or a note in the Notes box.

✦ **Tasks with Fixed Dates**: This filter displays all tasks that have an actual start date and tasks to which you assign some constraint other than As Soon As Possible.

✦ **Tasks/Assignments with Overtime:** This filter displays the tasks or assignments that have overtime.

✦ **Top Level Tasks:** This filter displays the highest-level summary tasks.

✦ **Unconfirmed**: This filter displays the tasks on which specified resources have *not* agreed to work.

✦ **Unstarted Tasks:** This filter displays tasks that haven't started.

✦ **Update Needed**: This filter displays tasks that have changes, such as revised start and finish dates or resource reassignments, and need to be sent for update or confirmation.

✦ **Using Resource**: This filter displays all tasks that use the resource you specify.

✦ **Using Resource in Date Range**: When you use this filter, you specify a resource, a start date, and a finish date. Project then displays the tasks assigned to the resource that start or finish after the first date and before the second date.

✦ **Work Overbudget:** This filter displays all tasks with scheduled work greater than baseline work.

Default resource filters

Use these filters to help you focus on a particular aspect of the resources on your project:

✦ **All Resources:** This filter displays all the resources in your project.

✦ **Confirmed Assignments:** This filter, available only in the Resource Usage view, displays only those tasks for which a resource has confirmed the assignment.

✦ **Cost Greater Than:** This filter displays the resources that exceed the cost you specify.

✦ **Cost Overbudget:** This calculated filter displays all resources with a cost that exceeds the baseline cost.

✦ **Date Range:** This interactive filter prompts you for two dates and then displays all tasks and resources with assignments that start after the earlier date and finish before the later date.

✦ **Group:** This filter prompts you for a group and then displays all resources belonging to that group.

✦ **In Progress Assignments:** This filter displays all tasks that have started but haven't finished.

✦ **Linked Fields**: This filter displays resources to which you have linked text from other programs.

✦ **Overallocated Resources:** This filter displays all resources that are scheduled to do more work than they have the capacity to do.

✦ **Resource Range:** This interactive filter prompts you for a range of ID numbers and then displays all resources within that range.

✦ **Resources with Attachments:** This filter displays resources that have objects attached or a note in the Notes box.

✦ **Resources/Assignments with Overtime:** This filter displays the resources or assignments that have overtime.

✦ **Should Start By:** This filter prompts you for a date and then displays all task and resources with assignments not yet begun that should have started by that date.

✦ **Should Start/Finish By:** This filter prompts you for two dates: a start date and a finish date. Then Project uses the filter to display those tasks or assignments that haven't started by the start date and those tasks or assignments that haven't finished by the finish date.

✦ **Slipped/Late Progress:** This filter displays two types of resources: those that have slipped behind their baseline scheduled finish date and those that are not progressing on schedule.

✦ **Slipping Assignments:** This filter displays all resources with uncompleted tasks that are behind schedule because the tasks have been delayed from the original baseline plan.

✦ **Unconfirmed Assignments:** This filter displays the assignments for which requested resources have *not yet* agreed to work.

✦ **Unstarted Assignments**: This filter displays confirmed assignments that have not yet started.

✦ **Work Complete:** This filter displays resources that have completed all of their assigned tasks.

✦ **Work Incomplete:** This filter displays all resources with baseline work greater than scheduled work.

✦ **Work Overbudget**: This filter displays all resources with scheduled work greater than baseline work.

Applying a filter to a view

By applying a filter to a view, you specify criteria that Project uses to determine what tasks or resources should appear in that view. Project then selects information to display and either highlights the selected information or hides the rest of the information. To apply a filter and hide all other information, follow these steps:

1. Display the view you want to filter.

2. Choose Project⇨Filtered for.

3. Choose the filter you want from the Filtered For side menu.

Note

Because Project allows you to apply task filters to task views only and resource filters to resource views only, the Filtered for side menu shows either All Task or All Resources, depending on the view you displayed before starting these steps.

If you want to apply a filter that doesn't appear on the list, or you want to apply a highlighting filter, follow these steps:

1. Display the view you want to filter.

2. Choose Project⇨Filtered for⇨More Filters. Project displays the More Filters dialog box (see Figure 6-36).

3. Click on the Task option button to select and apply a task filter; select the Resource option button to select and apply a resource filter.

Tip

Remember, Project won't let you apply a task filter to a resource view or a resource filter to a task view.

4. Select a filter name in the Filters list.

5. Click on Apply to apply the filter or click on Highlight to apply a highlighting filter.

If the filter you want to apply is an interactive filter, type the requested values.

6. Click on OK.

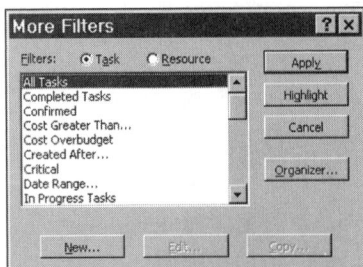

Figure 6-36: Use the More Filters
dialog box to apply a filter that
doesn't appear on the Filtered
For list or to apply a highlighting filter.

Tip

To turn off a filter, choose Project➪Filtered for. Then choose All Tasks or All
Resources, as appropriate.

Creating custom filters

If none of Project's default filters meet your needs, you can create a new filter or
modify an existing filter by customizing a filter's criteria from the More Filters
dialog box. To edit an existing filter, follow these steps:

1. Display the view you want to filter.

2. Choose Project➪Filtered for➪More Filters to open the More Filters dialog box.

3. Select the option button of the type of filter you want to use: Task or Resource.

4. Highlight the filter you want to modify and then click on the Edit button at
the bottom of the dialog box. Project displays a Filter Definition dialog box
similar to the one in Figure 6-37.

5. Click in the Field Name box; Project displays a list box arrow to the right of
the field.

6. Select a field from the list.

7. Repeat steps 5 and 6 for the Test box and supply a comparison operator.

8. Repeat steps 5 and 6 in the Value (s) box and supply a filtering value.

9. Repeat steps 5 through 8 for each criterion you want to create; also supply an
And/Or operator if you supply additional criteria. Remember, *And* means that
the filter displays information only if the task or resource meets *all* criteria,
whereas *Or* means that the filter displays information if a task or resource
meets *any* of the criteria.

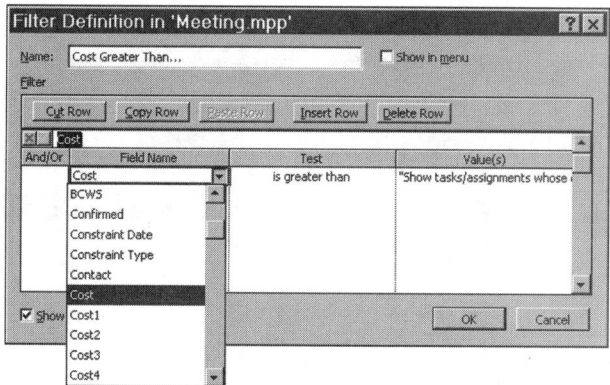

Figure 6-37: The Filter Definition dialog box enables you to edit an existing filter.

10. Click OK to redisplay the More Filters dialog box.

11. Click Apply to apply the filter.

Note

To create a new filter, click the New button in step 4. In the Filter Definition dialog box, the name Filter 1 appears in the Name box and no information appears at the bottom of the box. You need to supply a name for the new filter and some filtering criteria. If you want your new filter to appear in the Filtered for list, place a check in the Show in menu check box.

Each line you create in this dialog box is called a statement. If you want to evaluate certain statements together, but separate from other statements in your filter, group the statements into a set of criteria. To group statements, leave a blank line between sets of criteria, and select either operator in the And/Or field for the blank row.

New Feature

If your filter contains three or more statements within one criteria group, Project evaluates all And statements before evaluating Or statements. Because earlier versions of Project did not work this way, using filters you created in earlier versions of Project may produce unanticipated results. Also note, however, that, across groups, Project evaluates And conditions in the order that they appear.

Using AutoFilters

New Feature

AutoFilters are similar to regular Project filters, but you can access them directly on the sheet of any sheet view instead of using a menu or a dialog box. By default, the AutoFilters option is off when you create a project, but you can enable it by clicking on the AutoFilter button on the Formatting toolbar.

When you enable AutoFilters, a list box appears at the right edge of every column name in a sheet view. When you open the drop-down list, Project displays filters appropriate to the column (see Figure 6-38).

AutoFilter button

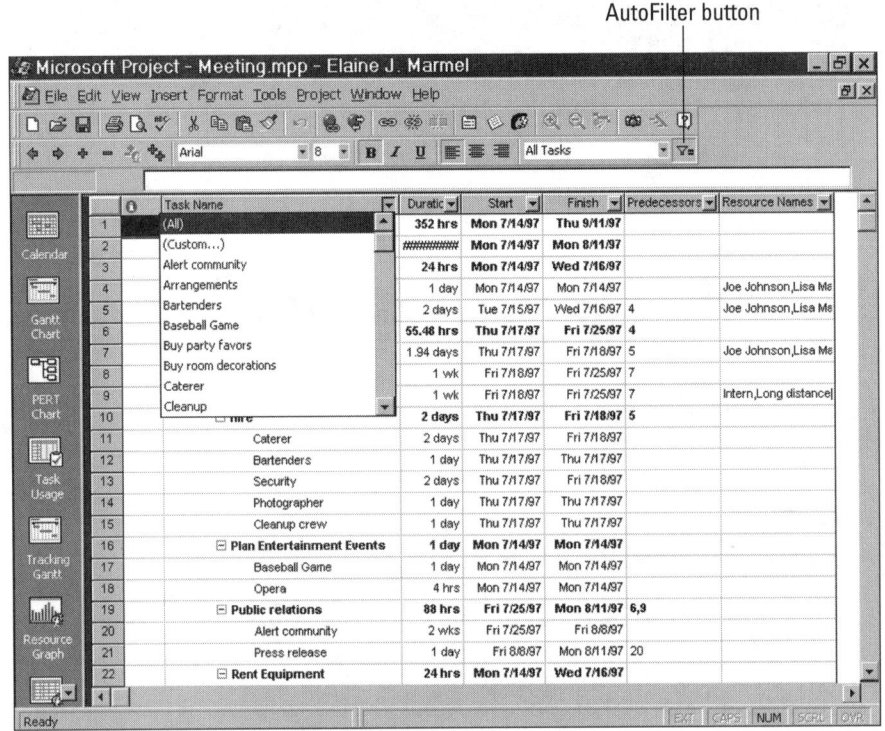

Figure 6-38: The Task Sheet view with AutoFilters enabled.

Tip

You can turn on AutoFilters automatically for new projects that you create. Choose Tools⇨Options and click on the General tab. Place a check in the Set AutoFilter on for new projects check box.

Printing Your Project

When you print a project, you are printing a view. So, before you do anything, select the view you want to print. If you're printing a sheet view, the number of columns you see onscreen determines the number of columns that print. If the printed product requires more than one page, Project prints down and across; that is, the entire left side of your project prints before the right side prints.

Printing in Project is very similar to printing in any other Microsoft product. You can use the Print button on the Standard toolbar to print using default settings. And what are the default settings? They appear in two dialog boxes that you can view if you *don't* use the Print button.

Choose File⇨Print to open the Print dialog box shown in Figure 6-39.

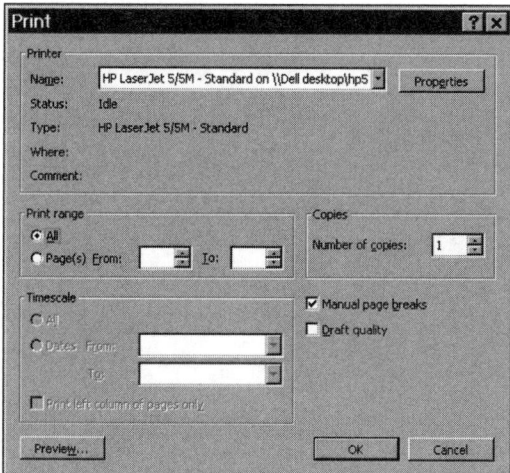

Figure 6-39: From the Print dialog box, you can control, for example, the printer to which you print and the number of copies you print.

Note

You can also preview before printing either by clicking on the Preview button in the Print dialog box or by clicking on the Print Preview button on the Standard toolbar.

You cannot open the Page Setup dialog box (see Figure 6-40) from the Print dialog box, but you can open the Page Setup dialog box either by choosing File⇨Page Setup or by clicking on the Page Setup button that is available in Print Preview. From the Page tab, you can set orientation and scaling. Using scaling, you may be able to fit the printed text onto one page.

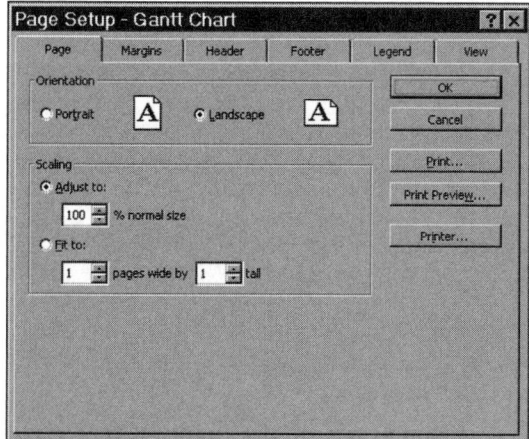

Figure 6-40: The Page tab of the Page Setup dialog box.

From the Margins tab (see Figure 6-41), you can change the margins for your printed text and determine whether a border should appear.

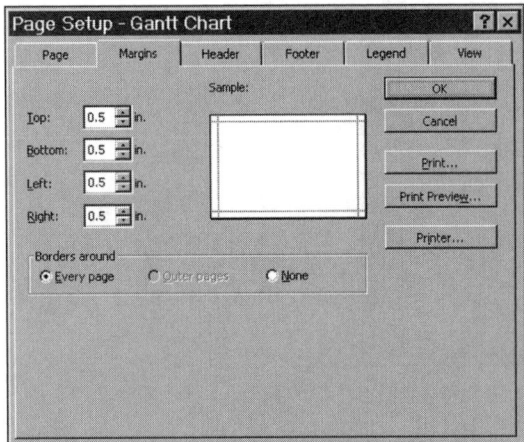

Figure 6-41: The Margins tab of the Page Setup dialog box.

From the Header tab (see Figure 6-42), you can define and align header information to appear on the top of every page you print. Use either the buttons at the bottom of the box or the list box to add information that you want Project to update automatically, such as page numbers.

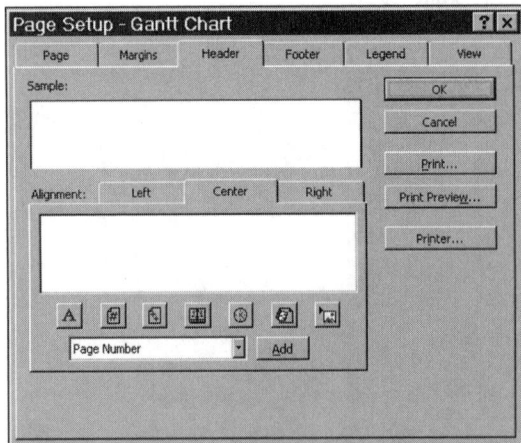

Figure 6-42: The Header tab of the Page Setup dialog box.

The Footer tab (see Figure 6-43) works just like the Header tab. You can align and include the same kind of updating information in the footer on each page of your printed text.

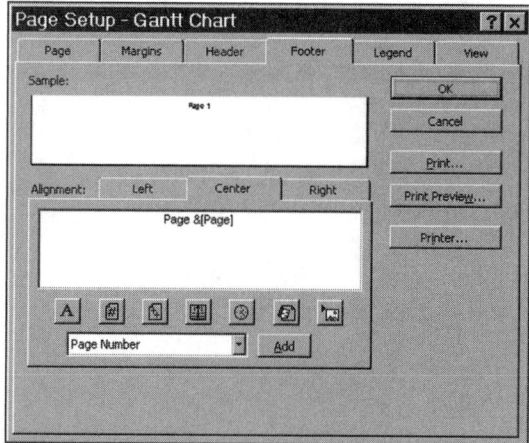

Figure 6-43: The Footer tab of the Page Setup dialog box.

The Page Setup dialog box changes just slightly, depending on the view you were using when you opened the dialog box. For example, the Legend tab is available only when you're printing a Calendar, Gantt Chart view, or PERT Chart view (see Figure 6-44). The Legend tab works just like the Header and Footer tabs, and you can align and include the same kind of updating information.

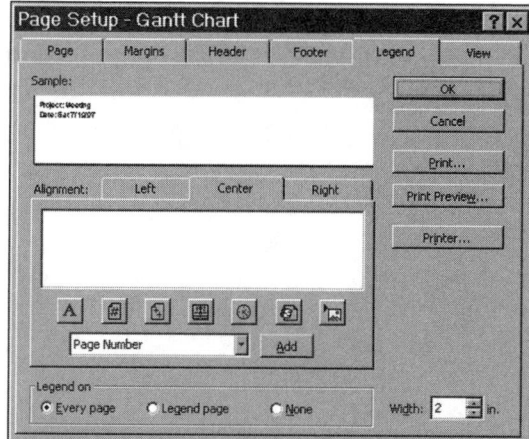

Figure 6-44: The Legend tab of the Page Setup dialog box.

The View tab enables you to control what Project prints, such as all or only some columns (see Figure 6-45).

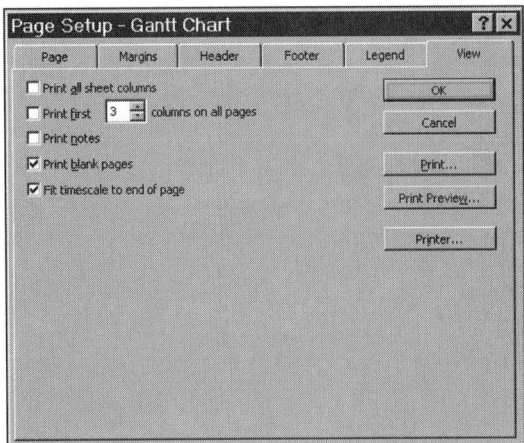

Figure 6-45: The View tab of the Page Setup dialog box.

Summary

In this chapter you learned how to use the views in Project. You also:

✦ Learned methods for filtering information while working

✦ Learned how to print in Project

Chapter 7 explains how to change the appearance of your project by formatting elements and inserting drawings and objects.

✦   ✦   ✦

Modifying the Appearance of Your Project

◆   ◆   ◆   ◆

In This Chapter

Use the GanttChart-
Wizard to format
your entire project
quickly

Learn how to format
text in your schedule

Modify chart
elements, including
task bars, PERT boxes,
gridlines, and layouts

Add drawings and
insert objects into
your schedule

◆   ◆   ◆   ◆

After you enter the information for your project, the next step is to fine-tune that information to resolve any conflicts and set a baseline. First, however, you should take the time to format the individual elements of the schedule. After all, you might be working with this project for months or even years. Why not get it to look just right?

Project has dozens of ways to format the appearance of elements from text to task bars, link lines and PERT nodes. Some of these changes are practical; others simply provide shapes or styles that might be more pleasing to you. You can also use color and insert drawings or pictures into your schedule to make a visual point. So get ready: This chapter is where you can get creative!

Why Change the Way Project Looks?

Beyond the obvious motivation of making the lines and colors in your schedule more appealing, you might have a practical reason for modifying a schedule's appearance.

You might, for example, want to do any of the following to make information about your project more accessible:

◆ Display information, such as the start and end dates or resources assigned to the task, in text form alongside task bars. This technique is especially useful in longer schedules where a task bar may appear on the printed page far to the right of the task name in the Gantt table.

✦ Use a bolder color on any tasks on the critical path (tasks that, if delayed, would delay the final completion of the project). This method helps you to keep an eye on tasks that are vital to meeting your deadline.

✦ Modify the display of your baseline timing estimate versus actual progress on tasks so that you can more clearly see any divergence.

✦ Display or don't display dependency lines between tasks. In a project with many complex dependency relationships, multiple lines can obscure task bar elements or PERT nodes.

In short, beyond mere cosmetics, paying attention to the format of your schedule elements can help you focus on your project. Keep in mind that these changes pertain only to the currently open schedule, and any changes you make to the format of these elements appear both onscreen and on any corresponding printouts.

Tip

You can change formats whenever you like and then change them back again without changing the data in your project. For example, you might decide not to display dependency lines to print out a report of resource assignments for your boss, because printing the lines can obscure the list of resources next to each task bar. You can always redisplay the dependency lines later.

Using the GanttChartWizard

You can make changes to specific elements in several Project views. However, the Gantt Chart view has its own wizard to help you format the various pieces. Running through the GanttChartWizard highlights some of the options.

Note

A *wizard* is an interactive series of dialog boxes that require you to answer questions or make selections. Project uses your input to create or modify some aspect of your project (in this case, the formatting applied to your Gantt chart). The Microsoft Office family of products uses wizards to automate many functions.

The GanttChartWizard is available in either the Gantt Chart view or the Tracking Gantt view. (GanttChartWizard changes apply only to the project file that's open when you run the wizard.) Start by displaying the project you want to format. Then follow these steps:

1. Click on the GanttChartWizard button on the Standard toolbar. (You can also choose Format⇨GanttChartWizard to initiate the wizard.) The dialog box in Figure 7-1 appears.

   The four buttons at the bottom of this dialog box appear at the bottom of each wizard dialog box. You can click on Cancel to leave the wizard without saving any settings, Back to move back one step, and Finish to complete the wizard based on your input to that point.

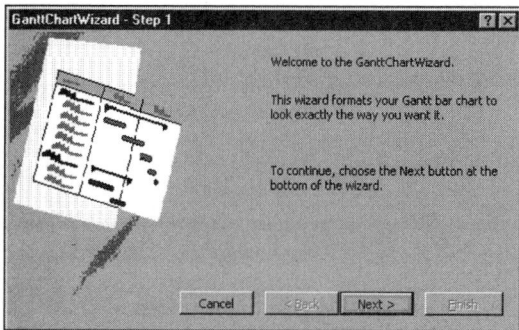

Figure 7-1: Step 1 of the wizard simply greets you and tells you what the wizard does.

2. Click on Next to move to the next step.

   The second wizard dialog box (see Figure 7-2) is where you indicate the category of information you want to display. You can select only one item here. Try clicking on each of these choices to see a preview of its style on the left of the dialog box.

   • **Standard:** Shows blue task bars, black summary task bars, and a black line superimposed over the task bars to indicate progress on tasks

   • **Critical path:** The Standard layout with critical path tasks in red

   • **Baseline:** Displays baseline task bars and progress task bars separately, rather than superimposed as with the Standard setup (see Figure 7-2)

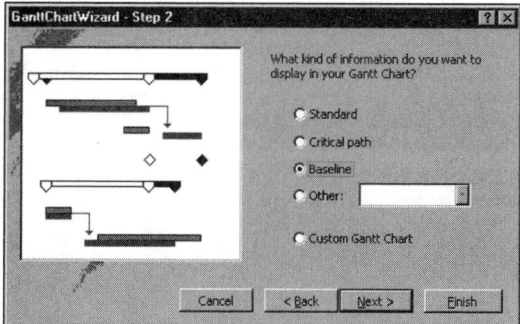

Figure 7-2: The preview gives you an idea of the way each option formats your Gantt chart.

   • **Other:** Displays a drop-down list that contains several alternative, predefined chart styles for the categories of Standard, Critical Path, Baseline, and Status

- **Custom Gantt Chart:** Causes the wizard to display several additional screens to allow you to create a highly customized Gantt chart

3. Click on the control button for Custom Gantt Chart and then click on the Next button.

Note

If you select any of the other options in the GanttChartWizard - Step 2 dialog box, the remaining wizard dialog boxes deal with the elements you want to display with the task bars, such as resource names, dates or custom information. You also have an opportunity to designate whether Project should display lines between task bars to indicate dependencies.

The third wizard dialog box appears, as shown in Figure 7-3. The only choice here is whether to differentiate between critical and noncritical tasks.

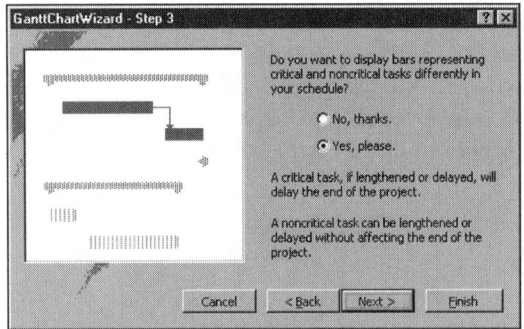

Figure 7-3: Formatting critical and noncritical tasks differently can help you spot potential scheduling problems early.

4. Leave the default setting of Yes, and click on Next to open the Step 4 dialog box, shown in Figure 7-4. Here you can select a color, pattern, and end shape for critical subtask bars.

Tip

Highlighting critical tasks in a project helps you pay special attention to them when reviewing or tracking progress. If you don't want to format the Gantt chart to treat critical tasks differently, another option is to use a filter to temporarily filter out all but critical tasks, as you learned to do in Chapter 6.

5. Click on each drop-down box and select the style options you desire. When you're done, click on Next. The Step 5 dialog box (not shown) resembles the dialog box in Figure 7-4 except that the choice of color, pattern, and end shapes here is for normal (noncritical) subtask bars.

Caution

Be careful about selecting a solid pattern for task bars: Superimposed progress lines are typically a solid color (black) and might be hard to see against a solid task bar.

6. Pick a combination that you can differentiate easily from your critical task bar choices and then click on Next.

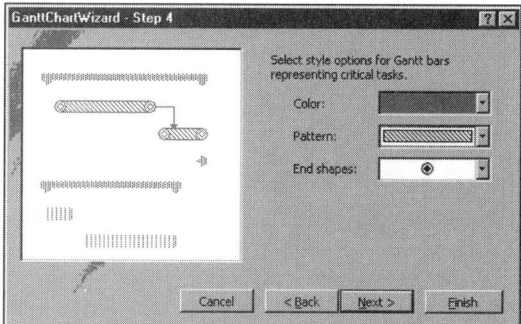

Figure 7-4: End shapes delineate the two ends of task bars.

Figure 7-5 shows the wizard's Step 6 dialog box. Here you select styles for summary task bars. The additional choice here of Bar style relates to the thickness of the bar.

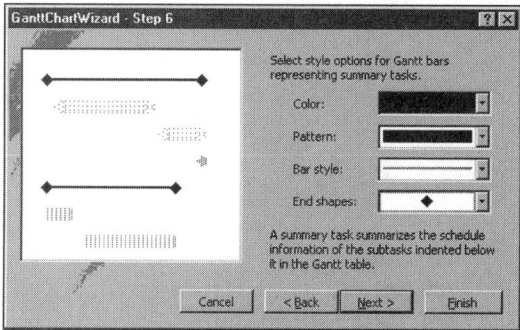

Figure 7-5: The thicker bar styles obscure the end shapes. If seeing end shapes is important, use the thinner style shown here.

Be sure to make choices here that differentiate summary task bar styles from the choices you made for normal and critical subtasks.

7. Click on Next to open the Step 7 dialog box (see Figure 7-6) where you can select the color, pattern, and shape of milestone symbols.

8. Select a shape for milestones that is different from the end shapes you've chosen for task bars so that the milestones stand out clearly. Make any modifications you like and then click on Next to open the Step 8 dialog box (see Figure 7-7).

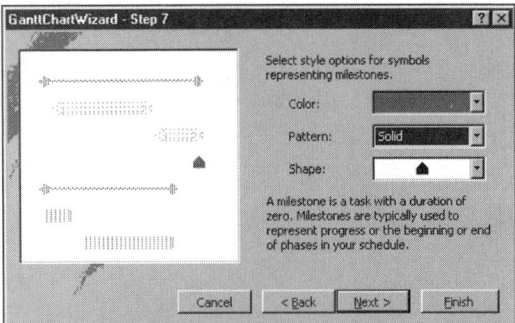

Figure 7-6: Solid patterns make a milestone stand out; consider a bright color to make them easy to spot.

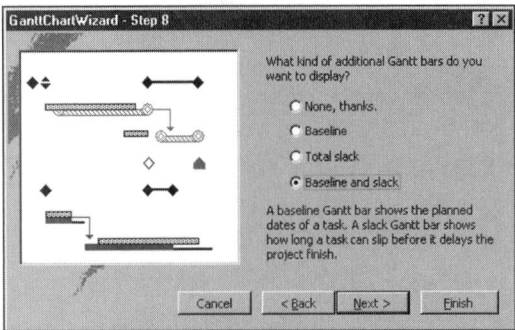

Figure 7-7: You can begin to see how your choices will look by the time you reach this preview.

Consistency counts

Displaying so many elements on a schedule can be a mixed blessing — for example, highlighting critical tasks, adding end shapes to task bars, and showing both the baseline and actual lines, as well as slack can result in a chart that is confusing. Remember that you're not formatting elements to satisfy your particular penchant for one color or another, but to make project information easier to read.

One way to help everyone in your organization read and understand Project schedules is to make the formatting consistent across your organization. The more your coworkers and management see the same formatting in various schedules, the more quickly they'll learn to read the symbols and the less likely they are to misread a schedule. Set standards for formatting projects in your workgroup, your division — even across your whole company — and stick to them.

9. Select the Baseline and slack option to tell the wizard what kind of additional Gantt bars to display. *Baseline* is a picture of the plan before you began tracking actual progress, and *slack* is any extra time a task can use up before it moves onto the critical path.

10. Click on Next to open the Step 9 dialog box.

When enough is too much

If you select Custom task information in the GanttChartWizard - Step 9 dialog box (see Figure 7-8), the wizard opens three consecutive dialog boxes. These dialog boxes prompt you to display one set of information alongside normal subtask bars, another set on summary task bars, and a third next to milestone tasks, respectively. The wizard also prompts you to display one set of data to the left of each task bar, one set to the right, and one inside the task bar itself. You could end up with nine pieces of information in and around your various task bars!

You make your selections from drop-down lists in these three dialog boxes. The information ranges from the task name, duration, and priority to percentage of work complete and types of constraints.

Obviously, if you display nine sets of data in and around task bars, your Gantt chart would become unreadable. However, you might consider this scenario: Put the task name inside both summary and subtask bars, put the start date to the left and the finish date to the right of subtask bars, and put the cost of summary tasks to the right of their bars. (The final element is a total of the cost of all subtasks beneath the summary tasks.)

You can also modify the information that is available to someone viewing your schedule by changing the columns displayed in the Gantt table pane of the Gantt Chart view.

11. Tell the wizard what task information to display with your Gantt bars. In Figure 7-8 Project displays the start date and end date for each subtask in the task bar area. (Click on Dates to select this option.) This setting means that you don't have to show the corresponding columns for start date and end date in the Gantt table, so this option can help you modify the size of your schedule printout. The other choices in the Step 9 dialog box are to include Resources and dates (the end date only); Resources only; None of the choices, or to display Custom task information.

12. Click on Next to continue.

13. Complete the Step 13 dialog box (not shown), telling the wizard whether or not to show link lines between tasks to represent dependency relationships.

    Leave the default setting — to display the lines — and click on Next.

    The GanttChartWizard Step 14 dialog box (see Figure 7-9) previews your formatting options. You can use the Back button to go back and make change.

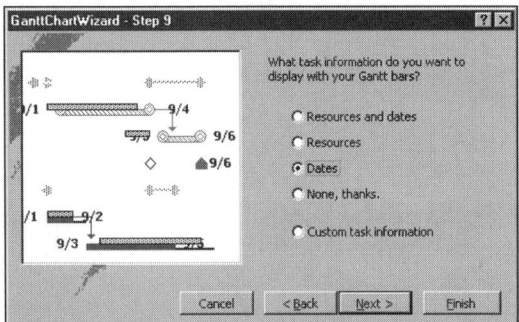

Figure 7-8: Placing text alongside task bars can be very useful with larger schedules.

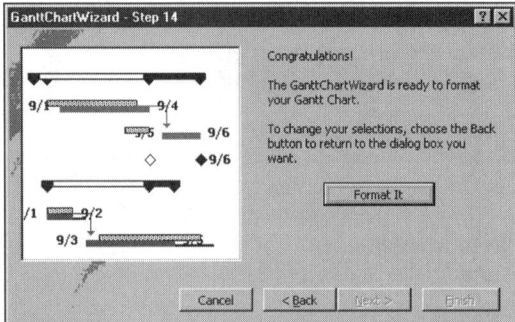

Figure 7-9: If you don't like what you see, move back to the dialog box where you made the setting, change it, and then move forward to this dialog box again.

14. Click on the Format It button to apply your choices.

A final dialog box tells you that your formatting is complete.

15. Click on the Exit Wizard button to close the dialog box and see your changes.

Formatting Elements One by One

The GanttChartWizard enables you to make changes to several common elements, such as summary task bars or the use of dependency lines. But Project also lets you format each of these elements separately, and to format them with even more options. You can change the style of many other elements in Project, including

✦ Text used in your charts

✦ Boxes used in the PERT chart view

✦ Gridlines displayed in various views

Working with text

You may want to change text to be more readable; some people prefer a larger font, for example, to make charts easy to read. Perhaps you want to use boldface for row and column titles or a distinctive font for summary tasks.

You can make all these changes and more in Project. You can even change all text in a certain category, or simply change the attributes of a single, selected piece of text in any Project table. For example, you may want to apply boldface to the task name of the milestone Grand Opening, but not to all milestone task names.

The Undo function is not available when you make changes to fonts and other formatting features. You have to manually return the text to its original settings if you're unhappy with the change.

Formatting selected text

To format selected text, follow these steps:

1. Move to any view with a table of columns in it (the Gantt Chart, Task Usage, or Resource Sheet, for example).

2. Click on the cell containing the text you want to format. To format more than one adjacent cell, click on the first cell. Then click and drag your mouse to highlight cells above, below, or to the left or right.

3. Choose Format⇨Font to open the Font dialog box, shown in Figure 7-10.

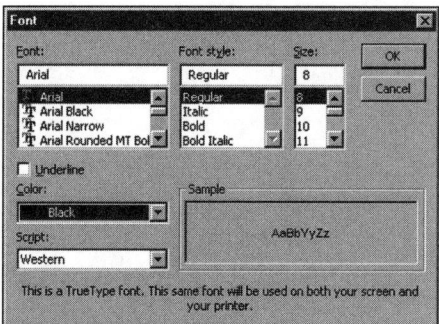

Figure 7-10: Project uses the standard Windows font dialog box, so many settings are probably familiar.

You can make selections from the three lists across the top of this dialog box: select a new Font; select a Font style such as Italic or Bold (Regular is normal text that has neither italic nor bold applied); or change the Font size. You can also click on the Underline check box to apply underlining to text, or select a color from the Color drop-down palette. The options in the Script drop-down list vary according to the font you select; for example, with Bookman Old Style you can apply script styles ranging from Greek to Cyrillic. A preview of your selections appears in the Sample area.

4. Make your choices and click on OK to apply them.

Note

You can also use buttons on the Formatting toolbar to change font and font size or to apply bold, italic, or underline styles. Using this method, you must apply the formats one at a time. Unlike the Font dialog box, the Formatting toolbar does not have a preview feature.

Applying formatting to categories of text

You can use *text styles* to change the format of text for one cell in a table or to apply a unique format to an entire category of information, for example all task names for milestones. Text styles are identical to the formatting options for text described in the preceding section, but you can apply text styles to specific categories of text.

Follow these steps use text styles to modify text:

1. Choose Format⇨Text Styles to open the Text Styles dialog box, shown in Figure 7-11.

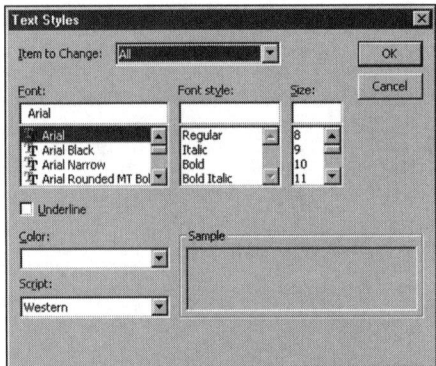

Figure 7-11: The default Item to Change is All (text in your project schedule).

2. Click on the down arrow next to the Item to Change field to display the options. (This field is the only element that distinguishes the Text Styles dialog box from the Font dialog box you saw earlier.)

3. Use the scroll bar to move down the list. You can format text for categories such as row and column titles, summary tasks, tasks on the critical path, and milestones. Click on one category to select it.

4. Select the settings you want for the text, including the font, font size, style, color, and script. When you're done, click on OK to apply the formatting.

You can format categories of text to add emphasis to certain key items, like critical tasks and milestones, or to make your schedule more readable by enlarging text or choosing easy-to-read fonts. Figure 7-12 shows a schedule with text styles applied to various elements, such as row and column headings, critical and noncritical tasks, and summary tasks.

		Task Name	Duration	Start	
	1	⊟ **Book Meeting Space**	**1 day**	**Fri 5/9/97**	
	2	⊟ **Locate facility**	**1 day**	**Fri 5/9/97**	
	3	*Contact local hotels*	*1 day*	*Fri 5/9/97*	
	4	*Obtain brochures*	*1 day*	*Fri 5/9/97*	
	5	⊞ **Confirm space**	**1 day**	**Fri 5/9/97**	
	8	Schedule Speakers	1 day	Fri 5/9/97	
	9	⊟ **Order Food**	**1 day**	**Mon 5/12/97**	
	10	*Get caterer bids*	*1 day*	*Mon 5/12/97*	
	11	⊟ **Approve menu**	**1 day**	**Mon 5/12/97**	
	12	*Obtain sample menus*	*1 day*	*Mon 5/12/97*	
	13	⊟ **Get executive approval**	**1 day**	**Mon 5/12/97**	
	14	*John Stall*	*1 day*	*Mon 5/12/97*	
	15	*Mary St. Clair*	*1 day*	*Mon 5/12/97*	
	16	*CEO*	*1 day*	*Mon 5/12/97*	
	17	*Request purchase order*	*1 day*	*Mon 5/12/97*	
	18	*Order Flowers*	*1 day*	*Tue 5/13/97*	
	19	*Send Invitations*	*1 day*	*Wed 5/14/97*	

Figure 7-12: Italic indicates critical tasks; summary tasks are bold.

Caution

Good advice bears repeating: Don't go overboard with multiple fonts on a single schedule. You can actually make a project harder to read by using too many fancy fonts. Avoid using more than one or two fonts in your schedule, and vary the text by using bold or italic or by modifying the font size between categories, rather than using many different fonts. Also, try to set up company standards for formatting so that all your project schedules have a consistent, professional look.

Changing task bars and PERT boxes

In addition to changing text styles in your schedule, you can modify the look of the task bars and PERT nodes in your schedule. You considered some of these changes when you went through the GanttChartWizard. You can make changes to the shape, pattern, and color of bars, as well as to the style of shape that appears on either end of the task bar.

With a PERT node box, you can adjust the thickness of the line that defines the box, the color of that line, and what information Project displays in the node.

You can also modify the style of text placed near task bars and within PERT boxes.

Working with task bars

Formatting task bars is similar to formatting text. You can format either an individual task bar or a category of task bars, such as milestones or critical tasks. You click on a particular task and reach the dialog box for formatting just that task bar by choosing Format⇨Bar. Alternatively, you can open the dialog box for formatting categories of task bars by choosing Format⇨Bar Styles. The actual settings you can modify are the same either way.

Tip You can open the Bar Styles dialog box by right-clicking on the task bar area of the Gantt chart and choosing Bar Styles from the shortcut menu that appears.

Figure 7-13 shows the Format Bar dialog box, and Figure 7-14 shows the Bar Styles dialog box. The bottom half of the Bar Styles dialog box has two tabbed sheets called Text and Bars. Counterparts to these tabbed sheets appear in the Format Bar dialog box with the names of Bar Shape and Bar Text. The Bar Styles dialog box has an additional area where you can designate the category of task bar you want to modify.

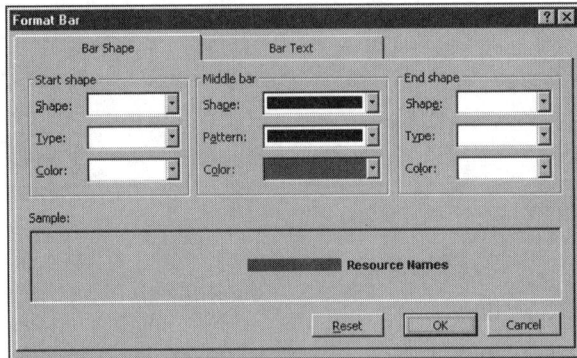

Figure 7-13: You can modify the appearance of an individual task bar to draw attention to it.

You can use the Bars tab at the bottom of the Bar Styles dialog box to set the shape, type or pattern, and color for the bar and its end shapes, as you did when you used the GanttChartWizard. Follow these steps:

1. Click on the Text tab to select the information you want to display to the left, right, above, below, or inside the selected category of task bar (see Figure 7-15).

2. Click on the blank line next to the location label, and open a drop-down list (use the arrow that appears to the right of this line).

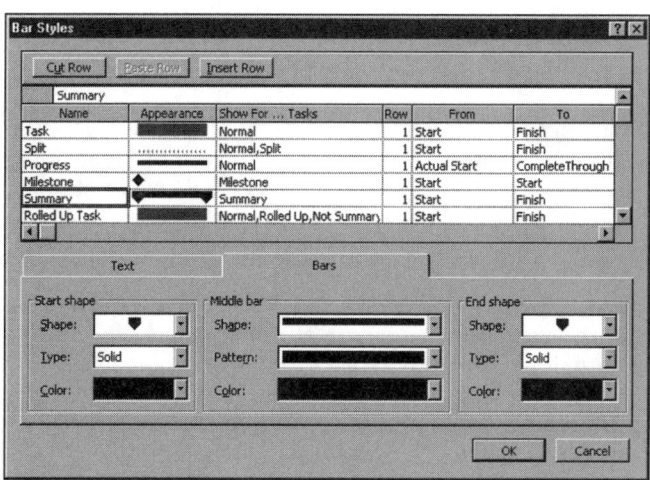

Figure 7-14: Use the Bar Styles dialog box to change the appearance of an entire category of tasks.

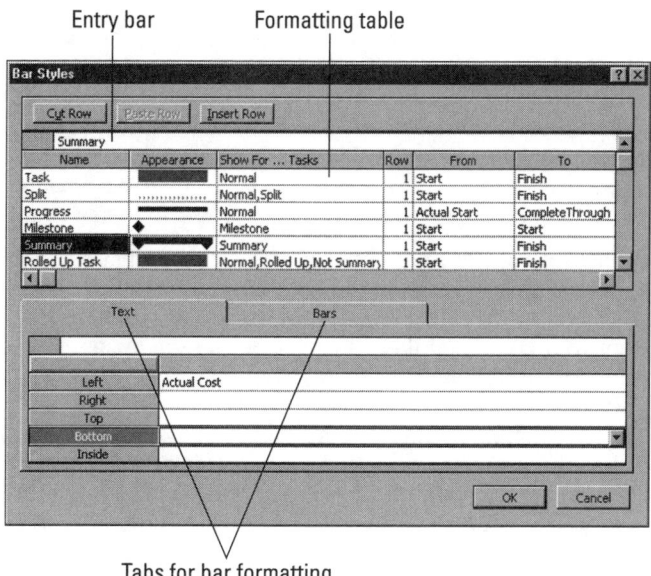

Figure 7-15: Be careful not to place too much information around task bars to avoid creating a cluttered, illegible Gantt chart.

Note
You can place text in more locations around a task bar from the Bar Styles dialog box than you can by using the GanttChartWizard. This dialog box also enables you to place many more pieces of information near task bars.

Here's what the columns in the Bar Styles table represent:

✦ **Name:** This column specifies the task bar category. To create a new task bar category name, click on the Insert Row button at the top of the dialog box and type in any name you like. This name appears in a legend for your chart when you print it.

✦ **Appearance**: Column 2 is a sample of the current formatting settings for the bar.

✦ **Show For ... Tasks:** This column defines the types of tasks that the specified formatting affects. You can specify the type of task to affect by selecting the category from a drop-down list or by typing a category name in the entry bar. If you want to specify more than one category, add a backslash after the first type in the entry bar above the table and then select or type a second category. For example, to specify Normal tasks that are critical and in progress as a new category of task bar style, type **Normal\Critical, In Progress** in the entry bar.

Note
What if you want to format tasks that *aren't* milestones and have started late? You can type **Not** before Milestone in the entry bar for the Show For Tasks field.

✦ **Row:** The Row column specifies how many rows of bars (as many as four) you want to display for each task. If you have only one row and you are showing a bar for both the baseline timing and progress, the bars overlap each other. If you want two separate bars, you need two rows. You can also add extra rows to accommodate text above or below task bars. Figure 7-16 shows a schedule with expanded rows; the baseline duration is displayed beneath normal task bars, and the baseline finish date appears to the right of summary task bars.

Tip
If a task fits in several categories, what happens? Project tries to display multiple formatting settings. (For example if one category is solid blue and the other is a pattern, you get a blue pattern.) If Project can't display the formats together, whichever item is higher in this listing takes over. To modify the formatting precedence, use the Cut Row and Paste Row features to rearrange the rows.

✦ **From and To:** These columns define the time period shown by the bar. The Progress bar, for example, shows the actual date the task started and the amount of task completed through today. Select the time frames from drop-down lists in each of these fields.

The settings in the Bar Styles dialog box enable you to modify the contents of your schedule and how Project displays or prints it in great detail. If you print a legend along with your schedule, it reflects these changes. However, remember that modifying task bar colors won't be of much use in black and white printouts of schedules, and creating too many kinds of formatting with too many variables can make your schedule difficult to read. The earlier advice about standardizing these settings across your organization holds for changes you make to task bar formatting as well.

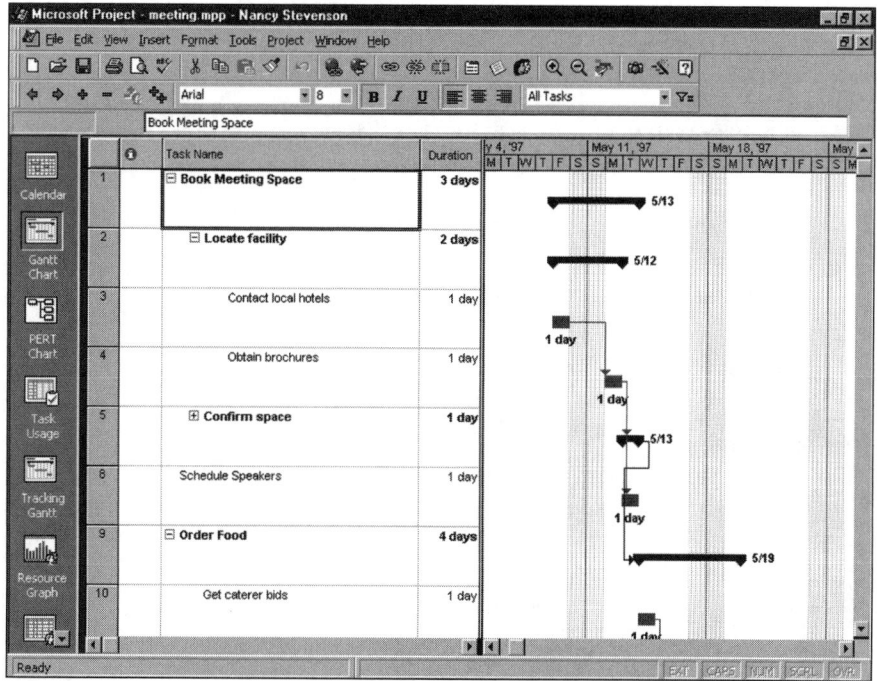

Figure 7-16: Adding rows to each task can make your schedule easier to read.

Formatting PERT nodes

You can make modifications to the boxes that form the various nodes displayed in the PERT Chart view. The only changes you can make to the box itself are color and line style, but you can use these simple changes to draw the reader's attention to categories of nodes you want to emphasize. Because the PERT view doesn't convey project timing as well as the Gantt view does, this feature enables you to delineate timing more clearly by reformatting tasks that are running late or that are in progress.

Just as with task text and task bars in the Gantt Chart view, you should be careful about keeping track of changes you make: The Undo feature doesn't work here. Project has its own color and line scheme for various types of tasks, and you run the risk of formatting one category to look just like another category by mistake. Because interpreting the information in a Project chart is so key to success, be very careful in changing formatting defaults.

PERT nodes display the following information by default: Task Name, ID, Start and Finish dates, and Duration. However, you can display any five pieces of information you wish. For example, to focus on costs in today's staff meeting, change the PERT information to Task Name, Baseline Cost, Actual Cost, Actual Overtime Cost, and Cost Variance. If your manager wants a PERT Chart report so that he or she can see whether the project schedule is on track, change this information to Task Name, Critical, Free Slack, Early Finish, and Late Finish.

You can't change the formatting of PERT boxes individually as you can with selected text or task bars in the Gantt Chart view. You must make global changes to the boxes. To do so, follow these steps:

1. Move to the PERT Chart view by clicking on its icon in the View bar.

2. Choose Format⇨Box Styles to open the Box Styles dialog box in Figure 7-17. If the Borders tab shown in this figure isn't active, select it now.

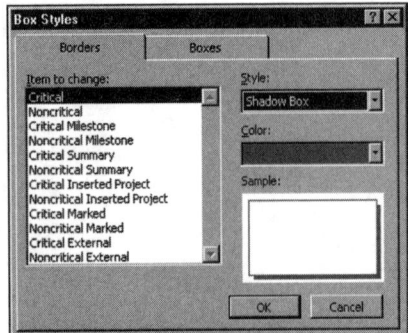

Figure 7-17: You can modify many task categories with two simple settings in the Border tab of the Box Styles dialog box.

3. Select an Item to change in the list on the left.

4. Open the Style drop-down list and click on a line style to select it. The Sample box reflects the new formatting.

5. Select a new color from the Color drop-down palette.

6. Click on the Boxes tab. Project displays the information fields shown in Figure 7-18.

7. Click on any of the five information drop-down lists. To display a piece of information from any list in the corresponding area of the node, click on the desired item.

Tip

You should usually make the Name one of the pieces of information you display. Otherwise, the flow of tasks in the PERT chart is nearly incomprehensible.

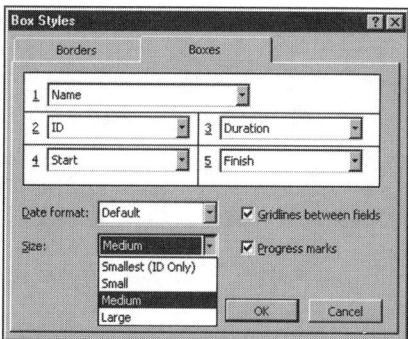

Figure 7-18: Use the Boxes tab of the Box Styles dialog box to change the information you show in all the PERT nodes.

8. Modify the format of any dates used in these information fields by choosing a format from the Date format drop-down list.

9. Change the size of the font used to display the specified information by selecting a preset Size in the drop-down list near the bottom left of the dialog box.

10. Choose to display or not to display Gridlines between fields (of information) and Progress marks (to indicate activity on tasks) by selecting or deselecting those check boxes.

11. Click on OK to apply the changes you've made to PERT nodes. Your changes apply to this Project file only.

Changing gridlines

Gridlines are those lines in your Gantt chart and the Gantt table that mark off periods of time, rows and columns, pages in your schedule, and regular intervals in the chart. In Figure 7-19 lines called *gridlines* mark off regular intervals down the rows of the chart; this format can help you read across the page on a long schedule. Also, the vertical line that marks the current date appears as a dashed line, rather than as the typical small-dotted line that you've seen in other figures in this chapter.

To modify gridlines, choose Format⇨Gridlines. The dialog box in Figure 7-20 appears. In the Line to change listing, the options Gantt Rows, Sheet Rows, and Sheet Columns enables you to set gridlines at regular intervals. For example, the project in Figure 7-20 has the Gantt Rows set to show every four rows. You can modify the other choices in the Line to change listing for line type and color only. To modify these settings, highlight the kind of line you want to change and then select the desired settings from the Type and Color drop-down lists.

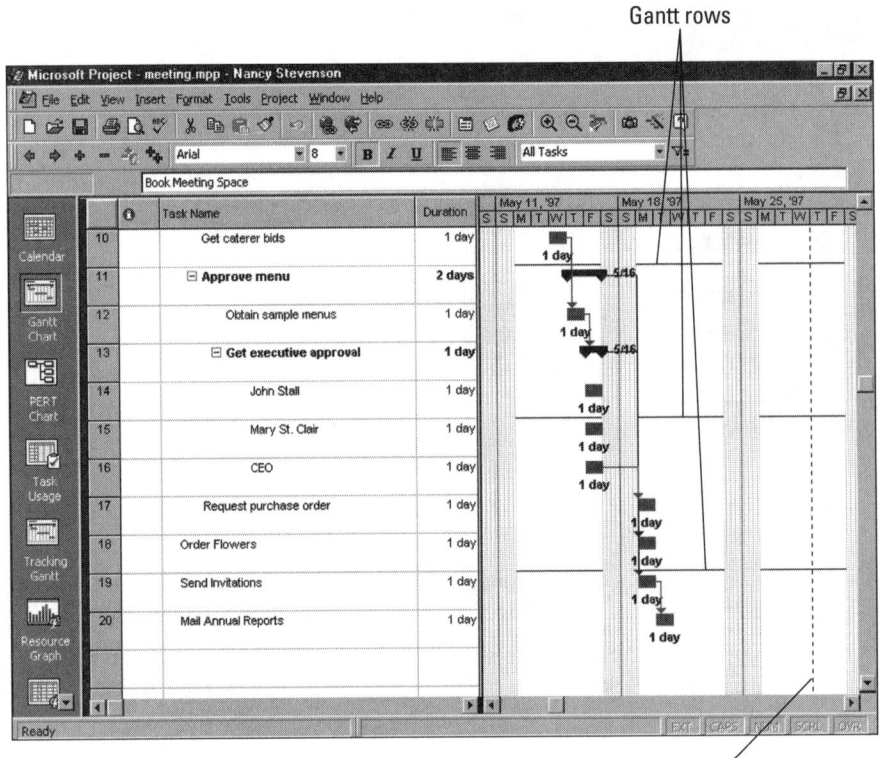

Figure 7-19: Displaying additional gridlines can make a schedule easier to read.

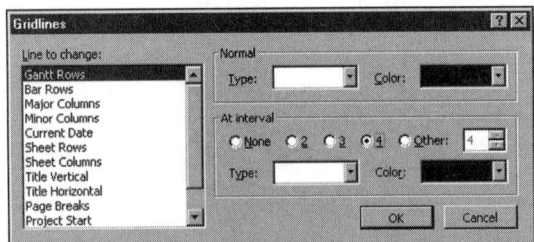

Figure 7-20: Only a few types of lines can be set at regular intervals.

Tip

If you do make substantial changes in the Gridlines dialog box, consider saving the file as a template for everyone else in your organization to use for their projects. This template not only saves you and your coworkers from having to repeat the changes but also helps to enforce consistency throughout the organization.

Changing the layout

The *layout* of a Gantt chart refers to the appearance of link lines, date formats used for information displayed near task bars, the height of task bars, and how Project displays certain characteristics of task bars.

Note

In views other than the Gantt Chart view, layout deals with slightly different elements. For example, in the PERT Chart view, layout deals with link lines and how Project handles page breaks. In the Calendar view, layout affects the order in which Project lists multiple tasks on a singular calendar day and how it splits date bars.

To modify the layout, choose Format⇨Layout. In the Gantt Chart view, the Layout dialog box shown in Figure 7-21 appears. (This version of the Layout dialog box is slightly different from the Layout dialog box associated with the PERT or Calendar views.)

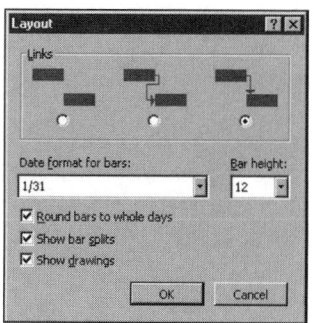

Figure 7-21: If you have a short schedule with many tasks running only hours in length, don't round task bars to whole days.

Here are the choices to make for the Gantt chart layout:

✦ **Links:** Click on one of these control buttons to display either no link lines or to use one of the available styles. Remember, link lines graphically display dependency relationships among tasks. If you want to take a quick look at your schedule with no dependency information showing, use the no link lines choice in this dialog box.

✦ **Date format for bars:** Use this drop-down list to select a date or time format. Two interesting date formats include a week number (W5/5 and W5/5/97) of the year and the day of the week; therefore, W2/2/97 is January 7, 1997 (the second day of the second week of the year, 1997).

✦ **Bar height:** Select a height in points for the bars in your Gantt chart.

✦ The three check boxes at the bottom of the Layout dialog box deal with rounding bars to whole days (good on longer schedules, not so good on schedules whose tasks tend to run in hourly or half day increments); showing bar splits; and showing drawings that you've inserted on your chart.

Note Split tasks are tasks that start, then stop for a time, and start again. For example, if you expect to begin hiring employees for the project, but know that your company imposes a two-week hiring freeze during the last two weeks of the year for accounting purposes, you could create a split task (see Chapter 8). The setting for splits in the Layout dialog box simply allows you to show the split task as one continuous task bar or two separate task bars.

Make any choices in the Layout dialog box and click on OK to implement them.

Inserting Drawings and Objects

We're living in the age of multimedia and MTV. Visual elements have a way of getting a message across that simple text often can't match. In Project you can insert graphic images (photos, illustrations or diagrams, for example) in four places:

✦ In a Gantt chart, in the task bar area

✦ In notes (task, resource, or assignment)

✦ In headers, footers, and chart legends

✦ In resource or task forms

Using visuals in schedules

Because project management is often a serious, information-oriented business, you don't want to overdo the visuals. Pictures of bunnies and curly doodads aren't likely to sit well with the head of your engineering division. However, used judiciously, images can reinforce the information about your project and lend a professional look to your reports.

Consider using graphics in these ways:

✦ Add a company logo to the header of your schedule so it appears at the top of every page.

✦ Add a photograph of each of your key resources in their resource note. The photo helps you get to know all the team members on a large-scale project so that you can address them by name in meetings and in the hallway.

✦ If a particular task involves a schematic or diagram of a product, place a copy of the diagram in the task notes for reference.

Caution Placing graphics in a schedule can take up a big chunk of memory, making your file larger and possibly making calculation time longer; for this reason, use graphics on an as-needed basis.

✦ If your schedule has a key milestone, place a graphic suggesting success or accomplishment next to the milestone in the Gantt chart. Every time you review your schedule with your team, you'll subconsciously focus on that goal and how close you're getting to it, which can boost morale.

Note

Graphic objects can include a variety of file formats, depending on the type of graphic and the program in which it was. You can use scanned images, photo files, illustrations like clip art, a chart you've created in a program like Excel, a Word for Windows table, and even a video clip. Look on the Internet for some sources for graphics files, or use the images available to the Microsoft Office Family products.

Inserting visual objects

To insert an object into a header, footer, or legend, choose File⇨Page Setup and click on the appropriate tab. Use the Insert Picture button to open a dialog box that allows you to select a file to insert. For task notes, double-click on the task to open the Task Information dialog box, select the Notes tab, and use the Insert Object button to insert a file.

You can use the Microsoft Clip Gallery that comes with Project (and all Microsoft Office Family products) to practice placing a graphic in a Project file. *Clip art* is a collection of line drawings in various styles. These images come in assorted categories, such as Business, Maps, Office, and Transportation.

To insert a piece of clip art in the Gantt chart portion of a schedule, with the Gantt Chart view displayed, follow these steps:

   1. Choose Insert⇨Object to open the Insert Object dialog box shown in Figure 7-22.

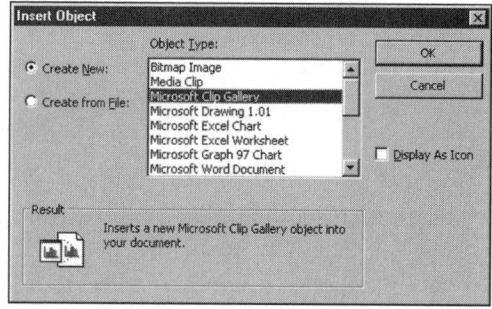

Figure 7-22: You can select various types of objects to insert from this list, such as Excel spreadsheets and even video clips.

Tip

To insert a graphic file, click on the Create from File control button in the Insert Object dialog box, click on the Browse button and locate your file using the File Open dialog box that appears. You can insert into your schedule any type of file listed in the Insert Object dialog box. With Microsoft products that take advantage of the Object Linking and Embedding (OLE) technology, after you insert an object from another program into Project, you can open the object for editing in the original program from within Project by double-clicking on the object.

2. Click on Microsoft Clip Gallery in the Object Type list and then click on OK. The Clip Gallery shown in Figure 7-23 appears.

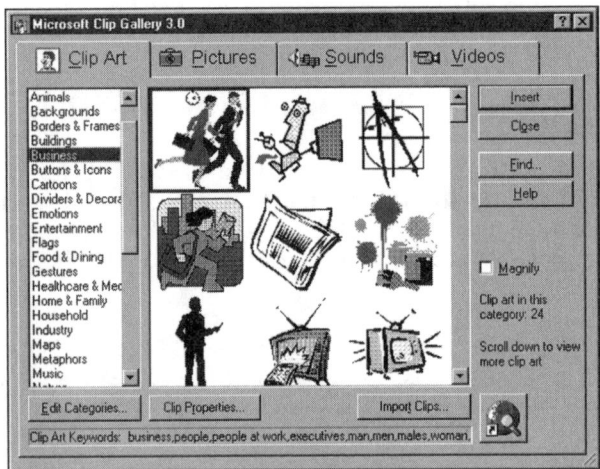

Figure 7-23: The various tabs of the Clip Gallery dialog box offer different kinds of media files to insert, although the only tabs with images built in are Clip Art and Pictures.

3. Click on a category in the list on the left.

4. Use the scrollbar to the right of the preview of the images to see more images in that category.

5. Click on the Insert button when you find a piece of clip art you want to use. (Alternatively, you can click on the Close button to close the dialog box without placing a picture on your schedule.)

The image appears in your Gantt chart area. You will probably have to resize it and move it around, which you learn to do shortly. For now, look at the image placed in the Gantt chart in Figure 7-24 to see how you can use a piece of clip art to mark a key milestone in a schedule.

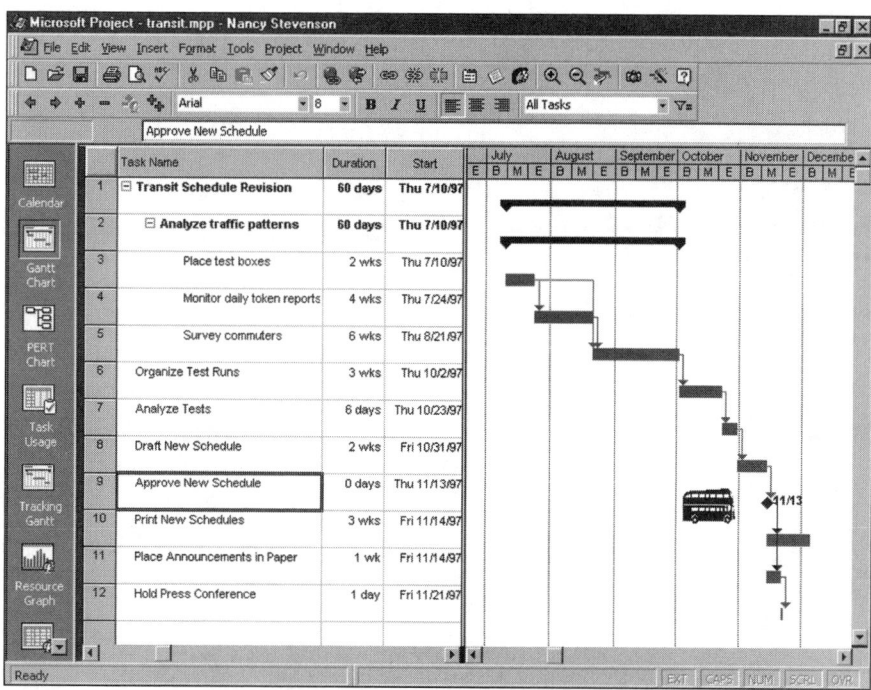

Figure 7-24: The approval of the new transit schedule is a key moment in this project, and the small image of a transit bus calls attention to it.

Using the Drawing toolbar

Project also has a Drawing feature that you can use to build simple diagrams or add shapes or text boxes to the Gantt chart area of your Project file. For example, you might want to draw a circle around an important task bar in your schedule to draw attention to it in a presentation, or draw a line through a task and include a note suggesting you cut it from the project to make your point (see Figure 7-25). The formatting methods you learned earlier in this chapter enable you to create settings so that predefined information appears next to task bars in your schedule. However, you must use the Drawing Text Box tool to enter your own text.

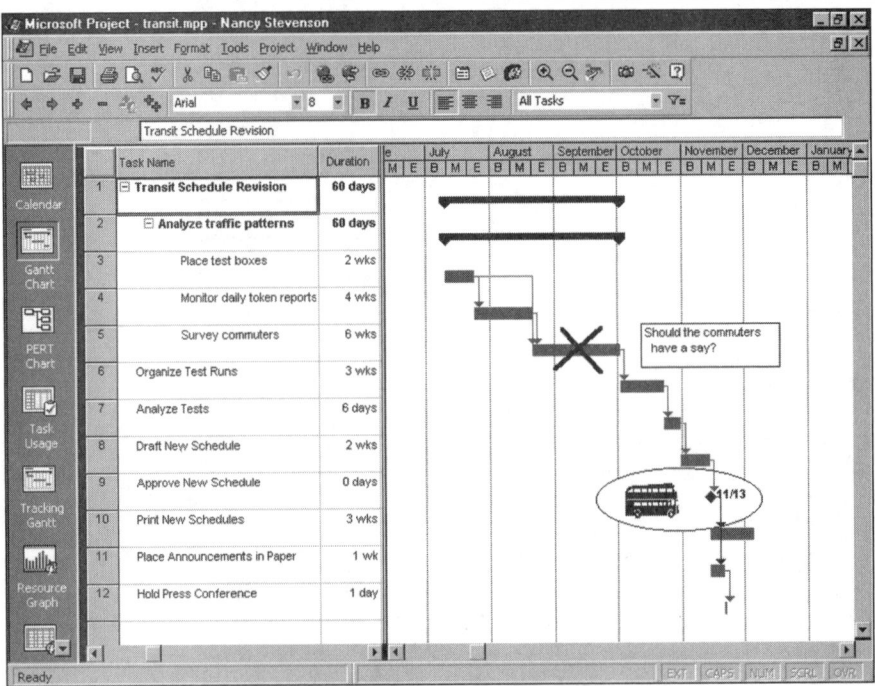

Figure 7-25: Consider using these kinds of drawings to display a project onscreen using an LCD panel, or at a trade show.

To display the Drawing toolbar shown in Figure 7-26, you can choose either View⇨ Toolbars and select the Drawing toolbar for display, or choose Insert⇨Drawing.

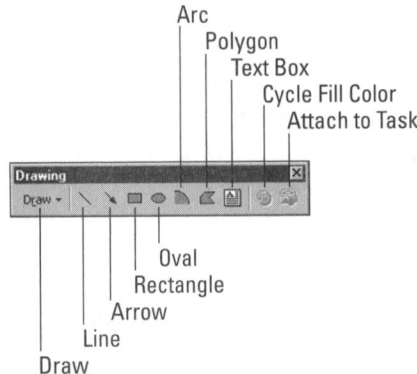

Figure 7-26: The Drawing toolbar is a floating toolbar; drag it up near the Formatting toolbar if you want to dock it at the top of your screen, or click on the dark blue bar at the top and drag to move it around your screen.

Here's how you can use the tools on the Drawing toolbar:

✦ To draw an object, click on the Line, Arrow, Rectangle, Oval, Arc, or Polygon buttons and then click on the task bar area of the Gantt chart. Holding down your mouse, drag to draw the shape. When using the Polygon tool, you need to drag several segments to define the multisided shape. With all the other tools, the shape appears automatically when you drag in one direction and release your mouse.

✦ To create text anywhere around your task bar, click on the Text Box button and drag to draw a box. Your insertion point appears in the box whenever you select the box; you can type any text you like.

✦ To fill an object with color, click on the Cycle Fill Color button on the Drawing toolbar repeatedly until you see the color you want.

✦ To anchor a drawing object in the Gantt chart to a particular task bar — so that if you move the task in the schedule the graphic moves with it — select the object and click on the Attach to Task button on the Drawing toolbar. Click on the Attach to task control button in the Format Drawing dialog box (see Figure 7-27), enter a task ID number, and enter the settings for the point on the task bar at which you want to attach the object. Then click on OK. (You can reach the Format Drawing dialog box at any time by choosing Format⇨Drawing⇨Properties.)

Tip

You can also use three tools on the Drawing toolbar with other types of graphic objects that you insert: the Draw, Cycle Fill Color, and Attach to Task buttons work with any selected object, such as clip art.

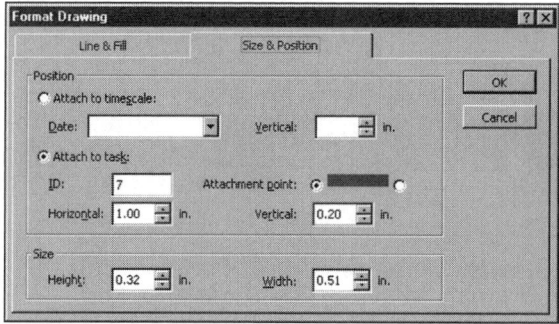

Figure 7-27: You could also attach a graphic to a position on the timescale, rather than attaching it to a particular task. Place a graphic at a particular date on the timescale, for example.

When you no longer need the Drawing toolbar, click on the close button in its upper-right corner to remove it.

Modifying graphics and drawings

You can also use the Format Drawing dialog box shown in Figure 7-27 to format graphic object styles. To open this dialog box, right-click on any object, choose Properties from the shortcut menu, and click on the Line & Fill tab to see the choices in Figure 7-28.

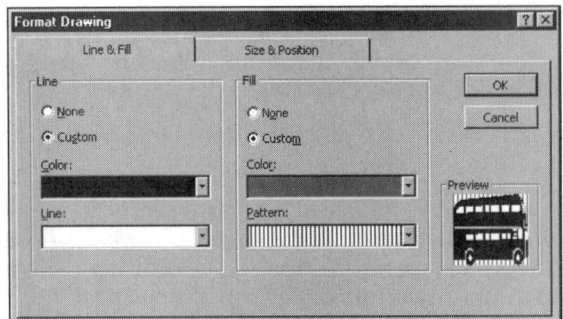

Figure 7-28: Rather than cycling through fill colors using the button on the Drawing toolbar, you can select a fill color from a drop-down palette in the Line & Fill tab of the Format Drawing dialog box.

Use the Color and Line drop-down options on the left to assign a style of thickness and color to lines. Use the Fill Color and Pattern options to place a color and pattern, such as solid or thatched lines, inside an object.

Tip   Fill color and pattern fills the inside of a drawn object and the background area of a clip art or other predrawn graphic object. The Preview box in Figure 7-28 shows you how a fill pattern surrounds the clip art object, filling the background of the object, rather than filling the object itself.

Resizing and moving drawings and other objects is similar to working with objects in other programs:

✦ **To resize an object**: Click on the object to select it. Click on any of the eight selection handles; drag inward to make the object smaller or drag outward to make the object larger.

✦ **To move an object**: Move your mouse pointer over the object until your cursor changes to four arrows. Click on the object, hold down your mouse button, and drag the object anywhere in the Gantt chart area. Release the mouse to place the object.

Summary

In this chapter you learned many ways to

✦ Format text for individual selections or globally by category of task

✦ Format task bars and the information displayed near them

✦ Use different styles for PERT node boxes and change the information that you display in the PERT Chart view

✦ Modify the way that your layout and gridlines appear in the Gantt chart

✦ Insert graphic objects and drawings in the Gantt chart and in notes, or as a header and footer

Chapter 8 explains how to fine-tune timing to resolve scheduling conflicts.

✦   ✦   ✦

Resolving Scheduling Problems

Scheduling conflicts are the bane of the project manager's existence. This chapter focuses on identifying scheduling problems and resolving them.

Understanding Why Scheduling Conflicts Occur

Scheduling conflicts typically fall into two categories:

✦ Your project is taking longer than you had planned.

✦ Your resources are overassigned.

This chapter considers the first problem; Chapter 9 focuses on the second.

Scheduling conflicts announce themselves in a number of ways. Changing views and filtering information using the techniques described in Chapter 6 may identify some glaring problem inherent in your original logic. For example, if you filter your project to view only incomplete tasks or slipping tasks, you may spot some problems. More likely, however, you'll unknowingly create a problem by using a task constraint, as the next section explains.

Resolving Scheduling Conflicts

Project provides several techniques that you can use to resolve scheduling conflicts. This section covers the following strategies:

✦ Adding resources

✦ Using overtime

✦ Adding time

✦ Adjusting Slack

✦ Changing constraints

✦ Adjusting dependencies

✦ Splitting a task

Adding resources to tasks

Adding resources to a task can decrease the time necessary to complete the task. Using the Advanced tab of the Task Information dialog box (see Figure 8-1), make sure to set the task type to Fixed Units; in this case adding resources to the task reduces the duration of the task. Also remember that a check appears by default in the Effort Driven check box of the Task Information dialog box. When you use the Effort Drive option, Project reallocates the work among the assigned resources.

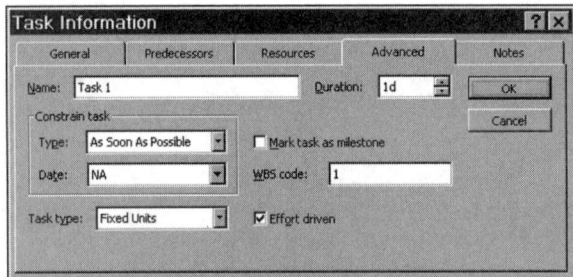

Figure 8-1: The Advanced tab of the Task Information dialog box controls the task type and whether the task is effort driven.

In the best of all possible worlds, you have unlimited resources — but now you need to consider reality. If you don't have unlimited resources, adding resources may not be an option for you. But you might be able to use overtime to shorten a task's duration, which is the next strategy you can use to resolve scheduling problems.

For information on resolving resource conflicts, see Chapter 9.

Using overtime

Overtime in Project is the amount of work scheduled beyond an assigned resource's regular working hours. Overtime hours are charged at the resource's overtime rate. Overtime work does *not* represent additional work on a task; instead, it represents the amount of time spent on a task outside regular hours. For example, if you assign 30 hours of work and 12 hours of overtime, the total work is still 30 hours. Of the 30 hours, 18 hours are worked during the regular work schedule (and charged to the project at the regular rate), and 12 hours are worked during off hours (and charged to the project at an overtime rate). You can use overtime, therefore, to shorten the time a resource takes to complete a task.

To enter overtime, follow these steps:

1. Select the Gantt Chart view from the View Bar.

2. Choose Window⇨Split to reveal the Task Form in the bottom pane.

3. Click on the Task Form to make it the active pane.

4. Choose Format⇨Details⇨Resource Work. Project adds the Ovt. Work column to the Task form (see Figure 8-2).

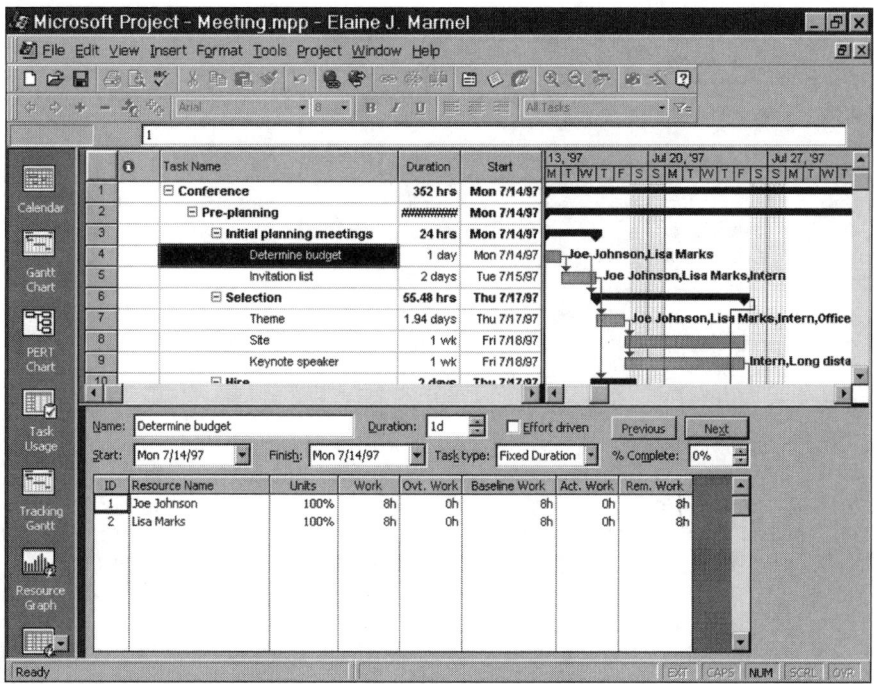

Figure 8-2: Use the Task form and display the Overtime column to add overtime.

5. Move to the top pane and select the task to which you want to assign overtime.

6. Move to the bottom pane and fill in the overtime amount for the appropriate resource.

Tip   When you finish entering overtime, you can hide the Task form by choosing Window⇩Remove Split.

Adding time to tasks

You can also solve scheduling conflicts by increasing the duration of a task. Again, in the best of all possible worlds, you have this luxury. In reality, you may not. But if you can increase the duration of a task, you may find scarce resources available to complete the task given its new timing.

As you know, you can change the duration from several different views, such as the Task Usage view or the Gantt Chart view. Or you can use the Task Information dialog box (see Figure 8-3). To open the Task Information dialog box, double-click on the task and use the Duration box to change the duration.

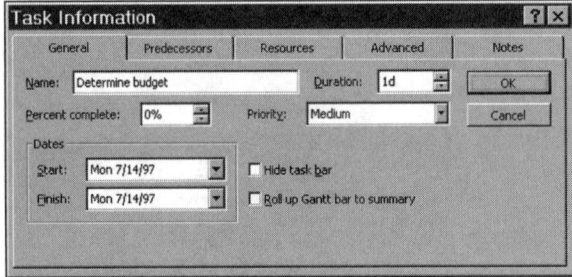

Figure 8-3: Change the duration from the Task Information dialog box.

Adjusting slack

Slack time is the amount of time a task can slip before it affects another task's dates or the finish date of the project. *Free slack* is the amount of time a task can be delayed without delaying any other task. Most projects contain noncritical tasks with slack, and these tasks can start late without affecting the schedule. If you have slack in your schedule, you might be able to move tasks around to balance phases of the schedule that have no slack with phases that have too much slack. That way, you can use tasks with slack to compensate for tasks that take longer than planned or to help resolve resource overallocations.

Note

Slack values can also help you identify inconsistencies in the schedule. For example, you'll see a negative slack value when one task has a finish-to-start dependency with a second task, but the second task has a Must Start On constraint that is earlier than the end of the first task.

Almost by definition, you create slack time if you use the Must Start On constraint when you create your task. As you learned in Chapter 4, you set constraints on the Advanced tab of the Task Information dialog box (see Figure 8-4); to display the Task Information dialog box, double-click on the task in your schedule. When the dialog box appears, select the Advanced tab.

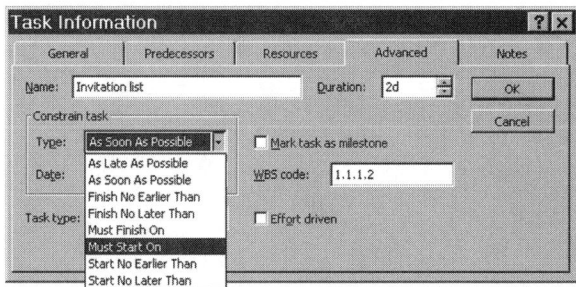

Figure 8-4: Constraints can often create slack time.

To avoid creating slack time, use the As Soon As Possible constraint as much as you can. To find tasks with slack time, follow these steps:

1. Choose View⇨More Views to open the More Views dialog box.

2. Select Detail Gantt from the list, and then click on Apply.

Tip

You can identify slack on the Gantt bars. Slack appears as thin lines extending from the regular Gantt bars.

3. Right-click on the Select All button and select Schedule from the list of tables.

4. Drag the divider bar to the right to view more of the table. Now you can see the Free Slack and Total Slack fields shown in Figure 8-5.

Slack on the Gantt chart

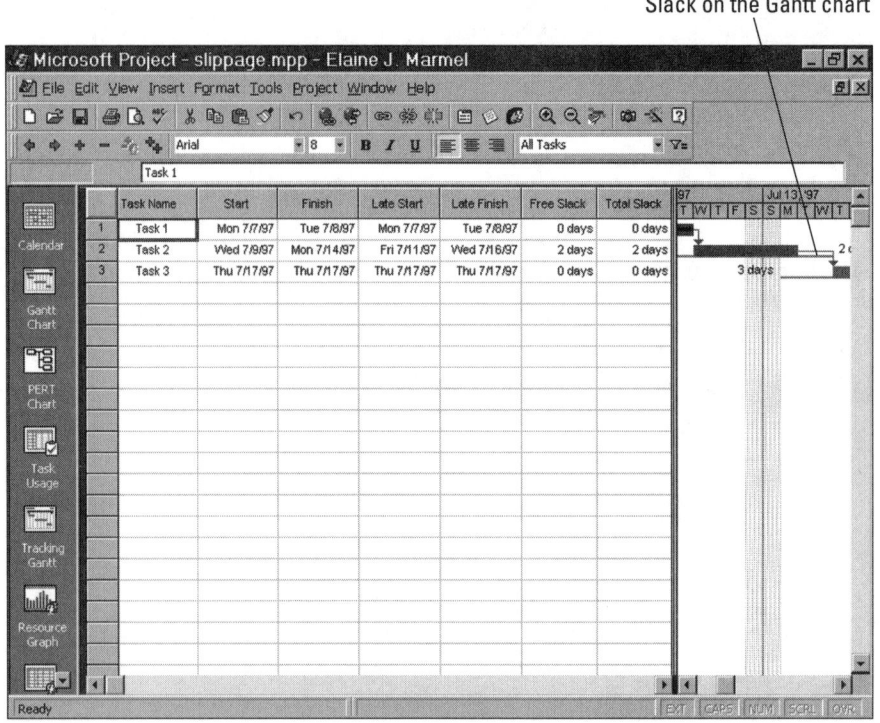

Figure 8-5: You can find slack time on tasks using the Detail Gantt view and the Schedule table.

Changing task constraints

Task constraints are the usual culprits when projects fall behind schedule. By default, Project uses the Planning Wizard to warn you when you are about to take an action that is likely to throw your project off schedule. For example, if you impose a Must Start On task constraint, Project displays the Planning Wizard dialog box in Figure 8-6.

Similarly, if you impose an illogical Start Date on a task when recording actual dates, Project displays a Planning Wizard dialog box that resembles the one in Figure 8-7. Suppose, for example, that you accidentally enter a start date for Task 4, and Task 4 is linked to and succeeds Task 3. Further suppose that you have not yet started Task 3.

You learn more about entering actual dates in Chapter 11.

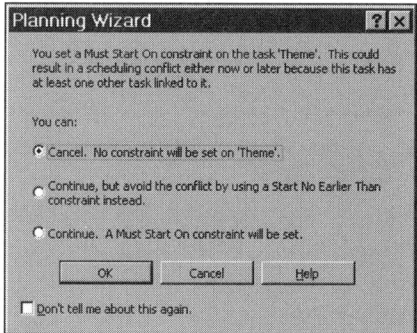

Figure 8-6: The Planning Wizard appears, by default, when you apply a constraint that is likely to lengthen your project schedule.

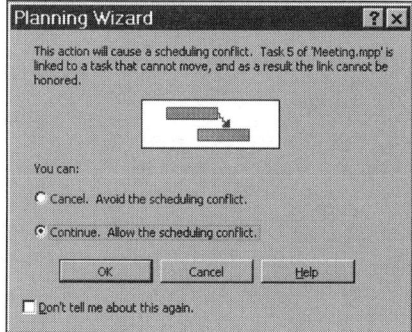

Figure 8-7: The Planning Wizard also warns you if you try to record an actual start date that will cause a scheduling conflict.

Notice that you can turn off the Planning Wizard warnings by placing a check in the Don't tell me about this again check box at the bottom of the Planning Wizard dialog box. (Some people just don't like to have Wizards popping up all the time.)

If you turn off the Planning Wizard, Project still warns you as you take actions that cause scheduling problems. Instead of the Planning Wizard, Project displays the more traditional message in Figure 8-8.

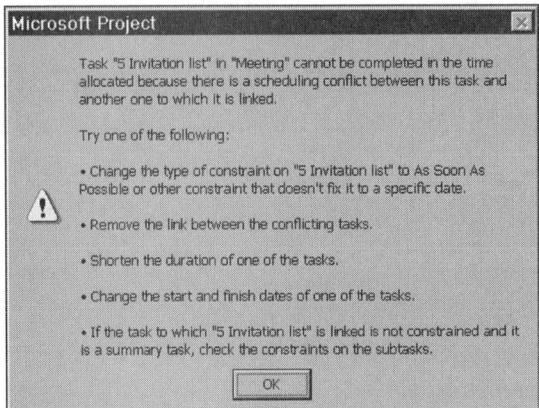

Figure 8-8: When you disable the Planning Wizard and take an action that might cause a scheduling problem, Project displays this warning message.

The message in Figure 8-8 refers to the Invitation List task, which is the predecessor task of the Theme task in Figure 8-6. Project makes suggestions concerning actions you can take to avoid the conflict — and the suggestions all refer to the predecessor task. Notice also that, unlike the Planning Wizard, this message box does *not* give you the option of canceling your action.

So, although you may find the Planning Wizard annoying at some levels, it can actually save you effort at other levels. Sorry you turned it off? To turn it on again, choose Tools⇨Options and click on the General tab (see Figure 8-9).

Place a check in the Advice from Planning Wizard check box. (You also can control the other types of advice you receive in the same location.)

Adjusting dependencies

By changing task dependencies, you can tighten up the schedule and eliminate scheduling conflicts. If you inadvertently link tasks that don't need to be linked, you could create a situation in which you don't have the resources to complete the tasks and the project schedule falls behind. If you discover unnecessary links, you can remove them. When you remove the dependencies, you may find holes in the project schedule where work could be performed but isn't. After you remove unnecessary dependencies, you may be able to move tasks around and fill those holes.

Reviewing dependencies is easiest if you use the Task PERT view in the bottom pane of the Gantt view (see Figure 8-10). The Task PERT view shows you the selected task and its immediate predecessor and successor.

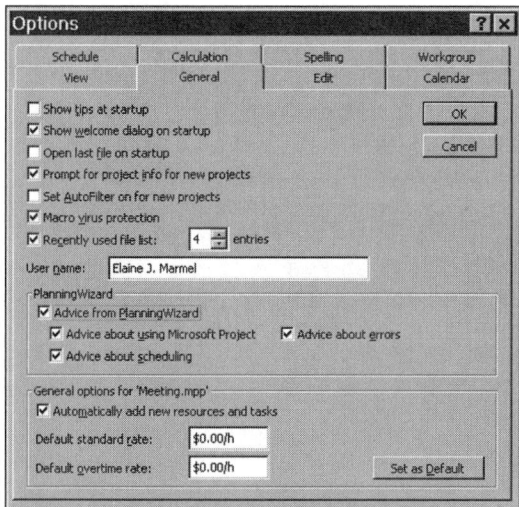

Figure 8-9: You can control whether the Planning Wizard appears from the General tab in the Options menu.

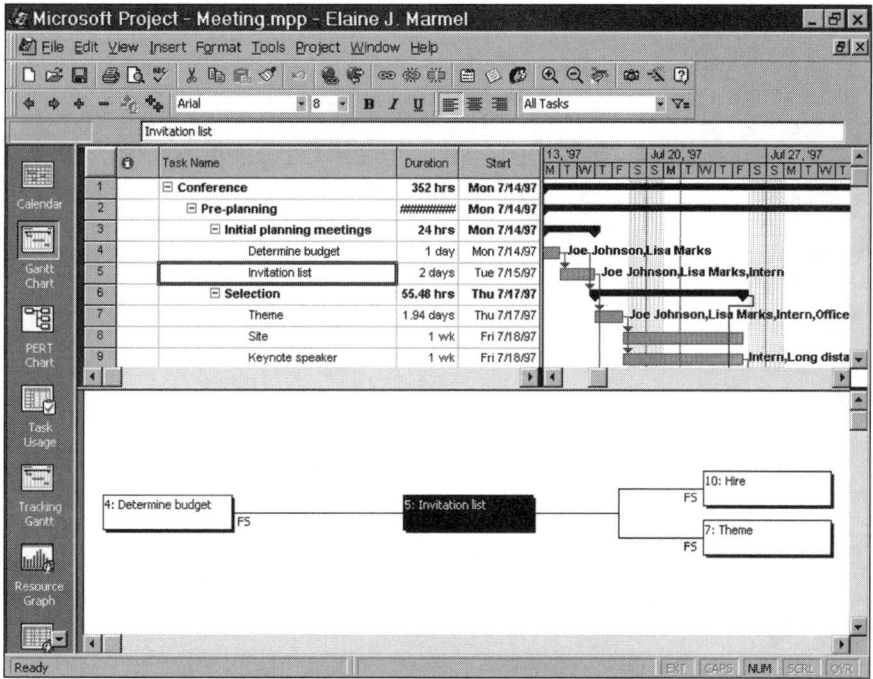

Figure 8-10: Use the Task PERT view to review task dependencies.

As you review the tasks, ask yourself these questions: Do I really need to complete A before B begins? Could I perform them concurrently? Could I do one of them later without harming the project?

Splitting a task

Splitting a task can sometimes be the best way to resolve a scheduling conflict. You may not be able to complete the task on consecutive days, but you can start the task, stop work on it for a period of time, and then come back to the task. Project allows you to split a task any time you determine you need to make this type of adjustment. Remember, splitting a task creates a gap. You'll see the gap in the task's Gantt bar. Follow these steps to split a task:

1. Switch to the Gantt Chart view using the View bar.

2. Click on the Split Task button on the Standard toolbar. The button appears to be pressed, the mouse pointer changes shape, and a screen tip tells you how to split a task (see Figure 8-11).

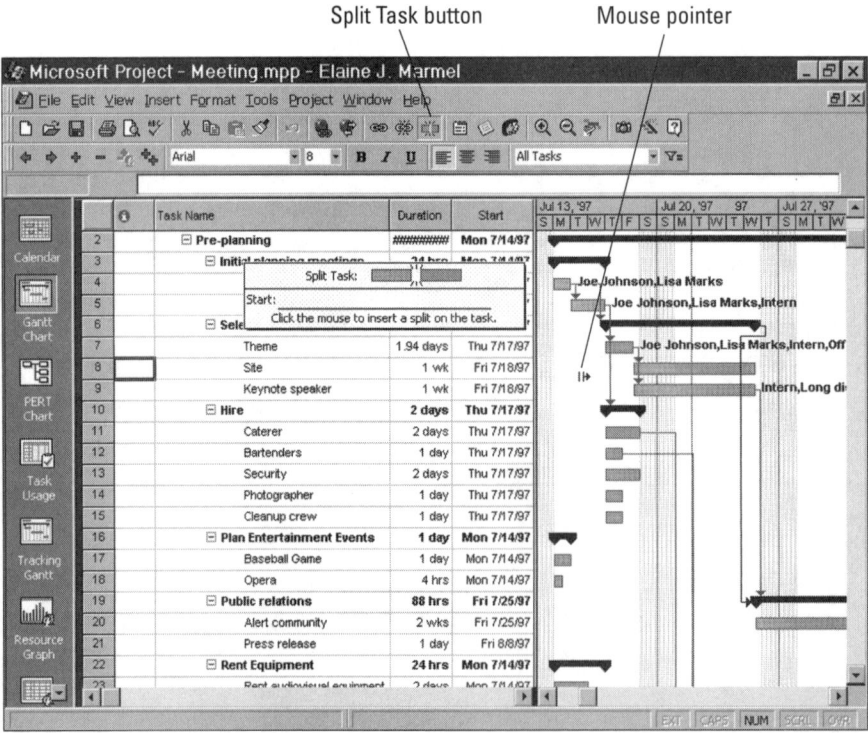

Figure 8-11: Use the Split Task button to divide a task.

3. Move the mouse pointer along the bar of the task you want to split. As the mouse pointer moves, dates representing the split date appear in the screen tip.

4. Click when the screen tip shows the date you want to split the task; Project inserts a one-day split.

 Tip

If you want the split to last longer than one day, drag to the right instead of clicking.

After you split a task, it looks like the task in Figure 8-12, with dotted lines appearing between the two portions of the split. If you decide that you want to remove a split, drag the inside portions of the split together so that they touch.

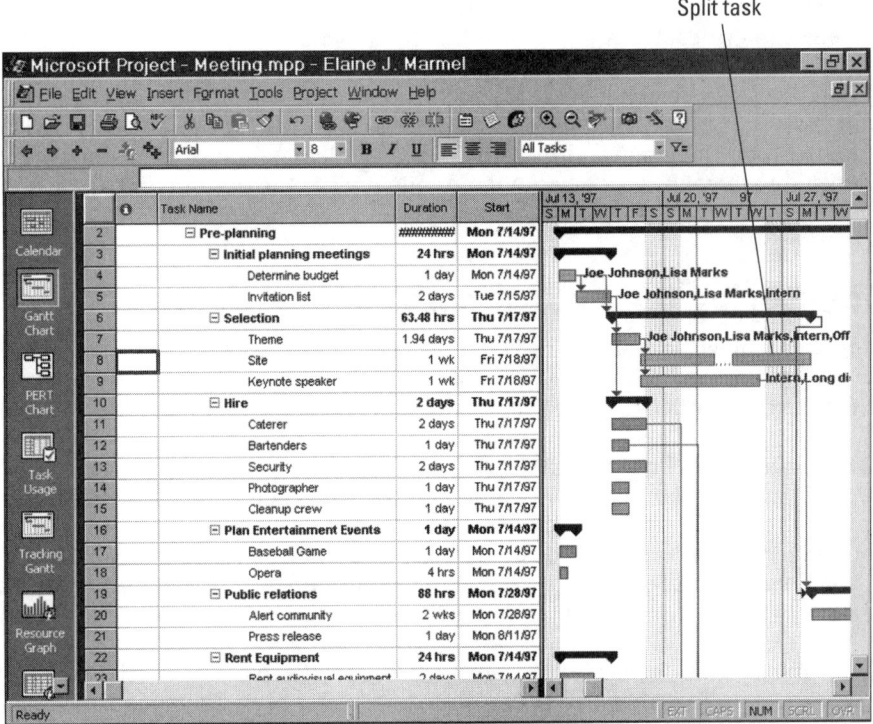

Figure 8-12: This Gantt chart shows a split task.

Using the Critical Path to Shorten a Project

The first part of this chapter examined ways to resolve scheduling conflicts that develop for one reason or another. But what about being a hero and simply shortening the time frame you originally allotted for the entire project? How would you approach that task? You'd evaluate — and try to shorten — the critical path.

The *critical path* shows the tasks in your project that must be completed on schedule for the entire project to finish on schedule — and these tasks are called *critical tasks.* Most tasks in a project have some slack, and you can delay them some without affecting the project finish date. However, if you delay critical tasks, you affect the project finish date. As you use the techniques described earlier in this chapter to modify tasks to resolve scheduling problems, be aware that changes to critical tasks affect your project finish date.

Note

Noncritical tasks can become critical if they slip too much. You can control how much slack Project allows for a task before defining the task as a critical task. Choose Tools⇨Options and then click on the Calculation tab. In the box labeled Tasks are critical if slack is less than or equal to, at the bottom of the tab, enter the number of slack days.

Identifying the critical path

You'll see the critical path best if you use the GanttChartWizard to display the critical path in red. This discussion of the GanttChartWizard focuses on displaying the critical path; see Chapter 7 for a more complete description of that wizard.

On the View bar, click on the Gantt Chart view to select it. Then click on the GanttChartWizard button on the Standard toolbar (second button from the right edge) or choose Format⇨ GanttChartWizard. The first GanttChartWizard dialog box welcomes you to the GanttChartWizard. Click on Next to move on to the GanttChartWizard Step 2 dialog box (shown in Figure 8-13). Then select Critical Path to describe the kind of information you want to display on the Gantt Chart.

Subsequent dialog boxes in the GanttChartWizard enable you to select other types of information to display, such as resources and dates on Gantt bars and links between dependent tasks. All other choices you make while running the GanttChartWizard are a matter of personal preference.

When you view the Gantt chart, all tasks in the project still appear, but tasks on the critical path appear in red.

Note

After you use the GanttChartWizard, you can switch to any view. Critical tasks appear in red. Try the PERT Chart view, for example; the critical tasks are red boxes.

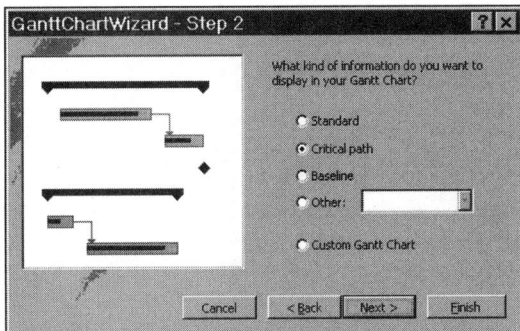

Figure 8-13: Select Critical Path when you run the GanttChartWizard.

You can also use formatting to identify critical tasks. When you apply formatting to critical and noncritical tasks, this formatting appears on all views in which you can see task bars. The formatting identifies critical tasks with a Yes in or near the bar of the tasks and noncritical tasks with a No.

To apply formatting, follow these steps:

1. Display the Gantt Chart view.

2. Choose Format⇨Bar Styles. Project displays the Bar Styles dialog box.

3. Select Task from the list at the top of the Bar Styles dialog box to apply formatting to noncritical tasks.

4. Click on the Text tab.

5. Select a position for the formatting. When you click on a position, a list box arrow appears.

6. Click on the list box arrow and scroll to select Critical (see Figure 8-14).

7. Select Critical Task from the list at the top of the box.

8. Repeat steps 5 and 6 once to apply formatting to critical tasks.

9. Click on OK.

After you apply the formatting, the Gantt chart shows critical and noncritical tasks and should resemble the Gantt chart in Figure 8-15.

Text tab

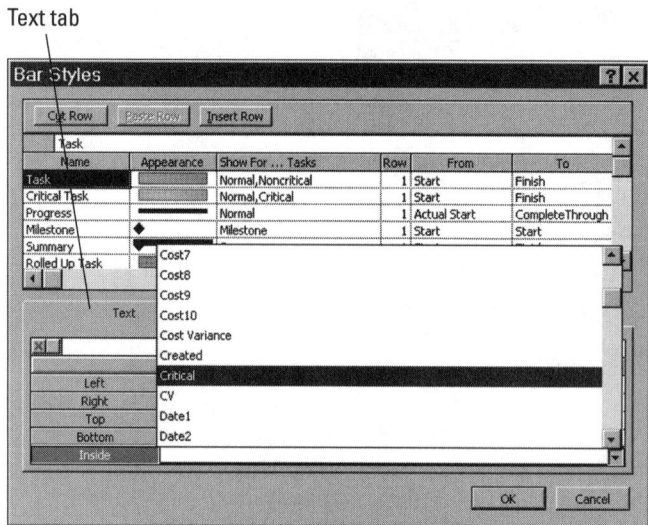

Figure 8-14: Use the Text tab of the Bar Styles dialog box to apply formatting that distinguishes critical from noncritical tasks.

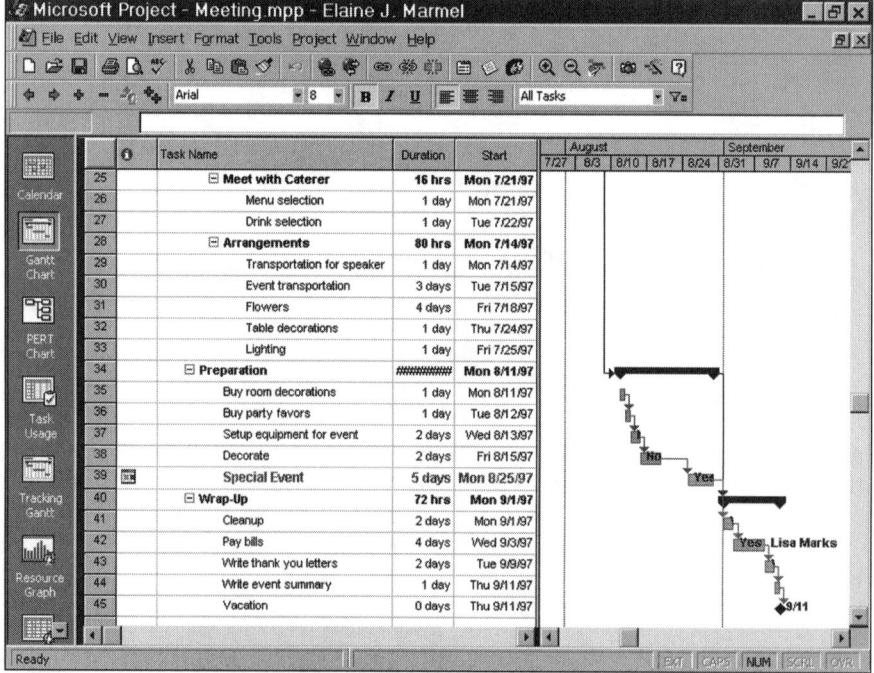

Figure 8-15: The formatting in this Gantt chart identifies critical and noncritical tasks.

Even with formatting, this approach to identifying the critical path can be cumbersome if your project contains many tasks. As an alternative, you can identify the critical path by filtering for it. As Chapter 6 explains, you can apply the Critical filter to any task view to display *only* critical tasks (see Figure 8-16). To apply the filter, display the view you want to filter and choose Project⇨Filtered for⇨Critical.

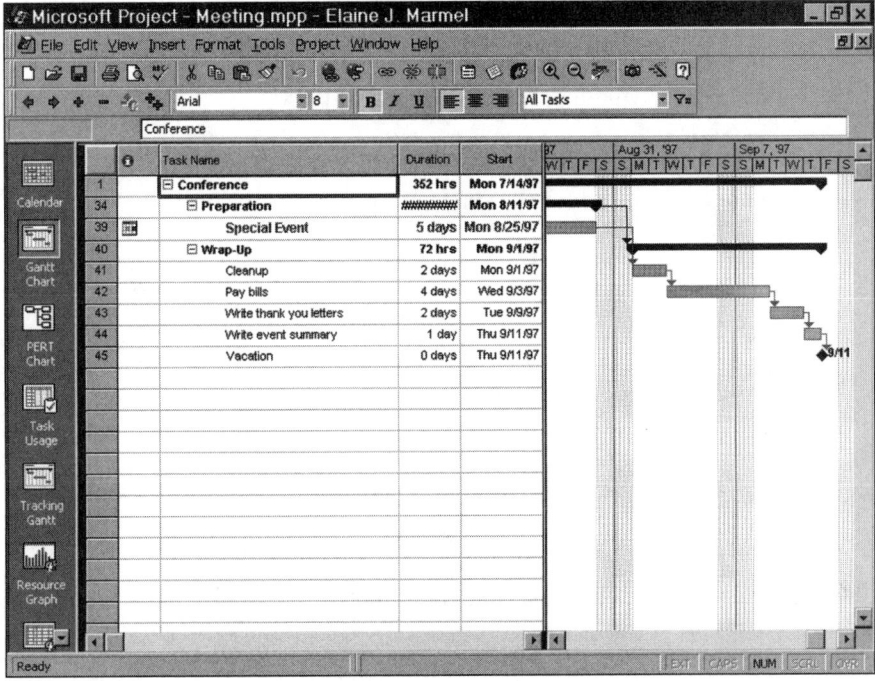

Figure 8-16: Filter to display only critical tasks.

Tip

Filtering is a very effective tool to display only certain aspects of the project, but sometimes you need to view all the tasks in your project and still identify the critical ones. If you use formatting, you can always identify critical and noncritical tasks, even if you are viewing all the tasks in your project.

Shortening the critical path

Shortening the time allotted on the critical path shortens your project's duration. The converse is also true; lengthening the time allotted on the critical path lengthens the project. In all probability, you, as project manager, are also responsible, at least to some extent, for the cost of a project — and typically, the longer a project goes on, the more it costs. Therefore, shortening the critical path is often the project manager's goal.

The result of shortening a project's duration can be finishing earlier. But it also can be starting later. Obviously, the second alternative is riskier, particularly if you are not confident of your estimates. If you are new to project management, you probably should not plan to start later; instead, use project management tools to help you evaluate the accuracy of your estimating skills. Over time (and multiple projects), you'll know how accurate your estimates are and can then take the risk of starting a project later than initially planned.

Here are some ways to reduce the time allotted on the critical path:

✦ You can reduce the duration of critical tasks.

✦ You can overlap critical tasks to reduce the overall project duration.

Here are some ways to reduce the duration of critical tasks:

✦ You can reassess estimates and use a more optimistic task time. The PERT Analysis views can help you here.

✦ You can add resources to a critical task. Remember, though that the task must not be a fixed-duration task — adding resources to a fixed-duration task does not reduce the time of the task.

✦ You can add overtime to a critical task.

Here are some ways to overlap critical tasks:

✦ You can adjust dependencies and task date constraints.

✦ You can redefine a finish-to-start relationship to either a start-to-start or a finish-to-finish relationship.

Now that you know the techniques you can apply to adjust the critical path, you need to ask the important question: What's the best way to identify tasks you want to change and then make changes? The answer: Select a view and filter it for critical tasks only. The Task Entry view is the best view to use because the top pane displays a graphic representation of your project and the bottom pane displays most of the fields you might want to change (see Figure 8-17).

To select the Task Entry view, right-click on the View bar and choose More Views from the shortcut menu. Then select Task Entry from the More Views dialog box and click on the Apply button. To filter for critical tasks, choose Project⇨Filtered for⇨Critical. Evaluate each critical task and make changes in the Task Entry form at the bottom of the screen.

Tip

You also can sort your critical tasks by duration. That way, the critical tasks are in order from the longest to the shortest, and you can focus on trying to shorten longer tasks.

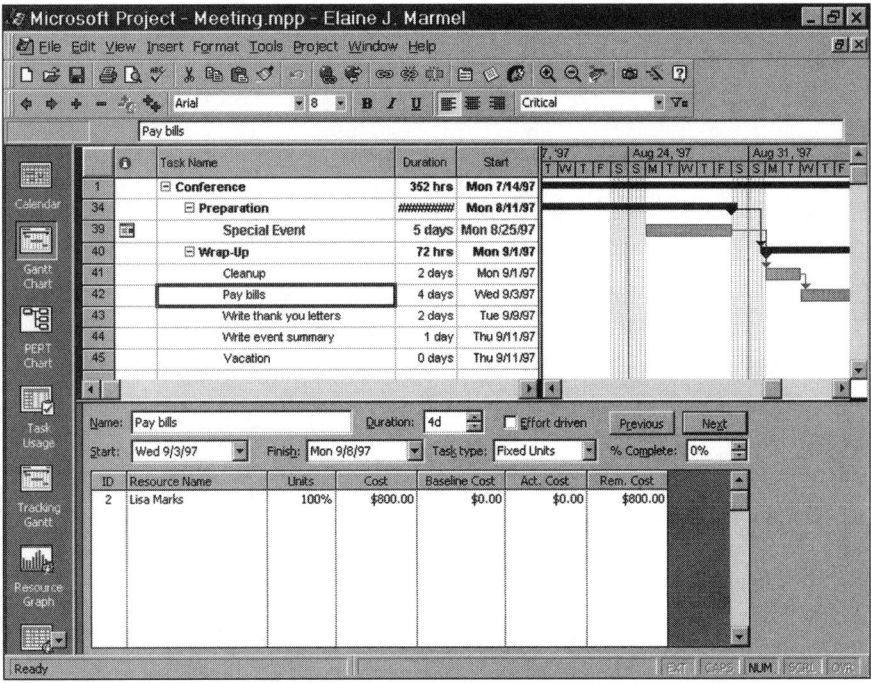

Figure 8-17: The Task Entry view, filtered for critical tasks, is probably the easiest view in which to work.

Summary

This chapter describes the techniques you can use to resolve scheduling conflicts and to shorten the length of your project:

✦ Adding resources to tasks

✦ Using overtime

✦ Adjusting slack

✦ Changing task constraints and dependencies

In Chapter 9 you learn how to resolve conflicts that occur with resources.

✦   ✦   ✦

Resolving Resource Problems

Resource allocation is the process of assigning resources to tasks in a project. Because the potential for resource overallocation always accompanies resource assignment, this chapter explores the causes of resource overallocation and introduces methods to resolve the conflicts.

Understanding How Resource Conflicts Occur

As you assign resources to tasks, Project checks the resource's calendar to make sure that the resource is working. Note, however, that Project doesn't care whether the resource is already obligated when you assign the resource to a new task; Project allows you to make the assignment. However, the additional assignment could lead to overallocating the resource. *Overallocation* occurs when you assign more work to the resource than the resource can accomplish in the given time period.

For example, if you assign Mary full-time to two tasks that start on the same day, you actually assign Mary to 16 hours of work in an 8-hour day — not possible. On the other hand, if you have a group of three mechanics and you assign two mechanics to work on a task, you still have one spare Mechanic and no overallocation.

Figure 9-1 shows a series of tasks that begin on the same day. By assigning the same resource to all of them, an overallocation is inevitable. Overallocations can cause delays in the project schedule.

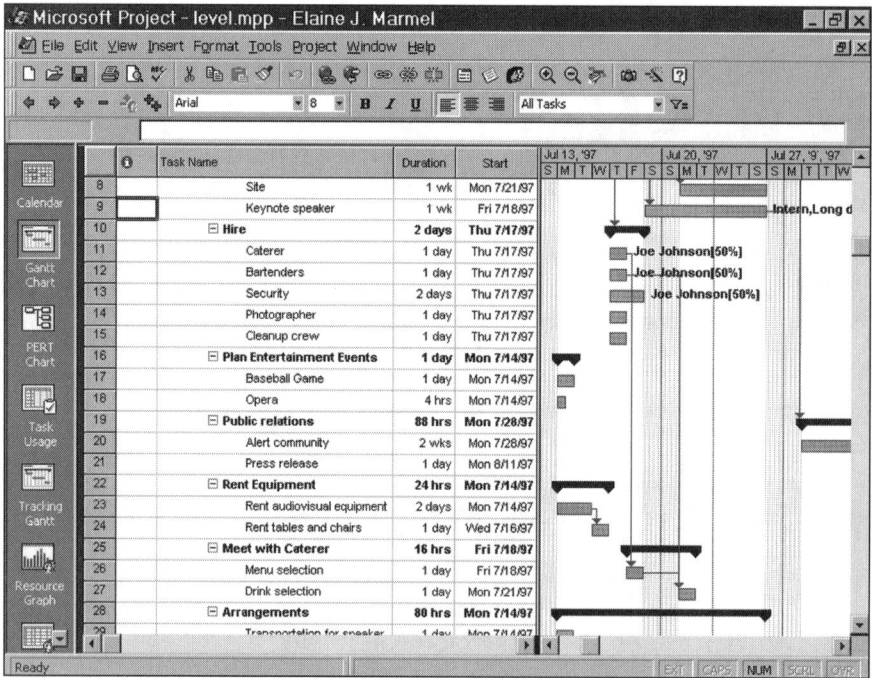

Figure 9-1: Assigning the same resource to tasks that run simultaneously causes an overallocation.

To calculate the scheduled start date for a task, Project checks factors such as the task's dependencies and constraints. Then Project checks the resource's calendar to identify the next regular workday and assigns that date as the start date for the task. If you haven't assigned resources to the task, Project uses the project's calendar to calculate the next regular workday. But when it calculates the task start date, Project does not consider other commitments the resource might have.

Spotting Resource Conflicts

Before you can resolve resource conflicts, you need to spot them. You can use views or filters to help you identify resource overallocation problems.

Using views to spot resource conflicts

Use a resource view, such as the Resource Sheet view or the Resource Usage view, to find resource conflicts. On these views, overallocated resources appear in red. In addition, an Indicator icon displays an overassigned message if you point at the icon with the mouse. To display the Resource Usage view shown in Figure 9-2, select Resource Usage from the View bar.

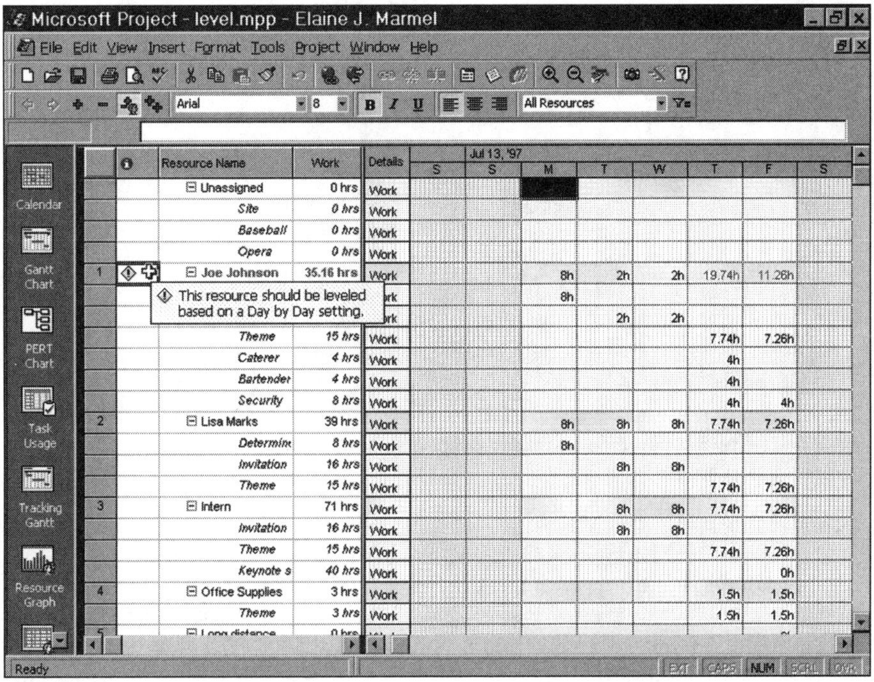

Figure 9-2: The Resource Usage view displays overallocated resources in red, and an icon appears in the Indicator column.

You also can see a graphic representation of a resource's allocation by switching to the Resource Graph view. To display the view shown in Figure 9-3, select Resource Graph from the View bar.

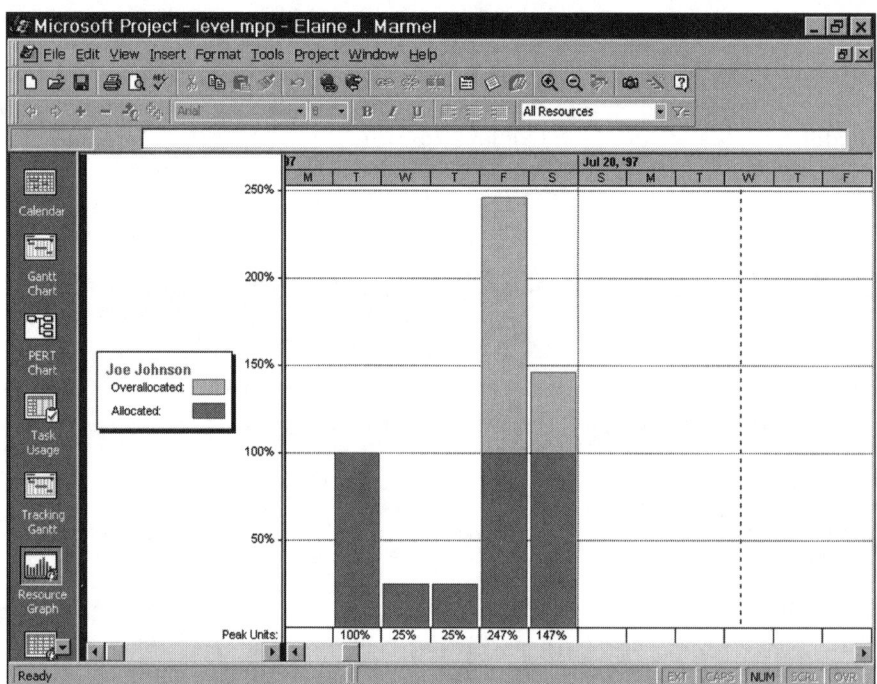

Figure 9-3: The Resource Graph view presents a pictorial representation of a resource's allocation.

The Resource Allocation view in Figure 9-4 is useful for working with overallocations — a Gantt chart in the lower pane shows the tasks assigned to the resource you select in the top pane. Tasks that start at the same time overlap in the Gantt Chart pane; this view helps you pinpoint the tasks that are causing the resource's overallocation.

Resource Management toolbar

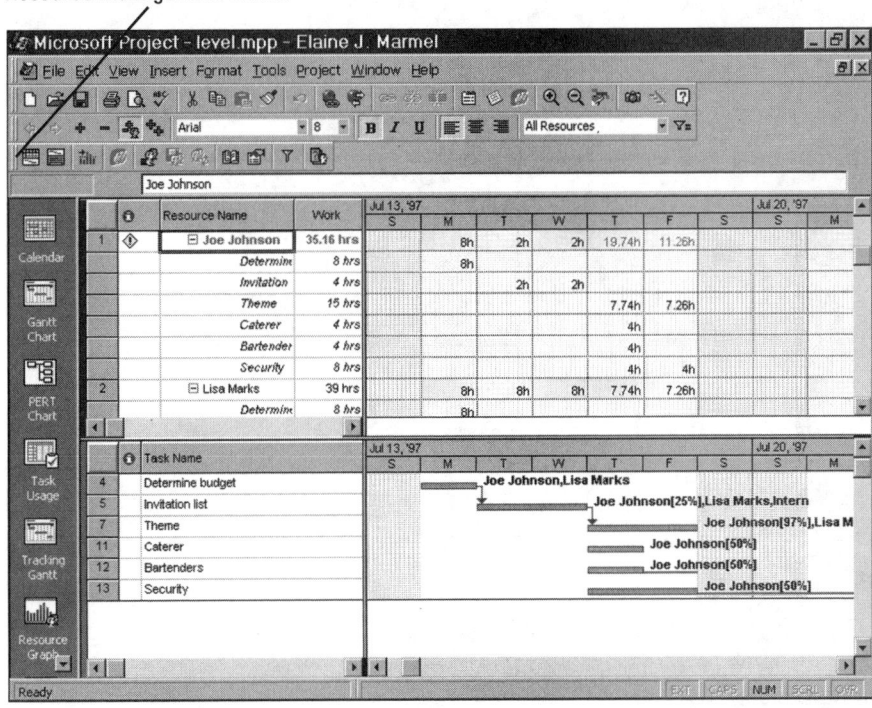

Figure 9-4: The Resource Allocation view uses the Gantt chart format to show the tasks assigned to the resource selected in the top pane.

To switch to the Resource Allocation view, use the first button on the Resource Management toolbar, which contains several tools to help you adjust resource allocations. You can display the Resource Management toolbar by choosing View⇨ Toolbars. From the list that appears, select Resource Management.

Tip

To find the next resource conflict, click on the Go To Next Overallocation button on the Resource Management toolbar. It's the third button from the left edge of the toolbar.

Using filters to spot resource conflicts

Filtering is another simple technique you can use to help you work on resource conflict problems. If you filter the Resource Usage view (shown in Figure 9-5) to display *only* overallocated resources, the problems become even more obvious. To filter the view, switch to it first. Then choose Project⇨Filtered⇨Overallocated Resources.

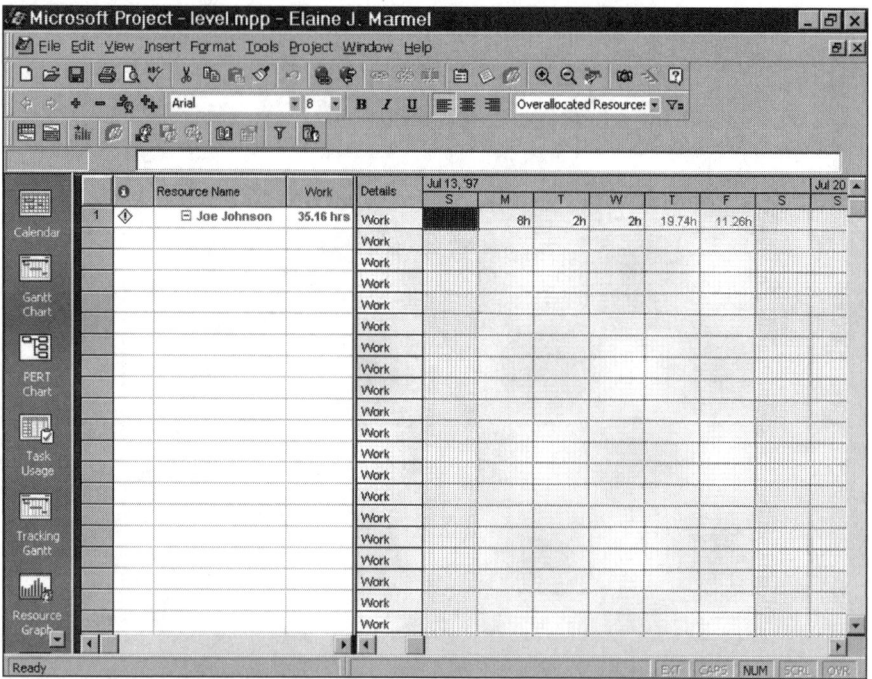

Figure 9-5: You can filter the Resource Usage view to show overallocated resources only.

Next add the Overallocation field to the view to identify the extent of the resource's overallocation. Choose Format⇨Details Overallocation. As Figure 9-6 shows, Project adds a line to the timescale portion of the view to show you the number of hours you need to eliminate to correct the overallocation.

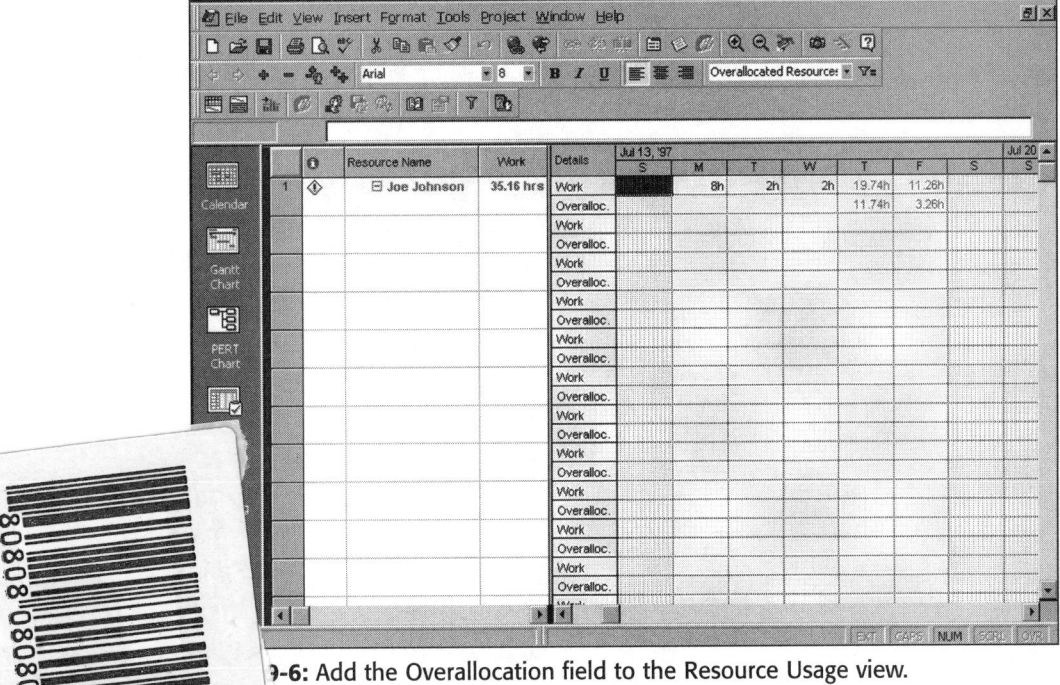

9-6: Add the Overallocation field to the Resource Usage view.

Resolving Conflicts

Project managers use several methods to resolve conflicts. The following discussion of these methods includes suggestions for techniques appropriate to each method.

Changing resource allocations

One obvious way to resolve a resource conflict is to play around with the resource allocations. Suppose Task 3 is an effort-driven task that has a resource conflict with Task 4; the two tasks don't run concurrently, but Task 3 is continuing when Task 4 is supposed to start. Further suppose that you need the same resource, Joe Johnson, to work on both tasks. Adding a resource (Lisa Marks) to Task 3 reduces the amount of time it takes to finish Task 3, which could eliminate Joe's conflict between Tasks 3 and 4. You can add a resource using the techniques described in Chapter 5, or you can add a resource to a task using the Resource Usage view (described next).

You also can solve resource conflicts by switching resources. You can use this technique when one resource is overallocated, but you have another resource capable of doing the job. You switch resources by adding one and deleting the other from the task in question. When you want to switch resources, work in the Resource Usage view (shown in Figure 9-7) where you can focus on resource conflicts.

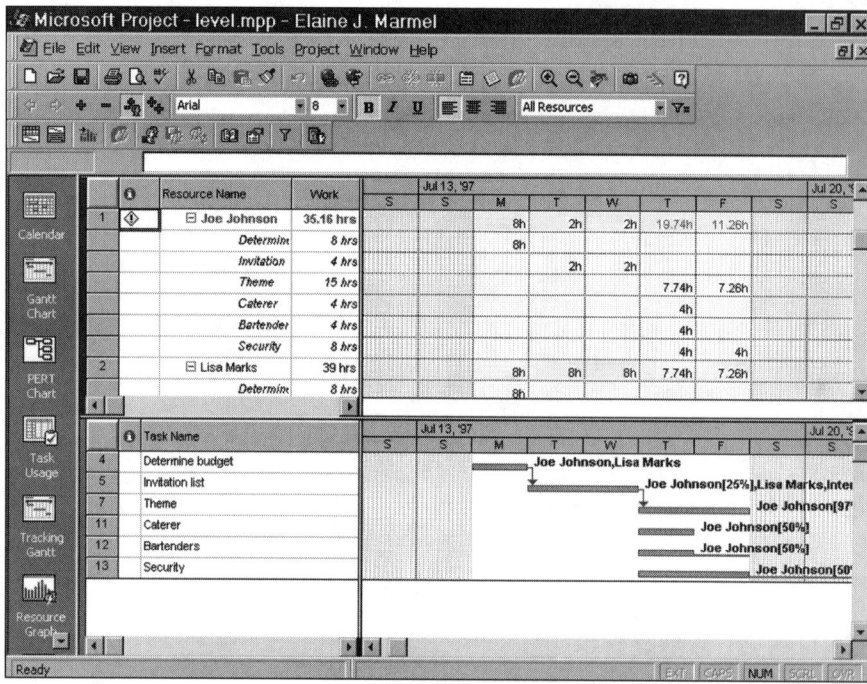

Figure 9-7: Use the Resource Usage view to switch resources.

First examine the resource with the conflict and find the task from which you want to remove that resource in the upper pane. Then click anywhere in the row of the task and press the Del key on your keyboard. Project removes the task from the assigned resource — and, with luck, indicates that the resource no longer has a conflict.

To add a task to a resource from the Resource Usage view, follow these steps:

1. Scroll down until you find the resource to which you want to add a task.

2. Click on the row of any task to which you have already assigned the resource.

3. Press the Ins key on your keyboard. Project inserts a blank line.

4. Fill in the task name, and Project fills in the default duration for the task.

You can add or delete a resource using a number of techniques. For example, you can work in the Gantt Chart view and then use the split bar to display the Task Entry view. Select a task in the Gantt Chart view and then:

✦ **To add a resource:** Select the resource from the list box that appears when you click on the Resource Name column of the Task Entry view.

✦ **To delete a resource:** Select the resource's ID number in the Task Entry view and press the delete key.

✦ **To switch resources:** Use the Replace Resource dialog box (see Chapter 5).

Working in the Gantt Chart view is effective, but the Resource Usage view helps you focus on resource conflicts.

Scheduling overtime

You also can resolve a resource conflict by scheduling overtime for the resource. Overtime in Project is the amount of work scheduled beyond an assigned resource's regular working hours, and Overtime hours are charged at the resource's overtime rate. Overtime work does *not* represent additional work on a task; instead, it represents the amount of time spent on a task during nonregular hours. By scheduling overtime, the resource may finish the task faster and therefore eliminate the conflict. As you learned in the last chapter, you assign overtime from the Gantt Chart view.

1. Select the Gantt Chart view from the View bar.

2. Choose Window⇨Split to reveal the Task Form in the bottom pane.

3. Click on the Task Form to make it the active pane.

4. Choose Format⇨Details⇨Resource Work. Project adds the Ovt. Work column to the Task form.

You can see the Ovt. Work column in Figure 9-8. 0h means that you have not yet assigned overtime.

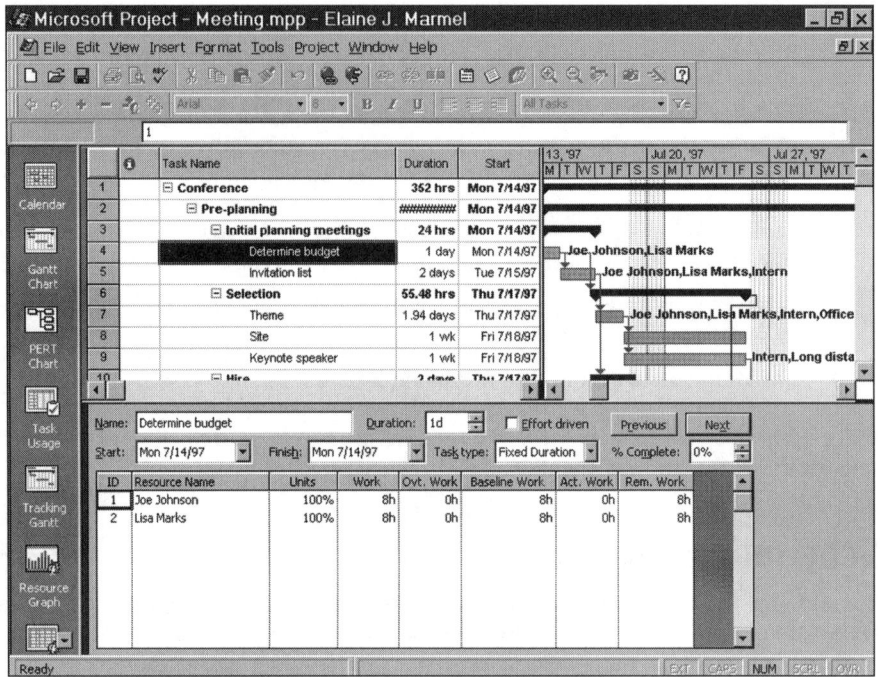

Figure 9-8: Use the Task Form and display the Overtime column to add overtime.

5. Select the task in the top pane to which you want to assign overtime.

6. Go to the bottom pane and fill in the overtime amount for the appropriate resource.

Tip

When you finish entering overtime, you can hide the Task form by choosing Window⇨Remove Split.

Redefining a resource's calendar

If your resource is a salaried resource, you may have the option of redefining a resource's calendar so that hours typically considered nonworking (and therefore charged at an overtime rate if worked) become working hours. If a resource has a conflict and the number of hours in conflict on a given day is low enough, you can eliminate the conflict by increasing the working hours for the resource for that day.

Note

You can make this kind of change to any resource — Project won't stop you. But you need to consider the effects on the cost of your project. If you are paying a resource at an overtime rate for working during nonworking hours, then you don't want to change nonworking hours to working hours in Project. If you do, you will understate the cost of your project.

To change a resource's working calendar, you can start in the Resource Usage view. Identify the resource that has a conflict, and note the number of hours the conflict involves. Double-click on the resource that has a conflict to open the Resource Information dialog box for that resource. Click on the Working Time tab to view that resource's calendar (see Figure 9-9).

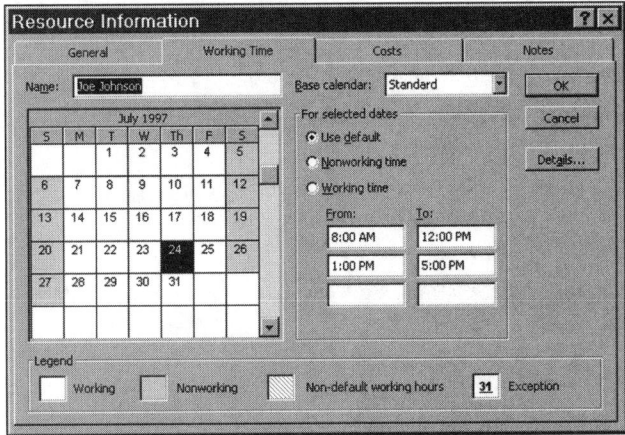

Figure 9-9: Use the Working Time tab of the Resource Information dialog box to change the standard working hours for the resource.

To change the standard working hours for a resource, follow these steps:

1. Click on the first date on which the resource is overallocated.

2. Click on the Working Time option button.

3. Use the From and To boxes to set up nonstandard working hours for that day.

4. Repeat this process for each day for which you want to change the working schedule for a particular resource.

Assigning part-time work

Suppose a resource is assigned to several concurrent tasks and is also overallocated. And further suppose that you don't want to add other resources or switch to a different resource or add overtime. You could assign the resource to work part-time on each of the tasks to solve the conflict. The tasks may take longer to complete using this method, or you may want to use this method in conjunction with additional resources to make sure that you can complete the task on time.

To assign a resource to work part-time, you can change the number of units you apply to the task. By default, Project sets task types to Fixed Units; therefore, Project changes the duration of the task accordingly if you change the amount a resource works on the task. If you want to retain the duration and assign a resource to work part-time on a task, you should change the task type to Fixed Duration.

To change the task type to Fixed Duration, follow these steps:

1. Select the Resource Usage view from the View bar.

2. Click on the task you want to change in the upper pane. Project displays that task in Gantt format in the lower pane.

3. Double-click on the task you want to change in the lower pane. Project displays the Task Information dialog box (see Figure 9-10).

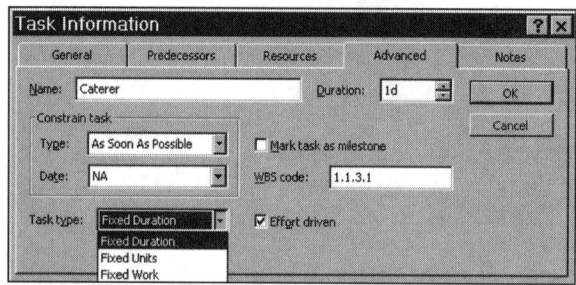

Figure 9-10: Use the Advanced tab of the Task Information dialog box to change the task type.

4. Click on the Advanced tab.

5. Open the Task Type list box and select Fixed Duration.

6. Click on OK.

Now you can assign resources to work part-time on this task without changing the task's duration. Follow these steps:

1. Select the Resource Usage view from the View bar.

2. Go to the top pane and select a task to which the overallocated resource is assigned.

3. Click on the Assignment Information button on the Standard toolbar or double-click on the task to open the Assignment Information dialog box. You can see the General tab in Figure 9-11.

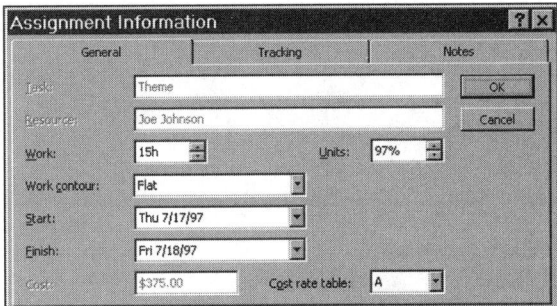

Figure 9-11: Use the Assignment Information dialog box to change a resource's workload to part-time.

4. Change the Units box to reflect the percentage of time you want the resource to spend on the task.

5. Click on OK.

Controlling when resources start working on a task

In cases where a task has more than one resource assigned to it, consider staggering the times the resources start working on the task to resolve resource conflicts. When you delay a resource's start on a task, Project recalculates the start date and time for that resource's work on the task. To stagger start times for resources, work in the Task Usage view and follow these steps:

1. Click on Task Usage on the View bar.

2. Select the resource in the Task Name column whose working time you want to delay.

3. Click on the Assignment Information button or double-click on the resource. Project opens the Assignment Information dialog box. You can see the General tab in Figure 9-12.

4. Change the dates in the Start or Finish boxes.

5. Click on OK.

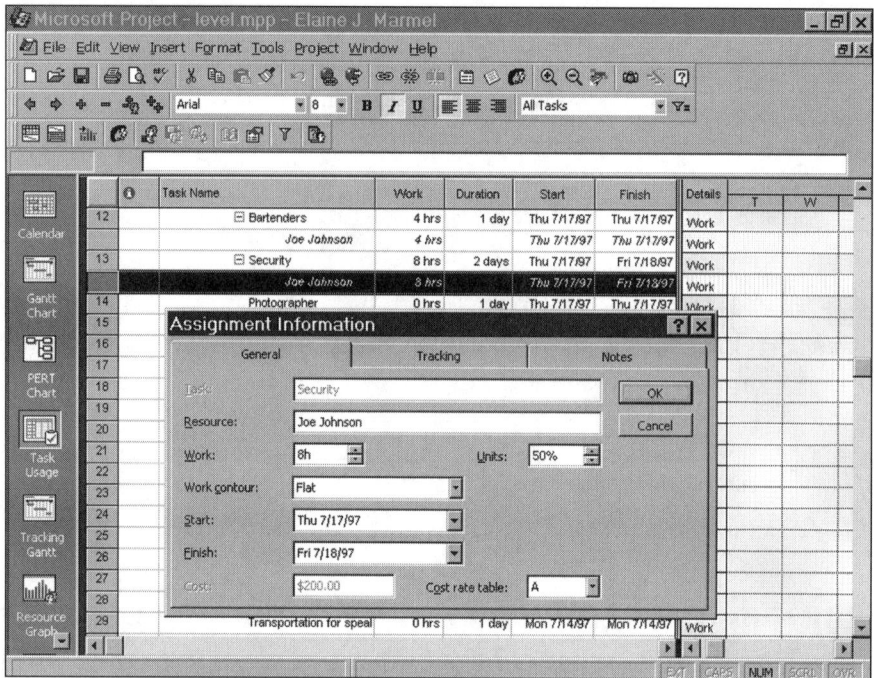

Figure 9-12: Use the General tab of the Assignment Information dialog box to delay a resource's start or finish date on a task.

Delaying tasks by leveling resource work loads

If you have scheduled several tasks to run concurrently and you now find resource conflicts in your project, you can delay some of these tasks to *level* or spread out the demands you're making on your resources. You can ask Project to select the tasks to delay, using its leveling feature, or you can delay tasks manually by examining the project to identify tasks you want to delay. *Leveling* is the process of resolving resource conflicts by delaying or splitting tasks.

Automatic leveling

When Project does the leveling for you, it redistributes the resource's selected assignments and reschedules them according to the resource's working capacity, assignment units, and calendar. Project also considers the task's duration and constraints.

In some circumstances you want Project to level some tasks before it levels others. You can do so by assigning different priority levels to tasks. By default, Project assigns all tasks a priority of Medium. The higher the priority level you assign, the longer Project waits before leveling a task. So, before you start to use the automatic-leveling feature, consider how you can prioritize tasks.

1. Click on the Gantt Chart view from the View bar.

2. Go to the Task Name field and select the task for which you want to set a priority.

3. Double-click on the task or click on the Task Information button on the Standard tool bar. Project displays the Task Information dialog box.

4. Use the General tab to select a priority from the list box (see Figure 9-13).

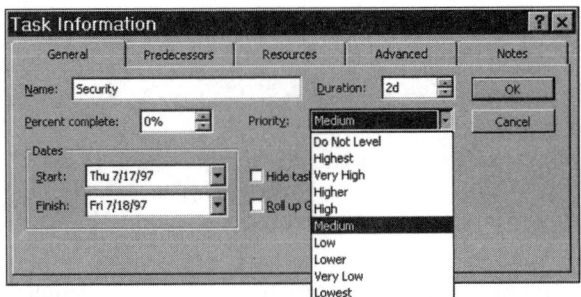

Figure 9-13: Use the Priority list box to select a priority for the task.

After you prioritize tasks, you can sort them by priority to view, before leveling, the tasks that Project is most likely to level.

To level tasks automatically, follow these steps:

1. Choose Tools⇨Resource Leveling to open the Resource Leveling dialog box shown in Figure 9-14.

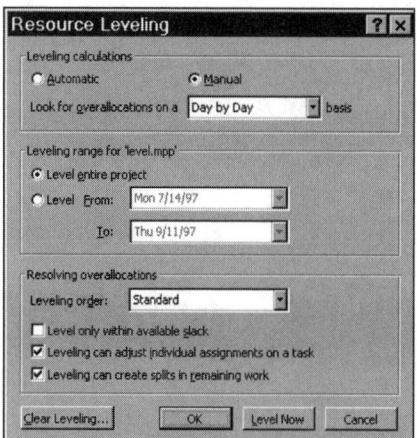

Figure 9-14: From the Resource Leveling dialog box, you can set resource leveling options.

2. Select Automatic to have Project automatically level resources, if necessary, whenever you make a change to your schedule. Select Manual to perform leveling only when you select Level Now from this dialog box.

3. Use the Look for overallocations on a ... basis list box to select a basis. The basis is a time frame, such as Day by Day or Week by Week. (The Indicator box in the Resource Usage view may contain a note suggesting the appropriate basis.)

   The basis you select is the only basis on which Project performs leveling; Project does not change tasks requiring any other basis.

4. Move to the Leveling range for section and select either to level the entire project or to level only for specified dates.

5. Move to the Leveling order drop-down list and select the order you want Project to consider when leveling your project. For example, if you've set priorities, select Standard.

6. Place a check next to any of the following options:

   ✦ Level only within available slack to avoid changing the end date of your project.

   ✦ Leveling can adjust individual assignments on a task to have leveling adjust one resource's work schedule on a task independent of other resources working on the same task.

   ✦ Leveling can create splits in remaining work if you want leveling to split tasks to resolve resource conflicts.

7. Click on Level Now to apply leveling.

You can review the effects of leveling from the Leveling Gantt Chart view shown in Figure 9-15. Choose Views⇨More Views⇨Leveling Gantt and then click on Apply. Project adds green bars to your Gantt Chart to represent leveled tasks. Depending on the nature of your project, Project may build more slack into your tasks.

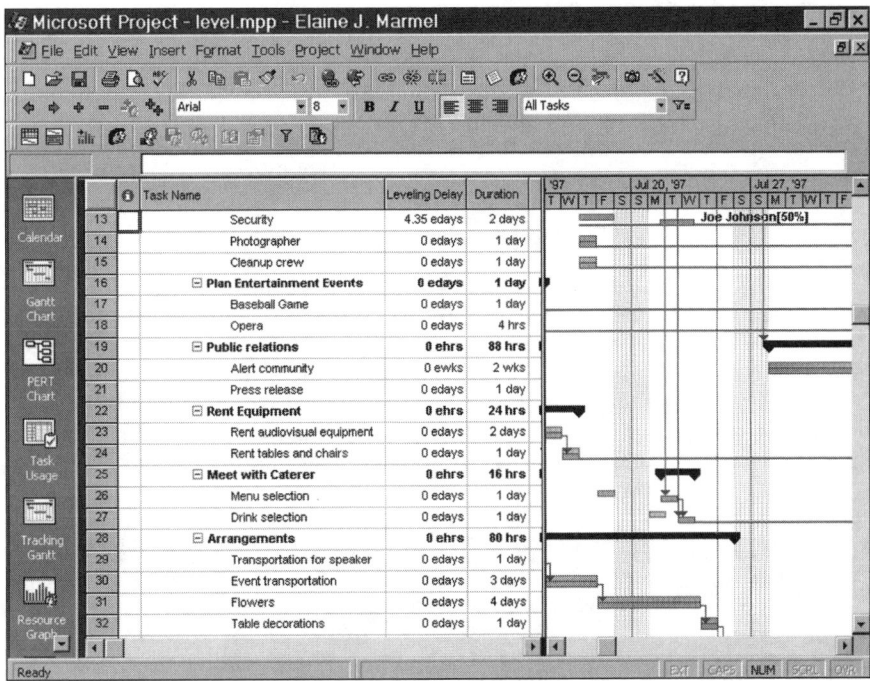

Figure 9-15: The Leveling Gantt Chart view shows how leveling affects your project.

To remove the effects of leveling immediately after you level, use the Undo button. However, you can undo the effects of the last leveling operation if you reopen the Resource Leveling dialog box (choose Tools⇨Resource Leveling) and select Clear Leveling. A subsequent dialog box enables you to clear leveling for the entire project or for selected tasks only.

New Feature

In previous versions of Project, you could not level resource assignments if you were scheduling your project from a finish date. Project 98 eliminates this restriction. If you are scheduling from a finish date, you still can level to resolve resource conflicts. Project calculates the delay by subtracting it from a task's or assignment's finish date, causing the finish date to occur earlier.

Manual leveling

Manual leveling is especially handy when automatic leveling doesn't provide acceptable results. Manual leveling is also useful when you have just a few resource conflicts to resolve.

To manually level resources in Project, use the Resource Allocation view. Follow these steps:

1. Choose View➪ More Views. From the More Views dialog box, highlight Resource Allocation and click on Apply.

2. Drag the vertical split bar to display the Leveling Delay column in the bottom pane.

3. Highlight the task you want to delay in the top pane.

4. Move to the bottom pane, and enter an amount in the Leveling Delay field. Project delays the task accordingly and reduces the resource's conflict.

Figures 9-16 and 9-17 show before and after pictures for manual leveling of the Caterer task. Notice the differences in the two figures between the total overallocated hours on Thursday (19.74 hours in Figure 9-16 and 15.74 hours in Figure 9-17) as well as the delay in the bottom pane that appears in Figure 9-17.

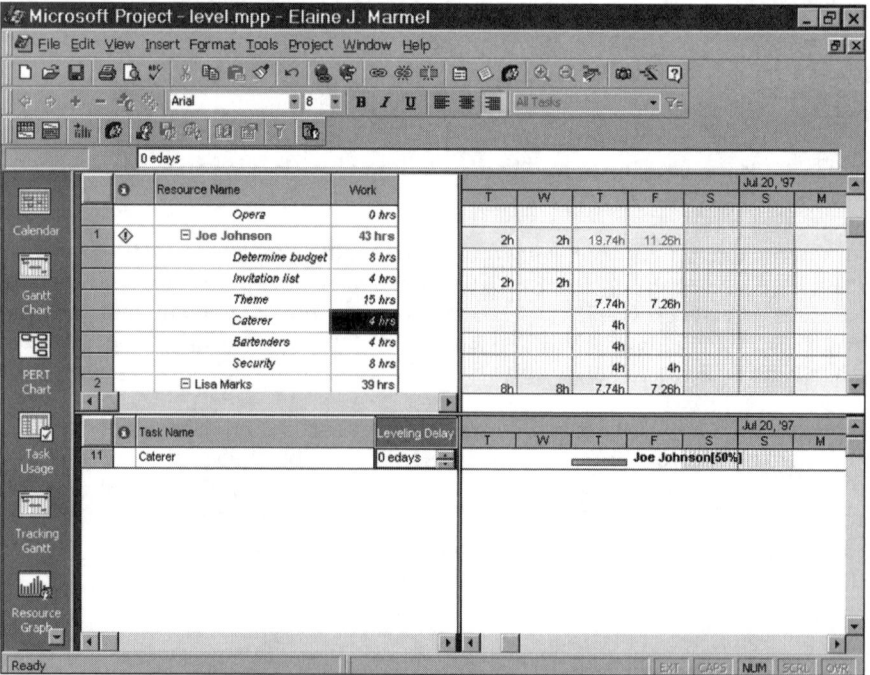

Figure 9-16: The Resource Allocation view before including a delay for the Caterer task.

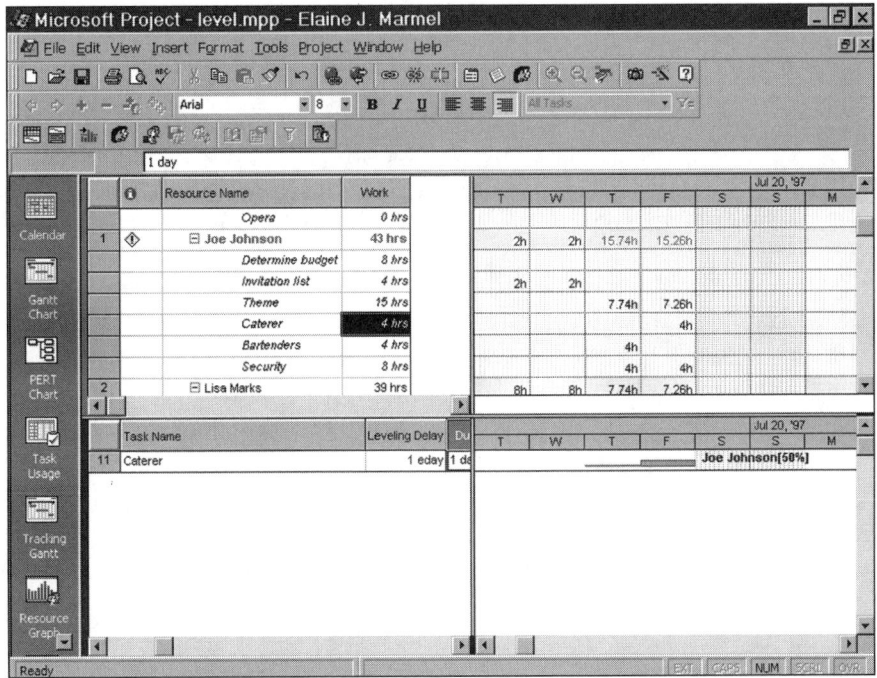

Figure 9-17: The Resource Allocation view after including a delay for the Caterer task.

Contouring resources

Contour is the term Project uses to refer to the shape of a resource's work assignment over time. Contours come in several flavors, the most common being flat, back loaded, front loaded, and bell. The default contour is flat, which means that a resource works on a task for the maximum number of hours that he or she is assigned to a task for the duration of the assignment. You can use different contours to control how much a resource works on a task at a given time — and possibly resolve a conflict.

Tip   Add the Peak Units field to the Resource Usage view to display the maximum effort, as distributed over time, a resource is expected to work. This field is particularly useful when you have selected a contour other than the default (Flat).

Understanding contours

As you've already learned, Project uses a flat contour by default; this contour assigns a resource to work the maximum number of hours per time period throughout the duration of the task. By changing the contour, you can more accurately reflect the actual work pattern for the resource while working on a task.

When you think of contours, think of dividing each task into ten equal time slots. Using the various contours, Project assigns percentages of work to be done in each time slot. The charts in Figures 9-18 through 9-24 show how a workload looks using various contours. The time period is on the x-axis of the chart, and the percentage of work is on the y-axis. The data table in each chart enables you to see the actual percentage of work Project allocates to each resource during each time period. The figures demonstrate how contours help you assign work to a task based on when the task requires the effort. For example, if a task requires less effort initially, consider using a back-loaded contour. If a task requires most effort in the middle of the task, consider using a bell, turtle, or even an early-peak contour.

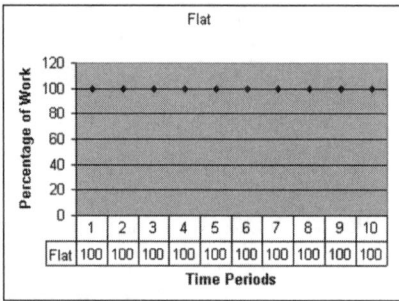

Figure 9-18: A flat contour.

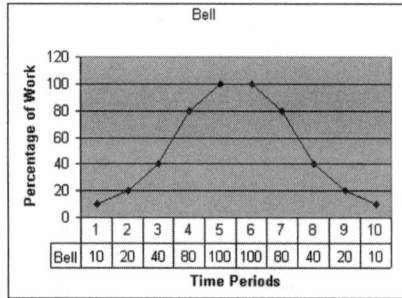

Figure 9-19: A bell contour.

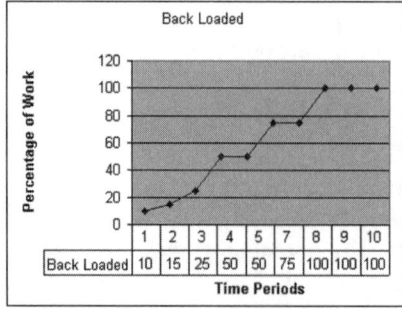

Figure 9-20: A back-loaded contour.

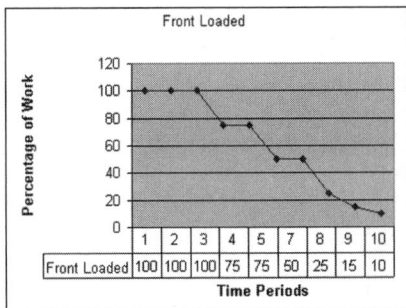

Figure 9-21: A front-loaded contour.

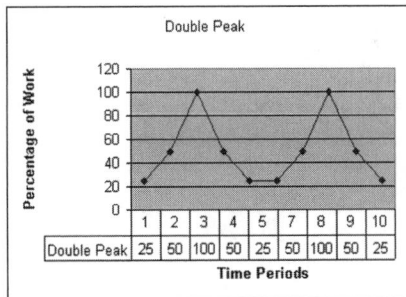

Figure 9-22: A double-peak contour.

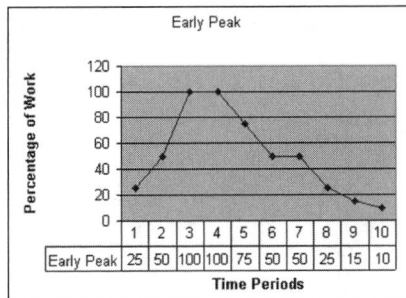

Figure 9-23: An early-peak contour.

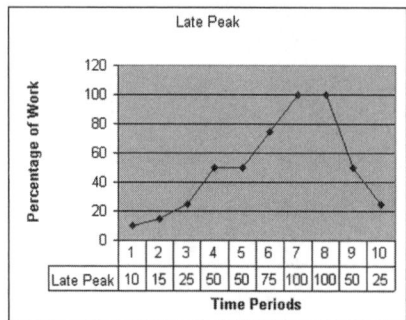

Figure 9-24: A late-peak contour.

Changing and viewing contour settings

If you start changing contours from the default flat contour, you could inadvertently create a resource conflict. Therefore, viewing the contours you set can help you resolve resource conflicts.

To set a contour pattern, follow these steps:

1. Click on the Task Usage view on the View bar.

   In the sheet portion of the view, Project displays each task in your project with the resources assigned to it below the task. The Details portion of the view shows the number of hours per day a resource is assigned to a task.

2. Select the resource in the Task Name column for which you want to apply a contour.

3. Double-click on the resource or click on the Assignment Information button on the Standard toolbar. Then click on the General tab of the Assignment Information dialog box (see Figure 9-25).

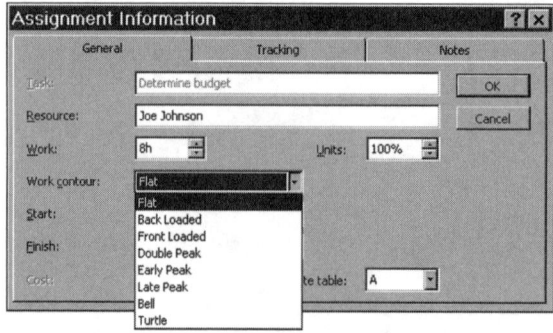

Figure 9-25: Use the General tab of the Assignment Information dialog box to select a contour.

4. Open the Work Contour list box and select a contour.

5. Click on OK.

Tip

To change the start and end dates for the resource's work on the task, use the Start and Finish list boxes.

When you select a contour other than Flat, an indicator appears next to the resource in the Indicator column. If you pass the mouse pointer over the indicator, Project identifies the contour applied to the resource (see Figure 9-26).

Tip

The same icon appears in the Indicator column in the Resource Usage view.

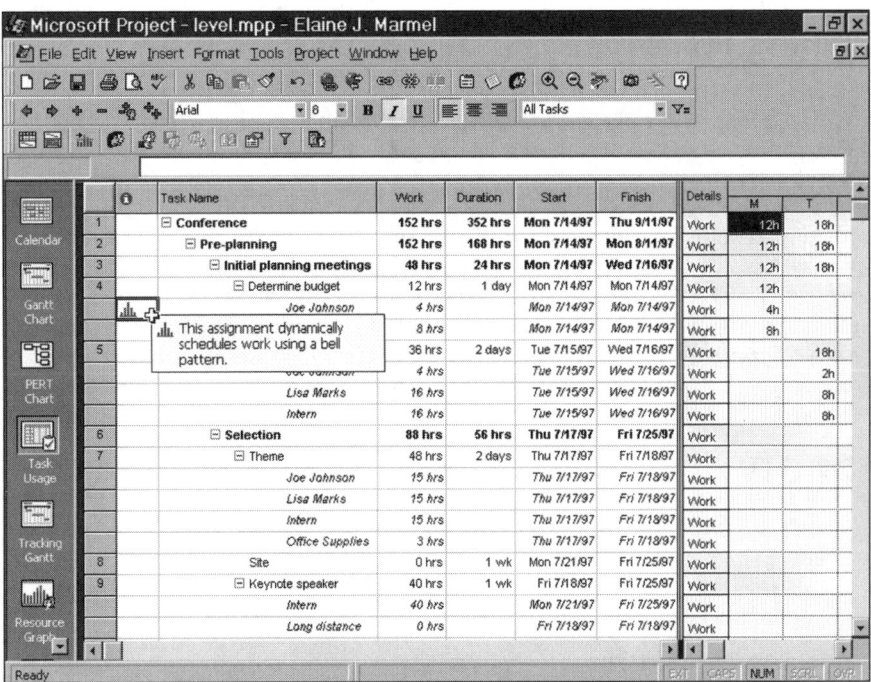

Figure 9-26: Project displays an icon in the Indicator column next to a resource for whom you have chosen a contour other than flat.

Here are a few points to keep in mind when you're working with contours:

✦ Suppose you apply a contour other than the default flat contour to a task and later you add new total work values to the task. Project automatically reapplies the contour pattern to the task and the resources by first distributing the new task work values across the affected time span and then assigning new work values to the resources working on the task.

✦ If you set a contour and then change the start date of the task or the start date of a resource's work on the task, Project automatically shifts the contour and reapplies it to include the new date, preserving the pattern of the original contour.

✦ If you increase the duration of a task, Project stretches the contour to include the new duration.

✦ Suppose you apply a contour other than the default contour to a task. If you manually edit a work value on the portion of a view displaying the contour, Project no longer applies the contour pattern automatically. However, you can reapply the contour to redistribute the new values.

✦ If you enter actual work and then change the task's total work or total remaining work, Project automatically redistributes the changes to the remaining work values and not to the actual work.

Pooling resources

The final way you can try to solve resource conflicts is by using a resource pool. A *resource pool* is a set of resources that are available to any project. You can use resources exclusively on one project, or you can share the resources among several projects.

Typically, resource pooling is useful only if you work with the same resources on multiple projects. Different project managers can share the same resources. Because resource pooling is so closely tied to the topic of managing multiple projects, further discussion is deferred until Chapter 15. The application of resource pooling to resolving resource conflicts will become apparent then.

Summary

This chapter explains how to identify and resolve resource conflicts that can delay a project. The techniques involve

✦ Changing resource allocations

✦ Scheduling overtime

✦ Redefining a resource calendar

✦ Assigning part-time work

✦ Controlling resource start times

✦ Leveling resource work loads

✦ Contouring resources

In the next chapter you learn the art of tracking your progress by comparing your project to its baseline.

✦   ✦   ✦

Tracking Your Progress

Understanding Tracking

This chapter marks something of a turning point in this book and in your use of Project. Up to now you've been in the planning phase: building a project schedule, entering tasks, adding resources, shifting things around so that resource assignments don't conflict and tasks have the proper relationships to each other. You've even tweaked details like text formatting and the appearance of task bars. You now have a workable, good-looking project in hand — and now you are ready to start the project.

Tracking, is the process of comparing what actually happens during your project to your estimates of what would happen. To perform tracking you need to take a picture of your project schedule at the moment your planning is complete, called a *baseline*. But you also have to understand what steps are involved in tracking and how to set up efficient procedures to handle them.

Understanding the Principles of Tracking

A good plan is only half the battle. How you execute that plan is key. Think of yourself as the quarterback in a football game. If you run straight down the field toward the goalpost, never swerving to avoid an oncoming opponent, you won't get very far. Project tracking is similar: If you don't swerve and make adjustments for changes in timing and costs that are virtually inevitable in any human endeavor, you're not playing the game correctly.

One of the strengths of computerized project management is that it enhances your ability to quickly see problems and revise the plan to minimize any damage. Project enables you to compare what you thought would happen to what actually happens over the course of the project.

Estimates versus actuals

The plan you've been building is an estimate of what could occur; it's your best guess (an educated one, we hope) about how long tasks might take, how one task affects another, how many resources you need to complete the work, and what costs you expect your project to incur. Good project managers keep good records of their estimates and actuals so that they can get to be better project managers. By comparing these two sets of data, you can see where your estimates were off and then use this information to make your next plan more realistic. You can also use data on actual costs and timing to make the changes in your strategy that are necessary to keep you on track and meet your current project's goals.

Tracking in Project consists of entering information about actuals, such as the actual start date, the actual finish date, and the actual duration of a task. You enter actual time worked by resources and actual costs incurred. When you enter information about actuals, Project shows you a revised schedule with projections of how the rest of the schedule is likely to play out, based on your actual activity.

Project managers usually track activity on a regular basis, for example, once a week or every two weeks. That tracking includes information about tasks in progress, as well as about tasks that have been completed.

Of course, one of the great benefits of this tracking activity is that is enables you to generate reports that show management where your efforts stand at any point in time. By showing managers the hard data on your project's status, rather than your best guess, you can make persuasive bids for more time, more resources, or a shift in strategy if things aren't going as you expected. Figure 10-1 shows a Tracking Gantt view and indicates some of the tracking information that's available to you.

Chapter 11 explains the specific steps for updating a project to reflect this kind of progress.

Timing information · Percentage of task complete

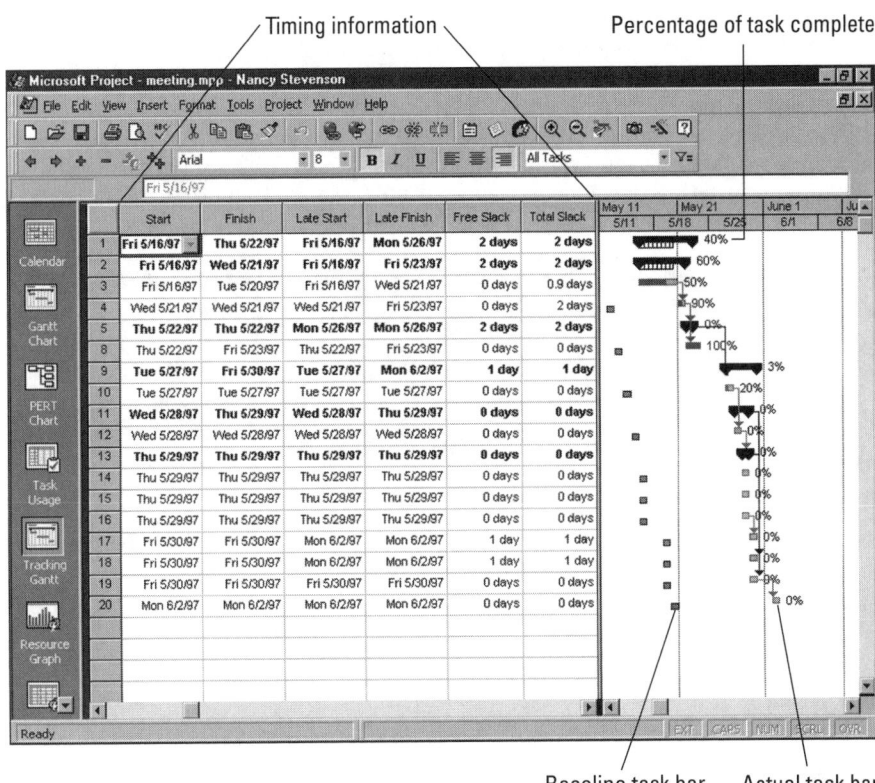

Baseline task bar · Actual task bar

Figure 10-1: Use the Tracking Gantt view to display the progress of your project.

Making adjustments as you go

Tracking isn't something you leave to the end of the project, or even to the end of individual tasks. Tracking activity on a regular basis on tasks in progress helps you detect any deviation from your estimates. The earlier you spot a delay, the more time you have to make up for it.

For example, you estimated that a task would take three days. However, you have already put four days of effort into it, and it's still not complete. Project not only tells you that you're running late but also moves future tasks with dependency relationships to this task farther out in the schedule. Project also shows any resource conflicts that result from resources having to put in more work than you estimated in resource views (such as Resource Sheet and Resource Graph). Project clearly shows how one delay ripples through your schedule.

Project also shows the effect of unanticipated costs on the total budget. If the costs you track on early tasks are higher than anticipated, Project displays what your total costs might be, based on a combination of actual costs and the remaining estimates. Project shows you exactly how much of your budget is used up and how much you have remaining so that you can revise your resource allocations to stay within your overall budget. Figure 10-2 shows the kind of tracking information you can access after you track actual costs.

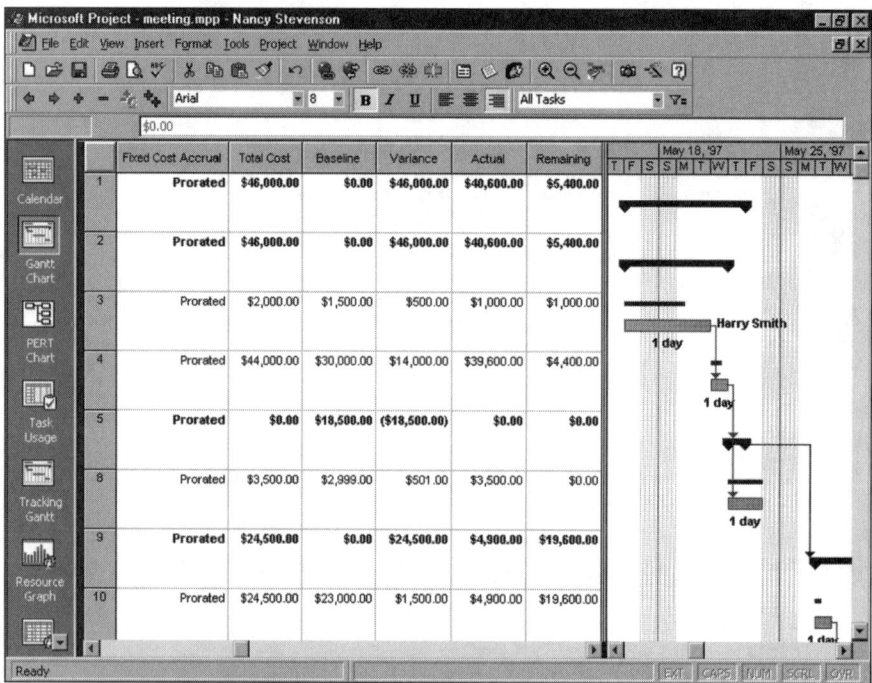

Figure 10-2: Save yourself from nasty budget surprises by using the information Project reveals about your project.

How much have you accomplished?

As Chapter 11 explains, you record activity on a task by entering an estimate of the percentage of the task that's complete, actual resource time spent on the task, and actual costs incurred (such as fees or equipment rentals paid). Estimating the percentage of the task that is complete is not an exact science, and different people use different methods.

With something concrete, like a building under construction, you can look at the actual building and make a fairly good estimate of how far along the project is. But most projects aren't so straightforward. How do you estimate how far along you are in more creative tasks, such as coming up with an advertising concept? You can sit in meetings for five weeks and still not find the right concept. Is your project 50 percent complete? Completion is hard to gauge from other, similar projects — perhaps on the last project you came up with the perfect concept in your very first meeting.

Don't fall into the trap of using money or time spent as a gauge. It's (unfortunately) easy to spent $10,000 on a task estimated to cost $8,000 and still be only 25 percent to completion. The bottom line is that you probably have to use the same gut instincts that put you in charge of this project to estimate the progress of individual tasks. Hint: If your project has individual deliverables that you can track, document them and use them consistently to help you make that estimate.

Using Baselines

You complete the planning phase of your project by setting a baseline. You have seen this term in previous chapters, but take a moment to grasp its significance in the tracking process.

What is a baseline?

A *baseline*, is a snapshot of your project when you complete the planning phase, or sometimes at the end of some other critical phase. The baseline is one set of data saved in the same file where you track actual progress data. Project allows you to save an initial baseline and up to ten interim baselines during your project; you can show a wide variety of information about your baseline, or you can choose not to display baseline information at all.

Some projects, particularly shorter ones that run only a few weeks or even a couple of months, may have one baseline set at the outset and proceed close enough to your estimates that they can run their course against that single baseline. Other projects, especially lengthier ones, may require you to set several baselines along the way. If the original estimate is so out of line with what's transpired in the project, the original is no longer useful. You can modify the entire baseline if changes are drastic and occur early in the project, or you can modify the baseline estimates only going forward from a particular point in the project.

For example, if your project is put on hold shortly after you complete the schedule and you actually start work three months later than you had planned, you would be wise to set a new baseline schedule before restarting. If, however, you're six months into your project and it is put on hold for three months, you might want to modify the timing of future tasks and reset the baseline only for tasks going forward.

As for costs, what if you save a baseline set to fit within a $50,000 budget and, before you start work, cost-cutting measures hit your company and your budget is cut to $35,000? You'd be wise to make the changes to your resources and costs and then reset your baseline. Setting interim baselines keeps your projects from looking wildly at variance with your estimates when mitigating circumstances come into play.

Setting the baseline

You can set the baseline by using either the Planning Wizard or the Tools menu.

In most cases you need to save the project file — without saving the baseline itself — several times during the planning phase. Every time you save the file (File⇨Save), Project displays the Planning Wizard option to save the file with or without a baseline. As you're planning, the appropriate step is to select the Save file without a baseline option. However, after you make your final changes to the project, you can go ahead and save the baseline with the help of the Planning Wizard. Saving the baseline this way replaces any existing baselines and sets the baseline for the entire project. Follow these steps:

1. Choose File⇨Save. If you never saved the file before, the Save As dialog box appears.

2. Select the location where you want to save the file, enter a file name, and click on OK. If you have saved the file before, the Planning Wizard dialog box in Figure 10-3 appears.

3. Click on the Save the file with a baseline control button and then click on OK. The baseline is set.

Tip

If it drives you crazy to have this dialog box appear every time you save a project, click on the Don't tell me about this again check box in the Planning Wizard dialog box and use the method explained in the next paragraph when you're ready to set a baseline.

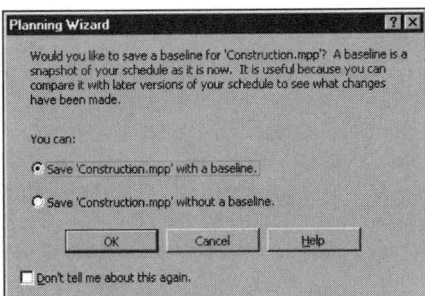

Figure 10-3: To save the file before you're ready to set a baseline, click on the appropriate control box.

The second way to set a baseline is to follow these steps:

1. Choose Tools⇨Tracking⇨Save Baseline to open the Save Baseline dialog box in Figure 10-4.

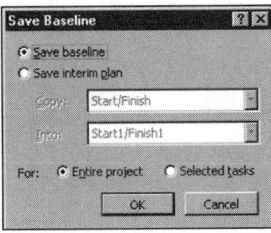

Figure 10-4: To save a baseline for the entire project, accept the default selection in the Save Baseline dialog box.

2. Click on OK to accept the default, that is, to save the entire project schedule as a baseline.

Project saves the baseline; any changes you make to the project now become part of the record of actual activity performed on the project.

Changing the Baseline

The whole idea of having a baseline is to not make changes to it. It's a moment frozen in time, a record against which you can compare your progress. If you change your original baseline on a regular basis, you are defeating its purpose.

That said, there are strategic times when you will need to modify the baseline and resave it, or to save a second or third baseline to document major shifts in the project. However, if you are overriding the original baseline, you must do so in a thoughtful and efficient way. This section discusses some of the times when changes to the baseline are necessary and explains how you can make those changes.

Adding a task to a baseline

The simplest modification to make to the baseline is to add a task to it or modify an existing task. This occurrence is fairly common: You set your baseline plan and then realize that you left out a step, or you decide to break one step into two. Perhaps your company institutes a new requirement or process, and you have to modify a task to deal with the change. You don't want to reset your whole project baseline, but you do want to save that one task along with the original baseline. This change can happen shortly after you save the original baseline, or even weeks or months later.

To add a task to your baseline so that you can track its progress, follow these steps:

1. Do one of the following:

   ✦ To add a new task to the schedule and then incorporate it into the baseline, first add the task in the Task Name column on your Gantt Chart and then select it.

   ✦ To save modifications to an existing task, first make the changes and then select the task.

2. Choose Tools⇨Tracking⇨Save Baseline. The Save Baseline dialog box appears.

3. Click on the Selected tasks check box, as in Figure 10-5.

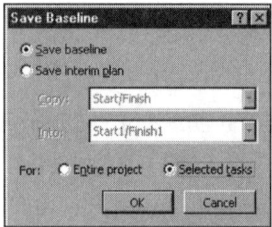

Figure 10-5: The choices in the Copy and Into lists enable you to save several versions of your baseline.

4. Click on OK to save the baseline, which now includes the new task.

Note

You can add tasks to the baseline by entering them in the Gantt table, using columns like Baseline Duration and Baseline Start or Finish. However, adding baseline data this way does not enable all baseline calculations. For example, adding a task at the end of the project with this method won't effect a change in the baseline finish date.

Using interim schedules

You can use the baseline in several ways. You can refer to it as your original estimate and compare it with actual results at the end of the project to see how well you guessed and to learn to guess better on future projects. But the baseline also has an important practical use during the project — it alerts you to shifts so that you can make changes to accommodate them.

The second use relates to the saving of interim baselines. The initial baseline may quickly take on more historical rather than practical interest. You should not change the initial baseline, because that record of your original planning process is important to retain. However, if timing shifts dramatically away from the baseline plan, all the little warning signs Project gives you about being off schedule become useless. A project that starts six months later than expected will show every task as late, every task as critical. Only by saving a second, third, or fourth interim baseline can you see how well you're meeting your revised goals.

You can set interim baseline schedules for all the tasks in the project. However, you would usually want to change the baseline only for tasks going forward. For example, if a labor strike bumps out a manufacturing project two months, you keep the baseline intact for all the tasks that were completed at the time the strike started and change the baseline for all the tasks still to perform when the strike ends.

You can set additional baselines by following these steps:

1. Select various tasks to save a second baseline for specific tasks, rather than for the whole project.

2. Choose Tools⇨Tracking⇨Save Baseline to open the Save Baseline dialog box.

3. Select the Entire project to set an interim baseline for the whole project, or select Selected tasks to save an interim baseline that saves the original baseline for nonselected tasks along with new baseline information for the tasks you've selected.

4. Click on the Save interim plan control button. Project makes the Copy and Into fields available.

Caution

Be very careful not to leave the Save baseline control button checked when saving interim schedules. If you do, Project overwrites the original baseline.

5. Click on the arrow to the right of the Copy field to display the drop-down list shown in Figure 10-6.

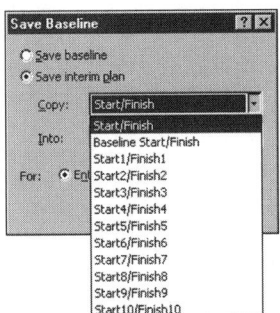

Figure 10-6: You can save up to ten baselines for your schedule, all in the same Project file.

6. Select Start/Finish from the Copy field drop-down list to copy current start to finish settings.

7. Open the drop-down list for the Into field and select a numbered item, such as Start1/Finish1, to set an interim baseline.

Don't select Baseline Start/Finish in these drop-down lists. This option copies the information over the original baseline, rather than into any of the ten interim baselines available to you.

8. Click on OK to save the interim baseline plan.

Remember, you can use the various numbered Start/Finish items to save up to 10 baselines plus the original, for a total of 11 baselines over the life of your project.

Viewing Progress with the Tracking Gantt

The whole point of having baselines is to be able to see how your estimates differ from actual activity in the project. Project allows you to see this variance both graphically, with baseline and actual task bars, and through data displayed in tables in various views. In Chapter 11 you learn how to enter tracking data. The next section briefly explains how to display a baseline and actual data and how you can use this feature to understand the status of your project.

Interpreting the Tracking Gantt

The view that is most useful in viewing progress against your baseline estimates is the Tracking Gantt view. (To open the Tracking Gantt view, click on its icon in the View bar.) This view shows the Tracking table by default. However, you can add or remove fields (columns), or you can display other tables of information. The columns displayed in Figure 10-7 include baseline information that I added to the Tracking table (using the procedure explained for modifying tables in Chapter 6).

Notice the Baseline Duration and Baseline Cost, as well as the Actual Duration and the Actual Cost fields, in the Tracking Gantt table. These fields help you compare estimated versus actual timing and costs.

You can modify this table so that the Baseline Duration column is next to the Actual Duration column and Baseline Cost is next to Actual Cost. (See Chapter 6 to review how to change the order of fields in tables.)

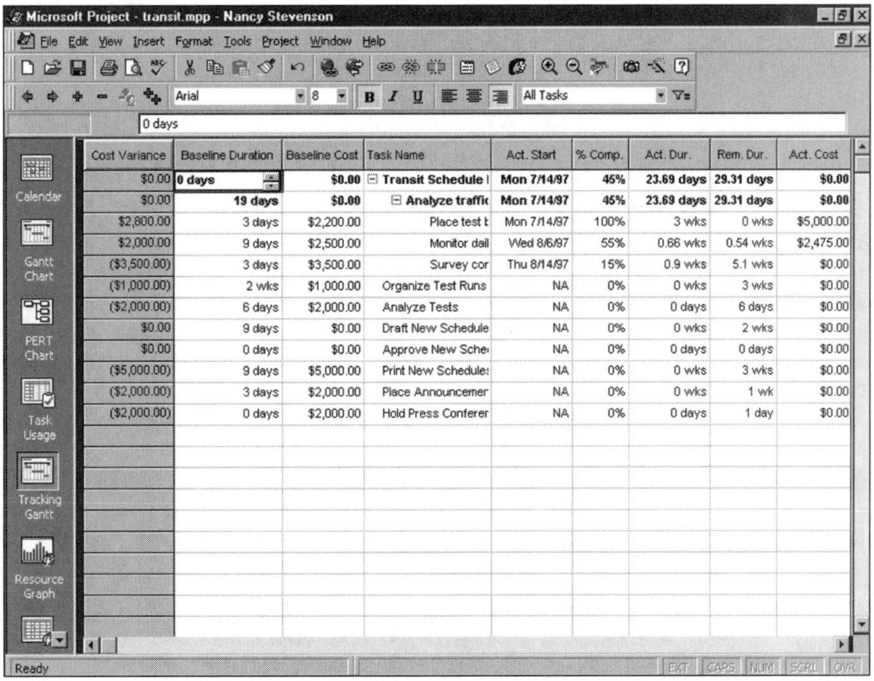

Figure 10-7: The Tracking Gantt table can display a wealth of information.

The Tracking Gantt table also contains the following information:

✦ **% Complete**: This field shows the progress of various tasks in the schedule. In Figure 10-7 only one task is complete.

✦ **Cost Variance**: This field is one of several that tells you the calculated difference between the baseline and actual information. For example, look at the task *Place test boxes* (slightly hidden on line 3). The Baseline cost was $2,200, the Actual Cost was $5,000, and the Cost Variance is $2,800, the difference between the two. Project calculates this amount automatically from baseline and actual data that you entered. You can display other fields that show calculations regarding variances; for example, several fields reflect variance in timing from estimated to actual.

You can also display the task bars by manipulating the divider between the table and chart areas to get a graphical view of progress on the project. Figure 10-8 adds task bars to the schedule shown in Figure 10-7. The various styles of task bar indicate progress on tasks in the project.

Notice that various graphic representations indicate progress on different types of tasks. Both summary tasks, *Transit Schedule Revision* and *Analyze traffic patterns*, have a white bar with black lines underneath their regular task bars. These lines indicate the progress (how much is complete) of the summary tasks. The noncritical task *Place text boxes* is solid blue: It is complete, so the dark blue of the progress bar fills out the lighter blue of the task bar. The task that follows is only partially filled in with the darker blue color, because it is only partially complete. Finally, the task *Survey commuters* is red. (Although you can't see the colors themselves in this black and white figure, you will when you track progress on screen.) A small section at the front of the line is solid, dark red to indicate progress on a critical task; the remainder of the task bar is a light, patterned red, showing the portion of the task not yet completed.

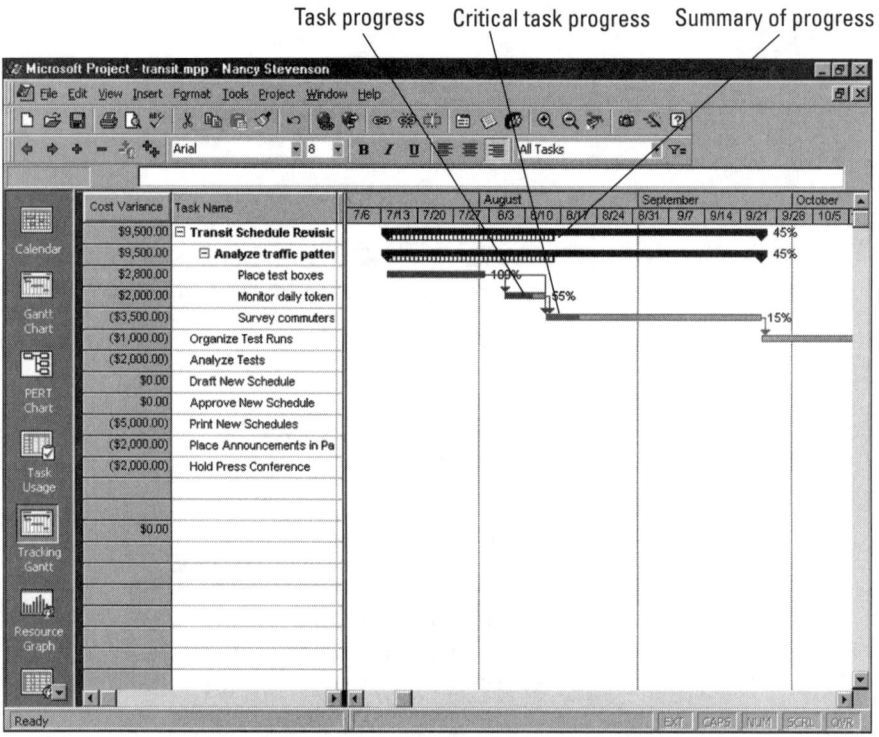

Figure 10-8: Various task bar styles and color codes display the project's progress and variances.

The Task Variance table

You can change the tables displayed in the Tracking Gantt view and see different information about your progress in the project. The Variance table, for example, highlights the variance in task timing between the baseline and actuals. To display this table, shown in Figure 10-9, right-click on the box in the upper-left corner of the table, where the row containing column headings and the task number column meet. Select Variance from the list of tables that appears.

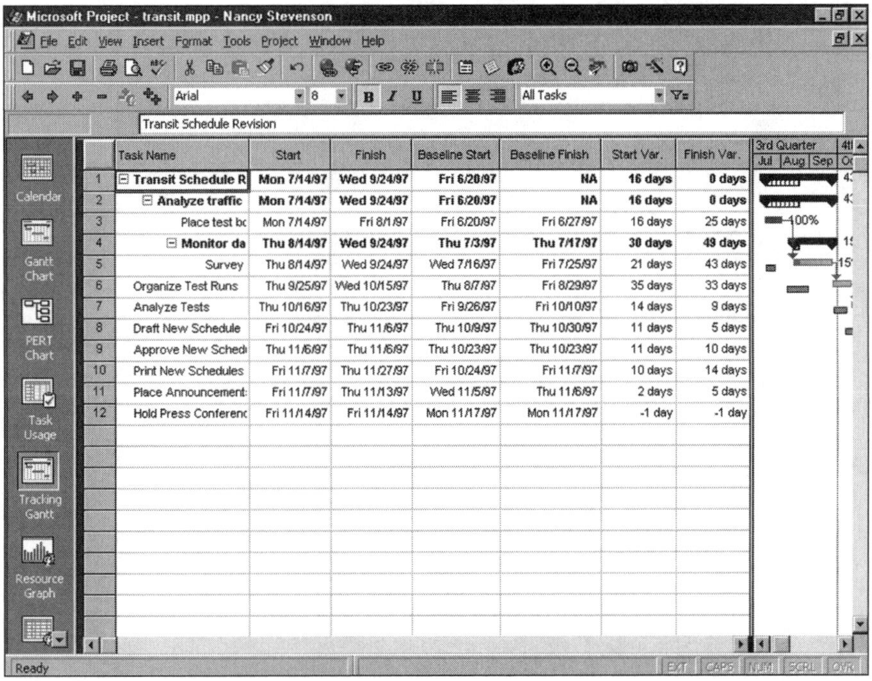

Figure 10-9: If you're behind schedule, you can see the awful truth easily in the Variance table.

You can easily compare the Baseline Start and Finish to the actual Start and Finish columns that show actual data for tasks on which you have tracked progress, as well as baseline data for tasks with no progress. This table also contains fields to show you the Start Variance (how many days late or early the task started) and the Finish Variance (how many days late or early the task ended). Notice that the last task of the project, *Hold Press Conference,* actually finished early — hence the negative number in the Variance fields.

With baseline and actual information displayed, you can compare the baseline task bars to the actual task bars in the chart side of the Gantt view, as shown in Figure 10-10.

Baseline task bar

Actual task bar with progress
bar superimposed on it

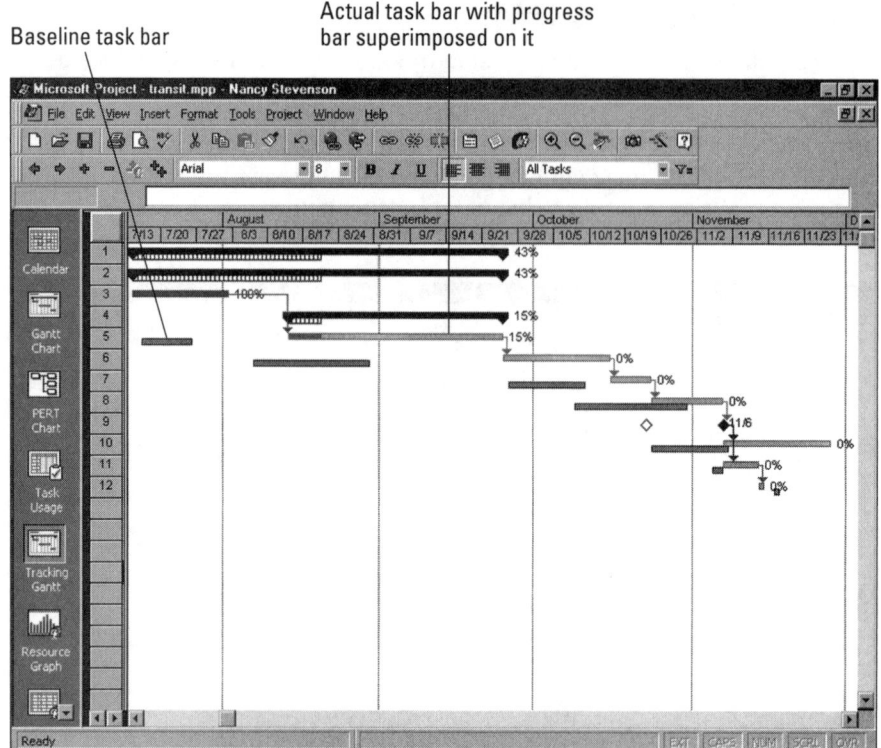

Figure 10-10: You can see how late you're running by how the baseline task bars lag behind the actual task bars.

The Task Cost table

The Task Cost table is most useful for pointing out variations in money spent on the project. Figure 10-11 shows the Task Cost table for the project shown in earlier figures. The project is in progress, with some costs incurred and others yet to be expended. At this point the task *Survey community,* which is taking much longer than its baseline duration (you can verify that in the Variance column shown for the task in Figure 10-10), is $28,500 over budget. The factors that Project takes into account in these calculations are the actual resource time worked, the estimate of days of resource time still to be expended to complete the task, and actual costs (such as fees and permits) that have been tracked on the task. Compared to a baseline estimate of $3,500, this task is way over budget.

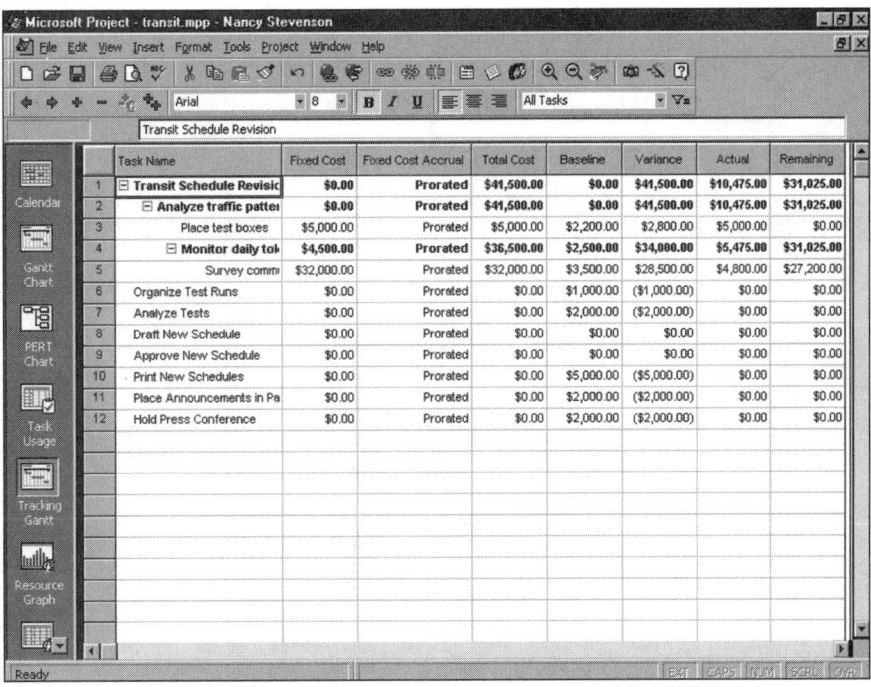

Figure 10-11: The Task Cost table shows where you've spent too much and where you have a lot more money to spend.

The Task Work table

One final table to look at in the Tracking Gantt view is the Task Work table shown in Figure 10-12. This table focuses on the number of work hours put in by resources working on tasks. For example, the baseline work for the task *Place test boxes* was 13 hours. However, the task is complete and took only five hours. Therefore, the Variance field (the difference between the baseline hours of work and the actual hours spent) shows a saving of eight hours. The parentheses around this number indicate fewer hours were used than estimated in the baseline.

You'll see many of these tables and more tracking views as you work through the next few chapters. For now, you should have a good idea of the types of information you can get by tracking progress on your project. Now take just a moment to consider your tracking procedures.

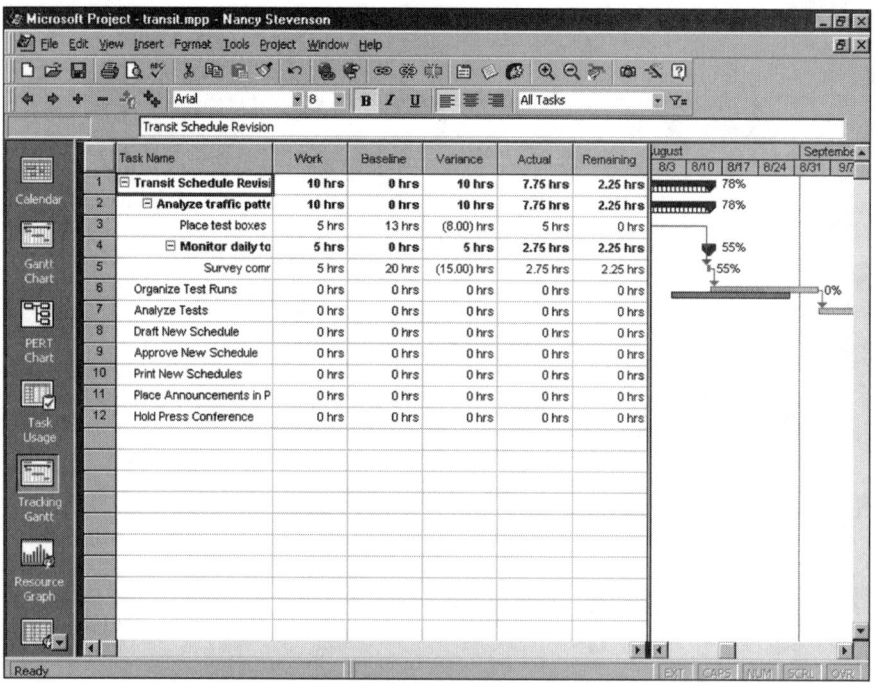

Figure 10-12: To determine whether a task is taking much more effort than you estimated, check the Task Work table.

Tracking Strategies

As you use Microsoft Project on real projects, your tracking skills will improve. However, if you follow certain basic principles of tracking from the start, you can save yourself a lot of aggravation in your first few projects.

Tackling the work of tracking

The first rule of tracking is to update frequently and at regular intervals. Many people see the task of tracking as monumental: All the details of each task's progress and duration, as well as all the resources and costs associated with each task have to be entered one by one. You have to gather that data through resource timecards, reports from other project participants, and vendor invoices. You have to type in all the information that you gather. I won't kid you: Tracking can be a big piece of work. The more often you track, the less the tracking data will pile up, and the less likely it is to overwhelm you.

Another way to get your arms around the tracking task is to assign pieces of the updating to various people in your project. If a particular resource is in charge of one phase of the project, have him or her track the activity on just that one phase. You can use various methods of compiling those smaller schedules into a master schedule.

Chapters 14 and 15 provide ideas for compiling several schedules and managing schedules with workgroups.

If you have a resource available, such as an administrative assistant, who can handle the tracking details, all the better. Make sure you provide this assistant with appropriate training (and a copy of this book) so that he or she understands the tracking process well enough to be accurate and productive. However, this resource probably does not need to be a Project expert to take on some of the work.

 To help you remember to track, enter tracking as a recurring task, occurring once every week or two, within your project file.

Keeping track of tracking

Another good strategy for effective tracking is to use task notes to record progress and changes. If an important change comes up, but not one that merits changing your baseline, use the task notes to record it. When you reach the end of the project, these notes help you document and justify everything from missed deadlines to cost overruns.

 Try to set some standards for tracking in your organization. For example, how do you determine when a task is complete? How do you measure costs, and what is the source of information on resource time spent on a task? Project becomes a much more effective management tool if each project manager uses identical methods of gauging progress and expenditures, just as your company's accounting department uses standards in tracking costs.

Setting multiple baselines is useful, but how do you decide when to save each iteration? One approach is to set a different baseline for each major milestone in your project. Even long projects usually have only four or five significant milestones, and they are likely to occur after you have accomplished a sizeable chunk of work.

Summary

This chapter explores some of the fundamental concepts of tracking activity on a project. You've learned the following:

✦ How to set and modify baselines

✦ How to view your baseline estimates against actual progress

Chapter 11 covers the mechanics of tracking, recording the actuals, and streamlining the entry of this data.

✦　　✦　　✦

Recording Actuals

Actuals represent what has, in fact, occurred during your project. In Microsoft Project you can record actual information about the cost of a task and about the time related to completing the task. By recording actual information, you accomplish several things:

+ You let Project automatically reschedule the remainder of your project.

+ You provide management with a way to measure how well your project is going.

+ You provide yourself with valuable information on your estimating skills — information that you can apply to your next project.

Organizing the Updating Process

Before you launch into the mechanics of updating a project, you should take a moment to examine the updating process. Updating a project can become complicated, particularly for large projects with many resources assigned to them. You need to establish efficient manual procedures for collecting information in a timely fashion and to determine the best ways to enter that information into Microsoft Project. This section examines ways to collect information.

Here are some questions that individuals working on tasks should answer regularly: Is it on schedule? How much is done? Is there a revised estimate on the duration of the task? Is there a revised estimate on the work required to complete the task?

You may want to create a form for participants to use for their regular reports. Their reports should provide the information you need to update Project. You might be able to use one of the reports in Project — or even customize one of Project's reports — to provide the necessary information. The rest of this chapter examines ways to decide what information you need to include on the data collection form.

You also should decide how often you need to receive the collection forms. If you receive the reports too frequently, your staff may spend more time reporting than working. If, on the other hand, you don't receive the reports often enough, you can't identify a trouble spot early enough to resolve it before it becomes a major crisis. As the manager, you must decide on the correct frequency for collecting actual information for your project.

Tip You can use the time-phased fields in Project to track actual costs on a daily or weekly basis. You can learn more about time-phased cost tracking in "Tracking work or costs regularly" later in this chapter.

When you receive the reports, you should evaluate them to identify unfinished tasks for which you need to adjust the planned duration, work, and costs. The easiest time to make these adjustments is before you record a task's actual dates or percentage of completion.

Also remember that recording actual information enables you to compare estimates to actuals; if you want to make this comparison, make sure you set a baseline for your project.

Updating Tasks to Reflect Actual Information

You update a project by filling in fields that track the progress of your project. For tasks, these fields include

- ✦ Actual start date
- ✦ Actual finish date
- ✦ Actual duration
- ✦ Remaining duration
- ✦ Percentage complete

In some cases when you enter information into one of these fields, Project calculates the values for the other fields. For example, if you enter a percentage complete for a task, Project calculates and supplies a start date, an actual duration, a remaining duration, and an actual work value.

Setting actual start and finish dates

The Gantt Chart view displays projected start and finish dates for tasks. To enter and view actual start and finish dates, you can use the Task Details view in Figure 11-1.

Actual option button

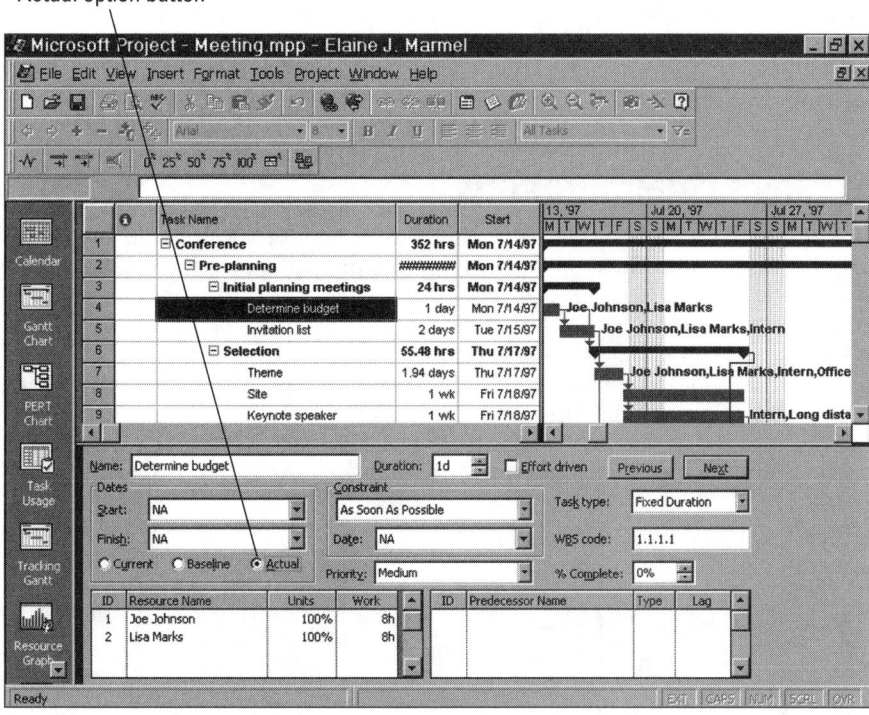

Figure 11-1: Use the Task Details form to enter actual information.

Starting from the Gantt Chart view, follow these steps to set up your screen:

1. Choose Window⇔Split to display the Task Form view.

2. Click on the bottom pane and then right-click on the View bar to display the shortcut menu.

3. Choose More Views to open the More Views dialog box.

4. Select Task Details Form and click on Apply.

5. Select the task in the top pane of the Task Details form for which you want to record actuals.

6. Click on the Actual option button in the bottom pane to identify the type of dates you want to enter.

7. Record either a Start or a Finish date.

Project initially sets the Actual Start Date and Actual Finish Date fields to NA to indicate that you have not yet entered a date. When you update your project to provide actual start and finish dates, Project changes the projected start and finish dates to the actual dates you enter. When you enter an actual start date, the only other field that Project changes is the projected start date. However, when you enter an actual end date, Project changes several other fields: the Percent Complete field, the Actual Duration field, the Remaining Duration field, the Actual Work field, and the Actual Cost field. If you didn't set an actual start date, Project also changes that field.

Setting actual durations

The actual duration of a task is the amount of time it took to complete the task. To use the Task Details form to record an actual duration, in the top pane select the task for which you want to record the duration. In the bottom pane click on the Actual option button. Then fill in the Duration field. If you prefer to use dialog boxes to perform updates, choose Tools⟹Tracking⟹Update Tasks. Alternatively, click on the Update Tasks button on the Tracking toolbar and display the Update Tasks dialog box, which appears in Figure 11-2.

Tip

You can display the Tracking toolbar by choosing View⟹Toolbars⟹Tracking.

Update Tasks button

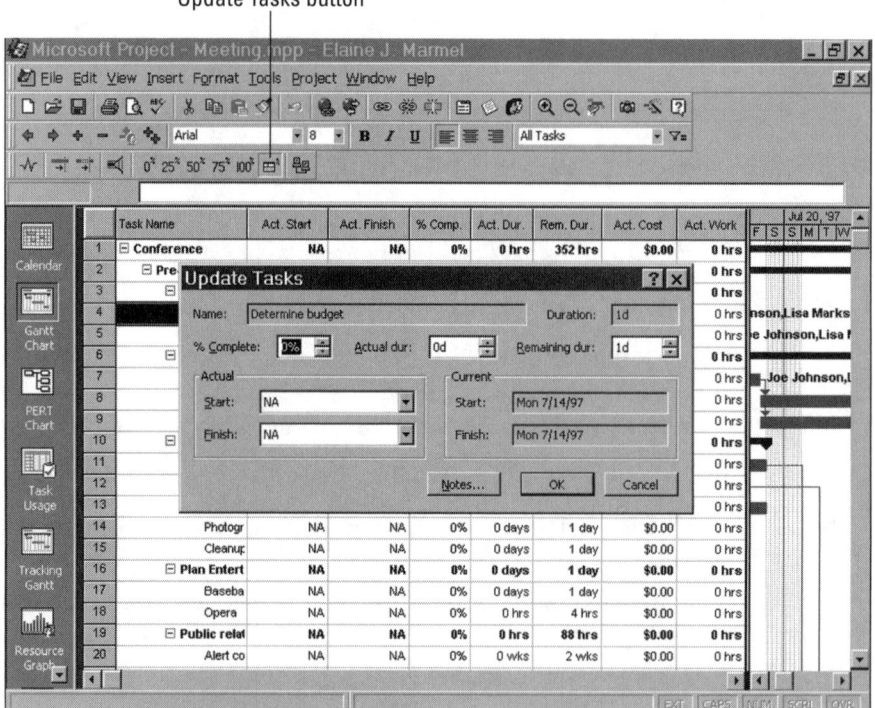

Figure 11-2: Use the Update Tasks dialog box to set the actual duration for a task by filling in the Actual dur field.

When you set an actual duration that is less than or equal to the planned duration, Project assumes the task is progressing on schedule. Therefore, Project sets the actual start date to the planned start date — unless you previously set the actual start date. In that case Project leaves the actual start date alone. In either case Project calculates the percentage complete and the remaining duration for the task.

If you set an actual duration that is greater than the planned duration, Project assumes that the task is finished but that it took longer than expected to complete. Project adjusts the planned duration to match the actual duration and changes the Percent Complete field to 100% and the Remaining Duration field to 0%.

You can use the Calculation tab on the Options dialog box (choose Tools⇨Options) to set Project to update the status of resources when you update a task's status. If you set this option and then supply an actual duration, Project also updates the work and cost figures for the resources. You learn more about this option in "Overriding resource cost valuations" later in this chapter.

Setting remaining durations

The Remaining dur field in the Update Tasks dialog box (refer to Figure 11-2) shows how much more time you need to complete a task. Although you can set the remaining duration for a task from the Update Tasks dialog box, you might prefer to enter actuals from the Tracking Table view shown in Figure 11-3. To display the Tracking Table view, start in the Gantt Chart and follow these steps:

1. Click on the top pane of the Gantt Chart.

2. Choose Window⇨Remove Split to display the standard Gantt chart.

3. Right-click on the Select All button and select Tracking. Project displays the Tracking Table view in the left portion of the Gantt Chart view.

To see all the fields available on the Tracking Table view, narrow the chart portion of the window.

If you enter a value into this field, Project assumes the work has begun on the task and will complete based on the remaining duration value. Therefore, Project sets the Act. Dur. (actual duration) and % Comp. (percent complete) fields based on a combination of the remaining duration value you supplied and the original planned duration. If necessary, Project also sets the actual start date; and, if you set Project's options to update the status of resources when you update a task's status, Project updates the work and cost figures for the resources on the task.

Entering 0 in the Rem. Dur. (remaining duration) field is the same as entering 100% in the Percent Complete field. Suppose you change the value in the Remaining Duration field so that it is larger than the existing figure. Project assumes you are changing the planned duration of the task instead of tracking actual progress for the task. In this case, Project adjusts the schedule based on the new planned duration. If the task has already started when you make this change, Project adds this new estimate to the previously calculated actual duration and adjusts the Percent Complete field.

Select All button

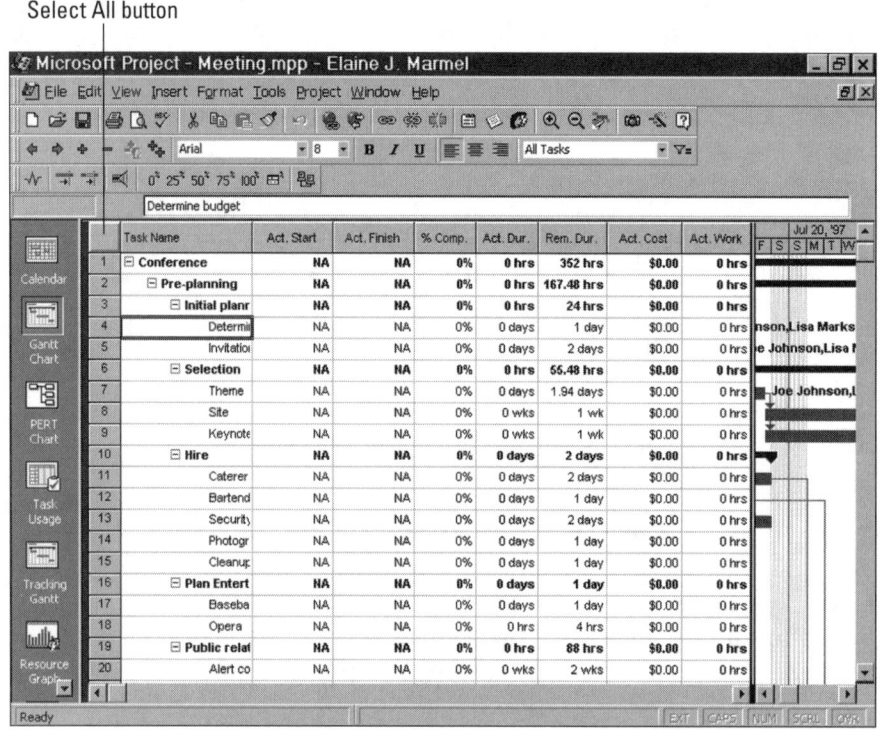

Figure 11-3: The Tracking Table view helps you view and enter actual values for tasks.

Setting percent complete

You can establish the amount of work performed on a task by assigned it a *percent complete* value. This value indicates progress on the task. Any value less than 100 indicates that the task is not complete. You can set percent complete from the Task Details form, from the Update Tasks dialog box, or from the Tracking Table view. Or you can select the task from any task view and use the percentage buttons on the Tracking toolbar (see Figure 11-4).

A value in the Percent Complete field also affects the actual duration and remaining duration values If you make an entry into any of these fields, Project automatically updates the others. When you set the Actual Duration value, Project calculates the value for the Percent Complete field by dividing the Actual Duration field by the original planned duration. If, alternatively, you set the Remaining Duration value, Project recalculates, if necessary, the Actual Duration value and the Percent Complete value.

Percentage buttons

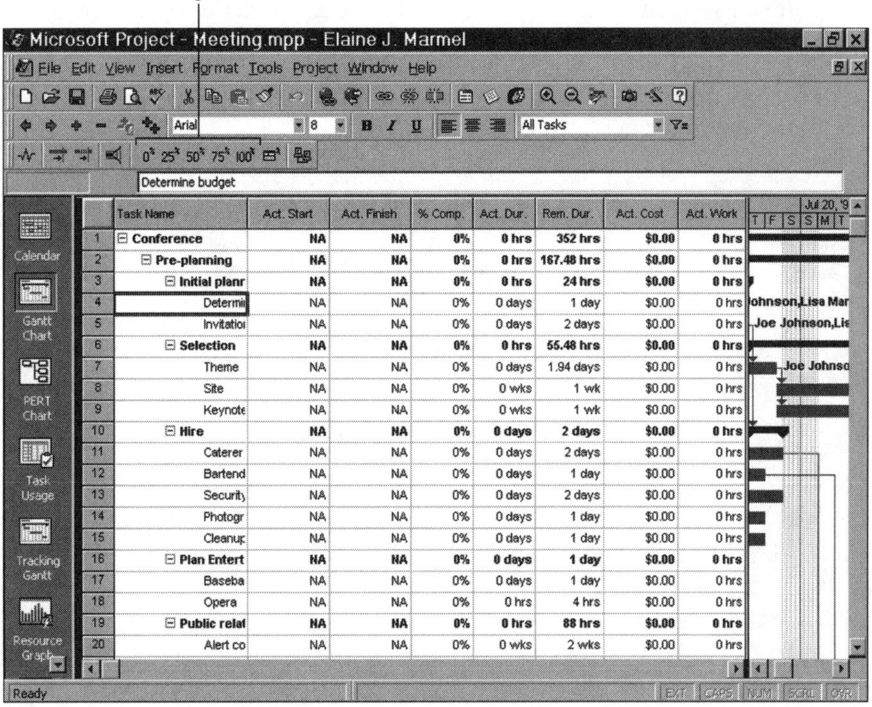

Figure 11-4: Use these buttons to set a task's actual progress at 0%, 25%, 50%, 75%, or 100% complete.

If you change the Percent Complete value, Project assigns an Actual Start Date (unless you had entered one previously). Project also calculates the Actual Duration and Remaining Duration fields. If you set your options to update resources when you update tasks, Project also calculates the Actual Cost and Actual Work fields. If you enter 100 into the Percent Complete field, Project assigns the planned finish date to the Actual Finish Date field. If this value is not correct, don't enter a Percent Complete; instead enter an Actual Finish Date.

Setting work completed

Sometimes, you must schedule tasks based on the availability of certain resources. In these cases updating the work completed is the easiest way to track progress on a task. Updating this value also updates the work that each resource is performing.

In the same way that Project calculates duration information when you fill in a duration field, Project updates the work remaining by subtracting the work performed from the total work scheduled.

Use the Tracking Table view to enter information into the Act. Work field, but start in the Task Usage view so that you can enter actual work performed for specific resources. Click on the Task Usage view in the View bar. Then right-click on the Select All button and choose Tracking from the side menu of tables. You'll probably need to drag the divider bar almost completely to the right edge of the screen to reveal the Act. Work field (see Figure 11-5).

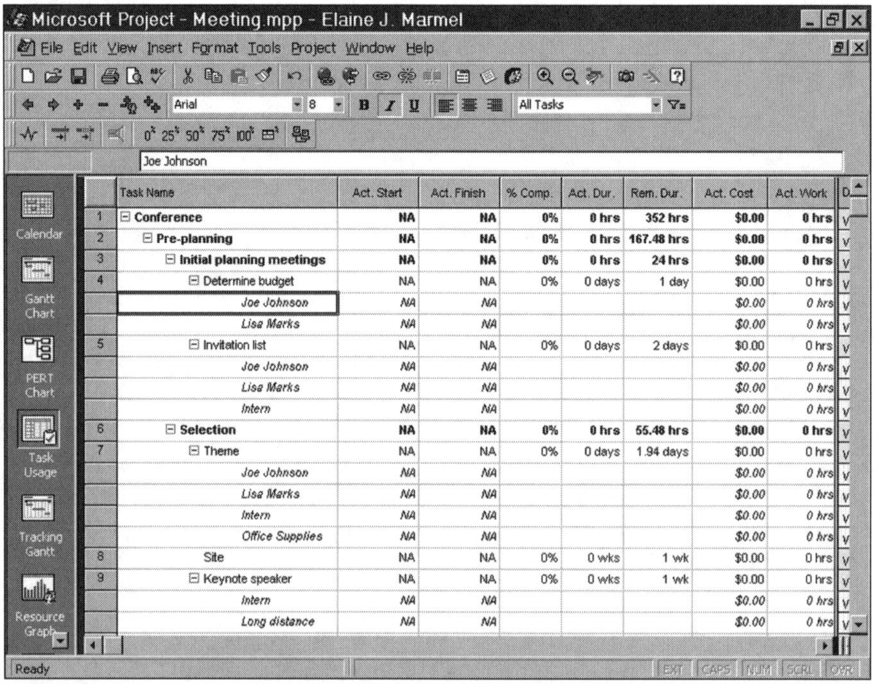

Task Name	Act. Start	Act. Finish	% Comp.	Act. Dur.	Rem. Dur.	Act. Cost	Act. Work	
1 ⊟ Conference	NA	NA	0%	0 hrs	352 hrs	$0.00	0 hrs	v
2 ⊟ Pre-planning	NA	NA	0%	0 hrs	167.48 hrs	$0.00	0 hrs	v
3 ⊟ Initial planning meetings	NA	NA	0%	0 hrs	24 hrs	$0.00	0 hrs	v
4 ⊟ Determine budget	NA	NA	0%	0 days	1 day	$0.00	0 hrs	v
Joe Johnson	NA	NA				$0.00	0 hrs	v
Lisa Marks	NA	NA				$0.00	0 hrs	v
5 ⊟ Invitation list	NA	NA	0%	0 days	2 days	$0.00	0 hrs	v
Joe Johnson	NA	NA				$0.00	0 hrs	v
Lisa Marks	NA	NA				$0.00	0 hrs	v
Intern	NA	NA				$0.00	0 hrs	v
6 ⊟ Selection	NA	NA	0%	0 hrs	55.48 hrs	$0.00	0 hrs	v
7 ⊟ Theme	NA	NA	0%	0 days	1.94 days	$0.00	0 hrs	v
Joe Johnson	NA	NA				$0.00	0 hrs	v
Lisa Marks	NA	NA				$0.00	0 hrs	v
Intern	NA	NA				$0.00	0 hrs	v
Office Supplies	NA	NA				$0.00	0 hrs	v
8 Site	NA	NA	0%	0 wks	1 wk	$0.00	0 hrs	v
9 ⊟ Keynote speaker	NA	NA	0%	0 wks	1 wk	$0.00	0 hrs	v
Intern	NA	NA				$0.00	0 hrs	v
Long distance	NA	NA				$0.00	0 hrs	v

Figure 11-5: The Tracking Table view with resources displayed.

Tip

If you are scheduling tasks based on the availability of resources generally, not on the availability of specific resources, you can still use this technique to record actual work. However, you need to enter the value on the same row as the task, rather than on the individual rows for the resources. Project divides the actual and remaining work among the resources.

Using Actuals and Costs

Except for fixed-cost tasks, Project uses the cost of the resources assigned to the task over the duration of the task to calculate a task's cost. Costs are accrued, and total project costs are the sum of all resource and fixed costs. Therefore, if you set up and assigned resources to your tasks, Project has been calculating and accruing the costs for you — all you need to do is review and analyze the costs.

Alternatively, you may have chosen not to assign resources to your tasks, or you may have changed your default options so that Project wouldn't calculate costs. How can you do that? Choose Tools⊅Options to display the Options dialog box. On the Calculation tab, look at the Calculation Options for your project (see Figure 11-6). If you *don't* see a check in the Updating task status updates resource status check box, Project has not been calculating your project's costs. Remember, however, that, by default, this check box contains a check, as you see in the figure.

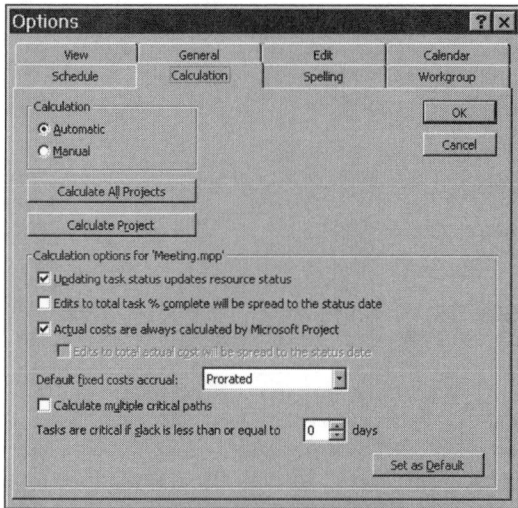

Figure 11-6: From the Calculation tab of the Options dialog box, you can tell whether Project has been calculating your project's costs.

If you did not assign resources or you changed the defaults, Project can't calculate the cost of your project unless you provide additional information after the task is completed. You can review and update your project's costs from one of two cost tables: the Cost table for tasks or the Cost table for resources. And you can override the costs Project assigns.

Using the Cost table for tasks

The Cost table for tasks in Figure 11-7 shows you cost information based on each task in your project. This table shows you the Baseline cost (the planned cost), the actual cost, the variance between planned and actual costs, and the remaining cost of the task.

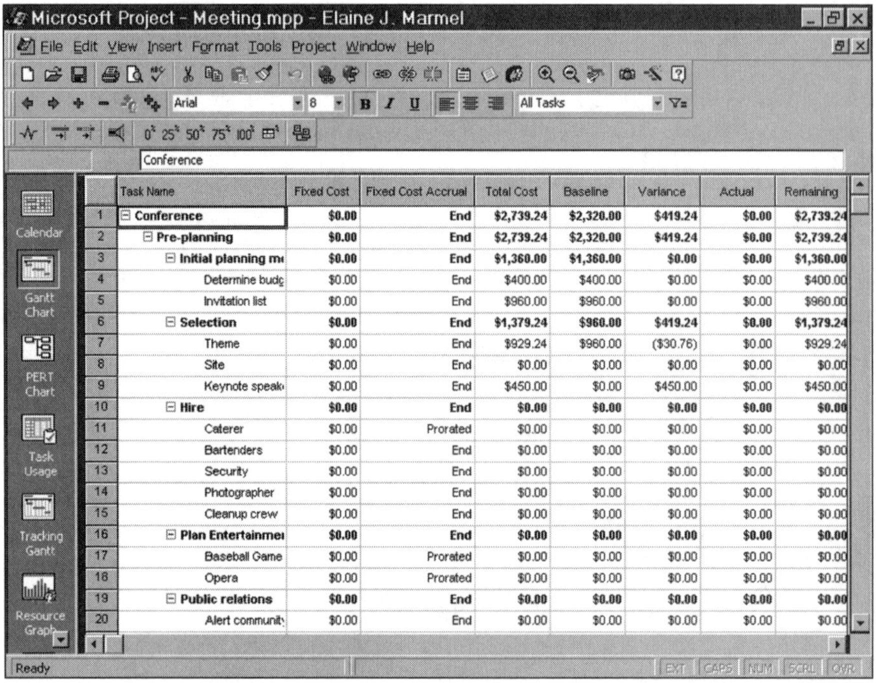

	Task Name	Fixed Cost	Fixed Cost Accrual	Total Cost	Baseline	Variance	Actual	Remaining
1	Conference	$0.00	End	$2,739.24	$2,320.00	$419.24	$0.00	$2,739.24
2	Pre-planning	$0.00	End	$2,739.24	$2,320.00	$419.24	$0.00	$2,739.24
3	Initial planning m	$0.00	End	$1,360.00	$1,360.00	$0.00	$0.00	$1,360.00
4	Determine budg	$0.00	End	$400.00	$400.00	$0.00	$0.00	$400.00
5	Invitation list	$0.00	End	$960.00	$960.00	$0.00	$0.00	$960.00
6	Selection	$0.00	End	$1,379.24	$960.00	$419.24	$0.00	$1,379.24
7	Theme	$0.00	End	$929.24	$960.00	($30.76)	$0.00	$929.24
8	Site	$0.00	End	$0.00	$0.00	$0.00	$0.00	$0.00
9	Keynote speak	$0.00	End	$450.00	$0.00	$450.00	$0.00	$450.00
10	Hire	$0.00	End	$0.00	$0.00	$0.00	$0.00	$0.00
11	Caterer	$0.00	Prorated	$0.00	$0.00	$0.00	$0.00	$0.00
12	Bartenders	$0.00	End	$0.00	$0.00	$0.00	$0.00	$0.00
13	Security	$0.00	End	$0.00	$0.00	$0.00	$0.00	$0.00
14	Photographer	$0.00	End	$0.00	$0.00	$0.00	$0.00	$0.00
15	Cleanup crew	$0.00	End	$0.00	$0.00	$0.00	$0.00	$0.00
16	Plan Entertainme	$0.00	End	$0.00	$0.00	$0.00	$0.00	$0.00
17	Baseball Game	$0.00	Prorated	$0.00	$0.00	$0.00	$0.00	$0.00
18	Opera	$0.00	Prorated	$0.00	$0.00	$0.00	$0.00	$0.00
19	Public relations	$0.00	End	$0.00	$0.00	$0.00	$0.00	$0.00
20	Alert communit	$0.00	End	$0.00	$0.00	$0.00	$0.00	$0.00

Figure 11-7: The Cost table for tasks.

If you assign a fixed cost to a task in this table, Project adds the fixed cost to the calculated cost for the task. To display this table, start in the Gantt Chart view. Then right-click on the Select All button to display the shortcut menu of tables and choose Cost. You may also need to slide the chart pane all the way to the right to see all the fields on the Cost table for tasks.

The Cost table for tasks is most useful if you saved a baseline view of your project because it enables you to compare baseline costs with actual costs.

Using the Cost table for resources

The Cost table for resources is very similar to the Cost table for tasks, with the breakdown of costs being displayed by resource rather than by task (see Figure 11-8).

To display this table, start with a resource view such as the Resource Sheet. Then right-click on the Select All button and choose Cost from the shortcut menu that appears.

Like the Cost table for tasks, the Cost table for resources is useful if you saved a baseline view of your project because it enables you to compare baseline costs with actual costs.

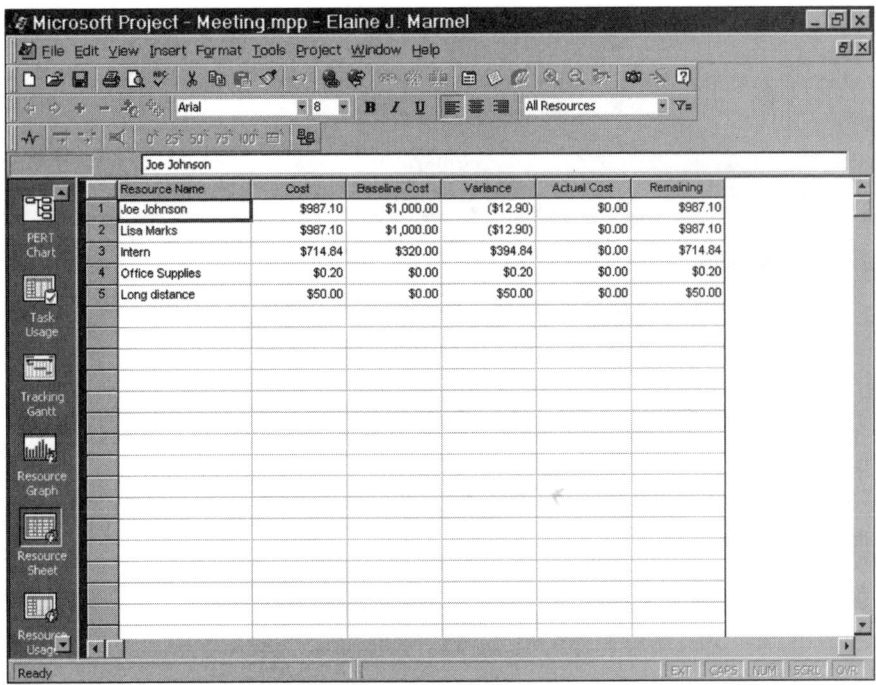

Figure 11-8: The Cost table for resources.

Overriding resource cost valuations

Project default settings automatically update costs as you record progress on a task. Project uses the accrual method you selected for the resource when you created the resource.

For more information about setting a resource's accrual method, see Chapter 5.

Alternatively, you can enter the actual costs for a resource assignment, or track actual costs separately from the actual work on a task. To do so, after the task is completed, you must enter costs manually to override Project's calculated costs. But before you can override the costs that Project calculated, you must turn off one of the default options. Follow these steps:

1. Choose Tools⇨Options to display the Options dialog box

2. Click on the Calculation tab.

3. Click on the bottom Calculation option — Actual costs are always calculated by Microsoft Project — to clear the check box (see Figure 11-9).

4. Click on OK.

5. Select the Task Usage view from the View bar.

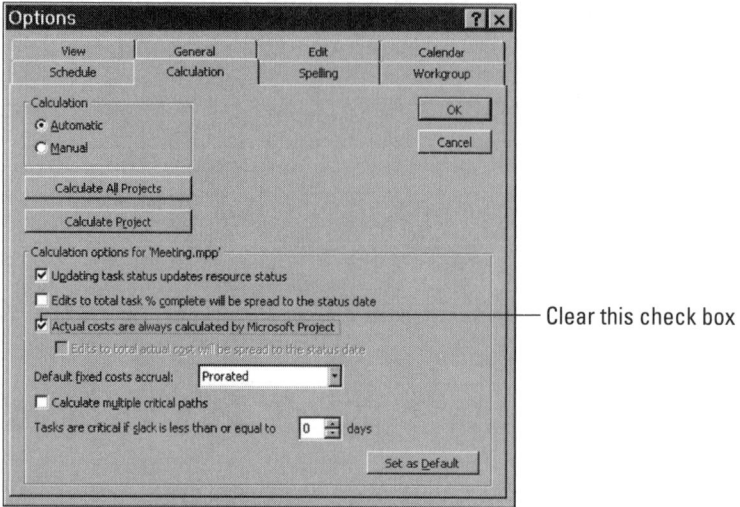

Figure 11-9: Revise the default settings to override Project's calculated costs.

6. Right-click on the Select All button to display the table shortcut menu and choose Tracking. Project displays the Tracking Table view shown in Figure 11-10.

7. Drag the divider bar to the right so that you can see all the fields.

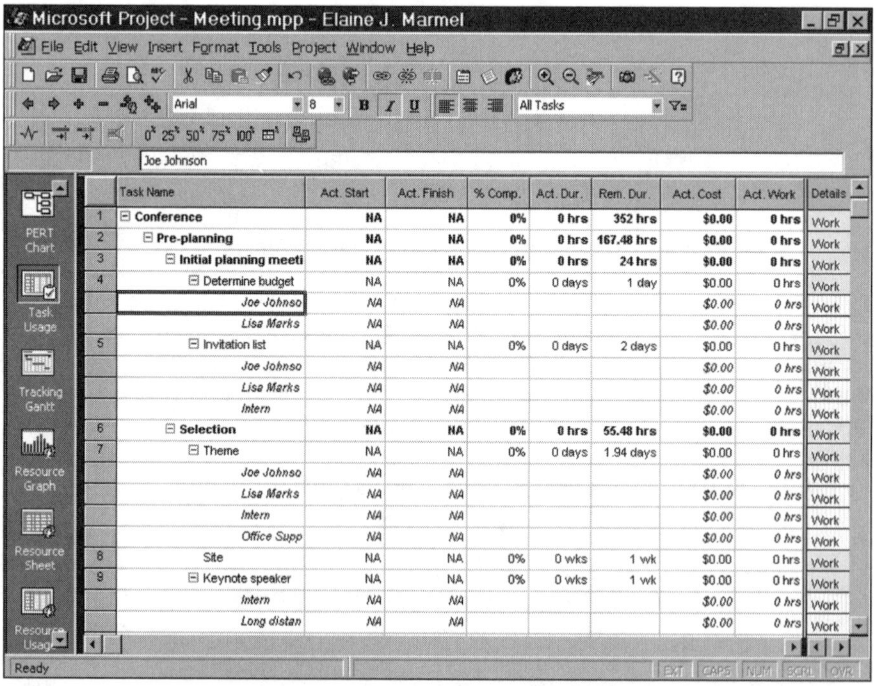

Figure 11-10: The Tracking Table view with the Actual Cost (Act. Cost) field visible.

8. Select the task or resource for which you want to assign a cost.

9. Enter the cost in the Act. Cost field.

Tip

If you change your mind and want Project to calculate costs as it originally did, repeat steps 1, 2, and 3 to restore the default calculation method. Project warns you that it will overwrite any manually entered costs when you click on OK.

Techniques and Tips for Updating

Project users can find ways to accelerate the updating process. For example, you can

✦ Use Project's timephased fields to easily update your project on some regular basis

✦ Update the progress of several tasks simultaneously

✦ Reschedule incomplete work so that it starts on the current date

Tracking work or costs regularly

Project's timephased fields enable you to update the progress on your project on some regular basis, such as daily or weekly. To use timephased fields to record progress information for resources, start by displaying the Resource Usage view (on the View bar, click on Resource Usage). Then right-click on the Select All button and select Work from the shortcut menu to change the table. Your screen should resemble Figure 11-11.

You're going to want to use most of the right side of the view, but on the left side of the view, you really need only the Actual Work column, which is hidden by the right side of the view. You could slide the divider bar over to the right, but then you'll lose the right side of the view. Or after sliding the divider bar, you could hide all the columns between the Resource Name column and the Actual Work column — but to redisplay them, you need to insert each of them.

To set up the left side of the view so that you can see the Actual Work column, add that column between the Resource Name column and the % Comp. (Percent Complete) column. To add the column:

1. Click on the title of the Percent Complete column to select the entire column.

2. Choose Insert➪Column to open the Column Definition dialog box shown in Figure 11-12.

3. Open the Field name drop-down list and select Actual Work.

4. Click on OK.

Project adds the Actual Work column to the right of the Resource Name column.

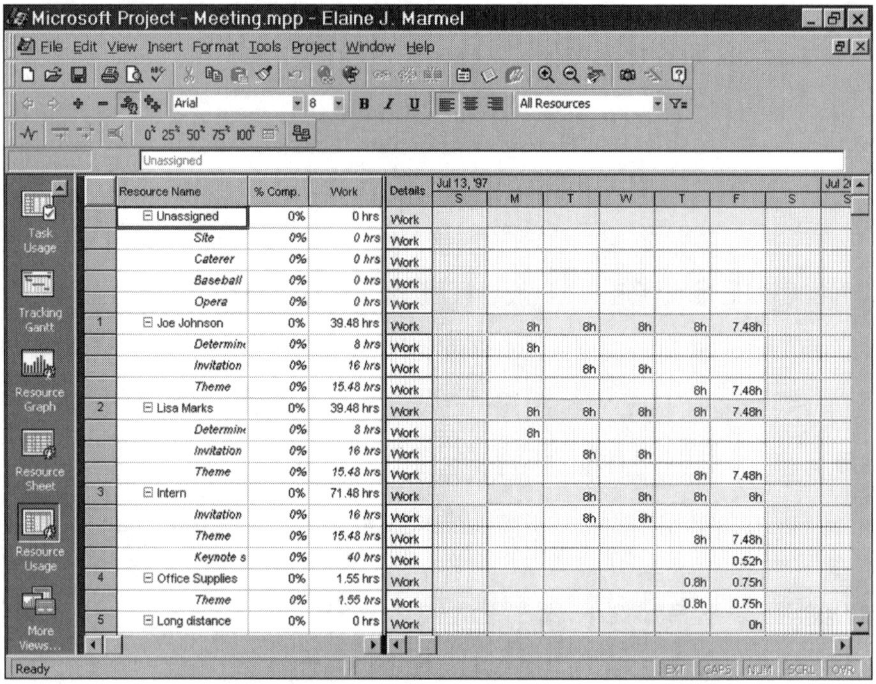

Figure 11-11: Setting up to use timephased fields.

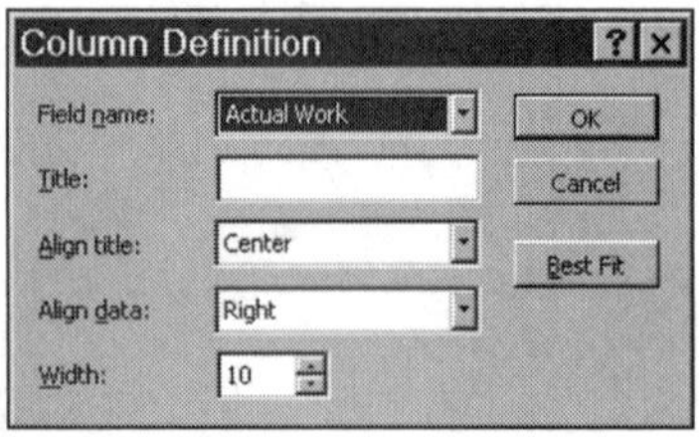

Figure 11-12: Add the Actual Work column from the Column Definition dialog box.

Next you should decide how often you want to update your project. If you want to update daily, you don't need to make any changes to the timescale on the right side of the screen. But if you want to update weekly (or some other frequency), you need to change the timescale. To change the timescale, choose Format⇨Timescale. Project opens the Timescale dialog box shown in Figure 11-13. This example doesn't require any timescale changes, but if you want to change the timescale to weekly, for example, open the Units list box in the Major scale box and select Months. Then open the Units list box in the Minor scale box and select Weeks.

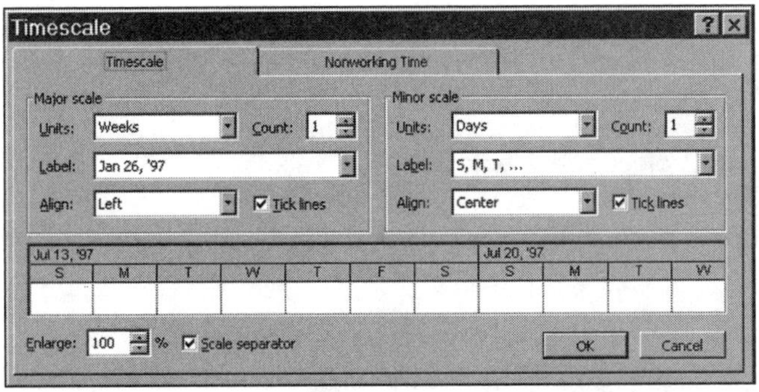

Figure 11-13: Use the Timescale dialog box to change the increments that appear on the right side of the Resource Usage view.

When you add a timephased field for Actual Work, you can see the results as you update the schedule. Choose Format⇨Details⇨Actual Work. Project adds a row for every task on the right side of the view. To enter hours worked for a particular day, click on the letter of the column representing that day to select the entire day, as you see in Figure 11-14. Then enter the hours for the correct resource and task in the Actual Work column you added on the left side of the view.

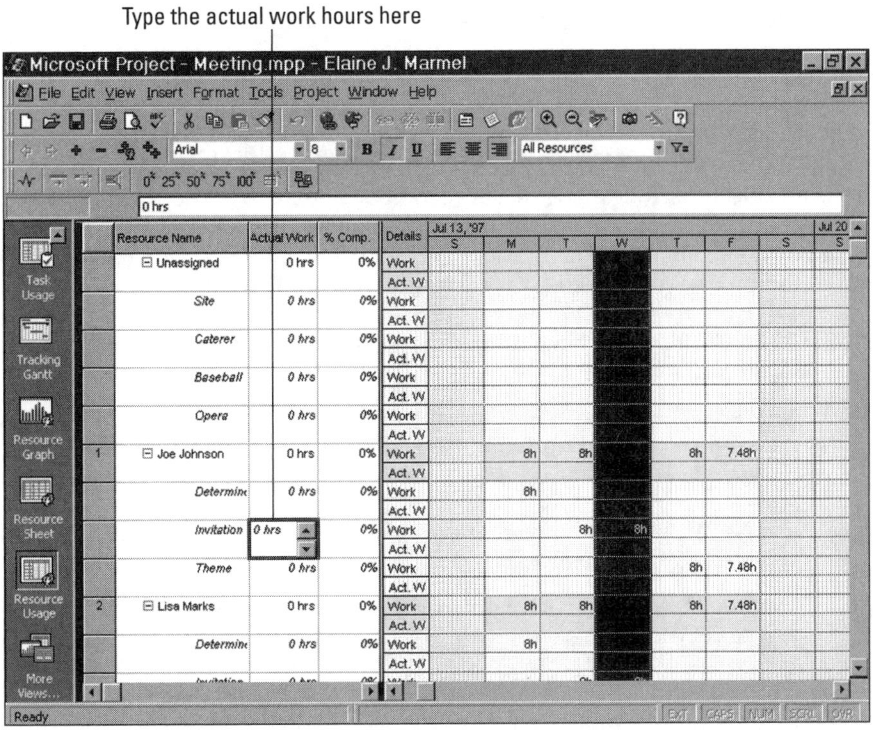

Figure 11-14: Add actual work information for a specific day.

Note   Remember, however, that you cannot add costs to override Project's automatically calculated costs unless you open the Options dialog box (choose Tools⇨Options), select the Calculation tab, and remove the check from the Actual costs are always calculated by Microsoft Project check box.

This entire process can also work if you are updating costs on a daily basis, with two minor changes:

✦ Start with the Task Usage view instead of the Resource Usage view.

✦ Add the Tracking table instead of the Work table.

Tip   To hide the Actual Work column you added to the left side of the view, select the entire column and then choose Edit⇨Hide Column. The left side of the view returns to its default appearance. To hide the Actual Work row you added to the right side of the view, choose Format⇨Details⇨Actual Work.

Accelerating the updating process

If you have several tasks that are on schedule or were completed on schedule, you can update these tasks all at once. Follow these steps:

1. Select the Gantt Chart view from the View bar.

Tip   If you want to update the entire project, don't select any tasks.

2. Go to the Task Name column and select the tasks you want to update. For example, Figure 11-15 shows four tasks selected for updating.

Note   You can select tasks using the same techniques you use in the Windows Explorer. To select two or more *contiguous* tasks, click on the first task. Then hold down the Shift key and click on the last task. To select two or more *noncontiguous* tasks, hold down the Ctrl key as you click on each task you want to select.

3. Choose Tools⇨Tracking⇨Update Project to display the Update Project dialog box shown in Figure 11-16.

4. Make sure that the correct date appears in the box next to the Update work as complete through option button.

5. Select one of the following:

✦ Set 0% - 100% complete if you want Project to calculate the Percent Complete for each task.

✦ Set 0% or 100% complete only if you want Project to mark completed tasks with 100% and incomplete tasks left at 0%.

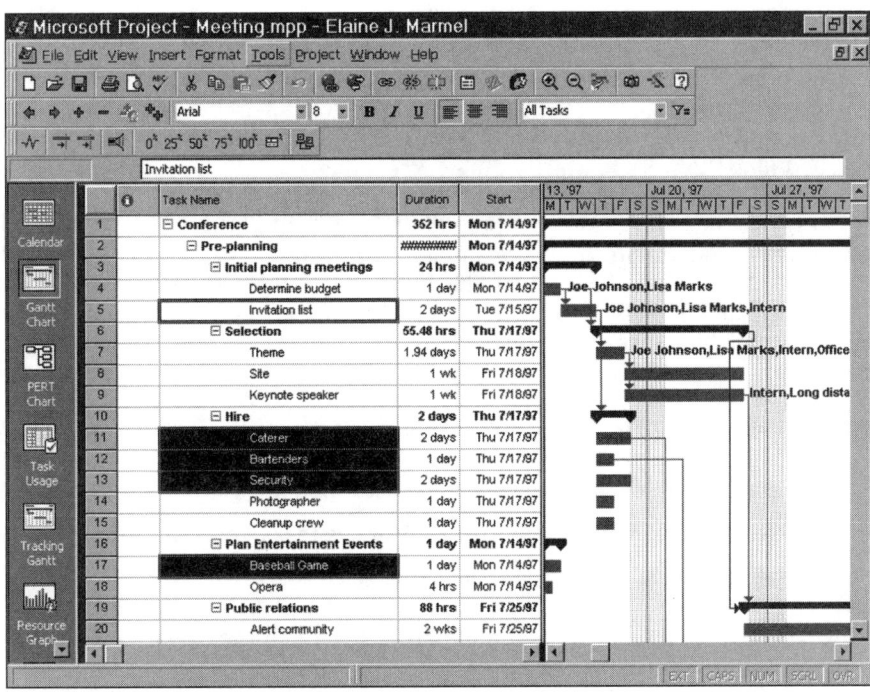

Figure 11-15: Selecting tasks to update.

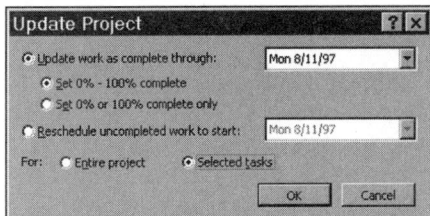

Figure 11-16: Use the Update Project dialog box to update your project.

6. Specify whether to update the Entire project or Selected tasks by selecting the appropriate option.

7. Click on OK.

When you update your project using this method, Project sets the project status date to the date you selected in step 4.

Letting Project reschedule uncompleted work

If you updated your project and you had partially completed tasks, you can guarantee that no remaining work is scheduled for dates that have already passed. You can make sure that all remaining work is scheduled for future dates by rescheduling the work to start on the current date.

Note   If you reschedule work using the technique described in this section, Project may remove task constraints you have applied. For example, suppose you reschedule the work of a task that has a Must Finish On constraint, and rescheduling moves the finish date beyond the constraint date. Project does not honor the constraint date; instead, it changes the constraint to As Soon As Possible. If you want to preserve a task's constraints, you should reschedule the remaining work manually.

Follow these steps to tell Project to reschedule remaining work for future dates:

1. Select the Gantt Chart view from the View bar.

2. Go to the Task Name column and select the tasks you want to update.

Tip   See the previous section for techniques you can use to select tasks.

3. Choose Tools⇨Tracking⇨Update Project to open the Update Project dialog box shown in Figure 11-17.

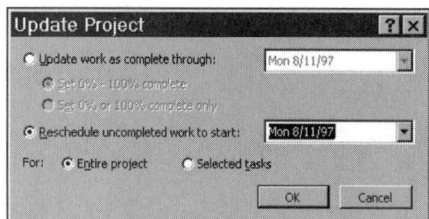

Figure 11-17: Use the Update Project dialog box to reschedule incomplete work to start today.

4. Click on the Reschedule uncompleted work to start option button and select the date from which you want to reschedule all unfinished work.

5. Specify whether to update the Entire project or Selected tasks by selecting the appropriate option button.

6. Click on OK.

Note   When you reschedule partially completed tasks using the technique just described, Project automatically splits the task between the completed portion and the remaining portion. Therefore, the Gantt Chart may display a split task that has a gap between its two parts because the completed portion may have finished some time before the remaining portion is scheduled to start.

Reviewing Progress

When you start recording actuals, you're going to want to review the progress of your project — and Project can help you.

Using the Tracking Gantt view

The Tracking Gantt view in Figure 11-18 probably provides the most effective picture of your project's progress. The bottom bar on the chart portion of the view (black hatching on your screen) represents the baseline dates for each task. The top bar shows either the scheduled start and finish dates or, if a task has been completed, the actual start and finish dates for each task.

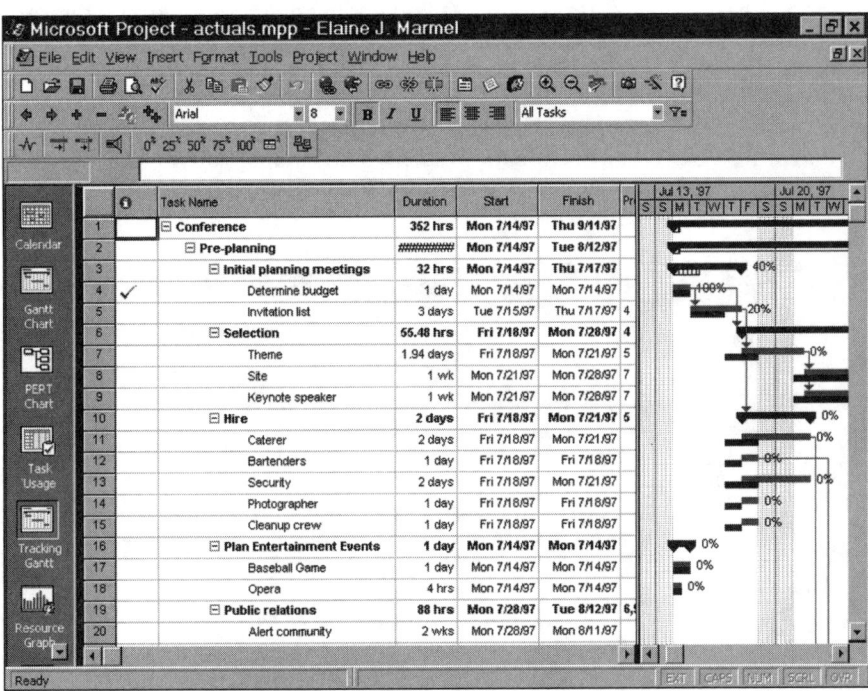

Figure 11-18: The Tracking Gantt view helps you understand the progress of your project.

Tip

If a task is finished, a check mark appears in the Indicator column on the left side of the view next to the task.

Project formats the task bar to indicate the task's status:

✦ If a task is scheduled, but not yet complete, the top bar appears as blue hatching.

✦ If the task is completed, the bar appears solid blue.

✦ If a task is partially complete, the complete portion appears as solid blue in the top bar, but the unfinished portion appears as blue hatching.

Using the Work table for tasks

The Work table for tasks in Figure 11-19 shows the total time required from all resources to complete the task. *Work* is different from a task duration:

✦ Work measures how many person hours are needed to complete a task.

✦ A task duration measures the number of days allotted to the task.

If the total work for a task is 16 hours but the task duration is only one day, you'll need to either add another resource (two people could complete the task in one day) or extend the task's duration.

The Work table for tasks includes baseline information so that you can compare your progress to your original estimate. For this table to be meaningful, therefore, you must have saved a baseline for your project. And as you might have guessed, you can enter information in the Work table for tasks.

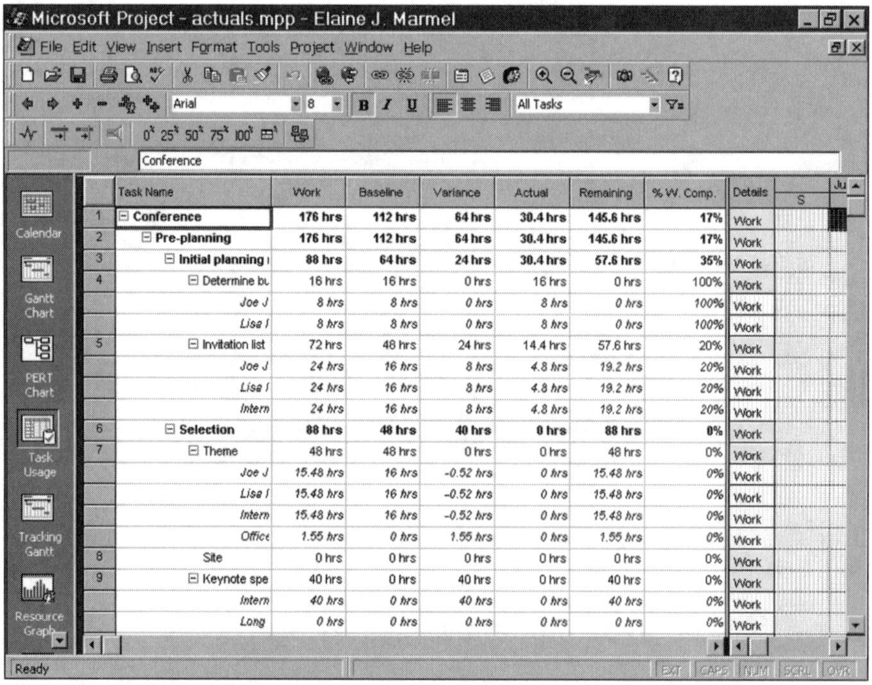

Figure 11-19: The Work table for tasks.

You can apply the Work table for tasks to any task sheet view. In Figure 11-19, for example, the Work table for tasks appears on the left side of the Task Usage view. Select the Task Usage view from the View bar; then right-click on the Select All button and choose Work.

Using the Work table for resources

The Work table for resources in Figure 11-20 shows work information for resources. Again, work represents the total time required from all resources to complete the task. The Work table for resources also includes baseline information so that you can compare your progress to your original estimate.

You can apply the Work table for resources to any resource sheet view. In Figure 11-20, for example, the Work table for resources appears on the left side of the Resource Usage view. Select the Resource Usage view from the View bar; then right-click on the Select All button and choose Work.

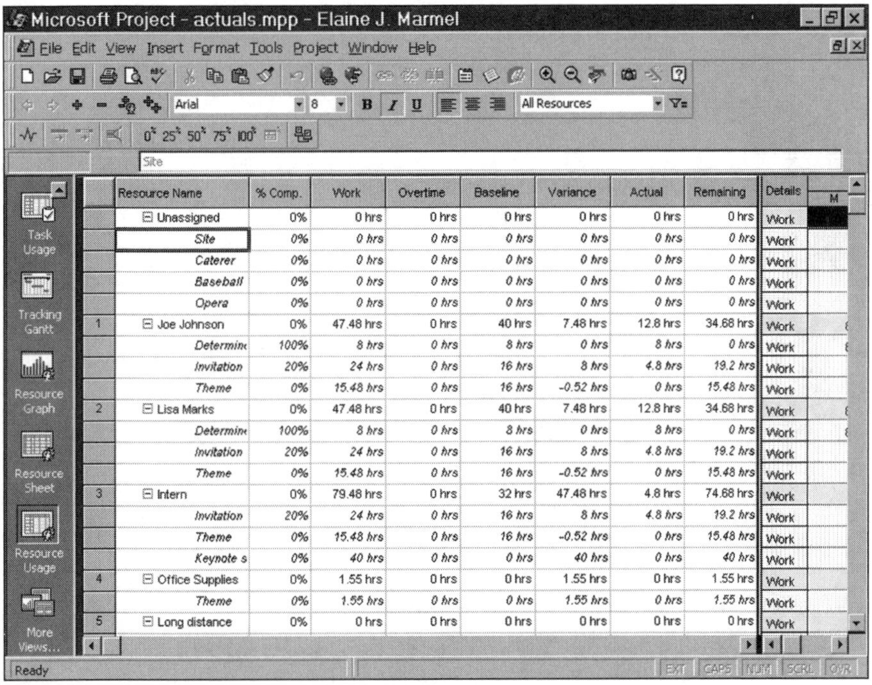

Figure 11-20: The Work table for resources.

Viewing progress lines

Project contains another tool that you can use to show the progress you're making on your project if you have saved a baseline of your project. If you add progress lines to the Gantt chart of your project, as you see in Figure 11-21, Project draws a line that connects in-progress tasks. The progress line creates a graph of your project, with peaks pointing to the right for work that is ahead of schedule and peaks pointing to the left for work that is behind schedule. The distance between the peaks and the line indicates the degree to which the task is ahead of or behind schedule.

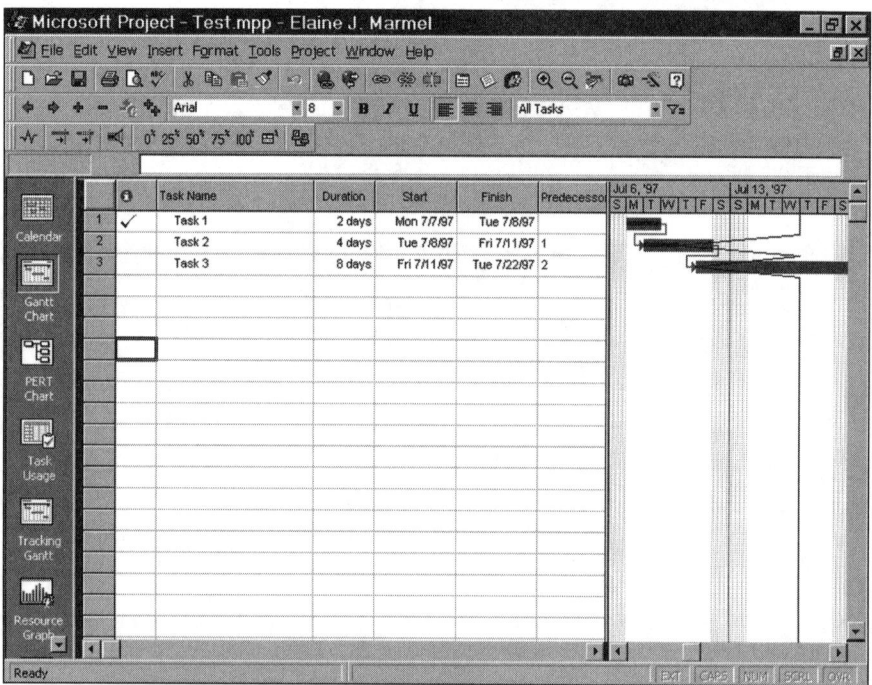

Figure 11-21: A Gantt chart with a progress line added.

To add a progress line, follow these steps:

1. Click on the Gantt Chart view in the View bar.

2. Choose Tools⇨Tracking⇨Progress Lines to open the Progress Lines dialog box and display the Dates and Intervals tab.

3. Place a check in the Display selected progress lines check box to activate the Progress Line Dates drop-down list.

4. Click once on the Progress Line Dates drop-down list. Project displays another list box arrow that you use to set the progress line's date.

5. Click on the list box arrow, and a small calendar appears (see Figure 11-22).

List box arrow you click to set a date

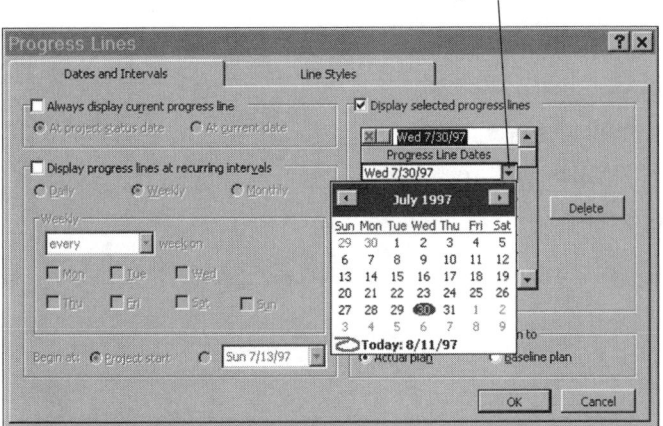

Figure 11-22: The Dates and Intervals tab of the Progress Lines dialog box.

6. Select a date for the progress line.

7. Select either Actual plan or Baseline plan in the Display progress lines in relation to box. This box is hidden behind the calendar in Figure 11-22.

8. Click on OK. Project adds the progress line to your Gantt chart that looks like the progress line you saw in Figure 11-21.

As you can imagine, a progress line on a project with a large number of tasks could begin to look messy. But if you decide you like progress lines, you can display them at varying intervals, as you can see from Figure 11-22. You can also add specific dates to the list box on the right side of the Progress Lines dialog box to display multiple progress lines on the Gantt Chart. If you decide to display more than one progress line, you may want to use the Line Styles tab of the Progress Lines dialog box to format the lines (for example, you can change colors) so that you can tell them apart.

To stop displaying progress lines, reopen the Progress Lines dialog box and remove any checks from the boxes on the Dates and Intervals tab.

Summary

In this chapter you learn how to record actual information about tasks and resources. For example, you learned how to

✦ Set start and finish dates

✦ Set actual and remaining durations

✦ Set the percent complete for a task

✦ Set the work completed for a task

✦ Use cost tables for tasks and resources

✦ Review the progress of your project

Chapter 12 shows you how to report on a project's progress.

✦   ✦   ✦

Reporting on Progress

Project contains various views that help you evaluate the progress of your project, identify areas with problems, and even resolve problems (see Chapter 6). Although you can print views, sometimes you need to present information in a format that is not available in any view. This chapter examines the use of reports to present your Project information.

Reporting Commonalities

All reports in Project have certain common characteristics. For example, you can print any report or you can review the report onscreen.

Note

Project organizes reports into categories of reports related to the same subject; that is, all the cost reports fall into the Costs category.

Here's how to display the reports available in a particular category:

1. Choose View⇨Reports to open the Reports dialog box (see Figure 12-1).

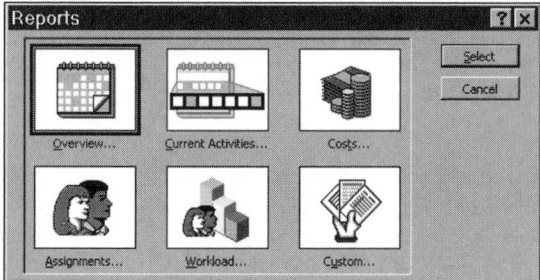

Figure 12-1: Select a report category from the Reports dialog box.

2. Click on the category of report you want.

3. Click on Select. Project displays the reports available in that category.

4. Select a report.

As you read through this chapter and see the reports available in each category, you can use the Edit button in report's dialog box to change the information that appears on the report. You can also use the Edit button to customize the report, as you learn at the end of this chapter.

5. Click on Select. Project displays the report onscreen in Print Preview mode, as you can see in Figure 12-2.

Zoom button

Scroll arrows | Full Page button   Multiple Pages button

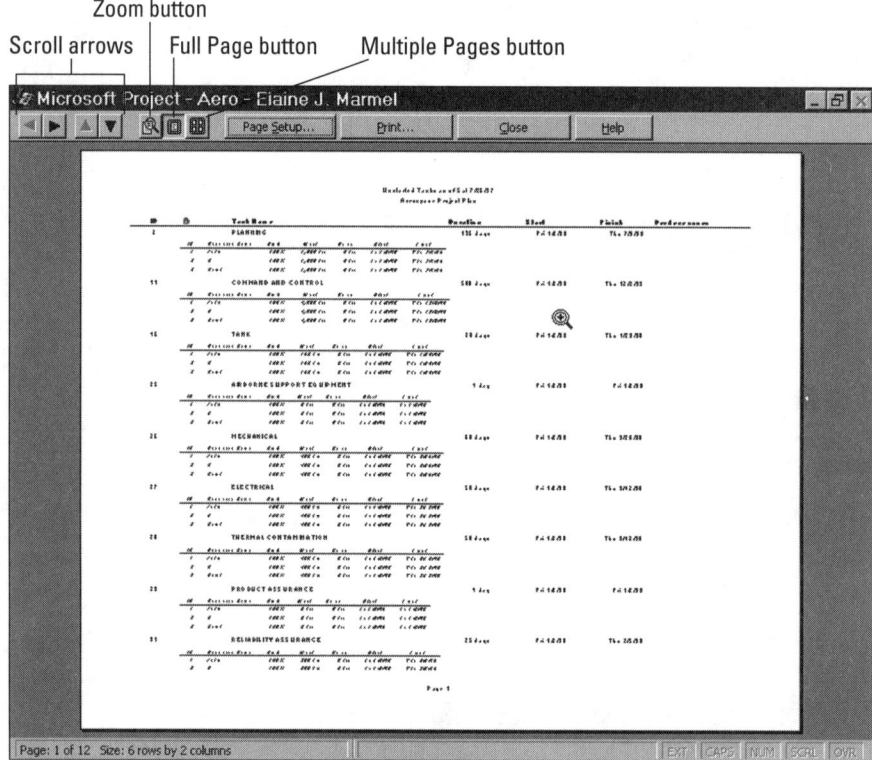

Figure 12-2: A report in Print Preview mode.

Use the scroll arrows on the toolbar at the top of the screen to move around the report. The Zoom button enlarges the view so that you can read the report's content onscreen. Or if you prefer, click on the portion of the report you want to enlarge — the shape of the mouse pointer indicates that it will zoom in on the area you click. To zoom out again, click on the Full Page button or click again on the report. To display more than one page at a time, click on the Multiple Pages button.

If you decide to print the report, you can review the page settings first. Click on the Page Setup button to display the Page Setup dialog box shown in Figure 12-3. Refer to Chapter 6 for a description of the tabs in this dialog box.

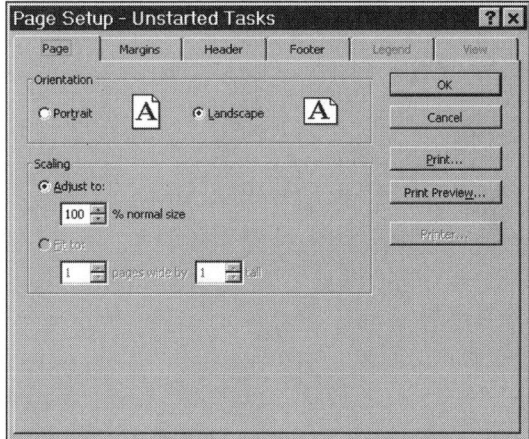

Figure 12-3: Use the Page Setup dialog box to set orientation, scaling, margins, and, if appropriate, header and footer information.

To print a report, click on the Print button. Project displays the Print dialog box you see in Figure 12-4.

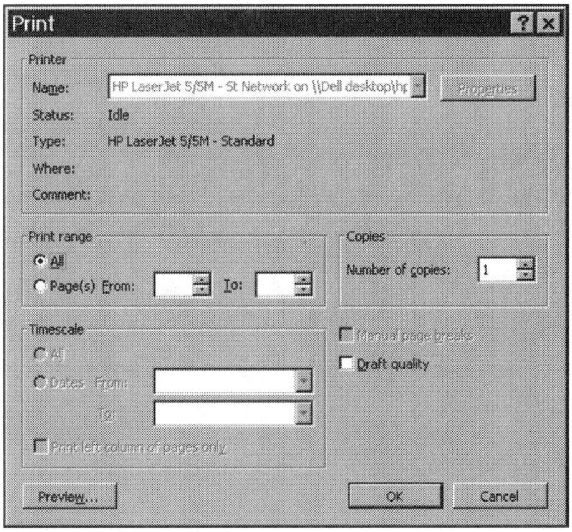

Figure 12-4: In the Print dialog box, select a print range for the report.

Alternatively, you can return to Project by clicking on the Close button.

Looking at the Big Picture

When you select Overview in the Reports dialog box, Project displays the top-level, summary-type reports (see Figure 12-5).

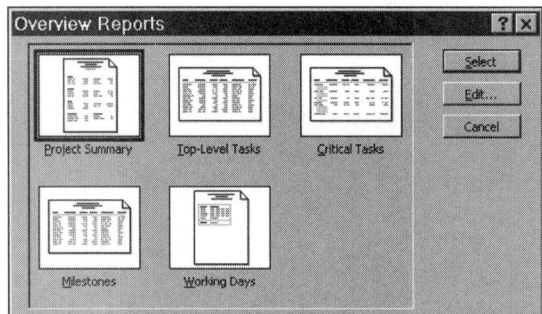

Figure 12-5: The reports available in the Overview category.

Project Summary

The Project Summary report (see Figure 12-6) shows top-level information about your project.

This report presents summarized information about dates, duration, work, costs, task status, and resource status.

Top-Level Tasks

The Top Level Tasks report (see Figure 12-7) shows, as of today's date, the summary tasks at the highest level in your project. You can see schedule start and finish dates, the percentage complete for each task, the cost, and the work required to complete the task.

Aerospace Project Plan

as of Sat 7/26/97

Dates

Start:	Fri 1/2/98	Finish:	Tue 6/12/01
Baseline Start:	Fri 1/2/98	Baseline Finish:	Tue 6/12/01
Actual Start:	NA	Actual Finish:	NA
Start Variance:	0 days	Finish Variance:	0 days

Duration

Scheduled:	898 days	Remaining:	898 days
Baseline:	898 days	Actual:	0 days
Variance:	0 days	Percent Complete:	0%

Work

Scheduled:	59,088 hrs	Remaining:	59,088 hrs
Baseline:	59,088 hrs	Actual:	0 hrs
Variance:	0 hrs	Percent Complete:	0%

Costs

Scheduled:	$1,319,632.00	Remaining:	$1,319,632.00
Baseline:	$1,319,632.00	Actual:	$0.00
Variance:	$0.00		

Task Status		Resource Status	
Tasks not yet started:	55	Resources:	0
Tasks in progress:	0	Overallocated Resources:	3
Tasks completed:	0		
Total Tasks:	55	Total Resources:	3

Figure 12-6: The Project Summary report.

Top Level Tasks as of Sat 7/26/97
Aerospace Project Plan

ID	Task Name	Duration	Start	Finish	% Comp.	Cost	Work
1	PROJECT MANAGEMENT	135 days	Fri 1/2/98	Thu 7/9/98	0%	$72,360.00	3,240 hrs
3	SYSTEM ENGINEERING	305 days	Fri 7/10/98	Thu 9/9/99	0%	$163,480.00	7,320 hrs
10	SPACECRAFT ENGINEERING	898 days	Fri 1/2/98	Tue 6/12/01	0%	$626,048.00	28,032 hrs
25	AIRBORNE SUPPORT EQUIPMEN	1 day	Fri 1/2/98	Fri 1/2/98	0%	$536.00	24 hrs
26	MECHANICAL	60 days	Fri 1/2/98	Thu 3/26/98	0%	$32,160.00	1,440 hrs
27	ELECTRICAL	50 days	Fri 1/2/98	Thu 3/12/98	0%	$26,800.00	1,200 hrs
28	THERMAL CONTAMINATION	50 days	Fri 1/2/98	Thu 3/12/98	0%	$26,800.00	1,200 hrs
29	PRODUCT ASSURANCE	1 day	Fri 1/2/98	Fri 1/2/98	0%	$536.00	24 hrs
30	QUALITY ASSURANCE	270 days	Fri 1/2/98	Thu 1/14/99	0%	$198,856.00	8,904 hrs
42	LAUNCH SYSTEM INTEGRATION	440 days	Fri 1/2/98	Thu 9/9/99	0%	$172,056.00	7,704 hrs

Figure 12-7: The Top Level Tasks report.

Critical Tasks

The Critical Tasks report (see Figure 12-8) shows the status of the tasks on the critical path of your project — those that will make or break your completing the project on time. This report displays each task's planned duration, start and finish dates, the resources assigned to the task, and the predecessors and successors of the task.

Figure 12-8: The Critical Tasks report.

Milestones

The Milestones report (see Figure 12-9) shows information about each milestone in your project. If you marked summary tasks to appear as milestones in the Task Information dialog box, summary tasks also appear on this report as milestones. For each milestone or summary task, Project displays the planned duration, start and finish dates, predecessors, and the resources assigned to the milestone.

Figure 12-9: The Milestones report.

Working Days

As you can see from Figure 12-10, the Working Days report shows the base calendar information for your project.

Figure 12-10: The Working Days report.

You can see the name of the base calendar for the project and the working hours established for each day of the week, along with any exceptions you defined.

Reports on Costs

When you select Costs in the Reports dialog box, Project displays thumbnail sketches of the reports that describe the costs associated with your project (see Figure 12-11).

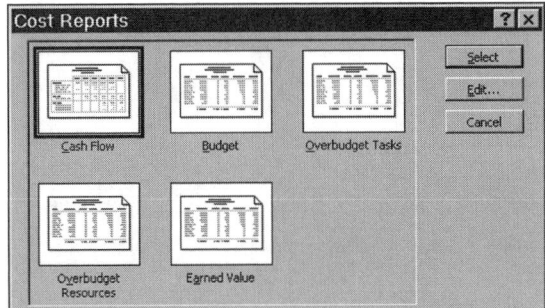

Figure 12-11: The reports available in the Cost category.

Cash Flow

The Cash Flow report (see Figure 12-12) is a tabular report that shows, by task, the costs for weekly time increments.

If you click on Cash Flow in the Cost Reports dialog box (refer to Figure 12-11) and then select Edit before you choose Select, Project opens the Crosstab Report dialog box shown in Figure 12-13. On the Definition tab, you can change the time increments.

Cash Flow as of Fri 8/15/97 Aerospace Project Plan								
	12/28/97	1/4/98	1/11/98	1/18/98	1/25/98	2/1/98	2/8/98	2/15/98
PROJECT MANAGEMENT								
PLANNING	$536.00	$2,680.00	$2,680.00	$2,680.00	$2,680.00	$2,680.00	$2,680.00	$2,680.00
SYSTEM ENGINEERING								
REQUIREMENTS								
ANALYSIS								
INTEGRATION								
MISSION OPERATIONS								
SYSTEM TEST PLANNING								
System Engineering Complete								
SPACECRAFT ENGINEERING								
COMMAND AND CONTROL	$536.00	$2,680.00	$2,680.00	$2,680.00	$2,680.00	$2,680.00	$2,680.00	$2,680.00
ATTITUDE CONTROL								
POWER								
THERMAL								
ORBIT ADJUST PROPULSION								
TANK	$536.00	$2,680.00	$2,680.00	$2,680.00	$2,144.00			
VALVES					$536.00	$2,680.00	$2,680.00	$2,680.00
THRUSTER								
DESIGN								
FABRICATE								
ASSEMBLE								
TEST								
CONTAINMENT SYSTEM								
Spacecraft Engineering Complete								
AIRBORNE SUPPORT EQUIPMENT	$536.00							
MECHANICAL	$536.00	$2,680.00	$2,680.00	$2,680.00	$2,680.00	$2,680.00	$2,680.00	$2,680.00
ELECTRICAL	$536.00	$2,680.00	$2,680.00	$2,680.00	$2,680.00	$2,680.00	$2,680.00	$2,680.00
THERMAL CONTAMINATION	$536.00	$2,680.00	$2,680.00	$2,680.00	$2,680.00	$2,680.00	$2,680.00	$2,680.00
PRODUCT ASSURANCE	$536.00							
QUALITY ASSURANCE								
RELIABILITY ASSURANCE	$536.00	$2,680.00	$2,680.00	$2,680.00	$2,680.00	$2,144.00		
PARTS CONTROLS	$536.00	$2,680.00	$2,680.00	$2,680.00	$2,680.00	$2,680.00	$2,680.00	$2,680.00
SYSTEM SAFETY	$536.00	$2,680.00	$2,680.00	$2,680.00	$2,144.00			
MATERIALS & PROCESSES CONTROLS	$536.00	$2,680.00	$2,680.00	$2,680.00	$2,680.00	$2,144.00		
INTEGRATION AND TEST						$536.00		
TEST FACILITIES							$2,680.00	$2,680.00
TEST SUPPORT								
GSC DESIGN								
POST RETRIEVAL REFURBISHMENT								
DATA REDUCTION								

Figure 12-12: The Cash Flow report.

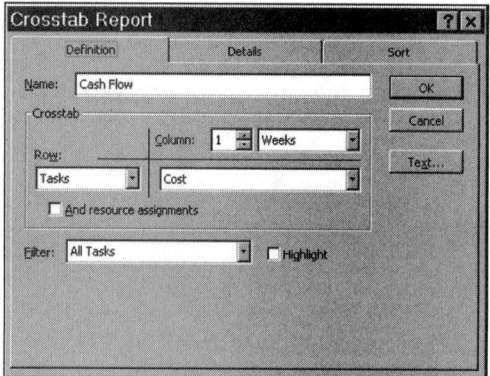

Figure 12-13: Use the Crosstab Report dialog box to change the default settings for the report.

See the section "Customizing Reports" at the end of this chapter for more about this dialog box.

Earned Value

The Earned Value report (see Figure 12-14) shows you the status of each task's costs when you compare planned to actual costs. Some of column headings in the report might seem cryptic; see Table 12-1 for translations.

Earned Value as of Fri 8/15/97
Aerospace Project Plan

ID	Task Name	BCWS	BCWP	ACWP	SV	CV	EAC	BAC	VAC
2	PLANNING	$0.00	$0.00	$0.00	$0.00	$0.00	$72,360.00	$72,360.00	$0.00
4	REQUIREMENTS	$0.00	$0.00	$0.00	$0.00	$0.00	$69,680.00	$69,680.00	$0.00
5	ANALYSIS	$0.00	$0.00	$0.00	$0.00	$0.00	$21,440.00	$21,440.00	$0.00
6	INTEGRATION	$0.00	$0.00	$0.00	$0.00	$0.00	$24,120.00	$24,120.00	$0.00
7	MISSION OPERATIONS	$0.00	$0.00	$0.00	$0.00	$0.00	$16,080.00	$16,080.00	$0.00
8	SYSTEM TEST PLANNING	$0.00	$0.00	$0.00	$0.00	$0.00	$32,160.00	$32,160.00	$0.00
9	System Engineering Complete	$0.00	$0.00	$0.00	$0.00	$0.00	$0.00	$0.00	$0.00
11	COMMAND AND CONTROL	$0.00	$0.00	$0.00	$0.00	$0.00	$268,000.00	$268,000.00	$0.00
12	ATTITUDE CONTROL	$0.00	$0.00	$0.00	$0.00	$0.00	$70,752.00	$70,752.00	$0.00
13	POWER	$0.00	$0.00	$0.00	$0.00	$0.00	$48,240.00	$48,240.00	$0.00
14	THERMAL	$0.00	$0.00	$0.00	$0.00	$0.00	$93,800.00	$93,800.00	$0.00
15	ORBIT ADJUST PROPULSION	$0.00	$0.00	$0.00	$0.00	$0.00	$536.00	$536.00	$0.00
16	TANK	$0.00	$0.00	$0.00	$0.00	$0.00	$10,720.00	$10,720.00	$0.00
17	VALVES	$0.00	$0.00	$0.00	$0.00	$0.00	$16,080.00	$16,080.00	$0.00
18	THRUSTER	$0.00	$0.00	$0.00	$0.00	$0.00	$18,760.00	$18,760.00	$0.00
19	DESIGN	$0.00	$0.00	$0.00	$0.00	$0.00	$10,720.00	$10,720.00	$0.00
20	FABRICATE	$0.00	$0.00	$0.00	$0.00	$0.00	$21,440.00	$21,440.00	$0.00
21	ASSEMBLE	$0.00	$0.00	$0.00	$0.00	$0.00	$10,720.00	$10,720.00	$0.00
22	TEST	$0.00	$0.00	$0.00	$0.00	$0.00	$10,720.00	$10,720.00	$0.00
23	CONTAINMENT SYSTEM	$0.00	$0.00	$0.00	$0.00	$0.00	$45,560.00	$45,560.00	$0.00
24	Spacecraft Engineering Complete	$0.00	$0.00	$0.00	$0.00	$0.00	$0.00	$0.00	$0.00
25	AIRBORNE SUPPORT EQUIPMENT	$0.00	$0.00	$0.00	$0.00	$0.00	$536.00	$536.00	$0.00
26	MECHANICAL	$0.00	$0.00	$0.00	$0.00	$0.00	$32,160.00	$32,160.00	$0.00
27	ELECTRICAL	$0.00	$0.00	$0.00	$0.00	$0.00	$26,800.00	$26,800.00	$0.00
28	THERMAL CONTAMINATION	$0.00	$0.00	$0.00	$0.00	$0.00	$26,800.00	$26,800.00	$0.00
29	PRODUCT ASSURANCE	$0.00	$0.00	$0.00	$0.00	$0.00	$536.00	$536.00	$0.00
31	RELIABILITY ASSURANCE	$0.00	$0.00	$0.00	$0.00	$0.00	$13,400.00	$13,400.00	$0.00
32	PARTS CONTROLS	$0.00	$0.00	$0.00	$0.00	$0.00	$32,160.00	$32,160.00	$0.00
33	SYSTEM SAFETY	$0.00	$0.00	$0.00	$0.00	$0.00	$10,720.00	$10,720.00	$0.00
34	MATERIALS & PROCESSES CONT	$0.00	$0.00	$0.00	$0.00	$0.00	$13,400.00	$13,400.00	$0.00
35	INTEGRATION AND TEST	$0.00	$0.00	$0.00	$0.00	$0.00	$536.00	$536.00	$0.00
36	TEST FACILITIES	$0.00	$0.00	$0.00	$0.00	$0.00	$48,240.00	$48,240.00	$0.00
37	TEST SUPPORT	$0.00	$0.00	$0.00	$0.00	$0.00	$32,160.00	$32,160.00	$0.00
38	GSC DESIGN	$0.00	$0.00	$0.00	$0.00	$0.00	$16,080.00	$16,080.00	$0.00
39	POST RETRIEVAL REFURBISHMEN	$0.00	$0.00	$0.00	$0.00	$0.00	$24,120.00	$24,120.00	$0.00
40	DATA REDUCTION	$0.00	$0.00	$0.00	$0.00	$0.00	$8,040.00	$8,040.00	$0.00
41	Assurance and Testing Complete	$0.00	$0.00	$0.00	$0.00	$0.00	$0.00	$0.00	$0.00
43	INTEGRATION ANALYSIS	$0.00	$0.00	$0.00	$0.00	$0.00	$13,400.00	$13,400.00	$0.00
44	LAUNCH PREPARATION	$0.00	$0.00	$0.00	$0.00	$0.00	$16,080.00	$16,080.00	$0.00
45	LAUNCH OPERATIONS	$0.00	$0.00	$0.00	$0.00	$0.00	$16,080.00	$16,080.00	$0.00
46	ABORT SUPPORT	$0.00	$0.00	$0.00	$0.00	$0.00	$10,720.00	$10,720.00	$0.00
47	RETRIEVAL	$0.00	$0.00	$0.00	$0.00	$0.00	$10,720.00	$10,720.00	$0.00
48	SOFTWARE	$0.00	$0.00	$0.00	$0.00	$0.00	$536.00	$536.00	$0.00
49	REQUIREMENTS ANALYSIS	$0.00	$0.00	$0.00	$0.00	$0.00	$16,080.00	$16,080.00	$0.00
50	DESIGN	$0.00	$0.00	$0.00	$0.00	$0.00	$16,080.00	$16,080.00	$0.00
51	CODE & CHECKOUT	$0.00	$0.00	$0.00	$0.00	$0.00	$40,200.00	$40,200.00	$0.00
52	DEVELOPMENT TESTING	$0.00	$0.00	$0.00	$0.00	$0.00	$16,080.00	$16,080.00	$0.00
53	DEVELOPMENT SUPPORT	$0.00	$0.00	$0.00	$0.00	$0.00	$16,080.00	$16,080.00	$0.00
54	Software Complete	$0.00	$0.00	$0.00	$0.00	$0.00	$0.00	$0.00	$0.00
55	Space Vehicle Completed	$0.00	$0.00	$0.00	$0.00	$0.00	$0.00	$0.00	$0.00
		$0.00	$0.00	$0.00	$0.00	$0.00	$1,319,632.00	$1,319,632.00	$0.00

Figure 12-14: The Earned Value report.

Table 12-1
Headings in the Earned Value Report

BCWS	Budgeted Cost of Work Scheduled
BCWP	Budgeted Cost of Work Performed
ACWP	Actual Cost of Work Performed
SV	Schedule Variance
CV	Cost Variance
BAC	Budgeted at Completion
EAC	Estimate at Completion
VAC	Variance at Completion

Project calculates BCWS, BCWP, ACWP, SV, and CV through the project status date. SV represents the cost difference between current progress and the baseline plan, and Project calculates this value as BCWP minus BCWS. CV represents the cost difference between actual costs and planned costs at the current level of completion, and Project calculates this value as BCWP minus ACWP. EAC shows the planned costs based on costs already incurred plus additional planned costs. VAC represents the variance between the baseline cost and the combination of actual plus planned costs for a task.

Budget

The Budget report (see Figure 12-15) lists all tasks and shows the budgeted cost as well as the variance between budgeted and actual costs.

Budget Report as of Fri 8/15/97
Meeting

ID	Task Name	Fixed Cost	Fixed Cost Accrual	Total Cost	Baseline	Variance	Actual	Remaining
7	Theme	$200.00	End	$1,129.24	$990.00	$169.24	$1,129.24	$0.00
8	Site	$1,000.00	End	$1,000.00	$0.00	$1,000.00	$1,000.00	$0.00
5	Invitation list	$0.00	End	$960.00	$960.00	$0.00	$0.00	$960.00
9	Keynote speaker	$0.00	End	$450.00	$0.00	$450.00	$450.00	$0.00
4	Determine budget	$0.00	End	$400.00	$400.00	$0.00	$0.00	$400.00
11	Caterer	$0.00	Prorated	$0.00	$0.00	$0.00	$0.00	$0.00
12	Bartenders	$0.00	End	$0.00	$0.00	$0.00	$0.00	$0.00
13	Security	$0.00	End	$0.00	$0.00	$0.00	$0.00	$0.00
14	Photographer	$0.00	End	$0.00	$0.00	$0.00	$0.00	$0.00
15	Cleanup crew	$0.00	End	$0.00	$0.00	$0.00	$0.00	$0.00
17	Baseball Game	$0.00	Prorated	$0.00	$0.00	$0.00	$0.00	$0.00
18	Opera	$0.00	Prorated	$0.00	$0.00	$0.00	$0.00	$0.00
20	Alert community	$0.00	End	$0.00	$0.00	$0.00	$0.00	$0.00
21	Press release	$0.00	End	$0.00	$0.00	$0.00	$0.00	$0.00
23	Rent audiovisual equipment	$0.00	End	$0.00	$0.00	$0.00	$0.00	$0.00
24	Rent tables and chairs	$0.00	End	$0.00	$0.00	$0.00	$0.00	$0.00
26	Menu selection	$0.00	End	$0.00	$0.00	$0.00	$0.00	$0.00
27	Drink selection	$0.00	End	$0.00	$0.00	$0.00	$0.00	$0.00
29	Transportation for speaker	$0.00	End	$0.00	$0.00	$0.00	$0.00	$0.00
30	Event transportation	$0.00	End	$0.00	$0.00	$0.00	$0.00	$0.00
31	Flowers	$0.00	End	$0.00	$0.00	$0.00	$0.00	$0.00
32	Table decorations	$0.00	End	$0.00	$0.00	$0.00	$0.00	$0.00
33	Lighting	$0.00	End	$0.00	$0.00	$0.00	$0.00	$0.00
35	Buy room decorations	$0.00	End	$0.00	$0.00	$0.00	$0.00	$0.00
36	Buy party favors	$0.00	End	$0.00	$0.00	$0.00	$0.00	$0.00
37	Setup equipment for event	$0.00	End	$0.00	$0.00	$0.00	$0.00	$0.00
38	Decorate	$0.00	End	$0.00	$0.00	$0.00	$0.00	$0.00
39	Special Event	$0.00	End	$0.00	$0.00	$0.00	$0.00	$0.00
41	Cleanup	$0.00	End	$0.00	$0.00	$0.00	$0.00	$0.00
42	Pay bills	$0.00	End	$0.00	$0.00	$0.00	$0.00	$0.00
43	Write thank you letters	$0.00	End	$0.00	$0.00	$0.00	$0.00	$0.00
44	Write event summary	$0.00	End	$0.00	$0.00	$0.00	$0.00	$0.00
45	Vacation	$0.00	End	$0.00	$0.00	$0.00	$0.00	$0.00
		$1,200.00		$3,939.24	$2,320.00	$1,619.24	$2,579.24	$1,360.00

Figure 12-15: The Budget Report.

This report won't have much meaning unless you have saved a baseline of your project; the values in the variance column change from $0.00 as you complete tasks.

Overbudget items

Project contains two overbudget reports: one for tasks and one for resources. Neither report prints if you have not yet indicated that some tasks are at least partially completed. Instead, you see the message that appears in Figure 12-16.

The Overbudget Tasks report (see Figure 12-17) shows cost, baseline, variance, and actual information about tasks that exceed their budgeted amounts.

The Overbudget Resources report (see Figure 12-18) displays resources whose costs are going to exceed baseline estimates based on the current progress of the project.

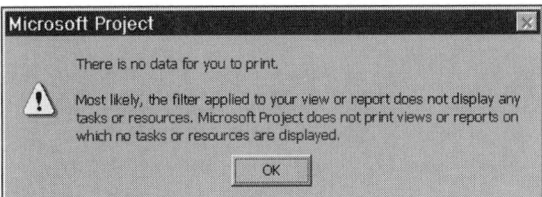

Figure 12-16: This message appears when you attempt to print an Overbudget report before you mark any tasks as at least partially complete.

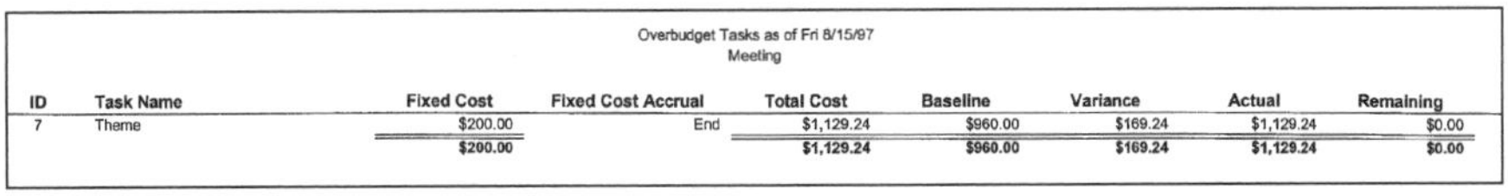

ID	Task Name	Fixed Cost	Fixed Cost Accrual	Total Cost	Baseline	Variance	Actual	Remaining
7	Theme	$200.00	End	$1,129.24	$960.00	$169.24	$1,129.24	$0.00
		$200.00		**$1,129.24**	**$960.00**	**$169.24**	**$1,129.24**	**$0.00**

Overbudget Tasks as of Fri 8/15/97 — Meeting

Figure 12-17: The Overbudget Tasks report.

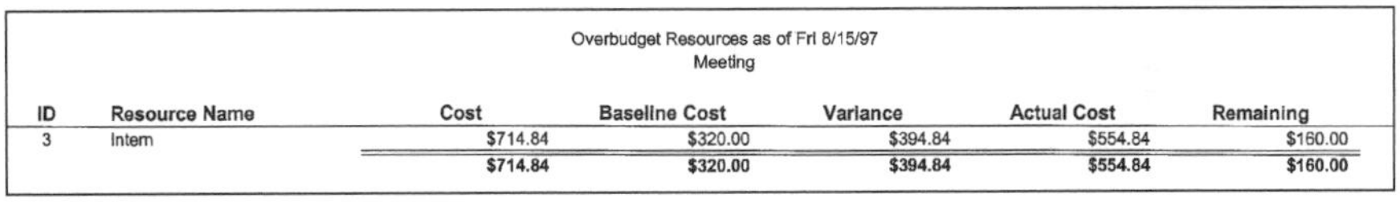

ID	Resource Name	Cost	Baseline Cost	Variance	Actual Cost	Remaining
3	Intern	$714.84	$320.00	$394.84	$554.84	$160.00
		$714.84	**$320.00**	**$394.84**	**$554.84**	**$160.00**

Overbudget Resources as of Fri 8/15/97 — Meeting

Figure 12-18: The Overbudget Resources report.

Reports on Time

Using the Current Activities reporting category, you can produce reports on the timing of your project. Select Current Activities to open the Current Activity Reports dialog box (see Figure 12-19) and view the reports available in this category.

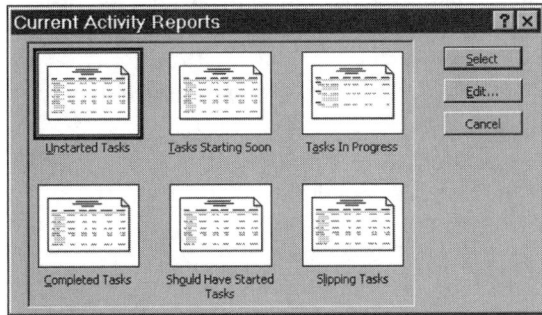

Figure 12-19: The reports available in the Current Activity category.

Unstarted Tasks

The Unstarted Tasks report (see Figure 12-20) lists the tasks that have not yet started, sorted by start date. For each task Project displays the duration, predecessor, and, if resources are assigned, resource information.

ID	O	Task Name	Duration	Start	Finish	Predecessors	Resource Names
4		Determine budget	1 day	Mon 7/14/97	Mon 7/14/97		Joe Johnson,Lisa Marks

	ID	Resource Name	Units	Work	Delay	Start	Finish
	1	Joe Johnson	100%	8 hrs	0 days	Mon 7/14/97	Mon 7/14/97
	2	Lisa Marks	100%	8 hrs	0 days	Mon 7/14/97	Mon 7/14/97

ID	O	Task Name	Duration	Start	Finish	Predecessors	Resource Names
17		Baseball Game	1 day	Mon 7/14/97	Mon 7/14/97		
18		Opera	4 hrs	Mon 7/14/97	Mon 7/14/97		
23		Rent audiovisual equipment	2 days	Mon 7/14/97	Tue 7/15/97		
29		Transportation for speaker	1 day	Mon 7/14/97	Mon 7/14/97		
5		Invitation list	2 days	Tue 7/15/97	Wed 7/16/97	4	Joe Johnson,Lisa Marks,Int

	ID	Resource Name	Units	Work	Delay	Start	Finish
	1	Joe Johnson	100%	16 hrs	0 days	Tue 7/15/97	Wed 7/16/97
	2	Lisa Marks	100%	16 hrs	0 days	Tue 7/15/97	Wed 7/16/97
	3	Intern	100%	16 hrs	0 days	Tue 7/15/97	Wed 7/16/97

ID	O	Task Name	Duration	Start	Finish	Predecessors	Resource Names
30		Event transportation	3 days	Tue 7/15/97	Thu 7/17/97	29	
24		Rent tables and chairs	1 day	Wed 7/16/97	Wed 7/16/97	23	
11		Caterer	2 days	Thu 7/17/97	Fri 7/18/97		
12		Bartenders	1 day	Thu 7/17/97	Thu 7/17/97		
13		Security	2 days	Thu 7/17/97	Fri 7/18/97		
14		Photographer	1 day	Thu 7/17/97	Thu 7/17/97		
15		Cleanup crew	1 day	Thu 7/17/97	Thu 7/17/97		
31		Flowers	4 days	Fri 7/18/97	Wed 7/23/97	30	
26		Menu selection	1 day	Mon 7/21/97	Mon 7/21/97	11	
27		Drink selection	1 day	Tue 7/22/97	Tue 7/22/97	26,12	
32		Table decorations	1 day	Thu 7/24/97	Thu 7/24/97	31	
33		Lighting	1 day	Fri 7/25/97	Fri 7/25/97	32	
20		Alert community	2 wks	Fri 7/25/97	Fri 8/8/97		
21		Press release	1 day	Fri 8/8/97	Mon 8/11/97	20	
35		Buy room decorations	1 day	Mon 8/11/97	Tue 8/12/97		
36		Buy party favors	1 day	Tue 8/12/97	Wed 8/13/97	35	
37		Setup equipment for event	2 days	Wed 8/13/97	Fri 8/15/97	36	
38		Decorate	2 days	Fri 8/15/97	Tue 8/19/97	37	
39		Special Event	5 days	Mon 8/25/97	Fri 8/29/97	38	
41		Cleanup	2 days	Mon 9/1/97	Tue 9/2/97	39	
42		Pay bills	4 days	Wed 9/3/97	Mon 9/8/97	41	
43		Write thank you letters	2 days	Tue 9/9/97	Wed 9/10/97	42	
44		Write event summary	1 day	Thu 9/11/97	Thu 9/11/97	43	
45		Vacation	0 days	Thu 9/11/97	Thu 9/11/97	44	

Figure 12-20: The Unstarted Tasks report.

Tasks Starting Soon

When you print the Tasks Starting Soon report (see Figure 12-21), Project displays the Date Range dialog boxes. The information you provide in these two dialog boxes tells Project the date range to use when selecting tasks for this report. In the first dialog box, specify the earlier date; Project includes tasks that start or finish after the date you specify. In the second dialog box, specify the later date; and Project includes tasks that start or finish before the date you specify.

Figure 12-21: The Tasks Starting Soon report.

The information that appears on the report is similar to the information you find on the Unstarted Tasks report: the duration, start and finish dates, predecessors, and, if resources are assigned, resource information. Completed tasks also appear on this report; the check mark that appears in the indicator column on the report identifies them.

Tasks In Progress

As you can see from Figure 12-22, the Tasks In Progress report Figure lists tasks that have started but not yet finished. You see the tasks' duration, start and planned finish dates, predecessors, and, if resources have been assigned, resource information.

Figure 12-22: The Tasks in Progress report.

Completed Tasks

The Completed Tasks report (see Figure 12-23) lists tasks that have completed. You can see the actual duration, the actual start and finish dates, the percent complete (always 100 percent — if a task is only partially complete, it won't appear on this report), the cost, and the work hours.

		Completed Tasks as of Fri 8/15/97 Meeting					
ID	Task Name	Duration	Start	Finish	% Comp.	Cost	Work
July 1997							
7	Theme	1.94 days	Thu 7/17/97	Fri 7/18/97	100%	$1,129.24	48 hrs
8	Site	0.2 wks	Fri 7/18/97	Mon 7/21/97	100%	$1,000.00	8 hrs
9	Keynote speaker	1 wk	Fri 7/18/97	Fri 7/25/97	100%	$450.00	40 hrs

Figure 12-23: The Completed Tasks report.

Should Have Started Tasks

When you print the Should Have Started Tasks report (see Figure 12-24), you must supply a date by which tasks should have started. Project uses this date to determine which tasks appear on the report.

		Should Have Started Tasks as of Fri 8/15/97 Meeting					
ID	Task Name	Start	Finish	Baseline Start	Baseline Finish	Start Var.	Finish Var.
1	Conference	Mon 7/14/97	Thu 9/11/97	Mon 7/14/97	Thu 9/11/97	0 days	0 days
2	Pre-planning	Mon 7/14/97	Mon 8/11/97	Mon 7/14/97	Mon 8/11/97	0 days	-0.06 days
	ID Successor Name Type Lag 34 Preparation FS 0 hrs						
3	Initial planning meetings	Mon 7/14/97	Wed 7/16/97	Mon 7/14/97	Wed 7/16/97	0 days	0 days
4	Determine budget	Mon 7/14/97	Mon 7/14/97	Mon 7/14/97	Mon 7/14/97	0 days	0 days
	ID Successor Name Type Lag 5 Invitation list FS 0 days 6 Selection FS 0 hrs						
16	Plan Entertainment Events	Mon 7/14/97	Mon 7/14/97	Mon 7/14/97	Mon 7/14/97	0 days	0 days
17	Baseball Game	Mon 7/14/97	Mon 7/14/97	Mon 7/14/97	Mon 7/14/97	0 days	0 days
18	Opera	Mon 7/14/97	Mon 7/14/97	Mon 7/14/97	Mon 7/14/97	0 days	0 days
22	Rent Equipment	Mon 7/14/97	Wed 7/16/97	Mon 7/14/97	Wed 7/16/97	0 days	0 days
23	Rent audiovisual equipment	Mon 7/14/97	Tue 7/15/97	Mon 7/14/97	Tue 7/15/97	0 days	0 days
	ID Successor Name Type Lag 24 Rent tables and chairs FS 0 hrs						
28	Arrangements	Mon 7/14/97	Fri 7/25/97	Mon 7/14/97	Fri 7/25/97	0 days	0 days
29	Transportation for speaker	Mon 7/14/97	Mon 7/14/97	Mon 7/14/97	Mon 7/14/97	0 days	0 days
	ID Successor Name Type Lag 30 Event transportation FS 0 hrs						

Figure 12-24: The Should Have Started Tasks report.

For each task on the report, Project displays planned start and finish dates, baseline start and finish dates, and variances for start and finish dates. Successor task information appears when a task on the report has a successor defined.

Slipping Tasks

The Slipping Tasks report (see Figure 12-25) lists the tasks that have been rescheduled from their baseline start dates.

		Slipping Tasks as of Fri 8/15/97 Meeting					
ID	Task Name	Start	Finish	Baseline Start	Baseline Finish	Start Var.	Finish Var.
1	Conference	Mon 7/14/97	Thu 9/11/97	Mon 7/14/97	Thu 9/11/97	0 days	0 days
2	Pre-planning	Mon 7/14/97	Mon 8/11/97	Mon 7/14/97	Mon 8/11/97	0 days	-0.06 days
	ID *Successor Name* *Type* *Lag*						
	34 Preparation FS 0 hrs						
10	Hire	Thu 7/17/97	Tue 7/29/97	Thu 7/17/97	Fri 7/18/97	0 days	7 days
11	Caterer	Mon 7/28/97	Tue 7/29/97	Thu 7/17/97	Fri 7/18/97	7 days	7 days
	ID *Successor Name* *Type* *Lag*						
	26 Menu selection FS 0 hrs						
25	Meet with Caterer	Wed 7/30/97	Thu 7/31/97	Mon 7/21/97	Tue 7/22/97	7 days	7 days
26	Menu selection	Wed 7/30/97	Wed 7/30/97	Mon 7/21/97	Mon 7/21/97	7 days	7 days
	ID *Successor Name* *Type* *Lag*						
	27 Drink selection FS 0 hrs						
27	Drink selection	Thu 7/31/97	Thu 7/31/97	Tue 7/22/97	Tue 7/22/97	7 days	7 days

Figure 12-25: The Slipping Tasks report.

This report has the same information as you saw on the Should Have Started Tasks report, but the presentation of the information changes the focus of your attention.

Reports on Work Assignments

Using the Assignments reporting category, you can produce reports on the resource assignments in your project. Select the Assignments category to open the Assignment Reports dialog box (see Figure 12-26) and view the reports available in this category.

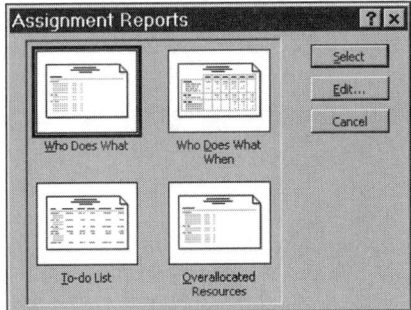

Figure 12-26: The reports available in the Assignments category.

Who Does What

The Who Does What report (see Figure 12-27) lists resources and the tasks to which they are assigned, the amount of work planned for each task, the planned start and finish dates, and any resource notes.

			Who Does What as of Sat 8/16/97			
			Meeting			

ID	ⓞ	Resource Name			Work	
1		Joe Johnson			39.48 hrs	

ID	Task Name	Units	Work	Delay	Start	Finish
4	Determine budget	100%	8 hrs	0 days	Mon 7/14/97	Mon 7/14/97
5	Invitation list	100%	16 hrs	0 days	Tue 7/15/97	Wed 7/16/97
7	Theme	100%	15.48 hrs	0 days	Thu 7/17/97	Fri 7/18/97

ID		Resource Name			Work	
2		Lisa Marks			39.48 hrs	

ID	Task Name	Units	Work	Delay	Start	Finish
4	Determine budget	100%	8 hrs	0 days	Mon 7/14/97	Mon 7/14/97
5	Invitation list	100%	16 hrs	0 days	Tue 7/15/97	Wed 7/16/97
7	Theme	100%	15.48 hrs	0 days	Thu 7/17/97	Fri 7/18/97

ID		Resource Name			Work	
3		Intern			87.48 hrs	

ID	Task Name	Units	Work	Delay	Start	Finish
5	Invitation list	100%	16 hrs	0 days	Tue 7/15/97	Wed 7/16/97
7	Theme	100%	15.48 hrs	0 days	Thu 7/17/97	Fri 7/18/97
9	Keynote speaker	100%	40 hrs	0 days	Fri 7/18/97	Fri 7/25/97
11	Caterer	100%	16 hrs	0 days	Mon 7/28/97	Tue 7/29/97

ID		Resource Name			Work	
4		Office Supplies			1.55 hrs	

ID	Task Name	Units	Work	Delay	Start	Finish
7	Theme	10%	1.55 hrs	0 days	Thu 7/17/97	Fri 7/18/97

ID		Resource Name			Work	
5		Long distance			0 hrs	

ID	Task Name	Units	Work	Delay	Start	Finish
9	Keynote speaker	0%	0 hrs	0 days	Fri 7/18/97	Fri 7/18/97

Figure 12-27: The Who Does What report.

Who Does What When

The Who Does What When report (see Figure 12-28) also lists resources and the tasks to which they are assigned, but the focus of this report is the daily work scheduled for each resource on each task.

				Who Does What When as of Sat 8/16/97 Meeting														
	7/13	7/14	7/15	7/16	7/17	7/18	7/19	7/20	7/21	7/22	7/23	7/24	7/25	7/26	7/27	7/28	7/29
Joe Johnson		8 hrs	8 hrs	8 hrs	8 hrs	#####											
Determine budget		8 hrs															
Invitation list			8 hrs	8 hrs													
Theme					8 hrs	#####											
Lisa Marks		8 hrs	8 hrs	8 hrs	8 hrs	#####											
Determine budget		8 hrs															
Invitation list			8 hrs	8 hrs													
Theme					8 hrs	#####											
Intern			8 hrs	8 hrs	8 hrs	8 hrs			8 hrs	8 hrs	8 hrs	8 hrs	#####			8 hrs	8 hrs
Invitation list			8 hrs	8 hrs													
Theme					8 hrs	#####											
Keynote speaker						#####			8 hrs	8 hrs	8 hrs	8 hrs	#####				
Caterer																8 hrs	8 hrs
Office Supplies					#####	#####											
Theme					#####	#####											
Long distance																	
Keynote speaker																	

Figure 12-28: The Who Does What When report.

Tip

You can use the Edit button in the Assignment Reports dialog box to change the timescale on the report from daily to some other increment, such as weekly. See "Customizing Reports" at the end of this chapter for more information.

To Do List

The To Do List report in Figure 12-29 lists, on a weekly basis, the tasks assigned to a resource you select. When you are ready to print this report, Project first displays the Using Resource dialog box, which contains the Show tasks using list box. When you open the list box, you see a list of your resources. Select a resource and click on OK. On the To-do List report shows the task ID number, duration, start and finish dates, predecessors, and a list of all of the resources assigned to each task.

ID	o	Task Name	Duration	Start	Finish	Predecessors	Resource Names
			To Do List as of Sat 8/16/97				
			Meeting				
Week of July 13							
4		Determine budget	1 day	Mon 7/14/97	Mon 7/14/97	4	Joe Johnson,Lisa Marks
5		Invitation list	2 days	Tue 7/15/97	Wed 7/16/97	4	Joe Johnson,Lisa Marks,Int
7	✓	Theme	1.94 days	Thu 7/17/97	Fri 7/18/97	5	Joe Johnson,Lisa Marks,Int
Week of July 20							
20		Alert community	2 wks	Fri 7/25/97	Fri 8/8/97		Joe Johnson
Week of July 27							
20		Alert community	2 wks	Fri 7/25/97	Fri 8/8/97		Joe Johnson
Week of August 3							
20		Alert community	2 wks	Fri 7/25/97	Fri 8/8/97		Joe Johnson

Figure 12-29: The To Do List report.

Overallocated Resources

The Overallocated Resources report shown in Figure 12-30 shows the overallocated resources, the tasks to which they are assigned, and the total hours of work assigned to them. You can also see the details of each task, such as the allocation, the amount of work, any delay, and the start and finish dates.

ID	o	Resource Name		Work			
		Overallocated Resources as of Sat 8/16/97					
		Meeting					
1	◈ ▨	Joe Johnson		131.48 hrs			
	ID	Task Name	Units	Work	Delay	Start	Finish
	4	Determine budget	100%	8 hrs	0 days	Mon 7/14/97	Mon 7/14/97
	5	Invitation list	100%	16 hrs	0 days	Tue 7/15/97	Wed 7/16/97
	7	Theme	100%	15.48 hrs	0 days	Thu 7/17/97	Fri 7/18/97
	20	Alert community	100%	80 hrs	0 days	Fri 7/25/97	Fri 8/8/97
	17	Baseball Game	100%	8 hrs	0 days	Mon 7/14/97	Mon 7/14/97
	18	Opera	100%	4 hrs	0 days	Mon 7/14/97	Mon 7/14/97
				131.48 hrs			

Figure 12-30: The Overallocated Resources report.

Reports on Workloads

You can use the Workload reporting category to produce reports on task and resource usage in your project. Click on Workload in the Reports dialog box to open the Workload Reports dialog box shown in Figure 12-31.

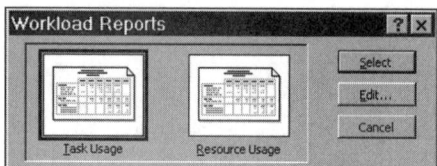

Figure 12-31: The Workload Reports dialog box.

Task Usage

The Task Usage report (see Figure 12-32) lists tasks and resources assigned to each task. It also displays the amount of work assigned to each resource in weekly time increments.

Tip You can change the time increment by clicking on Edit in the Workload Reports dialog box. See "Customizing Reports" later in this chapter for more information about editing reports.

	7/13/97	7/20/97	7/27/97	8/3/97	8/10/97	8/17/97	8/24/97	8/31/97	9/7/97	Total
Conference										
Pre-planning										
Initial planning meetings										
Determine budget	16 hrs									16 hrs
Joe Johnson	8 hrs									8 hrs
Lisa Marks	8 hrs									8 hrs
Invitation list	48 hrs									48 hrs
Joe Johnson	16 hrs									16 hrs
Lisa Marks	16 hrs									16 hrs
Intern	16 hrs									16 hrs
Selection										
Theme	48 hrs									48 hrs
Joe Johnson	15.48 hrs									#######
Lisa Marks	15.48 hrs									#######
Intern	15.48 hrs									#######
Office Supplies	1.55 hrs									1.55 hrs
Site	0.52 hrs	7.48 hrs								8 hrs
Keynote speaker	0.52 hrs	39.48 hrs								40 hrs
Intern	0.52 hrs	39.48 hrs								40 hrs
Long distance										
Hire										
Caterer			16 hrs							16 hrs
Intern			16 hrs							16 hrs
Bartenders										
Security										
Photographer										
Cleanup crew										
Plan Entertainment Events										
Baseball Game	8 hrs									8 hrs
Joe Johnson	8 hrs									8 hrs
Opera	4 hrs									4 hrs
Joe Johnson	4 hrs									4 hrs
Public relations										
Alert community		0.52 hrs	40 hrs	39.48 hrs						80 hrs
Joe Johnson		0.52 hrs	40 hrs	39.48 hrs						80 hrs
Press release										
Rent Equipment										
Rent audiovisual equipment										
Rent tables and chairs										
Meet with Caterer										
Menu selection										
Drink selection										
Arrangements										
Transportation for speaker										
Event transportation										
Flowers										

Task Usage as of Sat 8/16/97
Meeting

Figure 12-32: The Task Usage report.

Resource Usage

The Resource Usage report (see Figure 12-33) lists resources and the tasks to which they are assigned. Like the Task Usage report, this report shows the amount of work assigned to each resource for each task in weekly time increments, but in this report, the focus is on the resource.

	7/13/97	7/20/97	7/27/97	8/3/97	8/10/97	8/17/97	8/24/97	8/31/97	9/7/97	Total
Joe Johnson	51.48 hrs	0.52 hrs	40 hrs	39.48 hrs						131.48 hrs
Determine budget	8 hrs									8 hrs
Invitation list	16 hrs									16 hrs
Theme	15.48 hrs									15.48 hrs
Baseball Game	8 hrs									8 hrs
Opera	4 hrs									4 hrs
Alert community		0.52 hrs	40 hrs	39.48 hrs						80 hrs
Lisa Marks	39.48 hrs									39.48 hrs
Determine budget	8 hrs									8 hrs
Invitation list	16 hrs									16 hrs
Theme	15.48 hrs									15.48 hrs
Intern	32 hrs	39.48 hrs	16 hrs							87.48 hrs
Invitation list	16 hrs									16 hrs
Theme	15.48 hrs									15.48 hrs
Keynote speaker	0.52 hrs	39.48 hrs								40 hrs
Caterer			16 hrs							16 hrs
Office Supplies	1.55 hrs									1.55 hrs
Theme	1.55 hrs									1.55 hrs
Long distance										
Keynote speaker										
Total	124.52 hrs	40 hrs	56 hrs	39.48 hrs						260 hrs

Resource Usage as of Sat 8/16/97
Meeting

Figure 12-33: The Resource Usage report.

Customizing Reports

Project contains some custom reports; in addition to printing these custom reports, you can customize any of the other reports described in this chapter. Click on the Custom category in the Reports dialog box to open the Custom Reports dialog box shown in Figure 12-34.

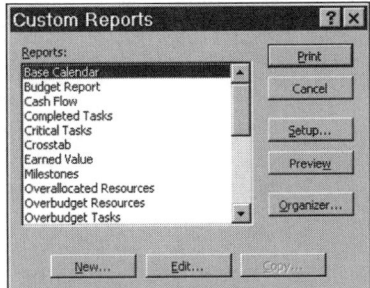

Figure 12-34: The Custom Reports dialog box.

Not all the reports listed in the Custom Reports dialog box are custom reports. But you can print any of the standard reports either from this dialog box or as described earlier in this chapter. However, you must use this dialog box to print the three custom reports.

Note

You can create your own reports by clicking on the New button in the Custom Reports dialog box shown in Figure 12-34. When you define a new custom report, Project offers you four formats. Three formats are based on the reports discussed in this section: the Task report format, the Resource report format, and the Crosstab report format. The fourth format is the Monthly Calendar format, and it functions just like the Working Days report you learned about earlier in this chapter.

Custom reports

Project contains three custom reports:

✦ The Task report

✦ The Resource report

✦ The Crosstab report

Task report

The Task report (see Figure 12-35) shows task information such as the ID number, the task name, indicator icons, the task duration, planned start and finish dates, predecessors, and, if resources have been assigned, resource names.

Task as of Sat 8/16/97
Meeting

ID	O	Task Name	Duration	Start	Finish	Predecessors	Resource Names
4		Determine budget	1 day	Mon 7/14/97	Mon 7/14/97		Joe Johnson,Lisa Marks
5		Invitation list	2 days	Tue 7/15/97	Wed 7/16/97	4	Joe Johnson,Lisa Marks,Int
7	✓	Theme	1.94 days	Thu 7/17/97	Fri 7/18/97	5	Joe Johnson,Lisa Marks,Int
8	✓	Site	0.2 wks	Fri 7/18/97	Mon 7/21/97	7	
9	✓	Keynote speaker	1 wk	Fri 7/18/97	Fri 7/25/97	7	
11		Caterer	2 days	Mon 7/28/97	Tue 7/29/97		Intern,Long distance[0%]
12		Bartenders	1 day	Thu 7/17/97	Thu 7/17/97		Intern
13		Security	2 days	Thu 7/17/97	Fri 7/18/97		
14		Photographer	1 day	Thu 7/17/97	Thu 7/17/97		
15		Cleanup crew	1 day	Thu 7/17/97	Thu 7/17/97		
17		Baseball Game	1 day	Mon 7/14/97	Mon 7/14/97		
18		Opera	4 hrs	Mon 7/14/97	Mon 7/14/97		Joe Johnson
20		Alert community	2 wks	Fri 7/25/97	Fri 8/8/97		Joe Johnson
21		Press release	1 day	Fri 8/8/97	Mon 8/11/97	20	Joe Johnson
23		Rent audiovisual equipment	2 days	Mon 7/14/97	Tue 7/15/97		
24		Rent tables and chairs	1 day	Wed 7/16/97	Wed 7/16/97	23	
26		Menu selection	1 day	Wed 7/30/97	Wed 7/30/97	11	
27		Drink selection	1 day	Thu 7/31/97	Thu 7/31/97	26,12	
29		Transportation for speaker	1 day	Mon 7/14/97	Mon 7/14/97		
30		Event transportation	3 days	Tue 7/15/97	Thu 7/17/97	29	
31		Flowers	4 days	Fri 7/18/97	Wed 7/23/97	30	
32		Table decorations	1 day	Thu 7/24/97	Thu 7/24/97	31	
33		Lighting	1 day	Fri 7/25/97	Fri 7/25/97	32	
35		Buy room decorations	1 day	Mon 8/11/97	Tue 8/12/97		
36		Buy party favors	1 day	Tue 8/12/97	Wed 8/13/97	35	
37		Setup equipment for event	2 days	Wed 8/13/97	Fri 8/15/97	36	
38		Decorate	2 days	Fri 8/15/97	Tue 8/19/97	37	
39	▤	Special Event	5 days	Mon 8/25/97	Fri 8/29/97	38	
41		Cleanup	2 days	Mon 9/1/97	Tue 9/2/97	39	
42		Pay bills	4 days	Wed 9/3/97	Mon 9/8/97	41	
43		Write thank you letters	2 days	Tue 9/9/97	Wed 9/10/97	42	
44		Write event summary	1 day	Thu 9/11/97	Thu 9/11/97	43	
45		Vacation	0 days	Thu 9/11/97	Thu 9/11/97	44	

Figure 12-35: The Task report.

Resource report

As you can see from the report sample shown in Figure 12-36, the Resource report shows resource information: resource ID numbers, indicator icons, resource names, initials, and groups, maximum units, rate information, accrual information, base calendar information, and, if any information exists, work breakdown structure code information. (Refer to the "Earned Value" section earlier in this chapter and Chapter 13.)

ID	ⓞ	Resource Name	Initials	Group	Max. Units	Std. Rate	Ovt. Rate	Cost/Use	Accrue At	Base Calendar	Code
1	✦✦	Joe Johnson	J		100%	$25.00/hr	$30.00/hr	$0.00	Prorated	Standard	
2		Lisa Marks	L		100%	$25.00/hr	$30.00/hr	$0.00	Prorated	Standard	
3		Intern	I		100%	$10.00/hr	$15.00/hr	$0.00	Prorated	Standard	
4		Office Supplies	O		300%	$0.00/hr	$0.00/hr	$2.00	Prorated	Standard	
5		Long distance	L		100%	$0.00/hr	$0.00/hr	$0.00	Prorated	Standard	

Resource as of Sat 8/16/97 — Meeting

Figure 12-36: The Resource report.

Crosstab report

The Crosstab report (see Figure 12-37) is a tabular report that shows task and resource information in rows and time increments in columns.

Crosstab as of Sat 8/16/97 Meeting	7/13	7/20	7/27	8/3	8/10	8/17	8/24	8/31	9/7
Conference									
Pre-planning									
Initial planning meetings									
Determine budget	$400.00								
Joe Johnson	$200.00								
Lisa Marks	$200.00								
Invitation list	$960.00								
Joe Johnson	$400.00								
Lisa Marks	$400.00								
Intern	$160.00								
Selection									
Theme	$1,129.24								
Joe Johnson	$387.10								
Lisa Marks	$387.10								
Intern	$154.84								
Office Supplies	$0.20								
Site		$1,000.00							
Keynote speaker	$55.17	$394.83							
Intern	$5.17	$394.83							
Long distance	$50.00								
Hire									
Caterer			$160.00						
Intern			$160.00						
Bartenders									
Security									
Photographer									
Cleanup crew									
Plan Entertainment Events									
Baseball Game	$200.00								
Joe Johnson	$200.00								
Opera	$100.00								
Joe Johnson	$100.00								
Public relations									
Alert community		$12.92	$1,000.00	$987.08					
Joe Johnson		$12.92	$1,000.00	$987.08					
Press release									
Rent Equipment									
Rent audiovisual equipment									
Rent tables and chairs									
Meet with Caterer									
Menu selection									
Drink selection									
Arrangements									

Figure 12-37: The Crosstab report.

Tip Much of the information on the Crosstab report also appears on the Task Usage report and the Resource Usage report. These reports give you more formatting options, such as the period covered by the report and the table used in the report.

Customizing an existing report

You can customize almost every report we've seen in this chapter. For a few reports, like the Working Days report, the only item you can change is the font information Project uses to print the report. For other reports, however, you can change the table or the task or resource filter to change the content of the report. Click on the Edit button when preparing to print the report to make these changes. When you click on the Edit button, Project opens the dialog box that relates to the report you selected. For example, if you select the Working Days report and then click on Edit in the Overview Reports dialog box, Project opens the Report Text dialog box shown in Figure 12-38. (The Report Text dialog box is covering the Edit button.)

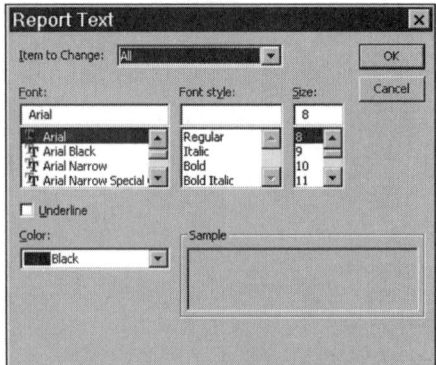

Figure 12-38: Use the Report Text dialog box to change the fonts report items.

Similarly, if you select the Tasks Starting Soon report and then click on Edit, Project opens the Definition tab of the Task Report dialog box in Figure 12-39.

From the Details tab (see Figure 12-40), select the information you want included on the report. You might want to display predecessors for tasks or place a grid line between details.

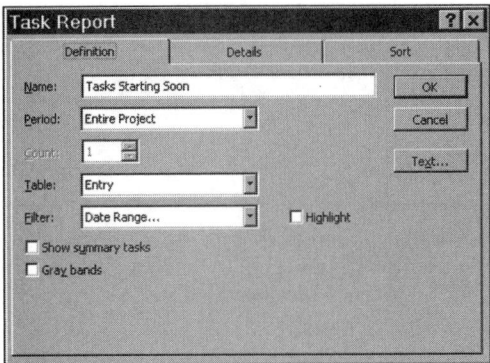

Figure 12-39: Use the Definition tab to change the report's filter or table.

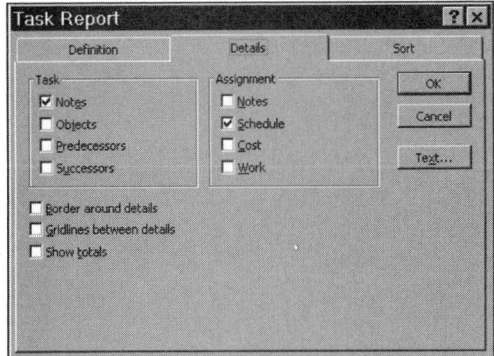

Figure 12-40: Use the Details tab to specify the information you want to include on the report.

From the Sort tab shown in Figure 12-41, select the sort orders for the report.

Remember that the type of report you select initially determines the dialog box you see when you click on Edit in the report's category dialog box (for example, the Overview Reports dialog box or the Cost Reports dialog box). In addition to the dialog boxes you've seen here, you may also see the Resource Report dialog box or the Crosstab Report dialog box, both of which contain slightly different options (primarily on the Definitions tab) than the Task Report dialog box. For example, when you edit the Who Does What report before printing it, Project opens a Resource Report dialog box. On the Definitions tab of this dialog box, you can select filters related to resources, whereas the filters in the Task Report dialog box pertain to tasks. Or if you edit the Cash Flow report before printing it, Project opens a Crosstab Report dialog box from which you can select the information you want to appear on each row; the default information is Tasks and Cost.

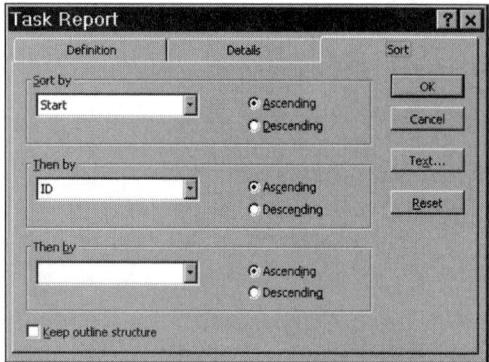

Figure 12-41: Select a sort order for the report.

Summary

In this chapter you learned how to produce reports in Project, and you examined samples of the reports available in each of Project's six report categories:

✦ Overview

✦ Current Activities

✦ Costs

✦ Assignments

✦ Workload

✦ Custom

In addition, you've learned how to customize any standard report in Project. The next chapter shows you how to analyze your project's progress.

✦   ✦   ✦

Analyzing Financial Progress

When you analyze the progress of your project, you must measure not only the progress of the schedule but also the progress based on the costs you incur. In Microsoft Project you measure the earned value of your project.

Understanding Earned Value

Earned value is the measure project managers use to evaluate the progress of a project based on the cost of work performed up to the project status date. When Project calculates earned value, it compares your original cost estimates to the actual work performed to show whether your project is on budget. You can think of earned value as a measure that indicates how much of the budget should have been spent when you compare the cost of the work that has been done so far to the baseline cost for the task, resource, or assignment.

To work with and use earned value information effectively, you must first:

1. Save a baseline for your project
2. Assign resources with costs to tasks in your project
3. Complete some work on your project

Using earned value tables to analyze costs

Project contains a series of earned value fields and two earned value tables that you can use to compare your expected costs with your actual costs. *Earned value fields* are currency fields that either appear on or can be added to the earned value tables; earned value fields measure various aspects of earned value.

The two earned value tables — Earned Value for Tasks and Earned Value for Resources — help you evaluate the relationship between work and costs. You can use the earned value tables to forecast whether a task will finish within the budget, based on the comparison of the actual costs incurred for the task to date and the baseline cost of the task.

Understanding earned value fields

The fields that appear as headings in the Earned Value report you saw in Chapter 12 also appear on earned value tables. The following table translates the acronyms Project uses to represent the earned value fields.

Earned Value Fields	
BCWS	Budgeted Cost of Work Scheduled
BCWP	Budgeted Cost of Work Performed
ACWP	Actual Cost of Work Performed
SV	Schedule Variance
CV	Cost Variance
BAC	Budgeted At Completion
EAC	Estimate At Completion
VAC	Variance At Completion

BCWS, BCWP, ACWP, SV, and CV are all calculated through today or through the project status date. SV represents the cost difference between current progress and the baseline plan, and Project calculates this value as BCWP minus BCWS. CV represents the cost difference between actual costs and planned costs at the current level of completion, and Project calculates this value as BCWP minus ACWP. EAC shows the planned costs based on costs already incurred plus additional planned costs. VAC represents the variance between the baseline cost and the combination of actual plus planned costs for a task.

Project uses BCWS, BCWP, ACWP, SV, and CV as task fields, resource fields, and assignment fields; Project also uses timephased versions of each field. BAC, EAC, and VAC, however, are task fields only.

Using the Earned Value table for tasks

When you use the Earned Value table for tasks, you can compare the relationship between work and costs for tasks. This table helps you evaluate your budget to estimate future budget needs and prepare an accounting statement of your project. You can use the information in the table to determine whether the work is getting done for the money you're paying or whether tasks need more money, less money, or perhaps should be cut. That is, the information in the Earned Value table helps you assess whether the money you're spending on a task is enough money, too much money, too little money, or perhaps wasted money.

To display the Earned Value table for tasks, start in any task view. You can get to the table in Figure 13-1, for example, by starting with the Task Sheet view. Right-click on the Select All button and choose More Tables from the shortcut menu. In the More Tables dialog box, select Earned Value and click on Apply.

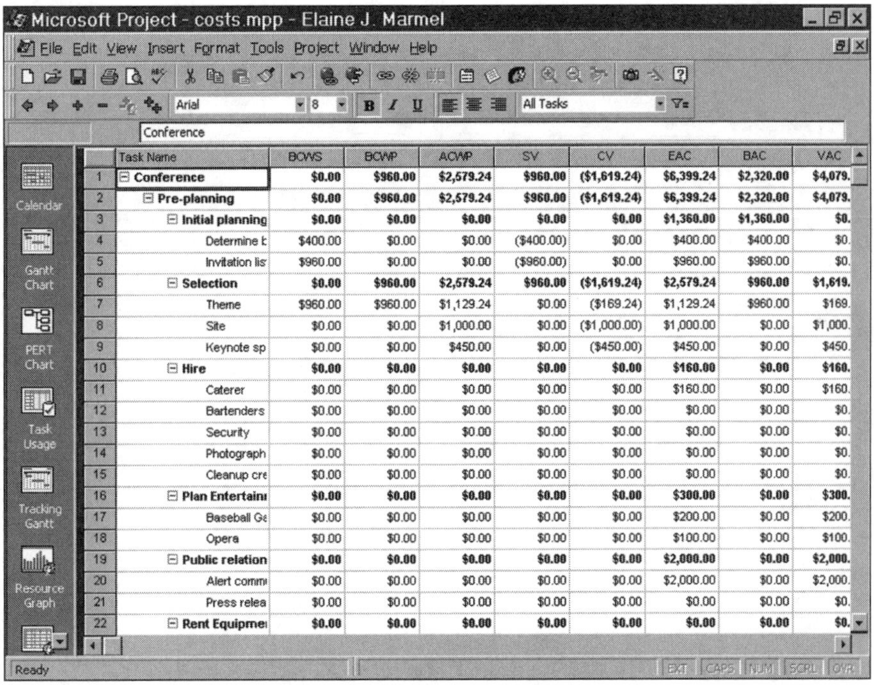

	Task Name	BCWS	BCWP	ACWP	SV	CV	EAC	BAC	VAC
1	**Conference**	**$0.00**	**$960.00**	**$2,579.24**	**$960.00**	**($1,619.24)**	**$6,399.24**	**$2,320.00**	**$4,079.**
2	**Pre-planning**	**$0.00**	**$960.00**	**$2,579.24**	**$960.00**	**($1,619.24)**	**$6,399.24**	**$2,320.00**	**$4,079.**
3	**Initial planning**	**$0.00**	**$0.00**	**$0.00**	**$0.00**	**$0.00**	**$1,360.00**	**$1,360.00**	**$0.**
4	Determine b	$400.00	$0.00	$0.00	($400.00)	$0.00	$400.00	$400.00	$0.
5	Invitation lis	$960.00	$0.00	$0.00	($960.00)	$0.00	$960.00	$960.00	$0.
6	**Selection**	**$0.00**	**$960.00**	**$2,579.24**	**$960.00**	**($1,619.24)**	**$2,579.24**	**$960.00**	**$1,619.**
7	Theme	$960.00	$960.00	$1,129.24	$0.00	($169.24)	$1,129.24	$960.00	$169.
8	Site	$0.00	$0.00	$1,000.00	$0.00	($1,000.00)	$1,000.00	$0.00	$1,000.
9	Keynote sp	$0.00	$0.00	$450.00	$0.00	($450.00)	$450.00	$0.00	$450.
10	**Hire**	**$0.00**	**$0.00**	**$0.00**	**$0.00**	**$0.00**	**$160.00**	**$0.00**	**$160.**
11	Caterer	$0.00	$0.00	$0.00	$0.00	$0.00	$160.00	$0.00	$160.
12	Bartenders	$0.00	$0.00	$0.00	$0.00	$0.00	$0.00	$0.00	$0.
13	Security	$0.00	$0.00	$0.00	$0.00	$0.00	$0.00	$0.00	$0.
14	Photograph	$0.00	$0.00	$0.00	$0.00	$0.00	$0.00	$0.00	$0.
15	Cleanup cre	$0.00	$0.00	$0.00	$0.00	$0.00	$0.00	$0.00	$0.
16	**Plan Entertain**	**$0.00**	**$0.00**	**$0.00**	**$0.00**	**$0.00**	**$300.00**	**$0.00**	**$300.**
17	Baseball Ga	$0.00	$0.00	$0.00	$0.00	$0.00	$200.00	$0.00	$200.
18	Opera	$0.00	$0.00	$0.00	$0.00	$0.00	$100.00	$0.00	$100.
19	**Public relation**	**$0.00**	**$0.00**	**$0.00**	**$0.00**	**$0.00**	**$2,000.00**	**$0.00**	**$2,000.**
20	Alert comm	$0.00	$0.00	$0.00	$0.00	$0.00	$2,000.00	$0.00	$2,000.
21	Press relea	$0.00	$0.00	$0.00	$0.00	$0.00	$0.00	$0.00	$0.
22	**Rent Equipme**	**$0.00**	**$0.00**	**$0.00**	**$0.00**	**$0.00**	**$0.00**	**$0.00**	**$0.**

Figure 13-1: The Earned Value table for tasks.

All the fields on this sheet are calculated except EAC and BAC — you can type values in those fields to change information in the table.

Using the Earned Value table for resources

When you use the Earned Value table for resources, you can compare the relationship between work and costs for resources. This table also helps you evaluate your budget to estimate future budget needs and prepare an accounting statement of your project. You can use the information in the table to determine whether the work is getting done for the money you're paying or whether you need more or less of a particular resource.

To display the Earned Value table for resources, follow these steps:

1. Start in any resource view, such as the Resource Sheet view.

2. Right-click on the Select All button and choose More Tables from the shortcut menu that appears.

3. Select Earned Value in the More Tables dialog box, and click on Apply. Your screen will look similar to the one you see in Figure 13-2.

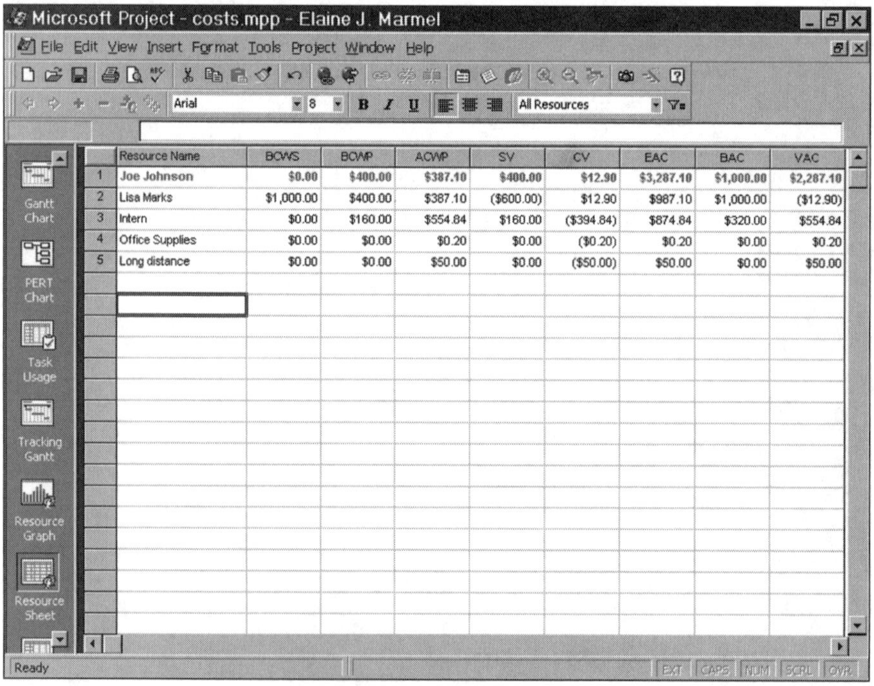

Figure 13-2: The Earned Value table for resources.

All the fields on this sheet are calculated except BAC — you can type values in this field to change information in the table.

Setting the date for earned value calculations

By default, Project uses today's date to calculate earned value information. But you can set a project status date for Project to use instead of today's date when it calculates earned value. From any view choose Project⇨Project Information to open the Project Information dialog box (see Figure 13-3).

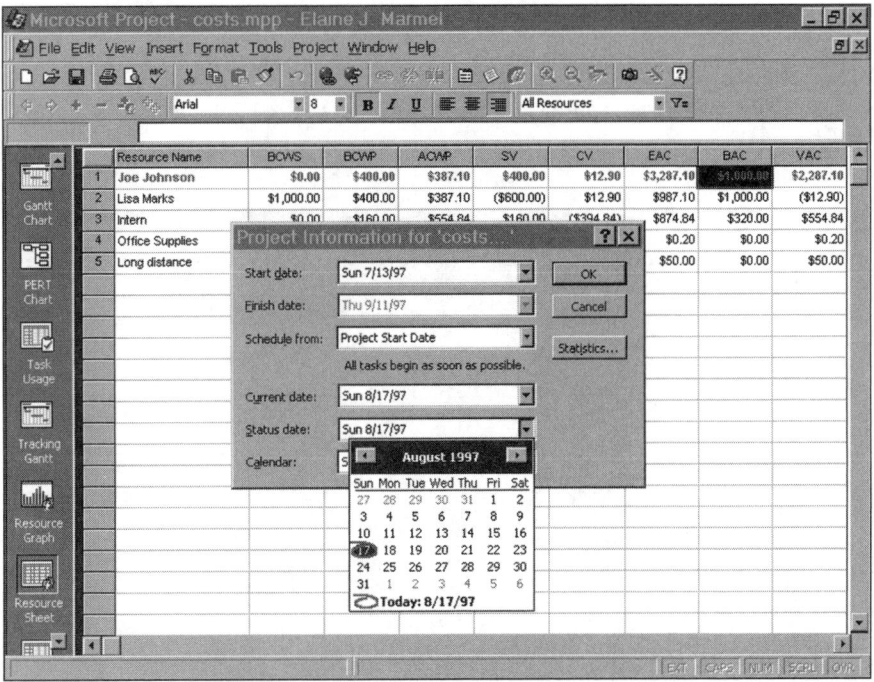

Figure 13-3: Use this dialog box to set a date for Project to use when calculating earned value.

Open the Status date list box, select the date you want Project to use when it calculates earned value, and click on OK.

Evaluating Cost Information

If you own Microsoft Excel, you can use it to help you evaluate cost information. By exporting information to Excel, you can chart earned value, analyze timescaled information, or create pivot tables.

Charting earned value

The saying goes: A picture is worth a thousand words. And when looking at earned value information, you might find it easier to understand the information if you use a picture rather than study Project's Earned Value tables. You can export the earned value information to Microsoft Excel (you must be using Excel version 5.0 or later) and then use Excel's ChartWizard to create charts of earned value information.

To learn more about Project's capabilities to export and import data, see Chapter 18.

When you export earned values from Project to Excel, you create an Excel workbook that contains each task ID, name, and the various earned values for each task (see Figure 13-4).

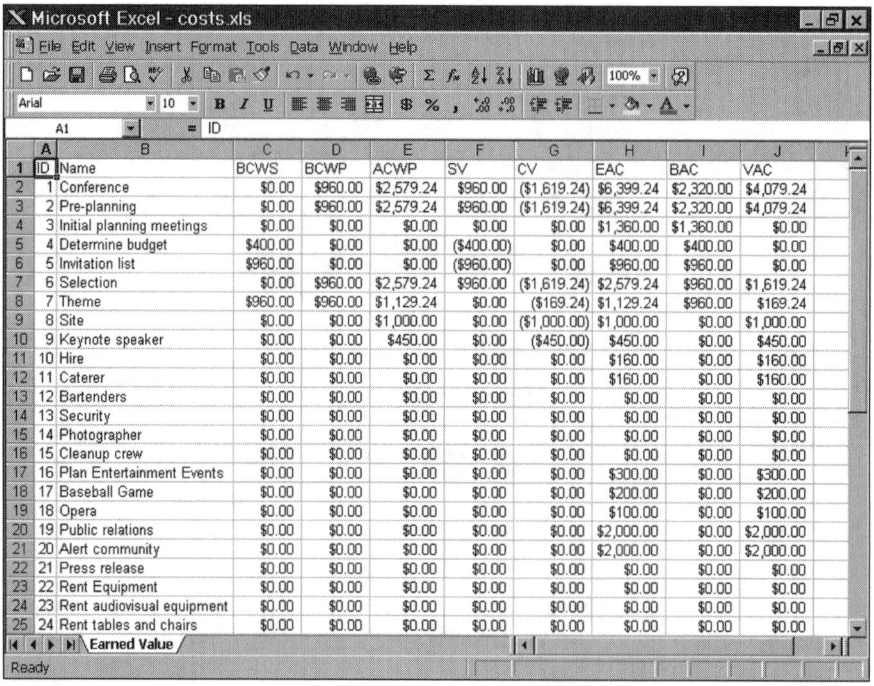

	A	B	C	D	E	F	G	H	I	J
1	ID	Name	BCWS	BCWP	ACWP	SV	CV	EAC	BAC	VAC
2	1	Conference	$0.00	$960.00	$2,579.24	$960.00	($1,619.24)	$6,399.24	$2,320.00	$4,079.24
3	2	Pre-planning	$0.00	$960.00	$2,579.24	$960.00	($1,619.24)	$6,399.24	$2,320.00	$4,079.24
4	3	Initial planning meetings	$0.00	$0.00	$0.00	$0.00	$0.00	$1,360.00	$1,360.00	$0.00
5	4	Determine budget	$400.00	$0.00	$0.00	($400.00)	$0.00	$400.00	$400.00	$0.00
6	5	Invitation list	$960.00	$0.00	$0.00	($960.00)	$0.00	$960.00	$960.00	$0.00
7	6	Selection	$0.00	$960.00	$2,579.24	$960.00	($1,619.24)	$2,579.24	$960.00	$1,619.24
8	7	Theme	$960.00	$960.00	$1,129.24	$0.00	($169.24)	$1,129.24	$960.00	$169.24
9	8	Site	$0.00	$0.00	$1,000.00	$0.00	($1,000.00)	$1,000.00	$0.00	$1,000.00
10	9	Keynote speaker	$0.00	$0.00	$450.00	$0.00	($450.00)	$450.00	$0.00	$450.00
11	10	Hire	$0.00	$0.00	$0.00	$0.00	$0.00	$160.00	$0.00	$160.00
12	11	Caterer	$0.00	$0.00	$0.00	$0.00	$0.00	$160.00	$0.00	$160.00
13	12	Bartenders	$0.00	$0.00	$0.00	$0.00	$0.00	$0.00	$0.00	$0.00
14	13	Security	$0.00	$0.00	$0.00	$0.00	$0.00	$0.00	$0.00	$0.00
15	14	Photographer	$0.00	$0.00	$0.00	$0.00	$0.00	$0.00	$0.00	$0.00
16	15	Cleanup crew	$0.00	$0.00	$0.00	$0.00	$0.00	$0.00	$0.00	$0.00
17	16	Plan Entertainment Events	$0.00	$0.00	$0.00	$0.00	$0.00	$300.00	$0.00	$300.00
18	17	Baseball Game	$0.00	$0.00	$0.00	$0.00	$0.00	$200.00	$0.00	$200.00
19	18	Opera	$0.00	$0.00	$0.00	$0.00	$0.00	$100.00	$0.00	$100.00
20	19	Public relations	$0.00	$0.00	$0.00	$0.00	$0.00	$2,000.00	$0.00	$2,000.00
21	20	Alert community	$0.00	$0.00	$0.00	$0.00	$0.00	$2,000.00	$0.00	$2,000.00
22	21	Press release	$0.00	$0.00	$0.00	$0.00	$0.00	$0.00	$0.00	$0.00
23	22	Rent Equipment	$0.00	$0.00	$0.00	$0.00	$0.00	$0.00	$0.00	$0.00
24	23	Rent audiovisual equipment	$0.00	$0.00	$0.00	$0.00	$0.00	$0.00	$0.00	$0.00
25	24	Rent tables and chairs	$0.00	$0.00	$0.00	$0.00	$0.00	$0.00	$0.00	$0.00

Figure 13-4: An Excel workbook created by exporting earned value information from Project to Excel.

To create an Excel workbook like the one you see in Figure 13-4, follow these steps:

1. Choose File⇨Save As to open the File Save dialog box.

2. Type a name for the Excel workbook in the File Name list box. Don't worry about the extension; Project supplies it.

3. Open the Save as type list box and select Microsoft Excel Workbook. The File Save dialog box should resemble Figure 13-5.

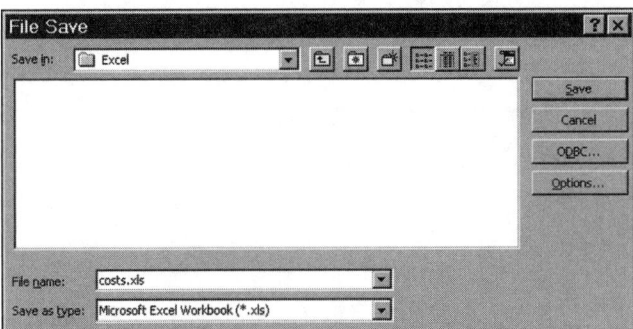

Figure 13-5: The File Save dialog box after you choose to save an Excel workbook file.

4. Click on Save to open the Export Format dialog box you see in Figure 13-6.

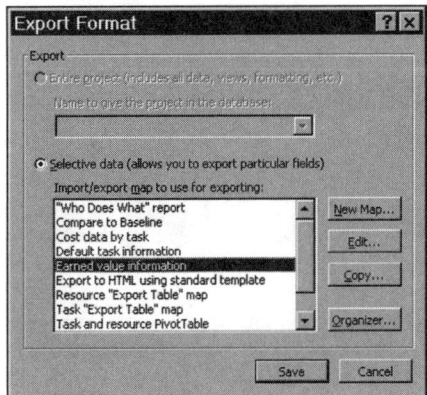

Figure 13-6: The Export Format dialog box.

5. Select Earned value information as the map to use for exporting.

6. Click on Save. Project saves your workbook in the folder you specified.

Open Microsoft Excel and then choose File⇨Open to open the workbook you just created. You can use Excel's ChartWizard to create as many charts from this data as you want. For example, the chart in Figure 13-7 shows all earned values for one task, and the chart in Figure 13-8 shows one earned value for selected tasks.

Note

If your project is small, you might be able to chart one earned value for all tasks, but if your project is large, Excel might display an error message if you try to chart one earned value for all tasks.

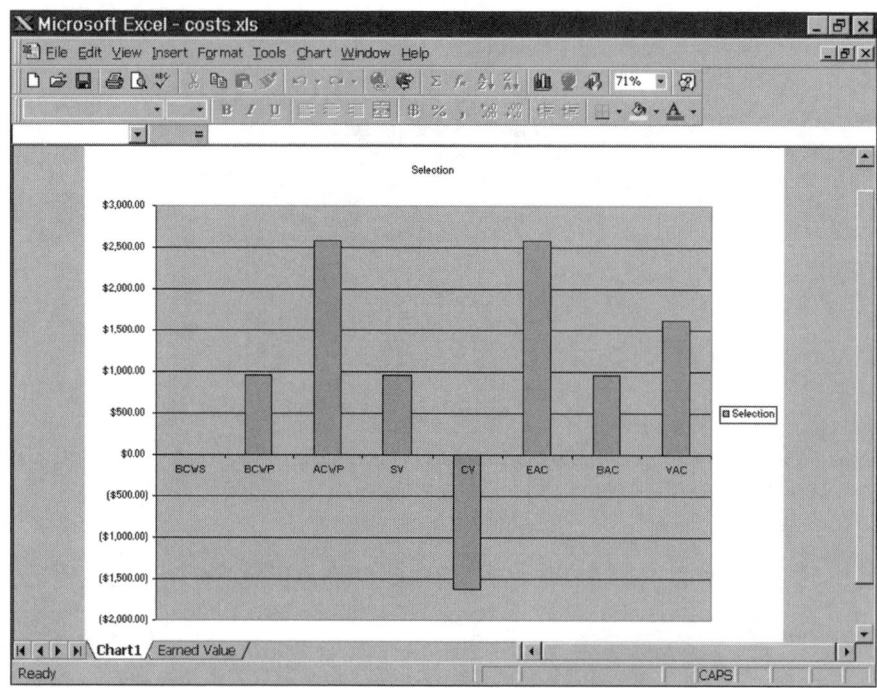

Figure 13-7: An Excel chart of all earned values for one task.

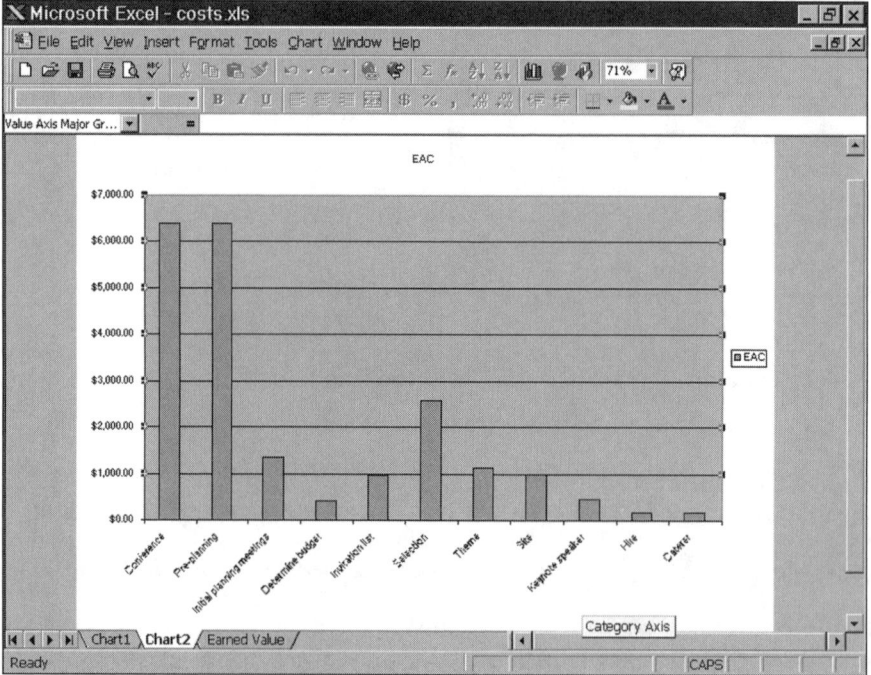

Figure 13-8: An Excel chart of one earned value for selected tasks.

To create a chart like the one in Figure 13-7 in Excel, follow these steps:

1. Click on the ChartWizard button on the Standard toolbar to start the ChartWizard. In the first ChartWizard dialog box, select the type of chart you want to create.

2. Click on Next to open the second ChartWizard dialog box (see Figure 13-9). In this dialog box, select Rows for the Series in option.

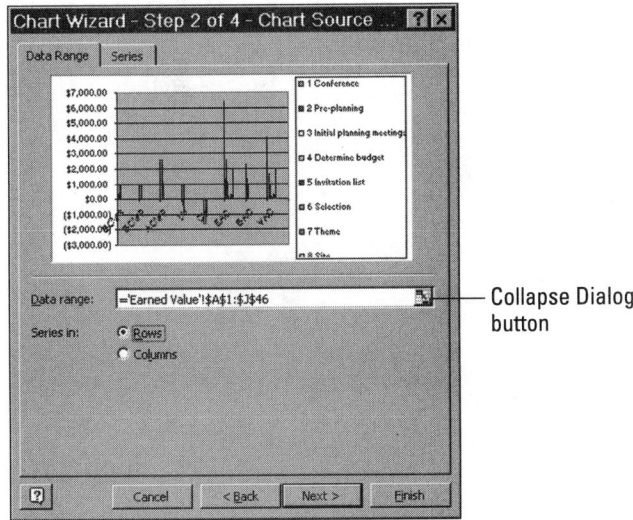

Figure 13-9: Chart the data by rows.

3. Click on the Collapse Dialog button at the right edge of the Data Range box to hide the ChartWizard so that you can select the task you want to chart from the worksheet.

4. Highlight (by dragging) the cells in the row containing the information you want to chart (see Figure 13-10).

Tip

Your chart will be more meaningful if you omit column A, which contains the task ID number.

5. Click on the Collapse Dialog button to redisplay the ChartWizard.

6. Click on the Series tab.

7. Click on the Collapse Dialog button to the right of the Category (X) axis labels box.

8. Select the headings in row 1 that contain the labels for the earned value fields. Your selection will probably include cells C1 through J1.

9. Click on the Collapse Dialog button to redisplay the ChartWizard. The Series tab should look similar to the one in Figure 13-11.

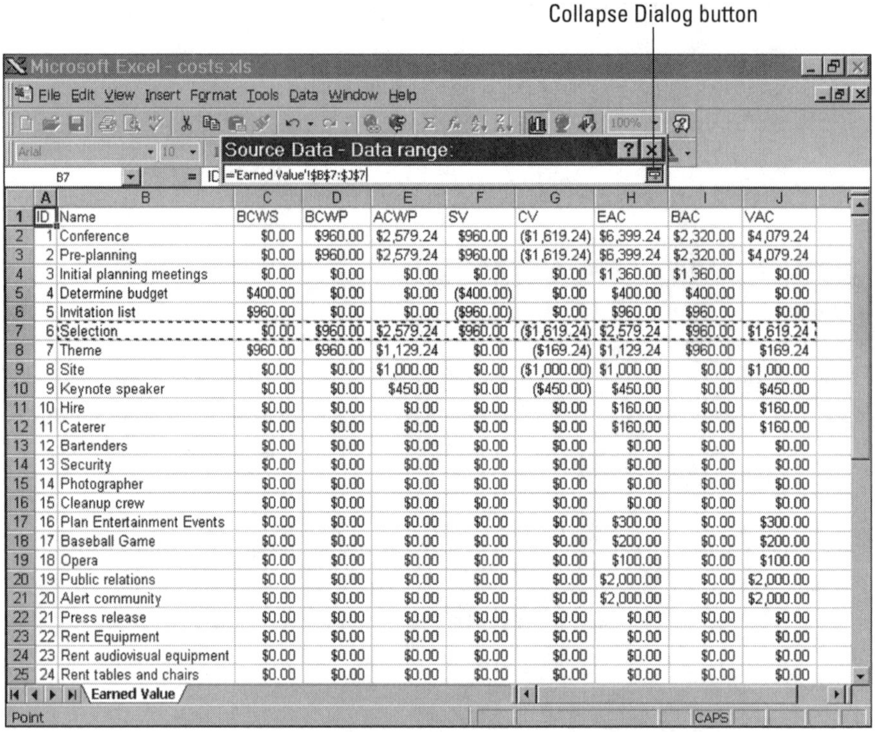

Collapse Dialog button

	A	B	C	D	E	F	G	H	I	J	
1	ID	Name	BCWS	BCWP	ACWP	SV	CV	EAC	BAC	VAC	
2	1	Conference	$0.00	$960.00	$2,579.24	$960.00	($1,619.24)	$6,399.24	$2,320.00	$4,079.24	
3	2	Pre-planning	$0.00	$960.00	$2,579.24	$960.00	($1,619.24)	$6,399.24	$2,320.00	$4,079.24	
4	3	Initial planning meetings	$0.00	$0.00	$0.00	$0.00	$0.00	$1,360.00	$1,360.00	$0.00	
5	4	Determine budget	$400.00	$0.00	$0.00	($400.00)	$0.00	$400.00	$400.00	$0.00	
6	5	Invitation list	$960.00	$0.00	$0.00	($960.00)	$0.00	$960.00	$960.00	$0.00	
7	6	Selection	$0.00	$960.00	$2,579.24	$960.00	($1,619.24)	$2,579.24	$960.00	$1,619.24	
8	7	Theme	$960.00	$960.00	$1,129.24	$0.00	($169.24)	$1,129.24	$960.00	$169.24	
9	8	Site	$0.00	$0.00	$1,000.00	$0.00	($1,000.00)	$1,000.00	$0.00	$1,000.00	
10	9	Keynote speaker	$0.00	$0.00	$450.00	$0.00	($450.00)	$450.00	$0.00	$450.00	
11	10	Hire	$0.00	$0.00	$0.00	$0.00	$0.00	$160.00	$0.00	$160.00	
12	11	Caterer	$0.00	$0.00	$0.00	$0.00	$0.00	$160.00	$0.00	$160.00	
13	12	Bartenders	$0.00	$0.00	$0.00	$0.00	$0.00	$0.00	$0.00	$0.00	
14	13	Security	$0.00	$0.00	$0.00	$0.00	$0.00	$0.00	$0.00	$0.00	
15	14	Photographer	$0.00	$0.00	$0.00	$0.00	$0.00	$0.00	$0.00	$0.00	
16	15	Cleanup crew	$0.00	$0.00	$0.00	$0.00	$0.00	$0.00	$0.00	$0.00	
17	16	Plan Entertainment Events	$0.00	$0.00	$0.00	$0.00	$0.00	$300.00	$0.00	$300.00	
18	17	Baseball Game	$0.00	$0.00	$0.00	$0.00	$0.00	$200.00	$0.00	$200.00	
19	18	Opera	$0.00	$0.00	$0.00	$0.00	$0.00	$100.00	$0.00	$100.00	
20	19	Public relations	$0.00	$0.00	$0.00	$0.00	$0.00	$2,000.00	$0.00	$2,000.00	
21	20	Alert community	$0.00	$0.00	$0.00	$0.00	$0.00	$2,000.00	$0.00	$2,000.00	
22	21	Press release	$0.00	$0.00	$0.00	$0.00	$0.00	$0.00	$0.00	$0.00	
23	22	Rent Equipment	$0.00	$0.00	$0.00	$0.00	$0.00	$0.00	$0.00	$0.00	
24	23	Rent audiovisual equipment	$0.00	$0.00	$0.00	$0.00	$0.00	$0.00	$0.00	$0.00	
25	24	Rent tables and chairs	$0.00	$0.00	$0.00	$0.00	$0.00	$0.00	$0.00	$0.00	

Source Data - Data range: ='Earned Value'!$B$7:$J$7

Figure 13-10: Select the cells containing the data you want to chart.

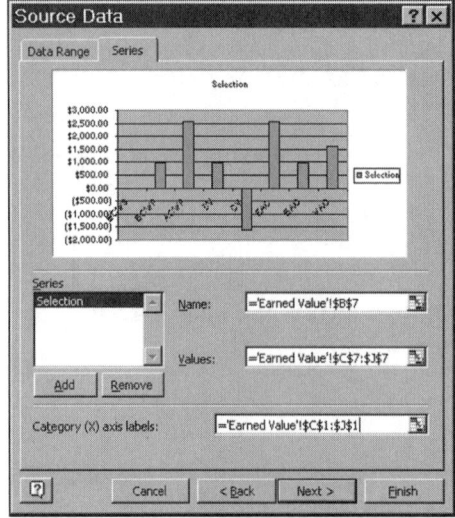

Figure 13-11: The Series tab after selecting X-axis labels.

10. Click on Next and fill in the other dialog boxes for the ChartWizard.

When you finish, your chart should resemble the chart in Figure 13-7, which displays all earned values for one task.

To create the chart in Figure 13-8, use the ChartWizard again and, in the second ChartWizard dialog box, use the following settings:

✦ On the Data Range tab select Columns for the Series in option. For the Data Range, select the cells containing the earned value information you want to chart.

✦ On the Series tab select the cells containing the task names (cells in column B in the pictured worksheet) for Set the Category (X) Axis Labels box.

Analyzing timescaled information

Project contains a wizard that helps you chart timescaled earned value data. You can use the Analyze Timescaled Data Wizard to automatically create a chart in Microsoft Excel of earned value information for the entire project. The chart you get when you complete the wizard looks similar to the one in Figure 13-12.

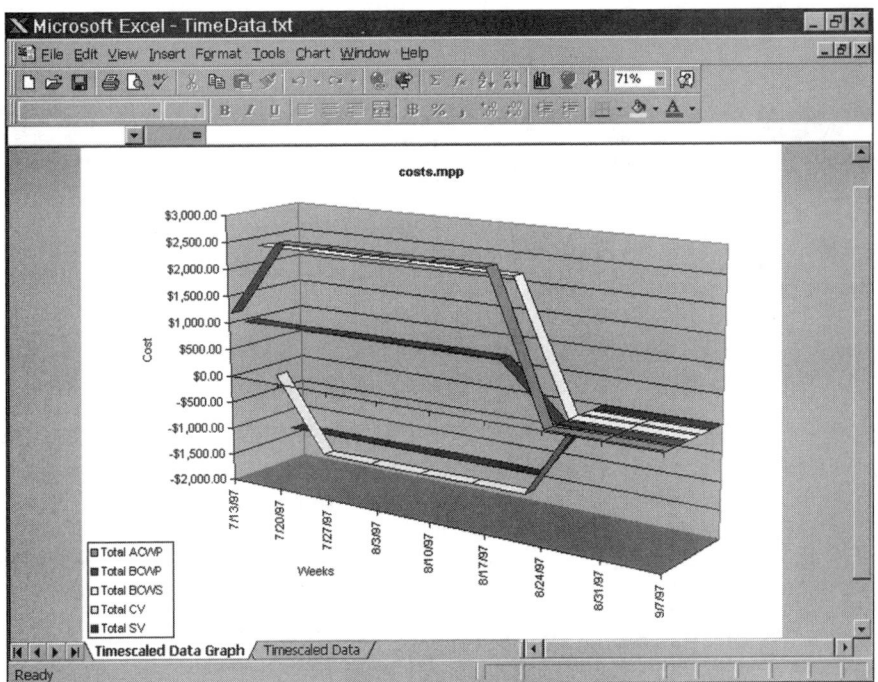

Figure 13-12: A chart of earned values created in Excel by using the Analyze Timescaled Data Wizard in Project.

To use the Timescaled Data Wizard in Project, follow these steps:

1. Click on the Gantt Chart icon in the View bar.

Tip

If you want to chart data for selected tasks, select them now.

2. Choose View➪Toolbars➪Analysis. Project displays the Analysis toolbar (see Figure 13-13).

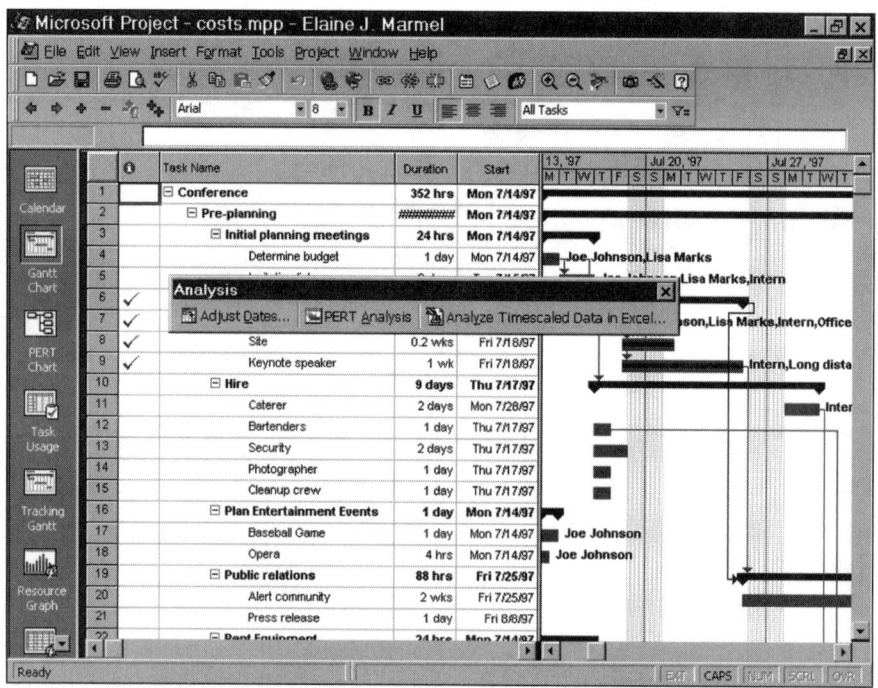

Figure 13-13: The Analysis toolbar.

3. Click on the Analyze Timescaled Data in Excel button. Project opens the first of five Analyze Timescaled Data Wizard dialog boxes (see Figure 13-14).

4. Select either Entire Project or Currently selected tasks and then click on Next to open the Step 2 dialog box.

5. Select the appropriate earned value fields from the Available fields list; click on Add to move the fields to the Fields to export list. Highlight the Work field in the Fields to export and click on the Remove button (see Figure 13-15). Click on Next.

6. Select the date range and time increments you want to use. The default time increment is days, but in Figure 13-16, I selected Weeks. Click on Next to open Step 4.

Figure 13-14: The first dialog box of the Analyze Timescaled Data Wizard.

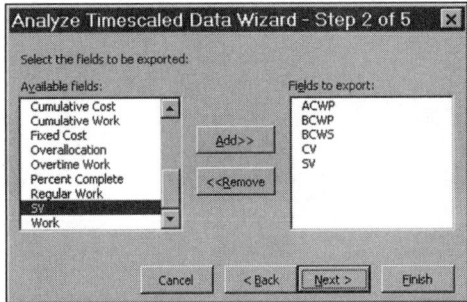

Figure 13-15: Select fields to export to Excel.

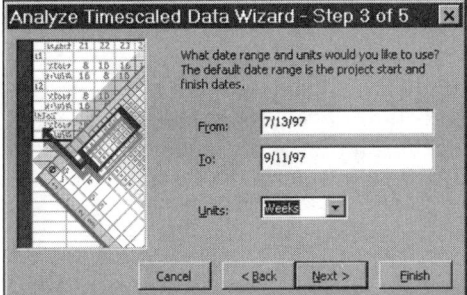

Figure 13-16: Select the date range and time increments for which you want to export data.

7. Select Yes, please if you want to graph the data. Otherwise, select No, thanks (see Figure 13-17). Click on Next to open the wizard's final dialog box.

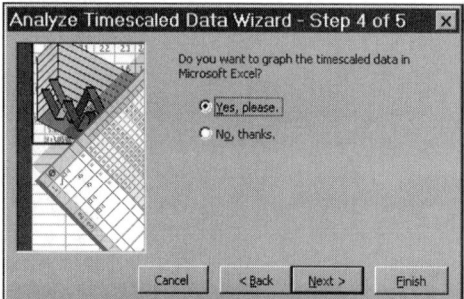

Figure 13-17: Tell Project whether or not to graph the data.

8. Click on Export Data to export the Project data into Microsoft Excel (see Figure 13-18).

Figure 13-18: Finish the process by exporting your data to Excel.

Excel starts up, processes your data, and then displays a chart similar to the one in Figure 13-12 at the beginning of this section. Excel also creates a worksheet in the workbook that you can view by clicking on the Timescaled Data tab (see Figure 13-19). The worksheet contains the earned value information that Excel used to create the chart in Figure 3-12.

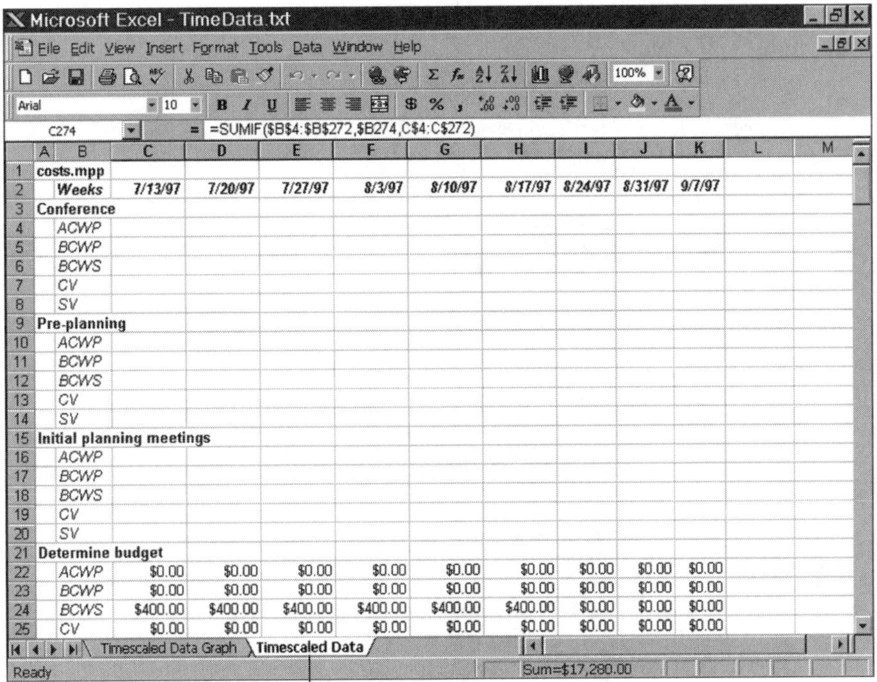

Figure 13-19: The worksheet Excel uses to create the chart.

Using PivotTables for analysis

Excel PivotTables are interesting tools to use when you want to analyze Project earned value data. The *PivotTable* is an interactive table that summarizes large amounts of data is a cross-tabular format. When you use Project to create a PivotTable in Excel, you get two PivotTables in the same workbook: a Task PivotTable and a Resource PivotTable. The Task PivotTable shows resources, tasks to which the resources are assigned, and costs for the resource per task. The Resource PivotTable summarizes resources by showing work assigned to each resource and the total cost of each resource. In addition to the PivotTable worksheets, the same Excel workbook also includes two worksheets that Excel uses to create these two PivotTables; their names are Tasks and Resources. To export Project information to create PivotTables in Excel, follow these steps:

1. Start in any view of your project.

2. Choose File⇨Save As to open the File Save dialog box.

3. Type a name for the Excel workbook you want to create in the File name box. Don't worry about the extension; Project supplies it.

4. Select Microsoft Excel PivotTable from the Save as type list box.

5. Click on Save to open the Export Format dialog box (see Figure 13-20).

6. Select Task and resource PivotTable and click on Save.

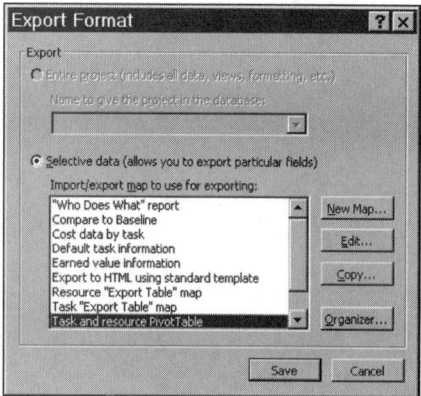

Figure 13-20: The Export Format dialog box.

You'll see the hourglass icon for the mouse pointer, indicating you should wait while action takes place. You'll also hear action on your hard disk. To view the PivotTables and their source data, start Excel and open the file you just created. The workbook contains four sheets that should resemble the sheets in Figures 13-21, 13-22, 13-23, and 13-24.

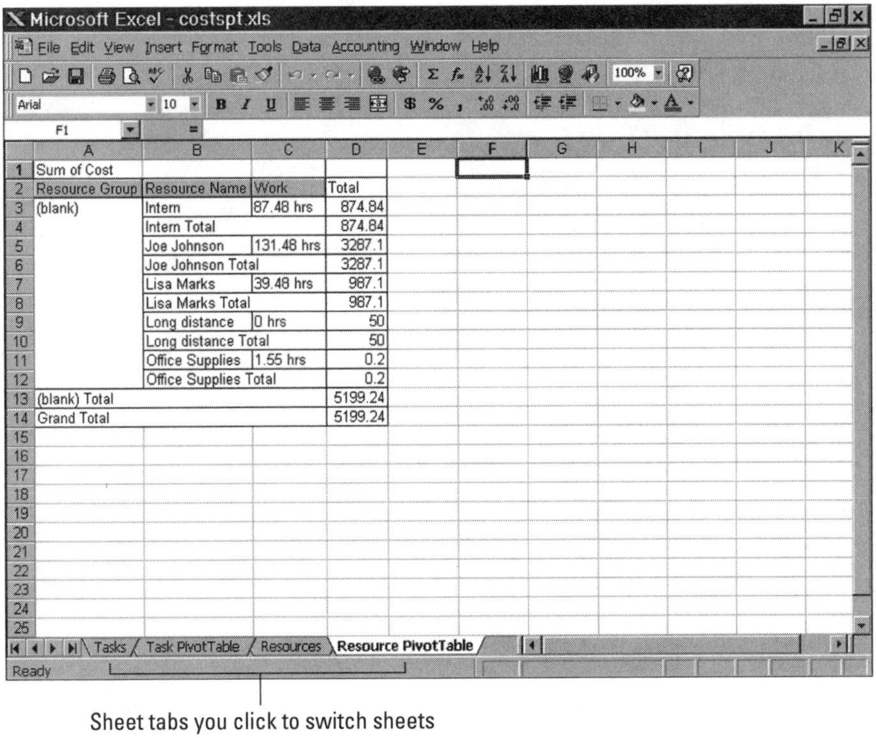

Sheet tabs you click to switch sheets

Figure 13-21: The Resource PivotTable.

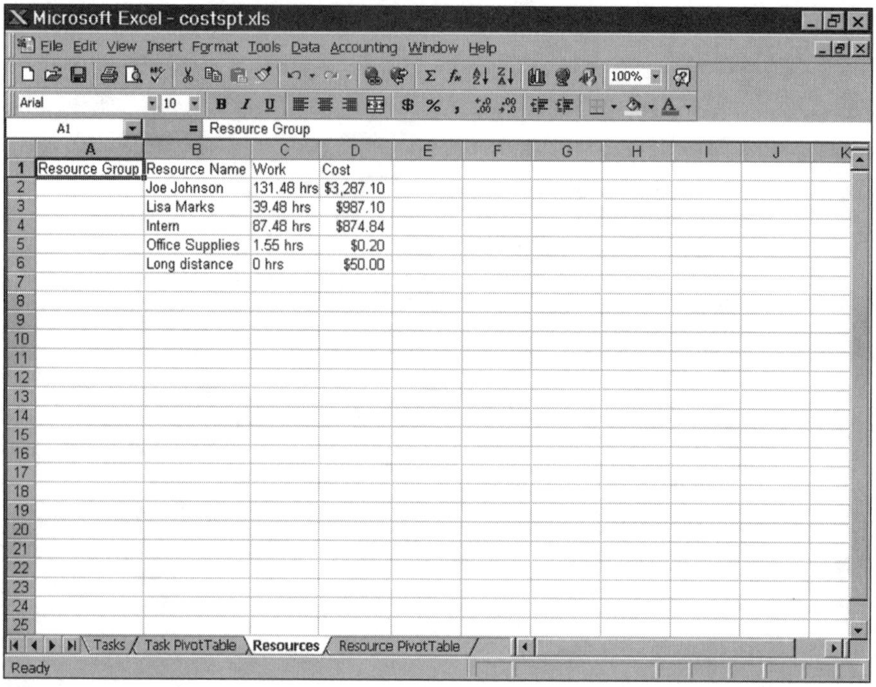

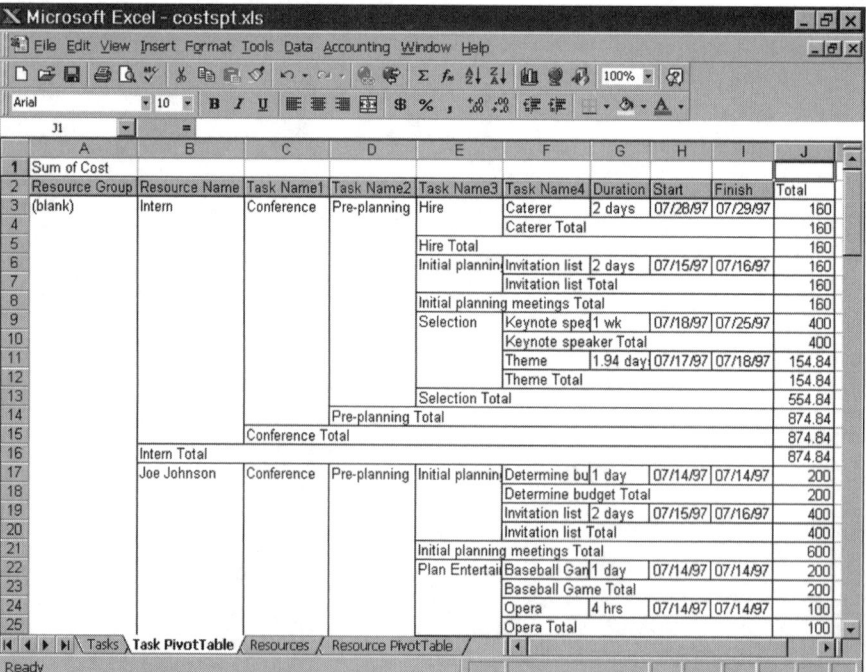

Figure 13-22: The Resources sheet that Excel used to create the Resource PivotTable.

Figure 13-23: The Task PivotTable.

	A	B	C	D	E	F	G	H	I	J
1	Resource G	Resource Name	Task Name1	Task Name2	Task Name3	Task Name4	Duration	Start	Finish	Cost
2		Joe Johnson	Conference	Pre-planning	Initial planning	Determine bu	1 day	07/14/97	07/14/97	$200.00
3		Lisa Marks	Conference	Pre-planning	Initial planning	Determine bu	1 day	07/14/97	07/14/97	$200.00
4		Joe Johnson	Conference	Pre-planning	Initial planning	Invitation list	2 days	07/15/97	07/16/97	$400.00
5		Lisa Marks	Conference	Pre-planning	Initial planning	Invitation list	2 days	07/15/97	07/16/97	$400.00
6		Intern	Conference	Pre-planning	Initial planning	Invitation list	2 days	07/15/97	07/16/97	$160.00
7		Joe Johnson	Conference	Pre-planning	Selection	Theme	1.94 days	07/17/97	07/18/97	$387.10
8		Lisa Marks	Conference	Pre-planning	Selection	Theme	1.94 days	07/17/97	07/18/97	$387.10
9		Intern	Conference	Pre-planning	Selection	Theme	1.94 days	07/17/97	07/18/97	$154.84
10		Office Supplies	Conference	Pre-planning	Selection	Theme	1.94 days	07/17/97	07/18/97	$0.20
11			Conference	Pre-planning	Selection	Site	0.2 wks	07/18/97	07/21/97	$1,000.00
12		Intern	Conference	Pre-planning	Selection	Keynote spea	1 wk	07/18/97	07/25/97	$400.00
13		Long distance	Conference	Pre-planning	Selection	Keynote spea	1 wk	07/18/97	07/25/97	$50.00
14		Intern	Conference	Pre-planning	Hire	Caterer	2 days	07/28/97	07/29/97	$160.00
15			Conference	Pre-planning	Hire	Bartenders	1 day	07/17/97	07/17/97	$0.00
16			Conference	Pre-planning	Hire	Security	2 days	07/17/97	07/18/97	$0.00
17			Conference	Pre-planning	Hire	Photographer	1 day	07/17/97	07/17/97	$0.00
18			Conference	Pre-planning	Hire	Cleanup crew	1 day	07/17/97	07/17/97	$0.00
19		Joe Johnson	Conference	Pre-planning	Plan Entertain	Baseball Gam	1 day	07/14/97	07/14/97	$200.00
20		Joe Johnson	Conference	Pre-planning	Plan Entertain	Opera	4 hrs	07/14/97	07/14/97	$100.00
21		Joe Johnson	Conference	Pre-planning	Public relation	Alert commun	2 wks	07/25/97	08/08/97	$2,000.00
22			Conference	Pre-planning	Public relation	Press release	1 day	08/08/97	08/11/97	$0.00
23			Conference	Pre-planning	Rent Equipme	Rent audiovisu	2 days	07/14/97	07/15/97	$0.00
24			Conference	Pre-planning	Rent Equipme	Rent tables a	1 day	07/16/97	07/16/97	$0.00
25			Conference	Pre-planning	Meet with Cate	Menu selectio	1 day	07/30/97	07/30/97	$0.00

Figure 13-24: The Tasks sheet that Excel used to create the Task PivotTable.

You may need to widen columns in Excel to see all the data. Double-click on the right border of the column letter.

Making Adjustments During the Project

Now that you've seen the various ways you can collect and analyze financial data about your project, you need to use that information to make improvements to your project. You can use many of the techniques you used to implement changes to your project because of scheduling problems (see Chapter 8) or resource conflicts (see Chapter 9).

Changing the schedule

After evaluating earned value information, you might want to change the schedule using techniques discussed in Chapter 8. For example, you might want to

- ✦ Add resources to tasks
- ✦ Use overtime
- ✦ Increase task duration
- ✦ Adjust slack
- ✦ Change task constraints
- ✦ Adjust dependencies
- ✦ Split tasks
- ✦ Adjust the critical path

You might also need to make changes to the baseline project you saved (see Chapter 10).

Modifying resource assignments

Your evaluation of earned value information may prompt you to make changes to resource assignments on your project using techniques discussed in Chapter 9. For example, you might need to

- ✦ Change resource allocations
- ✦ Schedule overtime
- ✦ Redefine a resource's calendar
- ✦ Assign part-time work
- ✦ Control when resources start working on a task
- ✦ Level work loads
- ✦ Contour resources
- ✦ Pool resources

Breaking a project into smaller projects

When you're working with an unusually large project, you may find it easier to break your project into smaller, more manageable portions called *subprojects*. In Project you can create subprojects and consolidate them into the larger project to see the larger picture (see Chapter 15).

Summary

This chapter explains how to analyze the costs in your project.

✦ You learned how to use Project's Earned Value tables.

✦ You learned to chart earned value information, to analyze timescaled information, and to use Microsoft Excel PivotTables.

✦ You reviewed how to make adjustments to your project.

In the next chapter you learn how Project can help when you work in groups.

✦   ✦   ✦

Working in Groups

Using Project in a Workgroup

To paraphrase John Donne, No project manager is an island. Most projects involve you and at least one other person. The people involved in your project constitute your workgroup, and the project manager is the workgroup manager. Workgroups can vary in their structure: On one project you might manage a project, coordinating activities of all its resources; on another you might be a member of a workgroup team that someone else is managing. In either case you'll be interacting with many people over the days, weeks, or months that it takes to reach your goal — and you need tools to make that interaction a success.

Project has many workgroup features to help you manage and work with other members of a project team. This chapter explores workgroup tools that you can use

- ✦ To communicate
- ✦ To make task assignments
- ✦ To keep your schedule up-to-date

Setting Up a Workgroup

With Project you set up a workgroup by establishing a workgroup manager and the members of the workgroup. You can then exchange workgroup messages through e-mail, your own organization's intranet, or the World Wide Web. The exchange of information enables the workgroup manager to alert workgroup members to task assignments through Project's *TeamAssign* feature. Workgroup members can return information to the workgroup manager, which he or she can use for tracking progress during the life of the project, using Project's *TeamStatus* feature. Finally, managers can use the *TeamUpdate* feature to notify workgroup members about shifts in the schedule or other project parameters.

Who's the boss?

The *workgroup manager* is the person who builds and maintains the project schedule and makes task assignments. The idea here is that one person creates the schedule, makes assignments, and uses communications from workgroup members to track their activities.

Regardless of whether your Project workgroup functions through e-mail, an intranet, or the Web, the workgroup manager must first install Project on his or her computer. Although workgroup members can also install Project on their computers, this step isn't absolutely necessary. Follow these steps to set up the workgroup manager's software:

1. Choose Tools⇨Options.

2. Click on the Workgroup tab to select it (see Figure 14-1).

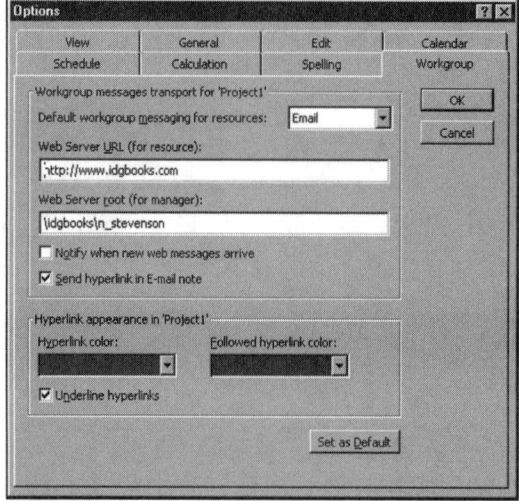

Figure 14-1: You can set the default messaging method for your workgroup and tell Project how to notify you when messages arrive in your inbox.

3. Select the default workgroup messaging method from the Default workgroup messaging for resources drop-down list. For e-mail only, select the Email option; for a Web server setup, including an intranet or the World Wide Web, select Web. To send messages both ways, select Email and Web.

4. Enter the URL for the Web server that resources should use to access workgroup messages in the Web Server URL field, along with the folder in which you want to keep your workgroup messages in the Web Server Root field. This Internet address points to your organizational server or to a server located on your own computer.

If your workgroup is using an intranet or the Internet for messaging, enter the path to access the Web server software, as well as a folder for Project, in the Web Server root (for manager) box.

5. Use the remaining check boxes and drop-down lists to set up Project to notify you when you receive messages, to enable the sending of hyperlinks in e-mail messages, and to format hyperlinks.

6. Click on the General tab of the Options dialog box and enter the User Name that should appear on messages that you send.

7. Click on OK to save your settings.

If you chose either the Web or the Email and Web method in step 3, Project tells you that it has to copy some files to your Web server. Click on Yes to continue.

Using e-mail

With an e-mail–based workgroup, in addition to loading Project on the workgroup manager's computer, you must complete a few other steps.

The manager and workgroup members must have access to a Messaging Application Programming Interface (MAPI) compliant, 32-bit e-mail setup. MAPI is a standard e-mail interface that Microsoft supports with products such as Outlook, Microsoft Exchange, and Microsoft Mail, but it is common to other major e-mail products as well.

In many cases not all members of your team will have Project on their computers. If some people on your team don't have Project on their computers, those members can run an executable file called Wgsetup.exe from the Project CD so they'll be able to send and receive messages. To run this file, follow these steps:

1. Copy the WGsetup folder from the CD to a drive on your network. Make sure that everyone in your workgroup can get to this drive using their MAPI-compliant e-mail interface.

2. Have each workgroup member open the folder and double-click on the file WGsetup.exe to run it. Project displays the Workgroup Message Handler Setup dialog box shown in Figure 14-2 and asks each user to confirm the location for the file.

When a user confirms that location, which is the location of the workgroup member's inbox, called the *TeamInbox*, Project automatically completes the installation.

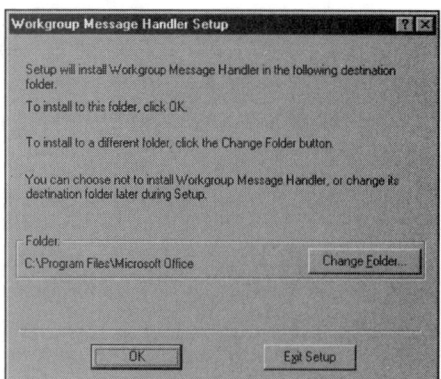

Figure 14-2: You can either accept the default location for the workgroup setup file or create a specially named folder for it.

Working with intranets

When managing workgroups across an organizational intranet, the workgroup manager's computer must have a copy of Project. In addition, you have to provide the manager and all team members with a Web browser, which provides an interface to display messages. Microsoft provides Internet Explorer with its Windows software, or as a free download, but you can also use browsers such as Netscape Navigator.

In addition, each person in the workgroup must be able to access either your organization's network or a TCP/IP network. Each workgroup member also needs a unique network identification. The workgroup features of Project require this unique identification to recognize and connect to workgroup members.

Finally, you must set up a share name for your workgroup on your organization's Web server. A *share name* is a chunk of space on the server set aside for your use. If you're in doubt about how to set up a share space on your network, talk to your Webmaster or IS contact.

Creating a workgroup on the Web

Setting up a workgroup on the Web is similar to setting up an intranet. The workgroup manager must have Project loaded on his or her computer, and each workgroup member must have a Web browser. In addition:

> ✦ Each workgroup member's computer must be able to connect to the Internet, either through a company server or an Internet Service Provider. Each workgroup member's computer must have an Internet address. This address serves the same purpose as the unique network identification on an intranet; that is, the Internet address enables Project to recognize workgroup members.

✦ As with an intranet, you must set up a share name for your group on your Web server. Again, the Webmaster is your most likely contact if you need help setting up this share name.

Tip

If you have Microsoft Personal Web Server, you can use your own computer as the Web server.

Building a Project Resource List

To use Project's workgroup communication features, you must assign resources to your project and designate them as being in your group. When you create these resources, you enter an online address so Project can communicate with them. Follow these steps to create a resource group:

1. Display the Resource Sheet view by clicking on it in the View bar.

2. Enter a resource name and any other pertinent information about the resource in the columns of the Resource Sheet.

3. Double-click on the resource name to open the Resource Information dialog box shown in Figure 14-3.

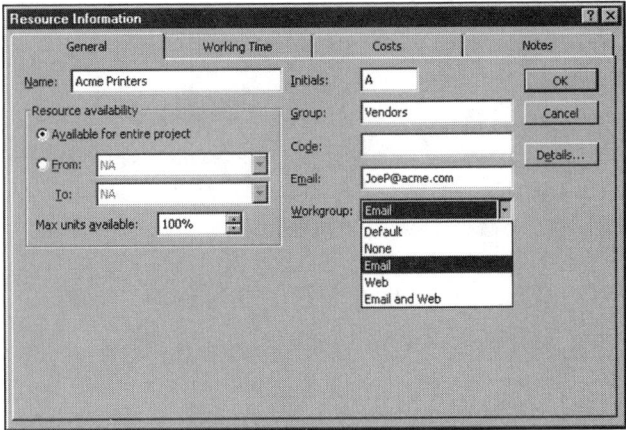

Figure 14-3: Enter a group name and e-mail address for every resource you want in your workgroup communications circle.

4. Enter a Group name in the Group field; this entry is required to use the workgroup features with this resource.

5. Enter an e-mail address in the Email field.

6. Select a workgroup (Email, Web, or Email and Web) from the Workgroup drop-down list. This choice should match the messaging method you chose when you set up the workgroup manager's connection.

7. Click on OK to save the resource, who is now part of the workgroup and is set up for workgroup communications.

Communicating with a Workgroup

After you set up a workgroup with a manager, the necessary network or Web connections, and resources with group affiliations, you are ready to use Project's workgroup communication features.

Managing messages with the WebInbox and TeamInbox

When a workgroup manager sends a message to his or her team, that message appears in each recipient's TeamInbox. When team members respond to a message, Project places that response in the workgroup manager's WebInbox, which is located within the manager's copy of Project. Project's inboxes, which are very similar to those in other e-mail programs, display lists of messages with information about the sender, project, subject, and date and time the message was received. Figure 14-4 shows a WebInbox.

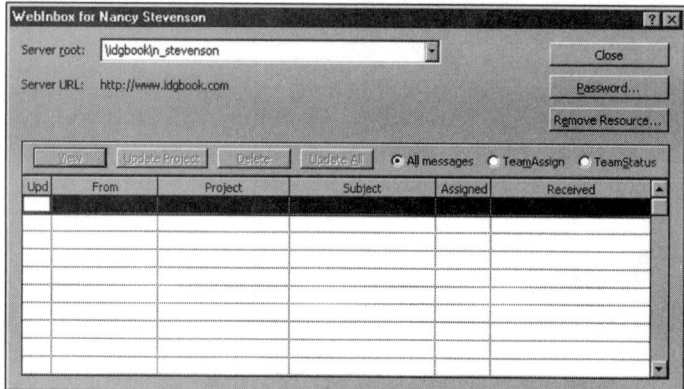

Figure 14-4: You can use the WebInbox to keep track of and manage messages from your workgroup.

You can use your WebInbox to send various types of messages to

✦ Make assignments (TeamAssign)

✦ Communicate about changes in dates (TeamUpdate)

✦ Get updated information about tasks that Project can automatically incorporate into your project schedule, saving you time in tracking progress (TeamStatus).

The tools on the Workgroup toolbar enable you to work with these messages.

Using the Workgroup toolbar

You can display the Workgroup toolbar by choosing View➪Toolbars➪Workgroup. The labels in Figure 14-5 identify the Workgroup toolbar in tools.

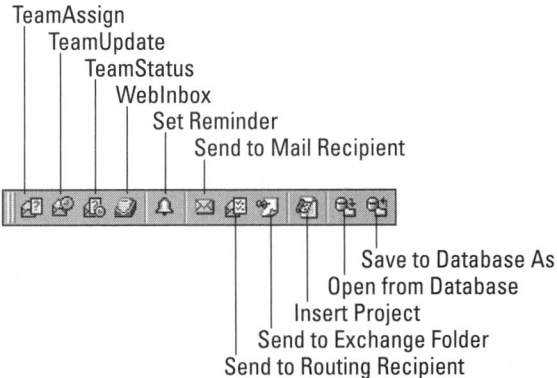

Figure 14-5: Use the Workgroup toolbar to access workgroup features that help you communicate with your team.

Here are some of the useful actions you can perform from the Workgroup toolbar:

✦ **Set Reminder:** Opens a dialog box that uses Microsoft Outlook's features to set reminders related to a task you selected in your schedule. For example, you can ask Project to remind you 15 minutes before a task involving a meeting or phone conference.

✦ **Send to Mail Recipient:** Sends an e-mail message to your team members or create a routing designation for the message consisting of any group of people you like.

✦ **Insert Project:** Places another project file into the currently open file.

✦ **Send to Exchange:** Opens a new Microsoft Exchange message box, with the file already included as an attachment. Just enter a recipient's address and any accompanying message, and send the e-mail through your e-mail system.

You can use also use the first three tools to create any of the team message types: TeamAssign, TeamUpdate, and TeamStatus.

TeamAssign

After you establish a workgroup, you can automatically generate messages notifying resources of assignments by selecting a task and clicking on the TeamAssign tool to open the Workgroup Mail dialog box shown in Figure 14-6.

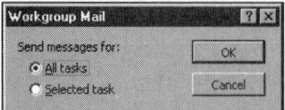

Figure 14-6: The Workgroup Mail dialog box is where you specify assignments by a single task or for all tasks in the project.

When you complete your schedule, you might want to send information about all tasks involving the resource to that resource. After the project begins and you periodically add the resource to a task or two, you can notify the resource about selected tasks only. You can use the Workgroup Mail dialog box to specify that you want to send a message to a team member for the currently selected task only or for all tasks in the project. Select one of the options and click on OK. Project displays the TeamAssign dialog box shown in Figure 14-7. You use this message form to enter specifics for messages concerning team assignments.

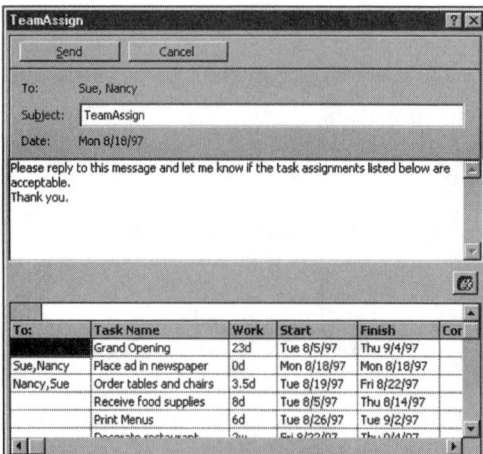

Figure 14-7: In this message, all tasks in the project are being forwarded to team members.

The recipient name in the To space at the top of the TeamAssign dialog box is the first resource assigned to the task (either the selected task, or the first task in your schedule if you selected to send a message for all tasks). The default Subject is TeamAssign, but you can modify that if you wish.

Project automatically generates a message that asks the recipient to indicate his or her acceptance of the assignment. You can either send this generic message or enter a message of your own.

Project lists the task or tasks to which the resource is assigned in a table below your message, indicating:

✦ The name of the task

✦ The amount of work time you expect from the resource on the task

✦ The task start and finish dates

✦ Any comments you entered into the Comments column of the Gantt table

Tip

You can modify the information in this table, as explained in "Customizing Your Workgroup" later in this chapter.

When the information in the TeamAssign dialog box is correct, click on the Send button at the top to send the message. The message a team member receives in his or her TeamInbox looks something like the message shown in Figure 14-8.

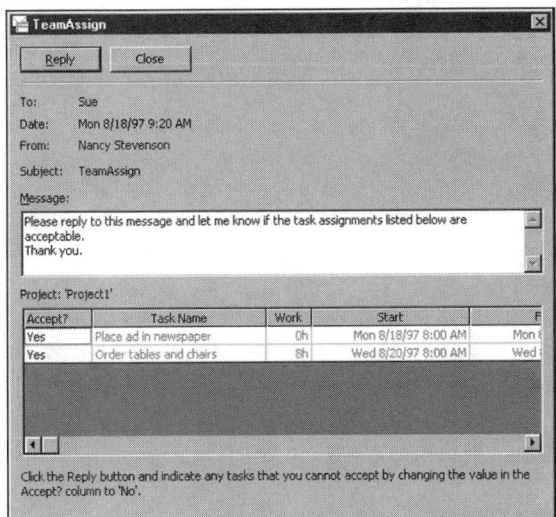

Figure 14-8: This message clearly asks the workgroup member to accept or decline the assignment.

To accept an assignment received through e-mail, the team member leaves the Yes in the Accept? column. To decline the assignment, the recipient types **No** in the Accept? column. To accept or reject an assignment received through the TeamInbox via the Web, the recipient selects or clears the Accept? check box as appropriate, enters a message (if desired), and clicks on Reply. Project places a team member's response, sent by any method, in the workgroup manager's WebInbox.

TeamUpdate

A TeamUpdate message is similar to a TeamAssign message, but the purpose of this message is to convey a change to the start or finish date of a task or tasks. You must have exchanged TeamAssign messages before you can send a TeamUpdate message because you are updating team members on changes to task timing that have occurred since a resource accepted the assignment.

When you click on the TeamUpdate button, Project opens the TeamUpdate dialog box shown in Figure 14-9. Type in a subject, type your message, and then click on Send to send a list of updated tasks.

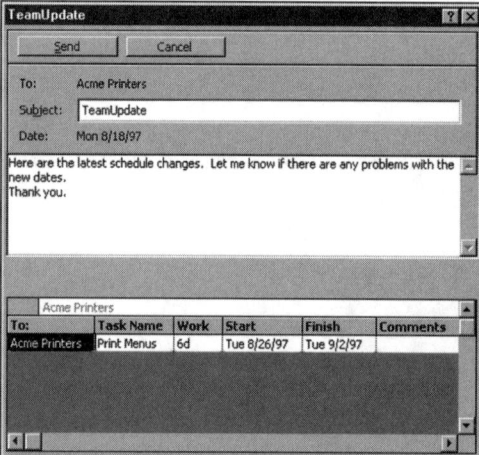

Figure 14-9: The table of information in this message notifies someone working on your project of a change in task timing.

Only tasks that involve the recipient (that resource) and that have changed appear in this list. The message appears either in a workgroup member's e-mail inbox or TeamInbox, depending on how you have set up the workgroup. To respond to a TeamUpdate message, click on Reply, type a message, and then click on Send.

TeamStatus

The third standard message type, TeamStatus, works similarly, but it goes beyond simple communication. You can use responses to your TeamStatus requests to automatically update your project. This feature saves you hours of time tracking and entering progress information manually.

With TeamStatus the message you send to team members asks them to update the workgroup manager as to the status of tasks. When you click on the TeamStatus button on the Workgroup toolbar, Project asks if this message is for All tasks or just the Selected tasks. Make your choice and click on OK. The dialog box in Figure 14-10 then appears.

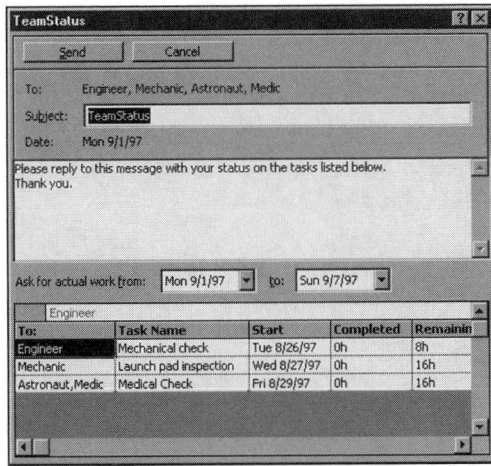

Figure 14-10: Similar to the TeamAssign dialog box, TeamStatus requests that the workgroup team member inform you of progress on tasks.

Follow these steps to complete a TeamStatus request:

1. Type another subject into the Subject line if desired.

2. Keep the default message, or delete it and enter one of your own.

3. Set a date range of the work period for which you want the recipient to respond.

4. Click on the Send button.

The team member receives a message that looks like the TeamStatus message in Figure 14-11.

Team members can edit the task information fields for Start, Completed, and Remaining. The team member enters information in the Remaining Work field reflecting actual work progress, optionally adds a return message about the status of the tasks, then clicks on Send to return the message to the workgroup manager. When the manager receives the response and clicks on the Update Project button at the top of the message (see Figure 14-12), Project uses the team member's entries to update the tasks in the actual schedule — automatically.

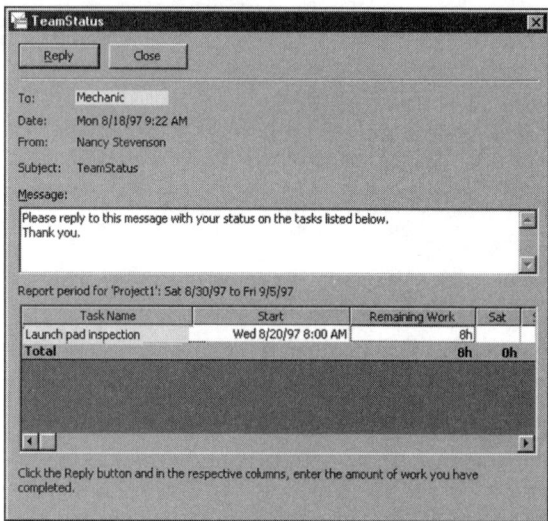

Figure 14-11: To respond to the request, the recipient clicks on the Reply button.

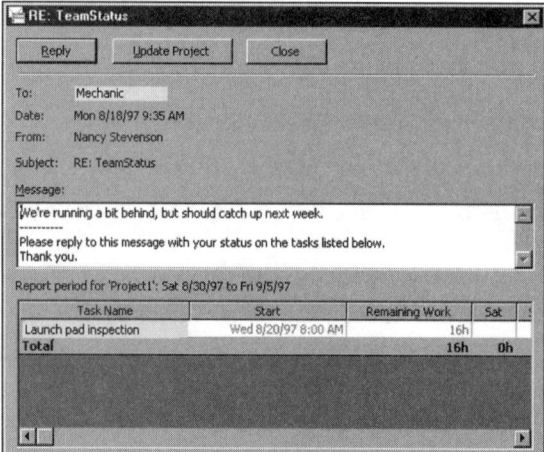

Figure 14-12: The TeamStatus feature helps to automate the sometimes laborious process of tracking progress on a project.

Customizing Your Workgroup

You can modify the task information that appears in your workgroup messages by using the customizing feature of Project. This feature enables you to add or delete items that appear in the task information fields, rearrange the fields, or request more detailed breakdowns of task timing.

Follow these steps to customize your messages:

1. Choose Tools⇨Customize⇨Workgroup to open the Customize Workgroup dialog box in Figure 14-13.

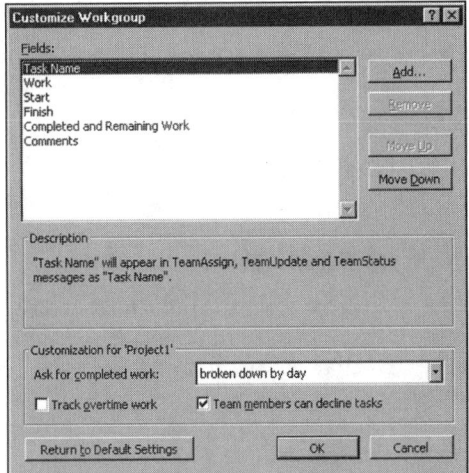

Figure 14-13: Use the Customize Workgroup dialog box to include the information most relevant to your project in your workgroup messages.

2. Make any of the following changes:

   ✦ **Add a field:** Click on the Add button, select a field from the drop-down list in the Add Field dialog box, and click on OK. The new field appears above whatever field was highlighted when you clicked on the Add button.

   ✦ **Delete a field:** Click on the name of the field you want to delete in the Fields list and then click on the Remove button. Note that you cannot delete the Task Name field.

   ✦ **Change the order of fields in the table of information:** Use the Move Up and Move Down buttons.

✦ **Designate how you want Project to break down status information:**
You can see status information by day, by week, or for the entire time
for which you are requesting information by making the appropriate
selection in the Ask for completed work drop-down list.

Tip   If you have made several changes and want to return to Project's standard settings
for workgroup messaging, click on the Return to Default Settings button in the
bottom left hand corner of the Customize Workgroup dialog box.

3. Click on OK to save the new settings.

Implementing Project Security in Workgroups

When you begin to pass around plans for a project, you may run into issues of
security. For example, you might have resource rate information you don't want
every Tom, Dick, and Mary to see. Maybe you want messages you receive on
project status to be for your eyes only. You can protect the contents of your
WebInbox or TeamInbox by assigning a password to it.

A word about passwords and security

The basic method of protecting project data is the password. You can set passwords
for your Team and Web inboxes. However, setting a password does not guarantee
safety; the procedures you use to devise an effective password and keep it from being
discovered are the real key to project security.

Whether for serious motives, like industrial espionage, or simple workplace
curiosity, people may try to peek at your project information. The computer world
has spawned a whole subculture of people, known as *crackers*, who have made an
art out of breaking into supposedly secure files.

Here are some guidelines for working with passwords:

✦ Don't use an easy-to-guess password. A clever cracker can find out your
spouse's name, your middle name, your phone extension, and your date of
birth in no time flat.

✦ Use the longest password that Project allows (up to 17 characters); the
longer the password, the harder it is to crack.

✦ Don't give your password to anybody. If you have to give it out, for example,
if you are away from the office and someone else must access data to keep
the project going, be sure to change your password as soon as you return.

✦ Create a password that is a random combination of letters and numbers. For
example, T2J773N is a good password; MyFile isn't.

✦ Change your password on a regular basis, even if you never give it to anyone. Crackers break passwords by trying out different options and combinations; it may take them a few sessions to break your code. The more often you change your password, the more times someone else will have to start from scratch to break it.

Setting your InBox password

To set a password, open your WebInbox or TeamInbox by choosing Tools⇨Workgroup and the appropriate inbox from the side menu that appears. (You can also click on the Inbox tool on the Workgroup toolbar.) Project displays the Password dialog box shown in Figure 14-14.

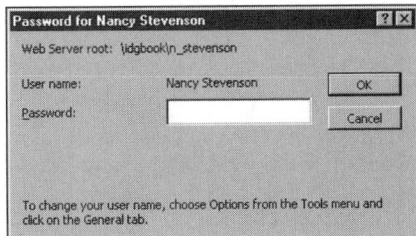

Figure 14-14: After you set a password, you must enter it in the Password dialog box to access your WebInbox or TeamInbox.

If you already entered a password, type it here to access your inbox. If you have not entered a password, leave the password field blank and click on OK. If you are the workgroup manager, Project displays the WebInbox shown in Figure 14-15; if you're not the workgroup manager, Project displays your TeamInbox.

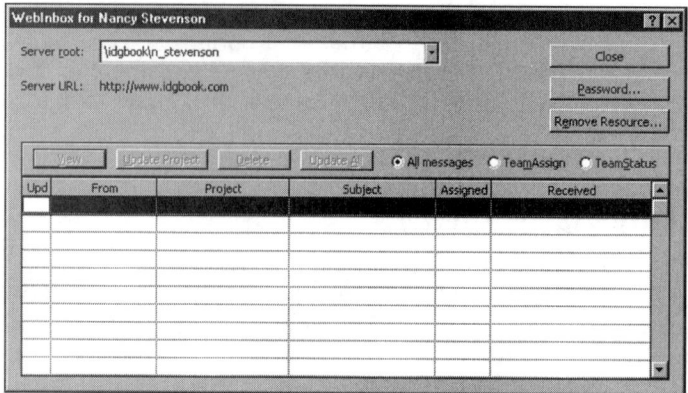

Figure 14-15: Like a standard e-mail inbox, the WebInbox displays a list of messages waiting for you and enables you to view them individually.

To set your password, click on the Password button. In the Change Password dialog box (see Figure 14-16), type your new password twice — first in the New password text box and then in the Confirm new password text box. If you make a mistake, Project asks you to enter the password again. Click on OK, and close your inbox. The next time you open this box, you must enter a password to access your messages.

Note

If you previously assigned a password, the Old password field is available. However, the first time you use the password feature, Project grays out this field.

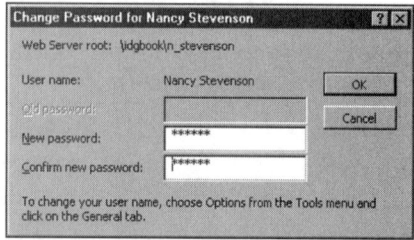

Figure 14-16: Project asks you to enter your new password twice. If you make an invisible typo, your password won't be what you expect.

Establishing Workgroup Management Procedures

If you are responsible for managing a workgroup, your job involves more than just setting up your group to send and receive workgroup messages. You also need to orchestrate those communications and manage project files efficiently to get the most out of the workgroup structure. Use these suggestions to guide you:

✦ Make sure all workgroup members understand how Project's workgroup features work. You (the workgroup manager) could well be the only person in the workgroup to have a copy of Project on your computer. Helping your team to understand not only how to use the workgroup features that are available to them but also why these features are important to using Project effectively is key.

✦ Set up a communication schedule with your workgroup. Make assignments and status requests on a regular basis, perhaps allowing a week or two of activity to occur before you perform updates. If workgroup members know they will receive requests for updates and status reports every Friday, for example, and that they must respond by end of day Tuesday, they can establish a routine to deliver the information in a timely way.

✦ Check your WebInbox on a regular basis. If you aren't being responsive to your workgroup's input, they'll stop being responsive to your requests.

Sending Notes and Files around a Workgroup

Project has two other tools that are most helpful in communicating with various resources assigned to a project, whether they are part of your designated workgroup or not. First, you can send a *project schedule note* to selected resources assigned to the project. Second, you can route a *project file* from one resource to another. The ability to route notes and files can be useful if you want each resource to add information to the file or note and then forward it to the next person for his or her comments.

Sending Project notes

To send a copy of your Project file, and perhaps a note to all resources — or a subset of resources on a project, whether or not they are part of your regular workgroup. Before beginning this procedure select a specific task, if you want to send a note concerning the resources assigned to that task only. Otherwise, don't have any specific task selected. To send a message through your MAPI-compliant e-mail system, follow these steps:

   1. Choose Tools⇨Workgroup⇨Send Schedule Note.

2. Select the people to whom you want to send the note in the Address message to field in the Send Schedule Note dialog box shown in Figure 14-17. Your choices include the Project manager, Resources for the selected task or entire project, or contacts. Then select the appropriate options:

✦ If you want everyone on the project to get this message, click on Entire project. If you want only the resources assigned to the task you selected before opening this dialog box, click on Selected tasks.

✦ If you want to attach the currently open Project file to your message, click on the File check box.

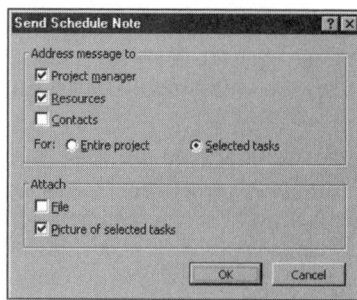

Figure 14-17: This dialog box gives you some flexibility for designating who should get this note: resources, the project manager, or various contacts for the project such as a vendor.

3. Click on OK. A new e-mail message form, like the one shown in Figure 14-18, appears, with a copy of the Project file attached.

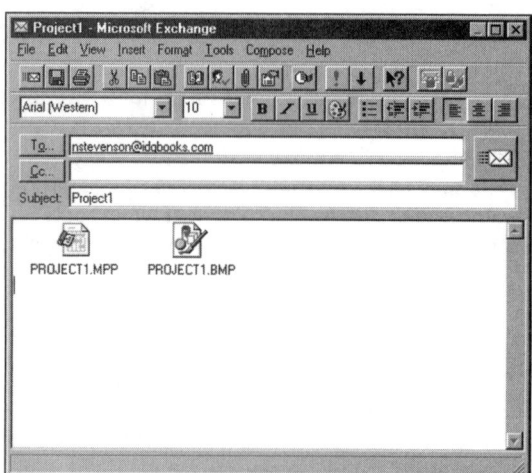

Figure 14-18: The e-mail form in your system may look different from this one, but you'll see some kind of blank message form. Icons represent the attachments.

4. Type your message in the large, blank message area.

5. Use your e-mail addressing method (for example, in the figure shown, you would click on the To: button to access saved lists of addresses in this e-mail software) to send the message to anyone other than the designated resources assigned to tasks who were automatically addressed when you created the message.

6. Send the message.

Routing a Project file

Another good way to keep workgroup members informed and involved in the project is to *route* a Project file to a group of people. Each person can add information that the next person on the route can build or comment on. Routing a file is a simple process. Follow these steps:

1. Choose File⇨Sent To⇨Routing Recipient to open the Routing Slip dialog box in Figure 14-19.

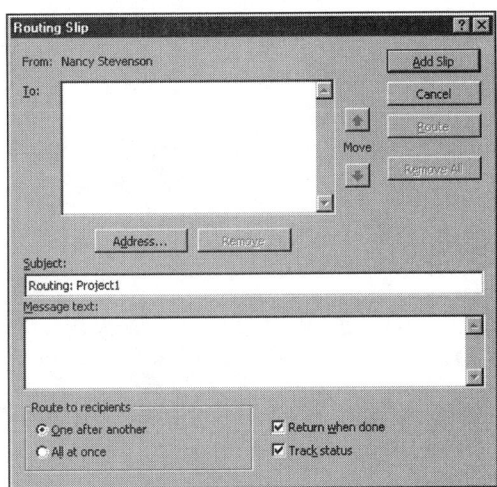

Figure 14-19: The Routing Slip dialog box enables you to track your message as it moves along its route by clicking on the Track status check box.

2. Click on the Address button to display the address dialog box for your e-mail software program.

Select as many addressees as you wish using this method and then click on OK to return to the Routing Slip dialog box.

3. Enter information for the Subject of the message.

4. Type your message in the Message text box.

5. Select one of the radio buttons in the Route to recipients box, choosing to route sequentially or all at once.

6. Check the Return when done check box if you want Project to return the file to you at the end of the route.

7. Check the Track status check box if you want Project to notify you each time the file moves to the next person on the routing list.

8. Click on Route to send the message.

Tip

If you're the last recipient of the routing, you can remove the routing slip from the Project file. Click on the Remove All button in the Routing Slip dialog box.

Summary

Because most projects are team efforts and successful teams communicate effectively, establishing good workgroup procedures in your projects is key. In this chapter, you learned how to

✦ Set up the workgroup manager and workgroup members to send and receive information

✦ Use TeamAssign, TeamStatus, and TeamUpdate to keep members informed and update the project file

✦ Use security methods to protect information shared with a group

✦ Route messages and files among team members

In addition to knowing how to use these features, you must know how to set up effective, consistent procedures for their use among your workgroup members.

Chapter 15 describes how to use Project to manage multiple projects or large projects that incorporate several smaller Project schedules.

✦   ✦   ✦

Coordinating Multiple Projects

Large projects are the most difficult to manage; organization is a cornerstone to good project management, and in a large project the sheer number of tasks makes the job more difficult than usual. In Microsoft Project you can use the concept of consolidated projects to facilitate the management of a large project.

Consolidating Projects

Whenever you're faced with a complex problem, finding the solution typically becomes easier if you can simplify the problem. Similarly, when you need to manage a complex project with many tasks, you may find it easier to organize the process if you deal with a limited number of tasks at one time.

In Microsoft Project you can take this approach to planning large complex projects by using Project's consolidation features. For example, you can create *subprojects*, which you can think of as the tasks that constitute one portion of your large project. When you create a subproject, you save it as a separate project file. You can assign resources, set up each subproject with links and constraints as if it were the entire project, and then consolidate the subprojects into one large project. When you consolidate, you actually insert one project into another project; therefore, subprojects are also called *inserted projects*.

When you work in a consolidated project, you can focus on just the portion of the project that you need. Subprojects appear as summary tasks in the consolidated project, and you can use Project's outlining tools to hide all tasks associated with any subproject. See Chapter 3 for more information on outlining.

From the consolidated project, you can view, print, and change information for any subproject just as if you were working with a single project.

The concept of consolidation in Project 98 is entirely different than it was in Project 95. In Project 95, for example, many project tools, such as copying and pasting, didn't work in consolidated projects. Project 95 used two techniques to work with multiple projects: one called *consolidation* and the other called *master projects and subprojects*. With the second technique you created a link between a placeholder task in the master project and the subproject.

In Project 98 you no longer need to think about master projects versus subprojects. Subprojects still exist as separate projects, but in Project 98 you include them in a consolidated project; in addition, you now have much greater flexibility in the consolidated project. You can think of the consolidated project as the host project into which you insert subprojects.

Setting up to use consolidation

Consolidation can help you achieve several objectives. For example:

✦ Tasks in projects managed by different people may depend on each other. Through consolidation, you can create the correct dependencies to accurately display the project's schedule and necessary resources.

✦ A project may be so large that breaking it into smaller pieces can help you organize it. You can use consolidation to combine the smaller pieces and then view the big picture.

✦ You may be pooling the resources of several projects and find you need to level the resources; consolidating enables you to link the projects sharing the resources so that you can level the resources.

You usually decide to use consolidation because:

✦ You realize right away that the project is too large.

✦ You discover that the project is bigger than you originally thought while you are working on it.

If you decide to use consolidation before you start your project, simply create separate Microsoft Project files for various portions of the project. These files act as subprojects when you consolidate. You need to set up each subproject file so that it is complete by itself, and create links as needed within each subproject file. This chapter explains techniques for consolidating the subprojects and linking them.

If you start a project and then decide that you want to use consolidation, you can create subprojects by following these steps:

1. Save your large project file.

2. Select all the tasks you want to save in your first subproject file and click on the Copy button.

3. Click on the New button to start a new project and use the Project Information dialog box that appears in Figure 15-1 to set basic Project Information, such as the project's start date and scheduling method.

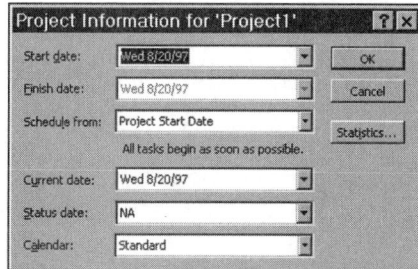

Figure 15-1: Use the Project Information dialog box to set basic project information such as the project's start date.

4. Click on the Paste button.

5. Save the subproject and close it.

6. Use the Window command to redisplay the large project file.

7. Select all the tasks you want to save in your second subproject file and click on the Copy button.

8. Repeat steps 3 through 7 until you have saved several separate files that contain portions of your larger project.

You may want to edit each subproject file you create to make it a complete project by itself. Then you can use the following techniques to consolidate the subprojects and link them.

Inserting a project

To consolidate project files into one large project, you insert projects into a host project file called the *consolidated project file*. Each project you insert appears as a summary task in the consolidated project file. As you can see from Figure 15-2, an icon in the Indicators field identifies an inserted project.

Inserted Project icon

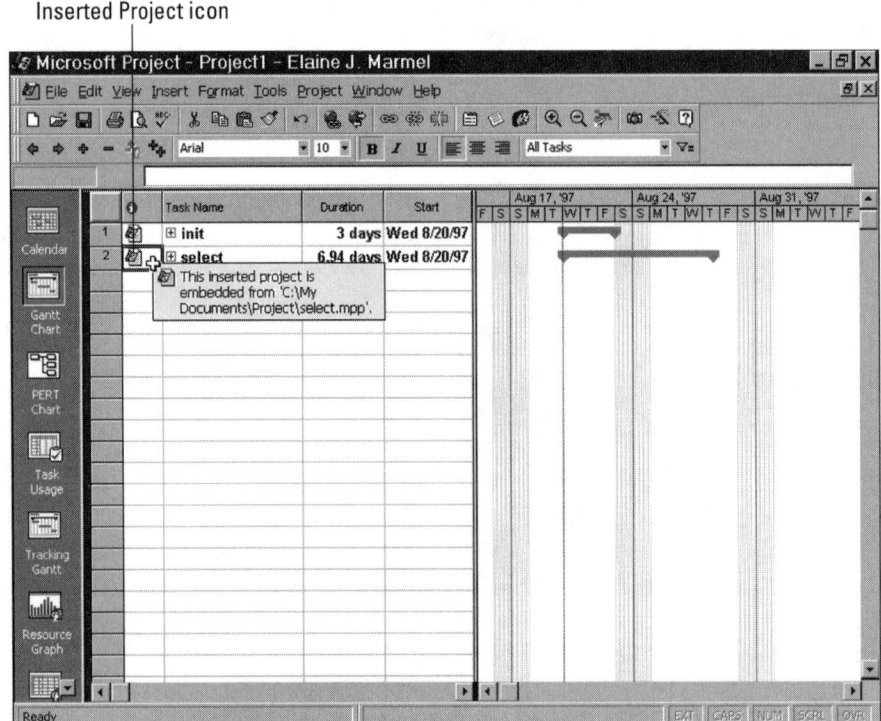

Figure 15-2: A special icon in the Indicators column identifies inserted projects.

You can insert projects at any outline level. The level at which an inserted project appears depends on the outline level that appears at the location where you intend to insert a project. Project inserts the project above the selected task at the same outline level as the task above the selected task, as you can see by comparing Figures 15-3, 15-4, and 15-5.

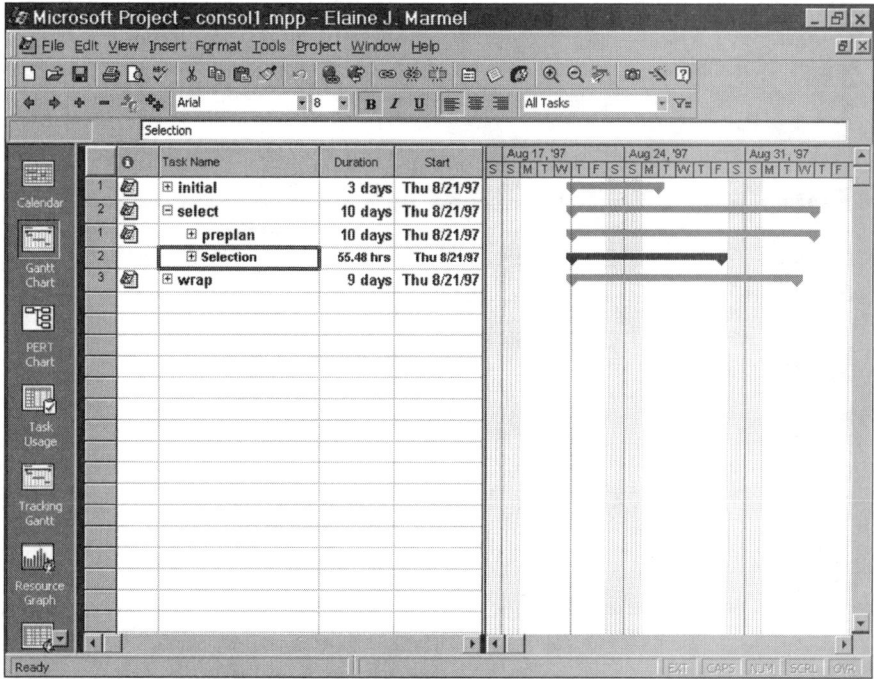

Figure 15-3: The Selection summary task was selected when you inserted the preplan project.

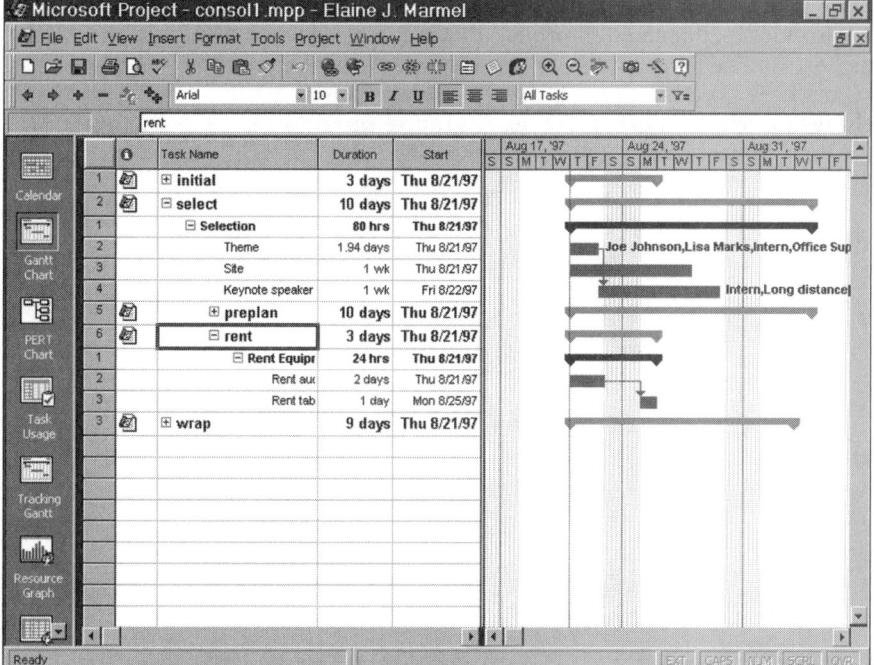

Figure 15-4: The Rent summary task was selected when you inserted the preplan project.

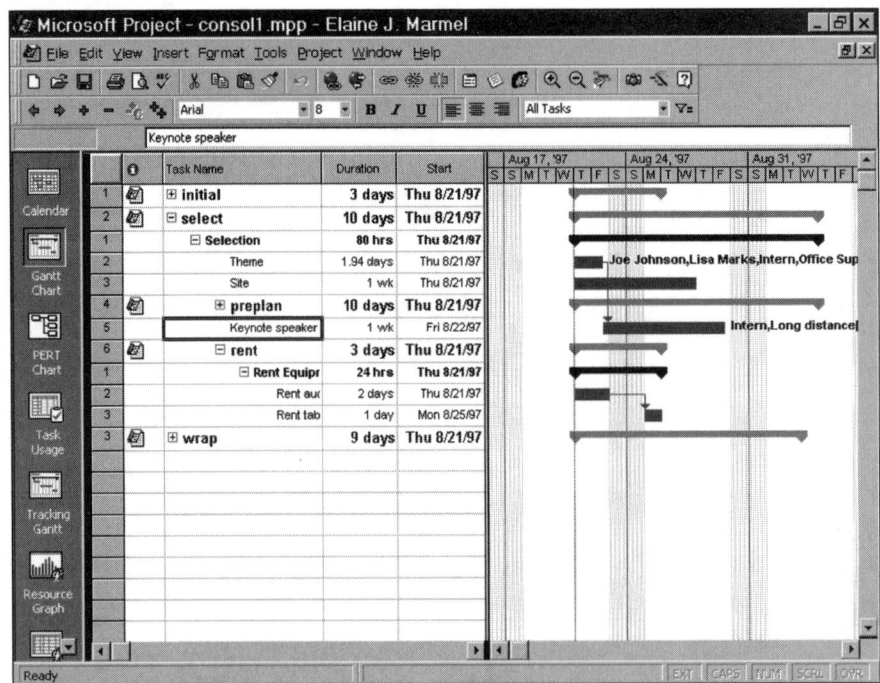

Figure 15-5: The Keynote Speaker task was selected when you inserted the preplan project.

To produce a consolidated project in which the inserted projects line up at the highest outline level as they do in Figure 15-6, make sure that you cannot see the tasks of the preceding inserted project when you insert the subproject. Project always inserts the new project above the selected row at the same outline level as the task immediately above the selected task.

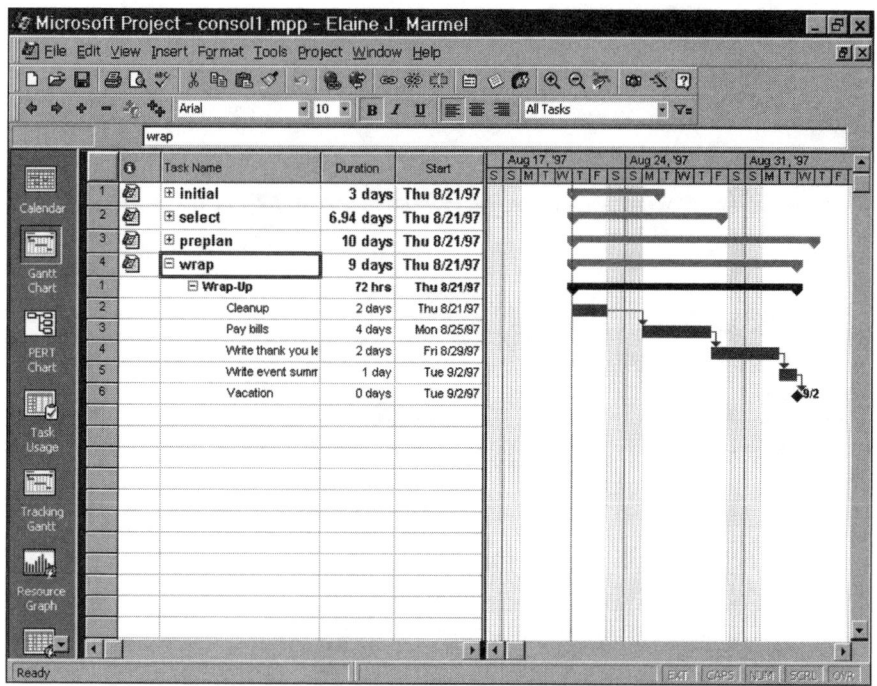

Figure 15-6: When the preplan task was inserted, the wrap summary task was selected and its subordinate tasks were visible, but the subordinate tasks of the select summary task were *not* visible.

To insert a project, follow these steps:

1. Open the project in which you want to store the consolidated project.

2. Click on the Gantt Chart icon in the View bar.

3. Click on the Task Name column on the row where you want the inserted project to begin.

Note

When you insert a project, Project places the project immediately above the selected row. Therefore, if your consolidated project already contains tasks, click on the task in the Task Name column that you want to appear below the subproject. You also can determine the outline level at which the inserted project appears in the host project. See Figures 15-3, 15-4, 15-5, and 15-6 that precede these steps for more information on where Project inserts a project.

4. Choose Insert⇨Project to open the Insert Project dialog box you see in Figure 15-7.

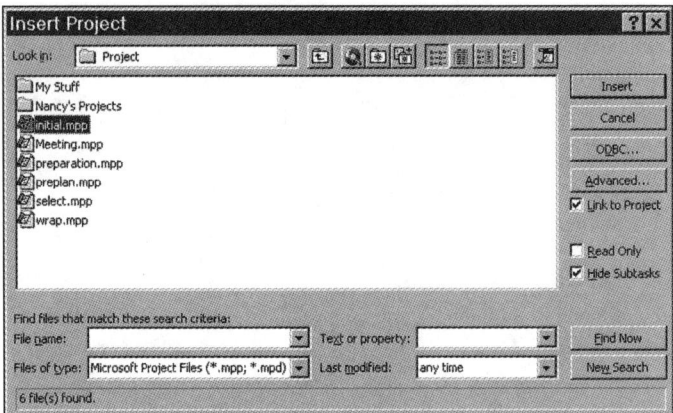

Figure 15-7: The Insert Project dialog box works like the Open dialog box.

5. Use the Look in list to navigate to the folder that contains the project you want to insert.

6. Highlight the file you want to insert.

7. Change any insert project options:

- If you remove the check from the Link to Project check box, the inserted project won't be linked to its source project.

- If you place a check in the Read Only check box, Project does not change the source project when you change the inserted project.

- If you remove the check from the Hide Subtasks check box, the inserted project's tasks appear in the consolidated project. You can also hide or show tasks after you insert the project by clicking on the summary task's outline symbol, as you can see in Figure 15-8.

8. Click on Insert. Project inserts the selected file into the open project. If you didn't change the Hide Subtasks option, the inserted file appears as a summary task, with its subordinate tasks hidden.

Click here to display task for a subproject

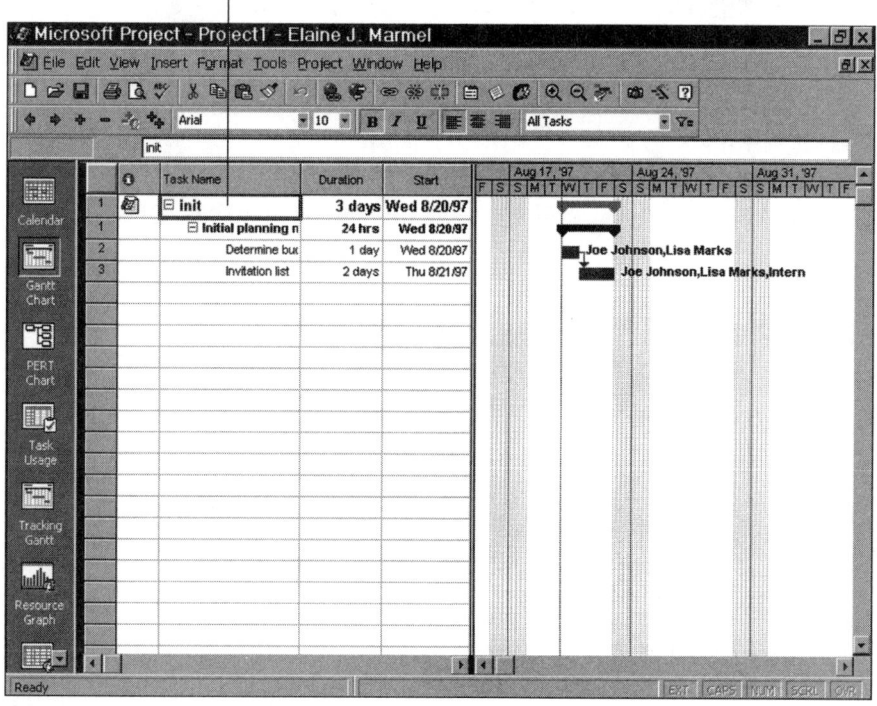

Figure 15-8: The tasks of an inserted project appear when you click on the outline symbol next to the summary task.

Using inserted projects and their source files

As you saw earlier when you inserted a project, Project enables you to link the inserted project to its source file. If you do not want to link an inserted project to its source file, any changes you make to the inserted project in the consolidated project file do not affect the source file. Similarly, any changes you make to the source file do not affect the consolidated project file containing the subproject. Why wouldn't you want to link the files? You may want to create a consolidated file just so that you can generate a report quickly.

Under many circumstances linking the files makes updating easier. Linking ensures that any changes you make in either the consolidated project or the subproject file affect the other file. When you insert a project and link it to its source file, you are creating a link between two files; that link works like any link you create between two files in a Windows environment. For example, if you move the subproject file, you need to update the link in the consolidated project; otherwise, the link does not work.

If you do move the file of a project that you have linked, follow these steps to update the link information in the consolidated project:

1. Open the consolidated project and display the Gantt Chart view.

2. Click on the inserted project in the Task Name column whose link you want to update.

3. Click on the Task Information button on the Standard toolbar to open the Inserted Project Information dialog box that appears in Figure 15-9.

4. Click on the Advanced tab.

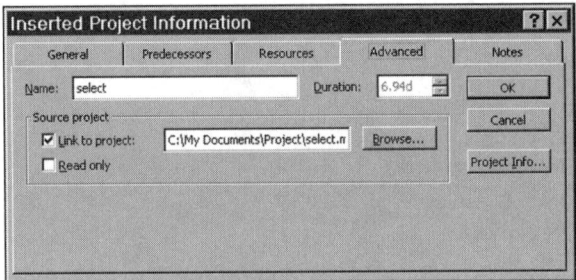

Figure 15-9: The Advanced tab of the Inserted Project Information dialog box.

5. Click on the Browse button to open a dialog box that looks and functions like the Open dialog box.

6. Navigate to the source file and click on OK.

Tip   You can also unlink subprojects from their source files using the Advanced tab of the Inserted Project Information dialog box. Remove the check from the Link to Project check box.

Consolidating all open projects: A shortcut

Here's how to consolidate several subprojects at the same time:

1. Open all the subprojects that you want to consolidate.

2. Choose Window➪New Window to open the New Window dialog box that appears in Figure 15-10.

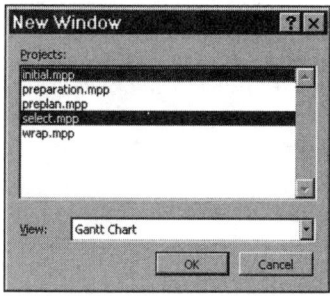

Figure 15-10: Use the New Window dialog box to quickly consolidate open projects.

3. Hold down the Ctrl key and click on each project you want to consolidate.

4. Click on OK.

Project creates a new consolidated project that contains the projects you selected in the New Window dialog box. Project inserts the subprojects into the consolidate project in the order in which the subprojects appear in the New Window dialog box.

New Feature

You can move subprojects around in the consolidated project by cutting a subproject row to delete it and then pasting the row where you want it to appear. When you select a summary row representing a subproject and click on the Cut button on the Standard toolbar, Project opens the Planning Wizard dialog box in Figure 15-11.

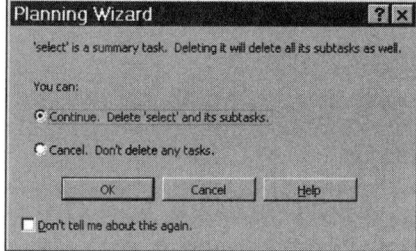

Figure 15-11: The Planning Wizard appears when you try to delete a summary task.

Click on the Continue option button and click on OK. The summary task representing the subproject and all its subordinate tasks disappears. When you paste the subproject, Project places the subproject immediately above the selected row. Therefore, in the Task Name column, you must click on the task you want to appear below the subproject. Then click on the Paste button on the Standard toolbar. Project reinserts the subproject at its new location.

Consolidated Projects and Dependencies

In a consolidated project you typically have tasks — either in the consolidated project or in one subproject — that are dependent on tasks in another subproject. You can create links between projects in a consolidated file, and if necessary, you can change the links you create.

Linking tasks across projects

New
Feature

When you create a dependency in Project 98, four types are available: finish-to-start, start-to-start, finish-to-finish, and start-to finish. In addition, these types support lead and lag time.

The actual process of linking tasks with dependencies across projects is much the same as the process of creating dependencies for tasks within the same project because you create the dependency in a consolidated project. Starting in the consolidated project file, follow these steps:

1. Click on the Gantt Chart on the View bar.

2. Select the tasks you want to link.

Tip

To select noncontiguous tasks, hold down the Ctrl key as you click on each task name.

3. Click on the Link Tasks button on the Standard toolbar. Project creates a finish-to-start link between the two tasks.

Tip

You can create the link in the consolidated project file by dragging from the middle of the Gantt bar of the predecessor task to the middle of the Gantt bar of the successor task.

You also can link tasks by typing in the Predecessor field, using the format **project name\ID#**; project name should include the path to the location of the file as well as the file name, and ID# should be the ID number of the task in that file. In Figure 15-12 the Theme task is linked to the Invitation List task, which is Task Number 3 in a Project file called INITIAL.MPP.

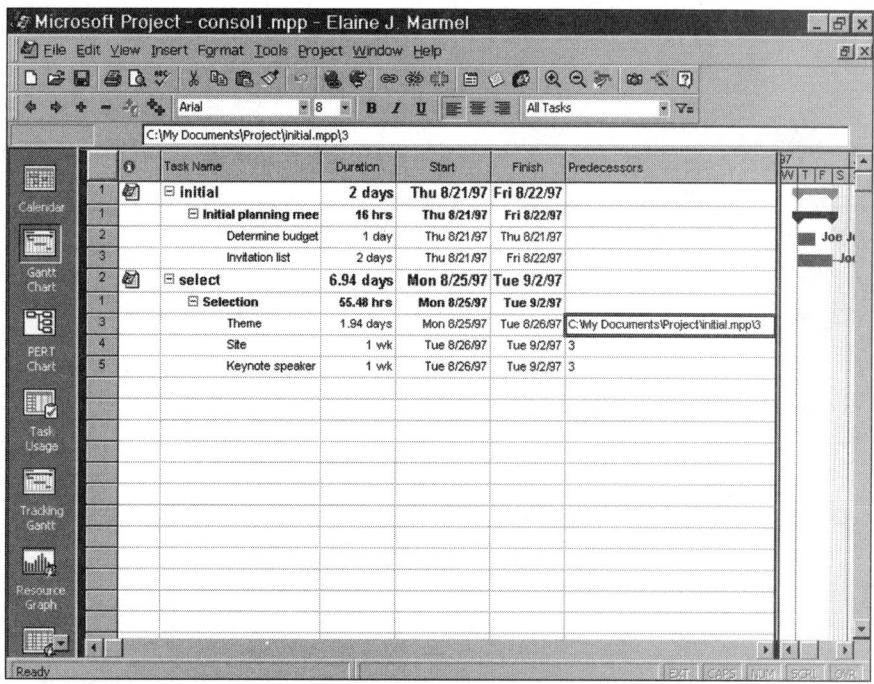

Figure 15-12: You can type in the Predecessor field to create a link between tasks across Project files.

New
Feature

When you link tasks between projects, the task links look like standard links in the consolidated project.

However, as Figure 15-13 shows, when you open the subproject file, Project has inserted an external link. the Task name of the inserted task appears gray, and the Gantt Chart bar also appears gray. If you click and hold the mouse button while pointing at the Gantt Chart bar, Project displays information about the task, including that it is an external task.

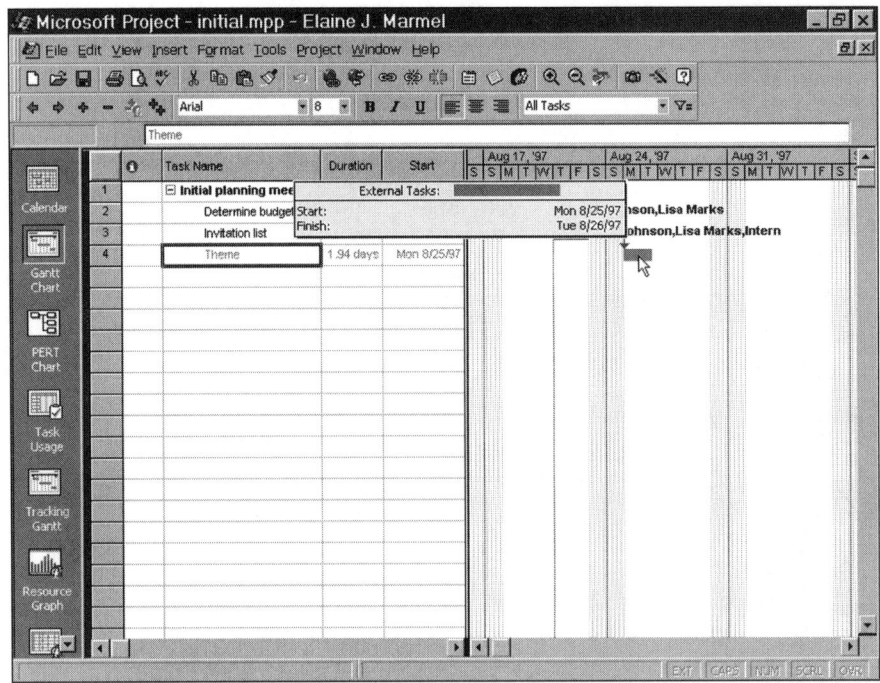

Figure 15-13: When you link tasks across files, Project inserts an external link in the subproject file.

If you double-click on the task name of the external task, Project displays the subproject containing the task to which the external is linked.

Changing links across projects

After you link tasks across projects, you may need to change information about the link. For example, you may want to change the type of dependency from the default finish-to-start link, or you may want to create lag time.

You can modify a link between tasks in different projects from either the consolidated project or from the subproject. In the consolidated project, double-click on the line that links the two tasks. In the subproject, double-click on the line that links an internal task to the external task (see Figure 15-14). Project displays the Task Dependency dialog box shown in Figure 15-15.

Double-click this line

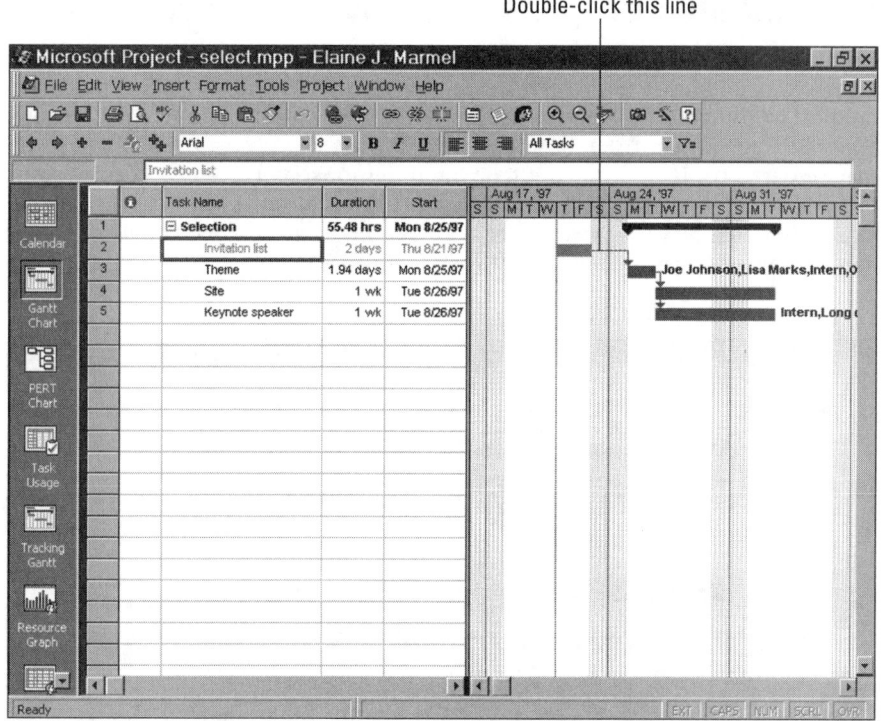

Figure 15-14: Double-click on the link line between the internal task and the external task.

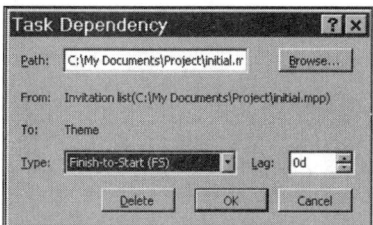

Figure 15-15: Use the Task Dependency dialog box to change the dependency information about tasks linked across projects.

Use the Path box to update the path between the linked files, the Type box to change the type of link, and the Lag box to change the amount of lag time between the link.

Consolidated projects — to save or not to save

You don't need to save consolidated project files unless you want them. You can create the consolidated project file using either the Window⇨New Window method or the Insert⇨Project method described in this chapter. You can use the consolidated project to create links and maybe even reports, and then close the consolidated project file without saving it. Suppose you created the consolidated project by inserting projects and the inserted projects are not open. When you close the consolidated project, Project asks whether you want to save changes you made to each inserted project (see Figure 15-16).

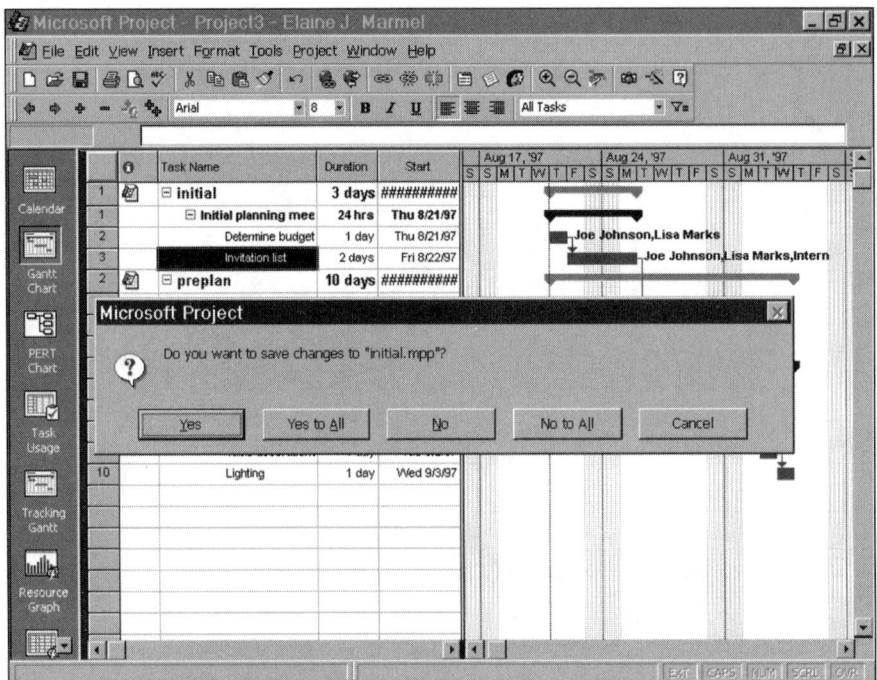

Figure 15-16: When you close a consolidated project you created by inserting projects, Project asks if you want to save changes, including links, you made to each subproject.

If you created the consolidated project using the Window⇨New Window method, Project asks you whether you want to save changes to the subprojects as you close them.

If you save the changes to the subprojects, whether or not you save the consolidated project, external tasks such as the one you saw in Figure 15-13 appear in the subproject files when you open them.

Viewing Multiple Projects

Creating a consolidated project makes your work easier because you can display and hide selected portions of your project.

The consolidated project in Figure 15-17 contains five inserted projects. As you can tell from the outline symbols, you can't see all the tasks in this consolidated project in the figure; the tasks for rent and wrap are hidden.

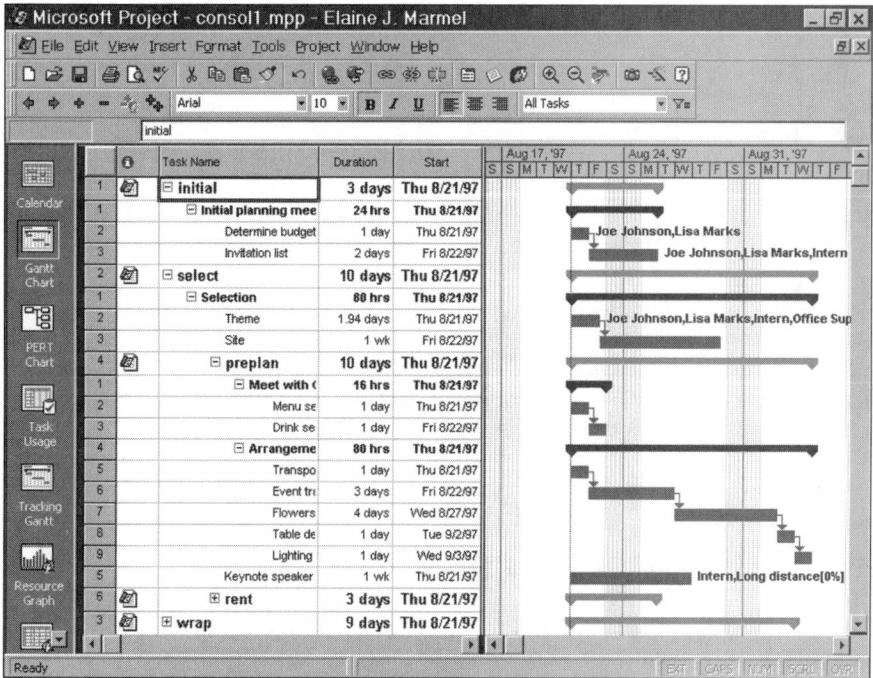

Figure 15-17: This consolidated project contains five inserted projects.

Suppose you need to focus on the initial portion of the project. As you can see in Figure 15-18, if you click on the outline symbols to the left of each summary task other than initial, you can easily focus on the portion of the project that currently needs your attention.

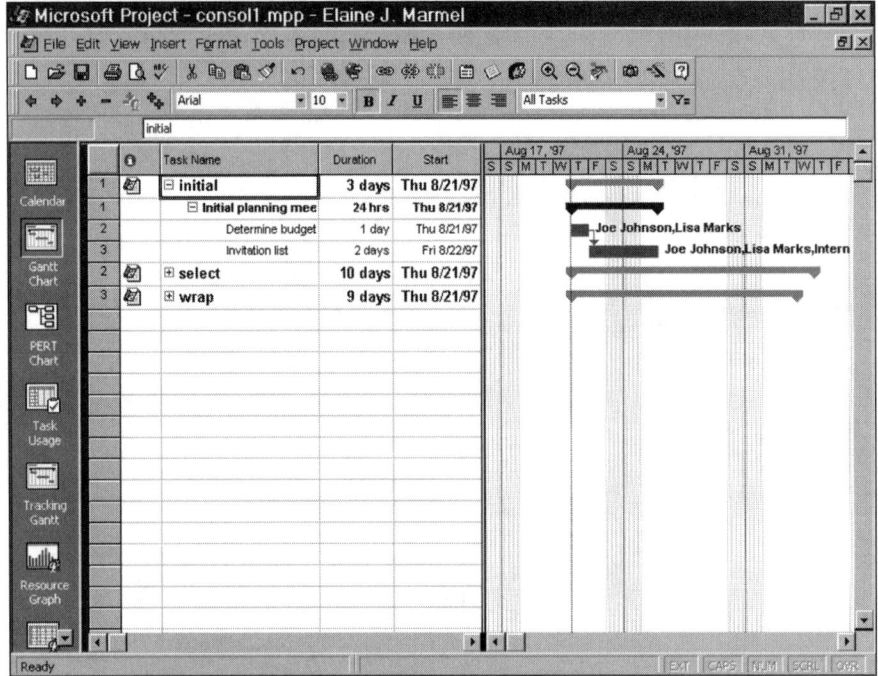

Figure 15-18: Close up inserted projects so that just their summary tasks appear when you want to focus on a portion of a consolidated project.

Using Multiple Critical Paths

Multiple critical paths can help you consolidate projects. By displaying multiple critical paths, you can see a critical path for each inserted project.

By default, Project displays only one critical path, but you can change this default. Choose Tools⇨Options and click on the Calculation tab to display the dialog box you see in Figure 15-19.

Place a check in the Calculate multiple critical paths check box and click on OK.

When you view your project in a view that displays critical paths, such as the Tracking Gantt view, you can see critical paths for each independent set of tasks. Project sets the late finish date of any task without a successor to the task's early finish date, giving the task no slack and making it critical. Figure 15-20 shows two critical paths; if you could see it onscreen in color, you would easily identify the critical paths because they are red.

Place a check in this box

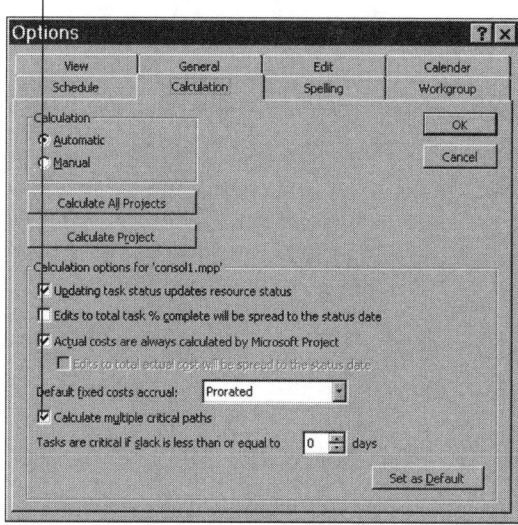

Figure 15-19: The Calculation tab of the Options dialog box.

Critical paths

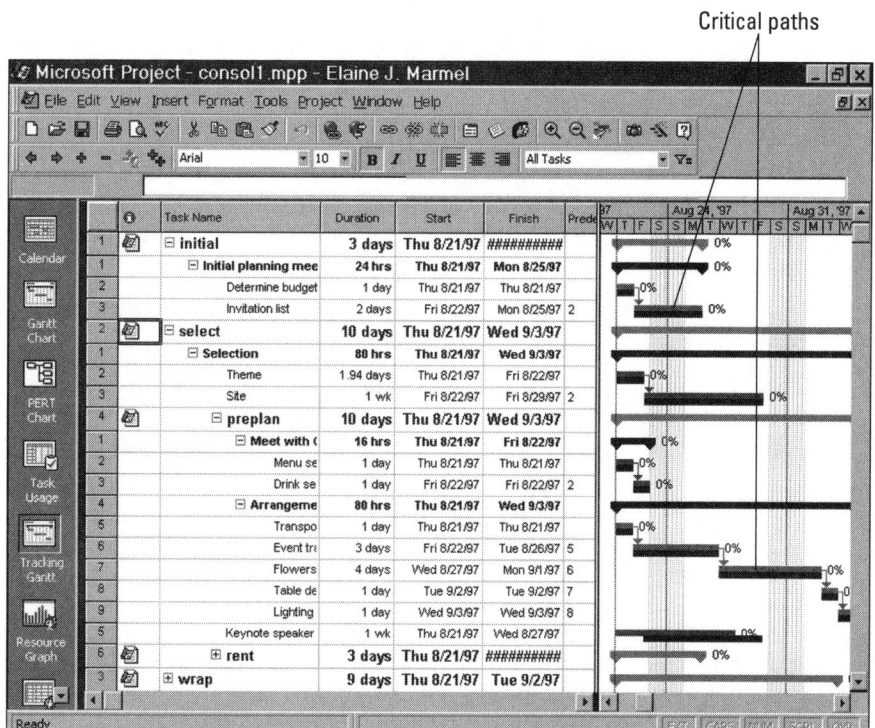

Figure 15-20: You can display multiple critical paths, which can be particularly effective when you work in a consolidated project.

Sharing Resources Among Projects

Creating a resource pool can be useful if you work with the same resources on multiple projects. A resource pool is a set of resources that are available to any project. You can use resources exclusively on one project, or you can share the resources among several projects.

If you work in an environment in which several project managers use the same set of resources on various projects, consider using a resource pool. Setting up a resource pool in Project can be a good way to schedule resources and resolve resource conflicts.

See Chapter 9 for more information on other techniques you can apply to resolve resource conflicts.

Creating a resource pool and sharing the resources

Setting up a resource pool in Project can facilitate resource management, especially for resources shared on several projects. To create a resource pool, you simply set up a project file that contains only resource information.

If you already have a project set up that contains all the resources available, you can use that project as a model. Just open it; you don't need to delete all its tasks.

After you identify a project that can serve as the resource pool, you designate it as the resource pool project in the following way:

1. Open the project that is to be the resource pool file.

2. Open the project that is to use the resource pool (that is, the project on which you want to work).

3. Choose Tools⇨Resources⇨Share Resources. Project displays the Share Resources dialog box (see Figure 15-21).

4. Click on the Use Resources option button; then use the From list box to select the resource pool project to indicate you want to use the resources defined in that project.

Note

If you open only the project on which you want to work, the Use own resources option button is the only choice available and you won't be able to share resources with the resource pool. The first time you want to enable resource sharing, you must open both the project on which you want to work and the project you determined would be the resource pool.

In addition, if you have any other projects open, they appear as candidates for the resource pool project when you open the From list box because Project allows you to select from any open project when you identify the resource pool.

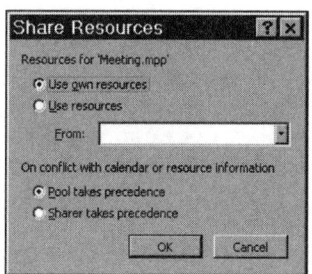

Figure 15-21: The Share Resources dialog box.

5. Tell Project how to handle calendar conflicts. If you select Pool takes precedence, the resource calendars in the resource pool file will take precedence when conflicts arise. If, however, you select Sharer takes precedence, the resource calendars in the file you're updating will take precedence over the resource calendars in the resource pool file when conflicts arise.

6. Click on OK.

If you switch to the Resource Sheet view of the file you want to update, Project displays all the resources contained in the resource pool file along with any resources you may have set up in your project file.

You can now continue working in your project, or you can save your project and close it. You can also close the resource pool file.

Opening a project that uses a resource pool

At some point you will save and close your file and then come back to work on it a second time. You don't need to open the resource pool file at that time. Instead, when you open your file *after* you have set it up to share resources, you see the dialog box that appears in Figure 15-22.

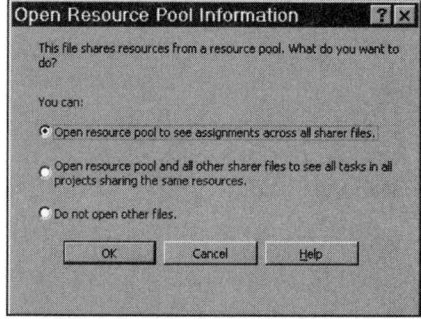

Figure 15-22: The Open Resource Pool Information dialog box.

Typically, if you select the first option button in this dialog box, Project gives you enough information to get to work. When you select the first option, Project opens your file and the resource pool file. When you select the second option, Project opens all files that are using the resource pool as well as the resource pool. If you select the last option, Project opens only your file; Project does not transfer any changes you make to the resources in your file to the resource pool because the resource pool file won't be open.

New Feature

When you select either the first or the second option, Project 98 automatically opens the resource pool file as a read-only file. This new functionality enables you to make changes to your project without tying up the resource pool file and, therefore, allows multiple users to simultaneously use the resource pool.

Updating information in the resource pool

If you make any changes to resource information while you're working on your project, you must update the resource pool file so that others using the resource pool have the most up-to-date information. To update the resource pool, make sure the resource pool file is open, even in read-only mode. Then choose Tools⇨Resources⇨Update Resource Pool (see Figure 15-23).

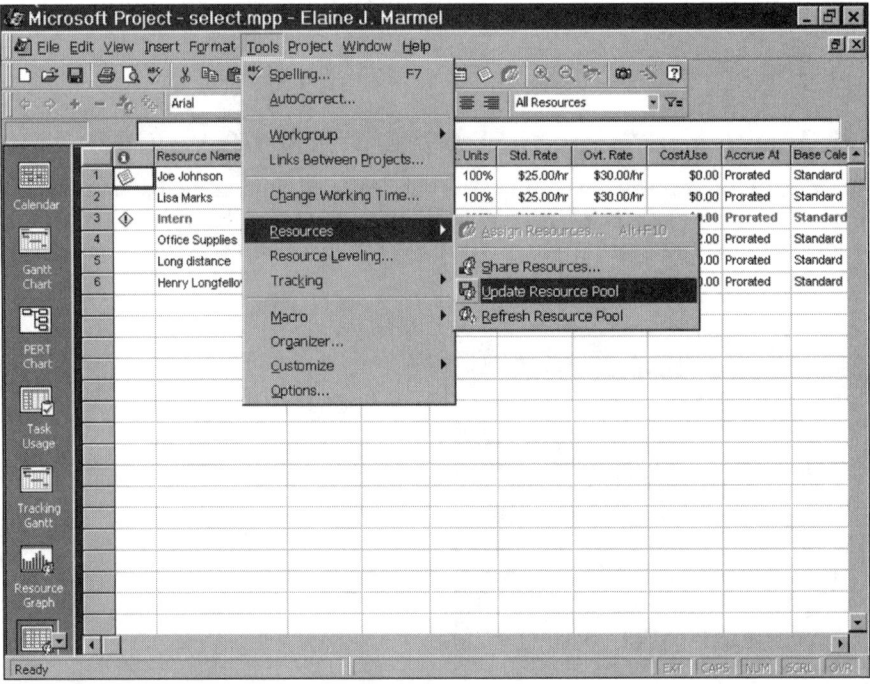

Figure 15-23: The Update Resource Pool command is available if you set up resource sharing and you make a change in your project while the resource pool file is open.

Note   If you opened only your project and made changes to the resources, this command is not available while working in your project. Further, if you opened only your project, saved and closed your project, and then open the resource pool file, this command *still* is not be available. To ensure that Project incorporates the changes you make to resources in your project in the resource pool, be sure to open the resource pool file in read-only mode when you open your file.

Tip   To ensure consistency and avoid arguments in the workplace, usually one group or person is responsible for updating the resource pool.

If you forget to update the resource pool after you make a change in your project that affects the resource pool, Project displays the message you see in Figure 15-24 when you close your project and save it.

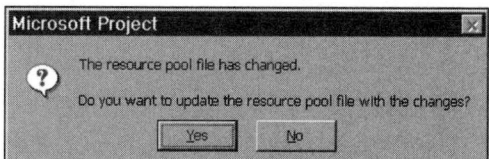

Figure 15-24: If you forget to update the resource pool, Project alerts you when you close and save your project.

Quit sharing resources

Suppose you decide that you no longer want to use the resource pool file. Follow these steps to disable the resource pool for a specific project:

1. Open that project.

2. Choose Tools⇨Resources⇨Share Resources.

3. Select the Use own resources option button in the Share Resources dialog box (refer to Figure 15-21).

But what if you decide that you want to disable the resource pool in general for all files. Do you need to open each file and disable resource sharing? No. Follow these steps to disable the resource pool file in general:

1. Open resource pool file in read-write mode.

2. Choose Tools⇨Resources⇨Share Resources. Project displays the Share Resources dialog box you see in Figure 15-25.

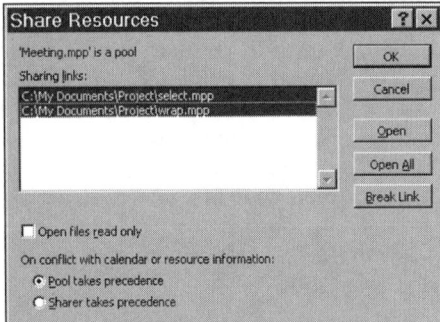

Figure 15-25: The Share Resources dialog box.

3. Select the project(s) you want to exclude from the resource pool. You can select multiple noncontiguous projects by holding Ctrl when you click or contiguous projects by holding Shift when you click.

4. Click on Break Link.

Summary

This chapter describes how to consolidate projects and pool resources. You learned how to

✦ Insert projects

✦ Understand and work with consolidated projects and dependencies

✦ Manage the view of a consolidated project

✦ Display multiple critical paths

✦ Share resources

The topic of Chapter 16 is customizing Microsoft Project to suit the way you work.

✦   ✦   ✦

Advanced
Microsoft Project

Customizing Microsoft Project to Suit Your Needs

◆ ◆ ◆ ◆

In This Chapter

Modifying toolbars

Customizing menus

Creating custom
views

Making changes
to tables

◆ ◆ ◆ ◆

After you have worked with Project for a while, you may want to change the way various elements appear on screen and how you use Project's tools and commands. For example, perhaps you use a particular command for sharing resources all the time — you could perform that action quickly if you could access it from a tool button on the standard toolbar. Or maybe you never use the Task Note tool and prefer to get it off screen and place its command on a menu. Perhaps none of Project's built-in views or tables contains quite the combination of information you use most often.

Luckily, Microsoft Project allows you to customize most of its elements. This chapter shows you how to make changes to toolbars, menus, views, tables, and reports to make Project work the way that's best for you.

Making Changes to Toolbars

Toolbars are to Windows software what remote controls are to television — effortless, hi-tech ways to take action. Toolbars are easy to use and always right at hand. However, you and Microsoft might not agree on which tools you use most often.

You can easily modify the arrangement of tools in Project — you can add or remove tools from a toolbar, change the function of a tool button, create your own set of tools, or even edit the look of tool buttons.

Note

You can make changes to your Project environment effective for your copy of Project alone, for those in a group, or across your company. Project saves your changes to a file named global.mpt and opens new projects based on the global file by default; consequently, your changes remain intact. You can use the Organizer to make the changed global file available to others.

Adding and deleting tools from a toolbar

Although toolbars include many commonly used functions, they aren't all inclusive. For example, the Formatting toolbar includes commands to change the font and font size; apply bold, italic and underline effects; and align tasks. But it doesn't include tools for modifying the timescale, gridlines, or bar styles. If you use those features often, you might want to add them. Alternatively, you might prefer to have a tool that appears on one toolbar by default appear on the Standard toolbar instead.

To add tools to any toolbar, locate the tool in the appropriate category and then drag it onto the toolbar where you want it to appear. Follow these steps to add a tool to a toolbar:

1. Choose View⇨Toolbars⇨Customize to open the Customize dialog box shown in Figure 16-1. The Toolbars tab is the default.

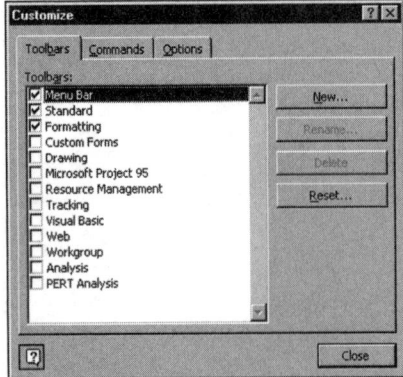

Figure 16-1: The toolbars that have a check mark here are currently displayed on screen.

2. Click on the check box for the toolbar on which you want to place the tool — so that Project displays that toolbar. For example, if you want to add the Paste as Hyperlink button to the Web toolbar, make sure the Web toolbar is displayed.

3. Click on the Commands tab, shown in Figure 16-2.

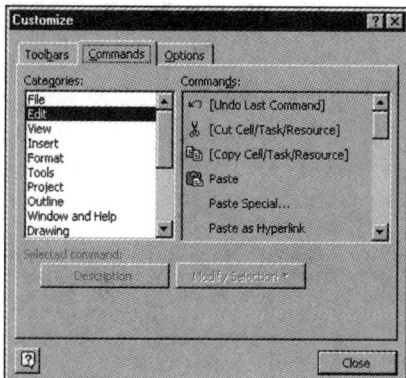

Figure 16-2: Categories of commands contain all the possible tools built into Project.

4. Click on the category of command that contains the tool you want to add to a toolbar. For example, the Paste as Hyperlink tool is in the Edit category because that category is where cutting, copying, and pasting tools typically reside.

Tip

If you don't know which category a tool command belongs to, use the scroll bar in the Categories list and select All Commands at the bottom of the list. The Commands list displays every available command in alphabetical order.

5. Click on the item in the Commands list, drag it from the dialog box onto your screen, and place it the toolbar of your choice.

You can also easily delete a tool from a toolbar. With the Customize dialog box open, display the toolbar that contains the tool you want to delete, click on the tool, and drag it off the toolbar.

Note

To restore a toolbar's original setting, open the Customize dialog box, select the Toolbars tab, click on the toolbar name in the list of toolbars, and click on Reset. Project restores the default tools.

Creating custom toolbars

Rather than modify some of Project's toolbars, you might prefer to create a custom toolbar that contains all the tools you use most often. You can also do that from the Customize dialog box by following these steps:

1. Display the Toolbars tab of the Customize dialog box.

2. Click on the New button. The New Toolbar dialog box shown in Figure 16-3 appears.

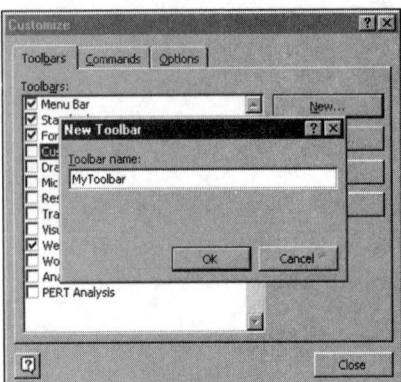

Figure 16-3: Name your toolbar anything you like — perhaps after your spouse, your pet, or your favorite movie star.

3. Type a Toolbar name and click on OK. A small toolbar, devoid of tools at the moment, appears. You can drag this floating toolbar to any location on the screen that's convenient for you.

4. Click on the Commands tab to select it.

5. Click on tools in any category and then drag them onto the new toolbar. The new toolbar resembles the toolbar in Figure 16-4.

Figure 16-4: Place these tools in any order you like; if you want to move a tool, drag it off the toolbar and place it again.

6. Add dividers (the thin gray lines that separate groups of tools) to your new toolbar. Select the tool that you want to place to the right of the divider and click on the Modify Selection button on the Commands tab. The menu shown in Figure 16-5 appears.

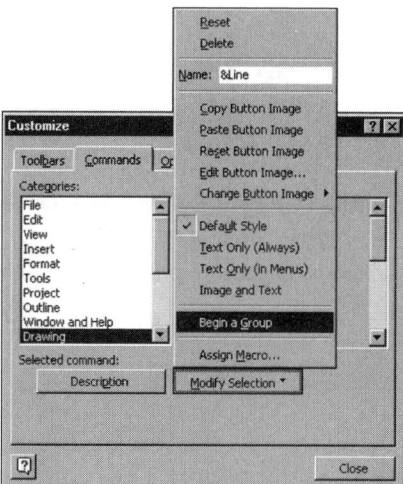

Figure 16-5: This menu offers options to work with button images, as well as options to modify other toolbar features.

7. Select the Begin a Group command from this menu to insert a divider in your toolbar, as shown in Figure 16-6.

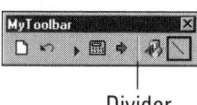

Divider

Figure 16-6: Place a divider on a toolbar to make logical groupings of tools that perform certain types of functions.

To delete a divider, select the tool to its right and, using the Modify Selection pop-up menu, select Begin a Group again to deselect that command.

Editing button images

Don't like the little pictures Microsoft assigned to its tool buttons? Feeling creative? Project allows you to select from a whole set of other button designs, from smiling faces to musical notes, or to edit a button image yourself with picture and color tools.

Caution

If anyone else uses your copy of Project, be cautious about changing tool images. Someone accustomed to Project's standard tool images might press a button unaware of its true function, doing damage or simply not being able to function with your copy of Project. And you aren't immune from forgetting the changes you made.

Choosing a new image

Here's how you can change the images that appear on tools:

1. Choose Views⇨Toolbars⇨Customize to open the Customize dialog box.

2. Click on the Commands tab to select it.

3. Click on a tool on any toolbar you have displayed. (If you need to display a toolbar, you can select it on the Toolbars tab of this dialog box.)

4. Click on the Modify Selection button and select Change Button Image. The pop-up palette of images shown in Figure 16-7 appears.

Figure 16-7: From coffee cups to the eight balls, these images are both clever and descriptive.

5. Click on an image you want to use.

To return an image to its original setting, choose Modify Selection⇨Reset Button Image.

6. Click on Close to close the Customize dialog box when you finish.

If you modify enough button images, you could end up with a toolbar that looks as unusual as the one in Figure 16-8. Just be sure you can remember what picture represents which command.

Figure 16-8: If a smiling face makes your day go faster, use it!

Tip

Tooltips still work with modified tool buttons and are a great help in remembering what button does which function. Just pass your mouse pointer over any tool, and its original name appears.

Editing an image

If you prefer, rather than replacing the button image with a predefined picture, you can edit the existing picture by modifying the pattern and colors on it. For example, if two tools seem similar to you, help yourself differentiate them by applying a bright red color to either one. Tool-button images comprise many tiny squares called *pixels*. By coloring in the pixels, you can form an image. You can use a color palette and the individual pixels to modify tool-button images or even draw an entirely new image.

To edit a tool-button image, follow these steps, starting from the Customize dialog box Commands tab:

1. Click on a tool button on any displayed toolbar and then click on Modify Selection.

2. Select the Edit Button Image command to open the Button Editor dialog box in Figure 16-9.

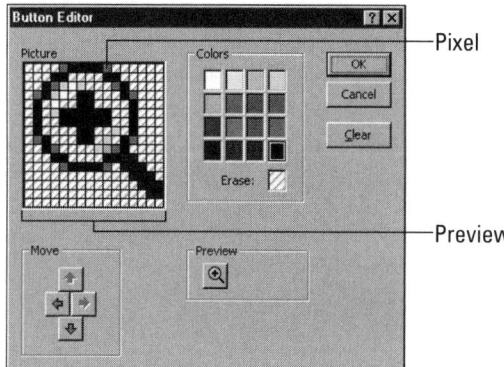

Figure 16-9: The small Preview helps you see how changes to individual picture pixels will appear on the tool-button image.

3. Try the following techniques:

   ✦ To make changes to an image, click on a color block in the Colors palette and then click on an individual pixel.

   ✦ To remove color from a pixel, click on the Erase square in the Colors palette and then click on the pixel.

   ✦ To see more of a (large) button that doesn't fit in the Picture box, use the Move arrows to move from side to side or up and down to display the images edges.

4. Click on OK to save your changes and to return to the Customize dialog box. Click on Close to return to your Project screen.

By modifying the location and color of pixels, you can modify an image or create a whole new image. For example, I added a yellow border around the outside of the button and changed the color of the magnifying glass handle to red in the image in Figure 16-10. This enhancement differentiates the Magnify and Zoom buttons.

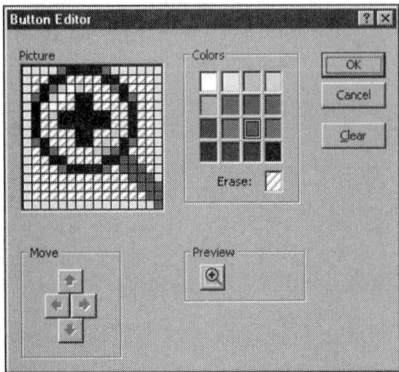

Figure 16-10: You can use colors to highlight buttons you frequently use.

Tip

To color in a large area of pixels, click on a color in the palette, then click on a pixel, and drag your cursor in any direction to color multiple pixels in one motion. Release your cursor to stop painting the pixels.

Customizing Project Menus

Toolbars aren't the only way to get things done in Project, and they aren't the only feature of Project that you can customize. You can also create new menus, and modify existing menus to your heart's content. For example, you could add a command to the File menu that changes the current view to the PERT Chart view and prints a report. You can add these functions because menu commands are actually *macros* — that is, recorded series of keystrokes or programming commands.

Note

Macros are really a form of computer programming. The macro-programming language for Microsoft products is Visual Basic. In a macro you save a string of commands that instruct the software to perform one action, or a series of actions. Project provides an easy method for selecting commands to associate with a macro and for saving the macro as a custom menu command. See Chapter 17 for more on macros.

When you select a menu command, you are really invoking a macro, telling Project to repeat the sequence of events that causes a dialog box to appear, copies a selected piece of text, and so on.

You can use your own macros and Project's built-in commands to customize Project by building new menus and changing the function of existing commands. Another way to customize Project is to delete menus or commands on menus that you don't need.

Adding menus

To add a new menu to your Project menu bar, you follow a process similar to that used to add a new toolbar. First you drag a new, blank menu to the menu bar, then you assign it a name, and finally you drag commands onto it.

Note
As with toolbars, Project adds new menus to your global file, the default file on which all project files are based. Therefore, changes you make to menus or the menu bar are in effect for all files you create with this copy of Project.

Follow these steps to add a new menu to Project:

1. Choose View⇨Toolbars⇨Customize to open the Customize dialog box.

2. Make sure the Menu Bar is showing on your screen; if it's not, click on the Menu Bar item on the Toolbars tab of the Customize dialog box.

3. Click on the Commands tab to select it.

4. Scroll to the bottom of the list of Categories and click on the category named New Menu. The single selection, New Menu, appears in the list of Commands, as in Figure 16-11.

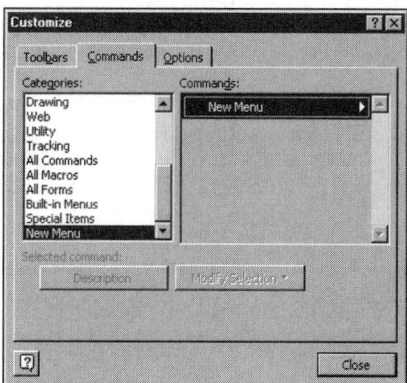

Figure 16-11: The New Menu category has only one command in it.

5. Click on the New Menu item in the Commands list and drag it up to the menu bar. When the dark vertical line of your cursor is where you want to place the new menu, release your mouse button. Project places a New Menu item on the menu bar.

6. Select the New Menu and click on Modify Selection. From the new pop-up menu (see Figure 16-12), highlight the name New Menu and type a specific menu name. Then click outside the Modify Selection menu to close it.

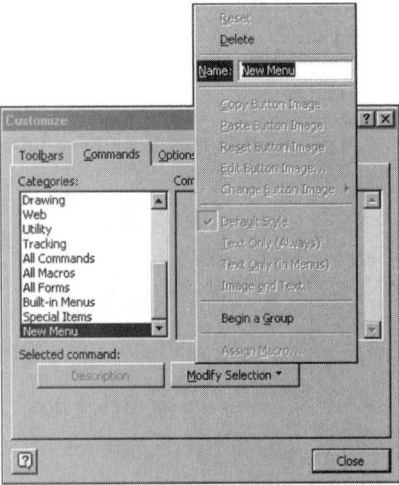

Figure 16-12: The menu name should help you remember what kinds of commands it contains.

7. Select a category of command that you want to place on the new menu. If you have created a macro and want to place it on the menu, select the category All Macros, which includes standard menu command macros as well as macros you've created.

8. Click on an item in the Commands list and drag it up to the New Menu on the menu bar. A small, blank box appears under the menu heading.

9. Place the cursor in that blank area and release the mouse button to place the command on the menu.

10. Click on Close to close the Customize dialog box.

You can repeat this process to build the new menu. The menu in Figure 16-13 has two macro commands.

Figure 16-13: To divide the menu into groups of commands, you can use the Modify Selection⟳ Begin a Group command to add dividing lines.

Assigning new commands

You might also want to modify the function of an existing menu command. For example, if you create a macro that invokes the Print command and accepts all the Print dialog box defaults for you, you could assign that macro to the Print command. That way you don't have the extra step of clicking on OK to accept print defaults every time you print. As always, be careful about replacing the function of one command with another, especially if other people will be using your copy of Project.

Tip

You can reinstate all the menu defaults by opening the Toolbars tab on the Customize dialog box, clicking on the Menu Bar item, and clicking on Reset.

To change the macro associated with a command, follow these steps:

1. Display the Customize dialog box (View➪Toolbars➪Customize).

2. Open the menu on which you want to edit a command.

3. Right-click on the command you want to change; the menu in Figure 16-14 appears.

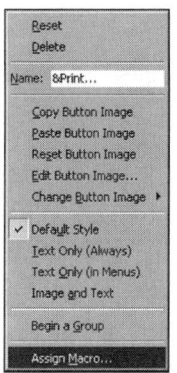

Figure 16-14: You can use this menu to add a tool-button image next to a menu command.

4. Select the Assign Macro command from this menu to open the Customize Tool dialog box shown in Figure 16-15.

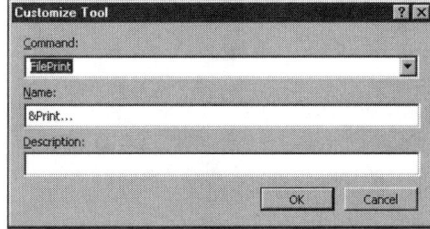

Figure 16-15: The Name entry in the Customize Tool dialog box is the name of the macro it invokes.

5. Click on the Command drop-down list and select the command you want to associate with the menu item.

6. Type a Description of what this command does (optional).

7. Click on OK to return to the Customize dialog box and then click on Close to save the new command with the menu item.

Deleting commands and menus

Is your screen getting cluttered with custom commands and menus? To remove a particular command or a whole menu, without resetting all the menu changes you've made, follow these steps:

1. Open the Customize dialog box.

2. Click on a menu name, or open the menu and click on a particular command.

3. Drag the item off the menu bar and close the Customize dialog box.

That's all there is to it!

Working with Views

As you've seen throughout this book, views display a variety of information: tables with several fields of data, task bars, PERT nodes, and so on. Microsoft has provided a plethora of views, meeting just about every information need. Nevertheless, you may want to create a variation on one of those views to look at information from a different perspective. For example, you could create a second PERT view in which you set the nodes to display an entirely different set of information than the standard PERT view. Then, rather than having to modify the nodes in the original PERT view all the time to see different information that you call on frequently, you can simply click on the new view to display the alternative PERT view. You can base an alternative view on any of the existing views and then change the information that Project displays by default to include only the information you need.

For information about displaying and using views and tables, refer to Chapter 6.

Adding views

You can select a view from the View bar along the left side of your screen, or you can right click on that bar and choose More Views from the shortcut menu. Project gives you dozens of alternative views to select from (see Figure 16-16). When you create a new view, you can include it on the View bar or make it available in the More Views dialog box only.

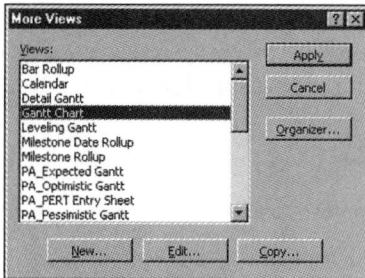

Figure 16-16: A wide selection of built-in views meets most informational needs.

To add a new view to your copy of Project, perform these steps:

1. Choose View⇨More Views (or right-click on the View bar and choose More Views from the shortcut menu).

2. Click on the New button in the More Views dialog box (refer to Figure 16-16). The Define New View dialog box shown in Figure 16-17 appears.

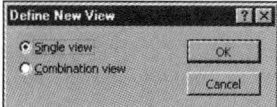

Figure 16-17: A simple choice awaits you in the Define New View dialog box: a single or combination view.

3. Click on the control button for a Single view. The View Definition dialog box in Figure 16-18 opens.

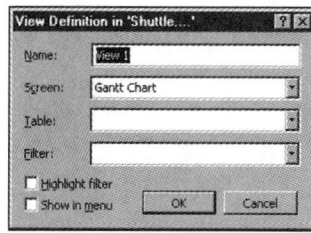

Figure 16-18: If you click on the Combination view control button, the View Definition dialog box requests slightly different information.

4. Enter the Name of the new view. Make it something that describes the information you'll show in the view.

5. Select a current view to base the new view on by clicking on the arrow to open the Screen drop-down list. Then click on a view name.

6. Do one of the following:

✦ If the screen you chose in step 5 gives you the option of selecting a table to include with it, select that table from the Table drop-down list shown in Figure 16-19.

✦ If the screen you chose in step 5 does not give you this option, go on to step 7.

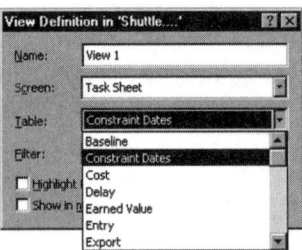

Figure 16-19: All the built-in tables and new tables that you have created appear on this list.

7. Click on the arrow to the right of the Filter field to open a drop-down list of filters to apply to the view. By default, Project applies the All Tasks filter; therefore, all tasks appear in the view. To apply a selective filter so that only filtered tasks are highlighted, click on the Highlight filter check box at the bottom of the View Definition dialog box.

Note

You can set filters to remove tasks from the display that don't meet the filtering criteria, or you can set filters to simply highlight the tasks that meet the criteria. If you want to reformat text that Project highlights as meeting filter criteria, choose Format➪Text Styles. Refer to Chapter 6 for more information on using filters.

8. Click on the Show in menu check box to make the new view available as a selection in the View bar and on the View menu. If you do not select this option, you must display the view by selecting it from the More Views dialog box.

9. Click on OK and then click on Apply to save the new view and display it on screen.

Defining a combination view

You've just seen how to create a single view. But what if you want a combination view? Figure 16-20 shows the dialog box that appears if you select the Combination view option in the Define New View dialog box.

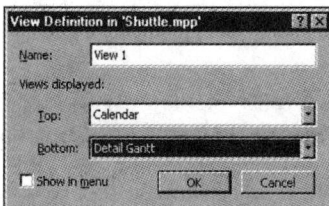

Figure 16-20: The only option in the combination view View Definition dialog box is which two views to place on screen.

Using these settings you would simply name the view and designate which view should appear on top of the screen and which view should appear at the bottom. You can either display these two views at the same time in a split screen or hide the bottom one temporarily.

Modifying views

If you're constantly changing the information that you're displaying in a view, you should probably create a second view. For example, if you are constantly editing a PERT view that contains information about the schedule to show information about resources, a second PERT view could save you time. However, if you almost never use the information provided by default in the PERT view, maybe you should just edit the original view to present the data you use most often.

You edit a view by modifying the information it displays, using the same dialog boxes you used to create a new view in the preceding section. Follow these steps to modify an existing view:

1. Choose View➪More Views to open the More Views dialog box.

2. Click on the view you want to edit and then click on the Edit button. The View Definition dialog box shown in Figure 16-21 appears.

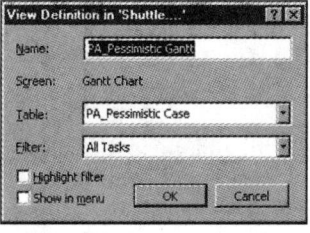

Figure 16-21 In views that don't contain tables, the table choice is not available to edit.

Note

You cannot modify the screen on which this view is based — you made that selection before opening the View Definition dialog box. However, you can make adjustments to the name, table of information displayed, and filter applied. If your goal is to make this view available in the View bar, select the Show in menu check box.

3. Click on OK when you are finished with the settings and then click on Apply to see the edited view.

To make new views available to other Project schedules, click on the Organizer feature in the More Views dialog box (refer to Figure 16-16). From the Organizer dialog box, shown in Figure 16-22, you can select a view from the current file list and copy it to the global.mpt file. That view becomes available to all schedules created with your copy of Project.

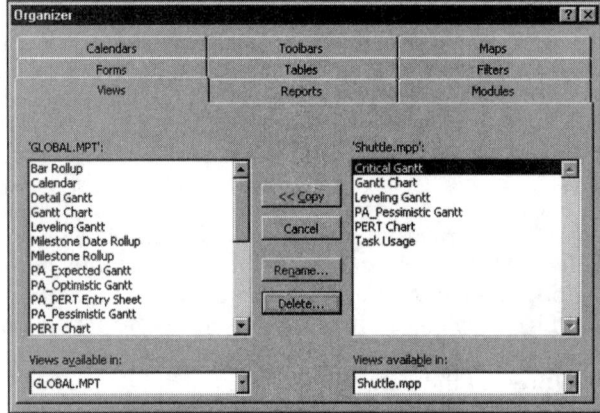

Figure 16-22: All views in the global.mpt file are available to every file based on the global.mpt file.

Changing Tables

Tables don't appear in every view. For example, neither the PERT view nor the Resource Graph view has a table displaying columns of information. However, views that have tables, such as any Gantt view or the Task Usage view shown in Figure 16-23, also have a table selection button. Right-click on the table selection button to list the standard tables you can display, as well as the More Tables options.

The More Tables option enables you to modify the fields of information displayed in the columns of tables, and even to create new tables. As with views, Project has dozens of tables built in, with a wide variety of information included to help you focus on issues of schedule, resources, tracking, and so on. However, your project may require different fields of information; for example, your boss might want a special combination of schedule and resource information that doesn't exist in any current Project table.

Note

How do you decide whether to create a new table or to modify an existing one? If you can find a predefined table with a similar focus that has several of the fields you want to include, start with that table. Then delete, rearrange, or add fields as needed. If you can't find an appropriate model, you may need to create a new table.

However, if you edit an existing table, instead of creating a new one, someone else using your schedule may expect to find different fields on the table. The best approach is to edit a copy of the original table and leave the original for others to use.

Table selection button   Shortcut menu of tables   Table fields displayed in columns

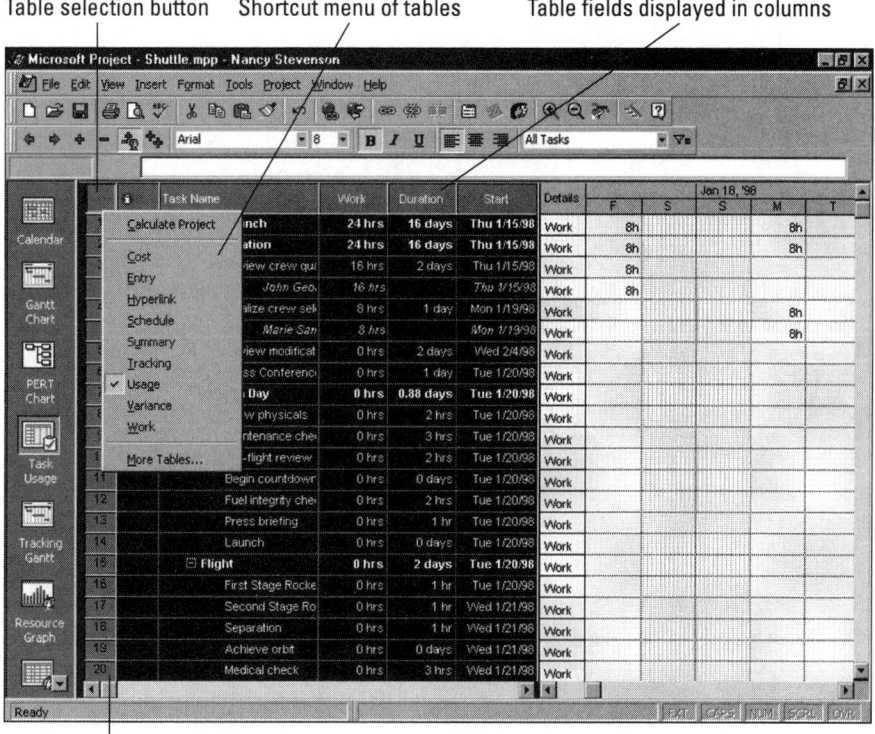

Locked first column

Figure 16-23: Display another table by selecting it from this shortcut menu.

Creating new tables

Because of Microsoft's consistency of design, creating new tables in Project is remarkably similar to several of the other procedures you've worked through in this chapter. You open a dialog box to see more tables and then use a Table Definition dialog box to define the fields you want to include.

Tip

Many tables list baseline information first and then list actual information resulting in this sequence of columns: Baseline Start, Baseline Finish, Actual Start, Actual Finish. Comparing this information might be easier if you create a table that presents the information this way: Baseline Start, Actual Start, Baseline Finish, Actual Finish, and so on.

To create a new table, follow these steps:

1. Choose View➪Table➪More Tables to open the More Tables dialog box in Figure 16-24.

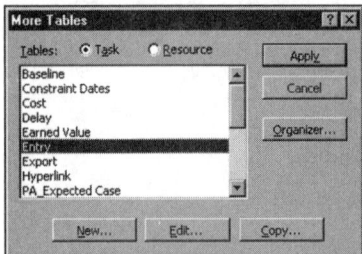

Figure 16-24: This dialog box looks much like the More Views dialog box and serves a similar purpose.

2. Click on New to display the Table Definition dialog box shown in Figure 16-25.

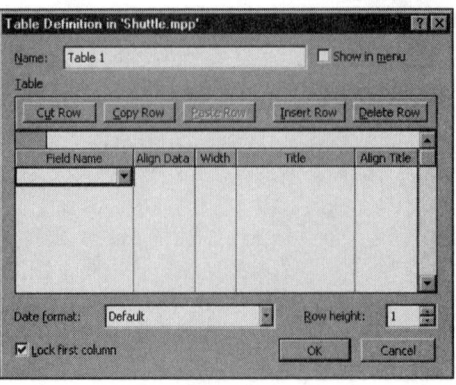

Figure 16-25: Be sure to give the table a meaningful name.

3. Enter a name for the table in the Name field. If you want to show this table in the shortcut menu that appears when you click on the table selection button, select the Show in menu check box.

4. Click on the area under the Field Name column; a cell with an arrow on its right side is defined.

5. Click on the arrow to display the drop-down list shown in Figure 16-26. Notice that an entry bar opens above the column.

6. Select a field name and then click on the Align Data column. The default settings for alignment of data and title, as well as the width of the column, appear.

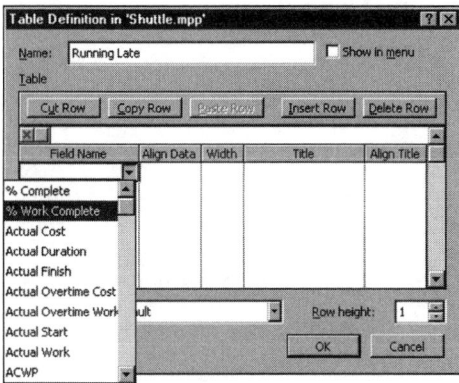

Figure 16-26: You can select fields of predefined information to build the columns in your table.

7. Click on the arrow to the right of the Align Data default; then select Left, Center, or Right alignment for the data in the column.

8. Click on the Width column and use the spin controls to modify the width of the column to accommodate the type of information you think will typically go there.

Tip If you aren't sure about the ideal column width, just accept the default. You can easily adjust column widths when the table is onscreen by clicking on the edge of the column heading and dragging to the right or left.

9. Click on the Title field and enter a title for the column if you don't want to use the default field name. Otherwise, skip this step.

10. Click on the Align Title column and select a different alignment for the column title if you like.

11. Repeat steps 4 through 10 to add more fields to your table. You can use the Cut Row, Copy Row, Insert Row, Paste Row, and Delete Row buttons to reorganize the order of fields in your table.

Note

If you have included any columns that include dates, such as Start or Finish information, you can modify the date format using the drop-down list of choices in the Date format field. You can also modify the height of all the rows with the Row height setting.

If you want the first column of your table to remain on screen while you scroll across your page, select the Lock first column check box. Typically, the Task ID column is the column locked in place in a table. (You can see a sample of a locked first column in Figure 16-23.)

12. Click on OK when you are finished, as you did for the new view definition. Then click on Apply to display the new table on your screen.

Making changes to existing tables

Just as you can edit existing views, menus, and toolbars, you can edit tables in Project, too. You might want to reorganize the order of columns in the table. Or perhaps you'd like to add the table to the list of tables on the shortcut menu that appears when you click on the table selection button. You may even want to add or delete some fields of information from the table. You can either edit an existing table or make a copy of it and edit the copy.

Tip

If you want to hide a particular column in a table you can temporarily remove it from view, rather than edit it out of the table. Simply click on the right edge of the column's title and drag to the left to shrink it to zero column width. To see the column again, choose View⇨Tables⇨More Tables, edit the table, and increase the column width again. When you save that change and return to the screen, the column has reappeared.

Perform these steps to edit an existing table:

1. Choose View⇨Table⇨More Tables.

2. Select a table you want to edit; you can use the Task or Resource choices at the top of the dialog box to categorize the type of table you need. Then click on either the Edit button to edit the original table or the Copy button to edit a copy of the table. The Table Definition dialog box, shown in Figure 16-27, appears.

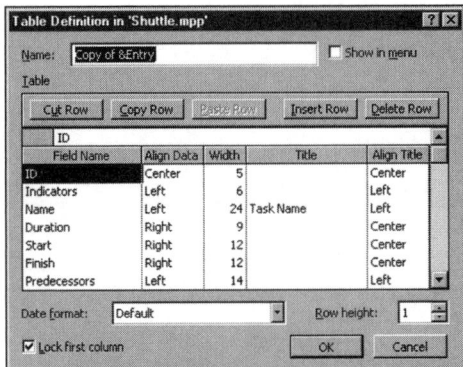

Figure 16-27: The Name field starts with the word Copy if you are editing a copy of the original table.

    3. Do any of the following:

        ✦ Click on a field name and click on the Delete Row button to remove a field

        ✦ Click on a field name and click on the Insert Row button to insert a new field above it

        ✦ Type a new Name for the table, and select the option to display it in the menu

        ✦ Change the Date format or Row height for all fields in the table

        ✦ Lock or unlock the first column of information

        ✦ Use the Cut Row and Paste Row buttons to change the order of fields displayed in the table

    4. Click on OK when you're done editing the table. Then click on Apply to display the edited table on screen.

Caution

The More Tables dialog box does not have a Table reset button; consequently, any changes you make are permanent. My advice is to always make a copy of a table to modify, rather than editing the original table. That way the original tables remain intact.

Note

Once again, if you want new or edited tables to be available to other schedules, you must use the Organizer function in the More Tables dialog box to copy them to the global.mpt file.

Summary

In this chapter you've learned

✦ How to customize the features you use to get things done (toolbars and menus)

✦ How to make changes to Project's informational displays (views and tables)

You can use the skills you've learned here to make Project work in the way that's most comfortable for you.

In the next chapter you learn details about creating your own macros, which can form the basis for new tools and menus and streamline the repetitive tasks you perform to create and track a schedule.

✦   ✦   ✦

Using Macros to Speed Your Work

Macros are small programs that carry out tasks you perform on a regular basis. You may have used macros in a word processing program; macros work the same way in Project as they do in your word processor.

Don't let the word *program* in the preceding paragraph deter you from learning about macros. Although you can actually work with the macro programming code, Project provides an easier way for you to write a macro, as you learn in this chapter.

Why Use Macros?

Macros are most useful when you need to perform any repetitive task. In particular, you can use Project macros to

✦ Display or hide frequently used toolbars

✦ Display frequently used tables

✦ Display frequently used views

✦ Switch to a custom view

✦ Generate standard reports

As you learn to use Project, you'll identify the steps you take over and over again; these tasks are excellent candidates for macros.

Recording Macros

Project stores macros in the Visual Basic for Applications programming language. And if you're adept at programming, you can actually write your macro in the Visual Basic for Applications programming language. A sample of the instructions stored in a macro in the Visual Basic for Applications language appears in Figure 17-1.

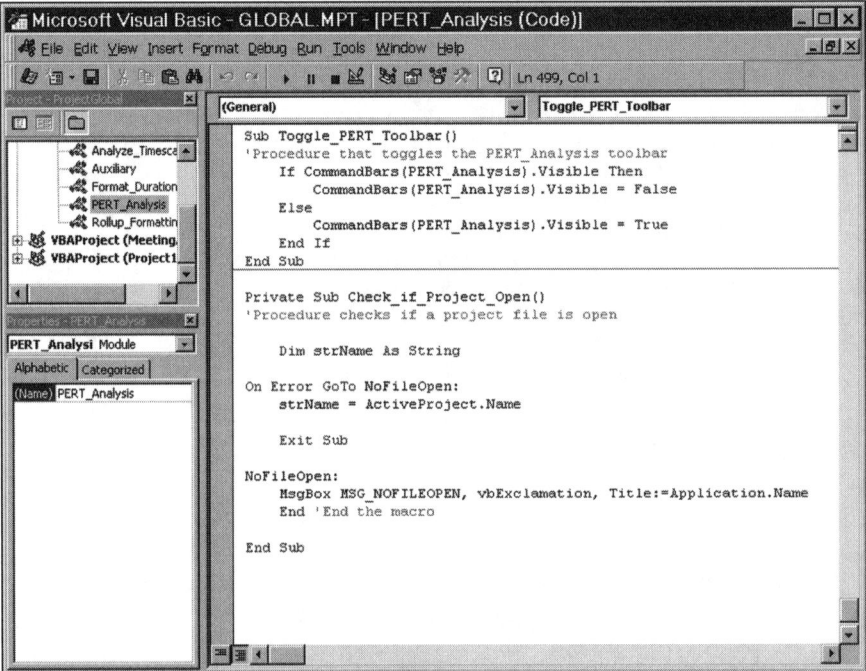

Figure 17-1: A sample set of instructions stored in a macro.

Most people prefer to record a macro. *Recording* a macro is a way to have Project memorize the steps you want to take and store those steps. When you record a macro, you *do* whatever you want Project to do; Project converts those actions in Visual Basic statements and stores the statements in a macro. Later, when you want to take that action again, you run your macro, which you learn how to do in the next section.

Before you record a macro, you should run through the steps you want to take. You might even want to write down the steps. That way, you are less likely to make (and record) mistakes.

Suppose you want to create a macro that displays the Task Details Form in the bottom pane when you display the Gantt Chart view. Here are the steps you need to record in this macro:

1. Click on Gantt Chart in the View bar.

Tip

By selecting the view first, you force Project to start your macro from the Gantt Chart view, regardless of the view you were using before you ran your macro.

2. Use the split bar (or choose Window⇨Split) to open the bottom pane that shows, by default, the Task Form view.

3. Click on the bottom pane and choose View⇨More Views to open the More Views dialog box.

4. Select the Task Details Form.

5. Click on Apply.

Now that you know what you're going to record, use these steps to record the macro:

1. Choose Tools⇨Macro⇨Record New Macro to open the Record Macro dialog box you see in Figure 17-2.

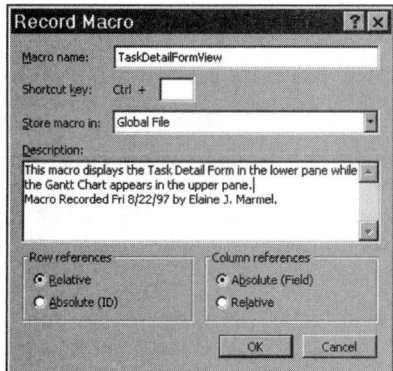

Figure 17-2: The Record Macro dialog box.

2. Enter a name for the macro in the Macro name box.

The first character of the macro name must be a letter, but the other characters can be letters, numbers, or underscore characters. You cannot include a space in a macro name, so try using an underscore character as a word separator in a macro name or capitalize the first letter of each word in the macro name.

3. (Optional) To assign the macro to a keyboard shortcut, type a letter in the Shortcut key box.

The letter you assign can be any letter key on your keyboard, but it cannot be a number or a special character.

You cannot assign a key combination that is already used by Microsoft Project; if you select a reserved letter, Project displays see the warning message shown in Figure 17-3 when you click on OK.

Note Keyboard shortcuts are only one way you can run a macro. Later in this chapter you learn the other methods to play back a macro as well as how to assign a keyboard shortcut after you record and store your macro.

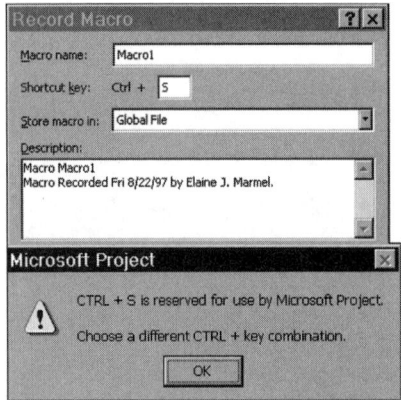

Figure 17-3: Project displays this warning message if you select a keyboard shortcut already in use.

4. Open the Store macro in box and click on the location where you want to store the macro. You can store the macro in the Global File or in the current project. To make a macro available to all projects, select Global File.

Note The Global File is also called the Global template, and it acts like the Normal template in Word or the Book1 template in Excel. Any customized features, such as macros, toolbars, or menus, that you store in the Global File are available to any project file. On the other hand, customized features you store in an individual project file are available only to that file.

5. Type a description of the purpose of the macro or the function it performs in the Description box. This description appears whenever you run the macro from the Macro dialog box.

6. Use the options in the Row references and Column references boxes to control the way the macro selects rows and columns if you select cells while running a macro. For rows, the macro always selects rows regardless of the position of the active cell because it records relative references to rows. If you want a macro to always select the same row, regardless of which cell is first selected, select Absolute (ID).

For columns, the macro always selects the same column each time it is run, regardless of which cell is first selected, because it records absolute references to columns. If you want a macro to select columns regardless of the position of the active cell when you run the macro, select Relative.

7. Click on OK. Project redisplays your project, and you won't notice any differences, but Project is now recording each action you take.

8. Take all the actions you want to record.

9. Choose Tools➪Macro➪Stop Recorder (see Figure 17-4) to stop recording.

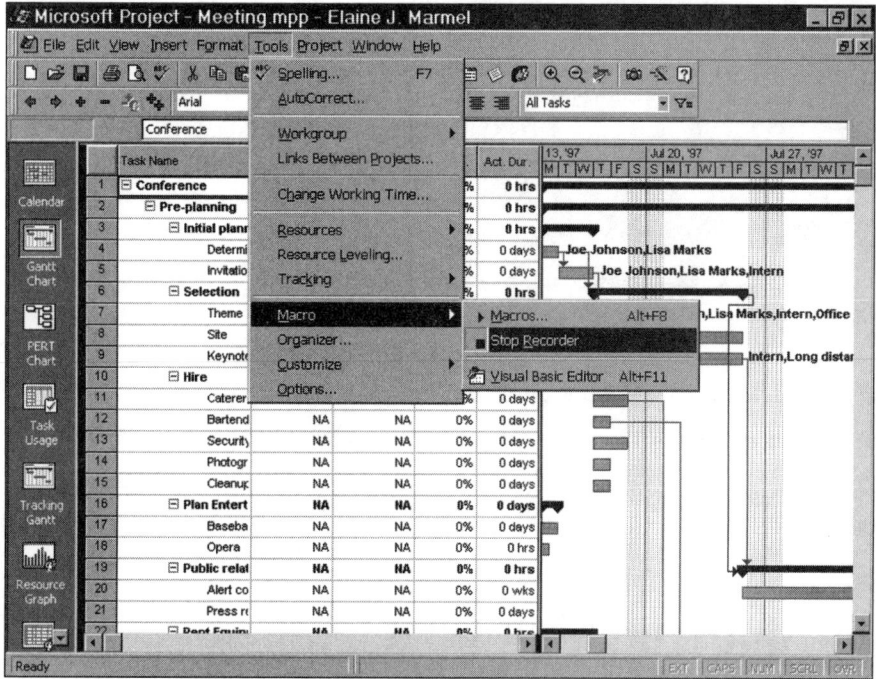

Figure 17-4: When you're recording a macro, the Stop Recorder command is available.

Running Macros

To use a macro that you have recorded, you run the macro. Some people refer to this action as "playing back" the macro because they associate recording and playing back with the process of recording a TV program on a VCR and then playing back the recording.

If your macro makes substantial changes to your project, you should save the project before you run the macro. You can't undo the effects of a macro easily. To run a macro, follow these steps:

1. Open the project that contains the macro.

2. Choose Tools➪Macro➪Macros to open the Macros dialog box you see in Figure 17-5.

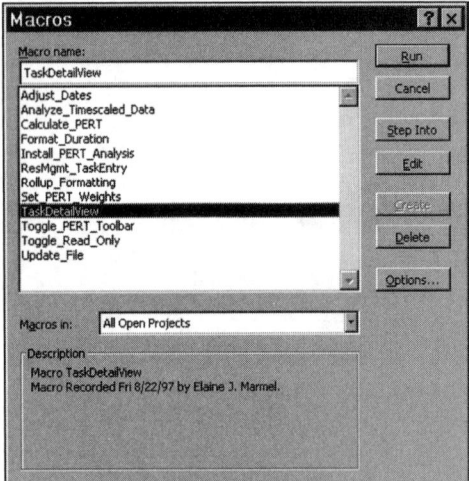

Figure 17-5: The Macros dialog box.

3. Select the macro you want to run from the Macro name list.

4. Click on Run. Project performs the steps you recorded in the macro.

If your macro is long and you want to stop it while it's still running, press Ctrl+Break. If your macro is short, it will probably finish before you can stop it.

Using Shortcuts to Run Macros

Although you can run macros by selecting them from the Macro dialog box, if you use a macro on a regular basis, you might want to shorten the method for running the macro. You can

✦ Create a toolbar button that runs the macro

✦ Create a menu command that runs the macro

✦ Create a keyboard shortcut that runs the macro

Assigning a macro to a toolbar button

Suppose you're a fan of toolbar buttons, and you create a macro that you use a lot. You find yourself wishing, "Gee, wouldn't it be great if I could just click on a toolbar button to make my macro run?" Well, you can get your wish by adding a button to a toolbar and assigning your macro to that button.

Caution

Adding buttons to the toolbars that come with Project isn't always a good idea. If you add a toolbar button to one of the toolbars that comes with Project and you reset that toolbar, the button you added disappears.

The following steps explain how to add a button assigned to a macro to the Standard toolbar, but you can also add toolbar buttons for macros to a custom toolbar you create. Chapter 16 explains how to create a custom toolbar.

1. Check to see whether the toolbar to which you want to add a button appears on screen. If it does, go to step 2. Otherwise, display the toolbar by right-clicking on any toolbar button and choosing the toolbar from the shortcut menu that appears.

2. Choose View⇨Toolbars⇨Customize to open the Customize dialog box.

   You can also open the Customize dialog box by choosing Tools⇨ Customize⇨Toolbars.

3. Choose Commands to display the Commands tab shown in Figure 17-6.

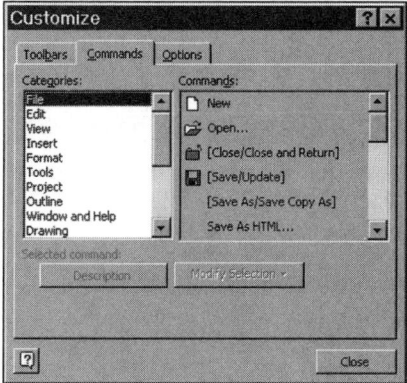

Figure 17-6: From the Commands tab of the Customize dialog box, you can add macros as buttons to toolbars.

4. Scroll down the Categories list and select All Macros. Project displays a list of macros in the Commands list on the right side of the dialog box.

5. Drag the macro you want to add onto the desired toolbar (see Figure 17-7). As you drag, the mouse pointer image changes to include a small button and a plus sign. As you move the mouse pointer over a toolbar, a large insertion point marks the location where the button appears when you release the mouse button.

Mouse pointer

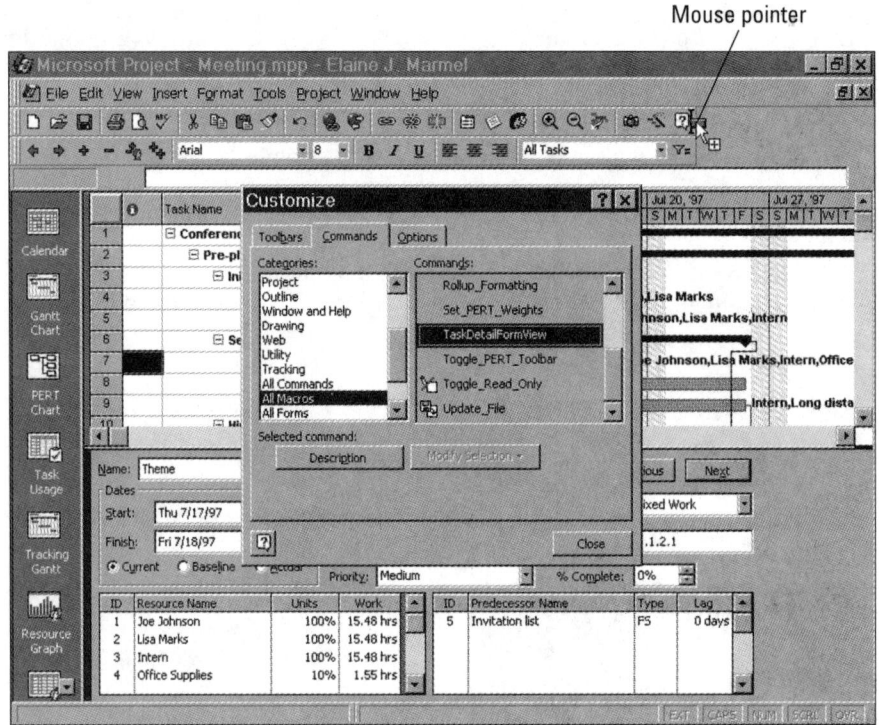

Figure 17-7: The image of the mouse pointer icon changes as you drag a macro onto the Standard toolbar.

When you release the mouse button, a new button appears on the toolbar, as shown in Figure 17-8.

Macro button

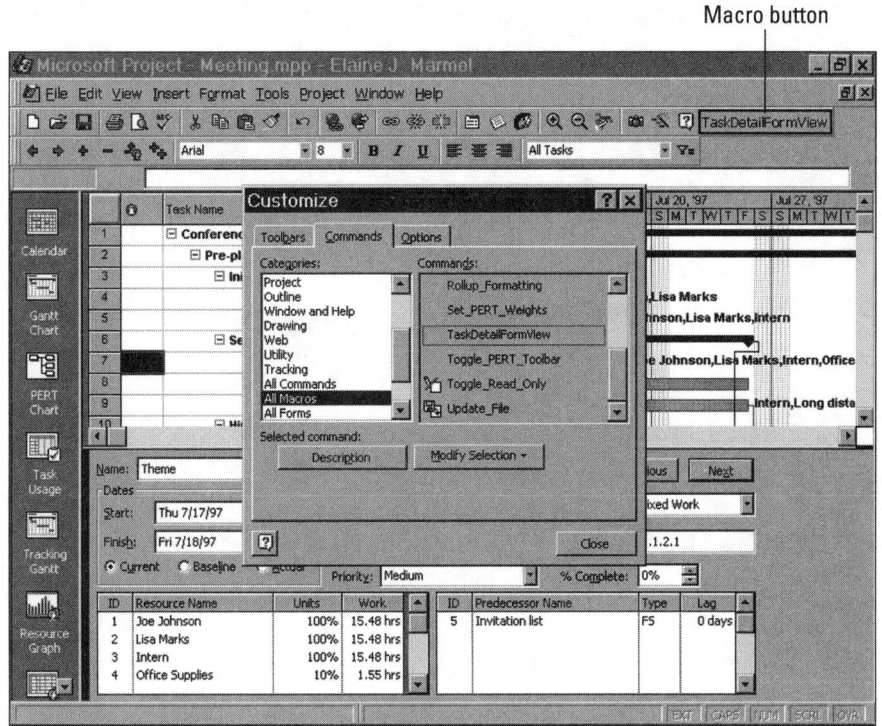

Figure 17-8: The new button after dropping it on the toolbar.

6. To change the name on the toolbar button, click on Modify Selection in the Customize dialog box to open the pop-up menu shown in Figure 17-9.

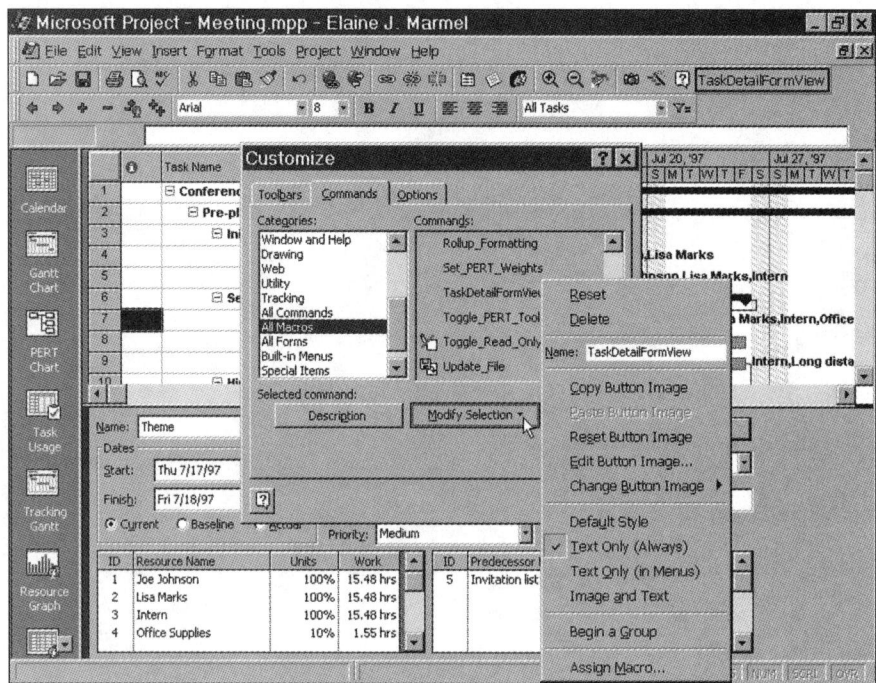

Figure 17-9: The menu that appears when you click on the Modify Selection button to change a macro button's name.

7. Type the name, exactly as you want it to appear on the toolbar button, into the Name box. You can include spaces.

8. Press Enter. The pop-up menu disappears, and Project renames the macro toolbar button, as shown in Figure 17-10.

Macro button

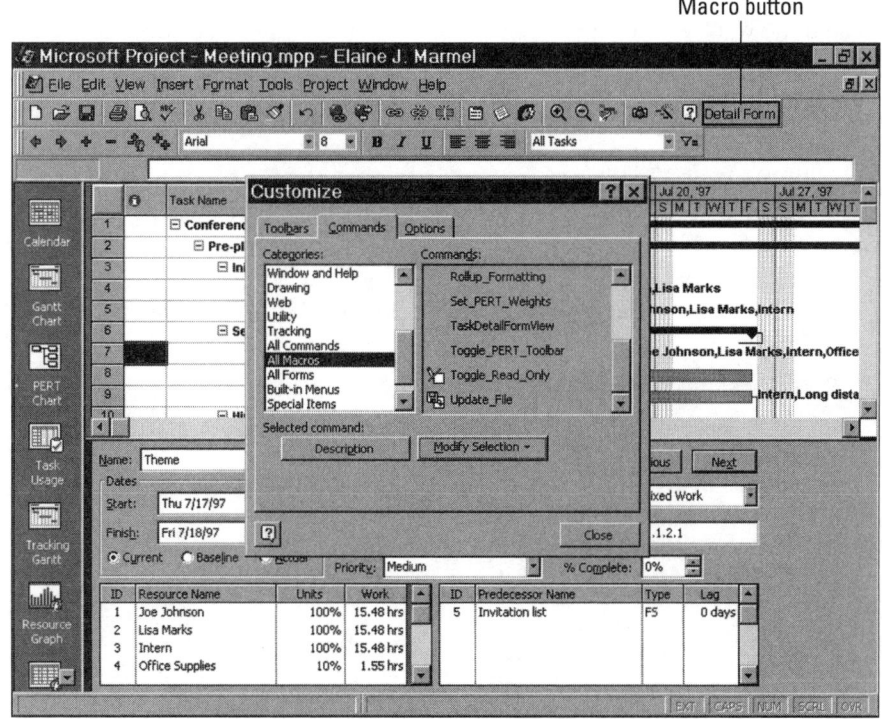

Figure 17-10: The toolbar button after renaming it.

9. Close the Customize dialog box.

When you add a toolbar button to an existing toolbar, Microsoft Project saves it in your global file. Any other project files you open on your computer using that global file contain the new toolbar button.

Assigning a macro to a menu command

Maybe you're not a toolbar person, or maybe you just prefer to use menu commands. The following steps demonstrate how to add a command assigned to a macro to the Tools menu; you can also add commands for macros to a custom menu you create.

Caution

As with toolbars, be aware that adding commands to the menus that come with Project isn't always a good idea. If you add a command to one of the standard menus and you reset that menu, the command you added will disappear.

See Chapter 16 for information on creating a custom menu.

Tip

If you don't want your custom menu to appear all the time, you can create a custom toolbar and drag menus onto it. Then you can hide or display the toolbar as needed.

Follow these steps to add a command that runs your macro from a menu:

1. Choose View⇨Toolbars⇨Customize to open the Customize dialog box.

Tip

You also can open the Customize dialog box by choosing Tools⇨Customize⇨ Toolbars.

2. Choose Commands to display the Commands tab you see in Figure 17-11.

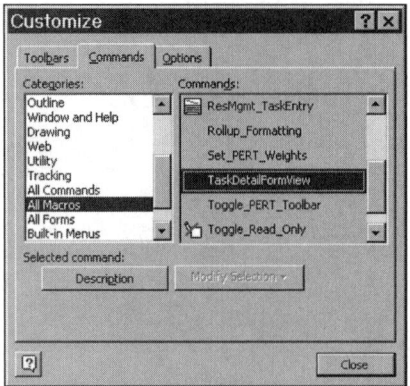

Figure 17-11: From the Commands tab of the Customize dialog box, you can add macros as commands on menus.

3. Scroll down the Categories list and select All Macros. Project displays a list of macros in the Commands list on the right.

4. Drag the macro you want to add to the desired menu (see Figure 17-12). As you drag, the mouse pointer image changes to include a small button and a plus sign. As you move the mouse pointer over a menu, the menu opens; a large horizontal insertion point marks the location where the button appears when you release the mouse button.

5. Release the mouse button. The macro appears on the menu (see Figure 17-13).

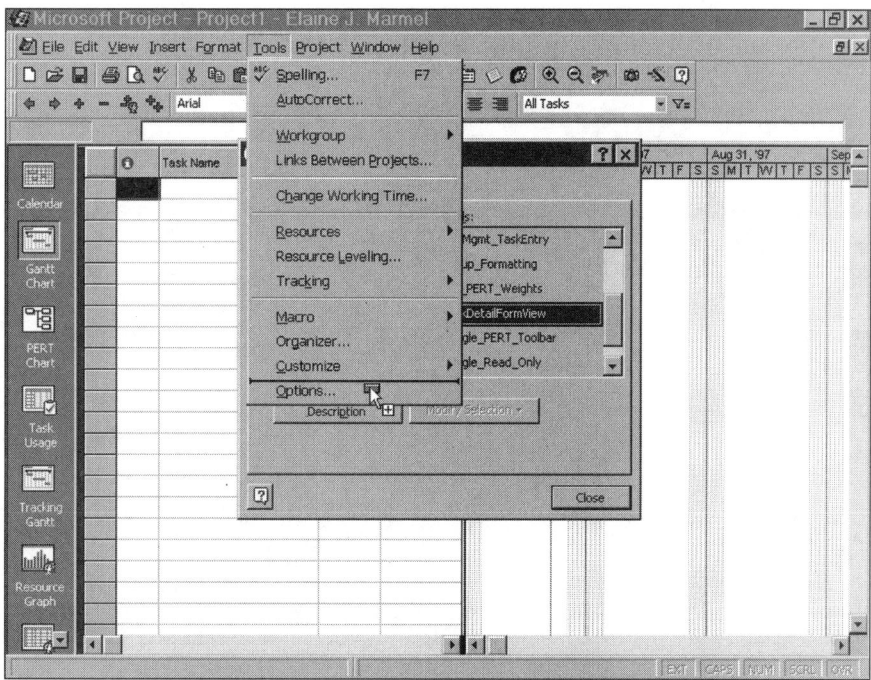

Figure 17-12: The image of the mouse pointer icon changes as you drag a macro onto a menu.

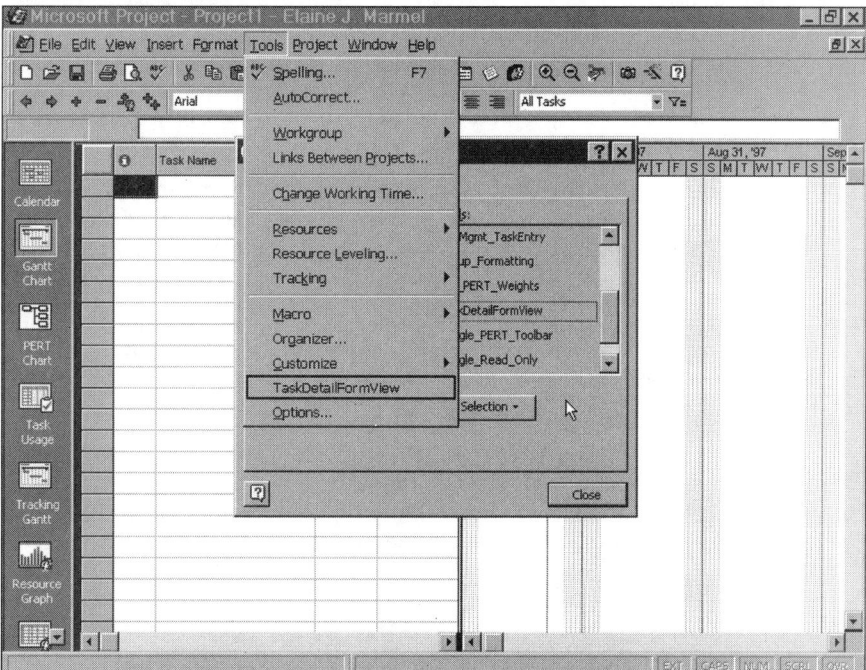

Figure 17-13: A macro placed on the Tools menu.

6. To change the name on the toolbar button, click on Modify Selection in the Customize dialog box to open the pop-up menu shown in Figure 17-14.

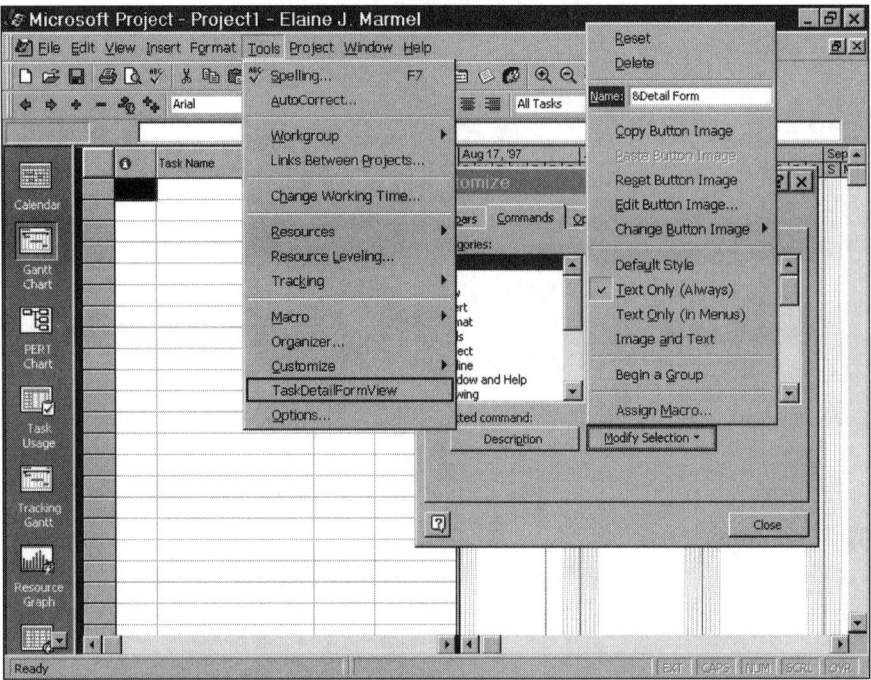

Figure 17-14: Modifying the command name on the menu.

7. Type the name (including spaces) exactly as you want it to appear on the toolbar button in the Name box.

   To provide a hotkey for your macro name, place an ampersand (&) immediately before the character you want to be the hot key. Make sure that the letter you select is not already in use by some other command on the same menu.

8. Press Enter. The pop-up menu disappears, and Project renames the menu command. As Figure 17-15 shows, the command includes your hot key if you added an ampersand.

9. Close the Customize dialog box.

When you add a command to one of the default menus, Microsoft Project saves the command and the menu in your global file. Any other project file you open on your computer using that global file contains the new menu command.

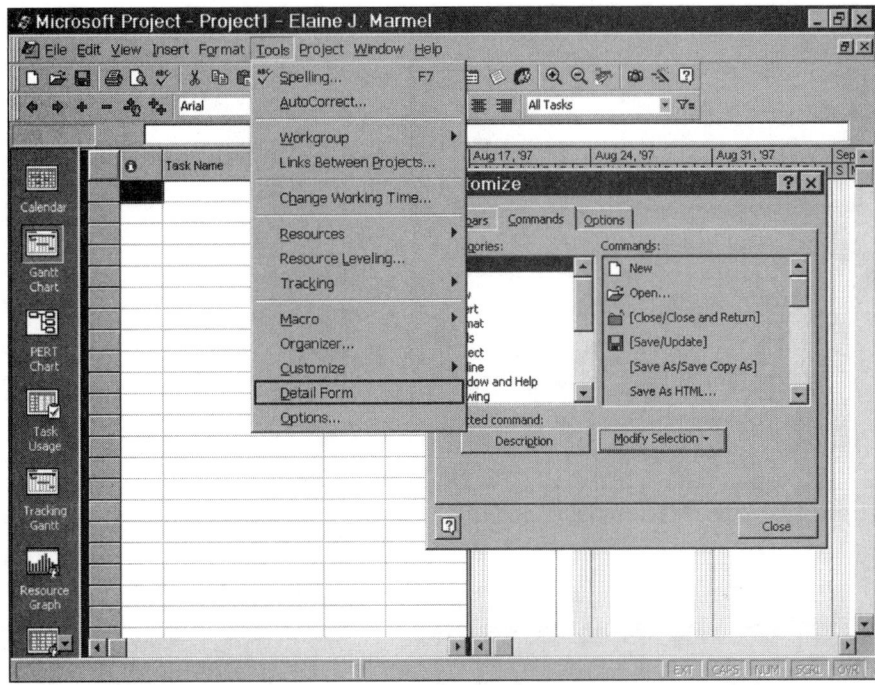

Figure 17-15: The command after renaming it and assigning a hot key.

Assigning a keyboard shortcut to a macro

So, suppose after you experiment, you decide that you really want to run your macro from a keyboard shortcut. Further suppose that you didn't set a shortcut when you created the macro. Follow these steps to add a keyboard shortcut to the macro after you create it:

1. Open the project containing the macro.

2. Choose Tools⇨Macro⇨Macros to open the Macros dialog box shown in Figure 17-16.

   You can press Alt+F8 to display the Macros dialog box.

3. Highlight the macro to which you want to add a keyboard shortcut.

4. Click on Options to open the Macro Options dialog box that appears in Figure 17-17.

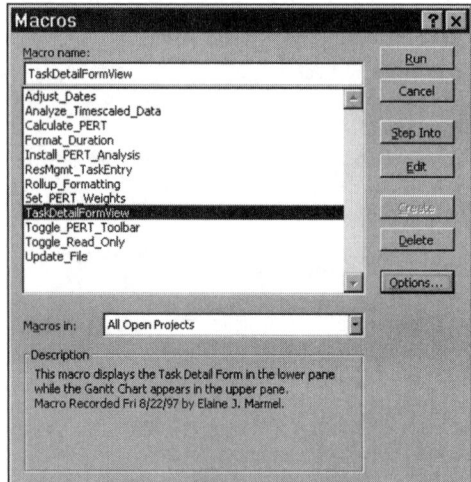

Figure 17-16: The Macros dialog box.

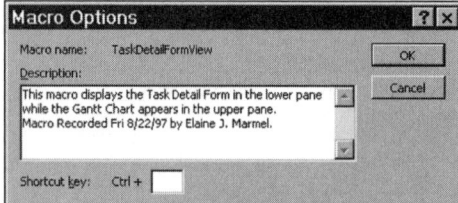

Figure 17-17: Set a keyboard shortcut for a macro from the Macro Options dialog box.

5. Place the insertion point in the Shortcut key box and type a letter.

6. Click on OK. If the combination you selected (Ctrl plus the letter you typed) is *not* in use by Project, Project displays the Macros dialog box again. If Project *is* using the combination you selected, even for another macro, Project asks you to try a different combination.

7. Close the Macros dialog box.

To run your macro, press the keyboard combination you assigned. If you decide that you don't want to run your macro using this keyboard combination, you can change the combination using the preceding steps, or you can remove the keyboard combination you assigned completely by reopening the Macro Options dialog box and deleting the letter from the Shortcut key box.

Summary

In this chapter you learned about using macros in Project. You've learned how to

✦ Create macros

✦ Use macros

✦ Copy macros to other projects

Chapter 18 explains how to import and export Project data.

✦   ✦   ✦

Importing and Exporting Project Information

♦ ♦ ♦ ♦

In This Chapter

Working with import/export maps

Importing and Exporting information

Understanding and solving importing and exporting problems

♦ ♦ ♦ ♦

Sometimes you need to move information in and out of Project. You can import information using various file formats. You also can export information to various file formats, including exporting a Project schedule as a graphic image to use in a graphics program, on a Web page, or to print on a plotter. You can also move information into and out of Project by copying and pasting the information.

Creating and Editing Import/Export Maps

When you import information into Project or export information from Project to another program, you usually use an import/export map. Project comes with a series of useful import/export maps, which you can also edit, or you can create a custom map.

An *import/export map* defines the information you want to import or export and allows you to describe how to match the information in the Project file with the information in the other program's file. For example, when you charted earned value in Excel in Chapter 13, you selected the Earned Value Information export map to send the data to Excel. This mapping information told Project what data to send to Excel for charting and how to identify the information in Excel.

Preliminary steps for mapping

To view, copy, or edit any of the predefined import/export maps or to create your own map, you must simulate importing or exporting a file. In the following steps, you simulate exporting a file to an Excel workbook:

1. Open any Project file.

2. Choose File⇨Save As to open the File Save dialog box.

3. Type a name in the File name list box for the file you want to simulate exporting.

4. Open the Save as type list box and select Microsoft Excel Workbook. Or you can select any file type other than Microsoft Project.

5. Click on Save. Project opens the Export Format dialog box shown in Figure 18-1.

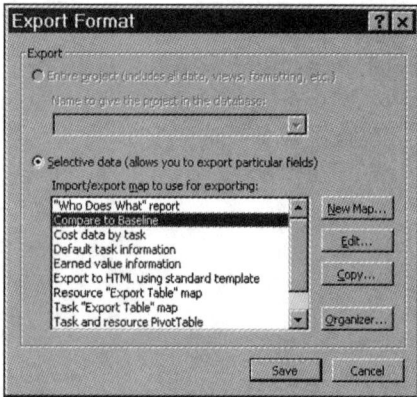

Figure 18-1: The Export Format dialog box.

You can now create your own map by selecting New Map. Or you can edit or copy an existing map by highlighting the map you want to use and then selecting Edit or Copy. If you simply want to view a map, select Edit and don't save any changes you might make while looking at the map. If you select Copy, Project creates a copy of the highlighted map, so if you make changes and save them, you won't affect any of Project's default maps.

Creating a new map

Note

Although this section talks about defining a new map for Excel, the concepts and steps are almost identical for defining a new map for another program. You simply wouldn't have some of the Excel-specific options, such as the Destination Worksheet Name on the Task Mapping tab or the Microsoft Excel check boxes on the Options tab.

When you select New Map, the Options tab of the Define Import/Export Map dialog box appears. Provide a name for the new map in the Import/Export map name text box. This name appears in the list in the Export Format dialog box. As you can see in Figure 18-2, you can use the Options tab to select the type of data to import or export. The boxes you check determine which mapping tab becomes available.

Tip

If you want your Excel workbook to contain assignments listed under tasks or resources, similar to the Task Usage or Resource Usage views, place a check in the Include assignment rows in output check box.

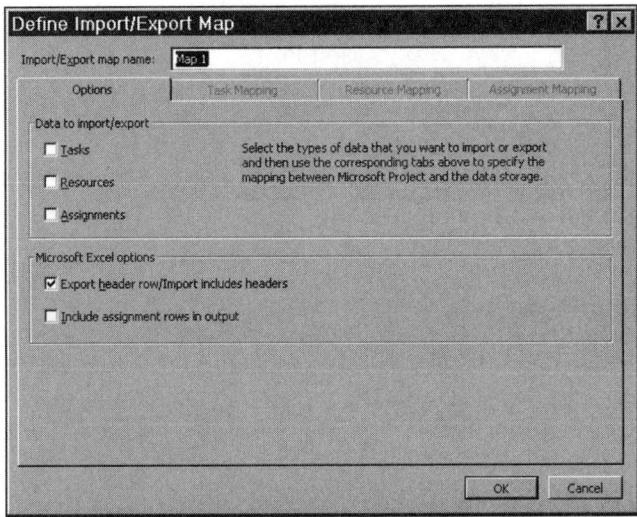

Figure 18-2: The Options tab of the Define Import/Export Map dialog box for an Excel file type.

After you select the type of data to import or export on the Options tab, some or all of the mapping tabs become available. All three mapping tabs in this dialog box and the Task Mapping tab in Figure 18-3 work the same way.

Note

The titles in the box refer to exporting because you simulated the export process to open this dialog box. If you had simulated importing, the titles in the box would refer to importing.

The Destination worksheet name box contains the name that is assigned in the Excel workbook. You can change this name.

Use the Export filter list box to select the tasks you want to export. By default, Project assumes you want to export all tasks, but you can export, for example, just completed tasks.

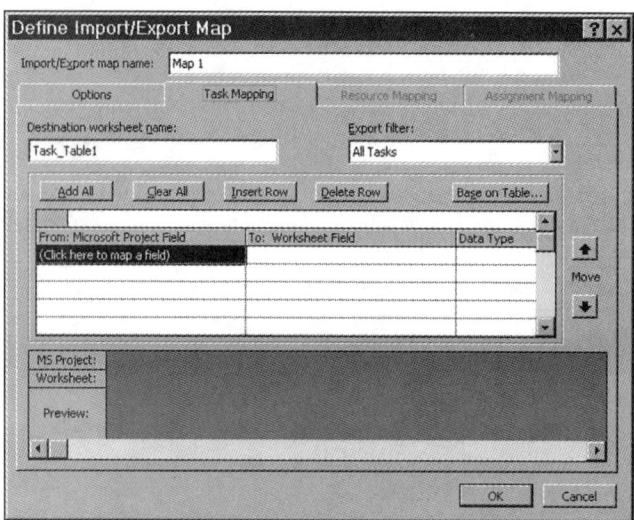

Figure 18-3: The Task Mapping tab where you identify the task fields you want to import or export.

To add fields to export one at a time, click on the phrase (Click here to map a field) that appears in the From: Microsoft Project Field column. After you click, you can use the list box arrow to view a list of fields available for exporting and to select a field.

After you select a field to export, click on the To: Worksheet Field column next to the field you added. Project suggests a column heading for the field in the Excel worksheet; you can change this heading. However, you cannot change the data type for the field in the destination program, which appears in the Data Type column.

To quickly add all the fields in the Project file, click on the Add All button. To add all the fields in a particular Project table, such as the Entry table or the Cost table, click on the Base on Table button. Project displays the Select Base Table for Field Mapping dialog box, from which you can select a table. When you click on OK, Project adds all fields contained in that table to the list of fields you want to export. As you add fields, the Preview box shows you how the Excel worksheet will appear (see Figure 18-4).

If you decide to add a field between two existing fields, click on the row you want to appear below the new field. Then click on the Insert Row button, and Project inserts a blank row above the selected row. You can use the Move buttons on the right side of the dialog box to reorder fields. Click on the field you want to move and then click on either the Move up arrow or the Move down arrow. To delete a field, click anywhere in the row containing the field and click on the Delete Row button.

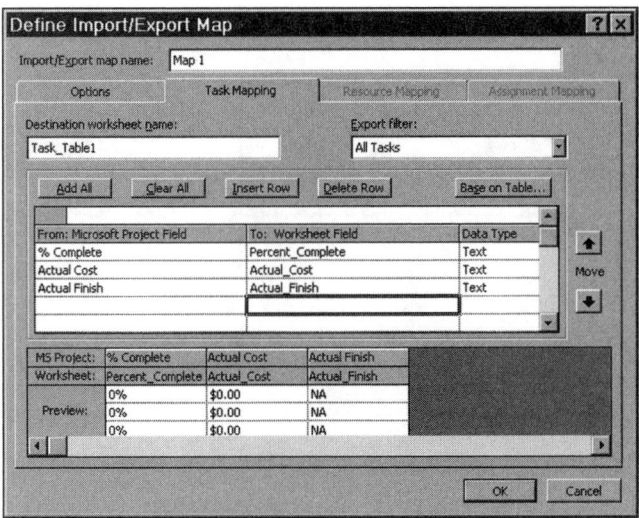

Figure 18-4: As you add fields, a preview of the Excel worksheet you will create appears at the bottom of the Define Import/Export Map dialog box.

To remove all the fields you added, click on the Clear All button.

When you click on OK to save your map, Project redisplays the Export Format dialog box. Your map appears in the Selective data list box.

Note

If you don't want to export information at this time, click on Close. Project retains the map you created but cancels the export operation.

Viewing, copying, or editing import/export maps

You must simulate the process of exporting or importing to view, copy, or edit an import/export map. The process for creating a new map and viewing, copying, or editing an existing map are essentially the same; the slight differences in the Define Import/Export Map dialog box depend on the action you select.

For example, if you highlight an existing map and select Copy in the Export Format dialog box, you still see the Define Import/Export Map dialog box. However, the name of the map indicates that it's a copy, and when you view the map (task, resource, or assignment), the fields are already inserted, as shown in Figure 18-5.

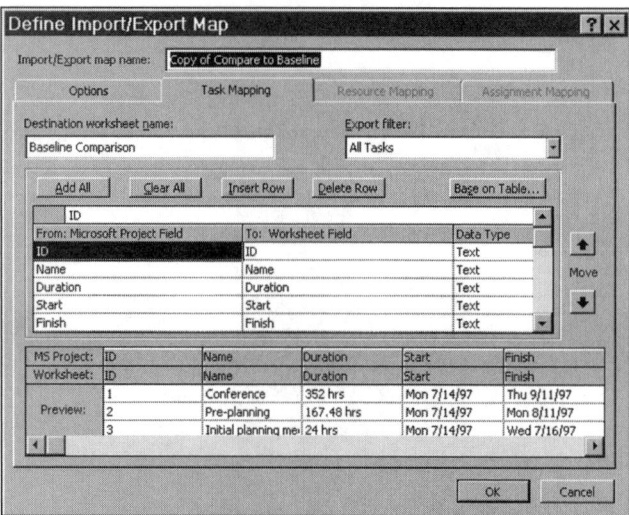

Figure 18-5: When you copy an existing map, the word *Copy* appears in its default name.

You can use the Edit button to view an existing map or to make changes to the map. If you highlight an existing map and select Edit in the Export Format dialog box, you can still see the Define Import/Export Map dialog box with the title of the map you selected. As you would expect, when you view the map (task, resource, or assignment), you see fields already inserted (see Figure 18-6).

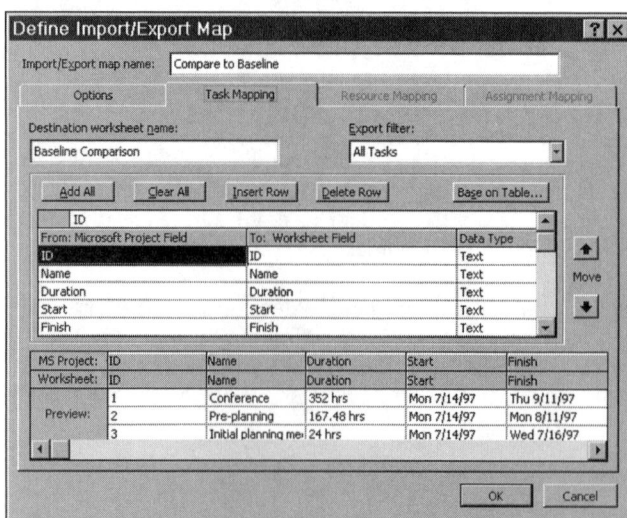

Figure 18-6: When you edit a map, the dialog box looks the same as when you copy an existing map except for the map name.

Tip   Although you can edit an existing map, if you make a copy of the map and edit the copy, you don't change the original version.

Exporting Information

Exporting is the process of sending data from one program to another program by transferring the information electronically. You can export information to Microsoft Office products such as Excel workbooks, Access databases, or Word documents. You also can export some Project information to graphic images that you can use in any graphics program or as an image on a Web page. And you can export information to any program that can read text (TXT) files or comma-separated value (CSV) files.

Exporting to Office files

You can use import/export maps to export information to Excel workbooks or to Access databases. You also can include Project information in Word, but you won't use the import process.

Sending Project data to Excel

In Chapter 13 you learned how to export information to Excel when you learned about analyzing cost information. And earlier in this chapter you saw how to create or edit a map to export Project information to Excel. Rather than repeat this information, consider the overview of the process:

1. Open the Project file containing the information you want to export.

2. Save the file as either an Excel workbook or an Excel PivotTable.

Note   When you create an Excel PivotTable file, Project creates two sheets in the workbook for each type of data you export. One sheet contains the data used in the PivotTable, and the other sheet contains the PivotTable. Project uses the last field in each map as the default field for the PivotTable, and all the other fields appear as rows in the PivotTable.

3. Select a map or create a new map from the Export Format dialog box.

4. Click on Save. Project exports the data specified in the map to the Excel workbook you specified.

Sending Project data to an Access database

You can export some or all of the information in a Project file to an Access 97 database file using an import/export map. If none of the existing maps can export data into the proper fields in your Access database, you might need to create a new map.

When you export to any database format, Project makes the following changes to the names of some fields in the database to ensure compatibility with database field naming conventions:

✦ Underscores replace spaces and forward slashes (/).

✦ The string "Percent" replaces the percent sign (%).

✦ Periods are deleted.

✦ Start changes to Start_Date.

✦ Finish changes to Finish_Date.

✦ Group changes to Group_Name.

✦ Work changes to Scheduled_Work.

Note You can append Project information to an existing Access database. However, you should make sure you have a backup copy of the database, just in case the information doesn't appear the way it should in Access. You may even want to create a testing copy of your database and use the copy to ensure that Project information appears in the correct fields.

Follow these steps to export Project information to a file in Microsoft Access database format:

1. Open the Project file containing the data you want to export.

2. Choose File➪Save As to open the File Save dialog box.

3. Open the Save as type list box and select Microsoft Access 8.0 Database.

4. Type a name in the File name box for the file you are exporting.

5. Click on Save. If you selected an existing Access database, Project displays the message that appears in Figure 18-7. To add information to the database, click on Append. To replace the existing database, click on Overwrite. To select a different file, click on Cancel.

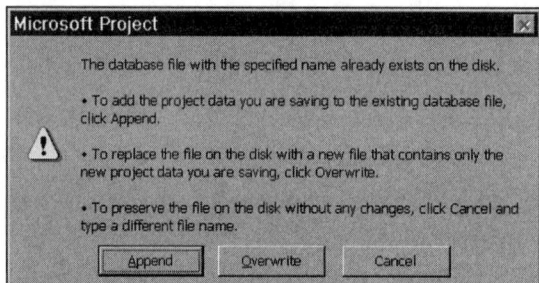

Figure 18-7: The message that appears when you select an existing Access database as the export file.

After you select an export file, Project opens the Export Format dialog box shown in Figure 18-8.

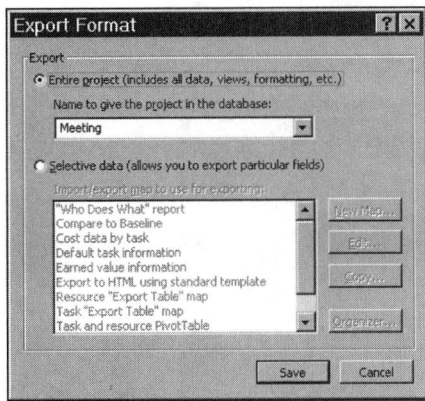

Figure 18-8: When you export to an Access database, the Export Format dialog box enables you to export some or all of your Project information.

6. Tell Project whether to export all or some of the data in your project:

✦ **To export all the data in your project:** Leave the Entire project option button selected and type a name for the project in the Name to give the project in the database box.

✦ **To export only some the data in your project:** Select Selective data and select the import/export map you want to use for exporting your data.

7. Click on Save.

Sending Project data to Microsoft Word

Although you can't export Project data directly to Word, you can use the Windows Copy and Paste commands to incorporate Project text or table data in a Word file. For example, you can copy the columns in any table to a Word document. Start in Project and follow these steps:

1. Open the file containing the information you want to incorporate in a Word document.

2. Select the information; you can copy text information from the Notes tab of either the Task Information dialog box or the Resource Information dialog box or, as you see in Figure 18-9, you can copy table columns.

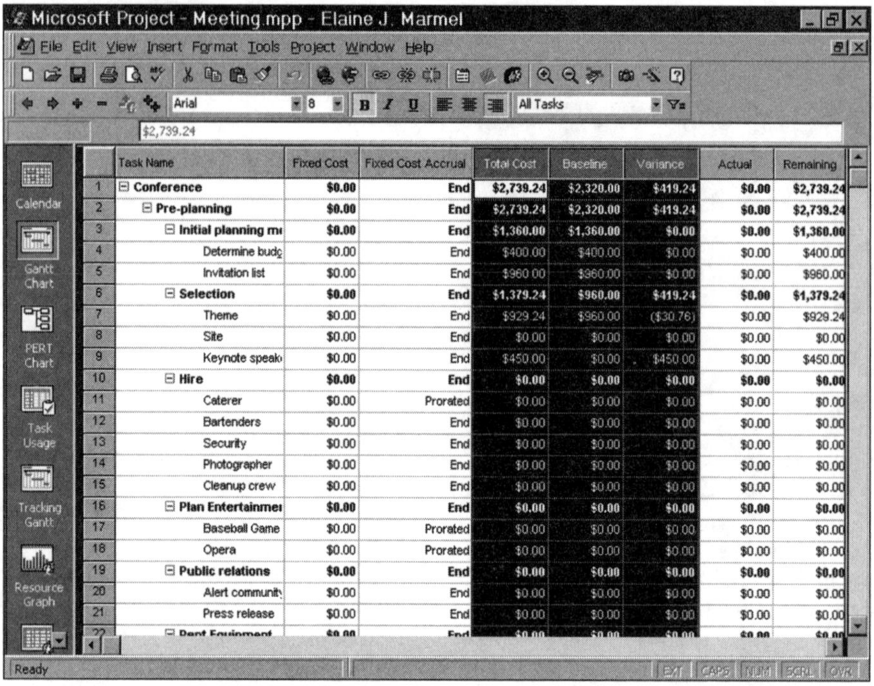

Figure 18-9: Select information to copy to Word.

3. Click on the Copy button on the Standard toolbar.

4. Open or switch to Word.

5. Position the insertion point where you want the Project information to begin.

6. Click on Paste. The Project information appears in Word.

As you can see from Figure 18-10, table information appears in Word as tab-separated columns; using Word's Convert Text to Table feature, you can convert the information into a Word table.

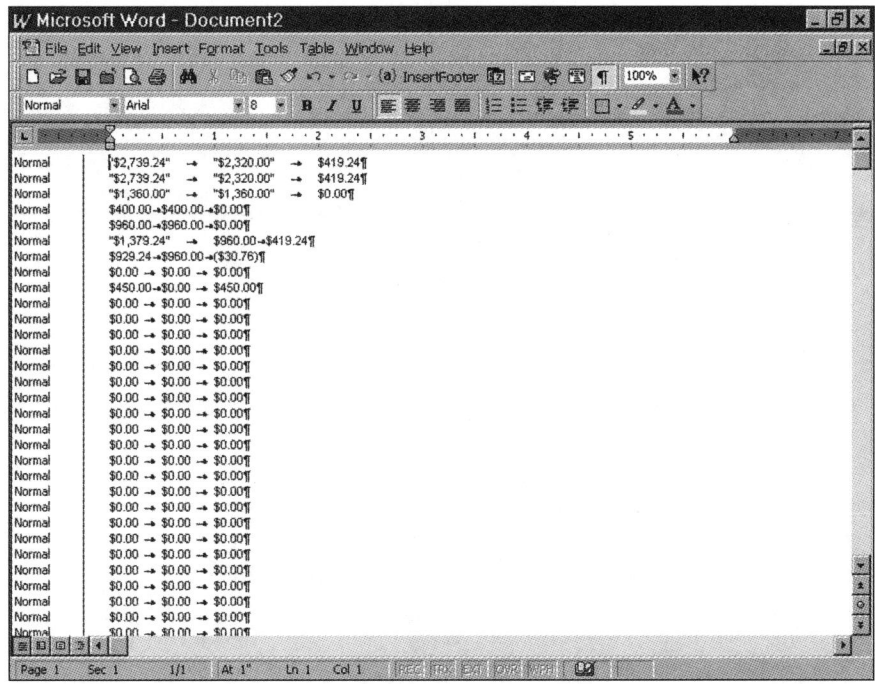

Figure 18-10: Project table information as it appears when you copy it into Word.

Exporting Project information to a graphic image

You can create a picture from your Project information and view the picture in any graphics program or save the picture in a Web-compatible file format. When you use the following technique, you copy Project information to the Windows Clipboard; you can copy all or part of any view except the Task PERT, Task Form, and Resource Form views.

1. Select the view of which you want a picture.

2. Tell Project how much of your plan to copy. To copy all visible portions of your plan, click on the Copy Picture button on the Standard toolbar. The Copy Picture dialog box appears (see Figure 18-11). To copy only a portion of your plan, select the information you want to copy.

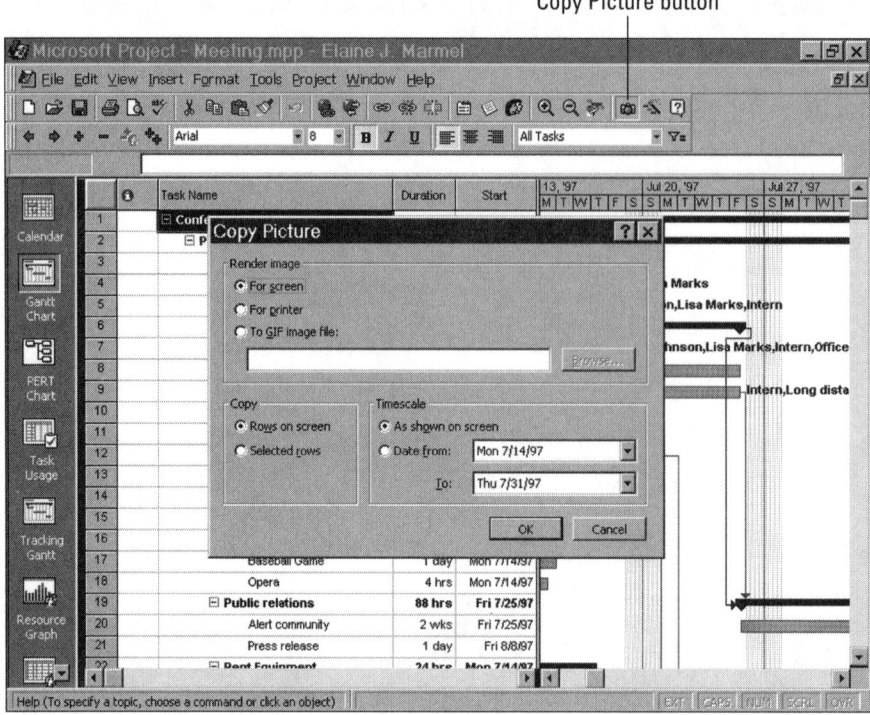

Figure 18-11: Use the Copy Picture dialog box to describe how you want to copy the picture.

3. Select an option button to specify how you want Project to copy the picture:

✦ Select For screen to copy the information for display on a computer screen.

✦ Select For printer to copy the information for a printer to use.

✦ Select To GIF image file to save the information as a image you can use on a Web page and in other programs. Be sure to specify the path and filename in the box below this option.

4. (Optional) If you selected rows before you started this process because you want to copy only those rows, select Selected Rows.

5. (Optional) If you want to copy information for a range of dates other than those currently displayed, click on the Date option button and then enter From and To dates.

6. Click on OK.

To view an image that you copied as a screen or printer image, switch to the program in which you want to display the Microsoft Project information and then paste the picture using the program's Paste command. A copied image in Microsoft Paint appears in Figure 18-12.

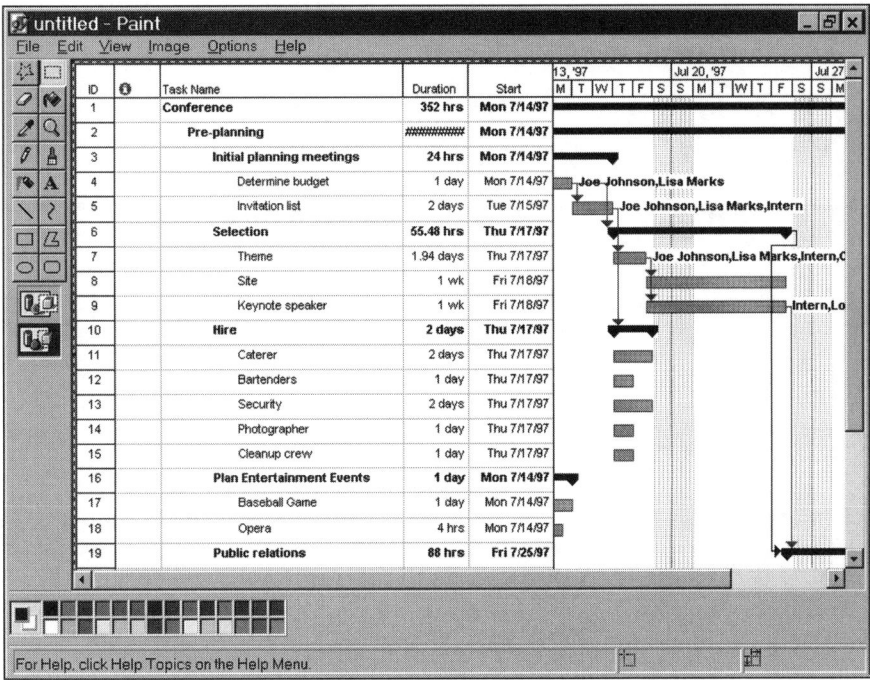

Figure 18-12: A Project image pasted into Microsoft Paint.

Exporting to other formats

If the information you want to export is going to a program that can read either text files or Microsoft Project Exchange Files, you can create an export file that the receiving program can read. Text files are a common format and are also called *comma-separated values files* (CSV). Microsoft Project Exchange format (MPX) is an ASCII, record-based file format.

Exporting to text files

If you have a program that can read either a text file or a CSV file, you can export information from Project to that program. You need to save the information you want to export as either a text file or a CSV file (also called an ASCII, comma-delimited file) in Project.

To export information to a text file, you need to use an import/export map. To ensure that Project information appears correctly in the program into which you want to import it, you may need to create or edit an import/export map.

If the program to which you want to export information supports the Microsoft Access database format (MDB), you should use that format for the best results when you import the information that you exported from Project.

Follow these steps to export information to a text file:

1. Open the Project file containing the information you want to export.

2. Choose File⇨Save As to open the File Save dialog box.

3. Select Text or CSV, whichever format works best in the program to which you're exporting, in the Save as type box.

4. Type a name in the File name box for the file you are exporting.

5. Click on Save. The Export Format dialog box appears.

6. Highlight the name of the map you want to use in the Import/export map to use for exporting list box.

7. Click on Save. Project saves the information.

Exporting to other project management software

You can use the MPX file format to export Project 98 information to older versions of Project. Some other project management software packages also support MPX, so if you need to export Project 98 information to another project management software package, you can save it as an MPX file.

Exporting an MPX file is similar to importing an Excel workbook or an Access database except that you don't use an import/export map. Choose File⇨Save As. In the File Save dialog box, open the Files of type list box and select MPX. In the File name box, supply a name for the file you want to export. Click on Save, and Project saves the file.

Note

The Microsoft Project database (MPD) format is a good format to use whenever possible. MPD has replaced the MPX format, and you can use it with any program that supports either the MPD format or Microsoft Access database formats.

Exporting to HTML

You can include information from a Microsoft Project schedule in an HTML document by exporting data from the Project file to HTML format. Like exporting Excel workbooks and Access databases, you use an import/export map. If necessary, edit the HTML import/export map to create a map that can handle the information you want to export. Remember, you can copy the existing map and then modify it.

To export a file to HTML format, follow these steps:

1. Open the file containing the information you want to export to HTML format.

2. Choose File⇨Save As HTML to open File Save dialog box.

   If necessary, use the Save in box to navigate to the location where you want to save the HTML file and its associated image files.

If necessary, change the name for the exported file that appears in the File name box.

3. Click on Save. The Export Format dialog box appears.

4. Highlight the name of the map you want to use in the Import/export map to use for exporting list box, or select Export to HTML using standard template.

5. Click on Save. Project saves the file in HTML format and creates any associated image files.

Importing Information

You can bring information into Project from another Project file or from Microsoft Excel, Microsoft Access, or Microsoft Word. You also can import information created in any program that can save text (TXT) files or comma-separated value (CSV) files. When you import a Project file, you actually consolidate two Project files. When you import non-Project files, you use an import/export map to define the data you want to import.

Inserting another project

When you import one project file into another, you *don't* use an import/export map. Instead, importing one Project file into another Project file is the same as consolidating Project files, which you learned about in Chapter 15. This section reviews the process of consolidating projects by inserting one project into another project.

When you consolidate project files, you insert one project into another Project file. Each project you insert appears as a summary task in the consolidated project file, as you can see in Figure 18-13. In addition, an icon in the Indicators field tells you, at a glance, that you're looking at an inserted project.

You can insert projects at any outline level. The level at which an inserted project appears depends on the outline level that appears at the location where you intend to insert a project. Project inserts the project above the selected task at the same outline level as the selected task.

For more information about inserting projects at different outline levels, see Chapter 15.

To insert a project, follow these steps:

1. Open the project into which you want to insert another project.

2. Click on Gantt Chart in the View bar.

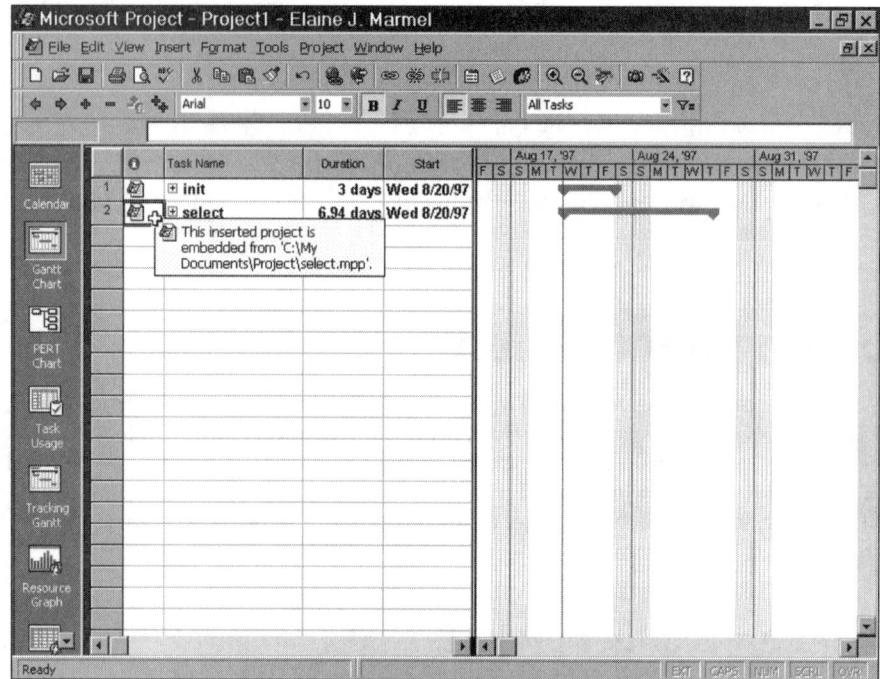

Figure 18-13: When you insert one project into another, a special icon appears in the Indicators column.

3. Click on the Task Name column on the row where you want the inserted project to begin.

Note

When you insert a project, Project places the project immediately above the selected row. Therefore, if your consolidated project already contains tasks, click on the task in the Task Name column that you want to appear below the subproject. You also can determine the outline level at which the inserted project appears in the consolidated project based on the outline level visible when you insert a project.

4. Choose Insert⇨Project to open the Insert Project dialog box that you see in Figure 18-14.

5. Use the Look in list to navigate to the folder that contains the project you want to insert.

6. Highlight the file you want to insert.

7. Change any inserted project options:

✦ If you remove the check from the Link to Project check box, the inserted project won't be linked to its source project.

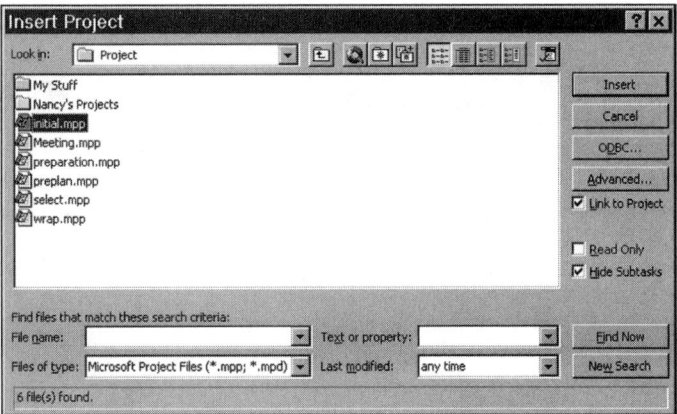

Figure 18-14: Use the Insert Project dialog box the same way you use the Open dialog box.

If you do not link an inserted project to its source file, any changes you make to the inserted project in the consolidated project file do not affect the source file. Similarly, any changes you make to the source file do not affect the consolidated project file containing the subproject.

Under many circumstances linking the files makes updating easier. When you link an inserted project to its source file, you are creating a link between two files that works like any two linked files in a Windows environment. If you move the inserted project file, you need to update the link in the consolidated project; otherwise, the link won't work.

For more information on updating links between Project files, see Chapter 15.

✦ If you place a check in the Read Only check box, the changes you make to the inserted project *do not* affect its source project.

✦ If you remove the check from the Hide Subtasks check box, the inserted project's tasks appear in the consolidated project. You can also hide or show tasks after you insert the project by clicking on the outline symbol (the plus sign) next to the summary task. You can see the inserted project's tasks in Figure 18-15.

8. Click on Insert. Project inserts the selected file into the open project. If you didn't change the Hide Subtasks option, the inserted project file appears as a summary task.

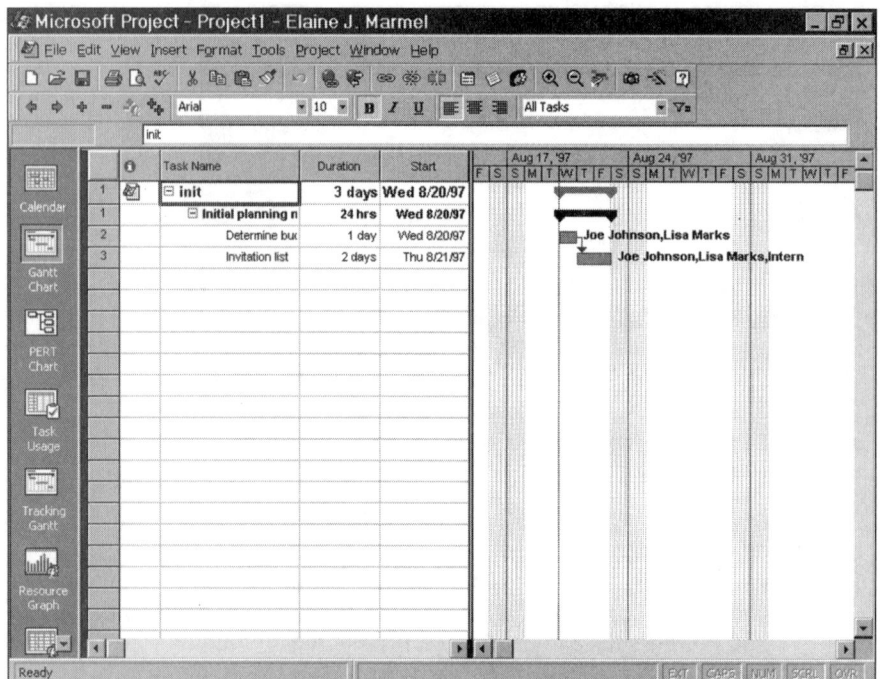

Figure 18-15: When you click on the outline symbol next to an inserted project's summary task, the tasks of the inserted project appear.

Importing Office files

Importing is the process of including data from one program in another program by transferring the information electronically. You can import information from Excel workbooks or Access databases by using maps that define the way the information should be viewed by Project. You also can include information from Word, but you won't use the import process.

Bringing Excel workbook information into Project

You can use an import/export map to transfer information from Microsoft Excel workbooks to Microsoft Project files. Project contains predefined import/export maps that tell Project how to treat the information you import. This section shows you how to use a predefined map; earlier in this chapter you learned how to edit a map and create your own map.

Note   You can use any of the existing import/export maps to either import to or export from an Excel workbook, but you cannot import an Excel PivotTable into Project.

   1. Choose File⇨Open or click on the Open button on the Standard toolbar.

2. Open the Files of type list box and select Microsoft Excel Workbooks (see Figure 18-16).

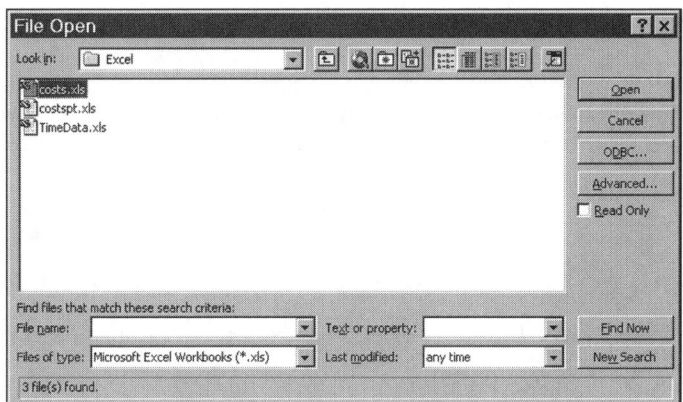

Figure 18-16: Set the type of file you want to import to Microsoft Excel Workbooks.

3. Use the Look In list box to navigate to the folder containing the Excel workbook you want to import.

4. Highlight the workbook and click on Open. Project displays the Import Format dialog box (see Figure 18-17).

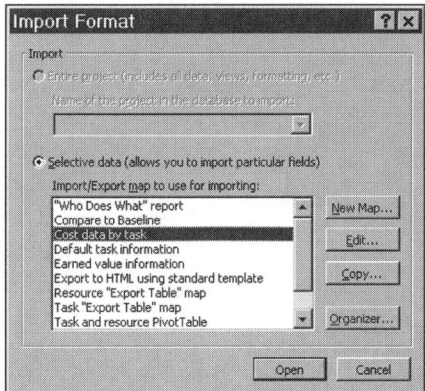

Figure 18-17: Use the Import Format dialog box to select a map for the imported data.

5. Select the Selective data option button, and highlight the map you want Project to use while importing your data.

6. Click on Open. Project opens the data contained in your Excel workbook in a Project file.

Bringing Access database information into Project

Importing Access databases into Project is similar to importing Excel workbooks except that you can import all or part of an Access database into a Project file. Again, you use an import/export map to describe to Project the type of data you're importing. If the map you need doesn't exist, you must create it; earlier in this chapter, you learned how to create maps.

To import some or all of an Access database into Project, follow these steps:

1. Choose File➪Open or click on the Open button on the Standard toolbar.

2. Open the Files of type list box and select Microsoft Access Databases.

3. Use the Look In list box to navigate to the folder containing the Access database you want to import.

4. Highlight the workbook and click on Open. Project displays the Import Format dialog box (see Figure 18-18).

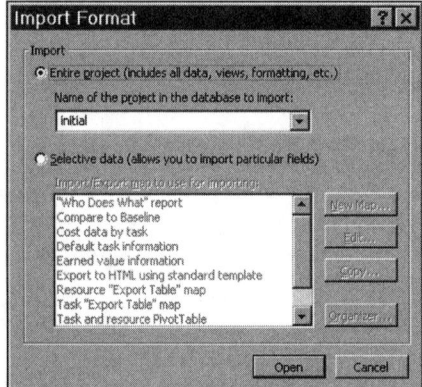

Figure 18-18: You can import all or part of the database into Project from Access.

5. Select one of Project's import options. (By default, Project suggests that you import the entire database.)

✦ Entire project imports the entire database.

✦ Selective data imports a subset of the database. If you click on this option, select an import/export map to use.

6. Click on Open.

Bringing Word document information into Project

Unlike other types of files, you cannot import Word files directly into Project. You can, however, include information in Word documents in a Project file using one of two techniques:

✦ You can paste information.

✦ You can link or embed information.

Pasting information from Word into Project

When you use the paste method, you can paste the information either into a table view or into a note in Project. Pasting eliminates the extra step of retyping information.

If you paste text into blank rows, Microsoft Project treats the information as new tasks or resources. If you paste information into fields that already contain information, Microsoft Project replaces the information in those fields with the pasted information. However, you cannot paste information into Project fields that contain calculated values, such as calculated values in a cost table.

Note

You can use the following technique to paste information from an Excel workbook into a Project table view, but first you must organize the information in your workbook to match the organization of a Microsoft Project table. For example, suppose you want to paste information into a resource sheet with the Entry table applied. Your workbook has 3 columns, but the resource sheet has 12 columns; and you want to paste the information into columns 2, 5, and 8. To paste this information, you need to create and apply a table in Project that displays only the fields you intend to paste from your workbook. Make sure that the order and type of columns in the Project table match the order and type of information being pasted.

To paste information from Word into a Project table, follow these steps:

1. Open the Word document from which you want to copy information and then copy the information to the Windows Clipboard (see Figure 18-19).

2. Switch to Microsoft Project.

3. Switch to the view into which you want to paste the information. If necessary, use the View bar to click on More Views. From the More Views dialog box that appears, select the view you need and then click on Apply.

4. Apply the table into which you want to paste information by choosing View⇨Table⇨More Tables. Select the table you want from the More Tables dialog box and then click on Apply.

5. (Optional) If the table you select has columns you don't need or is missing columns you do need, then add or hide columns. Also add rows if necessary.

6. Click on the first field in which you want information to appear after you paste.

7. Click on the Paste button on the Standard toolbar. The information stored on the Windows Clipboard appears in the Project table (see Figure 18-20).

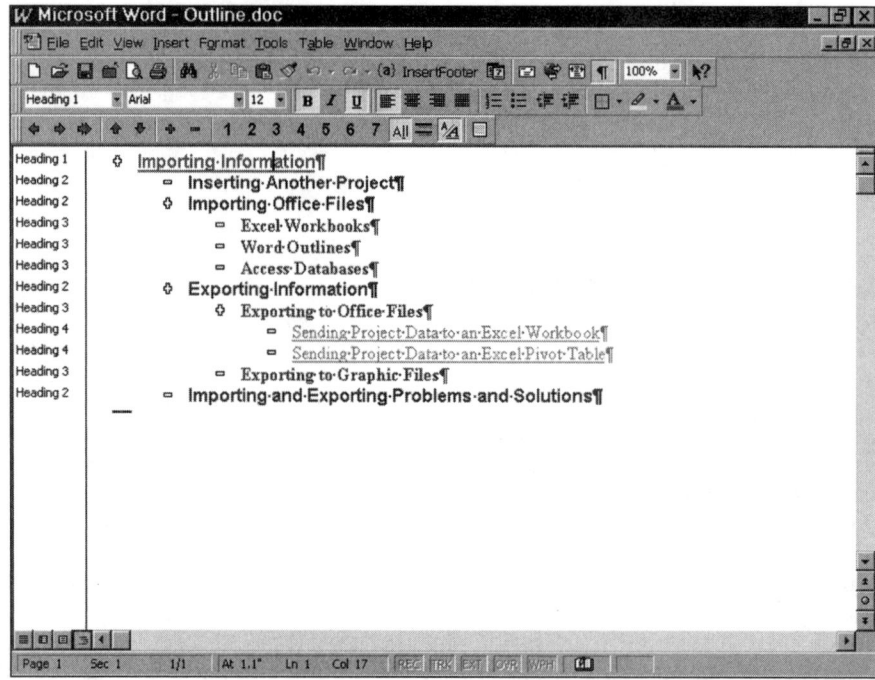

Figure 18-19: A Word document you can paste into a Project table.

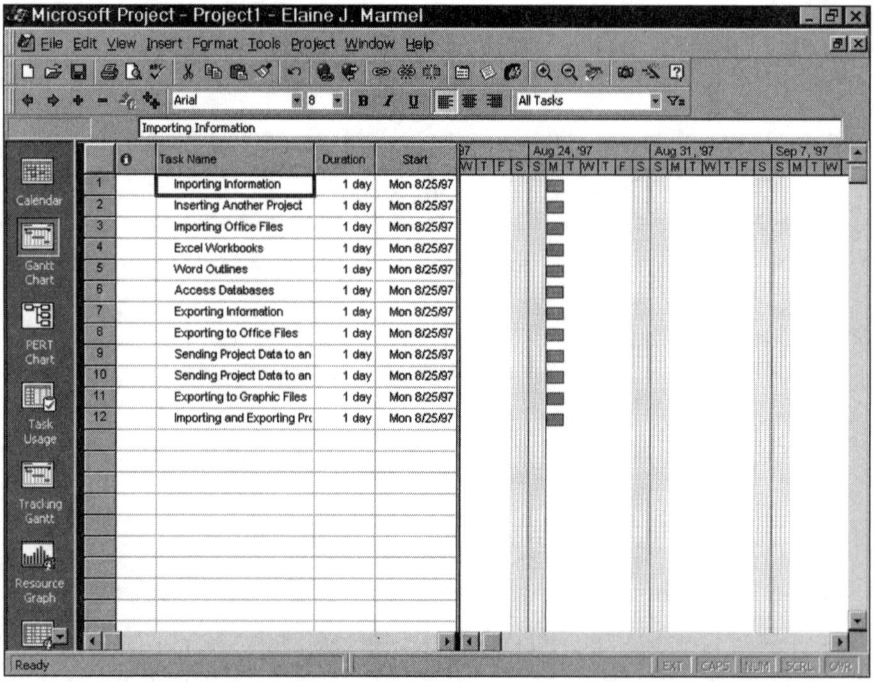

Figure 18-20: The information from the Word document appears in Project.

You can paste information from a Word document into a note in Project using the same technique. Copy the information in Word to the Windows Clipboard. Switch to Project and double-click on either the task or the resource to which you want to add a note. In the Task Information or Resource Information dialog box that appears, click on the Notes tab. Then right-click on the Notes area to display a shortcut menu (see Figure 18-21), and choose Paste. The information from Word appears in the Notes area.

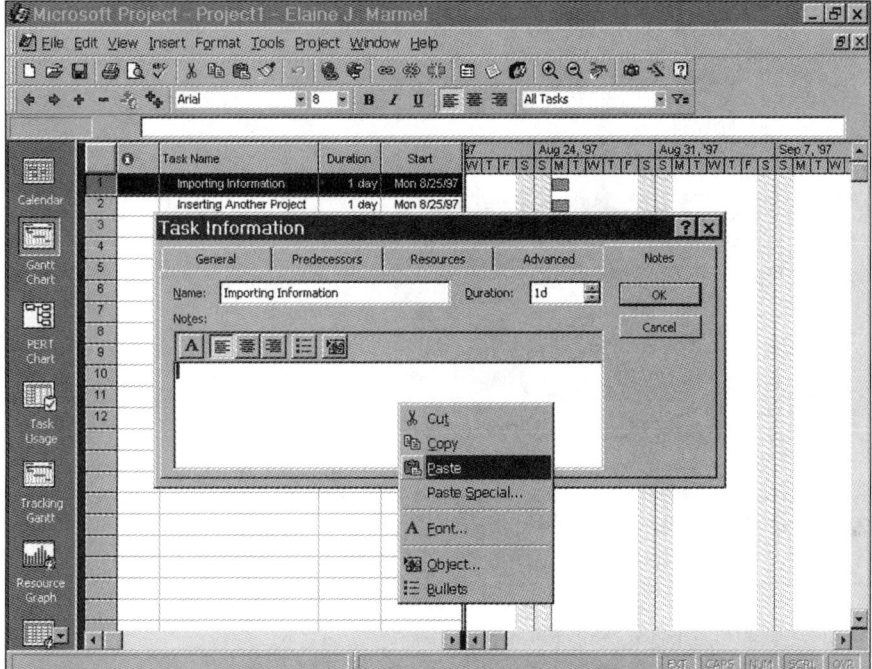

Figure 18-21: You can use a shortcut menu to paste information from the Windows Clipboard into a task or resource note.

Linking or embedding a Word document in Project

When you link or embed a Word document in Project, you actually insert the document as an object in your Project schedule.

✦ When you link a Word document to a Project file, the Project file reflects any changes you make to the Word document.

✦ When you embed a Word document in a Project file, the Project file *does not* reflect subsequent updates to the Word document.

Project views objects you insert as graphics; therefore, you can link or embed a Word document as a graphic element in any graphics area of a Project file. A graphics area is any area in Project that can display picture information, including task, resource, or assignment notes; headers, footers, and legends in views; headers and footers in reports; the chart portion of the Gantt view; and the Objects box in a task or resource form.

To insert a Word document as a linked or embedded object, follow these steps:

1. Open a Microsoft Project file and display the graphics area into which you want to insert a document.

2. Open the Insert Object dialog box shown in Figure 18-22.

   To open the Insert Object dialog box in a task, resource, or assignment note, right-click to display a shortcut menu and choose Object. To open the Insert Object dialog box in the Gantt Chart view or Objects box, choose Insert➪Object.

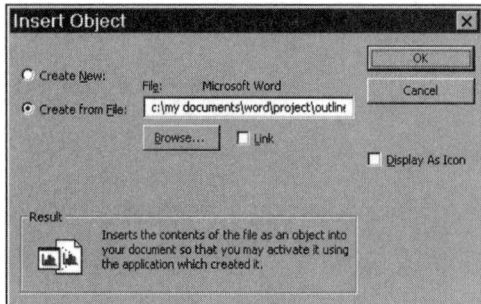

Figure 18-22: Use the Insert Object box to link or embed a Word document in a Project file.

3. Select the Create from File option.

4. Type in the path and filename of the document you want to insert, or click on Browse to locate and select the file.

5. Do one of the following:

   ✦ To link the object to the source document, place a check in the Link check box.

   ✦ To embed the object, leave the Link check box unselected.

   By default, Project displays the contents of the file you insert rather than an icon representing the file. To display the object as an icon, place a check mark next to Display As Icon.

6. Click on OK. Project displays a graphic image of your file, as you can see in Figure 18-23.

You can use the handles around the image in the Task Information dialog box to move or resize the image.

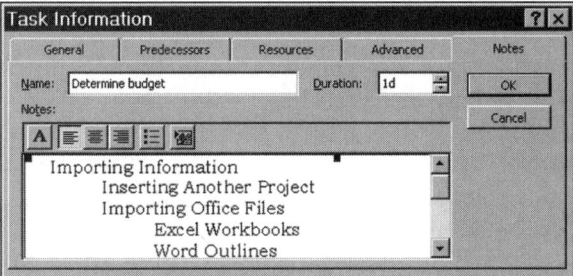

Figure 18-23: A Word document inserted as a graphic image in a task note.

Tip

You can delete the object by making sure you see the handles surrounding it and pressing the Delete key on your keyboard.

After you click on OK, an icon appears in the Indicator column. When you slide the mouse over that icon, however, you won't see the contents of the note because it is a graphic image. Instead, you see a pair of single quotation marks (see Figure 18-24).

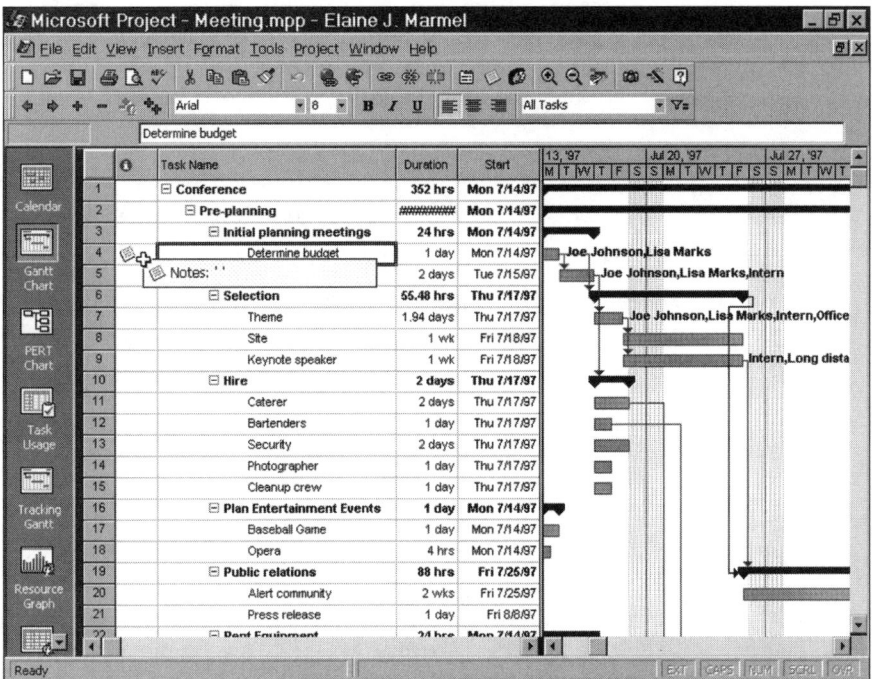

Figure 18-24: When you link or embed an object in the note of a task or resource, you can't reveal the contents of the note with the mouse pointer.

Importing other files

If the information you want to import comes from a program that can produce either text files or Microsoft Project Exchange Files, you can import that information. Text files are a common format and are also called comma-separated values files (CSV). Microsoft Project Exchange format (MPX) is an ASCII, record-based file format.

Importing Microsoft Project Exchange Files

You can use the MPX file format to import information from older versions of Project into Project 98. Some other project management software packages also support MPX, so if you need to import information from another project management software package, you can save it as an MPX file and import it into Project.

Importing an MPX file is similar to importing an Excel workbook or an Access database, except that you don't use an import/export map. Choose File⇨Open. In the Open dialog box, open the Files of type list box and choose MPX. Use the Look in list box to navigate to the file and click on Open.

Importing text files

If you have a program that can create either a text file or a comma-separated value file, you can import information from that program into Project. You need to save the information you want to import as either a text file or a CSV file in the native program. Again, you use an import/export map to describe to Project the type of data you're importing. If the map you need doesn't exist, you need to create it.

Follow these steps in Project to import the information:

1. Choose File⇨Open or click on the Open button on the Standard toolbar.

2. Open the Files of type list box and choose Text (*.txt) or CSV (*.csv)

3. Use the Look in list box to navigate to the folder containing the file you want to import.

4. Highlight the file and click on Open. Project displays the Import Format dialog box.

5. Choose the map you want to use and click on Open.

Troubleshooting

Importing and exporting can be tricky operations. Little things go wrong that cause these operations to fail. This section suggests ways to solve some of the problems you might encounter while importing or exporting.

Project imports incorrect times in data from Microsoft Excel

In Excel, when you assign a date to a cell, Excel assigns a default time to the cell of 12:00 a.m. You may not see that time, but Excel has attached it to the cell. If the data you import from Microsoft Excel to Microsoft Project contains dates without specific times, Project automatically uses Excel's default time of 12:00 a.m.

Objects are missing in imported or exported data

If the data you are importing or exporting contains linked or embedded objects, Project does not import or export those objects when exchanging data with Microsoft Excel, Microsoft Access, HTML, MPX, or text files. You need to link or embed the objects again in the file after you complete the import or export operation.

The export file contains more or less information than expected

The information you find in your exported file depends on the import/export map you select, the table you choose, and the filter you apply. If you export more or less information than you expect, check the map, table, and filter. Choose File⇨Save As and specify a filename and file type to display the Export Format dialog box. Highlight the map you want to use and click on Edit. Click on the appropriate mapping tab; then use the map to inspect the fields you selected for export, the table you selected, and the filter you applied.

Project imports invalid information

Project checks data you import to ensure that the data types for each field are valid. If necessary, Project may modify the values of some fields to handle inconsistencies.

If Project warns that you are trying to import invalid data, check the import/export map you've selected to make sure you are importing the correct type of information into a Project field. Also check the data in the import file and make sure that the field values are valid and within the acceptable range for the Project field into which you intend to import the data.

The values of imported information change

This situation is similar to the previous one, where Project determines that the information you're trying to import is invalid. Project checks — and changes if necessary — the data that you import to ensure that the data types and the values for each field are valid. Project may also change data to make sure that it falls within ranges valid for Project fields and won't create inconsistencies between fields that depend on each other. Project also overrides values you attempt to import into calculated fields by replacing the imported data with the calculated value.

The imported project is empty

As you know, importing depends on the import/export map you select. If you choose the wrong map, no data may import. Also, make sure you're looking at the correct view after importing; if you import task information, you may not see it if you're looking at a resource view.

Project displays imported information in the wrong fields

When imported information appears in the wrong Project field, you should check the import/export map. Make sure you select the correct map and that the table you used contains the correct fields. Finally, check the mapping of the fields between the import file and your Project file.

Summary

In this chapter you learned how to import and export information in Microsoft Project. You learned to

✦ Create and edit import/export maps

✦ Export information to Excel, Access, and Word

✦ Export information to graphics files, text files, HTML files, and other project management software files

✦ Import information from another project; from Excel, Access or Word; or from text files

✦ Solve common problems that occur when you export or import information

Chapter 19 describes how Microsoft Project works with the Web.

✦   ✦   ✦

Project on the Web

B y now you realize that the world of project management has moved beyond the traditional pencil-and-ruler war room and into the world of technology. Nowhere is this shift more evident than in the many ways project managers can take advantage of the Internet to communicate with others, present information, and gather data.

Project includes a few useful tools that help you access the World Wide Web. These tools enable you to

♦ Save Project files in a Web-compatible format so that you can place your information on a Web page

♦ Place hyperlinks in a project file to quickly take you to another location

Using the Web to Manage Projects

The Internet itself is a large network of computers that you can use to send and retrieve information, images, and messages around the globe. The World Wide Web is perhaps the biggest success story on the Internet — this graphical Internet service enables you to move around the Web using a programming language called *Hypertext Markup Language* (HTML). With HTML you can jump between Web locations by clicking on images or text linked to a specific online address. These links are *hyperlinks*.

Connectivity helps you manage projects more effectively in several ways. You can use Project's Web capabilities to

♦ Insert hyperlinks to Internet addresses within your project file so that you or someone using your schedule can move instantly to an area on the Web that contains related information or images. For example, if your project has to do with the design of a network for your company, you can insert a hyperlink in your schedule to the network software vendor's home page so that you can find answers to technical questions or order software.

✦ Navigate around the Internet using the Web toolbar. Rather than embedding a link to a site in your schedule, you can save lists of your favorite Web locations and go to a site on that list quickly using the Web toolbar. Your favorite sites might include your company's Web page, a newsgroup related to your industry, or a data source, such as a university library, that you search often for information related to your project.

✦ Save a view of your project as a graphic image in GIF format. You can use that image on a Web or distribute it via e-mail.

✦ Save your Project files in HTML format to publish project information as a Web page.

You can also use the Internet to send e-mail about your project. Chapter 14 covers this feature in more detail.

Using the Web Toolbar

Project has a special set of tools specifically designed for navigating around the World Wide Web. You can display this toolbar by clicking on the Web Toolbar button on the Standard toolbar or by choosing View⇨Toolbars⇨Web. Figure 19-1 shows you the tools that are available.

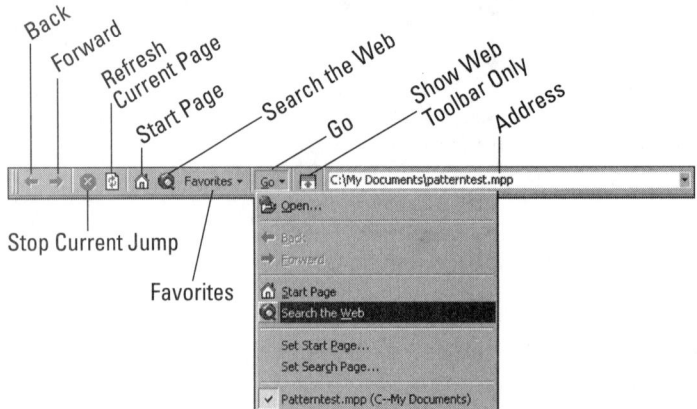

Figure 19-1: The Web toolbar appears just below the Formatting toolbar, though you can drag it away to be a floating toolbar if you prefer.

The tools here work with your Web browser to help you to navigate around either an organizational intranet or the Web. Table 19-1 briefly describes each tool.

Table 19-1 The Project Web Toolbar	
Tool	**Function**
Back	Takes you back to the last site visited during the current online session.
Forward	Moves you one site ahead in the list of sites visited during the current online session.
Stop Current Jump	Becomes active if you initiate a jump to a site; clicking on this button when it's active stops the hyperlink jump that's in progress.
Refresh Current Page	Refreshes or updates the contents of a currently displayed page, incorporating any changes made by the author as you're reading the page.
Start Page	Takes you to the home page that you have set your Web browser to access.
Search the Web	Takes you to whatever search page you have set your Web browser to use.
Favorites	Opens a list of favorite sites that you have saved into a favorites folder. Click on any site name in this list to go directly to that site.
Go	Displays a menu of common Web navigation commands.
Show Web Toolbar Only	Hides any other currently displayed toolbars, leaving only the Web toolbar visible on screen.
Address	Shows the address of the current site and, when opened by clicking on the arrow on the right, displays a drop-down list of recently visited sites.

To use these tools, you need an Internet connection and a Web browser. When all the elements are in place and you click on, for example, the Search tool button, Project connects with the Internet and opens the search page you have set up in your browser. When you are connected, you can use the Back and Forward buttons to move through the Web pages. You can use your browser's Favorites feature to save addresses of sites you like to visit often; Project also saves these addresses in its own Favorites list. Figure 19-2 shows the Web toolbar with the Show Web Toolbar Only button selected and the Favorites list displayed.

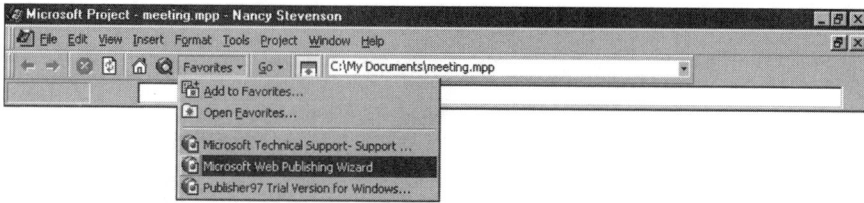

Figure 19-2: Notice that the Show Web Toolbar Only button is depressed: all other toolbars have disappeared.

Note

Microsoft provides its Internet Explorer browser with Project. You can install the browser from your Project CD. You can also download Internet Explorer from the Microsoft Web site at

```
http://www.microsoft.com/ie/default.asp
```

Taking a Picture of Your Project

You can take a picture of your project information as it displays on your screen in any view. It's like taking a snapshot of the project information on your computer screen that you can hand on to others. You might, for instance, want to send an image of a project schedule to someone who doesn't have Project loaded on her computer. Although she can't open a Project file, if she can view common graphics file formats, she can view or print this image of your schedule. You can also create a picture of your onscreen display and save it in GIF format; that's the format preferred for posting such a picture on a Web page.

To create a GIF image of your onscreen information, follow these steps:

1. Display the view you want to show, and set it up any way you like (for example, move the divider between the Gantt chart and table panes, or adjust the timescale to show different increments of time).

2. Click on the Copy Picture button on the Standard toolbar to open the Copy Picture dialog box in Figure 19-3.

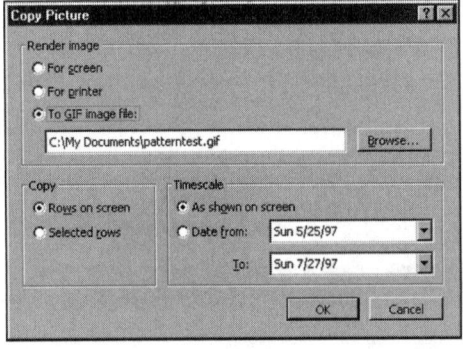

Figure 19-3: The Copy Picture dialog box enables you to take a picture of whatever is currently on screen.

3. Click on the To GIF image file control button. A path to the last folder to which you have saved a file and the filename with a .gif extension appear.

   Two other options for rendering the image are also available in the Copy Picture dialog box:

   ✦ The For screen option makes a copy of the screen just as it looks; you can then paste the copy into another program.

✦ The For printer option makes a copy of the schedule as it would look if printed. Use this option when you're not intending to show the image onscreen. Project uses your printer settings to format the printed option.

4. Select any or all of the following options:

✦ To save the file in a different directory or with a different name, click on the Browse button and use the settings in the Browse dialog box to save the file with different settings.

✦ To save a picture of specific rows of information, select the rows before opening this dialog box. Then click on the Selected rows control button.

✦ To save a certain date range from the timescale, click on the Date from control button and set a date range; otherwise, Project uses the range of data that is currently displayed on your screen.

5. Click on OK to copy the picture when you are satisfied with the settings.

Figure 19-4 shows a GIF image of a project opened in Internet Explorer. You can now use Web page design software to insert this picture file on a Web page.

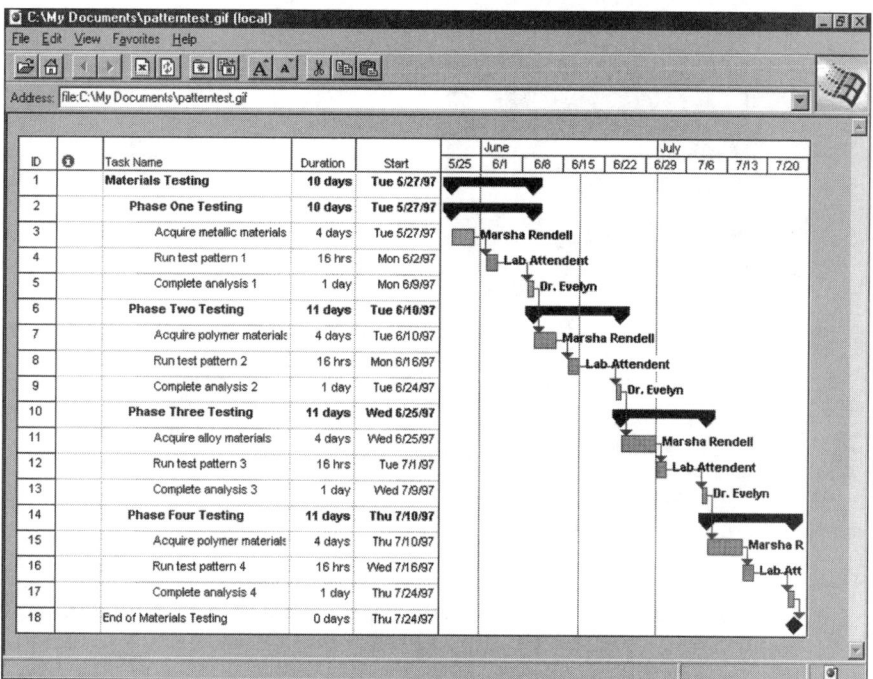

Figure 19-4: When you take a picture, you don't get a chart legend as you do when you print a project, but you get everything else.

Tip

Because of the many technologies being used in Web page design, some Web browsers won't be able to "see" certain images on a Web page. If you can't see your Project picture or if it appears corrupted in some way, take the file you've saved as HTML in Project and save it as HTML again from a Web editing program. Use the Refresh button to redisplay the page, and you should see your picture.

Saving Project Files as HTML

Suppose you want to include information from your schedule within an HTML document — say, as a page on a company intranet or a corporate Web site. To do so, you have to export the project file to HTML format. In Project you use *maps* to designate the fields that you want to export.

To export project information in HTML format, follow these steps:

1. Choose File⇨Save As HTML to open the Save dialog box.

2. Type a new filename or accept the default of your project filename with an .htm extension. Click on Save. The Export Format dialog box shown in Figure 19-5 appears.

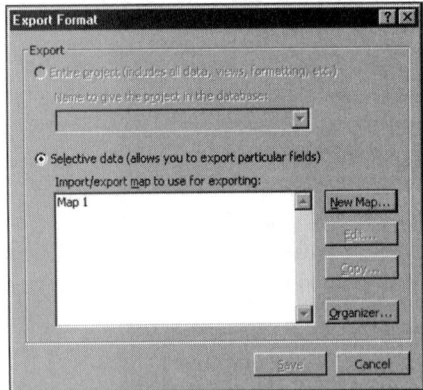

Figure 19-5: The Selective data option enables you to customize maps.

3. Select the Entire project option to save the whole file in HTML format. Click on the Selective data control button to create a map of fields to export.

Caution

The Entire project option usually doesn't fit well on the single page of the HTML format. It has more columns of information than can fit across the page and becomes very difficult to read.

4. Click on New Map to display the Define Import/Export Map dialog box shown in Figure 19-6 to display the Options tab. Project generates a map name (such as Map 1 or Map 2) in the Import/Export map name field.

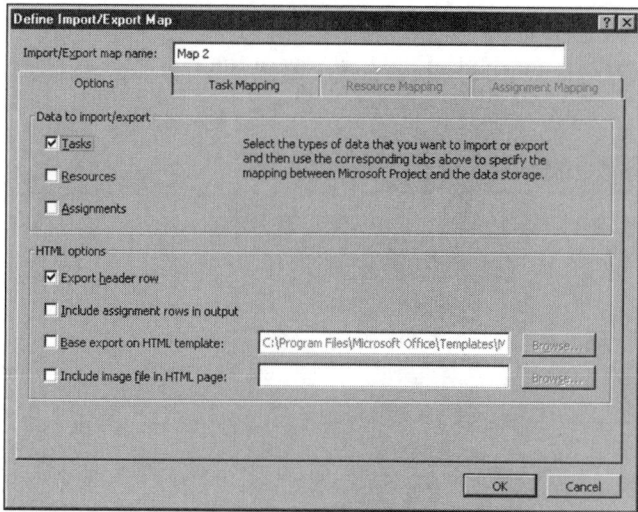

Figure 19-6: You can set your HTML export options here.

You can change the automatically generated map name to make it more informative. For example, you might want to create one map with mostly cost information and another with timing information, and call them Cost Map and Time Map, respectively. This type of naming convention helps everyone using your schedule locate the right map.

5. Click on one or more check boxes at the top of the Define Import/Export Map dialog box to designate what kind of information to export: Tasks, Resources, or Assignments. Depending on the options you select, additional tabs become available. Use the tabs to specify fields in those categories of data to include in the export file.

6. Click on any of the HTML options check boxes; here's what they do:

✦ **Export header row:** Includes the row of field titles in the HTML file

✦ **Include assignment rows in output:** Includes rows that contain information about resource assignments in the file

✦ **Base export on HTML template:** Enables you to use a template that applies a predesigned look to the HTML document

✦ **Include image file in HTML page:** Enables you include a graphic file on the HTML document

7. Click on the Task Mapping tab now. (Assuming you selected Tasks as one type of information to include, the Task Mapping tab should be available. If you chose a different category — Resource or Assignment — other related tabs that work in the same way are available.)

8. Click on the text Click here to map a field; an arrow appears.

9. Click on the arrow (on the right of the first row of the From: Microsoft Project Field column). The drop-down list shown in Figure 19-7 appears.

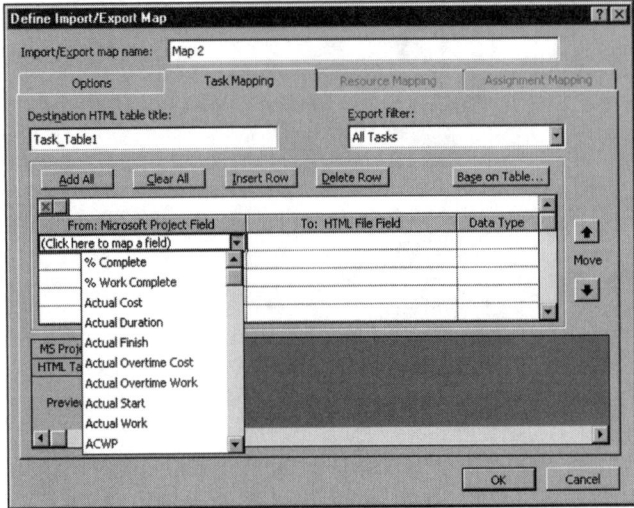

Figure 19-7: Build your own maps by using the settings on these tabs.

10. Select a field to include by clicking on it. (Use the scroll bar in the drop-down list to locate a field if necessary.) Project fills in a field name to export to in the HTML file and enters the data type (usually Text).

11. Repeat steps 8 and 9 to add other fields to your map.

Tip   The Task Mapping tab has several shortcuts for building maps. To include all the possible task fields, simply click on the Add All button. To apply a filter to tasks, for example, to export only critical task information, use the Export filter drop-down list to select a filter. To base the map on fields contained in a Project table, click on the Base on Table button and select the table name from the dialog box that appears.

12. Click on OK to save the map and then click on Save in the Define Import/Export Map dialog box to save the export file.

Figure 19-8 shows a Project file in HTML format. When you save a file in this format, you can publish the file as a Web page using any Web page design and management software.

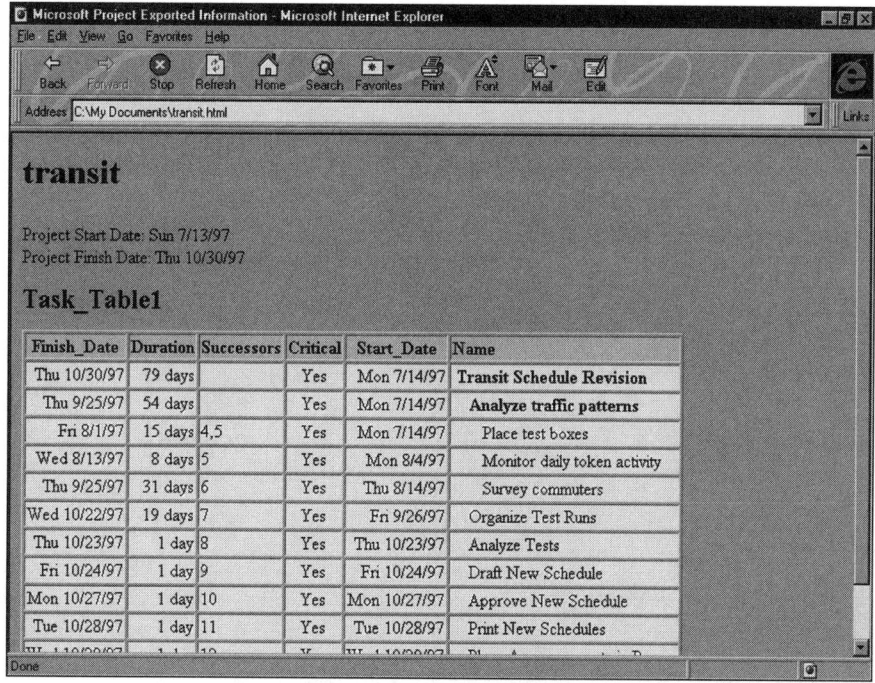

Figure 19-8: Project displays data saved in HTML format in columns across the page.

Working with Hyperlinks

A *hyperlink* is a mechanism that enables you to jump from the currently displayed document to another document on your hard drive or on a computer network, or to an Internet address (referred to as a Universal Resource Locator, or URL).

Here's an example of how you might use hyperlinks. You place a hyperlink in a schedule that deals with moving all equipment into your new manufacturing facility. This hyperlink connects to an Excel file on your company's network that contains the budget for the move to the new facility. The hyperlink appears as a little icon in the Indicators field of the Gantt chart. When you display the move schedule and click on that hyperlink, the Excel file appears so that you can check on the budgeted dollars for each aspect of the move.

You can also insert a hyperlink to an Internet address, for example, to link a research task to the Internet site where most of the research is performed.

Inserting a hyperlink

Here's how you insert a hyperlink in your project:

1. Select the task on which you want to place the hyperlink. (When you finish inserting the hyperlink, the link icon appears in the information field for the selected task.)

2. Choose Insert⊏ᗒHyperlink or click on the Insert Hyperlink button on the Standard toolbar. The Insert Hyperlink dialog box shown in Figure 19-9 appears.

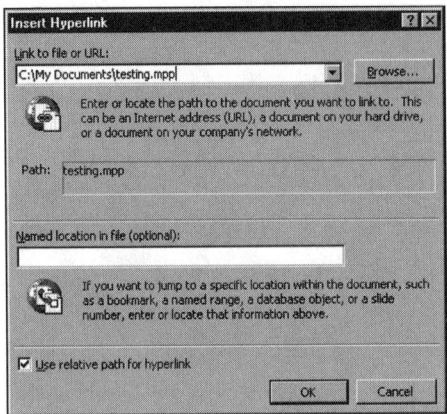

Figure 19-9: Enter a file path and name, or a URL, to set up the hyperlink.

3. Do any of the following:

   ✦ To link to an Internet address, type the URL in the Link to file or URL field (for example, `http://www.microsoft.com`).

   ✦ To link to a file on your hard drive or a network, click on Browse and locate the file, or type the path in the Link to file or URL field.

   ✦ To go to a particular location in a file, such as a named cell in an Excel spreadsheet or a bookmark in a Word file, enter that name in the Named location in file field. If you don't need to go to a particular location, just leave this field blank.

Caution

If you think you might move a file you're establishing a link to at some time in the future, select the Use relative path for hyperlink check box. That way, the link is not to a specific path, but is based on the location of the file where you're placing the hyperlink.

4. Click on OK to insert the hyperlink. A hyperlink icon, like the one shown in Figure 19-10, appears in the Indicators field to the left of the selected task.

Note

To remove a hyperlink, select the task where the link has been created and then choose Insert⇨Hyperlink. The dialog box, which was called Insert Hyperlink, appears with the name Edit Hyperlink. Click on the Remove Link button at the bottom of this dialog box to remove the link.

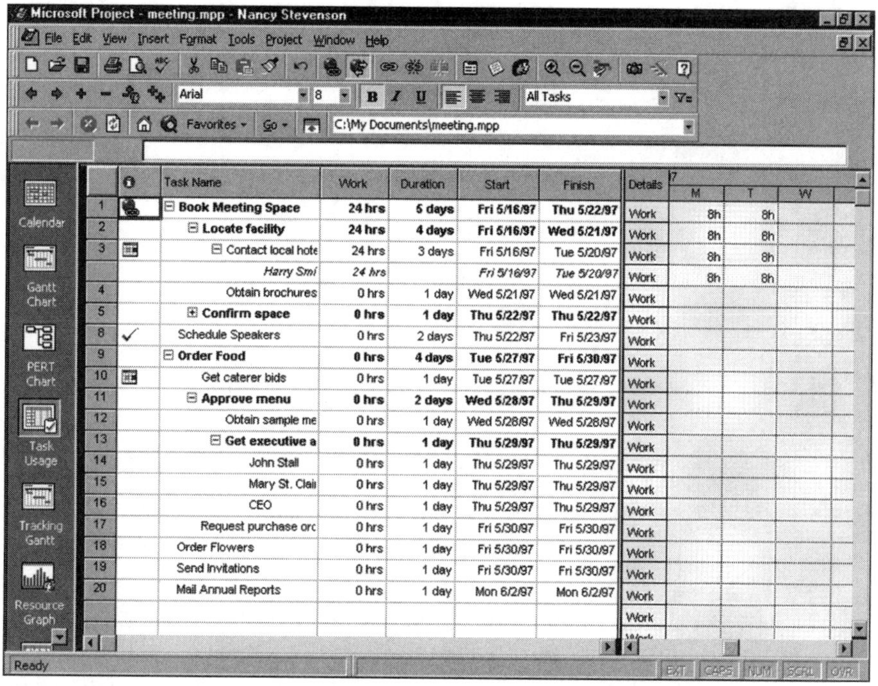

		🛈	Task Name	Work	Duration	Start	Finish	Details	M	T	W
1		🔖	⊟ **Book Meeting Space**	24 hrs	5 days	Fri 5/16/97	Thu 5/22/97	Work	8h	8h	
2			⊟ **Locate facility**	24 hrs	4 days	Fri 5/16/97	Wed 5/21/97	Work	8h	8h	
3		🔲	⊟ Contact local hote	24 hrs	3 days	Fri 5/16/97	Tue 5/20/97	Work	8h	8h	
			Harry Smi	24 hrs		Fri 5/16/97	Tue 5/20/97	Work	8h	8h	
4			Obtain brochures	0 hrs	1 day	Wed 5/21/97	Wed 5/21/97	Work			
5			⊞ **Confirm space**	0 hrs	1 day	Thu 5/22/97	Thu 5/22/97	Work			
8	✓		Schedule Speakers	0 hrs	2 days	Thu 5/22/97	Fri 5/23/97	Work			
9			⊟ **Order Food**	0 hrs	4 days	Tue 5/27/97	Fri 5/30/97	Work			
10		🔲	Get caterer bids	0 hrs	1 day	Tue 5/27/97	Tue 5/27/97	Work			
11			⊟ **Approve menu**	0 hrs	2 days	Wed 5/28/97	Thu 5/29/97	Work			
12			Obtain sample me	0 hrs	1 day	Wed 5/28/97	Wed 5/28/97	Work			
13			⊟ **Get executive a**	0 hrs	1 day	Thu 5/29/97	Thu 5/29/97	Work			
14			John Stall	0 hrs	1 day	Thu 5/29/97	Thu 5/29/97	Work			
15			Mary St. Clai	0 hrs	1 day	Thu 5/29/97	Thu 5/29/97	Work			
16			CEO	0 hrs	1 day	Thu 5/29/97	Thu 5/29/97	Work			
17			Request purchase orc	0 hrs	1 day	Fri 5/30/97	Fri 5/30/97	Work			
18			Order Flowers	0 hrs	1 day	Fri 5/30/97	Fri 5/30/97	Work			
19			Send Invitations	0 hrs	1 day	Fri 5/30/97	Fri 5/30/97	Work			
20			Mail Annual Reports	0 hrs	1 day	Mon 6/2/97	Mon 6/2/97	Work			

Figure 19-10: To go to a URL or file, click on one of these hyperlink icons.

Editing hyperlinks

When you create a hyperlink, Project uses the path name to the file as a *hyperlink representation* (that is, a phrase that describes the link). However, a path and filename may not be the best description of that link. Perhaps finding your way around would be easier if, instead of \job\0563x3.xls, the hyperlink description read Sales Budget. You can edit the hyperlink representation to differ from the hyperlink address by following these steps:

1. Display a view that includes a table, such as the Gantt chart.

2. Choose View⇨Table⇨Hyperlink. The hyperlink table in Figure 19-11 shows columns of information relevant to any HTML links you've created for your project.

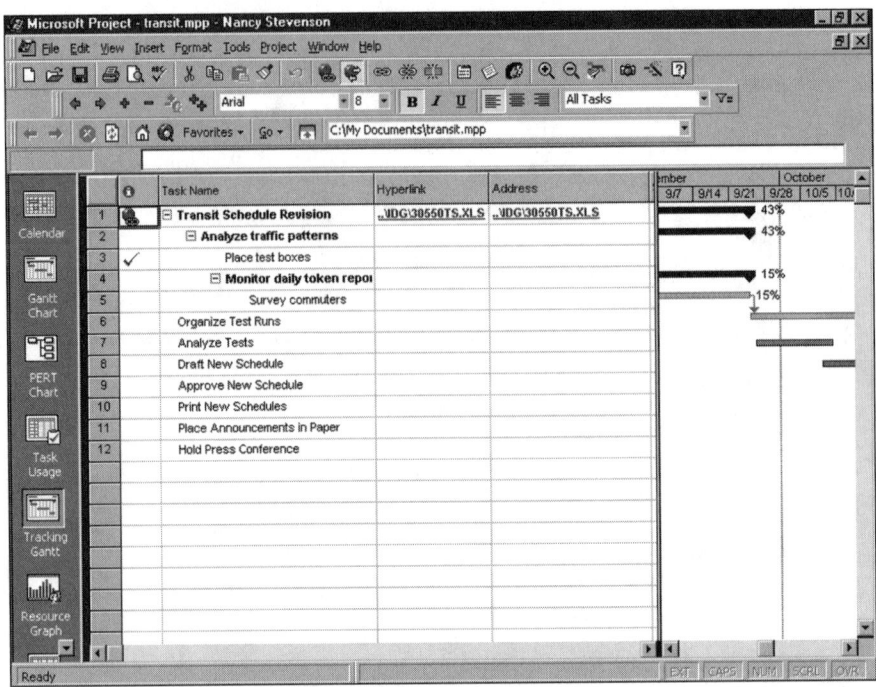

Figure 19-11: The hyperlink address and representation are two fields available here.

3. Click on a task name to select it, and use the right-arrow key to move to the Hyperlink cell you want to edit. Because the hyperlink cell contains hypertext, clicking on the field itself activates the link; you can also use this navigation method to reach the hyperlink.

4. Type the representation you want to use in the Entry bar.

If you want to edit the link itself, you can use this method to select and edit the path name using the Address field in the hyperlink table.

When hyperlinks don't work

After you establish a hyperlink, some things can happen to cause the link to not work. This condition usually involves a change in the location of the linked file or location. On a network or hard drive, a file could simply have been moved to another directory or deleted. Similarly, a Web site could have been moved to a new URL, or perhaps it no longer exists.

Another possibility is that you've mapped your hyperlink to a file on a network that is in a location to which you don't have access. Or perhaps you give a copy of your schedule to a coworker, and she doesn't have access to that location from her computer.

The best way to work around this problem is to use the relative address option, rather than an absolute address, when you create the hyperlink. You can also edit the address in the hyperlink table. For example, you could change the location f:\budget.xls with \\server\share\budget.xls. This change means that if your server changes from f:, the relative address to your server would still work. For more help with hyperlinks problems, check out the hyperlink/troubleshooting topic in Project's Help feature.

Moving or copying hyperlinks

You can also use the hyperlink table to move or copy a hyperlink. Follow these steps to do so:

1. Select the hyperlink cell you want to copy by clicking on its task name and then by using the right-arrow key to move to the hyperlink cell.

2. Press the Shift key and the right-arrow key to also select the address of the hyperlink.

3. Do one of the following:

   ✦ To move the link, click on the Cut button on the Standard toolbar, click on the hyperlink cell next to the task where you want to move the link, and click on the Paste button.

   ✦ To copy the link, select the link, click on the Copy button, click on the hyperlink cell next to the task where you want to place a copy of the link, and click on the Paste button.

As shown in Figure 19-12, Project can copy or move the link to the other task. However, note that the hyperlink representation is again the path name. To change the representation, use the techniques in the section on editing hyperlinks.

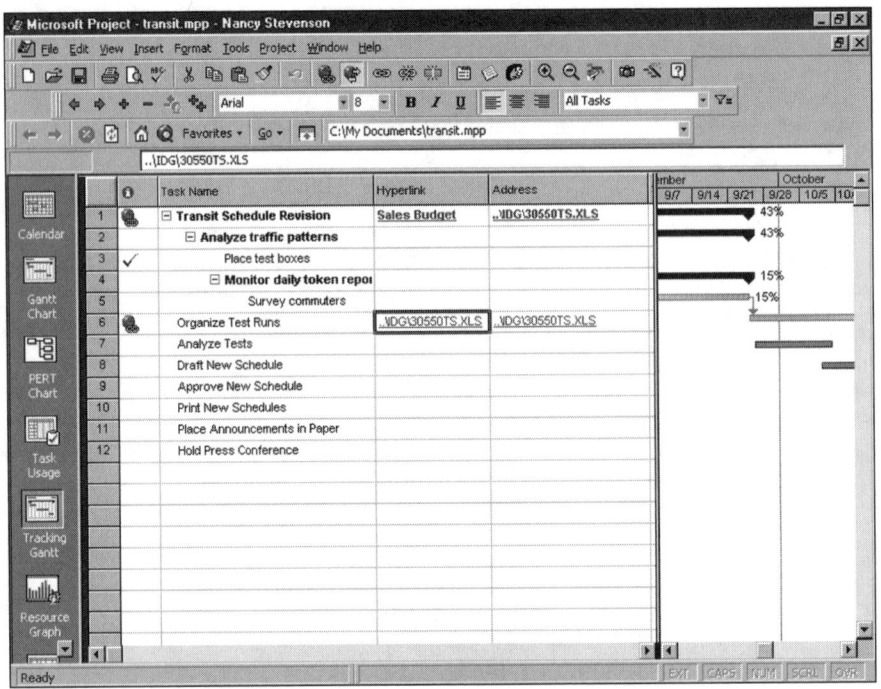

Figure 19-12: Notice that the hyperlink representation has returned to the original path name in the copied link.

Getting Help on the Web

The Office 95 family of products includes the Microsoft on the Web feature. This handy submenu is also available in Project 98. The Microsoft of the Web menu (see Figure 19-13) offers links to various Microsoft Web pages that provide support, information, and even free downloads of goodies like templates and graphics files to Project users. Refer to Chapter 3 for an in-depth discussion of the Microsoft on the Web Help feature.

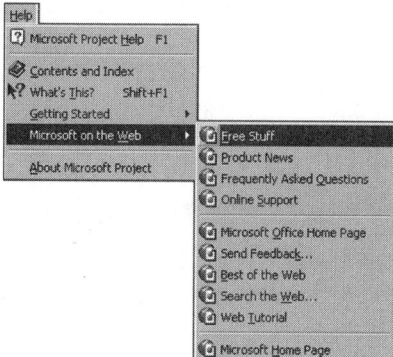

Figure 19-13: Try the Web tutorial if you want an overview of what Project can do. Free Stuff offers an assortment of downloadable items, such as graphics you can use in your work.

You should check the Product News Web page regularly to find out about enhancements or add-on products that make Project easier to use.

On the CD-ROM This book's companion CD-ROM contains several add-on products in demonstration or publisher editions. Add-on products can streamline your use of Project or add functions not available in the current version.

In addition, I encourage you to send feedback to Microsoft, using that option in the Microsoft on the Web menu, to suggest features or enhancements you would like to see in future versions of Project. Project is a very flexible software product; its specific uses vary according to your industry and project requirements. New features in every version of the software make it easier to use and provide new types of information useful in specific industry situations.

Summary

Project's Web capabilities enable you to post Project files on the Web, to use links among files, or to use links from a file to an Internet address. These simple Web features can help you communicate project information to coworkers or clients in an effective, high-tech way. No doubt, as Microsoft continues its focus on online support and communication, new Web-specific features will appear in future versions of Project.

In this chapter you learned to

    ✦ Save Project files in Web page format

    ✦ Take a picture of a project using the online graphics file format

    ✦ Insert hyperlinks

    ✦ Connect to Microsoft with Project's Microsoft on the Web feature

As you continue to use Project to create and manage schedules, you'll discover more about all the features described in this book. After a few projects, you'll be taking full advantage of this powerful software.

✦   ✦   ✦

Project Management Glossary

Note

The first nine terms are abbreviations that appear in the Microsoft Project selection lists for columns to include in views, reports, and so on.

ACWP (actual cost of work performed). Cost of actual work performed to date on the project plus any fixed costs.

ALAP (as late as possible). A constraint placed on a task's timing to make it occur as late as possible in the project schedule based on its dependency relationships.

ASAP (as soon as possible). A constraint placed on a task's timing to make it occur as early in the project as possible based on its dependency relationships.

BAC (budget at completion). The total of planned costs to complete a task (also referred to as baseline costs).

BCWP (budgeted cost of work performed). Also called earned value, this term refers to the value of work completed. A task with $1,000 of associated costs, when 75 percent complete, has a baseline value of $750.

BCWS (budgeted cost of work scheduled). The planned completion percentage times the planned cost. This calculated value reflects the amount of the task that is completed and the planned cost of the task.

CV (earned value cost variance). This variance indicates the difference between the planned costs (baseline costs) and the costs taking into account actual costs to date and estimated costs going forward (scheduled costs). The difference between these two values produces either a positive (overbudget) or negative (underbudget) cost variance.

EAC (estimate at completion). The total scheduled cost for a resource on a task. This calculation provides the costs incurred to date plus costs estimated for remaining work on the task.

WBS (work breakdown structure). Automatically assigned numbers for each task in a project outline that reflect that outline structure. Government project reports often includes WBS codes.

actual. A cost or percentage of work completed and tracked as having already occurred or been incurred.

actual cost of work performed. See ACWP.

as late as possible. See ALAP.

as soon as possible. See ASAP.

base calendar. The default calendar on which all new tasks are based unless a resource-specific calendar is applied.

baseline. The snapshot of a project plan against which actual work is tracked.

baseline cost. The total of all planned costs on tasks in a project before any actual costs have been incurred.

budget at completion. See BAC.

budgeted cost of work performed. See BCWP.

budgeted cost of work scheduled. See BCWS.

calendar. The various settings for hours in a workday, days in a work week, holidays, and nonworking days on which a project schedule is based.

circular dependency. A dependency among tasks that creates an endless loop that cannot be resolved.

collapse. Close a project outline to hide subtasks from view.

combination view. A Project view with the task details showing at the bottom of the screen.

constraint. A parameter that forces a task to fit a certain timing. For example, a task can be constrained to start as late as possible in a project.

cost. A cost can be applied to a task in a project by assigning resources, which can be equipment, materials, or people with associated hourly rates or fees.

critical path. The series of tasks that must occur on time in order for the overall project to meet its deadline.

critical task. A task on the critical path.

crosstab. A report format that compares two intersecting sets of data; for example, you can generate a crosstab report showing costs of critical tasks that are running late.

cumulative cost. The planned total cost for a resource to date on a particular task. This calculation provides the costs already incurred on the task plus the costs planned for the remaining, as yet uncompleted, portion of the task.

cumulative work. The planned total work of a resource on a particular task. This calculation provides the work already performed on the task plus the work planned for the remaining, as yet uncompleted, portion of the task.

current date line. The vertical line in a Gantt chart indicating today's date and time.

demote. To move a task to a lower level in the project outline hierarchy.

dependency. A timing relationship between two tasks in a project. A dependency can cause a task to happen after another task, to happen before another task, or to begin at some point during the life of the other task.

detail task. See subtask.

duration. The amount of time it takes to complete a task.

duration variance. A field displaying the variation between the planned (baseline) duration of a task and the current estimated task duration based on activity to date and remaining activity to be performed.

earned value. Also called budgeted cost of work performed. Earned value refers to the value of work completed. A task with $1,000 of associated costs, when 75 percent complete, will have a baseline value of $750.

earned value cost variance. See CV.

effort driven. An effort-driven task has an assigned amount of effort to complete it. When you add resources to these tasks, the effort is distributed among those resources.

elapsed duration. An estimate of how long it will take to complete a task based on a 24-hour day and seven-day week.

estimate at completion (EAC). The total scheduled cost for a resource on a task. This calculation provides the costs incurred to date plus costs estimated for remaining work on the task.

expand. Opening a project outline to reveal subtasks as well as summary tasks.

expected duration. This calculation estimates the actual duration of a task based on performance to date.

external task. When tasks are linked between projects, Project displays tasks from the external project in the current project. The external task represents the linked tasks without having to leave the current project.

finish date. The date on which a project will be completed.

finish-to-finish relationship. A dependency relationship in which two tasks must finish at the same time.

finish-to-start relationship. A dependency relationship in which one task must finish at the same time that another task starts.

fixed cost. A cost that does not increase or decrease based on the time a resource spends on a task. A consultant's fee or permit fee are examples of fixed costs.

fixed date. A task that must occur on a certain date. Fixed-date tasks do not move earlier or later in the schedule because of dependency relationships.

fixed duration. The length of time required for a task remains constant no matter how many resources are assigned to it. Travel time is a good example of a fixed-duration task.

float. See slack.

Gantt chart. A standard project management tracking device that displays task information alongside a chart that shows task timing in a bar chart format.

gap. See lag.

ID number. The number assigned to a task based on its sequence in the schedule.

lag. The result of dependency relationships among tasks. Lag is a certain amount of downtime between the end of one task and the start of another.

leveling. A process used by Microsoft Project to modify resource assignments to tasks to resolve resource conflicts.

linking. Establishing a connection between two tasks in separate schedules so that changes to tasks in the first schedule are reflected in the second. Linking is also a term applied to establishing dependencies among tasks in a project.

milestone. A task of zero duration that marks a moment of time in a schedule.

node. Boxes containing information about individual project tasks in the PERT Chart view.

nonworking time. Time when a resource on a project is not assigned to current task.

outline. The structure of summary and subordinate tasks in a project.

overallocation. When a resource is assigned to spend more time than its work calendar permits on a single task or combination of tasks occurring at the same point in time.

overtime. Any work scheduled above and beyond a resource's standard work hours; overtime work can have a different rate assigned to it than a resource's regular rate.

percent complete. The amount of work on a task that has already been accomplished, expressed as a percentage.

PERT chart. A standard project management tracking form that indicates work flow among the tasks in a project.

predecessor. In a dependency relationship, the task that is designated to occur before, or precede, another.

priorities. Project uses the priorities you assign to tasks when it performs resource leveling to resolve project conflicts; a higher priority task is less likely than a lower priority task to incur delay during the leveling process.

progress lines. Gantt chart bars that overlap the baseline task bar and indicate tracked actual progress on the task.

project. A series of steps to reach a specific goal. A project seeks to meet the triple constraints of time, quality, and cost.

project management. The discipline that studies various methods, procedures, and concepts used to control the progress and outcome of projects.

promote. To move a task to a higher level in a project's outline hierarchy.

recurring task. A task that is repeated during the life of a project. Typical recurring tasks are regular meetings of project teams or regular reviews of project output.

resource. A cost associated with a task; a resource can be a person, piece of equipment, materials, or a fee.

resource contouring. Changing the time when a resource begins work on a task. You can use contouring to vary the amount of work a resource does on a task over the life of that task.

resource driven. A task whose timing is determined by the number of resources assigned to it.

resource leveling. A process used by Project to modify resource assignments to resolve resource conflicts.

resource pool. A group of resources that can be assigned as a group to an individual task (for example, a pool of administrative workers assigned to generating a report).

roll up. The calculation by which all subtask values are "rolled up" or summarized in a summary task.

slack. Also called float. The time you have available to delay a task before that task becomes critical. You have used up slack on a task when any delay on that task will cause a delay in the overall project deadline.

split tasks. When progress on a task is interrupted or delayed because the task has been placed on hold, you can split the task into two tasks. When you split tasks, the downtime between the two is not allocated to the total time taken to complete the task.

start date. The date on which a project begins.

start-to-finish relationship. A dependency relationship in which one task cannot start until another task finishes.

start-to-start relationship. A dependency relationship in which two tasks must start at the same time.

subproject. An inserted copy of a second project that becomes a phase of the project in which it is inserted.

subtask. Also called a subordinate task. A task providing detail for a specific step in the project. This detail is rolled up into a higher-level summary task.

successor. In a dependency relationship a successor task is scheduled to begin after another task in the project.

summary task. A task in a project outline that has subordinate tasks beneath it. A summary task rolls up the details of its subtasks and has no timing of its own.

task. An individual step to be performed to reach a project's goal.

template. A format in which a Project file can be saved; the template saves elements like calendar settings, formatting, and tasks. New project files can be based on a template.

timescale. The area of a Gantt Chart view that indicates the units of time being displayed.

tracking. The act of recording actual progress in terms of both work completed and costs accrued on tasks in a project.

variable rate. A shift in resource cost that can be set to occur at specific times during a project. For example, if a resource is expected to receive a raise or if equipment lease rates are expected to increase, you can assign variable rates for those resources.

work breakdown structure. See WBS.

workload. The amount of work any resource is performing at any given point in time, taking into account all tasks to which the resource is assigned.

workspace. A set of files and project settings that can be saved and reopened together so that you can pick up work on a project or projects at the point at which you stopped.

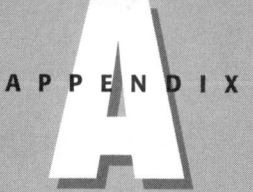

Project Management Resources

Project management is a detailed methodology and intricate system of requirements for various industries and disciplines that has evolved over many years. Project management as a topic encompasses concepts of leadership and team building, charting and analysis of data, cost and schedule control, and more.

Many useful resources for project management information, tools, and support can help you work with Microsoft Project. This appendix, contains five resource categories: Associations, Publications, Education, Online and Software Products. It provides phone numbers, and when available, address and fax information. As you see from this list, project management is a very international discipline — remember to dial country codes before any phone number outside the United States.

Associations

The following associations provide support and information for both general and industry-specific project management issues.

American Association of Cost Engineers counts among its membership those interested in cost engineering and cost estimating.

209 Prairie Ave., #100
Morgantown, WV 26505
Phone: 800 858-COST

Association of Proposal Management Professionals can assist you in developing proposals for your projects, whether you bid for government or industry contracts. APMP has local chapters as well as a newsletter and task force on Electronic Procurement.

P.O. Box 1172
Idyllwild, CA 92549-1172
Phone: 909 659-0789

Association for Project Management is based in England, with chapters in both the UK and Hong Kong. This association has a certification program for project management professionals.

85 Oxford Rd.
High Wycombe
Bucks, England HP112DX
Phone: 44 14 94 44 00 90
Fax: 44 14 94 52 89 37

American Society of Quality Control focuses on quality issues in project management. This organization offers certification in a variety of specializations related to quality.

P.O. Box 3005
Milwaukee, WI 53201-3005
Phone: 800-248-1946

Center for International Project and Program Management supports project and quality management with standards and education. This organization is based at the University of Michigan.

123 Charles
Jackson, MI 49203
E-mail: CIPPM@Free.org

Construction Management Association of America

Phone: 703 356-2622
Fax: 703 356-6388

Educational Society for Resource Management (formerly American Production & Inventory Control Society and still referred to as APICS) specializes in support and information for those wishing to improve or maximize their resource management skills.

500 W. Annandale Road
Falls Church, VA 22046
Phone: 800 444-2742

International Cost Systems Engineering Council is a global organization that supports those involved in product development and project management.

1168 Hidden Lake Drive
Granite Falls, NC 28630
Phone: 704 728-5287
Fax: 704 728-0048

IPMA Service Secretariat, based in Denmark, offers international conferences on project management.

Pia Dyhr
DiEU
Dr Neegarrds Vej 3
DK-2970 Hoersholm, Denmark
Phone: 45 45 76 46 76
Fax: 45 45 76 80 20
E-mail: 100113.240303@compuserve.com

Project Management Institute is the premier U.S. project management association It has chapters across the country, educational programs, a long list of publications, and online discussion forums. In addition, PMI has a monthly magazine called *PM Network* and a

quarterly called *Project Management Journal*. Its publication, *A Guide to the Project Management Body of Knowledge* (PMBOK Guide), is a bible in the project management world.

130 South State Road
Upper Darby, PA 19082
Phone: 610 734-3330

Software Program Managers Network provides information and guidance for those involved in software project management.

142 No. Central Avenue
Campbell, CA 95008
Phone: 408 378-4700
Fax: 408 378-5395

PMI Special Interest Groups

PMI offers a variety of special interest groups, or SIGs, that focus on different aspects of project management. SIG members are required to pay a small fee to support the group, and all members must also belong to PMI.

These SIGs are either currently available or under consideration:

Aerospace and Defense	Manufacturing
Automotive	Marketing and Sales
Design-Procurement-Construction	New Product Development
Diversity	Oil, Gas, and Petrochemical
Education and Training	Pharmaceutical
Environmental Management	Quality in Project Management
Financial Services	Risk Management
Government	Service and Outsourcing Projects
Information Management and Movement	Utility
Information Systems	Women in Project Management

Publications

A great many books, newsletters, and journals are devoted to project management and its many facets. Some of the publications in this list are from small presses or associations. You can use the ISBN number, a publishing industry code, to order many of the books from your local bookstore.

Books

The following books provide guidance on general project management principles and industry-specific project management advice.

Advanced Project Management, 3rd Edition
Author: F. L. Harrison
Publisher: Gower
ISBN:0-566-09100-3

A Guide to the Project Management Body of Knowledge
Authors: Project Management
    Institute Standards Committee
Publisher: Project Management
Institute
ISBN: 1-880410-12-5

A Practical Guide to Project Management
Authors: Celia Buron and
    Norma Michael
Publisher: Kogan Page
ISBN: 0-7494-0790-5

Construction Project Management Using Small Computers
Author: Glen Peters
Publisher: Architectural Press/
    Nichols Publishing
ISBN: 0-85139-776-X

Effective Project Management Through Applied Cost and Schedule Control
Authors: James A. Bent and
    Kenneth K. Humphreys
Publisher: Marcel Dekker, Inc.
ISBN: 0-8247-9715-9

Effective Project Planning and Management
Authors: W. Alan Randolph and
    Barry Z. Posner

Publisher: Prentice-Hall International
ISBN: 0-13-245101-8

Engineering Management
Author: Patrick D. T. O'Connor
Publisher: J. Wiley & Sons
ISBN: 0-471-93974-9

People and Project Management for IT
Authors: Sue Craig and Hadi Jassim
Publisher: McGraw-Hill
ISBN: 0-07-707844-5

Project Leadership
Authors: Wendy Briner, Colin Hastings,
    and Michael Geddes
Publisher: Gower
ISBN: 0-566-07785-X

Project Management: A Managerial Guide
Authors: Jack R. Merredith and
    Samuel J. Mantell, Jr.
Publisher: J. Wiley & Sons
ISBN: 0-471-50534-X

Software Project Management
Authors: Mike Cotterell and Bob Hughes
Publisher: International Thomson
ISBN: 1-85032-190-6

Value Management in Construction
Authors: Brian R. Norton and
    William C. McElligott
Publisher: Macmillan
ISBN: 0-333-60626-4

Journals and magazines

Many of the associations listed in the first section of this appendix publish magazines or journals. Some of those are listed here, along with a phone number to contact for additional information. Note that many of these publications are available only to members of the organization.

APICS: The Performance Advantage
Educational Society for Resource
  Management
Phone: 800-444-2742

Computing Canada (regular column
on project management)
Plesman Publications
Phone: 416-497-9562

*International Journal of Project
Management*
Elsevier Science
Phone: 212-633-3730

Journal of Quality Technology
American Society of Quality Control
Phone: 800-248-1946

Project Management Journal
Project Management Institute
Phone: 610-734-3330

Quality Engineering
American Society of Quality Control
Phone: 800-248-1946

Quality Management Journal
American Society of Quality Control
Phone: 800-248-1946

Technometrics
American Society of Quality Control
Phone: 800 248-1946

Education

Educational opportunities exist around the world for certification and degree programs in a variety of project management-related disciplines. Here are just a few.

Center for Management and Organization Effectiveness offers workshops relating to coaching and facilitation.

245 S. E. Madison
Bartlesville, OK 74006
Phone: 918 333-6609
Fax: 918 333-5102

Louisiana State University offers a week-long seminar through its Department of Executive Education. Go through this seminar to prepare for the PMI certification exam that will earn you the title of Project Management Professional.

One University Place
Shreveport, LA 71115-2399
Phone: 318-797-5000

Project Management Research Network runs out of a university in Austria and supports project management educational programs at many technical schools and universities throughout the world.

Extraordinariat Projektmanagement
University of Economics and
Business Administration
Franz Klein-Gasse 1
1190 Vienna, Austria
0043 1 313 52215

The University of Calgary in Alberta, Canada, has brought together its manufacturing and engineering courses and created a project management area of specialization.

Project Management Specialization
Department of Civil Engineering
The University of Calgary
2500 University Drive NW
Calgary, Alberta, Canada T2N 1N4
Phone: 403 220-4816

University of New England, New South Wales, Australia, offers a project management and operations management unit within its MBA degree program. You don't have to fly to Australia to take advantage of these courses (although it's a good excuse to!). The school offers these special programs throughout the world.

Phone: 61 67 733545
Fax: 61 67 733461

Western Carolina University confers a masters of project management degree from its College of Business.

College of Business
Cullowhee, NC 28723
Phone: 704 227-7401
Fax: 704 227-7414

Online

You could spend days online and never run through all the project management and project management associated Web sites. However, here are a few good places to start surfing. Please note that Web sites and addresses change frequently; those listed here were current as this book went to press.

American Society for Quality Control
http://www.asq@org

American Production and Inventory Control Society
http://www.apics.org

International Cost Engineering Council
http://206.100.228.200/icec
E-mail: icec@twave.net

Project World
http://www.projectworld.com/

Architecture, Engineering, Construction Business Center
http://www.aecinfo.com

Software Program Managers Network
http://www.icompe.com/

Acquisition Program Integration/Performance Management
http://www.acq.osd.mil/pm/

Center for Management and Organization Effectiveness
http://www.thecoach.com/cmoeright.html

Project Management Institute
http://www.pmi.org

Center for International Project and Program Management
http://www.iol.ie/~mattewar/CIPPM

WWW Guide to Project Management Research Sites
http://www.fek.umu.se/irnop/projweb.htm

Software Products

In addition to the excellent software products in demo or trial version form on the companion CD-ROM, here are some other project management tools to investigate.

Project Integrator (PI) is great for working with time and process management issues in a workgroup or team. It has tools for planning, tracking, and reporting on individual resource time expenditures on multiple projects.

System Solvers, Ltd.
30685 Barrington Avenue, Suite 100
Madison Heights, MI 48071-5133
Phone: 810 588-7400
Fax: 810 588-7170

TurboProject from IMSI in England is a higher-end project management software for design, testing, and production.

IMSI (UK) Ltd
IMSI House
Printing House Lane
Hayes, Middlesex, England UB31AP
Phone: 0181 581 2000
Fax: 00181 581 2200

Project Administration and Control System (PACS) is the project management portion of a larger financial software suite called Renaissance C/S Financial Applications. If you want to integrate your project costs into your general ledger, check this one out.

Herkemij & Partners
Cypresbaan 6
2908 LT Capelle a/d Ijssel
The Netherlands
Phone: 31 10 4580899
Fax: 31 10 4508233

Graneda is a professional graphics add-on package with which you can create exciting project charts. The application includes extensive printer and plotter drivers for printing your charts.

American Netronic, Inc.
5212 Katella Ave., Suite 104
Los Alamitos, CA 90720
Phone: 562 795-0147
Fax: 562 795-0152

ProjectView from the Artemis family of products helps with multiple projects management details, especially in a client/server environment.

CSC Artemis International
One Flint Hill
10530 RoseHaven Street
Fairfax, VA 22030
Phone/Fax: 703 298-7400

Project Exchange is used with MS Project for enterprisewide project management and information solutions.

IMS Information Management Services
549 Columbian Street
Weymouth, MA 02190
Phone: 617 340-4400
Fax: 617 340-4401

Multi-Project is another tool for multiple projects. Multi-Project extends MS Project to work with department or programwide project management. Using this software you can easily create links between projects for analysis and report generation.

Innate, Inc.
525 N. Manoa Rd.
Havertown, PA 19083
Phone: 610 853-2944

Cascade is an Oracle-based project and finance management tool for senior management. This software is especially helpful in decision analysis for mission-critical projects.

Mantix Systems, Inc.
12020 Sunrise Valley Drive
Reston, VA 22091
Phone: 703 715-2450
Fax: 703 715-2450

Production Control Outputs with Project

Octopus Technologies
301 Oxford Valley Rd., Suite 102A
Yardley, PA 19067
Phone: 215 321-8759

Risk+

Program Management Solutions
111 Sepulveda, Suite 333
Manhattan Beach, CA 94941
Phone: 310 374-0455
Fax: 310 374-2090

Project Management Worksheet

This appendix provides worksheets that allow you to plan every phase of a project. Feel free to make copies of these pages and fill them in as you work through your project to be sure you've covered all your bases in managing your project.

Phase I: Research

In this phase you are gathering information about the scope and goals of your project; determining parameters such as dates, resources, and money available for your project; and specifying deliverables.

1. Ask the following people or groups of people to define the goal of this project. Note any discrepancies in their goal statements and resolve them before you begin planning your project:

   ✦ Your manager

   ✦ Your staff

   ✦ The manager of finance

   ✦ The person who manages the product or service that pertains to your project. For example, if you are setting up a new manufacturing unit, contact the production line supervisor. If you are organizing the move to a new facility, contact the office or facilities manager.

Write the responses here:

_____

_____

_____

_____

2. In the space provided, sketch the organizational chart of those who will implement your project. Indicate who reports to whom within your general organization and then specifically for this project (these two hierarchies may differ slightly). Who will expect to receive reports, communications, and deliverables?

3. To help you begin to build a project team, list the resources you may have available for your project in Table B-1, noting each resource's department, expertise, and availability.

Table B-1
Project Resources

Resource	Department	Expertise	Availability

4. Research timing for this project and answer these questions:

✦ How long have similar projects taken in your organization or your experience?

_____

✦ Are any dates related to your project immutable, such as a yearly inspection by an outside organization or the end of your fiscal year? List them here.

_____

_____

_____

_____

✦ Rank the priority of the three major areas that typically affect a project: time, quality, and cost. In a crunch the criteria you rank highest here will take precedence.

___ Time

___ Quality

___ Cost

Phase II: Planning

In this phase you take some of the information you gathered in Phase I and begin to see how those details will come together to form a project plan that can be the basis of your project schedule.

1. Write a goal statement. This one sentence description states the desired end result of all the efforts in your project. A sample goal statement would be as follows: Our goal is to launch a new software product successfully into the marketplace.

_____

_____

_____

2. Write a scope statement. This statement should broadly outline the parameters of your project. A sample scope statement would be as follows: We will finalize the software according to our internal quality standards and launch it in three major markets by the end of this fiscal year at a cost not to exceed $1.2 million.

_____

_____

_____

_____

_____

3. List the major phases of your project:

_____

_____

_____

_____

_____

4. List any milestones in your project. Milestones are tasks that mark a moment or accomplishment in your project.

_____

_____

_____

_____

_____

_____

_____

_____

_____

5. Create a contact list for your project, including resource name, title, and department; the name of each resource's manager, contact information, hourly rate or fee; and any other information you consider useful. You can create this list in a word processor program, such as Word for Windows, or begin to enter this resource information in Microsoft Project. Use the entry below as a model:

Resource Name: John Smith

Title/Department: Engineer/manufacturing department

Manager: Sally Jones, manufacturing manager

Phone: (444) 555-1111

E-mail: jsmith@org.com

Rate: $35 per hour

Comments: Not available in December due to professional association commitments; assistant is Bob James, ext. 5567

_____

_____

_____

_____

_____

_____

_____

_____

_____

_____

_____

_____

_____

_____

_____

_____

_____

_____

_____

_____

_____

_____

_____

_____

_____

_____

6. Outline the standards you will use for entering information into Microsoft Project, including the following:

✦ How will you name resources (by name or title)?

_____

✦ Who will track progress and how often?

_____

✦ What are your organization's standard work hours and fiscal year? This information enables you to create an accurate calendar in Project.

_____

◆ What regular reports will you generate and who will they go to?

_____

_____

◆ How will you track and account for overtime?

_____

_____

Phase III: Creating Your Project Schedule

In this phase you enter information to begin building your project. Use this checklist to be sure you are creating a comprehensive and accurate schedule.

Checklist for Creating a Project Schedule

___ Enter general project information, such as the project name and start and finish dates.

___ Make any calendar settings for your project based on your organization's work day, week, or year.

___ Enter the names of major phases of your project

___ Enter the first level of individual tasks in each phase, including task name and timing. If this level task will have subtasks, do not bother to enter timing as the task timing will be derived from subtasks.

___ Enter any subtasks and include timing information.

___ Enter any regularly recurring tasks such as monthly project meetings.

___ Add resource information to individual tasks including costs and availability.

___ Establish dependencies between tasks.

___ Study and resolve resource conflicts using the resource leveling and contouring tools in Project.

___ Determine whether Project is giving you an acceptable finish date. If it is not, consider any of the following actions:

> ✦ Add resources to reduce timing. (However, this action is likely to add costs.)
>
> ✦ Request additional time to complete the project.
>
> ✦ Utilize resource downtime more efficiently.
>
> ✦ Adjust dependencies.
>
> ✦ Start the project earlier.

___ If possible, add some slack into tasks to allow for delays.

___ Set up any workgroup resources with whom you will be using Project's TeamAssign, TeamStatus, and TeamUpdate features.

___ When the project is acceptable, set the baseline and save the file.

Phase IV: Tracking Your Project

Tracking your project involves entering actual timing of tasks and resource time actually expended on tasks. Use this checklist to help in tracking projects. Don't forget to set a baseline before beginning to track activity on your project.

Tracking Procedures Checklist

___ Enter actual start and finish dates for tasks that have been completed.

___ Enter resource effort expended on tasks.

___ Enter actual fees or charges incurred on tasks.

___ Set remaining durations and percent complete for individual tasks.

___ Use various tracking views in Project, information about earned value and resource usage, and filters such as critical path to analyze the status of your project. Pay careful attention to how much time and money remains by comparing your original estimates and actual activity on the project.

___ Make any adjustments necessary to keep your project on track, such as reassigning resources, extending your final deadline, or reassessing the budget remaining to you for the rest of the project based on cost overruns.

___ Send out TeamStatus and TeamUpdate messages to keep your team informed of project progress.

Phase V: Preparing for the Next Project

Now that you've completed a project, don't forget to analyze what went on so you can improve on estimating and tracking your next project. Use this worksheet to analyze your complete project.

1. List your baseline start and finish dates and actual start and finish dates for your entire project here:

   ✦ Baseline start: _____

   ✦ Baseline finish: _____

   ✦ Actual start: _____

   ✦ Actual finish: _____

2. Write a statement about the major factor that affected your timing and a conclusion about whether you could have anticipated or avoided that factor. Be honest about your own failings. It's the best way to become better at what you do.

   _____

   _____

   _____

3. Enter your baseline total costs and actual total costs for the project here:

   ✦ Baseline costs: _____

   ✦ Actual costs: _____

4. Write a statement about the major factor or factors influencing your final costs, including what you can do to avoid cost overruns on a future project (or, if you're lucky, what you can do to have similar cost savings on future projects). What did you do or not do to keep costs in line?

   _____

   _____

   _____

5. Analyze how resources performed on your project; are there people or vendors you would not recommend for use on future projects? Are there people or vendors you feel did exceptionally well? Make a record of them here so that you and others in your company can plan resources for future projects appropriately.

✦ Vendor issues on current project:

_____

_____

_____

✦ Recommended resources for future projects:

_____

_____

_____

6. List three things you can do more efficiently as a project manager on your next project to improve performance and efficiency:

_____

_____

_____

7. List three things your manager or organization could provide you with to make your next project more successful:

_____

_____

_____

8. List three ways you can improve your tracking procedures on future projects:

_____

_____

_____

9. Write statements of what worked and didn't work in your management of resources in these areas:

◆ Communication:

_____

_____

_____

◆ Accuracy of time estimates for resources to complete tasks:

_____

_____

_____

◆ Resource management:

_____

_____

_____

What's on the CD-ROM

The CD-ROM that accompanies this book contains demos or trial versions of several of the most popular add-on products for use with Microsoft Project, as well as templates for four of the most common types of projects. Use these templates as time-savers when you begin building similar schedules.

Software on the CD-ROM

This appendix describes the contents of the CD-ROM and gives instructions for installing each program on your computer. You can use the trial or demonstration versions of these products to see how they fit your needs. Each listing includes contact information so that you can buy the software directly from the vendor.

In some cases these vendors did not have the fully updated version of their software for Project 98 ready in time for this book's publication. If you have access to Project 95, you can test the early version and then order the Project 98 version. If you no longer have access to Project 95, you can contact the companies to get an updated demo or more product information.

Milestones, Etc. 5.0

Company: Kidasa Software, 1114 Lost Creek Blvd., Suite 300, Austin, TX 78746

Phone; e-mail: (512) 328-0167; kidasa1@aol.com

Installation instructions: Double-click on the My Computer icon on your Windows desktop. Open the Milestones folder on the CD-ROM and double-click on the Milestones file. Follow the onscreen prompts to install the trial version of the program. Note that no serial number is required to install this trial version. When you are asked to enter this number, type **None** and proceed.

Running the program: Milestones, Etc. trial version is Project 98 compatible. To run Milestones, Etc. from the Windows Start menu, choose Programs⇨Milestones, Etc.

Milestones, Etc. is a front end for Microsoft Project. You can enter and manage project data in Milestones and then move (export) it into Project. You can also import Project data to Milestones. This approach enables you to better control the display of some Project data because you can make settings for the number of tasks per page, column and page layout, and OLE linking and embedding.

Milestones, Etc. can also be used as a stand-alone scheduler for creating and updating simple Gantt or timeline schedules without using the resource management features of Project.

PERT Chart EXPERT

Company: Critical Tools, 8004 Bottlebrush Drive, Austin, TX 78750

Phone; e-mail: (512) 342-2232; www.criticaltools.com

Installation instructions: Double-click on the My Computer icon on your Windows desktop. Open the PERTChart folder and double-click on the setup file.

Running the program: This trial version of PERT Chart EXPERT is Project 95 compatible. When you install this program, you can opt to add a toolbar to Project. Then simply open a Microsoft Project file and either select the PERT Chart EXPERT menu or click on the toolbar button to automatically generate a PERT chart. Alternatively, you can open the program from the Windows Start menu. Choose Programs⇨PERT Chart EXPERT⇨PERT Chart EXPERT. When the program window opens, choose File⇨Go to Project to open Project 95.

PERT Chart Expert is a Windows-based application that enables you to create PERT charts from existing Project schedules, text files, or spreadsheets. As an add-on to Microsoft Project, PERT Chart EXPERT integrates with Project to generate presentation-quality PERT chart diagrams.

Project Control

Company: Software Made Easy, 1038 Redwood Highway, B-7, Mill Valley, CA 94941

Phone; e-mail: (415) 381-9639; www.smez.com

Installation instructions: If you are using the Microsoft Office Manager toolbar, you must close it before running the installation. Close any other programs that are running. Double-click on the My Computer icon on the Windows desktop. Open the ProjectControl folder and double-click on the setup file. Follow the onscreen prompts to complete installation.

Running the program: You don't need any version of Project to run this demo. From the Windows Start menu, simply choose Programs⇨Project Control 2.0 demo⇨Project Control 2 demo. You can run through a series of screens such as the one shown in Figure C-1 to get an overview of Project Control.

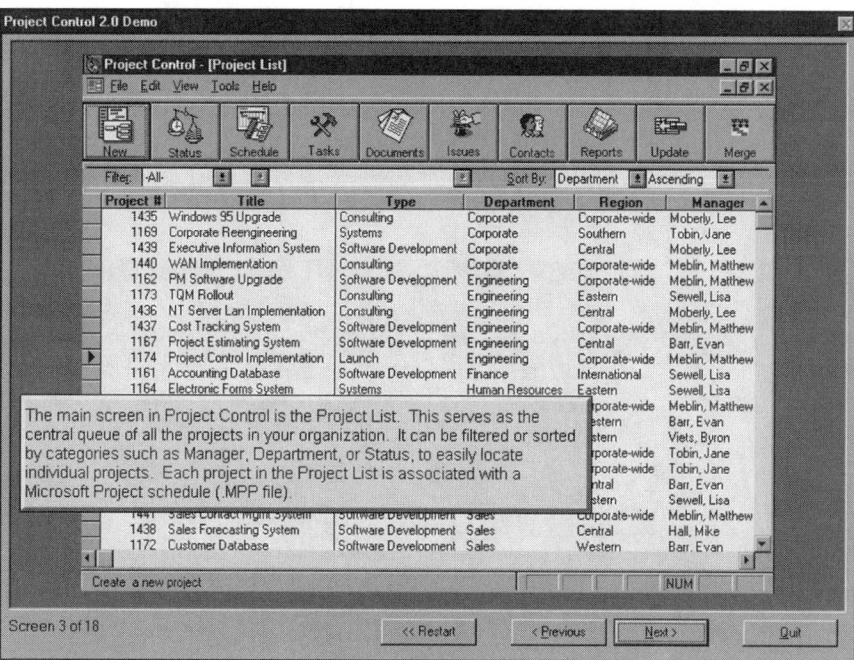

Figure C-1: You can see how Project Control interacts with Project to work with multiple projects.

Project Control uses a centralized database of information about all your projects to help you control multiple projects. You can update a single project or all your projects from this database. Project Control's document manager works with applications such as Word and Excel to help you track all documents associated with a project.

Project Kickstart

Company: Experience in Software, 2000 Hearst Avenue, Berkeley, CA 94709-2176

Phone; e-mail: (510) 644-0694; www.experienceware.com

Installation instructions: From the ProjectKickStart folder on the CD, double-click on the file pkstrial. The opening screen asks whether you want to install Project Kickstart version 2.02. Click on OK and then follow the prompts on the next few screens to designate a program folder for the file.

Running the program: This trial version of Project Kickstart is compatible with Project 98. Open the Project Kickstart folder on your hard drive and double-click on the Project Kickstart 2.0 icon. The first screen of this 20-day trial version gives you the option of purchasing the full program or running the trial version. From the main screen you can start to build a project outline with Project Kickstart's easy-to-use tools.

Project Kickstart is a front-end planning tool for project managers. With Project Kickstart you can outline your objectives, list things to do, and anticipate major project issues. The software has features to help you brainstorm, strategize, and organize the details of your project before you start to build your project schedule (see Figure C-2). An online planning Advisor and templates for project planning help you formulate your approach to your project. Then you can seamlessly output your data to Microsoft Project.

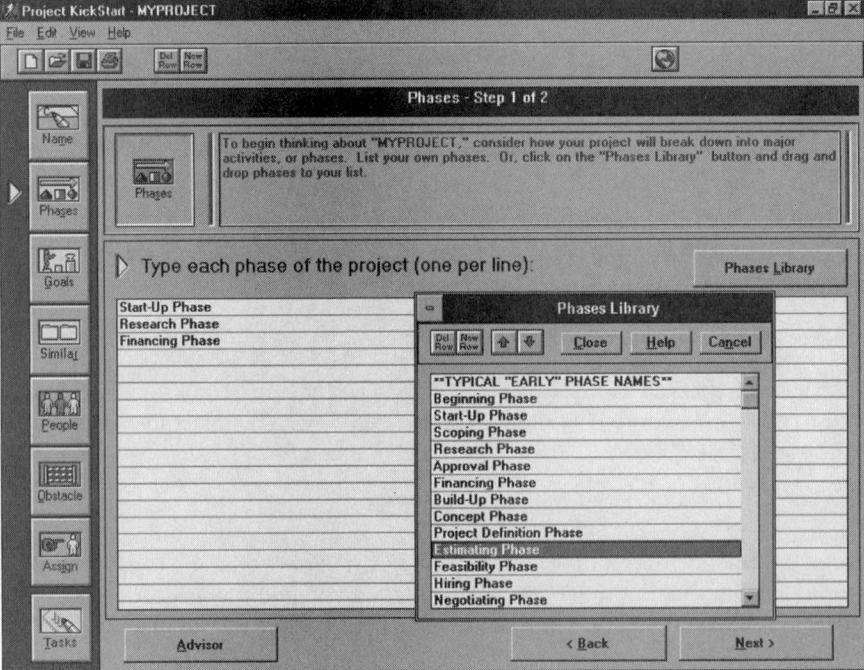

Figure C-2: Use predefined lists of project phases to begin to build your Project outline.

TimeSheet Professional

Company: Timeslips Corporation, 239 Western Avenue, Essex, MA 01929

Phone; e-mail: (508) 768-6100; `www.timeslips.com`

Installation instructions: Double-click on the My Computer icon on your Windows desktop. Open the TimeSheetPro folder and double-click on the setup file. Follow the onscreen prompts to complete installation.

Running the program: This 30-day trial version of TimeSheet Professional is Project 95 compatible. To run the software from the Windows Start menu, choose Programs⇨ TimeSheet Professional for Windows. When the TimeSheet window opens, double-click on the TimeSheet Professional icon. You may be asked to create a database; say Yes to proceed. When the database is ready, TimeSheet opens a new file ready for entry. The trial version includes sample files that highlight the intuitive TimeSheet Professional interface for entering data about resource time (see Figure C-3).

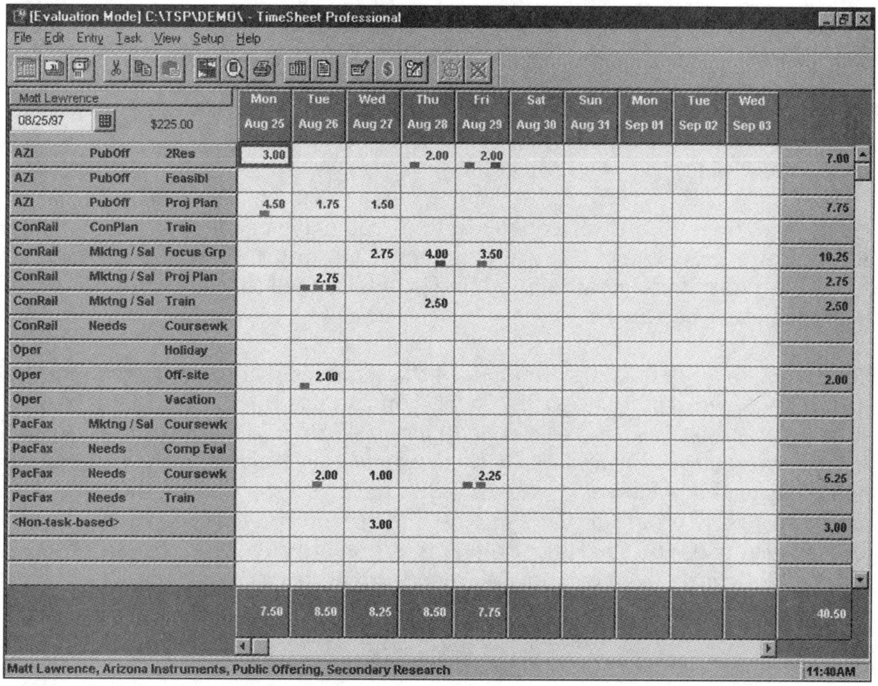

Figure C-3: Even people who don't know the first thing about using Project can track their time in TimeSheet.

TimeSheet Professional is an easy-to-use front end for tracking of resource time in Microsoft Project. If people working on your project don't have a copy of Project, they can enter the time they have spent on various tasks in TimeSheet Professional's simple calendar-like interface. The project manager can then import this information into a Project file, automatically updating resource effort expended on a task-by-task basis. You can also export TimeSheet information on resource time and expenses to a payroll system.

WBS Chart for Project

Company: Critical Tools, 8004 Bottlebrush Drive, Austin, TX 78750

Phone; e-mail: (512) 342-2232; www.criticaltools.com

Installation instructions: Double-click on the My Computer icon on the Windows desktop. Open the folder named WBSChart and then double-click on the setup.exe file. Follow instructions to complete installation.

This setup program needs access to Microsoft Project. If you are accessing Project through a network, you may not have Read/Write access to the GLOBAL.MPT file.

Running the program: WBS Chart for Project trial version is compatible with Project 95. When you install the program, you can choose to add a toolbar to Project 95. Then open Project and simply use the toolbar to run WBS Chart. Alternatively, you can open WBS Chart from the Windows Start menu. Choose Programs⇨WBS Chart for Project⇨WBS Chart. From the program window, choose File⇨Go to Project to open Project 95.

Depending on your hardware configuration, you may see messages about setup failure. However, because this is a demo, click OK or Continue; the program should install correctly. If you continue to have problems, call the tech support number that will appear on screen.

WBS Chart for Project is a planning tool that enables you to create projects using a work breakdown structure (WBS) chart. You can use this method to plan, manage, and display projects with a tree-style diagram. With WBS Chart for Project, you can sketch a project quickly and easily by dragging your mouse on the screen. You can then transfer the plans you create in WBS Chart for Project directly to Microsoft Project or to any program that can read a Microsoft Project file format (*.mpp). You can also use WBS Chart for Project to automatically generate presentation-quality WBS charts from existing Microsoft Project files.

Project Templates

The CD-ROM also contains four template files that give you a head start on typical projects. Open them; save them with your own project name; and then add, delete and change settings for the various tasks included here. You need to create your own resources and assign them to tasks and add timing and dependency relationships between tasks. The four templates are

✦ **Publication template (Publish.mpp):** This template (see Figure C-4) is useful for any kind of publishing project, from a simple brochure to a product documentation manual. Phases for writing and editing content, design, layout, printing, and distribution give you the basis for your own publishing project.

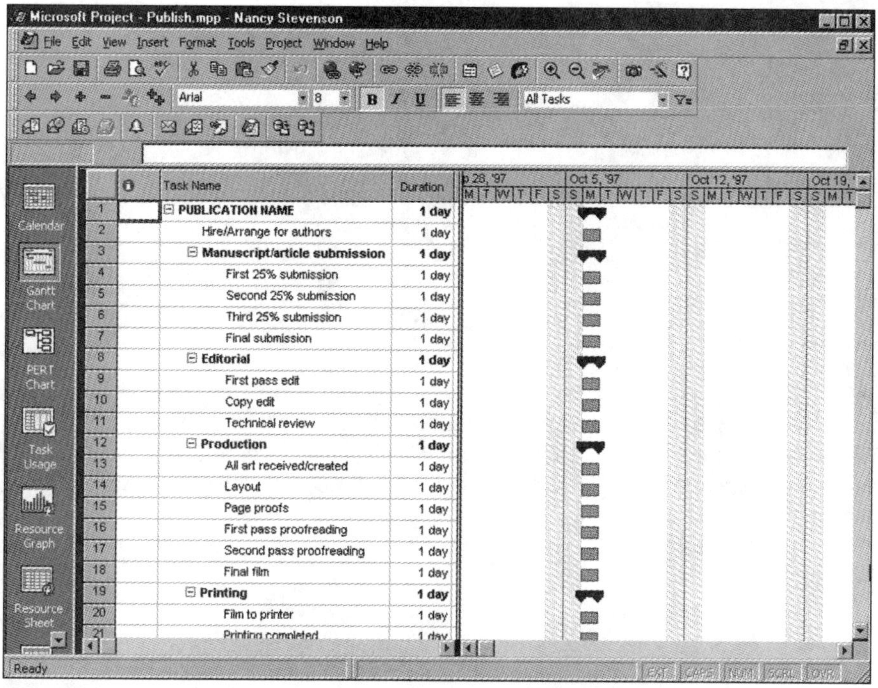

Figure C-4: Whether you're publishing product documentation or the company newsletter, many of these tasks will prove useful.

✦ **Meeting template (Meeting.mpp):** Everybody plans meetings. Whether it's a regular weekly staff meeting or your company's annual meeting, this template (see Figure C-5) provides the tasks you need to arrange for location, transportation and lodging, invitations, catering, equipment, and speakers.

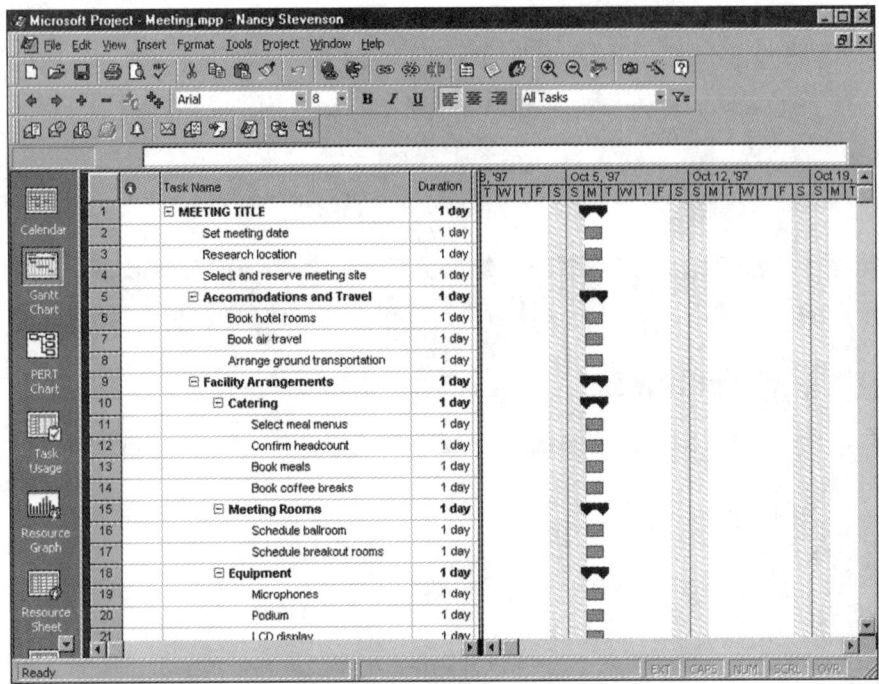

Figure C-5: All the details of arranging for meeting space, catering, equipment, and participant transportation and lodging are included here to give you a head start on planning your next meeting.

✦ **New Product template (NewProd.mpp):** From the early stages of design and prototype through market research and media promotion, this template (see Figure C-6) gives you the outline of any new product launch project. Customize it for your particular industry and product or service type.

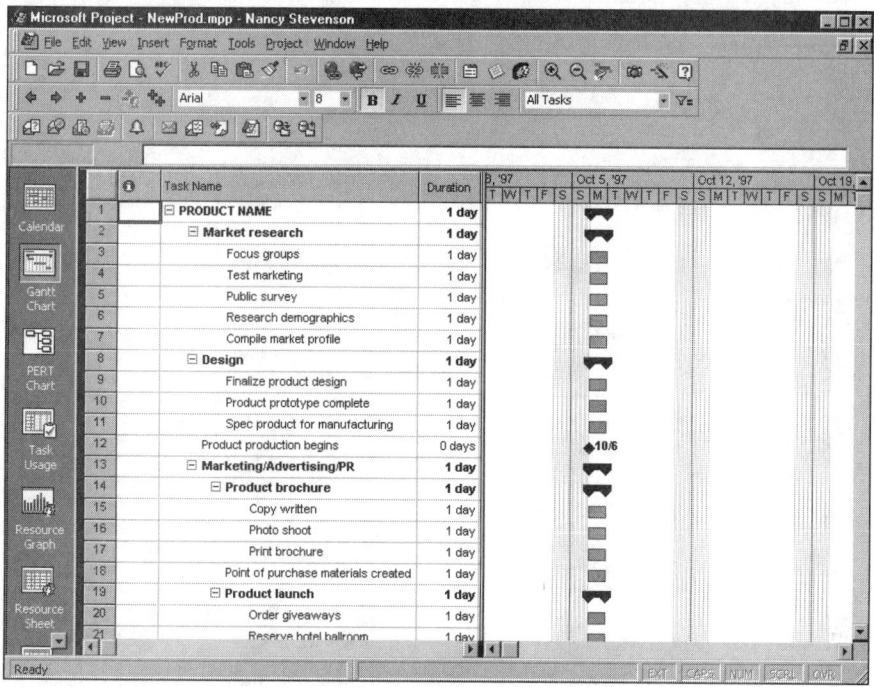

Figure C-6: When your next product is ready to launch, use this template to organize the marketing and promotional activities.

✦ **Facility template (Facility.mpp):** You can use this template (see Figure C-7) to set up a new facility or to move to a new space. Tasks include planning space, coordinating movers, managing utilities, and setting up computer networks.

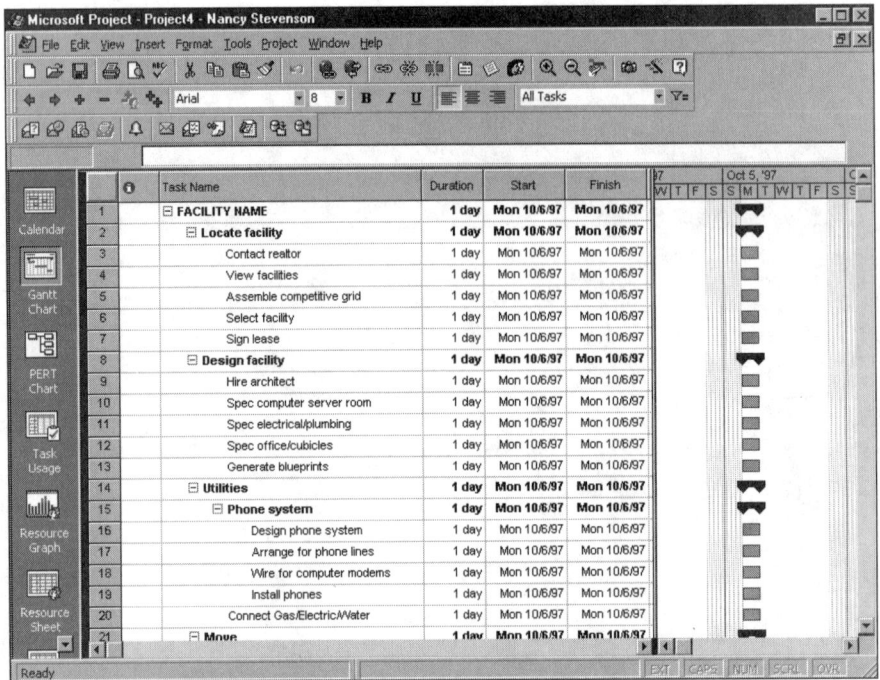

Figure C-7: Moving to a new facility or expanding an existing facility is a complex project — this template provides the basics.

Index

W

my2cents.idgbooks.com

Register This Book — And Win!

Visit **http://my2cents.idgbooks.com** to register this book and we'll automatically enter you in our monthly prize giveaway. It's also your opportunity to give us feedback: let us know what you thought of this book and how you would like to see other topics covered.

Discover IDG Books Online!

The IDG Books Online Web site is your online resource for tackling technology — at home and at the office.

Ten Productive and Career-Enhancing Things You Can Do at www.idgbooks.com

1. Nab source code for your own programming projects.

2. Download software.

3. Read Web exclusives: special articles and book excerpts by IDG Books Worldwide authors.

4. Take advantage of resources to help you advance your career as a Novell or Microsoft professional.

5. Buy IDG Books Worldwide titles or find a convenient bookstore that carries them.

6. Register your book and win a prize.

7. Chat live online with authors.

8. Sign up for regular e-mail updates about our latest books.

9. Suggest a book you'd like to read or write.

10. Give us your 2¢ about our books and about our Web site.

Not on the Web yet? It's easy to get started with *Discover the Internet,* at local retailers everywhere.

IT TAKES THE TIME OUT OF TIME SHEETS.

Designed for

Microsoft
Windows NT®
Windows® 95

It's Client/Server. It's Web Browser Enabled. It Links to Project® 98!
It's New TimeSheet Professional Version 5.5.

Thousands of hours are lost every week as people fill out paper time sheets. TimeSheet Professional puts those lost hours back in the day - easily. It's the most effective time and expense, budget and project tracking system available. And its seamless link to Project 98 makes it a must for any office which tracks time.

Works in tandem with Project 98.
TimeSheet Professional provides data import and export to Project 98. This allows you to import tasks from Project, track time for those tasks in TimeSheet Professional and export the actual hours back into Project - instantly. Once your project is laid out, you can use TimeSheet Professional to track your progress against the planned schedule. It's a seamless process that ends manual data collection and automates the updating of actuals in the project plan.

Client/Server means speed and performance.
Available as a Client/Server or standard Betrieve network product, TimeSheet Professional gives you flexibility for nearly every computing environment. Plus, its new browser interface allows anyone to enter

time into TimeSheet Professional through their Internet or Intranet browser.

Try it Free.
Call today for a Free Demo CD. See for yourself how TimeSheet Professional, combined with the power of Microsoft Project 98, can make it easier than ever to keep track of your projects. Call Today.

1-800-285-0999

www.timesheetprofessional.com
Be sure to mention offer code MSP98

TimeSheet Professional simplifies tracking your time.

IDG BOOKS WORLDWIDE, INC.
END-USER LICENSE AGREEMENT

READ THIS. You should carefully read these terms and conditions before opening the software packet(s) included with this book ("Book"). This is a license agreement ("Agreement") between you and IDG Books Worldwide, Inc. ("IDGB"). By opening the accompanying software packet, you acknowledge that you have read and accept the following terms and conditions. If you do not agree and do not want to be bound by such terms and conditions, promptly return the Book and the unopened software packet to the place you obtained them for a full refund.

1. **License Grant.** IDGB grants to you (either an individual or entity) a nonexclusive license to use one copy of the enclosed software program(s) (collectively, the "Software") solely for your own personal or business purposes on a single computer (whether a standard computer or a workstation component of a multiuser network). The Software is in use on a computer when it is loaded into temporary memory (i.e., RAM) or installed into permanent memory (e.g., hard disk, CD-ROM, or other storage device). IDGB reserves all rights not expressly granted herein.

2. **Ownership.** IDGB is the owner of all rights, titles, and interests, including copyright, in and to the compilation of the Software recorded on the CD-ROM. Copyright to the individual programs on the CD-ROM is owned by the author or other authorized copyright owner of each program. Ownership of the Software and all proprietary rights relating thereto remain with IDGB and its licensors.

3. **Restrictions on Use and Transfer.**

   (a) You may only (i) make one copy of the Software for backup or archival purposes, or (ii) transfer the Software to a single hard disk, provided that you keep the original for backup or archival purposes. You may not (i) rent or lease the Software, (ii) copy or reproduce the Software through a LAN or other network system or through any computer subscriber system or bulletin-board system, or (iii) modify, adapt, or create derivative works based on the Software.

   (b) You may not reverse engineer, decompile, or disassemble the Software. You may transfer the Software and user documentation on a permanent basis, provided that the transferee agrees to accept the terms and conditions of this Agreement and you retain no copies. If the Software is an update or has been updated, any transfer must include the most recent update and all prior versions.

4. **Restrictions on Use of Individual Programs.** You must follow the individual requirements and restrictions detailed for each individual program in Appendix C. These limitations are contained in the individual license agreements recorded on the CD-ROM. These restrictions may include a requirement that after using the program for the period of time specified in its text, the user must pay a registration fee or discontinue use. By opening the Software packet, you will be agreeing to abide by the licenses and restrictions for these individual programs. None of the material on this CD-ROM or listed in this Book may ever be distributed, in original or modified form, for commercial purposes.

5. Limited Warranty.

    (a) IDGB warrants that the Software and CD-ROM are free from defects in materials and workmanship under normal use for a period of sixty (60) days from the date of purchase of this Book. If IDGB receives notification within the warranty period of defects in materials or workmanship, IDGB will replace the defective CD-ROM.

    (b) IDGB AND THE AUTHOR OF THE BOOK DISCLAIM ALL OTHER WARRANTIES, EXPRESS OR IMPLIED, INCLUDING WITHOUT LIMITATION IMPLIED WARRANTIES OF MERCHANTABILITY AND FITNESS FOR A PARTICULAR PURPOSE, WITH RESPECT TO THE SOFTWARE, THE PROGRAMS, THE SOURCE CODE CONTAINED THEREIN, AND/OR THE TECHNIQUES DESCRIBED IN THIS BOOK. IDGB DOES NOT WARRANT THAT THE FUNCTIONS CONTAINED IN THE SOFTWARE WILL MEET YOUR REQUIREMENTS OR THAT THE OPERATION OF THE SOFTWARE WILL BE ERROR FREE.

    (c) This limited warranty gives you specific legal rights, and you may have other rights which vary from jurisdiction to jurisdiction.

6. Remedies.

    (a) IDGB's entire liability and your exclusive remedy for defects in materials and workmanship shall be limited to replacement of the Software, which may be returned to IDGB with a copy of your receipt at the following address: Disk Fulfillment Department, Attn: Microsoft Project 98 Bible, IDG Books Worldwide, Inc., 7260 Shadeland Station, Ste. 100, Indianapolis, IN 46256, or call 1-800-762-2974. Please allow 3-4 weeks for delivery. This Limited Warranty is void if failure of the Software has resulted from accident, abuse, or misapplication. Any replacement Software will be warranted for the remainder of the original warranty period or thirty (30) days, whichever is longer.

    (b) In no event shall IDGB or the author be liable for any damages whatsoever (including without limitation damages for loss of business profits, business interruption, loss of business information, or any other pecuniary loss) arising from the use of or inability to use the Book or the Software, even if IDGB has been advised of the possibility of such damages.

    (c) Because some jurisdictions do not allow the exclusion or limitation of liability for consequential or incidental damages, the above limitation or exclusion may not apply to you.

7. U.S. Government Restricted Rights. Use, duplication, or disclosure of the Software by the U.S. Government is subject to restrictions stated in paragraph (c) (1) (ii) of the Rights in Technical Data and Computer Software clause of DFARS 252.227-7013, and in subparagraphs (a) through (d) of the Commercial Computer—Restricted Rights clause at FAR 52.227-19, and in similar clauses in the NASA FAR supplement, when applicable.

8. General. This Agreement constitutes the entire understanding of the parties and revokes and supersedes all prior agreements, oral or written, between them and may not be modified or amended except in a writing signed by both parties hereto which specifically refers to this Agreement. This Agreement shall take precedence over any other documents that may be in conflict herewith. If any one or more provisions contained in this Agreement are held by any court or tribunal to be invalid, illegal, or otherwise unenforceable, each and every other provision shall remain in full force and effect.

CD-ROM Installation Instructions

The CD-ROM contains demo and trial versions of software, as well as Project templates for common project types.

Each software product is in its own, individual folder. You can install each software product using a setup file located in the corresponding folder. See the Appendix C for more detailed installation instructions for each program.

The Project templates are located in the folder named Templates. You can copy these to your hard drive, or open them from the CD and save them to a location of your choosing with your specific project's name.

STARTING OUT WITH

Visual Basic® 2010

Fifth Edition

Tony Gaddis
Haywood Community College

Kip Irvine
Florida International University

Addison-Wesley

Boston   Columbus   Indianapolis   New York   San Francisco   Upper Saddle River
Amsterdam   Cape Town   Dubai   London   Madrid   Milan   Munich   Paris   Montreal   Toronto
Delhi   Mexico City   Sao Paulo   Sydney   Hong Kong   Seoul   Singapore   Taipei   Tokyo

Editor in Chief: Michael Hirsch
Acquisitions Editor: Matt Goldstein
Editorial Assistant: Chelsea Bell
Managing Editor: Jeffrey Holcomb
Senior Production Project Manager: Marilyn Lloyd
Media Producer: Katelyn Boller and Daniel Sandin
Director of Marketing: Margaret Waples
Marketing Coordinator: Kathryn Ferranti
Senior Operations Supervisor: Alan Fischer
Cover, Art Director: Linda Knowles
Text and Cover Designer: Joyce Cosentino Wells
Cover Image: © Kitch Bain/Alamy
Project Management: Sherrill Redd/Aptara®, Inc.
Full Service Vendor: Aptara®, Inc.
Printer/Binder: Edwards Brothers

The interior of this book was composed in QuarkXPress 6.52. The main type face used in the text is Sabon. The display font is Stone Sans.

Library of Congress Cataloging-in-Publication Data
Gaddis, Tony.
   Starting out with Visual Basic 2010 / Tony Gaddis, Kip Irvine.—5th ed.
      p. cm.
   Includes bibliographical references and index.
      ISBN 0-13-611340-0 (978-0-13-611340-9 : alk. paper)   1. Microsoft
Visual BASIC.   2. BASIC (Computer program language) I.
R., 1951 - II. Title.
   QA76.73.B3G328 2010b
   005.2'768—dc22

2.

10 9 8 7 6 5 4 3 2 1—EB—14 13 12 11 10

Addison-Wesley
is an imprint of

PEARSON

Contents in Brief

Contents

Chapter 3   Variables and Calculations 109

Chapter 4   Making Decisions   205

Chapter 9   Files, Printing, and Structures 541

Chapter 10   Working with Databases 597

Chapter 11   **Developing Web Applications 673**

Chapter 12   **Classes, Collections, and Inheritance 729**

Preface

Welcome to *Starting Out with Visual Basic* 2010, Fifth Edition. This book is intended for use in an introductory programming course. It is designed for students who have no prior programming background, but even experienced students will benefit from its depth of detail and the chapters covering databases, Web applications, and other advanced topics. The book is written in clear, easy-to-understand language and covers all the necessary topics of an introductory programming course. The text is rich in concise, practical, and real-world example programs, so the student not only learns how to use the various controls, constructs, and features of Visual Basic, but also learns why and when to use them.

Changes in the Fifth Edition

- **The book is completely updated for Visual Basic 2010**—This book is designed for use with Visual Basic 2010 and Visual Studio 2010.
- **The tutorials have been simplified**—Many of the book's tutorials have been simplified, and several of them have been completely replaced. These changes were made so students can work through the text at a quicker pace, and concentrate more on the important topics in each chapter.
- **New VideoNotes to accompany many of the tutorials**—This edition provides new VideoNotes for many of the book's tutorials. The new VideoNotes explain the details of the code that the student writes and lead the student through the completion of the tutorials.
- **Implicit line continuation is now used**—In most situations where a statement continues across multiple lines, Visual Basic 2010 allows implicit line continuation. VB no longer requires the underscore character to be inserted to indicate a continued line. The programmer can simply press the Enter key where the underscore character was previously required. In this book we use implicit line continuation, which helps to further simplify code.
- **Message boxes introduced in Chapter 2**—In previous editions this book introduced message boxes in Chapter 3. In this edition we introduce message boxes as a simple way to display output in Chapter 2.
- **Field-level input validation has been moved from Chapter 5 to Appendix A**—In previous editions, Chapter 5 introduced field-level input validation using the CausesValidation property, the Validating event, and the Validated event. Because of the complexity of using this technique, many of our adopters prefer to use traditional input validation techniques instead. In this edition we have moved this material from Chapter 5 to Appendix A and use decision structures and standard exception handling for input validation.
- **Class-Level Variables introduced in Chapter 3**—Class-level variables are now introduced in Chapter 2 along with local variables.
- **Random numbers introduced in Chapter 5**—In previous editions random numbers were introduced in Chapter 8 and only briefly covered. In this edition random numbers are introduced in Chapter 5 and used in more examples.
- **Appendix A has been enhanced and expanded as a reference**—In this edition, Appendix A has been expanded as a reference for advanced user interface controls

and programming techniques. The appendix now provides short examples demonstrating the following controls:

- scroll bars
- TabControls
- WebBrowser controls
- ErrorProvider components
- DateTimePicker controls
- MonthCalendar controls.

Appendix A also describes programming techniques for selecting text in a TextBox using the SelectionStart and SelectionLength properties and discusses field-level validation using the CausesValidation property, the Validating event, and the Validated event. A section discussing user interface design guidelines also appears in this appendix.

- **A new appendix on the Windows Presentation Framework (WPF) has been added—** Appendix B is now an introduction to the Windows Presentation Framework (WPF). This appendix includes a tutorial in which the student creates a simple WPF application.

Visual Basic 2010 Express Edition

The book is bundled with Microsoft's Visual Basic 2010 Express Edition—a streamlined product that captures the best elements of Visual Studio in an ideal format for learning programming. The Express edition offers an impressive set of tools for developing and debugging Visual Basic Windows Forms applications and Web applications, applications, including those that work with databases and use SQL.

A Look at Visual Basic: Past and Present

The first version of Visual Basic was introduced in 1991. Prior to its introduction, writing a GUI interface for an application was no small task. Typically, it required hundreds of lines of C code for even the simplest *Hello World* program. Additionally, an understanding of graphics, memory, and complex system calls were often necessary. Visual Basic was revolutionary because it significantly simplified this process. With Visual Basic, a programmer could visually design an application's user interface. Visual Basic would then generate the code necessary to display and operate the interface. This allowed the programmer to spend less time writing GUI code and more time writing code to perform meaningful tasks.

The evolution of Visual Basic from version 1 to version 6 followed a natural progression. Each new release was an improved version of the previous release, providing additional features and enhancements. Visual Basic versions offered backward compatibility, where code written in an older version was compatible with a newer version of the Visual Basic development environment.

In 2002, Microsoft released a new object-oriented software platform known as .NET. The .NET platform consists of several layers of software that sit above the operating system and provide a secure, managed environment in which programs can execute. In addition to providing a managed environment for applications to run, .NET also provided new technologies for creating Internet-based programs and programs that provide services over the Web. Along with the introduction of the .NET platform, Microsoft introduced a new version of Visual Basic known as VB .NET 2002, which allowed programmers to write desktop applications or Web applications for the .NET platform.

VB .NET was not merely a new and improved version of VB 6, however. VB .NET was a totally new programming environment, and the Visual Basic language was dramatically revised. The changes were substantial enough that programs written in earlier versions of

Visual Basic were not compatible with VB .NET. Microsoft provided a utility that could be used to convert older Visual Basic applications to the new VB .NET syntax, but the results were not always perfect. Although this was frustrating for some Visual Basic developers, Microsoft reasoned the changes were necessary to ensure that Visual Basic continued to evolve as a modern, professional programming environment.

Microsoft has continued to enhance and improve Visual Basic by regularly releasing new versions. The versions, which are named after the year in which they were released, are Visual Basic 2003, Visual Basic 2005, Visual Basic 2008, and the most recent version, Visual Basic 2010.

This book is written for Visual Basic 2010. This version of Visual Basic includes several enhancements that make Visual Basic even more powerful as a professional programming system. Many of the new features are beyond the scope of this book, so we do not cover them all. The following list summarizes some of the most significant new features of VB 2010:

- Multiline lambda expressions and single-line sub lambda expressions
- Implicit line continuation
- Auto-implemented properties
- Collection initializers
- Array literals
- Nullable optional parameters
- Support for generic covariance and contravariance
- Interoperability with dynamic languages
- Ability to deploy programs using the Microsoft Object Model without requiring the Primary Interop Assemblies (PIAs)

Organization of the Text

The text teaches Visual Basic step-by-step. Each chapter covers a major set of programming topics, introduces controls and GUI elements, and builds knowledge as the student progresses through the book. Although the chapters can be easily taught in their existing sequence, there is some flexibility. The following diagram suggests possible sequences of instruction.

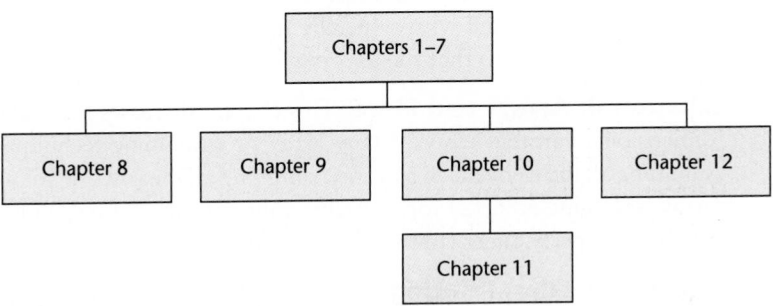

Chapters 1 through 7 cover the fundamentals of program design, flow control, modular programming, and the most important Visual Basic controls. The instructor may then continue in any order with Chapters 8, 9, 10, or 12. Part of Chapter 11 relies on database concepts, so it should be covered after Chapter 10.

Brief Overview of Each Chapter

Chapter 1: Introduction to Programming and Visual Basic. This chapter provides an introduction to programming, the programming process, and Visual Basic. GUI programming and the event-driven model are explained. The components of programs, such as keywords, variables, operators, and punctuation are covered, and tools such as flowcharts and pseudocode are presented. The student gets started using the Visual Basic environment in a hands-on tutorial.

Chapter 2: Creating Applications with Visual Basic. The student starts by creating a simple application that displays a graphic image. In the tutorials that follow, the student adds controls, modifies properties, and enables the application to respond to events. An introduction to the *Visual Basic Help* system, with a tutorial on debugging, is given.

Chapter 3: Variables and Calculations. Variables, constants, and the Visual Basic data types are introduced. The student learns to gather input and create simple arithmetic statements. The intricacies of GUI design are introduced as the student learns about grouping controls with group boxes, assigning keyboard access keys, and setting the tab order. The student is introduced to exceptions and learns to write simple exception handlers. Debugging techniques for locating logic errors are covered.

Chapter 4: Making Decisions. The student learns about relational operators and how to control the flow of a program with the `If...Then`, `If...Then...Else`, and `If...Then...ElseIf` statements. Logical operators are introduced, and the `Select Case` statement is covered. Important applications of these constructs are discussed, such as testing numeric values, strings, and determining if a value lies within a range, and validating user input. Several string-handling functions and string methods are discussed. Radio buttons and check boxes are also introduced.

Chapter 5: Lists and Loops. This chapter begins by showing the student how to use input boxes as a quick and simple way to gather input. Next, list boxes and combo boxes are introduced. The chapter covers repetition control structures: the `Do While`, `Do Until`, and `For...Next` loops. Counters, accumulators, running totals, and other loop-related topics are discussed. The student also learns how to generate random numbers.

Chapter 6: Procedures and Functions. The student learns how and why to modularize programs with general-purpose procedures and functions. Arguments, parameters, and return values are discussed. Debugging techniques for stepping into and over procedures are introduced.

Chapter 7: Multiple Forms, Modules, and Menus. This chapter shows how to add multiple forms to a project and how to create a module to hold procedures and functions that are not associated with a specific form. It covers creating a menu system, with commands and submenus that the user may select from.

Chapter 8: Arrays and More. This chapter discusses both single dimension and multi-dimensional variable arrays. Many array programming techniques are presented, such as summing all the elements in an array, summing all the rows or columns in a two-dimensional array, searching an array for a specific value, sorting arrays, and using parallel arrays. The Enabled property, timer controls, and control anchoring and docking are also covered.

Chapter 9: Files, Printing, and Structures. This chapter begins by discussing how to save data to sequential text files and then read the data back into an application. The OpenFileDialog, SaveFileDialog, FontDialog, and ColorDialog controls are introduced. The PrintDocument control is discussed, with a special focus on printing reports. The chapter shows the student how to create user-defined data types with structures.

Chapter 10: Working with Databases. This chapter introduces basic database concepts. The student learns how to display a database table in a DataGridView control and write applications that display, sort, and update database data. The Structured Query Language (SQL) is introduced. An application that shows how to display database data in list boxes, text boxes, labels, and combo box is presented. The chapter concludes with an overview of Language Integrated Query (LINQ).

Chapter 11: Developing Web Applications. This chapter shows the student how to create ASP.NET applications that run on Web Browsers such as Internet Explorer, Chrome, Firefox, and Safari. Using Microsoft Visual Studio, or Microsoft Visual Web Developer, the student learns how to use Web server controls and Web forms to build interactive, database-driven Web applications.

Chapter 12: Classes, Collections, and Inheritance. This chapter introduces classes as a tool for creating abstract data types. The process of analyzing a problem and determining its classes is discussed, and techniques for creating objects, properties, and methods are introduced. Collections are presented as structures for holding groups of objects. The *Object Browser*, which allows the student to see information about the classes, properties, methods, and events available to a project, is also covered. The chapter concludes by introducing inheritance, and shows how to create a class that is based on an existing class.

Appendix A: Advanced User Interface Controls and Techniques. Discusses many of the more advanced controls available in Visual Basic, as well as several helpful programming techniques. This appendix also provides a summary of common user interface design guidelines.

Appendix B: Windows Presentation Foundation (WPF). Introduces the student to the Windows Presentation Framework (WPF), and includes a tutorial in which the student creates a simple WPF application.

Appendix C: Converting Mathematical Expressions to Programming Statements. Shows the student how to convert a mathematical expression into a Visual Basic programming statement.

Appendix D: Answers to Checkpoints. Students may test their progress by comparing their answers to Checkpoints with the answers provided. The answers to all Checkpoints are included.

Appendix E: Glossary. Provides a glossary of the key terms presented in the text.

The following appendixes are located on the Student CD-ROM:

Appendix F: Visual Basic 2010 Function and Method Reference. Provides a reference for all the functions and methods that are covered in the text. The exceptions that may be caused by these functions and methods are also listed.

Appendix G: Binary and Random-Access Files. Describes programming techniques for creating and working with binary and random-access data files.

The following appendix is available on the Companion Website for this book at `http://www.pearsonhighered.com/gaddisvb/`.

Appendix H: Answers to Odd-Numbered Review Questions. Provides another tool that students can use to gauge their progress.

Features of the Text

Concept Statements. Each major section of the text starts with a concept statement. This statement concisely summarizes the meaning of the section.

 Tutorials. Each chapter has several hands-on tutorials that reinforce the chapter's topics. Many of these tutorials involve the student in writing applications that can be applied to real-world problems.

 VideoNotes. A series of online videos, developed specifically for this book, are available for viewing at `http://www.pearsonhighered.com/gaddisvb/`. Icons appear throughout the text alerting the student to videos about specific topics.

Checkpoints. Checkpoints are questions placed at intervals throughout each chapter. They are designed to query the student's knowledge immediately after learning a new topic. Answers to all the Checkpoints are provided in Appendix D.

 Notes. Notes are short explanations of interesting or often misunderstood points relevant to the topic being discussed.

 Tips. Tips advise the student on the best techniques for approaching different programming problems and appear regularly throughout the text.

 Warnings. Warnings caution the student about certain Visual Basic features, programming techniques, or practices that can lead to malfunctioning programs or lost data.

Review Questions and Exercises. In the tradition of all Gaddis texts, each chapter presents a thorough and diverse set of review questions and exercises. These include traditional fill-in-the-blank, true or false, multiple choice, and short answer questions. There are also unique tools for assessing a student's knowledge. For example, *Find the Error* questions ask the student to identify syntax or logic errors in brief code segments. *Algorithm Workbench* questions ask the student to design code segments to satisfy a given problem. There are also *What Do You Think?* questions that require the student to think critically and contemplate the topics presented in the chapter. The answers to the odd-numbered review questions appear in Appendix H, which can be found on the Companion Website for this book at http://www.pearsonhighered.com/gaddisvb/.

Programming Challenges. Each chapter offers a pool of programming exercises designed to solidify the student's knowledge of the topics at hand. In most cases, the assignments present real-world problems to be solved. When applicable, these exercises also include input validation rules.

Supplements

Student

The following supplementary material is bundled with the book:

- A Student CD-ROM containing the source code and files required for the chapter tutorials. The CD-ROM also contains Appendix F, *Visual Basic 2010 Function and Method Reference*, and Appendix G, *Binary and Random-Access Files*.
- Microsoft Visual Basic 2010 Express Edition

Instructor

The following supplements are available to qualified instructors:

- Answers to all Review Questions in the text
- Solutions for all Programming Challenges in the text
- PowerPoint presentation slides for every chapter
- Test bank
- Test generation software that allows instructors to create customized tests

For information on how to access these supplements, visit the Pearson Education Instructor Resource Center at http://www.pearsonhighered.com/irc/ or send e-mail to computing@aw.com.

Web Resources

Self-assessment quizzes, PowerPoint slides, source code files, glossary flashcards, and answers to odd-numbered review questions are available on the Companion Website for *Starting Out with Visual Basic 2010* at http://www.pearsonhighered.com/gaddisvb/.

Acknowledgments

There were many helping hands in the development and publication of this text. The authors would like to thank the following faculty reviewers for their helpful suggestions and expertise during the production of the manuscript:

Achla Agarwal, *Bossier Parrish Community College*

Douglas Bock, *Southern Illinois University at Edwardsville*

Robert Ekblaw, *SUNY Albany*

Rose M. Endres, *City College of San Francisco*

Mark Fienup, *University of Northern Iowa*

Tom Higginbotham, *Southeastern Louisiana University*

Dennis Higgins, *SUNY Oneonta*

Herb Kronholm, *Mid-State Technical College*

Gary Marrer, *Glendale Community College*

Joseph Merrell

Christopher J. Olson, *Dakota State University*

Malu Roldan, *San Jose State*

Judy Scholl, *Austin Community College*

Anne Spalding, *Mesa State College*

Reviewers of the Previous Editions

Ronald Bass, *Austin Community College*

Ronald Beauchemin, *Springfield Technical Community College*

Zachory T. Beers, *Microsoft Corporation*

Robert M. Benavides, *Collin County Community College District*

Skip Bottom, *J. Sargeant Reynolds Community College*

Harold Broberg, *Indiana Purdue University*

Nancy Burns. *Professor of Computer Science, Chipola College*

Mara Casado, *State College of Florida, Manatee-Sarasota*

Joni Catanzaro, *Louisiana State University*

Dr. Robert Coil, *Cincinnati State Community and Technical College*

Carol A. DesJardins, *St. Clair County Community College*

William J. Dorin, *Indiana University*

Jean Evans, *Brevard Community College*

Pierre M. Fiorini, PhD, *University of Southern Maine*

Arlene Flerchinger, *Chattanooga State Technical Community College*

Lawrence Fudella, *Erie Community College*

Gail M. Gehrig, *Florida Community College at Jacksonville*

Jayanta Ghosh, *Florida Community College*

Iskandar Hack, *Indiana University—Purdue University at Fort Wayne*

David M. Himes, *Oklahoma State University, Okmulgee*

Greg Hodge, *Northwestern Michigan College*

Corinne Hoisington, *Central Virginia Community College*

May-Chuen Hsieh, *Southwest Tennessee Community College*

Lee A. Hunt, *Collin County Community College*

Phil Larschan, *Tulsa Community College*

Art Lee, *Lord Fairfax Community College*

Joo Eng Lee-Partridge, *Central Connecticut State University*

Norman McNeal, *Dakota County Technical College*

Juan Marquez, *Mesa Community College*

Gary Marrer, *Glendale Community College*

George McOuat, *Hawaii Pacific University*

Sylvia Miner, *Florida International University*

Billy Morgan, *Holmes Community College*

Joan P. Mosey, *Point Park College*

Robert Nields, *Cincinnati State Community and Technical College*

Gregory M. Ogle

Merrill B. Parker, *Chattanooga State Technical Community College*

Rembert N. Parker, *Anderson University*

Carol M. Peterson, *South Plains Community College*

Anita Philipp, *Oklahoma City Community College*

T. N. Rajashekhara, *Camden County College*

Mark Reis, *University of Virginia*

Gurmukh Singh, *SUNY at Fredonia*

Angeline Surber, *Mesa Community College*

Robert L. Terrell, *Walters State Community College*

Margaret Warrick, *Allan Hancock College*

Elaine Yale Weltz, *Seattle Pacific University*

Floyd Jay Winters, *Program Director, Computer Science, College of Florida, Manatee-Sarasota*

Catherine Wyman, *DeVry Institute, Phoenix*

Sheri L. York, *Ball State University*

The authors would like to thank their families for their tremendous support throughout this project. We would also like to thank everyone at Pearson Addison-Wesley who was part of our editorial, production, and marketing team. We are fortunate to have Matt Goldstein as our editor for this book. He and Chelsea Bell, editorial assistant, guided us through the delicate process of revising the book. The production team did a tremendous job to make this book a reality, and included Marilyn Lloyd, Jeff Holcomb, Katelyn Boller, Daniel Sandin, Alan Fischer, Carol Melville, Linda Knowles, and John Lewis and Sherrill Redd of Aptara Corp. We would also like to thank Chris Rich for painstakingly checking the tutorials. You are all great people to work with!

About the Authors

Tony Gaddis is the principal author of the *Starting Out with* series of textbooks. Tony has nearly two decades of experience teaching computer science courses, primarily at Haywood Community College in North Carolina. He is a highly acclaimed instructor who was previously selected as North Carolina's Community College *Teacher of the Year*, and has received the *Teaching Excellence* award from the National Institute for Staff and Organizational Development. Besides Visual Basic books, the *Starting Out with* series includes introductory books on programming logic and design, Alice, the C++ programming language, Java™, Python, and Microsoft® C#®, all published by Pearson Addison-Wesley.

Kip Irvine holds M.S. (computer science) and D.M.A. (music composition) degrees from the University of Miami. He was formerly on the faculty at Miami-Dade Community College, and is presently a member of the School of Computing and Information Sciences at Florida International University. His published textbooks include *COBOL for the IBM Personal Computer*, *Assembly Language for Intel-Based Computers*, *C++ and Object-Oriented Programming*, and *Advanced Visual Basic .NET*.

Attention Students

Installing Visual Basic

To complete the tutorials and programming problems in this book, you need to install Visual Basic 2010 on your computer. When purchased new, this textbook is packaged with a Microsoft DVD that contains **Visual Basic 2010 Express Edition**. Install this on your computer before starting any of the book's tutorials.

If you plan to work through Chapter 11, you will also need to install **Visual Web Developer 2010 Express Edition**, which is available on the accompanying Microsoft DVD.

If your book does not have the accompanying Microsoft DVD, you can download both Visual Basic 2010 Express Edition and Visual Web Developer 2010 Express Edition from the following Web site:

http://www.microsoft.com/express/Downloads/

 NOTE: If you are working in your school's computer lab, there is a good chance that **Microsoft Visual Studio** has been installed, rather than Visual Basic Express Edition. Visual Studio is a professional development package that includes several programming languages and development tools, including Visual Basic. If this is the case, your instructor will show you how to start Visual Studio. The tutorials in this book can be completed with either Visual Studio 2010, or Visual Basic 2010 Express Edition.

Installing the Student Sample Program Files

When purchased new, your textbook is also packaged with a **Student Resource CD**. This CD contains a set of **Student Sample Program** files that you will need to copy to your computer's hard drive. These files are required for many of the book's tutorials. Simply copy the Student Sample Program files from the CD to a location on your hard drive where you can easily access them.

1

Introduction to Programming and Visual Basic

TOPICS

Microsoft Visual Basic is a powerful software development system for creating applications that run on the Windows operating system. With Visual Basic, you can do the following:

- Create applications with graphical windows, dialog boxes, and menus
- Create applications that work with databases
- Create Web applications and applications that use Internet technologies
- Create applications that display graphics

Visual Basic, which is commonly referred to as VB, is a favorite tool among professional programmers. It provides tools to visually design an application's appearance, a modern programming language, and access to the latest Microsoft technologies. Powerful applications can be created with Visual Basic in a relatively short period of time.

Before plunging into learning Visual Basic, we will review the fundamentals of computer hardware and software, and then become familiar with the Visual Studio programming environment.

1.1   Computer Systems: Hardware and Software

CONCEPT: Computer systems consist of similar hardware devices and hardware components. This section provides an overview of computer hardware and software organization.

Hardware

The term **hardware** refers to a computer's physical components. A computer, as we generally think of it, is not an individual device, but rather a system of devices. Like the instruments in a symphony orchestra, each device plays its own part. A typical computer system consists of the following major components:

1. The central processing unit (CPU)
2. Main memory
3. Secondary storage devices
4. Input devices
5. Output devices

The organization of a computer system is shown in Figure 1-1.

Figure 1-1 The organization of a computer system

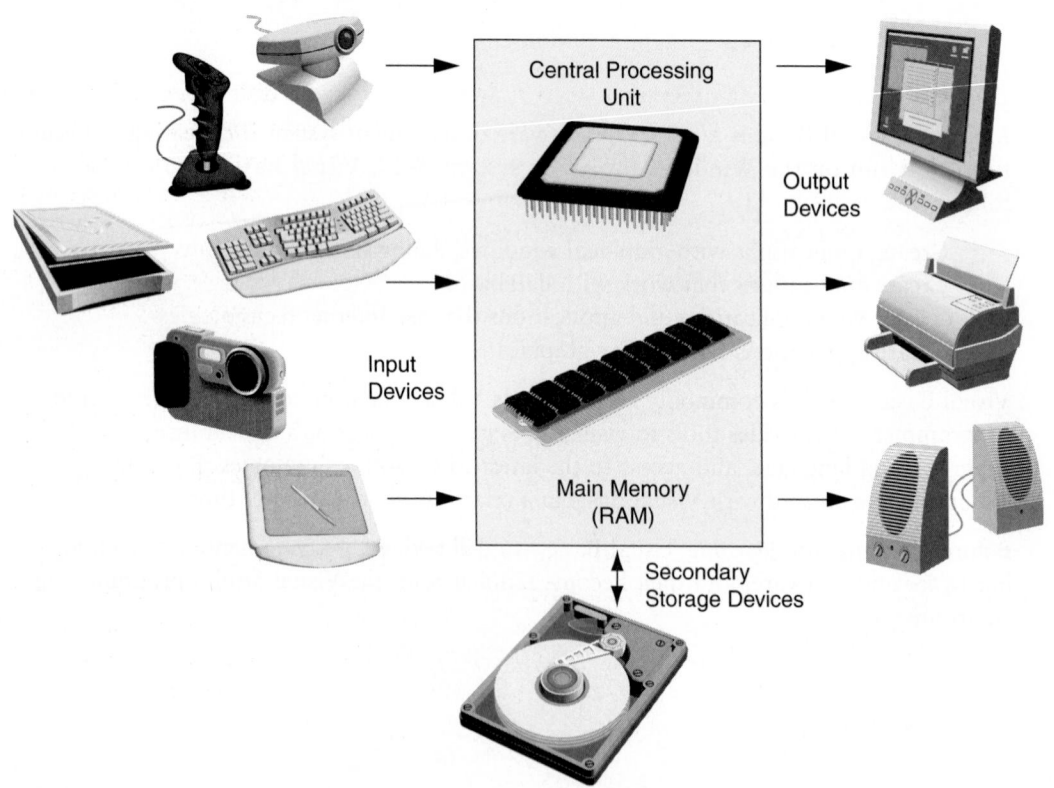

1. The CPU

When a computer is performing the tasks that a program tells it to do, we say that the computer is running or executing the program. The **central processing unit**, or CPU, is the part of a computer that actually runs programs. The CPU is the most important component in a computer because without it, the computer could not run software.

A **program** is a set of instructions that a computer's CPU follows to perform a task. The program's instructions are stored in the computer's memory, and the CPU's job is to fetch those instructions, one by one, and carry out the operations that they command. In memory, the instructions are stored as a series of **binary numbers**. A binary number is a sequence of 1s and 0s, such as

```
11011011
```

This number has no apparent meaning to people, but to the computer it might be an instruction to multiply two numbers or read another value from memory.

2. Main Memory

You can think of **main memory** as the computer's work area. This is where the computer stores a program while the program is running, as well as the data that the program is working with. For example, suppose you are using a word processing program to write an essay for one of your classes. While you do this, both the word processing program and the essay are stored in main memory.

Main memory is commonly known as **random-access memory**, or **RAM**. It is called this because the CPU is able to quickly access data stored at any random location in RAM. RAM is usually a volatile type of memory that is used only for temporary storage while a program is running. When the computer is turned off, the contents of RAM are erased. Inside your computer, RAM is stored in microchips.

3. Secondary Storage

The most common type of secondary storage device is the **disk drive**. A disk drive stores data by magnetically encoding it onto a circular disk. Most computers have a disk drive mounted inside their case. External disk drives, which connect to one of the computer's communication ports, are also available. External disk drives can be used to create backup copies of important data or to move data to another computer.

In addition to external disk drives, many types of devices have been created for copying data, and for moving it to other computers. For many years floppy disk drives were popular. A floppy disk drive records data onto a small floppy disk, which can be removed from the drive. The use of floppy disk drives has declined dramatically in recent years, in favor of superior devices such as USB drives. USB drives are small devices that plug into the computer's USB (universal serial bus) port, and appear to the system as a disk drive. USB drives, which use flash memory to store data, are inexpensive, reliable, and small enough to be carried in your pocket.

Optical devices such as the CD (compact disc) and the DVD (digital versatile disc) are also popular for data storage. Data is not recorded magnetically on an optical disc, but is encoded as a series of pits on the disc surface. CD and DVD drives use a laser to detect the pits and thus read the encoded data. Optical discs hold large amounts of data, and because recordable CD and DVD drives are now commonplace, they are good mediums for creating backup copies of data.

4. Input Devices

Input is any data the computer collects from the outside world. The device that collects the data and sends it to the computer is called an **input device**. Common input devices are the keyboard, mouse, scanner, and digital camera. Disk drives and CD drives can also be considered input devices because programs and data are retrieved from them and loaded into the computer's memory.

5. Output Devices

Output is any data the computer sends to the outside world. It might be a sales report, a list of names, a graphic image, or a sound. The data is sent to an **output device**, which formats and presents it. Common output devices are monitors and printers. Disk drives and CD recorders can also be considered output devices because the CPU sends data to them in order to be saved.

Software

Software refers to the programs that run on a computer. There are two general categories of software: operating systems and application software. An **operating system** or **OS** is a set of programs that manages the computer's hardware devices and controls their processes. Windows, Mac OS, and Linux are all operating systems.

Application software refers to programs that make the computer useful to the user. These programs, which are generally called applications, solve specific problems or perform general operations that satisfy the needs of the user. Word processing, spreadsheet, and database packages are all examples of application software. As you work through this book, you will develop application software using Visual Basic.

 Checkpoint

    1.1 List the five major hardware components of a computer system.

    1.2 What is main memory? What is its purpose?

    1.3 Explain why computers have both main memory and secondary storage.

    1.4 What are the two general categories of software?

 **1.2** **Programs and Programming Languages**

> **CONCEPT:** A program is a set of instructions a computer follows in order to perform a task. A programming language is a special language used to write computer programs.

What Is a Program?

Computers are designed to follow instructions. A computer program is a set of instructions that enables the computer to solve a problem or perform a task. For example, suppose we want the computer to calculate someone's gross pay—a *Wage Calculator* application. Figure 1-2 shows a list of things the computer should do.

Collectively, the instructions in Figure 1-2 are called an **algorithm**. An algorithm is a set of well-defined steps for performing a task or solving a problem. Notice these steps are sequentially ordered. Step 1 should be performed before Step 2, and so on. It is important that these instructions are performed in their proper sequence.

Figure 1-2 Program steps—*Wage Calculator* application

1. Display a message on the screen: *How many hours did you work?*
2. Allow the user to enter the number of hours worked.
3. Once the user enters a number, store it in memory.
4. Display a message on the screen: *How much do you get paid per hour?*
5. Allow the user to enter an hourly pay rate.
6. Once the user enters a number, store it in memory.
7. Once both the number of hours worked and the hourly pay rate are entered, multiply the two numbers and store the result in memory as the gross pay.
8. Display a message on the screen that shows the gross pay. The message must include the result of the calculation performed in Step 7.

States and Transitions

It is helpful to think of a running computer program as a combination of states and transitions. Each state is represented by a snapshot (like a picture) of the computer's memory. Using the *Wage Calculator* application example from Figure 1-2, the following is a memory snapshot taken when the program starts:

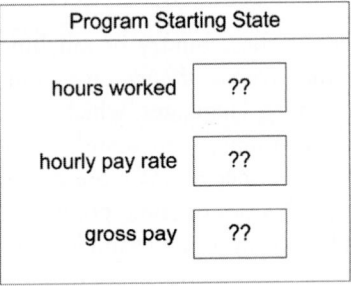

In Step 3, the number of hours worked by the user is stored in memory. Suppose the user enters the value 20. A new program state is created:

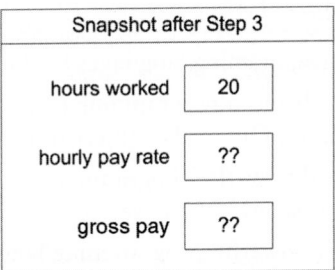

In Step 6, the hourly pay rate entered by the user is stored in memory. Suppose the user enters the value 25. The following memory snapshot shows the new program state:

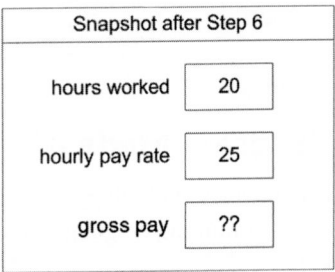

In Step 7, the application calculates the amount of money earned, saving it in memory. The following memory snapshot shows the new program state:

Snapshot after Step 7	
hours worked	20
hourly pay rate	25
gross pay	500

The memory snapshot produced by Step 7 represents the final program state.

Programming Languages

In order for a computer to perform instructions such as the wage calculator algorithm, the steps must be converted to a format the computer can process. As mentioned earlier, a program is stored in memory as a series of binary numbers. These numbers are known as **machine language instructions**. The CPU processes only instructions written in machine language. Our *Wage Calculator* application might look like the following at the moment when it is executed by the computer:

10101101110101000111100001101110100011110001110011010101110 *etc.*

The CPU interprets these binary or machine language numbers as commands. As you might imagine, the process of encoding an algorithm in machine language is tedious and difficult. **Programming languages**, which use words instead of numbers, were invented to ease this task. Programmers can write their applications in programming language statements, and then use special software called a **compiler** to convert the program into machine language. Names of some popular recent programming languages are shown in Table 1-1. This list is only a small sample—there are thousands of programming languages.

Table 1-1 Popular programming languages

Language	Description
Visual Basic, C#	Popular programming languages for building Windows and Web applications.
C, C++	Powerful advanced programmng languages that emphasize flexibility and fast running times. C++ is also object-oriented.
Java	Flexible and powerful programming language that runs on many different computer systems. Often used to teach object-oriented programming.
Python	Simple, yet powerful programming language used for graphics and small applications.
PHP	Programming language used for creating interactive Web sites.
JavaScript	Scripting language used in Web applications that provides rich user interfaces for Web browsers.

What Is a Program Made of?

All programming languages, including Visual Basic, have certain elements in common. Let's look at the major programming language elements that you will work with when writing a program.

Keywords (Reserved Words)

Each high-level language has its own set of words that the programmer must learn in order to use the language. The words that make up a high-level programming language are known as **keywords** or **reserved words**. Each keyword has a specific meaning, and cannot be used for any other purpose. As you work through this book you will learn many of the Visual Basic keywords, and how to use them in a program.

Operators

In addition to keywords, programming languages have **operators** that perform various operations on data. For example, all programming languages have math operators that perform arithmetic. In Visual Basic, as well as most other languages, the + sign is an operator that adds two numbers. The following would add 12 and 75:

```
12 + 75
```

Variables

Programs use variables to store data in memory. A **variable** is a storage location in memory that is represented by a name. When a value is stored in a variable, it is stored in the computer's memory.

Programmers make up the names for all the variables that they use in a program. You will learn specific rules and guidelines for naming variables in Chapter 3, but for now just remember that a variable's name is a single word that indicates what the variable is used for. For example, a program that calculates the sales tax on a purchase might use a variable named `tax` to hold that value in memory. And a program that calculates the distance from Earth to a star might use a variable named `distance` to hold that value in memory. When a program stores a value in a variable, the value is actually stored in memory at the location represented by the variable.

Syntax

In addition to keywords and operators, each language also has its own **syntax**, which is a set of rules that must be strictly followed when writing a program. The syntax rules dictate how keywords, operators, and various punctuation characters must be used in a program. When you are learning a programming language, you must learn the syntax rules for that particular language.

> **NOTE:** Human languages also have syntax rules. Do you remember when you took your first English class, and you learned all those rules about infinitives, indirect objects, clauses, and so forth? You were learning the syntax of the English language.
>
> Although people commonly violate the syntax rules of their native language when speaking and writing, other people usually understand what they mean. Unfortunately, program compilers do not have this ability. If even a single syntax error appears in a program, the program cannot be compiled or executed.

Statements

The individual instructions that you write in a program are called **statements**. A programming statement can consist of keywords, operators, punctuation, and other allowable programming elements, arranged in the proper sequence to perform an operation. The statements that are written in a program are commonly called **source code**, or simply **code**.

Procedures

A **procedure** is a set of programming statements that exist within a program for the purpose of performing a specific task. The program executes the procedure when the task needs to be performed.

Comments (Remarks)

Not everything that the programmer writes in a program is meant to be executed by the computer. Some parts of a program are **comments**, or **remarks**, that help the human reader of a program understand the purposes of the program statements. In Visual Basic, any statement that begins with an apostrophe (') is considered a comment. When the Visual Basic compiler sees a statement that begins with an apostrophe, it recognizes it as a comment and it skips over it.

You should always add descriptive comments to your code. The extra time it takes is well spent. Sometimes you (the programmer) will have to reread and understand your own code. Comments are a great way to remind you of what you were thinking when you created the program. In addition, you may have to modify or maintain code written by another programmer and you will appreciate the time spent to write comments!

Graphical User Interfaces

When a computer program is needed to perform a task, the programmer is the person who develops the algorithm, and writes the programming statements that perform the algorithm's steps. Once the program is complete, it is made available to those who need to use it. The people who use the program are known as **users**.

Although the programmer works directly with a program's statements, users are typically not concerned with the program's inner workings. Users want to make sure that they know how to operate the program when it is running, and that the program works as it should. The part of a program that users interact with is known as the **user interface**. On modern operating systems such as Windows, most of the programs that people use have a **graphical user interface**, or GUI (pronounced *gooey*). A graphical user interface typically consists of one or more windows that appear on the computer screen. A **window** is a rectangular area that contains other visual elements such as text, buttons that can be clicked with the mouse, boxes that accept keyboard input, and so forth. Let's look at an example. Follow the steps in Tutorial 1-1 to run a program that was copied to your system from the Student CD that accompanies this book.

Tutorial 1-1:

Running the *Wage Calculator* application

Step 1: On your computer, navigate to the folder containing the student sample programs that you copied from the textbook's Student CD. If you are working in your school's computer lab, your instructor will tell you where the files are located.

Step 2: Inside the folder containing the student sample programs, go to the *Chap1* folder. Double-click the file *Wage Calculator.exe* (the *.exe* filename extension may not be visible). The program's window should display as shown in Figure 1-3. Leave the program running as you continue to read. We will perform operations with the program in Tutorial 1-2.

Figure 1-3 A graphical user interface

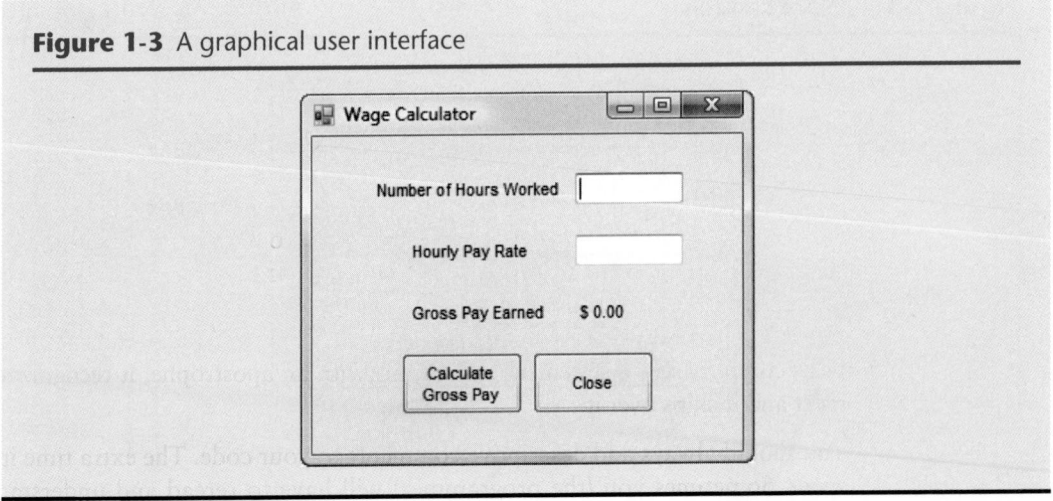

The program that you executed in Tutorial 1-1 calculates an employee's gross pay. Notice that inside the program's window (shown in Figure 1-3) there are boxes for entering the number of hours worked and the hourly pay rate. There is also a button that calculates the gross pay when it is clicked with the mouse, and a button that closes the program (stops its execution). All of these elements are part of the program's GUI, and anyone operating the program will interact with these elements.

In addition to being a programming language, Visual Basic is also a programming environment that provides tools for creating an application's graphical user interface. With Visual Basic you can design the appearance of an application's GUI, and write the code that makes the application work.

Objects and Controls

As a student studying Visual Basic, you will frequently encounter two terms: object and control. An **object** is an item in a program that contains data and has the ability to perform operations. The data that an object contains is referred to as **properties,** or **attributes.** The operations that an object can perform are called **methods.** (Recall that earlier we mentioned that a procedure is a set of programming statements that exist within a program for the purpose of performing a specific task. A method is a special type of procedure that belongs to an object.)

In the beginning of your studies you will learn how to use many different objects that are provided by Visual Basic to perform various operations in your programs. In Chapter 12, you will learn to define your own objects.

VideoNote

Forms,
Controls, and
Properties

A **control** is a specific type of object that usually appears in a program's graphical user interface. For example, each of the elements that appear in the user interface in Figure 1-3 is a control. The window that contains the other elements is known as a **Form** control. The small boxes that accept keyboard input are known as **TextBox** controls. The areas that simply display text are known as **Label** controls. The buttons that perform operations when clicked with the mouse are known as **Button** controls. Figure 1-4 points out each of these controls in the user interface.

NOTE: Visual Basic is an **object-oriented programming (OOP)** language. A typical VB application uses numerous objects (such as GUI controls) that work together.

Figure 1-4 Types of controls

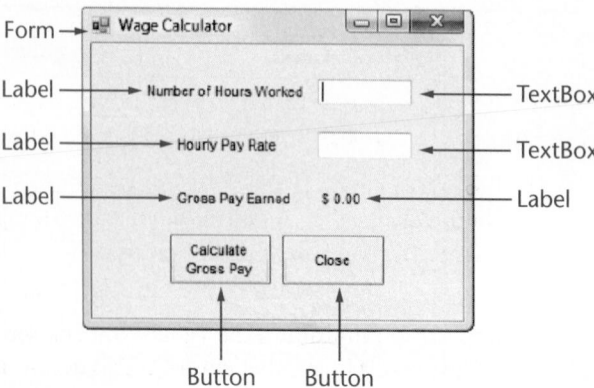

Properties

A GUI control's visual appearance is determined by the control's properties. A **property** is simply a piece of data that determines some characteristic of the control. For example, many controls have a **Text property** that determines the text that is displayed by the control. If you look at Figure 1-4, near the top of the form you see a Label control that displays the text *Number of Hours Worked*. That Label control's Text property is set to the value *Number of Hours Worked*. Just below that Label is another Label control, and its Text property is set to the value *Hourly Pay Rate*.

Button controls also have a Text property. In Figure 1-4, the leftmost button's Text property is set to the value *Calculate Gross Pay*, and the rightmost button's Text property is set to the value *Close*. Forms have a Text property too, which determines the text that is displayed in the title bar at the top of the form. In Figure 1-4, the form's Text property is set to *Wage Calculator*. Part of the process of creating a Visual Basic application is deciding what values to store in each object's properties.

VideoNote

Event-Driven
Programming

Event-Driven Programming

Programs that operate in a GUI environment must be **event-driven**. An event is an action that takes place within a program, such as the clicking of a control. All Visual Basic controls are capable of detecting various events. For example, a Button control can detect when it has been clicked and a TextBox control can detect when its contents have changed.

Names are assigned to all of the events that can be detected. For instance, when the user clicks a Button control, a Click event occurs. When the contents of a TextBox control changes, a TextChanged event occurs. If you wish for a control to respond to a specific event, you must write a set of programming statements known as an **event handler**. An event handler is a special type of procedure that executes when a specific event occurs. (Event handlers are also known as **event procedures**.) If an event occurs, and there is no event handler to respond to that event, the event is ignored.

Part of the Visual Basic programming process is designing and writing event handlers. Tutorial 1-2 demonstrates an event handler using the *Wage Calculator* application you executed in Tutorial 1-1.

Tutorial 1-2:
Running an application that demonstrates event handlers

Step 1: With the *Wage Calculator* application from Tutorial 1-1 still running, enter the value **10** in the first TextBox control. This is the number of hours worked.

Step 2: Press the [Tab] key. Notice that the cursor moves to the next TextBox control. Enter the value **15**. This is the hourly pay rate. The window should look like that shown in Figure 1-5.

Step 3: Click the *Calculate Gross Pay* button. Notice that in response to the mouse click, the application multiplies the values you entered in the TextBox controls and displays the result in a Label control. This action is performed by an event handler that responds to the button being clicked. The window should look like that shown in Figure 1-6.

Figure 1-5 Text boxes filled in on the *Wage Calculator* form

Figure 1-6 Gross pay calculated

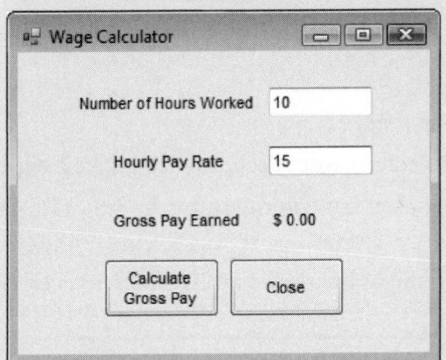

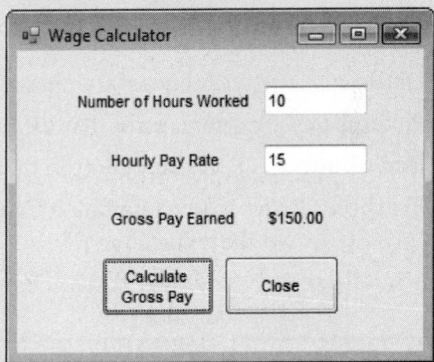

Step 4: Next, click the *Close* button. The application responds to this event by terminating. This is because an event handler closes the application when the button is clicked.

This simple application demonstrates the essence of event-driven programming. In the next section, we examine the controls and event handlers more closely.

1.3 More about Controls and Programming

CONCEPT: As a Visual Basic programmer, you must design and create an application's GUI elements (forms and other controls) and the programming statements that respond to and/or perform actions (event handlers).

While creating a Visual Basic application, you will spend much of your time doing three things: creating the controls that appear in the application's user interface, setting the properties of the controls, and writing programming language statements that respond to events and perform other operations. In this section, we take a closer look at these aspects of Visual Basic programming.

Visual Basic Controls

In the previous section, you saw examples of several GUI elements, or controls. Visual Basic provides a wide assortment of controls for gathering input, displaying information, selecting values, showing graphics, and more. Table 1-2 lists some of the commonly used controls.

Table 1-2 Visual Basic controls

Control Type	Description
Button	A rectangular button-shaped object that performs an action when clicked with the mouse
CheckBox	A box that is checked or unchecked when clicked with the mouse
ComboBox	A control that is the combination of a ListBox and a TextBox
Form	A window, onto which other controls may be placed
GroupBox	A rectangular border that functions as a container for other controls
HScrollBar	A horizontal scroll bar that, when moved with the mouse, increases or decreases a value
Label	A box that displays text that cannot be changed or entered by the user
ListBox	A box containing a list of items
PictureBox	A control that displays a graphic image
RadioButton	A round button that is either selected or deselected when clicked with the mouse
TextBox	A rectangular area in which the user can enter text, or the program can display text
VScrollBar	A vertical scroll bar that, when moved with the mouse, increases or decreases a value

If you have any experience using Microsoft Windows, you are already familiar with most of the controls listed in Table 1-2. The Student CD contains a simple demonstration program in Tutorial 1-3 that shows you how a few of them work.

Tutorial 1-3:

Running an application that demonstrates various controls

Step 1:   In Windows, navigate to the location where the sample program files have been copied from the Student CD.

Step 2:   Navigate to the the *Chap1* folder.

Step 3:   Double-click the file *Controls Demo.exe*. (The *.exe* extension may not be visible on your system.)

Step 4:   Once the program loads and executes, the window shown in Figure 1-7 should appear on the screen.

Figure 1-7 Control demonstration screen

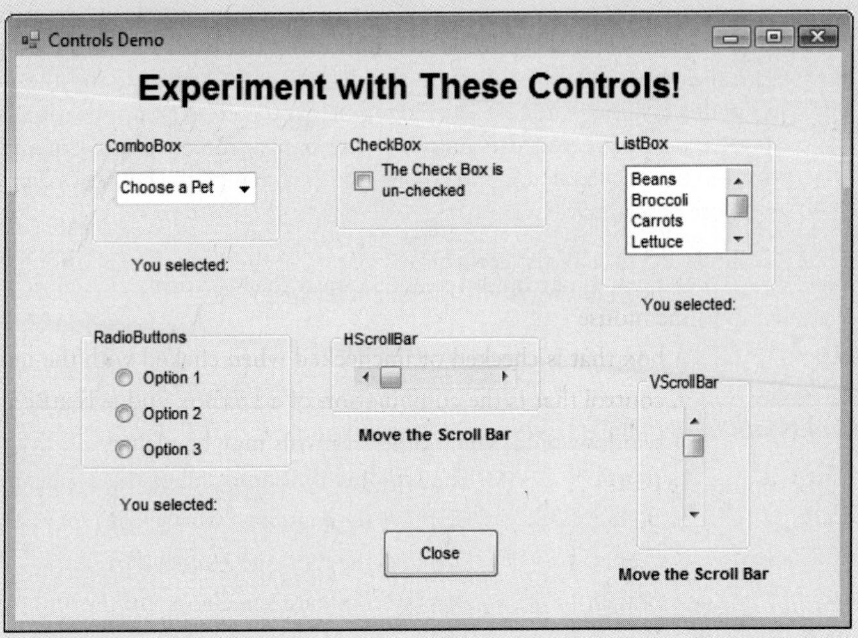

Step 5:   The program presents several Visual Basic controls. Experiment with each one, noticing the following actions, which are performed by event handlers:

- When you click the small down arrow ([▼]) in the ComboBox control, you see a list of pets. When you select one, the name of the pet appears below the combo box.
- When you click the CheckBox control, its text changes to indicate that the check box is checked or unchecked.
- When you click an item in the ListBox control, the name of that item appears below the list box.
- When you select one of the RadioButton controls, the text below them changes to indicate which one you selected. You may only select one at a time.
- You move the horizontal scroll bar (HScrollBar) and the vertical scroll bar (VScrollBar) by doing the following:
  - Clicking either of the small arrows at each end of the bar
  - Clicking inside the bar on either side of the slider
  - Clicking on the slider and while holding down the mouse button, moving the mouse to the right or left for the horizontal scroll bar, or up or down for the vertical scroll bar.

  When you move either of the scroll bars, the text below it changes to a number. Moving the scroll bar in one direction increases the number, and moving it in the other direction decreases the number.

Step 6:   Click the *Close* button to end the application.

The Name Property

The appearance of a control is determined by its properties. Some properties, however, establish nonvisual characteristics. An example is the control's **Name property**. When the programmer wishes to manipulate or access a control in a programming statement, he or she must refer to the control by its name.

When you create a control in Visual Basic, it automatically receives a default name. The first Label control created in an application receives the default name `Label1`. The second Label control created receives the default name `Label2`, and the default names continue in this fashion. The first TextBox control created in an application is automatically named `TextBox1`. As you can imagine, the names for each subsequent TextBox control are `TextBox2`, `TextBox3`, and so on. You can change the control's default name to something more descriptive.

Table 1-3 lists all the controls, by name, in the *Wage Calculator* application (Section 1.2), and Figure 1-8 shows where each is located.

Table 1-3 *Wage Calculator* controls

Control Name	Control Type	Description
Form1	Form	The window that holds all of the application's other controls
Label1	Label	Displays the message *Number of Hours Worked*
Label2	Label	Displays the message *Hourly Pay Rate*
Label3	Label	Displays the message *Gross Pay Earned*
txtHoursWorked	TextBox	Allows the user to enter the number of hours worked
txtPayRate	TextBox	Allows the user to enter the hourly pay rate
lblGrossPay	Label	Displays the gross pay, after the btnCalcGrossPay button has been clicked
btnCalcGrossPay	Button	When clicked, multiplies the number of hours worked by the hourly pay rate
btnClose	Button	When clicked, terminates the application

Figure 1-8 *Wage Calculator* controls

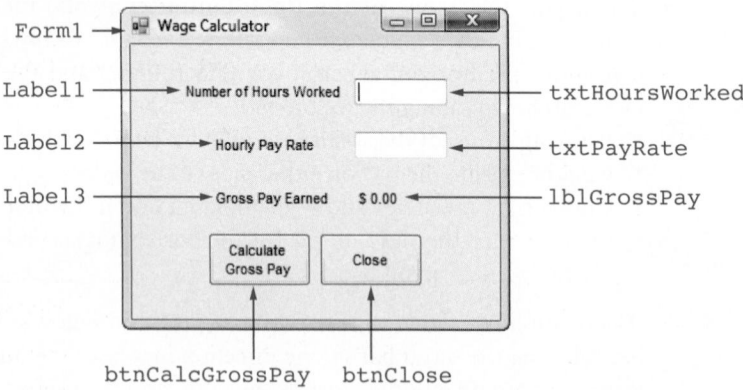

Control Naming Rules and Conventions

Four controls shown in Figure 1-8 (`Form1`, `Label1`, `Label2`, and `Label3`), still have their default names. The other five controls have programmer-defined names because those controls play an active role in the application's event handlers, and their names appear in the application's programming statements. Any control whose name appears in a programming statement should have a descriptive, programmer-defined name.

NOTE: Some programmers prefer to give all the controls in their application meaningful names, including ones whose names do not appear in programming statements.

Although you have a great deal of flexibility in naming controls, you must follow these mandatory rules:

- The first character of a control name must be a letter or an underscore character (_).
- After the first character, the remaining characters may be letters, digits, or underscore (_) characters.

It's important to remember that control names must be one word. They cannot contain spaces. Punctuation marks and other special symbols are also prohibited in control names.

In addition to these mandatory rules, there are three conventions that you should follow when naming controls:

1. The first three letters of the name should be a lowercase prefix indicating the control's type. In the *Wage Calculator* application, programmer-defined names use the following standard three-letter prefixes:
   - `lbl` indicates a Label control.
   - `txt` indicates a TextBox control.
   - `btn` indicates a Button control.
   There are standard prefixes for other controls as well. They are discussed in Chapter 2.
2. The first letter after the prefix should be uppercase. In addition, if the name consists of multiple words, the first letter of each word should be capitalized. This makes the name more readable. For example, `txtHoursWorked` is easier to read than `txthoursworked`.
3. The part of the control name that appears after the three-letter prefix should describe the control's purpose in the application. This makes the control name very helpful to anyone reading the application's programming statements. For example, it is evident that the `btnCalcGrossPay` control is a button that calculates the gross pay.

These are not mandatory rules, but they are standard conventions that many Visual Basic programmers follow. You should use these guidelines when naming the controls in your applications as well. Table 1-4 describes several fictitious controls and suggests appropriate programmer-defined names for them.

Table 1-4 Programmer-defined control name examples

Control Description	Suggested Name
A text box in which the user enters his or her age	`txtAge`
A button that, when clicked, calculates the total of an order	`btnCalcTotal`
A label that is used to display the distance from one city to another	`lblDistance`
A text box in which the user enters his or her last name	`txtLastName`
A button that, when clicked, adds a series of numbers	`btnAddNumbers`

 **Checkpoint**

1.5 What is an algorithm?

1.6 Why were computer programming languages invented?

1.7 What is an object? What is a control?

1.8 What does event-driven mean?

1.9 What is a property?

1.10 Why should the programmer change the name of a control from its default name?

1.11 If a control has the programmer-defined name `txtRadius`, what type of control is it?

1.12 What is the default name given to the first TextBox control created in an application?

1.13 Is `txtFirst+LastName` an acceptable control name? Why or why not?

1.4 The Programming Process

CONCEPT: The programming process consists of several steps, which include designing, creating, testing, and debugging activities.

Imagine building a bridge without a plan. How could it be any easier to create a complex computer program without designing its appearance and behavior? In this section, we introduce some of the most important knowledge you will gain from this book—how to begin creating a computer application. Regardless of which programming language you use in the future, good program design principles always apply.

Steps for Developing a Visual Basic Application

1. Clearly define what the application is to do.
2. Visualize the application running on the computer and design its user interface.
3. Determine the controls needed.
4. Define the values of each control's relevant properties.
5. Determine the event handlers and other code needed for each control.
6. Create a flowchart or pseudocode version of the code.
7. Check the flowchart or pseudocode for errors.
8. Start Visual Basic and create the forms and other controls identified in Step 3.
9. Use the flowcharts or pseudocode from Step 6 to write the actual code.
10. Attempt to run the application. Correct any syntax errors found and repeat this step as many times as necessary.
11. Once all syntax errors are corrected, run the program with test data for input. Correct any runtime errors. Repeat this step as many times as necessary.

These steps emphasize the importance of planning. Just as there are good ways and bad ways to paint a house, there are good ways and bad ways to write a program. A good program always begins with planning.

With the *Wage Calculator* application as our example, let's look at each of these steps in greater detail.

1. Clearly define what the application is to do.

This step requires that you identify the purpose of the application, the information to be input, the processing to take place, and the desired output. For example, the requirements for the *Wage Calculator* application are as follows:

Purpose: To calculate the user's gross pay
Input: Number of hours worked, hourly pay rate
Process: Multiply number of hours worked by hourly pay rate. The result is the user's gross pay
Output: Display a message indicating the user's gross pay

2. Visualize the application running on the computer and design its user interface.

Before you create an application on the computer, first you should create it in your mind. Step 2 is the visualization of the program. Try to imagine what the computer screen will look like while the application is running. Then, sketch the form or forms in the application. For instance, Figure 1-9 shows a sketch of the form presented by the *Wage Calculator* application.

Figure 1-9 Sketch of the *Wage Calculator* form

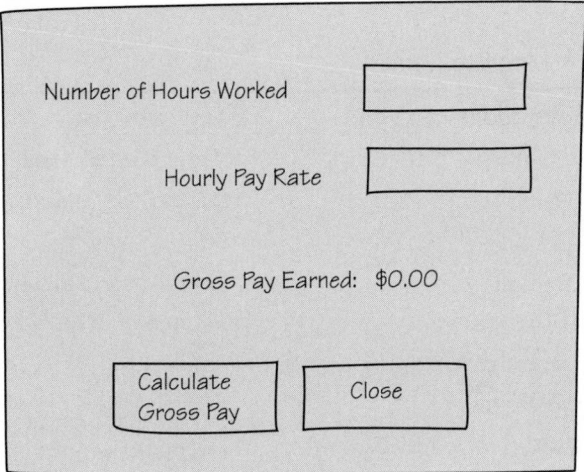

3. Determine the controls needed.

The next step is to determine the controls needed on each of the application's forms. You should assign names to all controls that will be accessed or manipulated in the application. Table 1-5 lists the controls in the *Wage Calculator* application.

Table 1-5 *Wage Calculator* controls

Control Type	Control Name	Description
Form	(Default)	A small form that will serve as the window onto which the other controls will be placed
Label	(Default)	Displays the message *Number of Hours Worked*
Label	(Default)	Displays the message *Hourly Pay Rate*
Label	(Default)	Displays the message *Gross Pay Earned*
TextBox	txtHoursWorked	Allows the user to enter the number of hours worked
TextBox	txtPayRate	Allows the user to enter the hourly pay rate
Label	lblGrossPay	Displays the gross pay, after the btnCalcGrossPay button has been clicked
Button	btnCalcGrossPay	When clicked, multiplies the number of hours worked by the hourly pay rate; stores the result in a variable and displays it in the lblGrossPay label
Button	btnClose	When clicked, terminates the application

4. Define the values of each control's relevant properties.

Other than Name, Text is the only control property modified in the *Wage Calculator* application. Table 1-6 lists the value of each control's Text property.

Table 1-6 *Wage Calculator* control values

Control Type	Control Name	Text Property
Form	(Default)	"Wage Calculator"
Label	(Default)	"Number of Hours Worked"
Label	(Default)	"Hourly Pay Rate"
Label	(Default)	"Gross Pay Earned"
Label	lblGrossPay	"$0.00"
TextBox	txtHoursWorked	" "
TextBox	txtPayRate	" "
Button	btnCalcGrossPay	"Calculate Gross Pay"
Button	btnClose	"Close"

5. Determine the event handlers and other code needed for each control.

Next, you should list the event handlers and other code that you will write. There are only two event handlers in the *Wage Calculator* application. Table 1-7 lists and describes them. Notice the Visual Basic names for the event handlers. btnCalcGrossPay_Click is the name of the event handler invoked when the btnCalcGrossPay button is clicked and btnClose_Click is the event handler that executes when the btnClose button is clicked.

Table 1-7 *Wage Calculator* event handlers

Event Handler Name	Description
btnCalcGrossPay_Click	Multiplies the number of hours worked by the hourly pay rate; these values are retrieved from the txtHoursWorked and txtPayRate TextBox controls and the result of the multiplication is stored in the lblGrossPay label's Text property
btnClose_Click	Terminates the application

6. Create a flowchart or pseudocode version of the code

A **flowchart** is a diagram that graphically depicts the flow of a method. It uses boxes and other symbols to represent each step. Figure 1-10 shows a flowchart for the btnCalcGrossPay_Click event handler.

Figure 1-10 Flowchart for btnCalcGrossPay_Click event handler

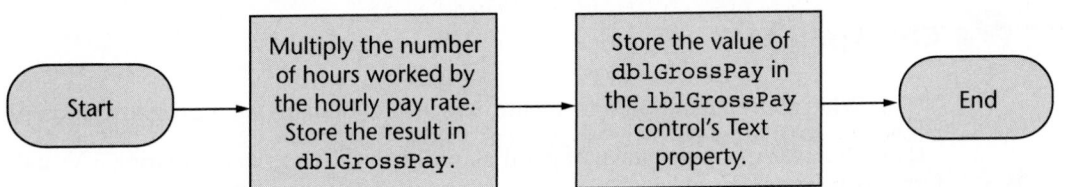

There are two types of boxes in the flowchart shown in Figure 1-10: ovals and rectangles. The flowchart begins with an oval labeled *Start* and ends with an oval labeled *End*. The rectangles represent a computational process or other operation. Notice that the symbols are connected with arrows that indicate the direction of the program flow.

Many programmers prefer to use pseudocode instead of flowcharts. **Pseudocode** is a cross between human language and a programming language. Although the computer can't understand pseudocode, programmers often find it helpful to plan an algorithm in a language that's almost a programming language but still very readable by humans. The following is a pseudocode version of the btnCalcGrossPay_Click event handler:

> *Store Number of Hours Worked × Hourly Pay Rate in the grossPay variable.*
> *Store the value of the grossPay variable in the* lblGrossPay *control's Text property.*

7. Check the code for errors.

In this phase the programmer reads the flowcharts and/or pseudocode from the beginning and steps through each operation, pretending that he or she is the computer. The programmer jots down the current contents of variables and properties that change and sketches what the screen looks like after each output operation. By checking each step, a programmer can locate and correct many errors.

8. Start Visual Studio and create the forms and other controls identified in Step 3.

This step is the first actual work done on the computer. Here, the programmer uses Visual Studio to create the application's user interface and arrange the controls on each form.

9. Use the flowcharts or pseudocode from Step 6 to write the actual code.

This is the second step performed on the computer. The flowcharts or pseudocode that was developed in Step 6 may be converted into code and entered into the computer using Visual Studio.

10. Attempt to run the application. Correct any syntax errors found and repeat this step as many times as necessary.

If you have entered code with syntax errors or typing mistakes, this step will uncover them. A **syntax error** is the incorrect use of a programming language element, such as a keyword, operator, or programmer-defined name. Correct your mistakes and repeat this step until the program runs.

11. Once all syntax errors are corrected, run the program with test data for input. Correct any runtime errors. Repeat this step as many times as necessary.

Runtime errors (errors found while running the program) are mistakes that do not prevent an application from executing but cause it to produce incorrect results. For example, a mistake in a mathematical formula is a common type of **runtime error**. When runtime errors are found in a program, they must be corrected and the program retested. This step must be repeated until the program reliably produces satisfactory results.

 Checkpoint

1.14 What four items should be identified when defining what a program is to do?

1.15 Describe the importance of good planning in the process of creating a Visual Basic application.

1.16 What does it mean to visualize a program running? What is the value of such an activity?

1.17 What is a flowchart?

1.18 What is pseudocode?

1.19 What is a runtime error?

1.20 What is the purpose of testing a program with sample data or input?

1.21 How much testing should you perform on a new program?

1.5 Visual Studio and Visual Basic Express Edition (the Visual Basic Environment)

CONCEPT: Visual Studio and Visual Basic Express Edition consist of tools that you use to build Visual Basic applications. The first step in using Visual Basic is learning about these tools.

> **NOTE:** The programs in this book can be written using either Microsoft Visual Studio or Microsoft Visual Basic Express Edition. There are only minor differences between the two products. In cases where they work identically, we will refer to them as **Visual Studio**.

In Chapter 2 you will create your first Visual Basic application. First, you need to know how to start Visual Studio, set up the programming environment, and understand the environment's major components. Visual Studio is an **integrated development environment (IDE)**, which means that it provides all the necessary tools for creating, testing, and debugging software. The full version of Visual Studio can be used to create applications not only with Visual Basic, but also with other languages such as Visual C++ and C#.

Visual Studio is a customizable environment. If you are working in your school's computer lab, there's a chance that someone else has customized the programming environment to suit his own preferences. If this is the case, the screens that you see may not match the ones shown in this book. For that reason it's a good idea to reset the programming environment before you create a Visual Basic application. Tutorial 1-4 guides you through the process.

Tutorial 1-4:
Starting Visual Studio and Setting Up the Environment

VideoNote

Tutorial 1-4
Walkthrough

Step 1: Find out from your instructor whether you are using Visual Studio 2010 or Visual Basic 2010 Express Edition. Then, click the *Start* button, open the *All Programs* menu, and perform one of the following:

- If you are using Visual Studio, open the *Microsoft Visual Studio 2010* program group and then execute *Visual Studio 2010*.
- If you are using Visual Basic 2010 Express Edition, open the *Microsoft Visual Studio 2010 Express* program group and then execute *Visual Basic 2010 Express*.

> **TIP:** If you are using Visual Studio rather than Visual Basic Express Edition, the first time you run the software, you will see a window entitled *Choose Default Environment Settings*. Select *Visual Basic Development Settings* from the list and click the *Start Visual Studio* button.

Step 2: Figure 1-11 shows the Visual Studio environment. The screen shown in the figure is known as the *Start Page*. By default, the *Start Page* is displayed when you start Visual Studio, but you may or may not see it because it can be disabled.

Figure 1-11 Visual Studio *Start Page*

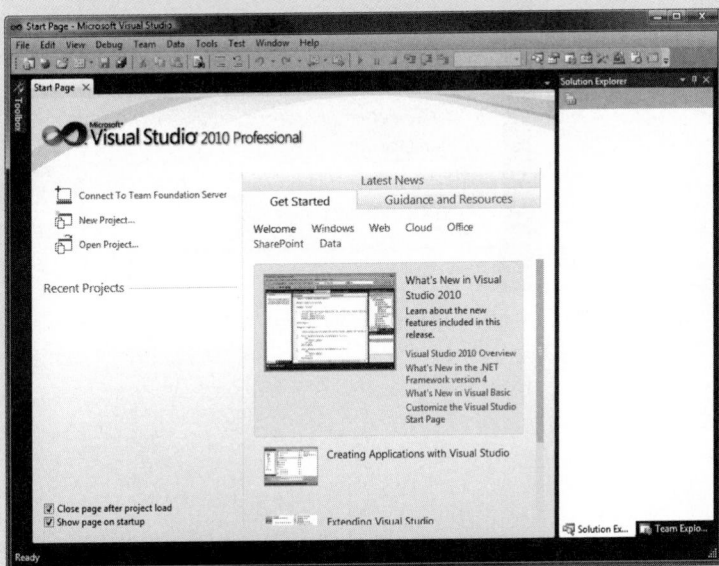

Notice the checkbox in the bottom left corner of the *Start Page* that reads *Show page on startup*. If this box is not checked, the *Start Page* will not be displayed when you start Visual Studio. If you do not see the *Start Page*, you can always display it by clicking *View* on the menu bar at the top of the screen, then clicking *Start Page*.

Step 3: This step is applicable *only* if you are using Visual Studio. If you are using Visual Basic Express Edition, skip to Step 4.

In a school computer lab, it is possible that the Visual Studio environment has been set up for a programming language other than Visual Basic. To make sure that Visual Studio looks and behaves as described in this book, you should make sure that Visual Basic is selected as the programming environment. Perform the following:

- As shown in Figure 1-12, click *Tools* on the menu bar and then click *Import and Export Settings . . .*
- On the screen that appears next, select *Reset all settings* and click the *Next >* button.
- On the screen that appears next, select *No, just reset settings, overwriting my current settings*, and then click the *Next >* button.
- The window shown in Figure 1-13 should appear next. Select *Visual Basic Development Settings* and then click the *Finish* button.
- After a moment you should see a *Reset Complete* window. Click the *Close* button and continue with the next step in the tutorial.

Figure 1-12 Select *Tools*, then *Import and Export Settings . . .*

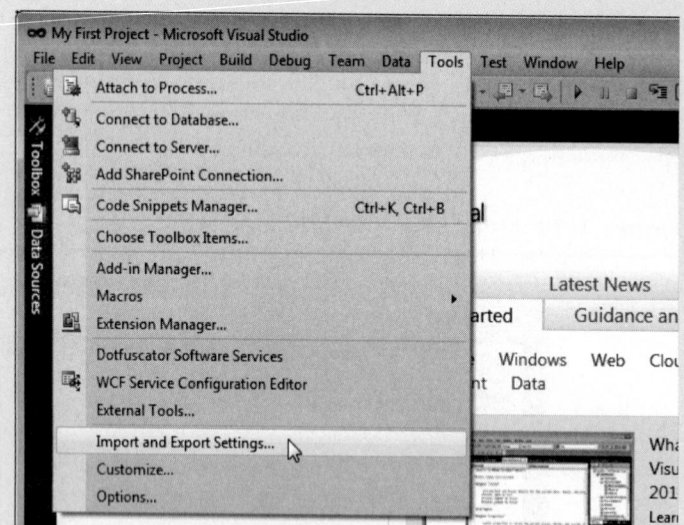

Figure 1-13 Select Visual Basic Development Settings

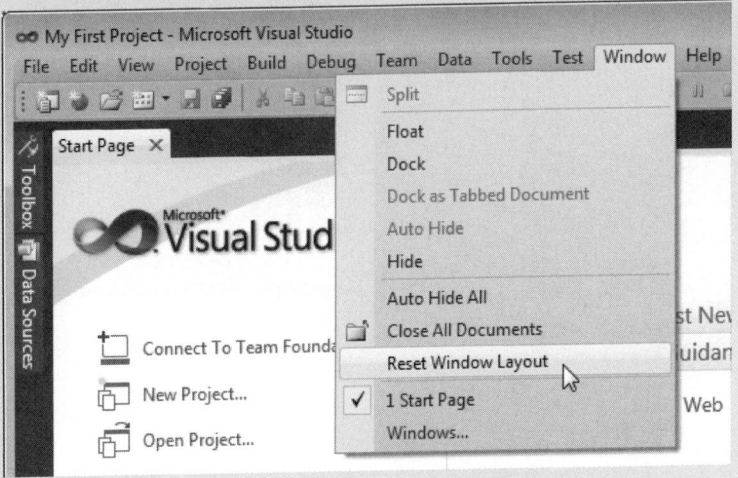

Step 4: Now you will reset Visual Studio's window layout to the default configuration. As shown in Figure 1-14, click *Window* on the menu bar and then click *Reset Window Layout*. Next you will see a dialog box asking *Are you sure you want to restore the default window layout for the environment?* Click *Yes*.

Figure 1-14 Resetting the window layout

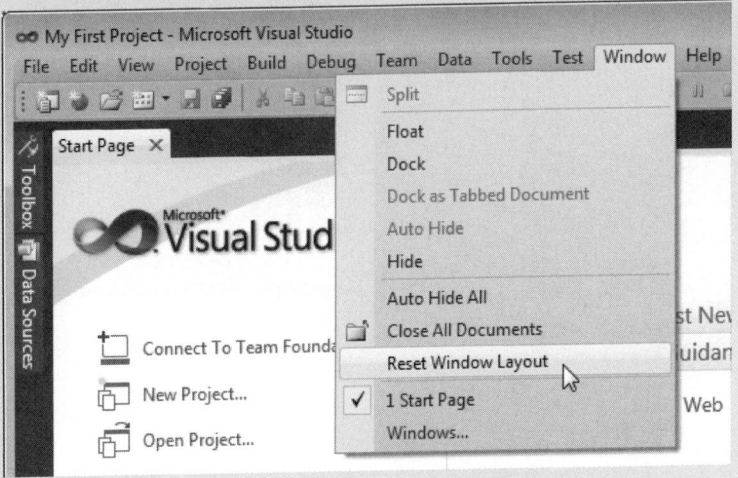

Step 5:   Visual Basic has two settings known as *Option Explicit* and *Option Strict*, which many programmers prefer to turn on because they prevent certain types of programming errors. Since you are a beginning programming student, it's a good idea that you turn these settings on, too. You will learn more about these settings in Chapter 3, but for now let's go through the process of turning them on. Click *Tools* on the menu bar at the top of the screen, and then click *Options*, as shown in Figure 1-15. This will display the *Options* window shown in Figure 1-16.

As shown in Figure 1-16, under *Projects and Solutions* (on the left side of the window), select *VB Defaults*. Then, set *Option Explicit* and *Option Strict* to *On*. After you make these settings, click *OK*.

The Visual Studio environment is now set up so you can follow the remaining tutorials in this book. If you are working in your school's computer lab, it is probably a good idea to go through these steps each time you start Visual Studio.

If you are continuing with the next tutorial, leave Visual Studio running. You can exit Visual Studio at any time by clicking *File* on the menu bar, and then clicking *Exit*.

Figure 1-15 Click *Tools*, and then *Options*

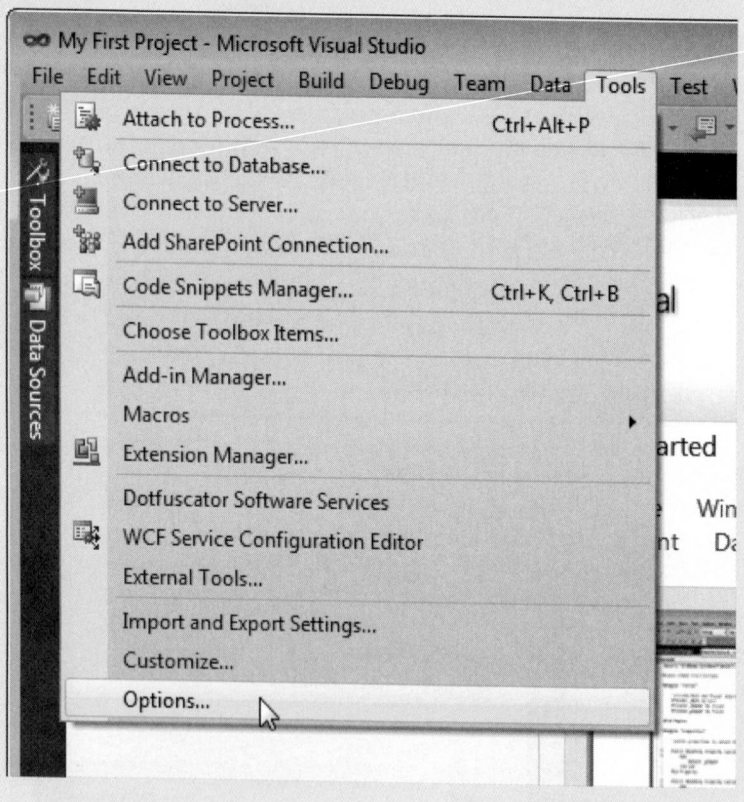

Figure 1-16 The *Options* window

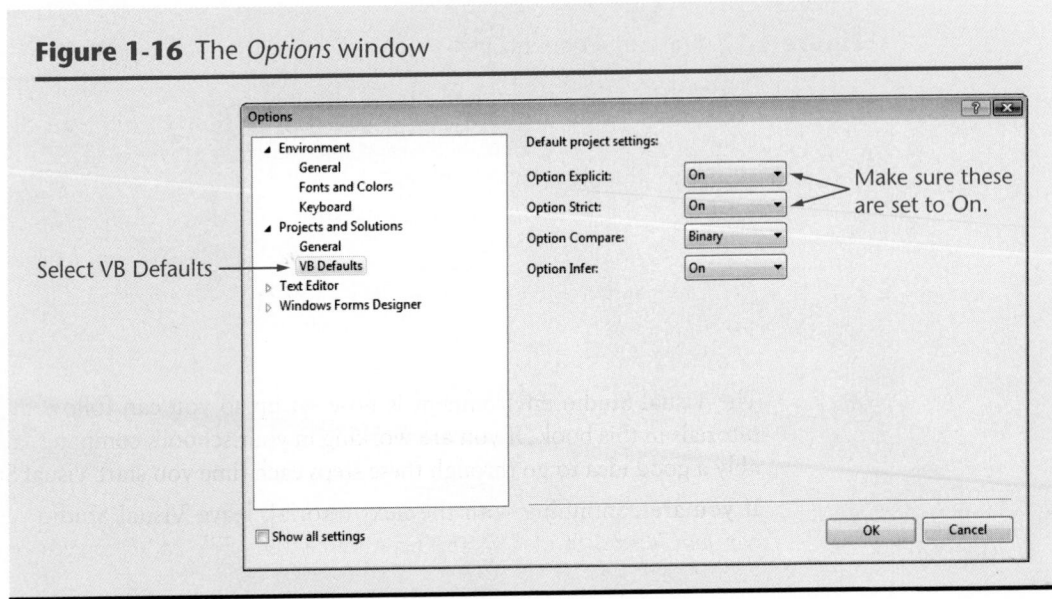

Starting a New Project

Each Visual Basic application that you create is called a **project**. When you are ready to create a new application, you start a new project. Tutorial 1-5 leads you through the steps of starting a new Visual Basic project.

Tutorial 1-5:
Starting a New Visual Basic Project

VideoNote

Tutorial 1-5
Walkthrough

Step 1: If Visual Studio is not already running, start it as you did in Tutorial 1-4.

Step 2: As shown in Figure 1-17, click *File* on the menu bar at the top of the screen, and then select *New Project*. After doing this, the *New Project* window shown in Figure 1-18 should be displayed.

Step 3: If you are using Visual Studio you will see *Installed Templates* at the left side of the window. Select *Visual Basic*. Then, select *Windows Forms Application*, as shown in Figure 1-18.

If you are using Visual Basic Express Edition, simply select *Windows Forms Application*.

Step 4: At the bottom of the *New Project* window you see a *Name* text box. This is where you enter the name of your project. Visual Studio automatically fills this box with a default name. In Figure 1-18 the default name is *WindowsApplication1*. Change the project name to *My First Project*, as shown in Figure 1-19, and click the *OK* button.

Figure 1-17 Starting a new project

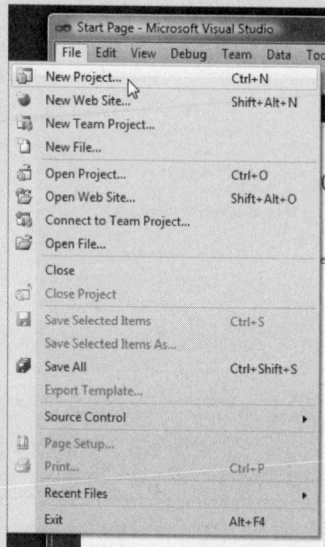

Figure 1-18 The *New Project* window

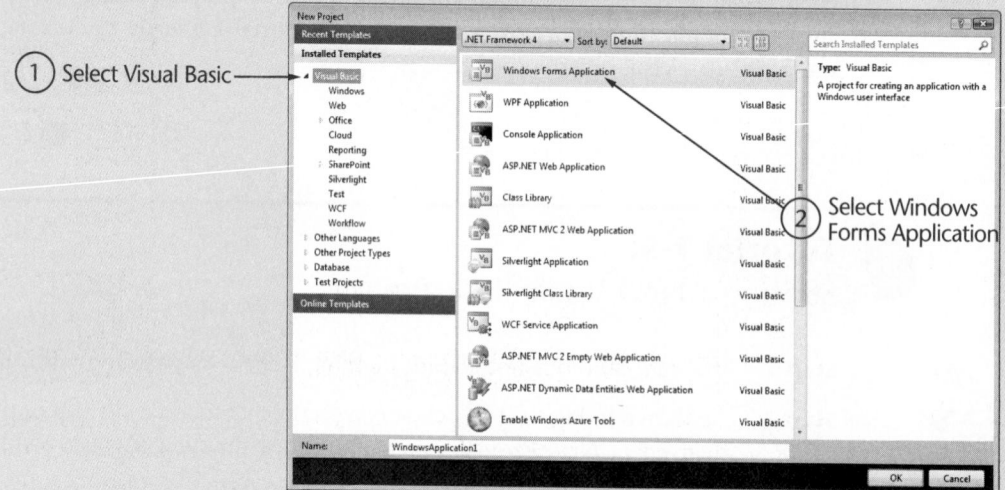

Figure 1-19 Changing the project name to *My First Project*

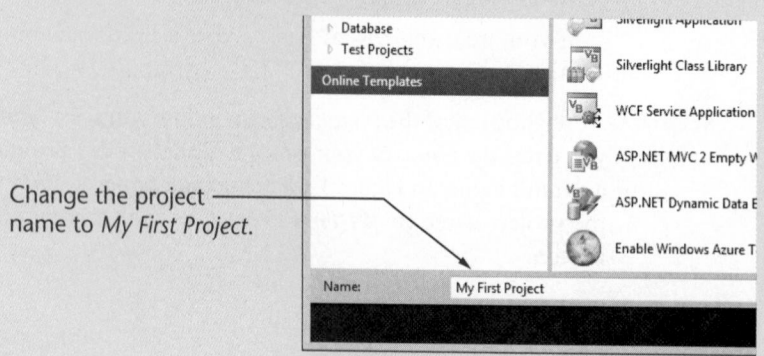

NOTE: As you work through this book you will create a lot of Visual Basic projects. As you do, you will find that default names such as *WindowsApplication1* do not help you remember what each project does. Therefore, you should always change the name of a new project to something that describes the project's purpose.

It might take a moment for the project to be created. Once it is, the Visual Studio environment should appear similar to Figure 1-20. Notice that the name of the project, *My First Project*, is displayed in the title bar at the top of the Visual Studio window.

Figure 1-20 The Visual Studio environment with a new project open

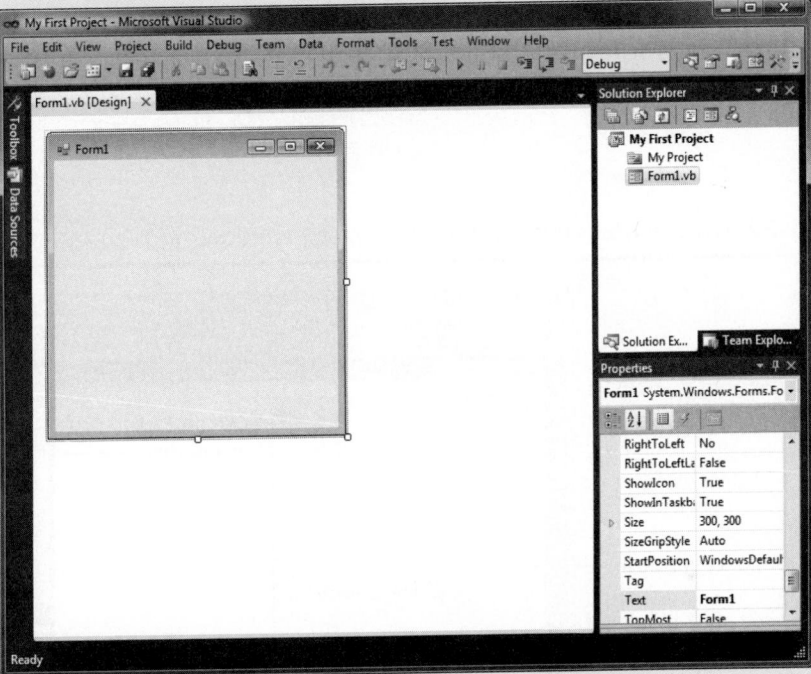

Step 5: Click *File* on the menu bar and then select *Save All*. The *Save Project* window will appear, as shown in Figure 1-21. The *Name* text box shows the project name that you entered when you created the project. The *Location* text box shows where a folder will be created on your system to hold the project. (The location shown on your system will be different than that shown in the figure.) If you wish to change the location, click the *Browse* button and select the desired drive and folder.

Click the *Save* button to save the project.

(Leave Visual Studio running so you can complete the next tutorial.)

Figure 1-21 The *Save Project* window

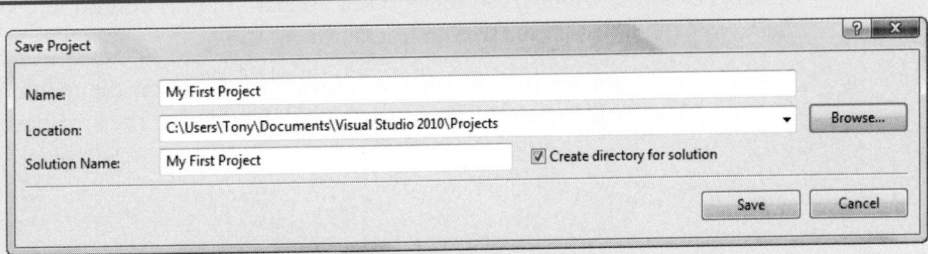

The Visual Studio Environment

The Visual Studio environment consists of a number of windows that you will use on a regular basis. Figure 1-22 shows the locations of the following windows that appear within the Visual Studio environment: the *Designer* window, the *Solution Explorer* window, and the *Properties* window. Here is a brief summary of each window's purpose:

- The *Designer* Window
  You use the *Designer* window to create an application's graphical user interface. The Designer window shows the application's form, and allows you visually design its appearance by placing the desired controls that will appear on the form when the application executes.
- The *Solution Explorer* Window
  A **solution** is a container for holding Visual Basic projects. When you create a new VB project, a new solution is automatically created to contain it. The *Solution Explorer* window allows you to navigate among the files in a Visual Basic project.
- The *Properties* Window
  When you are creating a VB application, you use the *Properties* window to examine and change a control's properties.

Figure 1-22 The *Designer* window, *Solution Explorer* window, and *Properties* window

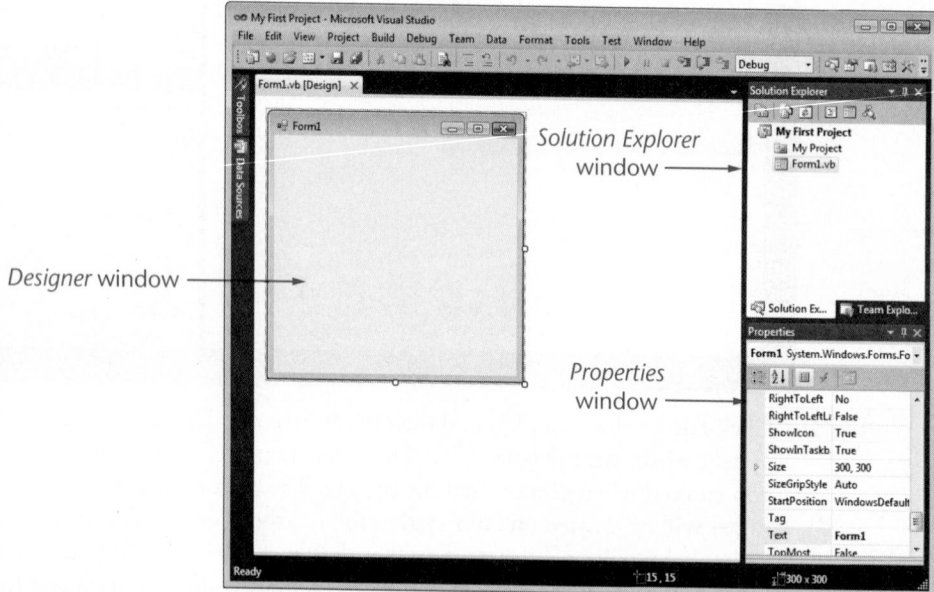

Remember that Visual Studio is a customizable environment. You can move these windows around, so they may not appear in the exact locations shown in Figure 1-22. You can also close the windows so they do not appear at all. If you do not see one or more of them, you can follow these steps to make them visible:

- If you do not see the *Designer* window, click *View* on the menu bar. On the *View* menu, click *Designer*. You can also press Shift+F7 on the keyboard.

- If you do not see the *Solution Explorer* window, click *View* on the menu bar. On the *View* menu, click *Solution Explorer*. (In Visual Basic Express Edition, click *View*, *Other Windows*, *Solution Explorer*.) You can also press Ctrl+Alt+L on the keyboard.
- If you do not see the *Properties* window, click *View* on the menu bar. On the *View* menu, click *Properties*. (In Visual Basic Express Edition, click *View*, *Other Windows*, *Properties*.) You can also press F4 on the keyboard.

Hidden Windows

Many windows in Visual Studio have a feature known as **Auto Hide**. When you see the pushpin icon in a window's title bar, as shown in Figure 1-23, you know that the window has Auto Hide capability. You click the pushpin icon to turn Auto Hide on or off for a window.

Figure 1-23 *Auto Hide* pushpin icon

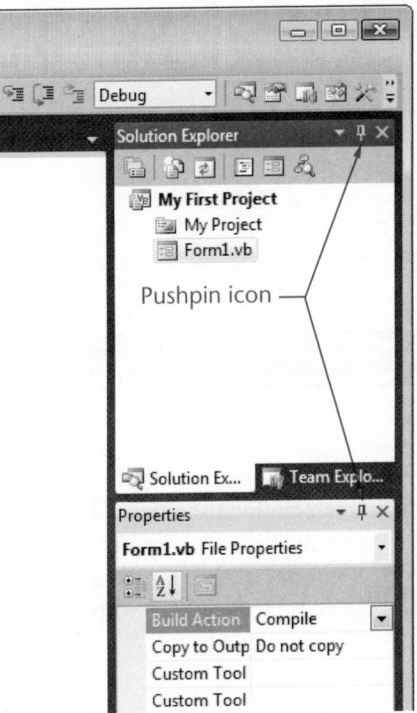

When Auto Hide is turned on, the window is displayed only as a tab along one of the edges of the *Visual Studio* window. This feature gives you more room to view your application's forms and code. Figure 1-24 shows how the *Solution Explorer* and *Properties* windows appear when their Auto Hide feature is turned on. Notice the tabs that read *Solution Explorer* and *Properties* along the right edge of the screen.

The Menu Bar and the Standard Toolbar

You've already used the Visual Studio menu bar several times. This is the bar at the top of the Visual Studio window that provides menus such as *File*, *Edit*, *View*, *Project*, and so forth. As you progress through this book, you will become familiar with many of the menus.

Figure 1-24 The *Solution Explorer* and *Properties* windows hidden

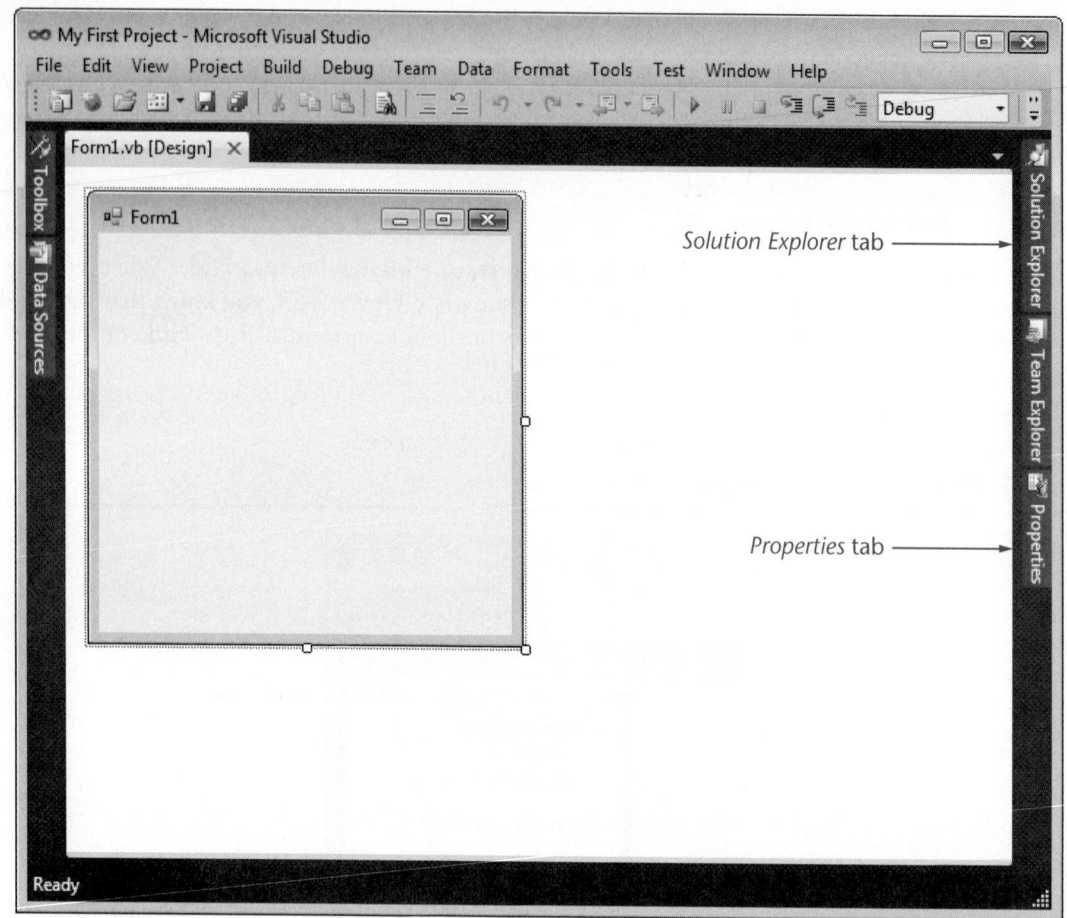

Below the menu bar is the standard toolbar. The **standard toolbar** contains buttons that execute frequently used commands. All commands that are displayed on the toolbar may also be executed from a menu, but the standard toolbar gives you quicker access to them. Figure 1-25 identifies the standard toolbar buttons and Table 1-8 gives a brief description of each.

Figure 1-25 Visual Studio standard toolbar buttons

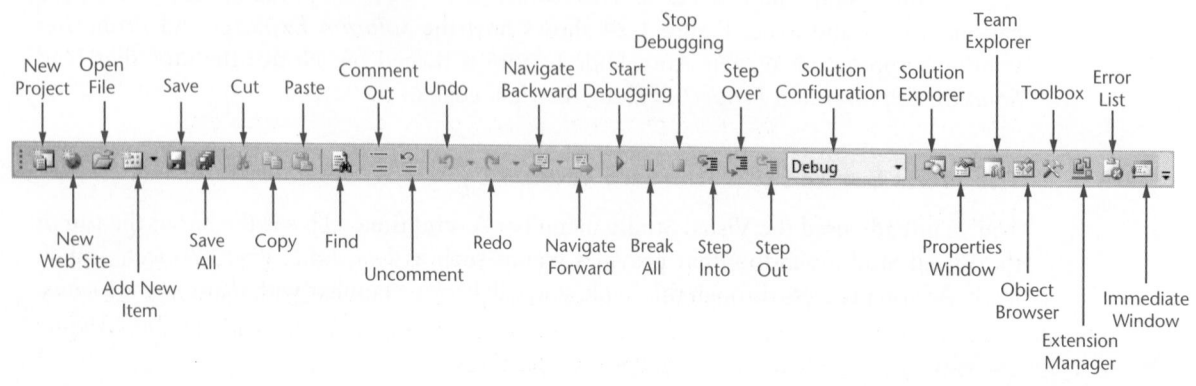

Table 1-8 Visual Studio toolbar buttons

Toolbar Button	Description
New Project	Starts a new project
New Web Site	Creates a new Web site (used in Web Forms applications)
Open File	Opens an existing file
Add New Item	Adds a new item such as a form to the current project
Save	Saves the file named by *filename*
Save All	Saves all of the files in the current project
Cut	Cuts the selected item to the clipboard
Copy	Copies the selected item to the clipboard
Paste	Pastes the contents of the clipboard
Find	Searches for text in your application code
Comment Out	Comments out the selected lines
Uncomment	Uncomments the selected lines
Undo	Undoes the most recent operation
Redo	Redoes the most recently undone operation
Navigate Backward	Moves to the previously active tab in the Designer window
Navigate Forward	Moves to the next active tab in the Designer window
Start Debugging	Starts debugging (running) your program
Break All	Pauses execution of your program
Stop Debugging	Stops debugging (running) your program
Step Into	Traces (steps) into the code in a procedure
Step Over	Executes the next statement without tracing into procedure calls
Step Out	Exits the current procedure while still debugging
Solution Configurations	Configures your project's executable code
Solution Explorer	Opens the *Solution Explorer* window
Properties Window	Opens the *Properties* window
Team Explorer	Opens the Team Explorer window, used in a professional development environment
Object Browser	Opens the *Object Browser* window
Toolbox	Opens the *Toolbox* window, displaying, for example, visual controls you can place on Windows forms
Extension Manager	Allows you to manage Visual Studio Extensions
Error List	Displays a list of most recent errors generated by the Visual Basic compiler
Immediate	Opens the *Immediate* window, which is used for debugging

 NOTE: Menu items and buttons cannot be used when they are grayed out.

The *Toolbox*

The *Toolbox* is a window that allows you to select the controls that you want to use in an application's user interface. When you want to place a Button, Label, TextBox, or other control on an application's form, you select it in the *Toolbox*. You will use the *Toolbox* extensively as you develop Visual Basic applications.

The *Toolbox* typically appears on the left side of the Visual Studio environment. If the *Toolbox* is in Auto Hide mode, its tab will appear as shown in Figure 1-26. Figure 1-27 shows the *Toolbox* opened, with Auto Hide turned off.

Figure 1-26 The *Toolbox* tab (Auto Hide turned on)

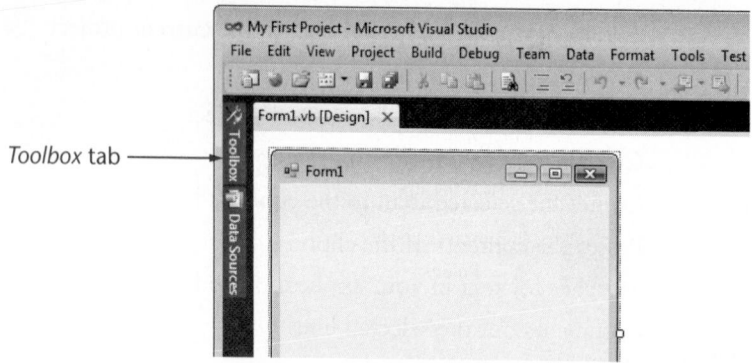

Toolbox tab

Figure 1-27 The *Toolbox* opened (Auto Hide turned off)

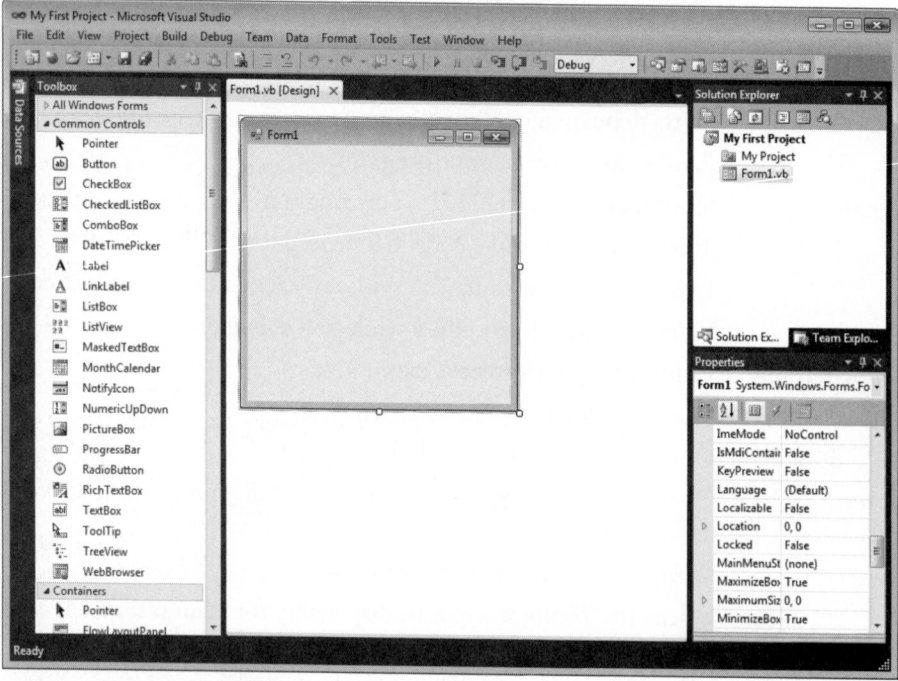

The *Toolbox* is divided into sections, and each section has a name. In Figure 1-27 you can see the *All Windows Forms*, *Common Controls*, and *Containers* sections. If you scroll the *Toolbox*, you will see many other sections. Each of the sections can be opened or closed. If you want to open a section of the *Toolbox*, you simply click on its name tab. To close the section, click on its name tab again. In Figure 1-27, the *Common Controls* section is open. You use the Common Controls section to access controls that you frequently need, such as Buttons, Labels, and TextBoxes. You can move any section to the top of the list by dragging its name with the mouse.

Using ToolTips

A **ToolTip** is a small rectangular box that pops up when you hover the mouse pointer over a button on the toolbar or in the *Toolbox* for a few seconds. The ToolTip box contains a short description of the button's purpose. Figure 1-28 shows the ToolTip that appears when the cursor is left sitting on the *Save All* button. Use a ToolTip whenever you cannot remember a particular button's function.

Figure 1-28 *Save All* ToolTip

Docked and Floating Windows

Figure 1-27 shows the *Toolbox*, *Solution Explorer* and *Properties* windows when they are **docked**, which means they are attached to one of the edges of the *Visual Studio* window. Alternatively, the windows can be **floating**. You can control whether a window is **docked** or floating as follows:

- To change a window from docked to floating, right-click its title bar and select *Float*.
- To change a window from floating to docked, right-click its title bar and select *Dock*.

Figure 1-29 shows Visual Studio with the *Toolbox*, *Solution Explorer* and *Properties* windows floating. When a window is floating, you can click and drag it by its title bar around the screen. You may use whichever style you prefer—docked or floating. When windows are floating, they behave as normal windows. You may move or resize them to suit your preference.

Figure 1-29 *Toolbox*, *Solution Explorer* and *Properties* windows floating

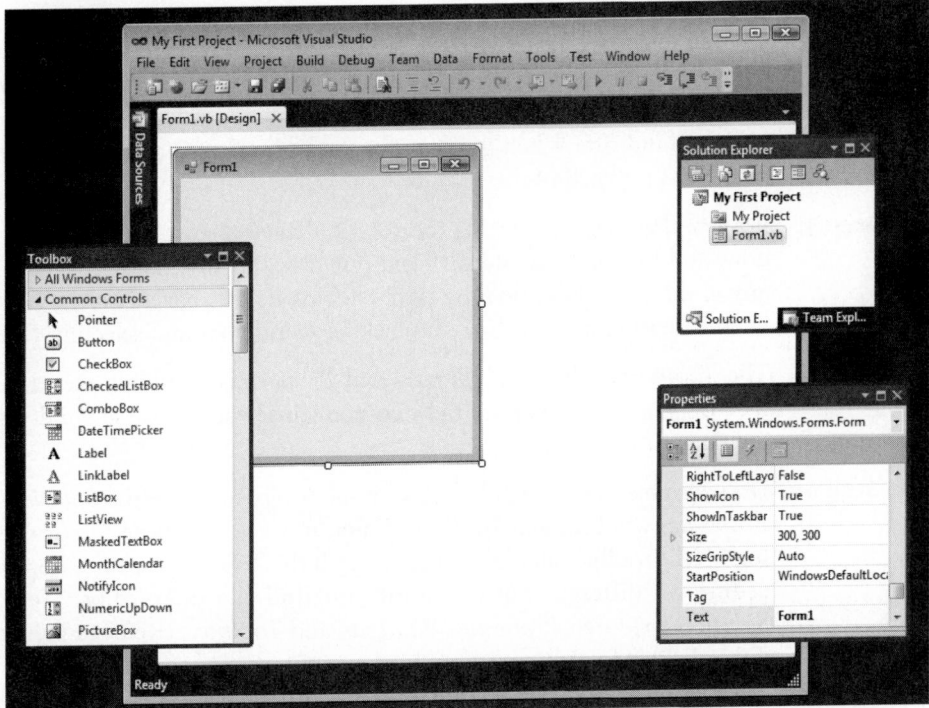

NOTE: A window cannot float if its Auto Hide feature is turned on.

TIP: Remember, you can always reset the window layout by clicking *Window* on the menu bar, and then selecting *Reset Window Layout*. If you accidentally close the Designer window, the *Solution Explorer* window, or the *Properties* window, you can use the *View* menu to redisplay them.

Accessing the Visual Studio Documentation

You can access the full documentation for Visual Studio by Clicking *Help* on the menu bar, and then selecting *View Help*. (Or, you can simply press Ctrl+F1.) This launches your Web browser and opens the online **Microsoft Developer Network (MSDN) library**. The MSDN library provides complete documentation for Visual Basic, as well as the other programming languages included in Visual Studio. You will also find code samples, tutorials, articles, and access to Microsoft Channel 9 Videos.

Tutorial 1-6:
Getting Familiar with the Visual Studio Environment

VideoNote

Tutorial 1-6
Walkthrough

This exercise will give you practice interacting with the *Solution Explorer* window, the *Properties* window, and the *Toolbox*.

Step 1: Visual Studio should still be running on your computer from the previous tutorial. If it is, continue to Step 2.

> If Visual Studio is not running on your computer, repeat the steps in Tutorial 1-5 to start a new project. This time, however, name the project *My Second Project*. (This is necessary because you've already created a project named *My First Project*.)

Step 2: Practice turning the *Auto Hide* feature on and off for the *Solution Explorer* window, the *Properties* window, and the *Toolbox*. Recall from our previous discussion that clicking the pushpin icon in each window's title bar turns *Auto Hide* on and off. When you are finished practicing, make sure Auto Hide is turned off for each of these windows. Your screen should look like Figure 1-27.

Step 3: Practice floating and docking the *Solution Explorer* window, the *Properties* window, and the *Toolbox*. Recall from our previous discussion that you can make any of these windows float by right-clicking its title bar and selecting *Float*. You dock a floating window by right-clicking its title bar and selecting *Dock*.

Step 4: The *Toolbox, Solution Explorer,* and *Properties* windows each have a *Close* button () in their upper right corner. Close each of these windows by clicking their *Close* button.

Step 5: Do you remember which buttons on the toolbar restore the *Solution Explorer*, *Properties* window, and *Toolbox*? If not, move your mouse cursor over any button on the toolbar, and leave it there until the ToolTip appears. Repeat this procedure on different buttons until you find the ones whose ToolTips read *Solution Explorer*, *Properties Window*, and *Toolbox*. (Refer to Figure 1-24 and Table 1-8 for further assistance.)

Step 6: Click the appropriate buttons on the toolbar to restore the *Solution Explorer*, the *Properties* window, and the *Toolbox*.

Step 7: Exit Visual Studio by clicking *File* on the menu bar, and then clicking *Exit*. You may see a dialog box asking you if you wish to save changes to a number of items. Click *Yes*.

Checkpoint

1.22 Briefly describe the purpose of the *Solution Explorer* window.

1.23 Briefly describe the purpose of the *Properties* window.

1.24 Briefly describe the purpose of the standard toolbar.

1.25 What is the difference between the toolbar and the *Toolbox*?

1.26 What is a ToolTip?

Summary

1.1 Computer Systems: Hardware and Software

- The major hardware components of a computer are the central processing unit (CPU), main memory, secondary storage devices, input devices, and output devices. Computer programs are stored in machine language, as a series of binary numbers.
- Main memory holds the instructions for programs that are running and data programs are working with. RAM is usually volatile, used only for temporary storage.
- The two general categories of software are operating systems and application software.

1.2 Programs and Programming Languages

- Although the computer can process only programs that written in machine language, programmers use languages such as Visual Basic to write programs. They then use a compiler to translate their programs to machine language.
- Keywords (reserved words), operators, variables, syntax, statements, and comments are some of the programming language elements that you will work with when writing a program.
- The part of the program that the user interacts with is called the user interface. Modern systems use graphical user interfaces.
- An object is an item in a program that contains data and has the ability to perform operations.
- A control is a type of object that usually appears in a program's graphical user interface.
- There are several types of controls available in Visual Basic. Applications in this chapter contained forms, Labels, TextBoxes, Buttons, CheckBoxes, RadioButtons, ListBoxes, ComboBoxes, and scroll bars.
- The appearance of a screen object, such as a form or other control, is determined by the object's properties.
- An event-driven program is one that responds to events or actions that take place while the program is running.

1.3 More about Controls and Programming

- All controls have a name. Programmers manipulate or access a control in a programming statement by referring to the control by its name. When the programmer creates a control in Visual Basic, it automatically receives a default name.
- Any control whose name appears in a programming statement should have a descriptive, programmer-defined name. Although programmers have a great deal of flexibility in naming controls, they should follow some standard guidelines.

1.4 The Programming Process

- This section outlines the steps for designing and creating a Visual Basic application.

1.5 Visual Studio and Visual Basic Express Edition (the Visual Basic Environment)

- The Visual Basic environment, which is part of Visual Studio, consists of tools used to build Visual Basic applications.
- Visual Basic can be used to create many different types of applications.

Key Terms

algorithm
application software
attributes
Auto Hide
binary number
Button
central processing unit (CPU)
CheckBox
code
ComboBox
comments
compiler
control
Designer window
disk drive
docked window
event-driven
event handler
floating window
flowchart
Form
graphical user interface (GUI)
GroupBox
hardware
HScrollBar
input
input device
integrated development
   environment (IDE)
keywords
Label
ListBox
machine language instructions
main memory
methods
Microsoft Developer Network
   (MSDN) library
Name property

object-oriented programming
   (OOP)
object
operand
operating system (OS)
operators
output
output device
PictureBox
procedure
program
programmer-defined name
programming languages
project
properties
Properties window
pseudocode
RadioButton
random-access memory (RAM)
remarks
reserved words
runtime error
secondary storage
software
source code
Solution Explorer window
standard toolbar
statement
syntax
Text property
TextBox
Toolbox window
ToolTip
user
user interface
variable
VscrollBar
window

Review Questions and Exercises

Fill-in-the-Blank

1. The job of the _____ is to fetch instructions, carry out the opera-
    tions commanded by the instructions, and produce some outcome or resultant
    information.

2. A(n) _____ is an example of a secondary storage device.

3. The two general categories of software are _____ and
    _____.

4. A program is a set of _____.

5. Since computers can't be programmed in natural human language, algorithms must be written in a(n) _____ language.

6. _____ is the only language computers really process.

7. Words that have special meaning in a programming language are called _____.

8. A(n) _____ is a name that represents a storage location in memory.

9. _____ are characters or symbols that perform operations on one or more operands.

10. A(n) _____ is part of an application's code but is ignored by the compiler. It is intended for documentation purposes only.

11. The rules that must be followed when writing a program are called _____.

12. _____ is information a program gathers from the outside world.

13. _____ is information a program sends to the outside world.

14. A(n) _____ is a set of well-defined steps for performing a task or solving a problem.

15. A(n) _____ is a diagram that graphically illustrates the flow of a program.

16. _____ is a cross between human language and a programming language.

17. A(n) _____ is a piece of data that determines some characteristic of a control.

18. If you do not see the *Solution Explorer* or *Properties* windows in Visual Studio, you may use the _____ menu to bring them up.

19. You click the pushpin icon in a window's title bar to turn the _____ feature on or off.

20. You use the _____ to place Buttons, Labels, TextBoxes, and other controls on an application's forms.

21. The _____ window allows you to navigate among the files in your project.

22. The _____ window allows you to examine and change a control's properties.

23. When windows are _____, it means they are attached to one of the edges of the Visual Studio main window.

24. To dock a floating window, right-click its title bar and then select _____.

25. To reset the Visual Studio window layout, you select *Reset Window Layout* from the _____ menu.

26. All commands executed by the _____ may also be executed from a menu.

27. The _____ window shows your application's form. This is where you design your application's user interface by placing controls on the form that appears when your application executes.

28. When you want to place a Button, Label, TextBox, or other control on an application's form, you select it in the _____, and drag it onto the form in the *Designer* window.

29. You can access the full documentation for Visual Studio by Clicking _____ on the menu bar, and then selecting *View Help*.

30. A(n) _____ is a small box that is displayed when you hold the mouse cursor over a button on the toolbar or in the *Toolbox* for a few seconds.

Short Answer

1. What is the difference between main memory and secondary storage?

2. What is the difference between operating system software and application software?

3. What is an object?

4. What is a control?

5. Briefly describe what an event-driven program is.

6. From what you have read in this chapter, describe the difference between a Label control and a TextBox control. When is it appropriate to use one or the other?

7. When creating a Visual Basic application, you will spend much of your time doing what three things?

8. What is a form?

9. Summarize the mandatory rules that you must follow when naming a control.

10. What is a keyword?

11. What is the purpose of inserting comments in a program?

12. What is language syntax?

13. What is a syntax error?

14. What is a runtime error?

15. What is an operator?

16. What is a flowchart?

17. What is pseudocode?

18. What default name will Visual Basic give to the first Label control that you place on a form? What default name will Visual Basic assign to the first TextBox control that you place on a form?

19. What property determines the text that is displayed by a Label control?

20. What is *Auto Hide*? How do you turn *Auto Hide* on or off?

21. What is the *Toolbox* window in Visual Studio?

22. What is the standard toolbar in Visual Studio?

23. What is a tooltip?

24. If you do not see the *Solution Explorer* window in Visual Studio, how do you display it?

25. If you do not see the *Properties* window in Visual Studio, how do you display it?

26. Figure 1-30 shows the Visual Studio IDE. What are the names of the four areas that are indicated in the figure?

Figure 1-30 The Visual Studio IDE

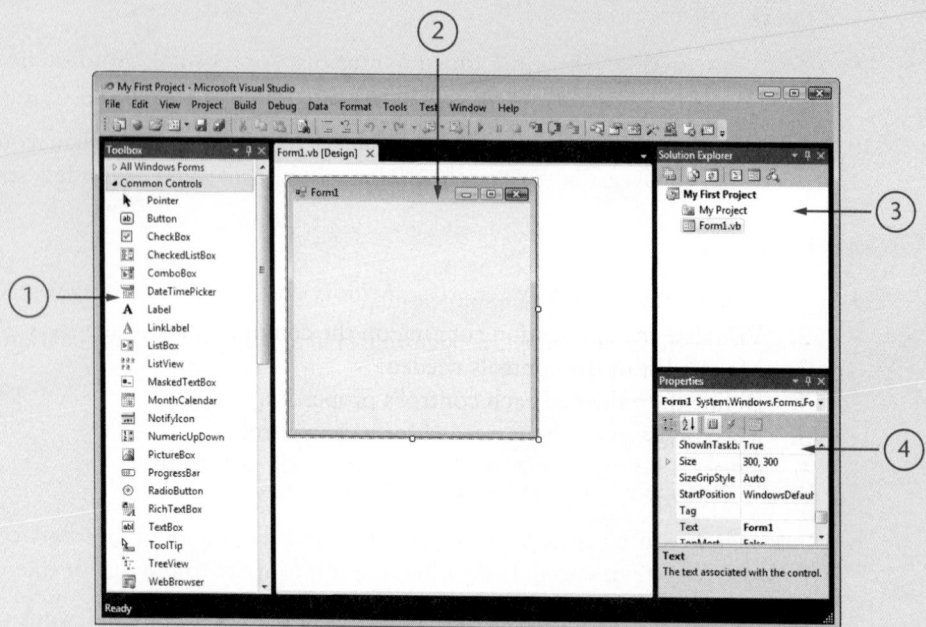

What Do You Think?

1. Are each of the following control names legal or illegal? If a name is illegal, indicate why.

   a. `txtUserName`
   b. `2001sales`
   c. `lblUser Age`
   d. `txtName/Address`
   e. `btnCalcSubtotal`

2. What type of control does each of the following prefixes usually indicate?

   a. `btn`
   b. `lbl`
   c. `txt`

3. For each of the following controls, make up a legal name that conforms to the standard control name convention described in this chapter.

   a. A TextBox control in which the user enters his or her last name
   b. A Button control that, when clicked, calculates an annual interest rate
   c. A Label control used to display the total of an order
   d. A Button control that clears all the input fields on a form

4. The following control names appear in a Visual Basic application used in a retail store. Indicate what type of control each is and guess its purpose.

   a. `txtPriceEach`
   b. `txtQuantity`
   c. `txtTaxRate`
   d. `btnCalcSale`
   e. `lblSubTotal`
   f. `lblTotal`

Programming Challenges

1. **Carpet Size**

   You have been asked to create an application for a carpet sales and installation business. The application should allow the user to enter the length and width of a room and calculate the room's area in square feet. The formula for this calculation is

   $$Area = Length \times Width$$

   In this exercise, you will gain practice using Steps 1 through 6 of the programming process described in Section 1.5:

   1. Clearly define what the application is to do.
   2. Visualize the application running on the computer and design its user interface.
   3. Make a list of the controls needed.
   4. Define the values of each control's properties.
   5. Make a list of methods needed for each control.
   6. Create a flowchart or pseudocode version of each method.

   Step 1: Describe the following characteristics of this application:

   > Purpose
   > Input
   > Process
   > Output

   Step 2: Draw a sketch of the application's form and place all the controls that are needed.

   Step 3: Make a list of the controls you included in your sketch. List the control type and the name of each control.

   Step 4: List the value of the Text property for each control, as needed. (Remember, some controls do not have a Text property.)

   Step 5: List each method needed. Give the name of each method and describe what each method does.

   Step 6: For each method you listed in Step 5, draw a flowchart or write pseudocode.

2. **Available Credit**

   A retail store gives each of its customers a maximum amount of credit. A customer's available credit is determined by subtracting the amount of credit used by the customer from the customer's maximum amount of credit. As you did in Programming Challenge 1, perform Steps 1 through 6 of the programming process to design an application that determines a customer's available credit.

VideoNote

Solving the
Sales Tax
Problem

3. **Sales Tax**

   Perform Steps 1 through 6 of the programming process to design an application that gets from the user the amount of a retail sale and the sales tax rate. The application should calculate the amount of the sales tax and the total of the sale.

4. **Account Balance**

   Perform Steps 1 through 6 of the programming process to design an application that gets from the user the starting balance of a savings account, the total dollar amount of the deposits made to the account, and the total dollar amount of withdrawals made from the account. The application should calculate the account balance.

2 Creating Applications with Visual Basic

TOPICS

In this chapter you will develop your first application, which displays a map and written directions to the Highlander Hotel. This application uses a form with labels, a PictureBox control, and buttons. You will write your first event handlers in Visual Basic code and then you will learn to use the Label control's AutoSize, BorderStyle, and TextAlign properties. You will be introduced to clickable images, context-sensitive help, and the debugging process.

2.1 Focus on Problem Solving: Building the *Directions* Application

CONCEPT: In this section you create your first Visual Basic application: a window that displays a map and road directions to a hotel. In the process you learn how to place controls on a form and manipulate various properties.

The desk clerks at the historic Highlander Hotel frequently receive calls from guests requesting driving directions. Some desk clerks are not familiar with the street numbers or exits, and inadvertently give unclear or incorrect directions. The hotel manager has asked you to create an application that displays a map to the hotel. The desk clerks can refer to the application when giving directions to customers over the phone. We will use the following steps to create the application:

1. Clearly define what the application is to do.
2. Visualize the application running on the computer and design its user interface.
3. Determine the controls needed.
4. Define the values of each control's relevant properties.
5. Start Visual Basic and create the forms and other controls.

Now we will take a closer look at each of these steps.

1. Clearly define what the application is to do.

Purpose: Display a map to the Highlander Hotel
Input: None
Process: Display a form
Output: Display on the form a graphic image showing a map

2. Visualize the application running on the computer and design its user interface.

Before you create an application on the computer, first you should create it in your mind. This step is the visualization of the program. Try to imagine what the computer screen will look like while the application is running. Then draw a sketch of the form or forms in the application. Figure 2-1 shows a sketch of the *Directions* form presented by this application.

Figure 2-1 Sketch of *Directions* form

3. Determine the controls needed.

In this step you list all the needed controls. You should assign names to all the controls that will be accessed or manipulated in the application code and provide a brief description of each control. Our application needs only three controls, listed in Table 2-1. Because none of the controls are used in code, we will keep their default names.

Table 2-1 *Directions* application controls

Control Type	Control Name	Description
Form	(Default Name: *Form1*)	A small form that will serve as the window onto which the other controls will be placed
Label	(Default Name: *Label1*)	Displays the message *Directions to the Highlander Hotel*
PictureBox	(Default Name: *PictureBox1*)	Displays the graphic image showing the map to the hotel

4. Define the values of each control's relevant properties.

Each control's property settings are listed in Table 2-2.

Table 2-2 *Directions* application control properties

Property	Value
Form	
Name	*Form1*
Text	*Directions*
Label	
Name	*Label1*
Text	*Directions to the Highlander Hotel*
Font	Microsoft sans serif, bold, 16 point
PictureBox	
Name	*PictureBox1*
Image	*HotelMap.jpg*
SizeMode	*StretchImage*

Notice that in addition to the Name and Text properties, we are also setting the Font property of the Label control. We will discuss this property in detail later.

In addition to its Name property, we are setting the PictureBox control's Image and Size-Mode properties. The Image property lists the name of the file containing the graphic image. We will use *HotelMap.jpg*, which is located in the student sample programs folder named *Chap2*. The **SizeMode property** is set to *StretchImage*, which allows us to resize the image. If the image is too small, we can enlarge it (stretch it). If it is too large, we can shrink it.

5. Start Visual Basic and create the forms and other controls.

Now you are ready to construct the application's form. Tutorial 2-1 gets you started.

Tutorial 2-1:
Beginning the *Directions* application

In this tutorial you begin the *Directions* application. You will create the application's form and use the *Properties* window to set the form's Text property.

Step 1: Start Visual Studio (or Visual Basic Express), as you did in Chapter 1. Perform *one* of the following actions to create a new project:

- On the *Start Page* click the *New Project* icon
- Click *File* on the menu bar and then select *New Project...*
- Press Ctrl+N on the keyboard

The *New Project* window will appear. If you are using Visual Studio, under *Installed Templates* select *Visual Basic*. Then, in either Visual Studio or Visual Basic Express select *Windows Forms Application*.

The default project name, such as *WindowsApplication1*, appears in the *Name* text box. Replace this name with **Directions**. Click the *OK* button to close the window.

Step 2: The Visual Basic environment should be open with a blank form named *Form1* in the *Designer* window, as shown in Figure 2-2. Click the form to select it.

Figure 2-2 *Form1* displayed in the *Designer* window

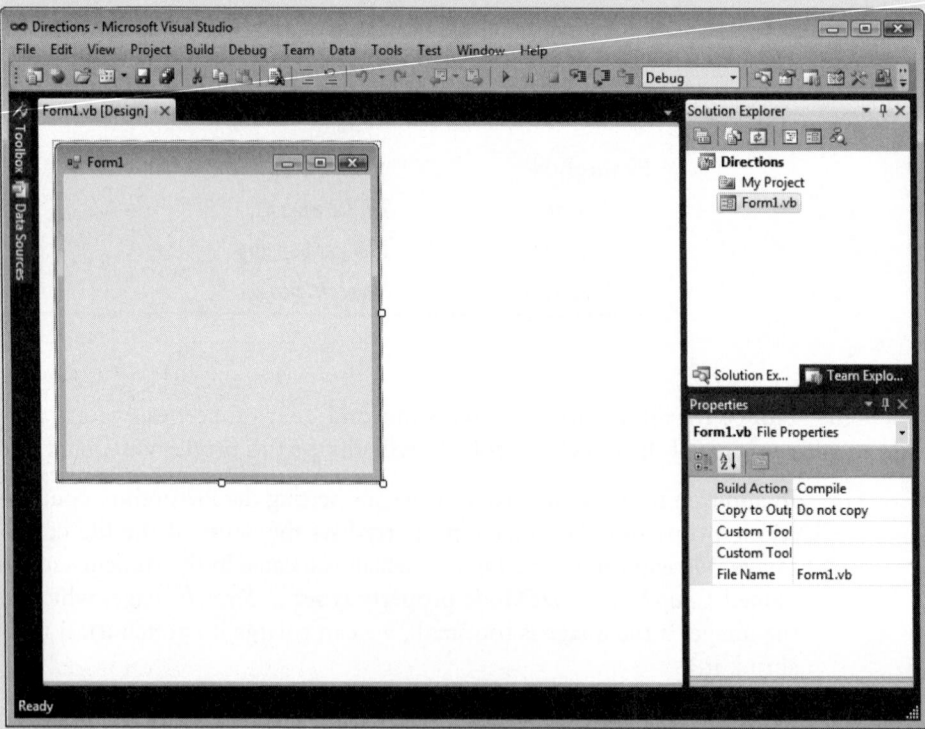

Step 3: Look at the *Properties* window. It should appear as shown in Figure 2-3.

Because you have selected *Form1*, the *Properties* window displays the properties for the *Form1* object. The drop-down list box at the top of the window shows the name of the selected object, *Form1*. Below that, the object's properties are displayed in two columns. The left column lists each property's name and the right column shows each property's value. The area at the bottom of the *Properties* window shows a brief description of the currently selected property.

> **TIP:** The *Properties* window has two buttons near the top that control the order of names in the window. The first (▦) sorts by category and the second (↕) sorts alphabetically. We will use the alphabetical sort in our examples.

The Text property is highlighted, which means it is currently selected. A form's Text property holds the text displayed in the form's title bar. It is initially set to the same value as the form name, so this form's Text property is set to *Form1*. Follow the instructions in Steps 4 and 5 to change the Text property to *Directions*.

Step 4: In the *Properties* window, double-click the word *Form1* inside the Text property.

Step 5: Delete the word *Form1* and type **Directions** in its place. Press the (Enter) key. Notice that the word *Directions* now appears in the form's title bar.

> **NOTE:** Remember, changing a form's Text property changes only the text that is displayed in the form's title bar. The form's name is still *Form1*.

Step 6: Perform *one* of the following actions to save the project:
- Click the Save All button (▣) on the standard toolbar
- Click File on the menu bar and then select Save All
- Press Ctrl+Shift+S on the keyboard

Because this is the first time you have saved the project, you will see the *Save Project* window. In that window, click the *Save* button to save the project at the specified location. Then, leave Visual Studio running for Tutorial 2-2, which takes you through the process of adding a Label control to the form.

Figure 2-3 *Properties* window showing *Form1*

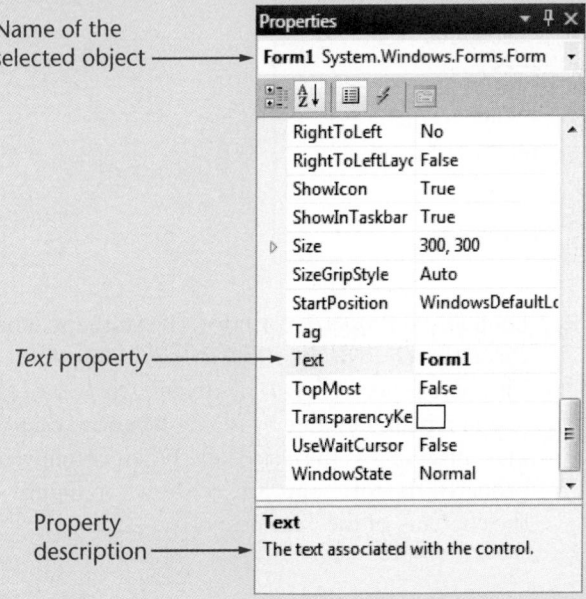

Tutorial 2-2:
Adding a Label control to the *Directions* application

VideoNote

Tutorial 2-2
Walkthrough

Step 1: Now you are ready to add the Label control to the form. Make sure the *Common Controls* tab is open in the *Toolbox* window, as shown in Figure 2-4, and double-click the *Label* control icon. The label appears on the form with a dotted line around it and a small white square in its upper left corner, as shown in Figure 2-5. The dotted-line rectangle is called a **bounding box**—it marks the tightest rectangle that contains all parts of the control.

Figure 2-4 Label control tool

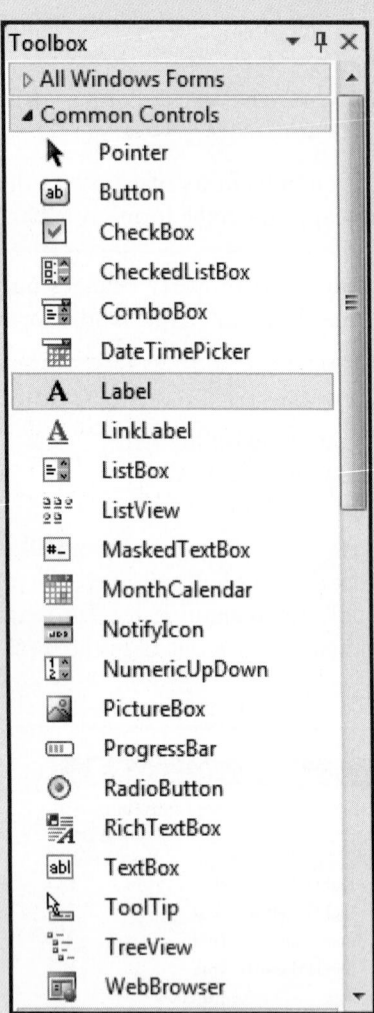

Figure 2-5 Label control on form

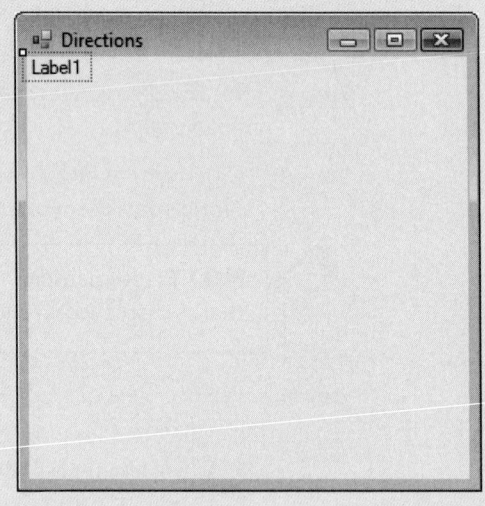

Step 2: Look at the *Properties* window. Because the label you just placed on the form is currently selected, the *Properties* window shows its properties (see Figure 2-6). The Text property is set, by default, to *Label1*. Double-click this value to select it, and replace its value by typing **Directions to the Highlander Hotel** in its place. Press the [Enter] key. When you have typed the new text into the Text property, the form appears, as shown in Figure 2-7. The label resizes itself to fit the contents of the Text property.

Figure 2-6 *Properties* window

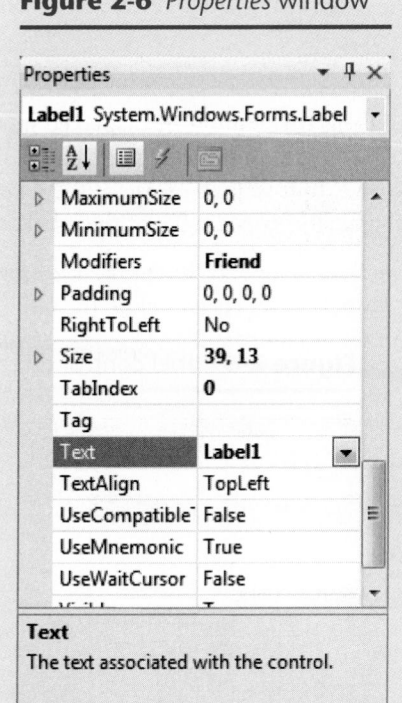

Figure 2-7 Label with new text property value

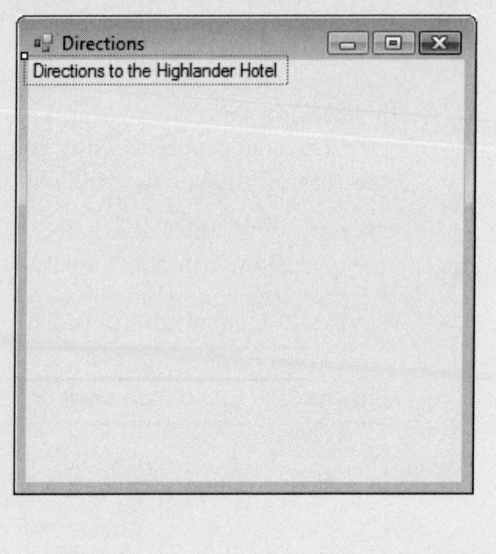

Step 3: Next, you will move the label to a new location on the form. Move the mouse over the label on the form. Notice that when the mouse pointer is over the label, it becomes a four-headed arrow (✥). Hold down the left mouse button, and drag the label to the top middle area of the form, as shown in Figure 2-8. From now on, we will refer to this type of operation as *dragging the control*.

Figure 2-8 After moving the Label control

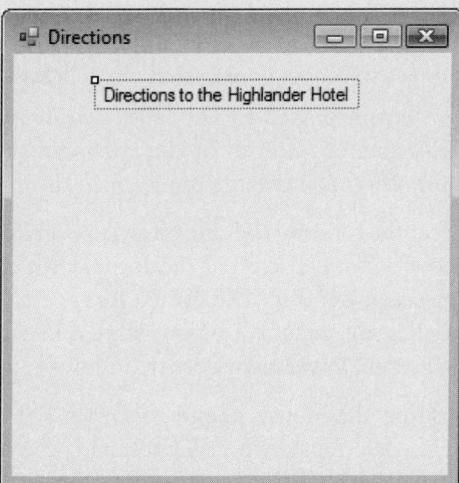

Step 4: Save the project. Leave Visual Studio running for Tutorial 2-3, which takes you through the process of changing the Label control's font size and style.

Tutorial 2-3:
Changing the Label's font size and style

In the planning phase, we indicated that the label's text should be displayed in a 16-point bold Microsoft sans serif font. These characteristics are controlled by the label's Font property. The **Font property** allows you to set the font, font style, and size of the label's text. In this tutorial you will use the Font property change the appearance of the label's text.

Step 1: With the Label selected, click the *Font* property in the *Properties* window. Notice that an ellipsis button (⊡) appears. When you click the ellipsis button, the *Font* dialog box appears, as shown in Figure 2-9.

Figure 2-9 *Font* dialog box

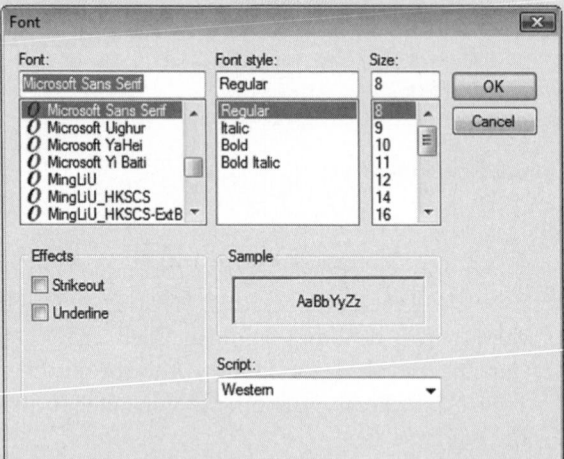

Step 2: *Microsoft Sans Serif* is already the selected font. Click *Bold* under *Font style*, and select *16* under *Size*. Notice that the text displayed in the *Sample* box changes to reflect your selections. Click the *OK* button.

The text displayed by the label is now in 16-point bold Microsoft sans serif. Unfortunately, not all of the label can be seen because it is too large for the form. You must enlarge the form so the entire label is visible.

Step 3: Select the form by clicking anywhere on it, except on the Label control. You will know you have selected the form when a thin dotted line with **sizing handles** appears around it. The dotted line is the form's bounding box, and the sizing handles are the small boxes, shown in Figure 2-10, that appear on the form's right edge, lower right corner, and bottom edge.

Step 4: Position the mouse pointer over the sizing handle that appears on the form's right edge. As shown in Figure 2-11, the mouse pointer becomes a two-headed arrow (⟷). Click and drag the sizing handle to widen the form. Then, select the label and move it so it appears similar to Figure 2-12.

Figure 2-10 The form selected, with sizing handles shown

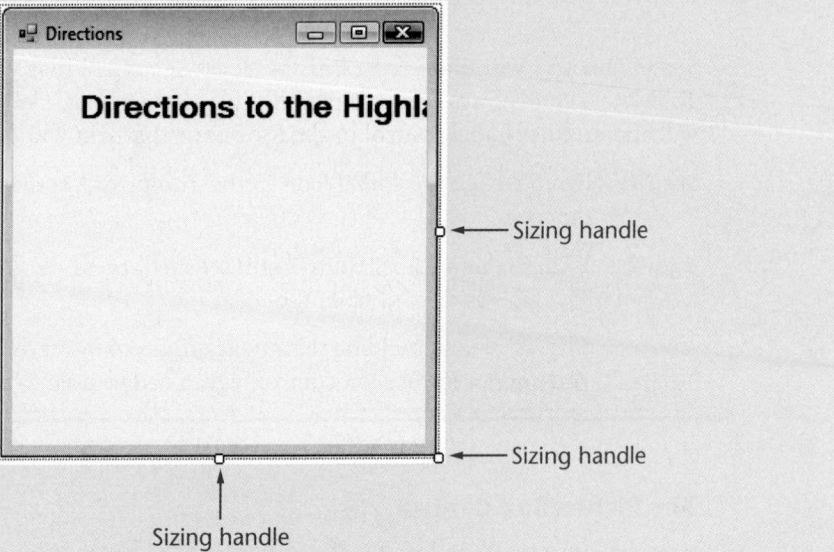

Figure 2-11 The mouse pointer positioned over the form's right edge sizing handle

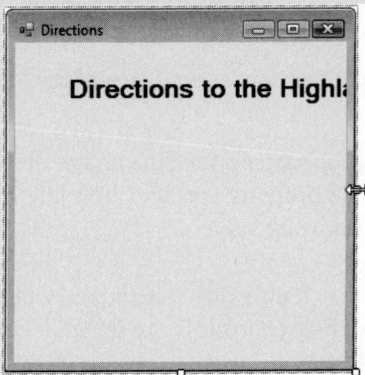

Figure 2-12 The form widened and the label repositioned

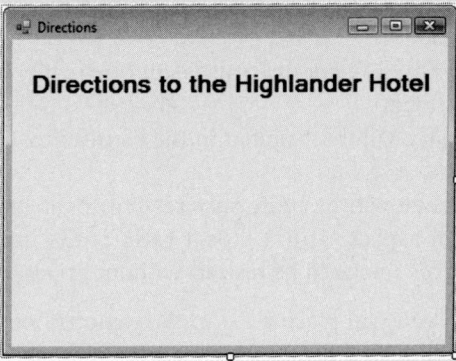

Step 5:   Save the project. Leave Visual Studio running for Tutorial 2-4, which takes you through the process of deleting a control.

Tutorial 2-4:
Deleting a control

Sometimes you will find it necessary to delete a control that you have placed on a form. To delete a control, select it and press the (Delete) key on the keyboard. In this tutorial you will add another Label control to the form (one that you will not need) and then delete it.

Step 1: Double-click the *Label* icon in the *Toolbox*. Another Label control appears on the form.

Step 2: With the new Label control still selected, press the (Delete) key on the keyboard. The label is deleted from the form.

The last step in building this application is to insert the street map. In Tutorial 2-5 you insert a PictureBox control, which can be used to display an image.

The PictureBox Control

If you want to display a graphic image on an application's form, you use a **PictureBox control**. A PictureBox control can display images that have been saved in the bitmap, GIF, JPEG, metafile, or icon graphics formats. When a PictureBox control is placed on a form, it appears as an empty rectangle in which the image will be displayed. You can adjust the PictureBox control's size to make the image any size that you want.

The PictureBox control has several properties, but the following two properties are of particular interest:

- The **Image property** specifies the image file that is to be displayed by the control.
- The **SizeMode property** specifies how the image is to be displayed. It can be set to one of the following values:
  - **Normal**
    This is the default value. The image will be positioned in the upper-left corner of the PictureBox control. If the image is too big to fit in the PictureBox control, it will be clipped.
  - **StretchImage**
    The image will be resized both horizontally and vertically to fit in the PictureBox control. If the image is resized more in one direction than the other, it will appear stretched.
  - **AutoSize**
    The PictureBox control will be automatically resized to fit the size of the image.
  - **CenterImage**
    The image will be centered in the PictureBox control, without being resized.
  - **Zoom**
    The image will be uniformly resized to fit in the PictureBox without losing its original aspect ratio. (**Aspect ratio** is the image's width to height ratio.) This causes the image to be resized without appearing stretched.

In Tutorial 2-5 you will place a PictureBox control on the application's form and set the control's properties so it displays the street map image.

Tutorial 2-5:
Inserting a PictureBox control

VideoNote

Tutorial 2-5
Walkthrough

Step 1: Locate the *PictureBox* icon in the *Toolbox*. You will find it in the Common Controls group. (The tools are listed in alphabetical order.) When you locate the *PictureBox* tool, double-click it.

An empty PictureBox control appears on the form. Move the control to a position approximately in the center of the form, as shown in Figure 2-13.

Figure 2-13 PictureBox control placed

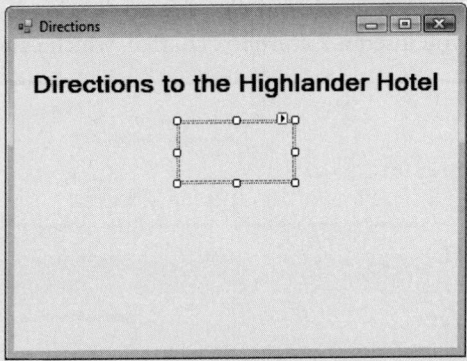

Step 2: Now you will specify the image that the PictureBox control will display. Locate the PictureBox control's Image property in the *Properties* window. The Image property is currently set to *(none)*, which means that no image is displayed. Click the property and notice that a browse button (...) appears next to the property setting. Click the browse button. The *Select Resource* window, shown in Figure 2-14 should appear.

Step 3: As indicated in Figure 2-14, in the *Select Resource* window select *Local Resource,* and then click the *Import* button. When the *Open* dialog box appears, navigate to the folder on your computer where the student sample files are located. Then, in the *Chap2* folder select the file named *HotelMap.jpg*. After you click the OK button, you should see the graphic shown in the *Select Resource* window, as shown in Figure 2-15. Click the OK button to accept the image, and you will see it displayed in the PictureBox control.

Your form should appear similar to Figure 2-16. As you can see from the figure, only part of the image is displayed. This is because the PictureBox control is smaller than the image, and the SizeMode property is set to its default value, *Normal*.

Figure 2-14 The Select Resource window

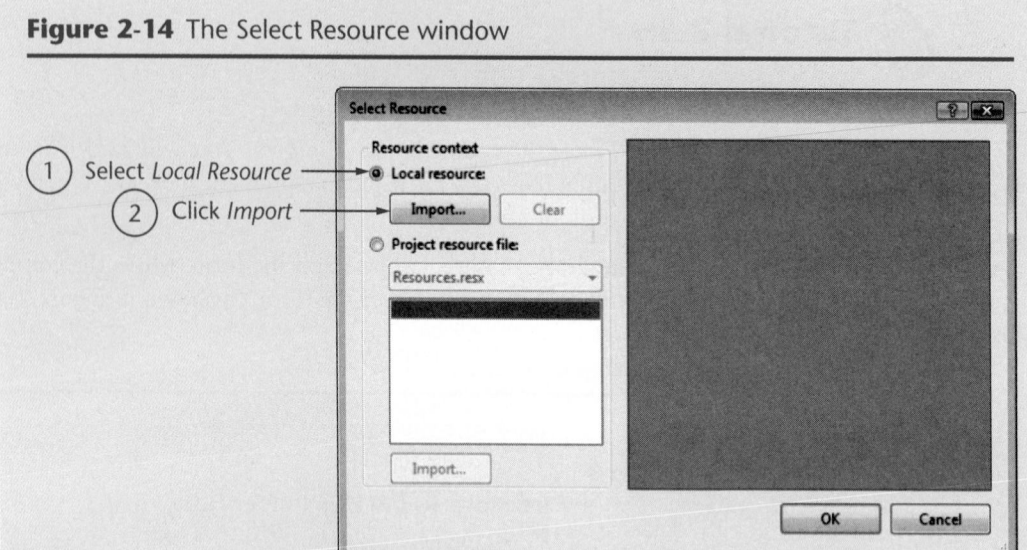

Figure 2-15 The HotelMap.jpg file selected

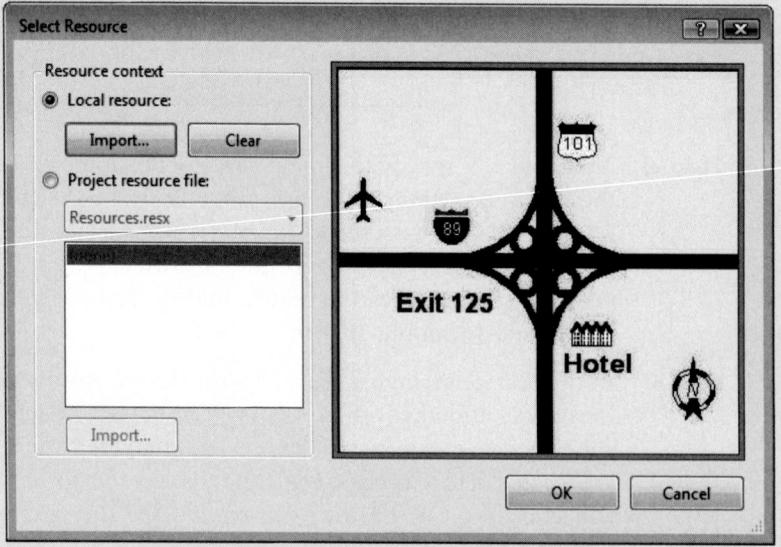

Figure 2-16 The HotelMap.jpg image partially displayed in the PictureBox control

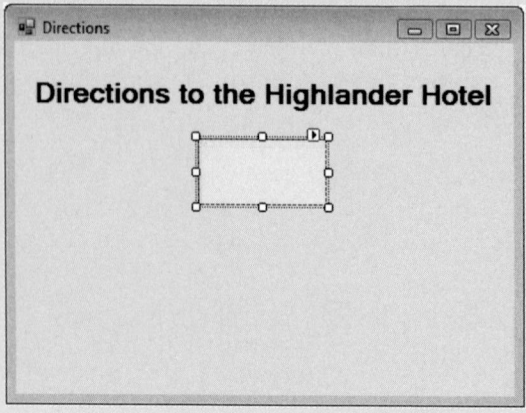

Step 4:   Make sure the PictureBox control is selected, and locate the SizeMode property in the Properties window. Notice that the SizeMode property is currently set to *Normal*. When you click the SizeMode property in the *Properties* window, a down arrow (⏷) appears next to the property value.

Click the down arrow and a drop-down list appears, as shown in Figure 2-17. The list shows all of the possible values for the SizeMode property. Select *Zoom* from the list. This setting will resize the image so it fits within the bounding box of the PictureBox control, without losing the image's original aspect ratio. (In other words, the image will not appear stretched.) Figure 2-18 shows an example of how the form will appear.

Figure 2-17 A drop-down list showing the possible values of the SizeMode property

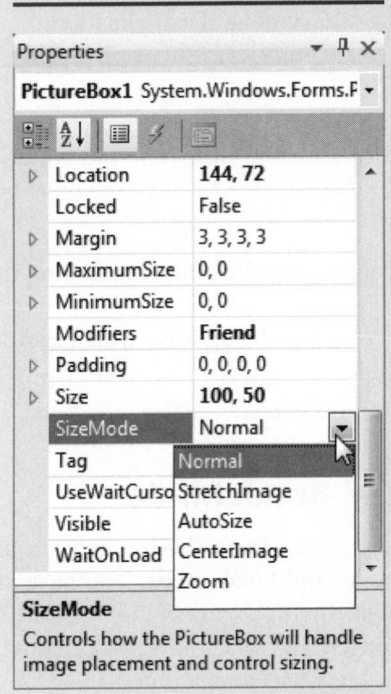

Figure 2-18 The image resized uniformly

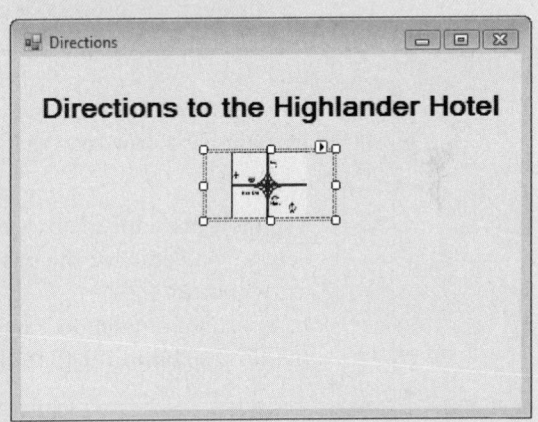

Step 5:   Although the image has been resized, the PictureBox shown in our example (in Figure 2-18) is too small. You can use the PictureBox's sizing handles to resize the PictureBox control so the image is displayed at the desired size. Resize and move the PictureBox control so the form appears similar to Figure 2-19.

Figure 2-19 The PictureBox control resized

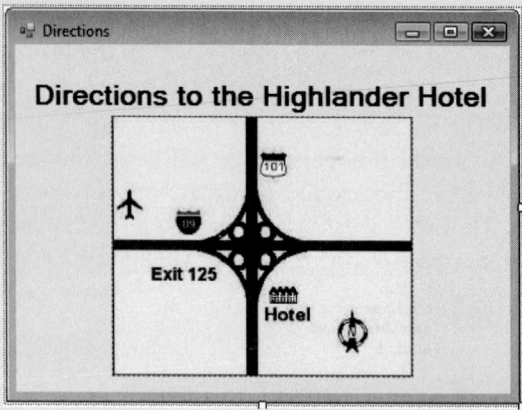

Step 6: Save the project. Leave Visual Studio running for Tutorial 2-6, which takes you through the process of compiling and running the application.

NOTE: You have now seen that properties are set in the *Properties* window in one of three ways:

- Typing a value for the property
- Selecting a value for the property from a drop-down list by clicking the down-arrow button ()
- Establishing a value for the property with a dialog box, which appears when the *Browse* button () is clicked

Design Mode, Run Mode, and Break Mode

Visual Basic has three modes in which it operates as you develop and test an application. The three modes are design mode, run mode, and break mode. You have already experienced **design mode**. This is the mode in which you create an application. When you are placing controls on an application's form or writing Visual Basic code, Visual Basic is operating in design mode. (Design mode is also known as **design time**.)

When you are ready to run an application that you are developing, you can execute it without leaving the Visual Studio environment. This puts Visual Basic in **run mode** (also known as **runtime**). The application will be running on the computer, and you can interact with it as the user. There are three ways to run an application from the Visual Studio environment:

- Click the *Start Debugging* button ( ) on the toolbar
- Click *Debug* on the menu bar, then select *Start Debugging*
- Press the F5 key

When you perform one of these actions, the Visual Basic compiler will begin compiling the application. If no errors are found, the application will begin executing and Visual Basic will enter run mode. You will experience run mode in the next tutorial.

Break mode is a special mode that allows you to momentarily suspend a running application for testing and debugging purposes. It is also the mode that Visual Basic enters when a running application encounters a runtime error. (Recall from Chapter 1 that a runtime error is an error that occurs while a program is running.) We will discuss break mode in Chapter 3.

Closing a Project

To close the current project, click *File* on the menu bar, and then click *Close Project*. If you have made changes to the project since the last time you saved it, you will see a window similar to Figure 2-20 asking you if you want to save your changes. If you want to save your changes (in most cases you do), click *Yes*.

Figure 2-20 *Save changes* window

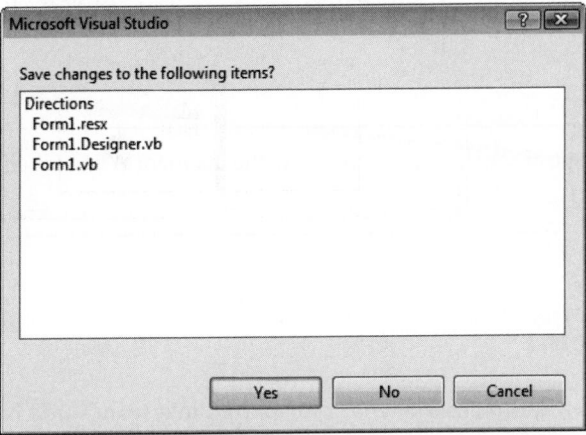

Tutorial 2-6:
Running the application

VideoNote

Tutorial 2-6
Walkthrough

Step 1: Now you will run the *Directions* application. It doesn't have any event handlers, so it will display only the PictureBox and Label when it runs. Perform one of the following actions to run the application:

- Click the *Start Debugging* button (▶) on the toolbar
- Click *Debug* on the menu bar, then select *Start Debugging*
- Press the F5 key

Step 2: The Visual Basic compiler will begin compiling the application. (Recall from Chapter 1 that the compiler translates the application to executable code.) After a few moments, the compiler will finish and the application will run. You should see the application's form appear on the screen, as shown in Figure 2-21.

Figure 2-21 The application running

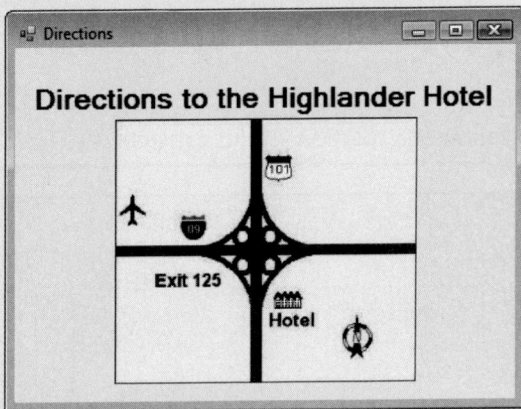

Step 3: Now you will stop the application (end its execution). Perform *one* of the following actions:

- Click the *Close* button ( ) on the application window
- Click *Debug* on the Visual Studio menu bar, then select *Stop Debugging*
- Press Ctrl+Alt+Break on the keyboard

The application will stop and Visual Studio will return to Design mode.

Step 4: If you have not recently saved the project, do so now. Then, close the project.

TIP: Save your work often to prevent the accidental loss of changes you have made to your project.

 Checkpoint

2.1 You want to change what is displayed in a form's title bar. Which of its properties do you change?

2.2 How do you insert a Label control onto a form?

2.3 What is the purpose of a control's sizing handles?

2.4 How do you delete a control?

2.5 What happens when you set a PictureBox control's SizeMode property to *StretchImage*?

2.6 What is the name of the dotted-line rectangle surrounding the Label control when looking at a form in Design mode?

2.7 What are the three modes in which Visual Studio operates?

How Solutions and Projects are Organized on the Disk

Now that you've created your first Visual Basic project, let's take a look at the way the project's files are organized on your computer's disk. A **solution** is a container that holds Visual Basic projects (see Figure 2-22). Each Visual Basic project must belong to a solution. Although it is possible for a solution to hold more than one project, each project that you will create in this book will be saved in its own solution. So, each time you create a new project, you will also create a new solution to hold it.

Figure 2-22 Organization of a solution and its projects

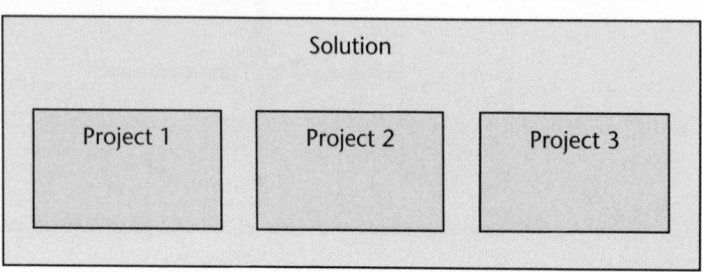

When you save a project the first time, you see the *Save Project* window shown in Figure 2-23. The window shows the project name, the location on the disk where the project will be saved, and the solution name. By default the solution's name will be the same as the project's name. Notice the *Browse . . .* button that appears next to the location. You can click this button to select a different location, if you wish.

Also notice the *Create directory for solution* check box. It is a good idea to leave this box checked. It causes a directory (folder) for the solution to be created at the specified location. Inside that directory, another directory (folder) will be created for the project.

Figure 2-23 The *Save Project* window

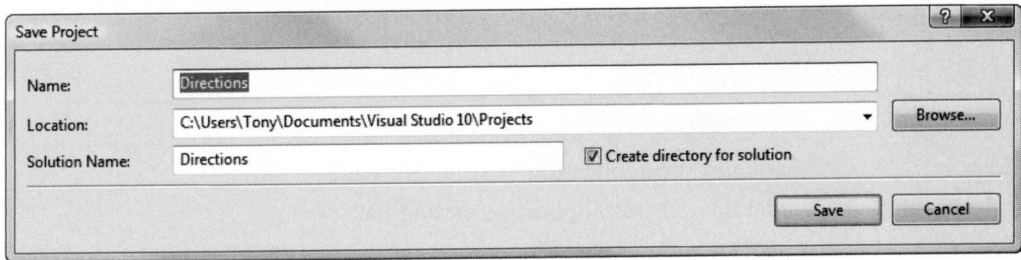

Let's use Figure 2-23 to see an example of how the files for the *Directions* project will be organized on the disk. Notice that the location specified is:

```
C:\Users\Tony\Documents\Visual Studio 10\Projects
```

At this location, a folder named *Directions* will be created to hold the solution. If we use Windows to look inside that folder we will see that it contains the two items shown in Figure 2-24. Notice that one of the items is another folder named *Directions*. That is the project folder. The *Directions.sln* file is the **solution file**. It contains information needed by Visual Studio about the solution. In Windows, you can double-click the solution file and the project will be loaded into Visual Studio.

Figure 2-24 Contents of the *Directions* solution folder

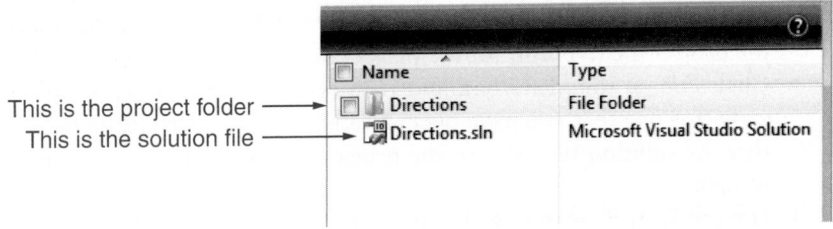

If we look inside the project folder, also named *Directions*, we will see the contents shown in Figure 2-25. There are several files and other folders in the project folder, which are briefly described in Table 2-3. These files and folders are all created and used by Visual Studio, so you will not have to directly manipulate them. It should be mentioned, however, that in Windows you can double-click the project file (in this case *Directions.vbproj*) to load the project into Visual Studio.

Figure 2-25 Contents of the *Directions* project directory

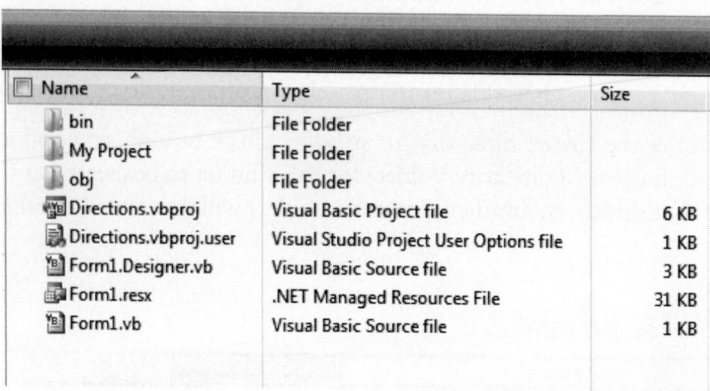

Table 2-3 Contents of the project folder

Item	Description
bin folder	contains the application's executable code
My Project folder	contains various application setting files
obj folder	holds temporary files that are created during the compilation process
Directions.vbproj	This is the project file. The **project file** contains information needed by Visual Studio about the *Directions* project. In Windows, you can double-click the project file and the project will be loaded into Visual Studio.
Directions.vbproj.user	This file contains information about Visual Studio's IDE settings.
Form1.Designer.vb	This file contains the Visual Basic code to generate the *Form1* form and all of the controls on it.
Form1.resx	This file contains information about various resources needed by *Form1* form.
Form1.vb	This file contains Visual Basic code that you write.

Opening an Existing Project

Once you've closed a Visual Basic project, you can open it again by performing any *one* of the following actions:

- Click *File* on the menu bar, and then select *Open Project . . .* The *Open Project* window will appear. Use the window to locate and select either the solution file (.sln) or the project file (.vbproj) for the project that you wish to open.
- Click *File* on the menu bar, and then select *Recent Projects and Solutions*. If the project is one that you have opened recently, it might be listed here. If it is, select either the solution file (.sln) or the project file (.vbproj) for the project that you wish to open.
- Use the *Start Page* to open the project. To display the *Start Page*, click *View* on the menu bar, then select *Start Page*. Then, as shown in Figure 2-26 either click the *Open Project* link to display the *Open Project* window, or select the name of project in the *Recent Projects* list.

Figure 2-26 Selecting a project from the *Recent Projects* list

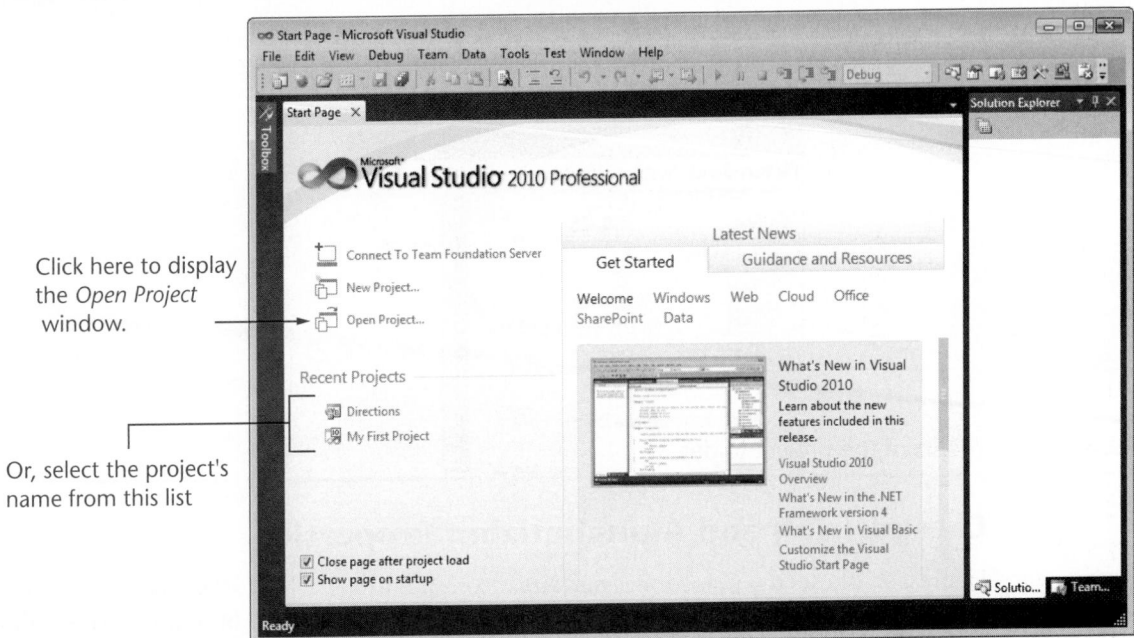

Click here to display the *Open Project* window.

Or, select the project's name from this list

Using the *Properties* Window to Select Controls

The box that appears at the top of the *Properties* window, shown in Figure 2-27, shows the name of the currently selected control. This is referred to as the **object box**. In the figure, the Label1 control is currently selected in the object box. If you click inside the object box, a drop-down list will appear showing the names of all of the objects in the form. Figure 2-28 shows an example. You can click the name of an object in the drop-down list to select it. This has the same effect as selecting a control in the *Designer* window. The selected object's properties will be displayed in the *Properties* window.

Figure 2-27 Name of the currently selected control

Name of the currently selected control

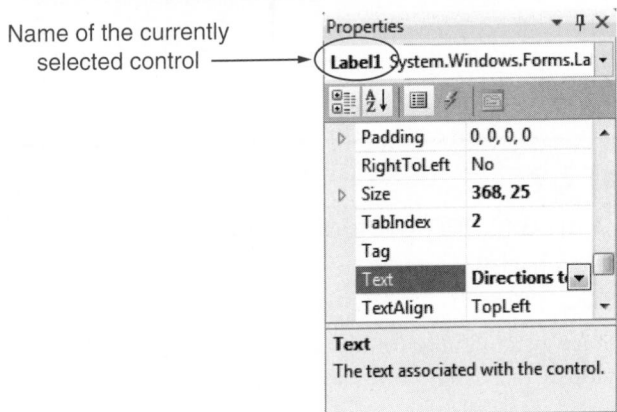

Figure 2-28 Drop-down list of the form's controls

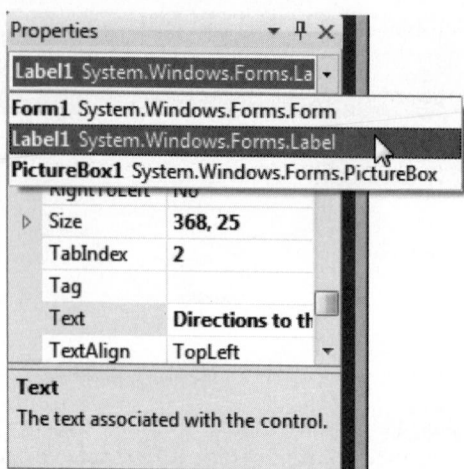

Categorizing and Alphabetizing Properties

Figure 2-29 shows the *Categorized* and *Alphabetical* buttons, which affect the way properties are displayed in the *Properties* window. When the **Alphabetical** button is selected, the properties are displayed in alphabetical order. When the **Categorized** button is selected, related properties are displayed together in groups. Most of the time, it will be easier for you to locate a specific property if the properties are listed in alphabetical order.

Perhaps you've noticed that a few of the properties shown in the *Properties* window, including the Name property, are enclosed in parentheses. Because these properties are used so often, the Visual Basic designers enclosed them in parentheses to make them appear at the top of the alphabetical list.

In Tutorial 2-7 you practice using these components of the *Properties* window.

Figure 2-29 The Categorized and Alphabetical buttons

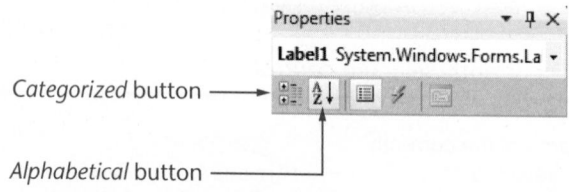

Tutorial 2-7:
Opening an existing project and becoming familiar with the *Properties* Window

Step 1: Start Visual Studio (or Visual Basic Express) and perform one of the actions previously discussed in this section to load the *Directions* project.

Step 2: Practice using the *Properties* window's drop-down list to select the *Label1*, *PictureBox1*, and *Form1* objects, as previously discussed in this section. Notice that as you select each object, its properties are displayed in the *Properties* window.

Step 3: Select the *Label1* control and click the *Categorized* button. Scroll through the list of properties displayed in the *Properties* window. Notice there are several categories of properties. When you are finished, click the *Alphabetical* button. Scroll through the list of properties and notice that they are listed in alphabetical order.

 **Checkpoint**

2.8 Describe three ways to open an existing project.

2.9 What are the two viewing modes for the *Properties* window? How do you select either of these modes? What is the difference between the two?

2.10 Open the *Directions* project. In the *Properties* window, arrange *Form1*'s properties in categorized order. Under what category does the Text property appear? Under what category does the Name property appear?

2.11 How can you select an object using only the *Properties* window?

2.2 Focus on Problem Solving: Responding to Events

CONCEPT: An application responds to events, such as mouse clicks and keyboard input, by executing code known as *event handlers*. In this section, you write event handlers for the *Directions* application.

VideoNote

Responding to Events

The manager of the Highlander Hotel reports that the *Directions* application has been quite helpful to the desk clerks. Some clerks, however, requested that the application be modified to display written directions as well as the map. Some also requested a more obvious way to exit the application, other than clicking the standard Windows *Close* button, located on the application's title bar.

You decide to add a button that is titled *Display Directions* to the application's form. When the user clicks the button, written directions to the hotel will appear in a Label control. You also decide to add an *Exit* button that the user can click to stop the application. Figure 2-30 shows the modified sketch of the form.

Figure 2-30 Modified *Directions* application sketch

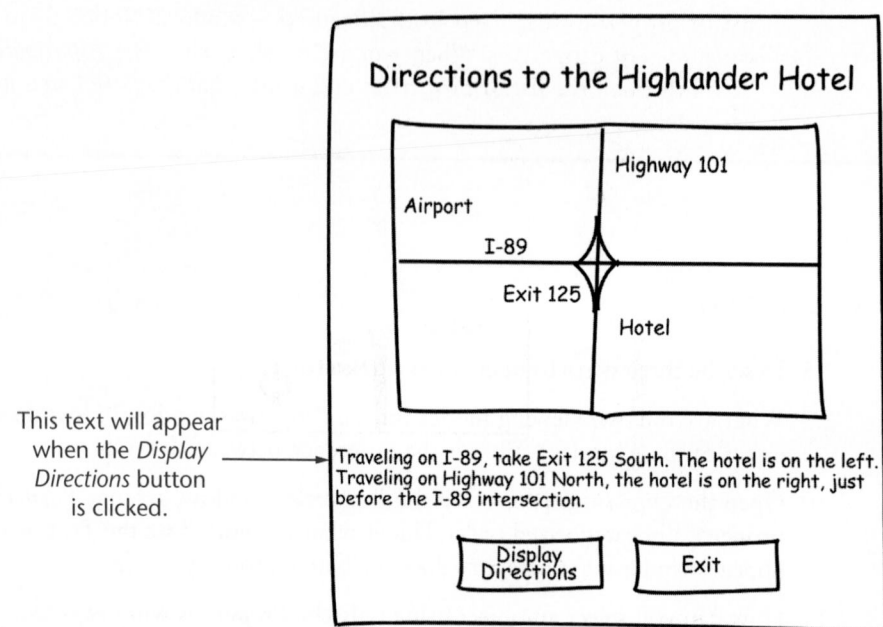

This text will appear when the *Display Directions* button is clicked.

When the application runs, the Label control that displays the written directions will initially be invisible. The Label control (and most other types of controls) has a property named Visible that determines whether it can be seen. The **Visible property** is a **Boolean property**, which means that it can hold only one of two values: True or False. If a control's Visible property is set to True, the control is visible. If a control's Visible property is set to False, however, the control is invisible. When we create the new Label control, to hold the written directions, we will use the Properties window to set its Visible property to False. This will cause it to initially be invisible when the application runs. Tutorial 2-8 leads you through the process.

Tutorial 2-8:
Adding a Label control for the written directions

VideoNote

Tutorial 2-8
Walkthrough

Step 1:   Start Visual Studio (or Visual Basic Express) and open the *Directions* project.

Step 2:   You will place the new controls at the bottom of the form, below the image of the map. Because the form is currently too small to accommodate the new controls, you will need to enlarge it. Select the form so its sizing handles are visible. Drag the bottom edge of the form down until it looks something like the one shown in Figure 2-31. (Don't worry about the exact size of the form. You can adjust it again later.)

Figure 2-31 *Directions* project with the form enlarged

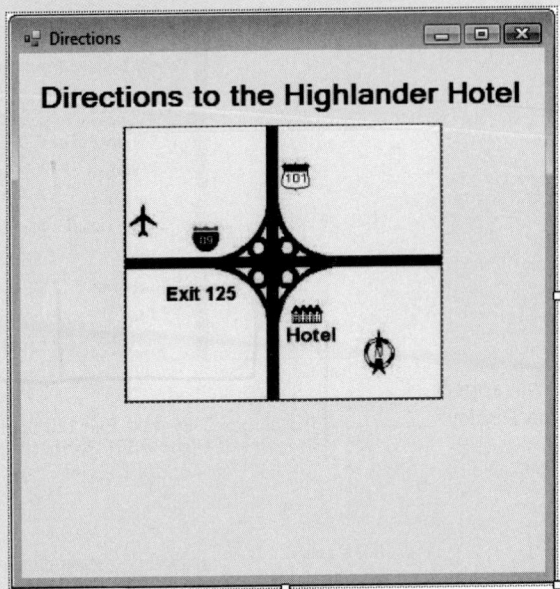

Step 3: Now you will add a new Label control to the form. Locate the Label control icon in the Toolbox and double-click it. This will create a new Label control positioned in the form's upper-left corner. Move the new Label control so it appears below the map image, at the approximate location shown in Figure 2-32.

Figure 2-32 New Label control moved below the map image

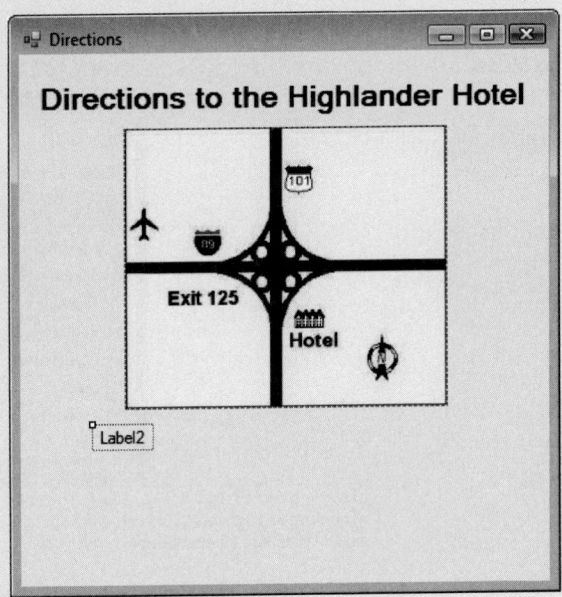

Step 4: Make sure the new Label control is still selected. In the *Properties* window, select the Text property, and then click the down-arrow button (⏷) that appears to the right of the property value. This opens an editing box as shown in Figure 2-33.

Figure 2-33 Editing box for the Label control's Text property

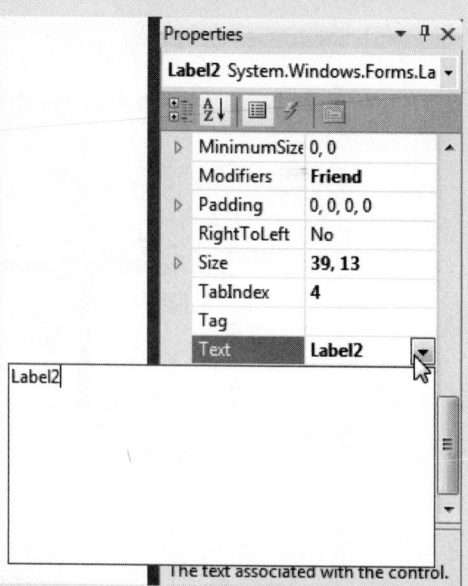

Step 5: Use the backspace key to delete the current contents of the editing box. Then type the following text. (Be sure to press Enter where specified.)

Traveling on I-89, take Exit 125 South. The hotel is on the left. ⌜Enter⌟ Traveling on Highway 101 North, the hotel is on the right, ⌜Enter⌟ just before the I-89 intersection.

The editing box should now appear as shown in Figure 2-34.

Figure 2-34 Editing box for the Label control's Text property

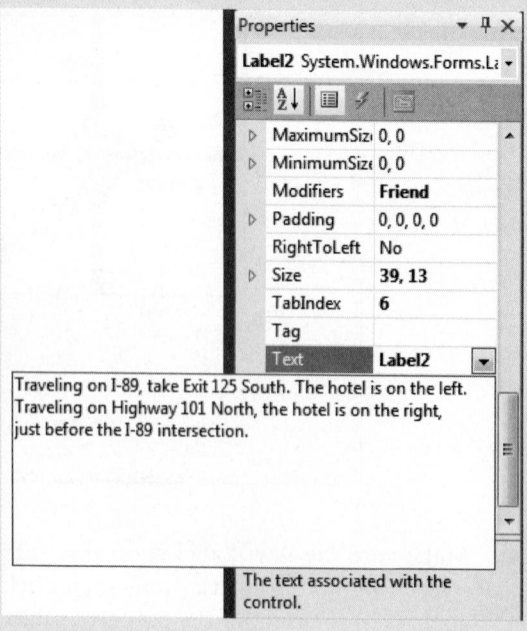

Step 6: Click the mouse anywhere outside of the editing box. This will cause the text you have typed to be saved in the Label control's Text property. The form should appear similar to Figure 2-35. (If necessary, move the Label control to match the approximate location shown in the figure.)

Figure 2-35 Label with the directions text entered

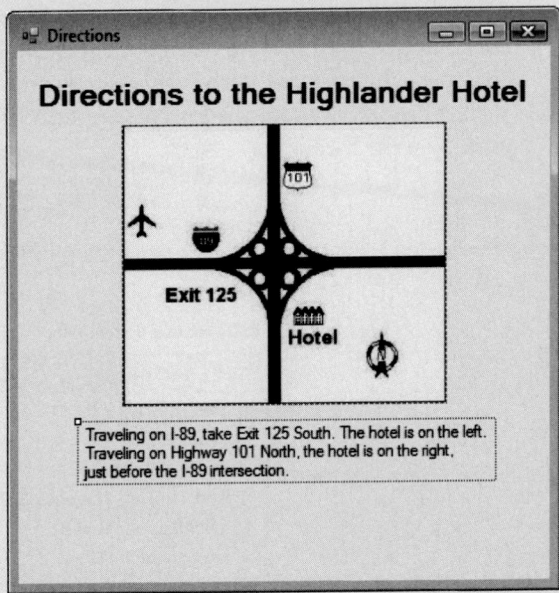

Step 7: Because we will refer to the new Label control in code, we should change the control's name to indicate its purpose. Make sure the Label control is still selected, and in the *Properties* window scroll up to the top of the property list. Near the top of the list, you will see the Name property. (Recall that the Name property is enclosed in parentheses so it appears near the top of the alphabetical listing.) Change the property's value to `lblDirections`, as shown in Figure 2-36. From this point forward we will refer to this label as the `lblDirections` control.

Figure 2-36 The Label control's name changed to `lblDirections`

Step 8: The last step is to change the `lblDirections` control's Visible property to False. With the control still selected, scroll down in the Properties window until you see the Visible property. Notice that the property is currently set to True. Click the down-arrow button (▾) that appears next to the property setting. A drop-down list containing the values *True* and *False* appears, as shown in Figure 2-37. Select *False*.

Even though you have set the `lblDirections` control's Visible property to False, notice that it is still visible in the *Designer* window. This is because all controls are displayed in the *Designer* window, regardless of the value of their Visible property. When you run the application, however, the control will not be visible on the form.

Figure 2-37 Setting the Visible property

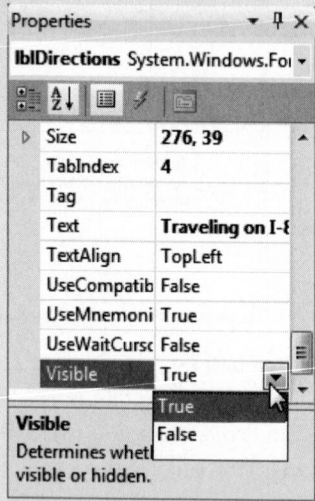

Step 9: Save the project. Leave Visual Studio running for Tutorial 2-9, which takes you through the process of adding a Button control and writing an event handler.

In the previous tutorial you added a Label control showing written directions to the hotel on the application's form. You named the control `lblDirections`, and you set its Visible property to False. Because its Visible property is set to False, the `lblDirections` control will not be visible on the form when the application runs. The next step is to add a Button control that, when clicked, causes the `lblDirections` control to appear at runtime. To make that happen, you will write an event handler that changes the `lblDirections` control's Visible property to True when the button is clicked. Tutorial 2-9 takes you through the process.

Tutorial 2-9:
Adding the *Display Directions* Button and its Click event handler

VideoNote
Tutorial 2-9
Walkthrough

Step 1: With the *Directions* project loaded into Visual Studio (or Visual Basic Express), click on the application's form in the *Designer* window to select it. Next, locate the Button control icon in the *Toolbox* and double-click it. This will create a new Button control positioned in the form's upper-left corner. Move the Button control so it appears at the approximate location shown in Figure 2-38.

Figure 2-38 New Button control added to the form

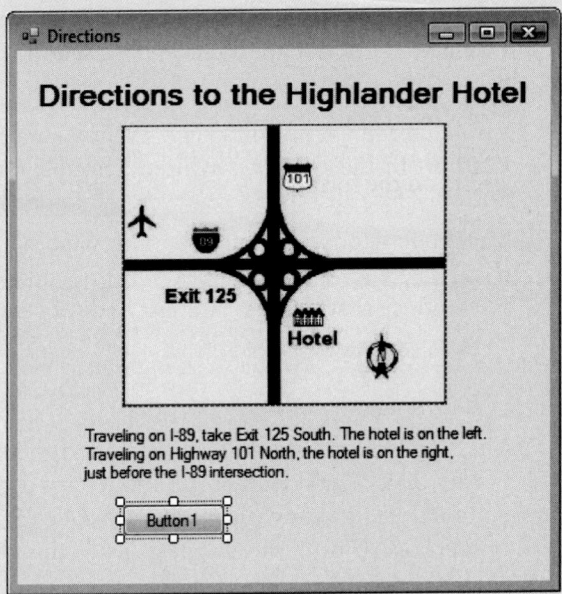

Step 2: With the button still selected, use the *Properties* window to change the button's Text property to *Display Directions*. This changes the text that is displayed on the face of the button.

Step 3: The button isn't quite large enough to accommodate this text, so use its sizing handles to increase its height, as shown in Figure 2-39.

Figure 2-39 Button control resized

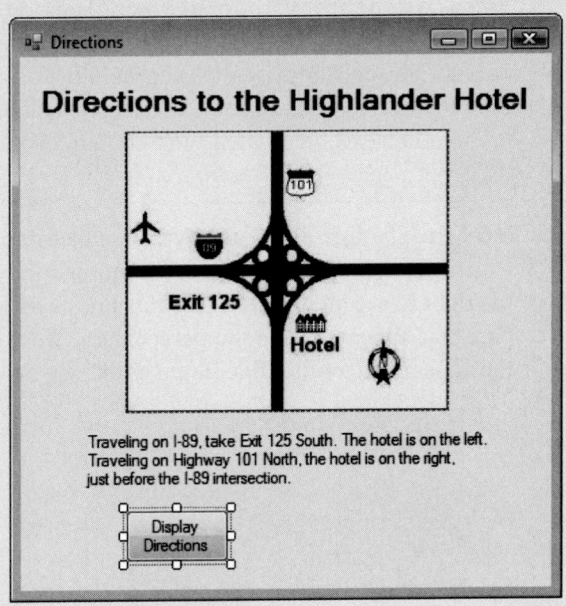

Step 4:   With the button still selected, scroll up in the *Properties* window and find the Name property. Notice that the button's name is currently set to `Button1`. Change the button's name to `btnDisplayDirections`.

Let's take a moment to think about why we changed the button's name. We did so because we will see the button's name appear in code later, and the default name, `Button1`, does not describe the control's purpose. The name `btnDisplayDirections` does describe the control: it is a button that displays directions.

Step 5:   Now you are ready to write the Click event handler for the `btnDisplayDirections` button. (A button's Click event handler executes when the user clicks the button.) In the *Designer* window, double-click the `btnDisplayDirections` button. This causes the *Code* window to open as shown in Figure 2-40.

The *Code* **window** is a text-editing window in which you write code. Notice that some code already appears in the window. Let's briefly discuss this code. First, notice that the first and last lines of code read:

```
Public Class Form1


End Class
```

These statements are the beginning and the end of a **class declaration** for the Form1 form. You'll learn more about class declarations in Chapter 12. For now, you just need to know that all of the code for the Form1 form (and all controls on the Form1 form) must appear inside this class declaration.

Next, notice that inside the class declaration, the following two lines of code appear:

We've left out the code that appears here.

```
Private Sub btnDisplayDirections_Click(…) Handles btnDisplayDirections.Click

End Sub
```

This is a **code template** for the `btnDisplayDirections` button's Click event handler. The template, which has been conveniently written for you, consists of the first and last lines of the event handler's code. Your job is to fill in the code that goes between these two lines. Any code that you write between these two lines will be executed when the `btnDisplayDirections` button is clicked.

> **NOTE:** The first line of the event handler template is a very long line of code. Unless you have a large monitor, you might have to scroll the *Code* window to the right to see all of it. Because this line of code is so long, we have left out the part that appears inside the parentheses. We will frequently do this to simplify the appearance of the code in the book.

Figure 2-40 The Code window opened with an event handler template

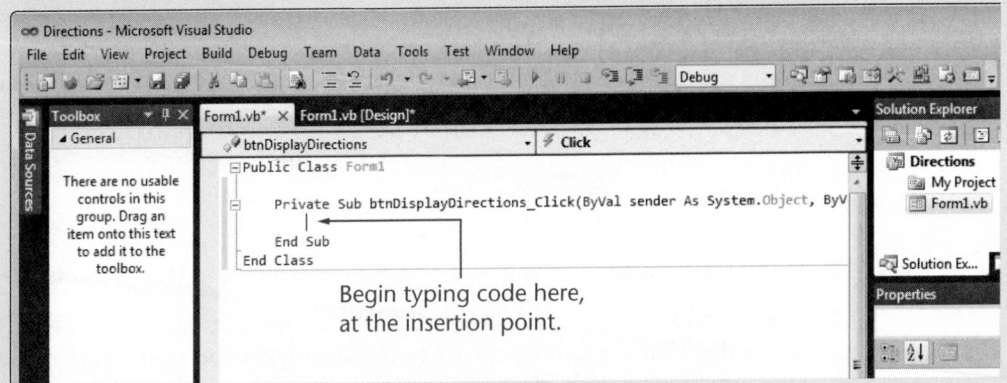

Step 6: Figure 2-40 shows the flashing cursor, known as the insertion point, appearing between the first and last lines of the event handler code template. If the insertion point is not located at the position shown in the figure, use the arrow keys on the keyboard to move it to this location. Then, type the following statement exactly as it appears here:

```
lblDirections.Visible = True
```

We will discuss this statement in greater detail after the tutorial, but here is a brief explanation: when this statement executes, it will set the lblDirections control's Visible property to True. As a result, the lblDirections control will become visible on the form.

After you have typed this statement, the *Code* window should appear as shown in Figure 2-41.

Figure 2-41 The statement written in the event handler

```
Public Class Form1

    Private Sub btnDisplayDirections_Click(ByVal sender As System
        lblDirections.Visible = True
    End Sub
End Class
```

Did you notice that as soon as you started typing the statement, a list box popped up on the screen? This is known as the **IntelliSense** list box. The contents of the list box changes as you type. Figure 2-42 shows the IntelliSense list box after you have typed the characters lbl.

IntelliSense is a feature of Visual Studio that helps you write code faster. As you type code, you will see these IntelliSense boxes popping up regularly. Later in this chapter we have included a section that explains more about IntelliSense. Until you've had time to read that section, just ignore the IntelliSense boxes.

Figure 2-42 IntelliSense list box displayed

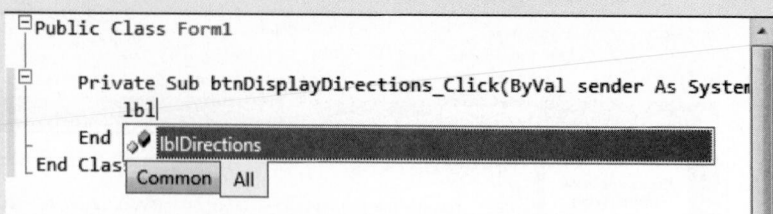

Step 7: This is a good time to save the project. Click the *Save All* button.

Step 8: Although you're not finished with the application, you can test the event handler that you just wrote. Click the *Start Debugging* button (▶) on the toolbar to run the application. After a moment the application will begin running and you will see the form displayed as shown in Figure 2-43. Notice that the written directions do not appear on the form.

Figure 2-43 The *Directions* application running

Step 9: Click the *Display Directions* button. The written directions appear on the form as shown in Figure 2-44.

Take a moment to review the following points about the application, and make sure you understand why it works the way that it does:

- When we created the lblDirections control, we set its Visible property to False in the *Properties* window. So, when the application starts, the control is not visible.
- When the btnDisplayDirections Button control is clicked, the event handler that you wrote sets the lblDirections control's Visible property to True, making it visible on the form.

Figure 2-44 The written directions displayed

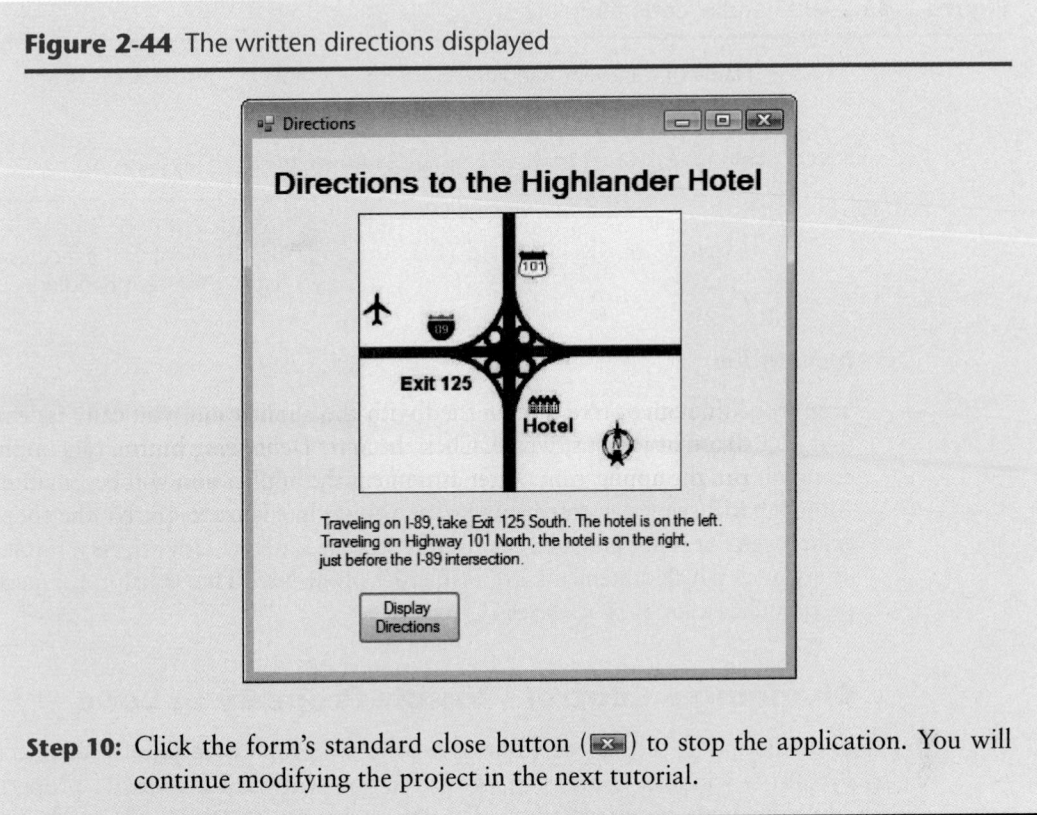

Step 10: Click the form's standard close button ( ) to stop the application. You will continue modifying the project in the next tutorial.

Before we finish developing the *Directions* application, let's discuss the concepts we covered in Tutorial 2-9 in greater depth.

Creating the Click Event Handler for
btnDisplayDirections

When a Button control appears on a form in the *Designer* window, you can double-click the Button control to edit the code for its Click event handler. You saw this happen in Step 5 of Tutorial 2-9. In that step, you double-clicked the btnDisplayDirections button. The *Code* window then opened, showing a code template for that button's Click event handler. Let's take a closer look at the code template, which is shown in Figure 2-45.

The first line starts with the keywords Private Sub. Following that is the name of the event handler, which in this case is btnDisplayDirections_Click. Following the name is some code that is enclosed in a set of parentheses. (As previously mentioned, we have left the contents of the parentheses out, here in the book, to simplify the figure.) After the parentheses are the words Handles btnDisplayDirections.Click. This tells us that the code handles the Click event when it happens to the btnDisplayDirections control.

The last line of the code template reads End Sub. These are keywords that mark the end of the event handler. Any code that you write between the first and last lines of the code template are executed, in the order in which they appear, when the event handler is invoked.

Figure 2-45 Event handler code template

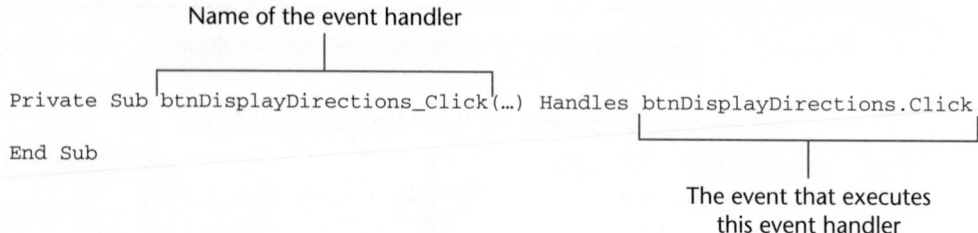

Name of the event handler

```
Private Sub btnDisplayDirections_Click(…) Handles btnDisplayDirections.Click

End Sub
```

The event that executes
this event handler

Indentation

You probably noticed in Tutorial 2-9 that Visual Studio automatically indented the code that you wrote inside the event handler. Indenting the statements inside a procedure is a common programming practice that makes code much easier for human eyes to read. Although indenting the statements inside a procedure is not required (the code will still execute, even if it is not indented), it visually sets the statements apart. As a result, you can tell at a glance which statements are inside the procedure. This is helpful, especially when a program has a lot of procedures.

Changing a Control's Visible Property in Code

In design mode, setting the value of a control's property is simple. You do so using the *Properties* window. Quite often, however, you will want a control's property to change while the application is running. The *Directions* project gives us a good example. While that application is running, the value of the `lblDirections` control's Visible property changes to True when the user clicks the *Display Directions* button. Recall from Tutorial 2-9 (Step 6) that you wrote code in the `btnDisplayDirections_Click` event handler to make that happen. Anytime you want a control's property to change during the application's runtime, you have to write code that performs the change.

Let's look again at the statement you wrote in the `btnDisplayDirections_Click` event handler in Tutorial 2-9:

```
lblDirections.Visible = True
```

This is called an **assignment statement**. The equal sign (=) is known as the **assignment operator**. It assigns the value that appears on its right side to the item that appears on its left side. In this example, the item on the left side of the assignment operator is the expression `lblDirections.Visible`. This simply means the `lblDirections` control's Visible property. The value on the right side of the assignment operator is the value True. When this statement executes, the value True is assigned to the `lblDirections` control's Visible property. As a result of this assignment statement, the `lblDirections` control becomes visible on the application form.

NOTE: In an assignment statement, the name of the item receiving the value must be on the left side of the = operator. The following statement, for example, is wrong:

```
True = lblDirections.Visible ← ERROR!
```

NOTE: The standard notation for referring to a control's property in code is *ControlName.PropertyName*. The period that appears between the control name and the property name is called a dot.

Switching Between the *Code* Window and the *Designer* Window

Before continuing with the next tutorial, we should discuss how to switch between the *Code* window and the *Designer* window. When developing a VB application you will often find yourself switching between these two windows.

When a form is created in a VB project, the code for that form is stored in a file with the same name as the form, followed by the .vb extension. For example, the form in the *Directions* project is named Form1, so its code will be stored in a file named Form1.vb. If you still have Visual Studio running from the previous tutorial, you should see the tabs shown in Figure 2-46 at the top of the *Code* window. One of the tabs reads *Form1.vb*, and another one reads *Form1.vb* [*Design*]. (The tabs on your screen might not be in this order.) In the figure, the tab that reads *Form1.vb* is highlighted, indicating that the *Code* window is currently opened. To switch to the *Designer* window, click the tab that reads *Form1.vb* [*Design*]. Then, to switch back to the *Code* window, click the tab that reads *Form1.vb*.

Figure 2-46 *Code* window and *Designer* window Tabs

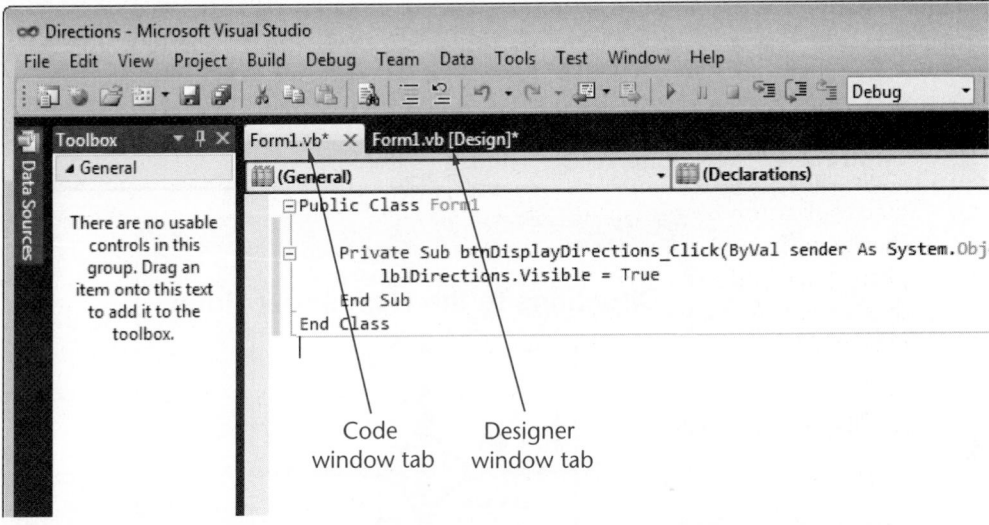

You can also use the *Solution Explorer* to switch between the *Code* window and the *Designer* window. First, make sure the form's code file is selected in the *Solution Explorer*. For example, in Figure 2-47 the Form1.vb file is selected. At the top of the *Solution Explorer* are two buttons that switch between the *Code* window and the *Designer* window: the *View Code* button (▤) and the *View Designer* button (▦).

Figure 2-47 *View Code* and *View Designer* buttons

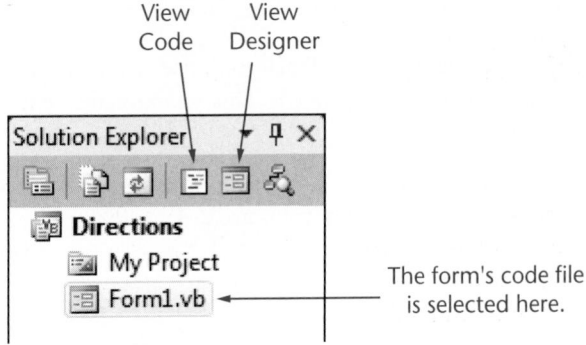

You can also perform any of the following actions to switch between the *Code* and *Designer* windows:

- Click *View* on the menu bar and then select either *Code* or *Designer*
- Press F7 on the keyboard to switch to the *Code* window, or Shift F7 to switch to the *Designer* window

VideoNote

Tutorial 2-10 Walkthrough

Tutorial 2-10:

Adding the *Exit* Button and its Click Event Handler

In this tutorial you will add the final control to the *Directions* application: an *Exit* button that causes the application to end when the user clicks it.

Step 1: When you finished the previous tutorial, the *Directions* project was loaded into Visual Studio (or Visual Basic Express), and the *Code* window was opened. Use one of the techniques previously discussed to switch to the *Designer* window.

Step 2: Select the form in the *Designer* window. Next, locate the Button control icon in the *Toolbox* and double-click it. This will create a new Button control positioned in the form's upper-left corner. Move the Button control so it appears at the approximate location shown in Figure 2-48.

Figure 2-48 New Button control added to the form

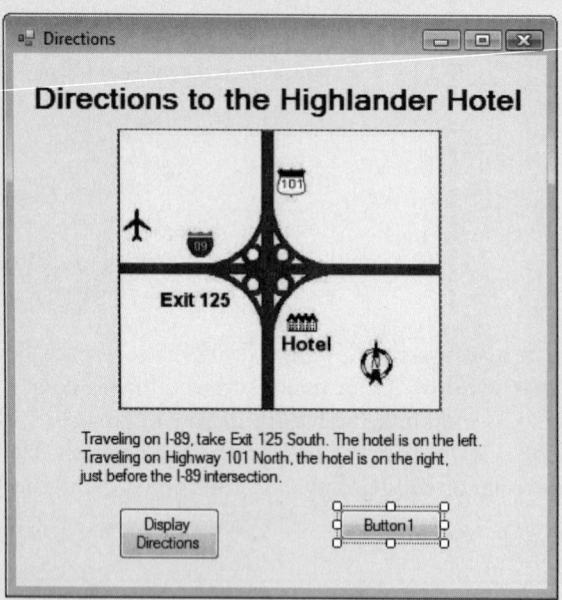

Step 3: With the new button still selected, use the *Properties* window to change the button's Text property to *Exit*. This changes the text displayed on the face of the button.

Step 4: Use the button's sizing handles to make it the same height as the *Display Directions* button, as shown in Figure 2-49.

Figure 2-49 Button control resized

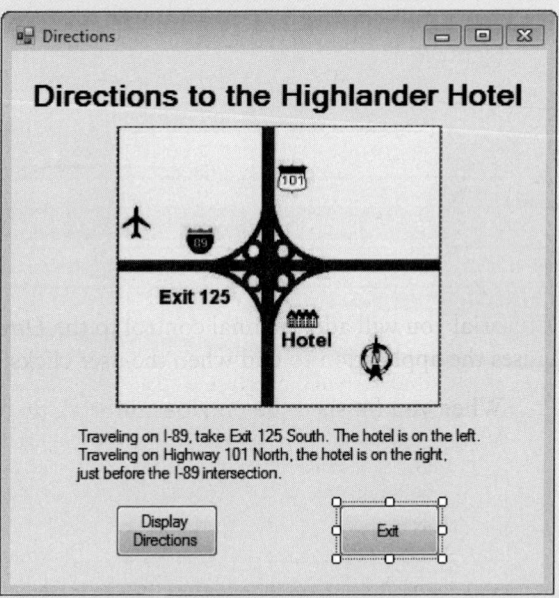

Step 5: With the button still selected, scroll up in the *Properties* window and find the Name property. Change the button's name to btnExit.

Step 6: Now you are ready to write the Click event handler for the btnExit button. In the *Designer* window, double-click the btnExit button. This causes the *Code* window to open as shown in Figure 2-50. Notice that a code template has been created for the btnExit_Click event handler.

Figure 2-50 The *Code* window opened with a new event handler code template

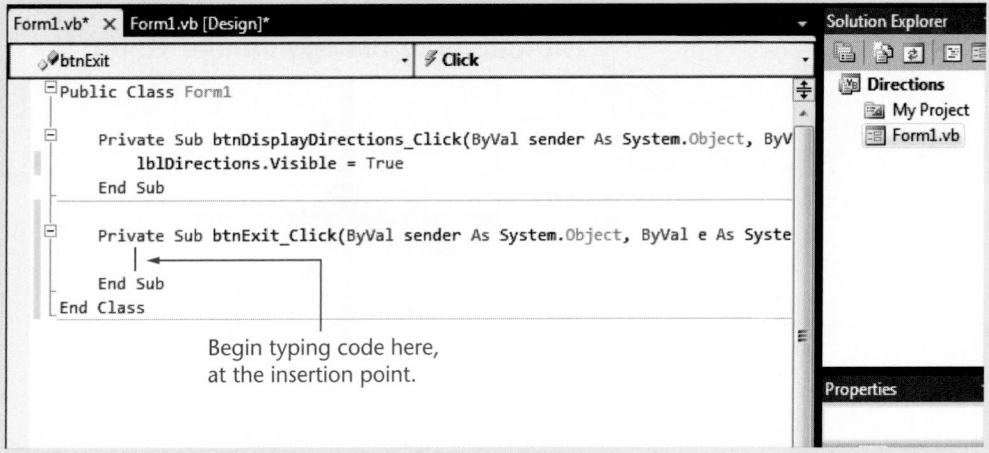

Step 7: At the current insertion point, between the first and last lines of the btnExit_Click event handler code template, type the following statement exactly as it is shown:

```
Me.Close()
```

When this statement executes, it will cause the form to close and the application to end. (We will discuss this statement in greater detail after the tutorial.) After you have typed this statement, the *Code* window should appear as shown in Figure 2-51.

Figure 2-51 The completed `btnExit_Click` event handler

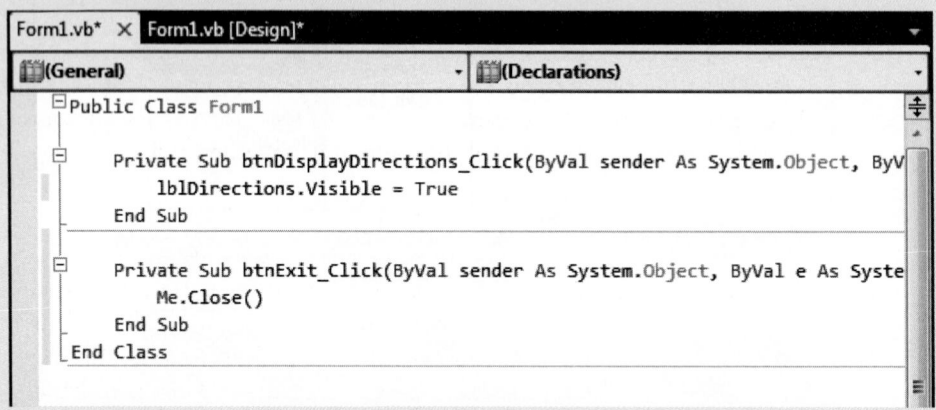

Step 8: Click the *Save All* button to save the project.

Step 9: Let's test the event handler that you just wrote. Click the *Start Debugging* button (▶) on the toolbar to run the application. After a moment the application will begin running and you will see the form displayed as shown in Figure 2-52.

Figure 2-52 The *Directions* application running

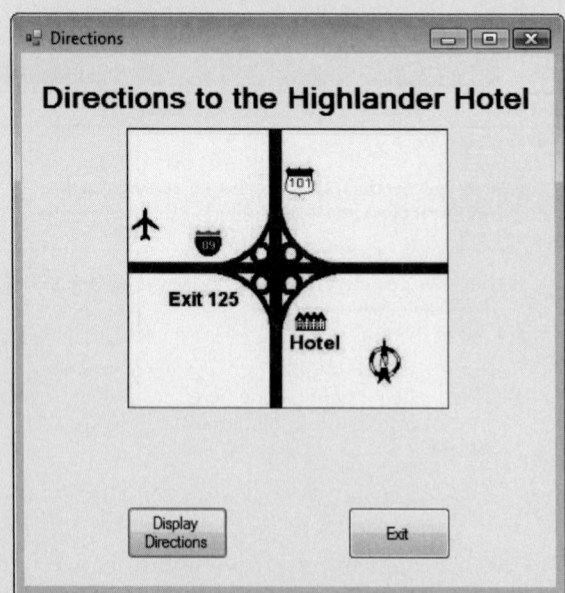

Step 10: Click the *Exit* button. The application should close.

Ending an Application with `Me.Close()`

You saw in the previous tutorial that when the statement `Me.Close()` executes, the application's form closes and the application ends. This statement is an example of a **method call**. Recall from Chapter 1 that objects have methods, which are operations that an object can perform. If you want to execute one of an object's methods, you have to call that method.

An application's form (which is an object) has a method named `Close`. When a form's `Close` method is called, it causes the form to close. If an application has only one form, as the *Directions* application does, closing the form also ends the application's execution.

In the statement `Me.Close()`, the keyword `Me`, which appears to the left of the period, is shorthand for referring to the current form. On the right side of the period, the word `Close` is the name of the method we are calling. Next is a set of parentheses, which always appear after the name of the method in a method call.

Comments

We mentioned in Chapter 1 that *comments*, which are also called *remarks*, are short notes that you can write in an application's code to explain what the code does. You should get into the habit of writing comments in your application code. The comments will almost certainly save you time in the future when you have to modify or debug the program. Even large and complex applications can be made easy to read and understand if they are properly commented.

In Visual Basic a comment starts with an apostrophe ('). Anything appearing after the apostrophe, to the end of the line, is ignored by the Visual Basic compiler. Here is an example of how we might use a comment to document a line of code:

```
' Make the directions visible.
lblDirections.Visible = True
```

The comment *Make the directions visible* explains in ordinary language what the next line of code does. In this example the comment uses an entire line, but it doesn't have to. A comment can be inserted at the end of a programming statement, like this:

```
lblDirections.Visible = True ' Make the directions visible.
```

In Tutorial 2-11 you will add comments to the code that you wrote in the *Directions* project.

Tutorial 2-11:
Adding comments to the *Directions* project code

Step 1: With the *Directions* project loaded into Visual Studio (or Visual Basic Express), use one of the techniques discussed earlier in this chapter to open the *Code* window.

Step 2: As shown in Figure 2-53, inside the `btnDisplayDirections_Click` event handler, insert the comment `' Make the directions visible.`

Figure 2-53 Comment inserted into the `btnDisplayDirections_Click` event handler

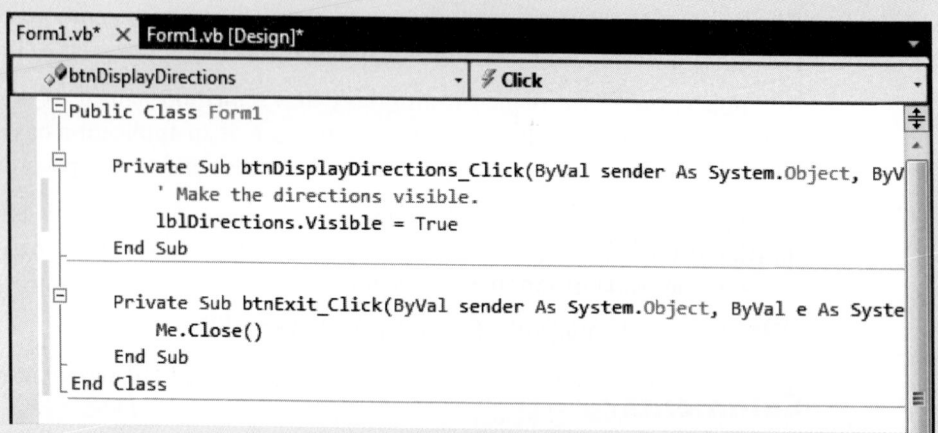

Step 3: As shown in Figure 2-54, inside the `btnExit_Click` event handler, insert the comment `' Close the form.`

Figure 2-54 Comment inserted into the `btnDisplayDirections_Click` event handler

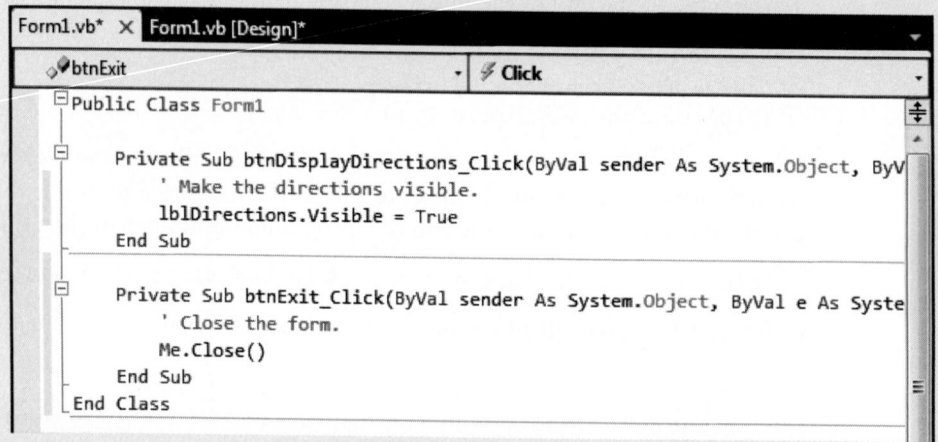

Step 4: Save the project.

 NOTE: From this point forward we will write comments as we write code. It's best to comment code as you write it because the code's purpose is fresh in your mind.

Checkpoint

2.12 How do you decide if you will keep a control's default name or assign it a new name?

2.13 What is a Boolean property?

2.14 Suppose an application has a button named btnShowName. The button has an event handler that executes when the user clicks it. What would the event handler be named?

2.15 Assume the following line appears in a button's Click event handler. What does the line cause the application to do?

```
lblGreeting.Visible = True
```

2.16 What is the purpose of a comment (or remark)?

2.17 Suppose an application has a Label control named lblSecretAnswer. Write an assignment statement that causes the control to be hidden. (*Hint*: Use the Visible property.)

2.18 What is the purpose of the Me.Close() statement?

Changing Text Colors

You have already learned that the font style and size of text on a control can be easily changed through the *Properties* window. You can also change the text background and foreground color with the **BackColor** and **ForeColor** properties. Tutorial 2-12 walks you through the process.

Tutorial 2-12:
Changing the text colors

Step 1: With the *Directions* project loaded, open the *Designer* window.

Step 2: Select the *Label1* control. This is the Label control whose Text property reads *Directions to the Highlander Hotel*.

Step 3: In the *Properties* window, look for the BackColor property. This is the property that establishes the background color for the label text. Click the property value. A down-arrow button (▾) appears.

Step 4: Click the down-arrow button (▾). A drop-down list of colors appears, as shown in Figure 2-55.

The drop-down list has three tabs: *Custom*, *Web*, and *System*. The *System* tab lists colors defined in the current Windows configuration. The *Web* tab lists colors displayed with consistency in Web browsers. The *Custom* tab displays a color palette, as shown in Figure 2-56.

Select a color from one of the tabs. Notice that the label text background changes to the color you selected.

Step 5: Now look for the **ForeColor property** in the *Properties* window. When you click it, a down-arrow button (▾) appears.

Step 6: Click the down-arrow button (▾) and notice the same drop-down list as you saw in Step 4. Once again, select a color from one of the tabs. Notice that the label's text foreground color changes to the color you selected.

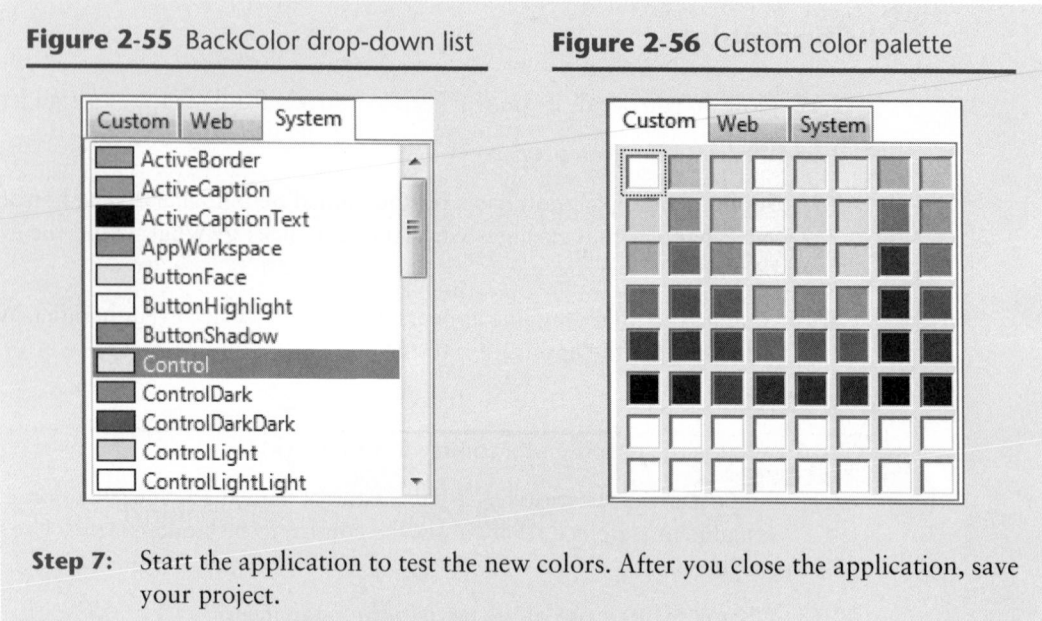

Figure 2-55 BackColor drop-down list

Figure 2-56 Custom color palette

Step 7:   Start the application to test the new colors. After you close the application, save your project.

Setting the FormBorderStyle Property and Locking Controls

The FormBorderStyle Property

Sometimes you want to prevent the user from resizing, minimizing, or maximizing a form, or from closing a form using its *Close* button (▣). You can control all of these actions by selecting an appropriate value for the form's **FormBorderStyle property**. Table 2-4 shows a list of the possible values for the FormBorderStyle property.

Table 2-4 Values for FormBorderStyle

Value	Description
Fixed3D	Displays a 3D border. The form's size is fixed and displayed with *Minimize*, *Maximize*, and *Close* buttons on its title bar. Although the form may be maximized and minimized, it may not be resized by its edges or corners.
FixedDialog	This type of border shows *Minimize*, *Maximize*, and *Close* buttons on its title bar. Although the form may be maximized and minimized, it may not be resized by its edges or corners.
FixedSingle	The form's size is fixed and uses a border that is a single line. The form is displayed with *Minimize*, *Maximize*, and *Close* buttons on its title bar. Although the form may be maximized and minimized, it may not be resized by its edges or corners.
FixedToolWindow	Intended for use with floating toolbars. Only shows the title bar with a *Close* button. May not be resized.
None	The form is displayed with no border at all. Subsequently, there is no title bar, and no *Minimize*, *Maximize*, and *Close* buttons. The form may not be resized.
Sizable	This is the default value. The form is displayed with *Minimize*, *Maximize*, and *Close* buttons on its title bar. The form may be resized, but the controls on the form do not change position.
SizableToolWindow	Like *FixedToolWindow*, but resizable.

Locking Controls

Once you have placed all the controls in their proper positions on a form, it is usually a good idea to lock them. When you lock the controls on a form, they cannot be accidentally moved at design time. They must be unlocked before they can be moved.

To lock all the controls on a form, place the cursor over an empty spot on the form and right-click. A small menu pops up. One of the selections on the menu is *Lock Controls*.

In Tutorial 2-13 we modify the value of the form's FormBorderStyle property so the user cannot minimize, maximize, or resize the window. We will also lock the controls on the form.

Tutorial 2-13:
Setting the FormBorderStyle property and locking the controls in the *Directions* application

Step 1: Open the *Directions* project in Visual Studio (or Visual Basic Express). Select the form and find the FormBorderStyle property in the *Properties* window.

Step 2: Click the FormBorderStyle property. A down-arrow button (⏷) appears. Click the down-arrow button (⏷) to see a list of values.

Step 3: Click *FixedSingle*.

Step 4: Start the application and test the new border style. Notice that you can move the window, but you cannot resize it by its edges or its corners.

Step 5: Click the *Exit* button to end the application.

Step 6: Now you will lock the controls. Place the cursor over an empty spot on the form and right-click. A small menu pops up.

Step 7: Click the *Lock Controls* command.

Step 8: Select any control on the form and try to move it. Because the controls are locked, you cannot move them.

Step 9: Save the project.

When you are ready to move the controls, just right-click over an empty spot on the form and select the *Lock Controls* command again. This toggles (reverses) the locked state of the controls.

WARNING: Be careful. Locked controls can still be deleted.

TIP: *A single control may be locked by setting its Locked property to True. It may be unlocked by setting its Locked property to False.*

Printing Your Code

To print a project's code, open the *Code* window, click *File* on the menu bar, and then click the *Print* command on the *File* menu.

Using IntelliSense

IntelliSense is a feature of Visual Studio that provides automatic code completion as you write programming statements. As you have worked through the tutorials in this chapter, you have probably noticed the IntelliSense list boxes that pop up as you write programming statements. For example, suppose you have the *Directions* project loaded, and you are about to type the following statement in the *Code* window:

```
lblDirections.Visible = True
```

As soon as you type the letter "l" an IntelliSense list box pops up, as shown in Figure 2-57. The IntelliSense system is anticipating what you are about to type. The list box shown in Figure 2-57 shows all the names starting with the letter "l" that might be a candidate for the statement you are typing. As you continue to type letters, the contents of the list box narrows. For example, after you have "lbl" the IntelliSense list box shows only one selection: lblDirections. This is shown in Figure 2-58. With that item selected, you can press the Tab key on the keyboard, and the lbl that you previously typed becomes lblDirections.

Figure 2-57 IntelliSense list box after typing the letter "l"

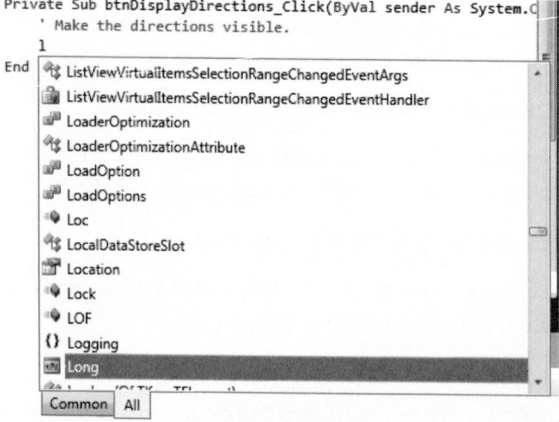

Figure 2-58 IntelliSense list box after typing "lbl"

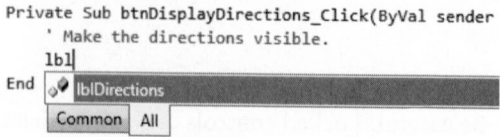

Next, when you type a period, an IntelliSense list pops up showing every property and method belonging to the lblDirections object. Type "vi" and the choice is narrowed down to the Visible property, as shown in Figure 2-59. At this point, when you press the Tab key to select the Visible property, your statement automatically becomes lblDirections.Visible.

Figure 2-59 IntelliSense list box after entering "lblDirections.vi"

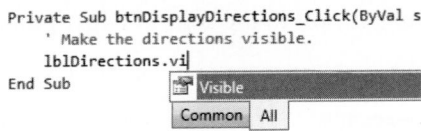

Next, if you type an = sign, another IntelliSense box appears, shown in Figure 2-60, show-ing the values False and True, which are the only possible values that can be assigned to the Visible property. Select True from the list and press the Tab key, and the statement is completed as `lblDirections.Visible = True`.

Now that you have an idea of how IntelliSense works, you are encouraged to experiment with it as you write code in future projects. With a little practice, it will become intuitive.

Figure 2-60 IntelliSense list box after entering "lblDirections.Visible="

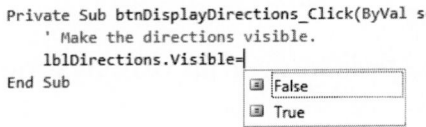

 **Checkpoint**

2.19 Which keyboard function key displays the *Code* window?

2.20 What three color categories are available when you edit a control's BackColor property?

2.21 What happens when you modify a Label control's BackColor property?

2.22 What happens when you modify a Label control's ForeColor property?

2.23 What property do you set in order to prevent a form from being resized when the application is running?

2.24 What happens when you lock the controls on a form?

2.25 How do you lock the controls on a form?

2.26 How do you unlock the controls on a form?

 **2.3** **Modifying a Control's Text Property with Code**

CONCEPT: Quite often, you will need to change a control's Text property with code. This is done with an assignment statement.

While building the *Directions* application, you learned that an assignment statement assigns a value to a property while the application is running. Recall that the following statement sets the `lblDirections` control's Visible property to *True*.

```
lblDirections.Visible = True
```

You use the same technique to modify a control's Text property. For example, assume an application has a Label control named lblMessage. The following statement assigns the sentence *Programming is fun!* to the control's Text property.

```
lblMessage.Text = "Programming is fun!"
```

Once the statement executes, the message displayed by the lblMessage control changes to

```
Programming is fun!
```

The quotation marks in the statement are not part of the message. They simply mark the beginning and end of the set of characters assigned to the property. In programming terms, a group of characters inside a set of quotation marks is called a **string literal**. You'll learn more about string literals in Chapter 3.

We usually display messages on a form by setting the value of a Label control's Text property. In Tutorial 2-14 you open and examine an application in the student sample programs folder that demonstrates this technique.

Tutorial 2-14:
Examining an application that displays messages in a Label control

Step 1: Start Visual Studio and open the *KiloConverter* project from the student sample programs folder named *Chap2\KiloConverter*.

Step 2: Open the *Designer* window, which displays *Form1*, as shown in Figure 2-61.

Step 3: Click the *Start Debugging* button (▶) to run the application.

Step 4: Once the application is running, click the *Inches* button. The form displays the number of inches equivalent to a kilometer, as shown in Figure 2-62.

Step 5: Experiment with the other buttons and observe the messages that are displayed when each is clicked.

Step 6: Click the *Exit* button to exit the application. Let's examine the application code. Figure 2-63 shows the *KiloConverter* application form with its controls labeled.

The buttons btnInches, btnFeet, btnYards, and btnMiles each change the lblMessage Text property when clicked. In the next step, you will view the *KiloConverter* event handlers.

Figure 2-61 *Kilometer Converter* form

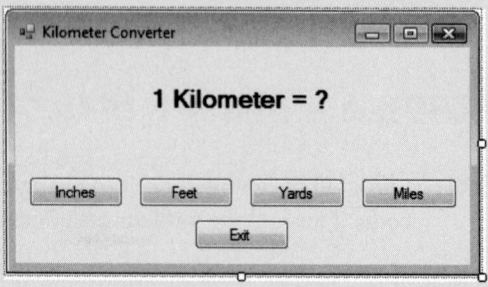

Figure 2-62 One kilometer converted to inches

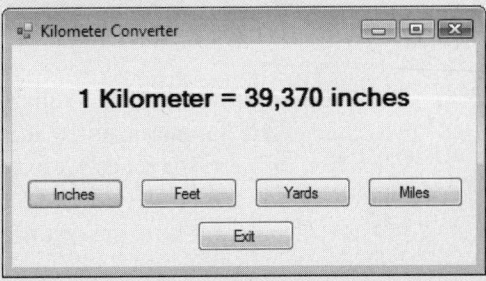

Figure 2-63 *KiloConverter* application controls

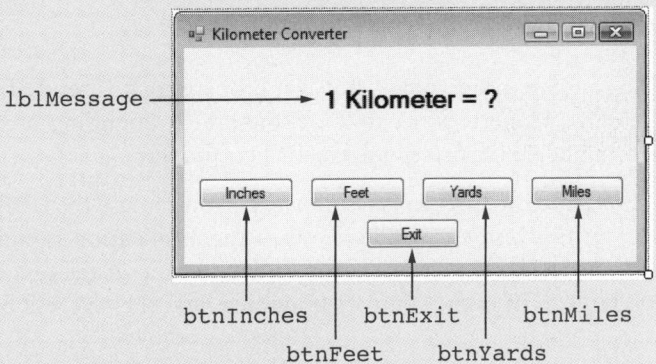

Step 7:   Click the *View Code* button ([⊞]) in the *Solution Explorer* window. The *Code* window appears, showing the following code. Examine each event handler and make sure you understand which Button control it works with, and how it changes the text that is displayed on the form.

```
Public Class Form1

    Private Sub btnExit_Click(...) Handles btnExit.Click
        ' End the application.
        Me.Close()
    End Sub

    Private Sub btnFeet_Click(...) Handles btnFeet.Click
        ' Display the conversion to feet.
        lblMessage.Text = "1 Kilometer = 3,281 feet"
    End Sub

    Private Sub btnInches_Click(...) Handles btnInches.Click
        ' Display the conversion to inches.
        lblMessage.Text = "1 Kilometer = 39,370 inches"
    End Sub

    Private Sub btnMiles_Click(...) Handles btnMiles.Click
        ' Display the conversion to miles.
        lblMessage.Text = "1 Kilometer = 0.6214 miles"
    End Sub

    Private Sub btnYards_Click(...) Handles btnYards.Click
        ' Display the conversion to yards.
        lblMessage.Text = "1 Kilometer = 1,093.6 yards"
    End Sub
End Class
```

2.4 The AutoSize, BorderStyle, and TextAlign Properties

CONCEPT: The Label control's AutoSize property determines whether a label will change size automatically to accommodate the amount of text in its Text property, or remain a fixed size. The BorderStyle property allows you to set a border around a Label control. The TextAlign property determines how the text is aligned within the label.

The Label control has three additional properties, AutoSize, BorderStyle, and TextAlign, which give you greater control over the label's appearance.

The AutoSize Property

The **AutoSize property** is a Boolean property that is set to *True* by default. When a label's AutoSize property is set to *True*, the label's bounding box will automatically resize to accommodate the text in the label's Text property.

When AutoSize is set to *False*, however, you can use the label's sizing handles to change its size in the *Designer* window. When the application is running, the Label control will remain the size that it was given at design time. If the text in the label's Text property is too large to fit in the control's bounding box, the text will be only partially displayed.

The BorderStyle Property

The Label control's **BorderStyle property** may have one of three values: *None*, *FixedSingle*, and *Fixed3D*. The property is set to *None* by default, which means the label will have no border. If BorderStyle is set to *FixedSingle*, the label will be outlined with a border that is a single pixel wide. If BorderStyle is set to *Fixed3D*, the label will have a recessed 3D appearance. Figure 2-64 shows an example of three Label controls: one with BorderStyle set to *None*, one with BorderStyle set to *FixedSingle*, and one with BorderStyle set to *Fixed3D*.

Quite often you will want to display output, such as the results of a calculation, in a Label control with a border. You will see many example applications in this book that use this approach.

Figure 2-64 *FixedSingle* and *Fixed3D* BorderStyle examples

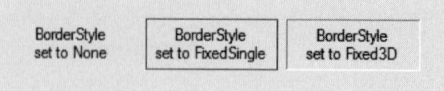

The TextAlign Property

When you set a label's AutoSize property to False and then manually resize the label, it sometimes becomes necessary to change the way the label's text is aligned. By default, a label's text is aligned with the top and left edges of the label's bounding box. For example, look at the label shown in Figure 2-65. When we created this label, we set the Text property to *Hello World*, we set the AutoSize property to False, and then we enlarged the size of the label as shown in the figure. Notice how the text is positioned in the label's upper-left corner.

Figure 2-65 Default text alignment

What if we want the text to be aligned differently within the Label? For example, what if we want the text to be centered in the label, or positioned in the lower-right corner? We can change the text's alignment in the label with the **TextAlign property**. The TextAlign property may be set to any of the following values: TopLeft, TopCenter, TopRight, MiddleLeft, MiddleCenter, MiddleRight, BottomLeft, BottomCenter, or BottomRight. Figure 2-66 shows nine Label controls, each with a different TextAlign value.

Figure 2-66 Text alignments

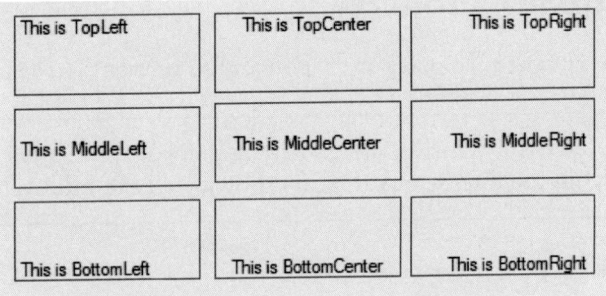

To change the TextAlign property, select it in the *Properties* window and then click the down-arrow button (⏷) that appears next to its value. This causes a dialog box with nine buttons, as shown in the left image in Figure 2-67, to appear. As shown in the right image in the figure, the nine buttons represent the valid settings of the TextAlign property.

Figure 2-67 Setting the TextAlign property with the *Properties* window

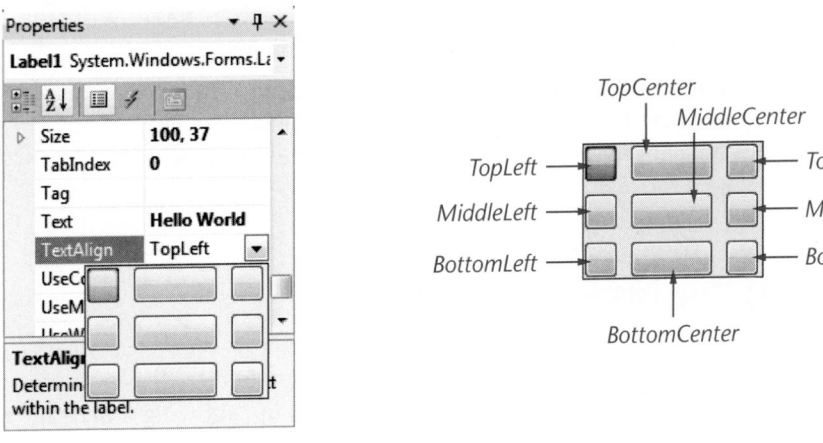

Changing a Label's TextAlign Property with Code

At design time, you set the TextAlign property's value in the *Properties* window. You can also set the property with code at runtime. You do this by using an assignment statement to assign one of the following values to the property:

```
ContentAlignment.TopLeft
ContentAlignment.TopCenter
ContentAlignment.TopRight
ContentAlignment.MiddleLeft
ContentAlignment.MiddleCenter
ContentAlignment.MiddleRight
ContentAlignment.BottomLeft
ContentAlignment.BottomCenter
ContentAlignment.BottomRight
```

For example, assume an application uses a Label control named `lblReportTitle`. The following statement aligns the control's text with the middle and center of the control's bounding box.

```
lblReportTitle.TextAlign = ContentAlignment.MiddleCenter
```

 TIP: When you write an assignment statement that stores a value in the TextAlign property, an Intellisense box appears showing all the valid values.

 Checkpoint

2.27   Suppose an application has a Label control named `lblTemperature`. Write a code statement that causes the label's Text property to display the message *48 degrees*.

2.28   What happens when a Label control's AutoSize property is set to *False*? When it is set to *True*?

2.29   What are the possible values for the Label control's BorderStyle property, and what result does each value produce?

2.30   Suppose an application has a Label control named `lblName`. Write the programming statements described by the following:

- A statement that aligns the label's text in the top right.
- A statement that aligns the label's text in the bottom left.
- A statement that aligns the label's text in the top center.

 **2.5** ## Displaying Message Boxes

CONCEPT: You can use the `MessageBox.Show` method to display a message box, which is a dialog box that pops up, showing a message to the user.

Sometimes you need a convenient way to display a message to the user. In Visual Basic, you can call the `MessageBox.Show` method to pop up a message box. A **message box** is a small window, sometimes referred to as a **dialog box**, that displays a message. Figure 2-68 shows an example of a message box, displaying the message *Hello World!* Notice that the message box also has an *OK* button. The user must click the *OK* button to close the message box.

Figure 2-68 A message box

The following statement shows an example of how you would call the `MessageBox.Show` method to display the message box shown in Figure 2-68:

```
MessageBox.Show("Hello World!")
```

Notice that the string `"Hello World!"` appears inside the parentheses. Any string that you type inside the parentheses will be displayed in the message box when the statement executes.

Tutorial 2-15:
Displaying Message Boxes

In the student sample programs folder named *Chap2\French Numbers,* you have a project named *French Numbers*. The project has been started for you, and in this tutorial you will complete it by writing the necessary event handlers.

When the project is complete, it will display the French words for the numbers 1 through 5, which are shown here:

1 un
2 deux
3 trois
4 quatre
5 cinq

The application's form has five button controls, displaying the numbers 1 through 5. The completed application will allow the user to click any of the buttons to select a number, and a message box will appear displaying the French word for the selected number. For example, if the user clicks the 2 button, a message box will appear displaying the word *deux*.

Step 1: Open the *French Numbers* project from the student sample programs folder named *Chap2\French Numbers*. Figure 2-69 shows the application's form, with the names of each Button control.

Figure 2-69 The *French Numbers* form

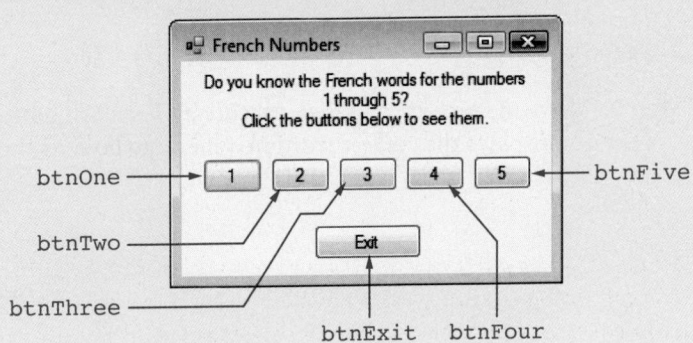

Step 2: Create Click event handlers for all of the button controls. When each button is clicked, it should display a message box showing the French word for the button's number, as described here:

- When the btnOne button is clicked, a message box should appear displaying *un*.
- When the btnTwo button is clicked, a message box should appear displaying *deux*.
- When the btnThree button is clicked, a message box should appear displaying *trois*.
- When the btnFour button is clicked, a message box should appear displaying *quatre*.
- When the btnFive button is clicked, a message box should appear displaying *cinq*.

In addition, write a Click event handler for the btnExit button that closes the form. When you have finished writing all of the event handlers, your code should be similar to the following. (Your event handlers might appear in a different order than those shown here, depending on the order in which you double-click each button in the *Designer* window.)

```
Public Class Form1

    Private Sub btnOne_Click(...) Handles btnOne.Click
        ' Display the French word for one.
        MessageBox.Show("un")
    End Sub

    Private Sub btnTwo_Click(...) Handles btnTwo.Click
        ' Display the French word for two.
        MessageBox.Show("deux")
    End Sub

    Private Sub btnThree_Click(...) Handles btnThree.Click
        ' Display the French word for three.
        MessageBox.Show("trois")
    End Sub

    Private Sub btnFour_Click(...) Handles btnFour.Click
        ' Display the French word for four.
        MessageBox.Show("quatre")
    End Sub

    Private Sub btnFive_Click(...) Handles btnFive.Click
        ' Display the French word for five.
        MessageBox.Show("cinq")
    End Sub

    Private Sub btnExit_Click(...) Handles btnExit.Click
        ' Close the form.
        Me.Close()
    End Sub
End Class
```

Step 3: Save the project, and then execute it. Test each button on the form to make sure it displays the correct word in a message box, as shown in Figure 2-70.

Figure 2-70 Message boxes that should be displayed by the *French Numbers* application

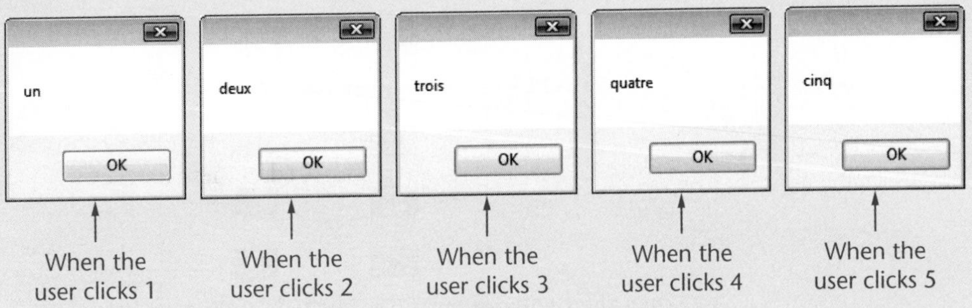

| un | deux | trois | quatre | cinq |
| OK | OK | OK | OK | OK |

When the user clicks 1 | When the user clicks 2 | When the user clicks 3 | When the user clicks 4 | When the user clicks 5

 Checkpoint

2.31 What is a dialog box?

2.32 Write a statement that displays a message box showing the message *Welcome to our hotel!*.

2.33 The following statement is not written correctly. What is wrong with it?

```
MessageBoxShow("Invalid password")
```

2.6 Clickable Images

CONCEPT: Controls other than buttons can have Click event handlers. In this section, you learn to create PictureBox controls that respond to mouse clicks.

In this chapter, you learned that buttons can have Click event handlers. A Click event handler is executed when the user clicks the button. Other controls, such as PictureBoxes and labels, may also have Click event handlers. In Tutorial 2-16 you write Click event handlers for a group of PictureBox controls.

 Tutorial 2-16:

Writing Click event handlers for PictureBox controls

Step 1: Open the *Flags* project from the student sample programs folder named *Chap2\Flags*.

Step 2: Open the *Designer* window and look at *Form1*. Figure 2-71 shows the form and the names of the controls on the form.

Step 3: Select the `lblMessage` control and set its TextAlign property to *MiddleCenter*, and its Font property to *Microsoft sans serif, bold, 8 points*.

Step 4: Change the form's Text property to **Flags**.

Step 5: `PictureBox1` shows the flag of the United States. Rename this control **picUSA**.

Figure 2-71 *Form1 of the Flags project*

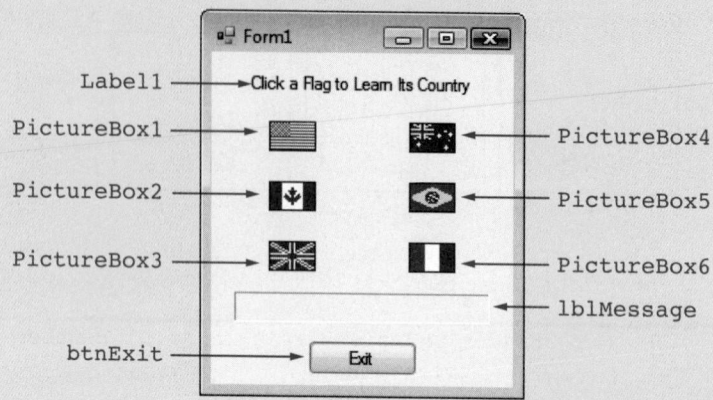

Step 6: PictureBox2 shows the flag of Canada. Rename this control **picCanada**.

Step 7: PictureBox3 shows the flag of the United Kingdom. Rename this control **picUK**.

Step 8: PictureBox4 shows the flag of Australia. Rename this control **picAustralia**.

Step 9: PictureBox5 shows the flag of Brazil. Rename this control **picBrazil**.

Step 10: PictureBox6 shows the flag of Italy. Rename this control **picItaly**.

Step 11: Double-click the picUSA control. The *Code* window opens with a code template generated for the picUSA_Click event handler. Complete the event handler by writing code that assigns the string "United States of America" to the lblMessge control's Text property. The code that you should write is shown in bold here:

```
Private Sub picUSA_Click(...) Handles picUSA.Click
    ' Display United States of America.
    lblMessage.Text = "United States of America"
End Sub
```

Step 12: Repeat the process that you followed in Step 11 for each of the other PictureBox controls. The Click event handler for each PictureBox control should assign the name of its flag's country to the lblMessage.Text property.

Next, double-click the btnExit button to create a code template for the btnExit_Click event handler. Complete the event handler so it closes the form.

When you have completed all of these event handlers, your code should look something like the following. Note that your event handlers might not appear in the same order as the ones shown, depending on the order in which you double-clicked the controls.

```
Public Class Form1

    Private Sub picUSA_Click(...) Handles picUSA.Click
        ' Display United States of America.
        lblMessage.Text = "United States of America"
    End Sub

    Private Sub picCanada_Click(...) Handles picCanada.Click
        ' Display Canada.
        lblMessage.Text = "Canada"
    End Sub
```

```
                Private Sub picUK_Click(...) Handles picUK.Click
                    ' Display United Kingdom.
                    lblMessage.Text = "United Kingdom"
                End Sub

                Private Sub picAustralia_Click(...) Handles picAustralia.Click
                    ' Display Australia.
                    lblMessage.Text = "Australia"
                End Sub

                Private Sub picBrazil_Click(...) Handles picBrazil.Click
                    ' Display Brazil.
                    lblMessage.Text = "Brazil"
                End Sub

                Private Sub picItaly_Click(...) Handles picItaly.Click
                    ' Display Italy.
                    lblMessage.Text = "Italy"
                End Sub

                Private Sub btnExit_Click(...) Handles btnExit.Click
                    ' Close the form.
                    Me.Close()
                End Sub
            End Class
```

Step 13: Save the project.

Step 14: Run the application. When you click any of the flags, you should see the name of the flag's country appear in the lblMessage Label control. For example, when you click the flag of Australia, the form should appear similar to the one shown in Figure 2-72.

Step 15: Exit the application.

Figure 2-72 *Flags* application identifying flag of Australia

Using Visual Studio Help

The documentation for Visual Studio and Visual Basic is contained in the MSDN (Microsoft Developer Network) Library. The MSDN Library contains a wealth of information, including code samples, tutorials, and technical articles. When you install Visual Studio, you have the option of installing the MSDN Library on your computer. If you choose not to install the MSDN Library on your computer, you can still access its content on the Web.

As shown in Figure 2-73, you can access the MSDN Library by Clicking *Help* on the Visual Studio menu bar, and then selecting *View Help*. (Or, you can simply press Ctrl+F1.) This opens the MSDN library in your Web browser.

Figure 2-73 Accessing the *Visual Studio Documentation*

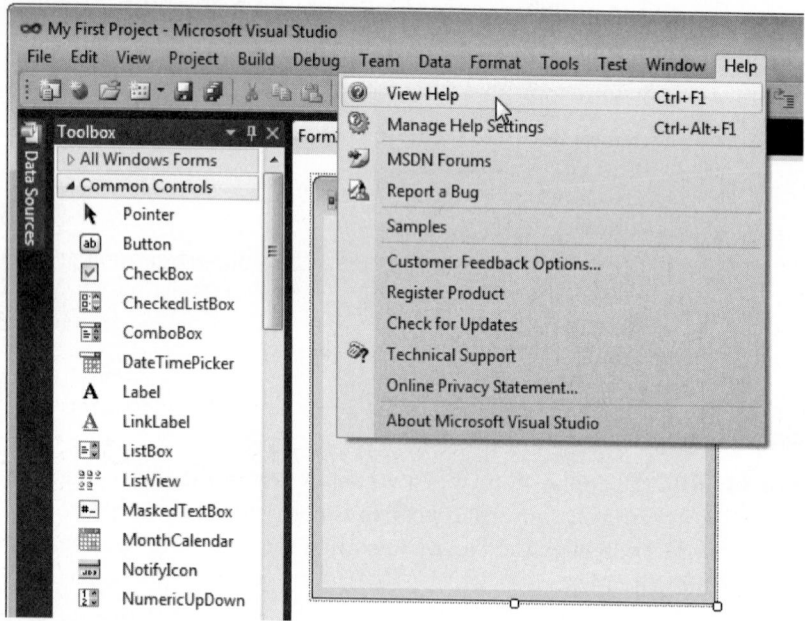

Context-Sensitive Help

The MSDN Library contains a vast amount of documentation on Visual Studio and Visual Basic. Because it contains so much information, it is often easier to find what you are looking for by using context-sensitive help. **Context-sensitive help** is help on a single topic that you are currently working on. You get context-sensitive help by selecting an item in the *Designer* window, *Code* window, *Properties* window, *Toolbox*, etc., and then pressing the F1 key. Your Web browser will launch, displaying help on the item that is selected.

For example, Figure 2-74 shows some code displayed in the *Code* window. Notice that the = operator has been selected (highlighted) in one of the lines of code. If we press the F1 key while the = operator is selected, we will see a help screen similar to Figure 2-75, displayed in a Web browser.

Notice that the left pane in the browser shows a list of topics that you can click on to get additional help. You can also use the search box that appears at the top of the left pane to search for help on specific items.

Figure 2-74 The = operator selected in the *Code* window

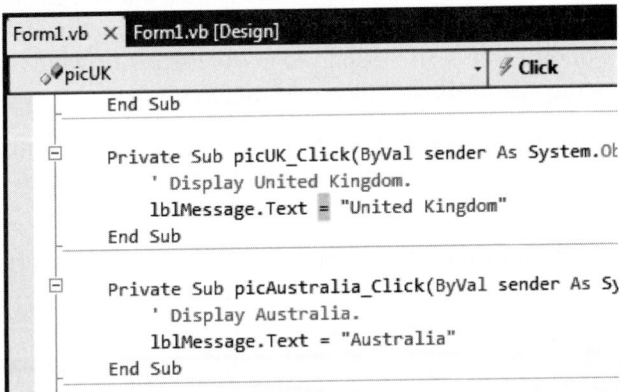

Figure 2-75 Help on the = operator

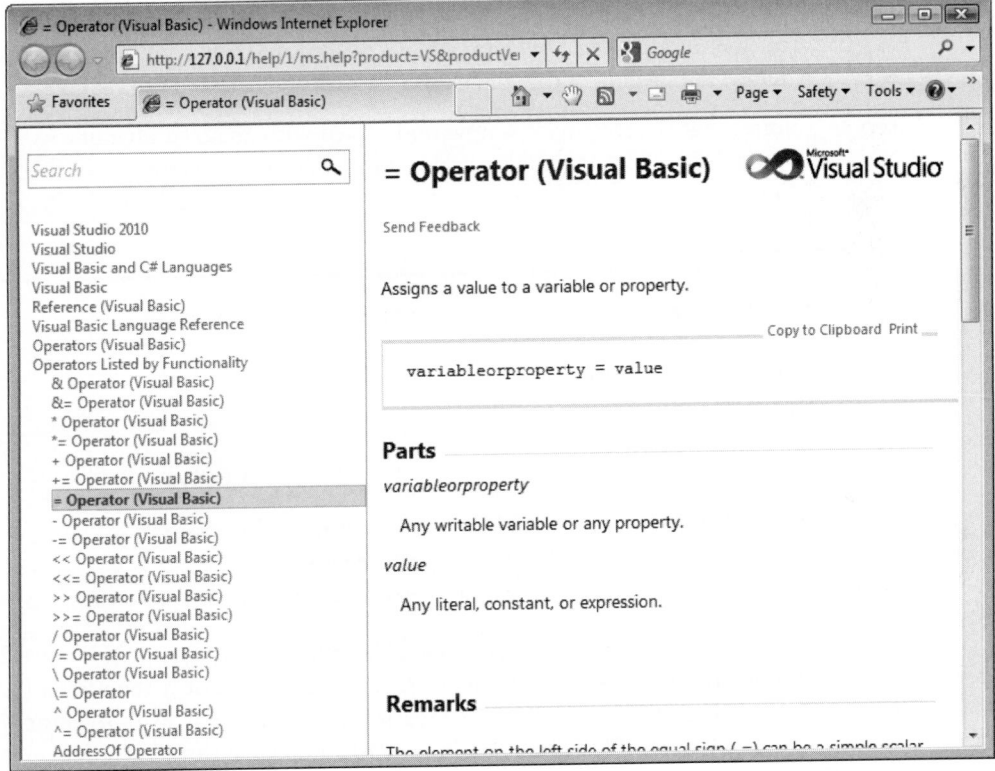

2.8 Debugging Your Application

CONCEPT: At some point, most applications contain bugs (errors) that prevent the application from operating properly. In this section, you learn fundamental debugging techniques.

Visual Basic reports errors in your project as soon as it finds them. In general, there are two types of errors: compile errors and runtime errors.

Compile errors are syntax errors, such as misspelled keywords or the incorrect use of operators or punctuation. Visual Basic checks each line of code for compile errors as soon as you enter it. When a compile error is found, it is underlined with a jagged blue line. A description of the error is also displayed in the *Error List* window. You display it by clicking *View* on the menu bar, and then selecting *Error List*.

Runtime errors are errors found while an application is running. They are not syntax errors but result if there is an attempt to perform an operation that Visual Basic cannot execute.

Tutorial 2-17 demonstrates how Visual Basic reports compile errors.

Tutorial 2-17:
Locating a compile error in Design mode

Step 1:   Open the *Directions* project and open the *Code* window.

Step 2:   You will modify the btnExit_Click procedure so it contains a syntax error. Change the spelling of the statement that reads Me.Close() to read Me.Clost().

Step 3:   Notice that the statement is now underlined with a jagged blue line as shown in Figure 2-76. This jagged blue underlining indicates an error.

Figure 2-76 Error underlined

```
Private Sub btnExit_Click(ByVal sender As System.Object,
    ' Close the form.
    Me.Clost()
End Sub
```

Step 4:   Perform *one* of the following actions to open the *Error List* window:
- Click View on the menu bar, then select Error List.
- Click the Error List button ( ) on the toolbar.
- Press Ctrl+W followed by Ctrl+E on the keyboard.

Look at the *Error List* window, which should appear similar to Figure 2-77. It shows an error message indicating that Clost is not a member of Directions.Form1. Notice that the location of the error is also given as line 10, column 9 of the file Form1.vb, in the *Directions* project.

Additionally, you can double-click the error message that appears in the Error List window, and the text editing cursor in the *Code* window will be positioned at the error.

Figure 2-77 The *Error List* window

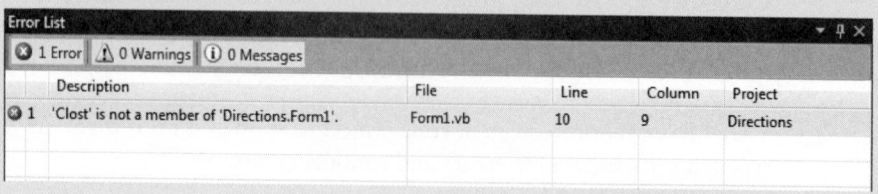

	Description	File	Line	Column	Project
1	'Clost' is not a member of 'Directions.Form1'.	Form1.vb	10	9	Directions

TIP: Sometimes you will see an error message you do not fully understand. When this happens, look at the area that shows the jagged underlining, and try to determine the problem. When you figure out what caused the error, consider how it relates to the error message.

Step 5: Correct the line of code that you changed in Step 2 so it reads `Me.Close()`.

 ## Checkpoint

2.34 What is context-sensitive help?

2.35 What are the two general types of errors in a Visual Basic project?

Summary

2.1 Focus on Problem Solving: Building the *Directions* Application

- The *Properties* window is used at design time to set control property values. The PictureBox control's SizeMode property determines how the control will place and size its image.
- Small squares (sizing handles) are used to enlarge or shrink the control. Once you place a control on a form, you can move it by clicking and dragging. To delete a control, select it and then press the [Delete] key.
- To run an application click the *Start Debugging* button on the toolbar, click the *Start Debugging* command on the *Debug* menu, or press the [F5] key. To end a running application, click the *Stop Debugging* command on the *Debug* menu or click the *Close* button on the application window.
- When you create a new project, Visual Studio automatically creates a solution with the same name as the project, and adds the project to the solution. The solution and the project are stored on the disk in a folder with the same name as the solution. The solution file ends with the *.sln* extension and the project file ends with the *.vbproj* extension.
- To open an existing project, click its name in the Recent Projects list on the *Start Page*, click *File* on the menu bar, then click *Open Project*, or click *File* on the menu bar, *Recent Projects and Solutions*, and then select the solution or project from the list.
- The *Properties* window's object box provides a drop-down list of the objects in the project. The *Alphabetical* button causes the properties to be listed alphabetically. The *Categorized* button causes related properties to be displayed in groups.

2.2 Focus on Problem Solving: Responding to Events

- The apostrophe (') marks the beginning of a comment in code. A comment is a note of explanation that is ignored by Visual Basic.
- The `Me.Close()` statement causes the current form to close. If the current form is the application's startup form, the application ends.
- To display the *Code* window, you click the *View Code* button on the *Solution Explorer* window, click *View* on the menu bar, then *Code*, or press the [F7] key on the keyboard.
- The color of a label's text is changed with the BackColor and ForeColor properties.
- Once you have placed all the controls in their proper positions on a form, it is a good idea to lock them.

2.3 Modifying a Control's Text Property with Code

- You may change a control's Text property with code. An assignment statement assigns a value into the property at runtime.

2.4 The AutoSize, BorderStyle, and TextAlign Properties

- The AutoSize property determines whether a label will change size automatically to accommodate the amount of text in its Text property, or remain a fixed size.
- The BorderStyle property allows you to set a border around a Label control.
- The TextAlign property determines how the text in a label is aligned, and may be set to any of the following values: TopLeft, TopCenter, TopRight, MiddleLeft, MiddleCenter, MiddleRight, BottomLeft, BottomCenter, or BottomRight.
- You can set the TextAlign property with code at runtime by using an assignment statement to store a valid value in the property.

2.5 Displaying Message Boxes

- A message box is a small window that displays a message.
- In Visual Basic you call the `MessageBox.Show` method to display a message.

2.6 Clickable Images

- Buttons are not the only controls that can have Click event handlers. Other controls, such as PictureBoxes and Labels, can also have Click event handlers that respond to mouse clicks.

2.7 Using Visual Studio Help

- You access the Visual Studio Documentation and the MSDN library by clicking *Help* on the menu bar.
- You can get context-sensitive help on a single item that is currently selected in the *Designer* window, *Code* window, *Properties* window, *Toolbox*, etc., and then pressing the F1 key.

2.8 Debugging Your Application

- Visual Basic checks each line of code for syntax errors as soon as you enter it. When a compile error is found, it is underlined with a jagged blue line.
- Runtime errors occur while an application is running. They are not syntax errors, but result if there is an attempt to perform an operation that Visual Basic cannot execute.

Key Terms

aspect ratio	ForeColor property
Alphabetical button	FormBorderStyle property
assignment operator	Image property
assignment statement	*Index* button
AutoSize property	IntelliSense
BackColor property	Method call
Boolean property	message box
BorderStyle property	object box
bounding box	PictureBox control
break mode	project file
Categorized button	run mode
class declaration	runtime
code template	runtime errors
Code window	*Search* button
compile errors	SizeMode property
Contents button	sizing handles
context-sensitive help	solution
Design mode	solution file
design time	string literal
dialog box	TextAlign property
Font property	Visible property

Review Questions and Exercises

Fill-in-the-Blank

1. The _____ property determines how a Label control's text is aligned.

2. A PictureBox control's _____ property lists the name of the file containing the graphic image.

3. A PictureBox control's _____ property determines how the graphic image will be positioned and scaled to fit the control's bounding box.

4. When set to _____, the TextAlign property causes text to appear in the bottom right area of a Label control.

5. The contents of a form's Text property is displayed on the form's _____ _____.

6. Anytime you select an existing control, _____ appear, which you use to resize the control.

7. A control's _____ is a transparent rectangular area that defines the control's size.

8. A Label control's _____ property establishes the font, style, and size of the label's displayed text.

9. To delete a control in the *Designer* window, select it and press the _____ _____ key.

10. The _____ control is used to display graphic images.

11. The SizeMode property of a PictureBox control is set to _____ by default.

12. When the _____ button is selected on the *Solution Explorer* window, it opens the *Code* window.

13. Clicking the _____ button in the *Properties* window causes related properties to be listed in groups.

14. Visible is a _____ property, which means it can only hold one of two values: *True* or *False*.

15. An apostrophe (') in code marks the beginning of a _____.

16. The equal sign (=) is known as the _____ operator. It copies the value on its right into the item on its left.

17. In an assignment statement, the name of the item receiving the value must be on the _____ side of the = operator.

18. Visual Basic automatically provides a code _____ , which is the first and last lines of an event handler.

19. The _____ statement causes the form to close.

20. The _____ property establishes the background color for a Label control's text.

21. The _____ property establishes the color of the type for a Label control's text.

22. The _____ property allows you to prevent the user from resizing, minimizing, or maximizing a form, or closing a form using its *Close* button.

23. When you _____ the controls on a form, they cannot be accidentally moved at design time.

24. You display text in a form's title bar by setting the value of the form's _____ property.

25. You commonly display words and sentences on a form by setting the value of a Label control's _____ property.

26. The _____ property causes the Label control to resize automatically to accommodate the amount of text in the Text property.

27. _____ errors are errors that are generated while an application is running.

True or False

Indicate whether the following statements are true or false.

1. T F: In the *Designer* window, sizing handles appear around a control that is currently selected.

2. T F: The PictureBox control has an ImageStretch property.

3. T F: The Visible property is Boolean.

4. T F: A control is hidden in the *Designer* window if its Visible property is set to *False*.

5. T F: You can delete a locked control.

6. T F: You set a control's name with its Text property.

7. T F: The TextAlign property causes a control to be aligned with other controls on the same form.

8. T F: Text is frequently the first property that the programmer changes, so it is listed in parentheses in the *Properties* window. This causes it to be displayed at the top of the alphabetized list of properties.

9. T F: Resizing handles are positioned along the edges of a control's bounding box.

10. T F: A label's text is *MiddleCenter* aligned by default.

11. T F: You can run an application in the Visual Studio environment by pressing the F5 key.

12. T F: The first line of an event handler identifies its name and the event it handles.

13. T F: You should be very cautious about, and even avoid, placing comments in your code.

14. T F: In an assignment statement, the name of the item receiving the value must be on the right side of the = operator.

15. T F: You can display the *Code* window by pressing the F7 key when the *Designer* window is visible.

16. T F: The BackColor property establishes the color of a Label control's text.

17. T F: A form's FormBorderStyle property can be used to prevent the user from resizing, minimizing, or maximizing a window, or closing the window using its *Close* button.

18. T F: When you lock the controls on a form, the user must enter a password before the application will run.

19. T F: You cannot modify a control's Text property with code.

20. T F: The *Properties* window only shows a control's properties that may be changed at design time.

21. T F: A Label control's AutoSize property is set to *True* by default.

22. T F: PictureBox controls can have a Click event handler.

Short Answer

1. Explain the difference between an object's Text property and its Name.

2. List three ways to run an application within the Visual Studio environment.

3. List three ways to display the *Code* window.

4. Why does Visual Studio indent the code between the first and last lines of an event handler?

5. How do you make a PictureBox control respond to mouse clicks?

What Do You Think?

1. Why, in the *Properties* window, do you change some properties with a drop-down list or a dialog box, while you change others by typing a value?

2. Why is it a good idea to equip a form with a button that terminates the application, if the form already has a standard Windows *Close* button in the upper right corner?

3. What is the benefit of creating PictureBox controls that respond to mouse clicks?

Find the Error

1. Open the *Error1* project from the student sample programs folder named *Chap2*\\ *Error1*. Run the application. When Visual Basic reports an error, find and fix the error.

2. Open the *Error2* project from the student sample programs folder named *Chap2*\\ *Error2*. Run the application. When Visual Basic reports an error, find and fix the error.

Programming Challenges

1. Welcome Screen Modification

   For this exercise, you will modify an application that displays a welcome screen for the First Gaddis Bank. After starting Visual Studio, open the *First Gaddis* project from the student sample programs folder named *Chap2\First Gaddis*. Figure 2-78 shows the application's form.

Figure 2-78 *First Gaddis* welcome screen, *Form1*

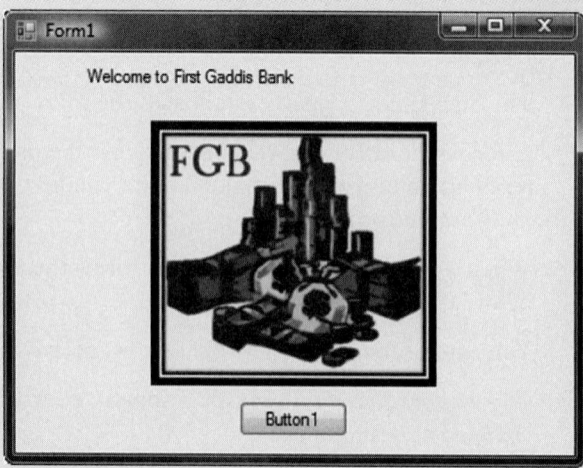

Make the following modifications to the application:

a. Change the form's title bar text to read *First Gaddis Bank*.

b. Change the label's Font property to *Microsoft sans serif, bold, 14.25 point*.

c. Change the label's text alignment to middle center.

d. Change the button's name to `btnExit`.

e. Change the button's text to read *Exit*.

f. Change the label's background color to a shade of light blue, or another color of your choice.

g. Change the form's background color to the same color you chose for the label.

h. Write a Click event handler for the button that closes the application window.

2. **Name and Address**

Create an application that displays your name and address when a button is clicked. The application's form should appear as shown in Figure 2-79 when it first runs. Once the *Show Info* button is clicked, the form should appear similar to the one shown in Figure 2-80.

Figure 2-79 Intitial *Name* and *Address* form

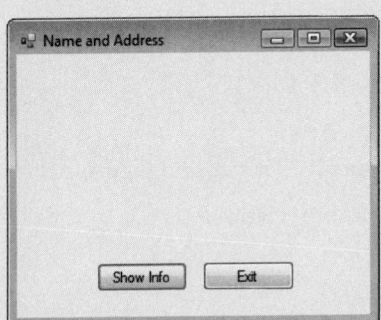

Figure 2-80 *Name and address* form after *Show Info* button is clicked

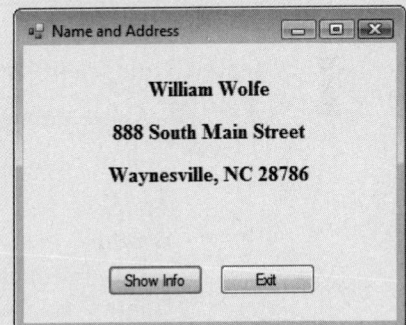

Here are the detailed property specifications:

a. The button that displays the name and address should be named `btnShowInfo`. Its text should read *Show Info*.

b. The button that closes the application should be named `btnExit`. Its text should read *Exit*.

c. The form should have three Label controls. The first will hold your name, the second will hold your street address, and the third will hold your city, state, and ZIP code. The labels should be named `lblName`, `lblStreet`, and `lblCityStateZip`, respectively. The labels' Font property should be set to *Times New Roman, bold, 12 point*. The labels' TextAlign property should be set to *MiddleCenter*.

d. The form's title bar should read *Name and Address*.

3. **Math Tutor Application**

You are to create a *Math Tutor* application. The application should display a simple math problem in a Label control. The form should have a button that displays the answer to the math problem in a second label, when clicked. It should also have a button that closes the application. Figure 2-81 shows an example of the application's form before the button is clicked to display the answer. Figure 2-82 shows the

Figure 2-81 Initial *Math Tutor* application

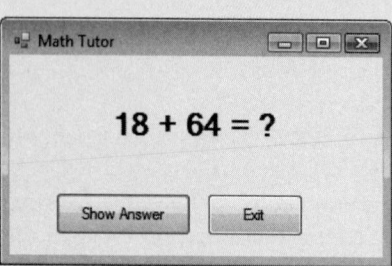

Figure 2-82 *Math Tutor* application after *Show Answers* button is clicked

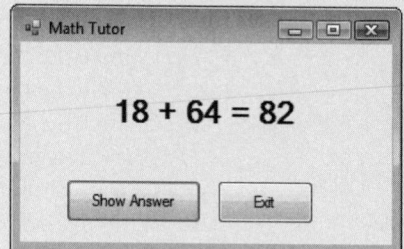

form after the *Show Answer* button is clicked. Here are the detailed property specifications:

a. The button that displays the answer should be named `btnShowAnswer`. Its Text property should read *Show Answer*.

b. The button that closes the application should be named `btnExit`. Its Text property should read *Exit*.

c. The label that displays the answer to the math problem should be named `lblAnswer`.

d. The form's title bar should read *Math Tutor*.

Design Your Own Forms

4. **State Abbreviations**

The following table shows lists of six states and their official abbreviations.

State	Abbreviation
Virginia	VA
North Carolina	NC
South Carolina	SC
Georgia	GA
Alabama	AL
Florida	FL

Create an application that allows the user to select a state, and then displays that state's official abbreviation. The form should have six buttons, one for each state. When the user clicks a button, the application displays the state's abbreviation in a Label control.

5. **Latin Translator**

Look at the following list of Latin words and their meanings.

Latin	English
sinister	left
dexter	right
medium	center

Create an application that translates the Latin words to English. The form should have three buttons, one for each Latin word. When the user clicks a button, the application should display the English translation in a Label control. When the user clicks the *sinister* button, the translation should appear with middle left alignment. When the user clicks the *dexter* button, the translation should appear with middle right alignment. When the user clicks the *medium* button, the translation should appear with middle center alignment.

6. **Clickable Images**

    In the *Chap2* folder, in the student sample programs, you will find the image files shown in Figure 2-83. Create an application that displays these images in PictureBox controls. The application should perform the following actions:

    *   When the user clicks the 1 image, the application should display the word *One* in a message box.
    *   When the user clicks the 2 image, the application should display the word *Two* in a message box.
    *   When the user clicks the 3 image, the application should display the word *Three* in a message box.
    *   When the user clicks the 4 image, the application should display the word *Four* in a message box.
    *   When the user clicks the 5 image, the application should display the word *Five* in a message box.

Figure 2-83 Image files

One.bmp   Two.bmp   Three.bmp   Four.bmp   Five.bmp

7. **Joke and Punch line**

    A joke typically has two parts: a setup and a punch line. For example, this might be the setup for a joke:

    How many programmers does it take to change a light bulb?

    And this is the punch line:

    None. That's a hardware problem.

    Think of your favorite joke and identify its setup and punch line. Then, create an application that has a Label and two buttons on a form. One of the buttons should read "Setup" and the other button should read "Punch line." When the *Setup* button is clicked, display the joke's setup in the Label. When the *Punch line* button is clicked, display the joke's punch line in the Label.

3 Variables and Calculations

TOPICS

This chapter covers the use of text boxes to gather input from users. It also discusses the use of variables, named constants, type conversion functions, and mathematical calculations. You will be introduced to the GroupBox control as a way to organize controls on an application's form. The *Format* menu commands, which allow you to align, size, and center controls are also discussed. You will learn about the form's Load event, which happens when a form is loaded into memory, and debugging techniques for locating logic errors.

3.1 Gathering Text Input

CONCEPT: In this section, we use the TextBox control to gather input the user has typed on the keyboard. We also alter a form's tab order and assign keyboard access keys to controls.

The programs you have written and examined so far perform operations without requiring information from the user. In reality, most programs ask the user to enter values. For example, a program that calculates payroll for a small business might ask the user to enter the name of the employee, the hours worked, and the hourly pay rate. The program then uses this information to print the employee's paycheck.

A **text box** is a rectangular area on a form that accepts keyboard input. As the user types, the characters are stored in the text box. In Visual Basic, you create a text box with a **TextBox control**. Tutorial 3-1 examines an application that uses a TextBox control.

Tutorial 3-1:
Using a TextBox control

Step 1: Open the *Greetings* project from the student sample programs folder named *Chap3\Greetings*.

Step 2: Click the *Start* button (▶) to run the application. The application's form appears, as shown in Figure 3-1. The TextBox control is the white rectangular area beneath the label that reads *Enter Your Name*.

Notice that the TextBox control shows a blinking text cursor, indicating it is ready to receive keyboard input.

Figure 3-1 *Greetings* project initial form

Figure 3-2 *Greetings* project completed form

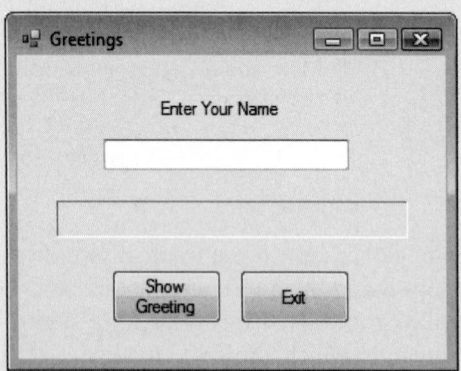

Step 3: Type your name. As you enter characters on the keyboard, they appear in the TextBox control.

Step 4: Click the *Show Greeting* button. The message *Hello* followed by the name you entered appears in a label below the TextBox control. The form now appears similar to the one shown in Figure 3-2.

Step 5: Click inside the TextBox control and use the [Delete] and/or [Backspace] key to erase the name you entered. Enter another name, and then click the *Show Greeting* button. Notice that the greeting message changes accordingly.

Step 6: Click the *Exit* button to exit the application. You have returned to Design mode.

Step 7: Look at the application's form in the *Designer* window. Figure 3-3 shows the form with its controls.

Notice that the name of the TextBox control starts with txt, which we use as the prefix for TextBox controls. Like the Label control, the TextBox control has a Text property. However, the Label control's Text property is only for displaying information—the user cannot directly alter its contents. The TextBox control's

Text property is for input purposes. The user can alter it by typing characters into the TextBox control. Whatever the user types into the TextBox control is stored, as a string, in its Text property.

Figure 3-3 *Greetings* project form with controls labeled

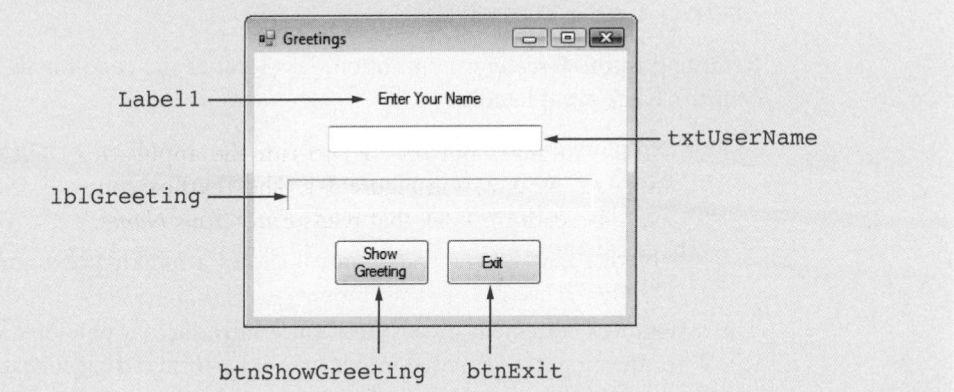

Using the Text Property in Code

You access a TextBox control's Text property in code the same way you access other properties. For example, assume an application has a Label control named `lblInfo` and a TextBox control named `txtInput`. The following statement assigns the contents of the TextBox control's Text property into the Label control's Text property.

```
lblInfo.Text = txtInput.Text
```

The following statement shows another example. It displays the contents of the `txtInput` control's Text property in a message box:

```
MessageBox.Show(txtInput.Text)
```

Clearing a Text Box

Recall from Chapter 1 that an object contains methods, which are actions the object performs. If you want to execute an object's method, you write a statement that calls the method. The general format of such a statement is

```
Object.Method
```

Object is the name of the object and *Method* is the name of the method that is being called.

A `TextBox` control is an object, and has a variety of methods that perform operations on the text box or its contents. One of these methods is `Clear`, which clears the contents of the text box's Text property. The general format of the `Clear` method is

```
TextBoxName.Clear()
```

TextBoxName is the name of the TextBox control. Here is an example:

```
txtInput.Clear()
```

When this statement executes, the Text property of `txtInput` is cleared and the text box appears empty on the screen.

You can also clear a text box by assigning the predefined constant `String.Empty` to its Text property. Here is an example:

```
txtInput.Text = String.Empty
```

Once this statement executes, the Text property of `txtInput` is cleared and the text box appears empty on the screen.

String Concatenation

Returning to the *Greetings* application, let's look at the code for the `btnShowGreeting` control's Click event handler:

```
Private Sub btnShowGreeting_Click(...) Handles btnShowGreeting.Click
    ' Display a customized greeting to the user
    ' in the lblGreeting control.
    lblGreeting.Text = "Hello " & txtUserName.Text
End Sub
```

The assignment statement in this procedure introduces a new operator: the ampersand (`&`). When the ampersand is used in this way, it performs **string concatenation**. This means that one string is appended to another.

The `&` operator creates a string that is a combination of the string on its left and the string on its right. Specifically, it appends the string on its right to the string on its left. For example, assume an application uses a Label control named `lblMessage`. The following statement assigns the string "Good morning Charlie" to the control's Text property:

```
lblMessage.Text = "Good morning " & "Charlie"
```

In our *Greetings* application, if the user types *Becky* into the `txtUserName` control, the control's Text property is set to *Becky*. So the statement

```
lblGreeting.Text = "Hello " & txtUserName.Text
```

assigns the string `"Hello Becky"` to `lblGreeting`'s Text property.

Look again at the assignment statement. Notice there is a space in the string literal after the word *Hello*. This prevents the two strings being concatenated from running together.

In a few moments, it will be your turn to create an application using TextBox controls and string concatenation. Tutorial 3-2 leads you through the process.

Aligning Controls in Design Mode

Visual Studio provides a convenient way to align controls on forms. When you drag a control to a position on a form that aligns with another control, guide lines automatically appear. In Figure 3-4, for example, a TextBox has been placed below an existing TextBox. The blue guide lines tell us the two controls are aligned vertically. If either control is dragged sideways, the guide lines disappear.

In Figure 3-5, two TextBox controls are aligned horizontally, indicated by lavender guide lines. In Figure 3-6, guide lines appear for simultaneous vertical and horizontal alignment. All in all, this feature of Visual Studio takes the guesswork out of aligning controls, saving you a lot of time. Tutorial 3-2 shows you how to build the *Date String* application.

Figure 3-4 Vertical guide lines align two TextBox controls

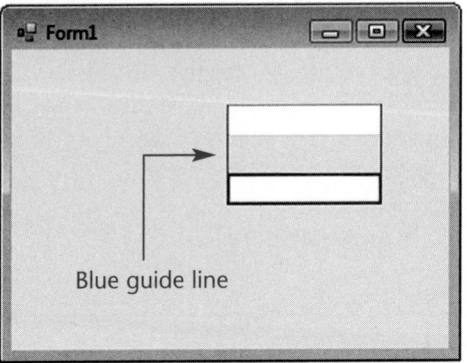

Figure 3-5 Horizontal guide lines align two TextBox controls

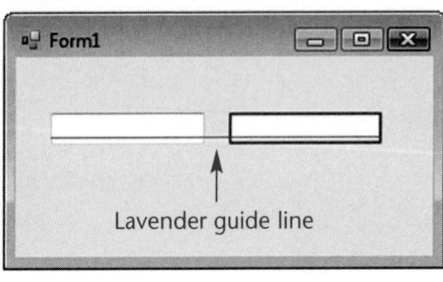

Blue guide line

Lavender guide line

Figure 3-6 Horizontal and vertical guide lines can be used together

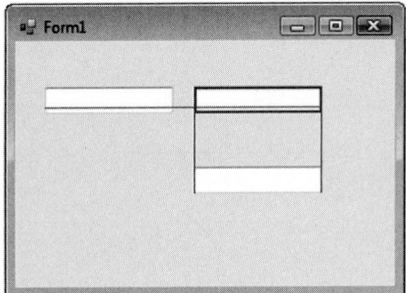

Tutorial 3-2:
Building the *Date String* application

VideoNote

Tutorial 3-2
Walkthrough

In this tutorial you will create an application that lets the user enter the following information about today's date:

- The day of the week
- The name of the month
- The numeric day of the month
- The year

When the user enters the information and clicks a button, the application displays a date string such as Friday, December 3, 2010.

Step 1:   Start Visual Studio and start a new Windows Forms Application named *Date String*.

Step 2:   Create the form shown in Figure 3-7, using the following instructions:

- You insert TextBox controls by double-clicking the TextBox icon in the Tool-Box. When a TextBox control is created, it will be given a default name. As with other controls, you can change a TextBox control's name by modifying its Name property.

- Give each control the name indicated in the figure. The labels that display *Enter the day of the week*, *Enter the month*, *Enter the day of the month*, and *Enter the year* will not be referred to in code, so they may keep their default names.
- Set the lblDateString label's AutoSize property to False, its BorderStyle property to *Fixed3D*, and its TextAlign property to *MiddleCenter*. Resize the label as shown in Figure 3-7, and delete the contents of the label's Text property.
- Set the form's Text property to *Date String*.

Figure 3-7 *Date String* form

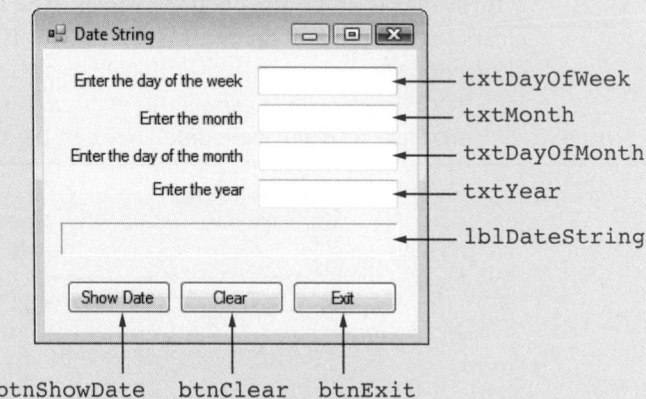

Step 3: Next, you will write code for the btnShowDate button's Click event handler. Double-click the button to create the code template, and then enter the lines shown in bold:

```
Private Sub btnShowDate_Click(...) Handles btnShowDate.Click
    ' Concatenate the input and build the date string.
    lblDateString.Text = txtDayOfWeek.Text & ", " &
        txtMonth.Text & " " &
        txtDayOfMonth.Text & ", " &
        txtYear.Text
End Sub
```

This example introduces a new programming technique: breaking up a long statement into multiple lines. Quite often, you will find yourself writing statements that are too long to fit entirely inside the *Code* window. Your code will be hard to read if you have to scroll the *Code* window to the right to view long statements. In addition, if you or your instructor chooses to print your code, the statements that are too long to fit on one line of the page will wrap around to the next line and make your code look unorganized. For these reasons, it is usually best to break a long statement into multiple lines.

When typing most statements, you can simply press the Enter key when you reach an appropriate point to continue the statement on the next line. Remember, however, that you cannot break up a keyword, quoted string, or a name (such as a variable name or a control name).

Step 4: Switch back to the *Designer* window and double-click the `btnClear` button to create a code template for its Click event handler. Then enter the following bold code to complete the event handler:

```
Private Sub btnClear_Click(...) Handles btnClear.Click
    ' Clear the Text Boxes and lblDateString.
    txtDayOfWeek.Clear()
    txtMonth.Clear()
    txtDayOfMonth.Clear()
    txtYear.Clear()
    lblDateString.Text = String.Empty
End Sub
```

Let's review this code. The `btnClear` button allows the user to start over with a form that is empty of previous values. The `btnClear_Click` event handler clears the contents of all the TextBox controls and the `lblDateString` label. To accomplish this, the procedure calls each TextBox control's `Clear` method, and then assigns the special value `String.Empty` to `lblDateString`'s Text property. (The value `String.Empty` represents an empty string. Assigning `String.Empty` to a label's Text property clears the value displayed by the label.)

Step 5: Switch back to the *Designer* window and double-click the `btnExit` button to create a code template for its Click event handler. Then enter the following bold code to complete the event handler:

```
Private Sub btnExit_Click(...) Handles btnExit.Click
    ' Close the form.
    Me.Close()
End Sub
```

Step 6: Save the project.

Step 7: Click the *Start* button (▶) to run the application. With the application running, enter the requested information into the TextBox controls and click the *Show Date* button. Your form should appear similar to the one shown in Figure 3-8.

Figure 3-8 Running the *Date String* application

Step 8: Click the *Clear* button to test it, and then enter new values into the TextBox controls. Click the *Show Date* button.

Step 9: Click the *Exit* button to exit the application.

The Focus **Method**

When an application is running and a form is displayed, one of the form's controls always has the **focus**. The control having the focus is the one that receives the user's keyboard input. For example, when a TextBox control has the focus, it receives the characters that the user enters on the keyboard. When a button has the focus, pressing the ⌊Enter⌋ key executes the button's Click event handler.

You can tell which control has the focus by looking at the form at runtime. When a TextBox control has the focus, a blinking text cursor appears inside it, or the text inside the TextBox control appears highlighted. When a button, radio button, or check box has the focus, a thin dotted line appears around the control.

NOTE: Only controls capable of receiving some sort of input, such as text boxes and buttons, may have the focus.

Often, you want to make sure a particular control has the focus. Consider the *Date String* application, for example. When the *Clear* button is clicked, the focus should return to the txtDayOfWeek TextBox control. This would make it unnecessary for the user to click the TextBox control in order to start entering another set of information.

In code, you move the focus to a control by calling the **Focus method**. The method's general syntax is:

```
ControlName.Focus()
```

where *ControlName* is the name of the control. For instance, you move the focus to the txtDayOfWeek TextBox control with the statement txtDayOfWeek.Focus(). After the statement executes, the txtDayOfWeek control will have the focus. In Tutorial 3-3, you add this statement to the *Clear* button's Click event handler so txtDayOfWeek has the focus after the TextBox controls and the lblDateString label are cleared.

Tutorial 3-3:
Using the Focus method

Step 1: Open the *Date String* project that you created in Tutorial 3-2.

Step 2: Open the *Code* window and add the statements shown in bold to the btnClear_Click event handler.

```
Private Sub btnClear_Click(...) Handles btnClear.Click
    ' Clear the Text Boxes and lblDateString
    txtDayOfWeek.Clear()
    txtMonth.Clear()
    txtDayOfMonth.Clear()
    txtYear.Clear()
    lblDateString.Text = String.Empty

    ' Give the focus to txtDayOfWeek.
    txtDayOfWeek.Focus()
End Sub
```

Step 3: Run the application. Enter some information into the TextBox controls, and then click the *Clear* button. The focus should return to the txtDayOfWeek TextBox control.

Step 4: Save the project.

Controlling a Form's Tab Order with the TabIndex Property

In Windows applications, pressing the Tab key changes the focus from one control to another. The order in which controls receive the focus is called the **tab order**. When you place controls on a form in Visual Basic, the tab order will be the same sequence in which you created the controls. In many cases this is the tab order you want, but sometimes you rearrange controls on a form, delete controls, and add new ones. These modifications often lead to a disorganized tab order, which can confuse and irritate the users of your application. Users want to tab smoothly from one control to the next, in a logical sequence.

You can modify the tab order by changing a control's TabIndex property. The **TabIndex property** contains a numeric value, which indicates the control's position in the tab order. When you create a control, Visual Basic automatically assigns a value to its TabIndex property. The first control you create on a form will have a TabIndex of 0, the second will have a TabIndex of 1, and so on. The control with a TabIndex of 0 will be the first control in the tab order. The next control in the tab order will be the one with a TabIndex of 1. The tab order continues in this sequence.

You may change the tab order of a form's controls by selecting them, one-by-one, and changing their TabIndex property in the *Properties* window. An easier method, however, is to click *View* on the menu bar, and then click *Tab Order*. This causes the form to be displayed in **tab order selection mode**. In this mode, each control's existing TabIndex value is displayed on the form. Then you establish a new tab order by clicking the controls in the order you want. When you are finished, exit tab order selection mode by pressing the Esc key. Tutorial 3-4 shows you how to change the tab order.

Tutorial 3-4:
Changing the tab order

In this tutorial, you rearrange the controls in the *Date String* application, and then change the tab order to accommodate the controls' new positions.

Step 1: Open the *Date String* project that you created in Tutorials 3-2 and 3-3.

Step 2: Open the application's form in the *Designer* window. Rearrange the controls to match Figure 3-9. (You might want to enlarge the form temporarily so you have

Figure 3-9 *Date String* form

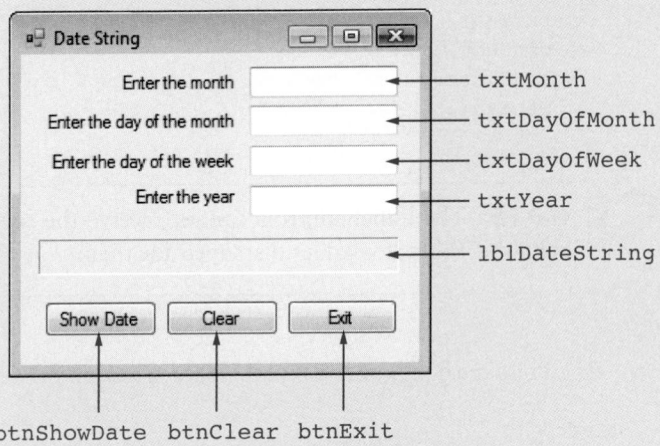

room to move some of the controls around. Don't forget to move the labels that correspond to the TextBox controls.)

Step 3: Run the application and notice which control has the focus. Press the ⌨Tab key several times and observe the tab order.

Step 4: Stop the application and return to Design mode.

Step 5: Click *View* on the menu bar, and then click *Tab Order*. The form should switch to tab order selection mode, as shown in Figure 3-10. The numbers displayed in the upper left corner of each control are the existing TabIndex values.

> **NOTE:** Your existing TabIndex values may be different from those shown in Figure 3-10.

Figure 3-10 Form in tab order selection mode

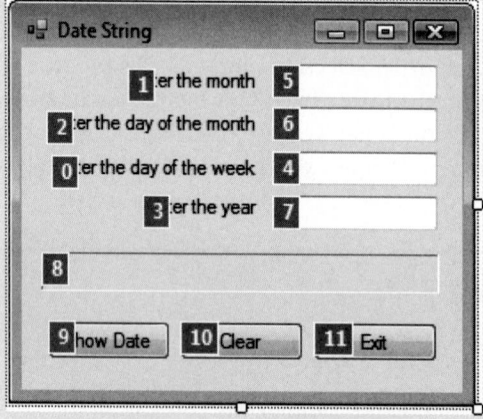

Step 6: Click the following controls in the order they are listed here: `txtMonth`, `txtDayOfMonth`, `txtDayOfWeek`, `txtYear`, `btnShowDate`, `btnClear`, `btnExit`.

Step 7: The controls you clicked should now have the following TabIndex values displayed:

```
txtMonth:        0
txtDayOfMonth:   1
txtDayOfWeek:    2
txtYear:         3
btnShowDate:     4
btnClear:        5
btnExit:         6
```

> **NOTE:** The Label controls cannot receive the focus, so do not be concerned with the TabIndex values displayed for them.

Step 8: Press the ⌨Esc key to exit tab order selection mode.

Step 9: Don't forget to change the `btnClear_Click` event handler so `txtMonth` gets the focus when the form is cleared. The code for the procedure is as follows, with the modified lines in bold:

```
Private Sub btnClear_Click(...) Handles btnClear.Click
  ' Clear the Text Boxes and lblDateString
  txtDayOfWeek.Clear()
  txtMonth.Clear()
  txtDayOfMonth.Clear()
  txtYear.Clear()
  lblDateString.Text = String.Empty

  ' Give the focus to txtMonth.
  txtMonth.Focus()
End Sub
```

Step 10: Run the application and test the new tab order.

Step 11: End the application and save the project.

Here are a few last notes about the TabIndex property:

- If you do not want a control to receive the focus when the user presses the `Tab` key, set its **TabStop property** to *False*.
- An error will occur if you assign a negative value to the TabIndex property in code.
- A control whose Visible property is set to *False* or whose Enabled property is set to *False* cannot receive the focus.
- GroupBox and Label controls have a TabIndex property, but they are skipped in the tab order.

Assigning Keyboard Access Keys to Buttons

An **access key**, also known as a **mnemonic**, is a key pressed in combination with the `Alt` key to access a control such as a button quickly. When you assign an access key to a button, the user can trigger a Click event either by clicking the button with the mouse or by using the access key. Users who are quick with the keyboard prefer to use access keys instead of the mouse.

You assign an access key to a button through its Text property. For example, assume an application has a button whose Text property is set to *Exit*. You wish to assign the access key `Alt`+`X` to the button, so the user may trigger the button's Click event by pressing `Alt`+`X` on the keyboard. To make the assignment, place an ampersand (&) before the letter *x* in the button's Text property: `E&xit`. Figure 3-11 shows how the Text property appears in the *Property* window.

Although the ampersand is part of the button's Text property, it is not displayed on the button. With the ampersand in front of the letter *x*, the letter will appear underlined as shown in Figure 3-12. This indicates that the button may be clicked by pressing `Alt`+`X` on the keyboard. (On many systems the underlining will not appear until the user presses the Alt key.)

Figure 3-11 Text property `E&xit`

Figure 3-12 Button with `E&xit` text

 NOTE: Access keys do not distinguish between uppercase and lowercase characters. There is no difference between [Alt]+X and [Alt]+x.

Suppose we had stored the value `&Exit` in the button's Text property. The ampersand is in front of the letter *E*, so [Alt]+[E] becomes the access key. The button will appear as shown in Figure 3-13.

Assigning the Same Access Key to Multiple Buttons

Be careful not to assign the same access key to two or more buttons on the same form. If two or more buttons share the same access key, a Click event is triggered for the first button created when the user presses the access key.

Displaying the & Character on a Button

If you want to display an ampersand character on a button use two ampersands (`&&`) in the Text property. Using two ampersands causes a single ampersand to display and does not define an access key. For example, if a button has the Text property `Save && Exit` the button will appear as shown in Figure 3-14.

Figure 3-13 Button with `&Exit` text

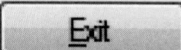

Figure 3-14 Button with text `Save && Exit`

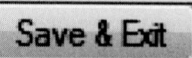

Accept Buttons and Cancel Buttons

An **accept button** is a button on a form that is automatically clicked when the user presses the ⎡Enter⎤ key. A **cancel button** is a button on a form that is automatically clicked when the user presses the ⎡Esc⎤ key. Forms have two properties, AcceptButton and CancelButton, which allow you to designate an accept button and a cancel button. When you select these properties in the *Properties* window, a down-arrow button (▾) appears, which allows you to display a drop-down list. The list contains the names of all the buttons on the form. You select the button that you want to designate as the accept button or cancel button.

Any button that is frequently clicked should probably be selected as the accept button. This will allow keyboard users to access the button quickly and easily. *Exit* or *Cancel* buttons are likely candidates to become cancel buttons. In Tutorial 3-5, you set access keys, accept, and cancel buttons.

Tutorial 3-5:
Setting access keys, accept, and cancel buttons

In this tutorial, you assign access keys to the buttons in the *Date String* application, and set accept and cancel buttons.

Step 1: Open the *Date String* project that you have worked on in Tutorials 3-2 through 3-4.

Step 2: Open the application's form in the *Designer* window.

Step 3: Select the *Show Date* button (`btnShowDate`) and change its text to read *Show &Date*. This assigns ⎡Alt⎤+⎡D⎤ as the button's access key.

Step 4: Select the *Clear* button (`btnClear`) and change its text to read *Clea&r*. This assigns ⎡Alt⎤+⎡R⎤ as the button's access key.

Step 5: Select the *Exit* button (`btnExit`) and change its text to read *E&xit*. This assigns ⎡Alt⎤+⎡X⎤ as the button's access key.

Step 6: Select the form, and then select the AcceptButton property in the *Properties* window. Click the down-arrow button (▾) to display the drop-down list of buttons. Select `btnShowDate` from the list.

Step 7: With the form still selected, select the CancelButton property in the *Properties* window. Click the down-arrow button (▾) to display the drop-down list of buttons. Select `btnExit` from the list.

Step 8: Run the application and test the buttons' new settings. Notice that when you press the ⎡Enter⎤ key, the *Show Date String* button's Click event hander is executed; when you press the ⎡Esc⎤ key, the application exits.

> **NOTE:** When the application executes, the access keys you assigned to the buttons might not be displayed as underlined characters until you press the ⎡Alt⎤ key.

Step 9: Save the project.

 **Checkpoint**

3.1 What TextBox control property holds text entered by the user?

3.2 Assume an application has a label named `lblMessage` and a TextBox control named `txtInput`. Write the statement that takes text the user entered into the TextBox control and assigns it to the label's Text property.

3.3 If the following statement is executed, what will the `lblGreeting` control display?

```
lblGreeting.Text = "Hello " & "Jonathon, " & "how are you?"
```

3.4 What is string concatenation?

3.5 What is meant when it is said that a control has the focus?

3.6 Write a statement that gives the focus to the `txtLastName` control.

3.7 What is meant by tab order?

3.8 How does the TabIndex property affect the tab order?

3.9 How does Visual Basic normally assign the tab order?

3.10 What happens when a control's TabStop property is set to *False*?

3.11 Assume a button's Text property is set to the text *Show &Map*. What effect does the & character have?

3.12 What is an accept button? What is a cancel button? How do you establish these buttons on a form?

 **3.2**   # Variables and Data Types

CONCEPT: Variables hold data that may be manipulated, used to manipulate other data, or remembered for later use.

VideoNote

Introduction to Variables

A **variable** is a storage location in computer memory that holds data while a program is running. It is called a variable because the data it holds can be changed by statements in the program.

In this chapter, you have seen programs that store data in properties belonging to Visual Basic controls. While properties hold values that are associated with a specific control, variables are used for general purpose data storage in memory. Generally speaking, you can do a number of things with variables:

- Copy and store values entered by the user so the values can be manipulated
- Perform arithmetic on numeric values
- Test values to determine that they meet some criterion
- Temporarily hold and manipulate the value of a control property
- Remember data for later use in a program

Think of a variable as a name that represents a location in the computer's random-access memory (RAM). When a value is stored in a variable, it is actually stored in RAM. You use the assignment operator (=) to store a value in a variable, just as you do with a control property. For example, suppose a program uses a variable named `intLength`. The following statement stores the value 112 in that variable:

```
intLength = 112
```

When this statement executes, the value 112 is stored in the memory location the name `intLength` represents. As another example, assume the following statement appears in a program that uses a variable named `strGreeting` and a TextBox control named `txtName`:

```
strGreeting = "Good morning " & txtName.Text
```

Suppose the user has already entered *Holly* into the `txtName` TextBox control. When the statement executes, the variable `strGreeting` is assigned the string `"Good morning Holly"`.

Declaring Variables

A **variable declaration** is a statement that creates a variable in memory when a program executes. The declaration indicates the name you wish to give the variable and the type of data the variable will hold. Here is the general form of a variable declaration:

```
Dim VariableName As DataType
```

Here is an example of a variable declaration:

```
Dim intLength As Integer
```

Let's look at each part of this statement, and its purpose:

- The `Dim` keyword tells Visual Basic that a variable is being declared.
- `intLength` is the name of the variable.
- `As Integer` indicates the variable's data type. We know it will be used to hold integer numbers.

You can declare multiple variables with one `Dim` statement, as shown in the following statement. It declares three variables, all holding integers:

```
Dim intLength, intWidth, intHeight As Integer
```

> **NOTE:** The keyword `Dim` stands for "dimension." This is a term for declaring a variable that goes back to some of the earliest programming languages.

Variable Names

It is your responsibility as the programmer to make up the names of the variables that you use in a program. You must follow these rules when naming a variable in Visual Basic:

- The first character must be a letter or an underscore character. (We do not recommend that you start a variable name with an underscore, but if you do, the name must also contain at least one letter or numeric digit.)
- After the first character, you may use letters, numeric digits, and underscore characters. (You cannot use spaces, periods, or other punctuation characters in a variable name.)
- Variable names cannot be longer than 1023 characters.
- Variable names cannot be Visual Basic keywords. Keywords have reserved meanings in Visual Basic, and their use as variable names would confuse the compiler.

Type Prefixes

In this book we normally begin variable names with a three- or four-letter prefix that indicates the variable's data type. For example, the variable name `intLength` begins with the three-letter prefix `int`, which indicates that it is an Integer variable. Earlier we used the name `strGreeting` as an example variable name. That name begins with the prefix `str`, indicating that it is a String variable.

The practice of beginning a variable name with a prefix is not required, but it is intended to make code more understandable. For example, when you are reading your own, or someone else's, code, and you see a variable name such as `intUnitsSold`, you immediately know that it is an Integer variable because of the `int` prefix.

The convention of using type prefixes in variable names has historically been popular among Visual Basic programmers, but not all programmers follow this practice. Your instructor may or may not require you to use them. Regardless of whether you use them or not, be consistent in the approach that you adopt.

Table 3-1 shows the prefixes that we use in this book, the Visual Basic data types that they are used with, and examples of each used in variable names. (We will discuss the commonly used data types in greater detail momentarily.)

Table 3-1 Recommended prefixes for variable names

Variable Type	Prefix	Examples
Boolean	bln	blnContinue, blnHasRows
Byte	byt	bytInput, bytCharVal
Char	chr	chrSelection, chrMiddleInitial
Date, DateTime	dat or dtm	datWhenPublished, dtmBirthDate
Decimal	dec	decWeeklySalary, decGrossPay
Double	dbl	dblAirVelocity, dblPlanetMass
Integer	int	intCount, intDaysInPayPeriod
Long	lng	lngElapsedSeconds
Object	obj	objStudent, objPayroll
Short	shrt	shrtCount
Single	sng	sngTaxRate, sngGradeAverage
String	str	strLastName, strAddress

Use Descriptive Variable Names

In addition to following the Visual Basic rules, you should always choose names for your variables that give an indication of what they are used for. For example, a String variable that holds a customer's name might be named `strCustomerName`, and an Integer variable that holds a car's speed might be named `intSpeed`. You may be tempted to give variables names like `x` and `b2`, but names like these give no clue as to what the variable's purpose is.

Because a variable's name should reflect the variable's purpose, programmers often find themselves creating names that are made of multiple words. For example, consider the following variable names:

```
inthoursworked
strcustomername
inthotdogssoldtoday
```

Unfortunately, these names are not easily read by the human eye because the words aren't separated. Because we can't have spaces in variable names, we need to find another way to separate the words in a multiword variable name, and make it more readable to the human eye.

One way to do this is to use the camel case naming convention. **Camel case** names are written in the following manner:

- The variable name starts with lowercase letters.
- The first character of the second and subsequent words is written in uppercase.

For example, the following variable names are written in camel case:

```
intHoursWorked
strCustomerName
intHotDogsSoldToday
```

This style of naming is called camel case because the uppercase characters that appear in a name may suggest a camel's humps. The camel case convention is widely used, not only in Visual Basic, but in other languages as well. We will use the camel case convention for variable names in this book.

Assigning Values to Variables

A value is put into a variable with an assignment statement. For example, the following statement assigns the value 20 to the variable `intUnitsSold`:

```
intUnitsSold = 20
```

The = operator is called the assignment operator. A variable name must always appear on the left side of the assignment operator. For example, the following would be incorrect:

```
20 = intUnitsSold
```

On the right side of the operator, you can put a literal, another variable, or a mathematical expression that matches the variable's type. In the following, the contents of the variable on the right side of the = sign is assigned to the variable on the left side:

```
intUnitsSold = intUnitsOnHand
```

Suppose `intUnitsOnHand` already equals 20. Then Figure 3-15 shows how the value 20 is copied into the memory location represented by `intUnitsSold`.

The assignment operator changes only the left operand. The right operand (or expression) does not change value. Sometimes your program will contain a series of statements that pass a value from one variable to the next. When the following statements execute, all three variables will contain the same value, 50:

```
Dim intA, intB, intC As Integer
intA = 50
intB = intA
intC = intB
```

Figure 3-15 Assigning `intUnitsOnHand` to `intUnitsSold`

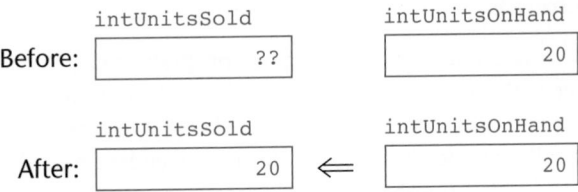

A variable can hold only one value at a time. If you assign a new value to the variable, the new value replaces the variable's previous contents. There is no way to "undo" this operation. For example:

```
Dim intA, intB As Integer
intA = 50
intA = 99
```

After the second assignment statement, `intA` equals 99. The value 50 no longer exists in memory.

Integer Data Types

Integers are whole numbers such as –5, 26, 12345, and 0. Visual Basic has four data types, listed in Table 3-2, for holding integers. (For your convenience the table also shows the type prefix that we will use for variables of each of these data types.) Unsigned integers can hold only positive values (zero is considered positive). Signed integers can hold both positive and negative values.

Table 3-2 Integer data types

Type	Naming Prefix	Description
Byte	byt	Holds an unsigned integer value in the range 0 to 255
Short	shrt	Holds a signed integer in the range –32,768 to +32,767
Integer	int	Holds a signed integer in the range –2,147,483,648 to +2,147,483,647
Long	lng	Holds a signed integer in the range –9,223,372,036,854,775,808 to +9,223,372,036,854,775,807

The following code example shows variables of the different integer types being declared and assigned values:

```
Dim bytInches As Byte
Dim shrtFeet as Short
Dim intMiles As Integer
Dim lngNationalDebt As Long

bytInches = 26
shrtFeet = 32767
intMiles = 2100432877
lngNationalDebt = 4000000000001
```

Each type has a different storage size and range of possible values it can hold. Most of the time, you will use the Integer data type for integer-type values. Its name is easy to remember, and Integer values are efficiently processed by the computer.

Integer Literals

When you write an integer literal in your program code, Visual Basic assumes the literal is type Integer if the value fits within the allowed range for the Integer data type. A value larger than that will be assumed to be type Long. On rare occasions you may want to override the literal's default type. You do this by appending one of the following special characters to the end of the number:

I Integer literal
L Long integer literal
S Short integer literal

In the following code example, an integer literal uses the L character to identify it as type Long:

```
Dim lngCounter As Long
lngCounter = 10000L
```

In the following, an integer literal uses the S character to identify it as type Short:

```
Dim shrtFeet as Short
shrtFeet = 1234S
```

 TIP: You cannot embed commas in numeric literals. The following, for example, causes an error: `intMiles = 32,767`

Floating-Point Data Types

Values that have fractional parts and use a decimal point must be stored in one of Visual Basic's floating-point data types. Table 3-3 lists the floating-point data types, showing their naming prefixes and descriptions.

Table 3-3 Floating-point data types

Type	Naming Prefix	Description
Single	sng	Holds a signed single precision real number with 7 significant digits, in the range of approximately plus or minus 1.0×10^{38}
Double	dbl	Holds a signed double precision real number with 15 significant digits, in the range of approximately plus or minus 1.0×10^{308}
Decimal	dec	Decimal real number, 29 significant digits. Its range (with no decimal places) is +/–79,228,162,514,264,337,593,543,950,335

Significant Digits

The significant digits measurement for each floating-point data type is important for certain kinds of calculations. Suppose you were simulating a chemical reaction and needed to calculate the number of calories produced. You might produce a number such as 1.234567824724. If you used a variable of type Single, only the first seven digits would be kept in computer memory, and the remaining digits would be lost. The last digit would be rounded upward, producing 1.234568. This loss of precision happens because the computer uses a limited amount of storage for floating-point numbers. If you did the same chemical reaction calculation using a variable of type Double, the entire result would be safely held in the number, with no loss of precision.

The Decimal data type is used in financial calculations when you need a great deal of precision. This data type helps prevent rounding errors from creeping into repeated calculations.

The following code demonstrates each floating-point data type:

```
Dim sngTemperature As Single
Dim dblWindSpeed As Double
Dim decBankBalance As Decimal

sngTemperature = 98.6
dblWindSpeed = 35.373659262
decBankBalance = 1234567890.1234567890123456789D
```

Notice that the last line requires a D suffix on the number to identify it as a Decimal literal. Otherwise, Visual Basic would assume that the number was type Double.

Floating-Point Literals

Floating-point literals can be written in either fixed-point or scientific notation. The number 47281.97, for example, would be written in scientific notation as 4.728197×10^4. Visual Basic requires the letter E just before the exponent in scientific notation. So, our sample number would be written in Visual Basic like this:

```
4.728197E+4
```

The + sign after the E is optional. Here is an example of a value having a negative exponent:

```
4.623476E-2
```

Scientific notation is particularly useful for very large numbers. Instead of writing a value such as 1234000000000000000000000000000.0, for example, it is easier to write 1.234E+31.

Boolean Data Type

A Boolean type variable can hold only one of two possible values: *True* or *False*. The values True and False are built-in Visual Basic keywords. The word Boolean is named after George Boole, a famous mathematician of the nineteenth century. (His Boolean algebra is the basis for all modern computer arithmetic.)

We use Boolean variables to hold information that is either true or false. The standard naming prefix for Boolean variables is `bln`. Here is an example:

```
Dim blnIsRegistered As Boolean
blnIsRegistered = True
```

We will begin using Boolean variables in Chapter 4.

Char Data Type

Variables of the Char data type can hold a single Unicode character. Unicode characters are the set of values that can represent a large number of international characters in different languages. To assign a character literal to a Char variable, enclose the character in double quotations marks, followed by a lowercase "c". The standard naming prefix for Char variables is `chr`. The following is an example:

```
Dim chrLetter As Char
chrLetter = "A"c
```

String Data Type

A variable of type String can hold between zero and about 2 billion characters. The characters are stored in sequence. A string literal, as you have seen earlier, is always enclosed in quotation marks. In the following code, a string variable is assigned various string literals:

```
Dim strName As String
strName = "Jose Gonzalez"
```

The standard naming prefix for String variables is `str`.

An empty string literal can be coded as `""` or by the special identifier named `String.Empty`:

```
strName = ""
strName = String.Empty
```

Date Data Type

A variable of the Date data type can hold date and time information. Date variables are assigned a prefix of dat or dtm. You can assign a date literal to a Date variable, as shown here:

```
Dim dtmBirth As Date
dtmBirth = #5/1/2010#
```

Notice that the Date literal is enclosed in # symbols. A variety of date and time formats is permitted. All of the following Date literals are valid:

```
#12/10/2010#
#8:45:00 PM#
#10/20/2010 6:30:00 AM#
```

A Date literal can contain a date, a time, or both. When specifying a time, if you omit AM or PM, the hours value is assumed to be based on a 24-hour clock. If you supply a date without the time, the time portion of the variable defaults to 12:00 AM.

In Tutorial 3-6, you will assign text to a variable.

Tutorial 3-6:
Assigning text to a variable

In this tutorial, you will modify a program that assigns the contents of text boxes to a string variable.

Step 1:   Open the *Variable Demo* project from the student sample programs folder named *Chap3\Variable Demo*.

Step 2:   View the *Form1* form in the *Designer* window, as shown in Figure 3-16.

Step 3:   Double-click the *Show Name* button, which opens the *Code* window and creates a template for the button's Click event handler. Type the following lines, shown in bold:

```
Private Sub btnShowName_Click(...) Handles btnShowName.Click
    ' Declare a string variable to hold the full name.
    Dim strFullName As String

    ' Combine the first and last names and assign the
    ' result to strFullName.
    strFullName = txtFirstName.Text & " " & txtLastName.Text

    ' Display the full name in the lblFullName label.
    lblFullName.Text = strFullName
End Sub
```

Figure 3-16 *Variable Demo* application, *Form1*

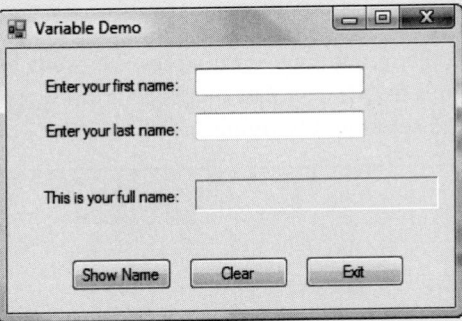

Step 4: In the *Designer* window, double-click the *Clear* button and insert the following lines in the *Code* window (shown in bold):

```
Private Sub btnClear_Click(...) Handles btnClear.Click
    ' Clear TextBox controls and the Label.
    txtFirstName.Clear()
    txtLastName.Clear()
    lblFullName.Text = String.Empty

    ' Set focus to txtfirstName.
    txtFirstName.Focus()
End Sub
```

Step 5: In the *Designer* window, double-click the *Exit* button and insert the following lines in the *Code* window (shown in bold):

```
Private Sub btnExit_Click(...) Handles btnExit.Click
    ' Close the form.
    Me.Close()
End Sub
```

Step 6: Save the project.

Step 7: Run the program, type in a name, and click the *Show Name* button. The output should look similar to that shown in Figure 3-17.

Figure 3-17 *Variable Demo* application, running

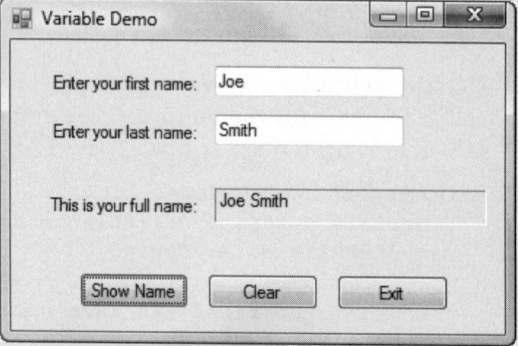

 TIP: Code outlining is a Visual Studio tool that lets you expand and collapse sections of code. As your programs get longer, it is sometimes helpful to collapse procedures you have already written. Then you can concentrate on new sections of code. For example, Figure 3-18 shows the btnShowName_Click procedure from the *Variable Demo* application. Notice that a minus sign (–) appears next to its heading.

If we click the minus sign, it collapses the event handler into a single line showing its name (Figure 3-19). You can modify outlining options by right-clicking in the *Code* window and selecting *Outlining*.

Figure 3-18 Expanded btnShowName_Click handler

Click here to collapse the event handler.

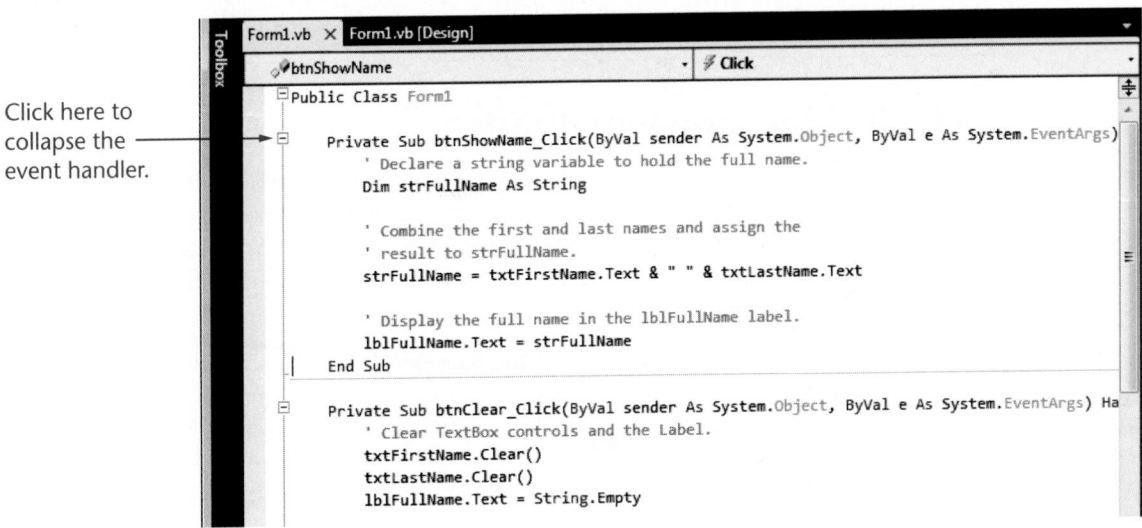

Figure 3-19 Collapsed btnShowName_Click handler

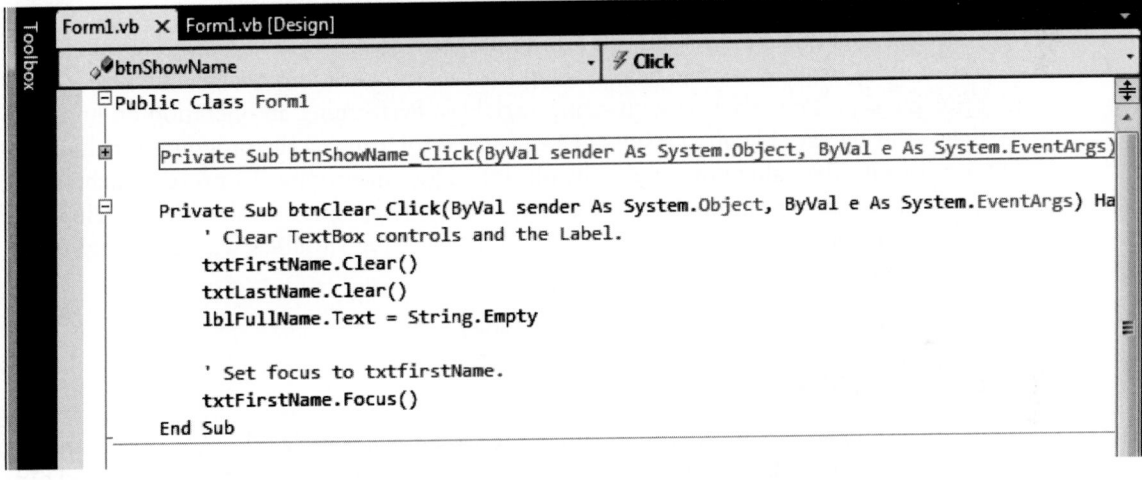

Variable Declarations and the IntelliSense Feature

When you are entering a variable declaration, Visual Studio's IntelliSense feature helps you fill in the data type. Suppose you begin to type a variable declaration such as the following:

```
Dim decPayRate As
```

If you press the (Spacebar) at this point, a list box appears with all the possible data types in alphabetical order. When the list box appears, type the first few letters of the data type name, and the box will highlight the data type that matches what you have typed. For example, after you type *dec* the Decimal data type will be highlighted. Press the (Tab) key to select the highlighted data type.

> **TIP:** You can use the arrow keys or the mouse with the list box's scroll bar to scroll through the list. Once you see the desired data type, double-click it with the mouse.

Default Values and Initialization

When a variable is first created it is assigned a default value. Variables with a numeric data type (such as Byte, Decimal, Double, Integer, Long, and Single) are assigned the value 0. Boolean variables are initially assigned the value False, and Date variables are assigned the value 12:00:00 AM, January 1 of year 1. String variables are automatically assigned a special value called `Nothing`.

You may also specify a starting value in the `Dim` statement. This is called **initialization**. Here is an example:

```
Dim intUnitsSold As Integer = 12
```

This statement declares `intUnitsSold` as an Integer and assigns it the starting value 12. Here are other examples:

```
Dim strLastName As String = "Johnson"
Dim blnIsFinished As Boolean = True
Dim decGrossPay As Decimal = 2500
Dim chrMiddleInitial As Char = "E"c
```

Forgetting to initialize variables can lead to program errors. Unless you are certain a variable will be assigned a value before being used in an operation, always initialize it. This principle is particularly true with string variables. Performing an operation on an uninitialized string variable often results in a runtime error, causing the program to halt execution because the value `Nothing` is invalid for many operations. To prevent such errors, always initialize string variables or make sure they are assigned a value before being used in other operations. A good practice is to initialize string variables with an empty string, as shown in the following statement:

```
Dim strName As String = String.Empty
```

Local Variables

In the examples we have looked at so far, the variables are declared inside event handlers. When a variable is declared inside of a procedure, such as an event handler, it is referred to as a **local variable**. A local variable belongs to the procedure in which it is declared, and only statements inside that procedure can access the variable. (The term local is meant to indicate that the variable can be used only locally, within the procedure in which it is declared.)

An error will occur if a statement in one procedure attempts to access a local variable that belongs to another procedure. For example, assume that an application has the following two event handlers:

```
Private Sub Button1_Click(...) Handles Button1.Click
    ' Declare an Integer variable named intValue.
    Dim intValue As Integer

    ' Assign a value to the variable.
    intValue = 25
End Sub

Private Sub Button2_Click(...) Handles Button2.Click
    ' Attempt to assign a value to the intValue variable.
    ' This will cause an error!
    intValue = 0
End Sub
```

The `intValue` variable that is declared inside the `Button1_Click` event handler is a local variable that belongs that procedure. However, the assignment statement inside the `Button2_Click` event handler attempts to store a value in `intValue` variable. This will cause an error because the `intValue` variable is local to the `Button1_Click` procedure, and statements outside that procedure cannot access it. If we try to compile this code, we still get the following error message: *Name 'intValue' is not declared.*

What if we declared `intValue` again in the `Button2_Click` event handler? Then the program would compile with no errors, but we would have created two different variables having the same name. Each variable is separate from the other:

```
Private Sub Button1_Click(...) Handles Button1.Click
    ' Declare an Integer variable named intValue.
    Dim intValue As Integer

    ' Assign a value to the variable.
    intValue = 25
End Sub

Private Sub Button2_Click(...) Handles Button2.Click
    ' Declare an Integer variable named intValue.
    Dim intValue As Integer

    ' Attempt to assign a value to the intValue variable.
    intValue = 0
End Sub
```

In this case, the `Button1_Click` event handler has a local variable named `intValue`, and the `Button2_Click` event handler has its own local variable named `intValue`. Variables in different procedures can have the same name because they are isolated from each other.

Scope

The term **scope** means the part of a program in which a variable may be accessed. Every variable has a scope, and a variable is visible only to statements in its scope. A local variable's scope begins at the `Dim` statement that declares the variable, and ends at the end of the procedure in which the variable is declared. The variable cannot be accessed by statements outside this region. That means that a local variable cannot be accessed by statements outside the procedure, or by statements that are inside the procedure but before the `Dim` statement that declares the variable.

For example, look at the following event handler code. This procedure attempts to assign a value to a variable before the variable is declared:

```
Private Sub Button1_Click(...) Handles Button1.Click
    strName = "Jane" 'ERROR!
    Dim strName As String
End Sub
```

If we try to compile this code, we will get the error message *Local variable 'strName' cannot be referred to before it is declared.*

Duplicate Variable Names

Earlier you saw that two variables with the same name can be declared in different procedures. That is because the scope of the two variables is separate. You cannot, however, declare two variables with the same name in the same scope. For example, look at the following event handler:

```
Private Sub Button1_Click(...) Handles Button1.Click
    ' Declare an Integer variable named intValue.
    Dim intValue As Integer = 0
```

```
        ' Declare another Integer variable named intValue.
        ' ERROR!
        Dim intValue As Integer = 25
    End Sub
```

This procedure declares two local variables named `intValue`. The second `Dim` statement will cause an error because a variable named `intValue` has already been declared. If we try to compile this code we will get the error message *Local variable 'intValue' is already declared in the current block*.

 Checkpoint

3.13 What is a variable?

3.14 Show an example of a variable declaration.

3.15 Which of the following variable names are written with the convention used in this book?
   a. `decintrestrate`
   b. `InterestRateDecimal`
   c. `decInterestRate`

3.16 Indicate whether each of the following is a legal variable name. If it is not, explain why.
   a. `count`
   b. `rate*Pay`
   c. `deposit.amount`
   d. `down_payment`

3.17 What default value is assigned to each of the following variables?
   a. Integer
   b. Double
   c. Boolean
   d. Byte
   e. Date

3.18 Write a Date literal for the following date and time: 5:35:00 PM on February 20, 2010.

3.19 *Bonus question*: Find out which famous Microsoft programmer was launched into space in early 2007. Was this programmer connected in any way to Visual Basic?

3.3 Performing Calculations

CONCEPT: Visual Basic has powerful arithmetic operators that perform calculations with numeric variables and literals.

There are two basic types of operators in Visual Basic: unary and binary. These reflect the number of operands an operator requires. A **unary operator** requires only a single operand. The negation operator, for example, causes a number to be negative:

VideoNote

Problem Solving with Variables

```
-5
```

It can be applied to a variable. The following line negates the value in `intCount`:

```
-intCount
```

A **binary operator** works with two operands. The addition operator (+) is binary because it uses two operands. The following mathematical expression adds the values of two numbers:

```
5 + 10
```

The following adds the values of two variables:

```
intA + intB
```

Table 3-4 lists the binary arithmetic operators in Visual Basic. Addition, subtraction, multiplication, division, and exponentiation can be performed on both integer and floating-point data types. Only two operations (integer division and modulus) must be performed on integer types.

Table 3-4 Arithmetic operators in Visual Basic

Operator	Operation
+	Addition
−	Subtraction
*	Multiplication
/	Floating-point division
\	Integer division
MOD	Modulus (remainder from integer division)
^	Exponentiation ($x\text{^}y = x^y$)

Addition

The addition operator (+) adds two values, producing a sum. The values can be literals or variables. The following are examples of valid addition expressions:

```
intA + 10

20 + intB
```

The question is, what happens to the result? Ordinarily, it is assigned to a variable, using the assignment operator. In the following statement, intC is assigned the sum of the values from intA and intB:

```
intC = intA + intB
```

This operation happens in two steps. First, the addition takes place. Second, the sum is assigned to the variable on the left side of the = sign.

The following example adds the contents of two Double variables that hold rainfall measurements for the months of March and April:

```
dblCombined = dblMarchRain + dblAprilRain
```

Subtraction

The subtraction operator (−) subtracts the right-hand operand from the left-hand operand. In the following, the variable intC will contain the difference between intA and intB:

```
intC = intA - intB
```

Alternatively, the difference might be assigned back to the variable intA:

```
intA = intA - intB
```

The following statement uses Decimal variables. It subtracts an employee's tax amount from his or her gross pay, producing the employee's net pay:

```
decNetPay = decGrossPay - decTax
```

Addition and Subtraction in Applications

How can addition and subtraction statements be useful in an application? Suppose a college registration program needs to add the credits completed by a student during two semesters (Fall and Spring). First, the variables would be declared:

```
Dim intFallCredits, intSpringCredits, intTotalCredits As Integer
```

Then the application would assign values to `intSpringCredits` and `intFallCredits`, perhaps by asking for their input from the user. Finally, the program would calculate the total credits for the year:

```
intTotalCredits = intFallCredits + intSpringCredits
```

Multiplication

The multiplication operator (*) multiplies the right-hand operand by the left-hand operand. In the following statement, the variable `intC` is assigned the product of multiplying `intA` and `intB`:

```
intC = intA * intB
```

The following statement uses Decimal variables to multiply an item's price by the sales tax rate, producing a sales tax amount:

```
decTaxAmount = decItemPrice * decTaxRate
```

Floating-Point Division

The floating-point division operator (/) divides one floating-point value by another. The result, called the quotient, is also a floating-point number. For example, the following statement divides the total points earned by a basketball team by the number of players, producing the average points per player:

```
dblAverage = dblTotalPoints / dblNumPlayers
```

 NOTE: If you divide a number by zero you get the special value `Infinity`.

Integer Division

The integer division operator (\) divides one integer by another, producing an integer result. For example, suppose we know the number of minutes it will take to finish a job, and we want to calculate the number of hours that are contained in that many minutes. The following statement uses integer division to divide the `intMinutes` variable by 60, giving the number of hours as a result:

```
intHours = intMinutes \ 60
```

Integer division does not save any fractional part of the quotient. The following statement, for example, produces the integer 3:

```
intQuotient = 10 \ 3
```

Modulus

The modulus operator (MOD) performs integer division and returns only the remainder. The following statement assigns 2 to the variable named `intRemainder`:

```
intRemainder = 17 MOD 3
```

Note that 17 divided by 3 equals 5, with a remainder of 2. Suppose a job is completed in 174 minutes, and we want to express this value in both hours and minutes. First, we can use integer division to calculate the hours (2):

```
intTotalMinutes = 174
intHours = intTotalMinutes \ 60
```

Next, we use the MOD operator to calculate the remaining minutes (54):

```
intMinutes = intTotalMinutes Mod 60
```

Now we know that the job was completed in 2 hours, 54 minutes.

Exponentiation

Exponentiation calculates a variable x taken to the power of y when written in the form x ^ y. The value it returns is of type Double. For example, the following statement assigns 25.0 to dblResult:

```
dblResult = 5.0 ^ 2.0
```

You can use integers as operands, but the result will still be a Double:

```
dblResult = intX ^ intY
```

Negative and fractional exponents are permitted.

Getting the Current Date and Time

Your computer system has an internal clock that calculates the current date and time. Visual Basic provides the functions listed in Table 3-5, which allow you to retrieve the current date, time, or both from your computer. We will discuss functions in greater detail later, but for now, you can think of functions as commands recognized by Visual Basic that return useful information.

Table 3-5 Date and time functions

Function	Description
Now	Returns the current date and time from the system
TimeOfDay	Returns the current time from the system, without the date
Today	Returns the current date from the system, without the time

The following code demonstrates how to use the Now function:

```
Dim dtmSystemDate As Date
dtmSystemDate = Now
```

After the code executes, dtmSystemDate will contain the current date and time, as reported by the system. The TimeOfDay function retrieves only the current time from the system, demonstrated by the following statement.

```
dtmSystemTime = TimeOfDay
```

After the statement executes, dtmSystemTime will contain the current time, but not the current date. Instead, it will contain the date January 1 of year 1. The Today function retrieves only the current date from the system, demonstrated by the following statement:

```
dtmSystemDate = Today
```

After the statement executes, dtmSystemDate will contain the current date, but will not contain the current time. Instead, it will contain the time 00:00:00.

> **TIP:** Later in this chapter you will see how to use the `ToString` method to display only the date value or time value inside a Date variable.

Combined Assignment Operators

Quite often, programs have assignment statements in the following form:

```
intNumber = intNumber + 1
```

On the right-hand side of the assignment operator, 1 is added to `intNumber`. The result is then assigned to `intNumber`, replacing the value that was previously stored there. Similarly, the following statement subtracts 5 from `intNumber`.

```
intNumber = intNumber - 5
```

Table 3-6 shows examples of similar statements. Assume that the variable x is set to 6 prior to each statement's execution.

Table 3-6 Assignment statements (Assume x = 6 prior to each statement's execution)

Statement	Operation Performed	Value of x after the Statement Executes
x = x + 4	Adds 4 to x	10
x = x - 3	Subtracts 3 from x	3
x = x * 10	Multiplies x by 10	60
x = x / 2	Divides x by 2	3

Assignment operations are common in programming. For convenience, Visual Basic offers a special set of operators designed specifically for these jobs. Table 3-7 shows the **combined assignment operators,** or **compound operators.**

Table 3-7 Combined assignment operators

Operator	Example Usage	Equivalent To
+=	x += 2	x = x + 2
-=	x -= 5	x = x - 5
*=	x *= 10	x = x * 10
/=	x /= y	x = x / y
\=	x \= y	x = x \ y
&=	strName &= lastName	strName = strName & lastName

Operator Precedence

It is possible to build **mathematical expressions** with several operators. The following statement assigns the sum of 17, x, 21, and y to the variable `intAnswer`.

```
intAnswer = 17 + x + 21 + y
```

Some expressions are not that straightforward, however. Consider the following statement:

```
dblOutcome = 12 + 6 / 3
```

What value will be stored in dblOutcome? If the addition takes place before the division, then dblOutcome will be assigned 6. If the division takes place first, dblOutcome will be assigned 14. The correct answer is 14 because the division operator has higher **precedence** than the addition operator.

Mathematical expressions are evaluated from left to right. When two operators share an operand, the operator with the highest precedence executes first. Multiplication and division have higher precedence than addition and subtraction, so 12 + 6 / 3 works like this:

- 6 is divided by 3, yielding a result of 2.
- 12 is added to 2, yielding a result of 14.

It can be diagrammed as shown in Figure 3-20.

Figure 3-20 dblOutcome = 12 + 6 / 3

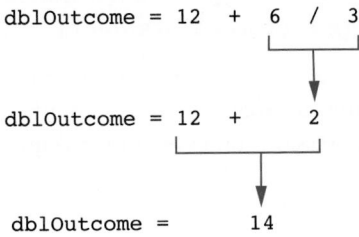

The precedence of the arithmetic operators, from highest to lowest, is as follows:

1. Exponentiation (the ^ operator)
2. Multiplication and division (the * and / operators)
3. Integer division (the \ operator)
4. Modulus (the MOD operator)
5. Addition and subtraction (the + and − operators)

The multiplication and division operators have the same precedence. This is also true of the addition and subtraction operators. When two operators with the same precedence share an operand, the operator on the left executes before the operator on the right.

Table 3-8 shows some example mathematical expressions with their values.

Table 3-8 Mathematical expressions and their values

Expression	Value
5 + 2 * 4	13
2^3 * 4 + 3	35
10 / 2 − 3	2
8 + 12 * 2 − 4	28
6 − 3 * 2 + 7 − 1	6

Grouping with Parentheses

Parts of a mathematical expression may be grouped with parentheses to force some operations to be performed before others. In the following statement, the sum of x, y, and z is divided by 3. The result is assigned to dblAverage.

```
dblAverage = (x + y + z) / 3
```

Without the parentheses, however, *z* would be divided by 3, and the result added to the sum of *x* and *y*. Table 3-9 shows more expressions and their values.

Table 3-9 Additional mathematical expressions and their values

Expression	Value
(5 + 2) * 4	28
10 / (5 – 3)	5
8 + 12 * (6 – 2)	56
(6 – 3) * (2 + 7) / 3	9

More about Mathematical Operations: Converting Mathematical Expressions to Programming Statements

In algebra, the mathematical expression $2xy$ describes the value 2 times *x* times *y*. Visual Basic, however, requires an operator for any mathematical operation. Table 3-10 shows some mathematical expressions that perform multiplication and the equivalent Visual Basic expressions.

Table 3-10 Visual Basic equivalents of mathematical expressions

Mathematical Expression	Operation	Visual Basic Equivalent
$6B$	6 times *B*	6 * B
(3)(12)	3 times 12	3 * 12
$4xy$	4 times *x* times *y*	4 * x * y

Checkpoint

3.20 What value will be stored in `dblResult` after each of the following statements executes?

   a. `dblResult = 6 + 3 * 5`
   b. `dblResult = 12 / 2 - 4`
   c. `dblResult = 2 + 7 * 3 - 6`
   d. `dblResult = (2 + 4) * 3`
   e. `dblResult = 10 \ 3`
   f. `dblResult = 6 ^ 2`

3.21 What value will be stored in `intResult` after each statement executes?

   a. `intResult = 10 MOD 3`
   b. `intResult = 47 MOD 15`

3.22 Write a statement that assigns the current time of day to the variable `dtmThisTime`.

3.23 Write a statement that assigns the current date and time to a variable named `dtmCurrent`.

3.24 How is integer division different from floating-point division?

3.25 What will be the final value of `dblResult` in the following sequence?

```
Dim dblResult As Double = 3.5
dblResult += 1.2
```

3.26 What will be the final value of `dblResult` in the following sequence?

```
Dim dblResult As Double = 3.5
dblResult *= 2.0
```

3.4 Mixing Different Data Types

Implicit Type Conversion

When you assign a value of one data type to a variable of another data type, Visual Basic attempts to convert the value being assigned to the data type of the receiving variable. This is known as an **implicit type conversion**. Suppose we want to assign the integer 5 to a variable of type Single named `sngNumber`:

```
Dim sngNumber As Single = 5
```

When the statement executes, the integer 5 is automatically converted into a single-precision real number, which is then stored in `sngNumber`. This conversion is a **widening conversion** because no data is lost.

Narrowing Conversions

If you assign a real number to an integer variable, Visual Basic attempts to perform a **narrowing conversion**. Often, some data is lost. For example, the following statement assigns 12.2 to an integer variable:

```
Dim intCount As Integer = 12.2    'intCount = 12
```

Assuming for the moment that Visual Basic is configured to accept this type of conversion, the 12.2 is rounded downward to 12. Similarly, the next statement rounds upward to the nearest integer when the fractional part of the number is .5 or greater:

```
Dim intCount As Integer = 12.5    'intCount = 13
```

Another narrowing conversion occurs when assigning a Double value to a variable of type Single. Both hold floating-point values, but Double permits more significant digits:

```
Dim dblOne As Double = 1.2342376
Dim sngTwo As Single = dblOne      'sngTwo = 1.234238
```

The value stored in `sngTwo` is rounded up to 1.234238 because variables of type Single can only hold seven significant digits.

Option Strict

Visual Basic has a configuration option named *Option Strict* that determines whether certain implicit data type conversions are legal. If you set *Option Strict* to *On*, only widening conversions are permitted (such as Integer to Single). Figure 3-21 shows how implicit conversion between numeric types must be in a left-to-right direction in the diagram. A Decimal value can be assigned to a variable of type Single, an Integer can be assigned to a variable of type Double, and so on. If, on the other hand, *Option Strict* is set to *Off*, all types of numeric conversions are permitted, with possible loss of data.

Figure 3-21 Conversions permitted with *Option Strict On*

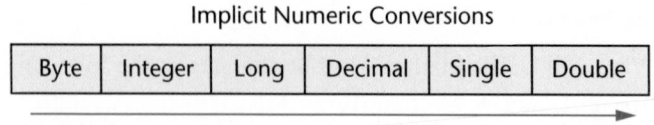

Implicit Numeric Conversions

Byte	Integer	Long	Decimal	Single	Double

To set *Option Strict* for a single project, right-click the project name in the *Solution Explorer* window, select *Properties*, and then select the *Compile* tab, as shown in Figure 3-22. From the *Option Strict* drop-down list, you can select *On* or *Off*.

We recommend setting *Option Strict* to *On*, so Visual Basic can catch errors that result when you accidentally assign a value of the wrong type to a variable. When set to *On*, *Option Strict* forces you to use a conversion function, making your intentions clear. This approach helps to avoid runtime errors.

Figure 3-22 *Project Properties* page

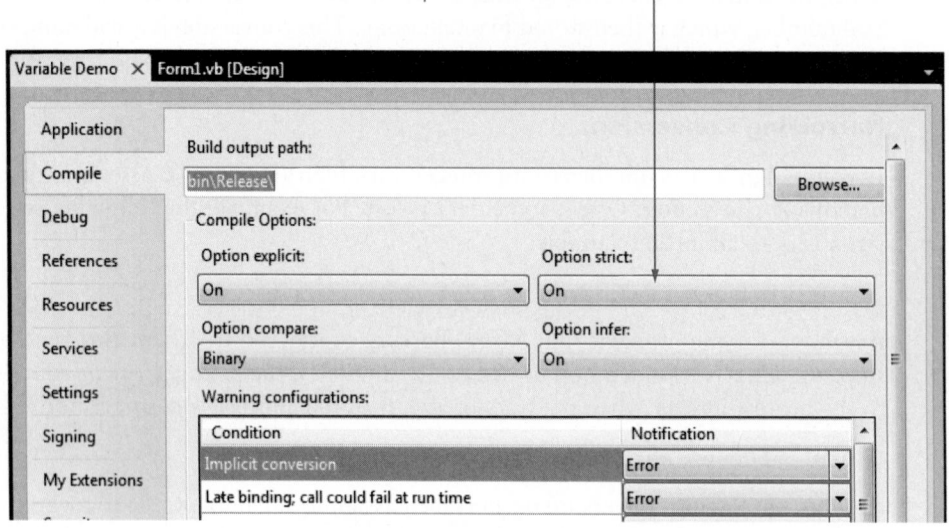

Type Conversion Runtime Errors

The following statement does not compile with *Option Strict* set to *On*:

```
Dim intCount As Integer = "abc123"
```

But if *Option Strict* has been set to *Off*, a program containing this statement will compile without errors. Then, when the program executes, it will stop when it reaches this statement because the string "abc123" contains characters that prevent the string from being converted to a number. The program will generate a runtime error message. Recall from Chapter 2 that runtime errors are errors that occur while the application is running. The type of error in this case is also known as a **type conversion error** or **type mismatch error**.

Runtime errors are harder to catch than syntax errors because they occur while a program is running. Particularly in programs where the user has a number of choices (mouse clicks, keyboard input, menus, and so on), it is very difficult for a programmer to predict when runtime errors might occur. Nevertheless, there are certain conversion functions shown in the next section that reduce the chance of this type of mishap.

> **TIP:** Can the best-trained programmers avoid runtime errors? To discover the answer to that question, spend some time using commercial Web sites and notice all the little things that go wrong. Software reliability is particularly hard to guarantee when users have lots of choices.

Literals

Literals (also known as constants) have specific types in Visual Basic. Table 3-11 lists the more common types. Many literals use a suffix character (*C*, *D*, *@*, *R*, *I*, *L*, *F*, *S*, !) to identify their type.

Table 3-11 Representing literals (constants) in Visual Basic

Type	Description	Example
Boolean	Keywords *True* and *False*	`True`
Byte	Sequence of decimal digits between 0 and 255	`200`
Char	Single letter enclosed in double quotes followed by the lowercase letter *C*	`"A"c`
Date	Date and/or time representation enclosed in # symbols	`#1/20/05 3:15 PM#`
Decimal	Optional leading sign, sequence of decimal digits, optional decimal point and trailing digits, followed by the letter *D* or *@*	`+32.0D` `64@`
Double	Optional leading sign, sequence of digits with a decimal point and trailing digits, followed by optional letter *R*	`3.5` `3.5R`
Integer	Optional leading sign, sequence of decimal digits, followed by optional letter *I*	`-3054I` `+26I`
Long	Optional leading sign, sequence of decimal digits, followed by the letter *L*	`40000000L`
Short	Optional leading sign, sequence of decimal digits, followed by the letter *S*	`12345S`
Single	Optional leading sign, sequence of digits with a decimal point and trailing digits, followed by the letter *F* or !	`26.4F` `26.4!`
String	Sequence of characters surrounded by double quotes	`"ABC"` `"234"`

It's important to know literal types because you often assign literal values to variables. If the receiving variable in an assignment statement has a different type from the literal, an implied conversion takes place. If *Option Strict* is *On*, some conversions are automatic and others generate errors. You need to understand why.

Most of the time, you will be inclined to use no suffix with numeric literals. As long as the receiving variable's data type is compatible with the literal's data type, you have no problem:

```
Dim lngCount As Long = 25          'Integer assigned to Long
Dim dblSalary As Double = 2500.0   'Double assigned to Double
```

In the following example, however, we're trying to assign a Double to a Decimal, which is not permitted when *Option Strict* is *On*:

```
Dim decPayRate As Decimal = 35.5          'Double to Decimal (?)
```

If you know how to create numeric literals, all you have to do is append a *D* to the number. The following is valid:

```
Dim decPayRate As Decimal = 35.5D
```

Named Constants

You have seen several programs and examples where numbers and strings are expressed as literal values. For example, the following statement contains the literal numeric value 0.129:

```
dblPayment = dblPrincipal * 0.129
```

Suppose this statement appears in a banking program that calculates loan information.

In such a program, two potential problems arise. First, it is not clearly evident to anyone other than the original programmer what the number 0.129 is. It appears to be an interest rate, but in some situations there are other fees associated with loan payments. How can you determine the purpose of this statement without painstakingly checking the rest of the program?

The second problem occurs if this number is used in other calculations throughout the program and must be changed periodically. Assuming the number is an interest rate, if the rate changes from 12.9% to 13.2% the programmer will have to search through the source code for every occurrence of the number.

Both of these problems can be addressed by using named constants. A **named constant** is like a variable whose content is read-only, and cannot be changed by a programming statement while the program is running. The following is the general form of a named constant declaration:

```
Const ConstantName As DataType = Value
```

Here is an example of a named constant declaration:

```
Const dblINTEREST_RATE As Double = 0.129
```

It looks like a regular variable declaration except for the following differences:

- The word Const is used instead of Dim.
- An initialization value is required.
- By convention, all letters after the prefix are capitals.
- Words in the name are separated by the underscore character.

The keyword Const indicates that you are declaring a named constant instead of a variable. The value given after the = sign is the value of the constant throughout the program's execution.

A value must be assigned when a named constant is declared or an error will result. An error will also result if any statements in the program attempt to change the contents of a named constant.

One advantage of using named constants is that they help make programs self-documenting. The statement

```
dblPayment = dblPrincipal * 0.129
```

can be changed to read

```
dblPayment = dblPrincipal * dblINTEREST_RATE
```

A new programmer can read the second statement and know what is happening. It is evident that `dblPrincipal` is being multiplied by the interest rate.

Another advantage to using named constants is that consistent changes can easily be made to the program. Let's say the interest rate appears in a dozen different statements throughout the program. When the rate changes, the value assigned to the named constant in its declaration is the only value that needs to be modified. If the rate increases to 13.2% the declaration is changed to the following:

```
Const dblINTEREST_RATE as Double = 0.132
```

Every statement that uses `dblINTEREST_RATE` will use the new value.

It is also useful to declare named constants for common values that are difficult to remember. For example, any program that calculates the area of a circle must use the value *pi*, which is 3.14159. This value could easily be declared as a named constant, as shown in the following statement:

```
Const dblPI as Double = 3.14159
```

Explicit Type Conversions

Let's assume for the current discussion that *Option Strict* is set to *On*. If you try to perform anything other than a widening conversion, your code will not compile. Visual Basic has a set of conversion functions to solve this problem.

What Is a Function?

A **function** is a special type of procedure. When you call a function, you typically send data to the function as input. The function performs an operation using that data, and then it sends a value back as output. Figure 3-23 illustrates this idea.

Figure 3-23 A function receives input and produces a single output

Input(s) ⟶ Function ⟶ Output

When we send a piece of data as input to a function, we typically say that we are passing the data as an **argument**. When a function sends a value back as output, we typically say that the function is **returning a value**.

For example, one of the Visual Basic conversion functions is named `CInt`. (You can think of this as standing for "Convert to Integer.") If you have a non-integer value that you need to convert to an integer, you can call the `CInt` function, passing the value as an argument. The `CInt` function will return that value, converted to an integer. Here is a code sample that shows how the `CInt` function works:

```
' Declare two variables.
Dim dblRealNumber as Double = 3.2
Dim intWholeNumber As Integer = 0

' Assign the Double value to the Integer variable.
intWholeNumber = CInt(dblRealNumber)
```

The last statement assigns the value of the Double variable, dblRealNumber, to the Integer variable, intWholeNumber. Let's take a closer look. On the right side of the = operator is the expression CInt(dblRealNumber). This expression calls the CInt function, passing the value of dblRealNumber, which is 3.2, as an argument.

The CInt function converts the value 3.2 to an integer by dropping the .2. (Dropping the fractional part of a number is called **truncation**.) The value 3 is then returned from the function. The assignment operator then assigns the value 3 to the intWholeNumber variable, as shown in Figure 3-24.

Figure 3-24 Using the CInt function

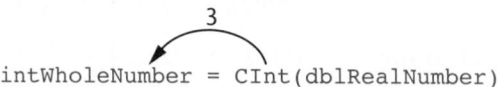

```
intWholeNumber = CInt(dblRealNumber)
```

The value 3 is returned from the CInt function and
assigned to the intWholeNumber variable.

Visual Basic Conversion Functions

Table 3-12 lists the Visual Basic conversion functions that we will use most often. The input to each conversion function is an expression, which is another name for a constant, a variable, or a mathematical expression (such as 2.0 + 4.2). The following situations require a conversion function:

- When assigning a wider numeric type to a narrower numeric type. In Figure 3-21 (page 142), the arrow pointing from left to right indicates automatic conversions. Any conversion in the opposite direction requires a call to a conversion function. Examples are Long to Integer, Decimal to Long, Double to Single, and Double to Decimal.
- When converting between Boolean, Date, Object, String, and numeric types. These all represent different categories, so they require conversion functions.

Table 3-12 Commonly used type conversion functions

Function	Description
CDate(*expr*)	Converts a String expression containing a valid date, such as "10/14/2010 1:30:00 PM", to a Date. Input can also be a Date literal, such as #10/14/2010 1:30:00 PM#.
CDbl(*expr*)	Converts an expression to a Double. If the input expression is a String, a leading currency symbol ($) is permitted, as are commas. The decimal point is optional.
CDec(*expr*)	Converts an expression to a Decimal. If the input expression is a String, a leading currency symbol ($) is permitted, as are commas. The decimal point is optional.
CInt(*expr*)	Converts an expression to an Integer. If the input expression is a String, a leading currency symbol ($) is permitted, as are commas. The decimal point is optional, as are digits after the decimal point.
CStr(*expr*)	Converts an expression to a String. Input can be a mathematical expression, Boolean value, a date, or any numeric data type.

Converting TextBox Input

The conversion functions listed in Table 3-12 are commonly used to convert values that the user has entered into TextBox controls. Anything entered by the user into a TextBox is stored as a string in the control's Text property. If the user has entered a numeric value into a TextBox, and you want to use that value in a calculation, you will have to convert it from a string to an appropriate numeric data type.

For example, suppose a payroll application uses a TextBox named `txtHoursWorked` to get the number of hours worked, and a TextBox named `txtPayRate` to get the hourly pay rate. If the application needs to use the values held in these controls in a calculation, the values must be converted to a numeric type. The following statement shows how we might get the value that has been entered into `txtHoursWorked`, convert that value to an Integer, and assign it to a variable named `intHoursWorked`:

```
intHoursWorked = CInt(txtHoursWorked.Text)
```

And, the following statement shows how we might get the value that has been entered into `txtPayRate`, convert that value to a Double, and assign it to a variable named `dblPayRate`:

```
dblPayRate = CDbl(txtPayRate.Text)
```

After these conversions have taken place, the `intHoursWorked` and `dblPayRate` variables can be used in calculations.

The value of a TextBox control's Text property can be converted to other values as well. For example, a TextBox can be used to get a date from the user, and then the control's Text property can be converted to the Date data type. For example, assume that an application has a TextBox named `txtBirthday`, and the user has entered a date such as *11/15/2010*. The following statement declares a Date variable named `datBirthday` and initialized it with the value in the TextBox:

```
Dim datBirthday As Date = CDate(txtBirthDay.Text)
```

Here's an example that declares a Decimal variable named `decAccountBalance`, and initializes it with the value entered into the `txtAccountBalance` TextBox:

```
Dim decAccountBalance As Decimal = CDec(txtAccountBalance.Text)
```

Converting Floating-Point Numbers to Integers

The `CInt` function is required when assigning any floating-point type to an integer. Here is an example showing a Double being converted to an integer:

```
Dim dblAmount As Double = 3.4
Dim intAmount As Integer = CInt(dblAmount)
```

Here is an example showing a Single being converted to an integer:

```
Dim sngAmount As Single = 1.2
Dim intAmount As Integer = CInt(sngAmount)
```

And, here is an example showing a Decimal being converted to an integer:

```
Dim decAmount As Decimal = 9.1
Dim intAmount As Integer = CInt(decAmount)
```

Converting Doubles and Singles to Decimals

As previously mentioned, when *Option Strict* is set to *On*, a Double value cannot be assigned directly to a Decimal variable. A Single value cannot be assigned directly to a Decimal, either. You can, however, use the `CDec` function to explicitly convert a Double or a

Single to a Decimal. The following shows an example with a Double being converted to a Decimal:

```
Dim dblAmount As Double = 123.45
Dim decAmount As Decimal = CDec(dblAmount)
```

And, the following shows an example with a Single being converted to a Decimal:

```
Dim sngAmount As Single = 4.5
Dim decAmount As Decimal = CDec(sngAmount)
```

If You Want to Know More: CInt and Rounding

The CInt function converts an expression to an Integer. If the input value contains digits after the decimal point, a special type of rounding occurs, called *banker's rounding*. Here's how it works:

- If the digit after the decimal point is less than 5, the digits after the decimal point are removed from the number. We say the number is *truncated*.
- If the digit after the decimal point is a 5, the number is rounded toward the nearest even integer.
- If the digit after the decimal point is greater than 5 and the number is positive, it is rounded to the next highest integer.
- If the digit after the decimal point is greater than 5 and the number is negative, it is rounded to the next smallest integer.

Invalid Conversions

What happens if you call a conversion function, passing a value that cannot be converted? Here's an example:

```
Dim dblSalary As Double
dblSalary = CDbl("xyz")
```

The program stops with a runtime error, displaying the dialog box shown in Figure 3-25. The specific type of error, also known as an **exception**, is called an *InvalidCastException*. The text inside the list box consists of hyperlinks, which take you to specific *Visual Studio Help* pages. Later in this chapter, you will learn how to catch errors like this so the program won't stop.

Figure 3-25 Error displayed when trying to perform an invalid conversion from String to Double

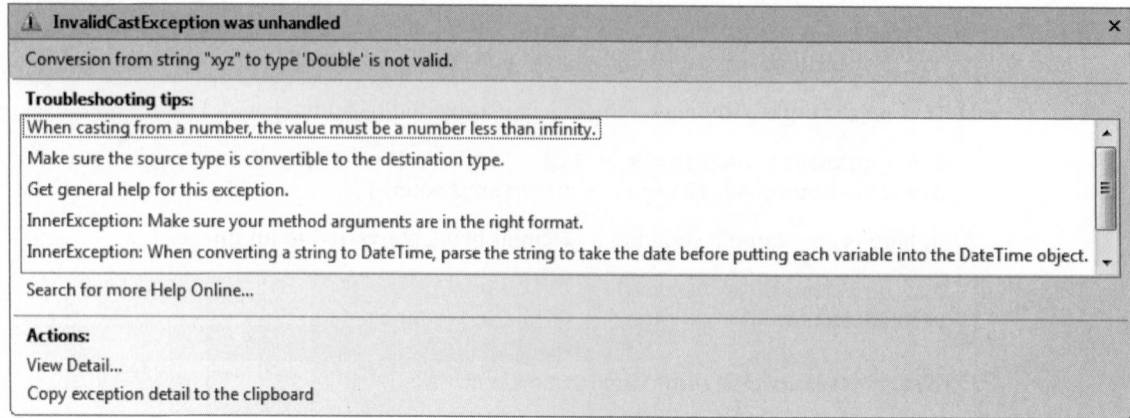

Tutorial 3-7:

Examining a *Simple Calculator* application

This tutorial examines an application that functions as a simple calculator. The application has two TextBox controls, into which you enter numbers. There are buttons for addition, subtraction, multiplication, division, exponentiation, integer division, and modulus. When you click one of these buttons, the application performs a math operation using the two numbers entered into the TextBox controls and displays the result in a label.

Step 1: Open the *Simple Calculator* project from the Chapter 3 sample programs folder named *Simple Calculator*.

Step 2: Click the *Start* button to run the application. The application's form appears, as shown in Figure 3-26.

Figure 3-26 *Simple Calculator* form

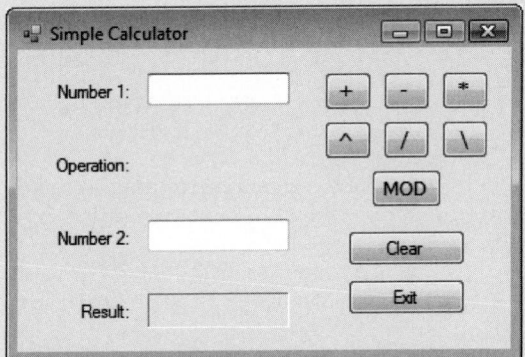

Step 3: Enter **10** into the *Number 1* TextBox control. (In the program source code, this TextBox control is named `txtNumber1`.)

Step 4: Enter **3** into the *Number 2* TextBox control. (In the program source code, this TextBox control is named `txtNumber2`.)

Step 5: Click the + button. Notice that next to the word *Operation* a large plus sign appears on the form. This indicates that an addition operation has taken place. (The plus sign is displayed in a label named `lblOperation`.) The result of 10 + 3 displays in the *Result* label, which is named `lblResult`. The form appears as shown in Figure 3-27.

Step 6: Click the – button. Notice that the `lblOperation` label changes to a minus sign and the result of 10 minus 3 displays in the `lblResult` label.

Step 7: Click the *, ^, /, \, and *MOD* buttons. Each performs a math operation using 10 and 3 as its operands and displays the result in the `lblResult` label.

Step 8: If you wish to experiment with other numbers, click the *Clear* button and continue.

Step 9: When you are finished, click the *Exit* button.

Figure 3-27 Result of 10 + 3

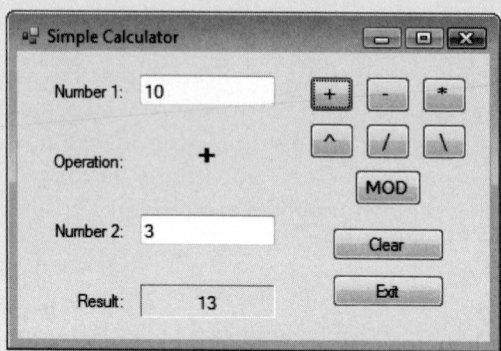

Step 10: Open *Form1* in the *Designer* window, if it is not already open. Double-click the + button on the application form. This opens the *Code* window, with the text cursor positioned in the `btnPlus_Click` event handler. The code is as follows:

```
Private Sub btnPlus_Click(...) Handles btnPlus.Click
    ' This event handler performs addition.
    ' Declare a variable to hold the result.
    Dim dblResult As Double

    ' Indicate "+" as the operation.
    lblOperation.Text = "+"

    ' Add the two numbers and store the result in dblResult.
    dblResult = CDbl(txtNumber1.Text) + CDbl(txtNumber2.Text)

    ' Display the result.
    lblResult.Text = CStr(dblResult)
End Sub
```

Step 11: Examine the other event handlers in this application. Most of the arithmetic operator button handlers are similar, except those for the Integer division and Modulus operators. In the Integer division operator handler, for example, the result variable is an integer, and the `CInt` function converts the contents of the TextBox controls:

```
Private Sub btnIntegerDivide_Click(...) Handles btnIntegerDivide.Click
    ' This event handler performs integer division.
    ' Declare a variable to hold the result.
    Dim intResult As Integer

    ' Indicate "\" as the operation.
    lblOperation.Text = "\"

    ' Integer-divide Number 1 by Number 2 and
    ' store the result in dblResult.
    intResult = CInt(txtNumber1.Text) \ CInt(txtNumber2.Text)

    ' Display the result.
    lblResult.Text = CStr(intResult)
End Sub
```

If You Want to Know More: Full Set of VB Conversion Functions

Table 3-12, shown earlier (p. 146), lists the Visual Basic conversion functions that you will use most frequently. For your reference, Table 3-13 contains a more complete list of Visual Basic conversion functions, including some that you will use only occasionally.

Table 3-13 Visual Basic type conversion functions

Function	Description
CBool(*expr*)	Converts an expression to a Boolean value. The expression must be a number, a string that represents a number, or the strings "True" or "False". Otherwise a runtime error is generated. If the expression is nonzero, the function returns *True*. Otherwise it returns *False*. For example, CBool(10) and CBool("7") return *True*, while CBool(0) and CBool("0") return *False*. If the argument is the string "True", the function returns *True*, and if the expression is the string "False", the function returns *False*.
CByte(*expr*)	Converts an expression to a Byte, which can hold the values 0 through 255. If the argument is a fractional number, it is rounded. If the expression cannot be converted to a value in the range of 0–255, a runtime error is generated.
CChar(*expr*)	Converts a string expression to a Char. If the string contains more than one character, only the first character is returned. For example, CChar("xyz") returns the character *x*.
CDate(*expr*)	Converts an expression to a Date. String expressions must be valid Date literals. For example, CDate("#10/14/2010 1:30:00 PM#") returns a Date with the value *1:30 PM, October 14th, 2010*. If the expression cannot be converted to a Date value, a runtime error is generated.
CDbl(*expr*)	Converts a numeric or string expression to a Double. If the expression converts to a value outside the range of a Double, or is not a numeric value, a runtime error is generated.
CDec(*expr*)	Converts a numeric or string expression to a Decimal. The CDec function can convert strings starting with a $ character, such as $1,200.00. Commas are also permitted. If the expression converts to a value outside the range of a Decimal, or is not a numeric value, a runtime error is generated.
CInt(*expr*)	Converts a numeric or string expression to an Integer. If the expression converts to a value outside the range of an Integer, or is not a numeric value, a runtime error is generated. Rounds to nearest integer.
CLng(*expr*)	Converts a numeric or string expression to a Long (long integer). If the expression converts to a value outside the range of a Long, or is not a numeric value, a runtime error is generated.
CObj(*expr*)	Converts an expression to an Object.
CShort(*expr*)	Converts a numeric or string expression to a Short (short integer). If the expression converts to a value outside the range of a Short, or is not a numeric value, a runtime error is generated.
CSng(*expr*)	Converts a numeric or string expression to a Single. If the expression converts to a value outside the range of a Single, or is not a numeric value, a runtime error is generated. The input expression may conatain commas, as in "1,234."
CStr(*expr*)	Converts a numeric, Boolean, Date, or string expression to a String. Input can be an arithmetic expression, a Boolean value, a date, or any numeric data type.

 **Checkpoint**

3.27 After the statement `dblResult = 10 \ 3` executes, what value will be stored in `dblResult`?

3.28 After each of the following statements executes, what value will be stored in `dblResult`?

    a. `dblResult = 6 + 3 * 5`
    b. `dblResult = 12 / 2 - 4`
    c. `dblResult = 2 + 7 * 3 - 6`
    d. `dblResult = (2 + 4) * 3`

3.29 What value will be stored in `dblResult` after the following statement executes?

    `dblResult = CInt("28.5")`

3.30 Will the following statement execute or cause a runtime error?

    `dblResult = CDbl("186,478.39")`

3.31 What is a named constant?

3.32 Assuming that `intNumber` is an integer variable, what value will each of the following statements assign to it?

    a. `intNumber = 27`
    b. `intNumber = CInt(12.8)`
    c. `intNumber = CInt(12.0)`
    d. `intNumber = (2 + 4) * 3`

3.33 Which function converts the string "860.2" to value of type Double?

3.34 How would the following strings be converted by the `CDec` function?

    a. `48.5000`
    b. `$34.95`
    c. `2,300`
    d. `Twelve`

3.5 Formatting Numbers and Dates

Users of computer programs generally like to see numbers and dates displayed in an attractive, easy to read format. Numbers greater than 999, for instance, should usually be displayed with commas and decimal points. The value 123456.78 would normally be displayed as "123,456.78".

 TIP: Number formatting is dependent on the locale that is used by the computer's Microsoft Windows operating system. *Localization* refers to the technique of adapting your formats for various regions and countries of the world. For example, in North America a currency value is formatted as 123,456.78. In many European countries, the same value is formatted as 123.456,78. In this book, we will display only North American formats, but you can find help on using other types of formats by looking for the topic named *localization* in Visual Studio help.

`ToString` Method

All numeric and date data types in Visual Basic contain the `ToString` method. This method converts the contents of a variable to a string. The following code segment shows an example of the method's use.

```
Dim intNumber As Integer = 123
lblNumber.Text = intNumber.ToString()
```

In the second statement the number variable's ToString method is called. The method returns the string "123", which is assigned to the Text property of lblNumber.

By passing a formatting string to the ToString method, you can indicate what type of format you want to use when the number or date is formatted. The following statements create a string containing the number 1234.5 in Currency format:

```
Dim dblSample As Double
Dim strResult As String
dblSample = 1234.5
strResult = dblSample.ToString("c")
```

When the last statement executes, the value assigned to strResult is "$1,234.50". Notice that an extra zero was added at the end because currency values usually have two digits to the right of the decimal point. The value "c" is called a format string. Table 3-14 shows the format strings used for all types of floating-point numbers (Double, Single, and Decimal), assuming the user is running Windows in a North American locale. The format strings are not case sensitive, so you can code them as uppercase or lowercase letters. If you call ToString using an integer type (Byte, Integer, or Long), the value is formatted as if it were type Double.

Table 3-14 Standard numeric format strings

Format String	Description
N or n	Number format
F or f	Fixed-point scientific format
E or e	Exponential scientific format
C or c	Currency format
P or p	Percent format

Number Format

Number format (n or N) displays numeric values with thousands separators and a decimal point. By default, two digits display to the right of the decimal point. Negative values are displayed with a leading minus (−) sign. Example:

```
–2,345.67
```

Fixed-Point Format

Fixed-point format (f or F) displays numeric values with no thousands separator and a decimal point. By default, two digits display to the right of the decimal point. Negative values are displayed with a leading minus (−) sign. Example:

```
–2345.67
```

Exponential Format

Exponential format (e or E) displays numeric values in scientific notation. The number is normalized with a single digit to the left of the decimal point. The exponent is marked by the letter e, and the exponent has a leading + or − sign. By default, six digits display to the right of the decimal point, and a leading minus sign is used if the number is negative. Example:

```
–2.345670e+003
```

Currency Format

Currency format (c or c) displays a leading currency symbol (such as $), digits, thousands separators, and a decimal point. By default, two digits display to the right of the decimal point. Negative values are surrounded by parentheses. Example:

```
($2,345.67)
```

Percent Format

Percent format (p or P) causes the number to be multiplied by 100 and displayed with a trailing space and % sign. By default, two digits display to the right of the decimal point. Negative values are displayed with a leading minus (−) sign. The following example uses −.2345:

```
-23.45 %
```

Specifying the Precision

Each numeric format string can optionally be followed by an integer that indicates how many digits to display after the decimal point. For example, the format n3 displays three digits after the decimal point. Table 3-15 shows a variety of numeric formatting examples, based on the North American locale.

Table 3-15 Numeric formatting examples (North American locale)

Number Value	Format String	ToString( ) Value
12.3	n3	12.300
12.348	n2	12.35
1234567.1	n	1,234,567.10
123456.0	f2	123456.00
123456.0	e3	1.235e+005
.234	p	23.40%
−1234567.8	c	($1,234,567.80)

Rounding

Rounding can occur when the number of digits you have specified after the decimal point in the format string is smaller than the precision of the numeric value. Suppose, for example, that the value 1.235 were displayed with a format string of n2. Then the displayed value would be 1.24. If the next digit after the last displayed digit is 5 or higher, the last displayed digit is rounded *away from zero*. Table 3-16 shows examples of rounding using a format string of n2.

Table 3-16 Rounding examples, using the n2 display format string

Number Value	Formatted As
1.234	1.23
1.235	1.24
1.238	1.24
−1.234	−1.23
−1.235	−1.24
−1.238	−1.24

Integer Values with Leading Zeros

Integer type variables (Byte, Integer, or Long) have a special format string, D (or d), that lets you specify the minimum width for displaying the number. Leading zeros are inserted if necessary. Table 3-17 shows examples.

Table 3-17 Formatting integers, using the D (d) format string

Integer Value	Format String	Formatted As
23	D	23
23	D4	0023
1	D2	01

Formatting Dates and Times

When you call the ToString method using a Date or DateTime variable, you can format it as a short date, short time, long date, and so on. Table 3-18 lists the most commonly used format strings for dates and times. The following example creates a string containing "8/10/2010", called the short date format.

```
Dim dtmSample As Date = "#8/10/2010#"
Dim strResult As String = dtmSample.ToString("d")
```

The following example gets the current date and formats it with a long date format.

```
Dim strToday As String = Today().ToString("D")
```

Date/time format strings are case sensitive.

Table 3-18 Common date/time formats

Format String	Description
d	Short date format, which shows the month, day, and year. An example is "8/10/2010".
D	Long date format, which contains the day of the week, month, day, and year. An example is "Tuesday, August 10, 2010".
t	Short time format, which shows the hours and minutes. An example is "3:22 PM".
T	Long time format, which contains the hours, minutes, seconds, and an AM/PM indicator. An example is "3:22:00 PM".
F	Full (long) date and time. An example is "Tuesday August 10, 2010 3:22:00 PM".

Tutorial 3-8 examines the *Format Demo* application.

Tutorial 3-8:

Examining the *Format Demo* application

Step 1: Open the *Format Demo* project from the Chapter 3 sample programs folder named *Format Demo*.

Step 2: Run the application, as shown in Figure 3-28. The five buttons on the left are used for formatting floating-point numeric values. The five buttons on the right are for formatting dates and times. The text in each button shows which format string is used when the `ToString` method is called.

Figure 3-28 *Format Demo* application

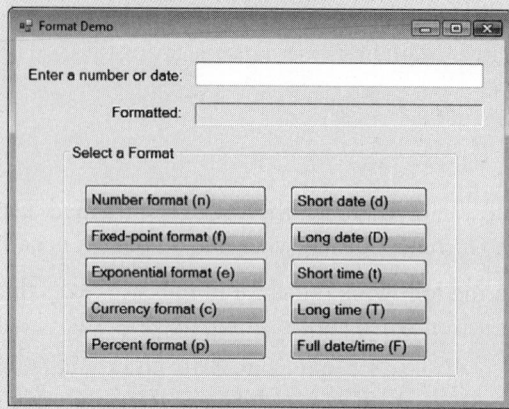

Step 3: Enter the value `67895.34926` into the TextBox control at the top of the form. Click the *Number format (n)* button. You should see the output shown in Figure 3-29.

Step 4: Click the *Fixed-point format (f)* button. Notice how the number next to the Formatted label changes its appearance.

Step 5: Click the remaining buttons on the left side. Change the value of the number in the TextBox control, and experiment with each of the format buttons on the left side.

Step 6: Enter the following date into the TextBox: *May 5, 2010 6:35 PM*.

Step 7: Click the *Short date (d)* button. You should see the date displayed as "5/5/2010".

Step 8: Click the other date and time buttons in the right-hand column. Notice all the ways the date and time can be displayed.

Step 9: Close the application window by clicking the (🗙) in the upper right corner. Open the form's code window and examine the code in each button's Click event handler.

Figure 3-29 Showing a Number format

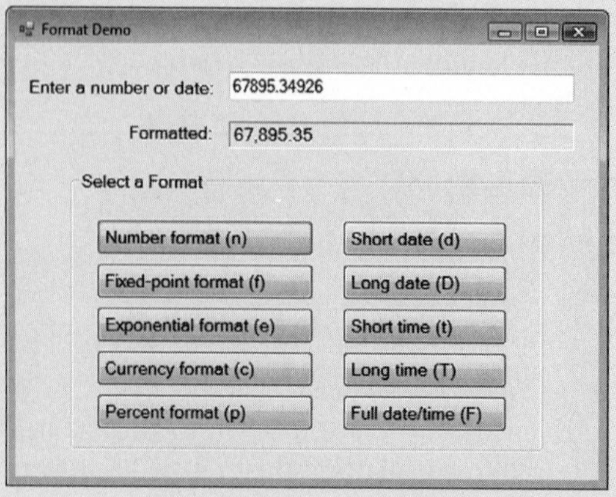

 **Checkpoint**

3.35 Write a statement that uses the `ToString` method to convert the contents of a variable named `dblSalary` to a Currency format.

3.36 For each of the following numeric formats, identify the format string used as the input parameter when calling the `ToString` method.
   a. Currency
   b. Exponential scientific
   c. Number
   d. Percent
   e. Fixed-point

3.37 How can you make the `ToString` method display parentheses around a number in Currency format when the number is negative?

3.38 In the following table, fill in the expected values returned by the `ToString` function when specific numeric values are used with specific format strings.

Number Value	Format String	`ToString( )` Value
12.3	n4	
12.348	n1	
1234567.1	n3	
123456.0	f1	
123456.0	e3	
.234	p2	
–1234567.8	c3	

3.39 Show an example of formatting a Date variable in Long Time format when calling the `ToString` method.

3.40 Show an example of formatting a Date variable in Long Date format when calling the `ToString` method.

 ## 3.6 Class-Level Variables

CONCEPT: Class-level variables are accessible to all procedures in a class.

Recall that a variable's scope is the part of the program in which the variable is visible. All of the variables you have created so far have had local scope, meaning that each was declared and used inside a procedure. Local variables are not visible to statements outside the procedure in which they are declared.

It's also possible to declare a class-level variable, which is accessible to all of the procedures in a class. Recall from Chapter 2 that a form's code appears inside a class. For example, suppose a project has a form named Form1. When you open the form in the *Code* window, you see that its code is contained inside a class declaration such as this:

```
Public Class Form1

    Event handlers appear here...

End Class
```

A class-level variable is declared inside a class declaration, but not inside any procedure. Class-level variables have class scope because they are visible to all statements inside the class. For example, look at the following code. The application's form has two Button controls: `btnSetValue` and `btnShowValue`.

```
 1 Public Class Form1
 2   ' Declare a class-level variable.
 3   Dim intValue As Integer
 4
 5   Private Sub btnSetValue_Click(...) Handles btnSetValue.Click
 6      intValue = 99
 7   End Sub
 8
 9   Private Sub btnShowValue_Click(...) Handles btnShowValue.Click
10      MessageBox.Show(intValue.ToString())
11   End Sub
12 End Class
```

Notice that the declaration of the intValue variable in line 3 is inside the class, but is not inside of either event handler. The variable has class scope, so it is visible to both of the event handlers. When the btnSetValue_Click procedure executes, the statement in line 6 assigns 99 to the variable. When the btnShowValue_Click procedure executes, the statement in line 10 displays the variable's value in a message box. (In the *Chap3* folder of student sample programs you will find the previously shown code in a project named *Class-Level Variable Demo*.)

Most programmers agree that you should not overuse class-level variables. Although they make it easy to share values between procedures, their use can also lead to problems. Here are some of the reasons:

- While debugging, if you find that the wrong value is being stored in a class-level variable, you will have to track down each statement in the class that uses the variable to determine where the bad value is coming from. In a class with lots of code, this can be tedious and time-consuming.
- When two or more procedures modify the same class-level variable, you must ensure that one procedure cannot upset the accuracy or correctness of another procedure by modifying the variable.
- Class-level variables can make a program hard to understand. A class-level variable can be modified by any statement in the class. If you are to understand any part of the class that uses a class-level variable, you have to be aware of all the other parts of the class that access that variable.

Class-Level Constants

Although you should be careful not to overuse class-level variables, it is generally acceptable to use class-level constants. A class-level constant is a named constant declared with the Const keyword, at the class level. Because a constant's value cannot be changed during the program's execution, you do not have to worry about many of the potential hazards that are associated with the use of class-level variables.

 Checkpoint

3.41 What is the difference between a class-level variable and a local variable?

3.42 Where do you declare class-level variables?

3.7 Exception Handling

CONCEPT: A well-engineered program should report errors and try to continue. Or, it should explain why it cannot continue, and then shut down. In this section, you learn how to recover gracefully from errors, using a technique known as exception handling.

An exception is an unexpected error that occurs while a program is running, causing the program to abruptly halt. Exceptions are typically caused by circumstances outside of the programmer's control. In Tutorial 3-9 you will run an application and deliberately cause an exception.

Tutorial 3-9:
Exception Demonstration

VideoNote

Exception
Demonstration

Step 1: Open the *Exception Demo* project from the Chapter 3 sample programs folder named *Exception Demo*. Figure 3-30 shows the application's form. The TextBox control's name is `txtSalary`, and the Button control's name is `btnOk`.

Figure 3-30 The *Exception Demo* application's form

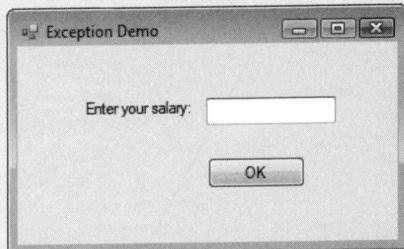

Step 2: Open the *Code* window and look at the `btnOk` button's Click event handler. The code is shown here, with line numbers inserted for reference purposes:

```
1 Private Sub btnOk_Click(...) Handles btnOk.Click
2   ' Declare a variable to hold the user's salary.
3   Dim decSalary As Decimal
4
5   ' Get the user's input and convert it to a Decimal.
6   decSalary = CDec(txtSalary.Text)
7
8   ' Display the user's salary.
9   MessageBox.Show("Your salary is " & decSalary.ToString("c"))
10 End Sub
```

Line 3 declares a Decimal variable named `decSalary`. Line 6 uses the `CDec` function to convert the `txtSalary` control's Text property to a Decimal, and assigns the result to the `decSalary` variable. Line 9 displays a message showing the value of `decSalary` formatted as currency.

Step 3: Run the application. Enter *4000* in the TextBox and click the *OK* button. You should see a message box with the message *Your salary is $4000.00*. Click the message box's *OK* button to dismiss it.

Step 4: Change the contents of the TextBox to *Four Thousand*, as shown in Figure 3-31.

Because the string *Four Thousand* cannot be converted by the `CDec` function, an exception will occur when you click the *OK* button. Go ahead and try it! Click the *OK* button. The application will halt and you will see the error window shown in Figure 3-32.

A lot of information is displayed in the error window. Before continuing, take note of the following:

- The window's title bar shows the message *InvalidCastException was unhandled*. All exceptions have a name, and the name of the exception that just occurred is InvalidCastException. Anytime a conversion function such as

Figure 3-31 *Four Thousand* entered into the TextBox

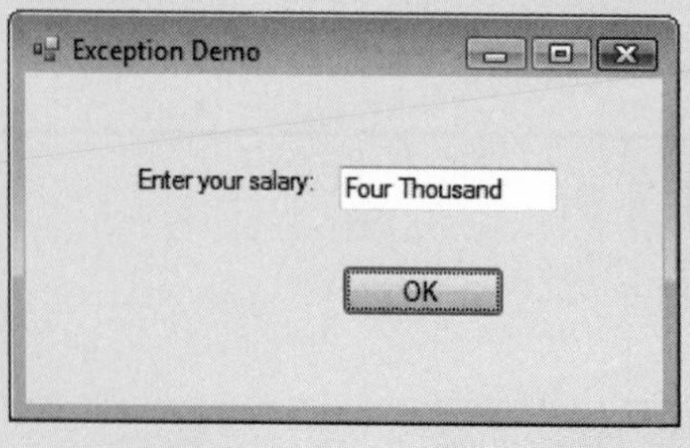

Figure 3-32 The resulting error window

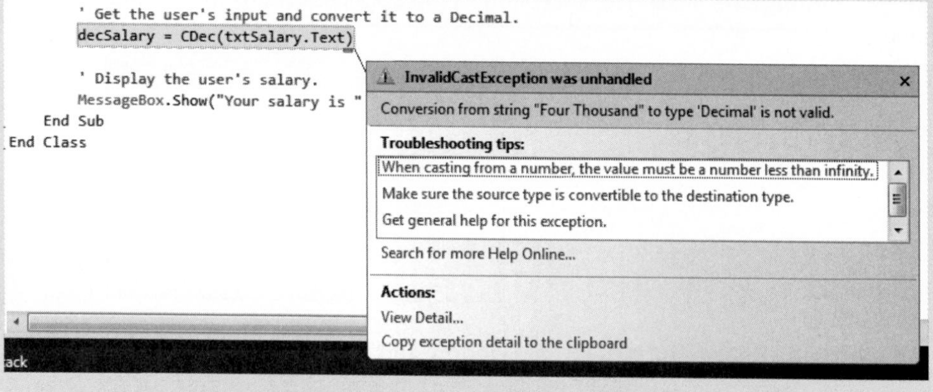

CDec fails to convert a value, it causes an InvalidCastException to occur. This message also tells us that the exception was *unhandled*. That means that the program doesn't have any code to take care of the exception. It simply allowed it to happen, and as a result the application halted.

- Just below the window's title bar you see the error message *Conversion from string "Four Thousand" to type 'Decimal' is not valid*. This tells us exactly what happened to cause the exception.
- In the *Code* window, the statement that caused the exception is highlighted.

Step 5: Close the error window. The application is now in Break mode, which is used for debugging. We will discuss break mode in greater detail later in this chapter. For now, just exit break mode by performing *one* of the following actions:

- Click the *Stop Debugging* button (▪) on the toolbar.
- Click *Debug* on the menu bar, and then select *Stop Debugging*.
- Press Ctrl+Alt+Break on the keyboard.

When an exception occurs, programmers commonly say an *exception was thrown*. As you were following the steps in Tutorial 3-9, an exception known as an InvalidCastException was thrown when the CDec function attempted to convert the string "Four Thousand" to a Decimal value. When an exception is thrown, it must be handled by the program. If the exception is unhandled (as was the case in Tutorial 3-9), the program halts.

Failure Can Be Graceful

Exceptions are typically thrown because of events outside the programmer's control. A disk file may be unreadable, for example, because of a hardware failure. The user may enter invalid data, as happened in Tutorial 3-9. Or, the computer may be low on memory.

Exception handling is designed to let programs recover from errors when possible. Or, if recovery is not possible, a program should fail gracefully, letting the user know why it failed. Under no circumstances should it just halt without warning. In this section we will show how you can handle exceptions.

Visual Basic, like most modern programming languages, allows you to write code that responds to exceptions when they are thrown, and prevents the program from abruptly crashing. Such code is called an **exception handler**, and is written with a **Try-Catch statement**. There are several ways to write a Try-Catch statement, but the following is a simplified general format:

```
Try
    statement
    statement
    statement
    etc...
Catch
    statement
    statement
    statement
    etc...
End Try
```

First the key word `Try` appears. Next, one or more statements appear which we will refer to as the **try block**. These are statements that can potentially throw an exception. After the last statement in the try block, a **Catch clause** appears. Beginning on the next line, one or more statements appear, which we will refer to as the **catch block**.

When the a `Try-Catch` block executes, the statements in the try block are executed in the order that they appear. If a statement in the try block throws an exception, the program immediately jumps to the `Catch` clause, and executes the statements in the catch block. After the last statement in the catch block has executed, the program resumes execution with any statement that appears after the `End Try` clause.

Let's see how a Try-Catch statement can be used in the *Exception Demo* application. A modified version of the `btnOk_Click` procedure is shown here, with line numbers inserted for reference:

```
 1 Private Sub btnOk_Click(...) Handles btnOk.Click
 2    ' Declare a variable to hold the user's salary.
 3    Dim decSalary As Decimal
 4
 5    Try
 6       ' Get the user's input and convert it to a Decimal.
 7       decSalary = CDec(txtSalary.Text)
 8
 9       ' Display the user's salary.
10       MessageBox.Show("Your salary is " & decSalary.ToString("c"))
11    Catch
12       ' Display an error message.
13       MessageBox.Show("Please try again, and enter a number.")
14    End Try
15 End Sub
```

In this code, when the statement in line 7 throws an exception, the program immediately jumps to the `Catch` clause in line 11 and begins executing the statements in the catch block. The catch block displays a message box in line 13, and that's the end of the `Try-Catch` statement. Figure 3-33 illustrates this sequence of events.

Figure 3-33 Sequence of events in the `Try-Catch` statement

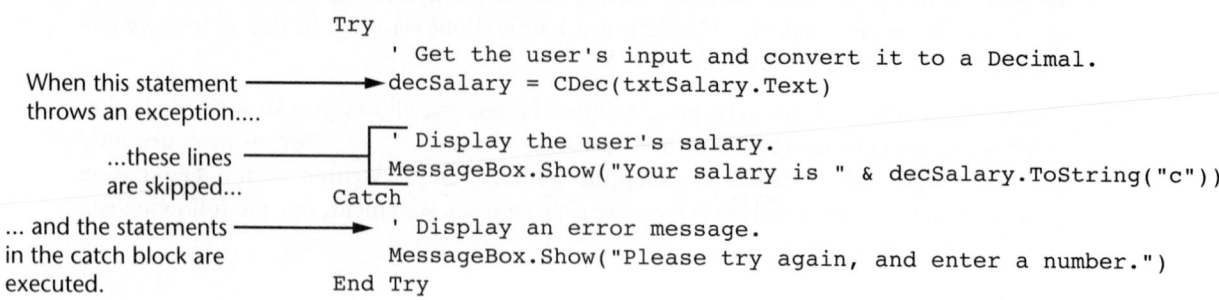

```
                           Try
                               ' Get the user's input and convert it to a Decimal.
When this statement  ───────► decSalary = CDec(txtSalary.Text)
throws an exception....
                               ' Display the user's salary.
    ...these lines  ─────────  MessageBox.Show("Your salary is " & decSalary.ToString("c"))
    are skipped...         Catch
... and the statements ───────► ' Display an error message.
in the catch block are         MessageBox.Show("Please try again, and enter a number.")
executed.                  End Try
```

We encourage you to modify the btnOk_Click procedure in the *Exception Demo* project by adding the Try-Catch statement as previously shown. Then, run the application again. If you enter 4000 in the TextBox and click the OK button, you will see a message box with the message *Your salary is $4000.00*, just as you did before. If you enter something that cannot be converted to a Decimal, such as the string *Four Thousand*, you will see the message box shown in Figure 3-34. This message box is displayed by the statement shown previously in line 13 (in the catch block).

Figure 3-34 Message displayed by the catch block code

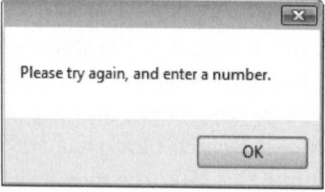

Tutorial 3-10:
Salary Calculator project with exception handling

VideoNote

Tutorial 3-10
Walkthrough

The student sample programs folder contains a partially completed project named *Salary Calculator*. When the project is complete, it will allow the user to input a person's annual salary and number of pay periods per year. With the click of a button, the program will calculate the amount of salary the user should receive per pay period.

In this tutorial you will complete the project. First, you will implement the program without exception handling, test it, and note how runtime errors occur. Then, you will add exception handling to the program and test it again.

Step 1: Open the *Salary Calculator* project from the Chapter 3 sample programs folder named *Salary Calculator*. Figure 3-35 shows the application's form with the names of the several controls.

Figure 3-35 *Salary Calculator* form

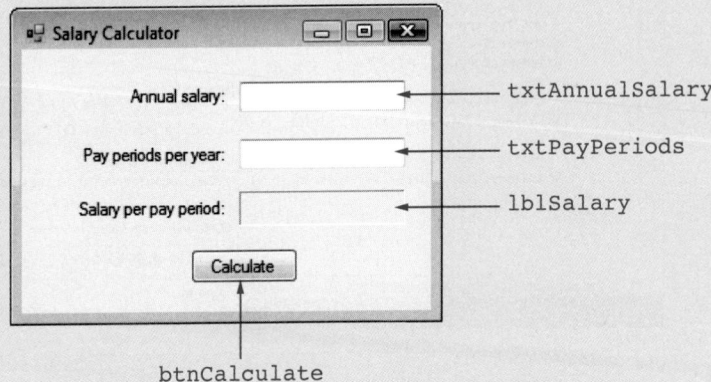

Step 2: Double-click the btnCalculate button to open the *Code* window. Insert the following bold code shown in the lines 2 through 14 into its Click event handler. (Don't enter the line numbers! They are shown only for reference.)

```
1 Private Sub btnCalculate_Click(...) Handles btnCalculate.Click
2    Dim decAnnualSalary As Decimal ' Annual salary
3    Dim intPayPeriods As Integer    ' Number of pay periods
4    Dim decSalary As Decimal        ' Salary per pay period
5
6    ' Get the annual salary and number of pay periods.
7    decAnnualSalary = CDec(txtAnnualSalary.Text)
8    intPayPeriods = CInt(txtPayPeriods.Text)
9
10   ' Calculate the salary per pay period.
11   decSalary = decAnnualSalary / intPayPeriods
12
13   ' Display the salary per pay period.
14   lblSalary.Text = decSalary.ToString("c")
15 End Sub
```

Let's go over the code that you just wrote:

- Lines 2 through 4 declare the local variables used in the procedure.
- Line 7 uses the CDec function to convert the value of the txtAnnual-Salary control's Text property to a Decimal , and assigns the result to the decAnnualSalary variable.
- Line 8 uses the CInt function to convert the value of the txtPayPeriods control's Text property to an Integer, and assigns the result to the intPayPeriods variable.
- Line 11 divides decAnnualSalary by intPayPeriods to calculate the salary per pay period. The result is assigned to the decSalary variable.
- Line 14 uses the ToString("c") method to convert decSalary to a string, formatted as currency. The resulting string is assigned to the lblSalary control's Text property.

Step 3: Save and run the program. Enter **75000** for the annual salary, and **26** for the pay periods per year. When you click *Calculate*, the output should be $2,884.62.

Step 4: Now you will purposely cause an exception. Erase the contents of the *Pay periods per year:* text box and click the *Calculate* button. You should see an error window appear, like the one shown in Figure 3-36, saying *InvalidCastException*

Figure 3-36 Exception reported

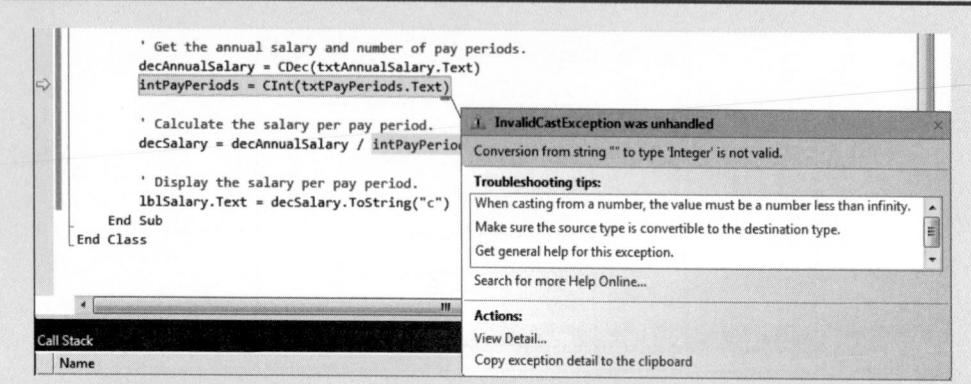

was unhandled. Notice the error message in the window reads *Conversion from string "" to type Integer is not valid.* Also notice the statement that caused the error. (Line 8 in the previously shown code.)

Close the error window and click the *Stop Debugging* button (▶) on the Visual Studio toolbar. The program should return to Design mode.

Step 5:   Your next task is to add exception handling to the program to prevent the type of runtime error you just saw. You never want a program to halt like this when the user enters bad data. Revise the code in the `btnCalculate_Click` procedure so it looks like the following. (The new code is shown in bold. As before, don't enter the line numbers. They are shown only for reference.)

```
 1 Private Sub btnCalculate_Click(...) Handles btnCalculate.Click
 2     Dim decAnnualSalary As Decimal ' Annual salary
 3     Dim intPayPeriods As Integer   ' Number of pay periods
 4     Dim decSalary As Decimal       ' Salary per pay period
 5
 6     Try
 7         ' Get the annual salary and number of pay periods.
 8         decAnnualSalary = CDec(txtAnnualSalary.Text)
 9         intPayPeriods = CInt(txtPayPeriods.Text)
10
11         ' Calculate the salary per pay period.
12         decSalary = decAnnualSalary / intPayPeriods
13
14         ' Display the salary per pay period.
15         lblSalary.Text = decSalary.ToString("c")
16     Catch
17         ' Display an error message.
18         MessageBox.Show("Error: Be sure to enter nonzero " &
19                         "numeric values.")
20     End Try
21 End Sub
```

Now, the statements that can potentially throw an exception are placed inside the try block:

- Line 8 can throw an InvalidCastException if the `txtAnnualSalary` control contains invalid data.
- Line 9 can throw an InvalidCastException if the `txtPayPeriods` control contains invalid data.

- Line 12 can also throw an exception if the `intPayPeriods` variable is set to 0. When division by zero happens, if one of the operands is a Decimal, an exception known as DivideByZeroException occurs.

If any of these exceptions occurs, the program will immediately jump to the `Catch` clause. When that happens, the statement shown in lines 18 and 19 will display an error message.

Step 6: Save and run the program. Enter *75000* for the annual salary, and leave the pay periods per year TextBox blank. When you click *Calculate*, you should see the message box shown in Figure 3-37. Click OK to dismiss the message box.

Figure 3-37 Error message box displayed

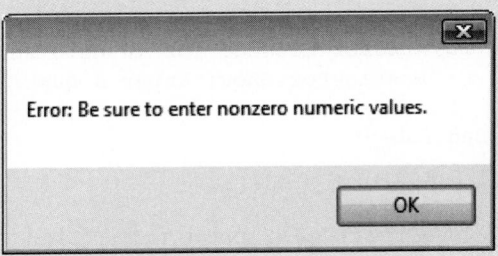

Error: Be sure to enter nonzero numeric values.

OK

Step 7: Now let's see what happens when the program divides by zero. Leave 75000 as the annual salary and enter *0* for the pay periods per year. When you click *Calculate*, you should again see the message box shown in Figure 3-37. Click OK to dismiss the message box, and then close the application.

Using Nested `Try-Catch` Statements

As you saw in Tutorial 3-10, a procedure might contain several statements that potentially can throw an exception. If you look back at Step 5 of that tutorial, you see that lines 8, 9, and 12 each can potentially throw an exception. Regardless of which line throws an exception, the catch block displays the same error message (in lines 18 and 19). If you want to handle the exceptions separately, with a unique error message displayed for each one, you can have a set of nested `Try-Catch` statements. (When we use the term "nested," we mean that one `Try-Catch` statement appears inside another.)

The following code shows how this can be done. This is a modified version of the `btnCalculate_Click` procedure in Tutorial 3-10.

```
1   Private Sub btnCalculate_Click(...) Handles btnCalculate.Click
2     Dim decAnnualSalary As Decimal ' Annual salary
3     Dim intPayPeriods As Integer   ' Number of pay periods per year
4     Dim decSalary As Decimal       ' Salary per pay period
5
6     Try
7       ' Get the annual salary and number of pay periods.
8       decAnnualSalary = CDec(txtAnnualSalary.Text)
9
10      Try
11        ' Get the number of pay periods.
12        intPayPeriods = CInt(txtPayPeriods.Text)
13
```

```
14        Try
15            ' Calculate the salary per pay period.
16            decSalary = decAnnualSalary / intPayPeriods
17
18            ' Display the salary per pay period.
19            lblSalary.Text = decSalary.ToString("c")
20        Catch
21            ' Error message for division-by-zero.
22            MessageBox.Show("Pay periods cannot be zero.")
23        End Try
24
25      Catch
26          ' Error message for invalid pay periods.
27          MessageBox.Show("Pay periods must be an integer.")
28      End Try
29
30    Catch
31        ' Error message for invalid salary.
32        MessageBox.Show("Enter a numeric value for salary.")
33    End Try
34  End Sub
```

Let's take a closer look at this code:

- The first Try statement appears in line 6. Inside the try block, line 8 attempts to convert txtAnnualSalary.Text to a Decimal. If an exception is thrown, the program will jump to the Catch clause in line 30. When that happens, line 32 displays an error message prompting the user to enter a numeric value for the salary, and the procedure ends.
- If txtAnnualSalary.Text is successfully converted to a Decimal in line 8, the program continues to the nested Try statement in line 10. Line 12 attempts to convert txtPayPeriods.Text to an Integer. If an exception is thrown, the program will jump to the Catch clause in line 25. When that happens, line 27 displays an error message indicating that pay periods must be an integer, and the procedure ends.
- If txtPayPeriods.Text is successfully converted to a Decimal in line 12, the program continues to the nested Try statement in line 14. Then, line 16 divides decAnnualSalary by intPayPeriods. If intPayPeriods happens to be zero, an exception is thrown and the program jumps to the Catch clause in line 20. When that happens, line 22 displays an error message indicating that pay periods cannot be zero, and the procedure ends.
- If the division operation in line 16 is successful, then line 19 displays the salary in the lblSalary control.

(In the *Chap3* folder of student sample programs you will find the previously shown code in a project named *Nested Try*.)

If You Want to Know More: Using Multiple Catch Clauses to Handle Multiple Types of Errors

Another way to handle different types of exceptions separately, with a unique error message displayed for each one, is to have a Catch clause for each type of exception.

The following code shows how this can be done. This is a modified version of the btnCalculate_Click procedure in Tutorial 3-10. Notice that the Try-Catch statement has two Catch clauses: one for InvalidCastExceptions (line 17) and one for

DivideByZeroExceptions (line 21). If the code inside the try block throws an InvalidCast-Exception, the program will jump to the Catch clause in line 17, perform its catch block, and then exit. If the code inside the try block throws a DivideByZeroException, the program will jump to the Catch clause in line 21, perform its catch block, and then exit.

```
 1 Private Sub btnCalculate_Click(...) Handles btnCalculate.Click
 2   Dim decAnnualSalary As Decimal ' Annual salary
 3   Dim intPayPeriods As Integer   ' Number of pay periods
 4   Dim decSalary As Decimal       ' Salary per pay period
 5
 6   Try
 7     ' Get the annual salary and number of pay periods.
 8     decAnnualSalary = CDec(txtAnnualSalary.Text)
 9     intPayPeriods = CInt(txtPayPeriods.Text)
10
11     ' Calculate the salary per pay period.
12     decSalary = decAnnualSalary / intPayPeriods
13
14     ' Display the salary per pay period.
15     lblSalary.Text = decSalary.ToString("c")
16
17   Catch ex As InvalidCastException
18     ' An invalid value as entered.
19     MessageBox.Show("Error: Input must be numeric.")
20
21   Catch ex As DivideByZeroException
22     ' 0 was entered for pay periods.
23     MessageBox.Show("Error: Enter nonzero values.")
24   End Try
25 End Sub
```

This is a more sophisticated way of handling exceptions, but it requires you to know the names of the exception types that you want to handle ahead of time. A simple way to do this is to run the program without the Try-Catch statement and deliberately cause the exceptions to occur. You can then see the name of the exception in the error window that appears. (In the *Chap3* folder of student sample programs you will find the previously shown code in a project named *Multiple Exceptions*.)

If You Want to Know More: Displaying an Exception's Default Error Message

It's possible for your program to retrieve the default error message for an exception. This is the error message that you see in the error window that appears when an exception is unhandled.

When an exception occurs, an object known as an **exception object** is created in memory. The exception object has various properties that contain data about the exception. When you write a Catch clause, you can optionally assign a name to the exception object, as shown here:

```
Catch ex As Exception
```

This Catch clause specifies that the name ex refers to the exception object. Inside the catch block, we can use the name ex to access the exception object's properties. One of these is the Message property, which contains the exception's default error message. The following code shows how this can be done. This is another modified version of the btnCalculate_Click procedure in Tutorial 3-10.

```
 1 Private Sub btnCalculate_Click(...) Handles btnCalculate.Click
 2   Dim decAnnualSalary As Decimal ' Annual salary
 3   Dim intPayPeriods As Integer   ' Number of pay periods
 4   Dim decSalary As Decimal       ' Salary per pay period
 5
 6   Try
 7     ' Get the annual salary and number of pay periods.
 8     decAnnualSalary = CDec(txtAnnualSalary.Text)
 9     intPayPeriods = CInt(txtPayPeriods.Text)
10
11     ' Calculate the salary per pay period.
12     decSalary = decAnnualSalary / intPayPeriods
13
14     ' Display the salary per pay period.
15     lblSalary.Text = decSalary.ToString("c")
16
17   Catch ex As Exception
18     ' Display the default error message.
19     MessageBox.Show(ex.Message)
20   End Try
21 End Sub
```

The statement in line 19 simply passes the exception object's Message property to the `MessageBox.Show` method. This causes the default error message to be displayed in a message box. Figure 3-38 shows some examples.

Figure 3-38 Message boxes showing default exception messages

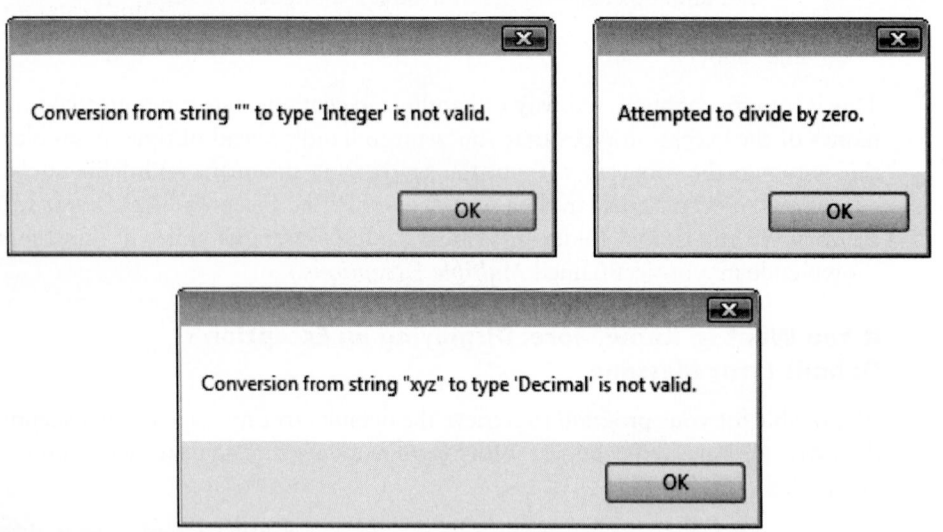

 **Group Boxes**

> **CONCEPT:** The GroupBox control is a container that is used to group other controls together.

Group Boxes

A group box is a rectangular border with an optional title that appears in the border's upper left corner. Other controls may be placed inside a group box. You can give forms a more organized look by grouping related controls together inside group boxes.

In Visual Basic, you use the **GroupBox control** to create a group box with an optional title. The title is stored in the GroupBox control's Text property. Figure 3-39 shows a GroupBox control. The control's Text property is set to *Personal Data*, and a group of other controls are inside the group box.

Figure 3-39 GroupBox containing other controls

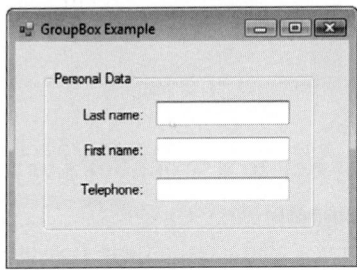

Creating a Group Box and Adding Controls to It

To create a group box, select the *GroupBox* control from the *Containers* section of the *Toolbox* window and then draw the group box at the desired size on the form. To add another control to the group box, select the GroupBox control that you placed on the form, and then double-click the desired tool in the Toolbox to place another control inside the group box.

The controls you place inside a group box become part of a group. When you move a group box, the objects inside it move as well. When you delete a group box, the objects inside it are also deleted.

Moving an Existing Control to a Group Box

If an existing control is not inside a group box, but you want to move it to the group box, follow these steps:

1. Select the control you wish to add to the group box.
2. Cut the control to the clipboard.
3. Select the group box.
4. Paste the control.

Group Box Tab Order

The value of a control's TabIndex property is handled differently when the control is placed inside a GroupBox control. GroupBox controls have their own TabIndex property and the TabIndex value of the controls inside the group box are relative to the GroupBox control's TabIndex property. For example, Figure 3-40 shows a GroupBox control displayed in tab order selection mode. As you can see, the GroupBox control's TabIndex is set to 2. The TabIndex of the controls inside the group box are displayed as 2.0, 2.1, 2.2, and so on.

NOTE: The TabIndex properties of the controls inside the group box will not appear this way in the *Properties* window. They will appear as 0, 1, 2, and so on.

Figure 3-40 Group box TabIndex values

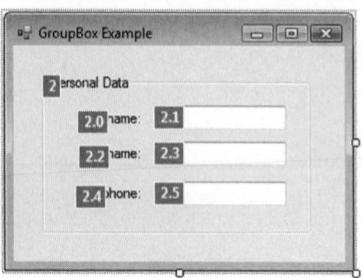

Assigning an Access Key to a GroupBox Control

Although GroupBox controls cannot receive the focus, you can assign a keyboard access key to them by preceding a character in their Text property with an ampersand (&). When the user enters the access key, the focus moves to the control with the lowest TabIndex value inside the group box.

Selecting and Moving Multiple Controls

It is possible to select multiple controls and work with them all at once. For example, you can select a group of controls and move them all to a different location on the form. You can also select a group of controls and change some of their properties.

Select multiple controls by using one of the following techniques:

- Position the cursor over an empty part of the form near the controls you wish to select. Click and drag a selection box around the controls. This is shown in Figure 3-41. When you release the mouse button, all the controls that are partially or completely enclosed in the selection box will be selected.
- Hold down the ⌈Ctrl⌋ key while clicking each control you wish to select.

After using either of these techniques, all the controls you have selected will appear with sizing handles. You may now move them, delete them, or use the *Properties* window to set many of their properties to the same value.

Figure 3-41 Selecting multiple controls by clicking and dragging the mouse

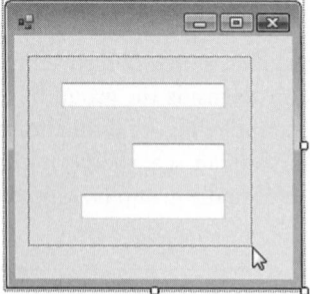

    TIP: In a group of selected controls, it is easy to deselect a control that you have accidentally selected. Simply hold down the ⌈Ctrl⌋ key and click the control you wish to deselect.

3.9 The Load Event

CONCEPT: When an application's form loads into memory, an event known as the Load event takes place. You can write an event handler for the Load event, and that handler will execute just before the form is displayed.

When you run an application, the application's form is loaded into memory and an event known as the **Load event** takes place. The Load event takes place before the form is displayed on the screen. If you want to execute some code at this point, you can write the code in the form's Load event handler.

To create a Load event handler for a form, simply double-click any area of the form in the *Designer* window, where there is no other control. The *Code* window will open with a template for the form's Load event handler. The following is an example of a Load event handler that displays a message box. When the application runs, the message box will appear before the Form1 form is displayed.

```
Private Sub Form1_Load(...) Handles MyBase.Load
    MessageBox.Show("Prepare to see the form!")
End Sub
```

(In the *Chap3* folder of student sample programs you will find a project named *Load Event Demo* that demonstrates this event handler.) In the next section you will develop an application that displays the current date and time on the application's form. You will accomplish this by writing code in the form's Load event handler that retrieves the date and time from the system.

 Checkpoint

3.43 How is a group box helpful when designing a form with a large number of controls?

3.44 When placing a new control inside an existing GroupBox control, what must you do before you double-click the new control in the *ToolBox*?

3.45 How is the clipboard useful when you want to move an existing control into a group box?

3.46 How does the tab order of controls inside a group box correspond to the tab order of other controls outside the group box?

3.47 What event happens just before a form is displayed on the screen?

3.10 Focus on Program Design and Problem Solving: Building the *Room Charge Calculator* Application

A guest staying at the Highlander Hotel may incur the following types of charges:

- Room charges, based on a per-night rate
- Room service charges
- Telephone charges
- Miscellaneous charges

The manager of the Highlander Hotel has asked you to create an application that calculates the guest's total charges. Figure 3-42 shows how the application's form should appear.

Figure 3-42 Sample output from the *Room Charge Calculator* application

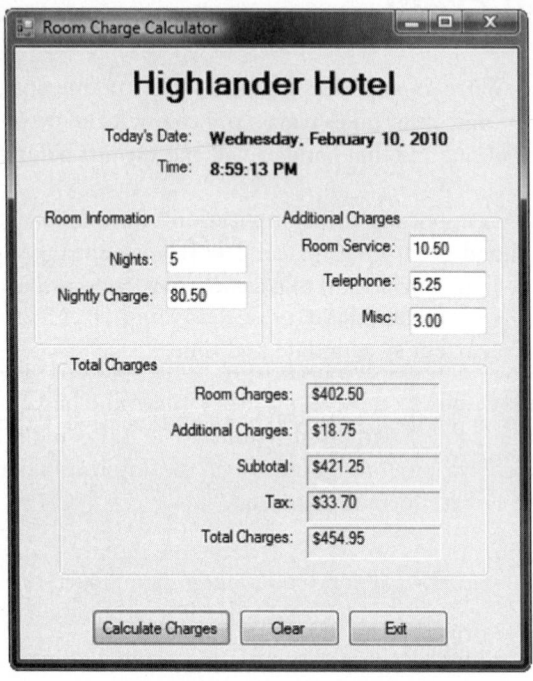

Figure 3-43 shows how the controls are arranged on the form with names. You can use this diagram when designing the form and assigning values to the Name property of each control. Table 3-20, located at the end of this section, can also be used as a reference.

Figure 3-43 Named controls

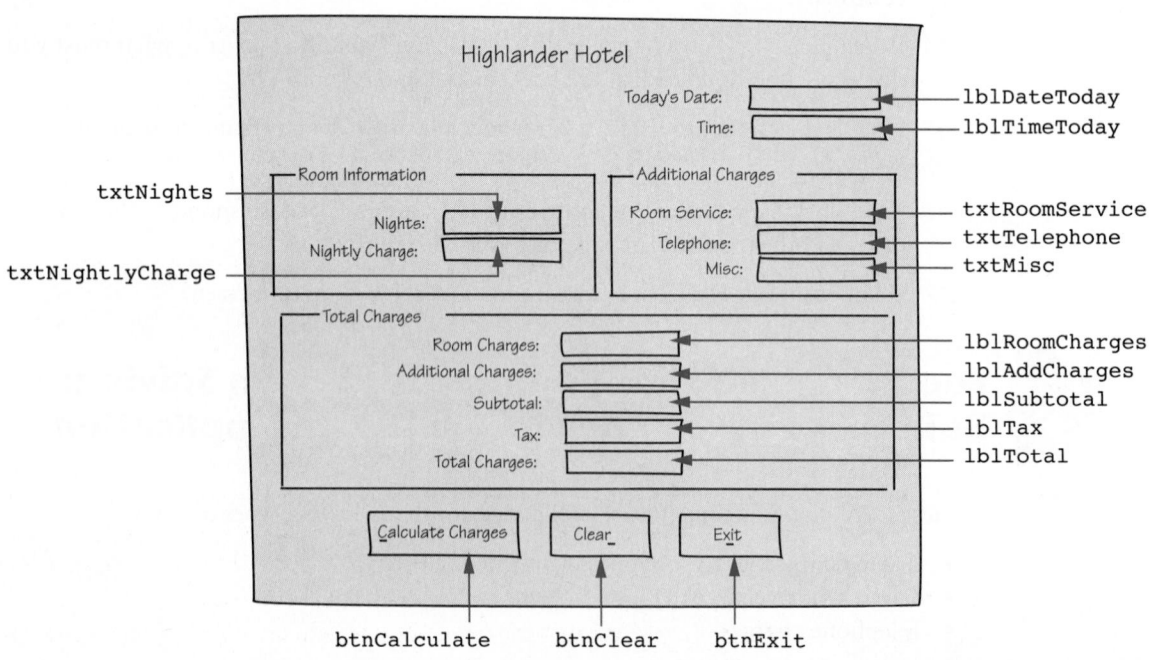

Table 3-19 lists and describes the event handlers needed for this application. Notice that a Load event handler is needed for the form.

Table 3-19 Event handlers in the *Room Charge Calculator* application

Method	Description
btnCalculate_Click	Calculates the room charges, additional charges, subtotal (room charges plus additional charges), 8% tax, and the total charges. These values are assigned to the Text properties of the appropriate labels.
btnClear_Click	Clears the TextBox controls, and the labels used to display summary charge information. This procedure also resets the values displayed in the lblDateToday and lblTimeToday labels.
btnExit_Click	Ends the application
Form1_Load	Initializes the lblDateToday and lblTimeToday labels with the current system date and time

Figure 3-44 shows the flowchart for the btnCalculate_Click procedure. The procedure uses the following Decimal variables:

    decRoomCharges
    decAddCharges
    decSubtotal
    decTax
    decTotal

The procedure also uses a named constant, decTAX_RATE, to hold the tax rate.

Figure 3-44 Flowchart for btnCalculate_Click

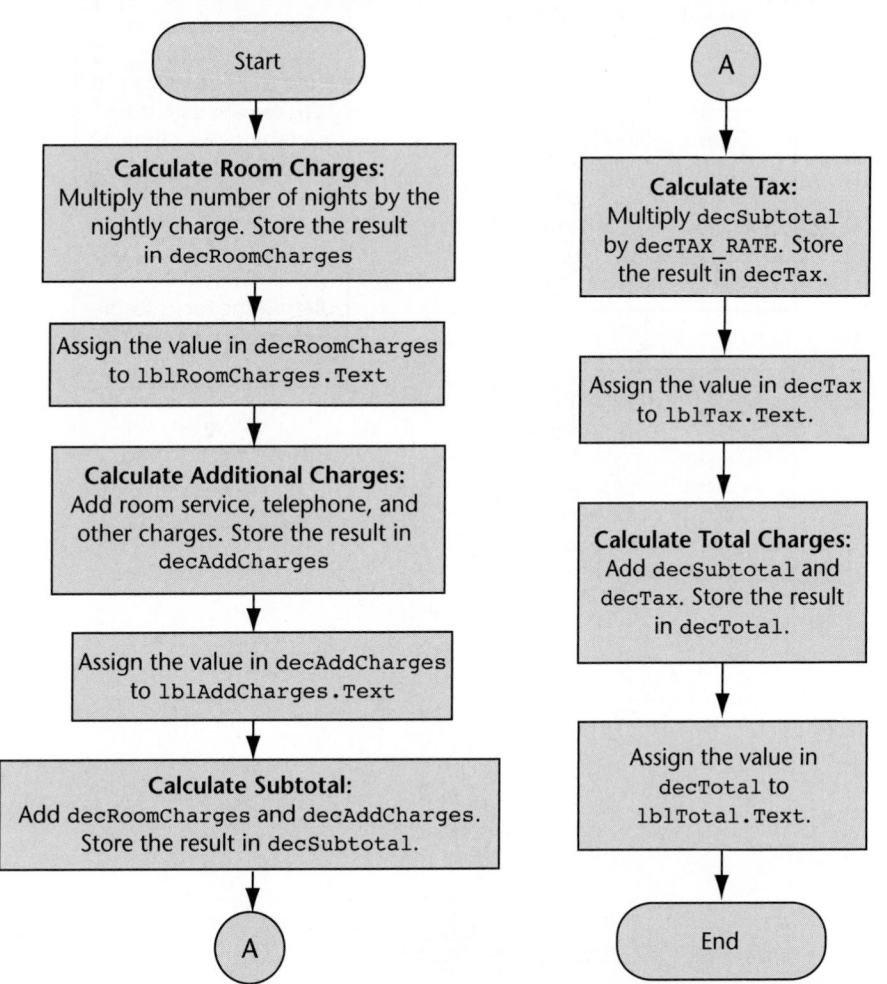

The flowchart in Figure 3-44 uses a new symbol: Ⓐ

This is called the **connector symbol** and is used when a flowchart is broken into two or more smaller flowcharts. This is necessary when a flowchart does not fit on a single page or must be divided into sections. A connector symbol, which is a small circle with a letter or number inside it, allows you to connect two flowcharts. In the flowchart shown in Figure 3-44, the Ⓐ connector indicates that the second flowchart segment begins where the first flowchart segment ends.

The flowcharts for the `btnClear_Click`, `btnExit_Click`, and `Form1_Load` procedures are shown in Figures 3-45, 3-46, and 3-47, respectively.

Recall that the form's `Load` procedure executes each time the form loads into memory. Tutorial 3-11 shows you how to create the *Room Charge Calculator* application.

Figure 3-45 Flowchart for `btnClear_Click`

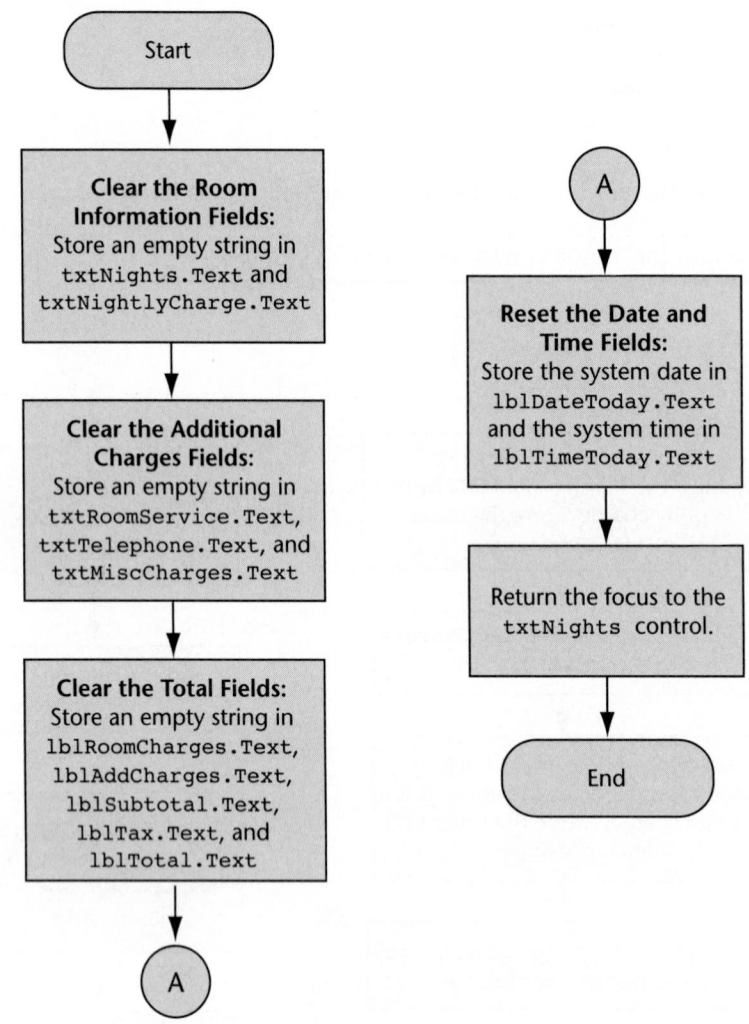

Figure 3-46 Flowchart for `btnExit_Click`

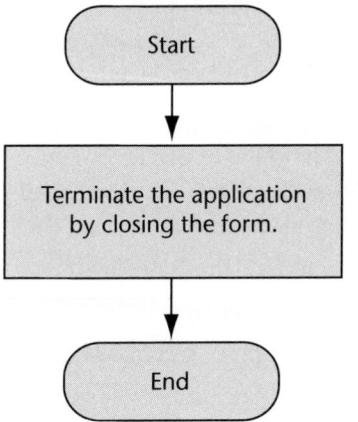

Figure 3-47 Flowchart for `Form1_Load` procedure

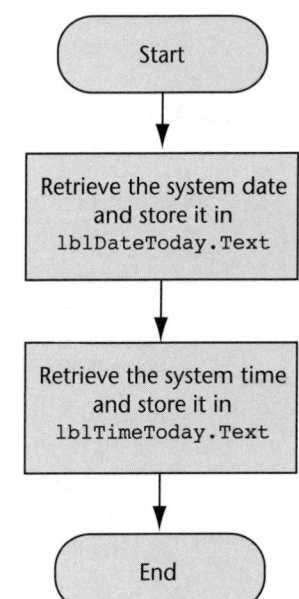

Tutorial 3-11:
Beginning the *Room Charge Calculator* application

Step 1:   Create a new Windows Forms Application project named *Room Charge Calculator*.

Step 2:   Figure 3-43 shows a sketch of the application's form and shows the names of the named controls. Refer to this figure as you set up the form and create the controls. Once you have completed the form, it should appear as shown in Figure 3-48.

Figure 3-48 The *Room Charge Calculator* form

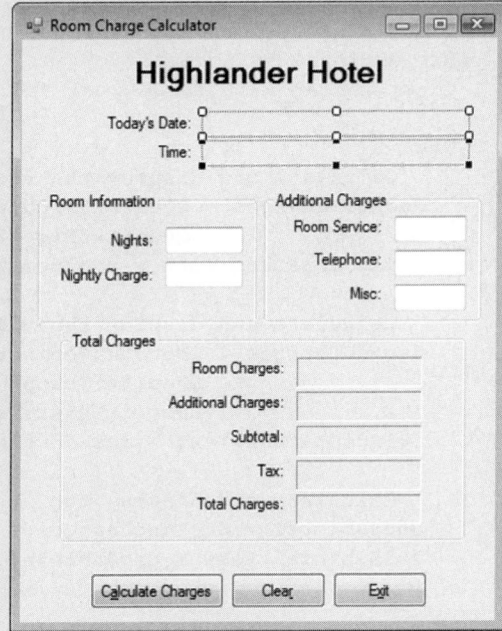

TIP: Most of the controls are contained inside group boxes. Refer to Section 3.8 for instructions on creating controls inside a group box.

TIP: The TextBox controls are all the same size, and all the Label controls that display output are the same size. If you are creating many similar instances of a control, it is easier to create the first one, set its size and properties as needed, copy it to the clipboard, and then paste it onto the form to create another one.

Step 3:   Table 3-20 (on page 179) lists the relevant property settings of all the controls on the form. Refer to this table and make the necessary property settings.

Step 4:   Now you will write the application's event handlers, beginning with the form's Load event handler. Double-click any area of the form not occupied by another control. The *Code* window should open with a code template for the Form1_Load procedure. Complete the procedure by typing the following code shown in bold:

```
Private Sub Form1_Load(...) Handles MyBase.Load
    ' Get today's date from the system and display it.
    lblDateToday.Text = Now.ToString("D")

    ' Get the current time from the system and display it.
    lblTimeToday.Text = Now.ToString("T")
End Sub
```

Step 5:   Double-click the *Calculate Charges* button. The *Code* window should open with a code template for the btnCalculate_Click procedure. Complete the procedure by typing the bold code shown in the following:

```
Private Sub btnCalculate_Click(...) Handles btnCalculate.Click
    ' Declare variables for the calculations.
    Dim decRoomCharges As Decimal       ' Room charges total
    Dim decAddCharges As Decimal        ' Additional charges
    Dim decSubtotal As Decimal          ' Subtotal
    Dim decTax As Decimal               ' Tax
    Dim decTotal As Decimal             ' Total of all charges
    Const decTAX_RATE As Decimal = 0.08D  ' Tax rate

    Try
        ' Calculate and display the room charges.
        decRoomCharges = CDec(txtNights.Text) *
                        CDec(txtNightlyCharge.Text)
        lblRoomCharges.Text = decRoomCharges.ToString("c")

        ' Calculate and display the additional charges.
        decAddCharges = CDec(txtRoomService.Text) +
                        CDec(txtTelephone.Text) +
                        CDec(txtMisc.Text)
        lblAddCharges.Text = decAddCharges.ToString("c")

        ' Calculate and display the subtotal.
        decSubtotal = decRoomCharges + decAddCharges
        lblSubtotal.Text = decSubtotal.ToString("c")
```

```
            ' Calculate and display the tax.
            decTax = decSubtotal * decTAX_RATE
            lblTax.Text = decTax.ToString("c")

            ' Calculate and display the total charges.
            decTotal = decSubtotal + decTax
            lblTotal.Text = decTotal.ToString("c")
        Catch
            ' Error message
            MessageBox.Show("All input must be valid numeric values.")
        End Try
    End Sub
```

Exception handling was used in this procedure to check for invalid input. If the user enters an invalid value in any of the text boxes, the message box shown in Figure 3-49 will appear, and then the user will be able to reenter the input. Imagine how much better this is than letting the program halt unexpectedly.

Figure 3-49 Message box displayed by the exception handler

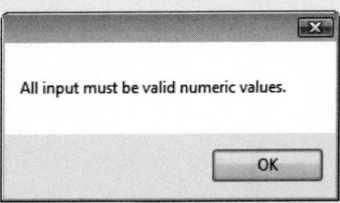

Step 6: Open the *Design* window and double-click the *Clear* button. The *Code* window should open with a code template for the `btnClear_Click` procedure. Complete the procedure by typing the following code shown in bold.

```
Private Sub btnClear_Click(...) Handles btnClear.Click
    ' Clear the room info fields.
    txtNights.Clear()
    txtNightlyCharge.Clear()

    ' Clear the additional charges fields.
    txtRoomService.Clear()
    txtTelephone.Clear()
    txtMisc.Clear()

    ' Clear the decTotal fields.
    lblRoomCharges.Text = String.Empty
    lblAddCharges.Text = String.Empty
    lblSubtotal.Text = String.Empty
    lblTax.Text = String.Empty
    lblTotal.Text = String.Empty

    ' Get today's date from the operating system and display it.
    lblDateToday.Text = Now.ToString("D")

    ' Get the current time from the operating system and display it.
    lblTimeToday.Text = Now.ToString("T")

    ' Reset the focus to the first field.
    txtNights.Focus()
End Sub
```

Step 7:   Open the *Design* window and double-click the *Exit* button. The *Code* window should open with a code template for the `btnExit_Click` procedure. Complete the procedure by typing the following code shown in bold.

```
Private Sub btnExit_Click(...) Handles btnExit.Click
    ' Close the form.
    Me.Close()
End Sub
```

Step 8:   Save the project.

Step 9:   Run the application. If there are errors, compare your code with that shown, and correct them. Once the application runs, enter test values, as shown in Figure 3-50 for the charges and confirm that it displays the correct output.

Figure 3-50 Sample output from the *Room Charge Calculator* application

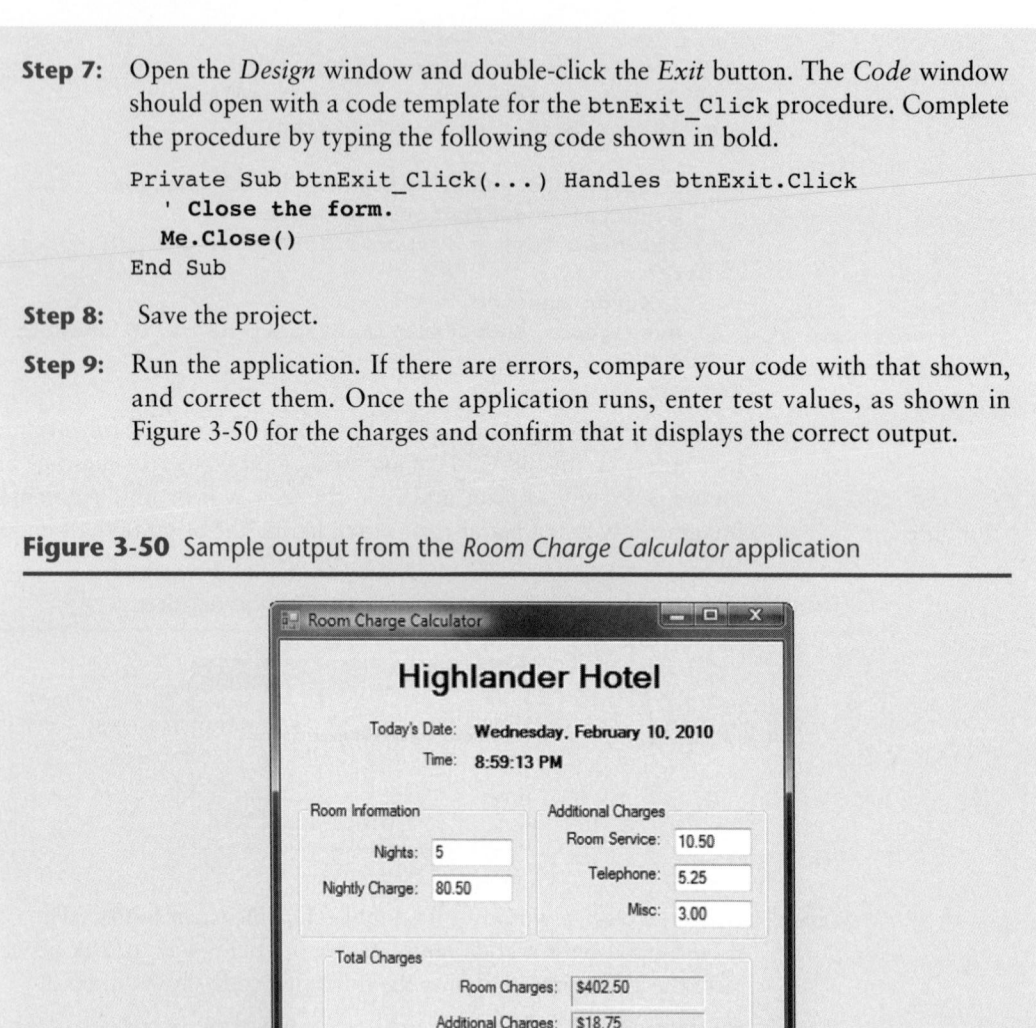

Table 3-20 lists each control, along with any relevant property values.

Table 3-20 Named controls in *Room Charge Calculator* form

Control Type	Control Name	Property	Property Value
Label	(Default)	Text: Font:	*Highlander Hotel* *MS sans serif, bold, 18 point*
Label	(Default)	Text:	*Today's Date:*
Label	lblDateToday	Text: AutoSize: Font.Bold:	(Initially cleared) *False* *True*
Label	(Default)	Text:	*Time:*
Label	lblTimeToday	Text: AutoSize: Font.Bold:	(Initially cleared) *False* *True*
Group box	(Default)	Text:	*Room Information*
Label	(Default)	Text:	*Nights:*
TextBox	txtNights	Text:	(Initially cleared)
Label	(Default)	Text:	*Nightly Charge:*
TextBox	txtNightlyCharge	Text:	(Initially cleared)
Group box	(Default)	Text:	*Additional Charges*
Label	(Default)	Text:	*Room Service:*
TextBox	txtRoomService	Text:	(Initially cleared)
Label	(Default)	Text:	*Telephone:*
TextBox	txtTelephone	Text:	(Initially cleared)
Label	(Default)	Text:	*Misc:*
TextBox	txtMisc	Text:	(Initially cleared)
Group box	(Default)	Text:	*Total Charges*
Label	(Default)	Text:	*Room Charges:*
Label	lblRoomCharges	Text: AutoSize: BorderStyle:	(Initially cleared) *False* *Fixed3D*
Label	(Default)	Text:	*Additional Charges:*
Label	lblAddCharges	Text: AutoSize: BorderStyle:	(Initially cleared) *False* *Fixed3D*
Label	(Default)	Text:	*Subtotal:*
Label	lblSubtotal	Text: AutoSize: BorderStyle:	(Initially cleared) *False* *Fixed3D*
Label	(Default)	Text:	*Tax:*
Label	lblTax	Text: AutoSize: BorderStyle:	(Initially cleared) *False* *Fixed3D*

(continued)

Table 3-20 Named controls in *Room Charge Calculator* form (*continued*)

Control Type	Control Name	Property	Property Value
Label	(Default)	Text:	*Total Charges:*
Label	lblTotal	Text: AutoSize: BorderStyle:	(Initially cleared) *False* *Fixed3D*
Button	btnCalculate	Text:	*C&alculate Charges*
Button	btnClear	Text:	*Clea&r*
Button	btnExit	Text:	*E&xit*

Changing Colors with Code (Optional Topic)

Chapter 2 showed how to change the foreground and background colors of a control's text by setting the ForeColor and BackColor properties in the *Properties* window. In addition to using the *Properties* window, you can also store values in these properties with code. Visual Basic provides numerous values that represent colors, and can be assigned to the ForeColor and BackColor properties in code. The following are a few of the values:

```
Color.Black
Color.Blue
Color.Cyan
Color.Green
Color.Magenta
Color.Red
Color.White
Color.Yellow
```

For example, assume an application has a Label control named lblMessage. The following code sets the label's background color to black and foreground color to yellow:

```
lblMessage.BackColor = Color.Black
lblMessage.ForeColor = Color.Yellow
```

Visual Basic also provides values that represent default colors on your system. For example, the value SystemColors.Control represents the default control background color and SystemColors.ControlText represents the default control text color. The following statements set the lblMessage control's background and foreground to the default colors.

```
lblMessage.BackColor = SystemColors.Control
lblMessage.ForeColor = SystemColors.ControlText
```

In Tutorial 3-12, you will modify the *Room Charge Calculator* application so that the total charges are displayed in white characters on a blue background. This will make the total charges stand out visually from the rest of the information on the form.

Tutorial 3-12:
Changing a label's colors

In this tutorial, you will modify two of the *Room Charge Calculator* application's event handlers: btnCalculate_Click and btnClear_Click. In the btnCalculate_Click procedure, you will add code that changes the lblTotal control's color settings just after the total charges are displayed. In the btnClear_Click procedure, you will add code that reverts lblTotal's colors back to their normal state.

Step 1: With the *Room Charge Calculator* project open, open the *Code* window and scroll to the btnCalculate_Click event handler.

Step 2: The btnCalculate_Click procedure is shown as follows. Add the three lines shown in bold:

```
Private Sub btnCalculate_Click(...) Handles btnCalculate.Click
    ' Declare variables for the calculations.
    Dim decRoomCharges As Decimal       ' Room charges total
    Dim decAddCharges As Decimal        ' Additional charges
    Dim decSubtotal As Decimal          ' Subtotal
    Dim decTax As Decimal               ' Tax
    Dim decTotal As Decimal             ' Total of all charges
    Const decTAX_RATE As Decimal = 0.08D   ' Tax rate

    Try
        ' Calculate and display the room charges.
        decRoomCharges = CDec(txtNights.Text) *
                        CDec(txtNightlyCharge.Text)
        lblRoomCharges.Text = decRoomCharges.ToString("c")

        ' Calculate and display the additional charges.
        decAddCharges = CDec(txtRoomService.Text) +
                       CDec(txtTelephone.Text) +
                       CDec(txtMisc.Text)
        lblAddCharges.Text = decAddCharges.ToString("c")

        ' Calculate and display the subtotal.
        decSubtotal = decRoomCharges + decAddCharges
        lblSubtotal.Text = decSubtotal.ToString("c")

        ' Calculate and display the tax.
        decTax = decSubtotal * decTAX_RATE
        lblTax.Text = decTax.ToString("c")

        ' Calculate and display the total charges.
        decTotal = decSubtotal + decTax
        lblTotal.Text = decTotal.ToString("c")

        ' Change the colors for the total charges.
        lblTotal.BackColor = Color.Blue
        lblTotal.ForeColor = Color.White
    Catch
        ' Error message
        MessageBox.Show("All input must be valid numeric values.")
    End Try
End Sub
```

Step 3: Add the following bold lines to the end of the btnClear_Click procedure, just before the line at the end that calls the Focus method. The existing line is shown to help you find the right location:

```
' Reset the lblTotal control's colors.
lblTotal.BackColor = SystemColors.Control
lblTotal.ForeColor = SystemColors.ControlText

' Reset the focus to the first field.
txtNights.Focus()
```

Step 4:   Save the project.

Step 5:   Run and test the application. When you click the *Calculate Charges* button, the value displayed in the lblTotal label should appear in white text on a blue background. When you click the *Clear* button, the color of the lblTotal label should return to normal.

3.11   More about Debugging: Locating Logic Errors

CONCEPT: Visual Studio allows you to pause a program, and then execute statements one at a time. After each statement executes, you may examine variable contents and property values.

A **logic error** is a mistake that does not prevent an application from running, but causes the application to produce incorrect results. Mathematical mistakes, assigning a value to the wrong variable, or assigning the wrong value to a variable are examples of logic errors. Logic errors can be difficult to find. Fortunately, Visual Studio provides you with debugging tools that make locating logic errors easier.

Visual Studio allows you to set breakpoints in your program code. A **breakpoint** is a line you select in your source code. When the application is running and it reaches a breakpoint, the application pauses and enters Break mode. While the application is paused, you may examine variable contents and the values stored in certain control properties.

Visual Studio allows you to **single-step** through an application's code once its execution has been paused by a breakpoint. This means that the application's statements execute one at a time, under your control. After each statement executes, you can examine variable and property values. This process allows you to identify the line or lines of code causing the error. In Tutorial 3-13, you single-step through an application's code.

Tutorial 3-13:
Single-stepping through an application's code at runtime

In this tutorial, you set a breakpoint in an application's code, run it in debugging mode, and single-step through the application's code to find a logic error.

Step 1:   Open the *Average Race Times* project from the student sample programs folder named *Chap3\Average Race Times*.

Step 2:   Run the application. The application's form appears, as shown in Figure 3-51.

Step 3:   This application allows you to enter the finishing times of three runners in a race, and then see their average time. Enter **25** as the time for all three runners.

Step 4:   Click the *Calculate Average* button. The application displays the incorrect value 58.3 as the average time. (The correct value should be 25.)

Figure 3-51 *Average Race Times* form

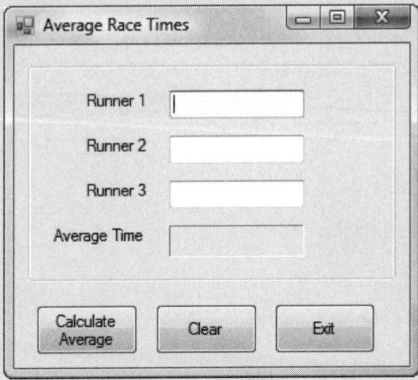

Step 5:   Click the *Exit* button to stop the application.

Step 6:   Open the *Code* window and locate the following line of code, which appears in the `btnCalculate_Click` event handler:

```
dblRunner1 = CDbl(txtRunner1.Text)
```

This line of code is where we want to pause the execution of the application. We must make this line a breakpoint.

Step 7:   Click the mouse in the left margin of the *Code* window, next to the line of code, as shown in Figure 3-52.

Figure 3-52 Click the mouse in the left margin of the *Code* window

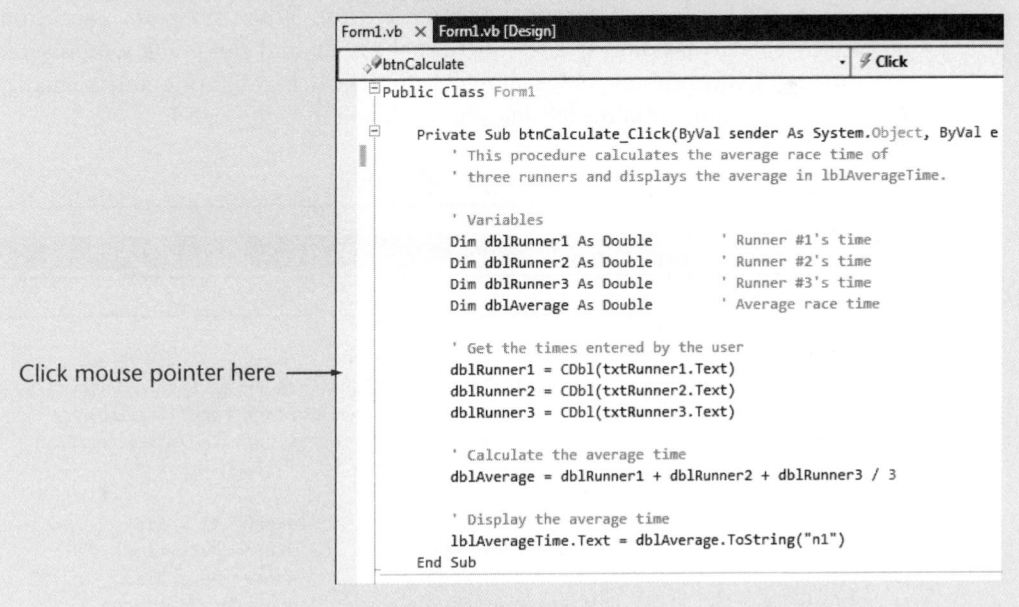

Step 8: Notice that a red dot appears next to the line in the left margin, and the line of code becomes highlighted. This is shown in Figure 3-53.

Figure 3-53 Breakpoint code highlighted

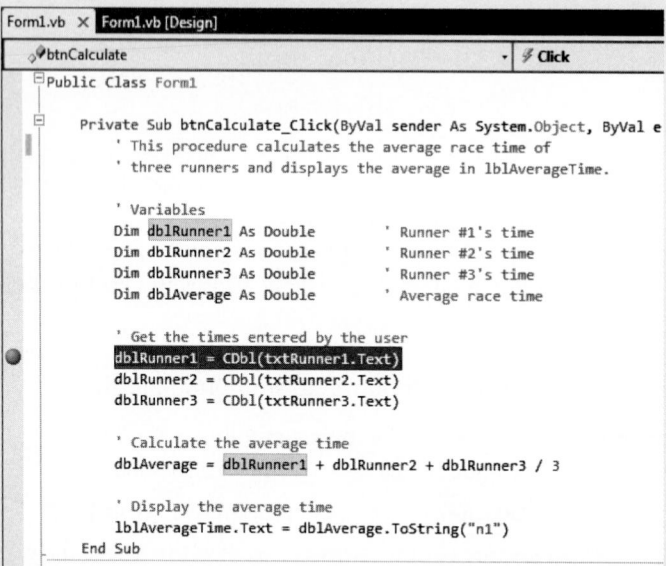

The dot indicates that a breakpoint has been set on this line. Another way to set a breakpoint is to move the text cursor to the line you wish to set as a breakpoint, and then press F9.

Step 9: Now that you have set the breakpoint, run the application. When the form appears, enter **25** as the time for each runner.

Step 10: Click the *Calculate Average* button. When program execution reaches the breakpoint, it goes into Break mode and the *Code* window reappears. The breakpoint line is shown with yellow highlighting and a small yellow arrow appears in the left margin, as shown in Figure 3-54.

Figure 3-54 Breakpoint during Break mode

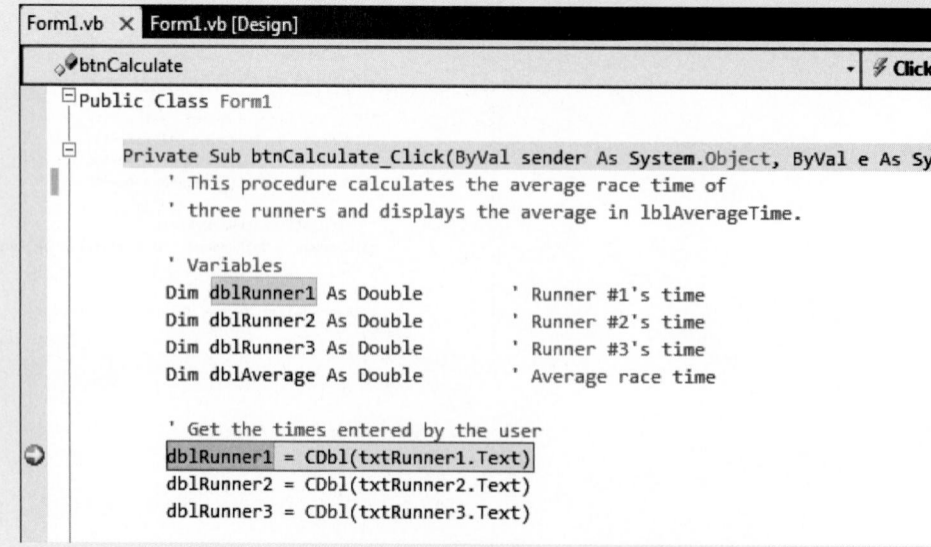

The yellow highlighting and small arrow indicate the application's current execution point. The **execution point** is the next line of code that will execute. (The line has not yet executed.)

 NOTE: If the highlighting and arrow appear in a color other than yellow, the color options on your system may have been changed.

Step 11: To examine the contents of a variable or control property, hover the cursor over the variable or the property's name in the *Code* window. A small box will appear showing the variable or property's contents. For example, Figure 3-55 shows the result of hovering the mouse pointer over the expression `txtRunner1.Text` in the highlighted line. The box indicates that the property is currently set to 25.

Figure 3-55 `txtRunner1.Text` property contents revealed

```
        ' Get the times entered by the user
        dblRunner1 = CDbl(txtRunner1.Text)
                                          txtRunner1.Text  🔍 ▾ "25" ⊟
        dblRunner2 = CDbl(txtRunner2.Te
        dblRunner3 = CDbl(txtRunner3.Text)

        ' Calculate the average time
        dblAverage = dblRunner1 + dblRunner2 + dblRunner3 / 3

        ' Display the average time
        lblAverageTime.Text = dblAverage.ToString("n1")
    End Sub
```

Step 12: Now hover the mouse pointer over the variable name `dblRunner1`. A box appears indicating that the variable is set to 0.0. Because the highlighted statement has not yet executed, no value has been assigned to this variable.

Step 13: You may also examine the contents of variables with the *Autos*, *Locals*, and *Watch* windows.

A description of each window follows:

- The *Autos* window (Visual Studio only) displays a list of the variables appearing in the current statement, the three statements before, and the three statements after the current statement. The current value and the data type of each variable are also displayed.
- The *Immediate* window allows you to type debugging commands using the keyboard. This window is generally used by advanced programmers.
- The *Locals* window displays a list of all the variables in the current procedure. The current value and the data type of each variable are also displayed.
- The *Watch* window allows you to add the names of variables you want to watch. This window displays only the variables you have added. Visual Studio lets you open multiple *Watch* windows, whereas Visual Basic Express offers only one *Watch* window.

You can open any of these windows by selecting *Debug* on the menu bar, then selecting *Windows*, and then selecting the window that you want to open. Use this technique to open the *Locals* window now.

The *Locals* window should appear, similar to Figure 3-56.

Figure 3-56 *Locals* window displayed

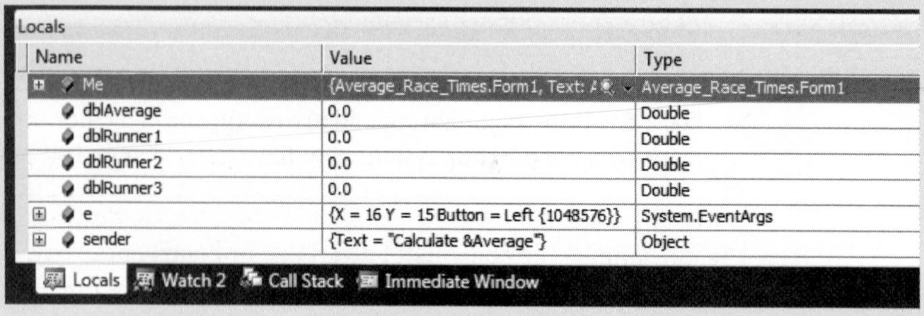

Locals		
Name	Value	Type
⊞ ♥ Me	{Average_Race_Times.Form1, Text: ⚡ ♥ ∨	Average_Race_Times.Form1
● dblAverage	0.0	Double
● dblRunner1	0.0	Double
● dblRunner2	0.0	Double
● dblRunner3	0.0	Double
⊞ ● e	{X = 16 Y = 15 Button = Left {1048576}}	System.EventArgs
⊞ ● sender	{Text = "Calculate &Average"}	Object

  🖳 Locals 🔲 Watch 2 📇 Call Stack 🖳 Immediate Window

Step 14: Now you are ready to single-step through each statement in the event handler. To do this, use the **Step Into** command. (The *Step Over* command, which is similar to *Step Into*, is covered in Chapter 6.) You activate the *Step Into* command by one of the following methods:

- Press the F8 key.
- Select *Debug* from the menu bar, and then select *Step Into* from the *Debug* menu.

When you activate the *Step Into* command, the highlighted statement is executed. Press the F8 key now. Look at the *Watch* window and notice that the dblRunner1 variable is now set to 25.0. Also notice that the next line of code is now highlighted.

Step 15: Press the F8 key two more times. The variables dblRunner1, dblRunner2, and dblRunner3 should display values of 25.0 in the *Locals* window.

Step 16: The following statement, which is supposed to calculate the average of the three scores, is now highlighted:

```
dblAverage = dblRunner1 + dblRunner2 + dblRunner3 / 3
```

After this statement executes, the average of the three numbers should display next to dblAverage. Press F8 to execute the statement.

Step 17: Notice that the *Locals* window now reports that dblAverage holds the value 58.333333333333336. This is not the correct value, so there must be a problem with the math statement that just executed. Can you find it? The math statement does not calculate the correct value because the division operation takes place before any of the addition operations. You must correct the statement by inserting a set of parentheses.

From the menu, select *Debug*, and then click *Stop Debugging* to halt the application. In the *Code* window, insert a set of parentheses into the math statement so it appears as follows:

```
dblAverage = (dblRunner1 + dblRunner2 + dblRunner3) / 3
```

Step 18: Next, you will clear the breakpoint so the application will not pause again when it reaches that line of code. To clear the breakpoint, use one of the following methods:

- Click the mouse on the breakpoint dot in the left margin of the *Code* window.
- Press Ctrl+Shift+F9.
- Select *Debug* from the menu bar, and then select *Delete All Breakpoints* from the *Debug* menu.

Step 19: Run the application again. Enter **25** as each runner's time, and then click the *Calculate Average* button. This time the correct average, 25.0, is displayed.

Step 20: Click the *Exit* button to stop the application.

If You Want to Know More: Debugging Commands in the Toolbar

Visual Studio provides a toolbar for debugging commands, shown in Figure 3-57.

Figure 3-57 *Debug* toolbar commands

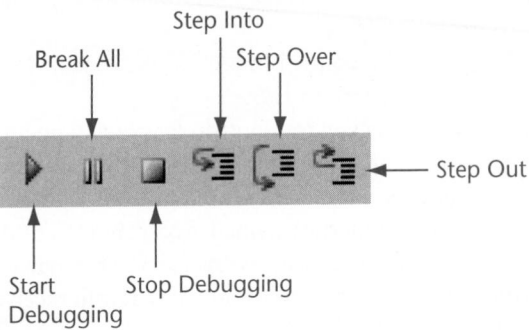

Checkpoint

3.48 What is the difference between a syntax error and a logic error?

3.49 What is a breakpoint?

3.50 What is the purpose of single-stepping through an application?

Summary

3.1 Gathering Text Input

- Words and characters typed into a TextBox control are stored in the control's Text property. The standard prefix for TextBox control names is txt.
- The & operator is used to perform string concatenation.
- The control that has the focus receives the user's keyboard input or mouse clicks. The focus is moved by calling the Focus method.
- The order in which controls receive the focus when the Tab key is pressed at runtime is called the tab order. When you place controls on a form, the tab order will be the same sequence in which you created the controls. You can modify the tab order by changing a control's TabIndex property.
- Tab order selection mode allows you to easily view the TabIndex property values of all the controls on a form.
- If you do not want a control to receive the focus when the user presses the Tab key, set its TabStop property to *False*.
- You assign an access key to a button by placing an ampersand (&) in its Text property. The letter that immediately follows the ampersand becomes the access key. That letter appears underlined on the button.
- Forms have two properties named AcceptButton and CancelButton. AcceptButton refers to the control that will receive a Click event when the user presses the Enter key. CancelButton refers to the control that will receive a Click event when the user presses the Esc key.

3.2 Variables and Data Types

- The assignment operator (=) is used to store a value in a variable, just as with a control property. A variable's data type determines the type of information that the variable can hold.
- Rules for naming variables are enforced by the Visual Basic compiler. Naming conventions, on the other hand, are not rigid—they are based on a standard style of programming.
- When a variable is first created in memory, Visual Basic assigns it an initial value, which depends on its data type. You may also initialize a variable, which means that you specify the variable's starting value.
- Variables of the Date (DateTime) data type can hold a date and time. You may store values in a Date variable with date literals, strings, or user input.
- Each Visual Basic data type has a method named ToString that returns a string representation of the variable calling the method.

3.3 Performing Calculations

- A unary operator has only one operand. An example is the negation operator (minus sign).
- A binary operator has two operands. An example is the addition operator (plus sign).
- The \ symbol identifies the integer division operator.
- The * symbol identifies the multiplication operator.
- The ^ symbol identifies the exponentiation operator.
- The MOD operator returns the remainder after performing integer division.
- When two operators share an operand, the operator with the highest precedence executes first. Parts of a mathematical expression may be grouped with parentheses to force some operations to be performed before others.
- A combined assignment operator combines the assignment operator with another operator.

- The Now function retrieves the current date and time from the computer system. The TimeOfDay function retrieves the current time. The Today function retrieves the current date.
- A variable's scope determines where a variable is visible and where it can be accessed by programming statements.
- A variable declared inside a procedure is called a local variable. This type of variable is only visible from its declaring statement to the end of the same procedure. If a variable is declared inside a class, but outside of any procedure, it is called a class-level variable. If a variable is declared outside of any class or procedure, it is called a global variable.

3.4 Mixing Different Data Types

- Implicit type conversion occurs when you assign a value of one data type to a variable of another data type. Visual Basic attempts to convert the value being assigned to the data type of the destination variable.
- A narrowing conversion occurs when a real number is assigned to one of the integer type variables. It also occurs when a larger type is assigned to a smaller type.
- A widening conversion occurs when data of a smaller type is assigned to a variable of a larger type. An example is when assigning any type of integer to a Double.
- The *Option Strict* statement determines whether certain implicit conversions are legal. When *Option Strict* is *On*, only widening conversions are permitted. When *Option Strict* is *Off*, both narrowing and widening conversions are permitted.
- A type conversion or type mismatch error is generated when an automatic conversion is not possible.
- An explicit type conversion is performed by one of Visual Basic's conversion functions. The conversion functions discussed in this chapter are CDate (convert to date), CDbl (convert to Double), CDec (convert to Decimal), CInt (convert to Integer), and CStr (convert to String).
- The CInt function performs a special type of rounding called bankers rounding.
- Visual Basic provides several type conversion functions, such as CInt and CDbl, which convert expressions to other data types.

3.5 Formatting Numbers and Dates

- Ordinarily, numeric values should be formatted when they are displayed. Formatting gives your programs a more professional appearance.
- The ToString method converts the contents of a variable into a string.
- You can pass a format string as an input argument to the ToString method. The format string can be used to configure the way a number or date is displayed.
- Number format (n or N) displays numeric values with thousands separators and a decimal point.
- Fixed-point format (f or F) displays numeric values with no thousands separator and a decimal point.
- Exponential format (e or E) displays numeric values in scientific notation. The number is normalized with a single digit to the left of the decimal point.
- Currency format (c or C) displays a leading currency symbol (such as $), digits, thousands separators, and a decimal point.
- Percent format (p or P) causes the number to be multiplied by 100 and displayed with a trailing space and % sign.
- You can use the ToString method to format dates and times. Several standard formats were shown in this chapter: short date, long date, short time, long time, and full date and time.

3.6 Class-Level Variables

- Class-level variables are declared inside a class declaration (such as a form's class), but not inside of any procedure.
- Class-level variables are accessible to all of the procedures in a class.

3.7 Exception Handling

- Exception handling is a structured mechanism for handling errors in Visual Basic programs.
- Exception handling begins with the `Try` keyword, followed by one or more `Catch` blocks, followed by `End Try`.
- Some types of errors are preventable by the programmer, such as dividing by zero. Other errors may be caused by user input, which is beyond the control of the programmer.
- When a program throws an exception, it generates a runtime error. An unhandled exception causes a program to terminate and display an error message.
- You can write exception handlers that catch exceptions and find ways for the program to recover. Your exception handler can also display a message to the user.
- Exception handlers can handle multiple types of exceptions by specifically identifying different types of exceptions with different catch blocks.

3.8 Group Boxes

- A GroupBox control, which is used as a container for other controls, appears as a rectangular border with an optional title. You can create the GroupBox first and then create other controls inside it. Alternatively, you can drag existing controls inside the GroupBox.
- In the *Designer* window, grid lines can be used to align controls. You can select and work with multiple controls simultaneously.
- Every form causes a Load event to happen when the form loads into memory. If you need to execute code before a form is displayed, place it in the form's Load event handler.

3.9 Focus on Program Design and Problem Solving: Building the *Room Charge Calculator* Application

- The *Room Charge Calculator* application calculates charges for guests at an imaginary hotel. It combines many of the techniques introduced in this chapter, such as type conversion functions, formatting numbers, and formatting dates.
- Visual Basic provides numerous values that represent colors. These values may be used in code to change a control's foreground and background colors.

3.10 More about Debugging: Locating Logic Errors

- A logic error is a programming mistake that does not prevent an application from compiling, but causes the application to produce incorrect results.
- A runtime error occurs during a program's execution—it halts the program unexpectedly.
- A breakpoint is a line of code that causes a running application to pause execution and enter Break mode. While the application is paused, you may perform debugging operations such as examining variable contents and the values stored in control properties.
- Single-stepping is the debugging technique of executing an application's programming statements one at a time. After each statement executes, you can examine variable and property contents.

Key Terms

accept button
access key
argument
Autos window
binary operator
breakpoint
cancel button
Camel case
catch block
catch clause
code outlining
combined assignment operators
compound operators
connector symbol
exception
exception handler
exception object
execution point
focus
`Focus` method
function
GroupBox control
Immediate window
implicit type conversion
initialization
Load event handler
local variable
Locals window
logic error

mathematical expression
mnemonic
named constant
narrowing conversion
Option Strict
precedence
returning a value
scope (of a variable)
single-step
Step Into command
string concatenation
tab order
tab order selection mode
TabIndex property
TabStop property
text box
TextBox control
`ToString` method
truncation
Try block
`Try-Catch` statement
type conversion error
type mismatch error
variable
variable declaration
unary operator
Watch window
widening conversion

Review Questions and Exercises

Fill-in-the-Blank

1. The _____ control allows you to capture input the user has typed on the keyboard.

2. _____ is the prefix for TextBox control names.

3. _____ means that one string is appended to another.

4. The _____ character allows you to break a long statement into two or more lines of code.

5. The _____ character is actually two characters: a space followed by an underscore.

6. The control that has the _____ is the one that receives the user's keyboard input or mouse clicks.

7. The order in which controls receive the focus is called the _____.

8. You can modify the tab order by changing a control's _____ property.

9. If you do not want a control to receive the focus when the user presses the Tab key, set its _____ property to *False*.

10. An access key is a key that you press in combination with the _____ key to access a control such as a button quickly.

11. You define a button's access key through its _____ property.

12. A(n) _____ is a storage location in the computer's memory, used for holding information while the program is running.

13. A(n) _____ is a statement that causes Visual Basic to create a variable in memory.

14. A variable's _____ determines the type of information the variable can hold.

15. A(n) _____ variable is declared inside a procedure.

16. A(n) _____ error is generated anytime a nonnumeric value that cannot be automatically converted to a numeric value is assigned to a numeric variable or property.

17. A(n) _____ is a specialized routine that performs a specific operation, and then returns a value.

18. The _____ function converts an expression to an integer.

19. The _____ format string, when passed to the `ToString` method, produces a number in Currency format.

20. A(n) _____ is information that is being passed to a function.

21. When two operators share an operand, the operator with the highest _____ executes first.

22. A(n) _____ is like a variable whose content is read-only; it cannot be changed while the program is running.

23. A(n) _____ appears as a rectangular border with an optional title.

24. A form's _____ procedure executes each time a form loads into memory.

25. A(n) _____ is a line of code that causes a running application to pause execution and enter Break mode.

True or False

Indicate whether the following statements are true or false.

1. T F: The TextBox control's Text property holds the text entered by the user into the TextBox control at runtime.

2. T F: You can access a TextBox control's Text property in code.

3. T F: The string concatenation operator automatically inserts a space between the joined strings.

4. T F: You cannot break up a word with the line-continuation character.

5. T F: You can put a comment at the end of a line, after the line-continuation character.

6. T F: Only controls capable of receiving input, such as TextBox controls and buttons, may have the focus.

7. T F: You can cause a control to be skipped in the tab order by setting its `TabPosition` property to *False*.

8. T F: An error will occur if you assign a negative value to the TabIndex property in code.

9. T F: A control whose Visible property is set to *False* still receives the focus.

10. T F: GroupBox and Label controls have a TabIndex property, but they are skipped in the tab order.

11. T F: When you assign an access key to a button, the user can trigger a Click event by typing [Alt]+ the access key character.

12. T F: A local variable may be accessed by any other procedure in the same Form file.

13. T F: When a string variable is created in memory, Visual Basic assigns it the initial value 0.

14. T F: A variable's scope is the time during which the variable exists in memory.

15. T F: A variable declared inside a procedure is only visible to statements inside the same procedure.

16. T F: The `CDbl` function converts a number to a string.

17. T F: If the `CInt` function cannot convert its argument, it causes a runtime error.

18. T F: The multiplication operator has higher precedence than the addition operator.

19. T F: A named constant's value can be changed by a programming statement, while the program is running.

20. T F: The statement `lblMessage.BackColor = Color.Green` will set `lblMessage` control's background color to green.

21. T F: You can select multiple controls simultaneously with the mouse.

22. T F: You can change the same property for multiple controls simultaneously.

23. T F: To group controls in a group box, draw the controls first, then draw the group box around them.

24. T F: While single-stepping through an application's code in Break mode, the highlighted execution point is the line of code that has already executed.

Multiple Choice

1. When the user types input into a TextBox control, in which property is it stored?
   a. Input
   b. Text
   c. Value
   d. Keyboard

2. Which character is the string concatenation operator?
   a. &
   b. *
   c. %
   d. @

3. In code, you move the focus to a control with which method?

   a. `MoveFocus`

   b. `SetFocus`

   c. `ResetFocus`

   d. `Focus`

4. Which form property allows you to specify a button to be clicked when the user presses the Enter key?

   a. DefaultButton

   b. AcceptButton

   c. CancelButton

   d. EnterButton

5. Which form property allows you to specify a button that is to be clicked when the user presses the Esc key?

   a. DefaultButton

   b. AcceptButton

   c. CancelButton

   d. EnterButton

6. You can modify a control's position in the tab order by changing which property?

   a. TabIndex

   b. TabOrder

   c. TabPosition

   d. TabStop

7. You assign an access key to a button through which property?

   a. AccessKey

   b. AccessButton

   c. Mnemonic

   d. Text

8. A group box's title is stored in which property?

   a. Title

   b. Caption

   c. Text

   d. Heading

9. You declare a named constant with which keyword?

   a. `Constant`

   b. `Const`

   c. `NamedConstant`

   d. `Dim`

10. Which of the following is the part of a program in which a variable is visible and may be accessed by programming statement?

   a. segment

   b. lifetime

   c. scope

   d. module

11. If a variable named `dblTest` contains the value 1.23456, then which of the following values will be returned by the expression `dblTest.ToString("N3")`?

    a. 1.23456
    b. 1.235
    c. 1.234
    d. +1.234

12. If the following code executes, which value is assigned to `strA`?

    ```
    Dim dblTest As Double = 0.25
    Dim strA As String = dblTest.ToString("p")
    ```

    a. "0.25"
    b. "2.50"
    c. "25.00%"
    d. "0.25"

Short Answer

1. Describe the difference between the Label control's Text property and the TextBox control's Text property.

2. How do you clear the contents of a text box?

3. What is the focus when referring to a running application?

4. Write a statement that sets the focus to the `txtPassword` control.

5. How does Visual Basic automatically assign the tab order to controls?

6. How does a control's TabIndex property affect the tab order?

7. How do you assign an access key to a button?

8. How does assigning an access key to a button change the button's appearance?

9. What is the difference between the Single and Integer data types?

10. Create variable names that would be appropriate for holding each of the following information items:

    a. The number of backpacks sold this week
    b. The number of pounds of dog food in storage
    c. Today's date
    d. An item's wholesale price
    e. A customer's name
    f. The distance between two galaxies, in kilometers
    g. The number of the month (1 = January, 2 = February, and so on)

11. Why should you always make sure that a string variable is initialized or assigned a value before it is used in an operation?

12. When is a local variable destroyed?

13. How would the following strings be converted by the `CDec` function?

    a. "22.9000"
    b. "1xfc47uvy"
    c. "$19.99"
    d. "0.05%"
    e. `String.Empty`

14. Briefly describe how the `CDec` function converts a string argument to a number.

15. Complete the following table by providing the value of each mathematical expression:

Expression	Value
5 + 2 * 8	_____
20 / 5 – 2	_____
4 + 10 * 3 – 2	_____
(4 + 10) * 3 – 2	_____

16. Assuming that the variable `dblTest` contains the value 67521.584, complete the following table, showing the value returned by each function call:

Function Call	Return Value
`dblTest.ToString("d2")`	_____
`dblTest.ToString("c2")`	_____
`dblTest.ToString("e1")`	_____
`dblTest.ToString("f2")`	_____

17. Describe one way to select multiple controls in Design mode.

18. Describe three ways to set a breakpoint in an application's code.

What Do You Think?

1. Why doesn't Visual Basic automatically insert a space between strings concatenated with the `&` operator?

2. Why would you want to use the line-continuation character to cause a statement to span multiple lines?

3. Why are Label controls not capable of receiving the focus?

4. Why should the tab order of controls in your application be logical?

5. Why assign access keys to buttons?

6. What is the significance of showing an underlined character on a button?

7. Generally speaking, which button should be set as a form's default button?

8. Why can't you perform arithmetic operations on a string, such as `"28.9"`?

9. Suppose a number is used in calculations throughout a program and must be changed every few months. What benefit is there to using a named constant to represent the number?

10. How can you get your application to execute a group of statements each time a form is loaded into memory?

11. How can you place an existing control in a group box?

12. Visual Basic automatically reports syntax errors. Why doesn't it automatically report logic errors?

Find the Error

1. Load the *Chap3\ Error1\ Error1* project from the student sample programs folder. The `btnSum_Click` event handler has an error. Fix the error so the application correctly displays the sum of the numbers.

2. Load the *Chap3\ Error2\ Error2* project from the student sample programs folder. The application has an error. Find the error and fix it.

3. Load the *Chap3\ Error3\ Error3* project from the student sample programs folder. The `btnCalculate_Click` procedure contains an unusual error. Find the error and fix it.

Algorithm Workbench

1. Create a flowchart that shows the necessary steps for making the cookies in the following recipe:

   Ingredients:

1/2 cup butter	1/2 teaspoon vanilla
1 egg	1/2 teaspoon salt
1 cup sifted all-purpose flour	1/2 teaspoon baking soda
1/2 cup brown sugar	1/2 cup chopped nuts
1/2 cup sugar	1/2 cup semisweet chocolate chips

   Steps:
   Preheat oven to 375°.
   Cream the butter.
   Add the sugar and the brown sugar to the butter and beat until creamy.
   Beat the egg and vanilla into the mixture.
   Sift and stir the flour, salt, and baking soda into the mixture.
   Stir the nuts and chocolate chips into the mixture.
   Shape the mixture into 1/2-inch balls.
   Place the balls about one inch apart on a greased cookie sheet.
   Bake for 10 minutes.

2. A hot dog, still in its package, should be heated for 40 seconds in a microwave. Draw a flowchart showing the necessary steps to cook the hot dog.

3. The following pseudocode algorithm for the event handler btnCalcArea_Click has an error. The event handler is supposed to calculate the area of a room's floor. The area is calculated as the room's width (entered by the user into txtWidth), multiplied by the room's length (entered by the user into in txtLength). The result is displayed with the label lblArea. Find the error and correct the algorithm.

   a. Multiply the intWidth variable by the intLength variable and store the result in the intArea variable.

   b. Assign the value in txtWidth.Text to the intWidth variable.

   c. Assign the value in txtLength.Text to the intLength variable.

   d. Assign the value in the intArea variable to lblArea.Text.

4. The following steps should be followed in the event handler btnCalcAvailCredit_Click, which calculates a customer's available credit. Construct a flowchart that shows these steps.

   a. Assign the value in the TextBox control txtMaxCredit to the variable decMaxCredit.

   b. Assign the value in the TextBox control txtUsedCredit to the variable decUsedCredit.

   c. Subtract the value in decUsedCredit from decMaxCredit. Assign the result to decAvailableCredit

   d. Assign the value in decAvailableCredit to the label lblAvailableCredit.

5. Convert the flowchart you constructed in Exercise 4 into Visual Basic code.

6. Design a flowchart or pseudocode for the event handler btnCalcSale_Click, which calculates the total of a retail sale. Assume the program uses txtRetailPrice, a TextBox control that holds the retail price of the item being purchased, and decTAX_RATE, a constant that holds the sales tax rate. The event handler uses the items above to calculate the sales tax for the purchase and the total of the sale. Display the total of the sale in a label named lblTotal.

7. Convert the flowchart or pseudocode you constructed in Exercise 6 into Visual Basic code.

Programming Challenges

VideoNote
The Miles per Gallon Calculator Problem

1. **Miles per Gallon Calculator**

   Create an application that calculates a car's gas mileage. The formula for calculating the miles that a car can travel per gallon of gas is:

   $$MPG = \frac{miles}{gallons}$$

   In the formula *MPG* is miles-per-gallon, *miles* is the number of miles that can be driven on a full tank of gas, and *gallons* is the number of gallons that the tank holds.

   The application's form should have TextBox controls that let the user enter the number of gallons of gas the tank holds, and the number of miles the car can be driven on a full tank. When the *Calculate MPG* button is clicked, the application should display the number of miles that the car can be driven per gallon of gas. The form should also have a *Clear* button that clears the input and results, and an *Exit* button that ends the application. The application's form should appear as shown in Figure 3-58.

Figure 3-58 *Miles per Gallon Calculator*

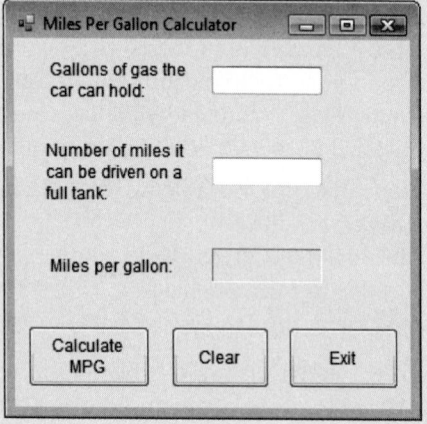

Use the following set of test data to determine if the application is calculating properly:

Gallons	Miles	Miles per Gallon
10	375	37.50
12	289	24.08
15	190	12.67

2. **Stadium Seating**

   There are three seating categories at an athletic stadium. For a baseball game, Class A seats cost $15 each, Class B seats cost $12 each, and Class C seats cost $9 each. Create an application that allows the user to enter the number of tickets sold for each class. The application should be able to display the amount of income generated from each class of ticket sales and the total revenue generated. The application's form should resemble the one shown in Figure 3-59.

Figure 3-59 *Stadium Seating* form

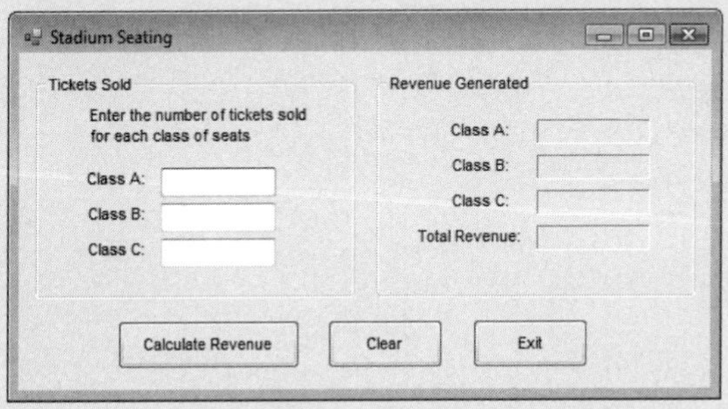

Use the following test data to determine if the application is calculating properly:

Ticket Sales	Revenue
Class A: 320	Class A: $4,800.00
Class B: 570	Class B: $6,840.00
Class C: 890	Class C: $8,010.00
	Total Revenue: $19,650.00
Class A: 500	Class A: $7,500.00
Class B: 750	Class B: $9,000.00
Class C: 1,200	Class C: $10,800.00
	Total Revenue: $27,300.00
Class A: 100	Class A: $1,500.00
Class B: 300	Class B: $3,600.00
Class C: 500	Class C: $4,500.00
	Total Revenue: $9,600.00

3. **Test Score Average**

Create an application that allows the user to enter five test scores. It should be able to calculate and display the average score. The application's form should resemble the one shown in Figure 3-60.

Figure 3-60 *Test Score Average* form

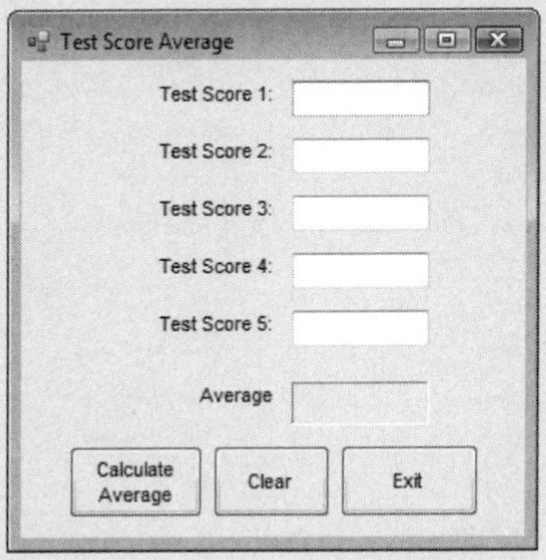

Use the following test data to determine if the application is calculating properly:

Test Scores	Averages
Test Score 1: 85	Average: 86.60
Test Score 2: 90	
Test Score 3: 78	
Test Score 4: 88	
Test Score 5: 92	
Test Score 1: 90	Average: 70.00
Test Score 2: 80	
Test Score 3: 70	
Test Score 4: 60	
Test Score 5: 50	
Test Score 1: 100	Average: 82.2
Test Score 2: 92	
Test Score 3: 56	
Test Score 4: 89	
Test Score 5: 74	

4. **Theater Revenue**

A movie theater only keeps a percentage of the revenue earned from ticket sales. The remainder goes to the movie company. Create an application that calculates and displays the following figures for one night's box office business at a theater:

a. *Gross revenue for adult tickets sold.* This is the amount of money taken in for all adult tickets sold.

b. *Net revenue for adult tickets sold.* This is the amount of money from adult ticket sales left over after the payment to the movie company has been deducted.

c. *Gross revenue for child tickets sold.* This is the amount of money taken in for all child tickets sold.

d. *Net revenue for child tickets sold.* This is the amount of money from child ticket sales left over after the payment to the movie company has been deducted.

e. *Total gross revenue.* This is the sum of gross revenue for adult and child tickets sold.

f. *Total net revenue.* This is the sum of net revenue for adult and child tickets sold.

The application's form should resemble the one shown in Figure 3-61.

Figure 3-61 *Theater Revenue* form

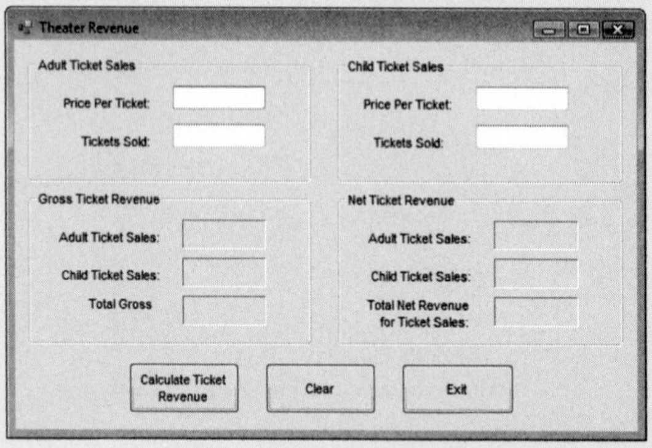

Assume the theater keeps 20% of its box office receipts. Use a named constant in your code to represent this percentage. Use the following test data to determine if the application is calculating properly:

Ticket Sales		Revenue	
Price per Adult Ticket:	$6.00	Gross Adult Ticket Sales:	$720.00
Adult Tickets Sold:	120	Gross Child Ticket Sales:	$288.00
Price per Child Ticket:	$4.00	Total Gross Revenue:	$1,008.00
Ticket Sales (*continued*)		Revenue (*continued*)	
Child Tickets Sold:	72	Net Adult Ticket Sales:	$144.00
		Net Child Ticket Sales:	$57.60
		Total Net Revenue:	$201.60

Design Your Own Forms

5. **How Many Widgets?**

   The Yukon Widget Company manufactures widgets that weigh 9.2 pounds each. Create an application that calculates how many widgets are stacked on a pallet, based on the total weight of the pallet. The user should be able to enter how much the pallet weighs alone and how much it weighs with the widgets stacked on it. The user should click a button to calculate and display the number of widgets stacked on the pallet. Use the following test data to determine if the application is calculating properly:

Pallet	Pallet and Widgets	Number of Widgets
100	5,620	600
75	1,915	200
200	9,400	1,000

6. **Celsius to Fahrenheit**

   Create an application that converts Celsius to Fahrenheit. The formula is $F = 1.8 * C + 32$ where F is the Fahrenheit temperature and C is the Celsius temperature. Use the following test data to determine if the application is calculating properly:

Celsius	Fahrenheit
100	212
0	32
56	132.8

7. **Currency**

   Create an application that converts U.S. dollar amounts to pounds, euros, and yen. The following conversion factors are not accurate, but you can use them in your application:

   1 dollar = 0.68 pound
   1 dollar = 0.83 euro
   1 dollar = 108.36 yen

   In your code, declare named constants to represent the conversion factors for the different types of currency. For example, you might declare the conversion factor for yen as follows:

   ```
   Const dblYEN_FACTOR As Double = 108.36
   ```

Use the named constants in the mathematical conversion statements. Use the following test data to determine whether the application is calculating properly:

Dollars	Conversion Values	
$100.00	Pounds:	68
	Euros:	83
	Yen:	10,836
$ 25.00	Pounds:	17
	Euros:	20.75
	Yen:	2,709
$ 1.00	Pounds:	0.68
	Euros:	0.83
	Yen:	108.36

8. **Monthly Sales Tax**

A retail company must file a monthly sales tax report listing the total sales for the month, and the amount of state and county sales tax collected. The state sales tax rate is 4% and the county sales tax rate is 2%. Create an application that allows the user to enter the total sales for the month. From this figure, the application should calculate and display the following:

a. The amount of county sales tax
b. The amount of state sales tax
c. The total sales tax (county plus state)

In the application's code, represent the county tax rate (0.02) and the state tax rate (0.04) as named constants. Use the named constants in the mathematical statements. Use the following test data to determine whether the application is calculating properly:

Total Sales	Tax Amounts	
9,500	County sales tax:	$190.00
	State sales tax:	$380.00
	Total sales tax:	$570.00
5,000	County sales tax:	$100.00
	State sales tax:	$200.00
	Total sales tax:	$300.00
15,000	County sales tax:	$300.00
	State sales tax:	$600.00
	Total sales tax:	$900.00

9. **Property Tax**

A county collects property taxes on the assessment value of property, which is 60% of the property's actual value. If an acre of land is valued at $10,000, its assessment value is $6,000. The property tax is then $0.64 for each $100 of the assessment value. The tax for the acre assessed at $6,000 will be $38.40. Create an application that displays the assessment value and property tax when a user enters the actual value of a property. Use the following test data to determine if the application is calculating properly:

Actual Property Value	Assessment and Tax	
100,000	Assessment value:	$ 60,000.00
	Property tax:	384.00
75,000	Assessment value:	45,000.00
	Property tax:	288.00
250,000	Assessment value:	150,000.00
	Property tax:	960.00

10. **Pizza Pi**

    Joe's Pizza Palace needs an application to calculate the number of slices a pizza of any size can be divided into. The application should do the following:

    a. Allow the user to enter the diameter of the pizza, in inches.
    b. Calculate the number of slices that can be cut from a pizza that size.
    c. Display a message that indicates the number of slices.

    To calculate the number of slices that can be cut from the pizza, you must know the following facts:

    a. Each slice should have an area of 14.125 inches.
    b. To calculate the number of slices, divide the area of the pizza by 14.125.

    The area of the pizza is calculated with the following formula:

    $$Area = \pi r^2$$

     NOTE: π is the Greek letter pi. 3.14159 can be used as its value. The variable r is the radius of the pizza. Divide the diameter by 2 to get the radius.

    Use the following test data to determine if the application is calculating properly:

Diameter of Pizza	Number of Slices
22 inches	27
15 inches	13
12 inches	8

11. **Distance Traveled**

    Assuming there are no accidents or delays, the distance that a car travels down the interstate can be calculated with the following formula:

    $$Distance = Speed \times Time$$

    Create a VB application that allows the user to enter a car's speed in miles-per-hour. When a button is clicked, the application should display the following:

    • The distance the car will travel in 5 hours
    • The distance the car will travel in 8 hours
    • The distance the car will travel in 12 hours

12. **Tip, Tax, and Total**

    Create a VB application that lets the user enter the food charge for a meal at a restaurant. When a button is clicked, it should calculate and display the amount of a 15 percent tip, 7 percent sales tax, and the total of all three amounts.

13. **Body Mass Index**

    Create a VB application that lets the user enter his or her weight (in pounds) and height (in inches). The application should calculate the user's body mass index (BMI). The BMI is often used to determine whether a person with a sedentary lifestyle is overweight or underweight for their height. A person's BMI is calculated with the following formula:

    $$BMI = weight \times 703/height^2$$

14. **How Much Insurance?**

    Many financial experts advise that property owners should insure their homes or buildings for at least 80 percent of the amount it would cost to replace the structure. Create a VB application that lets the user enter the replacement cost of a building and then displays the minimum amount of insurance he or she should buy for the property.

15. **How Many Calories?**

A bag of cookies holds 40 cookies. The calorie information on the bag claims that there are 10 "servings" in the bag and that a serving equals 300 calories. Create a VB application that lets the user enter the number of cookies they actually ate and then reports the number of total calories consumed.

16. **Automobile Costs**

Create a VB application that lets the user enter the monthly costs for the following expenses incurred from operating his or her automobile: loan payment, insurance, gas, oil, tires, and maintenance. The program should then display the total monthly cost of these expenses and the total annual cost of these expenses.

4 Making Decisions

TOPICS

In this chapter, you will learn how programs use If...Then, If...Then...Else, and If...Then...ElseIf statements to make decisions. You will learn how to compare values using relational operators and build complex comparisons using logical operators. You will be introduced to the Select Case statement, radio buttons (which allow the user to select one choice from many possible choices), and check boxes (which allow the user to make on/off or yes/no types of selections). You will learn more about message boxes, which display messages to the user, and the process of input validation.

4.1 The Decision Structure

CONCEPT: The decision structure allows a program's logic to have more than one path of execution.

In the programs you have written so far, statements execute sequentially. This means that statements are executed one after the other, in the order in which they appear.

You might think of sequentially executed statements as the steps you take as you walk down a road. To complete the journey, you must start at the beginning and take each step, one after the other, until you reach your destination. This is illustrated in Figure 4-1.

Figure 4-1 Sequence instruction

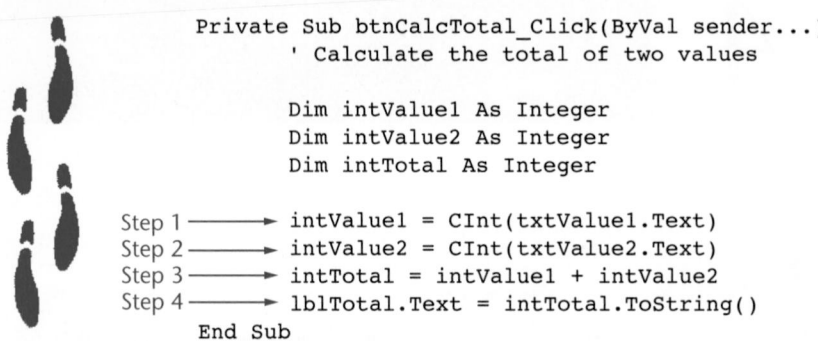

```
                    Private Sub btnCalcTotal_Click(ByVal sender...)
                        ' Calculate the total of two values

                        Dim intValue1 As Integer
                        Dim intValue2 As Integer
                        Dim intTotal As Integer

          Step 1 ————→  intValue1 = CInt(txtValue1.Text)
          Step 2 ————→  intValue2 = CInt(txtValue2.Text)
          Step 3 ————→  intTotal = intValue1 + intValue2
          Step 4 ————→  lblTotal.Text = intTotal.ToString()
                    End Sub
```

This type of code is called a **sequence structure** because the statements are executed in sequence, without branching in another direction. Programs often need more than one path of execution because many algorithms require a program to execute some statements only under certain circumstances. This can be accomplished with a **decision structure**.

Decision Structures in Flowcharts and Pseudocode

In a decision structure's simplest form, an expression is tested for a true or false value. If the expression is true, an action is performed. If the expression is false, the action is not performed. Figure 4-2 shows a flowchart segment for a decision structure. The diamond symbol represents a yes/no question, or a true/false expression. If the answer to the question is *yes* (or if the expression is true), the program follows one path. If the answer to the question is *no* (or the expression is false), the program follows another path.

In the flowchart, the action *Wear a coat* is performed only when it is cold outside. If it is not cold outside, the action is skipped. The action is **conditionally executed** because it is performed only when a certain condition (*cold outside*) exists. Figure 4-3 shows a more elaborate flowchart, where three actions are taken, only when it is cold outside.

Decision structures can also be expressed as pseudocode. For example, the decision structure shown in Figure 4-2 can be expressed as

> *If it is cold outside Then*
>   *Wear a coat.*
> *End If*

The *End If* statement marks the end of the decision structure in pseudocode. The statements appearing between *If...Then* and *End If* are executed only when it is cold outside. The decision structure shown in Figure 4-3, which conditionally executes three actions, can be expressed as

> *If it is cold outside Then*
>   *Wear a coat.*
>   *Wear a hat.*
>   *Wear gloves.*
> *End If*

Figure 4-2 Simple decision structure flowchart

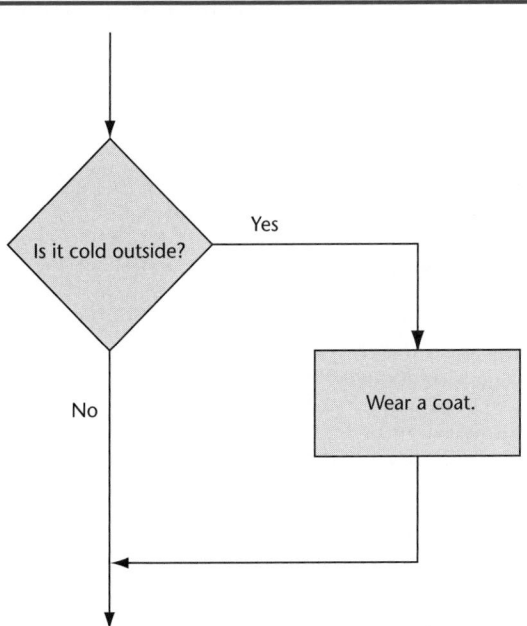

Figure 4-3 Three-action decision structure flowchart

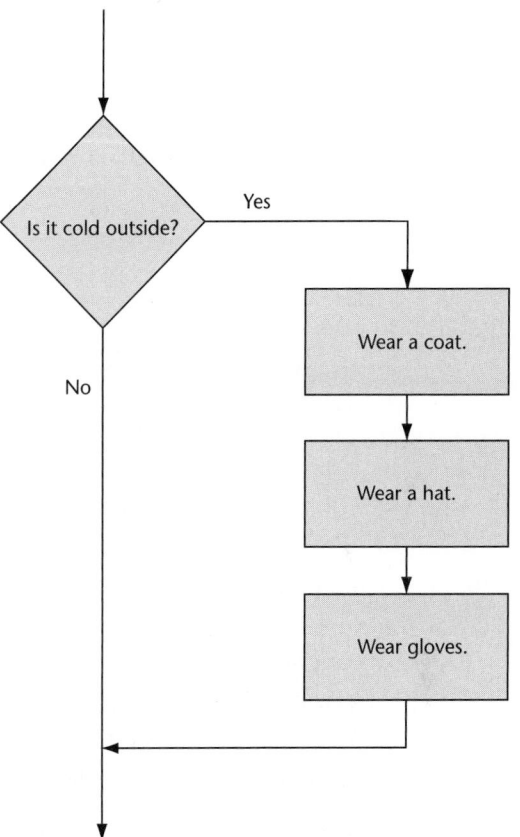

4.2 The If...Then **Statement**

CONCEPT: The If...Then statement causes other statements to execute only when an expression is true.

VideoNote

The If... Then Statement

One way to code a decision structure in Visual Basic is with the If...Then statement. Here is the general form of the If...Then statement.

```
If expression Then
    statement
    (more statements may follow)
End If
```

The If...Then statement is really very simple: if the *expression* is true, the statement or statements that appear between the If...Then and the End If are executed. Otherwise, the statements are skipped.

Boolean Expressions and Relational Operators

The expression that is tested in an If...Then statement can be either True or False. Such an expression is known as a **Boolean expression**. Special operators known as relational operators are commonly used in Boolean expressions. A **relational operator** determines whether a specific relationship exists between two values. For example, the greater-than operator (>) determines whether one value is greater than another value. The equal to operator (=) determines two values are the same. Table 4-1 lists the Visual Basic relational operators.

Table 4-1 Visual Basic relational operators

Relational Operator	Meaning
>	Greater than
<	Less than
=	Equal to
<>	Not equal to
>=	Greater than or equal to
<=	Less than or equal to

All relational operators are binary, which means they use two operands. Here is an example of an expression using the greater than operator:

```
length > width
```

This expression determines whether the value of `length` is greater than the value of `width`. If `length` is greater than `width`, the value of the expression is true. Otherwise, the value of the expression is false. Because the expression can be only true or false, it is a Boolean expression. The following expression uses the less than operator (<) to determine whether `length` is less than `width`:

```
length < width
```

Table 4-2 shows examples of several relational expressions that compare the variables x and y.

Table 4-2 Boolean expressions using relational operators

Relational Expression	Meaning
$x > y$	Is x greater than y?
$x < y$	Is x less than y?
$x >= y$	Is x greater than or equal to y?
$x <= y$	Is x less than or equal to y?
$x = y$	Is x equal to y?
$x <> y$	Is x not equal to y?

The = operator, when used in a relational expression, determines whether the operand on its left is equal to the operand on its right. If both operands have the same value, the expression is true. Assuming that a is 4, the expression $a = 4$ is true and the expression $a = 2$ is false.

There are two operators that can test more than one relationship at the same time. The >= operator determines whether the operand on its left is greater than or equal to the operand on the right. Assuming that a is 4, b is 6, and c is 4, the expressions $b >= a$ and $a >= c$ are true, and $a >= 5$ is false. When using this operator, the > symbol must precede the = symbol, with no space between them.

The `<=` operator determines whether the left operand is less than or equal to the right operand. Once again, assuming that *a* is 4, *b* is 6, and *c* is 4, both *a* <= *c* and *b* <= 10 are true, but *b* <= *a* is false. When using this operator, the < symbol must precede the = symbol, with no space between them.

The `<>` operator is the *not equal* operator. It determines whether the operand on its left is not equal to the operand on its right, which is the opposite of the = operator. As before, assuming *a* is 4, *b* is 6, and *c* is 4, both *a* <> *b* and *b* <> *c* are true because a is not equal to *b* and *b* is not equal to *c*. However, *a* <> *c* is false because *a* is equal to *c*. Values compared by a relational expression need not be exactly the same type. Suppose we compare a variable of type Single to an integer constant, as in the following:

```
sngTemperature > 40
```

In this example, the integer 40 is temporarily converted to a Single so the comparison can take place. You do not have to worry about doing this conversion. It is carried out automatically by the Visual Basic compiler. Similarly, we might want to compare a Double to a Single, as in the following:

```
dblTemperature < sngBoilingPoint
```

The value of `sngBoilingPoint` is automatically converted to type Double so the values can be compared.

Putting It All Together

Let's look at an example of an `If...Then` statement:

```
If decSales > 50000 Then
    MessageBox.Show("You've earned a bonus!")
End If
```

This statement uses the > operator to determine whether `decSales` is greater than 50000. If expression `decSales > 50000` is true, the message *You've earned a bonus!* is displayed in a message box.

The following example conditionally executes multiple statements.

```
If decSales > 50000 Then
    MessageBox.Show("You've earned a bonus!")
    decCommissionRate = 0.12
    intDaysOff = intDaysOff + 1
End If
```

Here are some specific rules to remember about the `If...Then` statement:

- The words `If` and `Then` must appear on the same line.
- Nothing other than a comment can appear after the `Then` keyword, on the same line.
- The `End If` statement must be on a line by itself. Only a comment may follow it on the same line.

Tutorial 4-1 examines an application that uses the `If...Then` statement.

Tutorial 4-1:

Examining an application that uses the `If...Then` statement

Step 1: Open the *Test Score Average 1* project from the student sample programs folder named *Chap4\Test Score Average 1*.

Step 2: Run the application. The form appears, as shown in Figure 4-4.

Step 3: Enter the following test scores in the three text boxes: **80, 90, 75**.

Step 4: Click the *Calculate Average* button. The average test score is displayed.

Step 5: Click the *Clear* button, and then enter the following test scores in the three text boxes: **100, 97, 99**.

Step 6: Click the *Calculate Average* button. This time, in addition to the average test score being displayed, the message *Congratulations! Great Job!* also appears. The form appears, as shown in Figure 4-5.

Figure 4-4 *Test Score Average* form

Figure 4-5 Average and message displayed

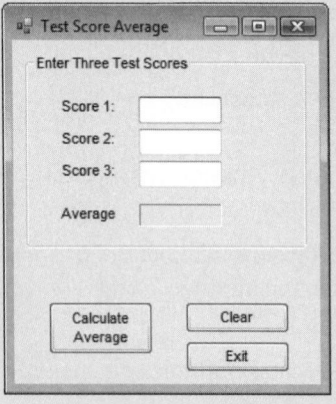

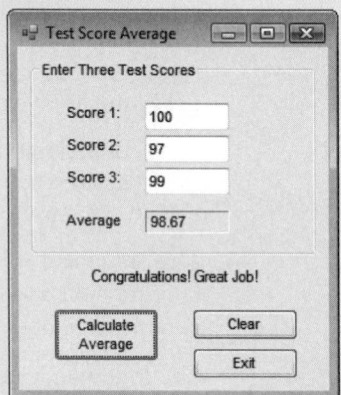

Step 7: Click the *Exit* button to terminate the application.

Step 8: Open the *Code* window and find the `btnCalculate_Click` event handler. The code is as follows:

```
Private Sub btnCalculate_Click(...) Handles btnCalculate.Click
    ' Variables to hold scores and the average score
    Dim dblScore1 As Double
    Dim dblScore2 As Double
    Dim dblScore3 As Double
    Dim dblAverage As Double

    ' Constant for a high score.
    Const dblHIGH_SCORE As Double = 95.0

    Try
        ' Copy the TextBox scores into the variables.
        dblScore1 = CDbl(txtScore1.Text)
        dblScore2 = CDbl(txtScore2.Text)
        dblScore3 = CDbl(txtScore3.Text)
```

```
        ' Calculate the average score.
        dblAverage = (dblScore1 + dblScore2 + dblScore3) / 3.0

        ' Display the average, rounded to 2 decimal places.
        lblAverage.Text = dblAverage.ToString("n2")

        ' If the score is high, compliment the student.
        If dblAverage > dblHIGH_SCORE Then
            lblMessage.Text = "Congratulations! Great Job!"
        End If
    Catch
        ' Display an error message.
        MessageBox.Show("Scores must be numeric.")
    End Try
End Sub
```

Notice that at the end of the try block, the following If...Then statement appears:

```
If dblAverage > 95 Then
    lblMessage.Text = "Congratulations! Great Job!"
End If
```

This statement determines whether the average is greater than 95, and if so, displays *Congratulations! Great Job!* in the lblMessage label.

Programming Style and the If...Then Statement

When you type an If...Then statement, Visual Studio automatically indents the conditionally executed statements. This is not a syntax requirement, but a programming style convention. For example, compare the following statements:

```
If decSales > 50000 Then
    MessageBox.Show("You've earned a bonus!")
    decCommissionRate = 0.12
    intDaysOff = intDaysOff + 1
End If
```

```
If decSales > 50000 Then
MessageBox.Show("You've earned a bonus!")
decCommissionRate = 0.12
intDaysOff = intDaysOff + 1
End If
```

Both If...Then statements produce the same result. The first example, however, is more readable to the human eye than the second because the conditionally executed statements are indented.

NOTE: If the automatic indenting feature has been turned off, you can turn it on by clicking *Tools* on the menu bar, then clicking *Options*. In the *Options* window, perform the following:

- Click the *Show all settings* check box. Then, click *Text Editor* in the left pane, then click *Basic*, then click *Tabs*. Make sure *Smart* is selected in the dialog box under *Indenting*.
- In the left pane, click *VB Specific*. Make sure *Automatic Insertion of end constructs* and *Pretty listing (reformatting) of code* are both checked.

Using Relational Operators with Math Operators

It is possible to use a relational operator and math operators in the same expression. Here is an example:

```
If intX + intY > 20 Then
    lblMessage.Text = "It is true!"
End If
```

When a relational operator appears in the same expression as one or more math operators, the math operators always execute first. In this statement, the + operator adds intX and intY. The result is compared to 20 using the > operator. Here is another example:

```
If intX + intY > intA - intB Then
    lblMessage.Text = "It is true!"
End If
```

In this statement, the result of intX + intY is compared, using the > operator, to the result of intA − intB.

Most programmers prefer to use parentheses to clarify the order of operations. Relying on operator precedence rules is risky because the rules are hard to remember. Here is a preferred way to write the foregoing If...Then statement:

```
If (intX + intY) > (intA − intB) Then
    lblMessage.Text = "It is true!"
End If
```

Using Function Calls with Relational Operators

It is possible to compare the return value of a function call with another value, using a relational operator. Here is an example:

```
If CInt(txtInput.Text) < 100 Then
    lblMessage.Text = "It is true!"
End If
```

This If...Then statement calls the CInt function to get the integer value of txtInput.Text. The function's return value is compared to 100 by the < operator. If the result of CInt(txtInput.Text) is less than 100, the assignment statement is executed.

Using Boolean Variables as Flags

A **flag** is a Boolean variable that signals when some condition exists in the program. When the flag is set to *False*, it indicates the condition does not yet exist. When the flag is set to *True*, it means the condition does exist. Look at the following code, which uses a Boolean variable named blnQuotaMet.

```
If blnQuotaMet Then
    lblMessage.Text = "You have met your sales quota"
End If
```

The preceding statement assigns the string "You have met your sales quota" to lblMessage.Text if the Boolean variable equals *True*. If blnQuotaMet is *False*, the assignment statement is not executed. It is not necessary to use the = operator to compare the variable to *True*. The statement is equivalent to the following:

```
If blnQuotaMet = True Then
    lblMessage.Text = "You have met your sales quota"
End If
```

 **Checkpoint**

4.1 Assuming *x* is 5, *y* is 6, and *z* is 8, indicate whether each of the following relational expressions equals *True* or *False*:

a. *x* = 5	T	F		e. *z* <> 4	T	F
b. 7 <= (*x* + 2)	T	F		f. *x* >= 6	T	F
c. *z* < 4	T	F		g. *x* <= (*y* * 2)	T	F
d. (2 + *x*) <> *y*	T	F				

4.2 In the following If...Then statement, assume that blnIsInvalid is a Boolean variable. Exactly what condition is being tested?

```
If blnIsInvalid Then
    ' Do something
End If
```

4.3 Do both of the following If...Then statements perform the same operation?

```
If decSales > 10000 Then
    decCommissionRate = 0.15
End If
If decSales > 10000 Then
decCommissionRate = 0.15
End If
```

4.4 Of the two If...Then statements shown in Checkpoint 4.3, which is preferred, and why?

4.3 The If...Then...Else **Statement**

CONCEPT: The If...Then...Else statement executes one group of statements if the Boolean expression is true and another group of statements if the Boolean expression is false.

VideoNote

The If...
Then...Else
Statement

The **If...Then...Else** statement is an expansion of the If...Then statement. Here is its format:

```
If condition Then
    statement
    (more statements may follow)
Else
    statement
    (more statements may follow)
End If
```

As in an If...Then statement, a Boolean expression is evaluated. If the expression is true, a statement or group of statements is executed. If the expression is false, a separate group of statements is executed, as in the following.

```
If dblTemperature < 40 Then
    lblMessage.Text = "A little cold, isn't it?"
Else
    lblMessage.Text = "Nice weather we're having!"
End If
```

The Else clause specifies a statement or group of statements to be executed when the Boolean expression is false. In the preceding example, if the expression dblTemperature < 40 is false, the statement appearing after the Else clause is executed.

The If...Then...Else statement follows only one of the two paths. If you think of the statements in a computer program as steps taken down a road, consider the If...Then...Else statement as a fork in the road. Instead of being a momentary detour, like an If...Then statement, the If...Then...Else statement causes the program execution to follow one of two exclusive paths. Figure 4-6 shows a flowchart for this type of decision structure.

Figure 4-6 Flowchart for If...Then...Else statement

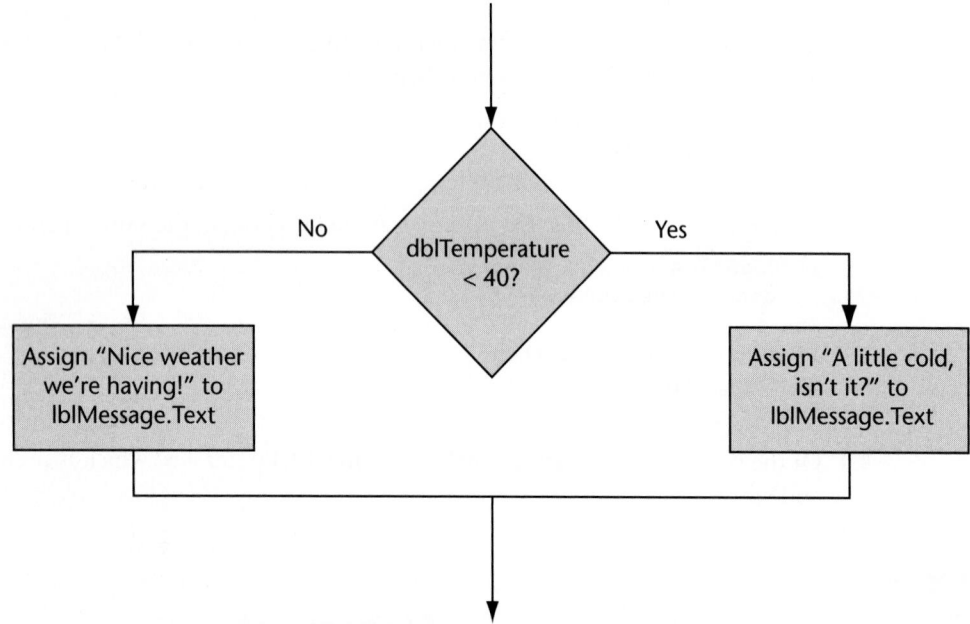

The logic shown in the flowchart in Figure 4-6 can also be expressed in pseudocode:

> *If temperature < 40 Then*
> *   Display the message "A little cold, isn't it?"*
> *Else*
> *   Display the message "Nice weather we're having!"*
> *End If*

In Tutorial 4-2 you complete an application that uses the If...Then...Else statement.

Tutorial 4-2:

Completing an application that uses the If...Then...Else statement

VideoNote

Tutorial 4-2
Walkthrough

Step 1: Open the *Test Score Average 2* project from the student sample programs folder named *Chap4\Test Score Average 2*. (This is a modification of the *Test Score Average 1* application from Tutorial 4-1.)

Step 2: Double-click the *Calculate Average* button. The *Code* window will open and show the btnCalculate_Click event handler, which is shown as follows. Complete the event handler by writing the code shown in bold:

```
Private Sub btnCalculate_Click(...) Handles btnCalculate.Click
    ' Variables to hold scores and the average score
    Dim dblScore1 As Double
    Dim dblScore2 As Double
    Dim dblScore3 As Double
    Dim dblAverage As Double
```

```
      ' Constant for a high score.
      Const dblHIGH_SCORE As Double = 95.0

      Try
         ' Copy the TextBox scores into the variables.
         dblScore1 = CDbl(txtScore1.Text)
         dblScore2 = CDbl(txtScore2.Text)
         dblScore3 = CDbl(txtScore3.Text)

         ' Calculate the average score.
         dblAverage = (dblScore1 + dblScore2 + dblScore3) / 3.0

         ' Display the average, rounded to 2 decimal places.
         lblAverage.Text = dblAverage.ToString("n2")

         ' If the score is high, give the student praise.
         ' Otherwise, give some encouragement.
         If dblAverage > dblHIGH_SCORE Then
            lblMessage.Text = "Congratulations! Great Job!"
         Else
            lblMessage.Text = "Keep trying!"
         End If
      Catch
         ' Display an error message.
         MessageBox.Show("Scores must be numeric.")
      End Try
   End Sub
```

Now the application will display one of two possible messages. If the user's average score is greater than 95, the message *Congratulations! Great Job!* will appear. Otherwise, the message *Keep trying!* will appear.

Step 3: Save the project.

Step 4: Run the application and input the following test scores in the three text boxes: **80, 90, 75**.

Step 5: Click the *Calculate Average* button. As shown in Figure 4-7, the average test score is displayed, and the message *Keep trying!* appears.

Figure 4-7 *Test Score Average* form with message displayed

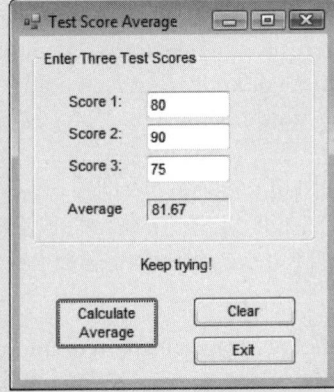

Step 6: Click the *Clear* button, and then enter the following test scores in the three text boxes: **100, 97, 99**.

Step 7: Click the *Calculate Average* button. This time, the message *Congratulations! Great job!* appears.

Step 8: Click the *Exit* button to terminate the application.

 Checkpoint

4.5 Look at each of the following code segments. What value will the `If...Then...Else` statements store in the variable `intY`?

a.
```
intX = 0
If intX < 1 Then
  intY = 99
Else
  intY = 0
End If
```

b.
```
intX = 100
If intX <= 1 Then
  intY = 99
Else
  intY = 0
End If
```

c.
```
intX = 0
If intX <> 1 Then
  intY = 99
Else
  intY = 0
End If
```

4.4 The `If...Then...ElseIf` Statement

CONCEPT: The `If...Then...ElseIf` statement is like a chain of `If...Then...Else` statements. They perform their tests, one after the other, until one of them is found to be true.

We make certain mental decisions by using sets of different but related rules. For example, we might decide which type of coat or jacket to wear by consulting the following rules:

- If it is very cold, wear a heavy coat
- Else, if it is chilly, wear a light jacket
- Else, if it is windy, wear a windbreaker
- Else, if it is hot, wear no jacket

The purpose of these rules is to decide on one type of outer garment to wear. If it is cold, the first rule dictates that a heavy coat must be worn. All the other rules are then ignored. If the first rule does not apply (if it isn't cold) the second rule is consulted. If that rule does not apply, the third rule is consulted, and so on.

 TIP: When logic rules are not expressed correctly by a program, the result is called a **logic error**. The Visual Studio Debugger can help you to identify logic errors by letting you walk through the program code, one line at a time.

The way these rules are connected is very important. If they were consulted individually, we might go out of the house wearing the wrong jacket or, possibly, more than one jacket. For instance, if it is windy, the third rule says to wear a windbreaker. What if it is both windy and very cold? Will we wear a windbreaker? A heavy coat? Both? Because of the order in which the rules are consulted, the first rule will determine that a heavy coat is needed. The remaining rules will not be consulted, and we will go outside wearing the most appropriate garment.

This type of decision making is also common in programming. In Visual Basic, it is accomplished with the **`If...Then...ElseIf`** statement. Here is its general format:

```
If condition Then
   statement
   (more statements may follow)
ElseIf condition Then
   statement
   (more statements may follow)
(put as many ElseIf statements as necessary)
Else
   statement
   (more statements may follow)
End If
```

This construction is like a chain of `If...Then...Else` statements. The `Else` part of one statement is linked to the `If` part of another. The chain of `If...Then...Else` statements becomes one long statement. In Tutorial 4-3, you complete an application that uses the `If...Then...ElseIf` statement.

Tutorial 4-3:

Completing an application that uses the `If...Then...ElseIf` statement

VideoNote

Tutorial 4-3 Walkthrough

In this tutorial, you will begin with the program from Tutorial 4-2 and add controls and program code that display the student's letter grade (*A, B, C, D, F*).

Step 1: Open the *Test Score Average 2* project you modified in Tutorial 4-2.

Step 2: Drag the form's border downward about one-half inch, and drag the `lblMessage` control and the three button controls downward on the form to make space for a new row of controls.

Step 3: Drag the lower border of the group box downward about one-half inch to make room for a label that will display the student's letter grade.

Step 4: Inside the group box add the new Label controls shown in Figure 4-8. When you add the label on the left, set its Text property to *Grade:*. When you add the label on the right, set its Name property to `lblGrade`, its AutoSize property to *False*, and set its BorderStyle property to *Fixed3D*.

Figure 4-8 Adding the *Grade* label inside the group box

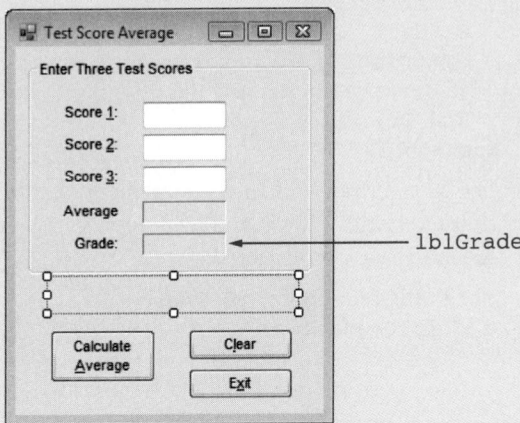

Step 5: Double-click the *Calculate Average* button. The *Code* window will open and show the `btnCalculate_Click` event handler, which is shown as follows. Complete the event handler by writing the code shown in bold:

```
Private Sub btnCalculate_Click(...) Handles btnCalculate.Click
    ' Variables to hold scores and the average score
    Dim dblScore1 As Double
    Dim dblScore2 As Double
    Dim dblScore3 As Double
    Dim dblAverage As Double

    ' Constant for a high score.
    Const dblHIGH_SCORE As Double = 95.0

    Try
        ' Copy the TextBox scores into the variables.
        dblScore1 = CDbl(txtScore1.Text)
        dblScore2 = CDbl(txtScore2.Text)
        dblScore3 = CDbl(txtScore3.Text)

        ' Calculate the average score.
        dblAverage = (dblScore1 + dblScore2 + dblScore3) / 3.0

        ' Display the average, rounded to 2 decimal places.
        lblAverage.Text = dblAverage.ToString("n2")

        ' Display the letter grade.
        If dblAverage < 60 Then
            lblGrade.Text = "F"
        ElseIf dblAverage < 70 Then
            lblGrade.Text = "D"
        ElseIf dblAverage < 80 Then
            lblGrade.Text = "C"
        ElseIf dblAverage < 90 Then
            lblGrade.Text = "B"
        ElseIf dblAverage <= 100 Then
            lblGrade.Text = "A"
        End If

        ' If the score is high, give the student praise.
        ' Otherwise, give some encouragement.
        If dblAverage > dblHIGH_SCORE Then
            lblMessage.Text = "Congratulations! Great Job!"
        Else
            lblMessage.Text = "Keep trying!"
        End If
    Catch
        ' Display an error message.
        MessageBox.Show("Scores must be numeric.")
    End Try
End Sub
```

The `If...Then...ElseIf` statement that you wrote has a number of notable characteristics. Let's analyze how it works. First, the Boolean expression `dblAverage < 60` is tested:

```
If dblAverage < 60 Then
    lblGrade.Text = "F"
```

If `dblAverage` is less than 60, *F* is assigned to `lblGrade.Text`, and the rest of the `ElseIf` statements are ignored. If `dblAverage` is not less than 60, the next `ElseIf` statement executes:

```
If dblAverage < 60 Then
    lblGrade.Text = "F"
ElseIf dblAverage < 70 Then
    lblGrade.Text = "D"
```

The first `If...Then` statement filtered out all grades less than 60, so when this `ElseIf` statement executes, `dblAverage` must be 60 or greater. If `dblAverage` is less than 70, *D* is assigned to `lblGrade.Text` and the remaining `ElseIf` statements are ignored. The chain of events continues until one of the expressions is true, or the `End If` statement is encountered. Figure 4-9 uses a flowchart to describe the logic.

Figure 4-9 Flowchart for determining the student's letter grade

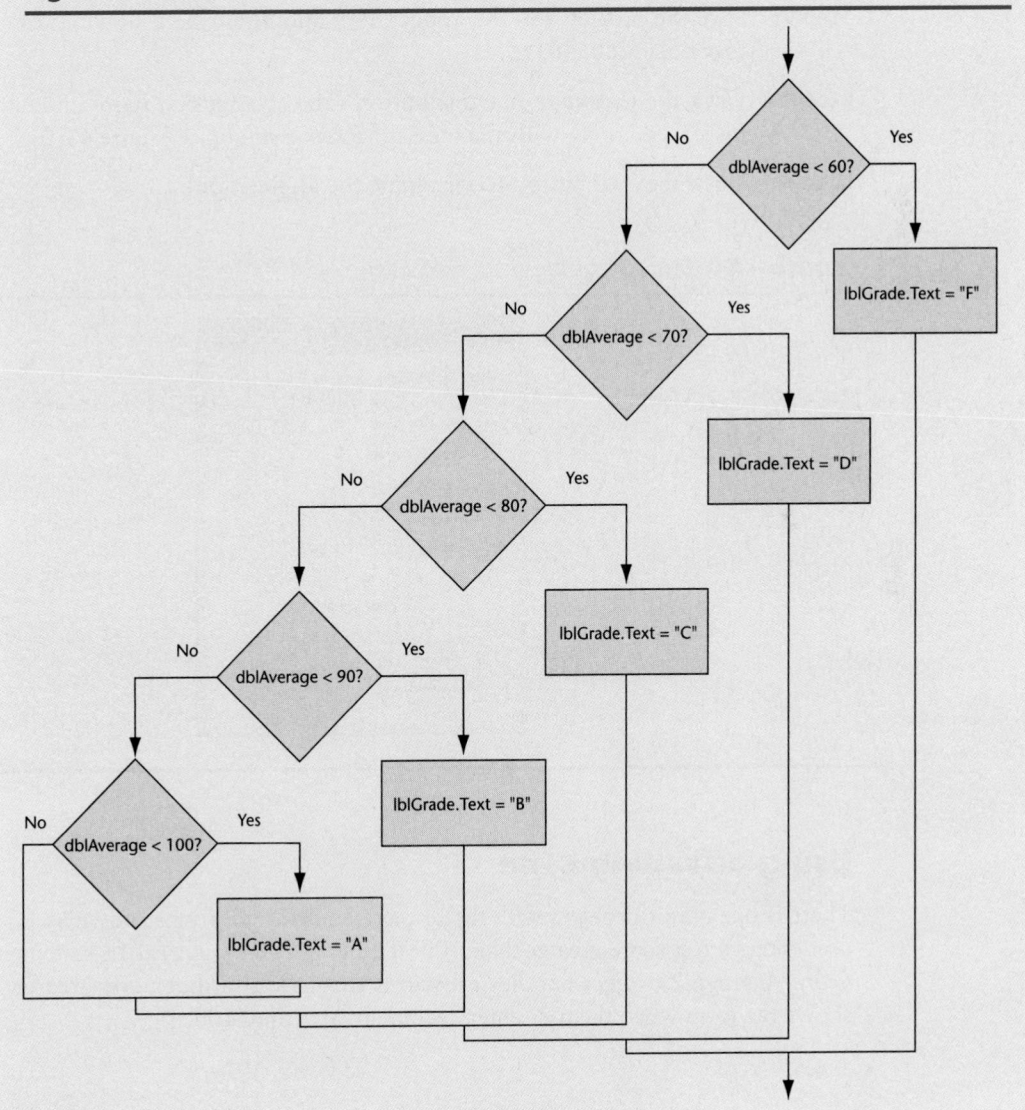

Step 6: Scroll down to the `btnClear_Click` event handler and add the statement shown here in bold:

```
Private Sub btnClear_Click(...) Handles btnClear.Click
  ' Clear the Text Boxes and Labels.
  txtScore1.Clear()
  txtScore2.Clear()
  txtScore3.Clear()
  lblAverage.Text = String.Empty
  lblMessage.Text = String.Empty
  lblGrade.Text = String.Empty

  ' Reset the focus.
  txtScore1.Focus()
End Sub
```

This statement will clear the contents of the `lblGrade` label when the user clicks the *Clear* button.

Step 7: Save the project, run the application, and input the following test scores in the text boxes: **80, 90, 75**.

Step 8: Click the *Calculate Average* button. The average test score and letter grade are displayed, along with the message *Keep trying!* (see Figure 4-10).

Step 9: Click the *Exit* button to terminate the application.

Figure 4-10 Student grade displayed

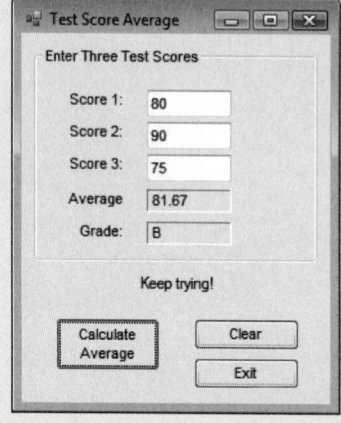

Using a Trailing `Else`

There is one minor problem with the test averaging applications shown so far: What if the user enters a test score greater than 100? The `If...Then...ElseIf` statement in the *Test Score Average 2* project handles all scores through 100, but none greater. Figure 4-11 shows the form when the user enters values greater than 100.

Figure 4-11 *Test Score Average 2* application showing values greater than 100

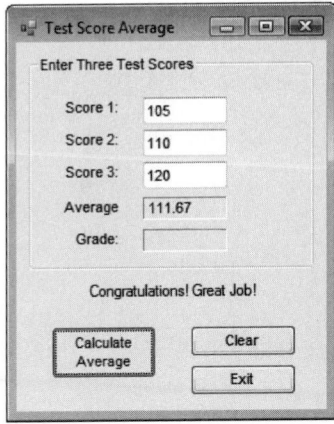

The program does not give a letter grade because there is no code to handle a score greater than 100. Assuming that any grade over 100 is invalid, we can fix the program by placing an `Else` at the end of the `If...Then...ElseIf` statement, as follows:

```
' Display the letter grade.
If dblAverage < 60 Then
    lblGrade.Text = "F"
ElseIf dblAverage < 70 Then
    lblGrade.Text = "D"
ElseIf dblAverage < 80 Then
    lblGrade.Text = "C"
ElseIf dblAverage < 90 Then
    lblGrade.Text = "B"
ElseIf dblAverage <= 100 Then
    lblGrade.Text = "A"
Else
    lblGrade.Text = "Invalid Score"
End If
```

The trailing `Else` catches any value that falls through the cracks. It provides a default response when the `If...Then` or none of the `ElseIf` statements finds a true condition.

> **TIP:** When writing an `If...Then...ElseIf` statement, code the structure of the statement first, identifying all the conditions to be tested. For example, the code in our example might initially be written as follows:
>
> ```
> If dblAverage < 60 Then
> ElseIf dblAverage < 70 Then
> ElseIf dblAverage < 80 Then
> ElseIf dblAverage < 90 Then
> ElseIf dblAverage <= 100 Then
> Else
> End If
> ```
>
> This creates the framework of the statement. Next, insert the conditionally executed statements, as shown in bold in the following code:
>
> ```
> If dblAverage < 60 Then
>     lblGrade.Text = "F"
> ```

```
    ElseIf dblAverage < 70 Then
        lblGrade.Text = "D"
    ElseIf dblAverage < 80 Then
        lblGrade.Text = "C"
    ElseIf dblAverage < 90 Then
        lblGrade.Text = "B"
    ElseIf dblAverage <= 100 Then
        lblGrade.Text = "A"
    Else
        lblGrade.Text = "Invalid Score"
    End If
```

A good design approach is to decide which conditions must be tested first, and then decide what actions must be taken for each condition.

Checkpoint

4.6 The following If...Then...ElseIf statement has several Boolean expressions that test the variable intX. Assuming intX equals 20, how many times will the following statement compare intX before it finds a Boolean expression that is true?

```
If intX < 10 Then
    intY = 0
ElseIf intX < 20 Then
    intY = 1
ElseIf intX < 30 Then
    intY = 2
ElseIf intX < 40 Then
    intY = 3
Else
    intY = -1
End If
```

4.7 In the following If...Then...ElseIf statement, if the variable intX equals 5, how many times will the code assign a value to intY?

```
If intX < 10 Then
    intY = 0
ElseIf intX < 20 Then
    intY = 1
ElseIf intX < 30 Then
    intY = 2
ElseIf intX < 40 Then
    intY = 3
End If
```

Look carefully at the following set of If...Then statements. If the variable intX equals 5, how many times will the code assign a value to intY?

```
If intX < 10 Then
    intY = 0
End If
If intX < 20 Then
    intY = 1
End If
If intX < 30 Then
    intY = 2
End If
If intX < 40 Then
    intY = 3
End If
```

4.5 Nested If Statements

CONCEPT: A nested If statement is an If statement in the conditionally executed code of another If statement. (In this section, we use the term If statement to refer to an **If ... Then, If...Then...Else, or If...Then...ElseIf** statement.)

A **nested If statement** is an If statement that appears inside another If statement. In Tutorial 4-4, you will examine an application that uses nested If statements. The application determines whether a bank customer qualifies for a special loan. The customer must meet one of the following qualifications:

- Earn $30,000 per year or more and have worked in his or her current job for more than two years.
- Have worked at his or her current job for more than five years.

Tutorial 4-4:
Completing an application with a nested If statement

VideoNote

Tutorial 4-4
Walkthrough

Step 1: Open the *Loan Qualifier* project from the student sample programs folder named *Chap4\Loan Qualifier*.

Step 2: Open *Form1* in the *Design* window. It should appear as shown in Figure 4-12.

Figure 4-12 *Loan Qualifier* application

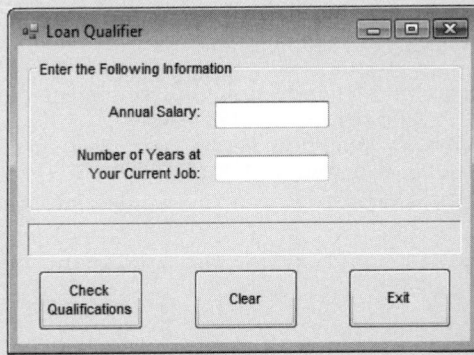

Step 3: Double-click the *Check Qualifications* button. The *Code* window will open and show the code template for the btnCheckQual_Click event handler. Complete the event handler by writing the code shown here in bold:

```
Private Sub btnCheckQual_Click(...) Handles btnCheckQual.Click
    ' Variables to hold input data.
    Dim dblSalary As Double
    Dim intYearsOnJob As Integer

    Try
        ' Get the user's input.
        dblSalary = CDbl(txtSalary.Text)
        intYearsOnJob = CInt(txtYearsOnJob.Text)

        ' Determine whether the applicant qualifies
        ' for the special loan.
        If dblSalary > 30000 Then
            If intYearsOnJob > 2 Then
                lblMessage.Text = "The applicant qualifies."
```

```
            Else
                lblMessage.Text = "The applicant does not qualify."
            End If
        Else
            If intYearsOnJob > 5 Then
                lblMessage.Text = "The applicant qualifies."
            Else
                lblMessage.Text = "The applicant does not qualify."
            End If
        End If

    Catch ex As Exception
        ' Display an error message.
        MessageBox.Show("Enter numeric data please.")
    End Try
End Sub
```

Step 4: Save and run the application. Enter **45000** for salary and **3** for years at current job. Click the *Check Qualifications* button. The message *The applicant qualifies* should appear on the form.

Step 5: Enter **15000** for salary and **3** for years at current job. Click the *Check Qualifications* button. The message *The applicant does not qualify* appears on the form.

Step 6: Experiment with other values. When you are finished, click the *Exit* button to terminate the application.

Examining the Nested **If** Statement in More Depth

In the *Loan Qualifier* project, the outermost **If** statement tests the following expression:

```
If dblSalary > 30000 Then
```

If this expression is true, the nested **If** statement shown in bold is executed:

```
If dblSalary > 30000 Then
    If intYearsOnJob > 2 Then
        lblMessage.Text = "The applicant qualifies."
    Else
        lblMessage.Text = "The applicant does not qualify."
    End If
Else
    If intYearsOnJob > 5 Then
        lblMessage.Text = "The applicant qualifies."
    Else
        lblMessage.Text = "The applicant does not qualify."
    End If
End If
```

However, if the expression `dblSalary > 30000` is not true, the `Else` part of the outermost `If` statement causes its nested `If` statement, shown in bold, to execute:

```
If dblSalary > 30000 Then
    If intYearsOnJob > 2 Then
        lblMessage.Text = "The applicant qualifies."
    Else
        lblMessage.Text = "The applicant does not qualify."
    End If
```

```
   Else
     If intYearsOnJob > 5 Then
       lblMessage.Text = "The applicant qualifies."
     Else
       lblMessage.Text = "The applicant does not qualify."
     End If
   End If
```

Figure 4-13 shows a flowchart for these nested If statements.

Figure 4-13 Flowchart of nested If statements

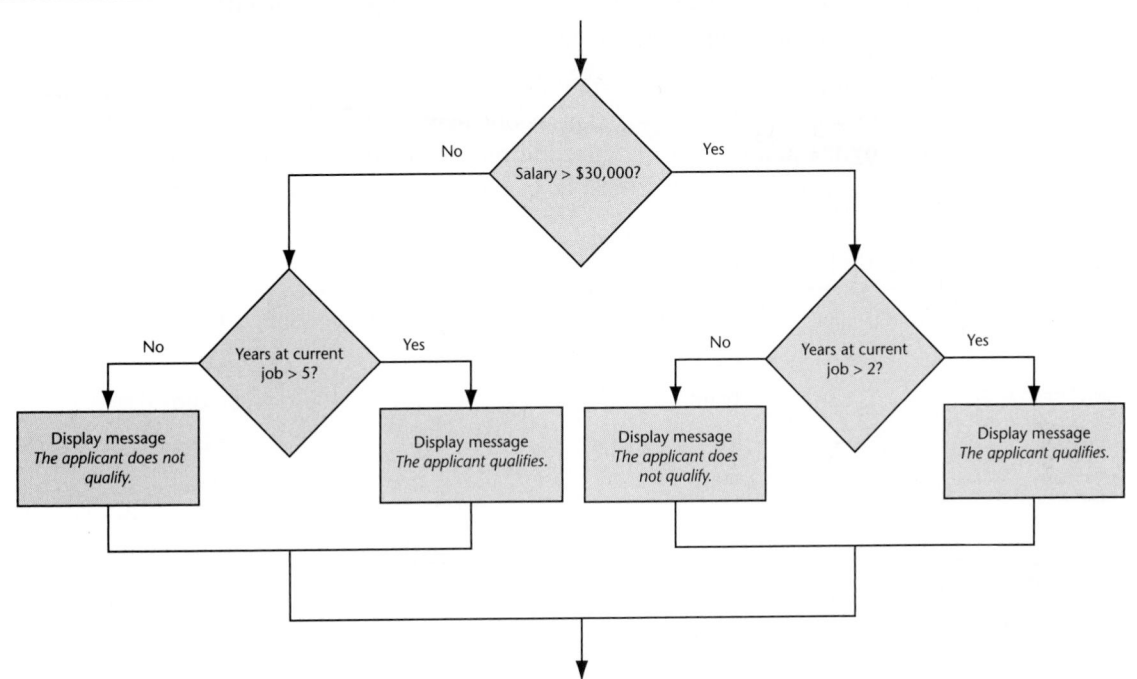

4.6 Logical Operators

CONCEPT: Logical operators combine two or more Boolean expressions into a single expression.

Logical operators can combine multiple Boolean expressions into a compound expression. Each individual Boolean expression might be very simple. But then, you can combine them using logical operators (also called Boolean operators) to make complex decisions. Table 4-3 lists Visual Basic's logical operators.

Table 4-3 Visual Basic logical operators

Operator	Effect
And	Combines two expressions into one. Both expressions must be true for the overall expression to be true.
Or	Combines two expressions into one. One or both expressions must be true for the overall expression to be true. It is only necessary for one to be true, and it does not matter which.
Xor	Combines two expressions into one. One expression (not both) must be true for the overall expression to be true. If both expressions are true, or both expressions are false, the overall expression is false.
Not	Reverses the logical value of an expression: makes a true expression false and a false expression true.

The And Operator

The **And operator** combines two expressions into one. Both expressions must be true for the overall expression to be true. The following If statement uses the And operator:

```
If intTemperature < 20 And intMinutes > 12 Then
    lblMessage.Text = "The temperature is in the danger zone."
End If
```

In this statement, the two relational expressions are combined into a single expression. The assignment statement is executed only if intTemperature is less than 20 and intMinutes is greater than 12. If either relational expression is false, the entire expression is false and the assignment statement is not executed.

Table 4-4 shows a truth table for the And operator. The truth table lists all the possible combinations of values that two expressions may have, followed by the resulting value returned by the And operator connecting the two conditions. As the table shows, both Expression 1 and Expression 2 must be true for the And operator to return value of *True*.

Table 4-4 Truth table for the And operator

Expression 1	Expression 2	Expression 1 **And** Expression 2
True	False	False
False	True	False
False	False	False
True	True	True

> **TIP:** You must provide complete expressions on each side of the And operator. For example, the following is not correct because the code on the right side of the And operator is not a complete expression:
>
> ```
> intTemperature > 0 And < 100
> ```
>
> The expression must be rewritten as follows:
>
> ```
> intTemperature > 0 And intTemperature < 100
> ```

Short-Circuit Evaluation with AndAlso

When the And operator appears in a compound Boolean expression, Visual Basic evaluates both expressions on the left and right side of the And operator. Consider the following example in which the first expression compares dblX to zero and the second expression calls a Boolean function named CheckValue:

```
If dblX > 0 And CheckValue(dblX) Then
    lblResult.Text = "Expression is True"
Else
    lblResult.Text = "Expression is False"
End If
```

When this code executes, the expression dblX > 0 will be tested, and then the CheckValue function is called. In some situations, however, it shouldn't be necessary to call the CheckValue function to determine the value of the compound Boolean expression. If the expression dblX > 0 is false, then we know that the compound expression is false, so the function call can be skipped. Such behavior is called **short-circuit evaluation**. In Visual

Basic you use the **AndAlso** operator to achieve short-circuit evaluation. In the following example, assuming that `dblX` is less than or equal to zero, `CheckValue` is not called and *Expression is False* is displayed:

```
If dblX > 0 AndAlso CheckValue(dblX) Then
    lblResult.Text = "Expression is True"
Else
    lblResult.Text = "Expression is False"
End If
```

See the *ShortCircuit* application in the student sample programs folder named *Chap4\ShortCircuit* for an example of the `AndAlso` operator.

The `Or` Operator

The **Or operator** combines two expressions into one. One or both expressions must be true for the overall expression to be true. It is only necessary for one to be true, and it does not matter which. The following `If` statement uses the `Or` operator:

```
If intTemperature < 20 Or intTemperature > 100 Then
    lblMessage.Text = "The temperature is in the danger zone."
End If
```

The assignment statement will be executed if `intTemperature` is less than 20 or `intTemperature` is greater than 100. If either relational test is true, the entire expression is true and the assignment statement is executed.

Table 4-5 is a truth table for the `Or` operator.

Table 4-5 Truth table for the `Or` operator

Expression 1	Expression 2	Expression 1 **or** Expression 2
True	False	True
False	True	True
False	False	False
True	True	True

All it takes for an `Or` expression to be true is for one of the subexpressions to be true. It doesn't matter if the other subexpression is true or false.

> **TIP:** You must provide complete Boolean expressions on both sides of the `Or` operator. For example, the following is not correct because the code on the right side of the `Or` operator is not a complete Boolean expression:
>
> ```
> intTemperature < 0 Or > 100
> ```
>
> The expression must be rewritten as follows:
>
> ```
> intTemperature < 0 Or intTemperature > 100
> ```

Short Circuit-Evaluation with `OrElse`

When the `Or` operator appears in a compound Boolean expression, Visual Basic evaluates both expressions on the left and right side of the `Or` operator. Consider the following example, in which the first expression compares dblX to zero; the second calls a Boolean function named CheckValue:

```
If dblX = 0 Or CheckValue(dblX) Then
    lblResult.Text = "Expression is True"
End If
```

When this code executes, the expression dblX = 0 will be tested, and then the CheckValue function is called. In some situations, however, it shouldn't be necessary to call the CheckValue function to determine the value of the compound expression. If the expression dblX = 0 is true, then we know that the compound expression is true, so the function call can be skipped. As previously mentioned, this type of evaluation is known as short-circuit evaluation, and it can be performed with the **OrElse** operator.

In the following example, if dblX equals zero, the CheckValue function is not called:

```
If dblX = 0 OrElse CheckValue(dblX) Then
    lblResult.Text = "Expression is True"
End If
```

See the *ShortCircuit* application in the student sample programs folder named *Chap4/ShortCircuit* for an example of the OrElse operator.

The Xor Operator

Xor stands for *exclusive or*. The **Xor operator** takes two expressions as operands and creates an expression that is true when one, but not both, of the subexpressions is true. The following If statement uses the Xor operator:

```
If decTotal > 1000 Xor decAverage > 120 Then
    lblMessage.Text = "You may try again."
End If
```

The assignment statement will be executed if decTotal is greater than 1000 or decAverage is greater than 120, but not both. If both relational tests are true, or neither is true, the entire expression is false. Table 4-6 shows a truth table for the Xor operator.

Table 4-6 Truth table for the Xor operator

Expression 1	Expression 2	Expression 1 **Xor** Expression 2
True	False	True
False	True	True
False	False	False
True	True	False

TIP: You must provide complete Boolean expressions on both sides of the Xor operator. For example, the following is not correct because the code on the right side of the Xor operator is not a complete Boolean expression:

```
value < 0 Xor > 100
```

The expression must be rewritten as follows:

```
value < 0 Xor value > 100
```

The `Not` Operator

The **Not operator** takes a Boolean expression and reverses its logical value. In other words, if the expression is true, the `Not` operator returns *False*, and if the expression is false, it returns *True*. The following `If` statement uses the `Not` operator:

```
If Not intTemperature > 100 Then
    lblMessage.Text = "You are below the maximum temperature."
End If
```

First, the expression `intTemperature > 100` is tested to be true or false. Then the `Not` operator is applied to that value. If the expression `intTemperature > 100` is true, the `Not` operator returns *False*. If it is false, the `Not` operator returns *True*. This example is equivalent to asking *Is intTemperature not greater than 100?* Table 4-7 shows a truth table for the `Not` operator.

Table 4-7 Truth table for the `Not` operator

Expression	**Not** Expression
True	False
False	True

Checking Numeric Ranges with Logical Operators

When your program is determining whether a number is inside a numeric range, it's best to use the `And` operator. For example, the following `If` statement checks the value in `intX` to determine whether it is in the range of 20 through 40:

```
If intX >= 20 And intX <= 40 Then
    lblMessage.Text = "The value is in the acceptable range."
End If
```

The expression in the `If` statement is true only when `intX` is greater than or equal to 20 *and* less than or equal to 40. The value in `intX` must be within the range of 20 through 40 for this expression to be true.

When your program is determining whether a number is outside a range, it's best to use the `Or` operator. The following statement determines whether `intX` is outside the range of 20 through 40:

```
If intX < 20 Or intX > 40 Then
    lblMessage.Text = "The value is outside the acceptable range."
End If
```

It is important not to get these logical operators confused. For example, the following expression cannot be true because no value exists that is both less than 20 and greater than 40.

```
If intX < 20 And intX > 40 Then
    lblMessage.Text = "The value is outside the acceptable range."
End If
```

If You Want to Know More about Using
`Not, And, Or, and Xor` Together

It is possible to write an expression containing more than one logical operator. For example, examine the following `If` statement:

```
If intX < 0 And intY > 100 Or intZ = 50 Then
    ' Perform some statement.
End If
```

Logical operators have an order of precedence. The Not operator has the highest precedence, followed by the And operator, followed by the Or operator, followed by the Xor operator. So, in the example statement, the following expression is evaluated first:

```
intX < 0 And intY > 100
```

The result of this expression is then applied to the Or operator to carry out the rest of the condition. For example, if the first expression (using And) is true, the remainder of the condition will be tested as follows:

```
True Or intZ = 50
```

If the first expression (using And) is false, however, the remainder of the condition will be tested as follows:

```
False Or intZ = 50
```

Always use parentheses in logical expressions to clarify the order of evaluation. The following If statement confirms that the And operator executes before the Or operator:

```
If (intX < 0 And intY > 100) Or intZ = 50 Then
    ' Perform some statement.
End If
```

You can use parentheses to force one expression to be tested before others. For example, look at the following If statement:

```
If intX < 0 And (intY > 100 Or intZ = 50) Then
    ' Perform some statement.
End If
```

In the statement, the expression (intY > 100 Or intZ = 50) is tested first.

If You Want to Know More about Using Math Operators with Relational and Logical Operators

It is possible to write expressions containing math, relational, and logical operators. For example, look at the following code segment:

```
intA = 5
intB = 7
intX = 100
intY = 30
If (intX > (intA * 10)) And (intY < (intB + 20)) Then
    ' Perform some statement.
End If
```

In statements containing complex conditions, math operators execute first. After the math operators, relational operators execute. Logical operators execute last. Let's use this order to step through the evaluation of the condition shown in our sample If statement. First, the math operators execute, causing the statement to become

```
If (intX > 50) And (intY < 27) Then
```

Next, the relational operators execute, causing the statement to become

```
If True And False Then
```

Since True And False equals *False*, the condition is false.

 **Checkpoint**

4.8 The following truth table shows various combinations of the values *True* and *False* connected by a logical operator. Complete the table by indicating whether the result of each combination is *True* or *False*.

Logical Expression	Result
`True And False`	_____
`True And True`	_____
`False And True`	_____
`False And False`	_____
`True Or False`	_____
`True Or True`	_____
`False Or True`	_____
`False Or False`	_____
`True Xor False`	_____
`True Xor True`	_____
`Not True`	_____
`Not False`	_____

 **4.7 Comparing, Testing, and Working with Strings**

CONCEPT: Visual Basic provides various methods in the `String` class that make it easy to work with strings. This section shows you how to use relational operators to compare strings, and discusses several functions and string methods that perform tests and manipulations on strings.

In the preceding examples, you saw how numbers can be compared using the relational operators. You can also use relational operators to compare strings. For example, look at the following code segment, in which `strName1` and `strName2` are string variables.

```
strName1 = "Mary"
strName2 = "Mark"
If strName1 = strName2 Then
   lblMessage.Text = "The names are the same"
Else
   lblMessage.Text = "The names are NOT the same"
End If
```

The = operator tests `strName1` and `strName2` to determine whether they are equal. Since the strings "Mary" and "Mark" are not equal, the `Else` part of the `If` statement will cause the message *The names are NOT the same* to be assigned to `lblMessage.Text`.

You can compare string variables with string literals as well. The following code sample uses the <> operator to determine if `strMonth` is not equal to *October*:

```
If strMonth <> "October" Then
   ' statement
End If
```

You can also use the >, <, >=, and <= operators to compare strings. Before we look at these operators, though, we must understand how characters are stored in memory.

Computers do not actually store characters, such as *A*, *B*, *C*, and so on, in memory. Instead, they store numeric codes that represent the characters. Visual Basic uses **Unicode**, which is a numbering system that represents all letters of the alphabet (lowercase and uppercase), the printable digits 0 through 9, punctuation symbols, and special characters. Each character is stored in memory as its corresponding Unicode number. When the computer is instructed to print the value on the screen, it displays the character that corresponds to the numeric code.

NOTE: Unicode is an international encoding system that is extensive enough to represent all the characters of most of the world's alphabets.

In Unicode, letters are arranged alphabetically. Because *A* comes before *B*, the numeric code for the letter *A* is less than the code for the letter *B*. In the following `If` statement, the relational expression `"A" < "B"` is true.

```
If "A" < "B" Then
   ' Do something
End If
```

TIP: When comparing strings, make sure they are consistent in their use of uppercase and lowercase letters. Avoid comparing `"jones"` to `"Adams"` or `"BAKER"`, for example. The ordering of strings is affected by the choice of uppercase and lowercase letters.

When you use relational operators to compare strings, the strings are compared character-by-character. For example, look at the following code segment:

```
strName1 = "Mary"
strName2 = "Mark"
If strName1 > strName2 Then
   lblMessage.Text = "Mary is greater than Mark"
Else
   lblMessage.Text = "Mary is not greater than Mark"
End If
```

The `>` operator compares each character in the strings `"Mary"` and `"Mark"`, beginning with the first, or leftmost characters, as shown in Figure 4-14.

Figure 4-14 String comparison

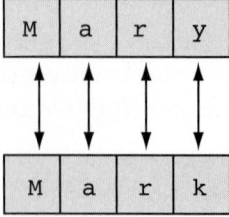

Here is how the comparison takes place:

1. The *M* in *Mary* is compared with the *M* in *Mark*. Since these are the same, the next characters are compared.
2. The *a* in *Mary* is compared with the *a* in *Mark*. Since these are the same, the next characters are compared.

3. The *r* in *Mary* is compared with the *r* in *Mark*. Since these are the same, the next characters are compared.

4. The *y* in *Mary* is compared with the *k* in *Mark*. Since these are not the same, the two strings are not equal. The character *y* is greater than *k*, so it is determined that *Mary* is greater than *Mark*.

NOTE: If one of the strings in a relational comparison is shorter in length than the other, Visual Basic treats the shorter character as if it were padded with blank spaces. For example, suppose the strings `"High"` and `"Hi"` were compared. The string `"Hi"` would be treated as if it were four characters in length, with the last two characters being spaces. Because the space character has a lower value than the alphabetic characters in Unicode, `"Hi"` would be less than `"High"`.

Testing for No Input

You can determine whether the user has entered a value into a text box by comparing the TextBox control's Text property to the predefined constant `String.Empty` as shown here:

```
If txtInput.Text = String.Empty Then
   lblMessage.Text = "Please enter a value"
Else
   ' The txtInput control contains input, so
   ' perform an operation with it here.
End If
```

The predefined constant `String.Empty` represents an **empty string**, which is a string that contains no characters.

The `If` statement copies the string *Please enter a value* to `lblMessage` if the `txtInput` control contains no input. The statements following the `Else` clause are executed only if `txtInput` contains a value. You can use this technique to determine whether the user has provided input for a required field before performing operations on that field.

NOTE: The technique we used in the preceding `If` statement does not detect a string that contains only spaces. A space is a character, just as the letter *A* is a character. If the user types only spaces into a text box, you will have to trim away the spaces to determine if any other characters were typed. Later in this section, we will discuss functions for trimming spaces from strings.

The `ToUpper` and `ToLower` Methods

The `ToUpper` and `ToLower` methods are both members of the `String` class, so they may be called with any string variable or expression. The **ToLower method** returns the lowercase equivalent of a string. Here is the method's general format:

```
StringExpression.ToUpper()
```

StringExpression can be any string variable or string expression. In the following example, `strLittleWord` and `strBigWord` are string variables:

```
strLittleWord = "Hello"
strBigWord = strLittleWord.ToUpper()
```

After the statement executes, strBigWord will contain "HELLO" in uppercase letters. Notice that the original string, "Hello" had one uppercase letter—the initial *H*. The ToUpper method converts only lowercase characters. Characters that are already uppercase and characters that are not alphabet letters are not converted.

 TIP: The ToUpper method does not modify the value of the string, but returns the string's uppercase equivalent. For example, after the statements in the previous example execute, strLittleWord still contains the original string "Hello".

The **ToLower method** works just like the ToUpper method, except it returns a lowercase version of a string. Here is the method's general format:

```
StringExpression.ToLower()
```

In the following example, strBigTown and strLittleTown are string variables:

```
strBigTown = "NEW YORK"
strLittleTown = strBigTown.ToLower()
```

After the statements execute, the variable strLittleTown contains the string "new york". The ToLower method converts only uppercase characters. Characters that are already lowercase, and characters that are not alphabet letters, are not converted.

 TIP: Like ToUpper, the ToLower method does not modify the original string.

You may also use the ToUpper and ToLower methods with a control's Text property. In the following example strLastName is a string variable:

```
strLastName = txtLastName.Text.ToUpper()
```

The ToUpper and ToLower methods are helpful in performing string comparisons. String comparisons in Visual Basic are *case sensitive*, meaning that uppercase letters are not considered the same as their lowercase counterparts. In other words, *A* is not the same as *a*. This can lead to problems when you construct If statements that compare strings. Tutorial 4-5 leads you through such an example.

 Tutorial 4-5:

Examining an application that performs string comparisons

Step 1: Open the *Secret Word* project from the student sample programs folder named *Chap4\Secret Word*.

Step 2: Run the application. The form shown in Figure 4-15 appears.

This application asks you to enter the secret word, which might be similar to a password in some programs. The secret word is *PROSPERO*.

Step 3: Enter **prospero** in all lowercase letters, and click the *Ok* button. You will see the message *Wrong! That is NOT the secret word!*

Figure 4-15 *Secret Word* form

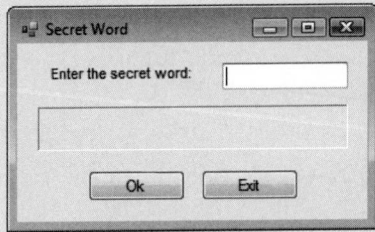

Step 4: Enter **Prospero** with an uppercase *P*, followed by all lowercase letters. Click the *Ok* button. Once again, you see the message *Wrong! That is NOT the secret word!*

Step 5: Enter **PROSPERO** in all uppercase letters and click the *Ok* button. This time you see the message *Congratulations! That is the secret word!*

Step 6: Click the *Exit* button to close the application.

Step 7: Open the *Code* window and look at the btnOk_Click event handler. The code is as follows:

```
Private Sub btnOk_Click(...) Handles btnOk.Click
    ' Compare the input entered with the secret word.
    If txtInput.Text = "PROSPERO" Then
        lblMessage.Text = "Congratulations! That " & _
                          "is the secret word!"
    Else
        lblMessage.Text = "Wrong! That is NOT the secret word!"
    End If
End Sub
```

The If...Then...Else statement compares the string entered by the user to *PROSPERO* in all uppercase letters. But what if the programmer intended to accept the word without regard to case? What if *prospero* in all lowercase letters is valid as well? One solution would be to modify the If statement to test for all the other possible values. However, to test for all the possible combination of lowercase and uppercase letters would require a large amount of code.

A better approach is to convert the text entered by the user to all uppercase letters, and then compare the converted text to *PROSPERO*. When the user enters the word *prospero* in any combination of uppercase or lowercase characters, this test will return *True*. Modify the code by adding a call to the ToUpper method, as shown bold in the following code.

```
If txtInput.Text.ToUpper() = "PROSPERO" Then
    lblMessage.Text = "Congratulations! That " & _
                      "is the secret word!"
Else
    lblMessage.Text = "Wrong! That is NOT the secret word!"
End If
```

Step 8: Run the application. When the form appears, Enter **prospero** in all lowercase letters and click the *Ok* button. This time you see the message *Congratulations! That is the secret word!* You can experiment with various combinations of uppercase and lowercase letters. As long as you type the word *prospero* the application will recognize it as the secret word.

Step 9: Close the project.

The ToLower method can also be used in Tutorial 4-5 to accomplish the same result, as shown in bold in the following code. Just make sure you compare the return value of the ToLower method to an all lowercase string.

```
If txtInput.Text.ToLower() = "prospero" Then
    lblMessage.Text = "Congratulations! That " &
                      "is the secret word!"
Else
    lblMessage.Text = "Wrong! That is NOT the secret word!"
End If
```

The IsNumeric Function

The **IsNumeric** function accepts a string as its argument and returns *True* if the string contains a number. The function returns *False* if the string's contents cannot be recognized as a number. Here is the function's general use:

```
IsNumeric(StringExpression)
```

Here is an example:

```
Dim strNumber As String
strNumber = "576"
If IsNumeric(strNumber) Then
    lblMessage.Text = "It is a number"
Else
    lblMessage.Text = "It is NOT a number"
End If
```

In this statement, the expression IsNumeric(strNumber) returns *True* because the contents of strNumber can be recognized as a number. In the following code segment, however, the expression returns *False*:

```
strNumber = "123abc"
If IsNumeric(strNumber) Then
    lblMessage.Text = "It is a number"
Else
    lblMessage.Text = "It is NOT a number"
End If
```

When you want the user to enter numeric data, the IsNumeric function is useful for checking user input and confirming that it is valid.

Determining the Length of a String

The **Length** property, a member of the String class, returns the number of characters in a string. Here is an example:

```
Dim strName As String = "Herman"
Dim intNumChars As Integer
intNumChars = strName.Length
```

The code stores 6 in intNumChars because the length of the string "Herman" is 6.

You can also determine the length of a control's Text property, as shown in the following code:

```
If txtInput.Text.Length > 20 Then
    lblMessage.Text = "Please enter no more than 20 characters."
End If
```

There are many situations in which `Length` is useful. One example is when you must display or print a string and have only a limited amount of space.

> **WARNING:** If you attempt to get the length of an uninitialized string variable, an exception (runtime error) occurs. You can prevent this error by initializing string variables with an empty string, as shown in the following statement:
>
> ```
> Dim str As String = String.Empty
> ```

Optional Topic: Trimming Spaces from Strings

Sometimes it is necessary to trim leading and/or trailing spaces from a string before performing other operations on the string, such as a comparison. A **leading space** is a space that appears at the beginning, or left side, of a string. For instance, the following string has three leading spaces:

```
"   Hello"
```

A **trailing space** is a space that appears at the end, or right side, of a string, after the non-space characters. The following string has three trailing spaces:

```
"Hello   "
```

The `String` class has three methods for removing spaces: `TrimStart`, `TrimEnd`, and `Trim`. Here is the general format of each method:

```
StringExpression.TrimStart()
StringExpression.TrimEnd()
StringExpression.Trim()
```

The **TrimStart** method returns a copy of the string expression with all leading spaces removed. The **TrimEnd** method returns a copy of the string expression with all trailing spaces removed. The **Trim** method returns a copy of the string expression with all leading and trailing spaces removed. The following is an example:

```
strGreeting = "   Hello   "
lblMessage1.Text = strGreeting.TrimStart()
lblMessage2.Text = strGreeting.TrimEnd()
lblMessage3.Text = strGreeting.Trim()
```

In this code, the first statement assigns the string "   Hello   " (with three leading spaces and three trailing spaces) to the named variable, `strGreeting`. In the second statement, the `TrimStart` method is called. Its return value, `"Hello   "`, is assigned to `lblMessage1.Text`. In the third statement, the `TrimEnd` method is called. Its return value, `"   Hello"`, is assigned to `lblMessage2.Text`. In the fourth statement, the `Trim` method is called. Its return value, `"Hello"`, is assigned to `lblMessage3.Text`.

These methods do not modify the string variable, but return a modified copy of the variable. To actually modify the string variable you must use a statement such as the following:

```
strGreeting = strGreeting.Trim()
```

After this statement executes, the `strGreeting` variable no longer contains leading or trailing spaces.

Like the `Length` property, these methods may also be used with a control's Text property. The following is an example:

```
Dim strName As String
strName = txtName.Text.Trim()
```

The `Substring` Method

The **Substring** method returns a substring, or a string within a string. There are two formats:

```
StringExpression.Substring(Start)
StringExpression.Substring(Start, Length)
```

The positions of the characters in `StringExpression` are numbered, with the first character at position 0. In the first format shown for the method, an integer argument, `Start`, indicates the starting position of the string to be extracted from `StringExpression`. The method returns a string containing all characters from the `Start` position to the end of `StringExpression`. For example, look at the following code:

```
Dim strLastName As String
Dim strFullName As String = "George Washington"
strLastName = strFullName.Substring(7)
```

After this code executes, the variable `strLastName` will contain the string `"Washington"` because `"Washington"` begins at position 7 in `strFullName`, and continues to the end of the string.

In the second format shown for `Substring`, a second integer argument, `Length`, indicates the number of characters to extract, including the starting character. For example, look at the following code:

```
Dim strFirstName As String
Dim strFullName As String = "George Washington"
strFirstName = strFullName.Substring(0, 6)
```

In this code, the `Substring` method returns the six characters that begin at position 0 in `strFullName`. After the code executes, the variable `strFirstName` contains the string `"George"`.

Optional Topic: The `IndexOf` Method

The **IndexOf** method searches for a character or a string within a string. The method has three general formats:

```
StringExpression.IndexOf(SearchString)
StringExpression.IndexOf(SearchString, Start)
StringExpression.IndexOf(SearchString, Start, Count)
```

In the first format, `SearchString` is the string or character to search for within `StringExpression`. The method returns the character position, or index, of the first occurrence of `SearchString` if it is found within `StringExpression`. If `SearchString` is not found, the method returns −1. For example, look at the following code:

```
Dim strName As String = "Angelina Adams"
Dim intPosition As Integer
intPosition = strName.IndexOf("e")
```

After this code executes, the variable position equals 3 because the character *e* is found at character position 3.

NOTE: With the `IndexOf` method, the first character position is 0.

In the second format shown for `IndexOf`, a second argument, *Start*, is an integer that specifies a starting position within *StringExpression* for the search to begin. The following is an example:

```
Dim strName As String = "Angelina Adams"
Dim intPosition As Integer
intPosition = strName.IndexOf("A", 1)
```

After the code executes, the variable `intPosition` equals 9. The `IndexOf` method begins its search at character position 1 (the second character), so the first *A* is skipped.

NOTE: The version of the `IndexOf` method used here performs a case sensitive search. When searching for *A* it does not return the position of *a*.

In the third format shown for `IndexOf`, a third argument, *Count*, is an integer specifying the number of characters within *StringExpression* to search. Here is an example:

```
Dim strName As String = "Angelina Adams"
Dim intPosition As Integer
intPosition = strName.IndexOf("A", 1, 7)
```

After the code executes, the variable position equals –1. The `IndexOf` method searches only 7 characters, beginning at character 1. Because *A* is not found in the characters searched, the method returns –1.

WARNING: An exception (runtime error) will occur if the starting position argument passed to `IndexOf` is negative or specifies a nonexistent position. Get the length of the string before calling `IndexOf`, to ensure the index is in a valid range.

The following code shows how to use the `IndexOf` method to determine if a search string exists within a string:

```
Dim strName As String = "Angelina Adams"
If strName.IndexOf("Adams") = -1 Then
   lblMessage.Text = "Adams is not found"
End If
```

Tutorial 4-6 completes a string searching application.

Tutorial 4-6:
Completing a string searching application

In this tutorial, you will write code that implements a string searching program. You will have an opportunity to try the `IsNumeric`, `Trim`, and `IndexOf` methods. The user interface is already created, so you can concentrate on the program code that makes it work. Here are its basic features:

- A string is shown at the top of the form, as shown in Figure 4-16, containing various character patterns (*abc, ABC, 00123,* and so on). It uses a blue font, which appears gray on the printed page.
- The user inputs a string into the text box, indicating which substring they want to find.
- The user clicks the *Go* button, as shown in Figure 4-17.

- The program displays the position in which the substring was found. You can verify the accuracy of the result by inspecting the numbers in the scale line below the string shown in blue.
- The user can change the starting index position of the search from 0 to another value. In Figure 4-18, the user has selected index position 4 to begin searching. The next matching occurrence of *ABC* is found at index 20.
- If the user enters a nonnumeric index, an error message box pops up, as shown in Figure 4-19.

Figure 4-16 *String Finder* application, when started

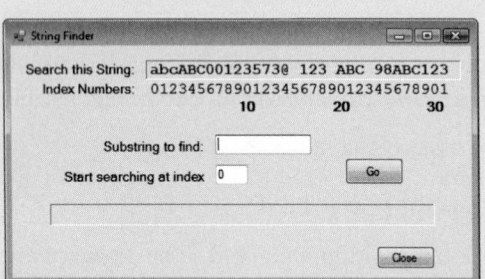

Figure 4-17 User enters substring they want to find, clicks *Go* button

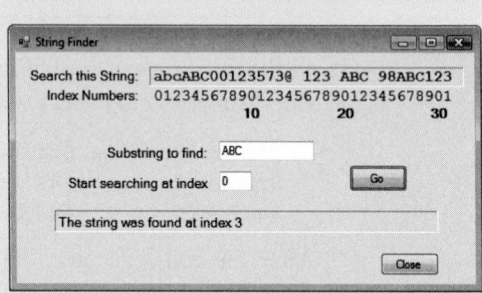

Figure 4-18 Searching for *ABC* starting at index position 4

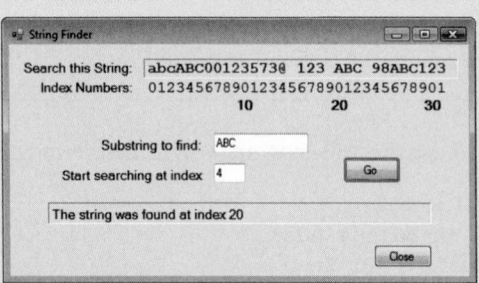

Figure 4-19 User has entered a nonnumeric index

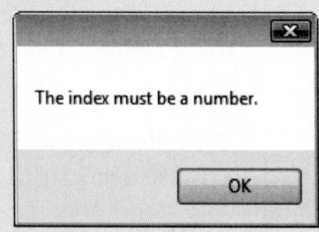

Step 1: Open the *String Finder* project from the student sample programs folder named *Chap4\String Finder*.

Step 2: Open *Form1* in the *Designer* window. Click each control and view its name in the *Properties* window. When you begin writing code, you will want to know the control names.

Step 3: Double-click the *Go* button. The *Code* window will open and show the code template for the btnGo_Click event handler. Complete the event handler by writing the code shown here in bold:

```
Private Sub btnGo_Click(...) Handles btnGo.Click
    ' Variable declarations
    Dim intStartIndex As Integer ' Starting index of the search
    Dim intFoundIndex As Integer ' Index of the found substring

    ' Determine whether the starting index is numeric.
    If IsNumeric(txtStartIndex.Text) Then

        ' Determine whether a string to search for was entered.
        If txtToFind.Text.Length > 0 Then
```

```
                     ' Get the starting index for the search.
                     intStartIndex = CInt(txtStartIndex.Text)

                     ' Search for the substring.
                     intFoundIndex = lblString.Text.IndexOf(txtToFind.Text,
                                                  intStartIndex)

                     ' Indicate whether the search string was found.
                     If intFoundIndex = -1 Then
                        lblResults.Text = "The string was not found."
                     Else
                        lblResults.Text = "The string was found at index " &
                                          intFoundIndex
                     End If

                  Else
                     ' Display an error message for an empty search string.
                     MessageBox.Show("Enter a string to search for.")
                  End If
               Else
                  ' Display an error message for a non-numeric index.
                  MessageBox.Show("The index must be a number.")
               End If
            End Sub
```

Step 4: Save and run the program. Search for the substring *ABC* starting at index 0. The program should find the string at position 3.

Step 5: Search for *ABC* starting at index 4. The program should find the string at position 20.

Checkpoint

4.9 Are each of the following relational expressions *True* or *False*?

a. "ABC" > "XYZ"   _____

b. "AAA" = "AA"   _____

c. "ABC123" < "abc123"   _____

4.10 Match the description in the right column with the method or function in the left column.

_____ IsNumeric   a. Returns the uppercase equivalent of a string.

_____ ToLower   b. Returns the number of characters in a string.

_____ ToUpper   c. Returns a copy of a string without trailing spaces.

_____ Length   d. Returns a copy of a string without leading or trailing spaces.

_____ TrimStart   e. Searches for the first occurrence of a character or string within a string.

_____ Substring   f. Accepts a string as its argument and returns *True* if the string contains a number.

_____ IndexOf   g. Returns the lowercase equivalent of a string.

_____ TrimEnd   h. Extracts a string from within a string.

_____ Trim   i. Returns a copy of a string without leading spaces.

4.8 More about Message Boxes

CONCEPT: Sometimes you need a convenient way to display a message to the user. This section discusses the `MessageBox.Show` method, which allows you to display a message in a dialog box.

A message box is a pop-up window that displays a message to the user. In Chapter 2 we briefly introduced the `MessageBox.Show` method, which displays a message box. In this section we will discuss the `MessageBox.Show` method in greater detail and you will learn more about its capabilities. We will discuss the following general formats of the method call:

```
MessageBox.Show(Message)
MessageBox.Show(Message, Caption)
MessageBox.Show(Message, Caption, Buttons)
MessageBox.Show(Message, Caption, Buttons, Icon)
MessageBox.Show(Message, Caption, Buttons, Icon, DefaultButton)
```

When `MessageBox.Show` executes, a message box (a Windows dialog box) pops up. For example, the following statement causes the message box shown in Figure 4-20 to appear:

```
MessageBox.Show("Operation complete.")
```

In the second format, *Caption* is a string to be displayed in the message box's title bar. The following statement causes the message box shown in Figure 4-21 to appear:

```
MessageBox.Show("Operation complete.", "Status")
```

Figure 4-20 Message box

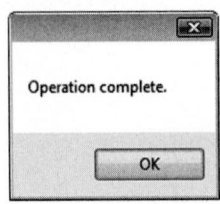

Figure 4-21 Message box with caption

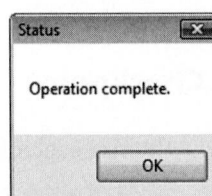

In both formats, the message box has only an *OK* button. In the third format, *Buttons* is a value that specifies which buttons to display in the message box. Table 4-8 lists the available values for *Buttons* and describes each.

Table 4-8 Message box button values

Value	Description
`MessageBoxButtons.AbortRetryIgnore`	Displays *Abort*, *Retry*, and *Ignore* buttons
`MessageBoxButtons.OK`	Displays only an *OK* button
`MessageBoxButtons.OKCancel`	Displays *OK* and *Cancel* buttons
`MessageBoxButtons.RetryCancel`	Displays *Retry* and *Cancel* buttons
`MessageBoxButtons.YesNo`	Displays *Yes* and *No* buttons
`MessageBoxButtons.YesNoCancel`	Displays *Yes*, *No*, and *Cancel* buttons

For example, the following statement causes the message box shown in Figure 4-22 to appear:

```
MessageBox.Show("Do you wish to continue?", "Please Confirm",
                MessageBoxButtons.YesNo)
```

Figure 4-22 Message box with caption and *Yes* and *No* buttons

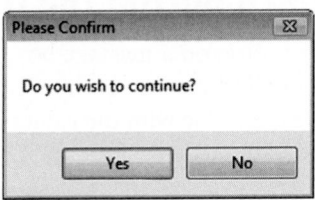

In some versions of `MessageBox.Show`, `Icon` is a value that specifies an icon to display in the message box. The available values for `Icon` are `MessageBoxIcon.Asterisk`, `MessageBoxIcon.Error`, `MessageBoxIcon.Exclamation`, `MessageBoxIcon.Hand`, `MessageBoxIcon.Information`, `MessageBoxIcon.Question`, `MessageBoxIcon.Stop`, and `MessageBoxIcon.Warning`. Figure 4-23 shows the icons matching each value. Note that some values display the same icon as others.

For example, the following statement causes the message box shown in Figure 4-24 to appear:

```
MessageBox.Show("Do you wish to continue?", "Please Confirm",
                MessageBoxButtons.YesNo, MessageBoxIcon.Question)
```

Figure 4-24 Message box with caption, *Yes* and *No* buttons, and *Question* icon

Figure 4-23 Message box icons

 MessageBoxIcon.Asterisk
MessageBoxIcon.Information

 MessageBoxIcon.Error
MessageBoxIcon.Hand
MessageBoxIcon.Stop

 MessageBoxIcon.Exclamation
MessageBoxIcon.Warning

 MessageBoxIcon.Question

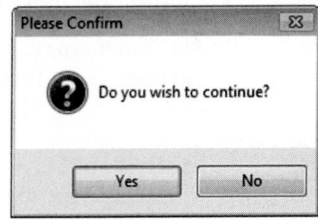

In one version of `MessageBox.Show`, the `DefaultButton` argument specifies which button to select as the default button. The default button is the button clicked when the user presses the [Enter] key. Table 4-9 lists the available values for this argument.

Table 4-9 *DefaultButton* values

Value	Description
`MessageBoxDefaultButton.Button1`	Selects the leftmost button on the message box as the default button
`MessageBoxDefaultButton.Button2`	Selects the second button from the left edge of the message box as the default button
`MessageBoxDefaultButton.Button3`	Selects the third button from the left edge of the message box as the default button

For example, the following statement displays a message box and selects `Button2` (the *No* button) as the default button:

```
MessageBox.Show("Do you wish to continue?", "Please Confirm",
                MessageBoxButtons.YesNo, MessageBoxIcon.Question,
                MessageBoxDefaultButton.Button2)
```

Determining Which Button the User Clicked

When the user clicks any button on a message box, the message box is dismissed. In code, the `MessageBox.Show` method returns an integer that indicates which button the user clicked. You can compare this value with the values listed in Table 4-10 to determine which button was clicked.

Table 4-10 `MessageBox.Show` return values

Value	Meaning
Windows.Forms.DialogResult.Abort	The user clicked the *Abort* button
Windows.Forms.DialogResult.Cancel	The user clicked the *Cancel* button
Windows.Forms.DialogResult.Ignore	The user clicked the *Ignore* button
Windows.Forms.DialogResult.No	The user clicked the *No* button
Windows.Forms.DialogResult.OK	The user clicked the *OK* button
Windows.Forms.DialogResult.Retry	The user clicked the *Retry* button
Windows.Forms.DialogResult.Yes	The user clicked the *Yes* button

The following code shows how an `If` statement can take actions based on which message box button the user clicked:

```
Dim intResult As Integer
intResult = MessageBox.Show("Do you wish to continue?",
            "Please Confirm", MessageBoxButtons.YesNo)

If intResult = Windows.Forms.DialogResult.Yes Then
    ' Perform an action here
ElseIf intResult = Windows.Forms.DialogResult.No Then
    ' Perform another action here
End If
```

Using `ControlChars.CrLf` to Display Multiple Lines

If you want to display multiple lines of information in a message box, use the constant **`ControlChars.CrLf`** (CrLf stands for *carriage return line feed*). Concatenate it with the string you wish to display, where you wish to begin a new line (as shown in this example):

```
MessageBox.Show("This is line 1" & ControlChars.CrLf &
                "This is line 2")
```

This statement causes the message box in Figure 4-25 to appear. When Visual Basic displays the string `"This is line 1" & ControlChars.CrLf & "This is line 2"`, it interprets `ControlChars.CrLf` as a command to begin a new line of output.

Figure 4-25 Message box displaying two lines

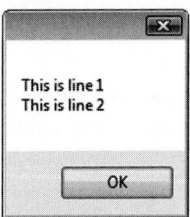

> **TIP:** In code, you can use `ControlChars.CrLf` to create multiple lines in label text too.

Checkpoint

4.11 Match each of the message boxes in Figure 4-26 with the statement it displays.

Figure 4-26 Message boxes

```
_____ MessageBox.Show("Are you sure?", "Confirm",
                      MessageBoxButtons.YesNo)
_____ MessageBox.Show("Are you sure?")
_____ MessageBox.Show("Are you sure?", "Confirm",
            MessageBoxButtons.YesNo, MessageBoxIcon.Question)
_____ MessageBox.Show("Are you sure?", "Confirm")
```

4.12 What value can you compare with the `MessageBox.Show` method's return value to determine if the user has clicked the *Abort* button?

4.13 The following statement displays *William Joseph Smith* in a message box. How would you modify the statement so that *William*, *Joseph*, and *Smith* appear on three separate lines?

```
MessageBox.Show("William Joseph Smith")
```

4.9 The `Select Case` Statement

CONCEPT: In a `Select Case` statement, one of several possible actions is taken, depending on the value of an expression.

The `If...Then...ElseIf` statement allows your program to branch into one of several possible paths. It performs a series of tests and branches when one of these tests is true. The `Select Case` statement, which is a similar mechanism, tests the value of an expression only once, and then uses that value to determine which set of statements to branch to. Following is the general format of the `Select Case` statement. The items inside the brackets are optional.

```
Select Case TestExpression
  [Case ExpressionList
    [one or more statements]]
  [Case ExpressionList
    [one or more statements]]
  ' Case statements may be repeated
  ' as many times as necessary.
  [Case Else
    [one or more statements]]
End Select
```

The first line starts with `Select Case` and is followed by a test expression. The test expression may be any numeric or string expression that you wish to test.

Starting on the next line is a sequence of one or more `Case statements`. Each Case statement follows this general form:

```
Case ExpressionList
  one or more statements
```

After the word `Case` is an expression list, so-called because it may hold one or more expressions. Beginning on the next line, one or more statements appear. These statements are executed if the value of the test expression matches any of the expressions in the `Case` statement's expression list.

A `Case Else` comes after all the `Case` statements. This branch is selected if none of the `Case` expression lists match the test expression. The entire `Select Case` construct is terminated with an `End Select` statement.

WARNING: The `Case Else` section is optional. If you leave it out, however, your program will have nowhere to branch to if the test expression doesn't match any of the expressions in the `Case` expression lists.

Here is an example of the `Select Case` statement:

```
Select Case CInt(txtInput.Text)
  Case 1
    MessageBox.Show("Day 1 is Monday.")
  Case 2
    MessageBox.Show("Day 2 is Tuesday.")
  Case 3
    MessageBox.Show("Day 3 is Wednesday.")
```

```
      Case 4
         MessageBox.Show("Day 4 is Thursday.")
      Case 5
         MessageBox.Show("Day 5 is Friday.")
      Case 6
         MessageBox.Show("Day 6 is Saturday.")
      Case 7
         MessageBox.Show("Day 7 is Sunday.")
      Case Else
         MessageBox.Show("That value is invalid.")
   End Select
```

Let's look at this example more closely. The test expression is `CInt(txtInput.Text)`. The `Case` statements `Case 1`, `Case 2`, `Case 3`, `Case 4`, `Case 5`, `Case 6`, and `Case 7` mark where the program is to branch to if the test expression is equal to the values 1, 2, 3, 4, 5, 6, or 7. The `Case Else` section is branched to if the test expression is not equal to any of these values.

Suppose the user has entered 3 into the `txtInput` text box, so the expression `CInt(txtInput.Text)` is equal to 3. Visual Basic compares this value with the first `Case` statement's expression list:

```
   Select Case CInt(txtInput.Text)
➡ Case 1
         MessageBox.Show("Day 1 is Monday.")
```

The only value in the expression list is 1, and this is not equal to 3, so Visual Basic goes to the next `Case`:

```
   Select Case CInt(txtInput.Text)
      Case 1
         MessageBox.Show("Day 1 is Monday.")
➡ Case 2
         MessageBox.Show("Day 2 is Tuesday.")
```

Once again, the value in the expression list does not equal 3, so Visual Basic goes to the next `Case`:

```
   Select Case CInt(txtInput.Text)
      Case 1
         MessageBox.Show("Day 1 is Monday.")
      Case 2
         MessageBox.Show("Day 2 is Tuesday.")
➡ Case 3
         MessageBox.Show("Day 3 is Wednesday.")
```

This time, the value in the `Case`'s expression list matches the value of the test expression, so the `MessageBox.Show` statement on the next line executes. (If there had been multiple statements appearing between the `Case 3` and `Case 4` statements, all would have executed.) After the `MessageBox.Show` statement executes, the program jumps to the statement immediately following the `End Select` statement.

The Select Case **Structure in Flowcharts and Pseudocode**

The flowchart segment in Figure 4-27 shows the general form of a `Case` structure. The diamond represents the test expression, which is compared to a series of values. The path of execution follows the value matching the test expression. If none of the values matches a test expression, the default path is followed (`Case Else`).

Figure 4-27 General form of a Case structure

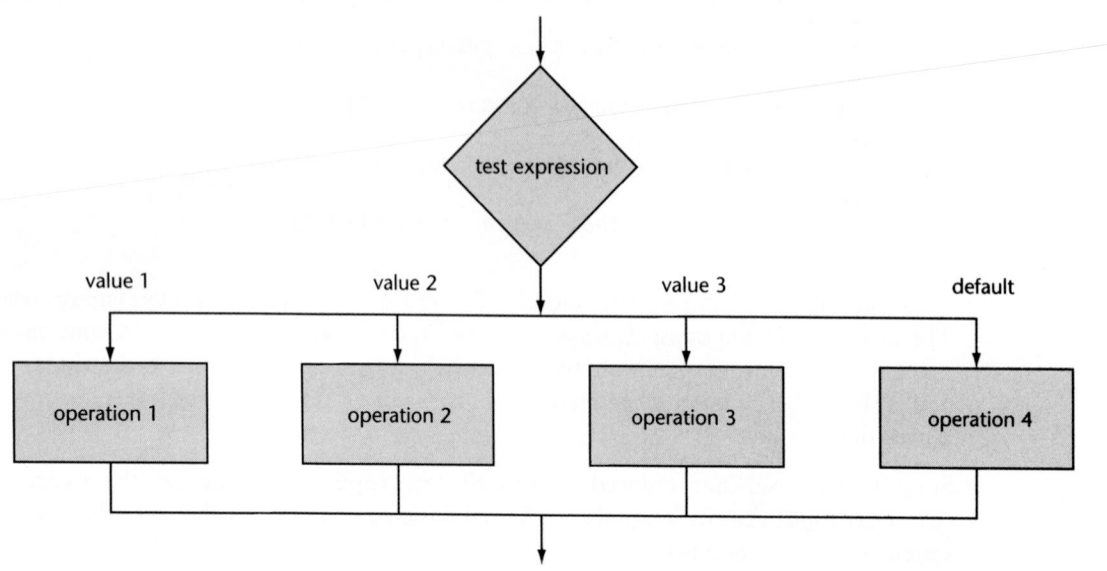

As with the `If` statement, the pseudocode for the `Select Case` statement looks very similar to the actual programming statements. The following is an example:

> *Select Case Input*
>   *Case 1*
>   *Display Message "Day 1 is Monday."*
>   *Case 2*
>   *Display Message "Day 2 is Tuesday."*
>   *Case 3*
>   *Display Message "Day 3 is Wednesday."*
>   *Case 4*
>   *Display Message "Day 4 is Thursday."*
>   *Case 5*
>   *Display Message "Day 5 is Friday."*
>   *Case 6*
>   *Display Message "Day 6 is Saturday."*
>   *Case 7*
>   *Display Message "Day 7 is Sunday."*
>   *Case Else*
>   *Display Message "That value is invalid."*
> *End Select*

More about the Expression List

The `Case` statement's expression list can contain multiple expressions, separated by commas. For example, the first `Case` statement in the following code compares `intNumber` to 1, 3, 5, 7, and 9, and the second `Case` statement compares it to 2, 4, 6, 8, and 10. In the following code, assume that `strStatus` is a string variable:

```
Select Case intNumber
   Case 1, 3, 5, 7, 9
     strStatus = "Odd"
   Case 2, 4, 6, 8, 10
     strStatus = "Even"
   Case Else
     strStatus = "Out of Range"
End Select
```

The `Case` statement can also test string values. In the following code, assume that `strAnimal` is a string variable:

```
Select Case strAnimal
   Case "Dogs", "Cats"
      MessageBox.Show("House Pets")
   Case "Cows", "Pigs", "Goats"
      MessageBox.Show("Farm Animals")
   Case "Lions", "Tigers", "Bears"
      MessageBox.Show("Oh My!")
End Select
```

You can use relational operators in the `Case` statement, as shown by the following example. The `Is` keyword represents the test expression in the relational comparison.

```
Select Case dblTemperature
   Case Is <= 75
      blnTooCold = True
   Case Is >= 100
      blnTooHot = True
   Case Else
      blnJustRight = True
End Select
```

Finally, you can determine whether the test expression falls within a range of values. This requires the `To` keyword, as shown in the following code.

```
Select Case intScore
   Case Is >= 90
      strGrade = "A"
   Case 80 To 89
      strGrade = "B"
   Case 70 To 79
      strGrade = "C"
   Case 60 To 69
      strGrade = "D"
   Case 0 To 59
      strGrade = "F"
   Case Else
      MessageBox.Show("Invalid Score")
End Select
```

The numbers used on each side of the `To` keyword are included in the range. So, the statement `Case 80 To 89` matches the values 80, 89, or any number in between.

> **TIP:** The `To` keyword works properly only when the smaller number appears on its left and the larger number appears on its right. You can write an expression such as `10 To 0`, but it will not function properly at runtime.

Tutorial 4-7 examines a sales commission calculator application.

Tutorial 4-7:
Examining *Crazy Al's Sales Commission Calculator* application

Crazy Al's Computer Emporium is a retail seller of personal computers. The sales staff at Crazy Al's works strictly on commission. At the end of the month, each salesperson's commission is calculated according to Table 4-11.

For example, a salesperson with $16,000 in monthly sales earns a 12% commission ($1,920.00). A salesperson with $20,000 in monthly sales earns a 14% commission ($2,800.00).

Table 4-11 Sales commission rates

Sales This Month	Commission Rate
Less than $10,000	5%
$10,000 – $14,999	10%
$15,000 – $17,999	12%
$18,000 – $21,999	14%
$22,000 or more	16%

Because the staff is paid once per month, Crazy Al's allows each employee to take up to $1,500 per month in advance pay. When sales commissions are calculated, the amount of each employee's advance pay is subtracted from the commission. If any salesperson's commission is less than the amount of the advance, he or she must reimburse Crazy Al's for the difference.

Here are two examples:

- Beverly's monthly sales were $21,400, so her commission is $2,996. She took $1,500 in advance pay. At the end of the month she gets a check for $1,496.
- John's monthly sales were $12,600, so his commission is $1,260. He took $1,500 in advance pay. At the end of the month he must pay back $240 to Crazy Al's.

In this tutorial, you examine the *Crazy Al's Commission Calculator* application used to determine a salesperson's commission.

Step 1: Open the *Crazy Al* project from the student sample programs folder named *Chap4\Crazy Al*.

Step 2: Run the application. The form shown in Figure 4-28 appears.

Step 3: Enter **16000** as the amount of sales for this month (first text box).

Figure 4-28 *Crazy Al's Commission Calculator* form

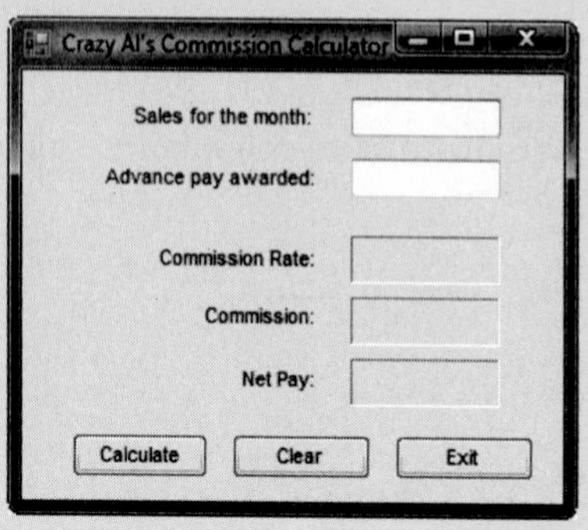

Step 4: Enter **1000** as the amount of advance pay taken (second text box). Click the *Calculate* button. You should see the commission rate, commission, and net pay information, as shown in Figure 4-29.

Step 5: Click the *Clear* button to reset the contents of the input and display fields.

Figure 4-29 Calculations filled in

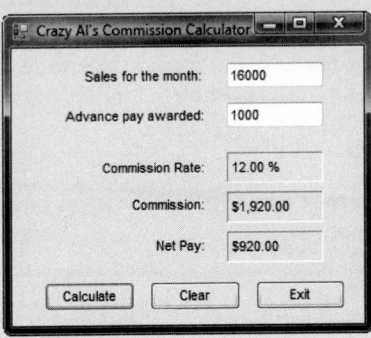

Experiment with other values for sales and advance pay.

Step 6: When you are finished, click the *Exit* button to end the application.

Step 7: Open the *Code* window and look at the btnCalculate_Click event handler. The code is as follows:

```
Private Sub btnCalculate_Click(...) Handles btnCalculate.Click
    ' Variable declarations
    Dim decSalesAmount As Decimal          ' Monthly sales amount
    Dim decAdvancePayAmount As Decimal     ' Advance pay taken
    Dim decCommissionRate As Decimal       ' Commission rate
    Dim decCommissionAmount As Decimal     ' Commission
    Dim decNetPay As Decimal               ' Net pay

    Try
        ' Get the amount of sales.
        decSalesAmount = CDec(txtSalesAmount.Text)

        ' Get the amount of advance pay.
        decAdvancePayAmount = CDec(txtAdvancePayAmount.Text)

        ' Determine the commission rate.
        Select Case decSalesAmount
          Case Is < 10000
            decCommissionRate = 0.05D

          Case 10000 To 14999
            decCommissionRate = 0.1D

          Case 15000 To 17999
            decCommissionRate = 0.12D

          Case 18000 To 21999
            decCommissionRate = 0.14D

          Case Is >= 22000
            decCommissionRate = 0.15D
        End Select
```

```
                ' Calculate the commission and net pay amounts.
                decCommissionAmount = decSalesAmount * decCommissionRate
                decNetPay = decCommissionAmount - decAdvancePayAmount

                ' Display the rate, commission, and net pay.
                lblCommissionRate.Text = decCommissionRate.ToString("p")
                lblCommissionAmount.Text = decCommissionAmount.ToString("c")
                lblNetPay.Text = decNetPay.ToString("c")

        Catch
            ' Display an error message.
            MessageBox.Show("Input must be numeric.")
        End Try
    End Sub
```

As you can see, the Select Case construct has a Case statement for each level of sales in the commission table.

Checkpoint

4.14 Convert the following If...Then...ElseIf statement into a Select Case statement.

```
If intQuantity >= 0 And intQuantity <= 9 Then
    decDiscount = 0.1
ElseIf intQuantity >= 10 And intQuantity <= 19 Then
    decDiscount = 0.2
ElseIf intQuantity >= 20 And intQuantity <= 29 Then
    decDiscount = 0.3
ElseIf intQuantity >= 30 Then
    decDiscount = 0.4
Else
    MessageBox.Show("Invalid Data")
End If
```

4.10 Introduction to Input Validation

CONCEPT: Input validation is the process of inspecting input values and determining whether they are valid.

The accuracy of a program's output is only as good as the accuracy of its input. Therefore, it is important that your applications perform input validation on the values entered by the user. **Input validation** is the process of inspecting input values and determining whether they are valid. In this section we will discuss ways of using decision structures to prevent data conversion exceptions, and determine whether numeric values entered by the user fall within an acceptable range.

Preventing Data Conversion Exceptions

In Chapter 3 you learned that an exception will occur if you try to convert the contents of a TextBox to a number, but the TextBox contains nonnumeric data. We introduced the Try-Catch statement, and you saw how to use it to handle those exceptions when they occur. Now that you know how to use the If...Then statement, you have more validation techniques at your disposal.

For example, suppose there is a way to determine whether a TextBox contains a value that can be successfully converted to a specific data type *before* you try to convert it to that data type. If that is possible, you can prevent data conversion exceptions from occurring in the first place. In Visual Basic, you can use a family of methods known as the **TryParse methods** to make this determination.

In computer science, the term **parse** typically means to analyze a string of characters for some purpose. The purpose of the TryParse methods is to parse a string, and try to convert the string's contents to a value of a specific data type. A TryParse method returns a Boolean value (True or False) to let you know if the conversion was successful. Table 4-12 describes several of the TryParse methods.

Table 4-12 TryParse methods

Method	Description
Integer.TryParse	Accepts two arguments: a string (argument 1) and an Integer variable (argument 2). The method attempts to convert the string (argument 1) to an Integer. If successful, the converted value is assigned to the Integer variable (argument 2) and the method returns True. If the conversion is not successful, the method returns False.
Double.TryParse	Accepts two arguments: a string (argument 1) and Double variable (argument 2). The method attempts to convert the string (argument 1) to a Double. If successful, the converted value is assigned to the Double variable (argument 2) and the method returns True. If the conversion is not successful, the method returns False.
Decimal.TryParse	Accepts two arguments: a string (argument 1) and a Decimal variable (argument 2). The method attempts to convert the string (argument 1) to a Decimal. If successful, the converted value is assigned to the Decimal variable (argument 2) and the method returns True. If the conversion is not successful, the method returns False.
Single.TryParse	Accepts two arguments: a string (argument 1) and a Single variable (argument 2). The method attempts to convert the string (argument 1) to a Single. If successful, the converted value is assigned to the Single variable (argument 2) and the method returns True. If the conversion is not successful, the method returns False.
Date.TryParse	Accepts two arguments: a string (argument 1) and a Date variable (argument 2). The method attempts to convert the string (argument 1) to a Date value. If successful, the converted value is assigned to the Date variable (argument 2) and the method returns True. If the conversion is not successful, the method returns False.

Because these methods return either True or False, they are commonly called as the Boolean expression in an If...Then statement. The following code snippet shows an example using the Integer.TryParse method. The lines are numbered for reference purposes. As you read the code, assume txtInput is the name of a TextBox control.

```
1 Dim intNumber As Integer
2
3 If Integer.TryParse(txtInput.Text, intNumber) Then
4     MessageBox.Show("Success!")
5 Else
6     MessageBox.Show("Error: Conversion failed.")
7 End If
```

The purpose of this code snippet is to convert the value of txtInput's Text property to an Integer and assign that value to the intNumber variable, which is declared in line 1. In line 3, the If...Then statement calls the Integer.TryParse method, passing txtInput.Text as argument 1 and intNumber as argument 2. Here's what happens:

- If txtInput.Text is successfully converted to an Integer, the resulting value is assigned to the intNumber variable, and the method returns True. That causes the statement in line 4 to execute.
- If txtInput.Text cannot be converted to an Integer, the method returns False. That causes the statement in line 6 (after the Else clause) to execute.

In Tutorial 4-8 you will look at a simple application that uses the Integer.TryParse and Decimal.TryParse methods to validate data entered by the user.

Tutorial 4-8:
Examining an application that uses `TryParse` for input validation

VideoNote

Validating Input with `TryParse`

Step 1: Open the *Gross Pay* project from the student sample programs folder named *Chap4\Gross Pay*. Figure 4-30 shows the application's form. This is a simple program that allows you to enter the number of hours worked and your hourly pay rate. When you click the *Calculate Gross Pay* button, your gross pay is calculated and displayed.

Step 2: Run the application. Enter an invalid value such as *xyz9* for the hours worked, and then click the *Calculate Gross Pay* button. Notice that a message box appears with the message *Enter a valid integer for hours worked*. Click the *OK* button to dismiss the message box.

Figure 4-30 The *Gross Pay* application's form

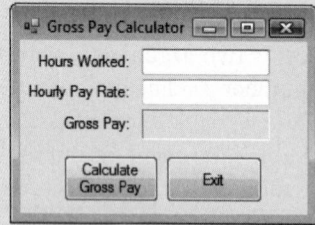

Step 3: Enter *40* for the hours worked (a valid number), and then enter an invalid value such as *abc44* for the hourly pay rate. Click the *Calculate Gross Pay* button. Notice that a message box appears, this time showing the message *Enter a valid value for hourly pay rate*. Click the *OK* button to dismiss the message box.

Step 4: With *40* still entered for the hours worked, change the hourly pay rate to *50*. Click the *Calculate Gross Pay* button. This time $2,000.00 is displayed as the gross pay.

Step 5: Click the *Exit* button to exit the application.

Step 6: Switch to the *Code* window and locate the btnCalculate_Click event handler. The code is shown here, with line numbers inserted for reference:

```
1 Private Sub btnCalculate_Click(...) Handles btnCalculate.Click
2    ' Declare variables
3    Dim intHours As Integer        ' Hours worked
4    Dim decPayRate As Decimal      ' Hourly pay rate
5    Dim decGrossPay As Decimal     ' Gross pay
6
7    ' Get the hours worked.
8    If Integer.TryParse(txtHours.Text, intHours) Then
9
10     ' Get the hourly pay rate.
11     If Decimal.TryParse(txtPayRate.Text, decPayRate) Then
12       ' Calculate the gross pay.
13       decGrossPay = intHours * decPayRate
14
15       ' Display the gross pay.
16       lblGrossPay.Text = decGrossPay.ToString("c")
17     Else
18       ' Display pay rate error message.
19       MessageBox.Show("Enter a valid value for hourly pay rate.")
20     End If
21
22   Else
23     ' Display hours worked error message.
24     MessageBox.Show("Enter a valid integer for hours worked.")
25   End If
26 End Sub
```

Let's take a closer look at the code:

- Lines 3 through 5 declare the variables intHours (to hold hours worked), decPayRate (to hold the hourly pay rate), and decGrossPay (to hold the gross pay).
- The If...Then statement that begins in line 8 calls Integer.TryParse to convert txtHours.Text to an Integer and assign the result to intHours. If the conversion fails, the program jumps to the Else clause in line 22, and the message *Enter a valid integer for hours worked* is displayed in line 24. If the conversion is successful, however, the program continues with the If...Then statement in line 11.
- The If...Then statement that begins in line 11 calls Decimal.TryParse to convert txtPayRate.Text to a Decimal and assign the result to decPayRate. If the conversion fails, the program jumps to the Else clause in line 17, and the message *Enter a valid value for hourly pay rate* is displayed in line 19. If the conversion is successful, however, the program continues with the calculation in line 13.
- Line 13 multiplies intHours by decPayRate and assigns the result to decGrossPay.
- Line 16 displays the value of decGrossPay, formatted as currency.

Checking Numeric Ranges

In addition to checking for valid conversions, you sometimes need to check numeric input values to make sure they fall within a range. For example, suppose you are running the *Gross Pay* application from Tutorial 4-8, and instead of entering 40 as the number of hours, you accidentally enter 400. The program doesn't know that you made a mistake, so it uses the bad data that you entered to calculate the gross pay.

This error could be avoided by having an `If...Then` statement that tests the number of hours to make sure it is a reasonable value. For example, there are 168 hours in a week, so the maximum number of hours that a person can work in a week is 168. The following `If...Then` statement determines whether the variable `intHours` is in the range of 0 through 168:

```
If intHours >= 0 And intHours <= 168 Then
   decGrosspay = intHours * decPayRate
Else
   MessageBox.Show("Invalid number of hours.")
End If
```

In this code, we used the `And` logical operator to create the following Boolean expression:

```
intHours >= 0 And intHours <= 168
```

This expression is true only if the value of `intHours` is within the range of 0 through 168.

It's also possible to enter an invalid value for the hourly pay rate. Suppose the company's maximum hourly pay rate is 45. Only values in the range of 0 through 45 are valid, so we could add another `If...Then` statement (shown here in bold) that validates the value of the `decPayRate` variable:

```
If intHours >= 0 And intHours <= 168 Then
   If decPayRate >= 0 And decPayRate <= 45.0 Then
     decGrosspay = intHours * decPayRate
   Else
     MessageBox.Show("Invalid pay rate.")
   End If
Else
   MessageBox.Show("Invalid number of hours.")
End If
```

In the previous examples we determined whether a value was within a range. Sometimes you want to know if a value is outside of a range. In that case it is better to use the `Or` operator to create a Boolean expression. For example, suppose you've written an application that is a car driving simulator, and the `intSpeed` variable holds the car's current speed. In the simulation, the minimum speed limit is 35 and the maximum speed limit is 60. To determine whether `intSpeed` is outside this range, we could use the following logic:

```
If intSpeed < 35 Or intSpeed > 60 Then
   MessageBox.Show("Speed violation!")
End If
```

It's important not to get the logic of the logical operators confused when testing for a range of values. For example, the Boolean expression in the following `If...Then` statement would never test true:

```
' This is an error!
If intSpeed < 35 And intSpeed > 60 Then
   MessageBox.Show("Speed violation!")
End If
```

Obviously, `intSpeed` cannot be less than 35 and at the same time be greater than 60.

4.11 Focus on GUI Design: Radio Buttons and Check Boxes

CONCEPT: Radio buttons appear in groups of two or more, allowing the user to select one of several options. A check box allows the user to select an item by checking a box, or deselect the item by unchecking the box.

Radio Buttons

Radio buttons are useful when you want the user to select one choice from several possible choices. Figure 4-31 shows a group of radio buttons.

A radio button may be selected or deselected. Each radio button has a small circle that appears filled in when the radio button is selected, and appears empty when the radio button is deselected.

Visual Basic provides the **RadioButton control**, which allows you to create radio buttons. Radio buttons are normally grouped in one of the following ways:

- All radio buttons inside a group box are members of the same group.
- All radio buttons on a form not inside a group box are members of the same group.

Figure 4-32 shows two forms. The form on the left has three radio buttons that belong to the same group. The form on the right has two groups of radio buttons.

At runtime, only one radio button in a group may be selected at a time, which makes them mutually exclusive. Clicking on a radio button selects it, and automatically deselects any other radio button in the same group.

Figure 4-31 Radio buttons

Figure 4-32 Forms with radio buttons

NOTE: The name *radio button* refers to the old car radios that had push buttons for selecting stations. Only one button could be pushed in at a time. When you pushed a button, it automatically popped out the currently selected button.

Radio Button Properties

Radio buttons have a Text property, which holds the text that is displayed next to the radio button's circle. For example, the radio buttons in the leftmost form in Figure 4-32 have their Text properties set to *Coffee*, *Tea*, and *Soft Drink*.

Radio buttons have a Boolean property named Checked. The **Checked property** is set to *True* when the radio button is selected and *False* when the radio button is deselected. Their default value is *False*.

Working with Radio Buttons in Code

The prefix that we use for radio button control names is `rad`. You determine if a radio button is selected by testing its Checked property. The following code shows an example. Assume that `radChoice1`, `radChoice2`, and `radChoice3` are radio buttons in the same group:

```
If radChoice1.Checked = True Then
    MessageBox.Show("You selected Choice 1")
ElseIf radChoice2.Checked = True Then
    MessageBox.Show("You selected Choice 2")
ElseIf radChoice3.Checked = True Then
    MessageBox.Show("You selected Choice 3")
End If
```

Radio Buttons have a **CheckedChanged** event that is triggered when the user selects or delelects a radio button. If you double-click a radio button in the *Designer* window, a code template for the `CheckedChange` event handler is created in the *Code* window.

Assigning a TabIndex Value and an Access Key to a Radio Button

Radio button controls have a position in the form's tab order, which may be changed with the TabIndex property. As with other controls, you can assign an access key to a radio button by placing an ampersand (&) in the Text property, just before the character you wish to serve as the access key. The character will appear underlined on the form. At runtime, when the user presses the [Alt]+*access key* combination, the focus shifts to the radio button, and the radio button is selected.

Selecting a Radio Button in Code

You can use code to select a radio button, using an assignment statement to set the desired radio button's Checked property to *True*, for example:

```
radChoice1.Checked = True
```

TIP: If you set a radio button's Checked property to *True* in Design mode (with the *Properties* window), it becomes the default radio button for that group. It is selected when the application starts up and it remains selected until the user or application code selects another radio button.

Check Boxes

A *check box* appears as a small box, labeled with a caption. An example is shown in Figure 4-33.

Figure 4-33 Check box

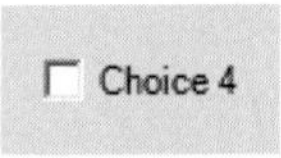

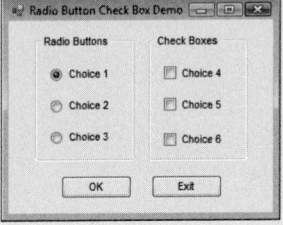

Visual Basic provides the **CheckBox control**, which allows you to create check boxes. Like radio buttons, check boxes may be selected or deselected at runtime. When a check box is selected, a small check mark appears inside the box. Unlike radio buttons, check boxes are not mutually exclusive. You may have one or more check boxes on a form or in a group box, and any number of them can be selected at any given time.

The prefix that we use for a CheckBox control's name is chk. Like radio buttons, check boxes have a Checked property. When a check box is selected, or checked, its Checked property is set to *True*. When a check box is deselected, or unchecked, its Checked property is set to *False*. Here is a summary of other characteristics of the check box:

- A check box's caption is stored in the Text property.
- A check box's place in the tab order may be modified with the TabIndex property. When a check box has the focus, a thin dotted line appears around its text. You can check or uncheck it by pressing the ⟨Spacebar⟩.
- You may assign an access key to a check box by placing an ampersand (&) in the Text property, just before the character that you wish to serve as the access key.
- You can use code to select or deselect a check box. Simply use an assignment statement to set the desired check box's Checked property, for example:

```
chkChoice4.Checked = True
```

- You may set a check box's Checked property at design time.
- Like radio buttons, check boxes have a CheckedChanged event that is triggered whenever the user changes the state of the check box. If you have written a CheckedChanged event handler for the check box, it will execute whenever the user checks or unchecks the check box.

In Tutorial 4-9, you complete the code for an application that demonstrates radio buttons and check boxes.

Tutorial 4-9:
Completing an application with radio buttons and check boxes

Step 1: Open the *Radio Button Check Box Demo* project from the student sample programs folder named *Chap4\Radio Button Check Box Demo*.

Step 2: Open *Form1* in *Design* mode, as shown in Figure 4-34.

Figure 4-34 *Radio Button Check Box Demo* form

Step 3: Double-click the *OK* button and insert the following bold code into the btnOk_Click event handler:

```
Private Sub btnOk_Click(...) Handles btnOk.Click
  ' Determine which radio button is selected.
  If radChoice1.Checked = True Then
    MessageBox.Show("You selected Choice 1.")
  ElseIf radChoice2.Checked = True Then
    MessageBox.Show("You selected Choice 2.")
  ElseIf radChoice3.Checked = True Then
    MessageBox.Show("You selected Choice 3.")
  End If

  ' Determine which check boxes are checked.
  If chkChoice4.Checked = True Then
    MessageBox.Show("You selected Choice 4.")
  End If

  If chkChoice5.Checked = True Then
    MessageBox.Show("You selected Choice 5.")
  End If

  If chkChoice6.Checked = True Then
    MessageBox.Show("You selected Choice 6.")
  End If
End Sub
```

Step 4: Save the project and run the application.

Step 5: Click *Choice 3*, *Choice 4*, and *Choice 6*. When you click the *OK* button you should see three message boxes, one after the other, indicating your selections. Experiment by clicking different radio buttons and check boxes. Note the results you see after clicking the *OK* button.

Checkpoint

4.15 In code, how do you determine whether a radio button has been selected?

4.16 If several radio buttons are placed on a form, not inside group boxes, how many of them may be selected at any given time?

4.17 In code, how do you determine whether a check box has been selected?

4.18 If several check boxes appear on a form, how many of them may be selected at any given time?

4.19 How can the user check or uncheck a check box that has the focus by using the keyboard?

4.12 Focus on Program Design and Problem Solving: Building the *Health Club Membership Fee Calculator* Application

CONCEPT: In this section you build the *Health Club Membership Fee Calculator* application. It will use features discussed in this chapter, including decision structures, radio buttons, and check boxes.

The Bay City Health and Fitness Club charges the following monthly membership rates:

Standard adult membership:	$40/month
Child (age 12 and under):	$20/month
Student:	$25/month
Senior citizen (age 65 and over):	$30/month

The club also offers the following optional services, which increase the base monthly fee:

Yoga lessons:	add $10 to the monthly fee
Karate lessons:	add $30 to the monthly fee
Personal trainer:	add $50 to the monthly fee

The manager of the club has asked you to create a *Health Club Membership Fee Calculator* application. It should allow the user to select a membership rate, select optional services, and enter the number of months of the membership. It should calculate the member's monthly and total charges for the specified number of months. The application should also validate the number of months entered by the user. An error message should be displayed if the user enters a number less than 1 or greater than 24. (Membership fees tend to increase every two years, so there is a club policy that no membership package can be purchased for more than 24 months at a time.)

Figure 4-35 shows a sketch of the application's form. The figure also shows the name of each control with a programmer-defined name.

Figure 4-35 Sketch of the *Health Club Membership Fee Calculator* form

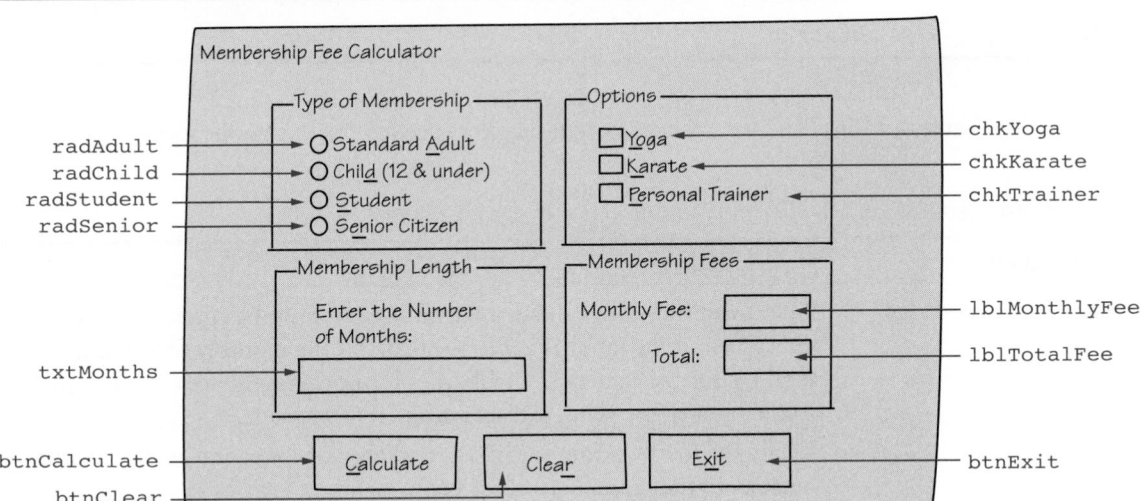

Table 4-13 lists each control, along with any relevant property settings.

Table 4-13 *Health Club Membership Fee Calculator* controls

Control Type	Control Name	Property	Property Value
Form	(Default)	Text:	*Membership Fee Calculator*
Group box	(Default)	Text:	*Type of Membership*
Radio button	`radAdult`	Text:	*Standard &Adult*
		Checked:	*True*
Radio button	`radChild`	Text:	*Chil&d (12 && under)*
Radio button	`radStudent`	Text:	*&Student*
Radio button	`radSenior`	Text:	*S&enior Citizen*
Group box	(Default)	Text:	*Options*
Check box	`chkYoga`	Text:	*&Yoga*
Check box	`chkKarate`	Text:	*&Karate*
Check box	`chkTrainer`	Text:	*&Personal Trainer*
Group box	(Default)	Text:	*Membership Length*
Label	(Default)	Text:	*Enter the Number of Months:*
Text box	`txtMonths`	Text:	
Group box	(Default)	Text:	*Membership Fees*
Label	(Default)	Text:	*Monthly Fee:*
Label	(Default)	Text:	*Total:*
Label	`lblMonthlyFee`	BorderStyle:	*Fixed3D*
		Text:	Initially cleared
		AutoSize:	*False*
Label	`lblTotalFee`	BorderStyle:	*Fixed3D*
		Text:	Initially cleared
		AutoSize:	*False*
Button	`btnCalculate`	Text:	*&Calculate*
Button	`btnClear`	Text:	*Clea&r*
Button	`btnExit`	Text:	*E&xit*

Table 4-14 lists and describes the event handlers needed for this application.

Table 4-14 *Health Club Membership Fee Calculator* event handlers

Event Handler	Description
`btnCalculate_Click`	First, this procedure validates the number of months entered by the user. Then, if the input is valid, it calculates the monthly fees and the total fee for the time period. Charges for optional services are included. If the input is not valid, it displays an error message.
`btnClear_Click`	Clears the text box, output labels, and check boxes, and resets the radio buttons so that `radAdult` is selected.
`btnExit_Click`	Ends the application.

Figure 4-36 shows a flowchart for the `btnCalculate_Click` event handler.

The number of months entered by the user is tested to determine whether it is valid. If the value is less than 1 or greater than 24, an error message is displayed. If the number of months is valid, the fees are calculated.

The first two processes in the calculation are (1) calculate the base monthly fee, and (2) calculate and add the cost of optional services. Each of these processes can be expanded into more detailed flowcharts. Figure 4-37 shows a more detailed view of the *calculate the base monthly fee* process.

Figure 4-36 Flowchart for `btnCalculate_Click`

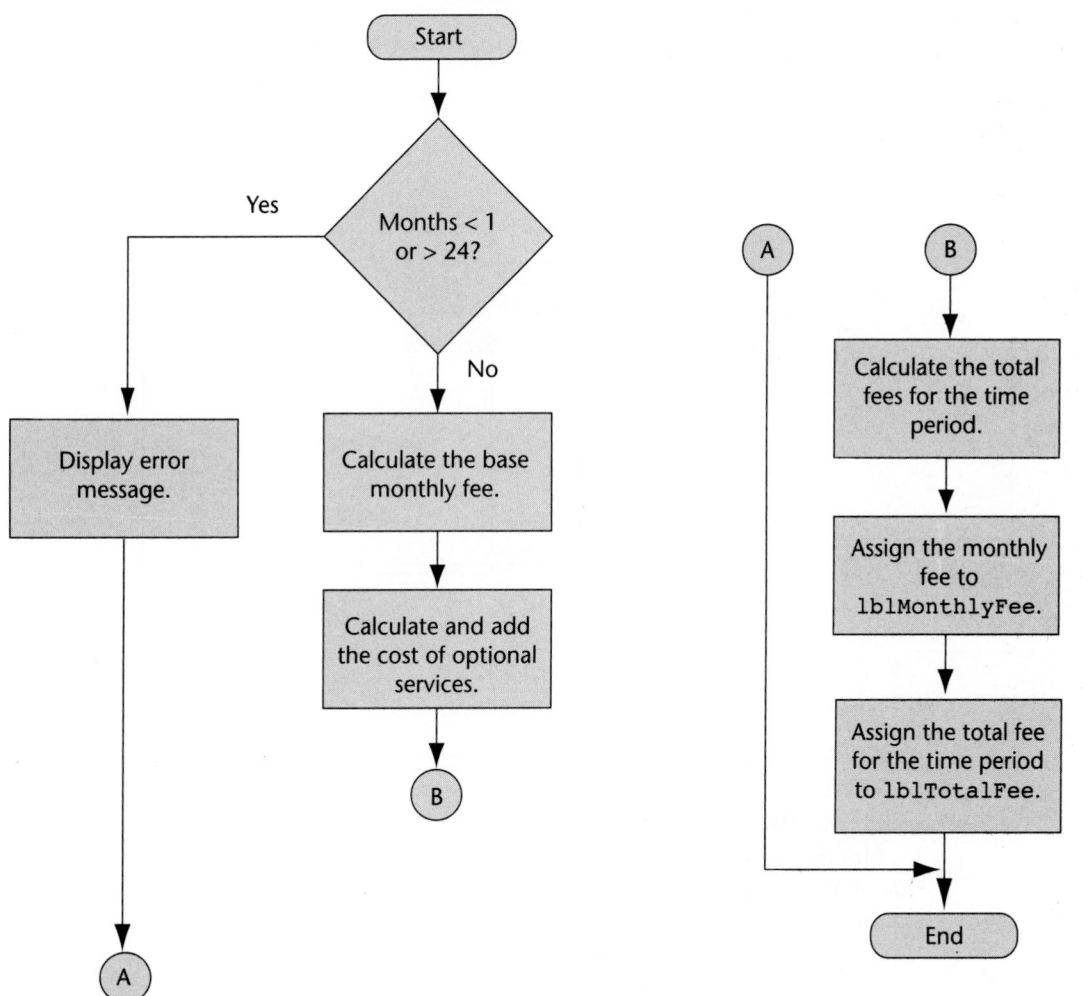

Figure 4-37 Flowchart of *calculate the base monthly fee* process

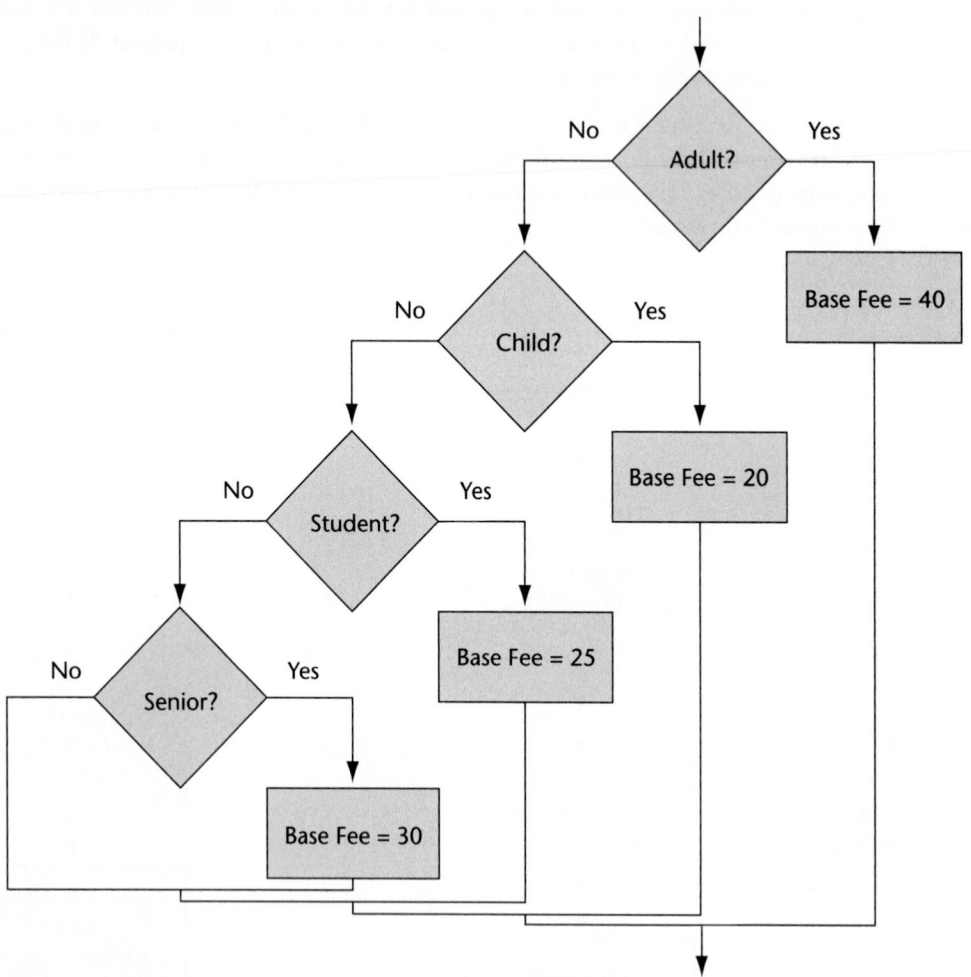

The logic in the flowchart can be expressed by the following pseudocode:

If Member is an Adult Then
  Monthly Base Fee = 40
ElseIf Member is a Child Then
  Montlhy Base Fee = 20
ElseIf Member is a Student Then
  Monthly Base Fee = 25
ElseIf Member is a Senior Citizen Then
  Monthly Base Fee = 30
End If

Figure 4-38 shows a more detailed view of the *calculate and add the cost of optional services* process.

Figure 4-38 Flowchart of *calculate and add the cost of optional services* process

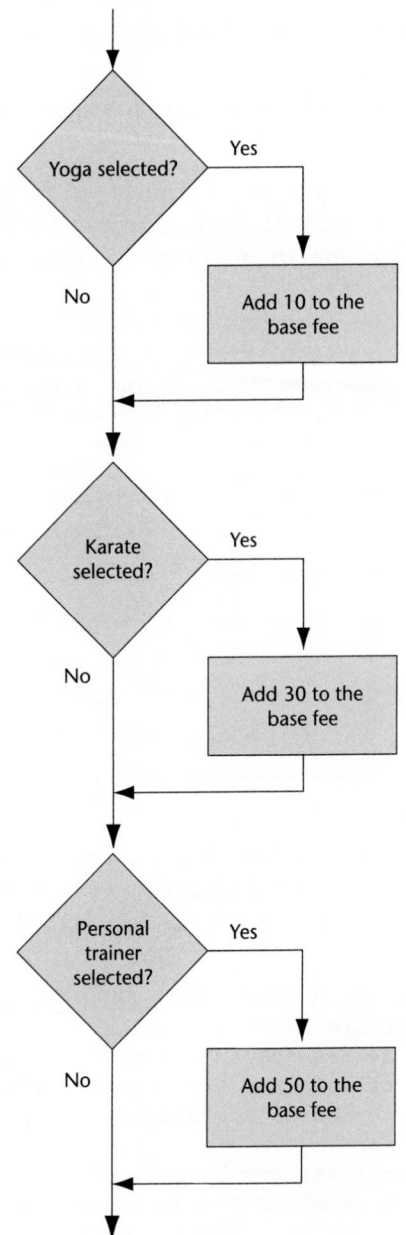

The logic in the flowchart can be expressed with the following pseudocode:

If Yoga is selected Then
    Add 10 to the monthly base fee
End If
If Karate is selected Then
    Add 30 to the monthly base fee
End If
If Personal Trainer is selected Then
    Add 50 to the monthly base fee
End If

Tutorial 4-10 builds the *Health Club Membership Fee Calculator* application.

Tutorial 4-10:

Building the *Health Club Membership Fee Calculator* application

Step 1: Create a new Windows application project named *Health Club Membership Fee Calculator*.

Step 2: Set up the form as shown in Figure 4-39. Create the group boxes, radio buttons, and check boxes. Refer to the sketch in Figure 4-35 for the control names and Table 4-13 for the relevant property settings of each control.

Figure 4-39 *Membership Fee Calculator* form

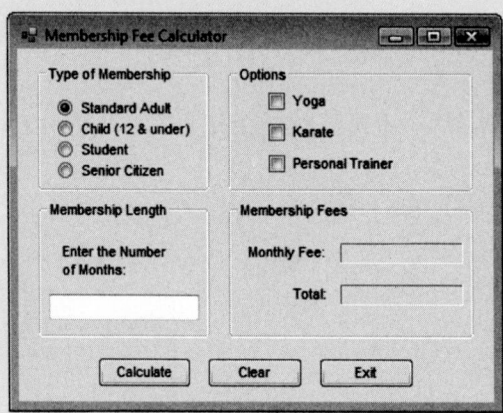

Step 3: In the *Designer* window, double-click the *Calculate* button to create the code template for the btnCalculate_Click event handler. Type the code shown here in bold. (Don't type the line numbers. We have inserted them for reference only.)

```
1 Private Sub btnCalculate_Click(...) Handles btnCalculate.Click
2     ' Declare local variables.
3     Dim decBaseFee As Decimal  ' Base Monthly Fee
4     Dim decTotalFee As Decimal ' Total Membership Fee
5     Dim intMonths As Integer   ' Number of months
6
7     ' Constants for base fees
8     Const decADULT_FEE As Decimal = 40D
9     Const decCHILD_FEE As Decimal = 20D
10     Const decSTUDENT_FEE As Decimal = 25D
11     Const decSENIOR_FEE As Decimal = 30D
12
13     ' Constants for additional fees
14     Const decYOGA_FEE As Decimal = 10D
15     Const decKARATE_FEE As Decimal = 30D
16     Const decTRAINER_FEE As Decimal = 50D
17
18     ' Get the number of months.
19     If Integer.TryParse(txtMonths.Text, intMonths) Then
20         ' Validate the number of months.
21         If intMonths >= 1 And intMonths <= 24 Then
22             ' Determine the base monthly fee.
23             If radAdult.Checked = True Then
24                 decBaseFee = decADULT_FEE
```

```
25        ElseIf radChild.Checked = True Then
26           decBaseFee = decCHILD_FEE
27        ElseIf radStudent.Checked = True Then
28           decBaseFee = decSTUDENT_FEE
29        ElseIf radSenior.Checked = True Then
30           decBaseFee = decSENIOR_FEE
31        End If
32
33        ' Look for additional services.
34        If chkYoga.Checked = True Then
35           decBaseFee += decYOGA_FEE
36        End If
37
38        If chkKarate.Checked = True Then
39           decBaseFee += decKARATE_FEE
40        End If
41
42        If chkTrainer.Checked = True Then
43           decBaseFee += decTRAINER_FEE
44        End If
45
46        ' Calculate the total fee.
47        decTotalFee = decBaseFee * intMonths
48
49        ' Display the fees.
50        lblMonthlyFee.Text = decBaseFee.ToString("c")
51        lblTotalFee.Text = decTotalFee.ToString("c")
52     Else
53        ' Error: Months is outside the range 1-24.
54        MessageBox.Show("Months must be in the range 1 - 24.")
55     End If
56  Else
57     ' Error: value entered for months is not an integer.
58     MessageBox.Show("Months must be an integer.")
59  End If
60 End Sub
```

Let's take a moment to go over this code. Lines 3 through 5 declare the following variables:

- The decBaseFee variable will hold the member's base monthly fee ($440 for an adult, $20 for a child, $25 for a student, or $30 for a senior citizen).
- The decTotalFee variable will hold the member's total monthly fee.
- The intMonths variable will hold the number of months of membership.

Lines 8 through 11 declare the following constants:

- decADULT_FEE specifies the monthly base fee for an adult membership.
- decCHILD_FEE specifies the monthly base fee for a child membership.
- decSTUDENT_FEE specifies the monthly base fee for a student membership.
- decSENIOR_FEE specifies the monthly base fee for a senior citizen membership.

Lines 14 through 16 declare the following constants:

- decYOGA_FEE specifies the additional monthly fee for yoga lessons.
- decKARATE_FEE specifies the additional monthly base fee for karate lessons.
- decTRAINER_FEE specifies the additional monthly base fee for a personal trainer.

The If...Then statement in line 19 calls Integer.TryParse to convert the value txtMonths.Text to an Integer, and assign the result to the intMonths variable. If the conversion fails, the program will branch to the Else clause in line 56, and the statement in line 58 displays an error message. If the conversion succeeds, the program continues to the If...Then statement in line 21.

Recall that the number of months must be in the range of 1 through 24. The If...Then statement in line 21 determines whether the value of intMonths falls within this range. If it does not, the program will branch to the Else clause in line 52, and the statement in line 54 displays an error message. If the conversion succeeds, the program continues to the If...Then...ElseIf statement that begins in line 23.

The user selects a radio button on the application's form to specify the type of membership. The If...Then...ElseIf statement that begins in line 23 determines which of the radio buttons is selected, and assigns the correct value to the decBaseFee variable.

Next, a series of three If...Then statements appears in lines 34 through 44. These statements determine whether any of the check boxes for additional services (yoga lessons, karate lessons, or a personal trainer) have been selected. If any have been selected, the decBaseFee variable is increased by the necessary amount.

Next, line 47 calculates the total fee by multiplying the monthly fee by the number of months. The result is assigned to the decTotalFee variable. Line 50 displays the monthly fee, and line 51 displays the total fee.

Step 4: Go back to the *Designer* window, and double-click the *Clear* button to create the code template for the btnClear_Click event handler. Type the code shown here in bold.

```
Private Sub btnClear_Click(...) Handles btnClear.Click
    ' Reset the Adult radio button.
    radAdult.Checked = True

    ' Clear the check boxes.
    chkYoga.Checked = False
    chkKarate.Checked = False
    chkTrainer.Checked = False

    ' Clear the number of months.
    txtMonths.Clear()

    ' Clear the fee labels.
    lblMonthlyFee.Text = String.Empty
    lblTotalFee.Text = String.Empty

    ' Give txtMonths the focus.
    txtMonths.Focus()
End Sub
```

Step 5: Go back to the *Designer* window, and double-click the *Exit* button to create the code template for the btnExit_Click event handler. Type the code shown here in bold.

```
Private Sub btnExit_Click(...) Handles btnExit.Click
    ' Close the form.
    Me.Close()
End Sub
```

Step 6: Save the project, and then run it. (If you mistyped something, and as a result have any syntax errors, correct them.)

Step 7: With the application running, enter the following test data and confirm that it displays the correct output.

Type of Membership	Monthly Fee	Total
Standard adult with yoga, karate, and personal trainer for 6 months	$130.00	$780.00
Child with karate for 3 months	$50.00	$150.00
Student with yoga for 12 months	$35.00	$420.00
Senior citizen with karate and personal trainer for 8 months	$110.00	$880.00

Step 8: End the application.

Summary

4.1 The Decision Structure

- Programs often need more than one path of execution. Many algorithms require a program to execute some statements only under certain circumstances. The decision structure accomplishes this.

4.2 The `If...Then` Statement

- The `If...Then` statement can cause other statements to execute under certain conditions.
- Boolean expressions, such as those created using relational operators, can be evaluated only as *True* or *False*.
- Math operators and function calls can be used with relational operators.

4.3 The `If...Then...Else` Statement

- The `If...Then...Else` statement executes one group of statements if a condition is true and another group of statements if the condition is false.

4.4 The `If...Then...ElseIf` Statement

- The `If...Then...ElseIf` statement is like a chain of `If...Then...Else` statements that perform their tests, one after the other, until one of them is found to be true.

4.5 Nested `If` Statements

- A nested `If` statement is an `If` statement in the conditionally executed code of another `If` statement.

4.6 Logical Operators

- Logical operators connect two or more relational expressions into one (using `And`, `Or`, `AndAlso`, `OrElse`, or `Xor`), or reverse the logic of an expression (using `Not`).
- When determining whether a number is inside a numeric range, it's best to use the `And` operator.
- When determining whether a number is outside a range, it's best to use the `Or` operator.

4.7 Comparing, Testing, and Working with Strings

- Relational operators can be used to compare strings.
- An empty string is represented by the constant `String.Empty`, or by two quotation marks, with no space between them.
- The `IsNumeric` function accepts a string as its argument and returns *True* if the string contains a number. The function returns *False* if the string's contents cannot be recognized as a number.
- The `Substring` method extracts a specified number of characters from within a specified position in a string.
- The `IndexOf` method is used to search for a character or a string within a string.

4.8 More about Message Boxes

- Message boxes are displayed with the `MessageBox.Show` method. The types of buttons and an icon to display in the message box can be specified.
- The return value of the `MessageBox.Show` method can be tested to determine which button the user clicked to dismiss the message box.

- The value `ControlChars.CrLf` can be concatenated with a string to produce multiple line displays.

4.9 The `Select Case` Statement

- The `Select Case` statement tests the value of an expression only once, and then uses that value to determine which set of statements to branch to.

4.10 Introduction to Input Validation

- The accuracy of a program's output depends on the accuracy of its input. It is important that applications perform input validation on the values entered by the user.

4.11 Focus on GUI Design: Radio Buttons and Check Boxes

- Radio buttons appear in groups and allow the user to select one of several possible options. Radio buttons placed inside a group box are treated as one group, separate and distinct from any other groups of radio buttons. Only one radio button in a group can be selected at any time.
- Clicking on a radio button selects it and automatically deselects any other radio button selected in the same group.
- Check boxes allow the user to select or deselect items. Check boxes are not mutually exclusive. There may be one or more check boxes on a form, and any number of them can be selected at any given time.

4.12 Focus on Program Design and Problem Solving: Building the *Health Club Membership Fee Calculator* Application

- This section outlines the process of building the *Health Club Membership Fee Calculator* application using the features discussed in the chapter.

Key Terms

And operator
`AndAlso` operator
Boolean expression
CheckBox control
`CheckedChanged` event
Checked property
conditionally executed (statement)
`ControlChars.CrLf`
decision structure
empty string
flag
`If...Then`
`If...Then...Else`
`If...Then...ElseIf`
`IndexOf` method
input validation
`IsNumeric` function
leading space
Length property
logic error

logical operators
nested `If` statement
`Not` operator
`Or` operator
`OrElse` operator
parse
RadioButton control
relational operator
`Select Case` statement
sequence structure
short-circuit evaluation
`Substring` method
`ToLower` method
`ToUpper` method
trailing space
`Trim` method
`TrimEnd` method
`TrimStart` method
Unicode
`Xor` operator

Review Questions and Exercises

Fill-in-the-Blank

1. A _____ structure allows a program to execute some statements only under certain circumstances.

2. A(n) _____ operator determines if a specific relationship exists between two values.

3. Boolean expressions can only be evaluated as _____ or _____.

4. A(n) _____ is a Boolean variable that signals when some condition exists in the program.

5. The _____ statement will execute one group of statements if the condition is true, and another group of statements if the condition is false.

6. The _____ statement is like a chain of `If...Then...Else` statements. They perform their tests, one after the other, until one of them is found to be true.

7. A _____ `If` statement is an `If` statement that appears inside another `If` statement.

8. _____ operators connect two or more relational expressions into one or reverse the logic of an expression.

9. The _____ method returns the uppercase equivalent of a string.

10. The _____ returns a lowercase version of a string.

11. The _____ function accepts a string as its argument and returns *True* if the string contains a number, or *False* if the string's contents cannot be recognized as a number.

12. The _____ method returns the number of characters in a string.

13. The _____ method returns a copy of a string without leading spaces.

14. The _____ method returns a copy of a string without trailing spaces.

15. The _____ method returns a copy of the string without leading or trailing spaces.

16. The _____ method extracts a specified number of characters from within a specified position in a string.

17. The value _____ can be concatenated with a string to produce multiple line displays.

18. A(n) _____ statement tests the value of an expression only once, and then uses that value to determine which set of statements to branch to.

19. _____ is the process of inspecting input values and determining whether they are valid.

20. _____ controls usually appear in groups and allow the user to select one of several possible options.

21. _____ controls may appear alone or in groups and allow the user to make yes/no, or on/off selections.

True or False

Indicate whether the following statements are true or false.

1. T F: It is not possible to write a Boolean expression that contains more than one logical operator.

2. T F: It is not possible to write Boolean expressions that contain math, relational, and logical operators.

3. T F: You may use the relational operators to compare strings.

4. T F: Clicking on a radio button selects it, and leaves any other selected radio button in the same group selected as well.

5. T F: Radio buttons that are placed inside a group box are treated as one group, separate and distinct from any other groups of radio buttons.

6. T F: When a group of radio buttons appears on a form (outside of a group box), any number of them can be selected at any time.

7. T F: You may have one or more check boxes on a form, and any number of them can be selected at any given time.

8. T F: The `If...Then` statement is an example of a sequence structure.

9. T F: An `If...Then` statement will not execute unless the conditionally executed statements are indented.

10. T F: The `Substring` method returns a lowercase copy of a string.

Multiple Choice

1. Relational operators allow you to _____ numbers.
   a. Add
   b. Multiply
   c. Compare
   d. Average

2. This statement can cause other program statements to execute only under certain conditions.
   a. `MessageBox.Show`
   b. `Decide`
   c. `If`
   d. `Execute`

3. This is a Boolean variable that signals when a condition exists.
   a. Relational operator
   b. Flag
   c. Arithmetic operator
   d. Float

4. This statement is like a chain of `If` statements. They perform their tests, one after the other, until one of them is found to be true.
   a. `If...Then`
   b. `If...Then...ElseIf`
   c. `Chain...If`
   d. `Relational`

5. When placed at the end of an `If...Then...ElseIf` statement, this provides default action when none of the `ElseIf` statements have true expressions.

   a. Trailing `If`
   b. Trailing `Select`
   c. Trailing `Otherwise`
   d. Trailing `Else`

6. When an `If` statement is placed inside another `If` statement, it is known as this type of statement.

   a. A nested `If`
   b. A complex `If`
   c. A compound `If`
   d. An invalid `If`

7. This operator connects two Boolean expressions into one. One or both expressions must be true for the overall expression to be true. It is only necessary for one to be true, and it does not matter which.

   a. `And`
   b. `Or`
   c. `Xor`
   d. `Not`

8. This operator connects two Boolean expressions into one. Both expressions must be true for the overall expression to be true.

   a. `And`
   b. `Or`
   c. `Xor`
   d. `Not`

9. This operator reverses the logical value of an Boolean expression. It makes a true expression false and a true expression true.

   a. `And`
   b. `Or`
   c. `Xor`
   d. `Not`

10. This operator connects two Boolean expressions into one. One, and only one, of the expressions must be true for the overall expression to be true. If both expressions are true, or if both expressions are false, the overall expression is false.

    a. `And`
    b. `Or`
    c. `Xor`
    d. `Not`

11. When determining whether a number is inside a numeric range, it's best to use this logical operator.

    a. `And`
    b. `Or`
    c. `Xor`
    d. `Not`

12. When determining whether a number is outside a range, it's best to use this logical operator.

    a. `And`
    b. `Or`
    c. `Xor`
    d. `Not`

13. In code you should test this property of a radio button or a check box to determine whether it is selected.
    a. Selected
    b. Checked
    c. On
    d. Toggle

14. This method attempts to convert a value to an Integer.
    a. `NumericConvert`
    b. `IntegerConvert`
    c. `Integer.TryParse`
    d. `Integer.TryConvert`

15. `strName` is a string variable. This expression returns the length of the string stored in `strName`.
    a. `Length(strName)`
    b. `strName.Length`
    c. `strName.StringSize`
    d. `CharCount(strName)`

16. Use this method to display a message box and determine which button the user clicked to dismiss the message box.
    a. `MessageBox.Show`
    b. `MessageBox.Button`
    c. `Message.Box`
    d. `MessageBox.UserClicked`

Short Answer

1. Describe the difference between the `If...Then...ElseIf` statement and a series of `If...Then` statements.

2. In an `If...Then...ElseIf` statement, what is the purpose of a trailing `Else`?

3. What is a flag and how does it work?

4. Briefly describe how the `And` operator works.

5. Briefly describe how the `Or` operator works.

6. How is the `Xor` operator different from the `Or` operator?

7. How is the `AndAlso` operator different from the `And` operator?

8. How is the `OrElse` operator different from the `Or` operator?

What Do You Think?

1. Why are the relational operators called relational?

2. When writing an `If...Then` statement to determine whether a number is inside a range, would you use the `And` operator, or the `Or` operator in the Boolean expression?

3. Why does Visual Studio automatically indent the conditionally executed statements in a decision structure?

4. Explain why you cannot convert the following `If...Then...ElseIf` statement into a `Select Case` statement.

```
If dblTemperature = 100 Then
    intX = 0
ElseIf intPopulation > 1000 Then
    intX = 1
ElseIf dblRate < .1 Then
    intX = -1
End If
```

Find the Error

1. What is syntactically incorrect in each of the following statements?

a.
```
If intX > 100
    MessageBox.Show("Invalid Data")
End If
```

b.
```
Dim str As String = "Hello"
Dim intLength As Integer
intLength = Length(str)
```

c.
```
If intZ < 10 Then
    MessageBox.Show("Invalid Data")
```

d.
```
Dim str As String = "123"
If str.IsNumeric Then
    MessageBox.Show("It is a number.")
End If
```

e.
```
Select Case intX
    Case < 0
        MessageBox.Show("Value too low.")
    Case > 100
        MessageBox.Show("Value too high.")
    Case Else
        MessageBox.Show("Value just right.")
End Select
```

Algorithm Workbench

1. Read the following instructions for cooking a pizza, and then design a flowchart with a decision structure that shows the necessary steps to cook the pizza with either thin and crispy or thick and chewy crust.

   a. For thin and crispy crust, do not preheat the oven. Bake pizza at 450 degrees for 15 minutes.

   b. For thick and chewy crust, preheat the oven to 400 degrees. Bake pizza for 20 minutes.

2. Write an `If...Then` statement that assigns 0 to `intX` when `intY` is equal to 20.

3. Write an `If...Then` statement that multiplies `decPayRate` by 1.5 when `intHours` is greater than 40.

4. Write an `If...Then` statement that assigns 0.2 to `decCommissionRate` when `decSales` is greater than or equal to $10,000.00.

5. Write an `If...Then` statement that sets the variable `intFees` to 50 when the Boolean variable `blnIsMax` equals *True*.

6. Write an `If...Then...Else` statement that assigns 1 to `intX` when `intY` is equal to 100. Otherwise it should assign 0 to `intX`.

7. The string variable `strPeople` contains a list of names, such as *Bill Jim Susan Randy Wilma* and so on. Write code that searches people for *Gene*. If *Gene* is found in `strPeople`, display a message box indicating that *Gene* was found.

8. Write an `If...Then` statement that prints the message *The number is valid* if the variable `sngSpeed` is within the range 0 through 200.

9. Write an `If...Then` statement that prints the message *The number is not valid* if the variable `sngSpeed` is outside the range 0 through 200.

10. Convert the following `If...Then...ElseIf` statement into a `Select Case` statement.

```
If intSelection = 1 Then
    MessageBox.Show("Pi times radius squared")
ElseIf intSelection = 2 Then
    MessageBox.Show("Length times width")
ElseIf intSelection = 3 Then
    MessageBox.Show("Pi times radius squared times height")
ElseIf intSelection = 4 Then
    MessageBox.Show("Well okay then, good bye!")
Else
    MessageBox.Show("Not good with numbers, eh?")
End If
```

Programming Challenges

1. **Larger and Smaller**

   Create an application that allows the user to enter two integers on a form similar to the one shown in Figure 4-40. The application should determine which value is larger than the other, or it should determine that the values are equal. Before comparing the numbers, use the `TryParse` method to verify that both inputs are valid integers. If an error is found, display an appropriate message to the user. Use a Label control to display all messages. The *Exit* button should close the window.

Figure 4-40 *Larger and Smaller* form

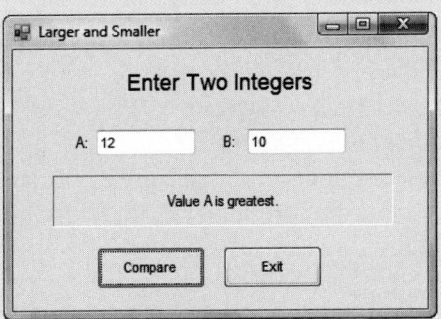

VideoNote

The Roman Numeral Converter Problem

2. **Roman Numeral Converter**

   Create an application that allows the user to enter an integer between 1 and 10 into a text box on a form similar to the one shown in Figure 4-41. Use a `Select Case` statement to identify which Roman numeral is the correct translation of the integer. Display the Roman numeral in a Label control. If the user enters an invalid value, display an appropriate error message and do not attempt the conversion. Include an *Exit* button that closes the window.

Figure 4-41 *Roman Numeral Converter* form

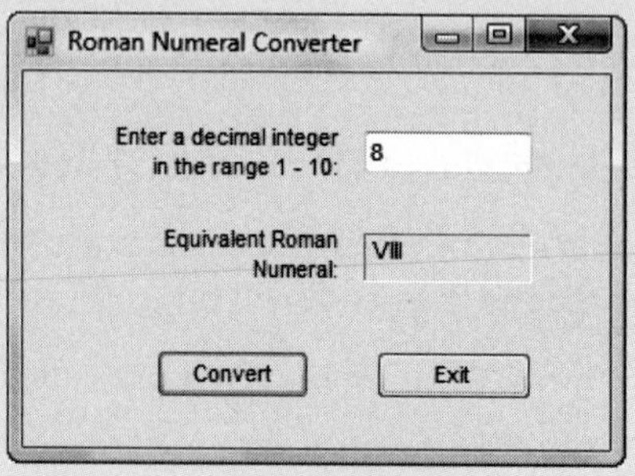

The following table lists the Roman numerals for the numbers 1 through 10.

Number	Roman Numeral
1	I
2	II
3	III
4	IV
5	V
6	VI
7	VII
8	VIII
9	IX
10	X

Input validation: Do not accept a number less than 1 or greater than 10. If the user enters a number outside this range, display an error message.

3. **Fat Percentage Calculator**

Create an application that allows the user to enter the number of calories and fat grams in a food. The application should display the percentage of the calories that come from fat. If the calories from fat are less than 30% of the total calories of the food, it should also display a message indicating the food is low in fat. (Display the message in a label or a message box.) The application's form should appear similar to the one shown in Figure 4-42.

One gram of fat has 9 Calories, so:
   *Calories from fat = fat grams * 9*

The percentage of calories from fat can be calculated as:
   Percentage of calories from fat = Calories from fat / total calories

Figure 4-42 *Fat Gram Calculator* form

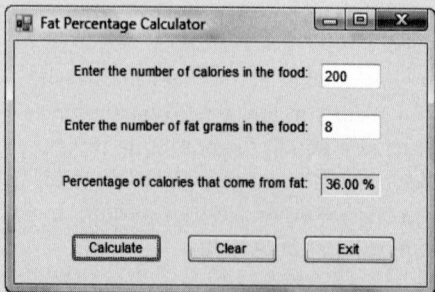

Input validation: Make sure the number of calories and fat grams are numeric, and are not less than 0. Also, the number of calories from fat cannot be greater than the total number of calories. If that happens, display an error message indicating that either the calories or fat grams were incorrectly entered.

Use the following test data to determine if the application is calculating properly:

Calories and Fat	Percentage Fat
200 calories, 8 fat grams	Percentage of calories from fat: 36%
150 calories 2 fat grams	Percentage of calories from fat: 12% (a low-fat food)
500 calories, 30 fat grams	Percentage of calories from fat: 54%

4. **Running the Race**

   Create an application that allows the user to enter the names of three runners and the time it took each of them to finish a race. The application should display who came in first, second, and third place. For simplicity, you can assume that the two runners will never have exactly the same finishing times. The application's form should appear similar to the one shown in Figure 4-43. The *Clear* button should clear all text boxes and calculated labels. The *Exit* button should close the form. Include the following input error checking: No runner name can be blank, and finishing times must be both numeric and positive.

   Use the following test data to determine if the application is calculating properly:

Names and Times	Results	
John, 87 seconds	First place:	Carol
Carol, 74 seconds	Second place:	John
Shelly, 94 seconds	Third place:	Shelly

Figure 4-43 *Race Results* form

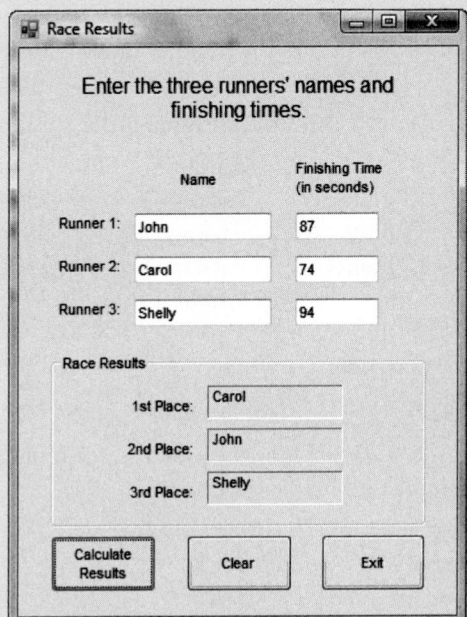

5. **Software Sales**

A software company sells three packages, Package A, Package B, and Package C, which retail for $99, $199, and $299, respectively. Quantity discounts are given according to the following table:

Quantity	Discount
10 through 19	20%
20 through 49	30%
50 through 99	40%
100 or more	50%

Create an application that allows the user to enter the number of units sold for each software package. The application's form should resemble Figure 4-44.

Figure 4-44 *Software Sales* form

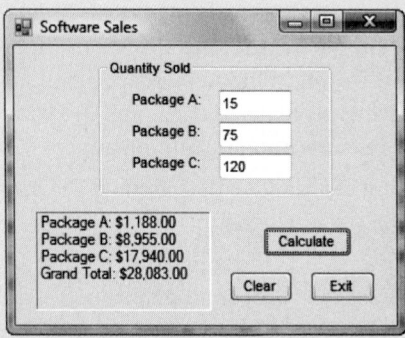

The application should calculate and display the order amounts and the grand total in a Label control. The *Clear* button must clear all text boxes and calculated labels. The *Exit* button must close the window.

Input validation: Make sure the number of units for each package is numeric, and is not negative.

Use the following test data to determine if the application is calculating properly:

Units Sold		Amount of Order	
Package A:	15 units	Package A:	$1,188.00
Package B:	75 units	Package B:	$8,955.00
Package C:	120 units	Package C:	$17,940.00
		Grand Total:	$28,083.00

Design Your Own Forms

6. **Bank Charges**

A bank charges $10 per month, plus the following check fees for a commercial checking account:

$0.10 each for less than 20 checks
$0.08 each for 20 through 39 checks
$0.06 each for 40 through 59 checks
$0.04 each for 60 or more checks

Create an application that allows the user to enter the number of checks written. The application should compute and display the bank's service fees for the month. All checks for the month are assigned the same charge, based on the total number of checks written during the month.

Input validation: Do not accept a negative value for the number of checks written. Ensure that all values are numeric. The *Clear* button must clear the text box and the label that displays the monthly service charge.

Use the following test data to determine if the application is calculating properly:

Number of Checks	Total Fees
15	$ 11.50
25	$ 12.00
45	$ 12.70
75	$ 13.00

7. **Shipping Charges**

The Fast Freight Shipping Company charges the rates listed in the following table.

Weight of the Package (in kilograms)	Shipping Rate per Mile
2 kg or less	$0.01
Over 2 kg, but not more than 6 kg	$0.015
Over 6 kg, but not more than 10 kg	$0.02
Over 10 kg, but not more than 20 kg	$0.025

Create an application that allows the user to enter the weight of the package and the distance it is to be shipped, and then displays the charges.

Input validation: Do not accept values of 0 or less for the weight of the package. Do not accept weights of more than 20 kg (this is the maximum weight the company will ship). Do not accept distances of less than 10 miles or more than 3000 miles. These are the company's minimum and maximum shipping distances. Suggestion: use the `OrElse` operator to combine the two range conditions that check for package weights that are too small or too large. Use exception handling to check for nonnumeric data.

Use the following test data to determine if the application is calculating properly:

Weight and Distance	Shipping Cost
1.5 Kg, 100 miles	$ 1.00
5 Kg, 200 miles	$ 3.00
8 Kg, 750 miles	$ 15.00
15 Kg, 2000 miles	$ 50.00

8. **Speed of Sound**

The following table shows the approximate speed of sound in air, water, and steel.

Medium	Speed
Air	1,100 feet per second
Water	4,900 feet per second
Steel	16,400 feet per second

Create an application that displays a set of radio buttons allowing the user to select air, water, or steel. Provide a text box to let the user enter the distance a sound wave will travel in the selected medium. Then, when the user clicks a button, the program should display the amount of time it will take. Format the output to two decimal places.

Input validation: Do not accept distances less than 0. Always check for nonnumeric data.

Use the following test data to determine if the application is calculating properly:

Medium and Distance	Speed of Sound
Air, 10,000 feet	9.09 seconds
Water, 10,000 feet	2.04 seconds
Steel, 10,000 feet	0.61 seconds

9. **Freezing and Boiling Points**

The following table lists, in degrees Fahrenheit, the freezing and boiling points of several substances. Create an application that allows the user to enter a temperature. The program should then display a list of the substances that freeze at that temperature, followed by a list of substances that will boil at the same temperature.

Substance	Freezing Point	Boiling Point
Ethyl alcohol	–173°	172°
Mercury	–38°	676°
Oxygen	–362°	–306°
Water	32°	212°

Use the following test data and sample outputs to determine if the application is calculating properly:

Temperature	Results
–20°	Water will freeze and oxygen will boil.
–50°	Mercury and water will freeze and oxygen will boil.
–200°	Ethyl alcohol, mercury, and water will freeze and oxygen will boil.
–400°	Ethyl alcohol, mercury, oxygen, and water will freeze.

10. **Long-Distance Calls**

A long-distance provider charges the following rates for telephone calls:

Rate Category	Rate per Minute
Daytime (6:00 a.m. through 5:59 P.M.)	$0.07
Evening (6:00 p.m. through 11:59 P.M.)	$0.12
Off-Peak (12:00 a.m. through 5:59 A.M.)	$0.05

Create an application that allows the user to select a rate category (from a set of radio buttons) and enter the number of minutes of the call, then displays the charges. Include a *Clear* button that clears the input and calculated values, and an *Exit* button that closes the window. Error checking: the minutes input by the user must be numeric, and it must be greater than zero.

Use the following test data to determine if the application is calculating properly:

Rate Category and Minutes	Charge
Daytime, 20 minutes	$ 1.40
Evening, 20 minutes	$ 2.40
Off-peak, 20 minutes	$ 1.00

11. **Internet Service Provider, Part 1**

An Internet service provider offers three subscription packages to its customers, plus a discount for nonprofit organizations:

a. Package A: 10 hours of access for $9.95 per month. Additional hours are $2.00 per hour.

b. Package B: 20 hours of access for $14.95 per month. Additional hours are $1.00 per hour.

c. Package C: Unlimited access for $19.95 per month.

d. Nonprofit Organizations: The service provider gives all nonprofit organizations a 20% discount on all packages.

The user should select the package the customer has purchased (from a set of radio buttons) and enter the number of hours used. A check box captioned *Nonprofit Organization* should also appear on the form. The application should calculate and display the total amount due. If the user selects the *Nonprofit Organization* check box, a 20% discount should be deducted from the final charges. Implementation note: all rates, limits, and discounts must be declared using symbolic constants (using the Const keyword).

Input validation: The number of hours used in a month cannot exceed 744. The value must be numeric.

Use the following data to determine if the application is calculating properly:

Package and Hours	The Monthly Charge
Package A, 5 hours, nonprofit	$ 7.96
Package A, 25 hours	$39.95
Package B, 10 hours, nonprofit	$11.96
Package B, 25 hours	$19.95
Package C, 18 hours, nonprofit	$15.96
Package C, 25 hours	$19.95

12. **Internet Service Provider, Part 2 (Advanced)**

Make a copy of your solution program from Programming Challenge 11. Then, using the copied program, modify it so the form has a check box captioned *Display Potential Savings*. When this check box is selected, the application should also display the amount of money that Package A customers would save if they purchased Package B or C, or the amount that Package B customers would save if they purchased Package C. If there would be no savings, the message should indicate that.

Use the following test data to determine if the application is calculating properly:

Package and Hours	Total Monthly Savings
Package A, 5 hours, nonprofit	$7.96, no savings with Packages B or C
Package A, 25 hours	$39.95, save $20.00 with Package B, and save $20.00 with Package C
Package B, 10 hours, nonprofit	$11.96, no savings with Package C
Package B, 25 hours	$19.95, no savings with Package C

13. **Mass and Weight**

Scientists measure an object's mass in kilograms and its weight in newtons. If you know the amount of mass of an object, you can calculate its weight, in newtons, with the following formula:

$$Weight = mass \times 9.8$$

Create a VB application that lets the user enter an object's mass and calculates its weight. If the object weighs more than 1000 newtons, display a message indicating that it is too heavy. If the object weighs less than 10 newtons, display a message indicating that it is too light.

14. **Book Club Points**

Serendipity Booksellers has a book club that awards points to its customers based on the number of books purchased each month. The points are awarded as follows:

- If a customer purchases 0 books, he or she earns 0 points.
- If a customer purchases 1 book, he or she earns 5 points.
- If a customer purchases 2 books, he or she earns 15 points.
- If a customer purchases 3 books, he or she earns 30 points.
- If a customer purchases 4 or more books, he or she earns 60 points.

  Create a VB application that lets the user enter the number of books that he or she has purchased this month and displays the number of points awarded.

15. **Body Mass Index Program Enhancement**

In Programming Challenge 13 in Chapter 3 you were asked to create a VB application that calculates a person's body mass index (BMI). Recall from that exercise that the BMI is often used to determine whether a person with a sedentary lifestyle is overweight or underweight for their height. A person's BMI is calculated with the following formula:

$$BMI = weight \times 703 / height^2$$

In the formula, weight is measured in pounds and height is measured in inches. Enhance the program so it displays a message indicating whether the person has optimal weight, is underweight, or is overweight. A sedentary person's weight is considered to be optimal if his or her BMI is between 18.5 and 25. If the BMI is less than 18.5, the person is considered to be underweight. If the BMI value is greater than 25, the person is considered to be overweight.

16. **Magic Dates**

The date June 10, 1960, is special because when we write it in the following format, the month times the day equals the year.

6/10/60

Create a VB application that lets the user enter a month (in numeric form), a day, and a two-digit year. The program should then determine whether the month times the day is equal to the year. If so, it should display a message saying the date is magic. Otherwise it should display a message saying the date is not magic.

17. **Time Calculator**

Create a VB application that lets the user enter a number of seconds and works as follows:

- There are 60 seconds in a minute. If the number of seconds entered by the user is greater than or equal to 60, the program should display the number of minutes in that many seconds.
- There are 3,600 seconds in an hour. If the number of seconds entered by the user is greater than or equal to 3,600, the program should display the number of hours in that many seconds.
- There are 86,400 seconds in a day. If the number of seconds entered by the user is greater than or equal to 86,400, the program should display the number of days in that many seconds.

5 Lists and Loops

TOPICS

This chapter begins by showing you how to use input boxes, which provide a quick and simple way to ask the user to enter data. List boxes and combo boxes are also introduced. Next, you learn to write loops, which cause blocks, or sequences of programming statements to repeat. You will also learn how to generate random numbers and use them for various purposes in a program. Finally, we cover the ToolTip control, which allows you to display pop-up messages when the user moves the mouse over controls.

5.1 Input Boxes

CONCEPT: Input boxes provide a simple way to gather input without placing a text box on a form.

An **input box** is a quick and simple way to ask the user to enter data. Figure 5-1 shows an example. In the figure, an input box displays a message to the user and provides a text box for the user to enter input. The input box also has *OK* and *Cancel* buttons.

You can display input boxes with the `InputBox` function. When the function is called, an input box such as the one shown in Figure 5-1 appears on the screen. Here is the general format:

```
InputBox(Prompt [, Title] [, Default] [, Xpos] [, Ypos])
```

Figure 5-1 Input box that requests the user's name

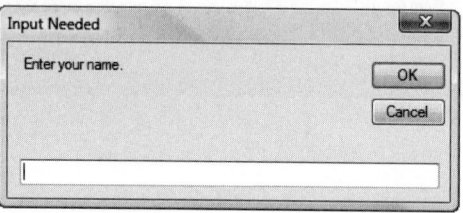

The brackets in the general format are shown around the *Title*, *Default*, *Xpos*, and *Ypos* arguments to indicate that they are optional. The first argument, *Prompt*, is a string that is displayed to the user in the input box. Normally, the string asks the user to enter a value. The optional arguments, *Title*, *Default*, *Xpos*, and *Ypos* are described as follows.

- *Title* is a string that appears in the input box's title bar. If you do not provide a value for *Title*, the name of the project appears.
- *Default* is a string to be initially displayed in the input box's text box. If you do not provide a value for *Default*, the input box's text box is left empty.
- *Xpos* and *Ypos* specify the input box's location on the screen. *Xpos* is an integer that specifies the distance of the input box's leftmost edge from the left edge of the screen. *Ypos* is an integer that specifies the distance of the topmost edge of the input box from the top of the screen. *Xpos* and *Ypos* are measured in pixels. If *Xpos* is omitted, Visual Basic centers the input box horizontally on the screen. If *Ypos* is omitted, the input box is placed near the top of the screen.

If the user clicks the input box's *OK* button or presses the [Enter] key, the function returns the string value from the input box's text box. If the user clicks the *Cancel* button, the function returns an empty string. To retrieve the value returned by the `InputBox` function, use the assignment operator to assign it to a variable. For example, the following statement displays the input box shown in Figure 5-2. Assume that `strUserInput` is a string variable that has already been declared.

```
strUserInput = InputBox("Enter your age.", "Input Needed")
```

Figure 5-2 Input box that requests the user's age

After this statement executes, the value the user entered in the input box is stored as a string in `strUserInput`. As another example, the following statement displays the input box shown in Figure 5-3.

```
strUserInput = InputBox("Enter the distance.", "Provide a Value",
                        "150")
```

Figure 5-3 Input box with default user input

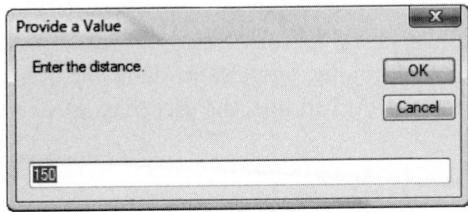

If the user clicks the *OK* button without entering a value in the text box, the input box function returns `"150"`.

 NOTE: In most applications, the `InputBox` function should not be used as the primary method of input because it draws the user's attention away from the application's form. It also complicates data validation, because the box closes before validation can take place. Despite these drawbacks, it is a convenient tool for developing and testing applications.

 **Checkpoint**

Carefully examine the input box in Figure 5-4 and complete Checkpoint items 5.1 and 5.2.

Figure 5-4 Input box that requests a number from the user

5.1 Write a statement that displays the input box at the default location on the screen.

5.2 Write a statement that displays the input box with its leftmost edge at 100 pixels from the left edge of the screen, and its topmost edge 300 pixels from the top edge of the screen.

5.2 List Boxes

> **CONCEPT:** List boxes display a list of items and allow the user to select an item from the list.

The ListBox Control

A **ListBox control** displays a list of items and also allows the user to select one or more items from the list. (Informally, we refer to this control as a *list box*.) Figure 5-5 shows a form with two list boxes. At runtime, the user may select one of the items, causing the item to appear selected.

Figure 5-5 List box examples

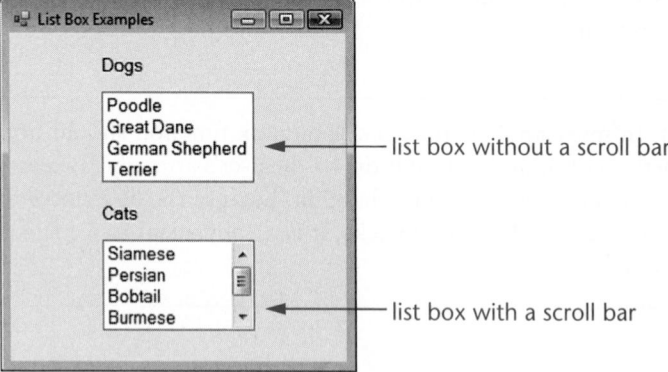

One of the list boxes in Figure 5-5 does not have a scroll bar, but the other one does. A scroll bar appears when the list box contains more items than can be displayed in the space provided. In the figure, the top list box has four items (Poodle, Great Dane, German Shepherd, and Terrier), and all items are displayed. The bottom list box shows four items (Siamese, Persian, Bobtail, and Burmese), but because it has a scroll bar, we know there are more items in the list box than those four.

Creating a ListBox Control

You create a ListBox control using either of the following methods:

- Double-click the ListBox icon in the *Toolbox* window to cause a ListBox control to appear on the form. Move the control to the desired location and resize it, if necessary.
- Click the ListBox icon in the *Toolbox* window and use the mouse to draw the List-Box control on the form with the desired location and size.

In Design mode, a ListBox control appears as a rectangle. The size of the rectangle determines the size of the list box. The prefix that we will use in a ListBox control's name is lst, where the first character is a lowercase letter L. Let's discuss some of the list box's important properties and methods.

The Items Property

The entries in a list box are stored in a property named Items. You can store values in the **Items property** (also known as the Items collection) at design time or at runtime. To store values in the Items property at design time, follow these steps:

1. Make sure the ListBox control is selected in the *Designer* window.
2. In the *Properties* window, the setting for the Items property is displayed as *(Collection)*. When you select the Items property, an ellipsis button (...) appears.
3. Click the ellipsis button. The *String Collection Editor* dialog box appears, as shown in Figure 5-6.
4. Type the values that are to appear in the list box into the *String Collection Editor* dialog box. Type each value on a separate line by pressing the ⏎ Enter key after each entry.
5. When you have entered all the values, click the *OK* button.

Figure 5-6 The *String Collection Editor* dialog box

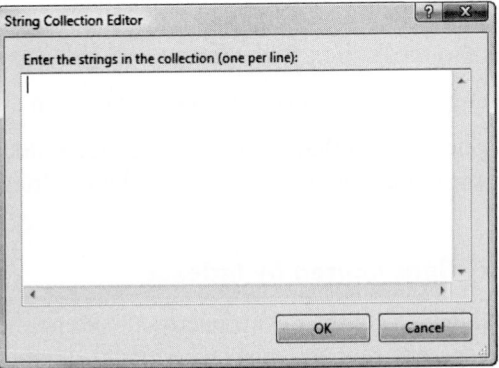

NOTE: Once you acquire the necessary skills, you will be able to fill the Items collection of list boxes from external data sources (such as databases).

The Items.Count Property

You can use the **Items.Count property** to determine the number of items stored in the list box. When there are no items in the Items property, the Items.Count property equals 0. For example, assume an application has a list box named `lstEmployees`. The following `If...Then` statement displays a message box when there are no items in the list box:

```
If lstEmployees.Items.Count = 0 Then
   MessageBox.Show("There are no items in the list!")
End If
```

The following statement assigns the number of items in the list box to the variable `intNumEmployees`:

```
intNumEmployees = lstEmployees.Items.Count
```

Item Indexing

The Items property is a collection of objects, in which each has an *index*, or number. The first object in the collection has index 0, the next has index 1, and so on. The last index value is $n - 1$, where n is the number of items in the collection. When you access the Items property in code, you must supply an index, using an expression such as the following:

```
lstEmployees.Items(0)
```

If you want to retrieve an item from a list box's Items property and assign it to a variable, you have to explicitly convert that item to the same data type as the variable. For example, suppose we want to get the first item that is stored in the lstEmployees list box and assign it to strName, which is a string variable. We would need to call the item's ToString method as shown here:

```
strName = lstEmployees.Items(0).ToString()
```

This statement gets the item that is stored at lstEmployees.Items(0), calls that item's ToString method, and assigns the resulting string to the strName variable.

Let's look at another example. Suppose an application has a list box named lstRoomNumbers that contains a list of room numbers. The following statement shows how you would assign the first item in the list box to the Integer variable intRoomNumber:

```
intRoomNumber = CInt(lstRoomNumbers.Items(0))
```

This statement gets the item that is stored at lstRoomNumbers.Items(0), converts it to an Integer with the CInt function, and assigns the resulting value to the intRoomNumber variable.

Handling Exceptions Caused by Indexes

When you use an index with the Item property, an exception is thrown if the index is out of range. Because indexes start at zero, the highest index number you can use is always one less than the collection size. You can use an exception handler to trap such an error. In the following code, assume that the variable intIndex contains a value that we want to use as an index. If the value in intIndex is out of range, the exception is handled. We display the Message property (Figure 5-7) of the exception object to give the user an idea of what went wrong.

```
Try
   strInput = lstMonths.Items(intIndex).ToString()
Catch ex As Exception
   MessageBox.Show(ex.Message)
End Try
```

Figure 5-7 Exception thrown by out of range index

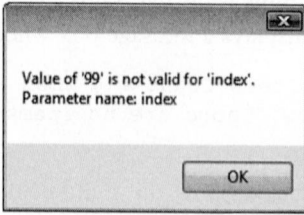

Many programmers prefer to handle indexing errors using an If statement. The following code is an example in which we compare the index (in a variable named intIndex) to the Count property of the Items collection:

```
If intIndex >= 0 And intIndex < lstMonths.Items.Count Then
   strInput = lstMonths.Items(intIndex).ToString()
Else
   MessageBox.Show("Index is out of range: " & intIndex)
End If
```

The SelectedIndex Property

When the user selects an item in a list box, the item's index is stored in the **SelectedIndex** property. If no item is selected, `SelectedIndex` is set to –1. You can use the SelectedIndex property to retrieve the selected item from the Items property. For example, assume an application has a list box named `lstLocations`. The following code segment uses an `If ...Then` statement to determine whether the user has selected an item in the list box. If so, it copies the item from the Items property to the string variable `strLocation`.

```
If lstLocations.SelectedIndex <> -1 Then
    strLocation = lstLocations.Items(lstLocations.SelectedIndex).
        ToString()
End If
```

 TIP: To prevent a runtime error, always test the SelectedIndex property to make sure it is not set to –1 before using it with the Items property to retrieve an item.

You can also use the SelectedIndex property to deselect an item by setting it to –1. For example, the following statement deselects any selected item in `lstLocations`:

```
lstLocations.SelectedIndex = -1
```

The SelectedItem Property

Whereas the SelectedIndex property contains the index of the currently selected item, the **SelectedItem** property contains the item itself. For example, suppose the list box `lstFruit` contains *Apples*, *Pears*, and *Bananas*. If the user has selected *Pears*, the following statement copies the string *Pears* to the variable `strSelectedFruit`:

```
strSelectedFruit = lstFruit.SelectedItem.ToString()
```

The Sorted Property

You can use the list box's **Sorted property** to cause the items in the Items property to be displayed alphabetically. This Boolean property is set to *False* by default, causing the items to be displayed in the order they were inserted into the list. When set to *True*, the items are sorted alphabetically.

The `Items.Add` Method

To store values in the Items property with code at runtime, use the **`Items.Add`** method. Here is the general format:

```
ListBox.Items.Add(Item)
```

ListBox is the name of the list box control. *Item* is the value to be added to the Items property. For example, suppose an application has a list box named `lstStudents`. The following statement adds the string "`Sharon`" to the end of the list box.

```
lstStudents.Items.Add("Sharon")
```

You can add virtually any type of values to list box, including objects. For example, the following statements add Integer, Decimal, and Date objects to list boxes.

```
Dim intNum As Integer = 5
Dim decGrossPay As Decimal = 1200D
Dim datStartDate As Date = #12/18/2010#
lstNumbers.Items.Add(intNum)
lstWages.Items.Add(decGrossPay)
lstDates.Items.Add(datStartDate)
```

When you add an object other than a string to a list box, the text displayed in the list box is the string returned by the object's `ToString` method.

The `Items.Insert` Method

To insert an item at a specific position, you must use the `Items.Insert` method. Here is the general format of the **`Items.Insert`** method:

```
ListBox.Items.Insert(Index, Item)
```

ListBox is the name of the list box control. *Index* is an integer argument that specifies the position where *Item* is to be placed in the Items property. *Item* is the item to add to the list.

For example, suppose the list box `lstStudents` contains the following items, in the order they appear: *Bill, Joe, Geri,* and *Sharon*. Since *Bill* is the first item, its index is 0. The index for *Joe* is 1, for *Geri* is 2, and for *Sharon* is 3. Now, suppose the following statement executes.

```
lstStudents.Items.Insert(2, "Jean")
```

This statement inserts *Jean* at index 2. The string that was previously at index 2 (*Geri*) is moved to index 3, and the string previously at index 3 (*Sharon*) is moved to index 4. The items in the Items property are now *Bill, Joe, Jean, Geri,* and *Sharon*.

The `Items.Remove` and `Items.RemoveAt` Methods

The **`Items.Remove`** and **`Items.RemoveAt`** methods both remove one item from a list box's Items property. Here is the general format of both methods:

```
ListBox.Items.Remove(Item)
ListBox.Items.RemoveAt(Index)
```

ListBox is the name of the list box control. With the `Items.Remove` method, *Item* is the item you wish to remove. For example, the following statement removes the string *Industrial Widget* from the `lstInventory` list box.

```
lstInventory.Items.Remove("Industrial Widget")
```

If you specify an item that is not in the list box, nothing is removed.

The `Items.RemoveAt` method removes the item at a specific index. For example, the following statement removes the item at index 4 from the `lstInventory` list box:

```
lstInventory.Items.RemoveAt(4)
```

 WARNING: If you specify an invalid index with the `Items.RemoveAt` method, an exception will occur.

The `Items.Clear` Method

The **`Items.Clear`** method erases all the items in the Items property. Here is the method's general format:

```
ListBox.Items.Clear()
```

For example, assume an application has a list box named `lstCars`. The following statement erases all items in the list.

```
lstCars.Items.Clear()
```

In Tutorial 5-1, you create an application with two list boxes.

Tutorial 5-1:
Creating list boxes

Step 1: Create a new Windows Forms Application project named *List Boxes*. Change the form's Text property to *List Box Demo*.

Step 2: On the form, create a list box as shown in Figure 5-8. Notice that the default name of the list box is `ListBox1`. Also notice that the name of the list box is displayed in the list box at design time. It will not appear there at runtime.

Step 3: Change the name of the list box to `lstMonths`.

Step 4: With the list box selected, click the Items property in the *Properties* window. Then click the ellipsis button (`...`) that appears.

Step 5: The *String Collection Editor* dialog box will appear. Type the following names of the months, with one name per line: **January**, **February**, **March**, **April**, **May**, **June**, **July**, **August**, **September**, **October**, **November**, and **December**. When you are finished, the dialog box should appear as shown in Figure 5-9. Click the *OK* button to close the dialog box.

Figure 5-8 A list box

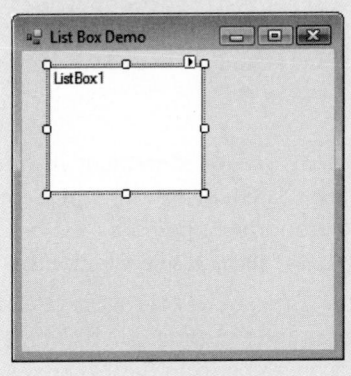

Figure 5-9 *String Collection Editor* with months filled in

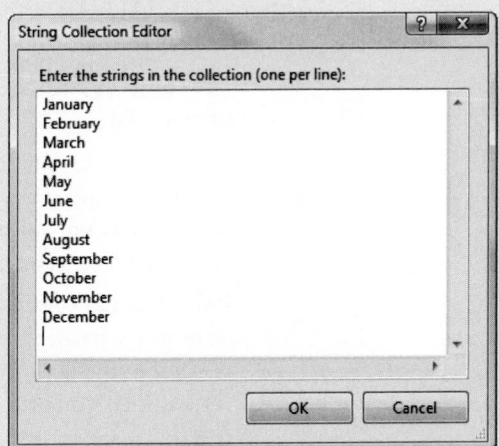

Step 6: Create another list box and make it the same size as the first one. Change its name to `lstYears`. Enter the following items in its Items property: **2008, 2009, 2010, 2011,** and **2012**.

Step 7: Create two buttons on the form. Name the first `btnOk`, and change its Text property to *OK*. Name the second `btnReset` and change its Text property to *Reset*. The form should look similar to Figure 5-10.

Figure 5-10 The form with two list boxes and two buttons

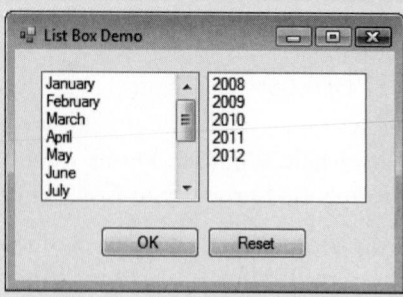

Step 8: Double-click the btnOk button to generate a Click event handler code template. Complete the event handler by writing the following bold code shown in lines 2 through 15.

```
 1 Private Sub btnOk_Click(...) Handles btnOk.Click
 2   Dim strInput As String ' Holds selected month and year
 3
 4   If lstMonths.SelectedIndex = -1 Then
 5     ' No month is selected
 6     MessageBox.Show("Select a month.")
 7   ElseIf lstYears.SelectedIndex = -1 Then
 8     ' No year is selected
 9     MessageBox.Show("Select a year.")
10   Else
11     ' Get the selected month and year
12     strInput = lstMonths.SelectedItem.ToString() &
13       " " & lstYears.SelectedItem.ToString()
14     MessageBox.Show("You selected " & strInput)
15   End If
16 End Sub
```

Let's take a closer look at the code. The If statement in line 4 determines whether lstMonths.SelectedIndex is equal to −1, which would mean that the user has not selected anything from the lstMonths list box. If that is true, line 6 displays a message box telling the user to select a month.

If the user has selected an item from lstMonths, the ElseIf clause in line 7 determines whether lstYears.SelectedIndex is equal to −1, which would mean that the user has not selected anything from the lstYears list box. If that is true, line 9 displays a message box telling the user to select a year.

If the user has selected items in both lstMonths and lstYears, the program jumps to the Else clause in line 10. The statement that appears in lines 11 and 12 creates a string containing the selected month, followed by a space, followed by the selected year. For example, if the user selected *April* in lstMonths and *2011* in lstYears, the string "April 2011" would be created and assigned to the strInput variable. Then line 14 displays the string in a message box.

Step 9: Double-click the btnReset button to add a Click event handler code template. Write the following code shown in bold:

```
Private Sub btnReset_Click(...) Handles btnReset.Click
  ' Reset the list boxes.
  lstMonths.SelectedIndex = -1
  lstYears.SelectedIndex = -1
End Sub
```

When this button is clicked, the SelectedIndex property of both list boxes is set to −1. This deselects any selected items.

Step 10: Run the application. Without selecting any item in either list box, click the *OK* button. A message box appears instructing you to *Select a month*.

Step 11: Select *March* in lstMonths, but do not select an item from lstYears. Click the *OK* button. This time a message box appears instructing you to *Select a year*.

Step 12: With *March* still selected in lstMonths, select *2012* in lstYears. Click the *OK* button. Now a message box appears with the message *You selected March 2012*. Click the message box's *OK* button to dismiss it.

Step 13: Click the *Reset* button. The items you previously selected in lstMonths and lstYears are deselected.

Step 14: Close the application and save it.

More about the Items Collection

You've learned that a list box's Items property is a special type of container known as a *collection*. Collections are commonly used to store groups of objects, and as you learn more about Visual Basic, you will see that collections are used in many places. What you have learned about a list box's Items collection applies to other collections as well. Table 5-1 lists several important methods and properties that collections have.

Table 5-1 Several methods and properties of collections

Method or Property	Description
Add (*item As Object*)	Method: adds *item* to the collection, returning its index position.
Clear ( )	Method: removes all items in the collection. No return value.
Contains (*value As Object*)	Method: returns *True* if *value* is found at least once in the collection.
Count	Property: returns the number of items in the collection. Read-only, so you can read it but not change it.
IndexOf (*value As Object*)	Method: returns the Integer index position of the first occurrence of *value* in the collection. If *value* is not found, the return value is −1.
Insert (*index As Integer, item As Object*)	Method: insert *item* in the collection at position *index*. No return value.
Item (*index As Integer*)	Property: returns the object located at position *index*.
Remove (*value As Object*)	Method: removes *value* from the collection. No return value.
RemoveAt (*index As Integer*)	Method: removes the item at the specified *index*. No return value.

You have already seen examples of the `Add`, `Clear`, `Insert`, `Remove`, and `RemoveAt` methods. Let's look at examples of the remaining methods and properties shown in the table. Assume that `lstMonths` is the same list box that you created in Tutorial 5-1. The following `If...Then` statement determines whether the `lstMonths` list box's Items property contains "March". If so, it displays the message "March is found in the list." Otherwise, it displays "March is NOT found in the list."

```
If lstMonths.Items.Contains("March") Then
    MessageBox.Show("March is found in the list.")
Else
    MessageBox.Show("March is NOT found in the list.")
End If
```

In the following statement, `intIndex` is assigned the value 2 because *March* is located at index 2 in the collection.

```
intIndex = lstMonths.Items.IndexOf("March")
```

In the following statement, `strMonth` is assigned the string "April" because it is at index position 3 in the collection.

```
Dim strMonth As String = lstMonths.Items.Item(3).ToString()
```

 Checkpoint

5.3 What is the index of the first item stored in a list box's Items property?

5.4 Which list box property holds the number of items stored in the Items property?

5.5 If a list box has 12 items stored in it, what is the index of the twelfth item?

5.6 Which list box property holds the item that has been selected from the list?

5.7 Which list box property holds the index of the item that has been selected from the list?

5.8 Assume `lstNames` is a list box with 15 items and `strSelectedName` is a string variable. Write a statement that assigns the second item in `lstNames` to `strSelectedName`.

5.3 Introduction to Loops: The `Do While` Loop

CONCEPT: A loop is a repeating structure that contains a block of program statements.

Chapter 4 introduced decision structures, which direct the flow of a program along two or more paths. A **repetition structure**, or **loop** causes one or more statements to repeat. Visual Basic has three types of loops: the `Do While` loop, the `Do Until` loop, and the `For...Next` loop. The difference among them is how they control the repetition.

VideoNote

The
Do While
Loop

The `Do While` Loop

The `Do While` loop has two important parts: (1) a Boolean expression that is tested for a *True* or *False* value, and (2) a statement or group of statements that is repeated as long as the Boolean expression is true. Figure 5-11 shows a flowchart of a `Do While` loop.

Figure 5-11 Flowchart of a Do While loop

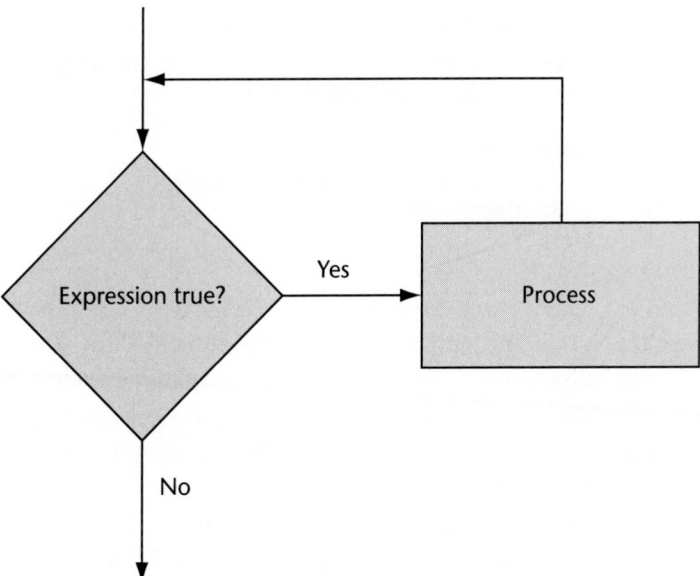

Notice the use of the diamond symbol for testing a Boolean expression. If the expression is true, the structure performs a process. Then it tests the Boolean expression again; if the expression is still true, the process is repeated. This continues as long as the Boolean expression is true when it is tested.

Here is the general format of the **Do While** loop in code:

```
Do While BooleanExpression
   statement
   (more statements may follow)
Loop
```

The statement that reads Do While is the beginning of the loop, and the statement that reads Loop is the end of the loop. The statements that appear between these two lines are known as the *body of the loop*. When the loop runs, the *BooleanExpression* is tested. If it is true, then the statements in the body of the loop are executed. Then the loop starts over and the *BooleanExpression* is tested again. If it is still true, the statements in the body of the loop are executed. This cycle repeats until the *BooleanExpression* is false.

Because the statements in the body of the loop are executed only under the condition that the Boolean expression is true, they are called **conditionally executed statements**. The Do While loop works like an If statement that executes over and over. As long as the Boolean expression is true, the conditionally executed statements will repeat. Each repetition of the loop is called an **iteration**. In Tutorial 5-2, you complete an application that demonstrates the Do While loop.

Tutorial 5-2:
Completing an application that uses the Do While loop

VideoNote

Tutorial 5-2
Walkthrough

Step 1: Open the *Do While Demo* project from the student sample programs folder named *Chap5\Do While Demo*.

Step 2: In the *Designer* window for *Form1*, double-click the *Run Demo* button to display the *Code* window.

Step 3: Complete the `btnRunDemo_Click` event handler by writing the following bold code shown in lines 2 through 7.

```
1 Private Sub btnRunDemo_Click(...) Handles btnRunDemo.Click
2    Dim intCount As Integer = 0
3
4    Do While intCount < 10
5        lstOutput.Items.Add("Hello")
6        intCount += 1
7    Loop
8 End Sub
```

Let's take a closer look at the code. Line 2 declares an Integer variable named `intCount`, and initializes it with the value 0. Line 4 is the beginning of a `Do While` loop that will execute as long as `intCount` is less than 10.

The first statement in the body of the loop appears in line 5. It adds the word *Hello* to the `lstOutput` list box. Then, line 6 uses the += combined assignment operator to add 1 to `intCount`.

The key word `Loop` appears in line 7. This marks the end of the `Do While` loop, and causes the loop to start over at line 4. Each time the loop starts over, the expression `intCount < 10` is tested. If the expression is true, the statements in the body of the loop (lines 5 and 6) are executed. If the expression is false, the loop stops and the program resumes with the statement that immediately follows the `Loop` statement in line 7. (In this code, the event handler ends immediately after the loop.)

Step 4: Save and run the application. Click the *Run Demo* button. The output should appear as shown in Figure 5-12.

Figure 5-12 Output from the *Do While Demo* application

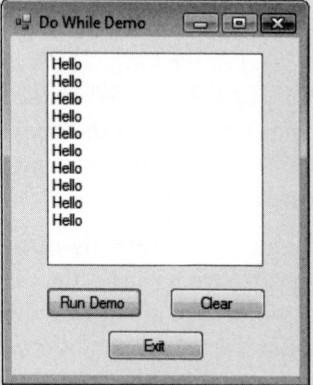

Infinite Loops

In all but rare cases, loops must contain within themselves a way to terminate. This means that something inside the `Do While` loop must eventually make the test expression false. The loop in the *Do While Demo* application stops when the variable `intCount` is no longer less than 10.

If a loop does not have a way of stopping, it is called an **infinite loop**. Infinite loops keep repeating until the program is interrupted. Here is an example:

```
intCount = 0
Do While intCount < 10
   lstOutput.Items.Add("Hello")
Loop
```

This loop will execute forever because it does not contain a statement that changes intCount. Each time the test expression is evaluated, intCount will still be equal to 0.

Programming Style and Loops

When you type the code for a loop, Visual Studio automatically indents the statements in the body of the loop. This is not a syntax requirement, but a programming style convention. For example, compare the following loops:

```
Do While intCount < 10
   lstOutput.Items.Add("Hello")
   intCount += 1
Loop

Do While intCount < 10
lstOutput.Items.Add("Hello")
intCount += 1
Loop
```

These two loops do the same thing, but the second one does not use proper indentation. In the first loop, you can quickly see which statements are repeated by the loop because they are indented.

NOTE: If the automatic indenting feature has been turned off, you can turn it on by clicking *Tools* on the menu bar, then clicking *Options*. In the *Options* window, perform the following:

- Click the *Show all settings* check box. Then, click *Text Editor* in the left pane, then click *Basic*, then click *Tabs*. Make sure *Smart* is selected in the dialog box under *Indenting*.
- In the left pane, click *VB Specific*. Make sure *Automatic Insertion of end constructs* and *Pretty listing (reformatting) of code* are both checked.

Counters

A **counter** is a variable that is regularly incremented or decremented each time a loop iterates. To increment a variable means to add 1 to its value. To decrement a variable means to subtract 1 from its value.

The following statements increment the variable intX:

```
intX = intX + 1
intX += 1
```

The following statements decrement the variable intX.

```
intX = intX − 1
intX -= 1
```

Often, a program must control or keep track of the number of iterations a loop performs. For example, the loop in the *Do While Demo* application adds *Hello* to the list box 10 times. Let's look at part of the code again.

```
Do While intCount < 10
   lstOutput.Items.Add("Hello")
   intCount += 1
Loop
```

In the code, the variable `intCount`, which starts at 0, is incremented each time through the loop. When `intCount` reaches 10, the loop stops. As a counter variable, it is regularly incremented in each iteration of the loop. In essence, `intCount` keeps track of the number of iterations the loop has performed.

TIP: `intCount` must be properly initialized. If it is initialized to 1 instead of 0, the loop will iterate only nine times.

Pretest and Posttest `Do While` Loops

The `Do While` loop can be written as a pretest loop or a posttest loop. The difference between these two types of loop is as follows:

- In a **pretest loop,** the Boolean expression is tested first. If the expression is true, the loop then executes the statements in the body of the loop. This process repeats until the Boolean expression is false.
- In a **posttest loop,** the statements in the body of the loop are executed first, and then the Boolean expression is tested. If the Boolean expression is true, the loop repeats. If the Boolean expression is false, the loop stops.

The examples that you have seen so far have all been pretest loops. An important characteristic of a pretest loop is that it will never execute if its Boolean expression is false to start with. For example, look at the following code:

```
Dim intCount As Integer = 100
Do While intCount < 10
   MessageBox.Show("Hello World!")
   intCount += 1
Loop
```

In this code the variable `intCount` is initialized with the value 100. When the `Do While` loop begins to execute, it tests the expression `intCount < 10`. Because this expression is false to start with, the loop immediately ends. The statements in the body of the loop never execute.

The `Do While` loop can also be written as a posttest loop, using the following general format:

```
Do
   Statement
   (More statements may follow)
Loop While BooleanExpression
```

Notice that in this general format, the `While BooleanExpression` clause appears at the end, after the `Loop` keyword. A loop written this way is a posttest `Do While` loop, and it tests its Boolean expression after each loop iteration. The flowchart in Figure 5-13 shows the logic of a posttest `Do While` loop.

Figure 5-13 Logic of the posttest Do While loop

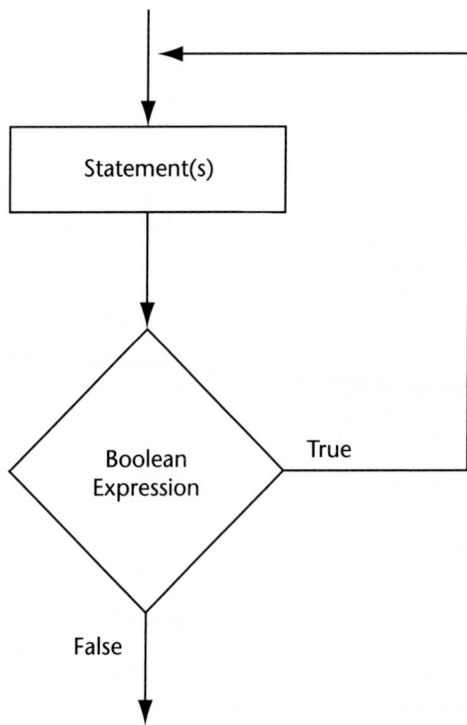

A posttest loop will always perform at least one iteration, even if its Boolean expression is false to start with. For example, look at the following code:

```
Dim intCount As Integer = 100
Do
    MessageBox.Show("Hello World!")
    intCount += 1
Loop While intCount < 10
```

In this code the variable intCount is initialized with the value 100. Then the loop begins to execute. Because this is a posttest loop, it first executes the statements in the body of the loop, and then tests the expression intCount < 10. The expression is false, so the loop stops after the first iteration.

In Tutorial 5-3, you will modify the *Do While Demo* application to use a posttest loop.

Tutorial 5-3:

Modifying the *Do While Demo* application to use a posttest loop

VideoNote

Tutorial 5-3
Walkthrough

Step 1: Open the *Do While Demo* project from the student sample programs folder named *Chap5\Do While Demo*.

Step 2: Open the *Code* window. When you wrote the btnRunDemo_Click event handler in Tutorial 5-2, you used a pretest Do While loop. In this step you will modify the loop so it is a posttest loop. Change the code to appear as follows. The modified lines of code are shown in bold.

```
      Private Sub btnRunDemo_Click(...) Handles btnRunDemo.Click
        Dim intCount As Integer = 0

        Do
            lstOutput.Items.Add("Hello")
            intCount += 1
        Loop While intCount < 10
      End Sub
```

Step 3: Run the application and click the *Run Demo* button. The loop should display *Hello* 10 times in the list box.

Step 4: Click the *Exit* button to end the application. Go back to the code for the `btnRunDemo_Click` event handler and change the less-than operator to a greater-than operator in the loop's Boolean expression. After doing this, the loop should appear as:

```
Do
    lstOutput.Items.Add("Hello")
    intCount += 1
Loop While intCount > 10
```

Although the expression `intCount > 10` is false to begin with, the statements in the body of the loop should execute once because this is a posttest loop.

Step 5: Run the application and click the *Run Demo* button. The loop should display *Hello* one time in the list box.

Step 6: Click the *Exit* button to end the application.

Keeping a Running Total

Many programming tasks require you to calculate the total of a series of numbers. For example, suppose you are writing a program that calculates a business's total sales for a week. The program would read the sales for each day as input and calculate the total of those numbers.

Programs that calculate the total of a series of numbers typically use two elements:

- A loop that reads each number in the series.
- A variable that accumulates the total of the numbers as they are read.

The variable that is used to accumulate the total of the numbers is called an **accumulator**. It is often said that the loop keeps a **running total** because it accumulates the total as it reads each number in the series. Figure 5-14 shows the general logic of a loop that calculates a running total.

When the loop finishes, the accumulator will contain the total of the numbers that were read by the loop. Notice that the first step in the flowchart is to set the accumulator variable to 0. This is a critical step. Each time the loop reads a number, it adds it to the accumulator. If the accumulator starts with any value other than 0, it will not contain the correct total when the loop finishes.

Let's look at an example. The application in Tutorial 5-4 calculates a company's total sales for five days by taking daily sales figures as input and keeping a running total of them as they are gathered.

Figure 5-14 Logic for calculating a running total

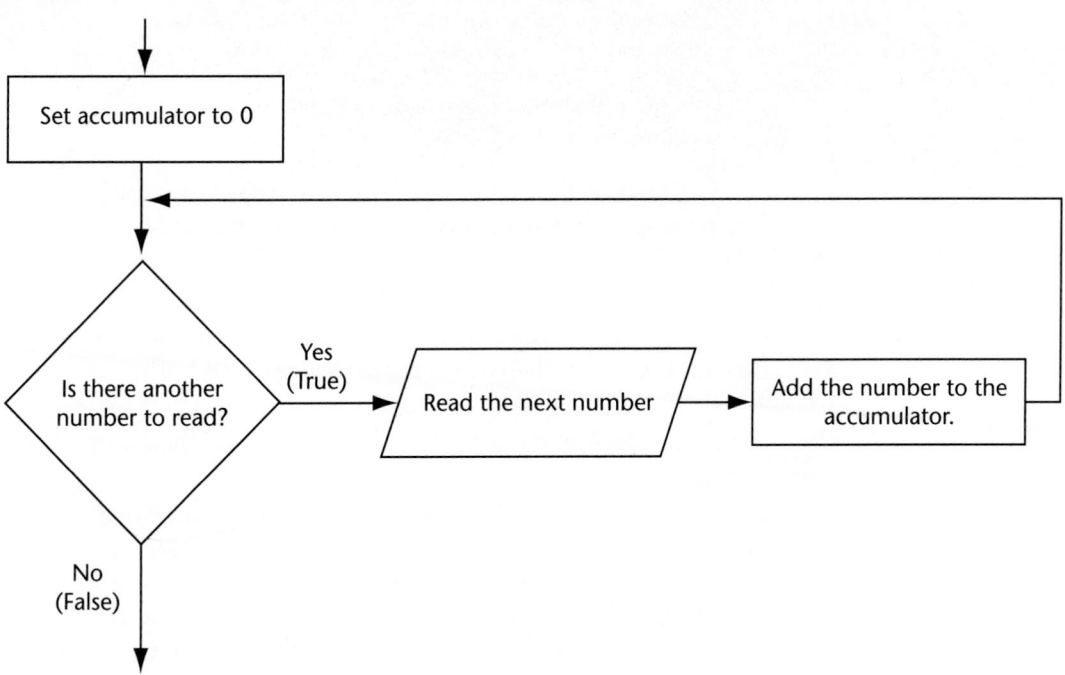

Tutorial 5-4:
Using a loop to keep a running total

In this tutorial, you will use an input box and a loop to enter five separate sales amount values. The values will be added to a total, which will be displayed.

Step 1: Open the *Running Total* project from the student sample programs folder named *Chap5\Running Total*.

Step 2: Open *Form1* in Design mode and double-click the *Enter Sales* button.

Step 3: Complete the btnEnterSales_Click event handler by writing the following bold code shown in lines 2 through 28.

```
 1 Private Sub btnEnterSales_Click(...) Handles btnEnterSales.Click
 2   Const intNUM_DAYS As Integer = 5  ' The number of days
 3   Dim intCount As Integer = 1       ' Loop counter
 4   Dim decSales As Decimal = 0       ' To hold daily sales
 5   Dim decTotal As Decimal = 0       ' To hold the total sales
 6   Dim strInput As String            ' To hold string input
 7
 8   ' Get the sales for each day.
 9   Do While intCount <= intNUM_DAYS
10     ' Get a daily sales amount from the user.
11     strInput = InputBox("Enter the sales for day " &
12                     intCount.ToString())
13
14     ' Convert the input to a Decimal.
```

```
15      If Decimal.TryParse(strInput, decSales) Then
16         ' Add the daily sales to the total sales.
17         decTotal += decSales
18
19         ' Add 1 to the loop counter.
20         intCount += 1
21      Else
22         ' Display an error message for invalid input.
23         MessageBox.Show("Enter a numeric value.")
24      End If
25   Loop
26
27   ' Display the total sales.
28   lblTotal.Text = decTotal.ToString("c")
29 End Sub
```

Let's take a closer look at the code. Here is a summary of the constant and variable declarations:

- Line 2 declares a constant named intNUM_DAYS, set to the value 5. This is the number of days of sales data we want to get from the user.
- Line 3 declares a variable named intCount that will be used as a loop counter. Notice that the variable is initialized with the value 1.
- Line 4 declares a variable named decSales that will be used to hold daily sales amounts.
- Line 5 declares a variable named decTotal that will hold the total sales. This is the accumulator variable. Notice that decTotal is initialized with the value 0. It is important that decTotal starts with the value 0 so the sum of all the sales amounts will be correct.
- Line 6 declares a variable named strInput that will hold the user's input, which is returned from the InputBox function.

The Do While loop that begins in line 9 executes as long as intCount is less than or equal to intNUM_DAYS. The statement in lines 11 and 12 displays an input box prompting the user to enter the sales for a specified day. (The first time the loop iterates, it will prompt the user to *Enter the sales for day 1*, the second time it will prompt *Enter the sales for day 2*, and so on.) The user's input is assigned, as a string, to the strInput variable.

Because the user's input is returned as a string, we need to convert it to a Decimal so we can perform math with it. That means that an exception will be thrown if the user has entered nonnumeric input. To prevent an exception, the If...Then statement in line 15 calls the Decimal.TryParse method to convert strInput to a Decimal, and store the result in the decSales variable. Recall from Chapter 4 that this method returns True if the conversion is successful, or False if the value cannot be converted to a Decimal. If the method returns False, the program will jump to the Else clause in line 21, display the error message in line 23, and then the loop starts over. If the user's input is successfully converted to a Decimal, however, decSales is added to the decTotal variable in line 17, and 1 is added to intCount in line 20. The loop then starts over.

After the loop finishes, line 28 displays the total sales in the lblTotal label.

Step 4: Save and run the program. Click the *Enter Sales* button. The input box shown in Figure 5-15 asks the user to enter the sales for day 1. Enter 1000, and click the *OK* button. (If you prefer, you may press the [Enter] key.)

Figure 5-15 Input box

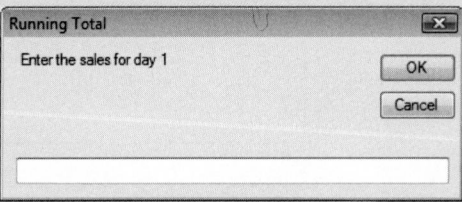

Step 5: The application will present input boxes asking for the sales for days 2, 3, 4, and 5. Enter the following amounts:

Day 2: **2000**
Day 3: **3000**
Day 4: **4000**
Day 5: **5000**

Step 6: After you enter the sales amount for all five days, the application should display the total sales as shown in Figure 5-16.

Step 7: End the program. You're finished.

Figure 5-16 Total sales displayed

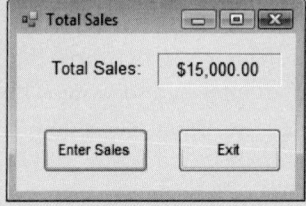

Letting the User Control the Loop

Sometimes the user must decide how many times a loop should iterate. In Tutorial 5-5, you examine a modification of the *Running Total* application. This version of the program asks the user how many days he or she has sales figures for. The application then uses that value to control the number of times the Do While loop repeats.

Tutorial 5-5:
Examining an application that uses a user-controlled loop

Step 1: Open the *User Controlled* project, from the student sample programs folder named *Chap5\User Controlled*.

Step 2: Run the application. When the form appears, click the *Enter Sales* button. The input box shown in Figure 5-17 appears.

Step 3: The input box asks you to enter the number of days you have sales figures for. Enter 3 and click the *OK* button (or press Enter).

Figure 5-17 Input box

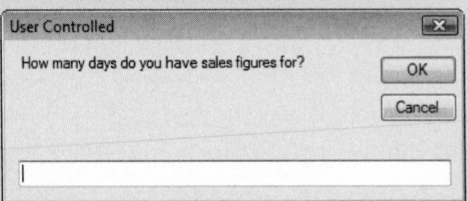

Step 4: Because you entered 3 for the number of days, the application presents three input boxes asking for the sales for days 1, 2, and 3. Enter the following values when asked:

Day 1: **1000**
Day 2: **2000**
Day 3: **3000**

Step 5: After you enter the sales figure for day 3, the application's form displays $6,000.00 as the total sales.

Step 6: Click the *Exit* button to terminate the application.

Step 7: Open the *Code* window and look at the btnEnterSales_Click event handler. Notice that this version of the code does not declare the constant intNUM_DAYS, as was used in Tutorial 5-4. This event handler has a new variable named intNumDays, declared as follows:

```
Dim intNumDays As Integer ' To hold the number of days
```

The following code that gets the number of days from the user, converts that input to an integer, and assigns the result to intNumDays:

```
' Get the number of days from the user.
strInput = InputBox("How many days do you have sales figures for?")

' Convert the user's input to an integer.
intNumDays = CInt(strInput)
```

After this code executes, intNumDays will hold the number of days specified by the user. Then, notice the first line of the Do While loop:

```
Do While intCount <= intNumDays
```

The loop repeats while intCount is less than or equal to intNumDays, the value specified by the user. As a result, the number of loop iterations will be equal to the number of days specified by the user.

Checkpoint

5.9 How many times will the following code segment display the message box?

```
Dim intCount As Integer = 0
Do While intCount < 10
  MessageBox.Show("I love Visual Basic!")
Loop
```

5.10 How many times will the following code segment display the message box?

```
Dim intCount As Integer = 0
Do While intCount < 10
  MessageBox.Show("I love Visual Basic!")
  intCount += 1
Loop
```

5.11 How many times will the following code segment display the message box?
```
Dim intCount As Integer = 100
Do
   MessageBox.Show("I love Visual Basic!")
   intCount += 1
Loop While intCount < 10
```

5.12 In the following code segment, which variable is the counter and which is the accumulator?
```
Dim intA As Integer
Dim intX As Integer
Dim intY As Integer
Dim intZ As Integer
Dim strInput As String
intX = 0
intY = 0
strInput = InputBox("How many numbers do you wish to enter?")
intZ = CInt(strInput)
Do While intX < intZ
   strInput = InputBox("Enter a number.")
   intA = CInt(strInput)
   intY += intA
   intX += 1
Loop
MessageBox.Show("The sum of those numbers is " & intY.ToString())
```

5.13 The following loop adds the numbers 1 through 5 to the lstOutput list box. Modify the loop so that instead of starting at 1 and counting to 5, it starts at 5 and counts backward to 1.
```
Dim intCount As Integer = 1
Do While intCount <= 5
   lstOutput.Items.Add(intCount)
   intCount += 1
Loop
```

5.14 Write a Do While loop that uses an input box to ask the user to enter a number. The loop should keep a running total of the numbers entered and stop when the total is greater than 300.

5.15 If you want a Do While loop always to iterate at least once, which form should you use, pretest or posttest?

5.4 The Do Until **and** For...Next **Loops**

CONCEPT: The Do Until loop iterates until its test expression is true. The For...Next loop uses a counter variable and iterates a specific number of times.

The Do Until **Loop**

The Do While loop iterates as long as a Boolean expression is true. Sometimes, however, it is more convenient to write a loop that iterates *until* an expression is true—that is, a loop that iterates as long as an expression is false, and then stops when the expression becomes true.

For example, consider a machine in an automobile factory that paints cars as they move down the assembly line. When there are no more cars to paint, the machine stops. If you were programming such a machine, you might want to design a loop that causes the machine to paint cars until there are no more cars on the assembly line.

A loop that iterates until a condition is true is known as a **Do Until** loop. The Do Until loop can be written as either a pretest or a posttest loop. Here is the general format of a pretest Do Until loop:

```
Do Until BooleanExpression
    Statement
    (More statements may follow)
Loop
```

Here is the general format of a posttest Do Until loop:

```
Do
    Statement
    (More statements may follow)
Loop Until BooleanExpression
```

In Tutorial 5-6, you examine an application that uses the Do Until loop. The application asks the user to enter test scores, and then displays the average of the scores.

Tutorial 5-6:
Examining an application that uses the Do Until loop

Step 1: Open the *Test Scores* project from the student sample programs folder named *Chap5\Test Scores*.

Step 2: Run the application. The form appears, as shown in Figure 5-18.

Step 3: Click the *Get Scores* button. The input box shown in Figure 5-19 appears.

Figure 5-18 *Test Score Average* form

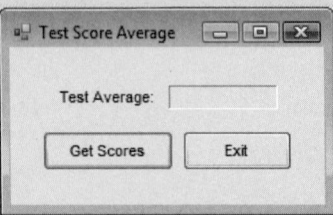

Figure 5-19 Input box

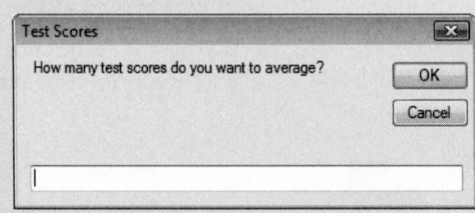

Step 4: Enter **5** for the number of test scores and click the *OK* button (or press Enter).

Step 5: Because you entered 5 for the number of test scores, the application presents five input boxes asking for scores 1, 2, 3, 4, and 5. Enter the following values when asked.

Test Score 1: **98**   Test Score 3: **100**   Test Score 5: **92**
Test Score 2: **87**   Test Score 4: **74**

Step 6: After you enter the fifth test score, the test score average 90.2 is displayed on the application form. Click the *Exit* button to end the application.

Step 7: Open the *Code* window. The application's code is shown, with line numbers for reference, at the end of the tutorial. Let's look at the `btnGetScores_Click` event handler in greater detail:

- Local variables are declared in lines 6 through 11. Notice that the `dblTotal` variable (line 8) is initialized to 0. This variable is used as an accumulator. Also notice that the `intCount` variable (line 11) is initialized to 1. This variable is used as a loop counter.
- Line 14 displays the input box prompting the user for the number of test scores. The input is assigned to `strInput`.
- The `If...Then` statement in line 17 uses the `Integer.TryParse` method to convert `strInput` to an Integer, and store the result in `intNumScores`. If the conversion is successful, the `Integer.TryParse` method returns `True` and the program continues to line 20. If the conversion fails (because of invalid input), the `Integer.TryParse` method returns `False`, and the program jumps to the `Else` clause in line 45. If this happens, line 47 displays an error message, and the event handler ends.
- The `Do Until` loop that begins in line 20 iterates until `intCount` is greater than `intNumScores`. Inside the loop, lines 22 and 23 prompt the user for a test score, storing the user's input in `strInput`. The `If...Then` statement in line 26 uses the `Double.TryParse` method to convert `strInput` to a Double, and store the result in `dblTestScore`. If the conversion is successful, the `Double.TryParse` method returns `True` and the program continues to line 29. If the conversion fails (because of invalid input), the `Double.TryParse` method returns `False`, and the program jumps to the `Else` clause in line 33. If this happens, line 35 displays an error message, and the event handler ends.
- Line 29 uses the `+=` operator to add `dblTestScore` to the accumulator variable `dblTotal`.
- Line 32 uses the `+=` operator to add 1 to the counter variable `intCount`.
- After the loop has finished, the `If...Then` statement in line 40 determines whether `intNumScores` is greater than 0. If so, line 41 calculates the average test score, and line 42 displays the average in the `lblAverage` label.

```
1 Public Class Form1
2
3    Private Sub btnGetScores_Click(...) Handles btnGetScores.Click
4        ' This procedure gets the test scores, then calculates and
5        ' displays the average.
6        Dim intNumScores As Integer    ' The number of test scores
7        Dim dblTestScore As Double     ' To hold a test score
8        Dim dblTotal As Double = 0     ' Accumulator, initialized to 0
9        Dim dblAverage As Double       ' The average of the test scores
10       Dim strInput As String         ' To hold user input
11       Dim intCount As Integer = 1    ' Counter variable, initialized to 1
12
13       ' Prompt the user for the number of test scores.
14       strInput = InputBox("How many test scores do you want to average?")
15
16       ' Convert the input to an integer.
17       If Integer.TryParse(strInput, intNumScores) Then
18
19          ' Get the test scores.
20          Do Until intCount > intNumScores
```

```
21          ' Prompt the user for a score.
22          strInput = InputBox("Enter test score " &
23                               intCount.ToString())
24
25          ' Convert the input to a Double.
26          If Double.TryParse(strInput, dblTestScore) Then
27
28              ' Add the score to the accumulator.
29              dblTotal += dblTestScore
30
31              ' Add 1 to the counter.
32              intCount += 1
33          Else
34              ' Invalid test score.
35              MessageBox.Show("Enter a numeric test score.")
36          End If
37      Loop
38
39      ' Calculate and display the average.
40      If intNumScores > 0 Then
41          dblAverage = dblTotal / intNumScores
42          lblAverage.Text = dblAverage.ToString()
43      End If
44
45    Else
46      ' Invalid number of test scores.
47      MessageBox.Show("Enter an integer value for number of test scores.")
48    End If
49  End Sub
50
51  Private Sub btnExit_Click(...) Handles btnExit.Click
52    ' Close the form.
53    Me.Close()
54  End Sub
55 End Class
```

The `For...Next` Loop

VideoNote

The
For...
Next Loop

The `For...Next` loop is ideal for situations that require a counter because it initializes, tests, and increments a counter variable. Here is the format of the **`For...Next`** loop:

```
For CounterVariable = StartValue To EndValue [Step Increment]
   statement
 (more statements may follow)
 Next [CounterVariable]
```

As usual, the brackets are not part of the syntax, but indicate the optional parts. Let's look closer at the syntax.

- *CounterVariable* is the variable to be used as a counter. It must be a numeric variable.
- *StartValue* is the value the counter variable will be initially set to. This value must be numeric.
- *EndValue* is the value the counter variable is tested against just prior to each iteration of the loop. This value must be numeric.
- The `Step` *Increment* part of the statement is optional. If it is present, *Increment* (which must be a numeric expression) is the amount added to the counter variable at the end of each iteration. If the `Step` *Increment* part of the statement is omitted, the counter variable is incremented by 1 at the end of each iteration.

- The Next [*CounterVariable*] statement marks the end of the loop and causes the counter variable to be incremented. Notice that the name of the counter variable is optional.

Here is an example of the For...Next loop:

```
For intCount = 1 To 10
    MessageBox.Show("Hello")
Next
```

This loop executes the MessageBox.Show("Hello") statement 10 times. The following steps take place when the loop executes.

1. intCount is set to 1 (the start value).
2. intCount is compared to 10 (the end value). If intCount is less than or equal to 10, continue to Step 3. Otherwise the loop is exited.
3. The MessageBox.Show("Hello") statement in the body of the loop is executed.
4. intCount is incremented by 1.
5. Go back to Step 2 and repeat this sequence.

The flowchart shown in Figure 5-20 shows loop's actions.

 WARNING: It is incorrect to place a statement in the body of the For...Next loop that changes the counter variable's value. For example, the following loop increments intX twice for each iteration.

```
' Warning!
For intCount = 1 To 10
    MessageBox.Show("Hello")
    intCount += 1
Next
```

Figure 5-20 Flowchart of For...Next loop

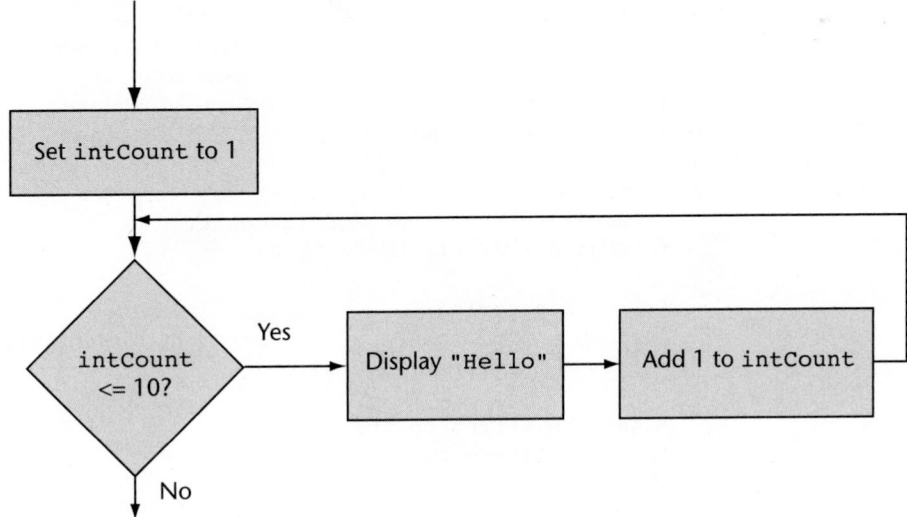

In Tutorial 5-7, you examine an application that demonstrates the For...Next loop.

 NOTE: Because the For...Next loop performs its test prior to each iteration, it is a pretest loop. Unlike the Do While and Do Until loops, this is the only form the For...Next loop may be written in.

Tutorial 5-7:
Examining an application that uses the `For...Next` loop

Step 1: Open the *For Next Demo 1* project from the student sample programs folder named *Chap5\For Next Demo 1*.

Step 2: Run the application. The form appears as shown in Figure 5-21.

Step 3: Click the *Run Demo* button. The form now appears as shown in Figure 5-22.

Figure 5-21 *For...Next Demo 1* form

Figure 5-22 Results of `For...Next` loop

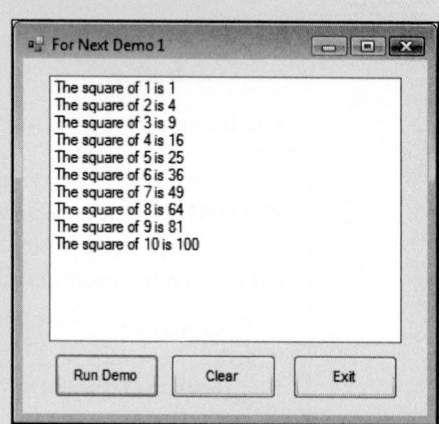

Step 4: Click the *Exit* button to terminate the application.

Step 5: Open the *Code* window and find the `btnRunDemo_Click` event handler. The code is as follows:

```
Private Sub btnRunDemo_Click(...) Handles btnRunDemo.Click
    Dim intCount As Integer        ' Loop counter
    Dim intSquare As Integer       ' To hold squares
    Dim strTemp As String          ' To hold output

    For intCount = 1 To 10
        ' Calculate the square of intCount.
        intSquare = CInt(intCount ^ 2)

        ' Create a string to display.
        strTemp = "The square of " & intCount.ToString() &
          " is " & intSquare.ToString()

        ' Add the string to the list box.
        lstOutput.Items.Add(strTemp)
    Next
End Sub
```

Figure 5-23 illustrates the order of the steps taken by the `For...Next` loop in this program.

Figure 5-23 Steps in For...Next loop

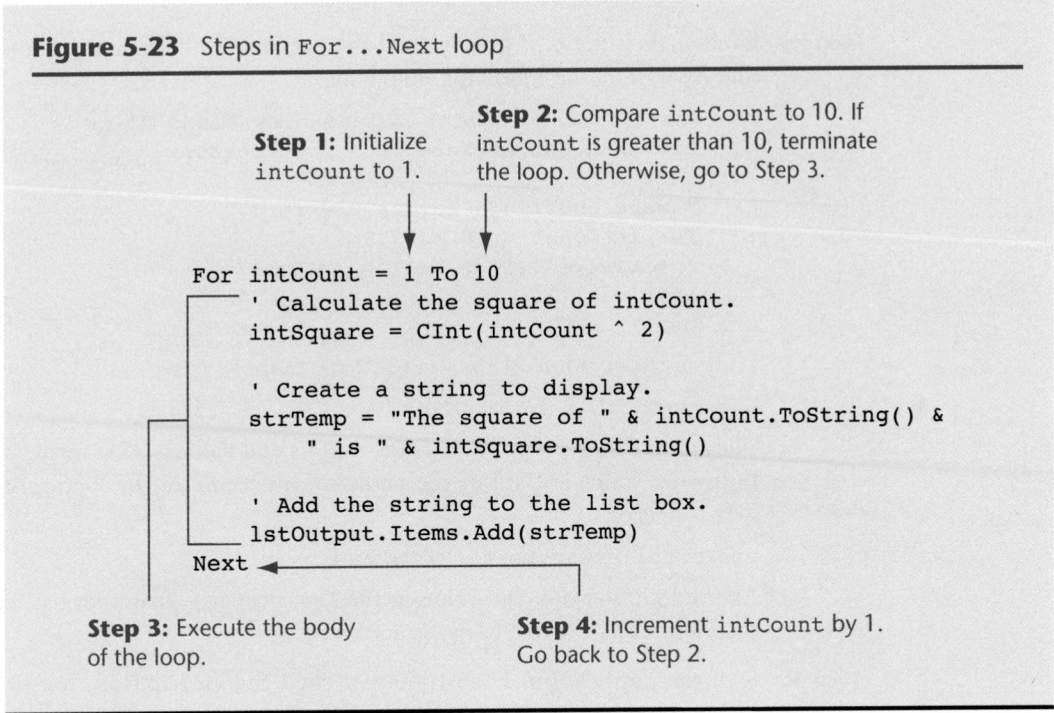

Step 1: Initialize intCount to 1.

Step 2: Compare intCount to 10. If intCount is greater than 10, terminate the loop. Otherwise, go to Step 3.

```
For intCount = 1 To 10
    ' Calculate the square of intCount.
    intSquare = CInt(intCount ^ 2)

    ' Create a string to display.
    strTemp = "The square of " & intCount.ToString() &
        " is " & intSquare.ToString()

    ' Add the string to the list box.
    lstOutput.Items.Add(strTemp)
Next
```

Step 3: Execute the body of the loop.

Step 4: Increment intCount by 1. Go back to Step 2.

In Tutorial 5-8, you complete a partially written application. The application will use a graphic image and a For...Next loop to perform a simple animation.

 Tutorial 5-8:

Completing an application that uses the For...Next loop

Step 1: Open the *For Next Demo 2* project from the student sample programs folder named *Chap5\For Next Demo 2*.

Step 2: Open the application's form, as shown in Figure 5-24.

Figure 5-24 *For Next Demo 2* form

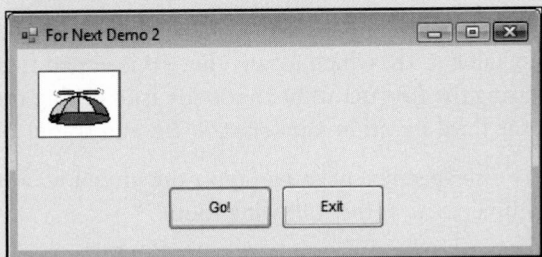

The propeller cap graphic is displayed by a PictureBox control. The PictureBox control has a Left property that specifies the distance from the left edge of the form to the left edge of the PictureBox control. (The distance is measured in pixels.) In this tutorial, you will write a For...Next loop that makes the image move across the form by increasing the value of the PictureBox control's Left property.

 NOTE: The PictureBox control's Left property does not appear in the Properties window. You access the Left property in code.

Step 3: Double-click the *Go!* button, and then complete the `btnGo_Click` event handler by writing the following bold code.

```
Private Sub btnGo_Click(...) Handles btnGo.Click
    Dim intCount As Integer ' Loop counter

    ' Move the image across the form.
    For intCount = 16 To 328
      picPropellerCap.Left = intCount
    Next
End Sub
```

Look at the first line of the `For...Next` loop:

```
For intCount = 16 To 328
```

The start value for `intCount` is 16, and its end value is 328. Inside the loop, the following statement stores the value of `intCount` in the PictureBox control's Left property:

```
picPropellerCap.Left = intCount
```

As the loop iterates, the value in the Left property grows larger, which causes the PictureBox control to move across the form.

Step 4: Run the application. Each time you click the *Go!* button, the propeller cap image should move from the form's left edge to its right edge.

Step 5: Click the *Exit* button to end the application. If you wish, open the *Code* window and experiment with different start and end values for the `For...Next` loop.

Specifying a Step Value

The **step value** is the value added to the counter variable at the end of each iteration of the `For...Next` loop. By default, the step value is 1. You can specify a different step value with the `Step` keyword. For example, look at the following code:

```
For intCount = 0 To 100 Step 10
   MessageBox.Show(intCount.ToString())
Next
```

In this loop, the starting value of `intCount` is 0 and the ending value of `intCount` is 100. The step value is 10, which means that 10 is added to `intCount` at the end of each iteration. During the first iteration `intCount` is 0, during the second iteration `intCount` is 10, during the third iteration `intCount` is 20, and so on.

You may also specify a negative step value if you want to decrement the counter variable. For example, look at the following loop:

```
For intCount = 10 To 1 Step -1
   MessageBox.Show(intCount.ToString())
Next
```

In this loop the starting value of `intCount` is 10 and the ending value of `intCount` is 1. The step value is -1, which means that 1 is subtracted from `intCount` at the end of each iteration. During the first iteration `intCount` is 10, during the second iteration `intCount` is 9, and so on.

Summing a Series of Numbers with the `For...Next` Loop

The `For...Next` loop can be used to calculate the sum of a series of numbers, as shown in the following code:

```
Dim intCount As Integer          ' Loop counter
Dim intTotal As Integer = 0      ' Accumulator

' Add the numbers 1 through 100.
For intCount = 1 To 100
    intTotal += intCount
Next

' Display the sum of the numbers.
MessageBox.Show("The sum of 1 through 100 is " & intTotal.ToString())
```

This code uses the variable `intTotal` as an accumulator, and calculates the sum of the numbers from 1 through 100. The counter variable, `intCount`, has a starting value of 1 and an ending value of 100. During each iteration, the value of `intCount` is added to `intTotal`.

You may also let the user specify how many numbers to sum, as well as the value of each number. For example, look at the following code:

```
1  Dim intCount As Integer          ' Loop counter
2  Dim intMaxCount As Integer       ' To hold the maximum count
3  Dim dblTotal As Double = 0.0     ' Accumulator
4  Dim strInput As String           ' To hold user input
5  Dim dblNum As Double             ' To hold a number
6
7  ' Get the number of numbers to sum.
8  strInput = InputBox("How many numbers to you want to sum?")
9  intMaxCount = CInt(strInput)
10
11 ' Add the user-specified numbers.
12 For intCount = 1 To intMaxCount
13     ' Get a number.
14     strInput = InputBox("Enter a number.")
15     dblNum = CDbl(strInput)
16
17     ' Add the number to the accumulator.
18     dblTotal += dblNum
19 Next
20
21 ' Display the sum of the numbers.
22 MessageBox.Show("The sum of those numbers is " &
23                 dblTotal.ToString())
```

For simplicity, we have left out exception handlers, or other code to validate the user input. Line 8 prompts the user for the number of numbers to sum, and line 9 stores the user's input in the `intMaxCount` variable. In line 12, which is the beginning of the `For...Next` loop, the `intCount` variable has a starting value of 1, and an ending value of `intMaxCount`. As a result, the number of iterations will be the value stored in `intMaxCount`.

In line 14, an input box is used to prompt the user for a number. In line 15, the value entered by the user is stored in the `dblNum` variable. Line 18 adds `dblNum` to the `dblTotal` variable, which is the accumulator.

Optional Topic: Breaking Out of a Loop

In rare circumstances, you might find it necessary to stop a loop before it goes through all of its iterations. Visual Basic provides the `Exit Do` statement, that allows you to prematurely break out of a Do While loop, and the Exit For statement, that allows you to prematurely break out of a For...Next loop. The way they work is simple:

- When a Do While loop is executing, if it encounters an Exit Do statement, the loop immediately ends.
- When a For...Next loop is executing, if it encounters an Exit For statement, the loop immediately ends.

You should do your best to avoid using these statements, however. They bypass the normal logic that terminates the loop, and make the code more difficult to understand and debug.

Deciding Which Loop to Use

Although most repetitive algorithms can be written with any of the three types of loops, each works best in different situations.

The Do While Loop

Use the Do While loop when you wish the loop to repeat as long as the test expression is true. You can write the Do While loop as a pretest or posttest loop. Pretest Do While loops are ideal when you do not want the code in the loop to execute if the test expression is false from the beginning. Posttest loops are ideal when you always want the code in the loop to execute at least once.

The Do Until Loop

Use the Do Until loop when you wish the loop to repeat until the test expression is true. You can write the Do Until loop as a pretest or posttest loop. Pretest Do Until loops are ideal when you do not want the code in the loop to execute if the test expression is true from the beginning. Posttest loops are ideal when you always want the code in the loop to execute at least once.

The For...Next Loop

The For...Next loop is a pretest loop that first initializes a counter variable to a starting value. It automatically increments the counter variable at the end of each iteration. The loop repeats as long as the counter variable is not greater than an end value. The For...Next loop is primarily used when the number of required iterations is known.

 Checkpoint

5.16 How many times will the code inside the following loop execute? What will be displayed in the message box?

```
intX = 0
Do Until intX = 10
    intX += 2
Loop
MessageBox.Show(intX.ToString())
```

5.17 Write a For...Next loop that adds every fifth number, starting at zero, through 100, to the list box lstOutput.

5.18 Write a For...Next loop that repeats seven times, each time displaying an input box that asks the user to enter a number. The loop should also calculate and display the sum of the numbers entered.

5.19 Which type of loop is best to use when you know exactly how many times the loop should repeat?

5.20 Which type of loop is best to use when you want the loop to repeat as long as a condition exists?

5.21 Which type of loop is best to use when you want the loop to repeat until a condition exists?

5.5 Nested Loops

CONCEPT: A loop that is contained inside another loop is called a nested loop.

A **nested loop** is a loop inside another loop. A clock is a good example of something that works like a nested loop. The second hand, minute hand, and hour hand all spin around the face of the clock. The hour hand, however, makes only one revolution for every 60 of the minute hand's revolutions. And it takes 60 revolutions of the second hand for the minute hand to make one revolution. This means that for every complete revolution of the hour hand, the second hand revolves 3,600 times.

The following is a code segment with a `For...Next` loop that partially simulates a digital clock. It displays the seconds from 0 through 59 in a label named `lblSeconds`.

```
For intSeconds = 0 To 59
    lblSeconds.Text = intSeconds.ToString()
Next
```

We can add a minutes variable and another label, and nest the loop inside another loop that cycles through 60 minutes:

```
For intMinutes = 0 To 59
    lblMinutes.Text = intMinutes.ToString()
    For intSeconds = 0 To 59
        lblSeconds.Text = intSeconds.ToString()
    Next
Next
```

To make the simulated clock complete, another variable, label, and loop can be added to count the hours:

```
For intHours = 0 To 23
    lblHours.Text = intHours.ToString()
    For intMinutes = 0 To 59
        lblMinutes.Text = intMinutes.ToString()
        For intSeconds = 0 To 59
            lblSeconds.Text = intSeconds.ToString()
        Next
    Next
Next
```

The innermost loop will iterate 60 times for each iteration of the middle loop. The middle loop will iterate 60 times for each iteration of the outermost loop. When the outermost loop has iterated 24 times, the middle loop will have iterated 1,440 times and the innermost loop will have iterated 86,400 times.

The simulated clock example brings up a few points about nested loops:

- An inner loop goes through all of its iterations for each iteration of an outer loop.
- Inner loops complete their iterations before outer loops do.
- To get the total number of iterations of a nested loop, multiply the number of iterations of all the loops.

 **Checkpoint**

5.22 What values will the following code segment add to the `lstNumbers` list box?

```
For intX = 1 To 3
    lstNumbers.Items.Add(intX)
    For intY = 1 To 2
        lstNumbers.Items.Add(intY)
    Next
Next
```

5.23 How many times will the value in `intY` be displayed in the following code segment?

```
For intX = 1 To 20
    For intY = 1 To 30
        MessageBox.Show(intY.ToString())
    Next
Next
```

5.6 Multicolumn List Boxes, Checked List Boxes, and Combo Boxes

CONCEPT: A multicolumn list box displays items in columns with a horizontal scroll bar, if necessary. A checked list box displays a check box next to each item in the list. A combo box performs many of the same functions as a list box, and it can also let the user enter text.

Multicolumn List Boxes

The ListBox control has a Multicolumn property that can be set to *True* or *False*. By default, it is set to *False*. If you set Multicolumn to *True*, it causes the list box to display its list in columns. You set the size of the columns, in pixels, with the ColumnWidth property. For example, suppose a form has a list box named `lstNumbers`, as shown in Figure 5-25.

The list box's Multicolumn property is set to *True*, and its ColumnWidth property is set to *30*. The following code adds the numbers 0 through 100 to a list box:

```
For intNumber = 0 To 100
    lstNumbers.Items.Add(intNumber)
Next
```

After the code executes, the list box appears as shown in Figure 5-26.

Notice that a horizontal scroll bar automatically appears in the list box. The user may scroll through the list and select a number.

Checked List Boxes

The CheckedListBox control is a variation of the ListBox control. It supports all ListBox properties and methods discussed in Section 5.2. Each item in a CheckedListBox control, however, is displayed with a check box next to it. Figure 5-27 shows an example.

An item in a checked list box may be selected and/or checked. Only one item in a checked list box may be selected at a given time, but multiple items may be checked.

Figure 5-25 List box

Figure 5-26 List box with multicolumn display

Figure 5-27 Checked list box

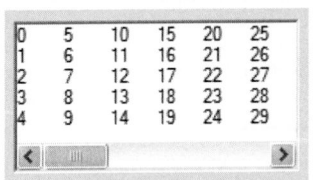

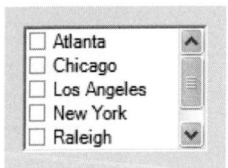

This is how the CheckOnClick property determines whether items become checked:

- When set to *False*, the user clicks an item once to select it, and then clicks it again to check it (or uncheck it, if it is already checked).
- When set to *True*, the user clicks an item only once to both select it and check it (or uncheck it, if it is already checked).

The CheckOnClick property is set to *False* by default. Because this setting makes working with the control a bit complicated, you may prefer setting it to *True* for most applications.

You can access the selected item in a checked list box exactly as you do with a regular list box: through the SelectedIndex and SelectedItem properties. These properties only indicate which item is selected, however, and do not report which items are checked. You access the checked items through the `GetItemChecked` method, which has the following general format:

```
CheckedListBox.GetItemChecked(Index)
```

`CheckedListBox` is the name of the CheckedListBox control. `Index` is the index of an item in the list. If the item is checked, the method returns *True*. Otherwise, it returns *False*. For example, assume an application has a checked list box name `clbCities`. (`clb` is the prefix for checked list boxes.) The following code counts the number of checked items:

```
Dim intIndex As Integer             ' List box index
Dim intCheckedCities As Integer = 0 ' To count the checked cities

' Step through the items in the list box, counting
' the number of checked items.
For intIndex = 0 To clbCities.Items.Count - 1
  If clbCities.GetItemChecked(intIndex) = True Then
    intCheckedCities += 1
  End If
Next

' Display the number of checked cities.
MessageBox.Show("You checked " & intCheckedCities.ToString() &
                " cities.")
```

As another example, assume an application uses the controls shown in Figure 5-28. The checked list box on the left is `clbCities` and the list box on the right is `lstChecked`. The *OK* button, `btnOk`, uses the following Click event handler:

```
Private Sub btnOk_Click(...) Handles btnOk.Click
  Dim intIndex As Integer ' List box index

  For intIndex = 0 To clbCities.Items.Count - 1
    If clbCities.GetItemChecked(intIndex) = True Then
      lstChecked.Items.Add(clbCities.Items(intIndex))
    End If
  Next
End Sub
```

The `btnOk_Click` event handler adds the items checked in the `clbCities` control to the `lstChecked` control. Figure 5-29 shows how the controls appear after the user has checked three cities and clicked the *OK* button.

Figure 5-28 Checked list box
and a list box

Figure 5-29 Cities checked

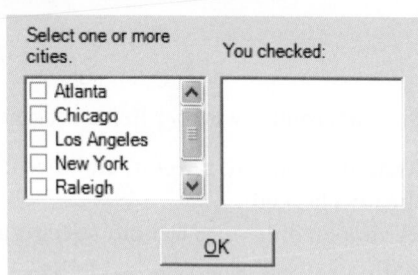

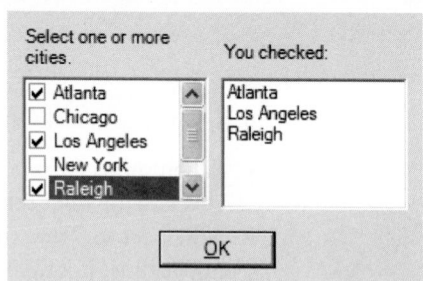

Combo Boxes

Combo boxes and list boxes are similar in the following ways:

- They both display a list of items to the user.
- They both have Items, Items.Count, SelectedIndex, SelectedItem, and Sorted properties.
- They both have `Items.Add`, `Items.Clear`, `Items.Remove`, and `Items.RemoveAt` methods.
- All of these properties and methods work the same with combo boxes and list boxes.

Additionally, a combo box has a rectangular area that works like a text box. The user may either select an item from the combo box's list or type text into the combo box's text input area.

Like a text box, the combo box has a Text property. If the user types text into the combo box, the text is stored in the Text property. Also, when the user selects an item from the combo box's list, the item is copied to the Text property.

The prefix that we use for combo box names is `cbo`.

Combo Box Styles

There are three different styles of combo boxes: the drop-down combo box, the simple combo box, and the drop-down list combo box. You can select a combo box's style with its DropDownStyle property. Let's look at the differences of each style.

The Drop-Down Combo Box

This is the default setting for the combo box DropDownStyle property. At runtime, a drop-down combo box appears like the one shown in Figure 5-30.

This style of combo box behaves like either a text box or a list box. The user may either type text into the box (like a text box) or click the down arrow (⏷). If the user clicks the down arrow, a list of items drops down, as shown in Figure 5-31.

Now the user may select an item from the list. When the user selects an item, it appears in the text input area at the top of the box, and is copied to the combo box's Text property.

NOTE: When typing text into the combo box, the user may enter a string that does not appear in the drop-down list.

Figure 5-30 A drop-down combo box

Figure 5-31 A list drops down when the user clicks the down arrow

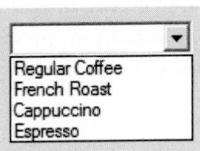

 TIP: When the combo box has the focus, the user may also press [Alt] + [↓] to drop the list down. This is also true for the drop-down list combo box.

The Simple Combo Box

With the simple style of combo box, the list of items does not drop down but is always displayed. Figure 5-32 shows an example.

As with the drop-down combo box, this style allows the user to type text directly into the combo box or select from the list. When typing, the user is not restricted to the items that appear in the list. When an item is selected from the list, it is copied to the text input area and to the combo box's Text property.

Drop-Down List Combo Box

With drop-down list combo box style, the user may not type text directly into the combo box. An item must be selected from the list. Figure 5-33 shows a drop-down list combo box.

When the user clicks the down arrow, a list of items appears, as shown in Figure 5-34.

Figure 5-33 The drop-down list combo box

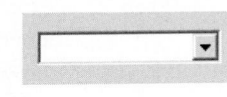

Figure 5-32 The simple combo box

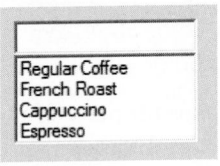

Figure 5-34 A list drops down when the user clicks the down arrow

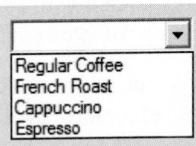

When the user selects an item from the list, it is copied to the text area at the top of the combo box and to the Text property. Because the user can only select items from the list, it is not possible to enter text that does not appear in the list.

Getting the User's Input from a Combo Box

As with the list box, you can determine which item has been selected from a combo box's list by retrieving the value in the SelectedIndex or SelectedItem properties. If the user has typed text into the combo box's text area, however, you cannot use the SelectedIndex or SelectedItem properties to get the text. The best way to get the user's input is with the Text property, which contains either the user's text input or the item selected from the list.

NOTE: The drop-down list combo box's Text property is read-only. You cannot change its value with code.

List Boxes versus Combo Boxes

The following guidelines help you decide when to use a list box and when to use a combo box.

- Use a drop-down or simple combo box when you want to provide the user a list of items to select from but do not want to limit the user's input to the items on the list.
- Use a list box or a drop-down list combo box when you want to limit the user's selection to a list of items. The drop-down list combo box generally takes less space than a list box (because the list doesn't appear until the user clicks the down arrow), so use it when you want to conserve space on the form.

In Tutorial 5-9, you create three styles of combo boxes.

Tutorial 5-9:

Creating combo boxes

In this tutorial, you will create each of the three styles of combo boxes.

Step 1: Create a new Windows Forms Application project named *Combo Box Demo*.

Step 2: Set up the form like the one shown in Figure 5-35. Create three combo boxes: cboCountries (drop-down combo box), cboPlays (simple combo box), and cboArtists (drop-down list combo box).

Step 3: Enter the following items into the Items property of the cboCountries combo box: **England, Ireland, Scotland,** and **Wales**. Set the combo box's Sorted property to *True*.

Step 4: Enter the following items into the Items property of the cboPlays combo box: **Hamlet, Much Ado about Nothing, Romeo and Juliet, A Comedy of Errors,** and **The Merchant of Venice.** Set the combo box's Sorted property to *True*.

Step 5: Enter the following items into the Items property of the cboArtists combo box: **Michelangelo, Raphael,** and **da Vinci.**

Figure 5-35 *Combo Box Demo* form

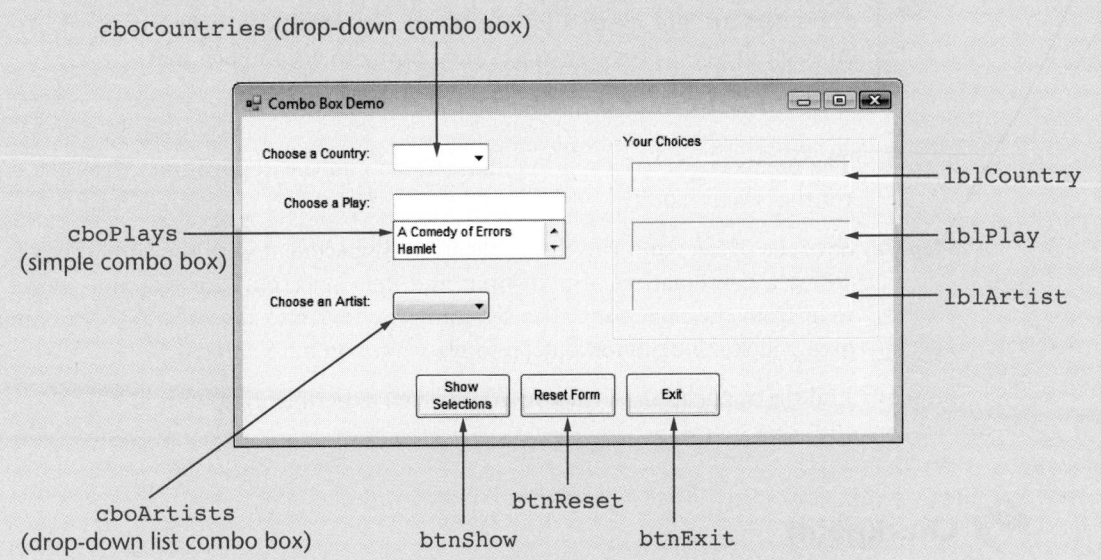

Step 6: The btnShow_Click event handler should perform the following tasks:
- Copy the selected item or typed text from the cboCountries combo box to the lblCountry.Text property.
- Copy the selected item or typed text from the cboPlays combo box to the lblPlay.Text property.
- Copy the selected item from the cboArtists combo box to the lblArtist.Text property.

Enter the following code shown in bold for the btnShow_Click event handler:

```
Private Sub btnShow_Click(...) Handles btnShow.Click
    ' Display the combo box selections.
    lblCountry.Text = cboCountries.Text
    lblPlay.Text = cboPlays.Text
    lblArtist.Text = cboArtists.Text
End Sub
```

Step 7: The btnReset_Click event handler should deselect any items that are selected in the combo boxes. As with list boxes, this is accomplished by setting the SelectedIndex property to –1. The procedure should also set the Text property of lblCountry, lblPlay, and lblArtist to String.Empty. Enter the following code, shown in bold, for the btnReset_Click event handler.

```
Private Sub btnReset_Click(...) Handles btnReset.Click
    ' Reset the combo boxes.
    cboCountries.SelectedIndex = -1
    cboCountries.Text = String.Empty
    cboPlays.SelectedIndex = -1
    cboPlays.Text = String.Empty
    cboArtists.SelectedIndex = -1
    ' Note: cboArtists.Text is read-only.

    ' Reset the labels.
    lblCountry.Text = String.Empty
    lblPlay.Text = String.Empty
    lblArtist.Text = String.Empty
End Sub
```

> **NOTE:** If the user types characters into a combo box's text input area, those characters are not cleared by setting the SelectedIndex property to –1. You must set the Text property to `String.Empty` to accomplish that.

Step 8: The `btnExit_Click` event handler should end the application. Write the code for that event handler.

Step 9: Save the project and run the application. Experiment with the combo boxes by trying a combination of text input and item selection. For example, select an item from the `cboCountries` list and type text into the `cboPlays'` text input area. Click the `btnShow` button to see what you have entered.

Step 10: End the application when you are finished experimenting with it.

Checkpoint

5.24 What is the index of the first item stored in a list box or combo box's Items property?

5.25 Which list box or combo box property holds the number of items stored in the Items property?

5.26 Which list box or combo box property holds the index of the item selected from the list?

5.27 What is the difference between a drop-down and drop-down list combo box?

5.28 What is the best method of getting the user's input from a combo box?

5.29 Suppose you want to place a list box on a form, but it would take up too much space. What other control might you use?

5.7 Random Numbers

CONCEPT: Visual Basic provides tools to generate random numbers and initialize the sequence of random numbers with a random seed value.

Computer applications such as games and simulations often create what appear to be random events. A program simulating a traffic intersection, for example, might generate random numbers of simulated vehicles. Based on information provided during the simulation, planners can estimate the average amount of time drivers spend waiting at the stoplight. Similarly, random numbers can simulate the movements of stock prices, using various rules about how stock prices change.

Unfortunately, computers aren't capable of generating truly random numbers (unless you have an old, malfunctioning computer—then it might fail from time to time, generating truly random results.) Instead, computers use carefully crafted formulas that are based on years of research to generate pseudo-random numbers. **Pseudo-random** numbers only seem to be random. For most applications that require random numbers, however, pseudo-random numbers work just as well.

To generate random numbers in Visual Basic, you have to create a special type of object known as a `Random` **object** in memory. `Random` objects have methods and properties that make generating random numbers fairly easy. Here is an example of a statement that creates a `Random` object:

```
Dim rand As New Random
```

This statement declares a variable named `rand`. The expression `New Random` creates a `Random` object in memory. After this statement executes, the `rand` variable will refer to the `Random` object. As a result, you will be able to use the `rand` variable to call the object's methods for generating random numbers. (There is nothing special about the variable name `rand` used in this example. You can use any legal variable name.)

The `Next` Method

Once you have created a `Random` object, you can call its `Next` method to get a random integer number. The following code shows an example:

```
' Declare an Integer variable.
Dim intNum As Integer

' Create a Random object.
Dim rand As New Random

' Get a random integer and assign it to intNum.
intNum = rand.Next()
```

After this code executes, the `intNum` variable will contain a random number. If you call the `Next` method with no arguments, as shown in this example, the returned integer is somewhere between 0 and 2,147,483,647. Alternatively, you can pass an argument that specifies an upper limit to the generated number's range. In the following statement, the value assigned to `intNum` is somewhere between 0 and 99:

```
intNum = rand.Next(100)
```

The random integer's range does not have to begin at zero. You can add or subtract a value to shift the numeric range upward or downward. In the following statement, we call the `Next` method to get a random number in the range of 0 through 9, and then we add 1 to it. So, the number assigned to `intNum` will be somewhere in the range of 1 through 10:

```
intNum = rand.Next(10) + 1
```

The following statement shows another example. It assigns a random integer to `intNum` between −50 and +49:

```
intNum = rand.Next(100) - 50
```

The `NextDouble` Method

You can call a `Random` object's `NextDouble` method to get a random floating-point number between 0.0 and 1.0 (not including 1.0). The following code shows an example:

```
' Declare a Double variable.
Dim dblNum As Double

' Create a Random object.
Dim rand As New Random

' Get a random number and assign it to dblNum.
dblNum = rand.NextDouble()
```

After this code executes, the `dblNum` variable will contain a random floating-point number in the range of 0.0 up to (but not including) 1.0. If you want the random number to fall within a larger range, multiply it by a scaling factor. The following statement assigns a random number between 0.0 and 500.0 to `dblNum`:

```
dblNum = rand.NextDouble() * 500.0
```

The following statement generates a random number between 100.0 and 600.0:

```
dblNum = (rand.NextDouble() * 500.0) + 100.0
```

In Tutorial 5-10 you will create a VB application that uses random numbers to simulate a coin toss.

Tutorial 5-10:
Creating the Coin Toss Application

In this tutorial you will create an application that simulates the tossing of a coin. Each time the user tosses the coin, the application will use a Random object to get a random integer in the range of 0 through 1. If the random number is 0, it means the tails side of the coin is up, and if the random number is 1, it means the heads side is up. The application will display an image of a coin showing either the heads side or the tails side, depending on the value of the random number.

Step 1: Create a new Windows Forms application named *Coin Toss*.

Step 2: Set up the form with two PictureBox controls and two buttons, like the one shown in Figure 5-36. In the student sample programs, in the *Chap5* folder, you will find two image files named Heads.bmp and Tails.bmp. Set the picHeads control's Image property to the Heads.bmp file, and set the picTails control's Image property to the Tails.bmp file.

Step 3: Set the Visible property to False for both the picHeads control and the picTails control. (You will still see the images on the form in the *Designer* window, but they will be invisible when the application runs.)

Figure 5-36 The *Coin Toss* form

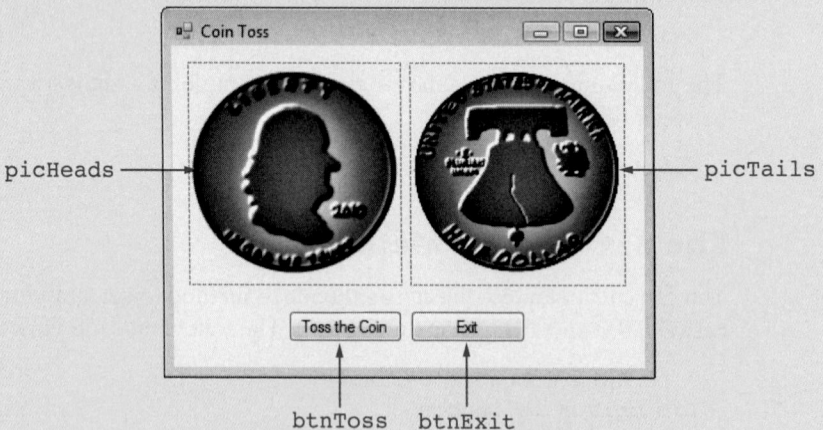

Step 4: Double-click the btnToss button to create a code template for its Click event handler. Complete the event handler by writing the following bold code shown in lines 2 through 20.

```
1 Private Sub btnToss_Click(...) Handles btnToss.Click
2    Dim intSideUp As Integer ' To indicate which side is up
3    Dim rand As New Random    ' Random number generator
4
```

```
 5    ' Get a random number in the range of 0 through 1.
 6    ' 0 means tails up, and 1 means heads up.
 7    intSideUp = rand.Next(2)
 8
 9    ' Display the side that is up.
10    If intSideUp = 0 Then
11        ' 0 means tails is up, so display the tails
12        ' image and hide the heads image.
13        picTails.Visible = True
14        picHeads.Visible = False
15    Else
16        ' 1 means heads is up, so display the heads
17        ' image and hide the tails image.
18        picHeads.Visible = True
19        picTails.Visible = False
20    End If
21 End Sub
```

Let's take a closer look at the code. Line 2 declares an Integer variable named intSideUp. This variable will hold a random number that indicates which side of the coin is up. Line 3 creates a Random object, using the name rand to refer to that object.

Line 7 calls the rand object's Next method, passing 2 as an argument. This means that the method will return a value in the range of 0 through 1. The random number is assigned to the intSideUp variable.

The If statement in line 10 determines whether intSideUp is equal to 0. If so, it means that the tails side of the coin is up, so line 12 makes the picTails control visible and line 13 makes the picHeads control invisible.

If the intSideUp variable is not equal to 0, then the heads side of the coin is up. In that case, the Else clause in line 15 takes over. Line 18 makes the picHeads control visible and line 19 makes the picTails control invisible.

Step 5: Write an event handler for the btnExit button. The button should close the form when it is clicked.

Step 6: Save the application, and then run it. Initially you will not see the coin on the form. When you click the *Toss the Coin* button, however, one of the two images (heads up or tails up) will be displayed, as shown in Figure 5-37. Click the button several times to simulate several coin tosses. When you are finished, exit the application.

Figure 5-37 The *Coin Toss* form with heads up and tails up

Random Number Seeds

The formula used to generate random numbers has to be initialized with a value known as a seed value. The **seed value** is used in the calculation that returns the next random number in the series. When a Random object is created in memory, it retrieves the system time from the computer's internal clock, and uses that as the seed value. The system time is an integer that represents the current date and time, down to a hundredth of a second.

If a Random object uses the same seed each time it is created, it will always generate the same series of random numbers. Because the system time changes every hundredth of a second, it is the preferred value to use as the seed in most cases. However, you can specify a different integer value as the seed, if you desire, when you create a Random object. Here is an example:

```
Dim rand As New Random(1000)
```

In this example, the Random object that is created uses 1000 as the seed value. Each time a Random object is created with this statement, it will generate the same series of random numbers. That may be desirable when running specific tests and validations, but decidedly boring if the program is a computer game or simulation.

 Checkpoint

5.30 What does a Random object's Next method return?

5.31 What does a Random object's NextDouble method return?

5.32 Write code that creates a Random object and then assigns a random integer in the range of 1 through 100 to the variable intRandomNumber.

5.32 Write code that creates a Random object and then assigns a random integer in the range of 100 through 400 to the variable intRandomNumber.

5.34 What does a Random object use as its seed value if you do not specify one?

5.35 What happens if the same seed value is used each time a Random object is created?

5.8 Simplifying Code with the With...End With Statement

CONCEPT: The With...End With statement allows you to simplify a series of consecutive statements that perform operations using the same object.

Sometimes you must write several consecutive statements that perform operations on the same control or other object. The following code shows an example of several operations being performed with a text box named txtName:

```
txtName.Clear()
txtName.ForeColor = Color.Blue
txtName.BackColor = Color.Yellow
txtName.BorderStyle = BorderStyle.Fixed3D
```

In Visual Basic you can simplify this code using the **With...End With** statement, as shown here:

```
With txtName
  .Clear()
  .ForeColor = Color.Blue
```

```
    .BackColor = Color.Yellow
    .BorderStyle = BorderStyle.Fixed3D
End With
```

Notice that the With...End With statement we refer to the txtName control only once, in the first line. That eliminates the need to repeatedly type txtName at the beginning of each line that appears inside the statement.

5.9 ToolTips

CONCEPT: ToolTips are a standard and convenient way of providing help to the users of an application. The ToolTip control allows you to assign pop-up hints to the other controls on a form.

A **ToolTip** is a small box displayed when the user holds the mouse cursor over a control. The box shows a short description of what the control does. Most Windows applications use ToolTips as a way of providing immediate and concise help to the user.

The **ToolTip control** allows you to create ToolTips for other controls on a form. Place a ToolTip control in your application just as you place other controls: double-click the ToolTip icon in the Toolbox. When you do so, a ToolTip control appears in an area at the bottom of the *Designer* window, as shown in Figure 5-38.

Figure 5-38 ToolTip control

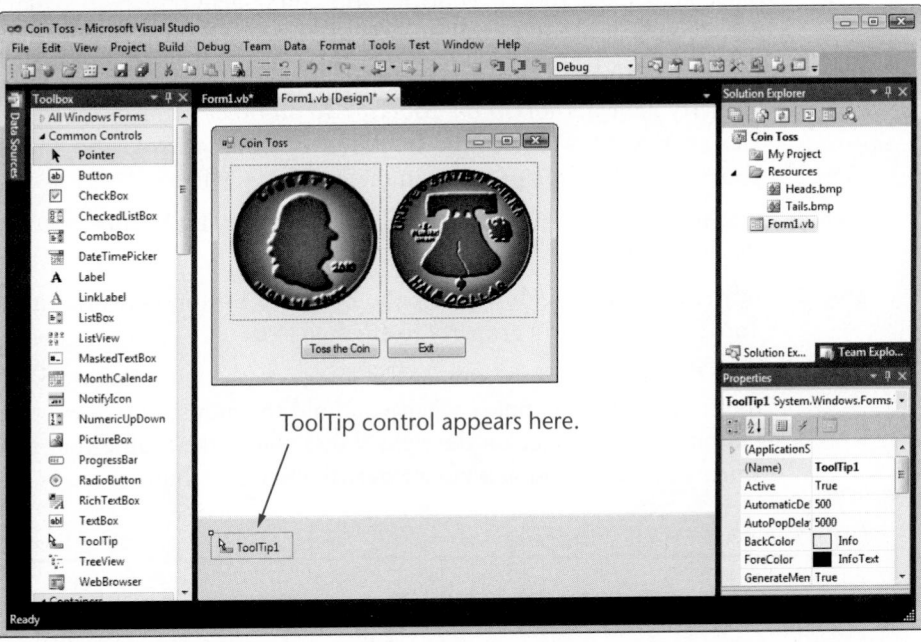

Because the ToolTip control is invisible at runtime, it does not appear on the form at design time. Instead, it appears in an area known as the component tray. The **component tray** is a resizable region at the bottom of the *Design* window that holds invisible controls.

When you add a ToolTip control to a form, a new property is added to all the other controls. The new property is named *ToolTip on ToolTipControl,* where *ToolTipControl* is the name of the ToolTip control. For example, suppose you add a ToolTip control to a form and keep the default name *ToolTip1.* The new property that is added to the other controls will be named *ToolTip on ToolTip1.* This new property holds the string that is displayed as the control's ToolTip.

ToolTip Properties

You can select the ToolTip control in the component tray and then examine its properties in the *Properties* window. The InitialDelay property determines the amount of time, in milliseconds, that elapses between the user pointing the mouse at a control and the ToolTip's appearance. The default setting is 500. (One millisecond is 1/1000th of a second, so 500 milliseconds is half of a second.)

The AutoPopDelay property is also a measure of time in milliseconds. It determines how long a ToolTip remains on the screen once it is displayed. The default setting is 5000. The ReshowDelay property holds the number of milliseconds that will elapse between the displaying of different ToolTips as the user moves the mouse from control to control. The default setting is 100.

You can set these properties individually, or set them all at once with the AutomaticDelay property. When you store a value in the AutomaticDelay property, InitialDelay is set to the same value, AutoPopDelay is set to 10 times the value, and ReshowDelay is set to one-fifth the value. In Tutorial 5-11, you add ToolTips to an application.

Tutorial 5-11:
Adding ToolTips to an application

Step 1: Load the *Coin Toss* project that you completed in Tutorial 5-10 and open the form in the *Designer* window.

Step 2: Scroll down in the Toolbox until you find the ToolTip icon (📑). Double-click the icon to add a ToolTip control to the component tray. Notice that the default name of the ToolTip control is *ToolTip1*.

Step 3: When you add the ToolTip1 control, Visual Basic automatically adds a new property named *ToolTip on ToolTip1* to all other controls on the form. In the *Designer* window select the btnToss Button control, and then locate the ToolTip on ToolTip1 property in the *Properties* window.

Step 4: Set the btnToss Button control's ToolTip on ToolTip1 property to *Click to toss the coin*.

Step 5: In the *Designer* window select the btnExit Button control, and then set its ToolTip on ToolTip1 property to *Click to exit*.

Step 6: Save the project and the run it. The image on the left in Figure 5-39 shows the tooltip that should appear when you hold the mouse cursor over the btnToss button, and the image on the right shows shows the tooltip that should appear when you hold the mouse cursor over the btnExit button.

Figure 5-39 Tooltips displayed

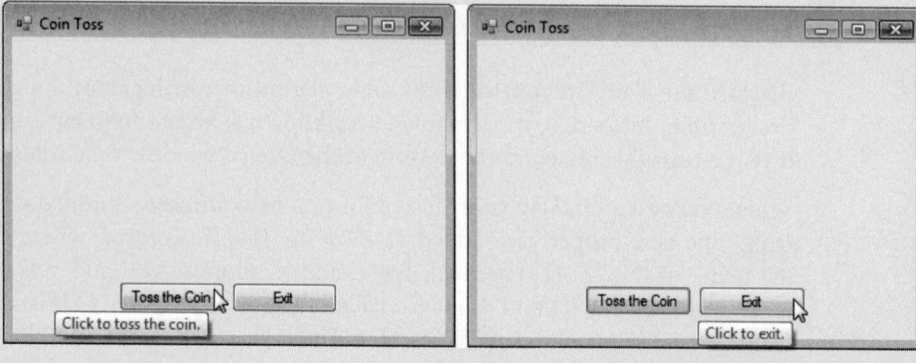

5.10 Focus on Program Design and Problem Solving: Building the *Vehicle Loan Calculator* Application

CONCEPT: In this section, you build the *Vehicle Loan Calculator* application. The application uses a loop, input validation, and ToolTips. This section also covers some of the Visual Basic intrinsic financial functions.

Visual Basic has several built-in functions for performing financial calculations. You will build a program named *Vehicle Loan Calculator*. It uses the following functions: Pmt, IPmt, and PPmt. Let's look at each function in detail before continuing with the case study.

The Pmt Function

The Pmt function returns the periodic payment amount for a loan. It assumes the loan has a fixed interest rate. Here is the general form of the **Pmt function** call:

```
Pmt(PeriodicInterestRate, NumberOfPeriods, —LoanAmount)
```

Descriptions of each argument follow:

1. *PeriodicInterestRate*: You usually know a loan's annual interest rate; this function, however, needs to know the loan's periodic interest rate. A loan is divided into periods, and you make a payment each period. The periodic interest rate is the rate of interest per period of the loan. For example, if you make monthly payments on a loan, the period is each month. If the annual interest rate is 9%, then the periodic interest rate is .09 divided by 12, which is .0075.
2. *NumberOfPeriods*: For a loan that requires monthly payments, this is the total number of months of the loan. For example, a three-year loan is given for 36 months.
3. *LoanAmount*: This is the amount being borrowed, which must be negative.

NOTE: The Pmt function can also be used to calculate payments on a savings plan. When using it for that purpose, specify the desired value of the savings as a positive number.

Here is an example of the function call:

```
dblPayment = Pmt(dblAnnInt / 12, 24, -5000)
```

In this statement, dblAnnInt contains the annual interest rate, 24 is the number of months of the loan, and the amount of the loan is $5,000. After the statement executes, dblPayment holds the fixed monthly payment amount.

The IPmt Function

The IPmt function returns the interest payment for a specific period on a loan. It assumes the loan has a fixed interest rate, with fixed monthly payments. Here is the general format of the **IPmt function** call:

```
IPmt(PeriodicInterestRate, Period, NumberOfPeriods, —LoanAmount)
```

Descriptions of each argument follow:

1. *PeriodicInterestRate*: As with the Pmt function, this function must know the periodic interest rate. (See the description of argument 1 for the Pmt function.)

2. *Period*: This argument specifies the period for which you wish to calculate the payment. The argument must be at least 1, and no more than the total number of periods of the loan.
3. *NumberofPeriods*: The total number of periods of the loan. (See the description of argument 2 for the Pmt function.)
4. *LoanAmount*: As with the Pmt function, the loan amount must be expressed as a negative number.

Here is an example of the function call:

```
dblInterest = IPmt(dblAnnInt / 12, 6, 24, -5000)
```

In this statement, dblAnnInt contains the annual interest rate, 6 is the number of the month for which you wish to calculate the payment, 24 is the number of months of the loan, and the amount of the loan is $5,000. After the statement executes, dblInterest holds the amount of interest paid in month 6 of the loan.

The PPmt Function

The PPmt function returns the principal payment for a specific period on a loan. It assumes the loan has a fixed interest rate, with fixed monthly payments. Here is the general format of the **PPmt function** call:

```
PPmt(PeriodicInterestRate, Period, NumberOfPeriods, -LoanAmount)
```

Descriptions of each argument follow:

1. *PeriodicInterestRate*: As with the Pmt function, this function must know the periodic interest rate. (See the description of argument 1 for the Pmt function.)
2. *Period*: This argument specifies the period for which you wish to calculate the payment. The argument must be at least 1, and no more than the total number of periods of the loan.
3. *NumberOfPeriods*: The total number of periods of the loan. (See the description of argument 2 for the Pmt function.)
4. *LoanAmount*: As with the Pmt function, the loan amount must be expressed as a negative number.

Here is an example of the function call:

```
dblPrincipal = PPmt(dblAnnInt / 12, 6, 24, -5000)
```

In this statement, dblAnnInt contains the annual interest rate, 6 is the number of the month for which you wish to calculate the payment, 24 is the number of months of the loan, and the amount of the loan is $5,000. After the statement executes, dblPrincipal holds the amount of principal paid in month 6 of the loan.

The Case Study

The Central Mountain Credit Union finances new and used vehicles for its members. A credit union branch manager asks you to write an application named Vehicle Loan Calculator that displays the following information for a loan:

- The monthly payment amount
- The amount of the monthly payment applied toward interest
- The amount of the monthly payment applied toward principal

The credit union currently charges 8.9% annual interest for new vehicle loans and 9.5% annual interest on used vehicle loans.

Figure 5-40 shows a sketch of the *Vehicle Loan Calculator* application's form.

Figure 5-40 Sketch of the *Vehicle Loan Calculator* form

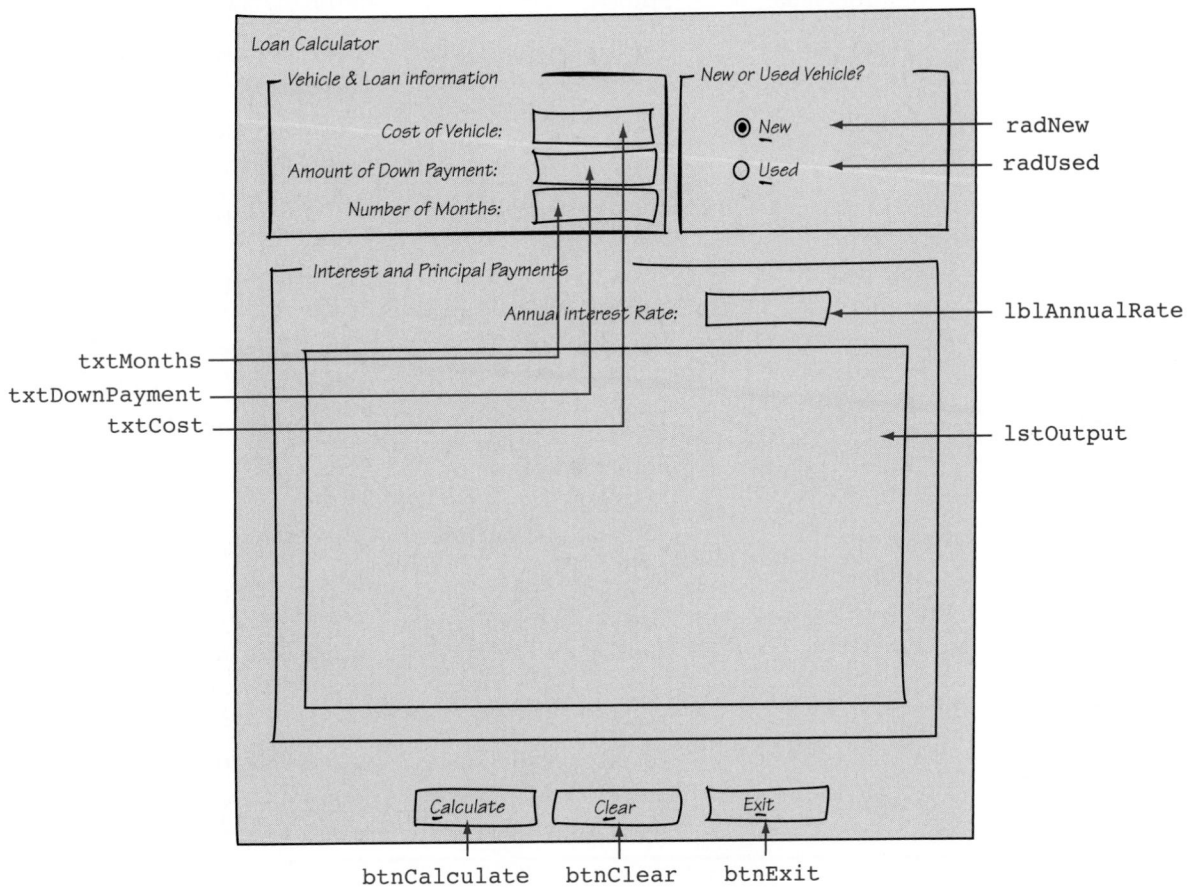

Table 5-2 lists each control, along with any relevant property settings.

Table 5-2 *Vehicle Loan Calculator* controls

Control Type	Control Name	Property	Property Value
Form	(Default)	Text:	*Loan Calculator*
ToolTip	(Default)		(Retain default property settings)
GroupBox	(Default)	Text: TabIndex:	*Vehicle && Loan Information* 0
Label	(Default)	Text:	*Cost of Vehicle:*
Text box	txtCost	ToolTip on ToolTip1:	*Enter the cost of the vehicle here.*
Label	(Default)	Text:	*Amount of Down Payment:*
Text box	txtDownPayment	ToolTip on ToolTip1:	*Enter the amount of the down payment here.*
Label	(Default)	Text:	*Number of Months:*

(*continued*)

Table 5-2 *Vehicle Loan Calculator* controls (*continued*)

Control Type	Control Name	Property	Property Value
Text box	txtMonths	ToolTip on ToolTip1:	*Enter the number of months of the loan here.*
GroupBox	(Default)	Text:	*New or Used Vehicle?*
RadioButton	radNew	Text:	*&New*
		ToolTip on ToolTip1: Checked	*Click here if the vehicle is new.* True
RadioButton	radUsed	Text:	*&Used*
		ToolTip on ToolTip1: Checked	*Click here if the vehicle is used.* False
GroupBox	(Default)	Text:	*Interest and Principal Payments*
Label	(Default)	Text:	*Annual Interest Rate:*
Label	lblAnnualRate	BorderStyle: AutoSize: ToolTip on ToolTip1:	*Fixed3D* *False* *Annual interest rate*
ListBox	lstOutput		
Button	btnCalculate	Text: ToolTip on ToolTip1:	*&Calculate* *Click here to calculate the payment data.*
Button	btnClear	Text: ToolTip on ToolTip1:	*C&lear* *Click here to clear the form.*
Button	btnExit	Text: ToolTip on ToolTip1:	*E&xit* *Click here to exit.*

Table 5-3 lists and describes the event handlers needed in this application.

Table 5-3 *Vehicle Loan Calculator* event handlers

Method	Description
btnCalculate_Click	Calculates and displays a table in the list box showing interest and principal payments for the loan
btnClear_Click	Resets the interest rate, clears the text boxes, and clears the list box
btnExit_Click	Ends the application
radNew_CheckedChanged	Updates the annual interest rate if the user selects a new vehicle loan
radUsed_CheckedChanged	Updates the annual interest rate if the user selects a used vehicle loan

The following pseudocode shows the general logic for the btnCalculate_Click event handler. Note that the pseudocode does not indicate input validation, and the actual arguments that need to be passed to the Pmt, IPmt, and PPmt functions are not shown.

Get VehicleCost from the form
Get DownPayment from the form
Get Months from the form

Loan = VehicleCost − DownPayment
MonthlyPayment = Pmt()

> *For Count = 0 To Months*
>   *Interest = IPmt()*
>   *Principal = PPmt()*
>   *Display Month, Payment, Interest, and Principal in list box*
> *Next*

These event handlers change the annual interest rate when the user clicks the `radNew` and `radUsed` radio buttons. Pseudocode for the `radNew_CheckedChanged` event handler is as follows:

> *If radNew is selected Then*
>   *Annual Interest Rate = 0.089*
>   *Display Annual Interest Rate in lblAnnInt*
> *End If*

Pseudocode for the `radUsed_CheckedChanged` event handler is as follows:

> *If radUsed is selected Then*
>   *Annual Interest Rate = 0.095*
>   *Display Annual Interest Rate in lblAnnInt*
> *End If*

In Tutorial 5-12 you build the *Vehicle Loan Calculator* application.

Tutorial 5-12:
Building the *Vehicle Loan Calculator* application

Step 1: Create a new Windows Forms Application project named *Loan Calculator*.

Step 2: Set up the form as shown in Figure 5-41. Refer to Figure 5-40 for the names of the programmer-defined control names, and Table 5-1 for the important property settings.

Figure 5-41 *Loan Calculator* form

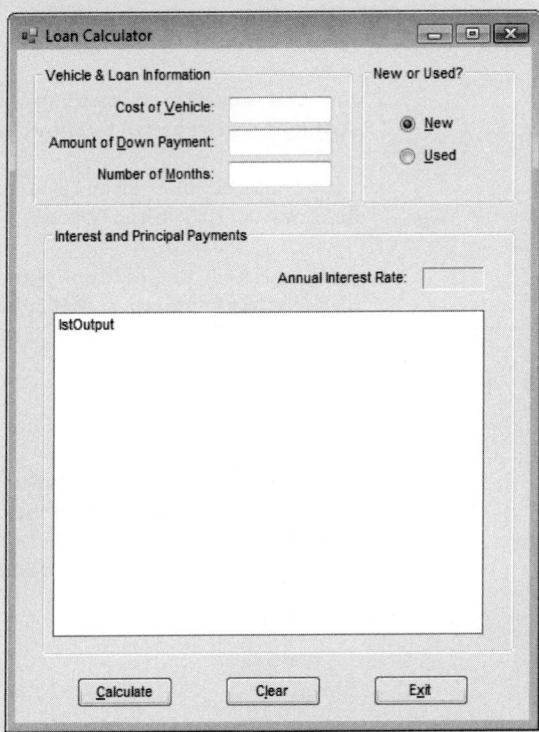

Step 3: Once you have placed all the controls on the form and set their properties, you can write the application's code. Open the *Code* window and write the comments and class-level variable declarations shown as follows in bold. This code should not appear inside of any event handler.

```
Public Class Form1
  ' Class-level constants
  Const dblMONTHS_YEAR As Double = 12 ' Months per year
  Const dblNEW_RATE As Double = 0.089 ' Interest rate, new cars
  Const dblUSED_RATE As Double = 0.095 ' Interest rate, used cars

  ' Class-level variable to hold the annual interest rate
  Dim dblAnnualRate As Double = dblNEW_RATE
End Class
```

The variable, dblAnnualRate, which holds the annual interest rate, is declared as a class-level variable because it will be accessed by multiple procedures. It is initialized with dblNEW_RATE because a new vehicle loan will be selected by default.

Step 4: Create the code template for the btnCalculate_Click event handler. Complete the event handler by writing the following bold code.

```
Private Sub btnCalculate_Click(...) Handles btnCalculate.Click
    Dim dblVehicleCost As Double      ' Vehicle cost
    Dim dblDownPayment As Double      ' Down payment
    Dim intMonths As Integer          ' Number of months for the loan
    Dim dblLoan As Double             ' Amount of the loan
    Dim dblMonthlyPayment As Double   ' Monthly payment
    Dim dblInterest As Double         ' Interest paid for the period
    Dim dblPrincipal As Double        ' Principal paid for the period
    Dim intCount As Integer           ' Counter for the loop
    Dim strOut As String              ' Used to hold a line of output

    ' Get the vehicle cost.
    If Double.TryParse(txtCost.Text, dblVehicleCost) Then

        ' Get the down payment.
        If Double.TryParse(txtDownPayment.Text, dblDownPayment) Then

            ' Get the number of months.
            If Integer.TryParse(txtMonths.Text, intMonths) Then

                ' Calculate the amount of the loan.
                dblLoan = dblVehicleCost - dblDownPayment

                ' Calculate the monthly payment
                dblMonthlyPayment = Pmt(dblAnnualRate / dblMONTHS_YEAR,
                                intMonths, -dblLoan)

                ' Clear the list box.
                lstOutput.Items.Clear()

                For intCount = 1 To intMonths
                    ' Calculate the interest for this period.
                    dblInterest = IPmt(dblAnnualRate / dblMONTHS_YEAR,
                                intCount, intMonths, -dblLoan)
```

```
                        ' Calculate the principal for this period.
                        dblPrincipal = PPmt(dblAnnualRate / dblMONTHS_YEAR,
                                            intCount, intMonths, -dblLoan)

                        ' Start building the output string with the month.
                        strOut = "Month: " & intCount.ToString()

                        ' Add the payment amount to the output string
                        strOut &= " Payment: " & dblMonthlyPayment.ToString("c")

                        ' Add the interest amount to the output string.
                        strOut &= " Interest: " & dblInterest.ToString("c")

                        ' Add the principal for the period.
                        strOut &= " Principal: " & dblPrincipal.ToString("c")

                        ' Add the output string to the list box
                        lstOutput.Items.Add(strOut)
                    Next

                Else
                    ' Error message for invalid months.
                    MessageBox.Show("Ener an integer for months.")
                End If
            Else
                ' Error message for invalid down payment.
                MessageBox.Show("Ener a numeric value for down payment.")
            End If
        Else
            ' Error message for invalid vehicle cost.
            MessageBox.Show("Ener a numeric value for vehicle cost.")
        End If
    End Sub
```

Step 5: Create the code template for the `btnClear_Click` event handler. Complete the event handler by writing the following bold code.

```
Private Sub btnClear_Click(...) Handles btnClear.Click
    ' Reset the interest rate, clear the text boxes
    ' and clear the list box. Set default interest
    ' rate for new car loans.

    radNew.Checked = True
    dblAnnualRate = dblNEW_RATE
    lblAnnualRate.Text = dblNEW_RATE.ToString("p")
    txtCost.Clear()
    txtDownPayment.Clear()
    txtMonths.Clear()
    lstOutput.Items.Clear()

    ' Reset the focus to txtCost.
    txtCost.Focus()
End Sub
```

Step 6: Create the code template for the `btnExit_Click` event handler. Complete the event handler by writing the following bold code.

```
Private Sub btnExit_Click(...) Handles btnExit.Click
    ' Close the form.
    Me.Close()
End Sub
```

Step 7:   Create the code template for the `radNew_CheckedChanged` event handler. (You can easily create the code template by opening the *Designer* window and double-clicking the radNew control.) Complete the event handler by writing the following bold code.

```
Private Sub radNew_CheckedChanged(...) Handles radNew.CheckedChanged
   ' If the New radio button is checked, then
   ' the user has selected a new car loan.
   If radNew.Checked = True Then
      dblAnnualRate   = dblNEW_RATE
      lblAnnualRate.Text = dblNEW_RATE.ToString("p")
   End If
End Sub
```

Step 8:   Create the code template for the `radUsed_CheckedChanged` event handler. (You can easily create the code template by opening the *Designer* window and double-clicking the radUsed control.) Complete the event handler by writing the following bold code.

```
Private Sub radUsed_CheckedChanged(...) Handles radUsed.CheckedChanged
   ' If the Used radio button is checked, then
   ' the user has selected a used car loan.
   If radUsed.Checked = True Then
      dblAnnualRate = dblUSED_RATE
      lblAnnualRate.Text = dblUSED_RATE.ToString("p")
   End If
End Sub
```

Step 9:   Attempt to run the application. If there are errors, compare your code and property settings with those listed to locate them.

Step 10:   Save the project.

Summary

5.1 Input Boxes

- Input boxes provide a simple way to gather input from the user.

5.2 List Boxes

- A list box control displays a list of items and allows the user to select one or more items from the list.

5.3 Introduction to Loops: The `Do While` Loop

- A repetition structure, or loop, causes one or more statements to repeat. Each repetition of a loop is called an iteration.
- The `Do While` loop has an expression that is tested for *True* or *False* value and a statement or group of statements that is repeated as long as an expression is true.

5.4 The Do Until and `For...Next` Loops

- The `Do Until` loop repeats until its test expression is true.
- The `For...Next` loop initializes, tests, and increments a counter variable.
- The `Do While` and `Do Until` loops may be written as either pretest or posttest loops. The `For...Next` loop is a pretest loop.
- The `Exit Do` and `Exit For` statements, when placed inside the body of a loop, stop the execution of the loop and cause the program to jump to the statement immediately following the loop.

5.5 Nested Loops

- A loop located inside another loop is called a nested loop. It is used when a task performs a repetitive operation and each iteration of that operation is itself a repetitive operation.

5.6 Multicolumn List Boxes, Checked List Boxes, and Combo Boxes

- A multicolumn list box displays items in columns with a horizontal scroll bar, if necessary.
- A checked list box displays a check box next to each item in the list.
- There are three different styles of combo box: the drop-down combo box, the simple combo box, and the drop-down list combo box. You select a combo box's style with its DropDownStyle property.

5.7 Random Numbers

- A `Random` object has methods that generate random sequences of numbers.
- A `Random` object's `Next` method returns the next random integer in a series.
- A `Random` object's `NextDouble` method returns a random value between 0.0 and 1.0.

5.8 Simplifying Code with the `With...End With` Statement

- The `With...End With` statement allows you to simplify a series of consecutive statements that perform operations using the same object.

5.9 ToolTips

- The ToolTip control allows you to create ToolTips (pop-up hints) for other controls on the same form.
- The ToolTip control is invisible at runtime; it appears in the component tray at design time.

5.10 Focus on Program Design and Problem Solving: Building the *Vehicle Loan Calculator* Application

- This section outlines the process of building the *Vehicle Loan Calculator* application using a loop.
- The Pmt function returns the periodic payment amount for a loan. The IPmt function returns the required interest payment for a specific period on a loan. The PPmt function returns the principal payment for a specific period on a loan.

Key Terms

accumulator
combo box
conditionally executed statements
counter
Do Until loop
Do While loop
Exit Do statement
Exit For statement
For...Next loop
infinite loop
input box
IPmt function
Items property
Items.Add method
Items.Count property
Items.Insert method
Items.Remove method
Items.RemoveAt method
iteration
ListBox control

loop
nested loop
Next method
NextDouble method
posttest loop
Pmt function
PPmt function
pretest loop
pseudo-random (numbers)
Random object
repetition structure
running total
Seed value
SelectedIndex property
SelectedItem property
Sorted property
step value
tooltip
ToolTip control
With...End With statement

Review Questions and Exercises

Fill-in-the-Blank

1. A(n) _____ provides a simple way to gather input without placing a text box on a form.

2. A(n) _____ displays a list of items and allows the user to select an item from the list.

3. A(n) _____ causes one or more statements to repeat.

4. If a loop does not have a way of stopping, it is called a(n) _____ loop.

5. A(n) _____ is a variable that is regularly incremented or decremented each time a loop iterates.

6. A(n)_____ loop evaluates its test expression after each iteration.

7. Each repetition of the loop is called a(n) _____.

8. The _____ statement, when placed inside the body of a Do While loop, stops the execution of the loop and causes the program to jump to the statement immediately following the loop.

9. A loop that is inside another loop is called a _____ loop.

10. A (n) _____ object has methods that can generate a sequence of random numbers.

11. The _____ method generates a random integer.

12. The _____ method generates a random floating-point value.

13. The _____ function returns the periodic payment amount for a loan.

14. The _____ function returns the principal payment for a specific period on a loan.

15. The _____ function returns the required interest payment for a specific period on a loan.

Multiple Choice

1. You display input boxes with this function.

   a. InBox
   b. Input
   c. InputBox
   d. GetInput

2. An input box returns the value entered by the user as this.

   a. String
   b. Integer
   c. Single
   d. Boolean

3. Visual Basic automatically adds this to a list box when it contains more items than can be displayed.

   a. Larger list box
   b. Scroll bar
   c. Second form
   d. Message box

4. A list box or combo box's index numbering starts at this value.

   a. 0
   b. 1
   c. −1
   d. any value you specify

5. This property holds the index of the selected item in a list box.

   a. Index
   b. SelectedItem
   c. SelectedIndex
   d. Items.SelectedIndex

6. This method erases one item from a list box.

   a. `Erase`
   b. `Items.Remove`
   c. `Items.RemoveItem`
   d. `Clear`

7. The `Do While` statement marks the beginning of a `Do While` loop, and the `Loop` statement marks the end. The statements between these are known as one of the following.

   a. Processes of the loop
   b. Functions of the loop
   c. Substance of the loop
   d. Body of the loop

8. This type of loop evaluates its test expression before each iteration.

   a. Out-test
   b. Pretest
   c. Posttest
   d. In-test

9. One of the following is a sum of numbers that accumulates with each iteration of a loop.

   a. Counter
   b. Running total
   c. Summation function
   d. Iteration count

10. This type of loop is ideal for situations that require a counter because it is specifically designed to initialize, test, and increment a counter variable.

    a. `Do While`
    b. `Do Until`
    c. `For...Next`
    d. `Posttest Do Until`

11. You do this to get the total number of iterations of a nested loop.

    a. Add the number of iterations of all the loops
    b. Multiply the number of iterations of all the loops
    c. Average the number of iterations of all the loops
    d. Get the number of iterations of the outermost loop

12. When this ListBox control's property is set to *True*, it causes the ListBox control to display its list in multiple columns.

    a. Columns
    b. Multicolumn
    c. ColumnList
    d. TableDisplay

13. This control has a rectangular area that functions like a text box.

    a. List box
    b. Drop-down list box
    c. Combo box
    d. Input label

14. This is the prefix that we use for combo box names.

    a. `cbo`
    b. `com`
    c. `cbx`
    d. `cob`

15. With this style of combo box, the list of items does not drop down, but is always displayed.

    a. Drop-down combo box
    b. Simple combo box
    c. Drop-down list combo box
    d. Simple drop-down combo list box

16. This combo box property will contain the user's text input or the item selected from the list.

    a. Input
    b. Caption
    c. List
    d. Text

17. Which of the following statements creates a `Random` object and initializes the sequence of random numbers with the seed value 25?

    a. `InitRandom(25)`
    b. `Rnd(25)`
    c. `Dim rand As New Seed(25)`
    d. `Dim rand As New Random(25)`

True or False

Indicate whether the following statements are true or false.

1. T F: If you do not provide a value for an input box's title, an error will occur.

2. T F: If the user clicks an input box's *Cancel* button, the function returns the number –1.

3. T F: The `Items.RemoveAt` method always removes the last item in a list box (the item with the highest index value).

4. T F: Infinite loops keep repeating until the program is interrupted.

5. T F: A loop's conditionally executed statements should be indented.

6. T F: A pretest loop always performs at least one iteration, even if the test expression is false from the start.

7. T F: The `Do While` loop may be written as either a pretest or posttest loop.

8. T F: In a `For...Next` loop, the *Counter Variable* must be numeric.

9. T F: The *Step Increment* part of the `For...Next` statement is optional.

10. T F: The `For...Next` loop is a posttest loop.

11. T F: In a nested loop, the inner loop goes through all of its iterations for each iteration of an outer loop.

12. T F: To create a checked list box, you draw a regular list box and set its Checked property to *True*.

13. T F: A drop-down list combo box allows the user to either select an item from a list or type text into a text input area.

14. T F: If a `Random` object is initialized with the same seed value each time it is created, it will produce the same series of random numbers each time.

Short Answer

1. What buttons automatically appear on an input box?

2. Where is an input box positioned if you leave out the Xpos and Ypos arguments?

3. Write a statement that adds *Spinach* to the list box lstVeggies at index 2.

4. Write a statement that removes the item at index 12 of the combo box cboCourses.

5. Describe the two important parts of a Do While loop.

6. In general terms, describe how a Do While loop works.

7. Why should you indent the statements in the body of a loop?

8. Describe the difference between pretest loops and posttest loops.

9. Why are the statements in the body of a loop called conditionally executed statements?

10. What is the difference between the Do While loop and the Do Until loop?

11. Which loop should you use in situations where you wish the loop to repeat as long as the test expression is true?

12. Which type of loop should you use in situations where you wish the loop to repeat until the test expression is true?

13. Which type of loop should you use when you know the number of required iterations?

14. What feature do combo boxes have that list boxes do not have?

15. With one style of combo box the user may not type text directly into the combo box, but must select an item from the list. Which style is it?

16. With one style of combo box the Text property is read-only. Which style?

17. What value does a Random object use as its seed if you do not specify a seed value?

What Do You Think?

1. Why is it critical that counter variables are properly initialized?

2. Why should you be careful not to place a statement in the body of a For...Next loop that changes the value of the loop's counter variable?

3. You need to write a loop that iterates until the user enters a specific value into an input box. Which type of loop should you choose? Why?

4. You need to write a loop that will repeat 224 times. Which type of loop will you choose? Why?

5. You need to write a loop that iterates as long as a variable has a specific value stored in it. Which type of loop will you choose? Why?

6. Why is a computer's system time a good source of random seed values?

7. You use the statement lstNames.Items.RemoveAt(6) to remove an item from a list box. Does the statement remove the sixth or seventh item in the list? Why?

8. What kind of control(s) do you use when you want to provide the user a list of items to select from, but do not want to limit the user's input to the items on the list?

9. What kind of control(s) do you use when you want to limit the user's selection to a list of items?

Find the Error

Identify the syntactically incorrect statements in the following:

1.
```
Loop
    intX = intX + 1
Do While intX < 100
```

2.
```
Do
    lstOutput.Items.Add("Hello")
    intX = intX + 1
While intCount < 10
```

3.
```
Loop Until intX = 99
    intX = intX + 1
Do
```

4.
```
For intX = 1
    lstOutput.Items.Add(intX)
Next
```

Algorithm Workbench

1. An event handler named `btnShow_Click` must add the numbers 1 through 20 to a list box named `lstNumbers`. Design a flowchart for this event handler.

2. Write the code that you would insert into the code template for the event handler described in Question 1.

3. Write a `Do While` loop that uses an input box to get a number from the user. The number should be multiplied by 10 and the result stored in the variable product. The loop should iterate as long as product contains a value less than 100.

4. Write a `Do While` loop that uses input boxes to get two numbers from the user. The numbers should be added and the sum displayed message box. An input box should ask the user whether he or she wishes to perform the operation again. If so, the loop should repeat; otherwise it should terminate.

5. Write a `For...Next` loop that adds the following set of numbers to the list box `lstNumbers`.

   0, 10, 20, 30, 40, 50 . . . 1000

6. Write a loop that uses an input box to get a number from the user. The loop should iterate 10 times and keep a running total of the numbers entered.

7. Convert the following pretest `Do While` loop to a posttest `Do While` loop:

```
intX = 1
Do While intX > 0
  strInput = InputBox("Enter a number")
  intX = CInt(strInput)
Loop
```

8. Convert the following `Do While` loop to a `Do Until` loop:

```
strInput = String.Empty
Do While strInput.ToUpper <> "Y"
  strInput = InputBox("Are you sure you want to quit?")
Loop
```

9. Convert the following `Do While` loop to a `For...Next` loop:

```
intCount = 0
Do While intCount < 50
  lstOutput.Items.Add(intCount)
  intCount += 1
Loop
```

10. Convert the following `For...Next` loop to a `Do While` loop:

```
For intX = 50 To 0 Step -1
   lstOutput.Items.Add(intX)
Next
```

11. Rewrite the following statements so they appear inside a `With` block:

```
txtName.Text = "(unknown)"
txtName.Font.Size = 10
txtName.BackColor = Color.Red
```

Programming Challenges

VideoNote

The Sum of
Numbers
Problems

1. **Sum of Numbers**

   Create an application that displays a form similar to the one shown in Figure 5-42. When the *Enter Numbers* button is clicked, the application should display the input box shown in Figure 5-43.

   The input box asks the user to enter a positive integer value. Notice that the default input value is 10. When the *OK* button is clicked, the application should display a message box with the sum of all the integers from 1 through the value entered by the user, as shown in Figure 5-44.

Figure 5-42 *Sum of Numbers* form

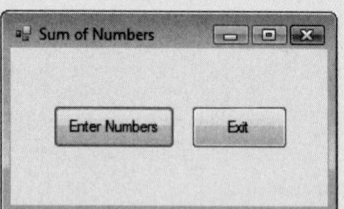

Figure 5-43 *Sum of Numbers* input box

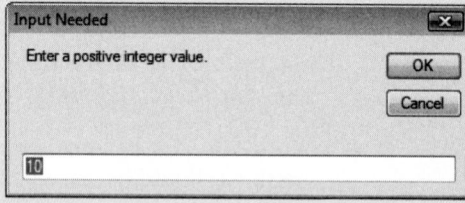

Figure 5-44 *Sum of Numbers* message box

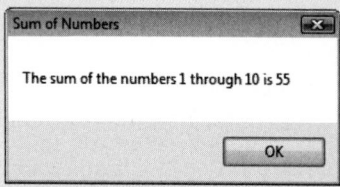

   If the user enters a negative value, the application should display an error message. Use the following test data to determine if the application is calculating properly:

Value	Sum
5	15
10	55
20	210
100	5050

2. **Distance Calculator**

   If you know a vehicle's speed and the amount of time it has traveled, you can calculate the distance it has traveled as follows:

   $$Distance = Speed * Time$$

For example, if a train travels 40 miles per hour for 3 hours, the distance traveled is 120 miles. Create an application with a form similar to the one shown in Figure 5-45.

When the user clicks the *Calculate* button, the application should display an input box asking the user for the speed of the vehicle in miles-per-hour, followed by another input box asking for the amount of time, in hours, that the vehicle has traveled. Then it should use a loop to display in a list box the distance the vehicle has traveled for each hour of that time period. Figure 5-46 shows an example of what the application's form should look like.

Figure 5-45 *Distance Calculator*

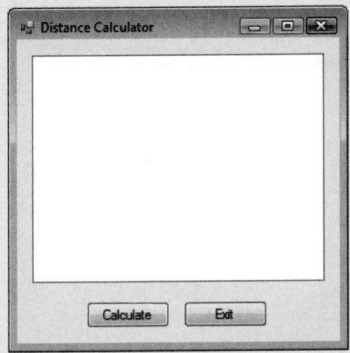

Figure 5-46 *Distance Calculator* completed

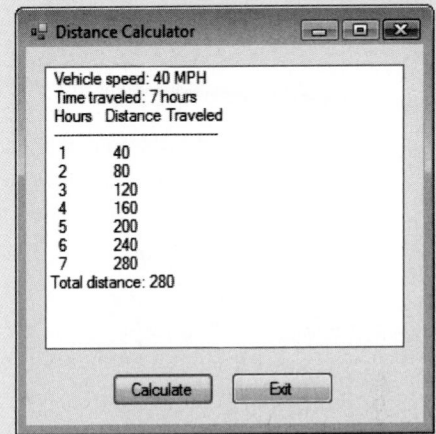

Use the following test data to determine if the application is calculating properly.

Vehicle Speed: 60
Hours Traveled: 7

Hour	Distance Traveled
1	60
2	120
3	180
4	240
5	300
6	360
7	420

3. **Workshop Selector**

Table 5-4 shows a training company's workshops, the number of days of each, and their registration fees.

Table 5-4 Workshops and registration fees

Workshop	Number of Days	Registration Fee
Handling Stress	3	$595
Time Management	3	$695
Supervision Skills	3	$995
Negotiation	5	$1,295
How to Interview	1	$395

The training company conducts its workshops in the six locations shown in Table 5-5. The table also shows the lodging fees per day at each location.

Table 5-5 Training locations and lodging fees

Location	Lodging Fees per Day
Austin	$95
Chicago	$125
Dallas	$110
Orlando	$100
Phoenix	$92
Raleigh	$90

When a customer registers for a workshop, he or she must pay the registration fee plus the lodging fees for the selected location. For example, here are the charges to attend the Supervision Skills workshop in Orlando:

Registration: $995
Lodging: $100 × 3 days = $300
Total: $1,295

Design an application with a form that resembles the one shown in Figure 5-47.

Figure 5-47 *Workshop Selector* form

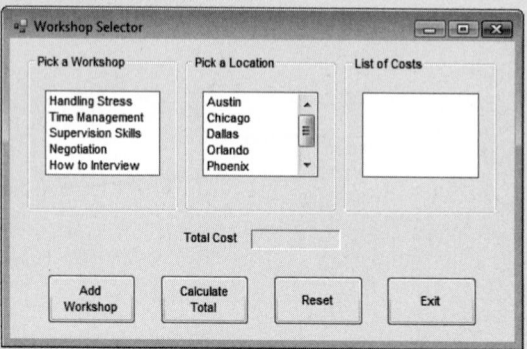

The application should allow the user to select a workshop from one list box and a location from another list box. When the user clicks the *Add Workshop* button, the application should add the total cost of the selected workshop at the selected location in the third list box. When the user clicks the *Calculate Total* button, the total cost of all the selected workshops should be calculated and displayed in the label. The *Reset* button should deselect the workshop and location from the first two list boxes, clear the third list box, and clear the total cost label.

4. **Hotel Occupancy**

The ElGrande Hotel has eight floors and 30 rooms on each floor. Create an application that calculates the occupancy rate for each floor, and the overall occupancy rate for the hotel. The occupancy rate is the percentage of rooms occupied, and may be calculated by dividing the number of rooms occupied by the number of rooms. For example, if 18 rooms on the first floor are occupied, the occupancy rate is as follows:

$$18 / 30 = .6 \text{ or } 60\%$$

The application's form should appear similar to the one shown in Figure 5-48.

Figure 5-48 *Hotel Occupancy* form

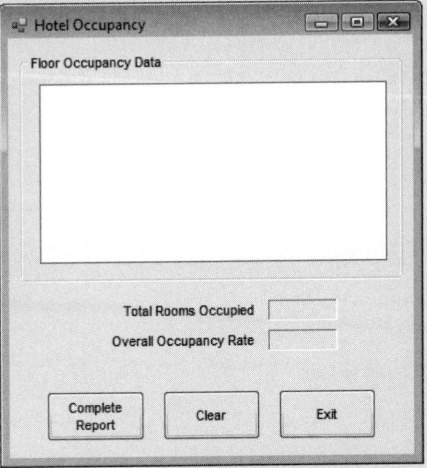

When the user clicks the *Complete Report* button, a loop should execute and iterate eight times. Each time the loop iterates, it should display an input box for one of the hotel's floors. The input box should ask the user to enter the number of rooms occupied on that floor. As the user enters a value for each floor, the loop should calculate the occupancy rate for that floor, and display the information for that floor in the list box. When the number of occupied rooms has been entered for all the floors, the application should display the total number of rooms occupied and the overall occupancy rate for the hotel. (The hotel has a total of 240 rooms.)

Figure 5-49 shows an example of the form after occupancy information has been provided for all the floors.

The *Clear* button should clear all the appropriate controls on the form. The *Exit* button should end the application. Use the values shown in Figure 5-49 to confirm that your application is performing the correct calculations.

Figure 5-49 Completed *Hotel Occupancy* form

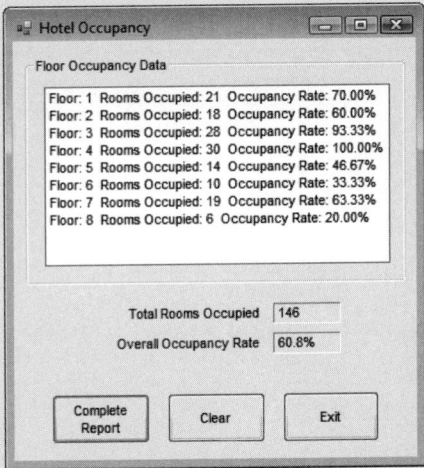

5. **Rainfall Statistics**

   Create an application that allows the user to enter each month's amount of rainfall (in inches) and calculates the total and average rainfall for a year. Figure 5-50 shows the application's form.

   Once the user has entered the amount of rainfall for each month, he or she may click the *Calculate* button to display the total and average rainfall. The *Clear* button should clear all the text boxes and labels on the form. The *Exit* button should end the application.

Figure 5-50 *Rainfall Statistics* form

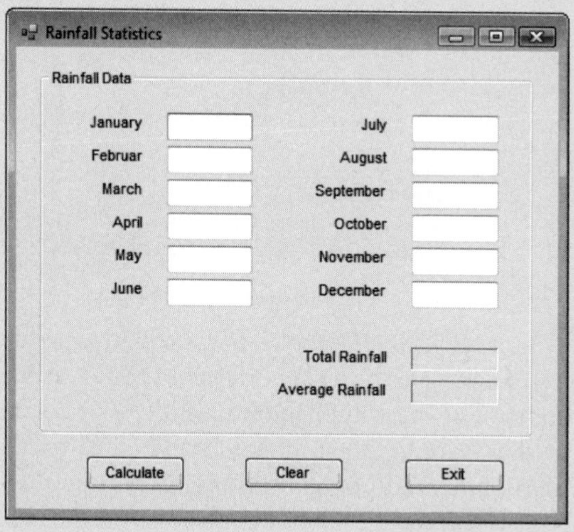

Rainfall Statistics				

Rainfall Data

January		July	
Februar		August	
March		September	
April		October	
May		November	
June		December	

Total Rainfall

Average Rainfall

Calculate   Clear   Exit

6. **Bar Chart**

   Create an application that prompts the user to enter today's sales for five stores. The program should then display a simple bar graph comparing each store's sales. Create each bar in the bar graph by displaying a row of asterisks (*) in a list box. Each asterisk in a bar represents $100 in sales.

   Figure 5-51 shows the form with the bar chart displayed. The sales data entered was $1000 for store #1, $1200 for store #2, $1800 for store #3, $800 for store #4, and $1900 for store #5.

Figure 5-51 *Bar Chart* form

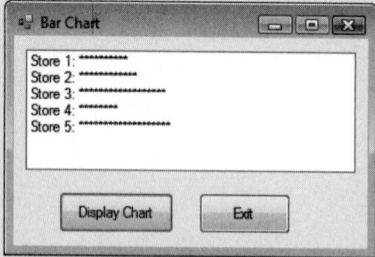

7. **Grade Report**

   Create an application that allows a teacher to enter three test scores each for three students. The application should calculate each student's average test score and assign a letter grade based on the following grading scale:

Average Test Score	Letter Grade
90 or greater	A
80 through 89	B
70 through 79	C
60 through 69	D
Below 60	F

   The application should prompt the user for each student's name and three test scores. Figure 5-52 shows an example of how the application's form might appear after all the data has been entered.

Figure 5-52 *Grade Report* form

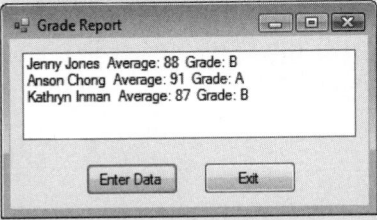

Design Your Own Forms

8. **Celsius to Fahrenheit Table**

   In Programming Challenge 6 of Chapter 3, you created an application that converts Celsius temperatures to Fahrenheit. Recall that the formula for performing this conversion is

   $$F = 1.8 * C + 32$$

   In the formula, *F* is the Fahrenheit temperature and *C* is the Celsius temperature.

   For this exercise, create an application that displays a table of the Celsius temperatures 0 through 20 and their Fahrenheit equivalents. The application should use a loop to display the temperatures in a list box.

9. **Population**

   Create an application that will predict the approximate size of a population of organisms. The user should select or enter the starting number of organisms in a combo box, enter the average daily population increase (as a percentage) in a text box, and select or enter the number of days the organisms will be left to multiply in another combo box. For example, assume the user enters the following values:

Starting number of organisms:	2
Average daily increase:	30%
Number of days to multiply:	10

The application should display the following table of data.

Day	Approximate Population
1	2
2	2.6
3	3.38
4	4.394
5	5.7122
6	7.42586
7	9.653619
8	12.5497
9	16.31462
10	21.209

Be sure to add appropriate ToolTips for each control on the form.

10. **Pennies for Pay**

Susan is hired for a job, and her employer agrees to pay her every day. Her employer also agrees that Susan's salary is one penny the first day, two pennies the second day, four pennies the third day, and continuing to double each day. Create an application that allows the user to select or enter into a combo box the number of days that Susan will work, and calculates the total amount of pay she will receive over that period of time.

11. **Payroll**

Create an application that displays payroll information. The application should allow the user to enter the following data for four employees:

- Number of hours worked
- Hourly pay rate
- Percentage to be withheld for state income tax
- Percentage to be withheld for federal income tax
- Percentage to be withheld for FICA

The application should calculate and display the following data for each employee in a list box:

- Gross pay (the number of hours worked multiplied by the hourly pay rate)
- State income tax withholdings (gross pay multiplied by state income tax percentage)
- Federal income tax withholdings (gross pay multiplied by federal income tax percentage)
- FICA withholdings (gross pay multiplied by FICA percentage)
- Net pay (the gross pay minus state income tax, federal income tax, and FICA)

When the calculations are performed, be sure to check for the following error:

- If any employee's state income tax plus federal tax plus FICA is greater than the employee's gross pay, display an error message stating that the withholdings are too great.

Be sure to add appropriate ToolTips for each control on the form.

12. **Ocean Levels**

Assuming the ocean's level is currently rising at about 1.5 millimeters per year, create an application that displays the number of millimeters that the ocean will have risen each year for the next 10 years.

13. **Calories Burned**

   Running on a particular treadmill you burn 3.9 calories per minute. Create an application that uses a loop to display the number of calories burned after 10, 15, 20, 25, and 30 minutes.

14. **Budget Analysis**

   Create an application that lets the user enter the amount that he or she has budgeted for a month. A loop should then use input boxes to prompt the user for his or her expenses for the month, and keep a running total. When the loop finishes, the program should display the amount that the user is over or under budget.

15. **Speed Conversion Chart**

   Your friend Amanda, who lives in the United States, just bought an antique European sports car. The car's speedometer works in kilometers per hour. The formula for converting kilometers per hour to miles per hour is:

   $$MPH = KPH * 0.6214$$

   In the formula, *MPH* is the speed in miles per hour and *KPH* is the speed in kilometers per hour. Amanda is afraid she will get a speeding ticket, and has asked you to write a program that displays a list of speeds in kilometers per hour with their values converted to miles per hour. The list should display the speeds from 60 kilometers per hour through 130 kilometers per hour, in increments of 5 kilometers per hour. (In other words, it should display 60 kph, 65 kph, 70 kph, and so forth, up through 130 kph.)

16. **Dice Simulator**

   Create an application that simulates rolling a pair of dice. When the user clicks a button, the application should generate two random numbers, each in the range of 1 through 6, to represent the value of the dice. Use PictureBox controls to display the dice. (In the student sample programs, in the *Chap5* folder, you will find six images named Die1.bmp, Die2.bmp, Die3.bmp, Die4.bmp, Die5.bmp, and Die6.bmp, that you can use in the PictureBoxes.)

17. **Addition Tutor**

   Create an application generates two random integers, each in the range of 100 through 500. The numbers should be displayed as an addition problem on the application's form, such as

   $$247 + 129 = ?$$

   The form should have a text box for the user to enter the problem's answer. When a button is clicked, the application should do the following:

   - Check the user's input and display a message indicating whether it is the correct answer.
   - Generate two new random numbers and display them in a new problem on the form.

18. **Random Number Guessing Game**

   Create an application that generates a random number in the range of 1 through 100, and asks the user to guess what the number is. If the user's guess is higher than the random number, the program should display "Too high, try again." If the user's guess is lower than the random number, the program should display "Too low, try again." The program should use a loop that repeats until the user correctly guesses the random number.

19. **Random Number Guessing Game Enhancement**

   Enhance the program that you wrote for Programming Challenge 18 so it keeps a count of the number of guesses that the user makes. When the user correctly guesses the random number, the program should display the number of guesses.

6 Procedures and Functions

A **procedure** is a collection of statements that performs a task. Event handlers, for example, are procedures. A **function** is a collection of statements that performs a task and then returns a value to the part of the program that executed it. You have already used many of Visual Basic's built-in functions such as `CInt` and `IsNumeric`.

This chapter discusses how to write general purpose procedures and functions. These procedures do not respond to events, but execute when they are called by statements. You will learn how to create, call, and pass arguments to these procedures as well as various techniques for debugging applications that use them.

In common object-oriented terminology, the term **method** is used to mean both procedures and functions.

6.1 Procedures

CONCEPT: You can write your own general purpose procedures that perform specific tasks. General purpose procedures are not triggered by events, but are called from statements in other procedures.

A procedure is a collection of statements that performs a task. An event handler or event procedure is a type of procedure that is executed when an event, such as a mouse click, occurs while the program is running. This section discusses general purpose procedures that are not triggered by events, but executed by statements in other procedures.

By writing your own procedures, you can **modularize** an application's code, that is, break it into small, manageable procedures. Imagine a book with a thousand pages that was not divided into chapters or sections. Finding a single topic in the book would be very difficult. Real-world applications can easily have thousands of lines of code, and unless they are modularized, they can be very difficult to modify and maintain.

Procedures can reduce the amount of duplicated code in a program. If a specific task is performed in several places, a procedure for performing that task can be written once and executed anytime it is needed.

Tutorial 6-1 walks you through an example application that uses a procedure.

Tutorial 6-1:
Examining an application with a procedure

Step 1: Open the *Procedure Demo* project from the student sample programs folder named *Chap6\Procedure Demo*. The application's form is shown in Figure 6-1. The form has a list box named `lstOutput` and two buttons: `btnGo` and `btnExit`.

Figure 6-1 *Procedure Demo* form

Step 2: Open the *Code* window and find the procedure named `DisplayMessage`, which is shown here:

```
Sub DisplayMessage()
    ' This is a procedure that displays a message.
    lstOutput.Items.Add("")
    lstOutput.Items.Add("Hello from the DisplayMessage procedure.")
    lstOutput.Items.Add("")
End Sub
```

The declaration of a procedure begins with a `Sub` statement and ends with an `End Sub` statement. The code that appears between these two statements is the body of the procedure. When the `DisplayMessage` procedure executes, it displays a blank line in the list box, followed by the string `"Hello from the DisplayMessage procedure."`, followed by another blank line.

Figure 6-2 shows the parts of the Sub statement.

Figure 6-2 First line of `DisplayMessage` procedure

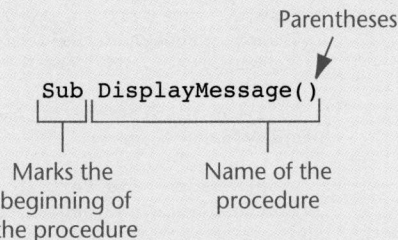

The first line of the procedure begins with the word `Sub`, followed by the name of the procedure, followed by a set of parentheses. In this procedure, the parentheses are empty. Later, you will see procedures having items inside the parentheses.

NOTE: An event handler is associated with a control, so its name is commonly prefixed with the control's name. For example, the `btnGo` button's Click event handler is named `btnGo_Click`. Since a general purpose procedure is not associated with a control, we do not usually prefix its name with any control name.

Step 3: General purpose procedures are not executed by an event. Instead, they must be called. Look at the following code for the `btnGo_Click` event handler. The statement in line 7 calls the `DisplayMessage` procedure.

```
1 Private Sub btnGo_Click(...) Handles btnGo.Click
2    ' Display some text in the list box.
3    lstOutput.Items.Add("Hello from the btnGo_Click procedure.")
4    lstOutput.Items.Add("Now I am calling the DisplayMessage procedure.")
5
6    ' Call the DisplayMessage procedure.
7    DisplayMessage()
8
9    ' Display some more text in the list box.
10   lstOutput.Items.Add("Now I am back in the btnGo_Click procedure.")
11 End Sub
```

This type of statement, known as a **procedure call**, causes the procedure to execute. A procedure call is simply the name of the procedure that is to be executed. Parentheses follow the name of the procedure. You can also use the `Call` keyword, as shown here:

```
Call DisplayMessage()
```

The `Call` keyword is optional, and is not used in this text.

When a procedure call executes, the application branches to the procedure and executes its body. When the procedure has finished, control returns to the procedure call and resumes executing at the next statement. Figure 6-3 illustrates how this application branches from the `btnGo_Click` procedure to the `DisplayMessage` procedure call, and returns to the `btnGo_Click` procedure.

Figure 6-3 Procedure call

```
Private Sub btnGo_Click(...) Handles btnGo.Click
    ' Display some text in the list box.
    lstOutput.Items.Add("Hello from the btnGo_Click procedure.")
    lstOutput.Items.Add("Now I am calling the DisplayMessage procedure.")

    ' Call the DisplayMessage procedure.
    DisplayMessage()

    ' Display some more text in the list box.
    lstOutput.Items.Add("Now I am back in the btnGo_Click procedure.")
End Sub


Sub DisplayMessage()
    ' This procedure displays a message in the list box.
    lstOutput.Items.Add("")
    lstOutput.Items.Add("Hello from the DisplayMessage procedure.")
    lstOutput.Items.Add("")
End Sub
```

Procedure is called / *Branch back*

Step 4: Run the application. Click the *Go* button. The form should appear as shown in Figure 6-4.

Figure 6-4 Results of *Procedure Demo*

As you can see, the statements in the `btnGo_Click` event handler executed up to the `DisplayMessage` procedure call. At that point, the application branched to the `DisplayMessage` procedure and executed all of its statements. When the `DisplayMessage` procedure finished, the application returned to the `btnGo_Click` event handler and resumed executing at the line following the `DisplayMessage` call.

Step 5: Click the *Exit* button to end the application.

Declaring a Procedure

The general format of a **procedure declaration** is as follows:

```
[AccessSpecifier] Sub ProcedureName ([ParameterList])
   [Statements]
End Sub
```

The items shown in brackets are optional. *AccessSpecifier* specifies the accessibility of the procedure. This is an important issue because some applications have more than one form. When you use the `Private` access specifier, the procedure may be accessed only by other procedures declared in the same class or form. When a procedure begins with `Public`, it may also be accessed by procedures declared in other forms. If you leave out the access specifier, it defaults to `Public`. We will begin to use access specifers in later chapters.

Following the keyword **Sub** is the name of the procedure. You should always give the procedure a name that reflects its purpose. You should also adopt a consistent style of using uppercase and lowercase letters. For procedure names, we use **Pascal casing**, which capitalizes the first character and the first character of each subsequent word in the procedure name. All other characters are lowercase. Using different styles of capitalization for variables and procedures lets the reader of your code know what type of entity a name belongs to.

Inside the parentheses is an optional *ParameterList*. A **parameter** is a special variable that receives a value being passed into a procedure. Later in this chapter, you will see procedures that use parameters to accept data passed into them.

The last line of a procedure declaration is the `End Sub` statement. Between the `Sub` statement and the `End Sub` statement, you write the statements that execute each time the procedure is called.

Tutorial 6-2 guides you through the process of writing procedures. In the tutorial, you will complete an application that uses two procedures, in addition to its event handlers.

VideoNote

Tutorial 6-2
Walkthrough

Tutorial 6-2:
Creating and Calling Procedures

The *Chap6* folder in the student sample programs contains a partially created project named *Lights*. In this tutorial you will complete the project so it simulates a light being turned off or on. The project's form is shown in Figure 6-5.

Figure 6-5 The *Lights* project's form

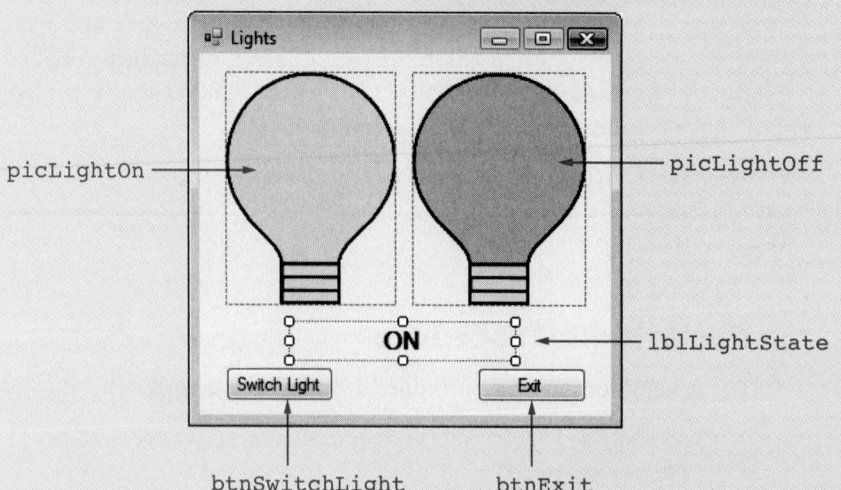

The form has the following controls:

- A PictureBox control named `picLightOn`, showing the image of a light bulb turned on. Initially, this PictureBox's Visible property is set to True.
- A PictureBox control name `picLightOff`, showing the image of a light bulb turned off. Initially, this PictureBox's Visible property is set to False.
- A Label control named `lblLightState` that will display either "ON" or "OFF". Initially, this control's Text property is set to "ON".
- A Button control named `btnSwitchLight` that turns the light off or on.
- A Button control named `btnExit` that closes the form.

When the user clicks the *Switch Light* button, the state of the light will be reversed. In other words, if the light is currently on, it will be turned off. If the light is currently off, it will be turned on.

When the light is turned on, the following actions will take place:

- The `picLightOn` control's Visible property is set to True
- The `picLightOff` control's Visible property is set to False.
- The `lblLightState` label's Text property is assigned the string "ON".

When the light is turned off, the following actions will take place:

- The `picLightOff` control's Visible property is set to True
- The `picLightOn` control's Visible property is set to False.
- The `lblLightState` label's Text property is assigned the string "OFF".

Step 1: Open the *Lights* project from the *Chap6* folder in the sample student programs.

Step 2: Open the *Code* window and type the following two procedures, shown in lines 3 through 23. (Don't type the line numbers. They are shown here for reference only.)

```
1 Public Class Form1
2
3   Sub TurnLightOn()
4     ' Display the "Light On" image.
5     picLightOn.Visible = True
6
```

```
 7         ' Hide the "Light Off" image.
 8         picLightOff.Visible = False
 9
10         ' Change the label text.
11         lblLightState.Text = "ON"
12     End Sub
13
14     Sub TurnLightOff()
15         ' Display the "Light Off" image.
16         picLightOff.Visible = True
17
18         ' Hide the "Light On" image.
19         picLightOn.Visible = False
20
21         ' Change the label text.
22         lblLightState.Text = "OFF"
23     End Sub
24 End Class
```

Before continuing, let's take a closer look at the code. Line 3 is the beginning of a procedure named TurnLightOn. The purpose of this procedure is to simulate the light turning on. When this procedure executes, line 5 makes the picLightOn control visible, line 8 hides the picLightOff control, and line 11 sets the lblLightState control's Text property to "ON".

Line 14 is the beginning of a procedure named TurnLightOff. The purpose of this procedure is to simulate the light turning off. When this procedure executes, line 16 makes the picLightOff control visible, line 19 hides the picLightOn control, and line 22 sets the lblLightState control's Text property to "OFF".

Step 3: Open the *Designer* window and double-click the btnSwitchLight button to create a code template for its Click event handler. Complete the event handler by writing the bold code, shown here in lines 2 through 7. (Don't type the line numbers. They are shown here for reference only.)

```
1 Private Sub btnSwitchLight_Click(...) Handles btnSwitchLight.Click
2     ' Reverse the state of the light.
3     If picLightOn.Visible = True Then
4         TurnLightOff()
5     Else
6         TurnLightOn()
7     End If
8 End Sub
```

Let's review this code. The If...Then statement in line 3 determines whether the picLightOn control is visible. If it is, it means the light is turned on, so the statement in line 4 calls the TurnLightOff procedure to turn the light off. Otherwise, the Else clause in line 5 takes over, and the TurnLightOn procedure is called on line 6 to turn the light on.

Step 4: Open the *Designer* window and double-click the btnExit button to create a code template for its Click event handler. Complete the event handler as shown here:

```
Private Sub btnExit_Click(...) Handles btnExit.Click
    ' Close the form.
    Me.Close()
End Sub
```

Step 5: Save the project, and then run the application. The form should initially appear as shown on the left in Figure 6-6. When you click the *Switch Light* button, the form should appear as shown on the right in the figure. Each time you click the *Switch Light* button, the state of the light should reverse.

Figure 6-6 Light on and off

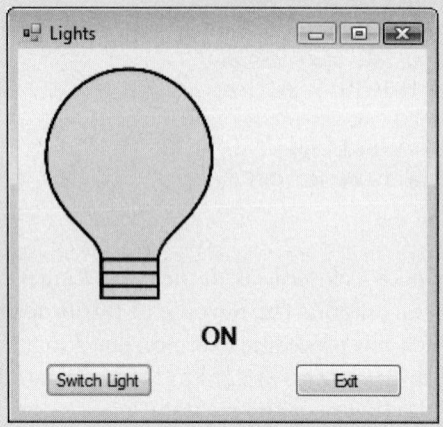
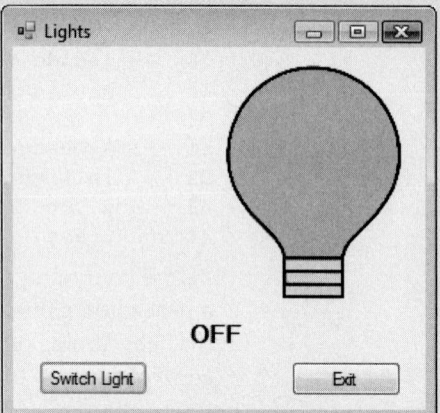

Step 6: When you are finished, exit the application.

If You Want to Know More: Static Local Variables

If a procedure is called more than once in a program, the values stored in the procedure's local variables do not remain between procedure calls. This is because the local variables are created in memory when the procedure starts, and destroyed when the procedure terminates. For example, look at the following procedure:

```
Sub ShowLocal()
    Dim intLocalNum As Integer
    MessageBox.Show(intLocalNum.ToString())
    intLocalNum = 99
End Sub
```

When this procedure is called, `intLocalNum` is created in memory and automatically initialized to 0, so the message box displays 0. Although the last statement in the `ShowLocal` procedure stores 99 in `intLocalNum`, the variable is destroyed when the procedure terminates. The next time this procedure is called, `intLocalNum` is recreated and initialized to 0 again. So, each time the procedure executes, it will display 0 in the message box.

Sometimes you want a procedure to remember the value stored in a local variable between procedure calls. This can be accomplished by making the variable static. **Static local variables** are not destroyed when a procedure terminates. They exist for the lifetime of the application, although their scope is only the procedure in which they are declared.

To declare a static local variable, replace `Dim` with `Static`. Here is the general format of a **Static** variable declaration.

```
Static VariableName As DataType
```

For example, look at the following procedure:

```
Sub ShowStatic()
   Static intStaticNum As Integer
   MessageBox.Show(intStaticNum.ToString())
   intStaticNum += 1
End Sub
```

Notice that `intStaticNum` is declared `Static`. When the procedure is called, `intStaticNum` is automatically initialized to 0 and its value is displayed in the message box. The last statement adds 1 to `intStaticNum`. Because the variable is static, it retains its value between procedure calls. The second time the procedure is called, `intStaticNum` equals 1. Likewise, the third time the procedure is called, `intStaticNum` equals 2, and so on.

NOTE: Static variables should only be used in those rare cases when a procedure must retain the value of a local variable between calls to the procedure. Also, you cannot declare a class-level variable using `Static`. Only variables declared inside a procedure may be static.

Checkpoint

6.1 Figure 6-7 shows an application's form.

The list box is named `lstOutput`. The buttons are named `btnGo` and `btnExit`. The application's procedures are as follows:

```
Private Sub btnGo_Click(...) Handles btnGo.Click
   Dim intNumber As Integer
   Dim strInput As String

   strInput = InputBox("Enter a number")
   intNumber = CInt(strInput)

   If intNumber < 10 Then
      Message1()
      Message2()
   Else
      Message2()
      Message1()

   End If
End Sub

Private Sub btnExit_Click(...) Handles btnExit.Click
   'Close the form.
   Me.Close()
End Sub

Sub Message1()
   lstOutput.Items.Add("Able was I")
End Sub

Sub Message2()
   lstOutput.Items.Add("I saw Elba")
End Sub
```

Suppose you run this application and click the `btnGo` button. What will the application display in the list box if you enter 10 in the input box? What if you enter 5?

Figure 6-7 *Checkpoint 6.1* application form

6.2 What is the difference between a regular local variable and a static local variable?

6.2 Passing Arguments to Procedures

CONCEPT: When calling a procedure, you can pass it values known as arguments.

VideoNote

Passing Arguments to Procedures

Values passed to procedures are called **arguments**. You are already familiar with how to use arguments. In the following statement, the `CInt` function is called and an argument, `txtInput.Text`, is passed to it:

```
intValue = CInt(txtInput.Text)
```

There are two ways to pass an argument to a procedure: by value or by reference. Passing an argument **by value** means that only a copy of the argument is passed to the procedure. Because the procedure has only a copy, it cannot make changes to the original argument. When an argument is passed **by reference**, however, the procedure has access to the original argument and can make changes to it.

In order for a procedure to accept an argument, it must be equipped with a parameter. A parameter is a special variable that receives an argument being passed into a procedure. Here is an example procedure that uses a parameter:

```
Sub DisplayValue(ByVal intNumber As Integer)
  ' This procedure displays a value in a message box.
  MessageBox.Show(intNumber.ToString())
End Sub
```

Notice the statement inside the parentheses in the first line of the procedure (repeated below).

```
ByVal intNumber As Integer
```

This statement declares the variable `intNumber` as an integer parameter. The **ByVal** keyword indicates that arguments passed into the variable are passed by value. This parameter variable enables the `DisplayValue` procedure to accept an integer argument.

TIP: The declaration of a parameter looks like a regular variable declaration, except the word `ByVal` is used instead of `Dim`.

Here is an example of how you would call the procedure and pass an argument to it:

```
DisplayValue(5)
```

The argument, 5, is listed inside the parentheses. This value is passed into the procedure's parameter variable, `intNumber`. This is illustrated in Figure 6-8.

Figure 6-8 Passing 5 to `DisplayValue`

```
DisplayValue(5)                    The value 5
                                is copied into the
                                parameter variable
                                    intNumber.


Sub DisplayValue(ByVal intNumber As Integer)
    ' This procedure displays a value in a message box.
    MessageBox.Show(intNumber.ToString())
End Sub
```

You may also pass variables and the values of expressions as arguments. For example, the following statements call the `DisplayValue` procedure, passing various arguments:

```
DisplayValue(intX)
DisplayValue(intX * 4)
DisplayValue(CInt(txtInput.Text))
```

The first statement passes the value in the variable `intX` as the argument. The second statement passes the value of the expression `intX * 4` as the argument. The third statement passes the value returned from `CInt(txtInput.Text)` as the argument. Tutorial 6-3 guides you through an application that demonstrates argument passing.

 Tutorial 6-3:
Examining an application that demonstrates passing an argument to a procedure

Step 1: Open the *Argument Demo* project from the student sample programs folder named *Chap6\Argument Demo*. The application's form is shown in Figure 6-9. The application's form has four buttons: `btnDemo1`, `btnDemo2`, `btnDemo3`, and `btnExit`.

Figure 6-9 *Argument Demo* form

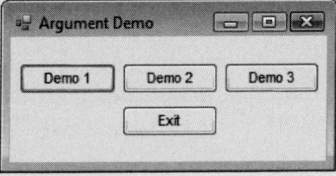

Step 2: In addition to the event handlers for each of the form's buttons, the application uses the DisplayValue procedure described earlier. Open the *Code* window and locate the btnDemo1_Click event handler. The code is as follows:

```
Private Sub btnDemo1_Click(...) Handles btnDemo1.Click
   'This event handler calls the DisplayValue procedure,
   'passing 5 as an argument.
   DisplayValue(5)
End Sub
```

This event handler calls DisplayValue with 5 as the argument.

Step 3: Locate the btnDemo2_Click event handler. The code is as follows:

```
Private Sub btnDemo2_Click(...) Handles btnDemo2.Click
   ' Call the DisplayValue procedure several times,
   ' passing different arguments each time.
   DisplayValue(5)
   DisplayValue(10)
   DisplayValue(2)
   DisplayValue(16)

   ' The value of an expression is passed to the
   ' DisplayValue procedure.
   DisplayValue(3 + 5)
End Sub
```

This event handler calls the DisplayValue procedure five times. Each procedure call is given a different argument. Notice the last procedure call:

```
DisplayValue(3 + 5)
```

This statement passes the value of an expression as the argument. When this statement executes, the value 8 is passed to DisplayValue.

Step 4: Locate the btnDemo3_Click event handler. The code is as follows:

```
Private Sub btnDemo3_Click(...) Handles btnDemo3.Click
   ' Use a loop to call the DisplayValue procedure
   ' passing a variable as the argument.
   Dim intCount As Integer

   For intCount = 1 To 10
      DisplayValue(intCount)
   Next
End Sub
```

This event handler has a local variable named intCount. It uses a For...Next loop to call the DisplayValue procedure ten times, each time passing the intCount variable as the argument.

Step 5: Run the application and click the *Demo 1* button. A message box appears displaying the value 5.

Step 6: Click the *Demo 2* button. Five successive message boxes are displayed, showing the values 5, 10, 2, 16, and 8.

Step 7: Click the *Demo 3* button. Ten successive message boxes are displayed, showing the values 1 through 10.

Step 8: Click the *Exit* button to end the application.

Passing Multiple Arguments

Often, it is useful to pass more than one argument to a procedure. For example, the following is a procedure that accepts two arguments:

```
Sub ShowSum(ByVal intNum1 As Integer, ByVal intNum2 As Integer)
   Dim intSum As Integer ' Local variable to hold a sum

   ' Get the sum of the two arguments.
   intSum = intNum1 + intNum2

   ' Display the sum.
   MessageBox.Show("The sum is " & intSum.ToString())
End Sub
```

Assuming that `intValue1` and `intValue2` are Integer variables, the following is an example call to the `ShowSum` procedure:

```
ShowSum(intValue1, intValue2)
```

When a procedure with multiple parameters is called, the arguments are assigned to the parameters in left-to-right order, as shown in Figure 6-10.

Figure 6-10 Multiple arguments passed to multiple parameters

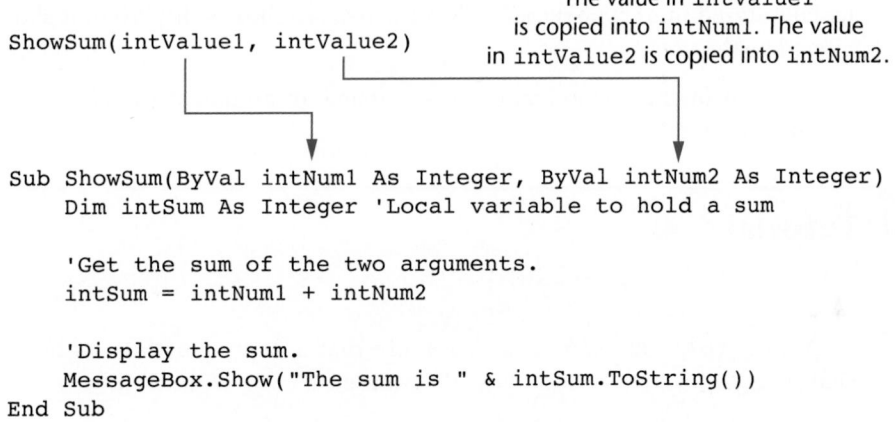

The following procedure call causes 5 to be assigned to the `intNum1` parameter and 10 to be assigned to `intNum2`:

```
ShowSum(5, 10)
```

However, the following procedure call causes 10 to be assigned to the `intNum1` parameter and 5 to be assigned to `intNum2`:

```
ShowSum(10, 5)
```

More about Passing Arguments by Reference

You have learned that when the `ByVal` keyword is used in the declaration of a parameter variable, an argument is passed by value to the parameter. This means that a copy of the argument is passed to the parameter variable. If the parameter's value is changed inside the procedure, it has no effect on the original argument.

When an argument is passed by reference, however, the procedure has access to the original argument. Any changes made to the parameter variable are actually performed on the original argument. Use the **ByRef** keyword in the declaration of a parameter variable to cause arguments to be passed by reference to the parameter. Here is an example:

```
Sub GetName(ByRef strName as String)
  ' Get the user's name
  strName = InputBox("Enter your name.")
End Sub
```

This procedure uses ByRef to declare the strName parameter. Any argument assigned to the parameter is passed by reference, and any changes made to strName are actually made to the argument passed into it. For example, assume the following code calls the procedure and displays the user name:

```
' Declare a string variable
Dim strUserName As String

' Get the user's name
GetName(strUserName)

' Display the user's name
MessageBox.Show("Your name is" & strUserName)
```

This code calls the GetName procedure and passes the string variable strUserName, by reference, into the strName parameter. The GetName procedure displays an input box instructing the user to enter his or her name. The user's input is stored in the strName variable. Because strUserName was passed by reference, the value stored in strName is actually stored in strUserName. When the message box is displayed, it shows the name entered by the user.

Tutorial 6-4 further demonstrates how passing an argument by reference differs from passing it by value.

Tutorial 6-4:
Working with ByVal and ByRef

In this tutorial, you examine a procedure that accepts a ByVal argument. Then you change ByVal to ByRef, to see how the procedure behaves differently.

Step 1: Open the *ByVal ByRef Demo* project from the student sample programs folder named *Chap6\ByVal ByRef Demo*. The application's form is shown in Figure 6-11. The form has a list box named lstOutput and two buttons named btnGo and btnExit.

Figure 6-11 *ByVal ByRef Demo* form

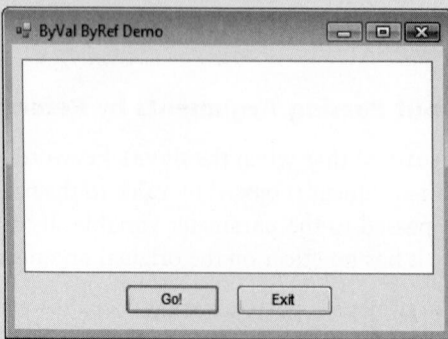

Step 2: Open the *Code* window and look at the btnGo_Click event handler.

```
Private Sub btnGo_Click(...) Handles btnGo.Click
    Dim intNumber As Integer = 100

    lstOutput.Items.Add("Inside btnGo_Click the value of " &
                        "intNumber is " &
                        intNumber.ToString())

    lstOutput.Items.Add("Now I am calling ChangeArg.")

    ChangeArg(intNumber)
    lstOutput.Items.Add("Now back in btnGo_Click, " &
                        "the value of intNumber is " &
                        intNumber.ToString())
End Sub
```

The variable intNumber is initialized to 100. This procedure calls the ChangeArg procedure and passes intNumber as the argument.

Step 3: Now look at the ChangeArg procedure. The code is as follows:

```
Sub ChangeArg(ByVal intArg As Integer)
    ' Display the value of intArg.
    lstOutput.Items.Add(" ")
    lstOutput.Items.Add("Inside the ChangeArg procedure, " &
                        "intArg is " & intArg.ToString())
    lstOutput.Items.Add("I will change the value of intArg.")

    ' Assign 0 to intArg.
    intArg = 0

    ' Display the value of intArg.
    lstOutput.Items.Add("intArg is now " & intArg.ToString())
    lstOutput.Items.Add(" ")
End Sub
```

Notice that the parameter variable, intArg, is declared ByVal.

Step 4: Run the application and click the *Go!* button. The form should appear as shown in Figure 6-12. Although the ChangeArg procedure sets intArg to 0, the value of intNumber did not change. This is because the ByVal keyword was used in the declaration of intArg. (intArg was passed by value).

Figure 6-12 Results with argument passed by value

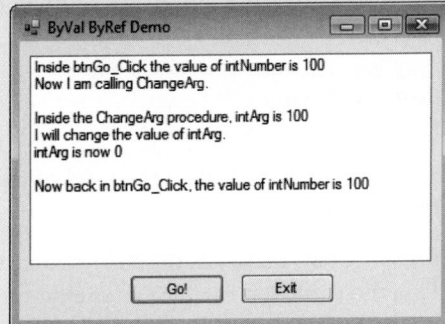

Step 5: Click the *Exit* button to end the application.

Step 6: Open the *Code* window. Change ByVal in the ChangeArg procedure to ByRef. The first line of the procedure should now look like this:

```
Sub ChangeArg(ByRef intArg As Integer)
```

Step 7: Run the application again and click the *Go!* button. The form should appear as shown in Figure 6-13. This time, when `ChangeArg` sets `intArg` to 0, it changes the value of `intNumber` to 0. This is because the `ByRef` keyword was used in the declaration of `intArg`.

Figure 6-13 Results with argument passed by reference

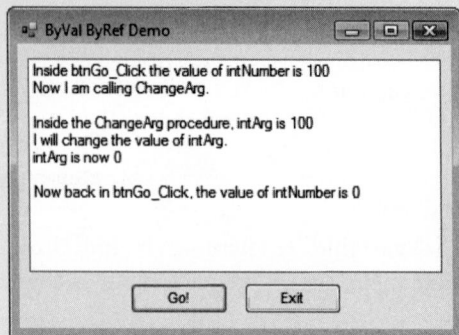

Step 8: Click the *Exit* button to end the application.

NOTE: You have learned how to pass variables as arguments to procedures. You can also pass constants and expressions as arguments to procedures. Although you can pass both variable and nonvariable arguments by reference, only variable arguments can be changed by the procedure receiving the arguments. If you pass a nonvariable argument by reference to a procedure, the procedure cannot change the argument.

Checkpoint

6.3 On paper, write the code for a procedure named `TimesTen`. The procedure must have an Integer parameter variable named `intValue`. The procedure must multiply the parameter by 10 and display the result in a message box.

6.4 Write a statement that calls the `TimesTen` procedure you wrote in Checkpoint 6.3. Pass the number 25 as the argument.

6.5 On paper, write the code for a procedure named `PrintTotal`. The procedure must have the following parameters:

```
intNum1 As Integer
intNum2 As Integer
intNum3 As Integer
```

The procedure must calculate the total of the three numbers and display the result in a message box.

6.6 Write a statement that calls the `PrintTotal` procedure you wrote in Checkpoint 6.5. Pass the variables `intUnits`, `intWeight`, and `intCount` as the arguments. The three arguments will be assigned to the `intNum1`, `intNum2`, and `intNum3` parameters.

6.7 Suppose you want to write a procedure that accepts an argument, and uses the argument in a mathematical operation. You want to make sure that the original argument is not altered. Should you declare the parameter `ByRef` or `ByVal`?

6.3 Functions

> **CONCEPT:** A function returns a value to the part of the program that called the function.

VideoNote
Functions

This section shows you how to write functions. Like a procedure, a function is a set of statements that perform a task when the function is called. In addition, a function returns a value that can be used in an expression.

In previous chapters, you called built-in Visual Basic functions many times. For instance, you used the CInt function to convert strings to integers. You also used the ToString function, which converts numbers to strings. Now you will learn to write your own functions that return values in the same way as built-in functions.

Declaring a Function

The general format of a function declaration is as follows:

```
[AccessSpecifier] Function FunctionName ([ParameterList]) As DataType
    [Statements]
End Function
```

A function declaration is similar to a procedure declaration. *AccessSpecifier* is optional, and specifies the accessibility of the function. As with procedures, you may use the keywords Private, Public, Protected, Friend, and Protected Friend as access specifiers. If you do not include an access specifier, it defaults to Public. Next is the keyword Function, followed by the name of the function. Inside the parentheses is an optional list of parameters. Following the parentheses is As *DataType*, where *DataType* is any data type. The data type listed in this part of the declaration is the data type of the value returned by the function.

The last line of a function declaration is the End Function statement. Between the Function statement and the End Function statements, are statements that execute when the function is called. Here is an example of a completed function:

```
1 Function Sum(ByVal dblNum1 As Double, ByVal dblNum2 As Double) As Double
2     Dim dblResult As Double
3
4     ' Add the two arguments.
5     dblResult = dblNum1 + dblNum2
6
7     ' Return the result.
8     Return dblResult
9 End Function
```

This code shows a function named Sum that accepts two arguments, adds them, and returns their sum. (Everything you have learned about passing arguments to procedures applies to functions as well.) The Sum function has two parameter variables, dblNum1 and dblNum2, both of the Double data type. Notice that the words As Double appear after the parentheses. This indicates that the value returned by the function will be of the Double data type.

Inside the function, the statement shown in line 2 declares a local variable named dblResult. The statement shown in line 5 adds the parameter variables dblNum1 and dblNum2, and assigns the result to dblResult. The Return statement in line 8 causes the function to end execution and return a value to the part of the program that called the function. The general format of the `Return` statement, when used to return a value from a function, is as follows:

```
Return Expression
```

Expression is the value to be returned. It can be any expression having value, such as a variable, a constant, or a mathematical expression. In this case, the `Sum` function returns the value in the `dblResult` variable. However, we could have eliminated the `dblResult` variable, and returned the expression `dblNum1 + dblNum2`, as shown in the following code:

```
Function Sum(ByVal dblNum1 As Double, ByVal dblNum2 As Double) As Double
    Return dblNum1 + dblNum2
End Function
```

The data type of the `Return` statement's expression should be the same as the function's return type, or convertible to the function's return type. For example, if the `Sum` function returns a Double, the value of the `Return` statement's expression must be Double, or a type that automatically converts to Double. If the return value cannot be converted to the function's return data type, a runtime error occurs.

Calling a Function

Assuming that `dblTotal`, `dblValue1`, and `dblValue2` are variables of type Double, here is an example of how you might call the `Sum` function:

```
dblTotal = Sum(dblValue1, dblValue2)
```

This statement passes the variables `dblValue1` and `dblValue2` as arguments. It assigns the value returned by the `Sum` function to the variable `dblTotal`. So, if `dblValue1` is 20.0 and `dblValue2` is 40.0, the statement assigns 60.0 to `dblTotal`.

Figure 6-14 illustrates how the arguments are passed to the function and how a value is returned from the function.

Figure 6-14 Arguments passed and a value returned

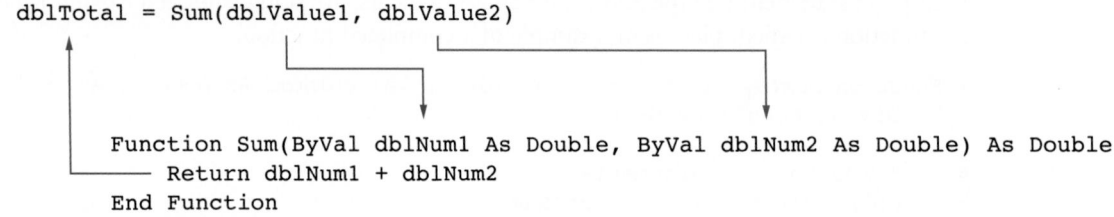

```
dblTotal = Sum(dblValue1, dblValue2)



    Function Sum(ByVal dblNum1 As Double, ByVal dblNum2 As Double) As Double
        Return dblNum1 + dblNum2
    End Function
```

In Tutorial 6-5, you will create a simple application that uses a function to calculate the sale price of a retail item.

Tutorial 6-5:
Creating and Calling a Function

VideoNote

Tutorial 6-5
Walkthrough

In this tutorial you will create an application that calculates the sale price of a retail item. The application will allow the user to enter the item's regular retail price and the discount percentage. It will then calculate the sale price using the following formula:

Sale Price = Retail Price − (Retail Price × Discount Percentage)

For example, if an item's retail price is $100 and the discount percentage is 25 percent (.25), then the sale price is $75.

In the application's code you will write a function named `SalePrice` that accepts the item's retail price and the discount percentage as arguments. The function will then return the sale price as a Decimal.

Step 1: Start a new Windows Forms Application project named *Sale Price Calculator*. Set up the application's form as shown in Figure 6-15.

Figure 6-15 *Sale Price Calculator* form

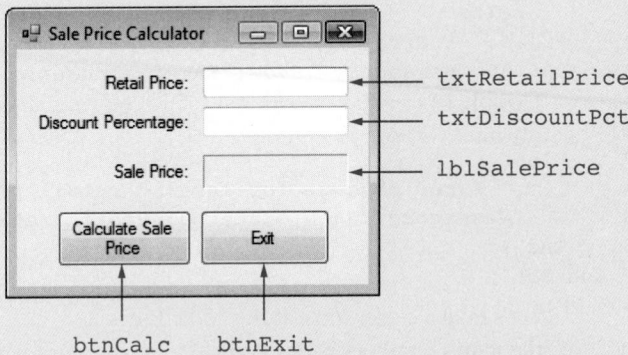

Step 2: Open the *Code* window and write the `SalePrice` function, as shown here in the bold code, in lines 3 through 12. (Don't type the line numbers. They are shown here for reference.)

```
1 Private Class Form1
2
3     Function SalePrice(ByVal decRetail As Decimal,
4                 ByVal decPercentage As Decimal) As Decimal
5         Dim decSalePrice As Decimal ' To hold the sale price
6
7         ' Calculate the sale price.
8         decSalePrice = decRetail - (decRetail * decPercentage)
9
10        ' Return the sale price.
11        Return decSalePrice
12    End Function
13 End Class
```

Let's take a closer look at the function's code. Notice that the function has two parameter variables: `decRetail` and `decPercentage`. When we call this function we will pass an item's retail price and the discount percentage as arguments. In line 5 we declare a local variable named `decSalePrice` that will be used to hold the sale price. Line 8 calculates the item's sale price, and assigns that value to the `decSalePrice` variable. Then, line 11 returns the value of the `decSalePrice` variable.

Step 3: Open the *Designer* window and double-click the `btnCalc` button. Complete the Click event handler with the bold code shown here in lines 2 through 26. (Don't type the line numbers. They are shown here for reference.)

```
1 Private Sub btnCalc_Click(...) Handles btnCalc.Click
2     Dim decRetail As Decimal      ' To hold the retail price
3     Dim decPercentage As Decimal ' To hold the discount percentage
4     Dim decSalePrice As Decimal   ' To hold the sale price
5
```

```
6      ' Get the retail price.
7     If Decimal.TryParse(txtRetailPrice.Text, decRetail) Then
8
9          ' Get the discount percentage.
10         If Decimal.TryParse(txtDiscountPct.Text, decPercentage) Then
11
12             ' Get the sale price.
13             decSalePrice = SalePrice(decRetail, decPercentage)
14
15             ' Display the sale price.
16             lblSalePrice.Text = decSalePrice.ToString("c")
17
18         Else
19             ' Error message for invalid discount percentage.
20             MessageBox.Show("Enter a numeric discount percentage.")
21         End If
22
23     Else
24         ' Error message for invalid retail price.
25         MessageBox.Show("Enter a numeric retail price.")
26     End If
27 End Sub
```

Let's take a closer look at the code. Lines 2, 3, and 4 declare local variables to hold the item's retail price (decRetail), the discount percentage (decPercentage), and the sale price (decSalePrice).

The If...Then statement in line 7 uses the Decimal.TryParse method to convert txtRetailPrice.Text to a Decimal, and stores the result in decRetail. If the conversion is successful, the Decimal.TryParse method returns True and the program continues to line 10. If the conversion fails (because of invalid input in the txtRetailPrice control), the Decimal.TryParse method returns False, and the program jumps to the Else clause in line 23. If this happens, line 25 displays an error message, and the event handler ends.

The If...Then statement in line 10 uses the Decimal.TryParse method to convert txtDiscountPct.Text to a Decimal, and stores the result in decPercentage. If the conversion is successful, the Decimal.TryParse method returns True and the program continues to line 13. If the conversion fails (because of invalid input in the txtDiscountPct control), the Decimal.TryParse method returns False, and the program jumps to the Else clause in line 18. If this happens, line 20 displays an error message, and the event handler ends.

Line 13 calls the SalePrice function, passing decRetail and decPercentage as arguments. The function uses these values to calculate a sale price, which is returned and assigned to decSalePrice. Line 16 displays the sale price in the lblSalePrice label.

Step 4:   Open the *Designer* window and double-click the btnExit button to create a code template for its Click event handler. Complete the event handler as shown here:

```
Private Sub btnExit_Click(...) Handles btnExit.Click
    ' Close the form.
    Me.Close()
End Sub
```

Step 5: Save the project, and then run the application. Enter **100** for the retail price and **.25** for the discount percentage. When you click the *Calculate Sale Price* button, the application should display $75.00 as the sale price, as shown in Figure 6-16.

Figure 6-16 Sale price calculated

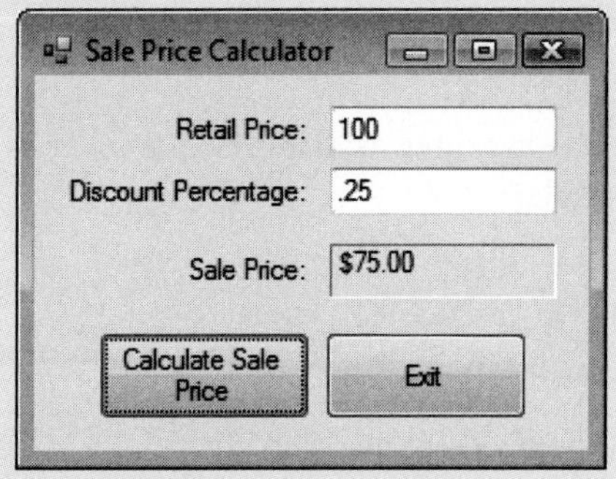

Step 6: When you are finished, exit the application.

If You Want to Know More about Functions: Returning Nonnumeric Values

When writing functions, you are not limited to returning numeric values. You can return nonnumeric values, such as strings and Boolean values. For example, here is the code for a function that returns a String:

```
Function FullName(ByVal strFirst As String,
                  ByVal strLast As String) As String
    ' Local variable to hold the full name
    Dim strName As String

    ' Append the last name to the first name and
    ' assign the result to strName.
    strName = strFirst & " " & strLast

    ' Return the full name.
    Return strName
End Function
```

Here is an example of a call to this function:

```
strCustomer = FullName("John", "Martin")
```

After this call, the string variable `strCustomer` will hold `"John Martin"`.

Here is an example of a function that returns a Boolean value:

```
Function IsValid(intNum As Integer) As Boolean
    Dim blnStatus As Boolean

    If intNum >= 0 And intNum <= 100 Then
      blnStatus = True
    Else
      blnStatus = False
    End If

    Return blnStatus
End Function
```

This function returns *True* if its argument is within the range 0 to 100. Otherwise, it returns *False*. The following code segment has an If...Then statement with an example call to the function:

```
intValue = 20
If IsValid(intValue) Then
    MessageBox.Show("The value is within range.")
Else
    MessageBox.Show("The value is out of range.")
End If
```

When this code executes, it displays *The value is within range.* in a message box. Here is another example:

```
intValue = 200
If IsValid(intValue) Then
    MessageBox.Show("The value is within range.")
Else
    MessageBox.Show("The value is out of range.")
End If
```

When this code executes, it displays *The value is out of range.* in a message box.

 **Checkpoint**

6.8   Look at the following function declaration and answer the questions below.
```
Function Distance(ByVal sngRate As Single,
                ByVal sngTime As Single) As Single
```
   a.   What is the name of the function?
   b.   When you call this function, how many arguments do you pass to it?
   c.   What are the names of the parameter variables and what are their data types?
   d.   This function returns a value of what data type?

6.9   Write the first line of a function named Days. The function should return an integer value. It should have three integer parameters: intYears, intMonths, and intWeeks. All arguments should be passed by value.

6.10   Write an example function call statement for the function described in Checkpoint 6.9.

6.11   Write the first line of a function named LightYears. The function should return a value of the Single data type. It should have one parameter variable, lngMiles, of the Long data type. The parameter should be declared so that the argument is passed by value.

6.12   Write an example function call statement for the function described in Checkpoint 6.11.

6.13   Write the entire code for a function named TimesTwo. The function should accept an integer argument and return the value of that argument multiplied by two.

6.4 More about Debugging: Stepping Into, Over, and Out of Procedures and Functions

CONCEPT: Visual Basic debugging commands allow you to single-step through applications with procedure and function calls. The *Step Into* command allows you to single-step through a called procedure or function. The *Step Over* command allows you to execute a procedure or function call without single-stepping through its lines. The *Step Out* command allows you to execute all remaining lines of a procedure or function you are debugging without stepping through them.

In Chapter 3 you learned to set a breakpoint in your application's code and to single-step through the code's execution. Let's find out how to step into or step over a procedure or function and step out of a procedure or function.

When an application is in Break mode, the **Step Into command** causes the currently high-lighted line (the execution point) to execute. If that line contains a call to a procedure or a function, the next highlighted line is the first line in that procedure or function. In other words, the *Step Into* command allows you to single-step through a procedure or function when it is called. Activate the *Step Into* command using one of the following methods:

- Press the F8 key
- Select *Debug* from the menu bar, and then select *Step Into* from the *Debug* menu
- Click the *Step Into* button (⬚) on the *Debug Toolbar*, if the toolbar is visible

Like the *Step Into* command, the **Step Over command** causes the currently highlighted line to execute. If the line contains a procedure or function call, however, the procedure or function is executed without stepping through its statements. Activate the *Step Over* command using one of the following methods:

- Press Shift+F8
- Select *Debug* from the menu bar, and then select *Step Over* from the *Debug* menu
- Click the *Step Over* button (⬚) on the *Debug Toolbar*, if the toolbar is visible

Use the **Step Out command** when single-stepping through a procedure or function, if you want the remainder of the procedure or function to complete execution without single-stepping. After the procedure or function has completed, the line following the procedure or function call is highlighted, and you may resume single-stepping. Activate the *Step Out* command using one of the following methods:

- Press Ctrl+Shift+F8
- Select *Debug* from the menu bar, and then select *Step Out* from the *Debug* menu
- Click the *Step Out* button (⬚) on the *Debug Toolbar* , if the toolbar is visible

In Tutorials 6-6, 6-7, and 6-8 you practice using each of these commands.

Tutorial 6-6:

Practicing the *Step Into command*

In this tutorial, you use the *Sale Price Calculator* project to practice single-stepping through procedures and functions.

Step 1: Open the *Sale Price Calculator* project from Tutorial 6-5.

Step 2: Open the *Code* window and set a breakpoint at the line in the `btnCalc_Click` event handler shown in Figure 6-17.

Figure 6-17 Location of breakpoint

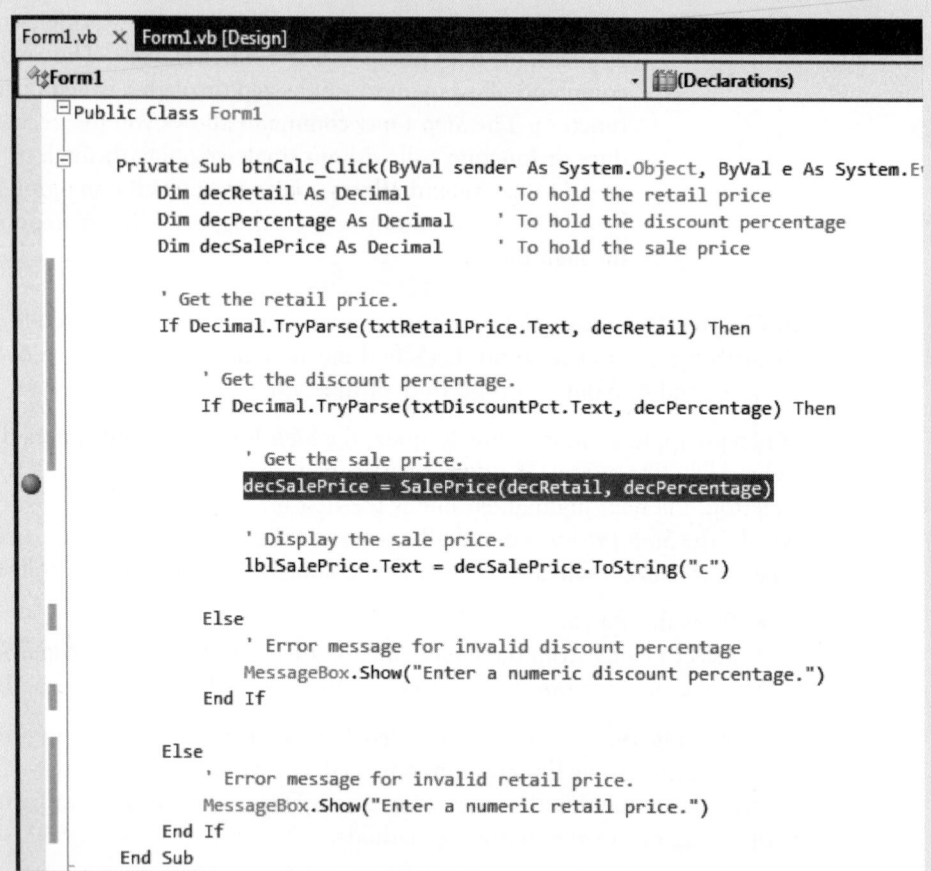

```vb
Form1.vb  ×  Form1.vb [Design]

Form1                                                    ▼  (Declarations)

  Public Class Form1

      Private Sub btnCalc_Click(ByVal sender As System.Object, ByVal e As System.E
          Dim decRetail As Decimal          ' To hold the retail price
          Dim decPercentage As Decimal      ' To hold the discount percentage
          Dim decSalePrice As Decimal       ' To hold the sale price

          ' Get the retail price.
          If Decimal.TryParse(txtRetailPrice.Text, decRetail) Then

              ' Get the discount percentage.
              If Decimal.TryParse(txtDiscountPct.Text, decPercentage) Then

                  ' Get the sale price.
                  decSalePrice = SalePrice(decRetail, decPercentage)

                  ' Display the sale price.
                  lblSalePrice.Text = decSalePrice.ToString("c")

              Else
                  ' Error message for invalid discount percentage
                  MessageBox.Show("Enter a numeric discount percentage.")
              End If

          Else
              ' Error message for invalid retail price.
              MessageBox.Show("Enter a numeric retail price.")
          End If
      End Sub
```

 TIP: Set a breakpoint by clicking the mouse while the pointer is positioned in the left margin, next to the line of code. You can also move the text cursor to the line you wish to set as a breakpoint, and then press F9

Step 3: Run the application in Debug mode, and enter 100 for the retail price and .25 for the discount percentage.

Step 4: Click the *Calculate Sale Price* button. The application enters Break mode with the breakpoint line highlighted.

Step 5: Notice that the highlighted line contains a call to the `SalePrice` function. Press F8 to execute the *Step Into* command.

Step 6: Because you pressed F8, the first line of the `SalePrice` function is highlighted next. You will now single-step through the statements inside the `SalePrice` function. Continue pressing the F8 key to single-step though the `SalePrice` function. When the `End Function` line is highlighted, press F8 once more to return to the line that called the function.

Step 7: Press F5 or click *Debug* on the menu bar and then click *Continue* to exit Break mode and resume normal execution. (Leave the project open in Visual Studio. You will use it in the next tutorial.)

Tutorial 6-7:
Practicing the *Step Over* command

Step 1: Make sure the *Sale Price Calculator* project is still open in Visual Studio from the previous tutorial. The breakpoint should still be set as shown in Figure 6-18.

Figure 6-18 Location of breakpoint

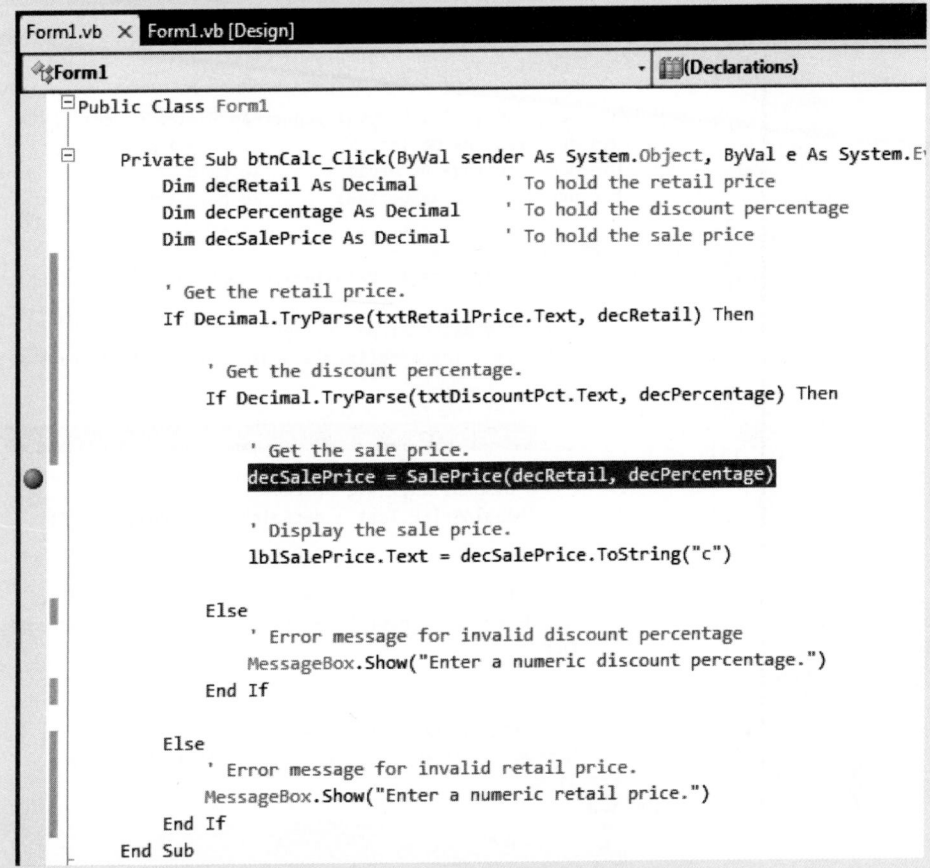

Step 2: Run the application in Debug mode and enter 100 for the retail price and .25 for the discount percentage.

Step 3: Click the *Calculate Sale Price* button. The application enters Break mode with the breakpoint line highlighted.

Step 4: Notice that the highlighted line contains a call to the `SalePrice` function. Press Shift+F8 to execute the *Step Over* command. This executes the function call without stepping through it. The next line is now highlighted.

Step 5: Press F5 or click *Debug* on the menu bar and then click *Continue* to exit Break mode and resume normal execution. (Leave the project open in Visual Studio. You will use it in the next tutorial.)

Tutorial 6-8:
Practicing the *Step Out* command

Step 1:   Make sure the *Sale Price Calculator* project is still open in Visual Studio from the previous tutorial. The breakpoint should still be set as shown in Figure 6-19.

Figure 6-19 Location of breakpoint

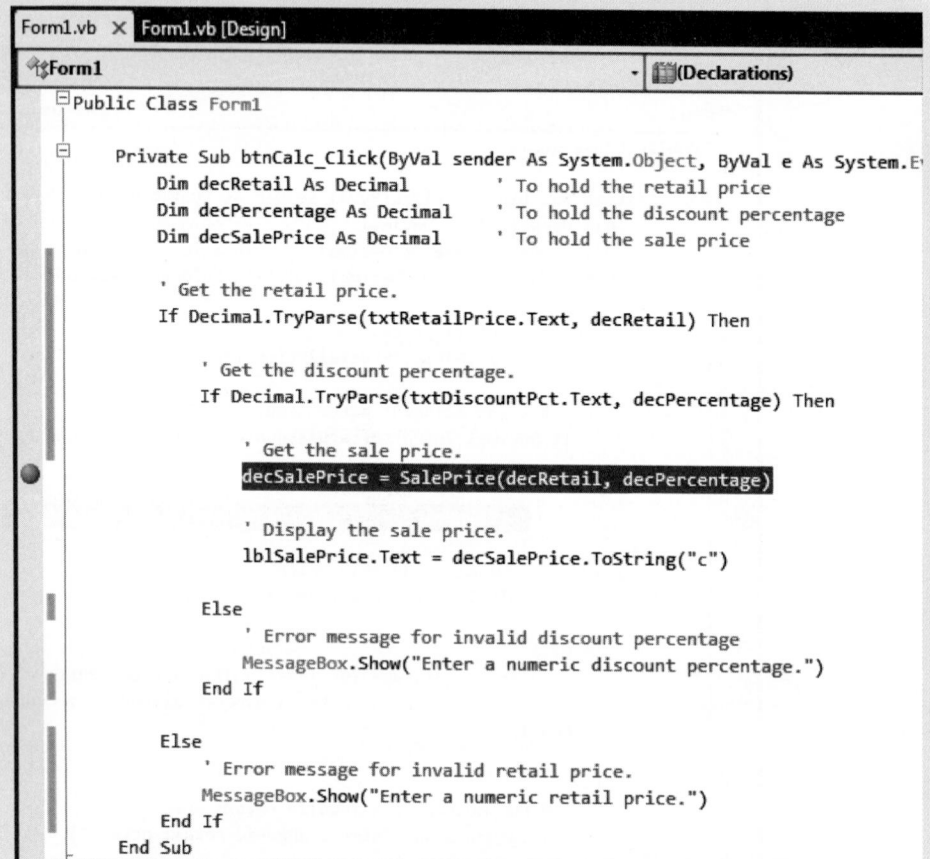

Step 2:   Run the application in Debug mode and enter **100** for the retail price and **.25** for the discount percentage.

Step 3:   Click the *Calculate Sale Price* button. The application enters Break mode with the breakpoint line highlighted.

Step 4:   Notice that the highlighted line contains a call to the `SalePrice` function. Press `F8` to execute the *Step Into* command.

Step 4:   Because you pressed `F8`, the first line of the `SalePrice` function is highlighted next. Press the `F8` key once again to advance to the next line in the function.

Step 5:   Instead of continuing to step through the function, you will now step out of the function. Press `Ctrl`+`Shift`+`F8` to execute the *Step Out* command. Single-stepping is suspended while the remaining statements in the `SalePrice` function execute. You are returned to the `btnCalc_Click` event handler, at the line containing the function call.

Step 6:   Press `F5` or click *Debug* on the menu bar and then click *Continue* to exit Break mode and resume normal execution.

TIP: When the current execution point does not contain a procedure or function call, the *Step Into* and *Step Over* commands perform identically.

 **Checkpoint**

6.14 Suppose you are debugging an application in Break mode, and are single-stepping through a function that has been called. If you want to execute the remaining lines of the function and return to the line that called the function, what command do you use? What key(s) do you press to execute this command?

6.15 Suppose you are debugging an application in Break mode and the current execution point contains a procedure call. If you want to single-step through the procedure that is being called, what command do you use? What key(s) do you press to execute this command?

6.16 Suppose you are debugging an application in Break mode, and the current execution point contains a function call. If you want to execute the line, but not single-step through the function, what command do you use? What key(s) do you press to execute this command?

 **6.5** **Focus on Program Design and Problem Solving: Building the *Bagel and Coffee Price Calculator* Application**

CONCEPT: In this section you build the *Bagel and Coffee Price* Calculator application. It uses procedures and functions to calculate the total of a customer order.

Brandi's Bagel House has a bagel and coffee delivery service for the businesses in her neighborhood. Customers may call in and order white and whole wheat bagels with a variety of toppings. Additionally, customers may order three different types of coffee. Here is a complete price list:

Bagels:
White bagel	$1.25
Whole wheat bagel	$1.50

Toppings:
Cream cheese	$0.50
Butter	$0.25
Blueberry jam	$0.75
Raspberry jam	$0.75
Peach jelly	$0.75

Coffee:
Regular coffee	$1.25
Cappuccino	$2.00
Café au lait	$1.75

(*Note:* Delivery for coffee alone is not offered.)

Brandi, the owner, has asked you to write an application that her staff can use to record an order as it is called in. The application should display the total of the order, including 6% sales tax. Figure 6-20 shows a sketch of the application's form and identifies all the controls with programmer-defined names.

Figure 6-20 Sketch of *Brandi's Bagel House* form

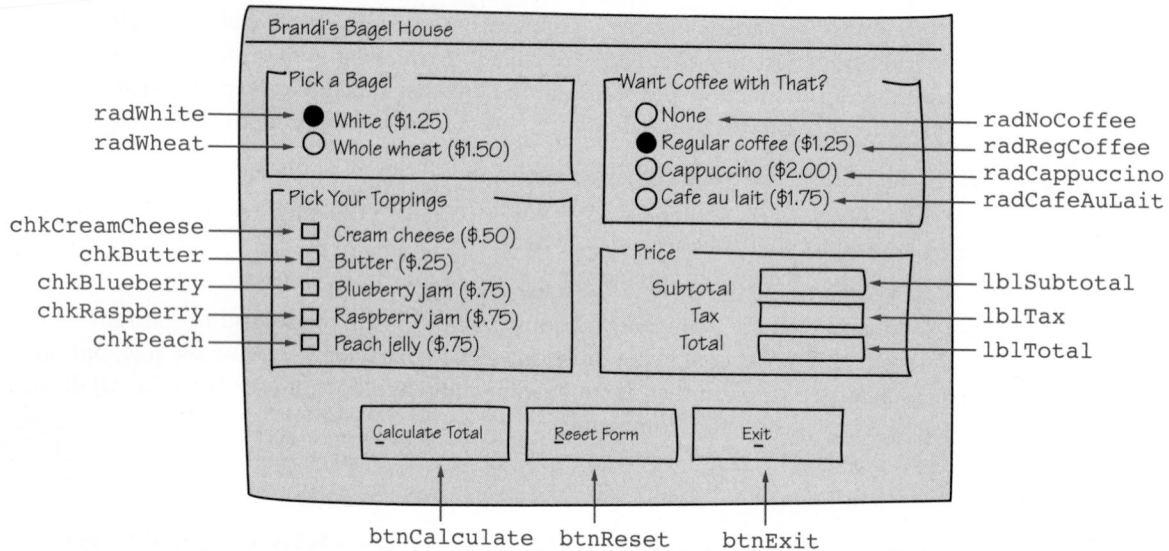

Table 6-1 lists each control, along with any relevant property settings.

Table 6-1 *Bagel and Coffee Calculator* controls

Control Type	Control Name	Property	Property Value
Form	(Default)	Text:	*Brandi's Bagel House*
ToolTip	(Default)		(Retain all default property settings.)
GroupBox	(Default)	Text:	*Pick a Bagel*
RadioButton	radWhite	Text:	*White ($1.25)*
		Checked:	*True*
		ToolTip on ToolTip1:	*Click here to choose a white bagel.*
RadioButton	radWheat	Text:	*Whole Wheat ($1.50)*
		ToolTip on ToolTip1:	*Click here to choose a whole wheat bagel.*
GroupBox	(Default)	Text:	*Pick Your Toppings*
CheckBox	chkCreamCheese	Text:	*Cream Cheese ($.50)*
		ToolTip on ToolTip1:	*Click here to choose cream cheese.*
CheckBox	chkButter	Text:	*Butter ($.25)*
		ToolTip on ToolTip1:	*Click here to choose butter.*
CheckBox	chkBlueberry	Text:	*Blueberry Jam ($.75)*
		ToolTip on ToolTip1:	*Click here to choose blueberry jam.*
CheckBox	chkRaspberry	Text:	*Raspberry Jam ($.75)*
		ToolTip on ToolTip1:	*Click here to choose raspberry jam.*

(continued)

Table 6-1 *Bagel and Coffee Calculator* controls (*continued*)

Control Type	Control Name	Property	Property Value
CheckBox	chkPeach	Text: ToolTip on ToolTip1:	*Peach Jelly ($.75)* *Click here to choose peach jelly.*
GroupBox	(Default)	Text:	*Want coffee with that?*
RadioButton	radNoCoffee	Text: ToolTip on ToolTip1:	None *Click here to choose no coffee.*
RadioButton	radRegCoffee	Text: Checked: ToolTip on ToolTip1:	*Regular Coffee ($1.25)* *True* *Click here to choose regular coffee.*
RadioButton	radCappuccino	Text: ToolTip on ToolTip1:	*Cappuccino ($2.00)* *Click here to choose cappuccino.*
RadioButton	radCafeAuLait	Text: ToolTip on ToolTip1:	*Cafe au lait ($1.75)* *Click here to choose cafe au lait.*
GroupBox	(Default)	Text:	*Price*
Label	(Default)	Text:	*Subtotal*
Label	lblSubtotal	Text: AutoSize: BorderStyle:	 *False* *Fixed3D*
Label	(Default)	Text:	*Tax*
Label	lblTax	Text: AutoSize: BorderStyle:	 *False* *Fixed3D*
Label	(Default)	Text:	*Total*
Label	lblTotal	Text: AutoSize: BorderStyle:	 *False* *Fixed3D*
Button	btnCalculate	Text: ToolTip on ToolTip1:	*&Calculate Total* *Click here to calculate the total of the order.*
Button	btnReset	Text: ToolTip on ToolTip1:	*&Reset Form* *Click here to clear the form and start over.*
Button	btnExit	Text: ToolTip on ToolTip1:	*E&xit* *Click here to exit.*

Table 6-2 lists and describes the methods (event handlers procedures, and functions) used in this application.

Table 6-2 Methods for *Bagel and Coffee Calculator*

Method	Type of Method	Description
btnCalculate_Click	Event handler	Calculates and displays the total of an order. Calls the following functions: BagelCost, CoffeeCost, ToppingCost, and CalcTax.
btnExit_Click	Event handler	Ends the application.

(*continued*)

Table 6-2 Methods for *Bagel and Coffee Calculator* (continued)

Method	Type of Method	Description
btnReset_Click	Event handler	Resets the controls on the form to their initial values. Calls the following procedures: ResetBagels, ResetToppings, ResetCoffee, ResetPrice.
BagelCost	Function	Returns the price of the selected bagel.
ToppingCost	Function	Returns the total price of the selected toppings.
CoffeeCost	Function	Returns the price of the selected coffee.
CalcTax	Function	Accepts the amount of a sale as an argument. Returns the amount of sales tax on that amount. The tax rate is stored in a class-level constant, decTAX_RATE.
ResetBagels	Procedure	Resets the bagel type radio buttons to their initial value.
ResetToppings	Procedure	Resets the topping check boxes to unchecked.
ResetCoffee	Procedure	Resets the coffee radio buttons to their initial values.
ResetPrice	Procedure	Sets the Text property of the lblSubtotal, lblTax, and lblTotal labels to String.Empty.

Figure 6-21 shows a flowchart for the btnCalculate_Click event handler. This procedure calculates the total of an order and displays its price. Notice that very little math is actually performed in this procedure, however. It calls the BagelCost, ToppingCost, CoffeeCost, and CalcTax functions to get the values it needs.

Notice that a new flowchart symbol, which represents a call to a procedure or function, is introduced.

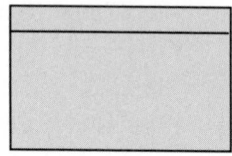

Pseudocode for the btnCalculate_Click procedure is as follows:

subtotal = BagelCost() + ToppingCost() + CoffeeCost()
tax = CalcTax(subtotal)
total = subtotal + tax

lblSubtotal.Text = subtotal
lblTax.Text = tax
lblTotal.Text = total

Figure 6-22 shows a flowchart for the btnReset_Click event handler. The purpose of this procedure is to reset all the radio buttons, check boxes, and labels on the form to their initial values. This operation has been broken into the following procedures: ResetBagels, ResetToppings, ResetCoffee, ResetPrice. When btnReset_Click executes, it simply calls these procedures.

Figure 6-21 Flowchart for
`btnCalculate_Click` event handler

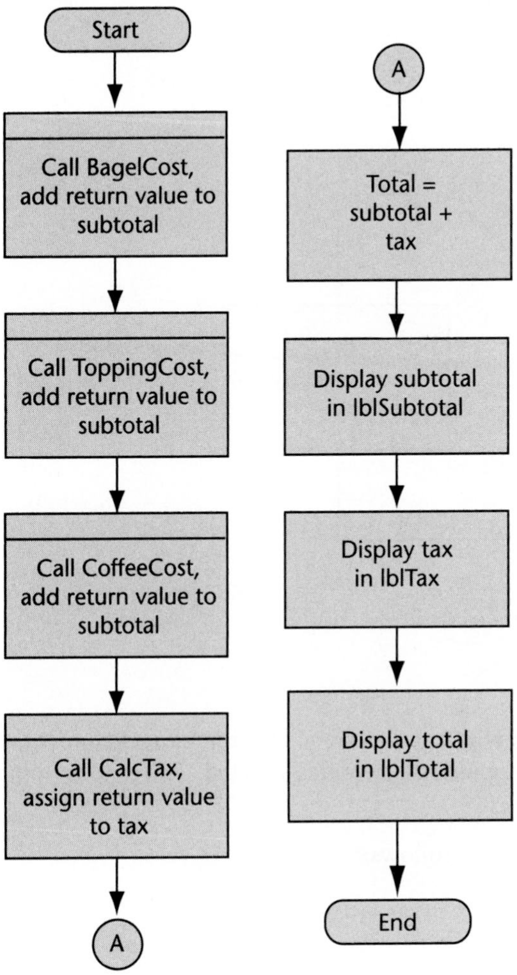

Figure 6-22 Flowchart for
`btnReset_Click` event handler

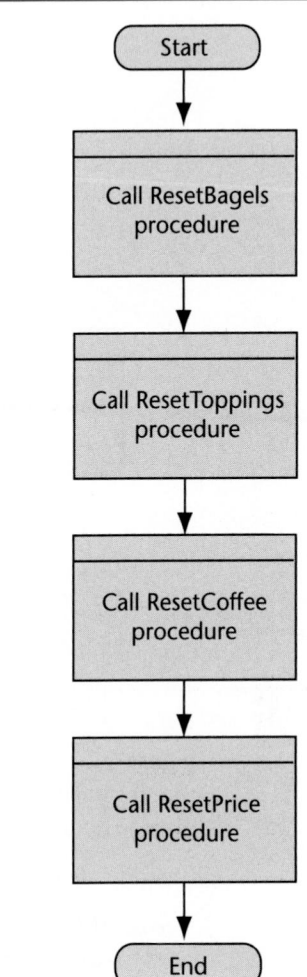

Pseudocode for the `btnReset_Click` procedure is as follows:

ResetBagels()
ResetToppings()
ResetCoffee()
ResetPrice()

Figure 6-23 shows a flowchart for the `BagelCost` function. This function determines whether the user has selected white or whole wheat, and returns the price of that selection.

Pseudocode for the `BagelCost` function is as follows:

If White Is Selected Then
　cost of bagel = 1.25
Else
　cost of bagel = 1.5
End If
Return cost of bagel

Figure 6-23 Flowchart for `BagelCost` function

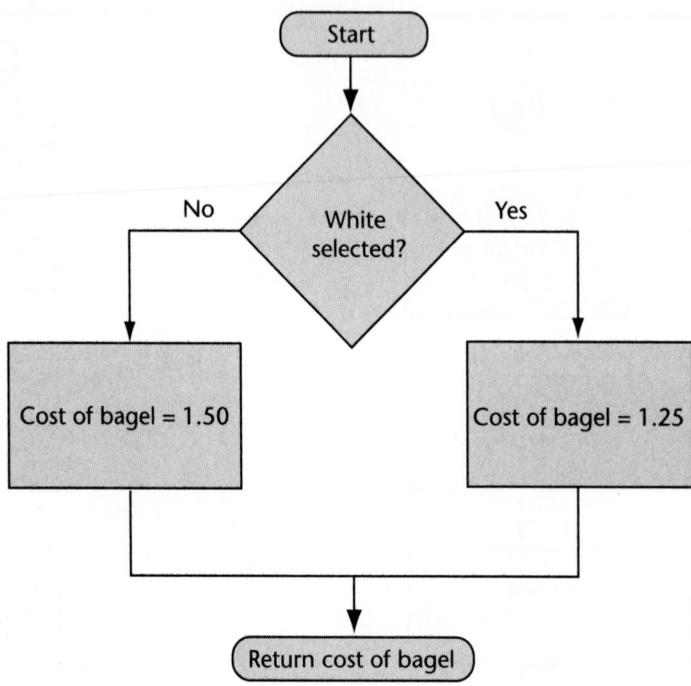

Figure 6-24 shows a flowchart for the `ToppingCost` function. This function examines the topping check boxes to determine which toppings the user has selected. The total topping price is returned.

Pseudocode for the `ToppingCost` function is as follows:

> *cost of topping = 0.0*
> *If Cream Cheese Is Selected Then*
>   *cost of topping += 0.5*
> *End If*
> *If Butter Is Selected Then*
>   *cost of topping += 0.25*
> *End If*
> *If Blueberry Is Selected Then*
>   *cost of topping += 0.75*
> *End If*
> *If Raspberry Is Selected Then*
>   *cost of topping += 0.75*
> *End If*
> *If Peach Is Selected Then*
>   *cost of topping += 0.75*
> *End If*
> *Return cost of topping*

Figure 6-24 Flowchart for `ToppingCost` function

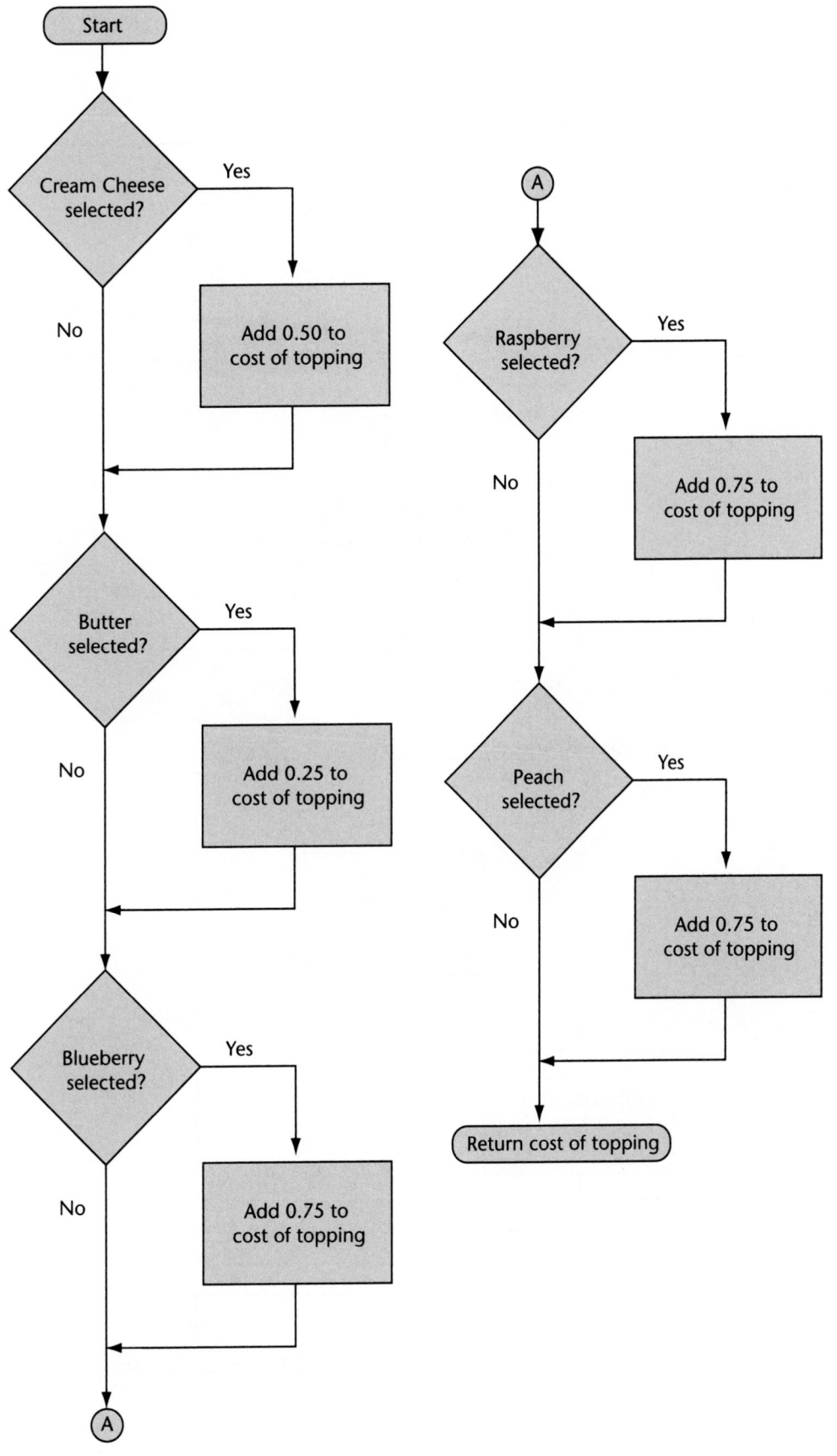

Figure 6-25 shows a flowchart for the `CoffeeCost` function. This function examines the coffee radio buttons to determine which coffee (if any) the user has selected. The price is returned.

Figure 6-25 Flowchart for `CoffeeCost` function

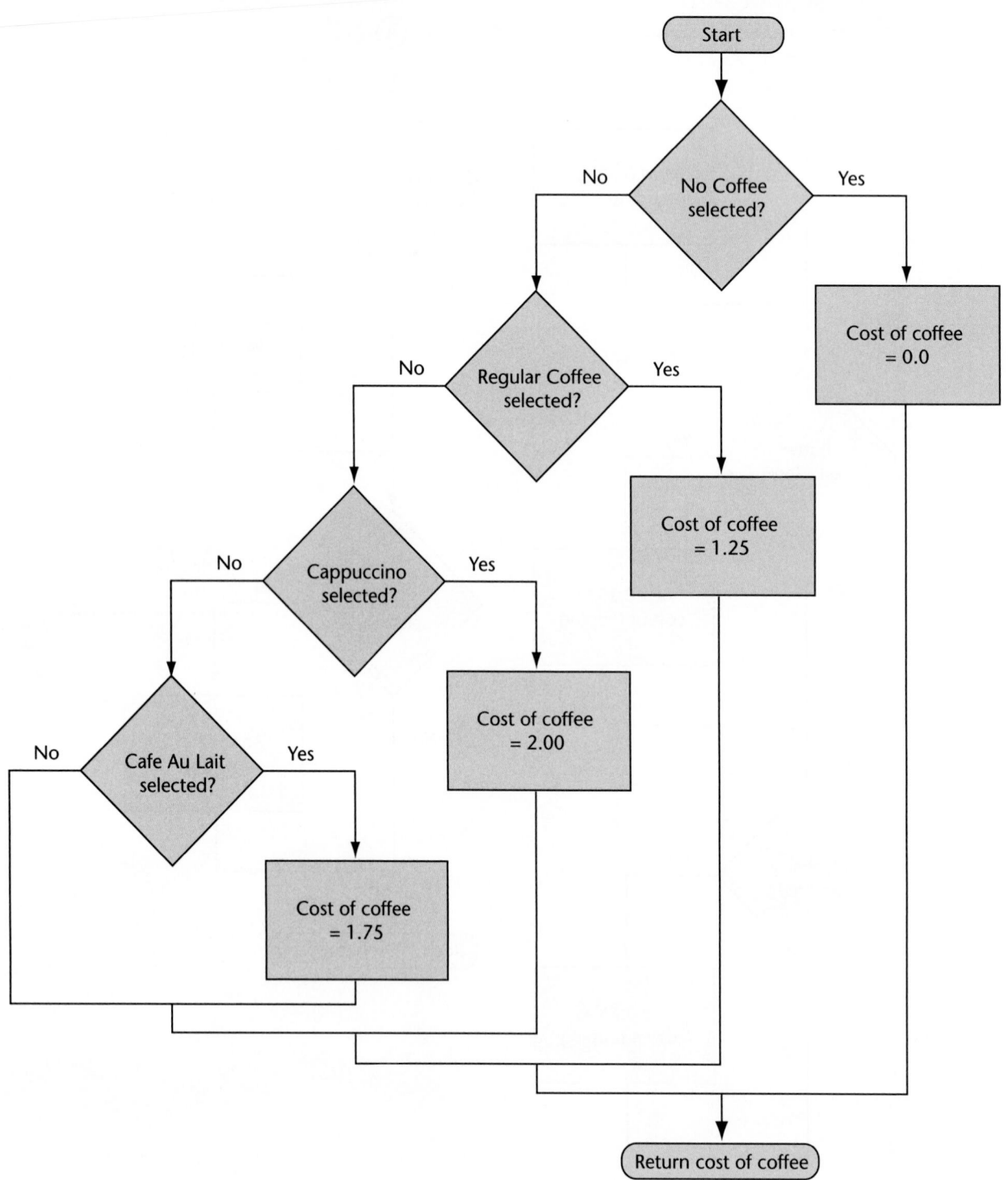

Pseudocode for the `CoffeeCost` function is as follows:

> *If No Coffee Is Selected Then*
>   *cost of coffee = 0*
> *ElseIf Regular Coffee Is Selected Then*
>   *cost of coffee = 1.25*
> *ElseIf Cappuccino Is Selected Then*
>   *cost of coffee = 2*
> *ElseIf Café Au Lait Is Selected Then*
>   *cost of coffee = 1.75*
> *End If*
> *Return cost of coffee*

Figure 6-26 shows a flowchart for the `CalcTax` function. Note that `CalcTax` accepts an argument, which is passed into the `amount` parameter variable. (The tax rate will be stored in a class-level constant.) The amount of sales tax is returned.

Pseudocode for the `CalcTax` function is as follows:

> *sales tax = amount * tax rate*
> *Return sales tax*

Figure 6-27 shows a flowchart for the `ResetBagels` procedure. This procedure resets the bagel radio buttons to their initial values.

Pseudocode for the `ResetBagels` procedure is as follows:

> *radWhite = Selected*
> *radWheat = Deselected*

Figure 6-26 Flowchart for `CalcTax` function

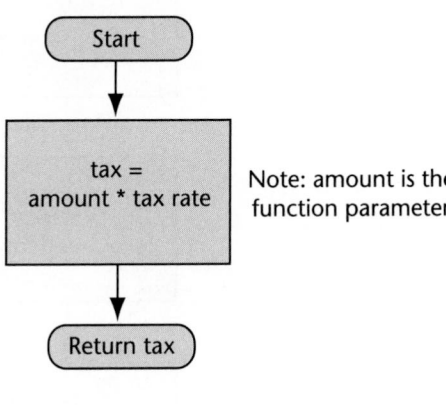

Figure 6-27 Flowchart for `ResetBagels` procedure

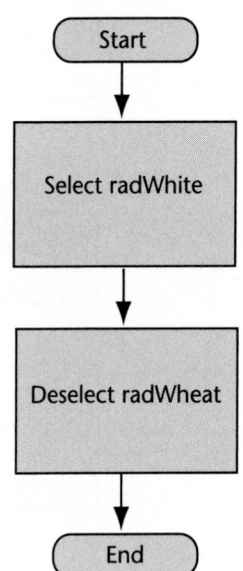

Figure 6-28 shows a flowchart for the `ResetToppings` procedure. This procedure unchecks all the topping check boxes.

Pseudocode for the `ResetToppings` procedure is as follows:

chkCreamCheese = Unchecked
chkButter = Unchecked
chkBlueberry = Unchecked
chkRaspberry = Unchecked
chkPeach = Unchecked

Figure 6-29 shows a flowchart for the `ResetCoffee` procedure. This procedure resets the coffee radio buttons to their initial values.

Pseudocode for the `ResetCoffee` procedure is as follows:

radNoCoffee = Deselected
radRegCoffee = Selected
radCappuccino = Deselected
radCafeAuLait = Deselected

Figure 6-28 Flowchart for `ResetToppings` procedure

Figure 6-29 Flowchart for `ResetCoffee` procedure

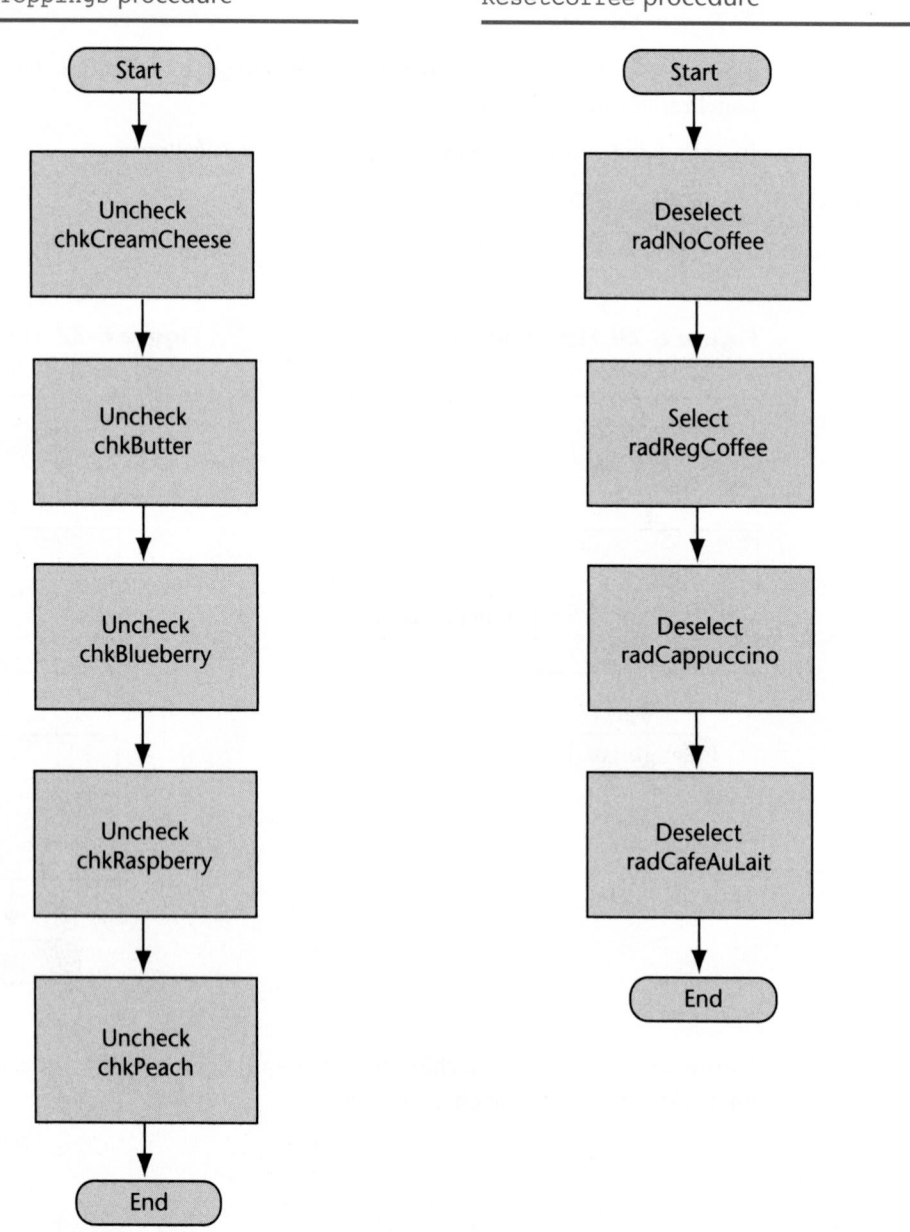

Figure 6-30 shows a flowchart for the `ResetPrice` procedure. This procedure copies an empty string to `lblSubtotal`, `lblTax`, and `lblTotal`.

Pseudocode for the `ResetPrice` procedure is as follows:

lblSubtotal.Text = String.Empty
lblTax.Text = String.Empty
lblTotal.Text = String.Empty

Figure 6-30 Flowchart for `ResetPrice` procedure

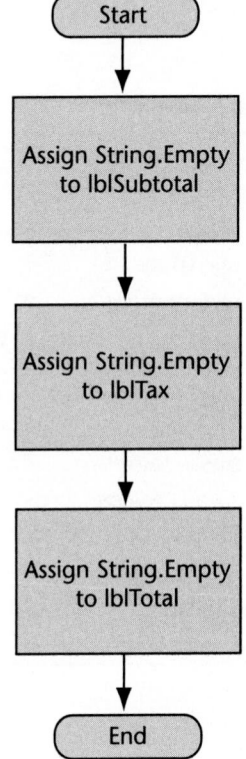

In Tutorial 6-9, you build the *Bagel House* application.

Tutorial 6-9:
Building the *Bagel House* application

Step 1: Create a new Windows Forms Application project named *Bagel House*.

Step 2: Set up the form as shown in Figure 6-31. Refer to Figure 6-20 and Table 6-1 for specific details about the controls and their properties.

Step 3: Once you have placed all the controls on the form and set their properties, you can begin writing the code. Start by opening the *Code* window and writing the class-level declarations shown in bold:

```
Public Class Form1

    ' Class-level declarations
    Const decTAX_RATE As Decimal = 0.06D        ' Tax rate
```

```
Const decWHITE_BAGEL As Decimal = 1.25D    ' Cost of a white bagel
Const decWHEAT_BAGEL As Decimal = 1.5D     ' Cost of a whole wheat bagel
Const decCREAM_CHEESE As Decimal = 0.5D    ' Cost of cream cheese topping
Const decBUTTER As Decimal = 0.25D         ' Cost of butter topping
Const decBLUEBERRY As Decimal = 0.75D      ' Cost of blueberry topping
Const decRASPBERRY As Decimal = 0.75D      ' Cost of raspberry topping
Const decPEACH As Decimal = 0.75D          ' Cost of peach topping
Const decREG_COFFEE As Decimal = 1.25D     ' Cost of regular coffee
Const decCAPPUCCINO As Decimal = 2D        ' Cost of cappuccino
Const decDAFE_AU_LAIT As Decimal = 1.75D   ' Cost of Cafe au lait

End Class
```

Figure 6-31 *Brandi's Bagel House form*

Step 4:   Now write the btnCalculate_Click, btnReset_Click, and btnExit_Click event handlers, as follows:

```
Private Sub btnCalculate_Click(...) Handles btnCalculate.Click
    ' This procedure calculates the total of an order.
    Dim decSubtotal As Decimal       ' Holds the order subtotal
    Dim decTax As Decimal            ' Holds the sales tax
    Dim decTotal As Decimal          ' Holds the order total

    decSubtotal = BagelCost() + ToppingCost() + CoffeeCost()
    decTax = CalcTax(decSubtotal)
    decTotal = decSubtotal + decTax

    lblSubtotal.Text = decSubtotal.ToString("c")
    lblTax.Text = decTax.ToString("c")
    lblTotal.Text = decTotal.ToString("c")
End Sub
```

```
Private Sub btnReset_Click(...) Handles btnReset.Click
  ' This procedure resets the controls to default values.
  ResetBagels()
  ResetToppings()
  ResetCoffee()
  ResetPrice()
End Sub

Private Sub btnExit_Click(...) Handles btnExit.Click
  ' Close the form.
  Me.Close()
End Sub
```

Step 5: Write the code for the following functions and procedures:

```
Function BagelCost() As Decimal
  ' This function returns the cost of the selected bagel.
  Dim decBagel As Decimal

  If radWhite.Checked = True Then
    decBagel = decWHITE_BAGEL
  Else
    decBagel = decWHEAT_BAGEL
  End If

  Return decBagel
End Function

Function ToppingCost() As Decimal
  ' This function returns the cost of the toppings.
  Dim decCostOfTopping As Decimal = 0D

  If chkCreamCheese.Checked = True Then
    decCostOfTopping += decCREAM_CHEESE
  End If

  If chkButter.Checked = True Then
    decCostOfTopping += decBUTTER
  End If

  If chkBlueberry.Checked = True Then
    decCostOfTopping += decBLUEBERRY
  End If

  If chkRaspberry.Checked = True Then
    decCostOfTopping += decRASPBERRY
  End If

  If chkPeach.Checked = True Then
    decCostOfTopping += decPEACH
  End If

  Return decCostOfTopping
End Function

Function CoffeeCost() As Decimal
  ' This function returns the cost of the selected coffee.
  Dim decCoffee As Decimal
```

```
            If radNoCoffee.Checked Then
              decCoffee = 0D
            ElseIf radRegCoffee.Checked = True Then
              decCoffee = decREG_COFFEE
            ElseIf radCappuccino.Checked = True Then
              decCoffee = decCAPPUCCINO
            ElseIf radCafeAuLait.Checked = True Then
              decCoffee = decDAFE_AU_LAIT
            End If

            Return decCoffee
        End Function

        Function CalcTax(ByVal decAmount As Decimal) As Decimal
            ' This function receives the sale amount and
            ' returns the amount of sales tax.
            Return decAmount * decTAX_RATE
        End Function

        Sub ResetBagels()
            ' This procedure resets the bagel selection.
            radWhite.Checked = True
        End Sub

        Sub ResetToppings()
            ' This procedure resets the topping selection.
            chkCreamCheese.Checked = False
            chkButter.Checked = False
            chkBlueberry.Checked = False
            chkRaspberry.Checked = False
            chkPeach.Checked = False
        End Sub

        Sub ResetCoffee()
            ' This procedure resets the coffee selection.
            radRegCoffee.Checked = True
        End Sub

        Sub ResetPrice()
            ' This procedure resets the price.
            lblSubtotal.Text = String.Empty
            lblTax.Text = String.Empty
            lblTotal.Text = String.Empty
        End Sub
```

Step 6: Save and run the program. If there are errors, use debugging techniques you have learned to find and correct them.

Step 7: When you're sure the application is running correctly, save it one last time.

Summary

6.1 Procedures

- The declaration for a procedure begins with a Sub statement and ends with an End Sub statement. The code that appears between these two statements is the body of the procedure.
- When a procedure call executes, the application branches to that procedure and executes its statements. When the procedure has finished, the application branches back to the procedure call and resumes executing at the next statement.
- Static local variables are not destroyed when a procedure returns. They exist for the lifetime of the application, although their scope is limited to the procedure in which they are declared.
- To declare a static local variable, substitute the word Static for Dim.

6.2 Passing Arguments to Procedures

- A parameter is a special variable that receives an argument value passed into a procedure or function. If a procedure or function has a parameter, you must supply an argument when calling the procedure or function.
- When a procedure or function with multiple parameters is called, arguments are assigned to the parameters in left-to-right order.
- There are two ways to pass an argument to a procedure: by value or reference. Passing an argument by value means that only a copy of the argument is passed to the procedure. Because the procedure has only a copy, it cannot make changes to the original argument. When an argument is passed by reference, however, the procedure has access to the original argument and can make changes to it.

6.3 Functions

- A function returns a value to the part of the program that called it. Similar to a procedure, it is a set of statements that perform a task when the function is called.
- A value is returned from a function by the Return statement.

6.4 More about Debugging: Stepping Into, Over, and Out of Procedures and Functions

- Visual Basic debugging commands (*Step Into*, *Step Over*, and *Step Out*) allow you to step through application code and through called procedures and function.

6.5 Focus on Program Design and Problem Solving: Building the *Bagel and Coffee Price Calculator* Application

- This section outlines the process of building the *Bagel and Coffee Price Calculator* application, with a focus on program design and problem solving.

Key Terms

arguments	parameter
by reference (pass argument)	Pascal casing
by value (pass argument)	procedure
ByRef	procedure call
ByVal	procedure declaration
Call keyword	Static
event handler	static local variables
event procedure	*Step Out* command
function	*Step Over* command
method	Sub keyword
modularize	

Review Questions and Exercises

Fill-in-the-Blank

1. A(n) _____ is a named block of code that performs a specific task and does not return a value.

2. A(n) _____ statement causes a procedure to be executed.

3. A(n) _____ is a named block of statements that executes and returns a value.

4. You return a value from a function with the _____ statement.

5. _____ local variables are not destroyed when a procedure returns.

6. Values passed to a procedure or function are called _____.

7. A(n) _____ is a special variable that receives an argument passed to a procedure or function.

8. When an argument is passed by _____ a copy of the argument is assigned to the parameter variable.

9. When an argument is passed by _____ the procedure has access to the original argument.

10. The _____ debugging command allows you to single-step through a called procedure or function.

Multiple Choice

1. Which of the following terms means to divide an application's code into small, manageable procedures?

   a. Break
   b. Modularize
   c. Parameterize
   d. Bind

2. Which type of statement causes a procedure to execute?

   a. Procedure declaration
   b. Access specifier
   c. Procedure call
   d. Step Into

3. What happens when a procedure finishes executing?

    a. The application branches back to the procedure call, and resumes executing at the next line
    b. The application terminates
    c. The application waits for the user to trigger the next event
    d. The application enters Break mode

4. In what way is a function different from a procedure?

    a. A procedure returns a value and a function does not
    b. A function returns a value and a procedure does not
    c. A function must be executed in response to an event
    d. There is no difference

5. What type of local variable retains its value between calls to the procedure or function in which it is declared?

    a. `Private`
    b. `Persistent`
    c. `Permanent`
    d. `Static`

6. What is an argument?

    a. A variable that a parameter is passed into
    b. A value passed to a procedure or function when it is called
    c. A local variable that retains its value between procedure calls
    d. A reason not to create a procedure or function

7. What keyword is used in a parameter declaration to specify that the argument is passed by value?

    a. `ByVal`
    b. `Val`
    c. `Value`
    d. `AsValue`

8. When an argument is passed to a procedure this way, the procedure has access to the original argument and may make changes to it.

    a. By value
    b. By address
    c. By reference
    d. By default

9. Which of the following is a debugging command that causes a procedure or function to execute without single-stepping through the procedure's or function's code?

    a. *Step Into*
    b. *Step Through*
    c. *Jump Over*
    d. *Step Over*

10. Which of the following is a debugging command that is used when you are stepping through a procedure's code and you wish to execute the remaining statements in the procedure without single-stepping through them?

    a. *Jump Out*
    b. *Step Through*
    c. *Step Out*
    d. *Step Over*

True or False

Indicate whether the following statements are true or false.

1. T F: A general purpose procedure is associated with a specific control.

2. T F: You must use the `Call` keyword to execute a procedure.

3. T F: The declaration of a parameter variable looks like a regular variable declaration, except `ByVal` or `ByRef` is used instead of `Dim`.

4. T F: You can pass more than one argument to a procedure or function.

5. T F: If you write a procedure or function with a parameter variable, you do not have to supply an argument when calling the procedure.

6. T F: If you are debugging an application in Break mode and you want to single-step through a procedure that will be called in the highlighted statement, you use the *Step Over* command.

Short Answer

1. Why do nonstatic local variables lose their values between calls to the procedure or function in which they are declared?

2. What is the difference between an argument and a parameter variable?

3. Where do you declare parameter variables?

4. If you are writing a procedure that accepts an argument and you want to make sure that the procedure cannot change the value of the argument, what do you do?

5. When a procedure or function accepts multiple arguments, does it matter what order the arguments are passed in?

6. How do you return a value from a function?

What Do You Think?

1. What advantage is there to dividing an application's code into several small procedures?

2. How would a static local variable be useful?

3. Give an example in which passing an argument by reference would be useful.

4. Suppose you want to write a procedure to perform an operation. How do you decide if the procedure should be a procedure or a function?

5. When debugging an application, why would you not want to single-step through every procedure or function?

Find the Error

Locate the errors in the following code examples:

1.
```
Sub DisplayValue(Dim intNumber As Integer)
    ' This displays a value.
    MessageBox.Show(intNumber.ToString())
End Sub
```

2. The following is a procedure:
```
Sub Greeting(ByVal strName As String)
    ' This procedure displays a greeting.
    MessageBox.Show("Hello " & strName)
End Sub
```

And the following is a call to the procedure:

```
Greeting()
```

3. The following is a function:

```
Function Product(ByVal intNum1 As Integer, ByVal intNum2
                  As Integer) As Integer
    Dim intResult As Integer
    intResult = intNum1 * intNum2
End Function
```

4. The following is a function:

```
Sub Sum(ByVal intNum1 As Single, ByVal intNum2 As Single)
        As Single
    Dim intResult As Single
    intResult = intNum1 + intNum2
    Return intResult
End Sub
```

Algorithm Workbench

1. The following statement calls a function named `Half` that returns a Decimal, which is half of the argument. Write the function.

```
intResult = Half(intNumber)
```

2. An application contains the following function:

```
Function Square(ByVal intValue As Integer) As Integer
    Return intValue ^ 2
End Function
```

Write a statement that passes the value 4 to this function and assigns its return value to a variable named `intResult`.

3. Write a procedure named `TimesTen` that accepts a single Integer argument. When the procedure is called, it should display the product of its argument multiplied by 10 in a message box.

4. An application contains the following procedure:

```
Sub Display(ByVal intArg1 As Integer, ByVal strArg2 As String,
          ByVal sngArg3 As Single)
    MessageBox.Show("Here are the values: " &
                      intArg1.ToString() & " " &
                      strArg2 & " " & sngArg3.ToString())
End Sub
```

Write a statement that calls the procedure and passes it the following variables:

```
Dim strName As String
Dim intAge As Integer
Dim sngIncome As Single
```

Programming Challenges

VideoNote

The Retail
Price
Calculator
Problem

1. **Retail Price Calculator**

Write an application that accepts from the user the wholesale cost of an item and its markup percentage. (For example, if an item's wholesale cost is $5 and its retail price is $10, then the markup is 100%.)

The program should contain a function named `CalculateRetail` that receives the wholesale cost and markup percentage as arguments, and returns the retail price of the item. The application's form should look something like the one shown in Figure 6-32.

Figure 6-32 *Retail Price Calculator* form

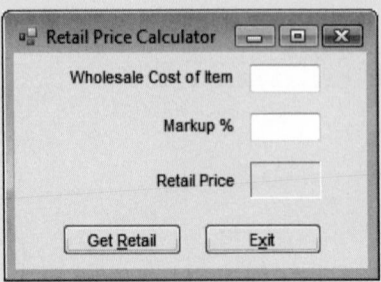

Figure 6-33 *Hospital Charges* form

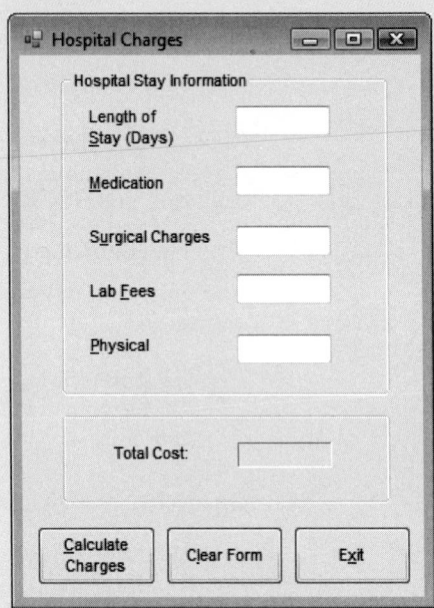

When the user clicks the *Get Retail* button, the program should do the following:

- Verify that the values entered by the user for the wholesale cost and the markup percent are numeric and not negative
- Call the `CalculateRetail` function
- Display the retail cost as returned from the function

2. **Hospital Charges**

Create an application that calculates the total cost of a hospital stay. The application should accept the following input:

- The number of days spent in the hospital
- The amount of medication charges
- The amount of surgical charges
- The amount of lab fees
- The amount of physical rehabilitation charges

The hospital charges $350 per day. The application's form should resemble the one shown in Figure 6-33.

Create the following functions:

`CalcStayCharges`   Calculates and returns the base charges for the hospital stay. This is computed as $350 times the number of days in the hospital.

`CalcMiscCharges`   Calculates and returns the total of the medication, surgical, lab, and physical rehabilitation charges.

`CalcTotalCharges`   Calculates and returns the total charges.

Input Validation: Do not accept a negative value for length of stay, medication charges, surgical charges, lab fees, or physical rehabilitation charges.

3. **Order Status**

The Middletown Wire Company sells spools of copper wiring for $100 each. The normal delivery charge is $10 per spool. Rush delivery costs $15 per spool. Create an application that displays the status of an order. The status should include the following:

- The number of spools ready to ship
- The number of spools on back order
- The shipping and handling charges
- The total amount due

The application's form should resemble the one shown in Figure 6-34.

Figure 6-34 *Order Status* form

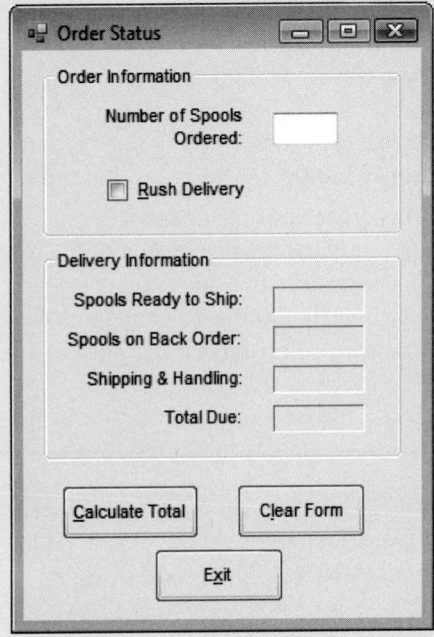

The user should enter the number of spools ordered into the text box, and check the *Rush Delivery* check box if rush delivery is desired. When the *Calculate Total* button is clicked, an input box should appear asking the user to enter the number of spools currently in stock. If the user has ordered more spools than are in stock, a portion of the order is back-ordered. For example, if the user orders 200 spools and there are only 150 spools in stock, then 150 spools are ready to ship and 50 spools are back-ordered.

The application should have the following functions, called from the *Calculate Total* button's Click event handler:

`GetInStock`	Displays an input box asking the user to enter the number of spools in stock. The function should return the value entered by the user.
`ReadyToShip`	Accepts the following arguments: the number of spools in stock and the number of spools ordered. The function returns the number of spools ready to ship.
`BackOrdered`	Accepts the following arguments: the number of spools in stock and the number of spools ordered. The function returns the number of spools on back order. If no spools are on back order, it returns 0.

ShippingCharges	Accepts the following arguments: the number of spools ready to ship and the per-spool shipping charges. The function returns the total shipping and handling charges.

The application should have the following procedures, called from the *Clear Form* button's Click event handler:

ResetSpools	Clears the text box and the check box.
ResetDelivery	Clears the labels that display the delivery information.

Input Validation: Do not accept orders for less than one spool.

4. **Joe's Automotive**

Joe's Automotive performs the following routine maintenance services:

- Oil change—$26.00
- Lube job—$18.00
- Radiator flush—$30.00
- Transmission flush—$80.00
- Inspection—$15.00
- Muffler replacement—$100.00
- Tire rotation—$20.00

Joe also performs other nonroutine services and charges for parts and labor ($20 per hour). Create an application that displays the total for a customer's visit to Joe's. The form should resemble the one shown in Figure 6-35. *Note*: Visual Studio lets you use an apostrophe in a project's name, but the apostrophe will prevent you from being able to run the project after it has been created.

Figure 6-35 *Joe's Automotive* form

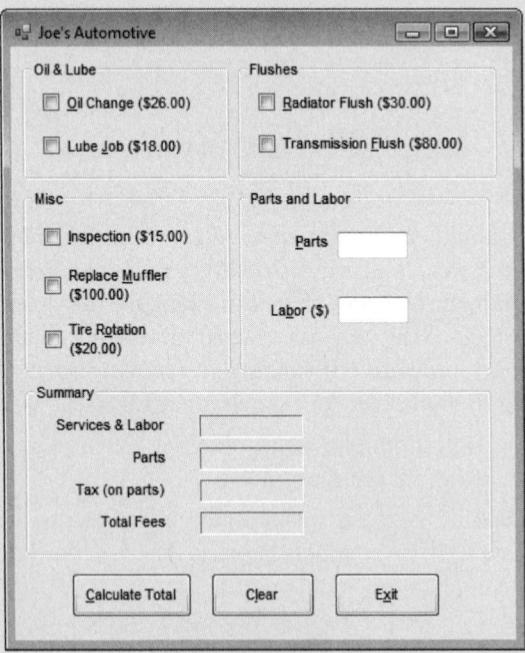

The application should have the following functions:

OilLubeCharges	Returns the total charges for an oil change and/or a lube job, if any.
FlushCharges	Returns the total charges for a radiator flush and/or a transmission flush, if any.

MiscCharges	Returns the total charges for an inspection, muffler replacement, and/or a tire rotation, if any.
OtherCharges	Returns the total charges for other services (parts and labor), if any.
TaxCharges	Returns the amount of sales tax, if any. Sales tax is 6%, and is only charged on parts. If the customer purchased services only, no sales tax is charged.
TotalCharges	Returns the total charges.

The application should have the following procedures, called when the user clicks the *Clear* button:

ClearOilLube	Clears the check boxes for oil change and lube job.
ClearFlushes	Clears the check boxes for radiator flush and transmission flush.
ClearMisc	Clears the check boxes for inspection, muffler replacement, and tire rotation.
ClearOther	Clears the text boxes for parts and labor.
ClearFees	Clears the labels that display the labels in the section marked *Summary*.

Input validation: Do not accept negative amounts for parts and labor charges.

Design Your Own Forms

5. **Password Verifier**

   You will develop a software package that requires users to enter their passwords. Your software requires users' passwords to meet the following criteria:

   - The password should be at least six characters long
   - The password should contain at least one numeric digit and at least one alphabetic character

   Create an application that asks the user to enter a password. The application should use a function named IsValid to verify that the password meets the criteria. It should display a message indicating whether the password is valid or invalid.

   The IsValid function should accept a string as its argument and return a Boolean value. The string argument is the password to be checked. If the password is valid, the function should return *True*. Otherwise, it should return *False*.

 TIP: Refer to Chapter 4 for more information about working with strings.

6. **Travel Expenses**

   Create an application that calculates and displays the total travel expenses for a business trip. The user must provide the following information:

   - Number of days on the trip
   - Amount of airfare, if any
   - Amount of car rental fees, if any
   - Number of miles driven, if a private vehicle was used
   - Amount of parking fees, if any
   - Amount of taxi charges, if any
   - Conference or seminar registration fees, if any
   - Lodging charges, per night

The company reimburses travel expenses according to the following policy:

- $37 per day for meals
- Parking fees, up to $10.00 per day
- Taxi charges up to $20.00 per day
- Lodging charges up to $95.00 per day
- If a private vehicle is used, $0.27 per mile driven

The application should calculate and display the following:

- Total expenses incurred by the business person
- The total allowable expenses for the trip
- The excess that must be paid by the business person, if any
- The amount saved by the business person if the expenses were under the total allowed

The application should have the following functions:

`CalcMeals`	Calculates and returns the amount reimbursed for meals.
`CalcMileage`	Calculates and returns the amount reimbursed for mileage driven in a private vehicle.
`CalcParkingFees`	Calculates and returns the amount reimbursed for parking fees.
`CalcTaxiFees`	Calculates and returns the amount reimbursed for taxi charges.
`CalcLodging`	Calculates and returns the amount reimbursed for lodging.
`CalcTotalReimbursement`	Calculates and returns the total amount reimbursed.
`CalcUnallowed`	Calculates and returns the total amount of expenses that are not allowable, if any. These are parking fees that exceed $10.00 per day, taxi charges that exceed $20.00 per day, and lodging charges that exceed $95.00 per day.
`CalcSaved`	Calculates and returns the total amount of expenses under the allowable amount, if any. For example, the allowable amount for lodging is $95.00 per day. If a business person stayed in a hotel for $85.00 per day for five days, the savings would $50.00.

Input validation: Do not accept negative numbers for any dollar amount or for miles driven in a private vehicle. Do not accept numbers less than 1 for the number of days.

7. **Paint Job Estimator**

A painting company has determined that for every 115 square feet of wall space, one gallon of paint and eight hours of labor are required. The company charges $18.00 per hour for labor. Create an application that allows the user to enter the number of rooms to be painted and the price of the paint per gallon. The application should use input boxes to ask the user for the square feet of wall space in each room. It should then display the following information:

- The number of gallons of paint required
- The hours of labor required
- The cost of the paint
- The labor charges
- The total cost of the paint job

Input validation: Do not accept a value less than 1 for the number of rooms. Do not accept a value less than $10.00 for the price of paint. Do not accept a negative value for square footage of wall space.

8. **Falling Distance**

    When an object is falling because of gravity, the following formula can be used to determine the distance the object falls in a specific time period:

    $$d = \tfrac{1}{2}\, gt^2$$

    The variables in the formula are as follows: d is the distance in meters, g is 9.8, and t is the amount of time in seconds that the object has been falling.

    Create a VB application that allows the user to enter the amount of time that an object has fallen and then displays the distance that the object fell. The application should have a function named `FallingDistance`. The `FallingDistance` function should accept an object's falling time (in seconds) as an argument. The function should return the distance in meters that the object has fallen during that time interval.

9. **Kinetic Energy**

    In physics, an object that is in motion is said to have kinetic energy. The following formula can be used to determine a moving object's kinetic energy:

    $$KE = \tfrac{1}{2}\, mv^2$$

    In the formula KE is the kinetic energy, m is the object's mass in kilograms, and v is the object's velocity in meters per second.

    Create a VB application that allows the user to enter an object's mass and velocity and then displays the object's kinetic energy. The application should have a function named `KineticEnergy` that accepts an object's mass (in kilograms) and velocity (in meters per second) as arguments. The function should return the amount of kinetic energy that the object has.

10. **Prime Numbers**

    A prime number is a number that can be evenly divided by only itself and 1. For example, the number 5 is prime because it can be evenly divided by only 1 and 5. The number 6, however, is not prime because it can be evenly divided by 1, 2, 3, and 6.

    Write a Boolean function named `IsPrime` which takes an integer as an argument and returns *true* if the argument is a prime number or *false* otherwise. Use the function in an application that lets the user enter a number and then displays a message indicating whether the number is prime.

> **TIP:** Recall that the MOD operator divides one number by another and returns the remainder of the division. In an expression such as `intNum1 MOD intNum2`, the MOD operator will return 0 if `intNum1` is evenly divisible by `intNum2`.

11. **Prime Number List**

    This exercise assumes you have already written the `IsPrime` function in Programming Challenge 10. Create another application that uses this function to display all of the prime numbers from 1 through 100 in a list box. The program should have a loop that calls the `IsPrime` function.

7 Multiple Forms, Modules, and Menus

TOPICS

This chapter shows how to add multiple forms to a project and how to create a module to hold procedures and functions. It also covers creating a menu system, as well as context menus, with commands and submenus that the user may select from.

7.1 Multiple Forms

CONCEPT: Visual Basic projects can have multiple forms. The startup form is the form that is displayed when the project executes. Other forms in a project are displayed by programming statements.

The applications you have created so far have only one form in their user interface. Visual Basic does not limit you to one form in a project, however. You may create multiple forms in a project to use as dialog boxes, display error messages, and so on. Then you can display these forms as they are needed.

A Windows Forms application typically has one form that is designated as the **startup form**. When the application executes, the startup form is automatically displayed. By default, the first form that you create in a Windows Forms application is the startup form. You will learn later in this chapter how to designate any form in a project as the startup form.

Form Files and Form Names

Each form in a Visual Basic project has a name that is stored in the form's Name property (viewable in the *Properties* window when the form is selected). As you already know, the first form in a project is automatically named Form1. When a form is created in a Visual

Basic project, the code associated with the form is stored in a file that has the same name as the form, followed by the *.vb* extension. So, the code for a form named Form1 will be stored in a file named *Form1.vb*. The *Solution Explorer* window shows an entry for each form file in a project. Figure 7-1 shows the *Solution Explorer* window with an entry for the form named *Form1.vb*.

Figure 7-1 *Solution Explorer* window with entry for *Form1.vb*

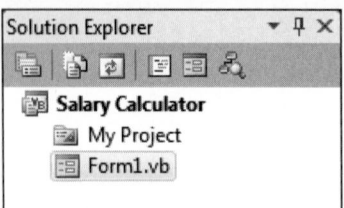

 NOTE: The code stored in a form file is the same code that you see when you open the form in the *Code* window.

Renaming an Existing Form File

If you use the *Solution Explorer* window to change a form's file name, the form's Name property changes automatically to match the file name. If, for example, you rename the file *Form1.vb* to *MainForm.vb*, the form's Name property changes from Form1 to MainForm.

On the other hand, if you change a form's Name property, the form's file name does not change automatically. To maintain consistency between the form's file name and its Name property, you should use the *Solution Explorer* to rename the form's file instead of changing the form's Name property. Here's how to rename a form file:

1. Right-click the form's file name in the *Solution Explorer* window.
2. A pop-up menu should appear, as shown in Figure 7-2. Select *Rename* from the pop-up menu.

Figure 7-2 Right-clicking the form file

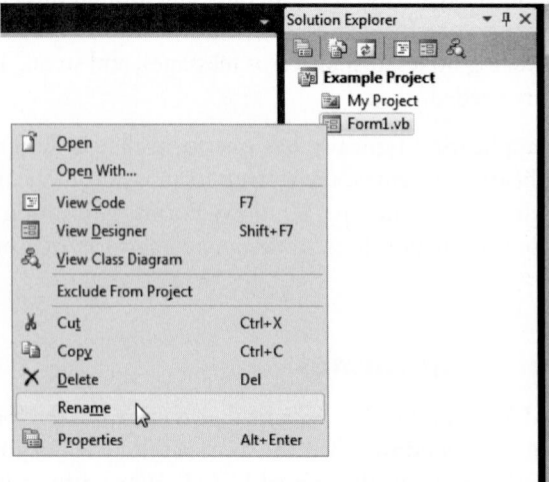

Figure 7-3 Form file renamed as *MainForm.vb*

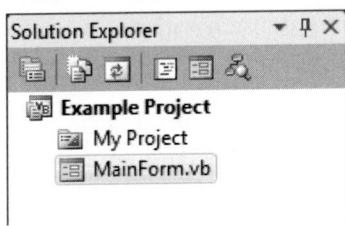

3. The name of the form file should be highlighted in the *Solution Explorer* window. Type the new name for the form file. Be sure to keep the *.vb* extension. Figure 7-3 shows an example where *Form1.vb* has been renamed *MainForm.vb*.

When you have multiple forms in an application, you should give each form a meaningful name. In a multi-form project, default form names such as Form1, Form2, etc., do not adequately describe the purpose of each form.

VideoNote

Creating and Displaying a Second Form

Adding a New Form to a Project

Follow these steps to add a new form to a project:

1. Click *Project* on the Visual Studio menu bar, and then select *Add Windows Form . . .* from the *Project* menu. The *Add New Item* window, shown in Figure 7-4, should appear.

Figure 7-4 *Add New Item* window

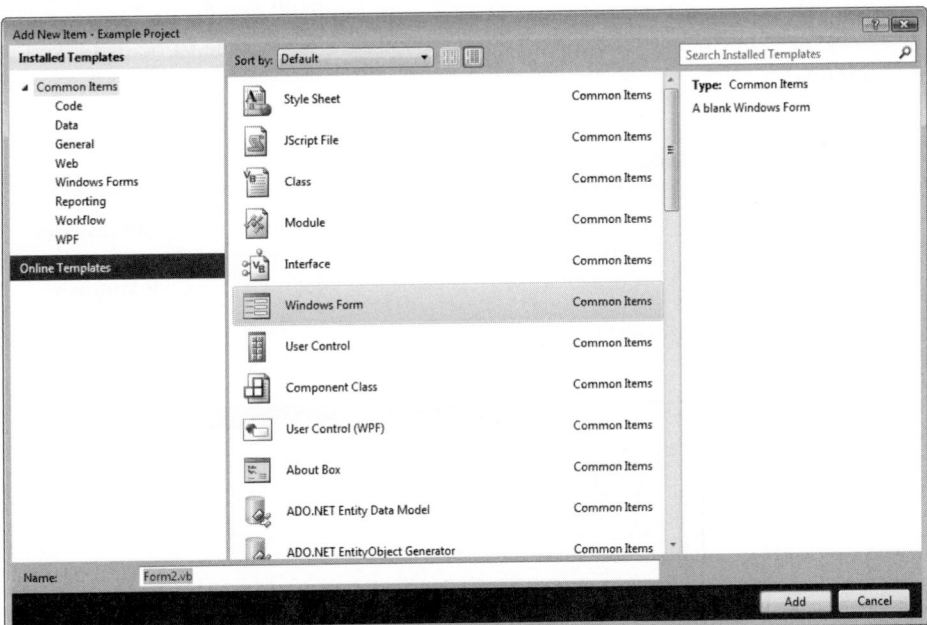

2. Near the bottom of the *Add New Item* window, a *Name* text box appears where you can specify the new form's file name. Initially, a default name will appear here. (Notice that in Figure 7-4 the default name *Form2.vb* appears. The actual name that appears on your screen may be different.) Change the default name that is displayed

in the *Name* text box to a more descriptive name. For example, if you wish to name the new form ErrorForm, enter **ErrorForm.vb** in the *Name* text box. (Make sure you specify the *.vb* extension with the file name that you enter!)

3. Click the *Add* button.

After completing these steps, a new blank form is added to your project. The new form is displayed in the *Designer* window and an entry for the new form's file appears in the *Solution Explorer* window. The *Solution Explorer* window in Figure 7-5 shows two form files: *ErrorForm.vb* and *MainForm.vb*.

Figure 7-5 *Solution Explorer* window showing two forms

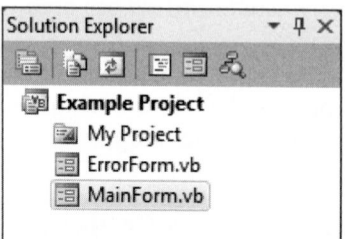

Switching between Forms and Form Code

At design time, you can easily switch to another form by double-clicking the form's entry in the *Solution Explorer* window. The form will be then displayed in the *Designer* window. You can also use the tabs that appear at the top of the *Designer* window to display different forms or their code. For example, look at Figure 7-6. It shows the tabs that appear for a project with two forms: ErrorForm and MainForm. The tabs that display the *[Design]* designator cause a form to be displayed in the *Designer* window. The tabs that appear without the designator cause a form's code to be displayed in the *Code* window.

Figure 7-6 *Designer* window tabs

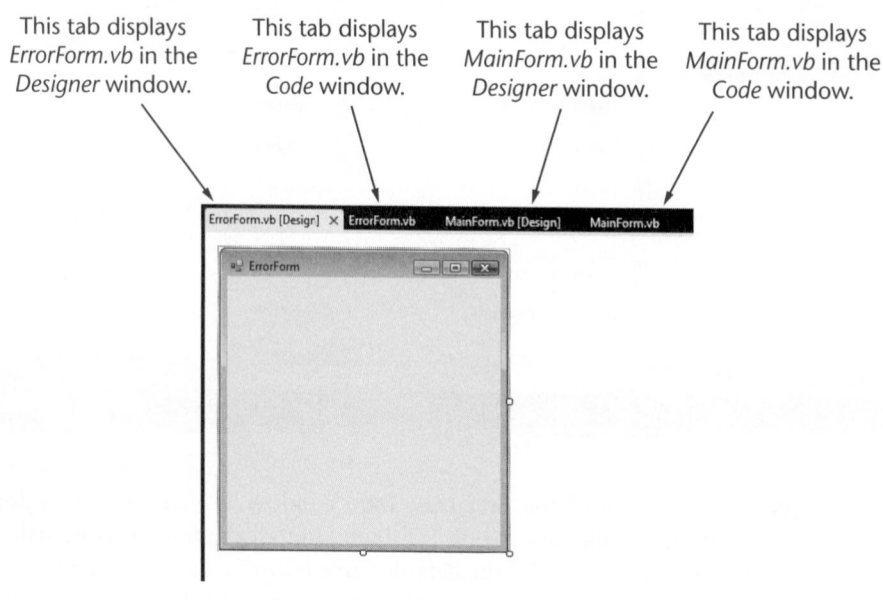

Removing a Form

If you wish to remove a form from a project and delete its file from the disk, follow these steps.

1. Right-click the form's entry in the *Solution Explorer* window.
2. On the pop-up menu, click *Delete*.

If you're using Visual Studio and you wish to remove a form from a project but you do not want to delete its file from the disk, follow one of these sets of steps. (This option is not available in Visual Basic Express.)

1. Right-click the form's entry in the *Solution Explorer* window.
2. On the pop-up menu click *Exclude From Project*.

or

1. Select the form's entry in the *Solution Explorer* window.
2. Click *Project* on the menu, and click *Exclude From Project*.

Designating the Startup Form

The first form you create is, by default, the startup form. It is automatically displayed when the application runs. To make another form the startup form, follow these steps:

1. In the *Solution Explorer* window, right click the project name. Figure 7-7 shows the location of the project name in the window.

Figure 7-7 Project name in *Solution Explorer* window

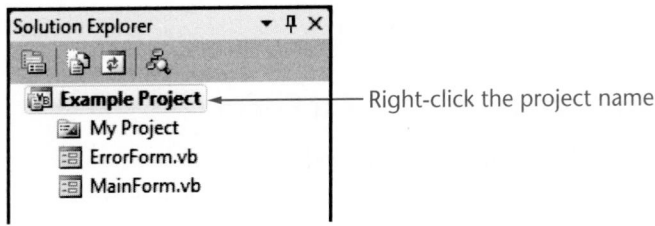

Right-click the project name

2. On the pop-up menu, click *Properties*. The project's properties page should appear, as shown in Figure 7-8.
3. Make sure the *Application* tab is selected at the left edge of the properties page, as shown in Figure 7-8. To change the startup form, click the down arrow (▼) in the *Startup Form* drop-down list. A list of all the forms in the project appears. Select the form that should display first when your program executes.
4. Save the project and click the Close button (✕) on the properties page tab.

Figure 7-8 Project's properties page

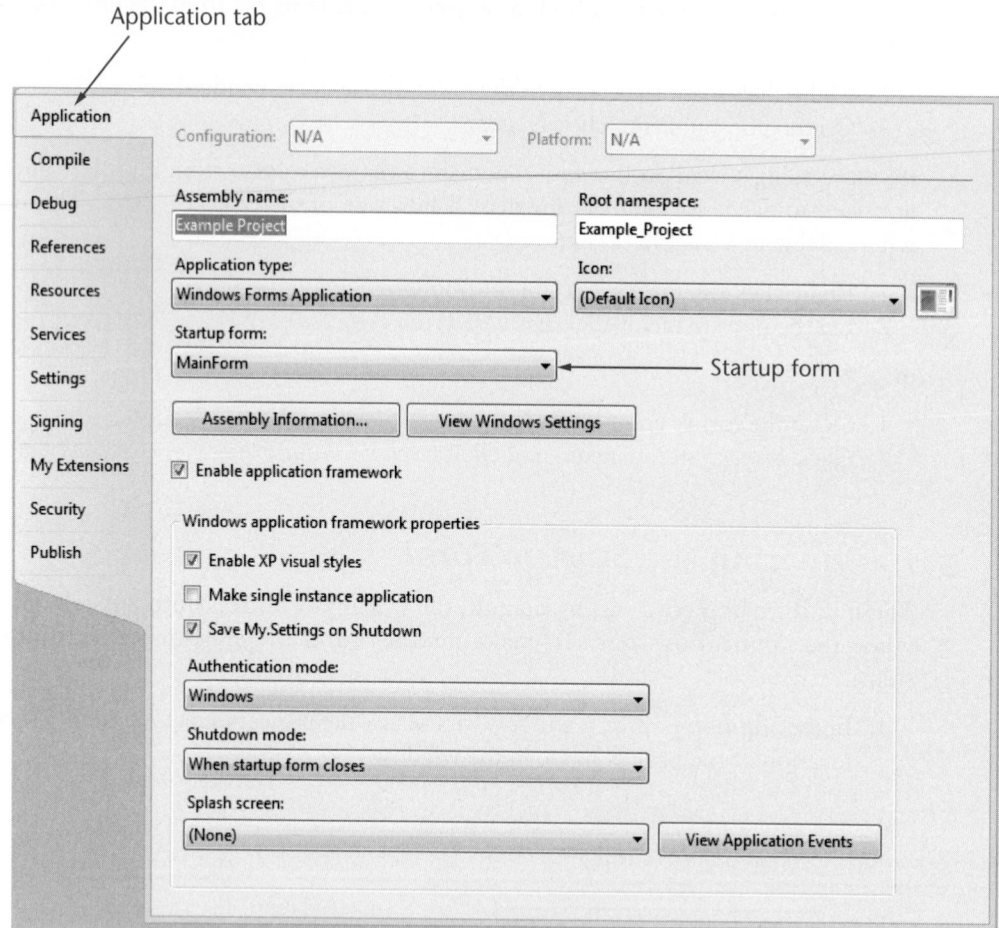

Creating an Instance of a Form

A form file contains all of a form's code. Recall that when you open a form in the *Code* window, the first and last lines of code look like the following:

```
Public Class FormName

End Class
```

In the first line, `FormName` is the form's name. Recall from Chapter 2 that these statements are the beginning and the end of a class declaration for the form. All of the code for the form (event handlers, procedures, functions, and class-level declarations) must appear inside this class declaration.

A form's class declaration by itself does not create a specific form, but is merely the description of a form. It is similar to the blueprint for a house. The blueprint itself is not a house, but is a detailed description of a house. When we use the blueprint to build an actual house, we can say we are building an instance of the house described by the blueprint. If we want, we can build several identical houses from the same blueprint. Each house is a separate instance of the house described by the blueprint. This idea is illustrated in Figure 7-9.

A form's class declaration serves a similar purpose. We can use it to create one or more instances of the form described by the class declaration, and then use the instance(s) to display the form on the screen.

Figure 7-9 Blueprints and instances of the blueprints

Blueprint that describes a house

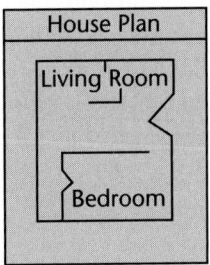

Instances of the house described by the blueprint

Displaying a Form

The first step in displaying a form is to create an instance of the form. You create an instance of a form with a Dim statement. The general format is as follows:

```
Dim ObjectVariable As New ClassName
```

ObjectVariable is the name of an object variable that references an instance of the form. An **object variable** is a variable that holds the memory address of an object and allows you to work with the object. *ClassName* is the form's class name. For example, assume that you have added a form to your project and named it ErrorForm. The following statement creates an instance of the form in memory:

```
Dim frmError As New ErrorForm
```

Let's examine what happens as a result of this statement. First, a variable named frmError is declared. Then, the part of the statement that reads New ErrorForm causes an instance of the ErrorForm form to be created in memory. The form's memory address is assigned to the frmError variable. (When an object variable holds the memory address of an object, we say that it references the object.) We may now use the frmError variable to perform operations with the form.

> **NOTE:** In this book we use the prefix frm in a variable name to indicate that the variable references a form.

This statement does not cause the form to be displayed on the screen. It only creates an instance of the form in memory and assigns its address to the object variable. To display the form on the screen, you must use the object variable to invoke one of the form's methods.

The `ShowDialog` and `Show` Methods

A form can be either modal or modeless. When a **modal form** is displayed, no other form in the application can receive the focus until the modal form is closed. The user must close the modal form before he or she can work with any other form in the application. A **modeless form**, on the other hand, allows the user to switch focus to another form while it is displayed. The **ShowDialog** method causes a form to be displayed as a modal form. When this method is called, the form is displayed and it receives the focus. The general format of the method call is as follows:

```
ObjectVariable.ShowDialog()
```

ObjectVariable is the name of an object variable that references an instance of a form. For example, the following code creates an instance of the ErrorForm form and displays it:

```
Dim frmError As New ErrorForm
frmError.ShowDialog()
```

To display a modeless form, use the **Show** method. The general format of the `Show` method is as follows:

```
ObjectVariable.Show()
```

ObjectVariable is the name of an object variable that references an instance of a form. For example, the following code creates an instance of the ErrorForm form and displays it as a modeless form:

```
Dim frmError As New ErrorForm
frmError.Show()
```

 TIP: Most of the time forms shoud be modal. It is common for a procedure to display a form, and then perform operations dependent on input gathered by the form. Therefore, you will normally use the `ShowDialog` method to display a form.

Closing a Form with the `Close` Method

Forms commonly have a button, such as *Close* or *Cancel*, which the user clicks to close the form. When the user clicks such a button, the form must call the `Close` method. The **Close method** closes a form and removes its visual part from memory.

When a form calls its own `Close` method, it typically does so with the `Me` keyword, as shown here:

```
Me.Close()
```

The word `Me` in Visual Basic is a special variable that references the currently executing object. For example, suppose a form has a Button control named `btnExit`, and the form's code contains the following event handler:

```
Private Sub btnExit_Click(...) Handles btnExit.Click
    Me.Close()
End Sub
```

Assume that an instance of the form has been created in memory and it is currently displayed on the screen. When this event handler executes, `Me` references the current instance of the form. So, the statement `Me.Close()` causes the current instance of the form to call its own `Close` method, thus closing the form.

The `Hide` Method

The `Hide` **method** makes a form or control invisible, but does not remove it from memory. It has the same effect as setting the Visible property to *False*. As with the `Close` method, a form uses the `Me` keyword to call its own `Hide` method, such as `Me.Hide()`. Use the `Hide` method when, instead of closing a form, you want to remove it temporarily from the screen. After hiding a form, you may redisplay it with the `ShowDialog` or `Show` methods.

Now that we've covered the basics of having multiple forms in a project, go through the steps in Tutorial 7-1. In the tutorial you will create a simple application that has two forms.

VideoNote

Tutorial 7-1
Walkthrough

Tutorial 7-1:
Creating an application with two forms

Step 1: Create a new *Windows Forms Application* project named *Multiform Practice*.

Step 2: In the *Solution Explorer* window, rename the *Form1.vb* file to *MainForm.vb*. (Right-click *Form1.vb* and then select *Rename* from the popup menu.) Changing the form's file name to *MainForm.vb* also changes the form's name to MainForm. The *Solution Explorer* window should appear as shown in Figure 7-10.

Step 3: In the *Designer* window, set up the MainForm form as shown in Figure 7-11. Name the *Display Form* Button control `btnDisplayForm` and the *Exit* Button control `btnExit`.

Figure 7-10 *Solution Explorer* after changing *Form1.vb* to *MainForm.vb*

Figure 7-11 MainForm

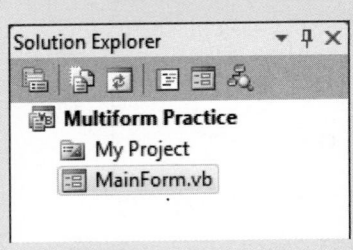

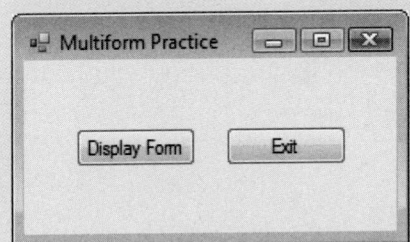

Step 4: Perform the following to create another form named MessageForm in the project:
- Click *Project* on the menu bar, then select *Add Windows Form . . .*
- The *Add New Item* window will appear. Enter *MessageForm.vb* as the name.
- Click the *Add* button.

  As shown in Figure 7-12, a new form named MessageForm will appear in the *Designer* window. Notice that an entry for *MessageForm.vb* appears in the *Solution Explorer*.

Figure 7-12 MessageForm added to the project

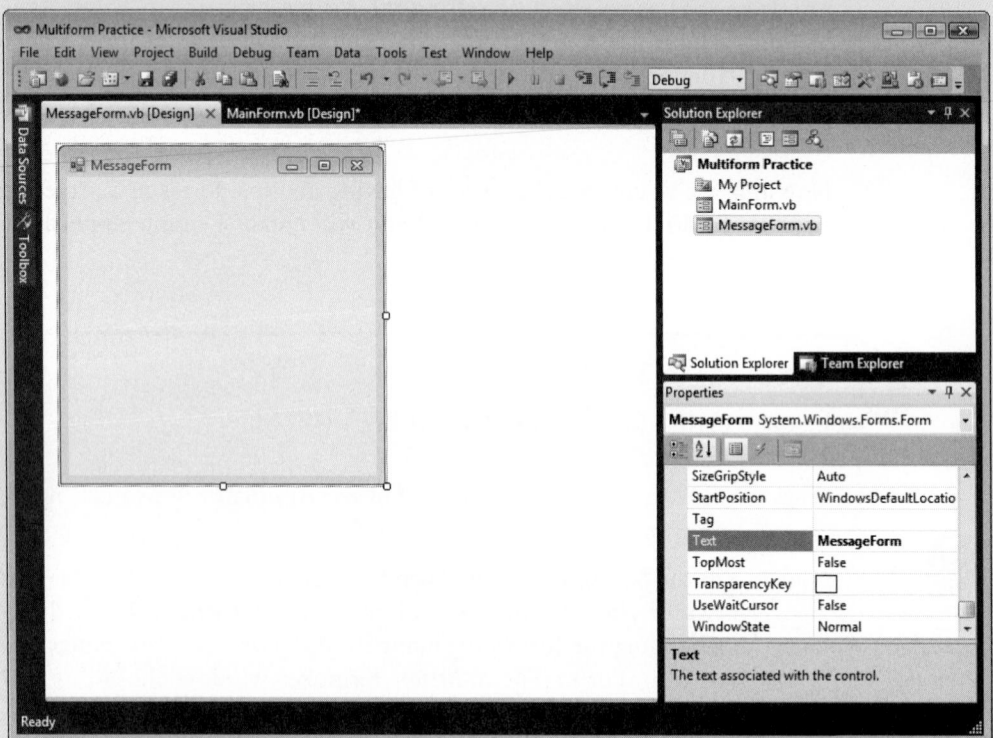

Step 5: In the *Designer* window, set up the MessageForm as shown in Figure 7-13. Name the Button control `btnClose`.

Figure 7-13 MessageForm

Step 6: Use the tabs at the top of the *Designer* window to switch to *MainForm.vb* [*Design*]. This brings up the MainForm in the *Designer* window.

Step 7: Double-click the `btnDisplayForm` button to create a code template for the button's Click event handler. Complete the event handler by writing the bold code shown here in lines 2 through 6. (Don't type the line numbers. They are shown for reference.)

```
1 Private Sub btnDisplayForm_Click(...) Handles btnDisplayForm .Click
2     ' Create an instance of MessageForm.
3     Dim frmMessage As New MessageForm
4
5     ' Display the form in modal style.
6     frmMessage.ShowDialog()
7 End Sub
```

Let's take a closer look at this code. Line 3 creates an instance of the MessageForm form in memory and assigns its address to the `frmMessage` variable. Line 6 uses the `frmMessage` variable to call the form's `ShowDialog` method. When this statement executes, it will display the form on the screen in modal style.

Step 8: Use the tabs at the top of the *Designer* window to switch back to *MainForm.vb* [*Design*]. This brings up the MainForm again in the *Designer* window.

Step 9: Double-click the `btnExit` button to create a code template for the button's Click event handler. Complete the event handler by writing the bold code shown here:

```
Private Sub btnExit_Click(...) Handles btnExit.Click
    ' Close the form.
    Me.Close()
End Sub
```

When this event handler executes, it will close the MainForm form, which will end the application.

Step 10: Use the tabs at the top of the *Designer* window to switch to *MessageForm.vb* [*Design*]. This brings up the MessageForm in the *Designer* window.

Step 11: Double-click the `btnClose` button to create a code template for the button's Click event handler. Complete the event handler by writing the bold code shown here:

```
Private Sub btnClose_Click(...) Handles btnClose.Click
    ' Close the form.
    Me.Close()
End Sub
```

When this event handler executes, it will close the MessageForm form.

Step 12: Save the project and then run it. The MainForm should appear, as shown on the left in Figure 7-14. Click the *Display Form* button. The MessageForm form should appear, as shown on the right in Figure 7-14.

Figure 7-14 The MainForm and the MessageForm forms displayed

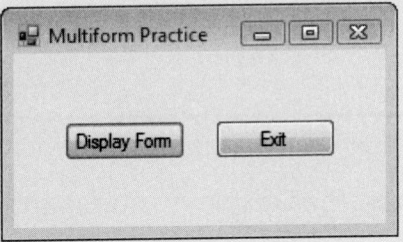
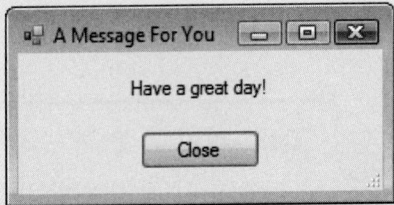

Step 13: On the MessageForm, click the *Close* button. This should close the Message-Form. Next, click the *Exit* button on the MainForm to end the application.

More about Modal and Modeless Forms

You have already learned that when a modal form is displayed, no other form in the application can receive the focus until the modal form is closed or hidden. There is another important aspect of modal forms. When a procedure calls the ShowDialog method to display a modal form, no subsequent statements in that procedure execute until the modal form is closed. This concept is illustrated in Figure 7-15.

Figure 7-15 Execution of statements after displaying a modal form

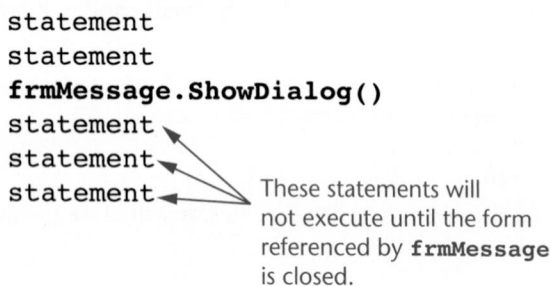

When a procedure calls the Show method to display a modeless form, however, statements following the method call continue to execute after the modeless form is displayed. Visual Basic does not wait until the modeless form is closed before executing these statements. This concept is illustrated in Figure 7-16. Tutorial 7-2 demonstrates this difference between modal and modeless forms.

Figure 7-16 Execution of statements after displaying a modeless form

```
statement
statement
frmMessage.Show()
statement
statement
statement
```
These statements will execute
immediately after the form
referenced by **frmMessage**
is displayed.

Tutorial 7-2:

Completing an application that displays modal and modeless forms

Step 1: Open the *Modal Modeless Demo* project from the student sample programs folder named *Chap7\Modal Modeless Demo*.

Step 2: Look at the *Solution Explorer* window, shown in Figure 7-17. The project has two forms, MainForm and MessageForm. MainForm is the startup form.

Step 3: Double-click the entry for *MainForm.vb* in the *Solution Explorer*. The form should appear in the *Designer* window, as shown in Figure 7-18.

Step 4: To look at the MessageForm form, double-click its entry in the *Solution Explorer* window, as shown in Figure 7-19. The *Close* button is named btnClose.

Figure 7-17 *Solution Explorer* window showing two forms

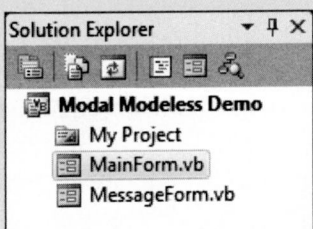

Figure 7-18 MainForm form

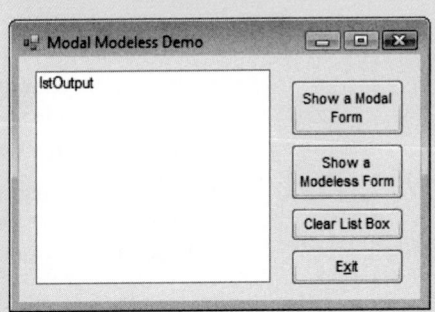

Figure 7-19 MessageForm form

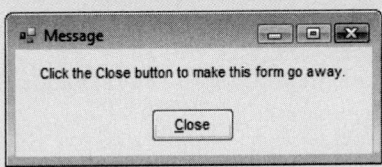

Step 5: Open the *Code* window to view the code for the `MessageForm` form. Look at the `btnClose_Click` event handler. Its code is as follows:

```
Private Sub btnClose_Click(...) Handles btnClose.Click
    ' Close the form.
    Me.Close()
End Sub
```

When this procedure executes, it closes the MessageForm form.

Step 6: Open MainForm in the *Designer* window and double-click the *Show a Modal Form* button. This will create a code template for the `btnShowModal_Click` event handler. Complete the event handler by typing the bold code shown in lines 2 through 12. (Don't type the line numbers. They are shown for reference.)

```
 1 Private Sub btnShowModal_Click(...) Handles btnShowModal.Click
 2     Dim intCount As Integer          ' Counter
 3     Dim frmMessage As New MessageForm ' Instance of MessageForm
 4
 5     ' Show the message form in modal style.
 6     frmMessage.ShowDialog()
 7
 8     ' Display some numbers in the list box on the MainForm.
 9     ' This will happen AFTER the user closes the MessageForm.
10     For intCount = 1 To 10
11         lstOutput.Items.Add(intCount.ToString())
12     Next
13 End Sub
```

Let's take a closer look at the code. Line 2 declares `intCount`, an Integer variable that will be used as a counter. Line 3 creates an instance of the MessageForm form in memory, and assigns its address to a variable named `frmMessage`.

Line 6 uses the `frmMessage` variable to call the form's `ShowDialog` method. This displays the MessageForm in modal style, which means that no other statements in this event handler will execute until the MessageForm closes.

After the MessageForm closes, the For...Next loop in lines 10 through 12 executes. The loop displays the numbers 1 through 10 in the lstOutput list box.

Step 7: Open MainForm in the *Designer* window again and double-click the *Show a Modeless Form* button. This will create a code template for the btnShowModeless_Click event handler. Complete the event handler by typing the bold code shown in lines 2 through 12. (Don't type the line numbers. They are shown for reference.)

```
1 Private Sub btnShowModeless_Click(...) Handles btnShowModal.Click
2    Dim intCount As Integer           ' Counter
3    Dim frmMessage As New MessageForm ' Instance of MessageForm
4
5    ' Show the message form in modeless style.
6    frmMessage.Show()
7
8    ' Display some numbers in the list box on the MainForm.
9    ' This will happen while the MessageForm is still on the screen.
10   For intCount = 1 To 10
11       lstOutput.Items.Add(intCount.ToString())
12   Next
13   End Sub
```

The btnShowModeless_Click event procedure basically performs the same operation as the btnShowModal_Click procedure: It displays the Message-Form form and then displays the numbers 1 through 10 in the lstOutput list box. The only difference is that line 6 displays the MessageForm in modeless style, using the Show method. Therefore, the For...Next loop in lines 10 through 12 executes immediately after the MessageForm is displayed. The program does not wait for the user to close the MessageForm before executing the loop.

Step 8: Run the application. On the main form, click the *Show a Modal Form* button. The MessageForm form is displayed. Figure 7-20 shows the forms, positioned so you can see both of them. Notice that the For...Next loop has not executed because you do not see the numbers 1 through 10 printed on the main form.

Figure 7-20 MainForm form and the modal MessageForm form

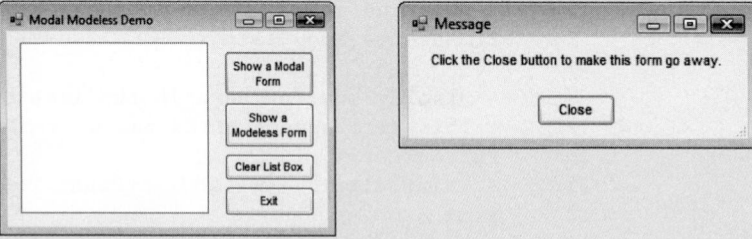

Step 9: Click the *Close* button on the MessageForm form to close the form. Now look at the MainForm form. As shown in Figure 7-21, the For...Next loop executes as soon as the MessageForm form is closed.

Figure 7-21 MainForm after the modal MessageForm form is closed

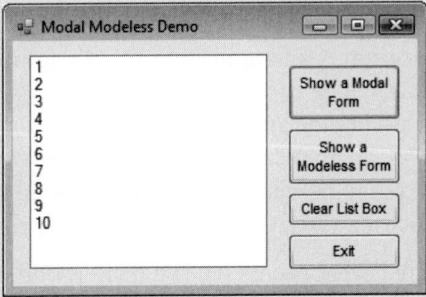

Step 10: Click the *Clear List Box* button to clear the numbers from the list box.

Step 11: Click the *Show a Modeless Form* button to display the MessageForm in modeless style. As shown in Figure 7-22, notice that the `For...Next` loop executes immediately after the form is displayed; it does not wait for you to click the MessageForm *Close* button.

Figure 7-22 MainForm form and the modeless MessageForm form

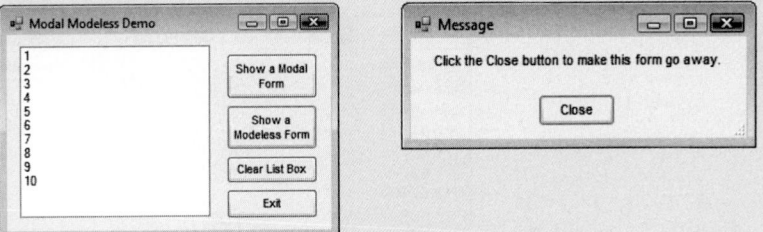

Step 12: Click the MessageForm *Close* button to close the form.

Step 13: Click the MainForm's *Exit* button to end the application.

The Load, Activated, FormClosing, and FormClosed Events

There are several events associated with forms. In this section we will discuss the Load, Activated, FormClosing, and FormClosed events.

The Load Event

The Load event was introduced in Chapter 3, but a quick review is in order. Just before a form is displayed, a Load event occurs. If you need to execute code automatically just before a form is displayed, you can create a Load event handler, which will execute in response to the Load event. To write code in a form's Load event handler, double-click any area of the form where there is no other control. The *Code* window appears with a code template similar to the following:

```
Private Sub MainForm_Load(...) Handles MyBase.Load

End Sub
```

Complete the template with the statements you wish the procedure to execute.

The Activated Event

A form's Activated event occurs when the user switches the focus to the form from another form or application. Here are two examples of how the Activated event occurs:

- Application A and application B are both running, and a form in application A has the focus. The user clicks application B's form. When this happens, the Activated event occurs for application B's form.
- Suppose an application has a main form and a second form, and the second form is displayed in modeless style. Then each time the user clicks a form that does not have the focus, an Activated event occurs for that form.

The Activated event occurs when a form is initially displayed, following the Load event. If you need to execute code in any of these situations, you can create an Activated event handler, which executes in response to the Activated event. To create an **Activated event handler**, follow these steps:

1. Click the class drop-down list, which appears at the top left of the *Code* window, as shown in Figure 7-23.
2. On the drop-down list, select *(FormName Events)*, where *FormName* is the name of the form. This is also shown in Figure 7-23.

Figure 7-23 Select *(FormName Events)* in the class drop-down list

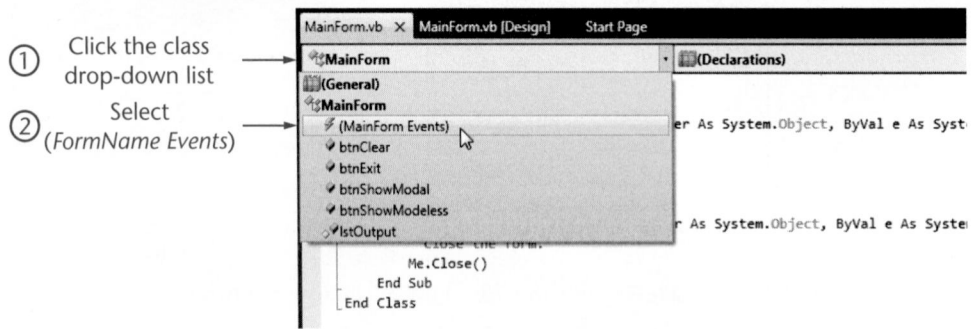

3. Click the method drop-down list, which appears at the top right of *Code* window, and select *Activated*, as shown in Figure 7-24.

Figure 7-24 Select *Activated* in the method name drop-down list

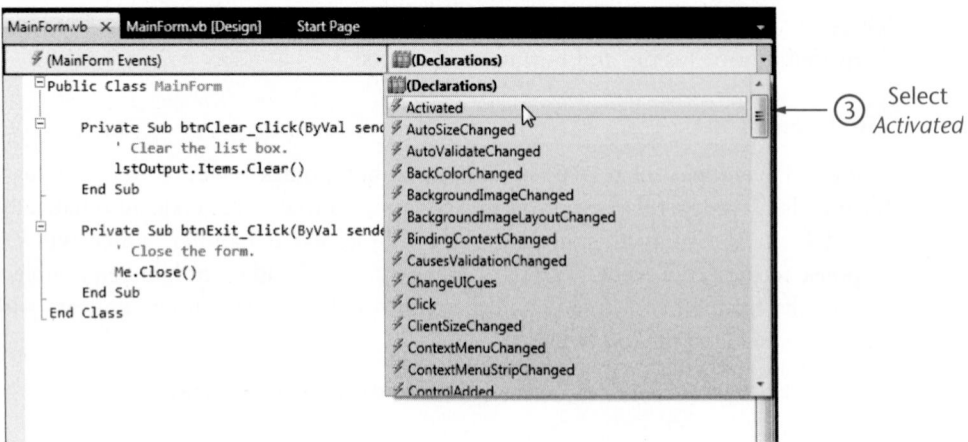

After completing these steps, a code template for the Activated event handler is created in the *Code* window.

The FormClosing Event

The FormClosing event occurs when a form is in the process of closing, but before it has closed. It might be in response to the Close method being executed, the user pressing the [Alt]+[F4] keys, or the user clicking the standard Windows Close button ( ) in the form's upper-right corner. To execute code in response to a form closing, such as asking the user if he or she really wants to close the form, create a **FormClosing** event handler. Here are the required steps:

1. Click the class drop-down list, which appears at the top left of the *Code* window.
2. On the drop-down list, select *(FormName Events)*, where *FormName* is the name of the form.
3. Click the method drop-down list, which appears at the top right of *Code* window, and select *FormClosing*.

After completing these steps, a code template for the FormClosing event handler is created in the *Code* window, as shown in the following example. Notice that we have shown the full parameter list that appears inside the event handler's parentheses:

```
Private Sub MainForm_FormClosing(ByVal sender As Object,
    ByVal e As System.Windows.Forms.FormClosingEventArgs)
    Handles Me.FormClosing

End Sub
```

One of the procedure parameters is named e. It has a Boolean property named *Cancel*. If you set e.Cancel to *True*, the form will not close. Code showing an example of this technique follows:

```
Private Sub MainForm_FormClosing(ByVal sender As Object,
    ByVal e As System.Windows.Forms.FormClosingEventArgs)
    Handles Me.FormClosing

    If MessageBox.Show("Are you Sure?", "Confirm",
        MessageBoxButtons.YesNo) = DialogResult.Yes Then
        e.Cancel = False  ' Continue to close the form.
    Else
        e.Cancel = True   ' Do not close the form.
    End If
End Sub
```

The FormClosed Event

The FormClosed event occurs after a form has closed. If you need to execute code immediately after a form has closed, create a **FormClosed** event handler by following these steps:

1. Click the class drop-down list, which appears at the top left of the *Code* window.
2. On the drop-down list, select *(FormName Events)*, where *FormName* is the name of the form.
3. Click the method drop-down list, which appears at the top right of *Code* window, and select *FormClosed*.

After completing these steps, a code template for the FormClosed event handler will be created in the *Code* window.

> **TIP:** You cannot prevent a form from closing with the FormClosed event handler. You must use the FormClosing event handler to prevent a form from closing.

When you use the `Me.Close( )` method to close an application's startup form, the application fires the FormClosing and FormClosed events.

Accessing Controls on a Different Form

Once you have created an instance of a form, you can access controls on that form in code. For example, suppose an application has a form named GreetingsForm, and Greetings-Form has a Label control named `lblMessage`. The following code shows how you can create an instance of GreetingsForm, assign a value to the `lblMessage` control's Text property, and then display the form in modal style:

```
Dim frmGreetings As New GreetingsForm
frmGreetings.lblMessage.Text = "Good day!"
frmGreetings.ShowDialog()
```

The first statement creates an instance of GreetingsForm and assigns its address to the `frmGreetings` variable. At this point the form exists in memory, but it has not been displayed on the screen. The second statement assigns the string `"Good day!"` to the `lblMessage` control's Text property. Notice that the control's name is preceded by `frmGreetings`, followed by a dot. This tells Visual Basic that the control is not on the current form, but on the form that is referenced by `frmGreetings`. The third statement calls the form's `ShowDialog` method to display the form on the screen. When the form appears on the screen, the `lblMessage` control will display the text *Good Day!*

In Tutorial 7-3 you get a chance to create a multiform application in which code on one form creates an instance of another form and assigns values to controls on that form.

Tutorial 7-3:
Accessing a Control on a Different Form

In this tutorial you will create an application that allows the user to select a food from the application's main form, and then display a second form that shows the selected food's nutritional information.

Step 1: Create a new *Windows Forms Application* project named *Food Facts*.

Step 2: In the *Solution Explorer* window, rename the *Form1.vb* file to *MainForm.vb*. (Right-click *Form1.vb* and then select *Rename* from the popup menu.) Changing the form's file name to *MainForm.vb* changes the form's name to MainForm. The *Solution Explorer* window should appear as shown in Figure 7-25.

Figure 7-25 *Solution Explorer* after changing *Form1.vb* to *MainForm.vb*

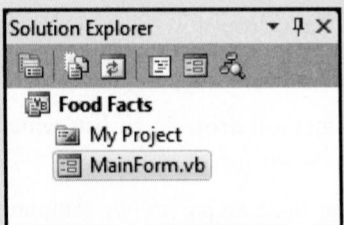

Step 3: In the *Designer* window, set up the MainForm form with the controls shown in Figure 7-26.

Figure 7-26 MainForm

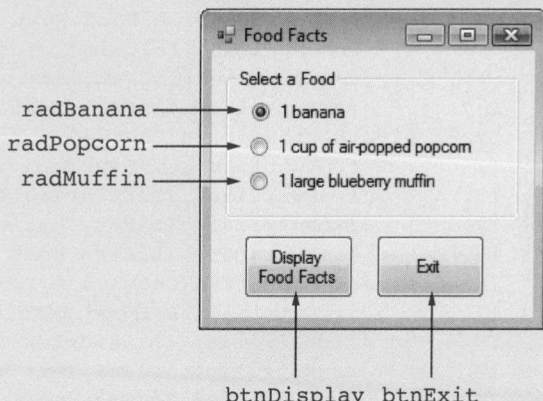

Step 4: Perform the following steps to create another form named NutritionForm in the project:

- Click *Project* on the menu bar, and then select *Add Windows Form...*
- The *Add New Item* window will appear. Enter *NutritionForm.vb* as the name.
- Click the *Add* button.

Step 5: In the *Designer* window, set up the NutritionForm form with the controls shown in Figure 7-27. The Label controls named lblFood, lblCalories, lblFat, and lblCarb have the following property settings:

- *AutoSize* is set to *False*
- *BorderStyle* is set to *Fixed3D*

Figure 7-27 NutritionForm

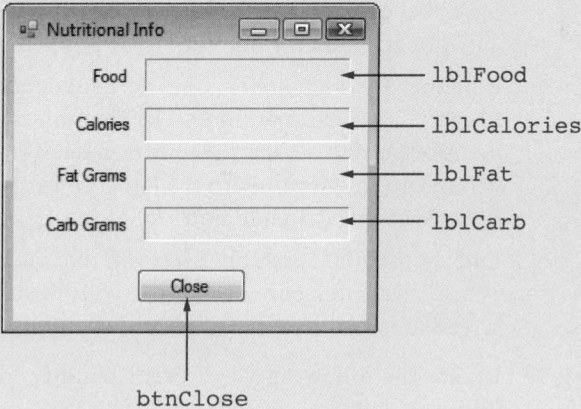

Step 6: Open MainForm in the *Designer* window, and double-click the *Display Food Facts* button to create a code template for the button's Click event handler. Complete the event handler by writing the following bold code, shown in lines 2 through 24. (Don't type the line numbers, they are shown for reference.)

```
1 Private Sub btnDisplay_Click(...) Handles btnDisplay.Click
2     ' Create an instance of the NutritionForm.
3     Dim frmNutrition As New NutritionForm
4
```

```
 5        ' Find the selected radio button.
 6        If radBanana.Checked = True Then
 7            frmNutrition.lblFood.Text = "1 banana"
 8            frmNutrition.lblCalories.Text = "100"
 9            frmNutrition.lblFat.Text = "0.4"
10            frmNutrition.lblCarb.Text = "27"
11        ElseIf radPopcorn.Checked = True Then
12            frmNutrition.lblFood.Text = "1 cup air-popped popcorn"
13            frmNutrition.lblCalories.Text = "31"
14            frmNutrition.lblFat.Text = "0.4"
15            frmNutrition.lblCarb.Text = "6"
16        ElseIf radMuffin.Checked = True Then
17            frmNutrition.lblFood.Text = "1 large blueberry muffin"
18            frmNutrition.lblCalories.Text = "385"
19            frmNutrition.lblFat.Text = "9"
20            frmNutrition.lblCarb.Text = "67"
21        End If
22
23        ' Display the NutritionForm.
24        frmNutrition.ShowDialog()
25 End Sub
```

Let's take a closer look at this code. Line 3 creates an instance of the Nutrition-Form form in memory and assigns its address to the frmNutrition variable. Keep in mind that although the form has been created in memory, it has not yet been displayed on the screen.

The If...Then statement in line 6 determines whether the radBanana radio button is selected. If so, the statements in lines 7 through 10 use the frmNutrition variable to assign values to the Label controls on the NutritionForm form. The values that are assigned are the nutritional values for a banana.

If the radBanana radio button is not selected, the ElseIf...Then clause in line 11 determines whether the radPopcorn radio button is selected. If so, the statements in lines 12 through 15 use the frmNutrition variable to assign values to the Label controls on the NutritionForm. The values that are assigned are the nutritional values for one cup of air-popped popcorn.

If neither the radBanana nor the radPopcorn radio buttons are selected, the ElseIf...Then clause in line 16 determines whether the radMuffin radio button is selected. If so, the statements in lines 17 through 20 use the frmNutrition variable to assign values to the Label controls on the NutritionForm. The values that are assigned are the nutritional values for one large blueberry muffin.

Line 24 uses the frmNutrition variable to call the form's ShowDialog method. When this statement executes, it will display the NutritionForm form on the screen in modal style.

Step 7: Create the following Click event handler for the MainForm form's btnExit button:

```
Private Sub btnExit_Click(...) Handles btnExit.Click
    ' Close the form.
    Me.Close()
End Sub
```

Step 8: Open NutritionForm in the *Designer* window, and double-click the *Close* button to create a code template for the button's Click event handler. Complete the event handler by writing the following bold code:

```
                Private Sub btnClose_Click(...) Handles btnClose.Click
                    ' Close the form.
                    Me.Close()
                End Sub
```

Step 9:   Save the project and then run it. The MainForm should appear, as shown on the left in Figure 7-28. With the *1 banana* radio button selected, click the *Display Food Facts* button. The NutritionForm form should appear, as shown on the right in Figure 7-28.

Figure 7-28 The MainForm and the NutritionForm forms displayed

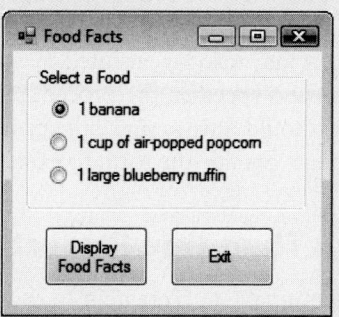
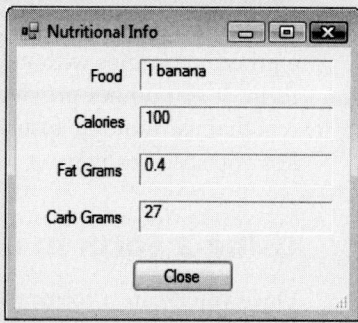

Step 10:   On the NutritionForm form, click the *Close* button. This should close the NutritionForm form. Try selecting the other radio buttons on the MainForm form and clicking the *Display Food Facts* button to see each item's nutritional information. When you are finished, click the *Exit* button on the MainForm form to end the application.

Class-Level Variables in a Form

Although a form's class-level variables are accessible to all statements in the form file, they are not accessible by default to statements outside the form file. For example, assume a project has a form named AmountForm, which has the following class-level variable declaration:

```
Dim dblTotal As Double          ' Class-level variable
```

The same project has another form that uses the following statements:

```
Dim frmAmount As New AmountForm
frmAmount.dblTotal = 100.0
```

Although the assignment statement has fully qualified the name of `dblTotal` by preceding it with the object variable name, the statement still cannot access it because class-level variables are private by default. The statement will cause an error when the project is compiled.

It is possible to make a class-level variable available to methods outside the class. This is done using the **Public** keyword. Here is an example:

```
Public dblTotal As Double            ' Class-level variable
```

Although class-level variables are automatically declared private by the `Dim` statement, you should explicitly declare them private with the **Private** keyword. Here is an example:

```
Private dblTotal As Double
```

> **NOTE:** Class-level variables should be declared `Private` unless a strong reason exists to do otherwise. By explicitly declaring private class-level variables with the `Private` keyword, you make your source code more self-documenting. Furthermore, programmers rarely make class variables public, because doing so would violate an important principle of object-oriented programming called *encapsulation*.

Using `Private` and `Public` Procedures in a Form

Recall from Chapter 6 that the declaration of a procedure or function may begin with an optional access specifier, such as `Public` or `Private`. When a procedure declaration begins with `Private`, the procedure may be executed only by statements in the same form. When a procedure begins with `Public`, it may also be executed by statements that are outside the form. If you do not provide an access specifier, the procedure defaults to `Public`. In projects that use multiple forms, you should always make the procedures in a form private unless you specifically want statements outside the form to execute the procedure.

Using a Form in More Than One Project

Once you create a form, you do not have to recreate it to use it in another project. After a form has been saved to a file, it may be used in other projects. Follow these steps to add an existing form to a project:

1. With the receiving project open in Visual Studio, click *Project* on the menu bar, and then click *Add Existing Item*.
2. The *Add Existing Item* dialog box appears. Use the dialog box to locate the form file that you want to add to the project. (Remember that form files end with the *.vb* extension.) When you locate the file, select it and click the *Open* button. A copy of the form is now added to the project.

 Checkpoint

7.1 How do you cause a form to be displayed automatically when your application executes?

7.2 What prefix do we use in this book when naming variables that will reference forms?

7.3 Describe the process of adding a new form to a project.

7.4 In Visual Studio only, describe the process of excluding a form from a project.

7.5 What is a form file? What file extension does a form file have?

7.6 What is the difference between a modal form and a modeless form?

7.7 Suppose a project has an object variable named `frmResults`, which references an instance of a form. Write the statement that uses the `frmResults` variable to display the form in modal style.

7.8 Write a statement that displays the form referenced by `frmResults` in modeless style.

7.9 In which event handler do you write code if you want it to execute when the user switches to a form from another form or from another application?

7.10 Suppose a project has a form named InfoForm with a label named `lblCustomer`. The following declaration statement appears in the MainForm form:

```
Dim frmInfo As New InfoForm:
```

The `frmInfo` variable references an instance of InfoForm. Write a statement that uses the `frmInfo` variable to copy *Jim Jones* to the `lblCustomer` Label control on the InfoForm form.

7.11 What is the `Me` keyword used for?

7.12 Suppose you want to declare a class-level variable of the Double data type named `dblAverage` in a form. Assuming you want code in other forms to access it, write the variable declaration.

7.2 Modules

CONCEPT: A module contains code—declarations and procedures—that are used by other files in a project.

When you create a large application with multiple forms, quite often you will find that the code in several different forms needs to call the same function or procedure. For example, suppose you are creating an application for a retail business and in one of the application's forms you write a function that calculates the sales tax on a purchase. Later you discover that event handlers in several other forms need to call the same function. Do you duplicate the sales tax function in each of the forms that need to call it? That's one approach. A better approach, however, is to store the sales tax function in some location where all the forms can access it. That would eliminate the duplication of the code, and make it easier to maintain the application if you ever need to modify the sales tax function. In Visual Basic, such a location is known as a module.

A **module** is a Visual Basic file that contains only code. That is to say, it contains only procedures, functions, and declarations of variables and constants. Any `Public` procedures, functions, and declarations that appear in a module are global, which means they are accessible to all of the forms in the same project. Modules are stored in files that end with the *.vb* extension, and when a module is added to a project, its entry appears in the *Solution Explorer* along with the entries for the project's form files.

NOTE: You do not write event handlers in a module. Modules are meant to contain general-purpose procedures, functions, and declarations that are available to all forms in a project.

Module Names and Module Files

The content of a module begins with a `Module` statement and ends with an `End Module` statement. The general format follows:

```
Module ModuleName
   [Module Contents]
End Module
```

ModuleName is the name of the module. This can be any valid identifier. If you have only one module in your project you should give it a name that clearly relates it to the project. For example, if a project is named *Order Entry*, then its module might be named `OrderEntryModule`. It is possible to have multiple modules in a project. For example, you might have one module containing math procedures and another module containing procedures for retrieving information from a database. If your project has multiple modules, give each module a name that describes its purpose.

When you create a module, its code is stored in a file that is named with the *.vb* extension. Normally, the name of the file is the same as the name of the module. Therefore, a module named `OrderEntryModule` should be saved to the file *OrderEntryModule.vb*.

Let's look at an example of a module. The following code shows the contents of a module named `RetailMath`. (The line numbers are not part of the module. They are shown only for reference.)

```
1 Module RetailMath
2     ' Global constant for the tax rate
3     Public Const decTAX_RATE As Decimal = 0.07D
4
5     ' The SalesTax function returns the sales tax on a purchase.
6     Public Function SalesTax(ByVal decPurchase As Decimal) As Decimal
7        Return decPurchase * decTAX_RATE
8     End Function
9 End Module
```

Line 3 declares a module-level constant named `decTAX_RATE`. (It's module-level because it is not declared inside any procedure or function.) Notice that the declaration begins with the word `Public`. This means that the constant is accessible to code outside the module. As a result, the code in any form in the same project has access to this constant.

In lines 6 through 8 a function named `SalesTax` appears. Notice that the function header in line 6 also begins with the word `Public`. This means that the function can be called by code outside the module. As a result, the code in any form in the same project may call this function.

Procedures, functions, and declarations can be declared as `Private`, which means that they can be accessed only by code in the same module.

Adding a Module

Follow these steps to add a module to a project.

1. Click *Project* on the menu bar and then click *Add Module*. The *Add New Item* window shown in Figure 7-29 should appear. Notice that in the figure, the name

Figure 7-29 *Add New Item* dialog box

Module1.vb appears in the *Name* text box. In this example, *Module1.vb* is the default name for the file that the module will be stored in and *Module1* is the default name for the module.

 NOTE: The default name may be different, depending on the number of modules already in the project.

2. Change the default name that is displayed in the *Name* text box to the name you wish to give the new module file. For example, if you wish to name the new module `MainModule`, enter *MainModule.vb* in the *Name* text box.
3. Click the *Add* button.

 NOTE: When you name the module file, be sure to keep the *.vb* extension.

A new, empty module will be added to your project. The module is displayed in the *Code* window, and an entry for the new module appears in the *Solution Explorer* window. The *Solution Explorer* window in Figure 7-30 shows two forms and one module: ErrorForm, MainForm, and ExampleProjectModule.

Figure 7-30 *Solution Explorer* window showing two forms and one module

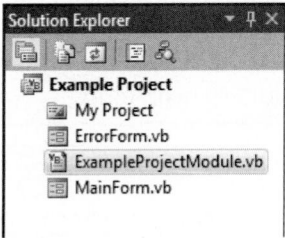

Once you have added a module to your project, you type code directly into it using the *Code* window.

Module-Level Variables

A variable declared inside a module, but not inside a procedure or function, is called a **module-level variable**. The same rules about the scope of class-level variables in a form apply to module-level variables in a module.

- A module-level variable in a module is accessible to any procedure or function in the module.
- If a module-level variable is declared with the `Dim` or `Private` keywords, the variable is not accessible to statements outside the module. Such a variable has **module scope**.
- If a module-level variable is declared with the `Public` keyword, it is accessible to statements outside the module.

A module-level variable declared `Public` is also known as a **global variable** because it can be accessed globally, by any statement in the application.

 TIP: Some programmers prefix the names of global variables with the characters `g_`. This documents the variable's scope. For example, a global Decimal variable that holds the amount of a purchase might be named `g_decPurchaseAmount`.

TIP: Although global variables provide an easy way to share data among procedures, forms, and modules, they should be used with caution. While debugging an application, if you find that the wrong value is being stored in a global variable, you will have to track down every statement that accesses it to determine where the bad value is coming from. Also, when two or more procedures modify the same variable, you must be careful that one procedure's actions do not upset the correctness of another procedure.

Tutorial 7-4 examines an application that uses a module.

Tutorial 7-4:
Examining an application that uses a module

In this tutorial you will examine the *Converter* application, which performs simple conversions between metric and English units. The application has three forms and a module that contains all of the conversion functions.

Step 1: Open the *Converter* project from the student sample programs folder named *Chap7\Converter*.

Step 2: Before we examine the application's code, let's see it in action. Run the application. The main form appears, as shown in Figure 7-31.

Figure 7-31 The application's main form

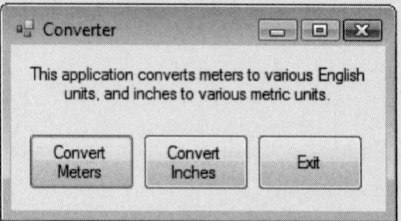

Step 3: Click the *Convert Meters* button. The *Meters To English* form appears, as shown on the right in Figure 7-32. This form has a TextBox for you to enter a number of meters. Enter a number in the TextBox, and then click the *Convert to Inches* button. A message box appears showing the equivalent number of inches. Close the message box, and then try the *Convert to Feet* and *Convert to Yards* buttons. When you are finished, click the *Close* button to close the *Meters To English* form.

Figure 7-32 The application's main form and the *Meters To English* form

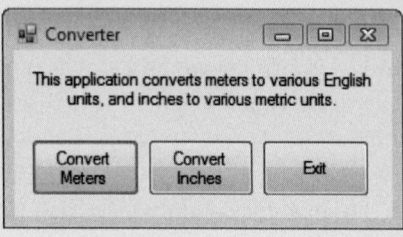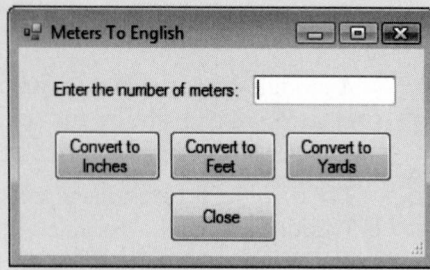

Step 4: Back on the main form, click the *Convert Inches* button. The *Inches To Metric* form appears, as shown on the right in Figure 7-33. This form has a TextBox for you to enter a number of inches. Enter a number in the TextBox, and then click the *Convert to Millimeters* button. A message box appears showing the equivalent number of millimeters. Close the message box, and then try the *Convert to Centimeters* and *Convert to Meters* buttons. When you are finished click the *Close* button to close the *Inches To Metric* form.

Figure 7-33 The application's main form and the *Inches To Metric* form

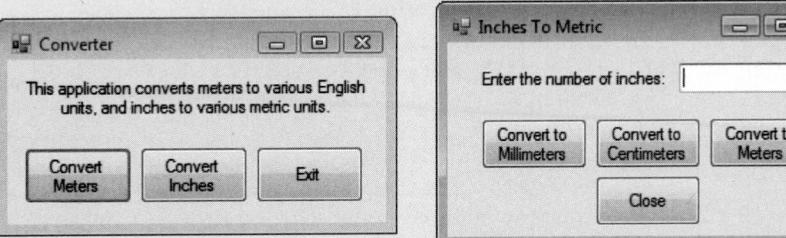

Step 5: Back on the application's main form, click the *Exit* button to end the application.

Step 6: Look in the *Solution Explorer*, as shown in Figure 7-34, and notice that the project has the following *.vb* files:

- *InchesToMetricForm.vb*–This is the form file for the form named InchesToMetricForm.
- *MainForm.vb*–This is the form file for the form named MainForm.
- *MathModule.vb*–This is a module file that contains functions and constants for the mathematical conversions.
- *MetersToEnglishForm.vb*–This is the form file for the form named MetersToEnglishForm.

Figure 7-34 Solution Explorer

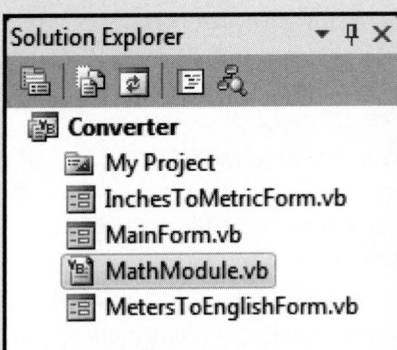

Step 7: Double-click the entry for *MathModule.vb* in the *Solution Explorer*. This opens the *MathModule.vb* file in the *Code* window. The file's contents are shown here, with line numbers added for reference:

```
1 Module MathModule
2     ' Constants for the meters to English conversion factors
3     Public Const dblMETERS_TO_INCHES As Double = 39.37
4     Public Const dblMETERS_TO_FEET As Double = 3.28
5     Public Const dblMETERS_TO_YARDS As Double = 1.09
6
```

```
 7    ' Constants for the inches to metric conversion factors
 8    Public Const dblINCHES_TO_MM As Double = 25.4
 9    Public Const dblINCHES_TO_CM As Double = 2.54
10    Public Const dblINCHES_TO_METERS As Double = 0.0254
11
12    ' The MetersToInches function accepts a number of meters as
13    ' an argument and returns the equivalent number of inches.
14    Public Function MetersToInches(ByVal dblMeters As Double) As Double
15        Return dblMeters * dblMETERS_TO_INCHES
16    End Function
17
18    ' The MetersToFeet function accepts a number of meters as
19    ' an argument and returns the equivalent number of feet.
20    Public Function MetersToFeet(ByVal dblMeters As Double) As Double
21        Return dblMeters * dblMETERS_TO_FEET
22    End Function
23
24    ' The MetersToYards function accepts a number of meters as
25    ' an argument and returns the equivalent number of yards.
26    Public Function MetersToYards(ByVal dblMeters As Double) As Double
27        Return dblMeters * dblMETERS_TO_YARDS
28    End Function
29
30    ' The InchesToMM function accepts a number of inches as
31    ' an argument and returns the equivalent number of millimeters.
32    Public Function InchesToMM(ByVal dblInches As Double) As Double
33        Return dblInches * dblINCHES_TO_MM
34    End Function
35
36    ' The InchesToCM function accepts a number of inches as
37    ' an argument and returns the equivalent number of centimeters.
38    Public Function InchesToCM(ByVal dblInches As Double) As Double
39        Return dblInches * dblINCHES_TO_CM
40    End Function
41
42    ' The InchesToMeters function accepts a number of inches as
43    ' an argument and returns the equivalent number of meters.
44    Public Function InchesToMeters(ByVal dblInches As Double) As Double
45        Return dblInches * dblINCHES_TO_METERS
46    End Function
47 End Module
```

The MathModule module contains all of the code for the application's conversion functions. A summary of the code follows. Note that all of the constants and functions in the file are declared as Public, which makes them globally accessible in the project.

- Lines 3 through 5 declare some constants that are used in the formulas to convert meters to English units.
- Lines 8 through 10 declare some constants that are used in the formulas to convert inches to metric units.
- The MetersToInches function appears in lines 14 through 16. This function accepts a number of meters as an argument and returns the equivalent number of inches.
- The MetersToFeet function appears in lines 20 through 22. This function accepts a number of meters as an argument and returns the equivalent number of feet.

- The `MetersToYards` function appears in lines 26 through 28. This function accepts a number of meters as an argument and returns the equivalent number of yards.
- The `InchesToCM` function appears in lines 38 through 40. This function accepts a number of inches as an argument and returns the equivalent number of centimeters.
- The `InchesToMeters` function appears in lines 44 through 46. This function accepts a number of inches as an argument and returns the equivalent number of meters.

Step 8: Now let's see how the functions in *MathModule.vb* are called by statements in the application's forms. Open the form MetersToEnglishForm in the Code window. (A fast way to do this is to right-click *MetersToEnglish.vb* in the *Solution Explorer*, and then select *View Code* from the pop-up menu.)

Figure 7-35 shows the `btnMetersToInches_Click` event handler. Notice the statement that calls the `MetersToInches` function, which is stored in the *MathModule.vb* file.

Figure 7-35 A call to the `MetersToInches` function

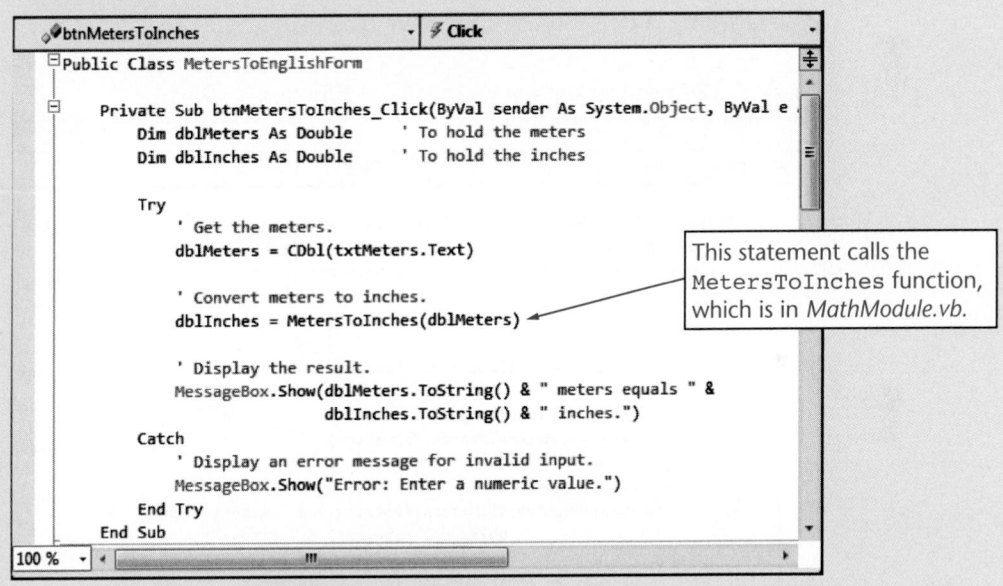

Scroll down to the the `btnMetersToFeet_Click` event handler, which is shown in Figure 7-36. Notice the statement that calls the `MetersToFeet` function, which is stored in the *MathModule.vb* file.

Now scroll down to the the `btnMetersToYards_Click` event handler, which is shown in Figure 7-37. Notice the statement that calls the `MetersToYards` function, which is stored in the *MathModule.vb* file.

Figure 7-36 A call to the `MetersToFeet` function

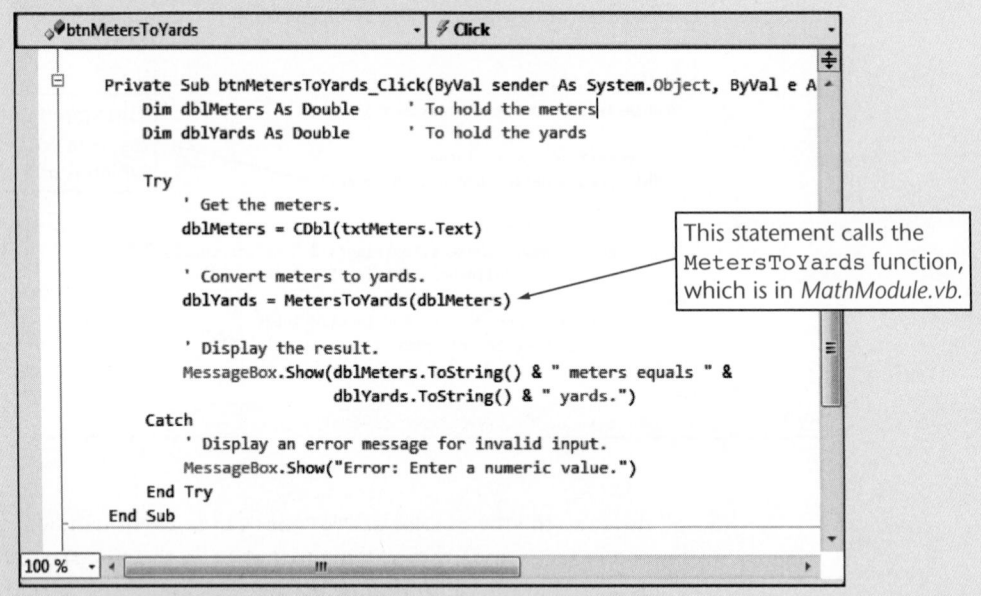

```
btnMetersToFeet                          ▼  ⨍ Click                        ▼

    Private Sub btnMetersToFeet_Click(ByVal sender As System.Object, ByVal e As
        Dim dblMeters As Double    ' To hold the meters
        Dim dblFeet As Double      ' To hold the feet

        Try
            ' Get the meters.
            dblMeters = CDbl(txtMeters.Text)

            ' Convert meters to feet.
            dblFeet = MetersToFeet(dblMeters)

            ' Display the result.
            MessageBox.Show(dblMeters.ToString() & " meters equals " &
                            dblFeet.ToString() & " feet.")
        Catch
            ' Display an error message for invalid input.
            MessageBox.Show("Error: Enter a numeric value.")
        End Try
    End Sub
End Sub

100 %   ▼  ◀          ⋯                              ▶
```

> This statement calls the `MetersToFeet` function, which is in *MathModule.vb*.

Figure 7-37 A call to the `MetersToYards` function

```
btnMetersToYards                         ▼  ⨍ Click                        ▼

    Private Sub btnMetersToYards_Click(ByVal sender As System.Object, ByVal e A
        Dim dblMeters As Double      ' To hold the meters
        Dim dblYards As Double       ' To hold the yards

        Try
            ' Get the meters.
            dblMeters = CDbl(txtMeters.Text)

            ' Convert meters to yards.
            dblYards = MetersToYards(dblMeters)

            ' Display the result.
            MessageBox.Show(dblMeters.ToString() & " meters equals " &
                            dblYards.ToString() & " yards.")
        Catch
            ' Display an error message for invalid input.
            MessageBox.Show("Error: Enter a numeric value.")
        End Try
    End Sub
End Sub

100 %   ▼  ◀          ⋯                              ▶
```

> This statement calls the `MetersToYards` function, which is in *MathModule.vb*.

Step 9:   Now let's see how the functions in *MathModule.vb* are called by statements in the InchesToMetricForm form. Open the form InchesToMetricForm in the Code window. At the top of the file you should see the `btnInchesToMM_Click` event handler as shown in Figure 7-38. Notice the statement that calls the `InchesToMM` function, which is stored in the *MathModule.vb* file.

Figure 7-38 A call to the `InchesToMM` function

btnInchesToMM
Click
Public Class InchesToMetricForm
Private Sub btnInchesToMM_Click(ByVal sender As System.Object, ByVal e As S
Dim dblInches As Double ' To hold the inches
Dim dblMillimeters As Double ' To hold the millimeters
Try
' Get the inches.
dblInches = CDbl(txtInches.Text)
' Convert inches to millimeters.
dblMillimeters = InchesToMM(dblInches)
' Display the result.
MessageBox.Show(dblInches.ToString() & " inches equals " &
dblMillimeters.ToString() & " millimeters.")
Catch
' Display an error message for invalid input.
MessageBox.Show("Error: Enter a numeric value.")
End Try
End Sub
100 %
This statement calls the InchesToMM function, which is in MathModule.vb.

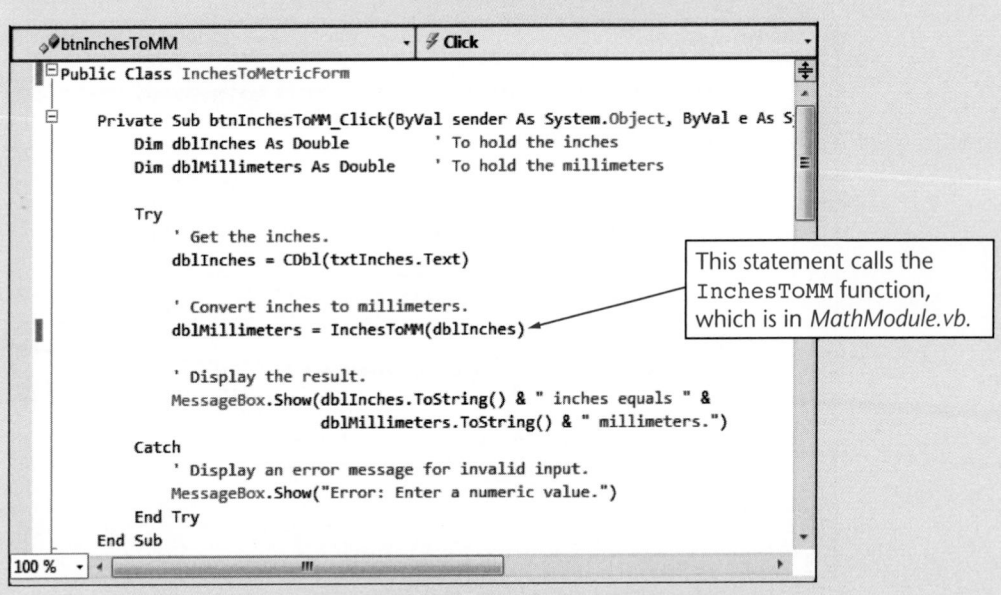

Scroll down to the the `btnInchesToCM_Click` event handler, which is shown in Figure 7-39. Notice the statement that calls the `InchesToCM` function, which is stored in the *MathModule.vb* file.

Figure 7-39 A call to the `InchesToCM` function

btnInchesToCM
Click
Private Sub btnInchesToCM_Click(ByVal sender As System.Object, ByVal e As S
Dim dblInches As Double ' To hold the inches
Dim dblCentimeters As Double ' To hold the centimeters
Try
' Get the inches.
dblInches = CDbl(txtInches.Text)
' Convert inches to centimeters.
dblCentimeters = InchesToCM(dblInches)
' Display the result.
MessageBox.Show(dblInches.ToString() & " inches equals " &
dblCentimeters.ToString() & " centimeters.")
Catch
' Display an error message for invalid input.
MessageBox.Show("Error: Enter a numeric value.")
End Try
End Sub
100 %
This statement calls the InchesToCM function, which is in MathModule.vb.

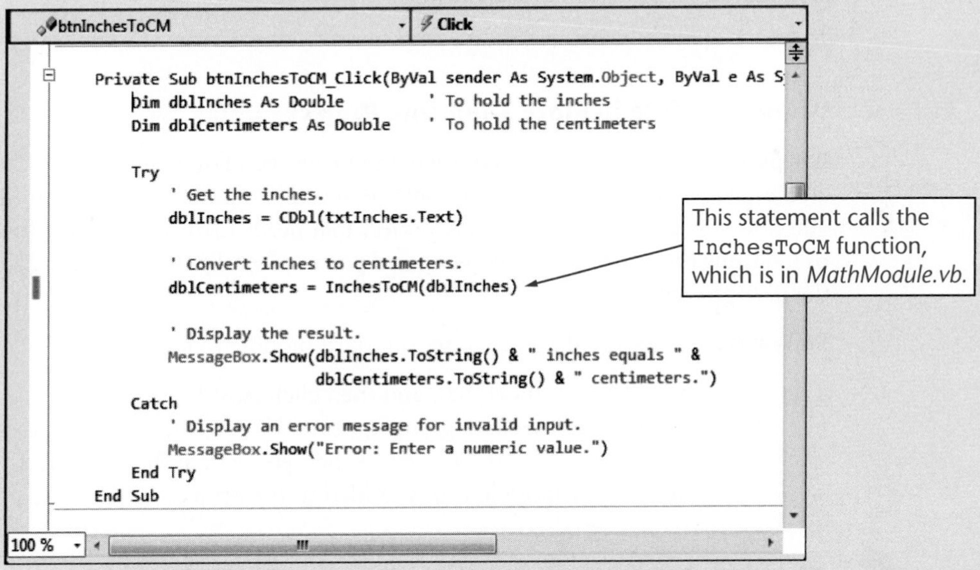

Now scroll down to the the `btnInchesToMeters_Click` event handler, which is shown in Figure 7-40. Notice the statement that calls the `InchesToMeters` function, which is stored in the *MathModule.vb* file.

Figure 7-40 A call to the `InchesToMeters` function

```
btnInchesToMeters                              Click

    Private Sub btnInchesToMeters_Click(ByVal sender As System.Object, ByVal e ...
        Dim dblInches As Double     ' To hold the inches
        Dim dblMeters As Double     ' To hold the millimeters

        Try
            ' Get the inches.
            dblInches = CDbl(txtInches.Text)

            ' Convert inches to millimeters.
            dblMeters = InchesToMeters(dblInches)

            ' Display the result.
            MessageBox.Show(dblInches.ToString() & " inches equals " &
                            dblMeters.ToString() & " meters.")
        Catch
            ' Display an error message for invalid input.
            MessageBox.Show("Error: Enter a numeric value.")
        End Try
    End Sub

100 %
```

> This statement calls the `InchesToMeters` function, which is in *MathModule.vb*.

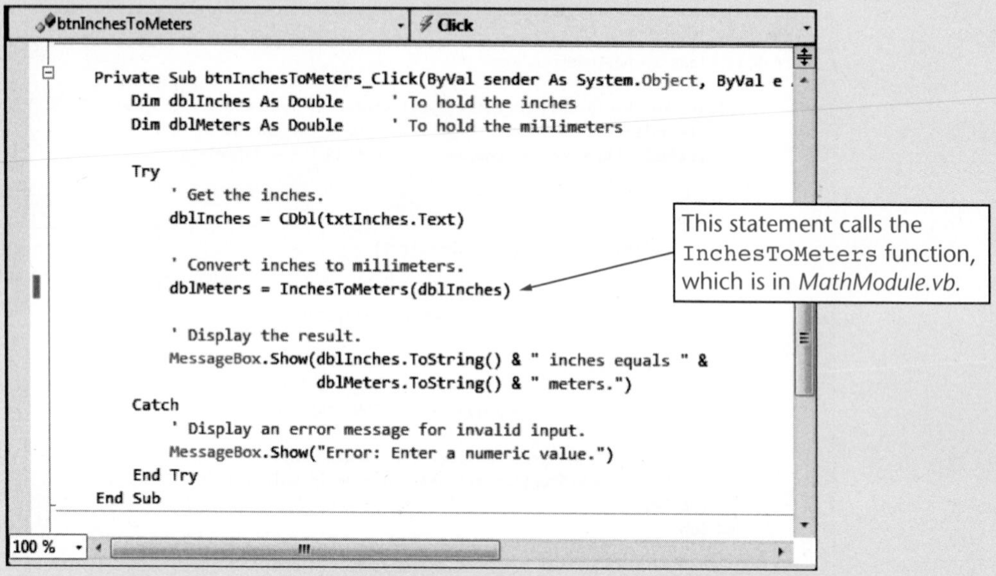

 NOTE: It's worth pointing out that the *Converter* application uses the *MathModule.vb* file not only for sharing common functions between two forms, but it is also for organizing all of the mathematical functions together, in the same module. It's possible to have multiple modules in the same application, with each module containing related procedures, functions, and declarations.

Using a Module in More Than One Project

It is possible to use a module in more than one project. For example, suppose you have created a project with a module that contains several commonly used math functions. Later, you find yourself working on a new project that needs many of the same functions. Instead of rewriting the functions, (or copying and pasting them) you can simply add the module to the new project.

Follow these steps to add an existing standard module to a project.

1. Click *Project* on the menu bar, and then click *Add Existing Item*.
2. The *Add Existing Item* dialog box appears. Use the dialog box to locate the module file you want to add to the project. When you locate the file, select it and click the *Open* button. The module is now added to the project.

 ## Checkpoint

7.13 What do modules contain?

7.14 With what file extension are modules saved?

7.15 Describe the steps you take to add a new module to a project.

7.16 How can modules be used to organize code in a multiform project?

7.17 How do you add an existing module to a project?

7.3 Menus

CONCEPT: Visual Basic allows you to create a system of drop-down menus for any form in your application. You use the menu designer to create a menu system.

VideoNote

Creating a Menu

In the applications you have studied so far, the user performs tasks primarily by clicking buttons. When an application has several operations for the user to choose from, a menu system is more commonly used than buttons. A **menu system** is a collection of commands organized in one or more drop-down menus. The **menu designer** allows you to visually create a custom menu system for any form in an application.

Before you learn how to use the menu designer, you must learn about the typical components of a menu system. Look at the Example Menu System shown in Figure 7-41.

Figure 7-41 Example Menu System

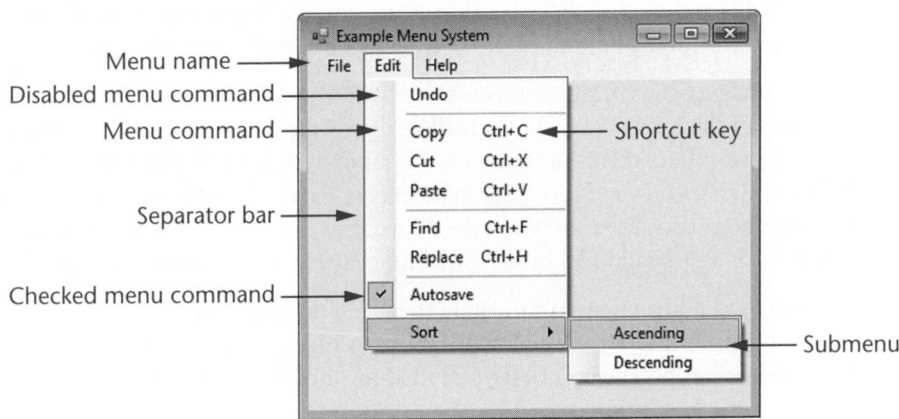

The menu system in the figure consists of the following items.

- **Menu names**—Each drop-down menu has a name. The menu names are listed on a menu strip that appears just below the form's title bar. The menu names in Figure 7-41 are *File*, *Edit*, and *Help*. The user may activate a menu by clicking the menu name. In the figure, the Edit menu has been activated. Menu items may also be assigned access keys (such as <u>F</u> for File, <u>E</u> for Edit, and <u>H</u> for Help). The user may also activate a menu by entering Alt + its access key.

- **Menu command**—Menus have commands. The user selects a command by clicking it, entering its access key, or entering its shortcut key.

- **Shortcut key**—A **shortcut key** is a key or combination of keys that cause a menu command to execute. Shortcut keys are shown on a menu to the right of their corresponding commands. For example, in Figure 7-41, Ctrl+C is the shortcut key for the *Copy* command. Here is the primary difference between a shortcut key and an access key: a menu command's access key works only while the menu is open, but a shortcut key may be executed at any time while the form is active.

- **Disabled menu command**—You can cause a menu command to be disabled when you do not want the user to select it. A disabled menu command appears in dim lettering (grayed out) and cannot be selected. In Figure 7-41, the *Undo* command is disabled.

- **Checked menu command**—A checked menu command is usually one that turns an option on or off. A check mark appears to the left of the command, indicating the option is turned on. When no check mark appears to the left of the command, the option is turned off. The user toggles a checked menu command each time he or she selects it. In Figure 7-41, *Autosave* is a checked menu command.

- **Submenu**—Some of the commands on a menu are actually the names of submenus. You can tell when a command is the name of a submenu because a right arrow (▶) appears to its right. Activating the name of a submenu causes the submenu to appear. For example, in Figure 7-41, clicking the *Sort* command causes a submenu to appear.

- **Separator bar**—A **separator bar** is a horizontal bar used to separate groups of commands on a menu. In Figure 7-41, separator bars are used to separate the *Copy*, *Cut*, and *Paste* commands into one group, the *Find* and *Replace* commands into another group, and the *Sort* command in a box by itself. Separator bars are used only as visual aids and cannot be selected by the user.

The MenuStrip Control

An application's menu system is constructed with a **MenuStrip control**. When your form is displayed in the *Designer* window, find the *Menus & Toolbars* section of the *Toolbox* window (Figure 7-42) and double-click the *MenuStrip* icon. A MenuStrip control will appear in the component tray at the bottom of the *Design* window, with a default name of `MenuStrip1`.

When the MenuStrip control is selected, you will see the words *Type Here* displayed in a strip at the top of the form. We will informally call this the menu designer, a tool that allows you to visually edit the contents of the menu. You simply click inside this strip and type the names of the items that you want to appear in the menu. Figure 7-43 shows an example where a *File* menu has been added. As shown in the figure, you can assign an access key to a menu name by typing an ampersand (&) before the character that is to become the access key.

Each time you add an item to a menu in the menu designer, you create a **ToolStripMenuItem object**. When you select a ToolStripMenuItem object, you see its properties listed in the *Properties* window. The text that you typed for the item in the Menu Designer will appear in the object's Text property.

ToolStripMenuItem objects are given default names (stored in their Name properties) when they are created, but it is recommended that you change these names to reflect each item's position in the menu system hierarchy. For example, look at the menu system sketch in Figure 7-44. Table 7-1 lists the recommended names of this menu system's ToolStripMenuItem objects, along with the contents of their Text properties.

Figure 7-42 *Menus & Toolbars* section of the *Toolbox*

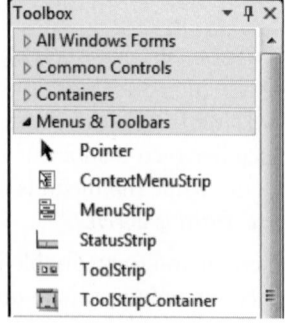

Figure 7-43 Inserting text into a menu item

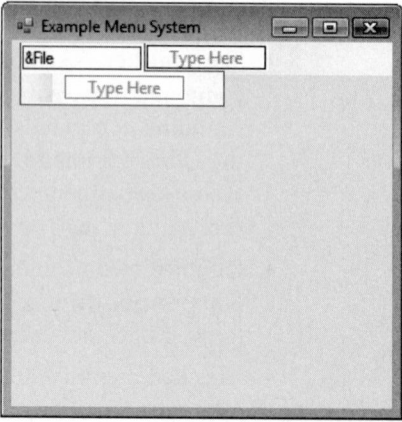

Figure 7-44 Example menu system sketch

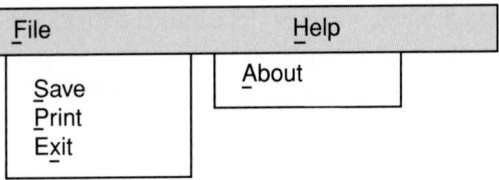

Table 7-1 ToolStripMenuItem objects and their Text properties

ToolStripMenuItem Name	Text Property
mnuFile	&File
mnuFileSave	&Save
mnuFilePrint	&Print
mnuFileExit	E&xit
mnuHelp	&Help
mnuHelpAbout	&About

The menu item names listed in Table Table 7-1 indicate where in the menu hierarchy each control belongs. The names of objects corresponding to commands on the *File* menu all begin with mnuFile. For example, the *Save* command on the *File* menu is named mnuFileSave. Likewise, the object for the *About* command on the *Help* menu is named mnuHelpAbout.

ToolStripMenuItem objects also respond to events. You can make a menu functional by writing Click event procedures for its objects.

How to Use the Menu Designer

Once you have placed a MenuStrip control in a form's component tray, you can use the menu designer to create menu items. Start the menu designer by selecting the MenuStrip control. Figure 7-45 shows a form with a MenuStrip control selected in the component tray, and the menu designer started. The designer appears on the form in the location that the menu system will appear.

Figure 7-45 MenuStrip control selected and menu designer started

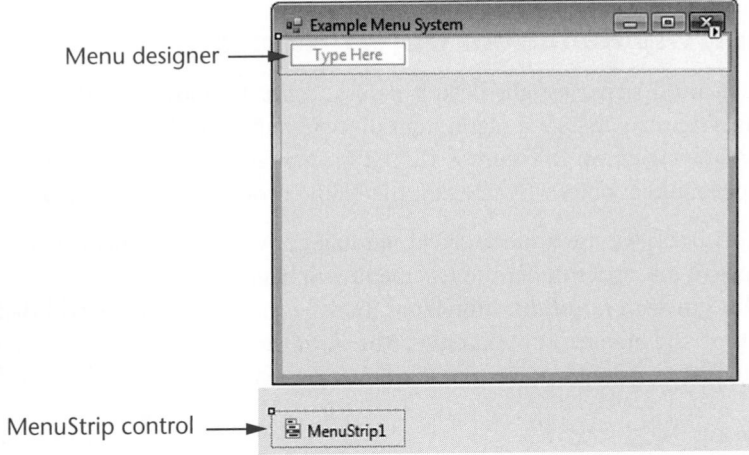

Notice in Figure 7-45 that the words *Type Here* appear in a small box in the menu designer. This marks the position of the first menu item. A ToolStripMenuItem object is automatically created when you type text into the box. The text you type is stored in the item's Text property, and is displayed on the menu strip. Figure 7-46 shows the menu designer after the word *File* has been typed as the text for the first menu item.

Figure 7-46 MenuStrip object with *File* as its text

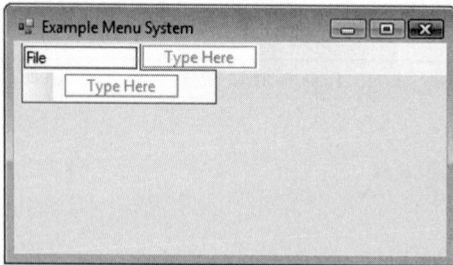

Notice that the menu designer now shows two new *Type Here* boxes, one below and one to the right of the first object. Simply click in one of the boxes to select it, and then type the text that you wish to appear at that position.

Figure 7-47 shows the menu designer with a more complete menu system. The menu system has a *File* and *Edit* menu. The *Edit* menu is displayed.

Figure 7-47 Menu designer with many items

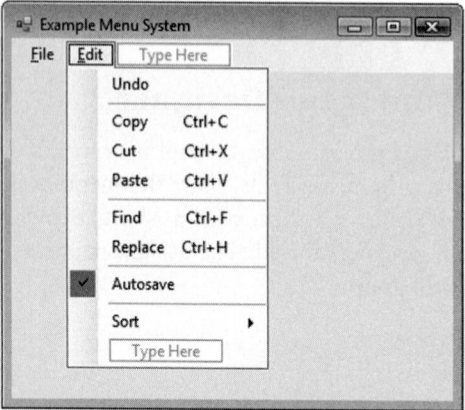

ToolStripMenuItem Object Names

The menu designer assigns default names to the ToolStripMenuItem objects as you create them. You can change a menu item object's name by changing its Name property in the *Properties* window. In Figure 7-48, the *Properties* window shows the properties of a ToolStripMenuItem object. Notice that the Name property has been changed to mnuEditCopy.

In this book we use a hierarchical naming convention for menu items. For example, the names of all entries under the *File* menu will begin with *mnuFile*. Entries in the *Edit* menu will begin with *mnuEdit*. Individual items within these menus will dictate the remaining part of the name. For example, the *Exit* item in the *File* menu is usually named *mnuFileExit*. The *Copy* item in the *Edit* menu is usually named *mnuEditCopy*.

Figure 7-48 *Properties* window showing a ToolStripMenuItem object's properties

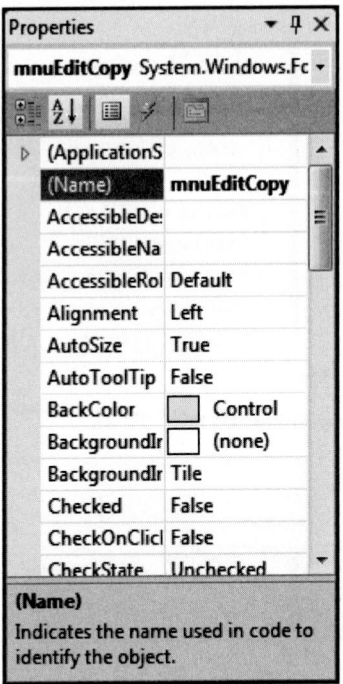

Shortcut Keys

As previously stated, a shortcut key is a key or combination of keys that cause a menu command to execute. Table 7-2 lists some commonly used shortcut keys in Windows applications.

Table 7-2 Some commonly used shortcut keys in Windows applications

Shortcut Key	Command
Ctrl + S	Save
Ctrl + P	Print
Ctrl + C	Copy
Ctrl + X	Cut
Ctrl + V or Shift + Insert	Paste

Shortcut keys are shown on a menu to the right of their corresponding commands. To create a shortcut key for a menu item, click the down arrow that appears next to the **ShortcutKeys property** in the *Properties* window. A dialog appears as shown in Figure 7-49. The *Key* drop-down list shows all the available shortcut keys, and allows you to select a key from the list. The dialog also allows you to select the Ctrl, Shift, or Alt key (or any combination of these). For example, if you want to assign Ctrl+S as a shortcut key, you would select the S key in the drop-down list and place a check next to Ctrl.

You must also make sure that the **ShowShortcut property** is set to *True*. When set to *False*, the item's shortcut key will not be displayed.

Checked Menu Items

Some programs have menu items that simply turn a feature on or off. For example, suppose you are creating an application that functions as an alarm clock, and you want the user to

Figure 7-49

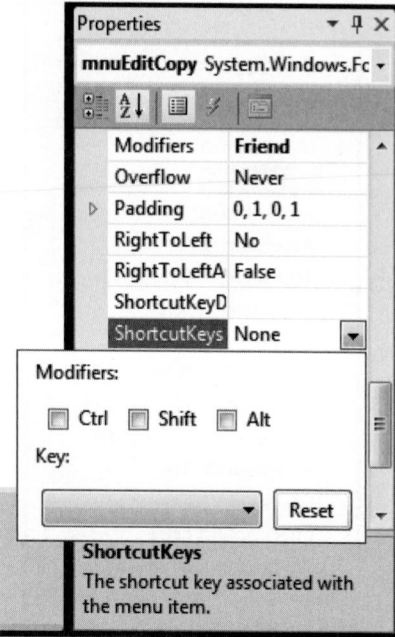

be able to turn the alarm on or off with a menu item. A common approach would be to have a checked menu item for the alarm. When a check mark appears next to the menu item, it indicates that the alarm is on. When the check mark is not displayed next to the menu item, it indicates that the alarm is off. When the user clicks the menu item, it toggles its state between on and off. This type of menu item is called a checked menu item.

To give a menu item the ability to become checked or unchecked when it is clicked by the user, you set the item's **CheckOnClick property** to *True*. You can then set the **Checked property** to either *True* or *False* to specify how the item should initially appear when the application runs. If you set the Checked property to *True*, the item will appear with a check mark next to it. If you set the Checked property to *False*, no check mark will be shown.

In code you can use the Checked property to determine whether a menu item is checked. If the Checked property is set to *True*, it means the item is checked. If the Checked property is set to *False*, it means the item is unchecked. The following code shows an example. This code tests the Checked property of a menu item named `mnuSettingsAlarm`. If the item is checked, a message box is displayed.

```
If mnuSettingsAlarm.Checked = True Then
   MessageBox.Show("WAKE UP!")
End If
```

Disabled Menu Items

A disabled menu item appears dimmed, or *grayed out*, and may not be selected by the user. You may disable a menu item by setting its Enabled property to *False*. For example, applications that provide *Cut*, *Copy*, and *Paste* commands usually disable the *Paste* command until something is cut or copied. So, the *Paste* menu item's Enabled property can be set to False at design time (in the *Properties* window), and then set to *True* in code after the *Cut* or *Copy* commands have been used. Assuming that the *Paste* menu item is named `mnuEditPaste`, the following code enables it:

```
mnuEditPaste.Enabled = True
```

Separator Bars

You can insert a separator bar into a menu in either of the following ways:

- Right-click an existing menu item. On the pop-up menu that appears, select *Insert*, and then select *Separator*. A separator bar will be inserted above the menu item.
- Type a hyphen (–) as a menu item's Text property.

Submenus

When an existing menu item is selected in the menu designer, a *Type Here* box is displayed to its right. Figure 7-50 shows an example. This box allows you to create a submenu item. When you create a submenu, a right arrow (▶) will automatically be displayed next to the menu item that is the parent of the submenu.

Figure 7-50 Creating a submenu

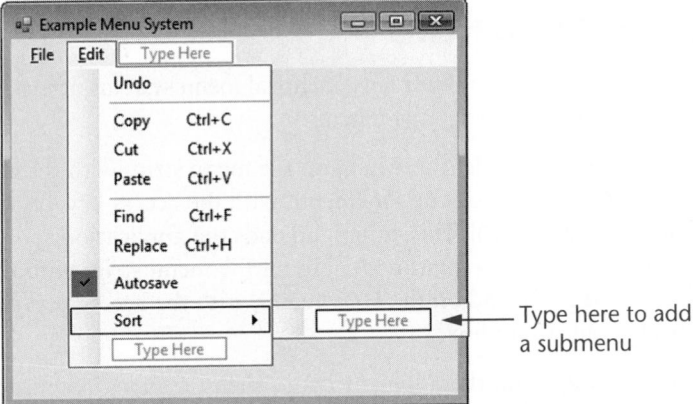

Inserting Menu Items in an Existing Menu

If you need to insert a new menu item above an existing menu item, start the menu designer and then right-click the existing menu item. On the pop-up menu that appears, select *Insert*, and then select *MenuItem*. A new menu item will be inserted above the existing menu item.

If you need to insert a new menu item at the bottom of an existing menu, start the menu designer and simply select the desired menu or submenu. A *Type Here* box automatically appears at the bottom.

Deleting Menu Items

To delete a menu item, start the menu designer and perform one of the following procedures:

- Right-click the menu item you wish to delete. On the pop-up menu, select *Delete*.
- Select the menu item you wish to delete, and then press the (Delete) key.

Rearranging Menu Items

You can move a menu item by clicking and dragging. Simply select it in the menu designer and drag it to the desired location.

ToolStripMenuItem Click Event

You do not have to write code to display a menu or a submenu. When the user clicks a menu item that displays a menu or a submenu, Visual Basic automatically causes the menu or submenu to appear.

If a menu item does not have a menu or submenu to display, you make it functional by providing a Click event procedure for it. For example, assume a menu system has a *File* menu with an *Exit* command, which causes the application to end. The menu item for the *Exit* command is named mnuFileExit. Here is the code for the object's Click event procedure:

```
Private Sub mnuFileExit_Click(...) Handles mnuFileExit.Click
    ' Close the form.
    Me.Close()
End Sub
```

To write a Click event procedure for a menu item, start the menu designer, then double-click the desired menu item. A code template for the Click event procedure will be created.

Standard Menu Items

Although all applications do not have identical menu systems, it is standard for most applications to have the following menu items:

- A *File* menu as the leftmost item on the menu strip, with the access key Alt+F.
- An *Exit* command on the *File* menu, with the access key Alt+X and optionally the shortcut key Alt+Q. This command ends the application.
- A *Help* menu as the rightmost item on the menu strip, with the access key Alt+H.
- An *About* command on the *Help* menu, with the access key Alt+A. This command displays an *About* box.

You should always add these items to your menu systems because most Windows users expect to see them. You should also assign shortcut keys to the most commonly used commands. Study the menu system in an application such as Microsoft Word or Microsoft Excel to become familiar with a typical menu design.

In Tutorial 7-5, you learn to use the menu designer by building a simple menu system.

Tutorial 7-5:
Building a menu

In this tutorial, you create an application that demonstrates how a label appears in different colors. You build a menu system that allows the user to select a color, which is then applied to a Label control. Figure 7-51 shows a sketch of the menu system.

Figure 7-51 Sketch of menu system

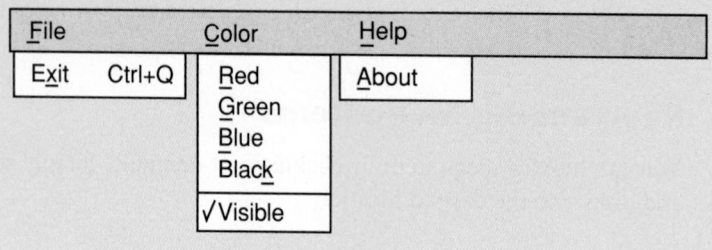

Step 1: Create a new Windows Forms Application project named *Menu Demo*.

Step 2: Change the form's Text property to **Menu Demo**. Place a label named **lblMessage** on the form and set its *Text* property to *Hello World!*, as shown in Figure 7-52.

Step 3: Double-click the *MenuStrip* tool in the *Toolbox* to add a MenuStrip control to the form.

The control, which appears in the component tray, should be selected. If it is not, select it. The menu designer should now be running, as shown in Figure 7-53.

Figure 7-52 *Menu Demo* form

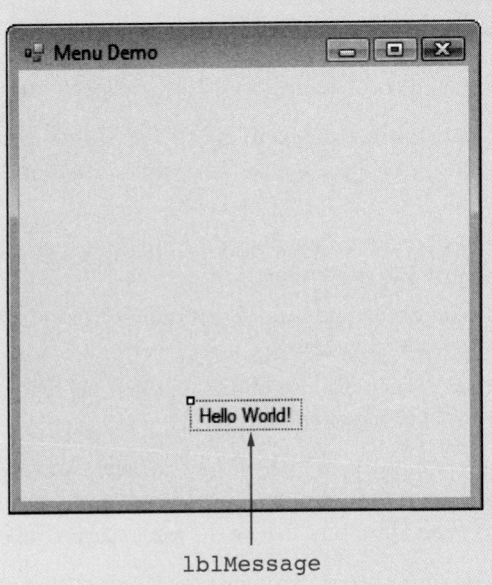

lblMessage

Figure 7-53 Form with menu designer running

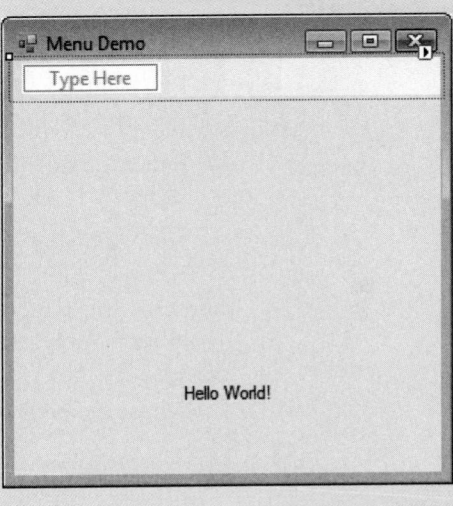

Step 4: First, you will create the *File* menu item. In the *Type Here* box, type **&File**. Press the Enter key to create the object. The text *File* should now appear on the menu strip.

Step 5: Set the Name property for the menu item you just created. Use the mouse to select the word *File* on the menu. The menu item's properties should be displayed in the *Properties* window. Change the Name property to **mnuFile**.

Step 6: Next, you will create the *Exit* menu item on the *File* menu. Use the mouse to select the *Type Here* box below the *File* menu item. Type **E&xit** and press Enter to create the object. The text *Exit* should now appear on the *File* menu, as shown in Figure 7-54.

Step 7: Next, you must set the properties for the menu item you just created. Use the mouse to select the word *Exit*. The menu item's properties should be displayed in the *Properties* window. Change the Name property to **mnuFileExit**. In the ShortcutKeys property select Ctrl+Q.

Step 8: Now you are ready to add the *Color* menu item. In the *Type Here* box shown in Figure 7-55 type **&Color** and press Enter.

Figure 7-54 *Exit* menu item created

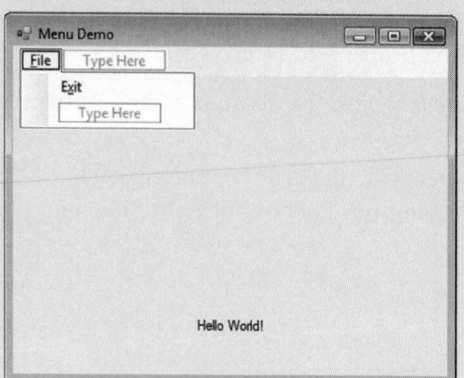

Figure 7-55 Where to type `&Color`

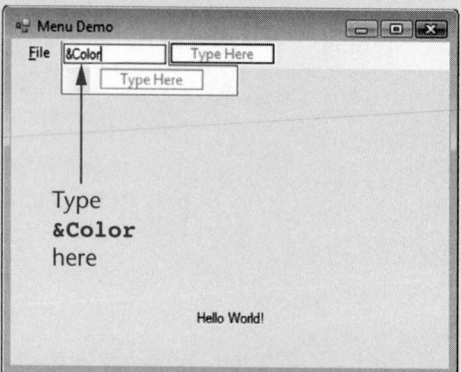

Type
`&Color`
here

Step 9: Set the Name property for the menu item you just created. Use the mouse to se-lect the word *Color* on the menu. The menu item's properties should be dis-played in the *Properties* window. Change the Name property to **mnuColor**.

Step 10: Next, you will add the first four menu items to the *Color* menu. Below the mnuColor menu item, add an object whose Text reads **&Red** and whose Name property is **mnuColorRed**.

Below the mnuColorRed object, add an object whose Text reads **&Green** and whose Name property is **mnuColorGreen**.

Below the mnuColorGreen object, add an object whose Text reads **&Blue** and whose Name property is **mnuColorBlue**.

Below the mnuColorBlue object, add an object whose Text reads **Blac&k** and whose Name property is **mnuColorBlack**.

Step 11: The menu sketch shown in Figure 7-51 (displayed earlier) shows a separator bar just below the word *Black* on the *Color* menu. Create the separator bar by typ-ing a hyphen (–) in the *Type Here* box below the mnuColorBlack object.

Step 12: Below the separator bar, add an object whose Text reads **Visible** and whose Name property is **mnuColorVisible**. This object's CheckOnClick and Checked properties should both be set to *True*. The *Color* menu should now appear as shown in Figure 7-56.

Step 13: To the right of the *Color* menu item, add the *Help* menu item with the text **&Help** and the name **mnuHelp**.

Step 14: Below the word *Help*, add a menu item with the text **&About** and the name **mnuHelpAbout**. When finished, the *Help* menu should appear as shown in Figure 7-57.

Figure 7-56 Completed *Color* menu

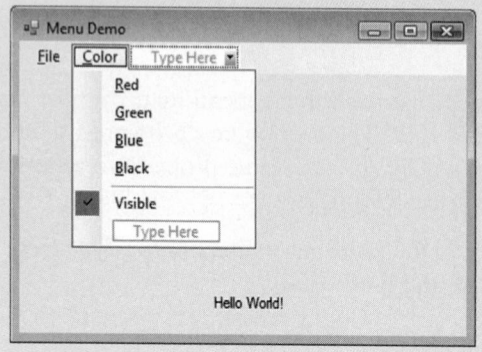

Figure 7-57 Completed *Help* menu

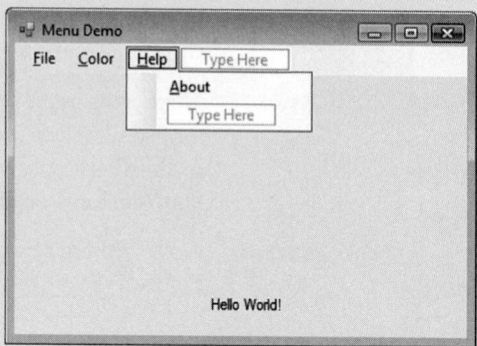

Step 15: Now you will write the Click event procedures for the appropriate menu items, starting with `mnuFileExit`. In the menu designer, double-click the word *Exit*, which is on the *File* menu. The *Code* window opens with a code template for the `mnuFileExit_Click` event procedure. Complete the procedure by typing the code shown in bold, as follows:

```
Private Sub mnuFileExit_Click(...) Handles mnuFileExit.Click
    ' Close the form.
    Me.Close()
End Sub
```

Step 16: Follow this same procedure to write the event procedures for the commands on the *Color* menu. The code for the event procedures is as follows:

```
Private Sub mnuColorRed_Click(...) Handles mnuColorRed.Click
    ' Set the label's foreground color to red.
    lblMessage.ForeColor = Color.Red
End Sub

Private Sub mnuColorGreen_Click(...) Handles mnuColorGreen.Click
    ' Set the label's foreground color to green.
    lblMessage.ForeColor = Color.Green
End Sub

Private Sub mnuColorBlue_Click(...) Handles mnuColorBlue.Click
    ' Set the label's foreground color to blue.
    lblMessage.ForeColor = Color.Blue
End Sub

Private Sub mnuColorBlack_Click(...) Handles mnuColorBlack.Click
    ' Set the label's foreground color to black.
    lblMessage.ForeColor = Color.Black
End Sub

Private Sub mnuColorVisible_Click(...) Handles mnuColorVisible.Click
    ' Make the label visible or invisible
    If mnuColorVisible.Checked = True Then
        lblMessage.Visible = True
    Else
        lblMessage.Visible = False
    End If
End Sub
```

Let's take a closer look at the `mnuColorVisible_Click` procedure. This procedure tests the `mnuColorVisible` object's Checked property to determine whether the menu item is checked. If it is checked, the user wants to make the label visible so the `lblMessage.Visible` property is set to *True*. Otherwise, the `lblMessage.Visible` property is set to *False*.

Step 17: The *Help* menu has one item: *About*. Most applications have this command, which displays a dialog box known as an *About* box. An **About** box usually shows some brief information about the application. Write the following code, shown in bold, for the `mnuHelpAbout` menu item's Click event procedure:

```
Private Sub mnuHelpAbout_Click(...) Handles mnuHelpAbout.Click
    ' Display a simple About box.
    MessageBox.Show("A Simple Menu System Demo")
End Sub
```

Step 18: Save the project and run it. Try selecting different colors to see how they make the label appear. Also test the *Visible* command and the *About* command. When finished, type Ctrl+Q to exit the application.

Context Menus

A **context menu**, or pop-up menu, is displayed when the user right-clicks a form or control. To create a context menu, you must add a ContextMenuStrip control to a form. You do this just as you add other controls: double-click the *ContextMenuStrip* icon in the *Toolbox* window. A ContextMenuStrip control is then created in the form's component tray. The first such control will have the default name `ContextMenuStrip1`, the second will have the default name `ContextMenuStrip2`, and so on.

Once you have added a ContextMenuStrip control to a form, you select it and then add items to it with the menu designer, just as you do with a regular menu. After you have built the context menu, you add Click event procedures for its menu items. Then, you associate the context menu with a control by setting the control's ContextMenuStrip property to the name of the ContextMenuStrip control. At runtime, the context menu will pop up when the user right-clicks the control. For example, Figure 7-58 shows a context menu displayed when the user right-clicks a Label control.

Figure 7-58 *Context* menu

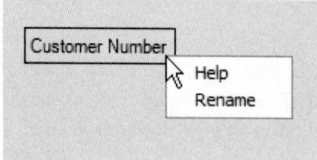

Checkpoint

7.18 Briefly describe each of the following menu system components:
   a.   Menu name
   b.   Menu command
   c.   Disabled menu command
   d.   Checked menu command
   e.   Shortcut key
   f.   Submenu
   g.   Separator bar

7.19 What is the difference between a menu item's access key and its shortcut key?

7.20 What prefix do we use for ToolStripMenuItem objects?

7.21 Suppose an application has a *File* menu with the following commands: *Save*, *Save As*, *Print*, and *Exit*. What name would you give each of the controls?

7.22 How do you assign an access key to a menu item?

7.23 What happens if you set a ToolStripMenuItem object's CheckOnClick property to *True*?

7.24 How do you disable a menu control in code?

7.25 How do you determine whether a check mark appears next to a menu item in code?

7.26 What event occurs when the user clicks on a menu item?

7.27 How does the user display a context menu?

7.28 How do you associate a context menu with a control?

7.4 Focus on Problem Solving: Building the *High Adventure Travel Agency Price Quote* Application

CONCEPT: In this section you build an application for the High Adventure Travel Agency. The application uses multiple forms, a module, and a menu system.

The High Adventure Travel Agency offers the following vacation packages for thrill-seeking customers.

- **Scuba Adventure:** This package provides six days at a Caribbean resort with scuba lessons. The price for this package is $3,000 per person.
- **Sky Dive Adventure:** This package provides individual sky diving lessons during a six-day vacation at a luxury lodge. The price for this package is $2,500 per person.

The travel agency gives a 10% discount for groups of five or more. You've been asked to create an application to calculate the charges for each package.

In Tutorial 7-6 you will create an application that has the following forms and modules:

- The MainForm form is the application's startup form. It will provide a menu that allows the user to select one of the vacation packages.
- The ScubaForm form will calculate the price of a scuba adventure travel package.
- The SkyDiveForm form will calculate the price of a sky dive adventure travel package.
- The PriceCalcModule module will contain global constants and a function that both the ScubaForm and SkyDiveForm forms will use to calculate discounts.

The MainForm

The MainForm form is shown in Figure 7-59. The beach photo shown on the form is located in the student sample files, in the *Chap7* folder in a file named *HighAdventure.bmp*. You will display this image in a PictureBox control. Notice that the form also has a Menu-

Figure 7-59 The *High Adventure* application's MainForm

Figure 7-60 The menu system

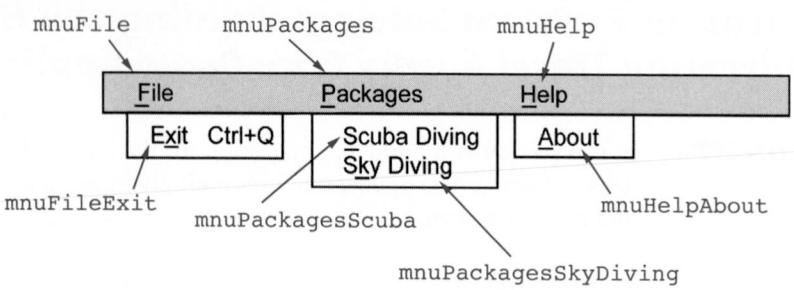

Strip control. Figure 7-60 shows a sketch of the menu system, along with the names that you will assign to each MenuItem control.

Here is a summary of the actions performed by the MenuItem controls:

- When the user clicks the `mnuFileExit` item, the application will end.
- When the user clicks the `mnuPackagesScuba` item, an instance of the ScubaForm form will be displayed. The ScubaForm form will calculate the price of a scuba adventure travel package.
- When the user clicks the `mnuPackagesSkyDiving` item, an instance of the SkyDive-Form form will be displayed. The SkyDiveForm form will calculate the price of a Sky dive adventure travel package.
- When the user clicks the `mnuHelpAbout` item, a simple *About* box will be displayed.

The ScubaForm

Figure 7-61 shows the ScubaForm form and lists the names that you will assign to various controls on the form. When you create the `lblDiscount` and `lblTotal` Label controls, you will set their AutoSize properties to False and their BorderStyle properties to FixedSingle. Here is a summary of the actions that the Button controls will perform:

- The `btnCalcTotal` button will use the value entered in the `txtNumberPeople` control to calculate and display the discount (if any) and the total cost for the scuba adventure vacation.
- The `btnReset` button will clear Text properties of the `txtNumberPeople`, `lblDiscount`, and `lblTotal` controls, and give the focus to `txtNumberPeople`.
- The `btnClose` button will close the form.

Figure 7-61 The ScubaForm form

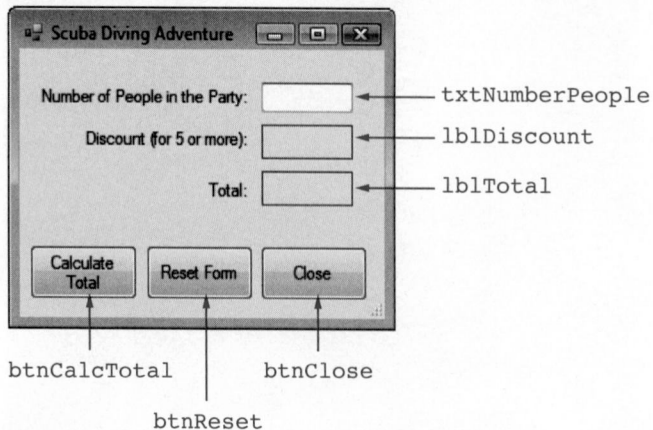

The SkyDiveForm

Figure 7-62 shows the SkyDiveForm form and lists the names that you will assign to various controls on the form. When you create the `lblDiscount` and `lblTotal` Label controls, you will set their AutoSize properties to False and their BorderStyle properties to FixedSingle. Here is a summary of the actions that the Button controls will perform:

- The `btnCalcTotal` button will use the value entered in the `txtNumberPeople` control to calculate and display the discount (if any) and the total cost for the sky dive adventure vacation.
- The `btnReset` button will clear Text properties of the `txtNumberPeople`, `lblDiscount`, and `lblTotal` controls, and give the focus to `txtNumberPeople`.
- The `btnClose` button will close the form.

Figure 7-62 The SkyDiveForm form

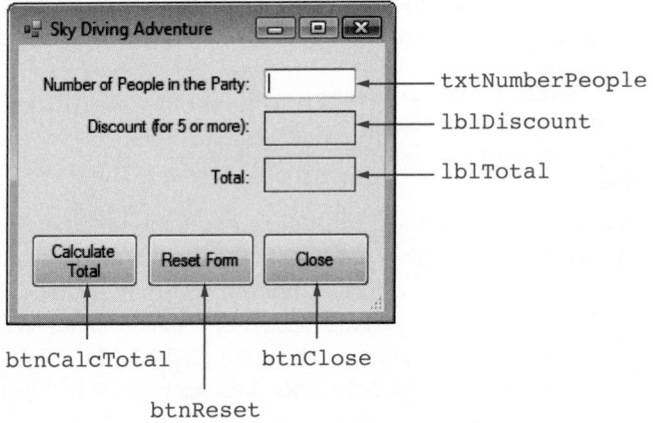

Tutorial 7-6:

Building the *High Adventure Travel Agency Price Quote* application

Step 1: Create a new Windows Forms Application project named *High Adventure*.

Step 2: Change the name of the Form1 form to MainForm.

Step 3: Place a MenuStrip control on the form and create the MenuItem objects shown previously in Figure 7-60. Refer to the Figure for the names of the MenuItem objects and the text that each object should display.

Step 4: Place a PictureBox control on the MainForm. Use the *HighAdventure.bmp* file, located in the *Chap7* folder of the student sample files, for the Image property.

Step 5: Create the ScubaForm form and place on it the controls shown previously in Figure 7-61. Refer to the figure for the names of the controls. When you create the `lblDiscount` and `lblTotal` Label controls, set their AutoSize properties to False and their BorderStyle properties to FixedSingle. (Don't worry about writing the event handlers for this form yet. You will do that at a later point.)

Step 6: Create the SkyDiveForm form and place on it the controls shown previously in Figure 7-62. Refer to the figure for the names of the controls. When you create the `lblDiscount` and `lblTotal` Label controls, set their AutoSize properties to False and their BorderStyle properties to FixedSingle. (Don't worry about writing the event handlers for this form yet. You will do that at a later point.)

Step 7: Create a module named *PriceCalcModule.vb*. Use the Code window to write the following code in the module. (Don't type the line numbers. They are shown only for reference.)

```
1 Module PriceCalcModule
2     ' Global constants
3     Public Const g_intMINIMUM_FOR_DISCOUNT As Integer = 5
4     Public Const g_decDISCOUNT_PERCENTAGE As Decimal = 0.1D
5
6     ' The DiscountAmount function accepts a package total
7     ' as an argument and returns the aount of discount
8     ' for that total.
9
10    Public Function DiscountAmount(ByVal decTotal As Decimal) As Decimal
11       Dim decDiscount As Decimal ' To hold the discount
12
13       ' Calculate the discount.
14       decDiscount = decTotal * g_decDISCOUNT_PERCENTAGE
15
16       ' Return the discount.
17       Return decDiscount
18    End Function
19 End Module
```

Let's take a closer look at the code in the module. Line 3 declares a global Integer constant named g_intMINIMUM_FOR_DISCOUNT. Recall from earlier in the chapter that when we declare a public constant in a module, we use the g_ prefix to indicate that it is globally accessible. This constant will be used for the minimum number of people required for a discount. Line 4 declares a global Decimal constant named g_decDISCOUNT_PERCENTAGE. It will be used for the percentage of the discount.

Lines 10 through 18 show a public function named DiscountAmount. This function accepts the total amount of a vacation package as an argument. Line 14 calculates the discount for that amount, and line 17 returns the discount. This function will be called by statements in both the ScubaForm and SkyDiveForm forms.

Step 8: Now you will write the event handlers for the ScubaForm form. Open the ScubaForm form in the Designer window and create the code templates for the btnCalcTotal, btnReset, and btnClose buttons. The following shows how the form's code should appear after you have completed the event handlers. (The line numbers are shown only for reference.)

```
1 Public Class ScubaForm
2
3     Private Sub btnCalcTotal_Click(...) Handles btnCalcTotal.Click
4         ' Constant for the price per person for this package
5         Const decSCUBA_PRICE_PER_PERSON As Decimal = 3000D
6
7         ' Local variables
8         Dim intNumberPeople As Integer ' Number of people
9         Dim decDiscount As Decimal ' Amount of discount
10        Dim decTotal As Decimal ' Total cost
11
12        Try
13            ' Get the number of people.
14            intNumberPeople = CInt(txtNumberPeople.Text)
15
```

```
16                  ' Get the total before any discount is applied.
17                  decTotal = intNumberPeople * decSCUBA_PRICE_PER_PERSON
18
19                  ' Determine whether a discount can be given.
20                  If intNumberPeople > = g_intMINIMUM_FOR_DISCOUNT Then
21                      ' Get the amount of the discount.
22                      decDiscount = DiscountAmount(decTotal)
23
24                      ' Subtract the discount from the total.
25                      decTotal = decTotal - decDiscount
26                  Else
27                      ' The discount is $0.
28                      decDiscount = 0D
29                  End If
30
31                  ' Display the results.
32                  lblDiscount.Text = decDiscount.ToString("c")
33                  lblTotal.Text = decTotal.ToString("c")
34              Catch ex As Exception
35                  ' Error message for invalid input.
36                  MessageBox.Show("Enter a valid integer for number of people.")
37              End Try
38      End Sub
39
40      Private Sub btnReset_Click(...) Handles btnReset.Click
41          ' Clear the text box and the display labels.
42          txtNumberPeople.Clear()
43          lblDiscount.Text = String.Empty
44          lblTotal.Text = String.Empty
45
46          ' Reset the focus.
47          txtNumberPeople.Focus()
48      End Sub
49
50      Private Sub btnClose_Click(...) Handles btnClose.Click
51          ' Close the form.
52          Me.Close()
53      End Sub
54 End Class
```

Let's take a closer look at the code. In the btnCalcTotal_Click event handler, line 5 declares the constant decSCUBA_PRICE_PER_PERSON to represent the price of the scuba package, per person. Line 8 declares the intNumberPeople variable to hold the number of people in the party. Line 9 declares the decDiscount variable to hold the discount, if one is given. Line 10 declares the decTotal variable to hold the total cost.

A Try-Catch statement begins in line 12. Inside the try block, line 13 reads the value entered by the user into the txtNumberPeople TextBox, converts it to an integer, and assigns the result to the intNumberPeople variable. If the user has entered an invalid value, an exception will be thrown and the program will jump to the Catch statement in line 34. If that happens, an error message is displayed by line 36 and the procedure ends.

If the value entered by the user is a valid integer, the total cost of the vacation (before any discount is given) is calculated in line 17 and assigned to the decTotal variable. Then the If...Then statement in line 20 determines whether five or more people are in the party. If so, the `DiscountAmount` function (which is stored in the module) is called in line 22 to get the amount of the discount. The value returned from the function is assigned to `decDiscount`. Then the discount is subtracted from the total in line 25. If there are less than five people in the party, the statement in line 28 sets `decDiscount` to 0. Line 32 displays the amount of the discount in the `lblDiscount` control, and line 33 displays the total cost in the `lblTotal` control.

The `btnReset_Click` event handler clears the Text properties of the `txtNumberPeople`, `lblDiscount`, and `lblTotal` controls in lines 42 through 44, and then gives the focus to the `txtNumberPeople` control in line 47.

The `btnClose_Click` event handler closes the form.

Step 9: Now you will write the event handlers for the SkyDiveForm form. Open the SkyDiveForm form in the *Designer* window and create the code templates for the `btnCalcTotal`, `btnReset`, and `btnClose` buttons. The following shows how the form's code should appear after you have completed the event handlers. (The line numbers are shown only for reference.)

```
1 Public Class SkyDiveForm
2
3     Private Sub btnCalcTotal_Click(...) Handles btnCalcTotal.Click
4         ' Constant for the price per person for this package
5         Const decSKYDIVE_PRICE_PER_PERSON As Decimal = 2500D
6
7         ' Local variables
8         Dim intNumberPeople As Integer ' Number of people
9         Dim decDiscount As Decimal ' Amount of discount
10        Dim decTotal As Decimal ' Total cost
11
12        Try
13            ' Get the number of people.
14            intNumberPeople = CInt(txtNumberPeople.Text)
15
16            ' Get the total before any discount is applied.
17            decTotal = intNumberPeople * decSKYDIVE_PRICE_PER_PERSON
18
19            ' Determine whether a discount can be given.
20            If intNumberPeople >= g_intMINIMUM_FOR_DISCOUNT Then
21                ' Get the amount of the discount.
22                decDiscount = DiscountAmount(decTotal)
23
24                ' Subtract the discount from the total.
25                decTotal = decTotal — decDiscount
26            Else
27                ' The discount is $0.
28                decDiscount = 0D
29            End If
30
31            ' Display the results.
32            lblDiscount.Text = decDiscount.ToString("c")
33            lblTotal.Text = decTotal.ToString("c")
34        Catch ex As Exception
35            ' Error message for invalid input.
36            MessageBox.Show("Enter a valid integer for number of people.")
```

```
37            End Try
38        End Sub
39
40        Private Sub btnReset_Click(...) Handles btnReset.Click
41            ' Clear the text box and the display labels.
42            txtNumberPeople.Clear()
43            lblDiscount.Text = String.Empty
44            lblTotal.Text = String.Empty
45
46            ' Reset the focus.
47            txtNumberPeople.Focus()
48        End Sub
49
50        Private Sub btnClose_Click(...) Handles btnClose.Click
51            ' Close the form.
52            Me.Close()
53        End Sub
54    End Class
```

This code is very similar to the code that you wrote in Step 8, but let's take a moment to go over it. In the btnCalcTotal_Click event handler, line 5 declares the constant decSKYDIVE_PRICE_PER_PERSON to represent the price of the sky diving package, per person. Line 8 declares the intNumberPeople variable to hold the number of people in the party. Line 9 declares the decDiscount variable to hold the discount, if one is given. Line 10 declares the decTotal variable to hold the total cost.

A Try-Catch statement begins in line 12. Inside the try block, line 13 reads the value entered by the user into the txtNumberPeople TextBox, converts it to an integer, and assigns the result to the intNumberPeople variable. If the user has entered an invalid value, an exception will be thrown and the program will jump to the Catch statement in line 34. If that happens, an error message is displayed by line 36 and the procedure ends.

If the value entered by the user is a valid integer, the total cost of the vacation (before any discount is given) is calculated in line 17 and assigned to the decTotal variable. Then the If...Then statement in line 20 determines whether five or more people are in the party. If so, the DiscountAmount function (which is stored in the module) is called in line 22 to get the amount of the discount. The value returned from the function is assigned to decDiscount. Then the discount is subtracted from the total in line 25. If there are less than five people in the party, the statement in line 28 sets decDiscount to 0. Line 32 displays the amount of the discount in the lblDiscount control, and line 33 displays the total cost in the lblTotal control.

The btnReset_Click event handler clears the Text properties of the txtNumberPeople, lblDiscount, and lblTotal controls in lines 42 through 44, and then gives the focus to the txtNumberPeople control in line 47.

The btnClose_Click event handler closes the form.

Step 10: Now you will write the event handlers for the MainForm form. Open the Main-Form form in the *Designer* window and create the code templates for each of the MenuItem objects. The following shows how the form's code should appear after you have completed the event handlers. (The line numbers are shown only for reference.)

```
 1 Public Class MainForm
 2
 3     Private Sub mnuFileExit_Click(...) Handles mnuFileExit.Click
 4         ' Close the form.
 5         Me.Close()
 6     End Sub
 7
 8     Private Sub mnuPackagesScuba_Click(...) Handles mnuPackagesScuba.Click
 9         ' Create an instance of the ScubaForm.
10         Dim frmScuba As New ScubaForm
11
12         ' Display the ScubaForm in modal style.
13         frmScuba.ShowDialog()
14     End Sub
15
16     Private Sub mnuPackagesSkyDiving_Click(...) Handles mnuPackagesSkyDiving.Click
17         ' Create an instance of the SkyDiveForm.
18         Dim frmSkyDive As New SkyDiveForm
19
20         ' Display the SkyDiveForm in modal style.
21         frmSkyDive.ShowDialog()
22     End Sub
23
24     Private Sub mnuHelpAbout_Click(...) Handles mnuHelpAbout.Click
25         ' Display a simple About box.
26         MessageBox.Show("High Adventure Travel Price Quote System Version 1.0")
27     End Sub
28 End Class
```

Let's take a closer look at the code. In the mnuFileExit_Click event handler, line 5 closes the form, thus ending the application.

In the mnuPackagesScuba_Click event handler, line 10 creates an instance of the ScubaForm form in memory and assigns its address to the frmScuba variable. Then line 13 displays the form on the screen in modal style.

In the mnuPackagesSkyDiving_Click event handler, line 18 creates an instance of the SkyDiveForm form in memory and assigns its address to the frmSkyDive variable. Then line 13 displays the form on the screen in modal style.

In the mnuHelpAbout_Click event handler, line 26 displays a message box as a simple About box.

Step 11: Save the project and test the application. Make sure all the menu items work properly, and try different numbers of people for each of the packages to make sure the calculations are correct.

Summary

7.1 Multiple Forms

- Visual Basic projects can have multiple forms; one form is the startup form, displayed when the project executes. Other forms are displayed by programming statements.
- When you create a form, the code for that form is stored in a file ending with a *.vb* extension. Normally, the name of the file is the same as the name of the form. The form file contains the form class declaration, which is code that describes the form's properties and methods.
- The Project's properties page allows you to designate a project's startup form.
- Before displaying a form, you must create an instance of the form. Then, you must call a method (Show or ShowDialog) to display the form. The Show method displays a form in modeless style. The ShowDialog method displays a form in modal style.
- When a modal form is displayed, no other form in the application can receive the focus until the modal form is closed. No other statements in the procedure that displayed the modal form will execute until the modal form is closed.
- A form's Close method removes it from the screen and from memory. A form typically uses the Me keyword to call its own Close method, as in Me.Close().
- The Load event occurs just before a form is displayed for the first time. A form's Activated event occurs when the user switches to the form from another form or another application. The FormClosing event occurs when a form is in the process of closing, but before it has closed. The FormClosed event is triggered after a form has closed. You may write event handlers that execute in response to any of these events.
- Code from one form can reference controls on a different form, as long as an instance of that form has been created in memory and its address has been assigned to a variable. You must fully qualify the name of the object by preceding it with the name of the variable that references the form, followed by a period.
- To make a form's class-level variable available to statements outside the form, declare it with the Public keyword. Although class-level variables are automatically declared private by the Dim statement, you should explicitly declare them private with the Private keyword.
- After a form has been saved to a form file, it may be used in other projects.

7.2 Modules

- A module contains code—declarations and procedures—that is used by other files in a project.
- A variable declared inside a module (between the Module and the End Module statements), but not inside a procedure or function, is a module-level variable. A module-level variable declared Public is also known as a global variable because it can be accessed globally by any statement in the application.
- You can use the same module in more than one project.

7.3 Menus

- The MenuStrip control lets you create a system of drop-down menus on any form. You place a MenuStrip control on the form and then use the menu designer to create a menu system.
- An application's menu system is constructed from ToolStripMenuItem objects. When you create menu items, you name them with the mnu prefix.
- If you do not want the user to be able to select a menu item, set the item's Enabled property to *False* (either in Design mode or in runtime code). When a menu control's CheckOnClick property is set to *True*, it will have the ability to become checked or

unchecked when clicked. When a menu control's Checked property equals *True*, a check mark appears on the menu next to the control's text.

- You make a ToolStripMenuItem object respond to clicks by providing it with a Click event handler.

7.4 Focus on Problem Solving: *Building the High Adventure Travel Agency Price Quote* Application

- This section outlines the process of building the *High Adventure Travel Agency Price Quote* application using multiple forms, a module, and a menu system.

Key Terms

About box	modeless form
Activated event handler	module
Checked property	module-level variable
CheckOnClick property	module scope
`Close` method	object variable
context menu	`Private` keyword
FormClosed event handler	`Public` keyword
FormClosing event handler	separator bar
global variable	shortcut key
`Hide` method	ShortcutKeys property
`Me` keyword	`Show` method
menu designer	`ShowDialog` method
menu system	ShowShortcut property
MenuStrip control	startup form
modal form	ToolStripMenuItem objects

Review Questions and Exercises

Fill-in-the-Blank

1. If a form is the _____, it is displayed first when the project executes.

2. When a _____ form is displayed, no other form in the application can receive the focus until the form is closed.

3. A _____ is a variable that holds the memory address of an object and allows you to work with the object.

4. The _____ method removes a form from the screen but does not remove it from memory.

5. The _____ method removes a form from the screen and releases the memory it is using.

6. The _____ method displays a form in modal style.

7. The _____ method displays a form in modeless style.

8. Modules contain no _____ procedures.

9. When a procedure declaration in a form file begins with _____, the procedure may only be accessed by statements in the same form.

10. To make a class-level variable available to statements outside the module, you declare it with the _____ keyword.

11. A module-level variable declared `Public` is also known as a _____ variable.

12. You can disable a menu control in code by setting its _____ property to *False*.

13. When a menu item's _____ property equals *True*, a check mark appears on the menu next to the item's text.

14. A _____ is a pop-up menu that is displayed when the user right-clicks a form or control.

Multiple Choice

1. Which of the following variable name prefixes do we use in this book for variables that reference forms?
   a. `fr`
   b. `frm`
   c. `for`
   d. `fm`

2. When this form is displayed, no other form in the application can receive the focus until the form is closed.
   a. Modal
   b. Modeless
   c. Startup
   d. Unloaded

3. When a form is displayed by a method call in this style, statements following the method call continue to execute after the form is displayed.
   a. Modal
   b. Modeless
   c. Startup
   d. Unloaded

4. What does the `Hide` method do?
   a. Removes a form from the screen and removes it from memory
   b. Removes a form from the screen but does not remove it from memory
   c. Positions one form behind another one
   d. Removes a form from memory but does not remove it from the screen

5. This method removes the visual part of a form from memory, making the form invisible.
   a. `Remove`
   b. `Delete`
   c. `Close`
   d. `Hide`

6. If you want to declare `g_intTotal` in a module as a global variable, which of the following declarations would you use?
   a. `Dim g_intTotal As Integer`
   b. `Public g_intTotal As Integer`
   c. `Global g_intTotal As Integer`
   d. `Private g_intTotal As Integer`

7. Just before a form is initially displayed, this event occurs.
   a. InitialDisplay
   b. Load

     c.   Display

     d.   Create

8.   This event occurs when the user switches to the form from another form or another application.

     a.   Activated

     b.   Load

     c.   Switch

     d.   Close

9.   This event occurs as a form is in the process of closing, but before it has closed.

     a.   FormClosed

     b.   StartClose

     c.   ShutingDown

     d.   FormClosing

10.   This event occurs after a form has closed.

     a.   FormClosed

     b.   EndClose

     c.   ShutDown

     d.   FormClosing

11.   A form uses this statement to call its own `Close` method.

     a.   `Form.Close()`

     b.   `Me.Close()`

     c.   `Close(Me)`

     d.   `ThisForm.Close()`

12.   If a procedure or variable is used by more than one form, where should it be declared?

     a.   Module

     b.   Form file

     c.   Multiprocess file

     d.   Project file

13.   If an application's menu system has a *Cut* command on the *Edit* menu, what should the MenuItem control for the command be named?

     a.   `mnuCut`

     b.   `mnuEdit`

     c.   `mnuCutEdit`

     d.   `mnuEditCut`

14.   A menu command's _____ only works while the menu is open, while a(n) _____ may be executed at any time while the form is active.

     a.   Shortcut key, access key

     b.   Access key, shortcut key

     c.   Function key, control key

     d.   Alternate key, control key

15.   Which of the following statements disables the `mnuFilePrint` object?

     a.   `mnuFilePrint.Disabled = True`

     b.   `mnuFilePrint.Enabled = False`

     c.   `mnuFilePrint.Available = False`

     d.   `Disable mnuFilePrint`

True or False

Indicate whether the following statements are true or false.

1. T F: By default, the first form you create is the startup form.

2. T F: The Show method displays a form in modeless style.

3. T F: Although the Hide method removes a form from the screen, it does not remove it from memory.

4. T F: If you have code that you want to execute every time a form displays, the form's Load event procedure is the best place to write it.

5. T F: The Activated event executes only once—when the form is initially displayed.

6. T F: The FormClosing event executes before a form has completely closed.

7. T F: It is not possible to access a control on another form in code.

8. T F: A menu command's shortcut key works only while the menu is open.

9. T F: If a menu control does not display a menu or submenu, you make it functional by providing a Click event handler for it.

10. T F: A context menu displays when the user double-clicks a control.

Short Answer

1. Describe the process of adding a new form to a project.

2. Describe the process of removing a form from a project, but not deleting the form file.

3. Describe the process of removing a form from a project, and deleting the form file.

4. Describe the process of changing the startup form to another form.

5. What does the statement Me.Close() do?

6. What is the difference between the Load event and the Activated event?

7. Suppose you want to execute code when a form is about to close, but has not fully closed. Where should you place the code?

8. Suppose you want to execute code when a form has fully closed. Where should you place the code?

9. Suppose you wish to declare a variable in a module so all the forms in the project have access to it. How should you declare the variable?

10. Describe the steps for adding a module to a project.

11. What is the difference between a menu control's access key and its shortcut key?

12. How do you create a checked menu item?

13. In code, how do you determine whether a check mark appears next to a menu item?

14. What is a disabled menu item? How do you make a menu item disabled?

What Do You Think?

1. If you want to display multiple forms on the screen at one time and be able to interact with any of them at any time, do you display them as modal or modeless forms?

2. You want to write code that removes a form from the screen, but you still want to access controls on the form in code. How do you accomplish this?

3. Suppose a form is referenced by a variable named `frmStatus`, and the form has a Label control named `lblArrivalGate`. Write a statement that stores the string `"D West"` in the label's Text property from another form.

4. Suppose you have written a function, named `CircleArea`, which returns the area of a circle. You call the function from numerous procedures in different form modules. Should you store the function in a form or a module?

5. The following code creates instances of three forms in memory and then displays them. After the code executes, will all three forms be on the screen at the same time? Why or why not?

```
Dim frmFirst As New OneForm
Dim frmSecond As New TwoForm
Dim frmThird As New ThreeForm
frmFirst.Show()
frmSecond.Show()
frmThird.Show()
```

Find the Error

What is wrong with the following statements?

1. `Hide Me`

2. *Class-level declaration in ResultsForm:*
   ```
   Dim intNumber as Integer
   ```
   Statements in another form:
   ```
   Dim frmResults as New ResultsForm
   frmResults.intNumber = 100
   ```

3. ```
   Dim frmError As ErrorForm
   frmError.ShowDialog()
   ```

4. ```
   Module TestModule
         ' Declare a GLOBAL variable.
         Dim g_intCount As Integer
   End Module
   ```

Algorithm Workbench

1. An application has two forms named MainForm and SecondForm. The SecondForm form has a public class-level integer variable named `intReading`, and the Main-Form form has a text box named `txtInput`. Assume the user has entered a value into the `txtInput` control on the MainForm form, and an event handler executes the following statement:

   ```
   Dim frmSecond As New SecondForm
   ```

   Write a statement that executes after this statement and stores the value entered in `txtInput` into the `intReading` variable (in the SecondForm form).

2. Here is the code template for a form's FormClosing event handler:

   ```
   Private Sub MainForm_FormClosing(ByVal sender As Object,
       ByVal e As System.Windows.Forms.FormClosingEventArgs)
       Handles Me.FormClosing


   End Sub
   ```

   Suppose you want the form to close only if the user knows the secret word, which is *water*. Write statements in this procedure to ask the user to enter the secret word. If the user enters the correct secret word, the form should close. Otherwise, the form should not close. (Perform a case-insensitive test for the secret word.)

Figure 7-71 *Family Plan* form

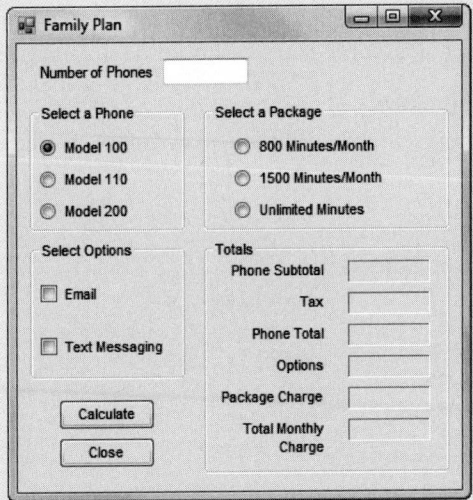

Design Your Own Forms

4. **Dorm and Meal Plan Calculator**

   A university has the following dormitories:

Allen Hall	$1,500 per semester
Pike Hall	$1,600 per semester
Farthing Hall	$1,200 per semester
University Suites	$1,800 per semester

   The university also offers the following meal plans:

7 meals per week	$ 560 per semester
14 meals per week	$1,095 per semester
Unlimited meals	$1,500 per semester

   Create an application with two forms. The startup form holds the names of the dormitories and the other holds the meal plans. When the user selects a dormitory and meal plan, the application should show the total charges for the semester on the startup form.

5. **Shade Designer**

   A custom window shade designer charges a base fee of $50 per shade. Additionally, charges are added for certain styles, sizes, and colors as follows:

   Styles:

Regular shades	Add $0
Folding shades	Add $10
Roman shades	Add $15

   Sizes:

25 inches wide	Add $0
27 inches wide	Add $2
32 inches wide	Add $4
40 inches wide	Add $6

   Colors:

Natural	Add $5
Blue	Add $0
Teal	Add $0
Red	Add $0
Green	Add $0

Create an application that allows the user to select the style, size, color, and number of shades from list boxes or combo boxes. If a combo box is used, set its Drop-DownStyle property in such a way that new items cannot be added to the customer list by the user. The total charges should be displayed on a second form.

6. **Skateboard Designer**

The Skate Shop sells the following skateboard products.

Decks:

The Master Thrasher	$60
The Dictator of Grind	$45
The Street King	$50

Truck assemblies:

7.75 axle	$35
8 axle	$40
8.5 axle	$45

Wheel sets:

51 mm	$20
55 mm	$22
58 mm	$24
61 mm	$28

Additionally, the Skate Shop sells the following miscellaneous products and services:

Grip tape	$10
Bearings	$30
Riser pads	$ 2
Nuts & bolts kit	$ 3
Assembly	$10

Create an application that allows the user to select one deck from a form, one truck assembly from a form, and one wheel set from a form. The application should also have a form that allows the user to select any miscellaneous product, using check boxes. The application should display the subtotal, the amount of sales tax (at 6%), and the total of the order. Do not apply sales tax to assembly.

7. **Astronomy Helper**

Create an application that displays the following data about the planets of the solar system. (For your information, the distances are shown in AUs, or astronomical units. 1 AU equals approximately 93 million miles. In your application simply display the distances as they are shown here, in AUs.)

VideoNote

The Astronomy Helper Problem

Mercury

Type	Terrestrial
Average distance from the sun	0.387 AU
Mass	3.31×10^{23} kg
Surface temperature	$-173°C$ to $430°C$

Venus

Type	Terrestrial
Average distance from the sun	0.7233 AU
Mass	4.87×10^{24} kg
Surface temperature	$472°C$

Earth

Type	Terrestrial
Average distance from the sun	1 AU
Mass	5.967×10^{24} kg
Surface temperature	$-50°$C to $50°$C

Mars

Type	Terrestrial
Average distance from the sun	1.5237 AU
Mass	0.6424×10^{24} kg
Surface temperature	$-140°$C to $20°$C

Jupiter

Type	Jovian
Average distance from the sun	5.2028 AU
Mass	1.899×10^{27} kg
Temperature at cloud tops	$-110°$C

Saturn

Type	Jovian
Average distance from the sun	9.5388 AU
Mass	5.69×10^{26} kg
Temperature at cloud tops	$-180°$C

Uranus

Type	Jovian
Average distance from the sun	19.18 AU
Mass	8.69×10^{25} kg
Temperature above cloud tops	$-220°$C

Neptune

Type	Jovian
Average distance from the sun	30.0611 AU
Mass	1.03×10^{26} kg
Temperature at cloud tops	$-216°$C

Pluto

Type	Low density
Average distance from the sun	39.44 AU
Mass	1.2×10^{22} kg
Surface temperature	$-230°$C

The application should have a separate form for each planet. On the main form, create a menu system that allows the user to select the planet he or she wishes to know more about.

8 Arrays and More

TOPICS

This chapter discusses arrays, which are like groups of variables that allow you to store sets of data. A single-dimensional array is useful for storing and working with a single set of data, while a multidimensional array can be used to store and work with multiple sets of data. This chapter presents many array programming techniques, such as summing and averaging the elements in an array, summing all columns in a two-dimensional array, searching an array for a specific value, and using parallel arrays. The Enabled, Anchor, and Dock properties, and Timer controls, are also covered.

8.1 Arrays

CONCEPT: An array is like a group of variables with one name. You store and work with values in an array by using a subscript.

Sometimes it is necessary for an application to store multiple values of the same type. Often it is better to create an array than several individual variables. An **array** is a like group of variables that have a single name. All of the values stored within an array are called **elements,** and all are of the same data type. You access the individual elements in an array through a subscript. A **subscript,** also known as an **index,** is a number that identifies a specific element within an array.

Subscript numbering begins at 0, so the subscript of the first element in an array is 0 and the subscript of the last element in an array is one less than the total number of elements. For example, consider an array of seven integers. The subscript of the first element in the array is 0 and the subscript of the last element in the array is 6.

Declaring an Array

You declare an array much like you declare a regular variable. Here is the general format of an array declaration:

```
Dim ArrayName (UpperSubscript) As DataType
```

Let's take a closer look at the syntax.

- *ArrayName* is the name of the array.
- *UpperSubscript* is the value of the array's highest subscript. This must be a positive integer, a positive Integer named constant, or an Integer variable containing a positive number.
- *DataType* is a Visual Basic data type.

Let's look at some examples.

```
Dim intHours(6) As Integer
```

This statement declares `intHours` as an array of integers. The number inside the parentheses, 6, indicates that the array's highest subscript is 6. Figure 8-1 shows that this array consists of seven elements with the subscripts 0 through 6. The figure shows that numeric array elements are initialized to the value 0.

Figure 8-1 `intHours` array

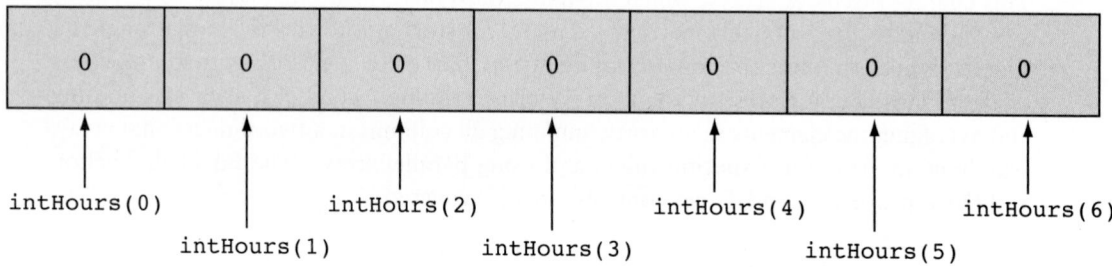

```
intHours(0)          intHours(2)          intHours(4)          intHours(6)
        intHours(1)          intHours(3)          intHours(5)
```

> **NOTE:** Like regular string variables, the uninitialized elements of a string array are set to the special value `Nothing`. Before doing any work with the elements of a string array, you must store values in them, even if the values are empty strings. Later you will see how to initialize arrays at the same time they are declared.

The following is another example of an array declaration:

```
Dim decPay(4) As Decimal
```

This statement declares `decPay` as an array of five Decimal values, as shown in Figure 8-2, with subscripts 0 through 4. The following example uses the contents of an Integer variable to specify the array size:

```
Dim intSize As Integer = 4
Dim decPay(intSize) As Decimal
```

Figure 8-2 `decPay` array

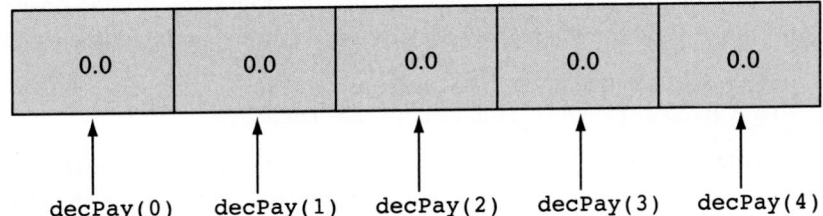

Implicit Array Sizing and Initialization

You can implicitly size an array by omitting the upper subscript in the declaration and providing an initialization list. An array initialization list is a set of numbers enclosed in a set of braces, with the numbers separated by commas. The following is an example of an array declaration that uses an initialization list:

```
Dim intNumbers() As Integer = { 2, 4, 6, 8, 10, 12 }
```

This statement declares `intNumbers` as an array of integers. The numbers 2, 4, 6, 8, 10, and 12 are stored in the array. The value 2 will be stored in element zero, 4 will be stored in element one, and so on. Notice that no upper subscript is provided inside the parentheses. The array is large enough to hold the values in the initialization list. In this example, the array has six elements, as shown in Figure 8-3.

Figure 8-3 `intNumbers` array

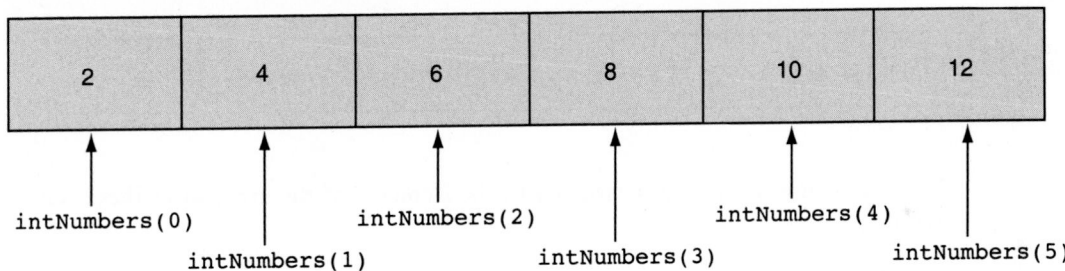

The following code declares an implicitly sized array of strings.

```
Dim strFriends() As String = { "Joe", "Geri", "Bill", "Rose" }
```

You can initialize an array with empty strings, as shown here.

```
Dim strFriends() As String = { "", "", "", "" }
```

It is a good idea to initialize a string array, particularly if there is a chance that your program will access its elements before any data has been stored there. Performing an operation on a string array element results in a runtime error if no data has been stored in the element.

 NOTE: You cannot provide both an initialization list and an upper subscript in an array declaration.

Using Named Constants as Subscripts in Array Declarations

To make programs easier to maintain and debug, programmers often use a named constant as the upper subscript in an array declaration, as shown in the following code:

```
Const intMAX_SUBSCRIPT As Integer = 100
Dim intArray(intMAX_SUBSCRIPT) As Integer
```

Quite often, when you write code that processes an array, you have to refer to the value of the array's upper subscript. You will see examples of this later in the chapter. When you declare a named constant to represent an array's upper subscript, you can use that constant any time that you need to refer to the array's last subscript in code. Then, if you ever need to modify the program so the array is a different size, you need only to change the value of the named constant.

Working with Array Elements

You can store a value in an array element with an assignment statement. On the left of the = operator, use the name of the array with the subscript of the element you wish to assign. For example, suppose `intNumbers` is an array of integers with subscripts 0 through 5. The following statements store values in each element of the array:

```
intNumbers(0) = 100
intNumbers(1) = 200
intNumbers(2) = 300
intNumbers(3) = 400
intNumbers(4) = 500
intNumbers(5) = 600
```

 TIP: The expression `intNumbers (0)` is pronounced *intNumbers sub zero.*

Figure 8-4 shows the values assigned to the elements of the array after these statements execute.

Figure 8-4 `intNumbers` array with assigned values

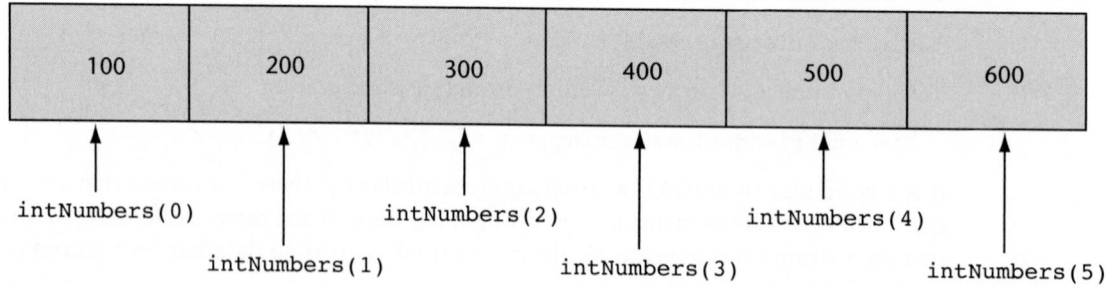

VideoNote

Accessing Array Elements with a Loop

Accessing Array Elements with a Loop

You can assign an integer to a variable and then use the variable as a subscript. This makes it possible to use a loop to cycle through an entire array, performing the same operation on each element. This can be helpful if you want to process the elements in a large array because writing individual statements would require a lot of typing.

For example, the following code declares `intSeries` as an array of 10 integers. The array's subscripts are 0 through 9. The `For...Next` loop stores the value 100 in each of its elements, beginning at subscript 0:

```
Const intMAX_SUBSCRIPT As Integer = 9
Dim intSeries(intMAX_SUBSCRIPT) As Integer
Dim intCount As Integer

For intCount = 0 To intMAX_SUBSCRIPT
   intSeries(intCount) = 100
Next
```

The variable `intCount`, used as the loop counter, takes on the values 0 through 9 as the loop repeats. The first time through the loop, `intCount` equals 0, so the statement `intSeries(intCount) = 100` assigns 100 to `intSeries(0)`. The second time the loop executes, the statement stores 100 in `intSeries(1)`, and so on. Figure 8-5 illustrates how the loop is set up so the counter variable begins with the first array subscript and ends with the last array subscript.

Figure 8-5 A `For...Next` loop using a counter variable to step through an array

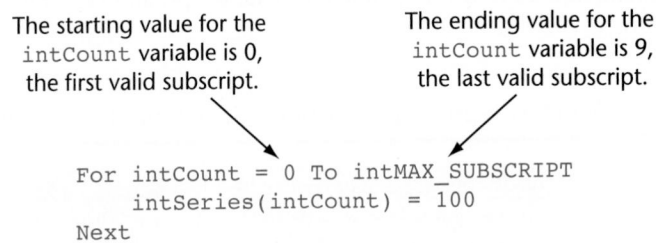

The following example uses a `Do While` loop to perform the same operation:

```
Const intMAX_SUBSCRIPT As Integer = 9
Dim intSeries(intMAX_SUBSCRIPT) As Integer
Dim intCount As Integer = 0

Do While intCount <= intMAX_SUBSCRIPT
   intSeries(intCount) = 100
   intCount += 1
Loop
```

We mentioned earlier that it is a good idea to initialize a string array if there is a chance that the program will access its elements before data has been stored there. It might be cumbersome, however, to provide a separate initializer for each array element. Instead, you can use a loop to initialize the array's elements. For example, the following code stores an empty string in each element of `strNames`, a 1000-element array of strings:

```
Const intMAX_SUBSCRIPT As Integer = 999
Dim strNames(intMAX_SUBSCRIPT) As String
Dim intCount As Integer

For intCount = 0 To intMAX_SUBSCRIPT
   strNames(intCount) = String.Empty
Next
```

Array Bounds Checking

The Visual Basic runtime system performs **array bounds checking**, meaning that it does not allow a statement to use a subscript outside the range of valid subscripts for an array. For example, in the following declaration, the array named `intValues` has a subscript range of 0 through 10:

```
Const intMAX_SUBSCRIPT As Integer = 10
Dim intValues(intMAX_SUBSCRIPT) As Integer
```

If a statement uses a subscript that is less than 0 or greater than 10 with this array, the program will throw an exception.

The compiler does not display an error message at design time when you write a statement that uses an invalid subscript. For example, the loop in the following code uses out-of-range subscripts:

```
Const intMAX_SUBSCRIPT As Integer = 10
Dim intValues(intMAX_SUBSCRIPT) As Integer
Dim intIndex As Integer

For intIndex = 0 To 20
  intValues(intIndex) = 99
Next
```

At runtime, this loop executes until `intIndex` equals 11. At that point, when the assignment statement tries to use `intIndex` as a subscript, an exception is thrown, as shown in Figure 8-6.

Figure 8-6 Exception window reporting index outside the bounds of the array

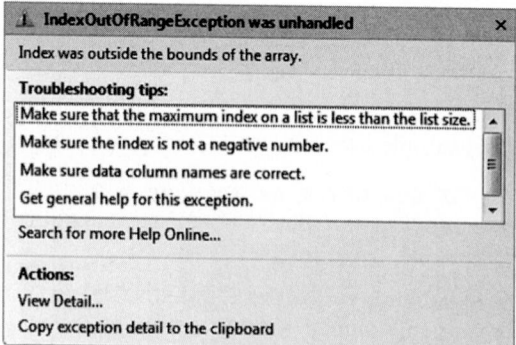

Tutorial 8-1:
Using an array to hold a list of random lottery numbers

In this tutorial you will create an application that randomly generates lottery numbers. When a button is clicked, the application will generate five 2-digit integer numbers and store them in an array. The contents of the array will then be displayed on the application's form in labels.

Step 1: Create a new Windows Forms Application project named *Lottery Numbers*.

Step 2: Set up the project's form with Label and Button controls as shown in Figure 8-7. Set the following properties for each of the Label controls:
- AutoSize = False
- BorderStyle = Fixed3D
- TextAlign = MiddleCenter
- Clear the Text property

Figure 8-7 The *Lottery Numbers* form

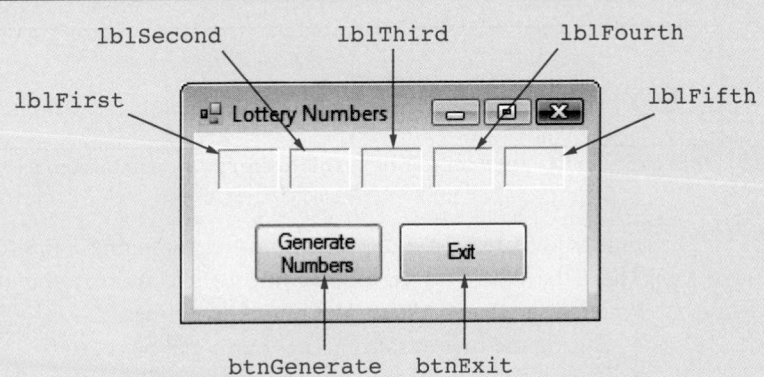

Step 3: Complete the code for the form's event handlers as shown in the following. (Don't type the line numbers. They are shown for reference.)

```
1 Public Class Form1
2
3     Private Sub btnGenerate_Click(...) Handles btnGenerate.Click
4         ' Create an array to hold five lottery numbers.
5         Const intMAX_SUBSCRIPT As Integer = 4        ' The maximum subscript
6         Dim intNumbers(intMAX_SUBSCRIPT) As Integer ' Array declaration
7         Dim intCount As Integer                      ' Loop counter
8
9         ' Create a Random object.
10        Dim rand As New Random
11
12        ' Fill the array with random numbers.
13        ' Each number will be in the range 0-99.
14        For intCount = 0 To intMAX_SUBSCRIPT
15            intNumbers(intCount) = rand.Next(100)
16        Next
17
18        ' Display the array elements in the labels.
19        lblFirst.Text = intNumbers(0).ToString()
20        lblSecond.Text = intNumbers(1).ToString()
21        lblThird.Text = intNumbers(2).ToString()
22        lblFourth.Text = intNumbers(3).ToString()
23        lblFifth.Text = intNumbers(4).ToString()
24    End Sub
25
26    Private Sub btnExit_Click(...) Handles btnExit.Click
27        ' Close the form.
28        Me.Close()
29    End Sub
30 End Class
```

Let's take a closer look at the code for the btnGenerate_Click event handler. Line 5 declares the constant intMAX_SUBSCRIPT, set to the value 4, and line 6 declares an Integer array named intNumbers. The constant intMAX_SUBSCRIPT is used as the upper subscript. As shown in Figure 8-8, the intNumbers array will have five elements, and their subscripts will be 0 through 4. Line 7 declares a variable named intCount that will be used as a loop counter.

Figure 8-8 The intNumbers array and its subscripts

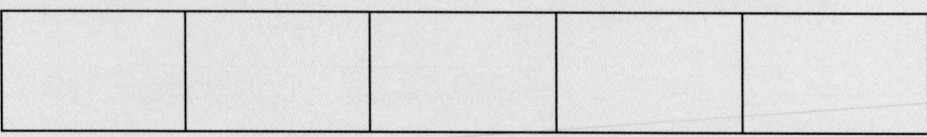

intNumbers(0) intNumbers(1) intNumbers(2) intNumbers(3) intNumbers(4)

Line 10 creates a Random object, using the name rand to refer to that object. Then, the For...Next loop in line 14 executes. If you study line 14 carefully you will see that the loop will iterate five times:

• During the first iteration, intCount will be set to 0.
• During the second iteration, intCount will be set to 1.
• During the third iteration, intCount will be set to 2.
• During the fourth iteration, intCount will be set to 3.
• During the fifth iteration, intCount will be set to 4.

The statement inside the loop in line 15 gets a random number in the range of 0 through 99 and assigns it to intNumbers(intCount). As a result,

• The first random number will be assigned to intNumbers(0).
• The second random number will be assigned to intNumbers(1).
• The third random number will be assigned to intNumbers(2).
• The fourth name random number will be assigned to intNumbers(3).
• The fifth random number will be assigned to intNumbers(4).

The statements in lines 19 through 23 display the values of the array elements by assigning their values to the Label controls. Notice that we call each array element's ToString method to convert its value to a string, as shown in line 19:

```
lblFirst.Text = intNumbers(0).ToString()
```

The value stored in intNumbers(0) is an integer, so the expression intNumbers(0).ToString() converts that value to a string. The resulting string is then assigned to the lblFirst control's Text property. This technique is used to convert the remaining array elements to strings and assign their values to the other Label controls in lines 20 through 23.

Step 4: Save the project, and run the application. Click the *Generate Numbers* button. You should see random numbers displayed in each of the Label controls, similar to Figure 8-9.

Figure 8-9 Array elements displayed in the Label controls

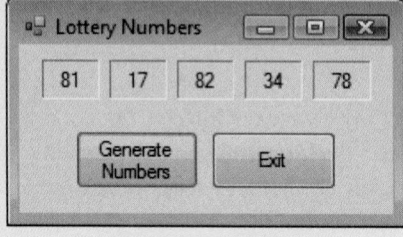

Using Array Elements to Store Input

Array elements can be used to hold data entered by the user. For example, the following code gets numbers from the user and stores them in the intSeries array:

```
Const intMAX_SUBSCRIPT As Integer = 9
Dim intSeries(intMAX_SUBSCRIPT) As Integer
Dim intCount As Integer

For intCount = 0 To intMAX_SUBSCRIPT
  intSeries(intCount) = CInt(InputBox("Enter a number."))
Next
```

In Tutorial 8-2 you will create an application that uses input boxes to read a sequence of strings as input, and stores those strings in an array.

VideoNote

Tutorial 8-2
Walkthrough

Tutorial 8-2:
Using an array to hold a list of names entered by the user

In this tutorial you will create an application that uses an array to hold five strings. The application will have a button that allows you to enter the names of five friends. It will store those names in the array, and then display the contents of the array in a list box.

Step 1: Create a new Windows Forms Application project named *Friend List*.

Step 2: Set up the project's form with a ListBox and two Button controls as shown in Figure 8-10.

Figure 8-10 The *Friend List* project's form

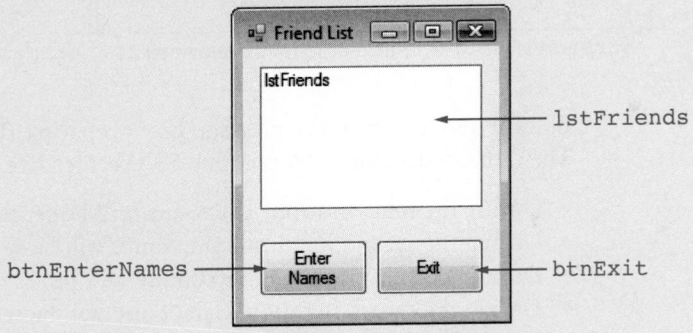

Step 3: Complete the code for the form's event handlers as shown in the following. (Don't type the line numbers. They are shown for reference.)

```
1 Public Class Form1
2
3     Private Sub btnEnterNames_Click(...) Handles btnEnterNames.Click
4         Const intMAX_SUBSCRIPT As Integer = 4     ' The max subscript
5         Dim strNames(intMAX_SUBSCRIPT) As String ' Array to hold names
6         Dim intCount As Integer                   ' Loop counter
7
8         ' Tell the user what we are about to do.
9         MessageBox.Show("I'm going to ask you to enter the names " &
10                        "of five friends.")
11
```

```
12              ' Get the names and store them in the array.
13              For intCount = 0 To intMAX_SUBSCRIPT
14                  strNames(intCount) = InputBox("Enter a friend's name.")
15              Next
16
17              ' Clear the list box of its current contents.
18              lstFriends.Items.Clear()
19
20              ' Display the contents of the array in the list box.
21              For intCount = 0 To intMAX_SUBSCRIPT
22                  lstFriends.Items.Add(strNames(intCount))
23              Next
24          End Sub
25
26          Private Sub btnExit_Click(...) Handles btnExit.Click
27              ' Close the form.
28              Me.Close()
29          End Sub
30      End Class
```

Let's take a closer look at the code for the `btnEnterNames_Click` event handler. Line 4 declares the constant `intMAX_SUBSCRIPT`, set to the value 4, and line 5 declares a `String` array named `strNames`. The constant `intMAX_SUBSCRIPT` is used as the upper subscript. As shown in Figure 8-11, the `strNames` array will have five elements, and their subscripts will be 0 through 4. Line 6 declares a variable named `intCount` that will be used as a loop counter.

Figure 8-11 The `strNames` array and its subscripts

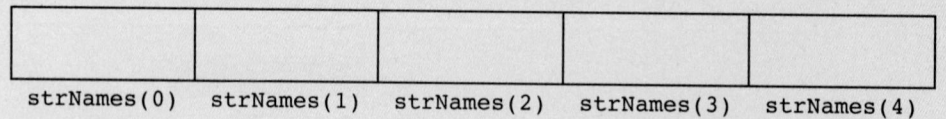

| strNames(0) | strNames(1) | strNames(2) | strNames(3) | strNames(4) |

Lines 9 and 10 display a message box preparing the user to enter five names. Then, the `For...Next` loop in line 13 executes five times:

- During the first iteration, `intCount` will be set to 0.
- During the second iteration, `intCount` will be set to 1.
- During the third iteration, `intCount` will be set to 2.
- During the fourth iteration, `intCount` will be set to 3.
- During the fifth iteration, `intCount` will be set to 4.

The statement inside the loop, in line 14, does the following: (1) It displays an input box prompting the user to enter a friend's name, and (2) it assigns the value entered by the user to `strNames(intCount)`. As a result,

- The first name the user enters will be assigned to `strNames(0)`.
- The second name the user enters will be assigned to `strNames(1)`.
- The third name the user enters will be assigned to `strNames(2)`.
- The fourth name the user enters will be assigned to `strNames(3)`.
- The fifth name the user enters will be assigned to `strNames(4)`.

Line 18 clears the contents of the `lstFriends` list box. Then, another `For...Next` loop executes in line 21. Just like the previous `For...Next` loop, this loop uses the `intCount` variable to step through the elements of the `strNames` array. When this loop executes, the statement in line 22 adds an array element to the `lstFriends` list box. After the loop has finished, each name that is stored in the `strNames` array will be displayed in the list box.

Step 4: Save the project, and run the application. Click the *Enter Names* button, and then enter five names in the resulting input boxes. After you enter the last one, you should see the names displayed in the list box, similar to Figure 8-12.

Figure 8-12 Names displayed in the list box

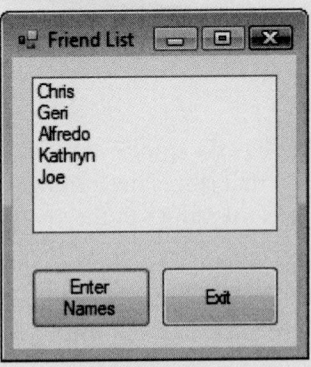

Getting the Length of an Array

Arrays have a Length property that holds the number of elements in the array. For example, assume the following declaration:

```
Dim strNames() As String = { "Joe", "Geri", "Rose" }
```

The `strNames` array has a total of 3 elements, with an upper subscript of 2. The array's Length property returns the value 3. The following is an example of code that uses the Length property:

```
For intCount = 0 to strNames.Length — 1
    MessageBox.Show(strNames(intCount))
Next
```

The code uses the expression `strNames.Length — 1` as the loop's upper limit, because the value in the Length property is 1 greater than the array's upper subscript. As you will learn later, it's possible to change an array's size while an application is running. You can use the Length property to get the current value of an array's size.

Processing Array Contents

You can use array elements just like regular variables in operations. For example, assuming `intHours` is an array of Integers, the following statement multiplies `intHours(3)` by the variable `decPayRate` and stores the result in `decGrossPay`:

```
decGrossPay = intHours(3) * decPayRate
```

Assuming `intTallies` is an array of Integers, the following statement adds 1 to `intTallies(0)`:

```
intTallies(0) += 1
```

And, assuming `decPay` is an array of Decimals, the following statement displays `decPay(5)` in a message box:

```
MessageBox.Show(decPay(5).ToString())
```

In Tutorial 8-3 you will complete an application that performs calculations using array elements.

Tutorial 8-3:
Completing an application that uses array elements in a calculation

JJ's House of Pizza has six employees, each paid $12 per hour. In this tutorial, you complete an application that stores the number of hours worked by each employee in an array. The application uses the values in the array to calculate each employee's gross pay.

VideoNote

Tutorial 8-3
Walkthrough

Step 1: Open the *Simple Payroll* project located in the student sample programs folder named *Chap8\Simple Payroll*. Figure 8-13 shows the project's form, which has already been created for you.

Figure 8-13 *Simple Payroll* form

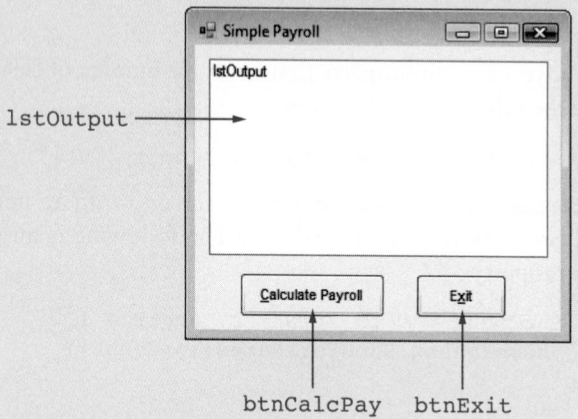

Step 2: Complete the code for the Button control event handlers as shown in the following. (Don't type the line numbers. They are shown for reference.)

```
1 Public Class Form1
2
3     Private Sub btnCalcPay_Click(...) Handles btnCalcPay.Click
4         ' Constants
5         Const decHOURLY_PAY_RATE As Decimal = 12D
6         Const intMAX_SUBSCRIPT As Integer = 5
7
```

```
 8          ' Array and other variables
 9          Dim dblHoursArray(intMAX_SUBSCRIPT) As Double
10          Dim intCount As Integer = 0   ' Loop counter
11          Dim decEmpPay As Decimal       ' To hold gross pay
12
13          ' Prepare the user to enter each employee's hours.
14          MessageBox.Show("I'm going to ask you for each " &
15                          "employee's hours worked.")
16
17          ' Get the hours worked by the employees.
18          Do While intCount < dblHoursArray.Length
19             Try
20                 dblHoursArray(intCount) =
21                     CDbl(InputBox("Employee number " &
22                                   (intCount + 1).ToString()))
23                 intCount += 1
24             Catch
25                 ' Display an error message for invalid hours.
26                 MessageBox.Show("Enter a valid number of " &
27                                 "hours for that employee.")
28             End Try
29          Loop
30
31          ' Clear the list box.
32          lstOutput.Items.Clear()
33
34          ' Calculate and display each employee's gross pay.
35          For intCount = 0 To dblHoursArray.Length - 1
36              decEmpPay = CDec(dblHoursArray(intCount) *
37                  decHOURLY_PAY_RATE)
38
39              lstOutput.Items.Add("Employee " &
40                                  (intCount + 1).ToString() &
41                                  " earned " &
42                                  decEmpPay.ToString("c"))
43          Next
44      End Sub
45
46      Private Sub btnExit_Click(...) Handles btnExit.Click
47          ' Close the form.
48          Me.Close()
49      End Sub
50 End Class
```

Let's take a closer look at the btnCalcPay_Click event handler. Here is a summary of the declarations that appear in lines 5 through 11:

- Line 5 declares the constant decHOURLY_PAY_RATE for the employee hourly pay rate.
- Line 6 declares the constant intMAX_SUBSCRIPT for the array's upper subscript.
- Line 9 declares dblHoursArray, an array of Doubles, to hold all of the employees' hours worked.
- Line 10 declares intCount, which will be used as a loop counter (initialized to 0), and to step through the dblHoursArray array.
- Line 11 declares decEmpPay, a Decimal to hold an employee's gross pay.

Lines 14 and 15 display a message box, letting the user know that we are about to ask for each employee's hours worked. The `Do While` loop that begins in line 18 uses the `intCount` variable to step through the `dblHoursArray` array. Recall that `intCount` was initialized with 0. The loop executes as long as `intCount` is less than `dblHoursArray.length`.

Inside the loop a `Try-Catch` statement is used to catch any exceptions that might occur if the user enters a non-numeric value. The statement that appears in lines 20 through 22 performs the following actions:

• It displays an input box prompting the user with an employee number.
• It uses the `CDbl` function to convert the user's input to a Double.
• It assigns the resulting value to the array element `dblHoursArray(intCount)`.

If the user enters an invalid value, the program will branch to the `Catch` clause in line 24, display an error message in lines 26 and 27, and then the loop starts over. If the user enters a valid value, however, line 23 adds 1 to the `intCount` variable. The loop then starts over.

Once the user has entered values for all of the array elements, line 32 clears the list box, and then the `For...Next` loop in line 35 begins. This loop also uses the `intCount` variable to step through each array element. Lines 36 and 37 use an array element to calculate an employee's gross pay, and lines 39 through 42 add a string to the list box reporting the employee's gross pay.

Step 3: Save the project, and run the application. Click the *Calculate Payroll* button. A series of input boxes should appear, asking you to enter the number of hours worked for employees 1 through 6. Enter the following values in order:

Employee 1:   **10**
Employee 2:   **40**
Employee 3:   **20**
Employee 4:   **15**
Employee 5:   **10**
Employee 6:   **30**

After you enter the hours for employee 6, the form should appear, as shown in Figure 8-14.

Step 4: Click the *Exit* button to end the program.

Figure 8-14 *Simple Payroll* application, after entering hours for all employees

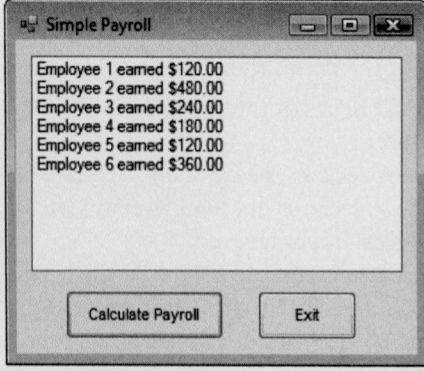

Accessing Array Elements with a For Each Loop

Visual Basic provides a special loop known as the For Each loop. The For Each loop can simplify array processing when your task is simply to step through an array, retrieving the value of each element. The loop can read the array elements, but it cannot modify their values. The For Each loop is written in the following general form:

```
For Each var As type In array
    statements
Next
```

In the general form, *var* is the name of a variable that will be created just for use with the loop, *type* is the data type of the array, and *array* is the name of an array. The loop will iterate once for every element in the array. Each time the loop iterates, it copies an array element to the *var* variable. For example, the first time the loop iterates, the *var* variable will contain the value of *array(0)*, the second time the loop iterates, the *var* variable will contain the value of *array(1)*, and so forth. This continues until the loop has stepped through all of the elements in the array.

For example, suppose we have the following array declaration:

```
Dim intArray() As Integer = {10, 20, 30, 40, 50, 60}
```

The following For Each loop displays all of the array values in a ListBox control named lstShow:

```
For Each intVal As Integer In intArray
    lstShow.Items.Add(intVal)
Next
```

Optional Topic: Using the For Each Loop with a ListBox

A For Each loop can also be used to process the items in a collection. Suppose we would like to search for a city name in the Items collection of a ListBox control named lstCities. We will assume that the user has entered a city name into a TextBox control named txtCity. Figure 8-15 shows an example of the program at runtime. Here are the statements that execute the search:

```
For Each strCity As String In lstCities.Items
  If strCity = txtCity.Text Then
    lblResult.Text = "The city was found!"
  End If
Next
```

Figure 8-15 Searching for a city name in a ListBox control

 **Checkpoint**

8.1 Write declaration statements for the following arrays:

    a. `intEmpNums`, an array of 100 integers
    b. `decPayRate`, an array of 24 Decimal variables
    c. `intMiles`, an array of integers initialized to the values 10, 20, 30, 40, and 50
    d. `strNames`, an array of strings with an upper subscript of 12
    e. `strDivisions`, an array of strings initialized to the values `"North"`, `"South"`, `"East"`, and `"West"`.

8.2 Identify the error in the following declaration:

```
Dim intNumberSet(4) As Integer = { 25, 37, 45, 60 }
```

8.3 Look at the following array declarations and indicate the number of elements in each array:

```
a. Dim dblNums(100) As Double
b. Dim intValues() As Integer = { 99, 99, 99 }
c. Dim intArray(0) As Integer
```

8.4 What is array bounds checking?

8.5 Assume that a procedure has the following array declaration:

```
Const intMAX_SUBSCRIPT As Integer = 25
Dim intPoints(intMAX_SUBSCRIPT) As Integer
```

Write a `For...Next` loop that displays each of the array's elements in message boxes.

8.6 Rewrite your answer to Checkpoint 8.5, using a `For Each` loop.

8.7 What values are displayed in the message boxes by the following code? (Use a calculator if necessary.)

```
Const dblRATE As Double = 0.1
Const intMAX_SUBSCRIPT As Integer = 3
Dim intBalance(intMAX_SUBSCRIPT) As Integer
Dim intCount As Integer
Dim dblResult As Double

intBalance(0) = 100
intBalance(1) = 250
intBalance(2) = 325
intBalance(3) = 500

For intCount = 0 To intMAX_SUBSCRIPT
    dblResult = intBalance(intCount) * dblRATE
    MessageBox.Show(dblResult.ToString())
Next
```

8.2 More about Array Processing

CONCEPT: There are many uses for arrays, and many programming techniques can be applied to them. You can total values and search for data. Related information may be stored in multiple parallel arrays. In addition, arrays can be resized at runtime.

How to Total the Values in a Numeric Array

To total the values in a numeric array, use a loop with an accumulator variable. The loop adds the value in each array element to the accumulator. For example, assume the following array declaration exists in an application, and values have been stored in the array:

```
Const intMAX_SUBSCRIPT As Integer = 24
Dim intUnits(intMAX_SUBSCRIPT) As Integer
```

The following code adds each array element to the `intTotal` variable:

```
Dim intTotal As Integer = 0
Dim intCount As Integer

For intCount = 0 To (intUnits.Length — 1)
   intTotal += intUnits(intCount)
Next
```

NOTE: The first statement in the previous example sets `intTotal` to 0. Recall from Chapter 5 that an accumulator variable must be set to 0 before it is used to keep a running total or the sum will not be correct. Although Visual Basic automatically initializes numeric variables to 0, this statement emphasizes that `intTotal` must equal 0 before the loop starts.

The previous example demonstrated how to use a `For...Next` loop to total all of the values in a numeric array. You can also use a `For Each` loop, as shown in the following code. Assume `intUnits` is an Integer array.

```
Dim intTotal As Integer = 0

For Each intVal As Integer In intUnits
    intTotal += intVal
Next
```

After the loop finishes, `intTotal` will contain the total of all the elements in `intUnits`.

Calculating the Average Value in a Numeric Array

The first step in calculating the average value in an array is to sum the values. The second step is to divide the sum by the number of elements in the array. Assume the following declaration exists in an application, and values have been stored in the array:

```
Const intMAX_SUBSCRIPT As Integer = 24
Dim intUnits(intMAX_SUBSCRIPT) As Integer
```

The following loop calculates the average value in the `intUnits` array. The average is stored in the `dblAverage` variable.

```
Dim intTotal As Integer = 0
Dim dblAverage As Double
Dim intCount As Integer

For intCount = 0 To (intUnits.Length - 1)
   intTotal += intUnits(intCount)
Next

' Use floating-point division to compute the average.
dblAverage = intTotal / intUnits.Length
```

The statement that calculates the average (`dblAverage`) must be placed after the end of the loop. It should execute only once.

Finding the Highest and Lowest Values in an Integer Array

Earlier in this chapter, when explaining For Each loops, we showed you how to find the largest value in an array. Let's look at a similar example that uses a For Next loop and accesses each array element using a subscript. Assume that the following array declaration exists in an application, and that values have been stored in the array:

```
Dim intUnits() As Integer = {1, 2, 3, 4, 5}
Dim intCount As Integer        ' Loop counter
Dim intHighest As Integer      ' To hold the highest value

' Get the first element.
intHighest = intNumbers(0)

' Search for the highest value.
For intCount = 1 To (intNumbers.Length - 1)
    If intNumbers(intCount) > intHighest Then
        intHighest = intNumbers(intCount)
    End If
Next
```

The code begins by assigning the value in the first array element to the variable `intHighest`. Next, the loop compares all remaining array elements, beginning at subscript 1, to `intHighest`. Each time it finds a value in the array greater than `intHighest`, the value is copied into `intHighest`. When the loop finishes, `intHighest` equals the largest value in the array.

Lowest Value

The following code, which finds the lowest value in the array, is very similar to the code for finding the highest value. When the loop finishes, `intLowest` equals the smallest value in the array.

```
Dim intUnits() As Integer = {1, 2, 3, 4, 5}
Dim intCount As Integer        ' Loop counter
Dim intLowest As Integer       ' To hold the lowest value

' Get the first element.
intLowest = intNumbers(0)

' Search for the lowest value.
For intCount = 1 To (intNumbers.Length - 1)
    If intNumbers(intCount) < intLowest Then
        intLowest = intNumbers(intCount)
    End If
Next
```

Copying One Array's Contents to Another

Assume that an application has the following statements:

```
Const intMAX_SUBSCRIPT As Integer = 2
Dim intOldValues(intMAX_SUBSCRIPT) As Integer
Dim intNewValues(intMAX_SUBSCRIPT) As Integer
intOldValues(0) = 10
```

```
intOldValues(1) = 100
intOldValues(2) = 200
```

Suppose we want to copy the contents of the intOldValues array to the intNewValues array. We might be tempted to use a single assignment statement, such as the following:

```
intNewValues = intOldValues
```

Although this statement compiles, it does not copy the intOldValues array to the intNewValues array. Instead it causes the names intNewValues and intOldValues to reference the same array in memory.

Arrays in Visual Basic are object variables. Recall from Chapter 7 that an object variable is a variable that holds a reference to an object. When you use the assignment operator to assign one array to another, the two array variables end up referencing to the same array. For example, after the statement intNewValues = intOldValues executes, the intNewValues variable refers to the same array as the intOldValues variable. This situation is illustrated in Figure 8-16.

Figure 8-16 State of the arrays before and after the assignment statement

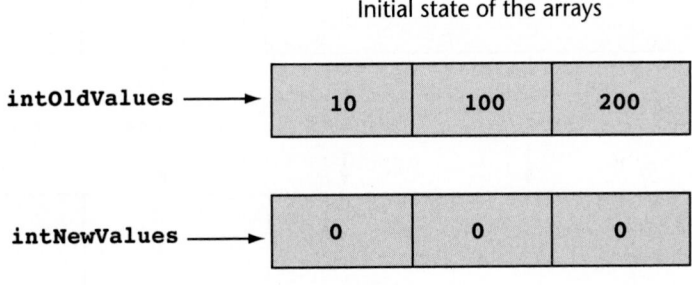

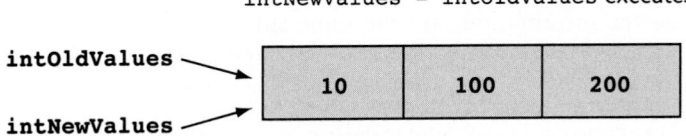

The danger of assigning intNewValues to intOldValues is that we are no longer working with two arrays, but one. If we were to change the value of any element in the intNewValues array, we would automatically be changing the same element of the intOldValues array. This action would probably be accidental, resulting in a program bug.

Rather than using a single assignment statement to copy an array, we would have to use a loop to copy the individual elements from intOldValues to intNewValues, as shown in the following code:

```
For intCount = 0 To (intOldValues.Length-1)
   intNewValues(intCount) = intOldValues(intCount)
Next
```

This loop copies intOldValue's elements to the intNewValues array. When finished, two separate arrays exist.

Parallel Arrays

Sometimes it is useful to store related data in two or more related arrays, also known as parallel arrays. For example, assume an application has the following array declarations:

```
Const intMAX_SUBSCRIPT As Integer = 4
Dim strNames(intMAX_SUBSCRIPT) As String
Dim strAddresses(intMAX_SUBSCRIPT) As String
```

The `strNames` array stores the names of five people, and the `strAddresses` array stores the addresses of the same five people. The information for one person is stored in the same relative location in each array. For instance, the first person's name is stored at `strNames(0)`, and the same person's address is stored at `strAddresses(0)`, as shown in Figure 8-17.

Figure 8-17 `strNames` and `strAddresses` parallel arrays

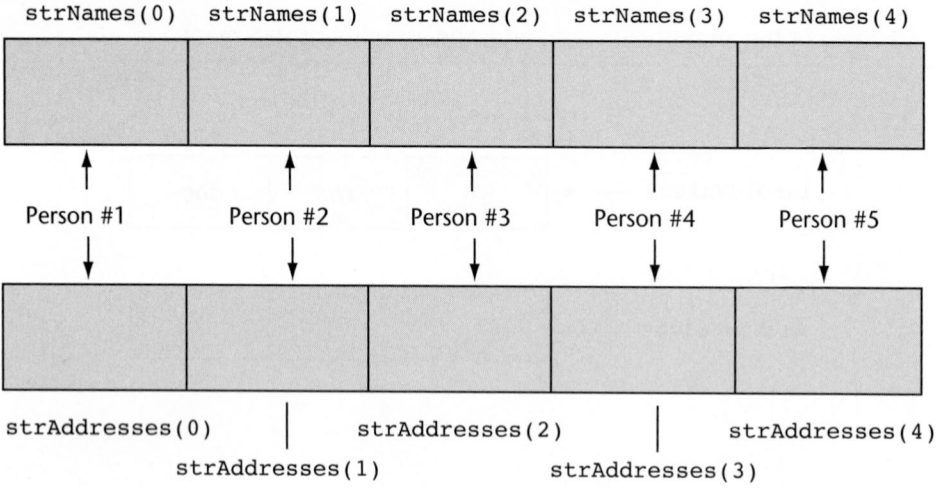

To access the information, use the same subscript with both arrays. For example, the following loop displays each person's name and address in a list box named `lstPeople`:

```
For intCount = 0 To intMAX_SUBSCRIPT
    lstPeople.Items.Add("Name: " & strNames(intCount) &
                        " Address: " & strAddresses(intCount))
Next
```

The arrays `strNames` and `strAddresses` are examples of parallel arrays. **Parallel arrays** are two or more arrays that hold related data. The related elements in each array are accessed with a common subscript. Parallel arrays are especially useful when the related data are of unlike types. For example, an application could store the names and ages of five people in the following arrays:

```
Const intMAX_SUBSCRIPT As Integer = 4
Dim strNames(intMAX_SUBSCRIPT) As String
Dim intAges(intMAX_SUBSCRIPT) As Integer
```

Tutorial 8-4 examines an application that uses parallel arrays: one to hold the names of the months, and one to hold the number of days in each month.

Tutorial 8-4:

Using parallel arrays

In this tutorial you will create an application that displays the number of days in each month. The application will use two parallel arrays: a String array that is initialized with the names of the months, and an Integer array that is initialized with the number of days in each month. When a button is clicked, the application will display its output in a list box.

Step 1: Create a new Windows Forms Application project named *Months and Days*.

Step 2: Set up the project's form with a ListBox and two Button controls as shown in Figure 8-18.

Figure 8-18 The *Months and Days* project's form

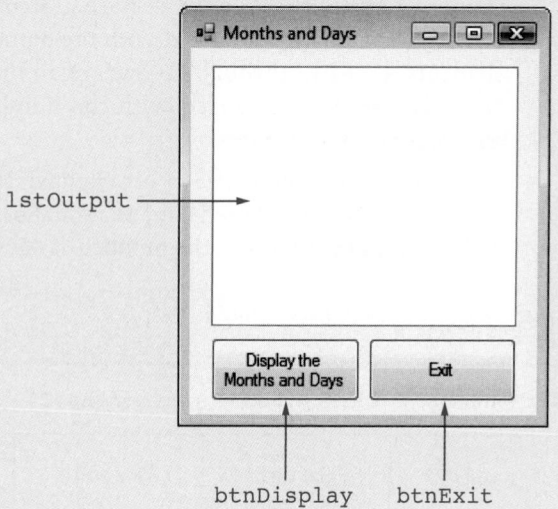

Step 3: Complete the code for the form's event handlers as shown in the following. (Don't type the line numbers. They are shown for reference.)

```
1 Public Class Form1
2
3     Private Sub btnDisplay_Click(...) Handles btnDisplay.Click
4         Dim intCount As Integer    ' Loop counter
5
6         ' Array with the names of the months
7         Dim strMonths() As String = {"January", "February", "March",
8                                      "April", "May", "June", "July",
9                                      "August", "September", "October",
10                                     "November", "December"}
11
12        ' Array with the days of each month
13        Dim intDays() As Integer = {31, 28, 31,
14                                    30, 31, 30,
15                                    31, 31, 30,
16                                    31, 30, 31}
```

```
17
18          ' Display a list of the months and days.
19          For intCount = 0 To strMonths.Length — 1
20              lstOutput.Items.Add(strMonths(intCount) & " has " &
21                                  intDays(intCount).ToString() &
22                                  " days.")
23          Next
24      End Sub
25
26      Private Sub btnExit_Click(...) Handles btnExit.Click
27          ' Close the form.
28          Me.Close()
29      End Sub
30  End Class
```

Let's take a closer look at the code for the `btnDisplay_Click` event handler. Line 4 declares the `intCount` variable that we will use as a loop counter. Lines 7 through 10 declare a String array named `strMonths`. The `strMonths` array is initialized with the names of the months, so it has twelve elements. Lines 13 through 16 declare an Integer array named `intDays`. The `intDays` array is initialized with the number of days in each month, so it also has twelve elements.

The `strMonths` and `intDays` arrays have the parallel relationship shown in Figure 8-19. In this relationship, `strMonths(n)` contains the name of a month, and `intDays(n)` contains the number of days in that same month.

Figure 8-19 Parallel arrays

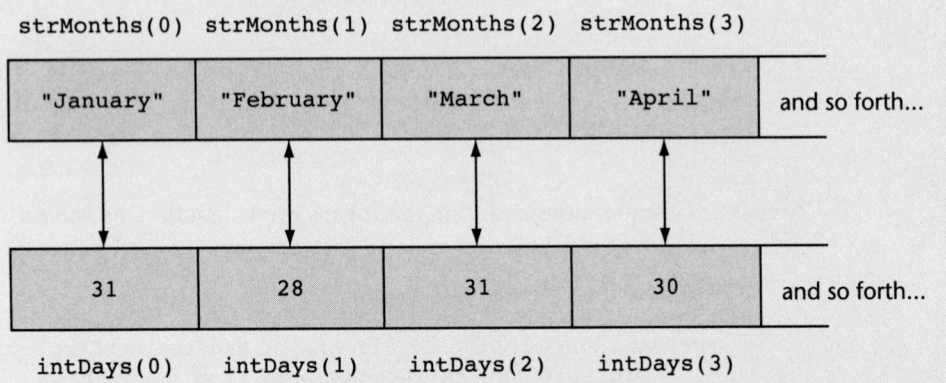

The `For...Next` loop that begins in line 19 uses the `intCount` variable to step through the parallel arrays, displaying a line of output in the `lstOutput` list box. In the first iteration the string "January has 31 days." will be added to the list box. In the second iteration the string "February has 28 days." will be added to the list box. This continues for each element in the arrays.

Step 4: Save the project, and run the application. Click the *Display the Months and Days* button. You should see the output shown in Figure 8-20.

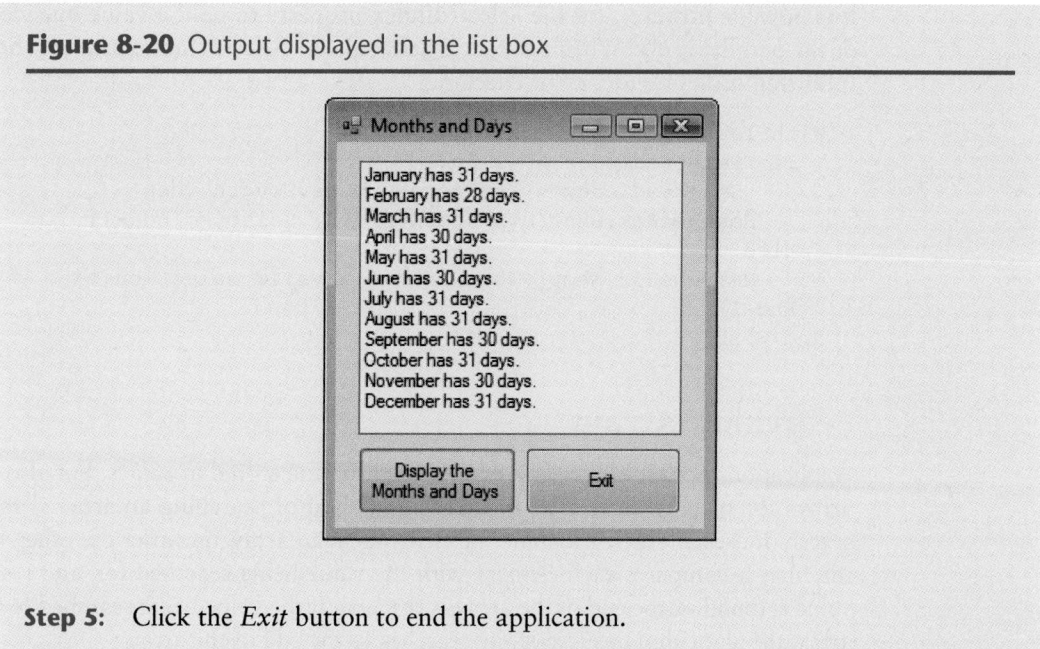

Figure 8-20 Output displayed in the list box

Step 5:   Click the *Exit* button to end the application.

Parallel Relationships between Arrays, List Boxes, and Combo Boxes

Items stored in a list box or a combo box have a built-in index. The index of the first item is 0, the index of the second item is 1, and so on. Because this indexing scheme corresponds with the way array subscripts are used, it is easy to create parallel relationships between list boxes, combo boxes, and arrays.

For example, assume that an application has a list box named lstPeople. The following statements store three names in the list box:

```
lstPeople.Items.Add("Jean James")
lstPeople.Items.Add("Kevin Smith")
lstPeople.Items.Add("Joe Harrison")
```

When these statements execute, "Jean James" is stored at index 0, "Kevin Smith" is stored at index 1, and "Joe Harrison" is stored at index 2. Also assume the application has an array of strings named strPhoneNumbers. This array holds the phone numbers of the three people whose names are stored in the list box. The following statements store phone numbers in the array:

```
strPhoneNumbers(0) = "555-2987"
strPhoneNumbers(1) = "555-5656"
strPhoneNumbers(2) = "555-8897"
```

The phone number stored at element 0 ("555-2987") belongs to the person whose name is stored at index 0 in the list box ("Jean James"). Likewise, the phone number stored at element 1 belongs to the person whose name is stored at index 1 in the list box, and so on. When the user selects a name from the list box, the following statement displays the person's phone number:

```
MessageBox.Show(strPhoneNumbers(lstPeople.SelectedIndex))
```

The SelectedIndex property holds the index of the selected item in the list box. This statement uses the index as a subscript in the strPhoneNumbers array.

It is possible however, for the SelectedIndex property to hold a value outside the bounds of the parallel array. When no item is selected, the SelectedIndex property holds –1. The following code provides error checking:

```
With lstPeople
   If .SelectedIndex > -1 And
      .SelectedIndex < strPhoneNumbers.Length Then
      MessageBox.Show(strPhoneNumbers(.SelectedIndex))
   Else
      MessageBox.Show("That is not a valid selection.")
   End If
End With
```

Searching Arrays

Applications not only store and process information stored in arrays, but also often search arrays for specific items. The most basic method of searching an array is the **sequential search**. It uses a loop to examine the elements in an array, one after the other, starting with the first. It compares each element with the value being searched for, and stops when the value is found or the end of the array is reached. If the value being searched for is not in the array, the algorithm unsuccessfully searches to the end of the array.

The pseudocode for a sequential search is as follows:

found = False
subscript = 0
Do While found is False and subscript < array's length
   If array(subscript) = search Value Then
      found = True
      position = subscript
   End If
   subscript += 1
End While

In the pseudocode, *found* is a Boolean variable, *position* and *subscript* are integers, *array* is an array of any type, and *search Value* is the value being searched for. When the search is complete, if the *found* variable equals *False*, the search value was not found. If *found* equals *True*, `position` contains the subscript of the array element containing the search value.

For example, suppose an application stores test scores in an array named *scores*. The following pseudocode searches the array for an element containing 100:

' Search for a 100 in the array.
found = False
count = 0
Do While Not found And count < scores.Length
   If scores(count) = 100 Then
      found = True
      position = count
   End If
   count += 1
Loop

' Was 100 found in the array?
If found Then
   Display "Congratulations! You made a 100 on test " & (position + 1)

> *Else*
> > *Display "You didn't score a 100, but keep trying!"*
> *End If*

Sorting an Array

Programmers often want to sort, or arrange the elements of an array in **ascending order**, which means its values are arranged from lowest to highest. The lowest value is stored in the first element, and the highest value is stored in the last element. To sort an array in ascending order, use the `Array.Sort` method. The general format is as follows:

```
Array.Sort(ArrayName)
```

ArrayName is the name of the array you wish to sort. For example, assume that the following declaration exists in an application:

```
Dim intNumbers() As Integer = {7, 12, 1, 6, 3}
```

The following statement will sort the array in ascending order:

```
Array.Sort(intNumbers)
```

After the statement executes, the array values are in the following order: 1, 3, 6, 7, 12.

When you pass an array of strings to the `Array.Sort` method, the array is sorted in ascending order according to the Unicode encoding scheme, which we discussed in Chapter 3. Generally, the sort occurs in alphabetic order. But to be more specific about the order, numeric digits are first, uppercase letters are second, and lowercase letters are last. For example, assume the following declaration:

```
Dim strNames() As String = {"dan", "Kim", "Adam", "Bill"}
```

The following statement sorts the array in ascending order:

```
Array.Sort(strNames)
```

After the statement executes, the values in the array appear in this order: `"Adam"`, `"Bill"`, `"Kim"`, `"dan"`.

Dynamically Sizing Arrays

You can change the number of elements in an array at runtime, using the `ReDim` statement. The general format of the `ReDim` statement is as follows:

```
ReDim [Preserve] Arrayname (UpperSubscript)
```

The word `Preserve` is optional. If it is used, any existing values in the array are preserved. If `Preserve` is not used, existing values in the array are destroyed. *Arrayname* is the name of the array being resized. *UpperSubscript* is the new upper subscript and must be a positive whole number. If you resize an array and make it smaller than it was, elements at the end of the array are lost.

For example, the following statement resizes `strNames` so that 25 is the upper subscript:

```
ReDim Preserve strNames(25)
```

After this statement executes, `strNames` has 26 elements. Because the `Preserve` keyword is used, any values originally stored in `strNames` will still be there.

When you do not know at design time the number of elements you will need in an array, you can declare an array without a size, and use the `ReDim` statement later to give it a size. For example, suppose you want to write a test-averaging application that averages any number of tests. You can initially declare the array with no size, as follows:

```
Dim dblScores() As Double
```

Currently, dblScores equals Nothing, but is capable of referencing an array of Double values. Later, when the application has determined the number of test scores, a ReDim statement will give the array a size. The following code shows an example of such an operation:

```
intNumScores = CInt(InputBox("Enter the number of test scores."))
If intNumScores > 0 Then
    ReDim dblScores (intNumScores - 1)
Else
    MessageBox.Show("You must enter 1 or greater.")
End If
```

This code asks the user to enter the number of test scores. If the user enters a value greater than 0, the ReDim statement sizes the array with intNumScores − 1 as the upper subscript. (Because the subscripts begin at 0, the upper subscript is intNumScores − 1.)

 **Checkpoint**

8.8 Suppose intValues is an array of 100 integers. Write a For...Next loop that totals all the values stored in the array.

8.9 Suppose intPoints is an array of integers, but you do not know the size of the array. Write code that calculates the average of the values in the array.

8.10 Suppose strSerialNumbers is an array of strings. Write a single statement that sorts the array in ascending order.

8.11 What is displayed by the message boxes in the following code segment? (You may need to use a calculator.)

```
Const intMAX_SUBSCRIPT As Integer = 4
Dim intTimes(intMAX_SUBSCRIPT) As Integer
Dim intSpeeds(intMAX_SUBSCRIPT) As Integer
Dim intDists(intMAX_SUBSCRIPT) As Integer
Dim intCount As Integer

intSpeeds(0) = 18
intSpeeds(1) = 4
intSpeeds(2) = 27
intSpeeds(3) = 52
intSpeeds(4) = 100

For intCount = 0 To 4
   intTimes(intCount) = intCount
Next

For intCount = 0 To 4
   intDists(intCount) = intTimes(intCount) * intSpeeds(intCount)
Next

For intCount = 0 To 4
   MessageBox.Show( intTimes(intCount).ToString() & " " &
                    intSpeeds(intCount).ToString() & " " &
                    intDists(intCount).ToString())
Next
```

8.12 Assume that decSales is an array of 20 Decimal values. Write a statement that resizes the array to 50 elements. If the array has existing values, they should be preserved.

8.13 Assume that intValidNumbers is an array of integers. Write code that searches the array for the value 247. If the value is found, display a message indicating its position in the array. If the value is not found, display a message indicating so.

8.3 Procedures and Functions That Work with Arrays

CONCEPT: You can pass arrays as arguments to procedures and functions. You can return an array from a function. These capabilities allow you to write procedures and functions that perform general operations with arrays.

Passing Arrays as Arguments

Quite often you will want to write procedures or functions that process the data in arrays. For example, procedures can be written to store data in an array, display an array's contents, and sum or average the values in an array. Usually such procedures accept an array as an argument.

The following procedure accepts an integer array as an argument and displays the sum of the array's elements:

```
' The DisplaySum procedure displays the sum of the elements in the
' argument array.

Sub DisplaySum(ByVal intArray() As Integer)
   Dim intTotal As Integer = 0 ' Accumulator
   Dim intCount As Integer      ' Loop counter

   For intCount = 0 To (intArray.Length - 1)
      intTotal += intArray(intCount)
   Next

   MessageBox.Show("The total is " & intTotal.ToString())
End Sub
```

The parameter variable is declared as an array with no upper subscript specified inside the parentheses. The parameter is an object variable that references an array that is passed as an argument. To call the procedure, pass the name of an array, as shown in the following code:

```
Dim intNumbers() As Integer = { 2, 4, 7, 9, 8, 12, 10 }
DisplaySum(intNumbers)
```

When this code executes, the `DisplaySum` procedure is called and the `intNumbers` array is passed as an argument. The procedure calculates and displays the sum of the elements in `intNumbers`.

Passing Arrays by Value and by Reference

Array parameters can be declared `ByVal` or `ByRef`. Be aware, however, that the `ByVal` keyword does not restrict a procedure from accessing and modifying the argument array's elements. For example, look at the following `SetToZero` procedure:

```
' Set all the elements of the array argument to zero.

Sub SetToZero(ByVal intArray() As Integer)
   Dim intCount As Integer ' Loop counter

   For intCount = 0 To intArray.Length - 1
      intArray(intCount) = 0
   Next
End Sub
```

This procedure accepts an integer array as its argument and sets each element of the array to 0. Suppose we call the procedure, as shown in the following code:

```
Dim intNumbers() As Integer = { 1, 2, 3, 4, 5 }
SetToZero(intNumbers)
```

After the procedure executes, the `intNumbers` array will contain the values 0, 0, 0, 0, and 0.

Although the `ByVal` keyword does not restrict a procedure from accessing and modifying the elements of an array argument, it does prevent an array argument from being assigned to another array. For example, the following procedure accepts an array as its argument, and then assigns the parameter to another array:

```
' Assign the array argument to a new array. Does this work?

Sub ResetValues(ByVal intArray() As Integer)
  Dim newArray() As Integer = { 0, 0, 0, 0, 0}
  intArray = newArray
End Sub
```

Suppose we call the procedure, as shown in the following code:

```
Dim intNumbers() As Integer = { 1, 2, 3, 4, 5 }
ResetValues(intNumbers)
```

After the procedure executes, the `intNumbers` array still contains the values 1, 2, 3, 4, and 5. If the parameter array had been declared with the `ByRef` keyword, however, the assignment would have affected the argument, and the `intNumbers` array would contain the values 0, 0, 0, 0, and 0 after the procedure executed.

Returning an Array from a Function

You can return an array from a function. For example, the following function prompts the user to enter four names. The names are then returned in an array.

```
' Get three names from the user and return them as an array
' of strings.

Function GetNames() As String()
  Const intMAX_SUBSCRIPT As Integer = 2
  Dim strNames(intMAX_SUBSCRIPT) As String
  Dim intCount As Integer

  For intCount = 0 To 3
    strNames(intCount) = InputBox("Enter name " &
      (intCount + 1).ToString())
  Next

  Return strNames
End Function
```

The function has a return type of `String()`, indicating that it returns an array of strings. The return value can be assigned to any array of strings. The following code shows the function's return value being assigned to `strCustomers`:

```
Dim strCustomers() As String
strCustomers = GetNames()
```

After the code executes, the `strCustomers` array contains the names entered by the user.

An array returned from a function must be assigned to an array of the same type. For example, if a function returns an array of integers, its return value can be assigned only to an array of integers. In Tutorial 8-5, you examine an application containing several functions that work with arrays.

Tutorial 8-5:
Examining an application that passes an array to procedures and functions

In this tutorial, you examine the *Sales Data* application, which asks the user for sales figures for five days. It calculates and displays the total sales, average sales, highest sales amount, and lowest sales amount.

Step 1: Open the *Sales Data* project located in the student sample programs folder named *Chap8\Sales Data*.

Step 2: Before we look at the code, let's see the application in action. Run the application. Figure 8-21 shows the project's form. Click the *Calculate Sales Data* button.

Figure 8-21 *Sales Data* form

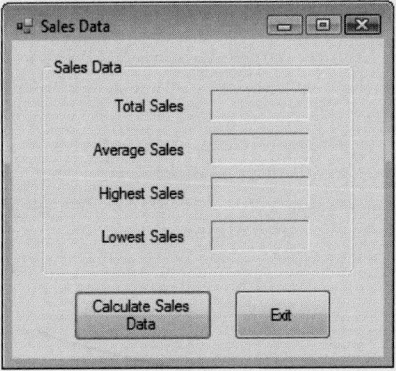

Step 3: A series of five input boxes will appear, asking you to enter the sales for days 1 through 5. Enter the following amounts for each input box:

Day 1: **1000**
Day 2: **2000**
Day 3: **3000**
Day 4: **4000**
Day 5: **5000**

After you enter the sales amount for day 5, the application's form should appear as shown in Figure 8-22.

Figure 8-22 *Sales Data* form with sales data displayed

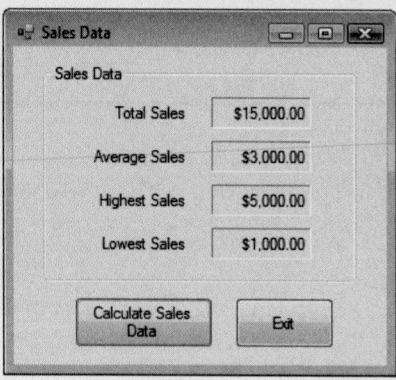

Step 4: Click the *Exit* button to end the application.

Step 5: Now we will examine the application's code. Open the *Code* window and look at the btnCalculate_Click event handler. The code is shown here, with line numbers for reference:

```
1 Public Class Form1
2
3       Private Sub btnCalculate_Click(...) Handles btnCalculate.Click
4           ' Create an array to hold sales amounts.
5           Const intMAX_SUBSCRIPT As Integer = 4
6           Dim decSales(intMAX_SUBSCRIPT) As Decimal
7
8           ' Other local variables
9           Dim decTotalSales As Decimal    ' To hold the total sales
10          Dim decAverageSales As Decimal ' To hold the average sales
11          Dim decHighestSales As Decimal ' To hold the highest sales
12          Dim decLowestSales As Decimal   ' To hold the lowest sales
13
14          ' Get sales amounts from the user.
15          GetSalesData(decSales)
16
17          ' Get the total sales, average sales, highest sales
18          ' amount and lowest sales amount.
19          decTotalSales = TotalArray(decSales)
20          decAverageSales = AverageArray(decSales)
21          decHighestSales = Highest(decSales)
22          decLowestSales = Lowest(decSales)
23
24          ' Display the results.
25          lblTotal.Text = decTotalSales.ToString("c")
26          lblAverage.Text = decAverageSales.ToString("c")
27          lblHighest.Text = decHighestSales.ToString("c")
28          lblLowest.Text = decLowestSales.ToString("c")
29      End Sub
30
```

Here is a summary of the declarations that appear in lines 5 through 12:
- Line 5 declares the constant intMAX_SUBSCRIPT, set to the value 4. This will be the upper subscript of the array that holds sales amount.

- Line 6 declares `decSales` as an array of Decimals, using `intMAX_SUB-SCRIPT` as the upper subscript. The array has five elements, one for each day of sales.
- Line 9 declares `decTotalSales` as a Decimal, to hold the total sales amount.
- Line 10 declares `decAverageSales` as a Decimal, to hold the average sales amount.
- Line 11 declares `decHighestSales` as a Decimal, to hold the highest sales amount.
- Line 12 declares `decLowestSales` as a Decimal, to hold the lowest sales amount.

Line 15 calls the `GetSalesData` procedure, passing the `decSales` array as an argument. The `GetSalesData` procedure displays the input boxes prompting the user to enter sales amounts for each day. It stores the amounts entered by the user in the array that is passed as an argument.

Line 19 calls the `TotalArray` function, passing the `decSales` array as an argument. The function returns the total of the values in the array, and that value is assigned to the `decTotalSales` variable.

Line 20 calls the `AverageArray` function, passing the `decSales` array as an argument. The function returns the average of the values in the array, and that value is assigned to the `decAverageSales` variable.

Line 21 calls the `Highest` function, passing the `decSales` array as an argument. The function returns the highest value in the array, and that value is assigned to the `decHighestSales` variable.

Line 22 calls the `Lowest` function, passing the `decSales` array as an argument. The function returns the lowest value in the array, and that value is assigned to the `decLowhestSales` variable.

The statements in lines 25 through 28 display the sales data in the Label controls on the application's form.

Just below the `btnCalculate_Click` event handler is the `GetSalesData` procedure, shown here with line numbers for reference:

```
31    ' The GetSalesData procedure accepts a Decimal array argument.
32    ' It fills the array with sales amounts entered by the user.
33
34    Sub GetSalesData(ByRef decSales() As Decimal)
35        Dim intCount As Integer = 0 ' Loop counter, set to 0
36
37        ' Fill the decSales array with values entered by the user.
38        Do While intCount < decSales.Length
39            Try
40                ' Get the sales for a day.
41                decSales(intCount) =
42                    CDec(InputBox("Enter the sales for day " &
43                                  (intCount + 1).ToString()))
44                ' Increment intCount.
45                intCount += 1
46            Catch
47                ' Display an error message for invalid input.
48                MessageBox.Show("Enter a valid numeric value.")
49            End Try
50        Loop
51    End Sub
52
```

Line 35 declares intCount, which will be used as a loop counter, and to step through the decSales array parameter. Notice that intCount is initialized to 0.

The Do While loop that begins in line 38 uses the intCount variable to step through the decSales array parameter. Recall that intCount was initialized with 0. The loop executes as long as intCount is less than decSales.length.

Inside the loop a Try-Catch statement is used to catch any exceptions that might occur if the user enters a non-numeric value. The statement that appears in lines 41 through 43 performs the following actions:

- It displays an input box prompting the user to enter the sales for a specific day.
- It uses the CDec function to convert the user's input to a Decimal.
- It assigns the resulting value to the array element decSales(intCount).

If the user enters an invalid value, the program will branch to the Catch clause in line 46, display an error message in line 48, and then the loop starts over. If the user enters a valid value, however, line 45 adds 1 to the intCount variable. The loop then starts over. When the loop is finished, the decSales array parameter will contain the sales amounts entered by the user, and the procedures ends.

Next is the TotalArray function, shown here with line numbers for reference. The function accepts a Decimal array as an argument. It uses a loop to step through the array's elements, adding their values to an accumulator variable. The total of the array's elements is then returned.

```
53      ' The TotalArray function accepts a Decimal array as an
54      ' argument and returns the total of its values.
55
56      Function TotalArray(ByVal decValues() As Decimal) As Decimal
57          Dim decTotal As Decimal = 0 ' Accumulator
58          Dim intCount As Integer      ' Loop counter
59
60          ' Calculate the total of the array's elements.
61          For intCount = 0 To (decValues.Length - 1)
62              decTotal += decValues(intCount)
63          Next
64
65          ' Return the total.
66          Return decTotal
67      End Function
68
```

Next is the AverageArray function, shown here with line numbers for reference. The function accepts a Decimal array as an argument, and returns the average of the array's values.

```
69      ' The AverageArray function accepts a Decimal array as an
70      ' argument and returns the total of its values.
71
72      Function AverageArray(ByVal decValues() As Decimal) As Decimal
73          Return TotalArray(decValues) / decValues.Length
74      End Function
75
```

Next is the Highest function, shown here with line numbers for reference. The function accepts a Decimal array as an argument, and returns the highest value found in the array.

```
76    ' The Highest function accepts a Decimal array as an
77    ' argument and returns the highest value it contains.
78
79    Function Highest(ByVal decValues() As Decimal) As Decimal
80        Dim intCount As Integer    ' Loop counter
81        Dim decHighest As Decimal ' To hold the highest value
82
83        ' Get the first value in the array.
84        decHighest = decValues(0)
85
86        ' Search for the highest value.
87        For intCount = 1 To (decValues.Length - 1)
88            If decValues(intCount) > decHighest Then
89                decHighest = decValues(intCount)
90            End If
91        Next
92
93        ' Return the highest value.
94        Return decHighest
95    End Function
96
```

Next is the `Lowest` function, shown here with line numbers for reference. The function accepts a Decimal array as an argument, and returns the lowest value found in the array.

```
97    ' The Lowest function accepts a Decimal array as an
98    ' argument and returns the lowest value it contains.
99
100   Function Lowest(ByVal decValues() As Decimal) As Decimal
101       Dim intCount As Integer   ' Loop counter
102       Dim decLowest As Decimal ' To hold the lowest value
103
104       ' Get the first value in the array.
105       decLowest = decValues(0)
106
107       ' Search for the lowest value.
108       For intCount = 1 To (decValues.Length - 1)
109           If decValues(intCount) < decLowest Then
110               decLowest = decValues(intCount)
111           End If
112       Next
113
114       ' Return the lowest value.
115       Return decLowest
116   End Function
117
```

Next is the `btnExit_Click` event handler, shown here with line numbers for reference:

```
118   Private Sub btnExit_Click(...) Handles btnExit.Click
119     ' Close the form.
120     Me.Close()
121   End Sub
122 End Class
```

8.4 Multidimensional Arrays

CONCEPT: You may create arrays with more than two dimensions to hold complex sets of data.

Two-Dimensional Arrays

The arrays presented so far have had only one subscript. An array with one subscript is called a **one-dimensional array**, and is useful for storing and working with a single set of data. Sometimes, though, it is necessary to work with multiple sets of data. For example, in a grade-averaging program, a teacher might record all of one student's test scores in an array. If the teacher has 30 students, that means there must be 30 arrays to record the scores for the entire class. Instead of declaring 30 individual arrays, it would be better to declare a two-dimensional array.

A **two-dimensional array** is like an array of arrays. It can be used to hold multiple sets of values. Think of a two-dimensional array as having rows and columns of elements, as shown in Figure 8-23. This figure shows an array having three rows (numbered 0, 1, and 2) and four columns (numbered 0, 1, 2, and 3). There are a total of 12 elements in the array.

Figure 8-23 Rows and columns

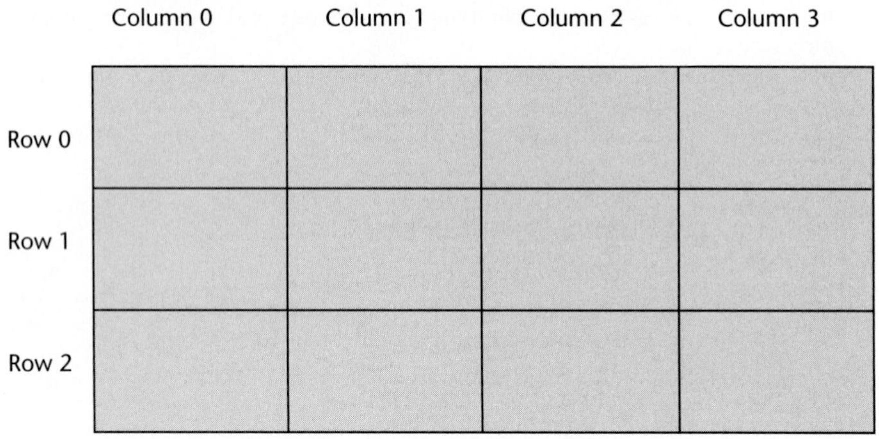

	Column 0	Column 1	Column 2	Column 3
Row 0				
Row 1				
Row 2				

To declare a two-dimensional array, two sets of upper subscripts are required, the first for the rows and the second for the columns. The general format of a two-dimensional array declaration is as follows:

```
Dim ArrayName (UpperRow,UpperColumn) As DataType
```

Let's take a closer look at the syntax.

- `ArrayName` is the name of the array.
- `UpperRow` is the value of the array's highest row subscript. This must be a positive integer.
- `UpperColumn` is the value of the array's highest column subscript. This must be a positive integer.
- `DataType` is a Visual Basic data type.

An example declaration of a two-dimensional array with three rows and four columns follows, and is shown in Figure 8-24. The highest row subscript is 2 and the highest column subscript is 3.

```
Dim dblScores (2, 3) As Double
```

Figure 8-24 Declaration of a two-dimensional array

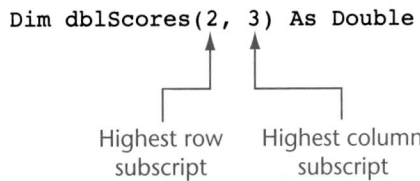

As with one-dimensional arrays, it is a good practice to use named constants to specify the upper subscripts. Here is an example:

```
Const intMAX_ROW As Integer = 2
Const intMAX_COL As Integer = 3
Dim dblScores(intMAX_ROW, intMAX_COL) As Double
```

When data in a two-dimensional array is processed, each element has two subscripts, the first for its row and the second for its column. Using the dblScores array as an example, the elements in row 0 are referenced as follows:

```
dblScores(0, 0)
dblScores(0, 1)
dblScores(0, 2)
dblScores(0, 3)
```

The elements in row 1 are referenced as follows:

```
dblScores(1, 0)
dblScores(1, 1)
dblScores(1, 2)
dblScores(1, 3)
```

The elements in row 2 are referenced as follows:

```
dblScores(2, 0)
dblScores(2, 1)
dblScores(2, 2)
dblScores(2, 3)
```

Figure 8-25 illustrates the array with the subscripts shown for each element.

Figure 8-25 Subscripts for each element of the dblScores array

	Column 0	Column 1	Column 2	Column 3
Row 0	dblScores(0, 0)	dblScores(0, 1)	dblScores(0, 2)	dblScores(0, 3)
Row 1	dblScores(1, 0)	dblScores(1, 1)	dblScores(1, 2)	dblScores(1, 3)
Row 2	dblScores(2, 0)	dblScores(2, 1)	dblScores(2, 2)	dblScores(2, 3)

To access one of the elements in a two-dimensional array, you must use two subscripts. For example, the following statement stores the number 95 in `dblScores(2, 1)`:

```
dblScores(2, 1) = 95
```

Programs often use nested loops to process two-dimensional arrays. For example, the following code prompts the user to enter a score, once for each element in the array:

```
For intRow = 0 To intMAX_ROW
    For intCol = 0 To intMAX_COL
        dblScores(intRow, intCol) = CDbl(InputBox("Enter a score."))
    Next
Next
```

And the following code displays all the elements in the `dblScores` array:

```
For intRow = 0 To intMAX_ROW
    For intCol = 0 To intMAX_COL
        lstOutput.Items.Add(dblScores(intRow, intCol).ToString())
    Next
Next
```

Implicit Sizing and Initialization of Two-Dimensional Arrays

As with a one-dimensional array, you may provide an initialization list for a two-dimensional array. Recall that when you provide an initialization list for an array, you cannot provide the upper subscript numbers. When initializing a two-dimensional array, you must provide the comma to indicate the number of dimensions. The following is an example of a two-dimensional array declaration with an initialization list:

```
Dim intNumbers(,) As Integer = { {1, 2, 3} ,
                                 {4, 5, 6} ,
                                 {7, 8, 9} }
```

Initialization values for each row are enclosed in their own set of braces. In this example, the initialization values for row 0 are {1, 2, 3}, the initialization values for row 1 are {4, 5, 6}, and the initialization values for row 2 are {7, 8, 9}. So, this statement declares an array with three rows and three columns.

The values are assigned to the `intNumbers` array in the following manner:

```
intNumbers(0, 0) is set to 1
intNumbers(0, 1) is set to 2
intNumbers(0, 2) is set to 3

intNumbers(1, 0) is set to 4
intNumbers(1, 1) is set to 5
intNumbers(1, 2) is set to 6

intNumbers(2, 0) is set to 7
intNumbers(2, 1) is set to 8
intNumbers(2, 2) is set to 9
```

Summing the Columns of a Two-Dimensional Array

You can use nested loops to sum the columns in a two-dimensional array. The following code sums each column of an array named `intValues`. The outer loop controls the column subscript and the inner loop controls the row subscript. The variable `intTotal` accumulates the sum of each column.

```
' Sum the columns.
For intCol = 0 To intMAX_COL
   ' Initialize the accumulator.
   intTotal = 0
   ' Sum all rows within this column.
   For intRow = 0 To intMAX_ROW
      intTotal += intValues(intRow, intCol)
   Next
   ' Display the sum of the column.
   MessageBox.Show("Sum of column " & intCol.ToString() &
                   " is " & intTotal.ToString())
Next
```

Tutorial 8-6:
Completing the *Seating Chart* application

In this tutorial, you will complete the *Seating Chart* application. When completed, the application will display an airplane seating chart and allow the user to select a seat number. The application will display the price of the selected seat.

Step 1: Open the *Seating Chart* project located in the student sample programs folder named *Chap8\Seating Chart*. Figure 8-26 shows the application's form, which has

Figure 8-26 The *Seating Chart* application's form

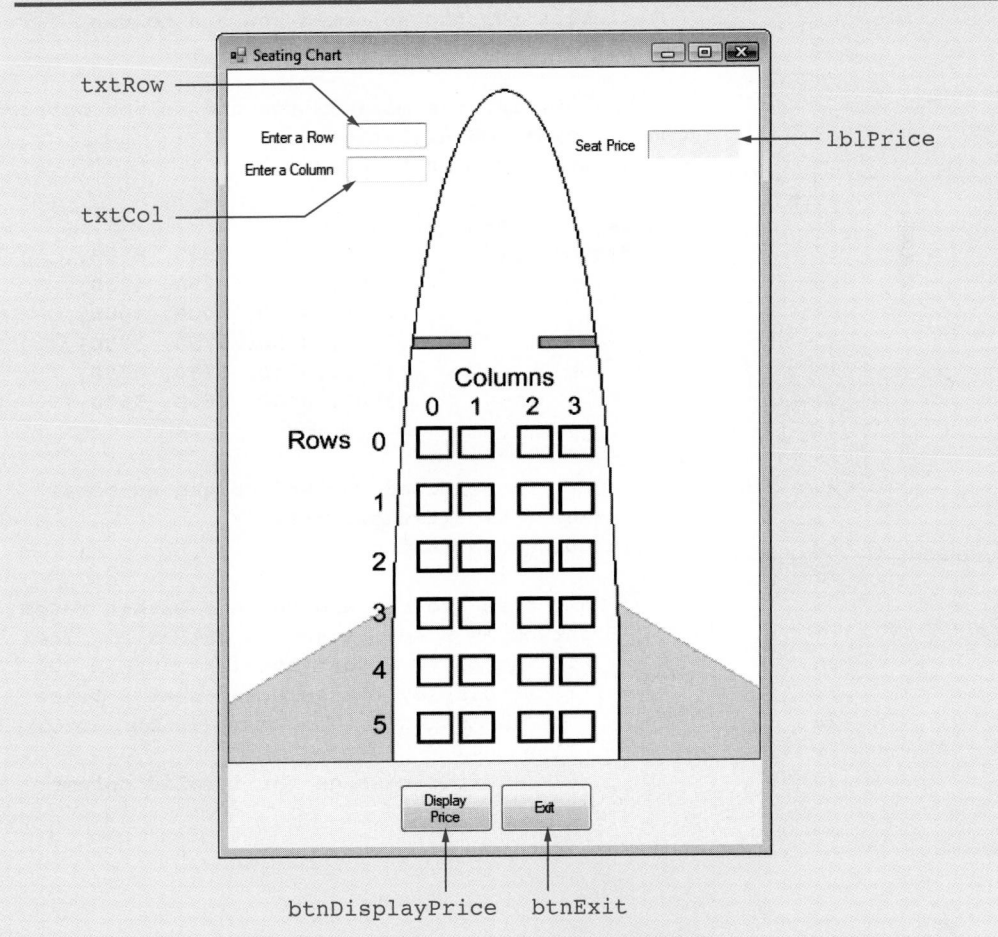

already been created for you. The seating chart image (which is displayed in a PictureBox control) shows the seats on the plane, arranged in rows and columns. When the completed application runs, the user will enter valid row and column numbers in the txtRow and txtCol text boxes, and then click the *Display Price* button. The price of the selected seat will be displayed in the lblPrice label.

The following table shows the seat prices:

	Columns			
	0	1	2	3
Row 0	$450	$450	$450	$450
Row 1	$425	$425	$425	$425
Row 2	$400	$400	$400	$400
Row 3	$375	$375	$375	$375
Row 4	$375	$375	$375	$375
Row 5	$350	$350	$350	$350

When you write the code for the application, you will create a two-dimensional array to hold these values.

Step 2: Complete the code for the form's event handlers as shown in the following. (Don't type the line numbers. They are shown for reference.)

```
1  Public Class Form1
2
3      Private Sub btnDisplayPrice_Click(...) Handles btnDisplayPrice.Click
4          ' Variables for the selected row and column
5          Dim intRow, intCol As Integer
6
7          ' Constants for the maximum row and column subscripts
8          Const intMAX_ROW As Integer = 5
9          Const intMAX_COL As Integer = 3
10
11         ' Array with seat prices
12         Dim decPrices(,) = {{450D, 450D, 450D, 450D},
13                             {425D, 425D, 425D, 425D},
14                             {400D, 400D, 400D, 400D},
15                             {375D, 375D, 375D, 375D},
16                             {375D, 375D, 375D, 375D},
17                             {350D, 350D, 350D, 350D}}
18
19         Try
20             ' Get the selected row and column numbers.
21             intRow = CInt(txtRow.Text)
22             intCol = CInt(txtCol.Text)
23
24             ' Make sure the row and col are within range.
25             If intRow >= 0 And intRow <= intMAX_ROW Then
26                 If intCol >= 0 And intCol <= intMAX_COL Then
27                     ' Display the selected seat's price.
28                     lblPrice.Text = decPrices(intRow, intCol).ToString("c")
29                 Else
30                     ' Error message for invalid column.
```

```
31                        MessageBox.Show("Column must be 0 through " &
32                                        intMAX_COL.ToString())
33                    End If
34                Else
35                    ' Error message for invalid row.
36                    MessageBox.Show("Row must be 0 through " &
37                                    intMAX_ROW.ToString())
38                End If
39            Catch
40                ' Error message for non-integer input.
41                MessageBox.Show("Row and column must be integers.")
42            End Try
43        End Sub
44
45        Private Sub btnExit_Click(...) Handles btnExit.Click
46            ' Close the form.
47            Me.Close()
48        End Sub
49    End Class
```

Let's take a closer look at the btnDisplayPrice_Click event handler. Line 5 declares the intRow and intCol variables. These will hold the row and column numbers that the user enters. Lines 8 and 9 declare the constants inMAX_ROW (set to 5) and intMAX_COL (set to 3). These values are the upper row and column numbers in the array that will hold the seat prices.

Lines 12 through 17 declare decPrices, a two-dimensional array of Decimals, initialized with the seat prices previously shown.

A Try-Catch statement begins in line 19, to deal with any non-numeric values entered by the user. In line 21 we get the row number entered by the user into the txtRow text box, convert it to an Integer, and store the result in the intRow variable. If an exception is thrown because of a non-numeric value, the program will jump to the Catch clause in line 39.

In line 22 we get the column number entered by the user into the txtCol text box, convert it to an Integer, and store the result in the intCol variable. If an exception is thrown because of a non-numeric value, the program will jump to the Catch clause in line 39.

Next we want to make sure the selected row and column numbers are within the correct range. The valid row numbers are 0 through 5, and the valid column numbers are 0 through 3. The If...Then statement in line 25 determines whether intRow is within the correct range. If it is not, the Else clause in line 34 displays an error message. If intRow is within the correct range, the If...Then statement in line 26 determines whether intCol is within the correct range. If it is not, the Else clause in line 29 displays an error message. Otherwise, the program continues with line 28. Line 28 uses intRow and intCol as subscripts, to retrieve the selected seat's price from the decPrices array, and then displays that value in the lblPrice label.

Step 3:   Save the project, and then run the application. Experiment by entering row and column numbers for different seats, and comparing the displayed price with the table previously shown. Figure 8-27 shows the application's form with row 2, column 3 selected. When you are finished, click the *Exit* button to end the application.

Figure 8-27 Row 2, column 3 selected

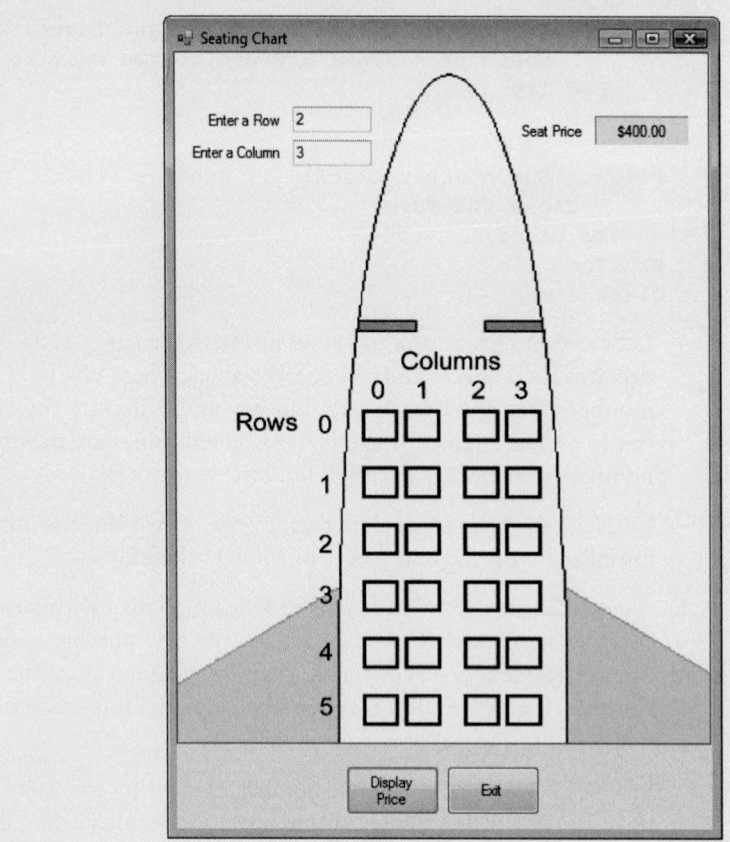

Three-Dimensional Arrays and Beyond

You can create arrays with up to 32 dimensions. The following is an example of a three-dimensional array declaration:

```
Dim decSeats(9, 11, 14) As Decimal
```

This array can be thought of as 10 sets of 12 rows, with each row containing 15 columns. This array might be used to store the prices of seats in an auditorium, in which there are 15 seats in a row, 12 rows in a section, and 10 sections in the room.

Figure 8-28 represents a three-dimensional array as pages of two-dimensional arrays.

Arrays with more than three dimensions are difficult to visualize but can be useful in some programming applications. For example, in a factory warehouse where cases of widgets are stacked on pallets, an array of four dimensions can store a part number for each widget. The four subscripts of each element can represent the pallet number, case number, row number, and column number of each widget. Similarly, an array with five dimensions could be used if there were multiple warehouses.

Figure 8-28 A three-dimensional array

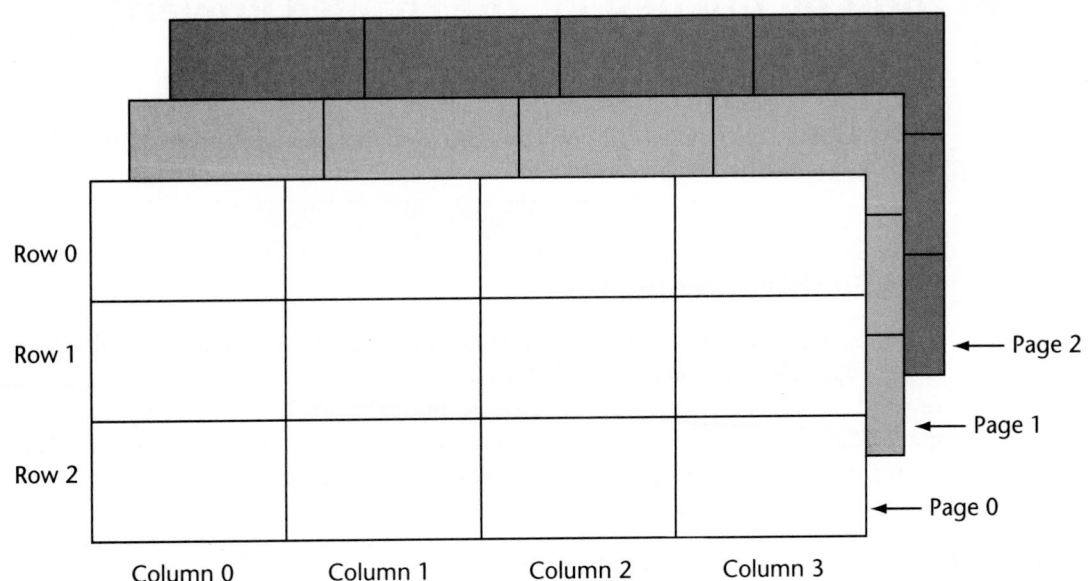

Row 0

Row 1 ← Page 2

Row 2 ← Page 1

← Page 0

Column 0   Column 1   Column 2   Column 3

Checkpoint

8.14 Declare a two-dimensional array of integers named intGrades. It should have 30 rows and 10 columns.

8.15 How many elements are in the following array?

```
Dim decSales(5, 3) As Decimal
```

8.16 Write a statement that assigns 56893.12 to the first column of the first row of the decSales array declared in Checkpoint 8.15.

8.17 Write a statement that displays in a message box the contents of the last column of the last row of the array decSales declared in Checkpoint 8.15.

8.18 Declare a two-dimensional Integer array named intSettings large enough to hold the following table of numbers:

```
12    24    32    21    42
14    67    87    65    90
19     1    24    12     8
```

8.19 How many rows and columns does the array declared in the following statement have?

```
Dim intMatrix(,) As Integer = { { 2, 4, 7, 0, 3} ,
   { 6, 5, 12, 8, 6} , { 9, 0, 14, 6, 0} ,
   { 16, 7, 9, 13, 10} }
```

8.20 A movie rental store keeps DVDs on 50 racks with 10 shelves each. Each shelf holds 25 DVDs. Declare a three-dimensional array of strings large enough to represent the store's storage system. Each element of the array holds a movie title.

8.5 Focus on GUI Design: The Enabled Property and the Timer Control

CONCEPT: You can disable controls by setting their Enabled property to *False*. The Timer control allows your application to execute a procedure at regular time intervals.

The Enabled Property

Most controls have a Boolean property named Enabled. When a control's **Enabled property** is set to *False*, it is considered disabled, which means it cannot receive the focus and cannot respond to events generated by the user. Additionally, many controls appear dimmed, or grayed out, when their Enabled property is set to *False*. For example, Figure 8-29 shows a form with three buttons that have their Enabled property set to *False*.

Figure 8-29 Controls with Enabled property set to *False*

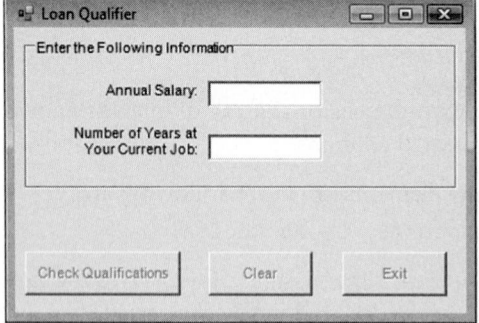

By default, a control's Enabled property is set to *True*. If you change a control's Enabled property to *False* at design time, the control is initially disabled when the application runs.

You can also change the Enabled property's value with code at runtime. For example, assume an application has a radio button named `radBlue`. The following statement disables the control:

```
radBlue.Enabled = False
```

Sometimes you do not want the user to access controls. For example, consider an application that calculates the price of two different models of a new car. One model comes only in red, yellow, and black, while the other model comes only in white, green, and orange. As soon as the user selects a model, the application can disable colors not available for that model.

The Timer Control

The **Timer control** allows an application to automatically execute code at regular time intervals. It is useful when you want an application to perform an operation at certain times or after an amount of time has passed. For example, a Timer control can perform simple animation by moving a graphic image across the screen, or it can cause a form to be hidden after a certain amount of time.

Double-click the Timer icon in the toolbox to place a Timer control on a form. (The Timer control is in the *Components* section of the toolbox.) Because the Timer control is invisible at runtime, it appears in the component tray at design time. The prefix that we will use for a Timer control's name is `tmr`.

Timer Events

When you place a Timer control on a form, it responds to Tick events as the application is running. A Tick event is generated at regular time intervals. If the control has a Tick event handler, it is executed each time a Tick event occurs. Therefore, the code that you write in the Tick event handler executes at regular intervals.

To create a Tick event handler code template, double-click a Timer control that has been placed in the form's component tray.

Timer Control Properties

The Timer control has two important properties: Enabled and Interval. When the Enabled property is set to *True*, the Timer control responds to Tick events. When the Enabled property is set to *False*, the Timer control does not respond to Tick events (code in the control's Tick event handler does not execute).

The **Interval property** can be set to a value of 1 or greater. The value stored in the Interval property is the number of milliseconds that elapse between timer events. A millisecond is a thousandth of a second, so setting the Interval property to 1000 causes a timer event to occur every second.

In Tutorial 8-7, you examine an application that demonstrates a Timer control.

Tutorial 8-7:
The *Timer Demo*

Step 1: Open the *Timer Demo* project from the sample student programs folder named *Chap8\Timer Demo*. The application's form is shown in Figure 8-30. Notice that the Timer control appears as a stopwatch in the component tray.

Figure 8-30 *Timer Demo* form

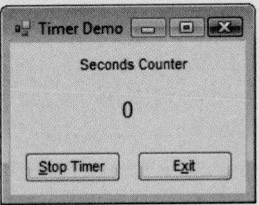

Step 2: Run the application. The form shown in Figure 8-31 appears.

Figure 8-31 *Timer Demo* application running

Step 3: The number appearing under the *Seconds Counter* label is initially set to 0, but it increments every second. After a few seconds, click the *Stop Timer* button to halt the timer.

Step 4: When you click the *Stop Timer* button, the button's text changes to *Start Timer*. Click the button again to start the timer.

Step 5: After a few seconds, click the *Exit* button to end the application.

Step 6: With the *Designer* window open, select the Timer control.

Step 7: With the Timer control selected, look at the *Properties* window. The name of the control is tmrSeconds. Its Enabled property is initially set to *True*, and its Interval property is set to *1000*.

Step 8: Open the *Code* window and notice that a class-level variable named intSeconds is declared.

Step 9: Look at the tmrSeconds_Tick event handler. The code is as follows:

```
Private Sub tmrSeconds_Tick(...) Handles tmrSeconds.Tick
    ' Update the seconds display by one second.
    intSeconds += 1
    lblCounter.Text = intSeconds.ToString()
End Sub
```

Each time the tmrSeconds_Tick event handler executes, it adds 1 to intSeconds and then copies its value to the lblCounter label. Because the Timer control's Interval property is set to *1000*, this event handler executes every second (unless the Timer control's Enabled property equals *False*).

Step 10: The button that stops and starts the timer is named btnToggleTimer. Look at the btnToggleTimer_Click event handler. The code is as follows:

```
Private Sub btnToggleTimer_Click(...) Handles btnToggleTimer.Click
  ' Toggle the timer.
  If tmrSeconds.Enabled = True Then
    tmrSeconds.Enabled = False
    btnToggleTimer.Text = "&Start Timer"
  Else
    tmrSeconds.Enabled = True
    btnToggleTimer.Text = "&Stop Timer"
  End If
End Sub
```

If tmrSeconds.Enabled equals *True*, the code sets it to *False* and changes the button's text to &*Start Timer*. Otherwise, it sets the property to *True* and changes the button's text to &*Stop Timer*.

In Tutorial 8-8 you will use a Timer control to create a game application.

Tutorial 8-8:
Creating the *Catch Me* game

In this tutorial you will create a game application that displays a button. Every second, the button will move to a new, random location on the application's form. The user wins the game when he or she clicks the button.

There are a few button and form properties that will prove useful:

- The current form is identified by the keyword Me.
- The width and height, in pixels, of a form or other control is controlled by its Width and Height properties.
- The position of a button within a form is controlled by its Top and Left properties. Vertical pixel coordinates start at 0 at the top of a form, and grow in a downward direction, as shown in Figure 8-32.

Figure 8-32 Pixel coordinates in a Visual Basic form

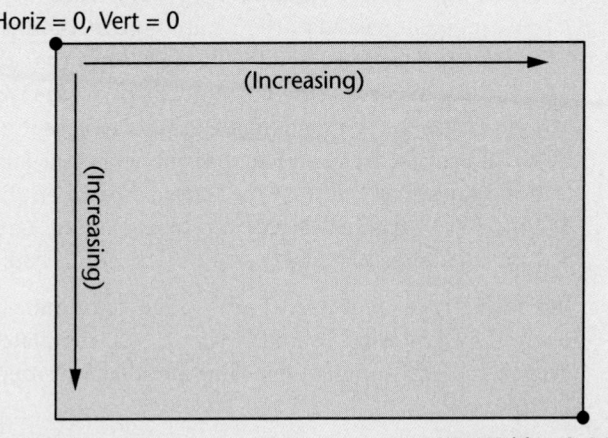

The *Catch Me* game application will have a Timer control with its Interval property set to 1000. As a result, it will generate a Tick event once every second. The Timer control's Tick event handler will generate two random numbers, and assign these random numbers to the Button control's Top and Left properties. As a result, the Button control will move to a random location on the form. The Button control's Click event handler will disable the Timer control (to stop the button from moving around on the form) and display a message indicating that the user won the game.

Step 1: Create a new Windows Forms Application project named *Catch Me*. Set up the application's form as shown in Figure 8-33. Name the Button control btnCatchMe, and center it vertically and horizontally in the form.

Figure 8-33 The Catch Me application's form

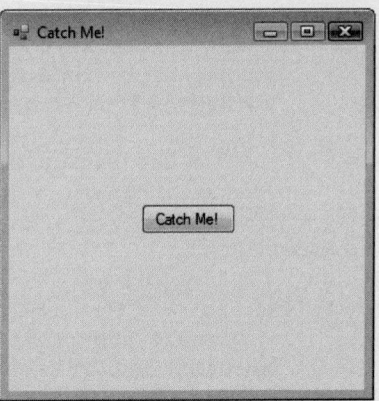

Step 2: Create a Timer control and name it tmrGameTimer. Set its Enabled property to *True* and its Interval property to 1000.

Step 3: The complete code for the application is shown at the end of this tutorial, with line numbers shown for reference. Double-click the `tmrGameTimer` control that you created in Step 2. This opens the *Code* window and creates a code template for the `tmrGameTimer_Tick` event handler. Complete the event handler by entering the code shown in lines 4 through 16.

Let's take a closer look at the code:

- Line 5 creates a `Random` object that we will use to generate random numbers.
- Line 8 declares two variables: `intNewLeft` and `intNewTop`. These variables will hold the random numbers for the button's new location.
- Line 11 generates a random integer and assigns it to `intNewLeft`. Notice that the argument passed to the `rand.Next` method is the expression `Me.Width - btnCatchMe.Width`. This will make sure that the random number is not a value that will place the Button control off the right edge of the form.
- Line 12 generates a random integer and assigns it to `intNewTop`. The expression `Me.Height - btnCatchMe.Height` will make sure that the random number is not a value that will place the Button control off the bottom edge of the form.
- Line 15 assigns `intNewLeft` to `btnCatchMe.Left`.
- Line 16 assigns `intNewTop` to `btnCatchMe.Top`.

Step 4: In the *Designer* window, double-click the `btnCatchMe` Button control. This opens the *Code* window and creates a code template for the `btnCatchMe_Click` event handler. Complete the event handler by entering the code shown in lines 20 through 24.

Let's take a closer look at the code:

- Line 21 sets the Timer control's Enabled property to *False*. This stops the Timer from generating Tick events.
- Line 24 displays a message box letting the user know he or she won.

Step 5: Save the project and run the application. After you've gotten good at the game, you can make it more challenging by changing the Timer control's Interval property to a lower value. This will decrease the amount of time between button moves.

```
 1 Public Class Form1
 2
 3  Private Sub tmrGameTimer_Tick(...) Handles tmrGameTimer.Tick
 4        ' Create a Random object.
 5        Dim rand As New Random
 6
 7        ' Variables to hold XY coordinates
 8        Dim intNewLeft, intNewTop As Integer
 9
10        ' Get random XY coordinates.
11        intNewLeft = rand.Next(Me.Width - btnCatchMe.Width)
12        intNewTop = rand.Next(Me.Height - btnCatchMe.Height)
13
14        ' Move the button to the new location.
15        btnCatchMe.Left = intNewLeft
16        btnCatchMe.Top = intNewTop
17  End Sub
18
19  Private Sub btnCatchMe_Click(...) Handles btnCatchMe.Click
20        ' Disable the timer.
21        tmrGameTimer.Enabled = False
22
23        ' Display a message.
24        MessageBox.Show("You win!")
25  End Sub
26 End Class
```

8.6 Focus on GUI Design: Anchoring and Docking Controls

CONCEPT: Controls have two properties, Anchor and Dock, which allow you to control the control's position on the form when the form is resized at runtime.

The Anchor Property

By default, when a user resizes a form at runtime, the positions of controls on the form do not change with respect to the top and left edges of the form. For example, in Figure 8-34, the image on the left shows the form before the user resizes it and the image on the right shows the form after the user resizes it.

Figure 8-34 A form before and after the user resizes it

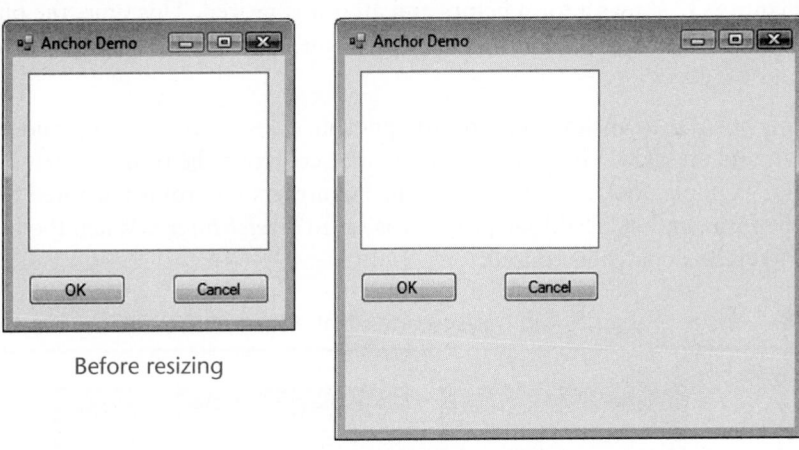

Before resizing

After resizing

When the user resizes the form, the positions of the list box and buttons do not change. Controls have an **Anchor property,** which allows you to anchor the control to one or more edges of a form. When a control is anchored to a form's edge, the distance between the control's edge and the form's edge remains constant when the form is resized at runtime.

When you click the Anchor property in the *Properties* window, the pop-up window shown in Figure 8-35 appears. Notice that the top and left bars are selected, indicating that the

Figure 8-35 Anchor property selected

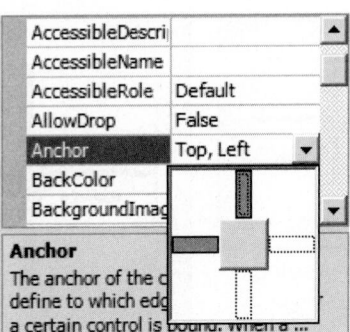

control is anchored to the top and left edges of the form. This is the Anchor property's default setting. To change the Anchor property's setting, select the bars that correspond to the edges of the form you wish to anchor the control to. For example, Figure 8-36 shows how the Anchor property appears when the control is anchored to the bottom and right edges.

Figure 8-36 Anchor property set to the bottom and right edges

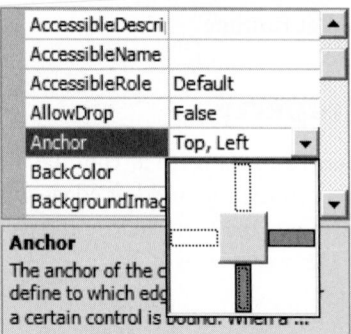

Figure 8-37 shows a form before and after it is resized. This time, the button controls are anchored to the bottom and right edges of the form and the list box is anchored to the top and left edges.

It is possible to anchor a control to opposing sides, such as the top and the bottom, or the left and the right. This approach causes the control to be resized when the form is resized. For example, look at Figure 8-38. The PictureBox control is anchored to all four edges of the form, and its SizeMode property is set to *StretchImage*. When the form is resized, the PictureBox control is resized.

Figure 8-37 Buttons anchored to the bottom and right edges of the form

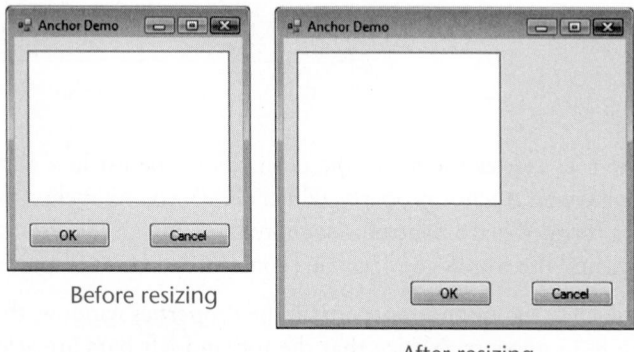

Figure 8-38 PictureBox control anchored to all four edges of the form

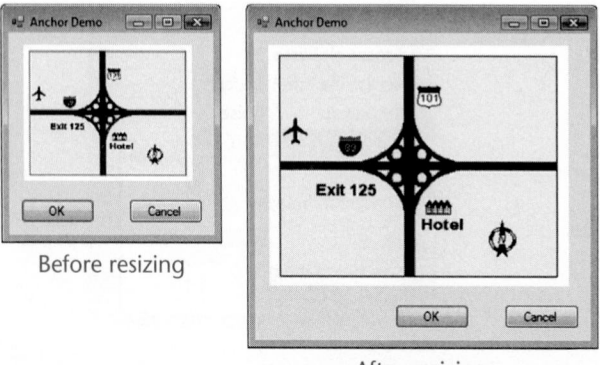

The Dock Property

When a control is docked, it is positioned directly against one of the edges of a form. Additionally, the length or width of a docked control is changed to match the length or width of the form's edge. For example, the form in Figure 8-39 has four docked buttons. A button is docked to each of the form's edges.

Figure 8-39 Form with docked buttons

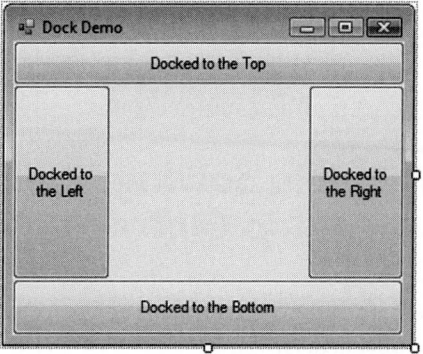

Buttons are automatically sized to fill up the edge to which they are docked. Use the **Dock property** to dock a control against a form's edge. In the *Properties* window, the pop-up window shown in Figure 8-40 appears. The figure illustrates how each button in the pop-up window affects the control. The square button in the center causes the control to fill the entire form.

Figure 8-40 Dock property selected

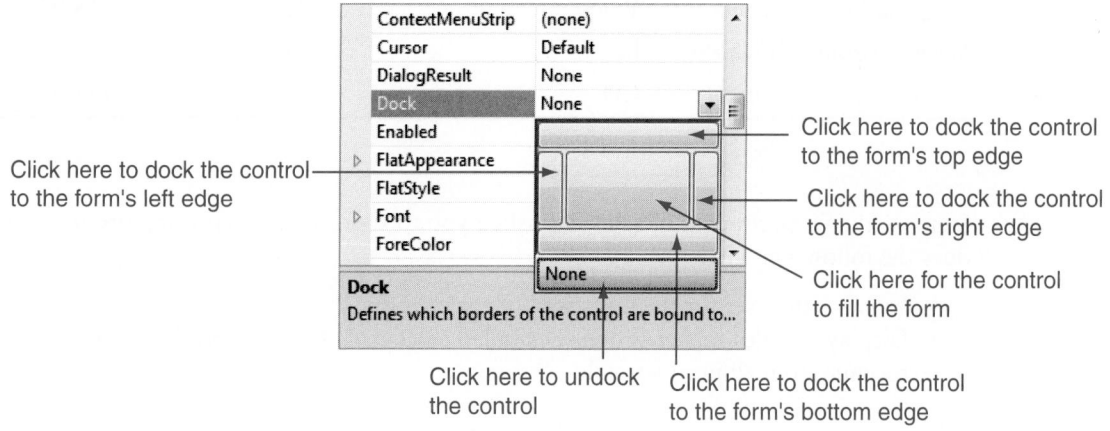

 **Checkpoint**

8.21 Suppose a form has check box controls named `chkFreePizza` and `chkFreeCola`, and a radio button control named `radLifeTimeMember`. Write code that enables the check boxes if the radio button is selected.

8.22 If you want a Timer control to execute its Tick event handler every half second, what value do you store in its Interval property?

8.23 What is the purpose of the Anchor property?

8.24 What is the purpose of the Dock property?

 **8.7**

Focus on Problem Solving: Building the *Demetris Leadership Center* Application

CONCEPT: In this section you build an application that uses data stored in parallel arrays.

The Demetris Leadership Center (DLC) publishes the books, videos, and CDs listed in Table 8-1.

Table 8-1 Demetris Leadership Center products

Product Title	Product Description	Product Number	Unit Price
Six Steps to Leadership	Book	914	$12.95
Six Steps to Leadership	CD	915	$14.95
The Road to Excellence	Video	916	$18.95
Seven Lessons of Quality	Book	917	$16.95
Seven Lessons of Quality	CD	918	$21.95

Suppose the vice president of sales has asked you to write a sales reporting program that does the following:

- Prompts the user for the units sold of each product
- Displays a sales report showing detailed sales data for each product and the total revenue from all products sold

The Application's Form

Figure 8-41 shows a sketch of the application's form with its controls labeled.

Table 8-2 lists each of the form's controls (excluding the menu controls) along with relevant property settings.

Figure 8-41 Sketch of the application's form

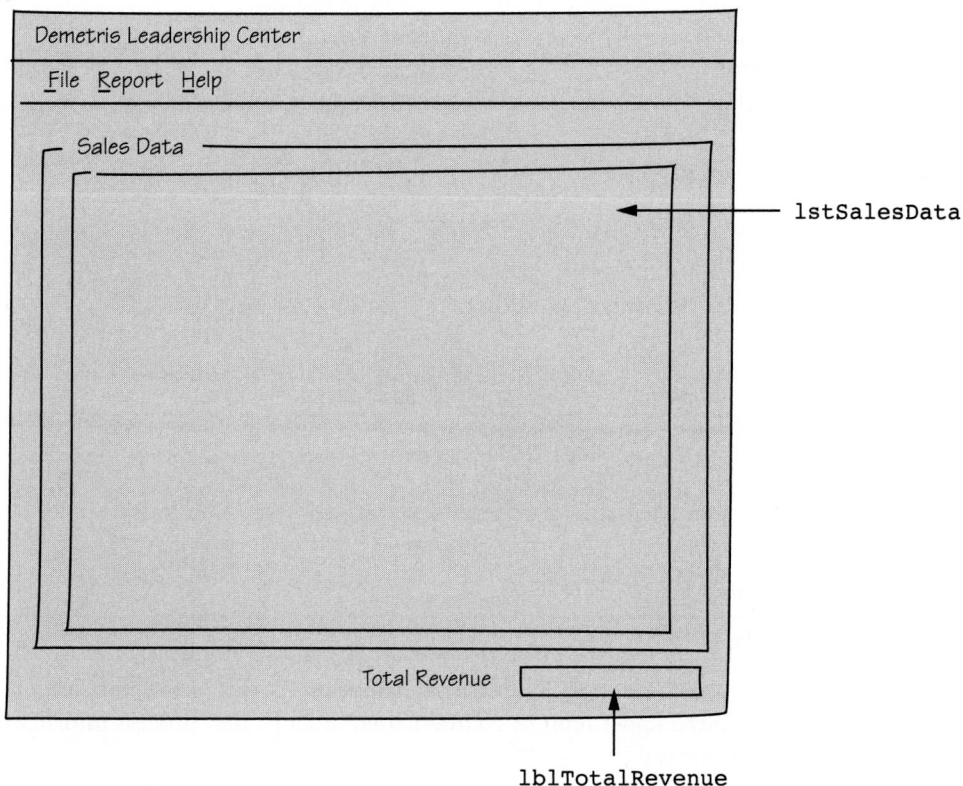

Table 8-2 Controls and property settings

Control Type	Control Name	Property	Property Value
Form	Form1 (default)	Text:	*Demetris Leadership Center*
GroupBox	(Default)	Text:	*Sales Data*
Label	(Default)	Text:	*Total Revenue*
Label	lblTotalRevenue	Text: AutoSize BorderStyle:	*False* *Fixed3D*
ListBox	lstSalesData	AutoSize	*False*
MenuStrip	(Default)		See Table 8-3 for details

Figure 8-42 shows a sketch of the menu system on the application's form.

Figure 8-42 Menu system

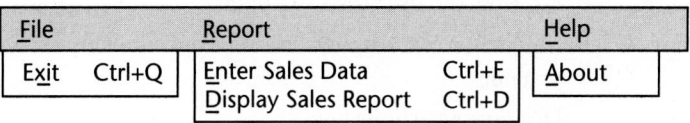

Table 8-3 lists the menu item object names, text, and shortcut keys.

Table 8-3 Menu item names, text properties, and shortcut keys

Menu Item Name	Text	Shortcut Key
mnuFile	&File	
mnuFileExit	E&xit	Ctrl + Q
mnuReport	&Report	
mnuReportData	&Enter Sales Data	Ctrl + E
mnuReportDisplay	&Display Sales Report	Ctrl + D
mnuHelp	&Help	
mnuHelpAbout	&About	

Table 8-4 describes the form's class-level declarations.

Table 8-4 Class-level declarations

Name	Description
IntMAX_SUBSCRIPT	A constant, set to 8, holding the upper subscript of the class-level arrays, and the upper limit of counters used in loops that process information in the arrays
strProdNames	An array of strings; this array holds the names of the DLC products
strDesc	An array of strings; this array holds the descriptions of the DLC products
intProdNums	An array of integers; this array holds the product numbers of the DLC products
decPrices	An array of Decimal variables; this array holds the prices of the DLC products
intUnitsSold	An array of integers; this array holds the number of units sold for each of the DLC products

The five arrays are parallel arrays, meaning that the same subscript can be used to access data relating to the same item. Table 8-5 lists and describes the methods in the form file.

Table 8-5 Methods

Method	Description
InitArrays	Procedure; assigns the names, descriptions, product numbers, and unit prices of the DLC products to the class-level arrays
mnuFileExit_Click	Ends the application
mnuReportData_Click	Prompts the user for sales data
mnuReportDisplay_Click	Calculates and displays the revenue for each product and the total revenue
mnuHelpAbout_Click	Displays an *About* box
Form1_Load	Calls the InitArrays procedure

In Tutorial 8-9, you build the *Demetris Leadership Center Sales Reporting* application.

Tutorial 8-9:
Building the *Demetris Leadership Center Sales Reporting* application

Step 1: Create a new Windows Forms Application project named *Demetris Sales*.

Step 2: Set up the form as shown in Figure 8-43.

Figure 8-43 The application's main form

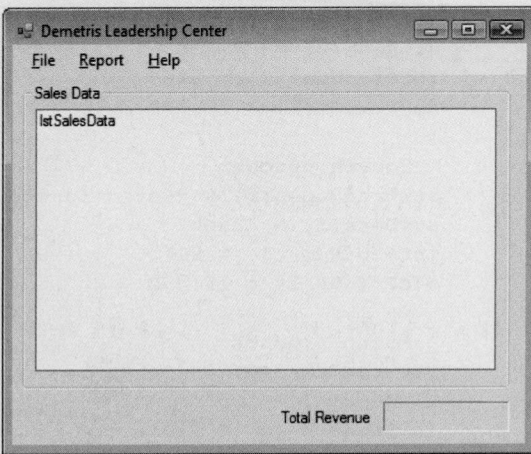

Refer to Table 8-2 for the control names and their property settings, and to Figure 8-41 for the locations of the controls in the control arrays. Refer to Figure 8-42 for the menu layout and to Table 8-3 for the menu item properties. Be sure to select frmMain as the startup object.

Step 3: The following shows the code for the application. Use this as a reference as you complete the application. (Don't type the line numbers. They are shown for reference.)

```
1 Public Class Form1
2      ' This application displays a sales report for the Demetris
3      ' Leadership Center.
4
5      ' Class-level declarations
6      Const intMAX_SUBSCRIPT As Integer = 4        ' Upper subscript
7      Dim strProdNames(intMAX_SUBSCRIPT) As String    ' Product names
8      Dim strDesc(intMAX_SUBSCRIPT) As String         ' Descriptions
9      Dim intProdNums(intMAX_SUBSCRIPT) As Integer    ' Product numbers
10     Dim decPrices(intMAX_SUBSCRIPT) As Decimal      ' Unit prices
11     Dim intUnitsSold(intMAX_SUBSCRIPT) As Integer   ' Units sold
12
13     Private Sub Form1_Load(...) Handles MyBase.Load
14         ' Initialize the arrays with product data.
15         InitArrays()
16     End Sub
17
```

```
18      Private Sub InitArrays()
19          ' Initialize the arrays.
20          ' First product
21          strProdNames(0) = "Six Steps to Leadership"
22          strDesc(0) = "Book"
23          intProdNums(0) = 914
24          decPrices(0) = 12.95D
25
26          ' Second product
27          strProdNames(1) = "Six Steps to Leadership"
28          strDesc(1) = "CD"
29          intProdNums(1) = 915
30          decPrices(1) = 14.95D
31
32          ' Third product
33          strProdNames(2) = "The Road to Excellence"
34          strDesc(2) = "Video"
35          intProdNums(2) = 916
36          decPrices(2) = 18.95D
37
38          ' Fourth product
39          strProdNames(3) = "Seven Lessons of Quality"
40          strDesc(3) = "Book"
41          intProdNums(3) = 917
42          decPrices(3) = 16.95D
43
44          ' Fifth product
45          strProdNames(4) = "Seven Lessons of Quality"
46          strDesc(4) = "CD"
47          intProdNums(4) = 918
48          decPrices(4) = 21.95D
49      End Sub
50
51      Private Sub mnuFileExit_Click(...) Handles mnuFileExit.Click
52          ' Close the form.
53          Me.Close()
54      End Sub
55
56      Private Sub mnuReportData_Click(...) Handles mnuReportData.Click
57          Dim intCount As Integer = 0 ' Loop counter
58
59          Do While intCount <= intMAX_SUBSCRIPT
60              Try
61                  ' Get the units sold for a product.
62                  intUnitsSold(intCount) = CInt(
63                      InputBox("Enter units sold of product number " &
64                              intProdNums(intCount)))
65
66                  ' Increment intCount.
67                  intCount += 1
68              Catch
69                  ' Error message for invalid input.
70                  MessageBox.Show("Enter a valid integer.")
71              End Try
72          Loop
73      End Sub
74
```

```
 75        Private Sub mnuReportDisplay_Click(...) Handles mnuReportDisplay.Click
 76             ' Calculates and displays the revenue for each
 77             ' product and the total revenue.
 78             Dim intCount As Integer
 79             Dim decRevenue As Decimal
 80             Dim decTotalRevenue As Decimal
 81
 82             ' Display the sales report header.
 83             lstSalesData.Items.Add("SALES REPORT")
 84             lstSalesData.Items.Add("-------------------")
 85
 86             ' Display sales data for each product.
 87             For intCount = 0 To intMAX_SUBSCRIPT
 88
 89                 ' Calculate product revenue.
 90                 decRevenue = intUnitsSold(intCount) * decPrices(intCount)
 91
 92                 ' Display the product data.
 93                 lstSalesData.Items.Add("Product Number: " &
 94                                     intProdNums(intCount))
 95                 lstSalesData.Items.Add("Name: " &
 96                                     strProdNames(intCount))
 97                 lstSalesData.Items.Add("Description: " &
 98                                     strDesc(intCount))
 99                 lstSalesData.Items.Add("Unit Price: " &
100                                     decPrices(intCount).ToString("c"))
101                 lstSalesData.Items.Add("Units Sold: " &
102                                     intUnitsSold(intCount).ToString())
103                 lstSalesData.Items.Add("Product Revenue: " &
104                                     decRevenue.ToString("c"))
105                 lstSalesData.Items.Add("")
106
107                 ' Accumulate revenue.
108                 decTotalRevenue = decTotalRevenue + decRevenue
109             Next
110
111             ' Display total revenue.
112             lblTotalRevenue.Text = decTotalRevenue.ToString("c")
113        End Sub
114
115        Private Sub mnuHelpAbout_Click(...) Handles mnuHelpAbout.Click
116             ' Display an About box.
117             MessageBox.Show("Displays a sales report for DLC.", "About")
118        End Sub
119 End Class
```

Step 4: Save the project.

Step 5: Run the application. On the application's form, click the *Report* menu, and then click *Enter Sales Data*. You will be prompted with input boxes to enter the units sold for each of the DLC products. Enter the following units' sold values:

Product number 914: **140**
Product number 915: **85**
Product number 916: **129**
Product number 917: **67**
Product number 918: **94**

Step 6: Click the *Report* menu, and then click *Display Sales Report.* Your form should now appear similar to the one shown in Figure 8-44. Scroll through the sales data displayed in the list box.

Figure 8-44 Sales report displayed

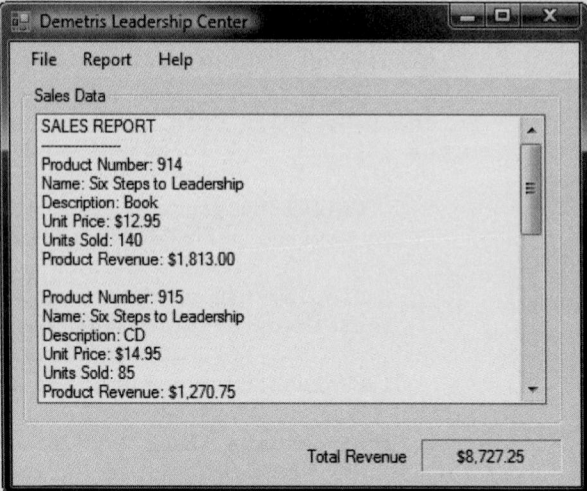

Step 7: Exit the application.

Summary

8.1 Arrays

- An array is a like group of variables with a single name. The variables within an array are called elements and are of the same data type.
- Individual variables in an array are accessed through a subscript, which is a number that pinpoints a specific element within an array. Subscript numbering begins at zero. When you declare an array you can specify the upper subscript.
- You can implicitly size an array by omitting the upper subscript in the declaration statement and providing an initialization list. An array initialization list is a set of numbers enclosed in a set of braces, with the numbers separated by commas.
- Array elements are processed in the same way as regular variables, but when working with array elements, you must provide a subscript.
- You can store a subscript number in a variable and then use the variable as a subscript. You can use a loop to cycle through an entire array, performing the same operation on each element.
- Visual Basic performs array bounds checking at runtime; it does not allow a statement to use a subscript outside the range of subscripts for an array.
- The `For Each` statement is a special loop designed specifically to access values from arrays and array-like structures.

8.2 More about Array Processing

- Arrays have a Length property that holds the number of elements in the array.
- To sum the numbers stored in an array, use a loop with an accumulator variable that adds all the elements. To average the numbers stored in an array, first sum all the values, and then divide the sum by the number of elements.
- To copy the values in one array to another, use a loop to copy the individual elements.
- You can create a parallel relationship between list boxes, combo boxes, and arrays.
- The sequential search algorithm uses a loop to examine the elements in an array. It compares each element with the value being searched for, and stops when the value is found or the end of the array is encountered. If the value being searched for is not in the array, the algorithm will unsuccessfully search to the end of the array.
- The `Array.Sort` method sorts the elements of an array in ascending order, which means the lowest value is stored in the first element and the highest value is stored in the last element.
- You can change the number of elements in an array at runtime with the `ReDim` statement.

8.3 Procedures and Functions That Work with Arrays

- Procedures and functions may be written to accept arrays as arguments. Functions may also be written to return arrays.

8.4 Multidimensional Arrays

- A single-dimensional array has one subscript, and is useful for storing and working with a single set of data. Two-dimensional arrays can hold multiple sets of values. Think of a two-dimensional array as having rows and columns of elements.
- To declare a two-dimensional array, two sets of upper subscripts are required: the first one for the rows and the second one for the columns. A two-dimensional array may be implicitly sized by omitting the upper subscripts from the declaration and providing an initialization list.

- When data in a two-dimensional array is processed, each element has two subscripts: one for its row and one for its column. Nested loops can be used to sum the rows or columns of a two-dimensional numeric array.
- The `For Each` loop can be used to sum all the values in a numeric two-dimensional array.
- Visual Basic allows arrays of up to 32 dimensions.

8.5 Focus on GUI Design: The Enabled Property and the Timer Control

- When a control's Enabled property is set to *False*, it is considered disabled, which means it cannot receive the focus, cannot respond to events generated by the user, and appears dimmed or grayed out on the form.
- The Timer control is invisible at runtime. At design time it appears in the component tray. The standard prefix for a Timer control's name is `tmr`.
- The Timer control responds to Tick events. When a Tick event occurs, the Tick event handler is executed.
- When the Timer control's Enabled property is set to *True*, the Timer control responds to Tick events. When the Enabled property is set to *False*, the Timer control does not respond to Tick events and the code in the Tick event handler does not execute.
- The Timer control's Interval property can be set to a positive nonzero value that is the number of milliseconds to elapse between Tick events.

8.6 Focus on GUI Design: Anchoring and Docking Controls

- When a control is anchored to a form's edge, the distance between the control's edge and the form's edge remains constant, even when the user resizes the form.
- When a control is docked, it is positioned directly against one of the edges of a form. Additionally, the length or width of a docked control is changed to match the length or width of the form's edge.

8.7 Focus on Problem Solving: Building the *Demetris Leadership Center* Application

- This section outlines the process of building the *Demetris Leadership Center* application, which processes data used in parallel arrays.

Key Terms

Anchor property
array
array bounds checking
ascending order
Dock property
elements
Enabled property
For Each loop

index
Interval property
one-dimensional array
parallel arrays
sequential search
subscript
Timer control
two-dimensional array

Review Questions and Exercises

Fill-in-the-Blank

1. You access the individual variables in an array through a(n) _____, which is a number that indentifies a specific element within an array.

2. The _____ loop is a special loop designed specifically to access values from arrays and array-like structures.

3. _____ arrays are two or more arrays that hold related data. The related elements in each array are accessed with a common subscript.

4. The _____ algorithm uses a loop to examine the elements in an array sequentially, starting with the first one.

5. The _____ statement resizes an array at runtime.

6. The _____ property holds the number of elements in an array.

7. Declaring a two-dimensional array requires two sets of _____.

8. When a control's _____ property is set to *False*, it is considered disabled.

9. The _____ property causes the distance between a control's edge and the form's edge to remain constant, even when the form is resized.

10. The _____ property causes a control to be positioned directly against one of the form's edges.

11. The _____ control allows an application to automatically execute code at regularly timed intervals.

12. The Timer control's _____ property specifies the number of milliseconds between timer events.

Multiple Choice

1. Which of the following describes the storage locations within an array?
   a. Boxes
   b. Elements
   c. Subvariables
   d. Intersections

2. Which of the following identifies a specific element within an array?
   a. Element specifier
   b. Determinator
   c. Locator
   d. Subscript

3. Which of the following is the lower subscript of an array?
   a. 1
   b. { }
   c. 0
   d. −1

4. When does array bounds checking occur?
   a. Runtime
   b. Design time
   c. Break time
   d. All of the above

5. Which of the following properties determines the number of elements in an array?

   a. Size

   b. Elements

   c. Length

   d. NumberElements

6. To access related data in a set of parallel arrays, how should you access the elements in the arrays?

   a. Using the same array name

   b. Using the same subscript

   c. Using the index −1

   d. Using the `GetParallelData` function

7. Which statement resizes the `intNumbers` array to 20 elements?

   a. `ReDim intNumbers(19)`

   b. `ReDim intNumbers(20)`

   c. `Resize intNumbers() To 19`

   d. `Resize intNumbers() To 20`

8. Which statement resizes the intNumbers array and does not erase the values already stored in the array?

   a. `ReDim intNumbers(99)`

   b. `ReDim Preserve intNumbers(99)`

   c. `Preserve intNumbers(99)`

   d. `ReSize Preserve intNumbers(99)`

9. Which of the following is an apt analogy for two-dimensional array elements?

   a. Feet and inches

   b. Books and pages

   c. Lines and statements

   d. Rows and columns

10. Which statement disables the control `lblResult`?

   a. `lblResult.Disabled = True`

   b. `Disable lblResult`

   c. `lblResult.Enabled = False`

   d. `lblResult.Dimmed = True`

11. The Timer control Interval property may be set to what type of value?

   a. 0 or greater

   b. A fractional number

   c. A negative number

   d. 1 or greater

12. Which of the following properties can you use to cause a control to fill an entire form?

   a. Fill

   b. Dock

   c. Anchor

   d. Stretch

True or False

Indicate whether the following statements are true or false.

1. T F: The upper subscript of an array must be a positive whole number.

2. T F: Numeric array elements are automatically initialized to −1.

3. T F: You may not use a named constant as a subscript in an array declaration.

4. T F: Visual Basic allows you to use a variable as a subscript when processing an array with a loop.

5. T F: You get an error message at design time when you write code that attempts to access an element outside the bounds of an array.

6. T F: The value stored in an array's Length property is the same as the array's upper subscript.

7. T F: You should use a loop to copy the values of one array to another array.

8. T F: Parallel arrays are useful when working with related data of unlike types.

9. T F: The ReDim statement may be used with any array.

10. T F: The value stored in the Timer control's Interval property specifies an interval in seconds.

11. T F: It is possible to anchor a control to a form's opposing edges.

12. T F: When a control is docked to a form's edge, the width or height of the control is adjusted to match the size of the form's edge.

Short Answer

1. Write code that declares a string array with three elements, and then stores your first, middle, and last names in the array's elements.

2. What values are displayed by the following code?
```
Const intMAX_SUBSCRIPT As Integer = 4
Dim intValues(intMAX_SUBSCRIPT) As Integer
Dim intCount As Integer

For intCount = 0 To intMAX_SUBSCRIPT
    intValues(intCount) = intCount + 1
Next

For intCount = 0 To intMAX_SUBSCRIPT
    MessageBox.Show(intValues(intCount).ToString())
Next
```

3. The following code segment declares a 20-element array of integers called intFish. When completed, the code should ask how many fish were caught by fisherman 1 through 20 and store this information in the array. Complete the program.
```
Sub FishCatchArray()
    Const intMAX_SUBSCRIPT As Integer = 19
    Dim intFish(intMAX_SUBSCRIPT) As Integer

    ' You must finish this procedure. It should ask how
    ' many fish were caught by fisherman 1 - 20 and
    ' store this information in the intFish array.
End Sub
```

4. What output is generated by the following code segment? (You may need to use a calculator.)
```
Const decRATE As Decimal = 0.1D
Const intMAX_SUBSCRIPT As Integer = 4
Dim decBalance(intMAX_SUBSCRIPT) As Decimal
Dim decDue As Decimal
Dim intCount As Integer

decBalance(0) = 100
decBalance(1) = 250
decBalance(2) = 325
decBalance(3) = 500
decBalance(4) = 1100
```

```
For intCount = 0 To intMAX_SUBSCRIPT
    decDue = decBalance(intCount) * decRATE
    MessageBox.Show(decDue.ToString())
Next
```

5. Write a statement that assigns 145 to the first column of the first row of the array declared in the following statement:

```
Dim intNumberArray(9, 11) As Integer
```

6. Write a statement that assigns 18 to the last column of the last row of the array declared in Question 5.

7. Assuming that an application uses a Timer control named `tmrClock`, write a statement that stops the timer from responding to timer events.

What Do You Think?

1. The following code totals the values in two Integer arrays: `intNumberArray1` and `intNumberArray2`. Both arrays have 25 elements. Will the code print the correct sum of values for both arrays? Why or why not?

```
Dim intTotal As Integer = 0      ' Accumulator
For intCount = 0 To 24
    intTotal += intNumberArray1(intCount)
Next
MessageBox.Show("Total for intNumberArray1 is " &
                intTotal.ToString())
For intCount = 0 To 24
    intTotal += intNumberArray2(intCount)
Next
MessageBox.Show("Total for intNumberArray2 is " &
                intTotal.ToString())
```

2. How many elements are in the following array?

```
Dim dblSales (5, 3) As Double
```

3. How many elements are in the following array?

```
Dim dblValues (3, 3) As Double
```

4. Suppose an application uses a Timer control named `tmrControl`. Write a programming statement that sets the time between timer events at three seconds.

Find the Error

1. ```
Dim intReadings(-99) As Integer
```

2. ```
Dim intTable(10) As Integer ' Stores 11 values
Dim intIndex As Integer
Dim intMaxNum As Integer = 11
For intIndex = 0 To intMaxNum
    intTable(intIndex) = CInt(InputBox("Enter the next value:"))
Next
```

3. ```
Dim intValues(3) = { 2, 4, 6 }
```

4. ```
' tmrTimer is a Timer control
tmrTimer.Interval = 0
```

Algorithm Workbench

1. Assume `strNames` is a string array with 20 elements. Write a `For Each` loop that prints each element of the array.

2. Suppose you need to store information about 12 countries. Declare two arrays that may be used in parallel to store the names of the countries and their populations.

3. Write a loop that uses the arrays you declared in Question 2 to print each country's name and population.

4. The arrays `intNumberArray1` and `intNumberArray2` have 100 elements. Write code that copies the values in `intNumberArray1` to `intNumberArray2`.

5. Write the code for a sequential search that determines whether the value –1 is stored in the array named `intValues`. The code should print a message indicating whether the value was found.

6. Suppose an application stores the following data about employees:
    *   Name, stored in a list box named `lstNames`
    *   Employee number, stored in an array of strings named `strEmpNums`

    There is a parallel relationship between the list box and the array. Assume that the user has selected an employee's name from the list box. Write code that displays (in a message box) the employee number for the selected employee.

7. Declare a two-dimensional array of integers named `intGrades`. It should have 30 rows and 10 columns.

8. Assume that `dblValues` is a two-dimensional array of Doubles with 10 rows and 20 columns. Write a `For Each` statement that sums all the elements in the array and stores the sum in the variable `dblTotal`.

9. Write nested code using `For...Next` loops that performs the same operation requested in Question 8.

10. Suppose an application uses a two-dimensional array named `intDays`. Write code that sums each row in the array and displays the result.

    ```
    Dim intDays(29, 5) As Integer
    ```

11. Write code that sums each column in the array in Question 10.

12. Write code that uses a `For Each` statement to sum all of the elements in the array in Question 10.

Programming Challenges

1. **Largest/Smallest Array Values**

    Create an application that lets the user enter 10 values into an array. The application should display the largest and smallest values stored in the array. Figure 8-45 shows an example of the application's form after all 10 values have been entered, with the largest and smallest values displayed.

Figure 8-45 *Largest/Smallest Array Values* form

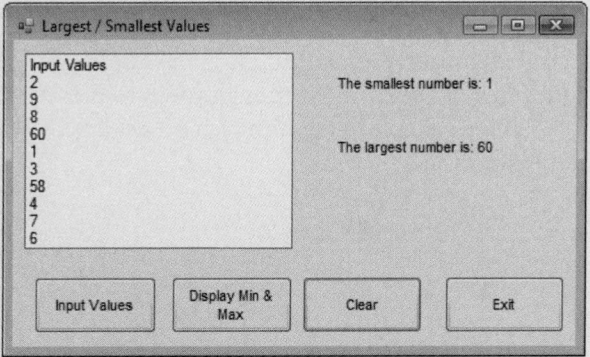

2. **Rainfall Statistics**

Create an application that lets the user enter the rainfall for each of 12 months into an array. The application should calculate and display the following statistics: total rainfall for the year, the average monthly rainfall, and the months with the highest and lowest amounts of rainfall. Figure 8-46 shows an example of the application's form after each month's rainfall amount has been entered and the statistics have been displayed.

Figure 8-46 *Rainfall Statistics* form

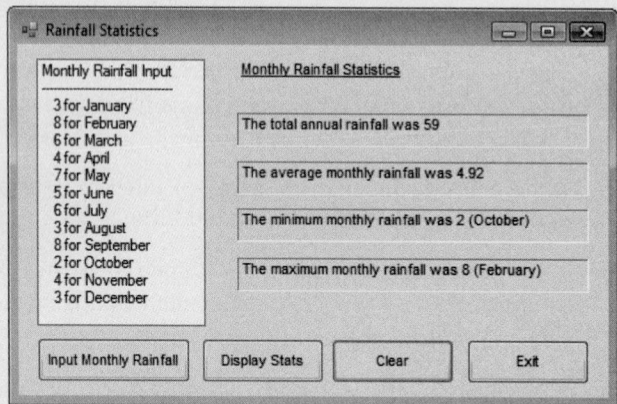

3. **Random Sentences**

Create an application that produces random sentences as output. Create five arrays of strings, one each for nouns, adjectives, verbs, prepositions, and articles. Each array should hold several words of that part of speech. For example, the `strArticles` array could hold the strings `"the"` and `"a"`; the `strNouns` array could hold `"Martian"`, `"baby"`, `"skunk"`, `"computer"`, and `"mosquito"`; the `strPrepositions` array could hold `"around"`, `"through"`, `"under"`, `"over"`, and `"by"`; and so on.

The application should generate sentences by randomly choosing eight words (randomly generating eight array indices) from these arrays, always constructing sentences by using the parts of speech in the following order: article, adjective, noun, verb, preposition, article, adjective, noun.

For example, a sentence might be "The shiny computer flew over a huge mosquito." In this example, "The" and "a" were randomly chosen from the articles array, "shiny" and "huge" from the adjectives array, "computer" and "mosquito" from the nouns array, "flew" from the verbs array, and "over" from the prepositions array. Be careful to produce sentences that have the proper spacing, uppercase and lowercase letters, and a period at the end.

Design your form with buttons to display the next sentence, to clear all sentences currently displayed, and to close the application. Display your sentences, one per line, in a list box. Allow enough room to display at least 10 sentences. Figure 8-47 shows an example of the form using a list box. The figure shows the form with three sentences generated.

Figure 8-47 *Random Sentences* form

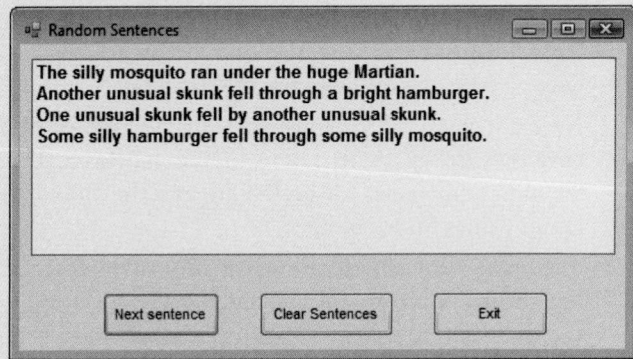

4. **Driver's License Exam**

    The local Registry of Motor Vehicles office has asked you to create an application that grades the written portion of the driver's license exam. The exam has 20 multiple choice questions. Here are the correct answers to the questions:

1.	B	6.	A	11.	B	16.	C
2.	D	7.	B	12.	C	17.	C
3.	A	8.	A	13.	D	18.	B
4.	A	9.	C	14.	A	19.	D
5.	C	10.	D	15.	D	20.	A

    Your application should store the correct answers in an array. A form, such as the one shown in Figure 8-48, should allow the user to enter answers for each question.

    When the user clicks the *Score Exam* button, the application should display another form showing whether each question was answered correctly or incorrectly, and whether the student passed or failed the exam. A student must correctly answer 15 of the 20 questions to pass the exam.

    Input validation: Only accept the letters A, B, C, or D as answers.

Figure 8-48 *Driver's License Exam* form

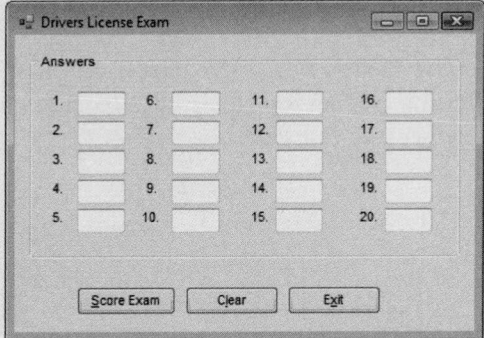

5. **PIN Verifier**

    The National Commerce Bank has hired you to create an application that verifies a customer personal identification number (PIN). A valid PIN is a seven-digit number that meets the following specifications:

    Digit 1: Must be in the range of 7 through 9
    Digit 2: Must be in the range of 5 through 7

Digit 3: Must be in the range of 0 through 4

Digit 4: Must be in the range of 0 through 9

Digit 5: Must be in the range of 6 through 9

Digit 6: Must be in the range of 3 through 6

Digit 7: Must be in the range of 4 through 8

Notice that each digit must fall into a range of numbers. Your application should have two arrays: intMinimum and intMaximum. The intMinimum array should hold the minimum values for each digit, and the intMaximum array should hold the maximum values for each digit.

The application should allow the user to enter seven digits on a form similar to the one shown in Figure 8-49. When the *Verify* button is clicked, the application should use the intMinimum and intMaximum arrays to verify that the numbers fall into acceptable ranges.

Figure 8-49 *PIN Verifier* form

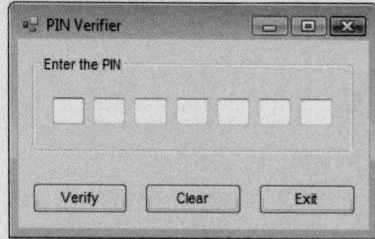

Design Your Own Forms

6. **Employee Directory**

    Create an employee directory application that shows employee names in a list box on the main form. When the user selects a name from the list box, the application should display the employee's ID number, department name, and telephone number on a separate form.

    The application should store all employee ID numbers, department names, and telephone numbers in separate arrays. The arrays and the list box should have a parallel relationship.

7. **Grade Book**

    Suppose a teacher has five students who have taken four tests. The teacher uses the following grading scale to assign a letter grade to a student, based on the average of his or her four test scores.

Test Score	Letter Grade
90–100	A
80–89	B
70–79	C
60–69	D
0–59	F

    Create an application that uses an array of strings to hold the five student names, an array of five strings to hold each student's letter grades, and five arrays of four single precision numbers to hold each student's set of test scores.

Equip the application with a menu or a set of buttons that allows the application to perform the following:

- Display a form that allows the user to enter or change the student names and their test scores.
- Calculate and display each student's average test score and a letter grade based on the average.

Input validation: Do not accept test scores less than zero or greater than 100.

8. **Grade Book Modification**

   Modify the *Grade Book* application in Programming Challenge 7 so it drops each student's lowest score when determining the test score averages and letter grades.

9. **Charge Account Validation**

   Create an application that allows the user to enter a charge account number. The application should determine whether the number is valid by comparing it to the numbers in the following list:

5658845	4520125	7895122	8777541	8451277	1302850
8080152	4562555	5552012	5050552	7825877	1250255
1005231	6545231	3852085	7576651	7881200	4581002

   The list of numbers should be stored in an array. A sequential search should be used to locate the number entered by the user. If the user enters a number that is in the array, the program should display a message indicating the number is valid. If the user enters a number that is not in the array, the program should display a message indicating the number is invalid.

VideoNote

The Lottery Application

10. **Lottery Application**

    Create an application that simulates a lottery. The application should have an array of five integers and should generate a random number in the range 0 through 9 for each element in the array. The array is permitted to contain duplicate values. The user should then enter five digits, which the application will compare to the numbers in the array. A form should be displayed showing how many of the digits matched. If all of the digits match, display a form proclaiming the user as a grand prize winner.

11. **Soccer Team Score Application**

    Suppose a soccer team needs an application to record the number of points scored by its players during a game. Create an application that asks how many players the team has, and then asks for the names of each player. The program should declare an array of strings large enough to hold the player names, and declare an array of integers large enough to hold the number of points scored by each player. The application should have a menu system or buttons that perform the following:

- Display a form allowing the user to enter the players' names.
- Display a form that can be used during a game to record the points scored by each player.
- Display the total points scored by each player and by the team.

Input validation: Do not accept negative numbers as points.

12. **Number Analysis Program**

Create an application that lets the user enter 10 numbers. The program should store the numbers in an array and then display the following data:

- The lowest number in the array
- The highest number in the array
- The total of the numbers in the array
- The average of the numbers in the array

13. **Phone Number Lookup**

Create an application that has two parallel arrays: a String array named strPeople that is initialized with the names of seven of your friends and a String array named strPhoneNumbers that is initialized with your friends' phone numbers. The program should allow the user to enter a person's name (or part of a person's name). It should then search for that person in the strPeople array. If the person is found, it should get that person's phone number from the strPhoneNumbers array and display it. If the person is not found in the strPeople array, the program should display a message indicating this.

14. **Rock, Paper, Scissors Game**

Create an application that lets the user play the game of "Rock, Paper, Scissors" against the computer. The program should work as follows:

(1) When the program begins, a random number in the range of 1 through 3 is generated. If the number is 1, then the computer has chosen rock. If the number is 2, then the computer has chosen paper. If the number is 3, then the computer has chosen scissors. (Don't display the computer's choice yet.)

(2) The user clicks a button to select his or her choice of rock, paper, or scissors.

(3) The computer's choice is displayed.

(4) A winner is selected according to the following rules:
- If one player chooses rock and the other player chooses scissors, then rock wins. (Rock smashes scissors.)
- If one player chooses scissors and the other player chooses paper, then scissors wins. (Scissors cuts paper.)
- If one player chooses paper and the other player chooses rock, then paper wins. (Paper covers rock.)
- If both players make the same choice, the game must be played again to determine the winner.

CHAPTER

9 Files, Printing, and Structures

TOPICS

9.1 Using Files

9.2 The OpenFileDialog, SaveFileDialog, FontDialog, and ColorDialog Controls

9.3 The PrintDocument Control

9.4 Structures

This chapter shows you how to save data to sequential text files and then read the data back into an application. You will learn how to use the OpenFileDialog, SaveFileDialog, ColorDialog, and FontDialog controls. You can use these to equip your application with standard Windows dialog boxes for opening and saving files and for selecting colors and fonts. We discuss the PrintDocument control and how to print reports from your application. Finally, you learn how to package units of data together into structures.

9.1 Using Files

CONCEPT: A file is a collection of data stored on a computer disk. Data can be saved in a file and later reused.

Applications you have created so far require you to re-enter data each time the program runs because the data kept in controls and variables is stored in RAM, and disappears once the program stops running. To retain data between the times it runs, an application must have a way of saving the data.

Data is saved in a **file**, on a computer disk. Once saved, the data remains after the program stops running, and can be retrieved and used at a later time. In this chapter, you write applications that create files to save data. These applications do not rely on the user to re-enter data each time the application runs.

The Process of Using a File

The following steps must be taken when a file is used by an application:

1. The file must be opened. If the file does not yet exist, opening it means creating it.
2. Data is written to the file or read from the file.
3. When the application is finished using the file, the file is closed.

When a Visual Basic application is actively working with data, the data is located in memory, usually in variables and/or control properties. When data is written to a file, it is copied from the variables or control properties, as shown in Figure 9-1.

Figure 9-1 Writing data to a file

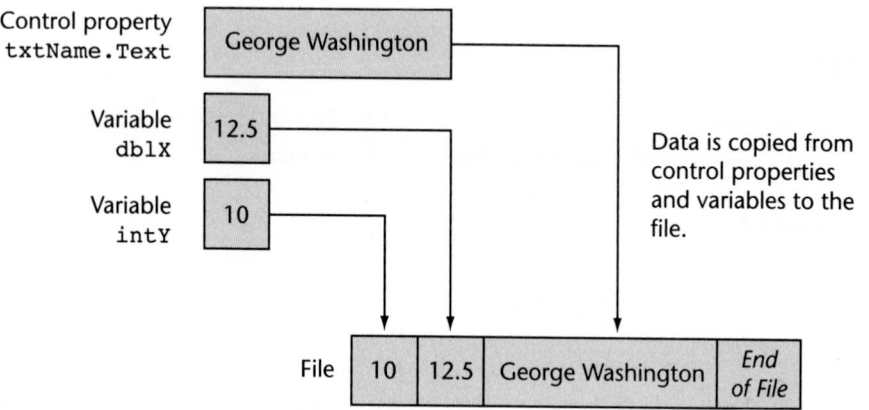

When data is read from a file, it is copied from the file into variables and/or control properties, as shown in Figure 9-2.

Figure 9-2 Reading data from a file

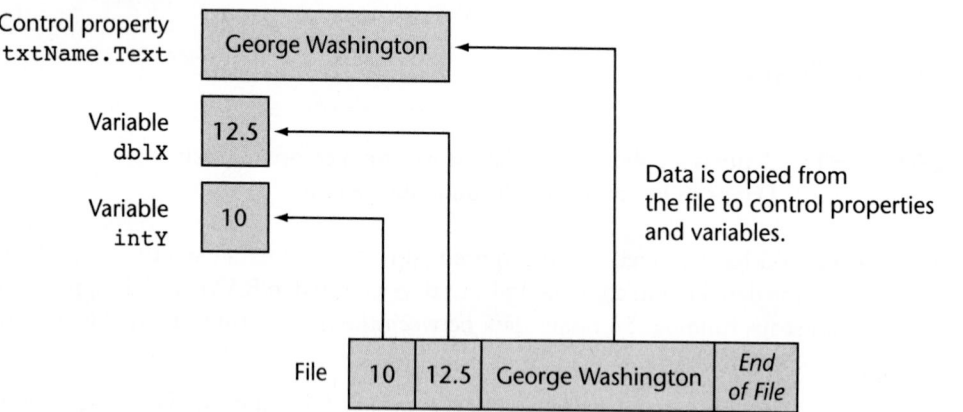

The terms input file and output file are often used. An **input file** is a file from which a program reads data. It is called an input file because the data stored in it serves as input to the program. An **output file** is a file into which a program writes data. It is called an output file because the program stores output in the file.

There are two types of files: text and binary. A **text file** contains plain text and may be opened in a text editor such as Windows Notepad. Data in **binary files** is stored as pure binary data; the content cannot usually be viewed with a text editor.

There are also two methods of accessing files: sequential-access and random-access. A **sequential-access file** is like a stream of data that must be read from its beginning to its end. To read an item stored in the middle or at the end of a sequential-access file, an application must read all the items in the file before it.

Data in a **random-access file** may be accessed in any order. An application can jump to any item in a random-access file without first reading the preceding items. The difference between sequential-access and random-access files is like the difference between a cassette tape and a CD. When listening to a CD, you don't need to listen to or fast-forward over unwanted songs. You simply jump to the track that you want to listen to.

Because most Visual Basic programmers prefer to use databases rather than random-access or binary files, we discuss only sequential-access text files in this chapter. Binary and random-access files are discussed in Appendix F, located on the Student Resources CD.

Writing to Files with StreamWriter Objects

There are two basic ways to open a text file so you can write data to it: You can create a new file, or you can open an existing file so data can be appended to it. The actual writing to the file is performed by a **StreamWriter** object. There are two required steps:

1. Declare a StreamWriter variable.
2. Call either the File.CreateText or File.AppendText method. If you want to create a new file, call File.CreateText and assign its return value to the StreamWriter variable. Or, to append to an existing text file, call File.AppendText and assign its return value to the StreamWriter variable.

Before using StreamWriter objects, you must insert the following Imports statement at the top of your form's code file. This will make the **StreamWriter classes** available to your program:

```
Imports System.IO
```

 NOTE: It is possible to omit the Imports System.IO statement, but then every reference to the StreamWriter class must use its fully qualified name, which is System.IO.StreamWriter.

Creating a Text File

First, we will show you how to create a new text file. Begin by declaring a StreamWriter variable, using the following general format:

```
Dim ObjectVar As StreamWriter
```

ObjectVar is the name of the object variable. You may use Private or Public in place of Dim if you are declaring the object variable at the class-level or module-level. Here's an example:

```
Dim phoneFile As StreamWriter
```

Next, call the **File.CreateText** method, passing it the name of a file. For example:

```
phoneFile = File.CreateText("phonelist.txt")
```

Notice how the return value from File.CreateText is assigned to the StreamWriter variable named phoneFile.

The filename that you pass to the `File.CreateText` method can optionally contain a complete path, such as *C:\data\vbfiles\phonelist.txt*. If you use only a filename with no path, Visual Basic assumes that the file will be created in the same location as the application's executable file, which by default is your project's *\bin\Debug* folder.

If the file cannot be created, the `File.CreateText` method will throw an exception. For example, an exception will occur if you specify a nonexistent path, or your application does not have the required permission to create a file in the specified location.

Opening an Existing File and Appending Data to It

If a text file already exists, you may want to add more data to the end of the file. This is called *appending* to the file. First, you declare a `StreamWriter` variable:

```
Dim phoneFile As StreamWriter
```

Then you call the **`File.AppendText`** method, passing it the name of an existing file. For example:

```
phoneFile = File.AppendText("phonelist.txt")
```

Any data written to the file will be written to the end of the file's existing contents.

If the file that you specify as an argument to the `File.AppendText` method does not exist, it will be created. If the file cannot be opened or created, the method will throw an exception. For example, an exception will occur if you specify a nonexistent path, or your application does not have the required permission to create a file in the specified location.

WARNING: It is possible to move an application's executable file to a location other than the project's *bin* directory. Doing so changes the default location where the files are created.

Writing Data to a File

The **`WriteLine`** method of the `StreamWriter` class writes a line of data to a file. The following is the general format of the method:

```
ObjectVar.WriteLine(Data)
```

ObjectVar is the name of a `StreamWriter` object variable. *Data* represents constants or variables whose contents will be written to the file. The `WriteLine` method writes the data to the file and then writes a newline character immediately after the data. A **newline character** is an invisible character that separates text by breaking it into another line when displayed on the screen.

NOTE: The newline character is actually stored as two characters: a carriage return (character code 13) and a linefeed character (character code 10).

To further understand how the `WriteLine` method works, let's look at an example. Assume that an application opens a file and writes three students' first names and their scores to the file with the following code:

```
Dim studentFile As StreamWriter

Try
    ' Open the file.
    studentFile = File.CreateText("StudentData.txt")

    ' Write data to the file.
    studentFile.WriteLine("Jim")
```

```
      studentFile.WriteLine(95)
      studentFile.WriteLine("Karen")
      studentFile.WriteLine(98)
      studentFile.WriteLine("Bob")
      studentFile.WriteLine(82)
   Catch
      MessageBox.Show("Error: The file cannot be created.")
   End try
```

You can visualize the data being written to the file in the following manner:

Jim*<newline>*95*<newline>*Karen*<newline>*98*<newline>*Bob*<newline>*82*<newline>*

The newline characters are represented here as *<newline>*. You do not actually see the newline characters, but when the file is opened in a text editor such as Notepad, its contents appear as shown in Figure 9-3. As you can see from the figure, each newline character causes the data that follows it to be displayed on a new line.

 TIP: Each time the `WriteLine` method executes, it writes a separate line of text to the file.

In addition to separating the contents of a file into lines, the newline character also serves as a delimiter. A **delimiter** is an item that separates other items. When you write data to a file using `WriteLine`, newline characters are the delimiters. Later, you will see that data must be separated in order for it to be read from the file.

Figure 9-3 File contents displayed in Notepad

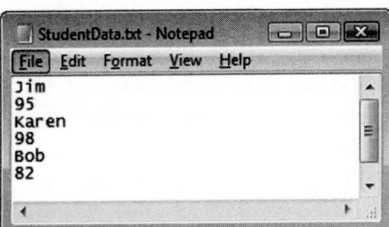

Writing a Blank Line to a File

The `WriteLine` method can write a blank line to a file by calling the method without an argument.

```
   textFile.WriteLine()
```

The `Write` Method

The **`Write` method**, a member of the `StreamWriter` class, writes an item of data to a file without writing a newline character. The general format is as follows:

```
   ObjectVar.Write(Data)
```

ObjectVar is the name of a `StreamWriter` object variable. *Data* represents the contents of a constant or variable that is to be written to the file. This method can be used to write data to a file without terminating the line with a newline character. For example, assume an application has a `StreamWriter` object variable named `outputFile`, as well as the following variables:

```
   Dim strName As String = "Jeffrey Smith"
   Dim intId As Integer = 47895
   Dim strPhone As String = "555-7864"
```

The contents of all three variables are written to a single line in the file:

```
outputFile.Write(strName)
outputFile.Write(" ")
outputFile.Write(intId)
outputFile.Write(" ")
outputFile.WriteLine(strPhone)
```

The first statement writes the `strName` variable to the file. The second statement writes a space character (`" "`), the third statement writes the `intId` variable, and the fourth statement writes another space. The last statement uses the `WriteLine` method to write the phone number, followed by a newline character. Here is a sample of the output:

```
Jeffrey Smith 47895 555-7864
```

Closing a File

The opposite of opening a file is closing it. The `StreamWriter` class has a method named `Close` that closes a file. The following is the method's general format:

```
ObjectVar.Close()
```

ObjectVar is a `StreamWriter` object variable. After the method executes, the file that was referenced by *ObjectVar* is closed. For example, `salesFile` is an object variable that references a `StreamWriter` object. The following statement closes the file associated with `salesFile`.

```
salesFile.Close()
```

To avoid losing data, your application should always close files after it is finished using them. Computers typically create one or more buffers (memory areas) when a file is opened. When an application writes data to a file, that data is first written to the **buffer**. When the buffer is filled, all data stored there is written to the file. This technique improves the system's performance because writing data to memory is faster than writing it to a disk. The **Close method** writes any unsaved information remaining in the file buffer and releases memory allocated by the `StreamWriter` object.

 NOTE: Once a file is closed, you must reopen it before performing any operations on it.

In Tutorial 9-1, you examine an application that writes data about three fictional persons to a file.

 ## Tutorial 9-1:
Completing an application that writes data to a file

Step 1: Open the *File WriteLine* demo project from the student sample programs folder named *Chap9\File WriteLine Demo*. The application form is shown in Figure 9-4.

Step 2: Complete the code for the form's event handlers as shown in the following. (Don't type the line numbers. They are shown for reference.) Be sure to write the `Imports` statement shown in line 1.

```
1 Imports System.IO
2
3 Public Class Form1
4
```

Figure 9-4 *File WriteLine Demo* form

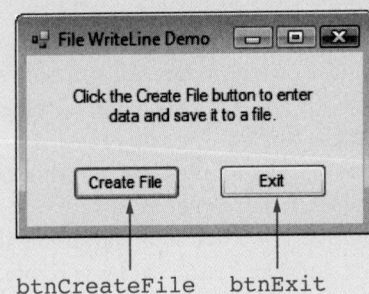

btnCreateFile   btnExit

```
5   Private Sub btnCreateFile_Click(...) Handles btnCreate File.Click
6      ' Constant for the number of friends
7      Const intNUM_FRIENDS As Integer = 3
8
9      ' Local variables
10     Dim strFilename As String        ' File name
11     Dim strFriend As String          ' Name of a friend
12     Dim strPhone As String           ' To hold a phone number
13     Dim intCount As Integer          ' Loop counter
14     Dim friendFile As StreamWriter   ' Object variable
15
16     ' Get the file name from the user.
17     strFilename = InputBox("Enter the filename.")
18
19     Try
20        ' Open the file.
21        friendFile = File.CreateText(strFilename)
22
23        ' Get the data and write it to the file.
24        For intCount = 1 To intNUM_FRIENDS
25           ' Get a friend's name.
26           strFriend = InputBox("Enter the name of friend " &
27                                "number " & intCount.ToString())
28
29           ' Get a friend's phone number.
30           strPhone = InputBox("Enter the that friend's " &
31                               "phone number.")
32
33           ' Write the data to the file.
34           friendFile.WriteLine(strFriend)
35           friendFile.WriteLine(strPhone)
36        Next
37
38        ' Close the file.
39        friendFile.Close()
40     Catch
41        ' Error message
42        MessageBox.Show("That file cannot be created.")
43     End Try
44   End Sub
45
46   Private Sub btnExit_Click(...) Handles btnExit.Click
47      ' Close the form.
48      Me.Close()
49   End Sub
50 End Class
```

Let's examine the btnCreateFile_Click event handler closer. Here is a summary of the declarations that appear in lines 7 through 14:

- Line 7: The intNUM_FRIENDS constant is set to 3. This is the number of friends for whom we will store data.
- Line 10: The strFilename variable will hold the path and filename of the file that the application will create.
- Line 11: The strFriend variable will hold the name of a friend.
- Line 12: The strPhone variable will hold a friend's phone number.
- Line 13: The intCount variable will be used as a loop counter.
- Line 14: The friendFile variable is an object variable that will be used to open the file and write data to it.

Line 17 uses an input box to prompt the user to enter a filename. The filename is assigned to the strFilename variable.

The Try–Catch statement that begins in line 19 will catch any exceptions that are thrown. Line 21 tries to create the file specified by the path and filename entered by the user. If the file cannot be created, an exception is thrown and the program jumps to the Catch clause in line 40. If the file is successfully created, the For...Next loop in line 24 begins to execute. As the loop is written, it will iterate three times, with the intCount variable taking on the values 1 through 3.

Inside the loop, the statement in lines 26 through 27 uses an input box to prompt the user for a friend's name. The name entered by the user is assigned to the strFriend variable. Then the statement in lines 30 through 31 uses an input box to prompt the user for that friend's phone number. The phone number entered by the user is assigned to the strPhone variable. Line 34 writes the friend's name to the file, and line 35 writes the phone number to the file. Then, the loop starts over.

When the loop is finished, line 39 closes the file.

Step 3: Save the project. Run the application and click the *Create File* button. When prompted to enter the filename, provide the path of a disk location that can be written to. For example, if you enter *C:\MyFriends.txt*, the application will create the file *MyFriends.txt* in the root directory of drive C. If you enter *C:\Temp\MyFriends.txt* the application will create the file *MyFriends.txt* in the *C:\Temp* folder. Enter a path and filename and make a note of it because you will use the same file later in this tutorial and again in Tutorial 9-2.

NOTE: If you are working in a school computer lab, you may be restricted to saving files only at certain disk locations. Ask your instructor or lab manager for these locations.

Step 4: Enter the following names, ages, and addresses as you are prompted for this data. After you have entered the data for the third friend, the application returns to the main form. Click the *Exit* button.

	Name	Phone
Friend 1	Jim Weaver	555-1212
Friend 2	Mary Duncan	555-2323
Friend 3	Karen Warren	555-3434

Step 5: In Windows, locate the file that was created when you ran the application. Double-click the file's name to open it in the Notepad text editor. The contents of the file should appear as shown in Figure 9-5.

Figure 9-5 Contents of the file displayed in Notepad

As you can see, each item is written to a separate line in the file because a newline character separates each item.

Step 6: Close the *Notepad* window that displays the text file.

Appending a File

When we **append** a file, we write new data immediately following existing data in the file. If an existing file is opened with the `AppendText` method, data written to the file is appended to the file's existing data. If the file does not exist, it is created.

For example, assume the file *MyFriends.txt* exists and contains the following data, from Tutorial 9-1:

```
Jim Weaver
555-1212
Mary Duncan
555-2323
Karen Warren
555-3434
```

The following statments open the file in append mode and write additional data to the file:

```
' Declare an object variable
Dim friendFile As StreamWriter
' Open the file.
friendFile = File.AppendText("MyFriends.txt")
' Write the data.
friendFile.WriteLine("Bill Johnson")
friendFile.WriteLine("555-4545")
' Close the file.
friendFile.Close()
```

After this code executes, the *MyFriends.txt* file will contain the following data:

Jim Weaver
555-1212
Mary Duncan
555-2323
Karen Warren
555-3434
Bill Johnson
555-4545

Reading Files with `StreamReader` Objects

VideoNote

Reading Data from a File

To read data from a sequential text file, use a **`StreamReader`** object. A `StreamReader` object is an instance of the **`StreamReader`** class, which provides methods for reading data from a file. The process of creating a `StreamReader` object is similar to that of creating a `StreamWriter` object, which we discussed in the previous section. First, you declare an object variable with a declaration statement in the following general format:

```
Dim ObjectVar As StreamReader
```

`ObjectVar` is the name of the object variable. As with other variables, you may use the `Private` or `Public` access specifier if you are declaring the object variable at the class level or module level.

You must create an instance of the `StreamReader` object and store its address in the object variable with the **`File.OpenText`** method. The method's general format is as follows:

```
File.OpenText(Filename)
```

`Filename` is a string or a string variable specifying the path and/or name of the file to open. This method opens the file specified by `Filename` and returns the address of a `StreamReader` object that may be used to write data to the file. If the file does not exist, or it cannot be opened for any reason, an exception will occur.

The following are examples:

```
Dim customerFile As StreamReader
customerFile = File.OpenText("customers.txt")
```

The first statement creates an object variable named `customerFile`. The second statement opens the file *customers.txt* and returns the address of a `StreamReader` object that may be used to read data from the file. The address of the `StreamReader` object is assigned to the `customerFile` variable.

As in the case of the `StreamWriter` class, you need to write the following `Imports` statement at the top of your code file:

```
Imports System.IO
```

Reading Data from a File

The **`ReadLine`** method in the `StreamReader` class reads a line of data from a file. The general format of the method is as follows:

```
ObjectVar.ReadLine()
```

`ObjectVar` is the name of a `StreamReader` object variable. The method reads a line from the file associated with `ObjectVar` and returns the data as a string. For example, assume that `customerFile` is a `StreamReader` object variable and `strCustomerName` is a string variable. The following statement reads a line from the file and stores it in the variable:

```
strCustomerName = customerFile.ReadLine()
```

Data is read in a forward-only direction. When the file is opened, its **read position,** the position of the next item to be read, is set to the first item in the file. As data is read, the read position advances through the file. For example, consider the file named *Quotation.txt,* as shown in Figure 9-6. As you can see from the figure, the file has three lines of text. Suppose a program opens the file with the following code:

```
Dim textFile As StreamReader
textFile = File.OpenText("Quotation.txt")
```

Figure 9-6 Text file with three lines

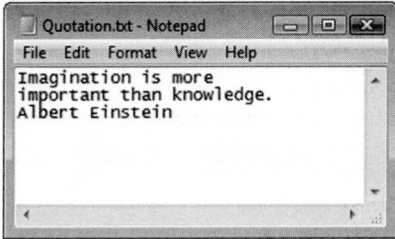

When this code opens the file, its read position is at the beginning of the first line, as illustrated in Figure 9-7.

Figure 9-7 Initial read position

Read position ⟶ Imagination is more
important than knowledge.
Albert Einstein

The following statement reads a line from the file, beginning at the current read position, and ending at the end-of-line marker:

```
strInput = textFile.ReadLine()
```

After the statement executes, the `strInput` variable contains the string `"Imagination is more"`. The invisible end-of-line marker is skipped, and the read position is placed at the beginning of the second line. Figure 9-8 illustrates the current read position.

Figure 9-8 Read position after first line is read

Imagination is more
Read position ⟶ important than knowledge.
Albert Einstein

If the `ReadLine` method is called again, the second line is read from the file and the file's read position is advanced to the third line. After all lines have been read, the read position will be at the end of the file.

Closing the File

Close an open `StreamReader` object by calling the `Close` method. The general format is as follows:

```
ObjectVar.Close()
```

In Tutorial 9-2, you complete an application that uses the `ReadLine` statement to read the file you created in Tutorial 9-1.

Tutorial 9-2:
Completing an application that reads a file

Step 1: Open the *File ReadLine Demo* project from the student sample programs folder named *Chap9\File ReadLine Demo*. The application's form, which has already been created for you, is shown in Figure 9-9.

Figure 9-9 *File ReadLine Demo* form

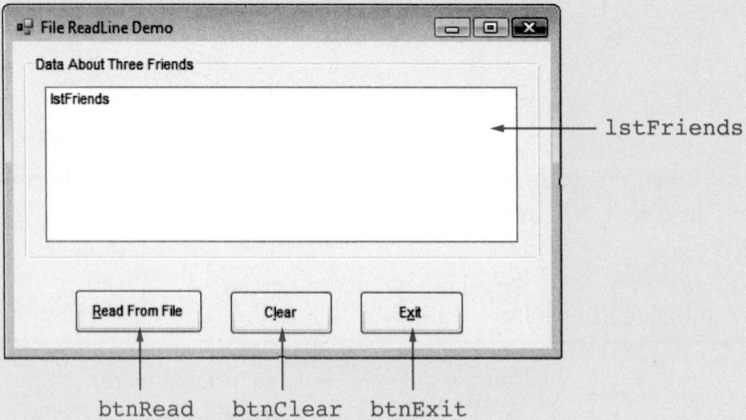

Step 2: Complete the code for the form's event handlers as shown in the following. (Don't type the line numbers. They are shown for reference.) Be sure to write the `Imports` statement shown in line 1.

```
1  Imports System.IO
2
3  Public Class Form1
4
5    Private Sub btnRead_Click(...) Handles btnRead.Click
6      ' Constant for the number of friends
7      Const intNUM_FRIENDS As Integer = 3
8
9      ' Local variables
10     Dim friendFile As StreamReader    ' Object variable
11     Dim strFilename As String         ' File name
12     Dim strFriend As String           ' Name of a friend
13     Dim strPhone As String            ' To hold a phone number
14     Dim intCount As Integer           ' Loop counter
15
16     ' Get the file name from the user.
17     strFilename = InputBox("Enter the filename.")
18
19     Try
```

```
20        ' Open the file.
21        friendFile = File.OpenText(strFilename)
22
23        ' Read the data.
24        For intCount = 1 To intNUM_FRIENDS
25          ' Read a name and phone number from the file.
26          strFriend = friendFile.ReadLine()
27          strPhone = friendFile.ReadLine()
28
29          ' Display the data in the list box.
30          lstFriends.Items.Add("Friend Number " & intCount.ToString())
31          lstFriends.Items.Add("Name: " & strFriend)
32          lstFriends.Items.Add("Phone: " & strPhone)
33          lstFriends.Items.Add("") ' Add a blank line
34        Next
35
36        ' Close the file.
37        friendFile.Close()
38      Catch
39        MessageBox.Show("That file cannot be opened.")
40      End Try
41    End Sub
42
43    Private Sub btnClear_Click(...) Handles btnClear.Click
44      ' Clear the list box.
45      lstFriends.Items.Clear()
46    End Sub
47
48    Private Sub btnExit_Click(...) Handles btnExit.Click
49      ' Close the form.
50      Me.Close()
51    End Sub
52 End Class
```

Let's examine the `btnRead_Click` event handler. Here is a summary of the declarations that appear in lines 7 through 14:

- Line 7: The `intNUM_FRIENDS` constant is set to 3. This is the number of friends for whom we will read data from the file.
- Line 10: The `friendFile` variable is an object variable that will be used to open the file and read data from it.
- Line 11: The `strFilename` variable will hold the path and filename of the file that the application will open.
- Line 12: The `strFriend` variable will hold the name of a friend that is read from the file.
- Line 13: The `strPhone` variable will hold a friend's phone number that is read from the file.
- Line 14: The `intCount` variable will be used as a loop counter.

Line 17 uses an input box to prompt the user to enter a filename. The filename is assigned to the `strFilename` variable.

The `Try-Catch` statement that begins in line 19 will catch any exceptions that are thrown. Line 21 tries to open the file specified by the path and filename entered by the user. If the file cannot be opened, an exception is thrown and the program jumps to the `Catch` clause in line 38. If the file is successfully created, the `For...Next` loop in line 24 begins to execute. As the loop is written, it will iterate three times, with the `intCount` variable taking on the values 1 through 3.

Inside the loop, the statement in line 26 reads a line of data from the file and assigns it to the `strFriend` variable, and line 27 reads the next line of data from the file and assigns it to the `strPhone` variable. Lines 30 through 33 add this friend's data to the list box, followed by a blank line. Then, the loop starts over. When the loop is finished, line 39 closes the file.

Step 3: Save the project. Run the application and click the *Read From File* button. An input box will appear asking for the filename. Enter the path and filename that you used to create the file in Step 3 of Tutorial 9-1. When you click the *OK* button on the input box, the data is read from the file and displayed in the list box, as shown in Figure 9-10. If you did not type the path and filename exactly as you did in Tutorial 9-1, you will see a message box indicating that the file was not found. In that case, click the *Read From File* button again, this time entering the correct path and filename.

Figure 9-10 Data displayed in the list box

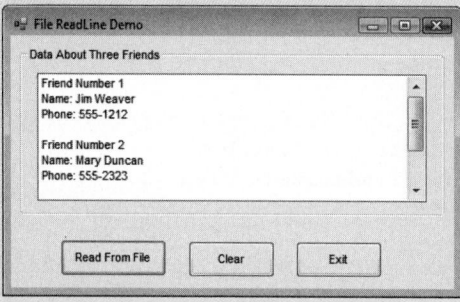

Step 4: Click the *Exit* button to end the application.

Determining Whether a File Exists

The `File.OpenText` method throws an exception if the file it is trying to open does not exist. To prevent an exception, you can call the **`File.Exists` method** to determine whether a file exists before you attempt to open it. The general format of the method is as follows:

```
File.Exists(Filename)
```

Filename is the name of a file, which may include the path. The method returns *True* if the file exists or *False* if the file does not exist. The following code shows an example of how to use the method to determine if a file exists prior to trying to open the file:

```
If File.Exists(strFilename) Then
    ' Open the file.
    inputFile = File.OpenText(strFilename)
Else
    MessageBox.Show(strFilename & " does not exist.")
End If
```

Using `vbTab` to Align Display Items

The predefined `vbTab` constant moves the print position forward to the next even multiple of 8. You can use it to align columns in displayed or printed output more effectively. The following is a simple example, displayed in a list box, of a reference line followed by three lines displaying tabs and characters:

```
ListBox1.Items.Add("012345678901234567890")
ListBox1.Items.Add("X" & vbTab & "X")
ListBox1.Items.Add("XXXXXXXXXXX" & vbTab & "X")
ListBox1.Items.Add(vbTab & vbTab & "X")
```

In the output in Figure 9-11, the vbTab constant in the second line moves the print position forward to column 8 before displaying the letter X. (Print positions are numbered starting at 0.) In lines three and four, the print position moves to column 16 before displaying the final letter X.

Figure 9-11 Demonstrating tabs in a list box

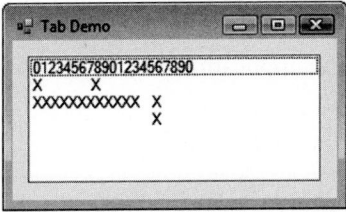

Briefly returning to the *ReadLine Demo* application from Tutorial 9-2, a slightly better way to display the person's information is to insert tabs between the labels and names in the list box. Here is the appropriately modified code from the loop inside the btnRead_Click event handler:

```
' Display the data in the list box.
lstFriends.Items.Add("Friend Number " & vbTab & intCount.ToString())
lstFriends.Items.Add("Name: " & vbTab & vbTab & strFriend)
lstFriends.Items.Add("Phone: " & vbTab & vbTab & strPhone)
lstFriends.Items.Add("") ' Add a blank line
```

The resulting output from this code appears in Figure 9-12.

Figure 9-12 *ReadLine Demo,* using tabs in the list box

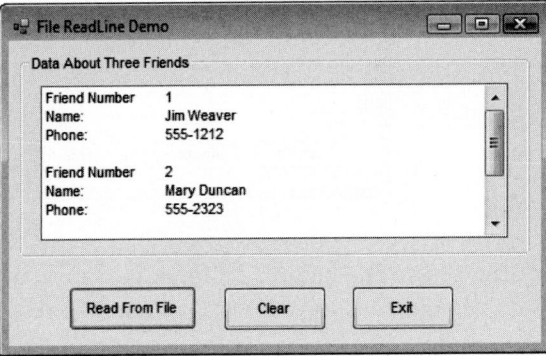

Detecting the End of a File

The *File ReadLine Demo* application in Tutorial 9-2 is designed to read exactly three records. This is because we know how many records are stored in the file. In many cases, however, the amount of data in a file is unknown. When this is the case, use the **Peek method** to determine when the end of the file has been reached. The general format of the Peek method is as follows:

ObjectVar.Peek

ObjectVar is an object variable referencing a `StreamReader` object. This method looks ahead in the file, without moving the current read position, and returns the next character that will be read. If the current read position is at the end of the file (where there are no more characters to read), the method returns –1. The following example uses a `Do Until` loop that uses the `Peek` method to determine when the end of the *Scores.txt* file has been reached. The loop reads all the lines from the file and adds them to the `lstResults` list box.

```
Dim scoresFile As StreamReader
Dim strInput As String
scoresFile = File.OpenText("Scores.txt")
Do Until scoresFile.Peek = -1
  strInput = scoresFile.ReadLine()
  lstResults.Items.Add(strInput)
Loop
scoresFile.Close()
```

Tutorial 9-3 examines an application that detects the end of a file.

Tutorial 9-3:
Examining an application that detects the end of a file

VideoNote

Tutorial 9-3
Walkthrough

Step 1: Open the *File Demo* project from the student sample program folder named *Chap9\File Demo*. Run the application. The form is shown in Figure 9-13.

Figure 9-13 *File Demo* form

Step 2: Click the *Create File* button. An input box appears and asks: *How many integers do you want to enter?* Enter **5** and press ⏎Enter.

Step 3: Because you indicated you want to enter five numbers, the application will prompt you five times with an input box to enter a number. Enter the following numbers: **2, 4, 6, 8,** and **10**. The application writes these numbers to a file.

Step 4: After you have entered the last number, click the *Read File* button. The application reads the numbers from the file and prints them in the list box, as shown in Figure 9-14. Click the *Exit* button to end the application.

Figure 9-14 *File Demo* form with numbers displayed

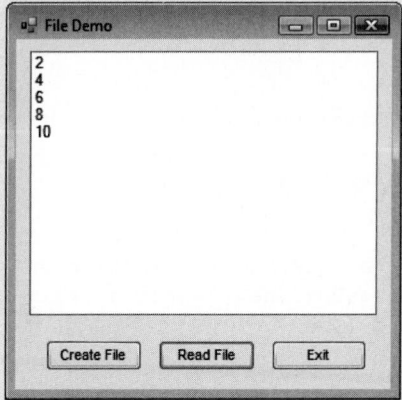

Step 5: Open the *Code* window. The first part of the form's class, including the btnCreate_Click event handler, are shown here with line numbers for reference.

```
1 Imports System.IO
2
3 Public Class Form1
4   ' Class-level constant for the filename
5   Private Const strFILENAME As String = "Numbers.txt"
6
7   Private Sub btnCreate_Click(...) Handles btnCreate.Click
8     ' Local variables
9     Dim outputFile As StreamWriter    ' Object variable
10    Dim intMaxNumbers As Integer      ' The number of values
11    Dim intCount As Integer = 0       ' Loop counter, set to 0
12    Dim intNumber As Integer          ' To hold user input
13
14    Try
15      ' Get the number of numbers from the user.
16      intMaxNumbers = CInt(InputBox("How many integers do " &
17                                    "you want to enter?"))
18
19      Try
20        ' Create the file.
21        outputFile = File.CreateText(strFILENAME)
22
23        ' Get the numbers and write then to the file.
24        Do While intCount < intMaxNumbers
25          Try
26            ' Get an integer.
27            intNumber = CInt(InputBox("Enter an integer."))
28
29            ' Write that integer to the file.
30            outputFile.WriteLine(intNumber)
31
32            ' Increment intCount.
33            intCount += 1
34          Catch
35            ' Error message for invalid integer.
36            MessageBox.Show("The last value you entered was not " &
37                            "a valid integer. Try again.")
38          End Try
```

```
39          Loop
40
41          ' Close the file.
42          outputFile.Close()
43
44      Catch
45          ' Error message for file creation error.
46          MessageBox.Show("Error creating the file " & strFILENAME)
47      End Try
48
49    Catch
50        ' Error message for invalid number of numbers.
51        MessageBox.Show("Enter a valid integer please.")
52    End Try
53 End Sub
54
```

Let's take a closer look at this code. Line 1 shows the `Imports System.IO` statement, and the form's class declaration begins in line 3. Line 5 declares a class-level constant named `strFILENAME` for the name of the file that we will be working with.

Here is a summary of the declarations that appear in lines 9 through 12:

- Line 9: The `outputFile` variable is an object variable that will be used to open the file and write data to it.
- Line 10: The `intMaxNumbers` variable will hold the number of integer values that will be written to the file.
- Line 11: The `intCount` variable will be used as a loop counter.
- Line 12: The `intNumber` variable will hold a number entered by the user, to be written to the file. Notice that we explicitly initialize `intCount` to 0.

Notice that a `Try-Catch` statement begins in line 14, and then lines 16 through 17 use an input box to prompt the user for the number of integer values that he or she wants to enter. If the user enters an invalid value, the `CInt` function in line 16 will throw an exception and the program will jump to the `Catch` clause in line 49.

If the user enters a valid integer value, the program can proceed to create the file. Notice that another `Try-Catch` statement begins in line 19, and then line 21 creates the file. If for any reason the file cannot be created, the `File.CreateText` method will throw an exception and the program will jump to the `Catch` clause in line 44.

If the file is successfully created, the program can proceed to get the numbers from the user and write them to the file. The `Do While` loop that begins in line 24 iterates as long as `intCount` is less than `intMaxNumbers`. Notice that inside the loop a `Try-Catch` statement begins in line 25, and then line 27 uses an input box to prompt the user for an integer. If the user enters an invalid value, the `CInt` function in line 27 will throw an exception and the program will jump to the `Catch` clause in line 34. If the user enters a valid integer, line 30 writes it to the file, and line 33 increments `intCount`. After the loop finishes, line 42 closes the file.

Step 6: Now scroll down and look at the `btnRead_Click` event handler, shown here with line numbers for reference:

```
55   Private Sub btnRead_Click(...) Handles btnRead.Click
56       ' Local variables
57       Dim inputFile As StreamReader ' Object variable
58       Dim strInput As String         ' To hold a line of input
59
60       Try
61           ' Open the file.
62           inputFile = File.OpenText(strFILENAME)
63
64           ' Clear the list box.
65           lstOutput.Items.Clear()
66
67           ' Read the file's contents.
68           Do Until inputFile.Peek = —1
69               ' Read a line from the file.
70               strInput = inputFile.ReadLine()
71
72               ' Add the line of input to the list box.
73               lstOutput.Items.Add(strInput)
74           Loop
75
76           ' Close the file.
77           inputFile.Close()
78       Catch
79           ' Error message for file open error.
80           MessageBox.Show(strFILENAME & " cannot be opened.")
81       End Try
82   End Sub
```

Let's take a closer look at this code. Here is a summary of the declarations that appear in lines 57 and 58:

- Line 57: The `inputFile` variable is an object variable that will be used to open the file and read data from it.
- Line 58: The `strInput` variable will hold a line of input that is read from the file.

Notice that a `Try-Catch` statement begins in line 60, and then line 62 opens the file. If the file cannot be opened, the `File.OpenText` method will throw an exception and the program will jump to the `Catch` clause in line 78. (This will happen, for example, if the user clicks the *Read File* button before the file has been created.)

If the file is successfully opened, line 65 clears the list box's contents. Then the `Do Until` loop in line 68 begins executing. The loop will iterate until the `inputFile.Peek` method returns –1, indicating that the end of the file has been reached. During each loop iteration, line 70 reads a line from the file and assigns it to the `strInput` variable, and line 73 adds `strInput` to the list box. After the loop finishes, line 77 closes the file.

Other `StreamReader` Methods

The `StreamReader` class also provides the `Read` and `ReadToEnd` methods, which we briefly discuss. The general format of the `Read` method is as follows:

```
ObjectVar.Read
```

ObjectVar is the name of a `StreamReader` object variable. The **Read method** reads only the next character from a file and returns the integer code for the character. To convert the integer code to a character, use the **Chr function**, as shown in the following code:

```
Dim textFile As StreamReader
Dim strInput As String = String.Empty
textFile = File.OpenText("names.txt")
Do While textFile.Peek <> −1
   strInput &= Chr(textFile.Read)
Loop
textFile.Close()
```

This code opens the *names.txt* file. The `Do While` loop, which repeats until it reaches the end of the file, executes the following statement:

```
strInput &= Chr(textFile.Read)
```

This statement gets the integer code for the next character in the file, converts it to a character with the `Chr` function, and concatenates that character to the string variable `strInput`. When the loop has finished, the string variable `strInput` contains the entire contents of the file *names.txt*.

The general format of the `ReadToEnd` method is as follows:

```
ObjectVar.ReadToEnd
```

ObjectVar is the name of a `StreamReader` object variable. The **ReadToEnd method** reads and returns the entire contents of a file, beginning at the current read position. The following is an example:

```
Dim textFile As StreamReader
Dim strInput As String
textFile = File.OpenText("names.txt")
strInput = textFile.ReadToEnd()
textFile.Close()
```

The statement `strInput = textFile.ReadToEnd()` reads the file's contents and stores it in the variable `strInput`.

Working with Arrays and Files

Saving the contents of an array to a file is easy. Use a loop to step through each element of the array, writing its contents to the file. For example, assume an application has the following array declaration:

```
Dim intValues() As Integer = {1, 2, 3, 4, 5, 6, 7, 8, 9, 10}
```

The following code opens a file named *Values.txt* and writes the contents of each element of the values array to the file:

```
Dim outputFile as StreamWriter
outputFile = File.CreateText("Values.txt")
For intCount = 0 To (intValues.Length − 1)
   outputFile.WriteLine(intValues(intCount))
Next
outputFile.Close()
```

Reading the contents of a file into an array is equally straightforward. The following code opens the *Values.txt* file and reads its contents into the elements of the intValues array:

```
Dim inputFile as StreamReader
inputFile = File.OpenText("Values.txt")
For intCount = 0 To (intValues.Length — 1)
  intValues(intCount) = CInt(inputFile.ReadLine())
Next
inputFile.Close()
```

 NOTE: This code does not check for the end of file, so it assumes the file contains enough values to fill the array. Also, an exception will be thrown by the CInt function if the file contains a value that cannot be converted to an integer.

 ## Checkpoint

9.1 What are the three steps in the process of using a file?

9.2 What type of object variable must you create to open a file for writing? For reading?

9.3 Write a statement that creates the file *Test.txt* so that you may write data to it. If the file already exists, its contents should be erased.

9.4 Write a statement that writes the contents of the variable intX to a line in the file you opened in Checkpoint 9.3.

9.5 Write a statement that opens the file *Test.txt* for reading.

9.6 Write a statement that reads a line from the file you opened in Checkpoint 9.5, into the variable intX.

9.7 How do you determine that a file already exists?

9.8 When reading a file, how does a program know it has reached end of the file?

 ## 9.2 The OpenFileDialog, SaveFileDialog, FontDialog, and ColorDialog Controls

CONCEPT: Visual Basic provides dialog controls that equip your applications with standard Windows dialog boxes for operations such as opening files, saving files, and selecting fonts and colors.

The OpenFileDialog and SaveFileDialog Controls

So far, the applications in this chapter that open a file either specify the filename as part of the code or require the user to enter the path and filename. Most Windows users, however, are accustomed to using a dialog box to browse their disk for a file to open or for a location to save a file. You can use the OpenFileDialog and SaveFileDialog controls to equip applications with standard dialog boxes used by most Windows applications.

The OpenFileDialog Control

The **OpenFileDialog control** displays a standard Windows *Open* dialog box, such as the one shown in Figure 9-15. The *Open* dialog box is useful in applications that work with files. It gives users the ability to browse for a file to open, instead of typing a long path and filename.

Figure 9-15 Windows *Open* dialog box

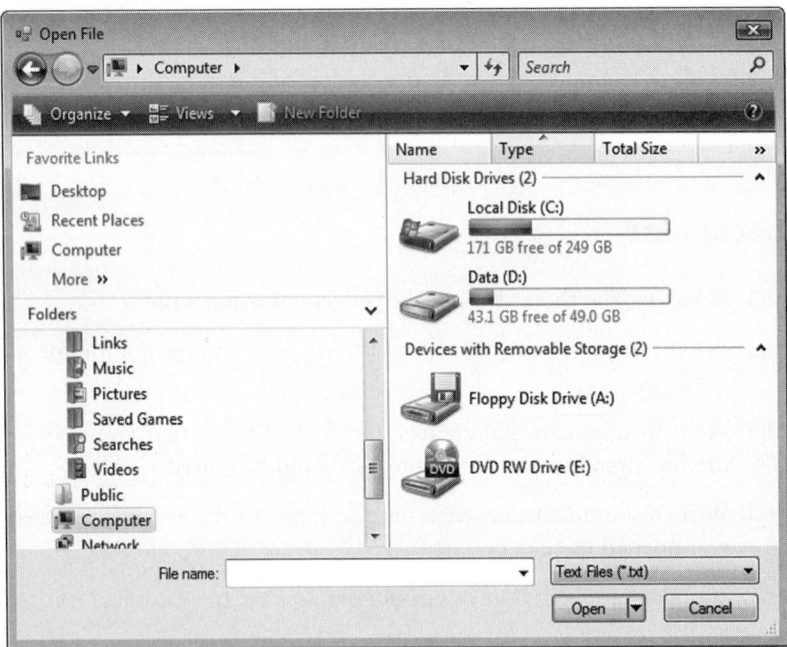

Adding the OpenFileDialog Control to Your Project

To place an OpenFileDialog control on a form, double-click the *OpenFileDialog* tool under the *Dialogs* tab in the *Toolbox* window. Because the control is invisible at runtime, it appears in the component tray at design time. We will use the prefix `ofd` when naming the control.

Displaying an Open Dialog Box

Display an *Open* dialog box by calling the OpenFileDialog control's `ShowDialog` method. The following is the method's general format:

```
ControlName.ShowDialog()
```

ControlName is the name of the OpenFileDialog control. For example, assuming `ofdOpenFile` is the name of an OpenFileDialog control, the following statement calls its `ShowDialog` method:

```
ofdOpenFile.ShowDialog()
```

`ShowDialog` returns one of the values `Windows.Forms.DialogResult.OK` or `Windows.Forms.DialogResult.Cancel`, indicating which button, *OK* or *Cancel*, the user clicked to close the dialog box. When the user selects a file with the *Open* dialog box, the file's path and name are stored in the control's **Filename property**.

The following code displays an *Open* dialog box and determines whether the user has selected a file. If so, the filename is displayed as follows:

```
If ofdOpenFile.ShowDialog() = Windows.Forms.DialogResult.OK Then
   MessageBox.Show(ofdOpenFile.FileName)
Else
   MessageBox.Show("You selected no file.")
End If
```

The Filter Property

The *Open* dialog box has a *Files of type* list box, which displays a filter that specifies the type of files visible in the dialog box. Filters typically use the wildcard character (*) followed by a file extension. For example, the *.txt filter specifies that only files ending in .txt (text files) are to be displayed. The *.doc filter specifies that only files ending in .doc (Microsoft Word files) are to be displayed. The *.* filter allows all files to be displayed.

The dialog box in Figure 9-16 shows a list box with *.txt and *.* filters.

Figure 9-16 *Open* dialog box with *.txt and *.* filters

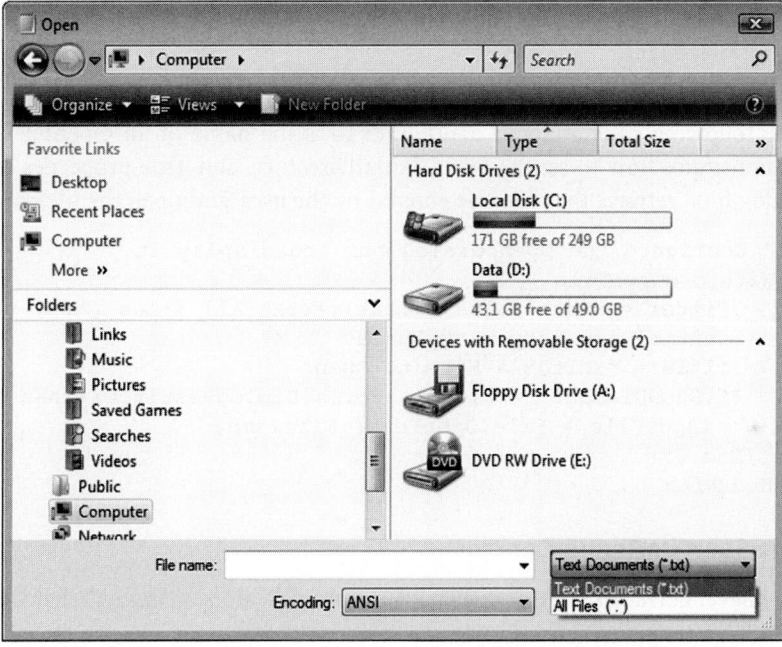

Use the **Filter property** to set the filters in the *Files of type* list box. This property can be set in the *Properties* window at design time, or by code at runtime. When storing a value in the Filter property, store a string containing a description of the filter and the filter itself. The description and the filter are separated with the pipe (|) symbol. For example, assuming an application has an OpenFileDialog control named ofdOpenFile, the following statement sets the Filter property for text files:

```
ofdOpenFile.Filter = "Text files (*.txt)|*.txt"
```

The part of the string appearing before the pipe symbol is a description of the filter, and is displayed in the *Files of type* list box. The part of the string appearing after the pipe symbol is the actual filter. In our example, the description of the filter is Text files (*.txt) and the filter is *.txt.

The pipe symbol is also used to separate multiple filters. For example, the following statement stores two filters in `ofdOpenFile.Filter`: `*.txt` and `*.*`:

```
ofdOpenFile.Filter = "Text files (*.txt)|*.txt|All Files (*.*)|*.*"
```

The description of the first filter is `Text files (*.txt)`, and the filter is `*.txt`. The description of the second filter is `All files (*.*)`, and the filter is `*.*`.

The InitialDirectory Property

By default, the *Open* dialog box displays the current directory (or folder). You can specify another directory to be initially displayed by storing its path in the **InitialDirectory** property. For example, the following code stores the path *C:\Data* in `ofdOpenFile.Initial-Directory` before displaying an *Open* dialog box:

```
ofdOpenFile.InitialDirectory = "C:\Data"
ofdOpenFile.ShowDialog()
```

When the *Open* dialog box is displayed, it shows the contents of the directory *C:\Data*.

The Title Property

You can change the default text displayed in the *Open* dialog box's title bar by storing a string in the control's **Title property**.

Using the *Open* Dialog Box to Open a File

The following code assumes `ofdOpenFile` is the name of an OpenFileDialog control. It demonstrates how to set the Filter, InitialDirectory, and Title properties, display the *Open* dialog box, retrieve the filename entered by the user, and open the file.

```
' Configure the Open dialog box and display it.
With ofdOpenFile
   .Filter = "Text files (*.txt)|*.txt|All files (*.*)|*.*"
   .InitialDirectory = "C:\Data"
   .Title = "Select a File to Open"
   If .ShowDialog() = Windows.Forms.DialogResult.OK Then
      inputFile = File.OpenText(.Filename)
   End If
End With
```

The SaveFileDialog Control

The **SaveFileDialog control** displays a standard Windows *Save As* dialog box. Figure 9-17 shows an example.

The *Save As* **dialog** box is useful in applications that work with files. It gives users the ability to browse their disks and to choose a location and name for the file.

The SaveFileDialog control has much in common with the OpenFileDialog control. Double-click the *SaveFileDialog* tool in the toolbox to place the control on a form. Because the control is invisible at runtime, it appears in the component tray at design time. We will use the prefix `sfd` when naming the control.

Display a *Save As* dialog box by calling the SaveFileDialog control's `ShowDialog` method. The following is the method's general format:

```
ControlName.ShowDialog()
```

ControlName is the name of the SaveFileDialog control. For example, assuming `sfdSaveFile` is the name of a SaveFileDialog control, the following statement calls its `ShowDialog` method:

```
sfdSaveFile.ShowDialog()
```

This method returns one of the values `Windows.Forms.DialogResult.OK` or `Windows.-Forms.DialogResult.Cancel` indicating which button, *OK* or *Cancel*, the user clicked to dismiss the dialog box.

Figure 9-17 Windows *Save As* dialog box

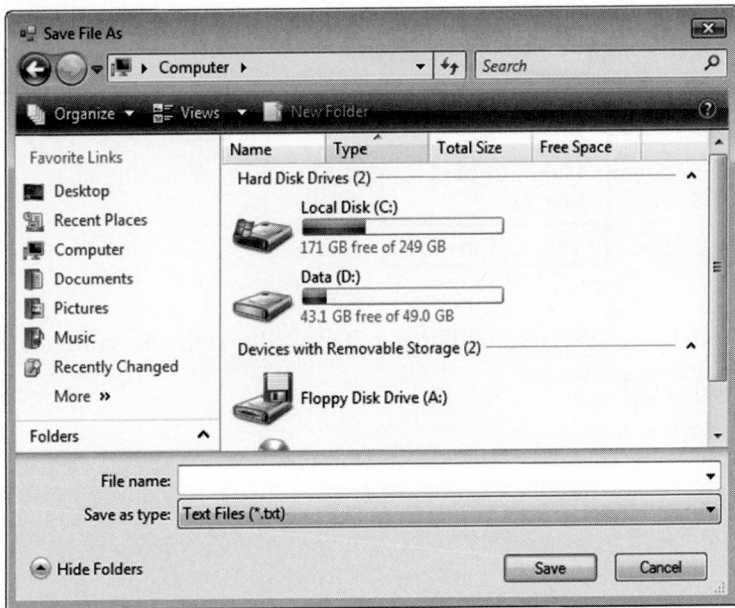

The Filename property holds the name of the file selected or entered by the user. The Filter, InitialDirectory, and Title properties work with the *Save As* dialog box the same way they do with the *Open* dialog box. The following code assumes that `sfdSaveFile` is the name of a common dialog control. It demonstrates how to set the Filter, InitialDirectory, and Title properties, display the *Save As* dialog box, retrieve the filename entered by the user, and open the file.

```
' Configure the Save As dialog box and display it.
With sfdSaveFile
   .Filter = "Text files (*.txt)|*.txt|All files (*.*)|*.*"
   .InitialDirectory = "C:\Data"
   .Title = "Save File As"
   ' If the user selected a file, open it for output.
   If.ShowDialog() = Windows.Forms.DialogResult.OK Then
      outputFile = System.IO.File.OpenText(.Filename)
   End If
End With
```

In Tutorial 9-4, you gain experience using the OpenFileDialog and SaveFileDialog controls by creating a simple text editor application. You will also learn about the TextBox control's MultiLine property, WordWrap property, and TextChanged event.

Tutorial 9-4:

Creating a simple text editor application

In this tutorial, you will create a simple text editing application that allows you to create documents, save them, and open existing documents. The application will use a Multiline TextBox control to hold the document text. It will also use the menu system shown in Figure 9-18.

Figure 9-18 Simple Text Editor menu system

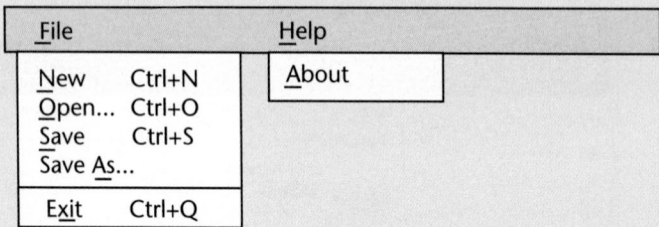

Table 9-1 lists the required menu items, showing the contents of their Text and ShortcutKeys properties.

Table 9-1 Menu items and their Text and ShortcutKeys properties

Menu Item Name	Text Property	ShortcutKeys Property
mnuFile	&File	(None)
mnuFileNew	&New	Ctrl+N
mnuFileOpen	&Open...	Ctrl+O
mnuFileSave	&Save	Ctrl+S
mnuFileSaveAs	Save &As...	(None)
mnuFileExit	E&xit	Ctrl+Q
mnuHelp	&Help	(None)
mnuHelpAbout	&About	(None)

Some of the menu item Text property values end with an ellipsis (. . .). It is a standard Windows convention for a menu item's text to end with an ellipsis if the menu item displays a dialog box.

Step 1: Create a new Windows Forms Application project named *Simple Text Editor*.

Step 2: Set the form's Text property to *Simple Text Editor*. Create a MenuStrip control on the form and add the menu items listed in Table 9-1. Set their Text and ShortcutKeys properties to the values shown in the table. The form should appear similar to the one shown in Figure 9-19.

Figure 9-19 Initial *Simple Text Editor* form

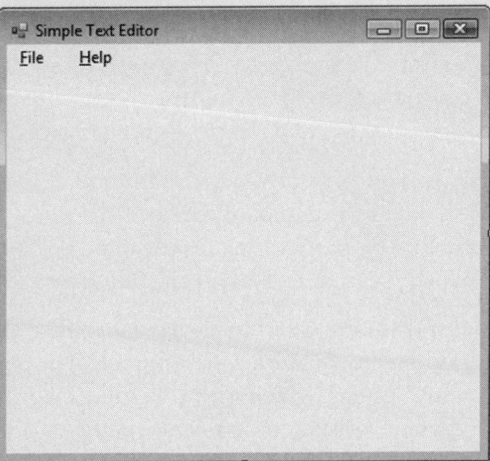

Step 3: Add a TextBox control to the form named `txtDocument`. TextBox controls have a Boolean property named **MultiLine**, which is set to *False* by default. When this property is set to *True*, the height of the TextBox control can be enlarged and its text can span multiple lines. Set the MultiLine property of the `txtDocument` control to *True*. TextBox controls also have a **WordWrap property** that, when set to *True*, causes long text lines to wrap around to the following line. By default, WordWrap is set to *True*.

Step 4: Enlarge the size of the `txtDocument` control so it fills most of the form, as shown in Figure 9-20.

Figure 9-20 *Simple Text Editor* form with text box enlarged

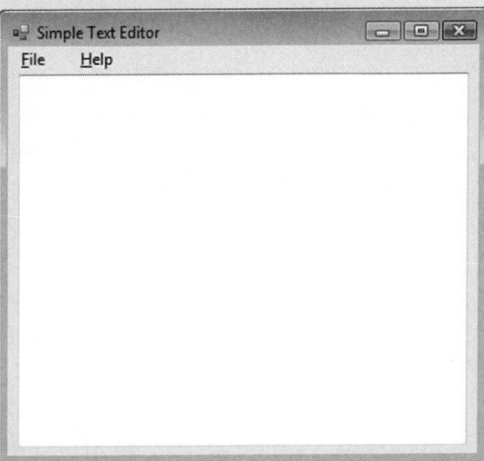

Step 5: Set the `txtDocument` control's Anchor property to *Top*, *Bottom*, *Left*, *Right*. This will cause the TextBox control to resize automatically if the user resizes the form.

Step 6: Add OpenFileDialog and SaveFileDialog controls to the form. (You will find these controls under the *Dialogs* group in the Toolbox.) Name the OpenFileDialog control **ofdOpenFile**. Name the SaveFileDialog control **sfdSaveFile**.

Step 7: Set the Title property of the `ofdOpenFile` control to *Open File*. Set the Title property of the `sfdSaveFile` control to *Save File As*. Set the Filter property to *Text Files (*.txt) | *.txt* for both controls.

Step 8: Now you are ready to write the code for the application. At the end of the tutorial you will find all of the code shown in one listing. (Don't type any of the line numbers. They are shown for reference only.) First, open the *Code* window and type the `Imports` statement shown in line 1.

Step 9: Inside the form's class declaration, type the comment and the class-level declarations shown in lines 4 through 6. The `strFilename` variable will hold the file-name under which the text box's contents are saved. The `blnIsChanged` variable is a flag to indicate whether the text box's contents have been changed since the last time they were saved. We need this flag so we can warn the user anytime he or she is about to clear the current document without saving it.

Step 10: Type the code for the `ClearDocument` procedure shown in lines 8 through 17. The `ClearDocument` procedure clears the `txtDocument` control's Text property, sets `strFilename` to an empty string, and sets `blnIsChanged` to *False*.

Step 11: Type the code for the `OpenDocument` procedure shown in lines 22 through 46. The `OpenDocument` procedure displays an *Open* dialog box, opens the file selected by the user, and reads its contents into the text box.

Step 12: Type the code for the `SaveDocument` procedure shown in lines 50 through 69. The `SaveDocument` procedure saves the contents of the text box to the file specified by the `strFilename` variable.

Step 13: Now you will write the code for the `txtDocument_TextChanged` event handler, shown in lines 71 through 74. This event handler will execute anytime the `txtDocument` TextBox control's Text property changes. When that happens, we want to set the `blnIsChanged` variable to *True* to indicate that the current document has changed. Here's how to write the event handler:

In the *Code* window, select *txtDocument* in the class drop-down list box (which is in the upper-left area of the *Code* window), and then select *TextChanged* in the method name drop-down list box (which is in the upper-right area of the *Code* window). This will create a code template for the event handler. Simply type the contents of lines 72 and 73 to complete the event handler.

Step 14: Next, write the Click event handlers for the menu items. The code for all of the event handlers is shown in lines 76 through 141.

Step 15: Last, you will write the code for the `Form1_FormClosing` event handler, shown in lines 143 through 157. The purpose of this event handler is to warn the user if he or she attempts to exit the application without saving the contents of the text box. Here's how to write the event handler:

In the *Code* window, select *(Form1 Events)* in the class drop-down list box (in the upper-left area of the *Code* window), and then select *FormClosing* in the method name drop-down list box (in the upper-right area of the *Code* window). This will create a code template for the event handler. Simply type the contents of lines 144 through 156 to complete the event handler.

Step 16: Save and run the application. If you entered all the code correctly, you should see the form shown in Figure 9-21. Enter some text into the text box. Experiment with each of the menu commands to see if the application operates correctly. When you are finished, exit the application.

Figure 9-21 *Simple Text Editor* form

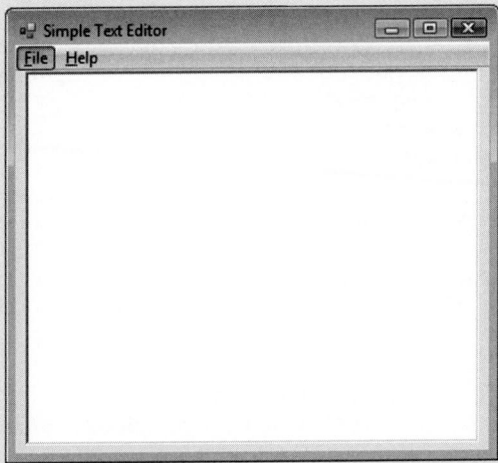

```
1  Imports System.IO
2
3  Public Class Form1
4      ' Class-level variables
5      Private strFilename As String = String.Empty ' Document filename
6      Dim blnIsChanged As Boolean = False          ' File change flag
7
8      Sub ClearDocument()
9        ' Clear the contents of the text box.
10       txtDocument.Clear()
11
12       ' Clear the document name.
13       strFilename = String.Empty
14
15       ' Set isChanged to False.
16       blnIsChanged = False
17     End Sub
18
19   ' The OpenDocument procedure opens a file and loads it
20   ' into the TextBox for editing.
21
22     Sub OpenDocument()
23       Dim inputFile As StreamReader ' Object variable
24
25       If ofdOpenFile.ShowDialog = Windows.Forms.DialogResult.OK Then
26         ' Retrieve the selected filename.
27         strFilename = ofdOpenFile.FileName
28
29         Try
30           ' Open the file.
31           inputFile = File.OpenText(strFilename)
```

```
32
33                  ' Read the file's contents into the TextBox.
34                  txtDocument.Text = inputFile.ReadToEnd
35
36                  ' Close the file.
37                  inputFile.Close()
38
39                  ' Update the isChanged variable.
40                  blnIsChanged = False
41             Catch
42                  ' Error message for file open error.
43                  MessageBox.Show("Error opening the file.")
44             End Try
45         End If
46     End Sub
47
48     ' The SaveDocument procedure saves the current document.
49
50     Sub SaveDocument()
51         Dim outputFile As StreamWriter ' Object variable
52
53         Try
54             ' Create the file.
55             outputFile = File.CreateText(strFilename)
56
57             ' Write the TextBox to the file.
58             outputFile.Write(txtDocument.Text)
59
60             ' Close the file.
61             outputFile.Close()
62
63             ' Update the isChanged variable.
64             blnIsChanged = False
65         Catch
66             ' Error message for file creation error.
67             MessageBox.Show("Error creating the file.")
68         End Try
69     End Sub
70
71     Private Sub txtDocument_TextChanged(...) Handles txtDocument.TextChanged
72         ' Indicate the text has changed.
73         blnIsChanged = True
74     End Sub
75
76     Private Sub mnuFileNew_Click(...) Handles mnuFileNew.Click
77         ' Has the current document changed?
78         If blnIsChanged = True Then
79             ' Confirm before clearing the document.
80             If MessageBox.Show("The current document is not saved. " &
81                                "Are you sure?", "Confirm",
82                                MessageBoxButtons.YesNo) =
83                     Windows.Forms.DialogResult.Yes Then
84                 ClearDocument()
85             End If
86         Else
```

```
 87                    ' Document has not changed, so clear it.
 88               ClearDocument()
 89           End If
 90      End Sub
 91
 92      Private Sub mnuFileOpen_Click(...) Handles mnuFileOpen.Click
 93          ' Has the current document changed?
 94          If blnIsChanged = True Then
 95              ' Confirm before clearing and replacing.
 96              If MessageBox.Show("The current document is not saved. " &
 97                                  "Are you sure?", "Confirm",
 98                                  MessageBoxButtons.YesNo) =
 99                                  Windows.Forms.DialogResult.Yes Then
100                  ClearDocument()
101                  OpenDocument()
102              End If
103          Else
104              ' Document has not changed, so replace it.
105              ClearDocument()
106              OpenDocument()
107          End If
108      End Sub
109
110      Private Sub mnuFileSave_Click(...) Handles mnuFileSave.Click
111          ' Does the current document have a filename?
112          If strFilename = String.Empty Then
113              ' The document has not been saved, so
114              ' use Save As dialog box.
115              If sfdSaveFile.ShowDialog = Windows.Forms.DialogResult.OK Then
116                  strFilename = sfdSaveFile.FileName
117                  SaveDocument()
118              End If
119          Else
120              ' Save the document with the current filename.
121              SaveDocument()
122          End If
123      End Sub
124
125      Private Sub mnuFileSaveAs_Click(...) Handles mnuFileSaveAs.Click
126          ' Save the current document under a new filename.
127          If sfdSaveFile.ShowDialog = Windows.Forms.DialogResult.OK Then
128              strFilename = sfdSaveFile.FileName
129              SaveDocument()
130          End If
131      End Sub
132
133      Private Sub mnuExit_Click(...) Handles mnuExit.Click
134          ' Close the form.
135          Me.Close()
136      End Sub
137
138      Private Sub mnuHelpAbout_Click(...) Handles mnuHelpAbout.Click
139          ' Display an about box.
140          MessageBox.Show("Simple Text Editor version 1.0")
141      End Sub
```

```
142
143    Private Sub Form1_FormClosing(...) Handles Me.FormClosing
144       ' If the document has not been changed, confirm
145       ' before exiting.
146       If blnIsChanged = True Then
147          If MessageBox.Show("The current document is not saved. " &
148                             "Do you wish to discard your changes?",
149                             "Confirm",
150                             MessageBoxButtons.YesNo) =
151                       Windows.Forms.DialogResult.Yes Then
152             e.Cancel = False
153          Else
154             e.Cancel = True
155          End If
156       End If
157    End Sub
158 End Class
```

The ColorDialog and FontDialog Controls

The ColorDialog Control

The **ColorDialog** control displays a standard Windows *Color* dialog box. Figure 9-22 shows a default *Color* dialog box, on the left. When the user clicks the *Define Custom Colors* button, the dialog box expands to become the fully open *Color* dialog box shown on the right.

Double-click the *ColorDialog* icon in the *Dialogs* section of the toolbox to place the control on a form. Because the control is invisible at runtime, it appears in the component tray at design time. We will use the prefix cd when naming the control.

Figure 9-22 Windows *Color* dialog box

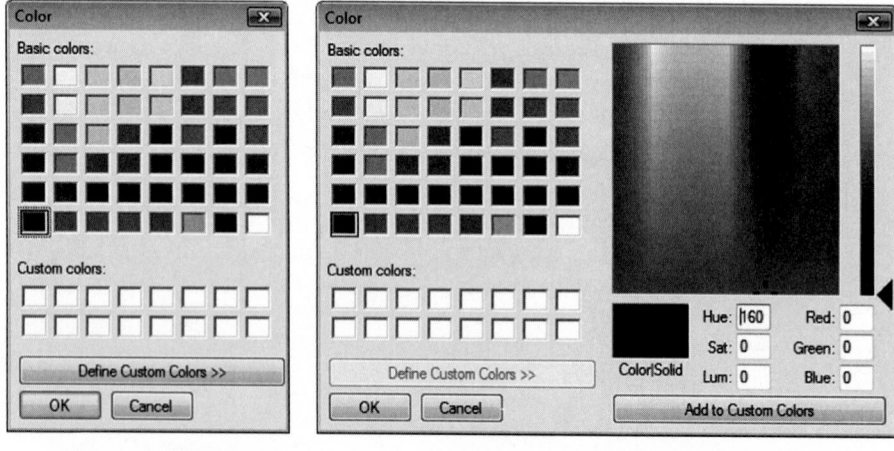

Color dialog box   Fully open *Color* dialog box

Display a *Color* dialog box by calling its `ShowDialog` method. For example, assuming `cdColor` is the name of a ColorDialog control, the following statement calls its `ShowDialog` method:

```
cdColor.ShowDialog()
```

This method returns one of the values, `Windows.Forms.DialogResult.OK` or `Windows.Forms.DialogResult.Cancel`, indicating which button, *OK* or *Cancel*, the user clicked to dismiss the dialog box. The Color property will hold a value representing the color selected by the user. This value can be used with control properties that designate color, such as ForeColor and BackColor. For example, the following code displays the *Color* dialog box and then sets the color of the text displayed by the `lblMessage` label to that selected by the user:

```
If cdColor.ShowDialog() = Windows.Forms.DialogResult.OK Then
    lblMessage.ForeColor = cdColor.Color
End If
```

By default, black is initially selected when the *Color* dialog box is displayed. If you wish to set the initially selected color, you must set the Color property to the desired color value. For example, the following code sets the initially selected color to blue:

```
cdColor.Color = Color.Blue
If cdColor.ShowDialog() = Windows.Forms.DialogResult.OK Then
    lblMessage.ForeColor = cdColor.Color
End If
```

The following code sets the initially selected color to the color of the `lblMessage` label before displaying the dialog box:

```
cdColor.Color = lblMessage.ForeColor
If cdColor.ShowDialog() = Windows.Forms.DialogResult.OK Then
    lblMessage.ForeColor = cdColor.Color
End If
```

The FontDialog Control

The **FontDialog control** displays a standard Windows *Font* dialog box. Figure 9-23 shows the default *Font* dialog box on the left, and a *Font* dialog box with a *Color* drop-down list on the right.

Figure 9-23 Windows *Font* dialog box

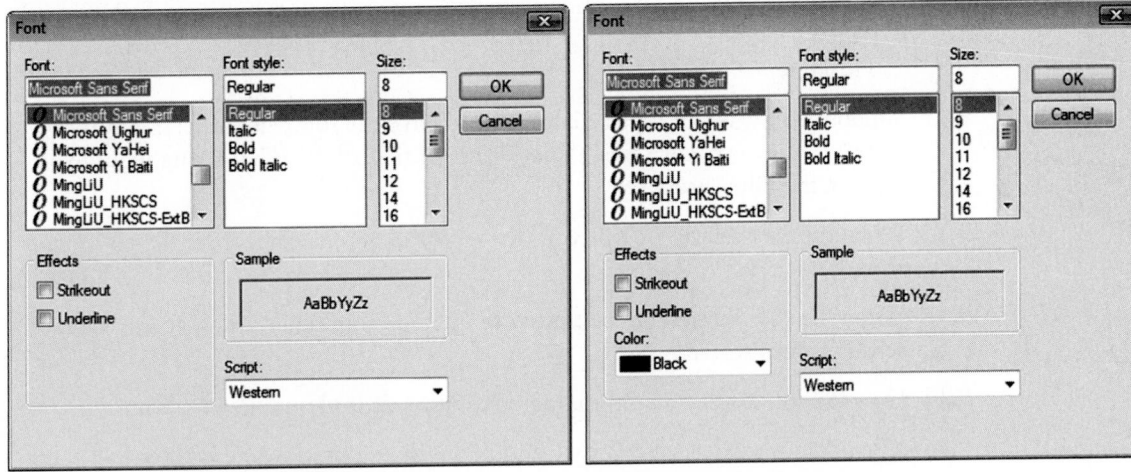

Default *Font* dialog box   *Font* dialog box with color choices displayed

Double-click the *FontDialog* icon in the *Dialogs* section of the toolbox to place the control on a form. Because the control is invisible at runtime, it appears in the component tray at design time. We will use the prefix `fd` when naming the control.

You display a *Font* dialog box by calling the FontDialog control's `ShowDialog` method. For example, assuming `fdFont` is the name of a FontDialog control, the following statement calls its `ShowDialog` method:

```
fdFont.ShowDialog()
```

By default, the *Font* dialog box does not allow the user to select a color. Color is controlled by the FontDialog control's ShowColor property, which can be set to *True* or *False*. When set to *True*, the *Font* dialog box appears with a *Color* drop-down list, shown on the right in Figure 9-23.

The `ShowDialog` method returns one of the values `Windows.Forms.DialogResult.OK` or `Windows.Forms.DialogResult.Cancel` indicating which button, *OK* or *Cancel*, the user clicked to dismiss the dialog box. The Font property will hold a value representing the font settings selected by the user. The Color property will hold a value representing the color selected by the user. For example, the following code displays the *Font* dialog box and then sets the `lblMessage` control's font to that selected by the user.

```
If fdFont.ShowDialog() = Windows.Forms.DialogResult.OK Then
    lblTest.Font = fdFont.Font
End If
```

The following code displays a *Font* dialog box with a drop-down list of colors. It then sets the `lblMessage` control's font and color to the values selected by the user.

```
fdFont.ShowColor = True
If fdFont.ShowDialog() = Windows.Forms.DialogResult.OK Then
    lblTest.Font = fdFont.Font
    lblTest.ForeColor = fdFont.Color
End If
```

Checkpoint

9.9 Why is it a good idea to use the *Open* and *Save As* dialog boxes in applications that work with files?

9.10 What is the purpose of the following OpenFileDialog and SaveFileDialog properties?

> Filter
> InitialDirectory
> Title
> Filename

9.11 Suppose you want an *Open* dialog box to have the following filters: text files (*.txt*), Microsoft Word files (*.doc*), and all files (*.* *). What string would you store in the Filter property?

9.12 When the user selects a color with the *Color* dialog box, where is the color value stored?

9.13 When the user selects font settings with the *Font* dialog box, where are the font setting values stored?

9.14 How do you display a *Font* dialog box with a drop-down list of colors?

9.15 When the user selects a color with the *Font* dialog box, where is the color value stored?

9.3 The PrintDocument Control

CONCEPT: The PrintDocument control allows you to send output to the printer.

The **PrintDocument control** gives your application the ability to print output on the printer. Double-click the *PrintDocument* tool in the Printing section of the *Toolbox* window to place a PrintDocument control on a form. Because the control is invisible at runtime, it appears in the component tray at design time. We will use the prefix pd when naming the control.

The `Print` Method and the `PrintPage` Event

The PrintDocument control has a **Print method** that starts the printing process. The method's general format is as follows:

```
PrintDocumentControl.Print()
```

When the `Print` method is called, it triggers a PrintPage event. You must write code in the PrintPage event handler to initiate the actual printing. To create a PrintPage event handler code template, double-click the PrintDocument control in the component tray. The following is an example:

```
Private Sub pdPrint_PrintPage(...) Handles pdPrint.PrintPage

End Sub
```

Inside the **PrintPage event handler**, you can write code that sends text to the printer using a specified font and color, at a specified location. We will use the following general format to call the `e.Graphics.DrawString` method:

```
e.Graphics.DrawString(String, New Font(FontName, Size,
    Style), Brushes.Black, HPos, VPos)
```

String is the string to be printed. *FontName* is a string holding the name of the font to use. *Size* is the size of the font in points. *Style* is the font style. Valid values are `FontStyle.Bold`, `FontStyle.Italic`, `FontStyle.Regular`, `FontStyle.Strikeout`, and `FontStyle.Underline`. *HPos* is the horizontal position of the output. This is the distance of the output, in points, from the left margin of the paper. *VPos* is the vertical position of the output. This is the distance of the output, in points, from the top margin of the paper. The `Brushes.Black` argument specifies that output should be printed in black.

The following PrintPage event handler prints the contents of a TextBox control, `txtInput`, in a regular 12 point Times New Roman font. The horizontal and vertical coordinates of the output are 10 and 10.

```
Private Sub pdPrint_PrintPage(...) Handles pdPrint.PrintPage
    e.Graphics.DrawString(txtInput.Text, New Font("Times New Roman",
                12, FontStyle.Regular), Brushes.Black, 10, 10)
End Sub
```

The following PrintPage event handler prints the string "Sales Report" in a bold 18 point Courier font. The horizontal and vertical coordinates of the output are 150 and 80.

```
Private Sub pdPrint_PrintPage(...) Handles pdPrint.PrintPage
    e.Graphics.DrawString("Sales Report", New Font("Courier",
                18, FontStyle.Bold), Brushes.Black, 150, 80)
End Sub
```

The following PrintPage event handler prints the contents of a file. Assume that `strFilename` is a class-level string variable containing the name of the file whose contents are to be printed.

```
Private Sub pdPrint_PrintPage(...) Handles pdPrint.PrintPage
    Dim inputFile As StreamReader ' Object variable
    Dim intX As Integer = 10      ' X coordinate for printing
    Dim intY As Integer = 10      ' Y coordinate for printing

    Try
        ' Open the file.
      inputFile = File.OpenText(strFilename)

        ' Read all the lines in the file.
      Do While inputFile.Peek <> -1
          ' Print a line from the file.
        e.Graphics.DrawString(inputFile.ReadLine(), New Font
            ("Courier", 10, FontStyle.Regular), Brushes.Black,
             intX, intY)

          ' Add 12 to intY.
        intY += 12
      Loop

        ' Close the file.
      inputFile.Close()
    Catch
        ' Error message for file open error.
      MessageBox.Show("Error: could not open file.")
    End Try
End Sub
```

The variables `intX` and `intY` specify the horizontal and vertical positions of each line of printed output. The statement `intY += 12` inside the loop increases the vertical distance of each line by 12 points from the top of the page. The output is printed in a 10 point font, so there are 2 points of space between each line.

In Tutorial 9-5, you will modify the *Simple Text Editor* application you created in Tutorial 9-4 by adding a *Print* command to the *File* menu.

Tutorial 9-5:
Adding printing capabilities to the *Simple Text Editor* application

Step 1:   Open the *Simple Text Editor* project you created in Tutorial 9-4.

Step 2:   Add a *Print* menu item and separator bar to the *File* menu, as shown in Figure 9-24. To add the *Print* menu item, right-click on the *Exit* MenuItem. From the pop-up menu, select *Insert*, then *MenuItem*. Set the Text property to &Print and the Name Property to `mnuFilePrint`. To add a separator bar, right-click on the *Exit* MenuItem, and select *Insert*, then *Separator*.

Step 3:   Add a PrintDocument control to the form. (The PrintDocument control is in the *Printing* section of the Toolbox.) Name the control `pdPrint`.

Step 4:   Double-click the `pdPrint` control to create a code template for the `pdPrint_PrintPage` event handler. Complete the event handler by entering the following code shown in bold:

```
Private Sub pdPrint_PrintPage(...) Handles pdPrint.PrintPage
    ' Print the contents of the text box.
    e.Graphics.DrawString(txtDocument.Text, New Font ("MS Sans Serif",
        12, FontStyle.Regular), Brushes.Black, 10, 10)
End Sub
```

Figure 9-24 Print menu item and separator bars added

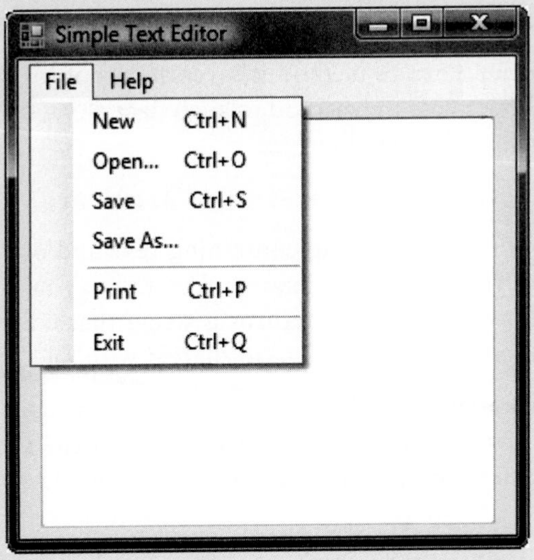

Step 5: Add the following `mnuFilePrint_Click` event procedure.

```
Private Sub mnuFilePrint_Click(...) Handles mnuFilePrint.Click
    ' Print the current document.
    pdPrint.Print()
End Sub
```

Step 6: Save and run the application. Enter some text into the text box or load an existing file. Test the new *Print* command. The contents of the text box should be printed on the printer.

Step 7: Exit the application.

Formatted Reports with `String.Format`

Reports typically contain the following sections:

- A **report header**, printed first, contains the name of the report, the date and time the report was printed, and other general information about the data in the report.
- The **report body** contains the report's data and is often formatted in columns.
- An optional **report footer** contains the sum of one or more columns of data.

Printing Reports with Columnar Data

Report data is typically printed in column format, with each column having an appropriate heading. To properly align printed data in columns, you can use a monospaced font to ensure that all characters occupy the same amount of space, and use the `String.Format` method to format the data into columns. Let's take a closer look at each of these topics.

Monospaced Fonts

Most printers normally use proportionally spaced fonts such as MS sans serif. In a proportionally spaced font, the amount of space occupied by a character depends on the width of the character. For example, the letters *m* and *w* occupy more space than the letters *i* and *j*. Using proportionally spaced fonts, you may have trouble aligning data properly in columns. To remedy the problem, you can select a monospaced font such as Courier New. All characters in a monospaced font use the same amount of space on the printed page.

Using `String.Format` to Align Data along Column Boundaries

The `String.Format` method is a versatile tool for formatting strings. In this section, we discuss how to use the method to align data along column boundaries. The method is used in the following general format:

```
String.Format(FormatString, Arg0, Arg1 [,...])
```

FormatString is a string containing text and/or formatting specifications. *Arg0* and *Arg1* are values to be formatted. The [,...] notation indicates that more arguments may follow. The method returns a string that contains the data provided by the arguments *Arg0*, *Arg1*, and so on, formatted with the specifications found in *FormatString*.

Let's look at an example of how *FormatString* can be used to format data into columns. The following code produces a string with the numbers 10, 20, and 30 aligned into columns of ten characters wide each. The resulting string is stored in the variable `strTemp`.

```
Dim strTemp As String
Dim intX, intY, intZ As Integer
intX = 10
intY = 20
intZ = 30
strTemp = String.Format("{0, 10} {1, 10} {2, 10} ", intX, intY, intZ)
```

The string "{0, 10} {1, 10} {2, 10}" is the format string. The variable `intX` is argument 0, the variable `intY` is argument 1, and the variable `intZ` is argument 2. This is illustrated in Figure 9-25.

Figure 9-25 Arguments of the `String.Format` method

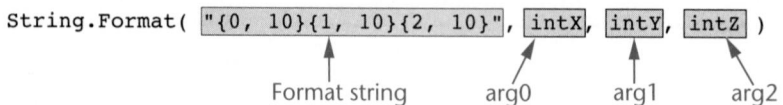

The contents of the format string specify how the data is to be formatted. In our example, the string has three sets of numbers inside curly braces. The first set is {0, 10}. This specifies that argument 0 (the variable `intX`) is to be placed in a column ten spaces wide. The second set is {1, 10}. This specifies that argument 1 (the variable `intY`) is to be placed in a column ten spaces wide. The third set, {2, 10}, specifies that argument 2 (the variable `intZ`) is to be placed in a column ten spaces wide. Figure 9-26 labels all these parts. There are no spaces between the sets.

Figure 9-26 Format specifications

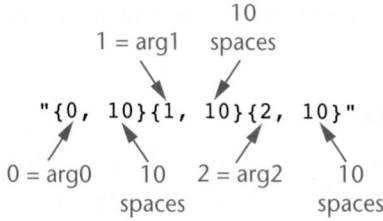

After the last statement in the previous code executes, the variable `strTemp` contains the string "   10   20   30". The numbers are placed in columns of ten spaces each, as illustrated in Figure 9-27. In our example, the numbers are right justified inside the columns. If you use a negative value for a column width in the format string, the column is left justified. For example, using the variables `intX`, `intY`, and `intZ` from the previous code example, the method call

```
String.Format("{0, -10} {1, -10} {2, -10} ", intX, intY, intZ)
```

produces the string "10   20   30   ".

Let's examine a code sample that prints a sales report with a header, two columns of data, and a footer. The data is printed from the following parallel arrays:

```
Dim strNames As String() = {"John Smith", "Jill McKenzie",
                            "Karen Suttles", "Jason Mabry",
                            "Susan Parsons"}
Dim decSales As Decimal() = {2500.0, 3400.0, 4200.0,
                             2200.0, 3100.0}
```

Figure 9-27 Column widths

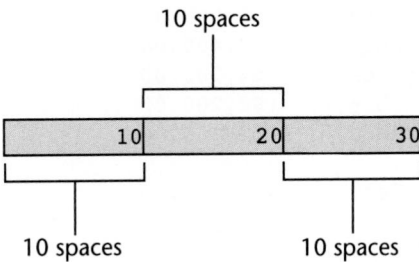

The `strNames` array contains five salespeople's names and the `decSales` array contains each salesperson's sales. The `For...Next` loop in the following event handler prints each line of data and uses an accumulator, `decTotal`, to sum the sales amounts. The contents of `decTotal` are printed in the footer to show the total sales.

```
Private Sub pdPrint_PrintPage(...) Handles pdPrint.PrintPage
    Dim intCount As Integer       ' Loop counter
    Dim decTotal As Decimal = 0   ' Accumulator
    Dim intVertPosition As Integer ' Vertical printing position

    ' Print the report header.
    e.Graphics.DrawString("Sales Report", New Font("Courier New", 12,
        FontStyle.Bold), Brushes.Black, 150, 10)

    e.Graphics.DrawString("Date and Time: " & Now.ToString(),
        New Font("Courier New", 12, FontStyle.Bold),
        Brushes.Black, 10, 38)

    ' Print the column headings.
    e.Graphics.DrawString(String.Format("{0, 20} {1, 20} ",
        "NAME", "SALES"), New Font("Courier New", 12,
        FontStyle.Bold), Brushes.Black, 10, 66)
```

```
' Print the body of the report.
intVertPosition = 82
For intCount = 0 To 4
    e.Graphics.DrawString(String.Format("{0, 20} {1, 20} ",
        strNames(intCount), decSales(intCount).ToString("c")),
        New Font("Courier New", 12, FontStyle.Regular),
        Brushes.Black, 10, intVertPosition)

    decTotal += decSales(intCount)
    intVertPosition += 14
Next

' Print the report footer.
e.Graphics.DrawString("Total Sales: " & decTotal.ToString("c"),
    New Font("Courier New", 12, FontStyle.Bold),
    Brushes.Black, 150, 165)
End Sub
```

The report printed by this code appears similar to the following:

```
        Sales Report

Date and Time: 10/14/2010 11:12:34 AM

            Name          Sales
      John Smith      $2,500.00
   Jill McKenzie      $3,400.00
   Karen Suttles      $4,200.00
     Jason Mabry      $2,200.00
   Susan Parsons      $3,100.00

   Total Sales:      $15,400.00
```

 **Checkpoint**

9.16 How do you trigger a PrinterDocument control's PrintPage event?

9.17 Assume an application has a PrintDocument control named pdPrint. Write a statement in the control's PrintPage event handler that prints your first and last name in an 18 point bold MS sans serif font. Print your name at 100 points from the page's left margin and 20 points from the page's top margin.

9.18 Name the three sections most reports have.

9.19 What is the difference between a proportionally spaced font and a monospaced font?

9.20 Assume that an application has a PrintDocument control named *pdPrint*. Write a statement in the control's PrintPage event handler that prints the contents of the variables a and b in a 12 point regular Courier New font. The contents of a should be printed in a column 12 characters wide, and the contents of b should be printed in a column 8 characters wide. Print the data 10 points from the page's left margin and 50 points from the page's top margin.

9.21 Rewrite the answer you wrote to Checkpoint 9.20 so the contents of the variable a are left justified.

9.4 Structures

CONCEPT: Visual Basic allows you to create your own data types, into which you may group multiple data fields.

So far you have created applications that keep data in individual variables. If you need to group items, you can create arrays. Arrays, however, require elements to be of the same data type. Sometimes a relationship exists between items of different types. For example, a payroll system might use the variables shown in the following declaration statements:

```
Dim intEmpNumber As Integer    ' Employee number
Dim strFirstName As String     ' Employee's first name
Dim strLastName As String      ' Employee's last name
Dim dblHours As Double         ' Number of hours worked
Dim decPayRate As Decimal      ' Hourly pay rate
Dim decGrossPay As Decimal     ' Gross pay
```

All these variables are related because they can hold data about the same employee. The `Dim` statements, however, create separate variables and do not establish relationships.

Instead of creating separate variables that hold related data, you can group the related data. A **structure** is a data type you can create that contains one or more variables known as fields. The fields can be of different data types. Once a structure has been created, variables of the structure may be declared.

You create a structure at the class- or module-level with the **Structure** statement:

```
[AccessSpecifier] Structure StructureName
    FieldDeclarations
End Structure
```

AccessSpecifier is shown in brackets, indicating that it is optional. If you use the `Public` access specifier, the structure is accessible to statements outside the class or module. If you use the `Private` access specifier, the structure is accessible only to statements in the same class or module. *StructureName* is the name of the structure. *FieldDeclarations* is one or more declarations of fields, as regular `Dim` statements. The following is an example:

```
Structure EmpPayData
    Dim intEmpNumber As Integer
    Dim strFirstName As String
    Dim strLastName As String
    Dim dblHours As Double
    Dim decPayRate As Decimal
    Dim decGrossPay As Decimal
End Structure
```

This statement declares a structure named `EmpPayData`, having six fields.

TIP: Structure names and class names should begin with uppercase letters. This serves as a visual reminder that the structure or class name is not a variable name.

> **TIP:** If you want a structure to be available to multiple forms in a project, place the `Structure` statement, with the `Public` access specifier, in a module.

The `Structure` statement does not create a variable—it creates a new data type by telling Visual Basic what the data type contains. You declare variables of a structure using `Dim` statements, just as you would with any other data type. For example, the following statement declares a variable called `deptHead` as an `EmpPayData` variable:

```
Dim deptHead As EmpPayData
```

The `deptHead` variable can store six values because the `EmpPayData` data type is made of six fields, as illustrated in Figure 9-28.

Access the fields with the dot operator. For example, the following statements assign values to all six fields of the `deptHead` variable.

```
deptHead.intEmpNumber = 1101
deptHead.strFirstName = "Joanne"
deptHead.strLastName = "Smith"
deptHead.dblHours = 40.0
deptHead.decPayRate = 25
deptHead.decGrossPay = CDec(deptHead.dblHours) *
                       deptHead.decPayRate
```

Figure 9-28 `deptHead` variable

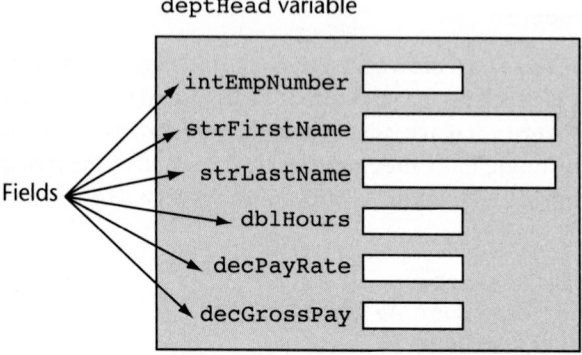

The following statement adds the `intEmpNumber` field to the `lstEmployeeList` list box:

```
lstEmployeeList.Items.Add(deptHead.intEmpNumber)
```

You can optionally use the `With` statement to simplify access to structure fields:

```
With deptHead
    .intEmpNumber = 1101
    .strFirstName = "Joanne"
    .strLastName = "Smith"
    .dblHours = 40.0
    .decPayRate = 25
    .decGrossPay = CDec(.dblHours) * .decPayRate
End With
```

Passing Structure Variables to Procedures and Functions

You may pass structure variables to procedures and functions. For example, the following procedure declares an `EmpPayData` parameter, passed by reference:

```
Sub CalcPay(ByRef employee As EmpPayData)
   ' This procedure accepts an EmpPayData variable
   ' as its argument. The employee's gross pay
   ' is calculated and stored in the grossPay
   ' field.
   With employee
      .decGrossPay =.dblHours * .decPayRate
   End With
End Sub
```

Arrays as Structure Members

Structures can contain array fields, but the arrays cannot be assigned initial sizes. An example is shown in the following statement:

```
Structure StudentRecord
   Dim strName As String
   Dim dblTestScores() As Double
End Structure
```

After declaring a structure variable, you can use the `ReDim` statement to establish a size for the array. Then you access the array elements with a subscript, as shown in the following example:

```
Dim student As StudentRecord
ReDim student.dblTestScores(4)
student.strName = "Mary McBride"
student.dblTestScores(0) = 89.0
student.dblTestScores(1) = 92.0
student.dblTestScores(2) = 84.0
student.dblTestScores(3) = 96.0
student.dblTestScores(4) = 91.0
```

Arrays of Structures

You may also declare an array of structures. For example, the following `statement` declares `employees` as an array of 10 `EmpPayData` variables:

```
Const intMAX_SUBSCRIPT As Integer = 9
Dim employees(intMAX_SUBSCRIPT) As EmpPayData
```

To access the individual elements in the array, use a subscript as shown in the following statement:

```
employees(0).intEmpNumber = 1101
```

When working with an array of structure variables in which the structure contains an array field, use the `ReDim` statement to establish a size for the array field of each element. For example, the `StudentRecord` discussed in the previous section has a field named `dblTestScores`, which is an array of five numbers. Suppose an application declares an array of `StudentRecord` variables as follows:

```
Const intMAX_SUBSCRIPT As Integer = 9
Dim students(intMAX_SUBSCRIPT) As StudentRecord
```

A loop, such as the following, can be used to set a size for each `testScores` array:

```
For intIndex = 0 To intMax_SUBSCRIPT
    ReDim students(intIndex).dblTestScores(4)
Next
```

You can use the array fields once they have been given a size. For example, the following statement stores 95 in `dblTestScores(0)` inside `students(5)`:

```
students(5).dblTestScores(0) = 95.0
```

Tutorial 9-6 examines an application that uses a structure.

Tutorial 9-6:
Examining an application with a structure

In this tutorial, you examine a modified version of the *File WriteLine Demo* project from Tutorial 9-1. This version of the project uses a structure to store the friend data.

Step 1: Open the *Structure File WriteLine Demo* project from the student sample programs folder named *Chap9\Structure File WriteLine Demo*.

Step 2: Open the *Code* window. The following statements declare the `FriendInfo` structure:

```
Structure FriendInfo
    Dim strName As String   ' To hold a name
    Dim strPhone As String  ' To hold a phone number
End Structure
```

Step 3: Look at the `btnCreateFile_Click` event handler. The procedure uses the structure variable `myFriend` to hold the names, ages, and addresses entered by the user. The `friendFile.WriteLine` statements write the contents of the structure variable's fields to the file.

```
Private Sub btnCreateFile_Click(...) Handles btnCreateFile.Click
    ' Constant for the number of friends
    Const intNUM_FRIENDS As Integer = 3

    ' Local variables
    Dim strFilename As String       ' File name
    Dim intCount As Integer         ' Loop counter
    Dim friendFile As StreamWriter  ' Object variable
    Dim myFriend As FriendInfo      ' Structure variable

    ' Get the file name from the user.
    strFilename = InputBox("Enter the filename.")

    Try
        ' Open the file.
        friendFile = File.CreateText(strFilename)

        ' Get the data and write it to the file.
        For intCount = 1 To intNUM_FRIENDS
            ' Get a friend's name.
            myFriend.strName = InputBox("Enter the name of friend " & _
                                "number " & intCount.ToString())
```

```
                  ' Get a friend's phone number.
                  myFriend.strPhone = InputBox("Enter the that friend's " &
                                               "phone number.")

                  ' Write the data to the file.
                  friendFile.WriteLine(myFriend.strName)
                  friendFile.WriteLine(myFriend.strPhone)
              Next

              ' Close the file.
              friendFile.Close()
          Catch
              ' Error message
              MessageBox.Show("That file cannot be created.")
          End Try
      End Sub
```

Step 4: Run the application and, as you did in Tutorial 9-1, click the *Save Data to File* button. Enter a filename and data for three of your friends. The procedure saves the data.

Step 5: Exit the application.

Checkpoint

9.22 Write a statement that declares a structure named Movie. The structure should have fields to hold the following data about a movie.

The name of the movie
The director of the movie
The producer of the movie
The year the movie was released

9.23 Write a statement that declares a variable of the Movie structure that you created in Checkpoint 9.22.

9.24 Write statements that store the following data in the variable you declared in Checkpoint 9.23. (Do not use the With statement.)

The name of the movie: *Wheels of Fury*
The director of the movie: *Arlen McGoo*
The producer of the movie: *Vincent Van Dough*
The year the movie was released: *2010*

9.25 Rewrite the statements you wrote in Checkpoint 9.24 using the With statement.

Summary

9.1 Using Files

- Data is saved in a file, which is stored on a computer's disk.
- For an application to use a file, the file must be opened (which creates the file if it does not exist), data is either written to the file or read from the file, and the file is closed.
- There are two types of files: text and binary. There are two methods of accessing data in files: sequential-access and random-access.
- When a sequential file is opened, its read position is set to the first item in the file. As data is read, the read position advances through the file.
- The contents of an array are saved to a file using a loop that steps through each element of the array, writing its contents to the file.
- By specifying a namespace with the Imports statement, you can refer to names in that namespace without fully qualifying them.
- The `File.CreateText` method creates a new file or replaces an existing one. The `File.AppendText` method opens a file so more data can be appended to the end of the file. The `File.OpenText` method opens a file for reading.

9.2 The OpenFileDialog, SaveFileDialog, FontDialog, and ColorDialog Controls

- The OpenFileDialog control displays a standard Windows *Open* dialog box. The SaveFileDialog control displays a standard Windows *Save As* dialog box. The ColorDialog control displays a standard Windows *Color* dialog box. The FontDialog control displays a standard Windows *Font* dialog box.

9.3 The PrintDocument Control

- The PrintDocument control allows your application to print output. You write the code that handles the printing in the `PrintPage` event handler. You trigger a Print-Page event by calling the `Print` method. You use the `e.Graphics.DrawString` method to send output to the printer.
- Reports typically have a header, body, and footer.
- To align printed data properly in columns, you must use a monospaced font to ensure that all characters occupy the same amount of space; you use the `String.Format` method to format the data into columns.

9.4 Structures

- A structure is a defined data type that you create, which contains one or more variables known as fields. Fields can be of different data types. You can create a structure with the `Structure` statement. Once you have defined a structure, you may declare instances of it.

Key Terms

append	delimiter
binary files	file
buffer	`File.AppendText` method
`Chr` function	`File.CreateText` method
`Close` method	`File.Exists` method
Color dialog box	`File.OpenText` method
ColorDialog control	Filename property

Filter property
Font dialog box
FontDialog control
InitialDirectory property
input file
MultiLine property
newline character
Open dialog box
OpenFileDialog control
output file
Peek method
Print method
PrintDocument control
PrintPage event handler
random-access file
Read method
read position
ReadLine method

ReadToEnd method
report body
report footer
report header
Save As dialog box
SaveFileDialog control
sequential-access file
StreamReader class
StreamReader object
StreamWriter class
StreamWriter object
structure
Structure statement
text file
Title property
Write method
WriteLine method

Review Questions and Exercises

Fill-in-the-Blank

1. Before a file can be used, it must be _____.

2. When a file is opened, a(n) _____ is created, which is a small holding section of memory that data is first written to.

3. When it is finished using a file, an application should always _____ it.

4. To write data to a sequential file, use a(n) _____ object.

5. To read data from a sequential file, use a(n) _____ object.

6. The _____ method writes a line to a file.

7. The _____ method reads a line from a file.

8. The _____ character is a delimiter that marks the end of a line in a file.

9. The _____ control allows you to print data directly to the printer.

10. You write code that handles printing in the _____ event handler.

11. All of the characters printed with a(n) _____ font occupy the same amount of space.

12. The _____ control displays an *Open* dialog box for selecting or entering a filename.

13. The _____ control displays a *Save As* dialog box for selecting or entering a file.

14. The _____ control displays a *Color* dialog box for selecting a color.

15. The _____ control displays a *Font* dialog box for selecting a font.

16. A(n) _____ is a data type that you create, containing one or more variables, which are known as fields.

Multiple Choice

1. Which two types of files are discussed in this chapter?
   a. Real and integer
   b. Microsoft Access and Microsoft Word
   c. Text and binary
   d. Encrypted and decrypted

2. You use this type of object to write data to a file.
   a. `FileWriter`
   b. `OuputFile`
   c. `File`
   d. `StreamWriter`

3. You use this type of object to read data from a file.
   a. `FileReader`
   b. `StreamReader`
   c. `File`
   d. `Inputfile`

4. This method creates a file if it does not exist, and erases the contents of the file if it already exists.
   a. `File.OpenText`
   b. `File.AppendText`
   c. `File.CreateText`
   d. `File.OpenNew`

5. This method creates a file if it does not exist. If it already exists, data written to it will be added to the end of its existing contents.
   a. `File.OpenText`
   b. `File.AppendText`
   c. `File.CreateText`
   d. `File.OpenNew`

6. This statement writes a line of data to a file, terminating it with a newline character.
   a. `WriteLine`
   b. `SaveLine`
   c. `StoreLine`
   d. `Write`

7. This statement writes an item of data to a file, and does not terminate it with a newline character.
   a. `WriteItem`
   b. `SaveItem`
   c. `StoreItem`
   d. `Write`

8. This statement reads a line from a file.
   a. `Read`
   b. `ReadLine`
   c. `GetLine`
   d. `Input`

9. You use this method to detect when the end of a file has been reached.

   a. `End`
   b. `Peek`
   c. `LastItem`
   d. `FileEnd`

10. You use this method to determine if a file exists.

    a. `System.File.Exists`
    b. `IO.Exists`
    c. `File.Exists`
    d. `Exists.File`

11. Assuming that `ofdOpen` is an OpenFileDialog control, the following statement displays the dialog box.

    a. `ofdOpen.Display()`
    b. `Show(ofdOpen)`
    c. `ofdOpen.OpenDialog()`
    d. `ofdOpen.ShowDialog()`

12. This property determines the types of files displayed in an *Open* or a *Save As* dialog box.

    a. FileTypes
    b. Filter
    c. Types
    d. FileDisplay

13. This property determines the directory, or folder first displayed in an *Open* or *Save As* dialog box.

    a. InitialDirectory
    b. InitialFolder
    c. Location
    d. Path

14. When the user selects a file with an *Open* or *Save As* dialog box, the file's path and name are stored in this property.

    a. Filename
    b. PathName
    c. File
    d. Item

15. When a PrintDocument control's `Print` method executes, it triggers this event.

    a. `StartPrint`
    b. `PrintPage`
    c. `PagePrint`
    d. `SendPage`

16. Inside the appropriate PrintDocument event handler you use this method to actually send output to the printer.

    a. `e.Graphics.DrawString`
    b. `e.PrintText`
    c. `e.Graphics.SendOutput`
    d. `Print`

17. You can use this method to align data into columns.
    a. `Align`
    b. `Format.Align`
    c. `Format.Column`
    d. `String.Format`

18. This statement allows you to create a data type that contains one or more variables, known as fields.
    a. `UserDefined`
    b. `DataType`
    c. `Structure`
    d. `Fields`

True or False

Indicate whether the following statements are true or false.

1. T F: A file must be opened before it can be used.

2. T F: An input file is a file that a program can write data to.

3. T F: To read a record stored in the middle or at the end of a sequential-access file, an application must read all records in the file before it.

4. T F: The `File.CreateText` method creates a `StreamReader` object and returns a reference to the object.

5. T F: If you specify only a filename when opening a file, Visual Basic will assume the file's location to be the same folder from which the application is running.

6. T F: In addition to separating the contents of a file into lines, the newline character also serves as a delimiter.

7. T F: If you call the `WriteLine` method with no argument, it writes a blank line to the file.

8. T F: A file's read position is set to the end of the file when a file is first opened.

9. T F: The `Peek` method causes the read position to advance by one character.

10. T F: The Title property holds the name of the file the user selected with an *Open* or *Save As* dialog box.

11. T F: You can specify the font to use when sending output to the printer.

12. T F: You must use a proportionally spaced font when aligning data in columns.

13. T F: A structure may hold variables of different data types.

14. T F: `Structure` statements can appear inside a procedure or function.

15. T F: Structures may not contain arrays.

16. T F: You may declare an array of structure variables.

Short Answer

1. What are the three steps that must be taken when a file is used by an application?

2. What happens when you close a file with the `Close` method?

3. What is a file's read position? Where is the read position when a file is first opened for reading?

4. What is the difference between the `WriteLine` method and the `Write` method?

5. What happens when you use the `File.OpenText` method to open a file that does not exist?

6. What has happened when the `Peek` method returns –1?

7. What does the `ReadLine` method return when it reads a blank line?

8. What does the `Read` method return?

9. What is the difference between the `Print` method and the `PagePrint` event handler?

10. Where must `Structure` statements appear?

What Do You Think?

1. How do you think a file buffer increases system performance?

2. Why should you call the `Peek` method before calling the `ReadLine` method?

3. You are using the `ReadLine` method to read data from a file. After each line is read, it is added to a list box. What error can potentially occur, and how do you prevent it?

4. An application has the forms MainForm and GetDataForm, and the module `MainModule`. You want a structure to be available only to procedures in the `MainModule` module. Where do you place the `Structure` statement, and which access specifier do you use: `Public` or `Private`?

5. Suppose an application properly aligns the contents of a report into columns using the `String.Format` method. But, when the same report is printed on paper, the columns do not align as they should. What is the most likely cause of the problem?

Find the Error

What is wrong with the following code?

1. ```
Dim myFile As System.IO.StreamReader
myFile = File.CreateText("names.txt")
```

2. ```
If Not System.Exists(strFilename) Then
    MessageBox.Show(strFilename & " does not exist.")
End If
```

3. ```
Do Until myFile.Peek = ""
    strInput = myFile.ReadLine()
    lstResults.Items.Add(strInput)
Loop
```

4. (Assume that `ofdOpen` is an OpenFileDialog control.)
   ```
   ofdOpen.Filter = "Text files (*.txt)&*.txt"
   ```

5. (Assume that `pdPrint` is a PrintDocument control.)
   ```
   Private Sub pdPrint_PrintPage(...) Handles pdPrint.PrintPage
       pdPrint.Print("Hello World!", New Font("Times New Roman",
           12, FontStyle.Regular), Brushes.Black, 10, 10)
   End Sub
   ```
   ```

6. The following Structure statement appears in a form:

```
Structure PersonInfo
   Dim strName As String
   Dim intAge As Integer
   Dim strPhone As String
End Structure
```

The following statement appears in the same form:

```
PersonInfo.strName = "Jill Smith"
```

Algorithm Workbench

1. Suppose a file named *DiskInfo.txt* already exists, and you wish to add data to the data already in the file. Write the statements necessary to open the file.

2. Suppose you wish to create a new file named *NewFile.txt* and write data to it. Write the statements necessary to open the file.

3. Assuming an application uses a list box named `lstInventory`, write code that writes the contents of the list box to the file *Inventory.txt*.

4. Assuming an application has an array of integers named `intNumbers`, write code that writes the contents of the array to the file *numbers.txt*.

5. Write a `Structure` statement that creates a structure to hold the following data about a savings account. The structure should be declared in a module and be available to all modules in the project.

```
Account number (String)
Account balance (Decimal)
Interest rate (Double)
Average monthly balance (Decimal)
```

6. Assume that `CustomerData` is a structure. The following statement declares customers as an array of ten `CustomerData` variables:

```
Dim customers(9) As CustomerData
```

Write a statement that stores `"Jones"` in the `strLastName` field of the `customers(7)`.

7. Using the variables: `strProductName`, `intProductNum`, and `decProductPrice`, write a `String.Format` statement that returns a string with `strProductName`'s value in a column of ten spaces, `intProductNum`'s value in a column of eight spaces, and `decProductPrice`'s value in a column of six spaces.

8. Assume an application uses an OpenFileDialog control named `ofdOpen`. Write statements that display an *Open* dialog box with the initial directory *C:\Becky\Images* and use the following filters: *JPEG images (*.jpg)* and *GIF images (*.gif)*.

Programming Challenges

1. **Employee Data, Part 1**

   Create an application that allows the user to enter the following employee data: First Name, Middle Name, Last Name, Employee Number, Department, Telephone Number, Telephone Extension, and E-mail Address. The valid selections for department are Accounting, Administration, Marketing, MIS, and Sales. Once the data is entered, the user should be able to save it to a file. Figure 9-29 shows an example of

Figure 9-29 *Employee Data* form for saving employee records

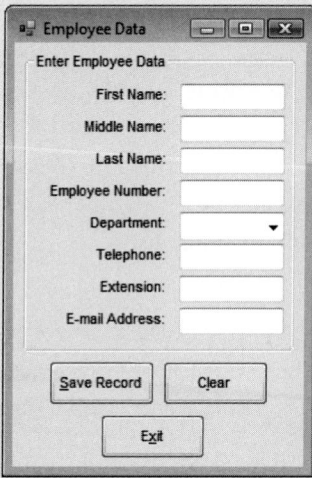

the application's form. The form shown in Figure 9-29 has a combo box for selecting the department; a *Save Record* button, which writes the record to a file; a *Clear* button, which clears the text boxes; and an *Exit* button. Write code in the `Form_Load` event handler that allows the user to enter the name of the file.

2. **Employee Data, Part 2**

Create an application that reads the records stored in the file created by Programming Challenge 1.

Write code in the form's Load event handler that allows the user to enter the name of the file, and opens the file. The form shown in Figure 9-30 has a *Next Record* button, which reads a record from the file and displays its fields; a *Clear* button, which clears the labels; and an *Exit* button. When the user clicks the *Next Record* button, the application should read the next record from the file and display it. When the end of the file is encountered, a message should be displayed.

Figure 9-30 *Employee Data* form for reading employee records

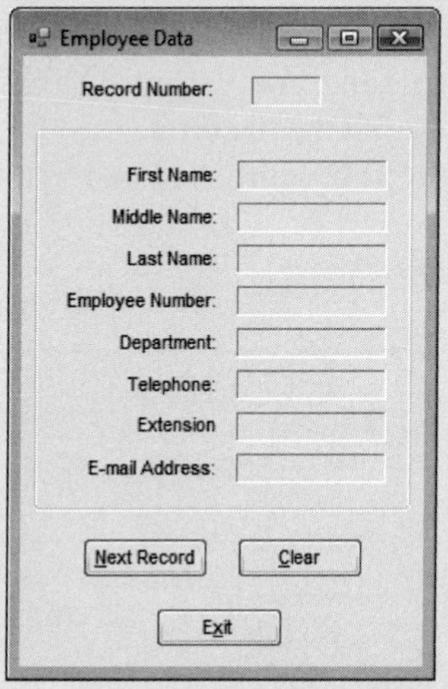

3. **Student Test Scores**

A teacher has six students and wants you to create an application that stores their grade data in a file and prints a grade report. The application should have a structure that stores the following student data: Name (a string), Test Scores (an array of five Doubles), and Average (a Double). Because the teacher has six students, the application should use an array of six structure variables.

The application should allow the user to enter data for each student, and calculate the average test score.

Figure 9-31 shows an example form.

Figure 9-31 *Student Test Scores* form

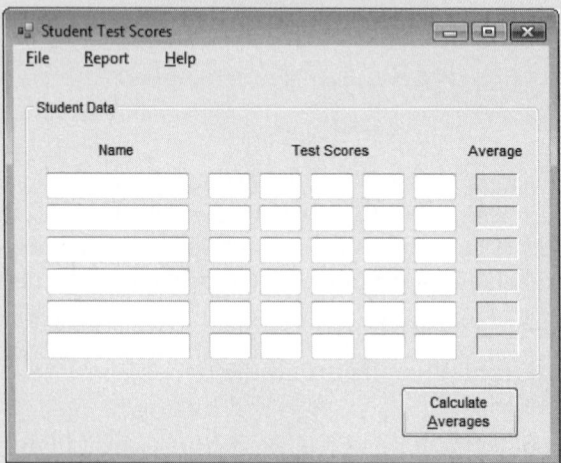

The user should be able to save the data to a file, read the data from the file, and print a report showing each student's test scores and average score. The form shown in Figure 9-31 uses a menu system. You may use buttons instead if you prefer.

Input validation: Do not accept test scores less than zero or greater than 100.

4. **Video Collection**

Create an application that stores data about your DVD collection in a file. The application should have a structure to hold the following fields: Video Name, Year Produced, Running Time, and Rating. The application should allow the user to save the data to a file, search the file for a video by name, and print a report listing all the video records in the file. Figure 9-32 shows an example form.

Figure 9-32 *Video Collection* form

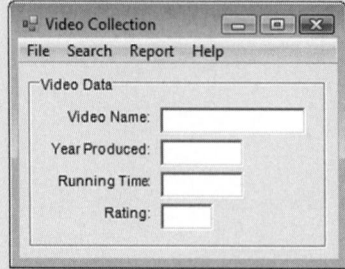

Design Your Own Forms

VideoNote

The Random
Number File
Generator
Problem

5. **Random Number File Generator**

   Create an application that generates a series of 100 random numbers in the range of 1 through 1,000. Save the series of numbers in a file.

6. **Number Analysis**

   Create an application that reads the numbers from the file your application created for Programming Challenge 5. (If you have not completed that assignment, use the file named *NumberSet.txt* in the *Chap9* folder on the student disk. It contains a series of 100 real numbers.) Your application should perform the following:

   • Display the total of the numbers
   • Display the average of the numbers
   • Display the highest number in the file
   • Display the lowest number in the file

7. **Font and Color Tester**

   Create an application that tests the way different fonts and color combinations appear. The application should display some text in a label, and have a menu with the items *Select Font* and *Select Color*.

   The *Select Font* menu item should display a *Font* dialog box with a *Color* drop-down list. The application should change the text displayed in the label to the font and color selected in the dialog box.

   The *Select Color* menu item should display a *Color* dialog box. The application should change the background color of the label to the color selected in the dialog box.

8. **Simple Text Editor Modification**

   Modify the *Simple Text Editor* application that you created in this chapter by adding a *View* menu to the menu system. The *View* menu should have two items: *Font* and *Color*.

   The *Font* menu item should display a *Font* dialog box with a *Color* drop-down list. The application should change the text displayed in the text box to the font and color selected in the dialog box.

   The *Color* menu item should display a *Color* dialog box. The application should change the background color of the text box to the color selected in the dialog box.

9. **Image Viewer**

   You can load an image into a PictureBox control at runtime by calling the `Image.FromFile` method. For example, assume that `picImage` is a PictureBox control and `filename` is a variable containing the name of a graphic file. The following statement loads the graphic file into the PictureBox control:

   ```
   picImage.Image = Image.FromFile(filename)
   ```

   Create an application that has a PictureBox control on a form. The PictureBox control should be configured so it fills the entire area of the form and resizes when the user resizes the form.

   The application should have a *File* menu with an *Open* command. The *Open* command should display an *Open* dialog box, displaying files of the following graphic types:

   • Bitmaps (**.bmp*)
   • JPEG images (**.jpg*)
   • GIF images (**.gif*)

   When the user selects a file with the *Open* dialog box, the application should display the image in the PictureBox control.

10. **Employee Data, Part 3**

    Create an application that performs the following operations with the employee file created by the application in Programming Challenge 1:

    - Uses an *Open* dialog box to allow the user to select the file
    - Allows the user to enter a new employee record and then saves the record to the file
    - Allows the user to enter an employee number and searches for a record containing that employee number. If the record is found, the record is displayed.
    - Displays all records, one after the other
    - Prints an employee record

    Equip your application with either a menu system or a set of buttons to perform these operations.

11. **Customer Accounts**

    Create an application that uses a structure to store the following data about a customer account: Last Name, First Name, Customer Number, Address, City, State, ZIP Code, Telephone Number, Account Balance, and Date of Last Payment. The application should allow the user to save customer account records to the file, search the file for a customer by last name or customer number, and print a report listing all the customer records in the file.

    Input validation: When entering a new record, make sure the user enters data for all fields. Do not accept negative numbers for the account balance.

12. **Rainfall Statistics File**

    In Programming Challenge 2 of Chapter 8, you created an application that allows the user to enter the amount of rainfall for each month and then displays rainfall statistics. Modify the application so it can save the monthly rainfall amounts entered by the user to a file and read the monthly rainfall amounts from a file.

13. **Charge Account Number File**

    In Programming Challenge 9 of Chapter 8, you created an application that allows the user to enter a charge account number. The program determines whether the account number is valid by comparing it to numbers in an array. Modify the application so it compares the number to the numbers in a file. Create the file using Notepad or another text editor.

10 Working with Databases

TOPICS

Most businesses store their company data in databases. In this chapter you will learn basic database concepts, and how to write Visual Basic applications that interact with databases. You will learn how to use a DataGridView control to display the data in a database. You will also learn how to sort and update database data. We will finish with an application that displays database data in list boxes, text boxes, labels, and combo boxes.

10.1 Database Management Systems

CONCEPT: Visual Basic applications use database management systems to make large amounts of data available to programs.

In Chapter 9 you learned how to perform input and output operations using simple text files. If an application needs to store only a small amount of data, those types of files work well. When a large amount of data must be stored and manipulated, however, they are not practical. Many businesses keep hundreds of thousands, or even millions of data items in files. When a text file contains this much data, simple operations such as searching, inserting, and deleting become slow, inefficient, and cumbersome.

When developing applications that work with a large amount of data, most developers prefer to use a database management system. A **database management system (DBMS)** is software that is specifically designed to store, retrieve, and manipulate large amounts of data in an organized and efficient manner. Once the data is stored using the database management system, applications may be written in Visual Basic or other languages to communicate with the DBMS. Rather than retrieving or manipulating the data directly, a Visual Basic application can send instructions to the DBMS. The DBMS carries out those instructions and sends the results back to the Visual Basic application. Figure 10-1 illustrates this.

Figure 10-1 A Visual Basic application interacts with a DBMS, which manipulates data

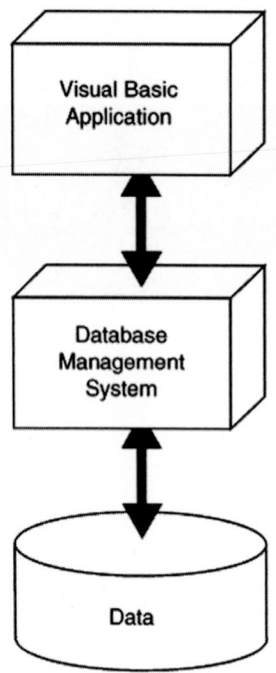

Although Figure 10-1 is greatly simplified, it illustrates the layered nature of an application that works with a database management system. The topmost layer of software, which in this case is written in Visual Basic, interacts with the user. It also sends instructions to the next layer of software, the DBMS. The DBMS works directly with the data, and sends the results of operations back to the application.

For example, suppose a company keeps all of its product records in a database. The company has a Visual Basic application that allows the user to search for information on any product by entering its product ID number. The Visual Basic application instructs the DBMS to retrieve the record for the product with the specified product ID number. The DBMS retrieves the product record and sends the data back to the Visual Basic application. The Visual Basic application displays the data to the user.

The advantage of this layered approach to software development is that the Visual Basic programmer does not need know about the physical structure of the data. He or she only needs to know how to interact with the DBMS. The DBMS handles the actual reading, writing, and searching of data.

Visual Basic is capable of interacting with many DBMSs. Some of the more popular DBMSs are Microsoft SQL Server, Oracle, DB2, and MySQL. In this chapter we will use Microsoft SQL Server Express, which is installed with Visual Basic.

10.2 Database Concepts

CONCEPT: A database is a collection of one or more tables, each containing data related to a particular topic.

A **database** is a collection of one or more tables, each containing data related to a particular topic. A **table** is a logical grouping of related information. A database might, for example, have a table containing information about employees. Another table might list information about weekly sales. Another table might contain a list of the items in a store's inventory. Let's look at a database table named *Departments*, shown in Table 10-1, which contains information about departments within a company. Each row of the table corresponds to a single department. The sample table contains the ID number, name, and number of employees in each department.

Table 10-1 *Departments* table

Dept_Id	Dept_Name	Num_Employees
1	Human Resources	10
2	Accounting	5
3	Computer Support	30
4	Research & Development	15

Each database record appears as a row in the table. In the *Departments* table, shown in Table 10-1, the first row contains 1, Human Resources, 10. When discussing a table, we refer to the columns by name. The columns in Table 10-1 are named Dept_Id, Dept_Name, and Num_Employees. Table columns are also called **fields**. Each table has a **design**, which specifies each column's name, data type, and field size and/or range of valid values. Table 10-2 contains the design of our sample *Departments* table.

Table 10-2 *Departments* table design

Field	Type	Range/Size
Dept_Id	Integer	–32,768 to +32,767
Dept_Name	String	30 characters
Num_Employees	Integer	–32,768 to +32,767

The *Dept_Id* column is called a **primary key** because it uniquely identifies each department. No two departments can ever have the same department ID. Primary keys can be either numbers or strings, but numeric values are processed by the database software more efficiently. In this table, the primary key is one column. Sometimes a primary key will consist of two or more combined columns, creating what is called a **composite key**.

SQL Server Column Types

When you use Visual Basic to read a database, your program copies values from a database table into program variables. Therefore, it is important to select variable types that match the type of data in the table. Table 10-3 compares SQL Server column types to Visual Basic data types. The varchar and nvarchar types permit variable-length strings. Their *n* parameter specifies the longest string that can be stored in the column.

Table 10-3 Comparing SQL Server column types to Visual Basic types

SQL type(s)	Usage	Visual Basic Type
bit	True/false values	Boolean
datetime, smalldatetime	Dates and times	Date, DateTime
decimal, money	Financial values in which precision is important	Decimal
float	Real-number values	Double
image	Pictures, Word documents, Excel files, PDF files	Array of Byte
int	Integer values	Integer
nvarchar(*n*)	Variable-length strings containing 16-bit Unicode characters	String
smallint	Integers between −32,768 and +32,767	Short
text	Strings longer than 8,000 characters	String
varchar(*n*)	Variable-length strings containing ANSI (8-bit) characters	String

Choosing Column Names

A **database schema** is the design of tables, columns, and relationships between tables in a database. Let's look at some of the elements that belong to a schema, beginning with tables. Suppose you want to create a database to keep track of club members. First, you should choose meaningful names for each column.

Let's assume you want to store each member's first and last names, phone number, E-mail address, date joined, number of meetings attended, and a column indicating whether the person is an officer. Table 10-4 contains a possible design. Choosing the lengths of varchar columns involves some guesswork because you don't want to cut off any of the values stored in these columns. Disk space is relatively inexpensive, so it's usually better to make the columns a little larger than they need to be.

In most cases, you should never embed spaces in column names. If you do that, all references to the column name in database queries must be surrounded by brackets, as in [Last Name]. As an alternative use an underscore character between words, as in Last_Name.

Table 10-4 *Members* table sample design

Column Name	Type	Remarks
Member_ID	int	Primary key
First_Name	varchar(40)	
Last_Name	varchar(40)	
Phone	varchar(30)	
Email	varchar(50)	
Date_Joined	smalldatetime	Date only, no time values
Meetings_Attended	smallint	
Officer	bit	True/False values

Table 10-5 *Employees* table with department names

Emp_Id	First_Name	Last_Name	Department
001234	Ignacio	Fleta	Accounting
002000	Christian	Martin	Computer Support
002122	Orville	Gibson	Human Resources
003000	Jose	Ramirez	Research & Development
003400	Ben	Smith	Accounting
003780	Allison	Chong	Computer Support

Avoiding Redundancy by Using Linked Tables

Most well-designed databases keep redundant data to a minimum. It might be tempting when designing a table of employees, for example, to include the complete name of the department in which an employee works. A few sample rows are shown in Table 10-5. There are problems with this approach. We can imagine that the same department name appears many times within the *Employees* table, leading to wasted storage space. Also, someone typing in employee data might easily misspell a department name. Finally, if the company decides to rename a department, it would be necessary to find and correct every occurrence of the department name in the *Employees* table (and possibly other tables).

Rather than inserting a department name in each employee record, a good designer would store a department ID number in each row of the *Employees* table, as shown in Table 10-6. A data entry clerk would require less time to input a numeric department ID, and there would be less chance of a typing error. One would then create a separate table named *Departments*, containing all department names and IDs, as shown in Table 10-7. When looking up the name of an employee's department, we can use the department ID in the *Employees* table to find the same ID in the *Departments* table. The department name will be in the same table row. Relational databases make it easy to create links (called relationships) between tables such as *Employees* and *Departments*.

Table 10-6 *Employees* table with department ID numbers

Emp_Id	First_Name	Last_Name	Dept_Id
001234	Ignacio	Fleta	2
002000	Christian	Martin	3
002122	Orville	Gibson	1
003000	Jose	Ramirez	4
003400	Ben	Smith	2
003780	Allison	Chong	3

Table 10-7 *Departments* table

Dept_Id	Dept_Name	Dept_Size
1	Human Resources	10
2	Accounting	5
3	Computer Support	30
4	Research & Development	15

One-to-Many Relationship

Databases are usually designed around a **relational model,** meaning that relations exist between tables. A **relation** is a link or relationship that relies on a common field value to join rows from two different tables. In the relationship diagram shown in Figure 10-2, *Dept_Id* is the common field that links the *Departments* and *Employees* tables. The primary key field is always shown in bold.

In the *Departments* table, *Dept_Id* is the primary key. In the *Employees* table, *Dept_Id* is called a **foreign key.** A foreign key is a column in one table that references a primary key in another table. There can be multiple occurrences of a foreign key in a table. Along the line connecting the two tables, the ⚷ and ∞ symbols indicate a **one-to-many relationship.** A particular *Dept_Id* (such as 4) occurs only once in the *Departments* table, but it can appear many times (or not at all) in the *Employees* table. At first, we will work with only one table at a time. Later, we will show how to pull information from two related tables.

Figure 10-2 One-to-many relationship between *Departments* and *Employees*

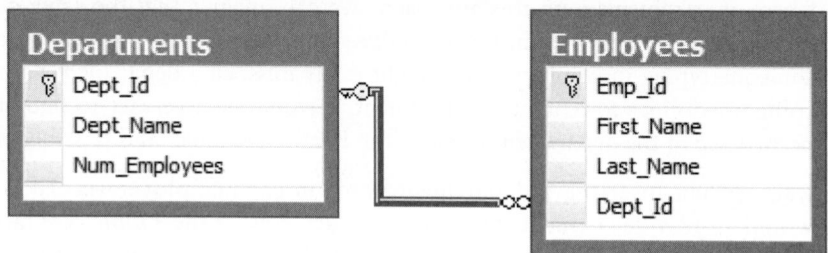

 **Checkpoint**

10.1 How is a table different from a database?

10.2 In a table of employees, what column would make a good primary key?

10.3 Which Visual Basic data type is equivalent to the *bit* column type in Microsoft SQL Server?

10.4 Why would we not want to spell out the name of each person's department in a table of employees?

10.5 How is a foreign key different from a primary key?

 **10.3 DataGridView Control**

CONCEPT: The DataGridView control allows you to display a database table in a grid. The grid can be used at runtime to sort and edit the contents of a table.

VideoNote
The
DataGridView
Control

Visual Basic provides easy-to-use tools for displaying database tables in Windows forms and Web forms. In this chapter, we will show how to display data on a Windows form, and in Chapter 11, we will demonstrate Web forms.

Visual Basic uses a technique called **data binding** to link database tables to controls on a program's forms. Special controls, called **components,** provide the linking mechanism.

When you decide to link a control to a database, a software tool named a **wizard** guides you through the process. Wizards are quite common in Microsoft Windows and many other applications such as Microsoft Word, so you have probably used one before.

We will use the following data-related components:

- **Data source.** A **data source** is usually a database, but can include text files, Excel spreadsheets, XML data, or Web services. Our data sources will be Microsoft SQL Server database files.
- **Binding source.** A **binding source** connects data bound controls to a dataset.
- **Table adapter.** A **table adapter** pulls data from one or more database tables and passes it to your program. It can select some or all table rows, add new rows, delete rows, and modify existing rows. It uses an industry standard language named **Structured Query Language (SQL)**, which is recognized by nearly all databases.
- **Dataset.** A **dataset** is an in-memory copy of the data pulled from database tables. The table adapter does the pulling, and it copies the data to the dataset. Your program can modify rows in the dataset, add new rows, and delete rows. None of your changes are permanent, unless you tell the table adapter to write the changes back to the database. Datasets can get data from more than one data source, and from more than one table adapter.

Figure 10-3 shows the relationship between the data source, binding source, table adapter, dataset, and application. Data from a data source travels all the way to the dataset and application. The dataset's contents can be modified and viewed by the application. Updates to the dataset can be written back to the data source. In Tutorial 10-1, you show a database table in a **DataGridView control**.

Figure 10-3 Data flow from the data source to an application

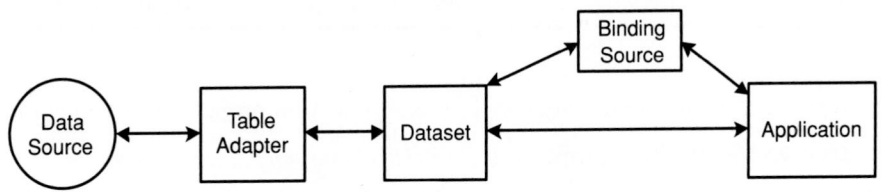

Tutorial 10-1:
Showing a database table in a DataGridView control

This tutorial leads you through the steps to display the contents of a database table in a DataGridView control. You will see all rows and columns of the data. You will see how easy it is for users of your program to sort on any column, delete rows, and insert new rows.

The *SalesStaff* table, located in the SQL Server database named *Company*, represents information collected about sales employees. Its design is shown in Table 10-8, and some sample rows are shown in Table 10-9.

Preparation Step: Make sure the *Company.mdf* file is located in the student sample programs folder named *Chap10*. This file must be located on your computer's hard drive, and not on a network drive. Visual Studio considers a network drive to be an unsafe location, and will display a warning message if you connect to a database on a network.

Table 10-8 *SalesStaff* table design

Column Name	Type
ID	int(primary key)
Last_Name	varchar(40)
First_Name	varchar(40)
Full_Time	bit
Hire_Date	smalldatetime
Salary	decimal

Table 10-9 Sample rows in the *SalesStaff* table

ID	Last_Name	First_Name	Full_Time	Hire_Date	Salary
104	Adams	Adrian	True	01/01/2010	$35,007.00
114	Franklin	Fay	True	08/22/2005	$56,001.00
115	Franklin	Adiel	False	03/20/2010	$41,000.00
120	Baker	Barbara	True	04/22/2003	$32,000.00
135	Ferriere	Henri	True	01/01/2010	$57,000.00
292	Hasegawa	Danny	False	05/20/2007	$45,000.00
302	Easterbrook	Erin	False	07/09/2004	$22,000.00
305	Kawananakoa	Sam	True	10/20/2009	$42,000.00
396	Zabaleta	Maria	True	11/01/2009	$29,000.00
404	Del Terzo	Daniel	True	07/09/2007	$37,500.00
407	Greenwood	Charles	False	04/20/2008	$23,432.00

Step 1: Create a new Windows Forms Application project named *SalesStaff 1.*

Step 2: Set the Text property of *Form1* to *Company Sales Staff Table.*

Step 3: Save your project by selecting *Save All* from the File menu.

Step 4: Drag a DataGridView control from the *Data* section of the *Toolbox* window onto the form. In the *Properties* window, set the DataGridView control's Dock property to *Fill.*

> **TIP:** If you select the DataGridView control and click on the Dock property in the *Properties* window, a small dialog window appears. Click on the center button, which causes the grid to fill the entire form.

Step 5: In the DataGridView control, click the small arrow (called a *smart tag*) pointing to the right in the upper right corner of the DataGridView. You should see a small pop-up window named *DataGridView Tasks*, as shown in Figure 10-4.

Step 6: Click the drop-down arrow next to *Choose Data Source.* In the dialog box that appears (see Figure 10-5), click *Add Project Data Source.*

Figure 10-4 *DataGridView Tasks* window

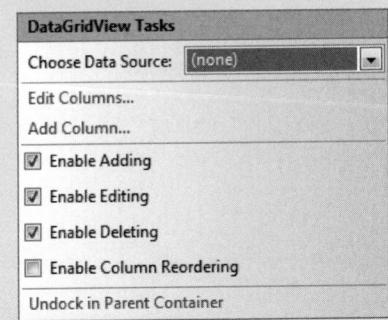

Figure 10-5 Choosing a data source, Step 1

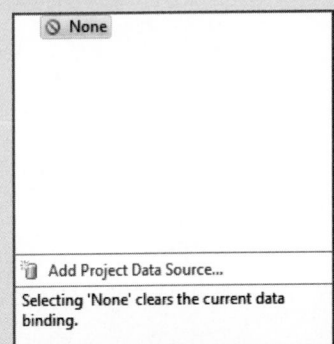

Step 7: When the *Data Source Configuration Wizard* displays, as shown in Figure 10-6, select the *Database* icon and click the *Next* button. (You may see fewer icons in this window if you are using Visual Basic Express Edition.)

Figure 10-6 Data Source Configuration Wizard

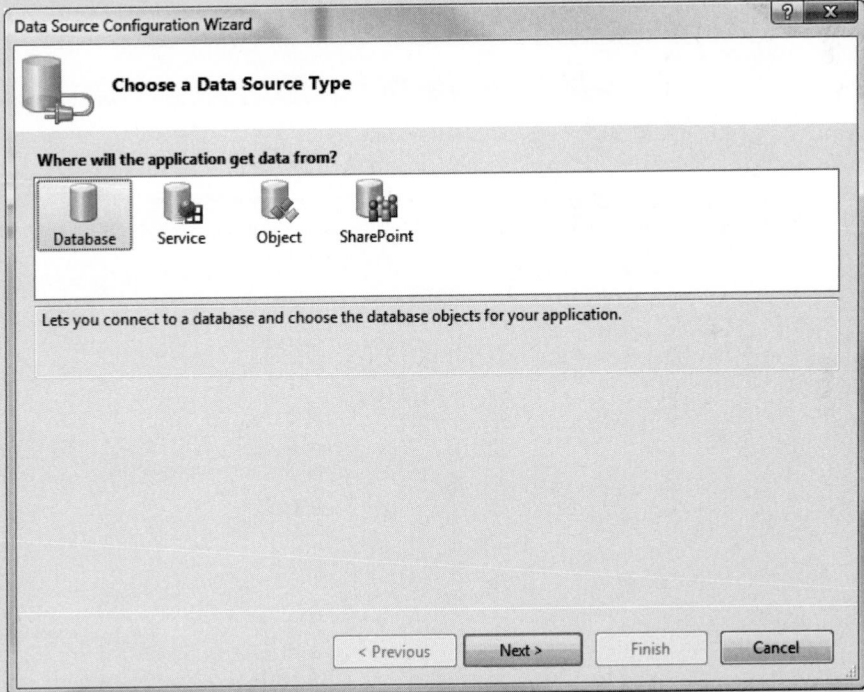

Step 8: Next, the wizard asks you to choose a database model, shown in Figure 10-7. Make sure the *Dataset* model is selected. Click the *Next* button to continue.

Step 9: Next, the wizard asks you to choose your data connection, as shown in Figure 10-8. If you had created data connections before, you could select one from the drop-down list. Because this is your first data connection, click the *New Connection* button.

Figure 10-7 Choose a database model

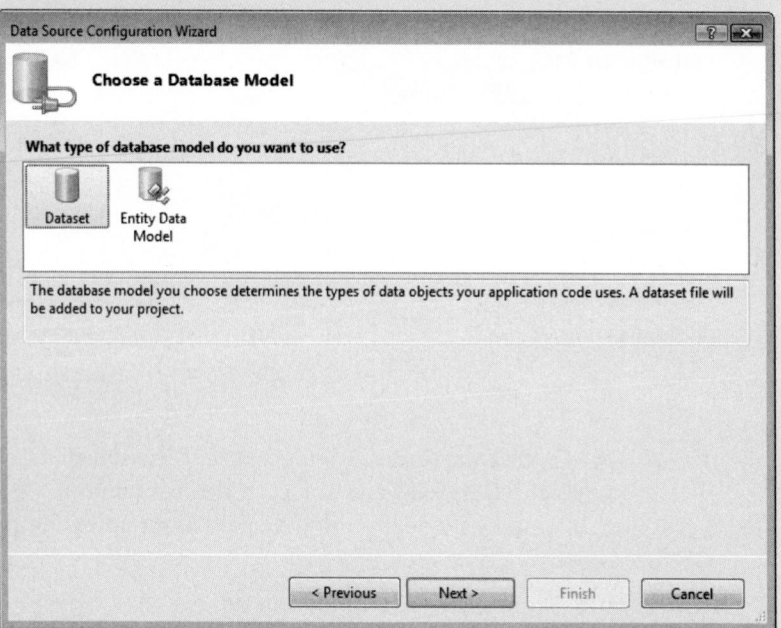

Figure 10-8 Choose your data connection

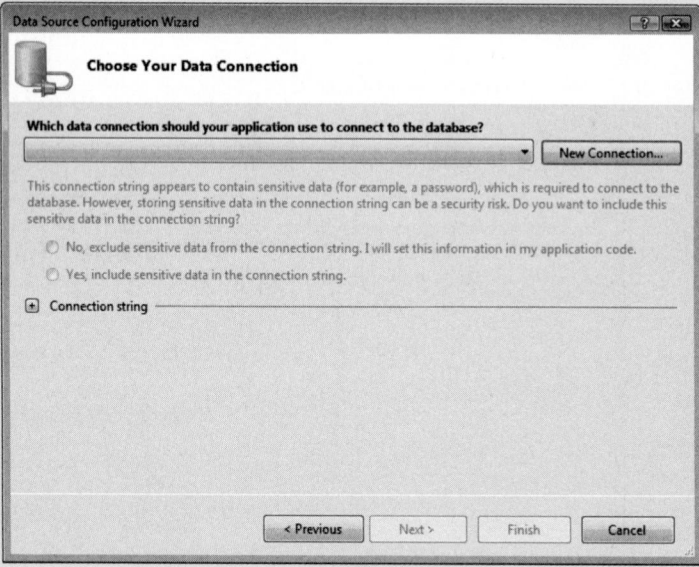

Step 10: The details of this step will differ, depending on whether you are using Visual Studio or Visual Basic Express Edition.

If you are using Visual Studio:

The *Add Connection* window shown in Figure 10-9 should appear. As shown in the figure, make sure *Microsoft SQL Server Database File (SqlClient)* is shown as the *Data source*. (If it is not, click the *Change . . .* button. In the window that appears next, select *Microsoft SQL Server Database File* and click *OK*.)

Next, click the *Browse . . .* button, as indicated in Figure 10-9. Navigate to student sample programs folder named *Chap10*, and select the *Company.mdf* database file. Figure 10-10 shows an example of the *Add Connection* window with the database file selected. (The path of the file shown on your system might look different.)

Figure 10-9 The Visual Studio *Add Connection* window

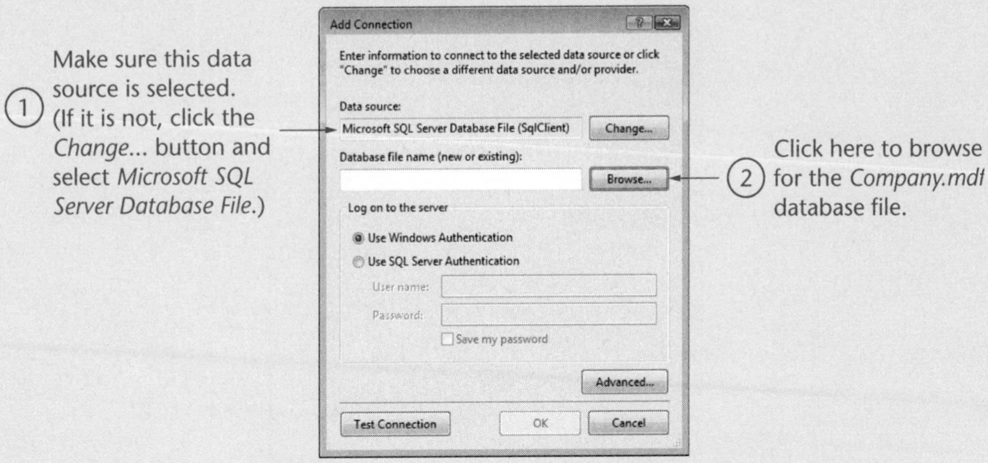

① Make sure this data source is selected. (If it is not, click the *Change...* button and select *Microsoft SQL Server Database File.*)

② Click here to browse for the *Company.mdf* database file.

Figure 10-10 The correct data source and database file selected in Visual Studio

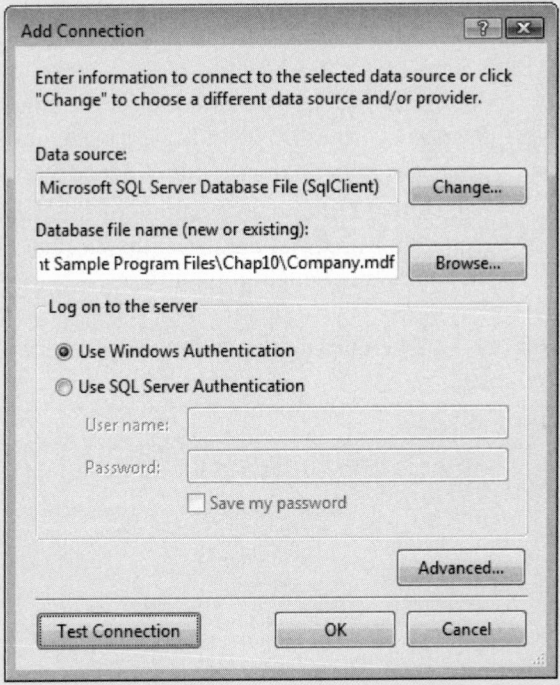

At this point you can optionally click the *Test Connection* button and wait for the message box that says *Test Connection Succeeded*. This message indicates that you successfully connected to the *Company.mdf* database file.

Click the *OK* button to close the *Add Connection* window, and go directly to Step 11.

If you are using Visual Basic Express Edition:

The *Add Connection* window shown in Figure 10-11 should appear. The default *Data source* for Visual Basic Express Edition is *Microsoft SQL Server Compact 3.5*, as shown in the figure. You need to change this to *Microsoft SQL Server Database File*. To make this change, click the *Change . . .* button. In the window that appears next, select *Microsoft SQL Server Database File* and click *OK*.

Figure 10-11 The Visual Basic Express Edition *Add Connection* window

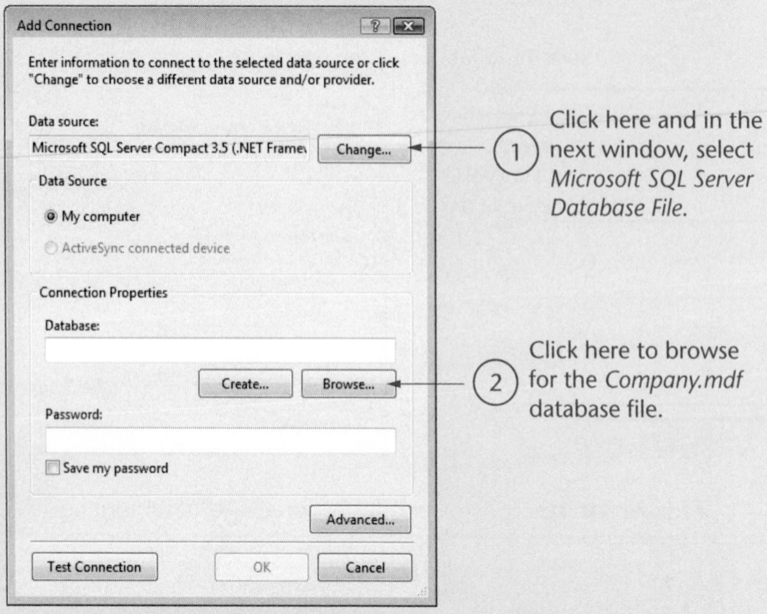

Next you will select the database file that you want to connect to. Click the *Browse* . . . button, as indicated in Figure 10-11. Navigate to student sample programs folder named *Chap10*, and select the *Company.mdf* database file.

Figure 10-12 shows an example of the *Add Connection* window with the correct data source and database file selected. (The path of the database file shown on your system might look different.)

Figure 10-12 The correct data source and database file selected in Visual Basic Express Edition

Figure 10-13 *Data Source Configuration Wizard* window with Company.mdf

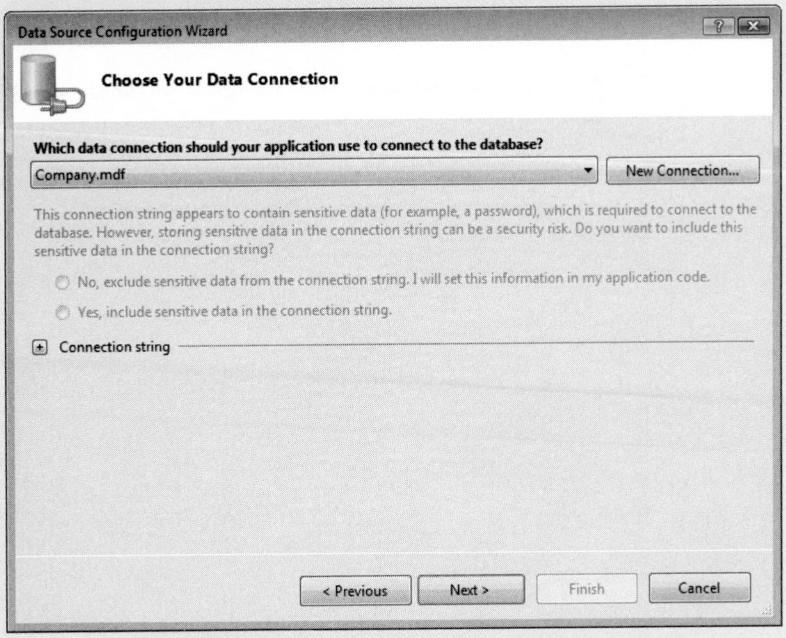

At this point you can optionally click the *Test Connection* button and wait for the message box that says *Test Connection Succeeded*. This message indicates that you successfully connected to the *Company.mdf* database file.

Click the *OK* button to close the *Add Connection* window.

Step 11: You will return to the *Data Source Configuration Wizard* window (in Figure 10-13), now showing the name of the connection as *Company.mdf*. Click the *Next* button to continue.

Step 12: Next you will see a dialog box with the following message:

> *The connection you selected uses a local data file that is not in the current project. Would you like to copy the file to your project and modify the connection?*

> *If you copy the data file to your project, it will be copied to the project's output directory each time you run the application. Press F1 for information on controlling this behavior.*

In a nutshell, this dialog box is asking you if you want to copy the database file to the project directory. If you click *Yes*, you will be more easily able to copy your program and its database to another computer. When you hand in programming projects, for example, it is a good idea to have the database stored with the project.

Click the *Yes* button to continue. After a moment, notice that an orange database icon with the name *Company.mdf* appears in your project's *Solution Explorer* window. This icon shows that the database file is now contained within your project.

Step 13: Next, the wizard asks if you want to save a named connection string to the application configuration file, as shown in Figure 10-14. This is a good idea, because it means that the application will remember the location of the database, and you could use it on other forms later on. You could possibly change the name of the connection string, but let's leave it as is.

Click the *Next* button to continue.

Figure 10-14 Saving the connection string

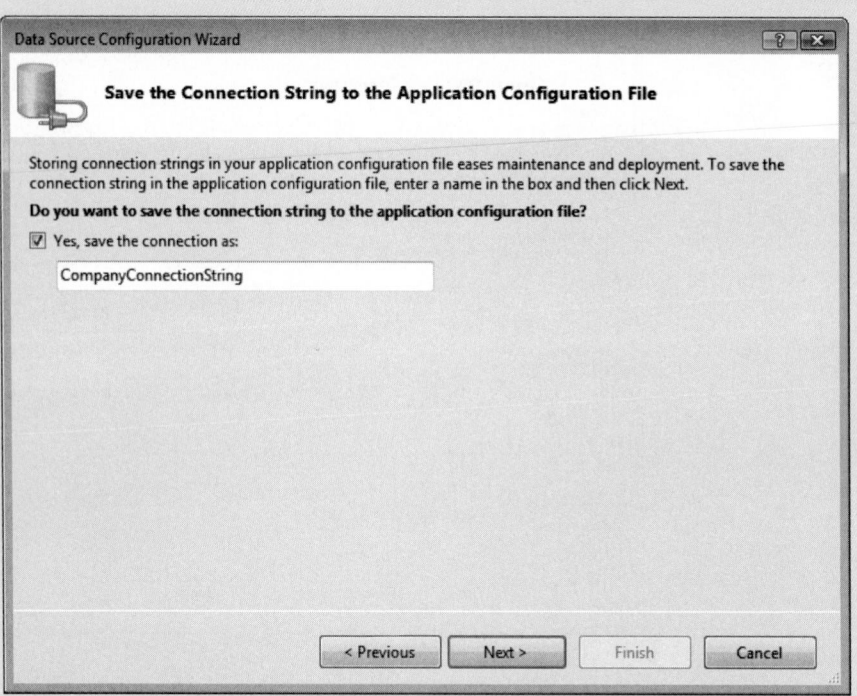

Step 14: Next, you are asked to select which database objects you want to include in your dataset. Expand the entry under *Tables*, place a check mark next to *SalesStaff*, and change the dataset name to *SalesStaffDataSet*, as shown in Figure 10-15. Ordinarily, we prefer the dataset name to be the same as the table name rather than the database. In some programs, we create multiple datasets that all refer to the same database.

Figure 10-15 Choosing the *SalesStaff* table and naming the dataset

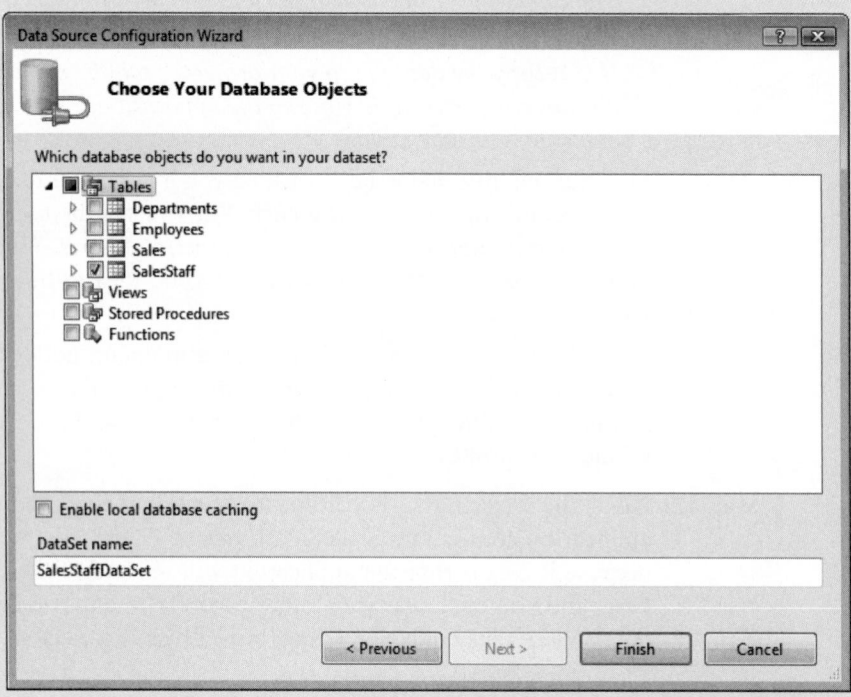

Click the *Finish* button to complete the wizard. If the *DataGridView Tasks* window appears next to the DataGridView, just click the mouse inside the grid to hide the tasks window.

Step 15: Now you should see column headings in the DataGridView control (Figure 10-16) that match the *SalesStaff* columns: *ID, Last_Name, First_Name, Full_Time, Hire_Date,* and *Salary.* If necessary, widen the form so the DataGridView control can expand.

Figure 10-16 Column headings in the DataGridView control

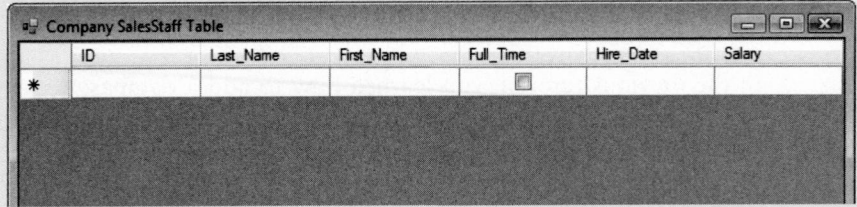

Step 16: Save and run the application. You should see all the rows of the *SalesStaff* table, as shown in Figure 10-17. Now you can experiment a bit while the application is running:

- Resize the form, and notice that the grid expands and contracts along with the form.
- Select individual rows in the grid by clicking on the buttons along the left side.
- Select multiple rows by holding down the Ctrl key or Shift key while clicking the selection buttons.
- Modify any of the cells by clicking the mouse inside the cell and typing new data.

When you are ready, close the window to exit the program.

Figure 10-17 Running the application, displaying the *SalesStaff* table

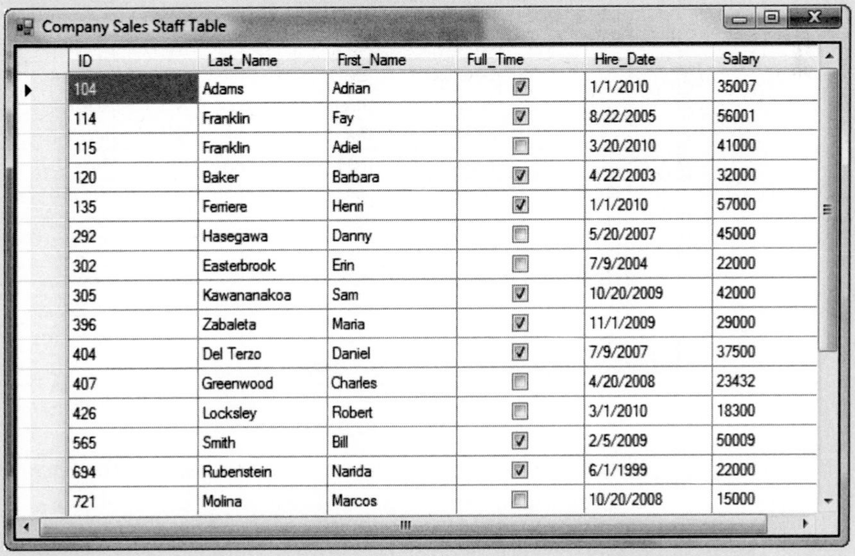

ID	Last_Name	First_Name	Full_Time	Hire_Date	Salary
104	Adams	Adrian	☑	1/1/2010	35007
114	Franklin	Fay	☑	8/22/2005	56001
115	Franklin	Adiel	☐	3/20/2010	41000
120	Baker	Barbara	☑	4/22/2003	32000
135	Ferriere	Henri	☑	1/1/2010	57000
292	Hasegawa	Danny	☐	5/20/2007	45000
302	Easterbrook	Erin	☐	7/9/2004	22000
305	Kawananakoa	Sam	☑	10/20/2009	42000
396	Zabaleta	Maria	☑	11/1/2009	29000
404	Del Terzo	Daniel	☑	7/9/2007	37500
407	Greenwood	Charles	☐	4/20/2008	23432
426	Locksley	Robert	☐	3/1/2010	18300
565	Smith	Bill	☑	2/5/2009	50009
694	Rubenstein	Narida	☑	6/1/1999	22000
721	Molina	Marcos	☐	10/20/2008	15000

In this tutorial, you have seen some of the power and convenience of the DataGridView control. This control, in fact, is the result of many years of evolution, through the different versions of Visual Basic. At one time, people had to write a great deal of code in order to display data in a grid. But now, it is possible without any coding at all. However, we have only touched the surface of what the DataGridView can do. In Tutorial 10-2, you will use the DataGridView control to sort columns, add rows, and delete rows from the *SalesStaff* table.

Tutorial 10-2:

Sorting and updating the *SalesStaff* table

In the previous tutorial, you learned how to add a database to a project and display a database table in a DataGridView control. Let's extend the application so you can learn more about the capabilities of DataGridView controls.

Step 1: Open the *SalesStaff 1* project you created in Tutorial 10-1.

Step 2: Run the application.

The Full_Time column holds True and False values—such columns are designed as type bit in the SQL Server database. The DataGridView control always displays bit values in a CheckBox control.

Step 3: Currently, the rows are listed in ascending order by ID number. Click the Last_Name column heading and watch the grid sort the rows in ascending order by last name (see Figure 10-18).

Figure 10-18 Sorting on the Last_Name column

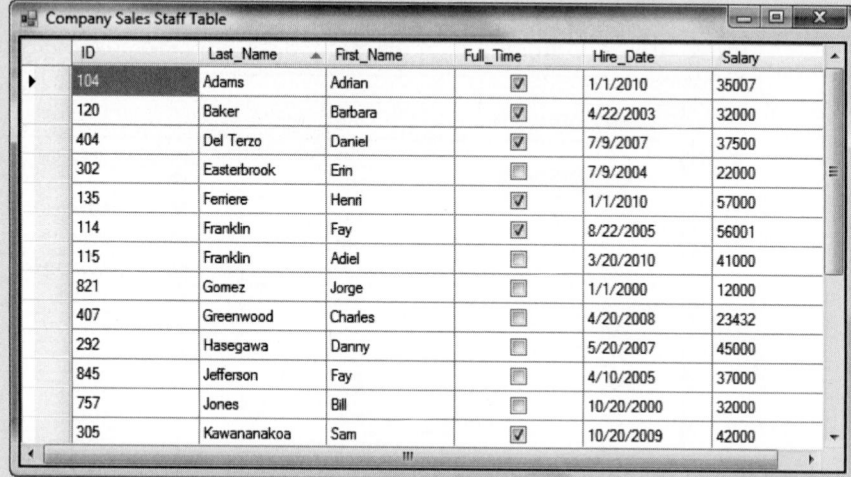

Step 4: Click the Last_Name column again and watch the rows sort in reverse on the same column.

Step 5: Place the mouse over the border between two column headings. When the mouse cursor changes to a horizontal arrow, press the mouse button and drag the border to the right or left. Doing this gives the user the opportunity to change the width of a column.

Step 6: Deleting rows: Click the button to the left of one of the grid rows. The entire row will be selected (highlighted), as shown in Figure 10-19. Press (Delete) and watch the row disappear. The row has been removed from the in-memory dataset, but not the database. Remember which row you deleted, because you will rerun the program soon and verify that the deleted row has been restored.

Figure 10-19 Selecting a DataGridView row

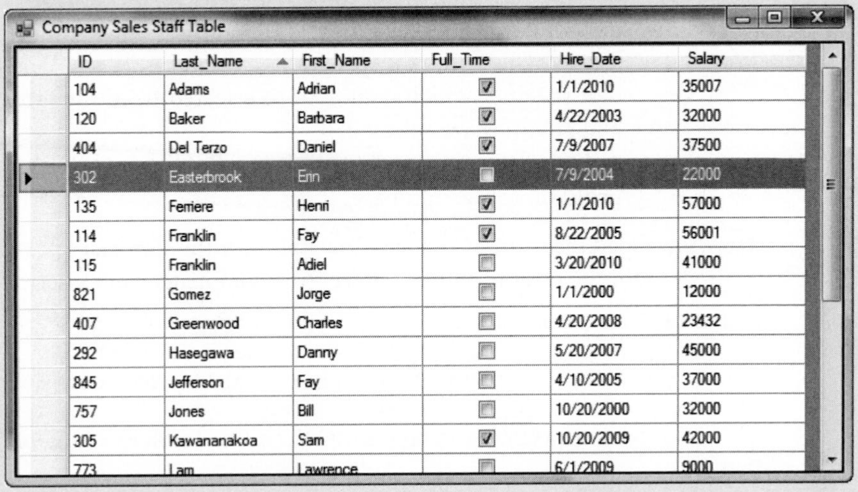

Step 7: Inserting rows: Scroll to the bottom row of the grid and enter the following information in the empty cells: 847, Jackson, Adele, (check Full_time), 6/1/2010, 65000. Figure 10-20 shows the new row added to the table. Press (Enter) to save your changes. Sort the grid on the Last_Name column and look for the row you inserted.

Figure 10-20 Adding a new row to the grid

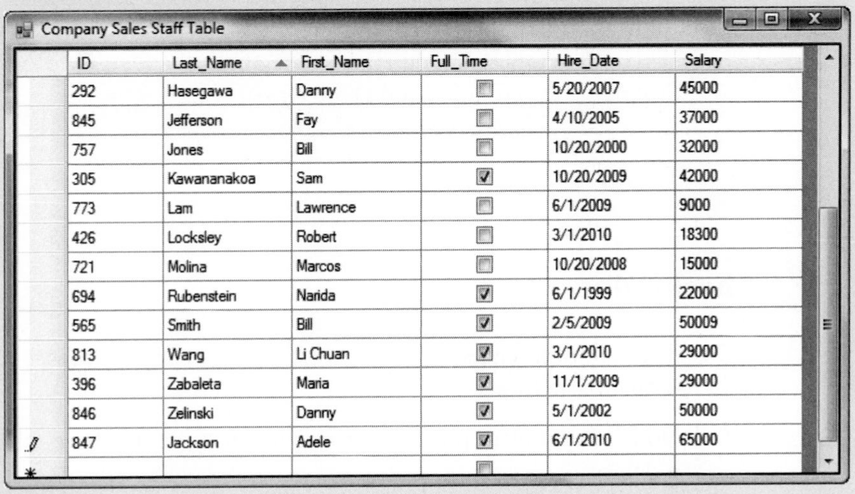

Step 8: Stop the program. Rerun the program, and notice that the changes you made to the dataset were not saved in the database. Later in the chapter we will show how to save changes directly into the database. The grid rows look exactly as they did when you first displayed the dataset.

Stop the program again.

Step 9: In the *Designer* window, look at the three components placed in the form's component tray by Visual Studio when you added the connection to the *SalesStaff* table:

⊞ SalesStaffDataSet   🔛 SalesStaffBindingSource   🗃 SalesStaffTableAdapter

- `SalesStaffDataSet` is the dataset object that holds the table data in memory and passes the data to the DataGridView control.
- `SalesStaffTableAdapter` is the TableAdapter object that pulls data from the database into your program. It contains a command called an SQL Query that specifies which data is to be selected from the table. By default, all rows and columns are selected.
- `SalesStaffBindingSource` is the BindingSource object that connects your program to the database.

Step 10: Open the form's *Code* window and note the statement in `Form_Load` that tells the table adapter to fill the dataset (the comments were inserted by Visual Studio):

```
Private Sub Form1_Load(. . .) Handles MyBase.Load
    'TODO: This line of code loads data into the
    'SalesStaffDataSet.SalesStaff' table. You can move,
    'or remove it, as needed.
    Me.SalesStaffTableAdapter.Fill(Me.SalesStaffDataSet.SalesStaff)
End Sub
```

The TableAdapter's `Fill` method opens the database connection, reads the data from the database into the dataset, and closes the connection. The `Me.` qualifier used when naming the `SalesStaffTableAdapter` just indicates that it belongs to the current form. The argument passed to the `Fill` method is the *SalesStaff* table inside the `SalesStaffDataSet`. It may seem unnecessary to specify a table name when the dataset contains only one table. But datasets can contain multiple tables, so we must identify which table is to be filled.

This tutorial shows how easy it is to display database data in a Windows form. The DataGridView control is the ideal tool for giving users a quick view of data. In our example, the column names and ordering were taken directly from the database table. As you learn more about the DataGridView, you will be able to rename the columns and change their order.

✅ Checkpoint

10.6 The technique called _____ links database tables to controls on Visual Basic forms.

10.7 Which component pulls data from one or more database tables and passes it into a dataset?

10.8 When changes are made to a dataset, what happens to the database that filled the dataset?

10.9 Which control displays datasets in a spreadsheet-like format?

10.10 What type of object connects a program to a database?

10.4 Data-Bound Controls

CONCEPT: Some controls can be bound to a dataset. A data-bound control can be used to display and edit the contents of a particular row and column.

VideoNote

Data-Bound
Controls

In this section, we will show you how to add new data sources to a project. Using a data source, you can bind its fields to individual controls such as text boxes, labels, and list boxes. **Data-bound controls** are convenient because they update their contents automatically when you move from one row to the next in a dataset. They can also be used to update the contents of fields. You will learn how to bind a DataGridView control to an existing dataset. You will also learn how to use a ListBox control to navigate between different rows of a dataset.

Adding a New Data Source

To add a new data source to an application, open the *Data Sources* window and click the *Add New Data Source* link, as shown in Figure 10-21. The *Data Source Configuration Wizard* window appears (see Figure 10-22), just as it did in Tutorial 10-1. Then you follow the steps to create a connection to a database, as was done in Tutorial 10-1. The data source entry added to the *Data Sources* window is shown in Figure 10-23.

TIP: If you cannot see the *Data Sources* window, select *Show Data Sources* from the *Data* menu. The Data Sources window usually appears in the same area of the screen as the *ToolBox*, or the *Solution Explorer*.

Figure 10-21 About to add a new data source

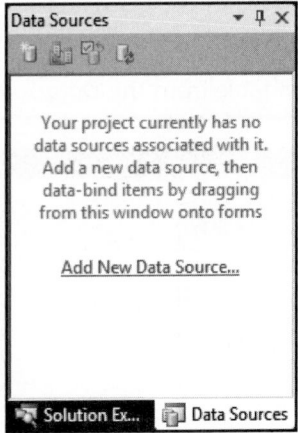

Figure 10-22 *Data Source Configuration Wizard*

Figure 10-23 *SalesStaff* table in the *Data Sources* window

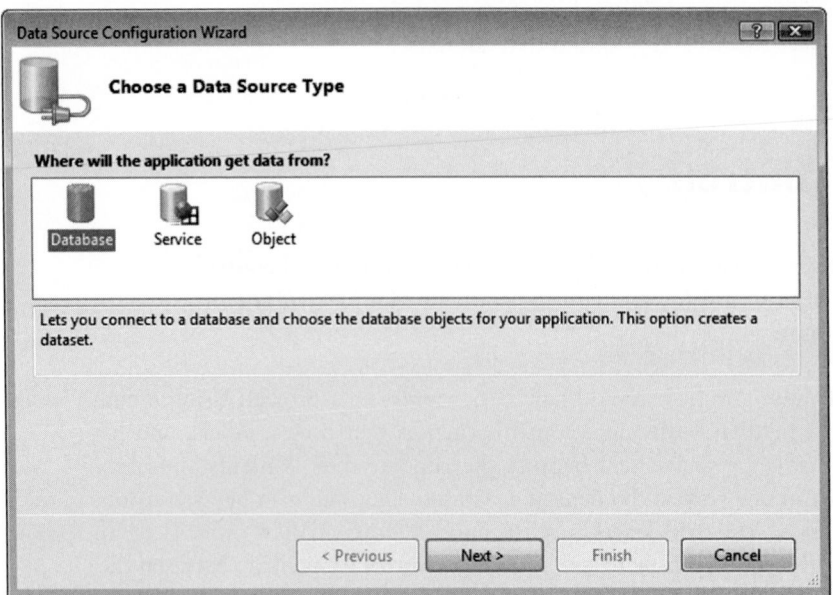

Deleting a Data Source

Suppose you were to create a data source and then later decide to rename it. Unfortunately, data sources are almost impossible to rename. But you can easily delete a data source and create a new one. To delete an existing data source, select its XSD file in the *Solution Explorer* window with the mouse, and then press Delete on the keyboard. A data source named *Employees*, for example, is defined by a file named *Employees.xsd*.

Binding the Data Source to a DataGridView Control

In Tutorial 10-1, you used the *DataGridView Tasks* window to guide you through creating a binding source, table adapter, and dataset. What if you already have a dataset, located in the *Data Sources* window? Then you can bind it to a DataGridView control just by dragging the *SalesStaff* table from the *Data Sources* window to the open area of a form, as shown in Figure 10-24. (The *Data Sources* window may be in a different location on your screen.) When you use this technique for data binding, Visual Studio adds a navigation toolbar to the form, as shown in Figure 10-25.

Figure 10-24 Dragging the *SalesStaff* table from the *Data Sources* window onto a form

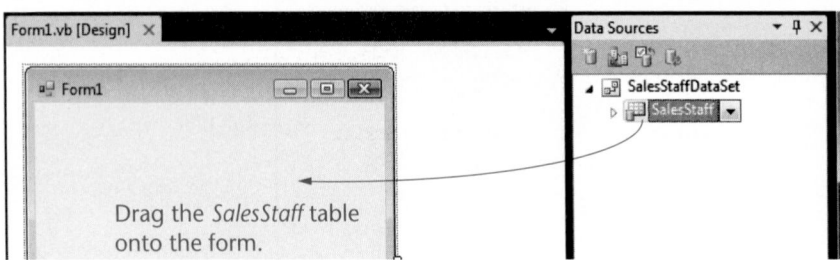

Figure 10-25 After dragging the *SalesStaff* table from the *DataSources* window onto a form

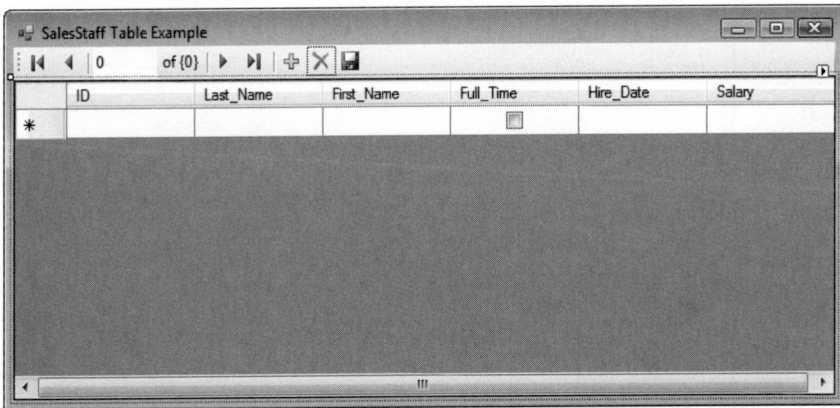

At the same time that Visual Studio builds a DataGridView on the form, it adds a number of important objects to the form's component tray, shown in Figure 10-26:

- *SalesStaffBindingNavigator*—Creates the ToolStrip at the top of the form, with buttons to carry out actions such as moving forward and backward, and adding and deleting rows.
- *SalesStaffDataSet*—An in-memory copy of the *SalesStaff* table
- *SalesStaffBindingSource*—Connects the DataGridView to the DataSet
- *SalesStaffTableAdapter*—Pulls data from the database and places it in the DataSet
- *TableAdapterManager*—A tool for saving data in related tables

 TIP: If you want to remove the ToolStrip from a form, all you have to do is select the SalesStaffBindingNavigator icon and press the Delete key on the keyboard.

Figure 10-26 Objects added to the form's component tray

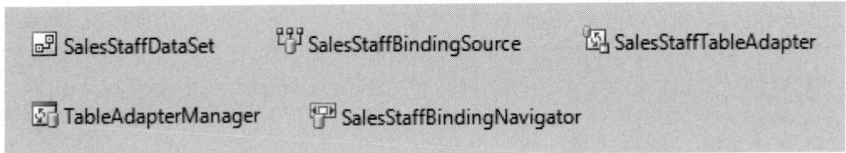

Binding Individual Fields to Controls

If you have an existing dataset in the *Data Sources* window, you can easily create an individual data-bound control for each field by dragging a table from the dataset onto a form that is visible in Design mode. First, click the arrow just to the right of the table name and select *Details* in the drop-down list associated with the table, as shown in Figure 10-27. (The default control type is DataGridView, which we've already used.) Then, when you drag the table name onto a form, a separate control is created for each field. As shown in Figure 10-28, a navigation toolbar is also added to the form. (You may have to wait a few seconds for the controls to appear.)

Figure 10-27 Selecting a table's binding control, in the *Data Sources* window

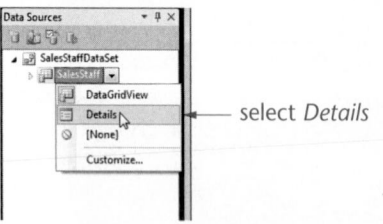

select *Details*

Figure 10-28 After dragging a dataset table onto the form

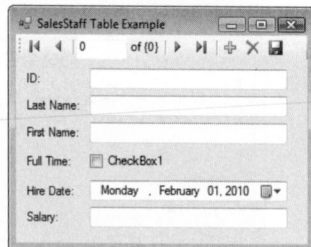

Although the dataset column names have underscores between words, as in *First_Name*, Visual Studio removes the underscore between words when generating the labels next to the controls. You may want to modify the appearance or properties of the controls. For example, if you want the *Hire_Date* column to display in *mm/dd/yyyy* format, set the DateTimePicker control's Format property to *Short*.

By default, numeric database columns are bound to TextBox controls, bit (Boolean) fields are bound to CheckBox controls, and datetime fields are bound to **DateTimePicker controls**. The DateTimePicker control displays a date in different formats, and lets the user select a date from a calendar-like popup dialog.

Suppose you would prefer not to let the user modify a protected field such as *ID*; then you can change the binding control type for individual fields in the *Data Sources* window. For example, if we click the *ID* field in the *SalesStaff* table in the *Data Sources* window, a list of control types appears (see Figure 10-29). If you choose a Label, the user can view the field, but cannot modify its contents.

In Figure 10-30, we show a sample of the same form with a Label control for the *ID* field, and some customizing of the appearance of the other controls. For example, we have cleared the Text property of the CheckBox control and shortened the Hire Date and

Figure 10-29 Selecting the control binding type for the *ID* field in the *Data Sources* window

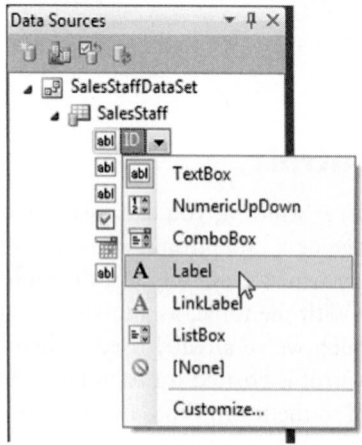

Figure 10-30 Displaying one row of the *SalesStaff* table in bound controls

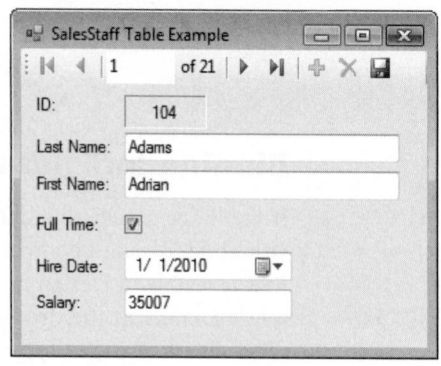

Salary fields. The DateTimePicker control's Format property has four choices: *Long, Short, Time,* and *Custom.* Changing the format to *Short* causes the dates to be displayed in *mm/dd/yyyy* format, or the equivalent for other world locales.

If you want to include only one or two bound controls from a dataset, you can drag individual columns from the *Data Sources* window onto a form. To run and modify this sample program, see the *Binding Example* program located in the student sample programs folder named *Chap10\Binding Example.* Tutorial 10-3 shows you how to bind a Data-GridView to the *SalesStaff* table.

Tutorial 10-3:
Binding a DataGridView to the *SalesStaff* table

In this tutorial, you will begin by adding a new data source to your application. Then you will bind the data source to a DataGridView control and tell Visual Studio to create a toolstrip with buttons that let the user navigate, insert, delete, and save database rows.

Step 1: Create a new Windows Forms Application project named *SalesStaff Databound.*

Step 2: Select *Show Data Sources* from the *Data* menu. This will cause the *Data Sources* window to appear. (The *Data Sources* window usually appears in the same area of the screen as either the *Solution Explorer,* or the *Toolbox.*)

Step 3: In the *Data Sources* window, click the *Add New Data Source* link.

Step 4: Repeat what you did in Tutorial 10-1, in steps 7 through 13 to select the Company.mdf database from the *Chap10* student samples folder.

Step 5: In the *Choose Your Database Objects* step of the *Data Source Configuration Wizard* window (Figure 10-31), select the *SalesStaff* table and name the dataset *SalesStaffDataSet.* Click the *Finish* button.

Figure 10-31 Data Source Configuration Wizard

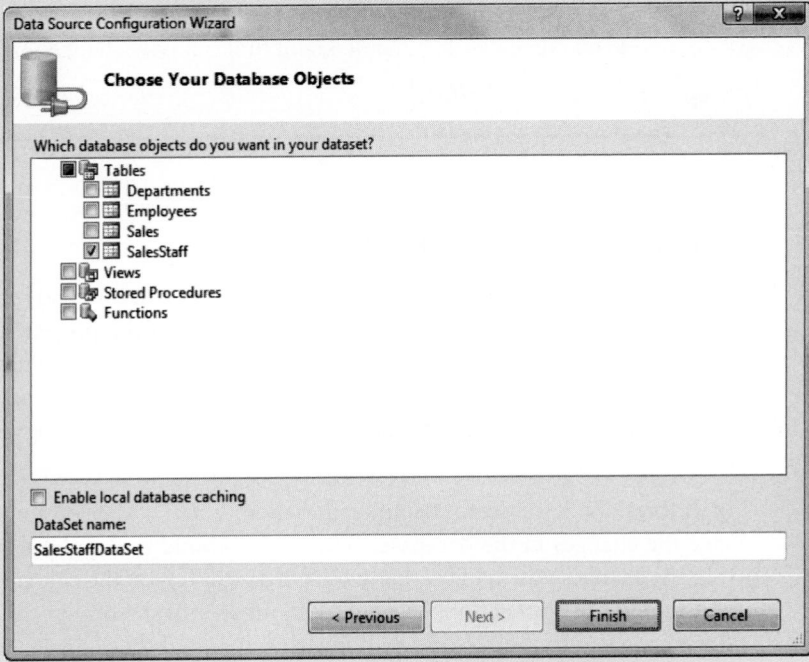

Step 6: Increase the width of the program's form to about 700 pixels and set its Text property to *SalesStaff Table*.

Step 7: Drag the *SalesStaff* table name from the *Data Sources* window onto your form. Notice how Visual Studio adds both a DataGridView control and a ToolStrip control to the form. The ToolStrip contains buttons that let the user perform operations on the DataGridView control's data.

Step 8: Set the DataGridView control's Dock property to *Fill*, so it anchors to all sides of the form.

Step 9: Save the project and run the application. You should see output similar to that shown in Figure 10-32.

Figure 10-32 Output from the *SalesStaff Databound* application

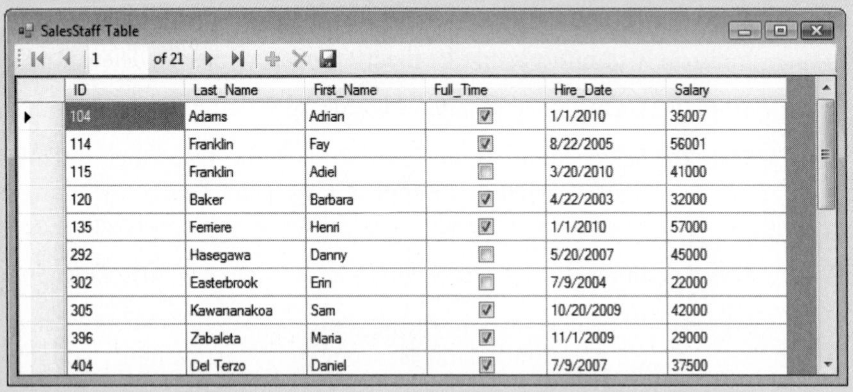

Step 10: Initially, the ID field of the first record is highlighted. Click the arrow buttons on the Navigation toolbar and notice that the highlighted selection bar moves from one record to the next. Experiment with the other toolbar buttons to see what they do. Modify one of the rows by clicking on the button just to the left of the ID number. Then, after you have changed the data in one of the row cells, click the *Save Data* button in the toolbar. In design mode, you can double-click this button to examine its Click handler, and find out how changes are saved to the database.

Step 11: Close the program.

Copying the Database

In Tutorial 10-1, when creating a new connection, a window, shown in Figure 10-33, asked if you wanted to copy the Company.mdf database to the project directory. In the second paragraph, it explains that each time you build the application, a new copy of the database file is copied to the project's output directory. If you only run the program without rebuilding, changes you make to the database while running your program will be saved in the database.

In Tutorial 10-3 you were encouraged to modify individual rows in the DataGridView and save the changes in the database. But, if you rebuild the application, it may have seemed that the changes you made earlier were not saved. If fact, the changes were saved, but when you rebuilt the application, Visual Studio made a fresh copy of the database and put it in the project's output directory. By doing this, it erased the changes you made to the data.

Figure 10-33 Copying a database to the project director

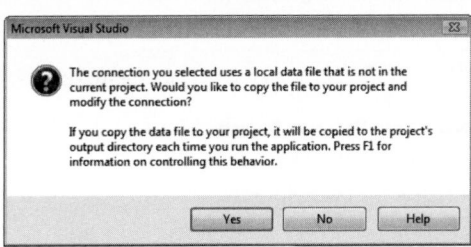

If you want changes to your database to be permanent, you can click the *No* button when the window in Figure 10-33 appears. This will cause Visual Studio to connect to the existing database rather than making a copy. There is only one disadvantage to this decision: If you give your project to another person (such as your instructor), the database will not be inside the project folder. Also, the database connection string in your project will have to be modified before the other person can execute your project. When creating a project to turn in for a grade, be sure to follow your instructor's instructions when answering either *Yes* or *No* in response to this window.

In Tutorial 10-4, you will display individual fields from the *SalesStaff* table.

VideoNote

Tutorial 10-4
Walkthrough

Tutorial 10-4:
Binding individual controls to the *SalesStaff* table

In this tutorial, you will select the *Details* option in the *Data Source* window so you can bind individual controls to fields in the *SalesStaff* table.

Step 1:   Create a new Windows Forms Application project named *SalesStaff Details*.

Step 2:   Set the form's Text property to *SalesStaff Details*.

Step 3:   Select *Show Data Sources* from the *Data* menu. This will cause the *Data Sources* window to appear.

Step 4:   In the *Data Sources* window, click the *Add New Data Source* link.

Step 5:   Select the *Company.mdf* database from the *Chap10* student sample programs folder. This is what you did in Steps 7 through 13 of Tutorial 10-1. When you are asked if the database should be copied to your project folder, answer *Yes*.

Step 6:   In the *Choose Your Database Objects* step of the *Data Source Configuration Wizard* (Figure 10-34), select the *SalesStaff* table and name the dataset *SalesStaffDataSet*. Click the *Finish* button.

Step 7:   In the *Data Sources* window, expand the list of fields under the *SalesStaff* table name by clicking the arrow to the left of the *SalesStaff* table name.

Step 8:   Drag the *Last_Name* field from the *Data Sources* window onto your form. When you do this, you should see a TextBox control appear on the form with a label to its left side. Notice that Visual Studio automatically removes the underscore character between the two words in the field name. You will also see a new ToolStrip control on the form. An example is shown in Figure 10-35.

Step 9:   Save the project and run the application. Click the navigation buttons in the tool strip and notice how the name changes. Also, the table's row number changes in the tool strip.

Figure 10-34 Data Source Configuration Wizard

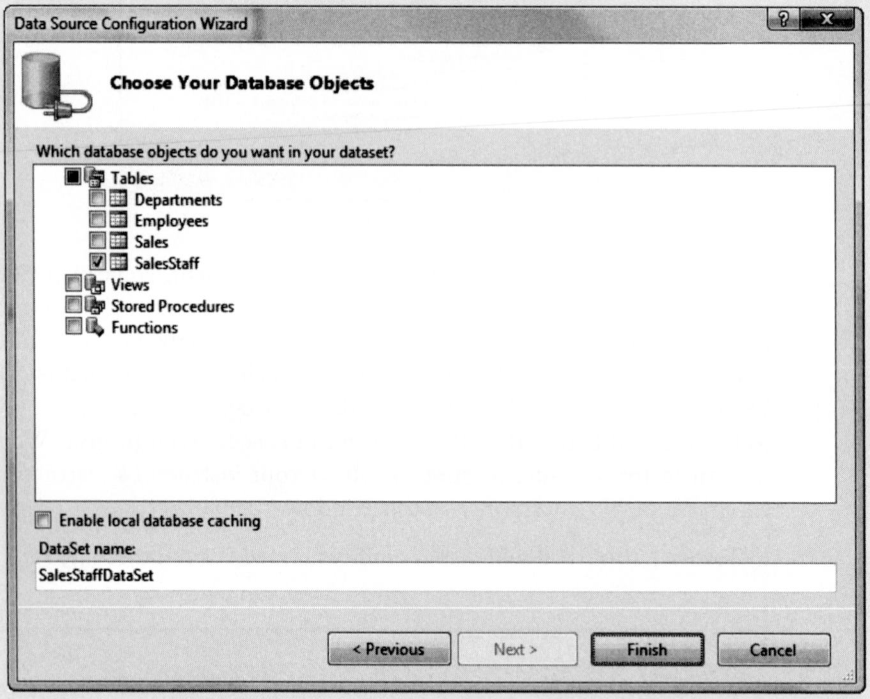

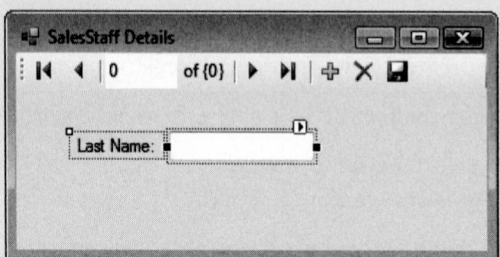

Figure 10-35 After dragging the *Last_Name* field onto the form

Step 10: Stop the application.

Step 11: Drag the remaining columns from the *SalesStaff* table onto the form. You might want to rearrange their order, expand some fields, remove the text from the Full Time checkbox, and change the *Hire_Date* control's Format property to *Short*. An example is shown in Figure 10-36.

Step 12: Save the project and run the application again. Notice how all the fields update at the same time when you click the navigation buttons on the tool strip.

Step 13: Experiment with adding, deleting, and editing individual rows from the table. Changes you make to individual fields will be saved only if you click the *Save Data* button on the tool strip.

Step 14: Close the application.

In this tutorial, you have seen how easy it is to work with data-bound tables in Visual Basic. You can display an entire table at once, or you can display each row of a table individually. Editing individual field values, which was a lot of work in previous versions of Visual Basic, has become remarkably easy.

Figure 10-36 After dragging all *SalesStaff* fields onto the form

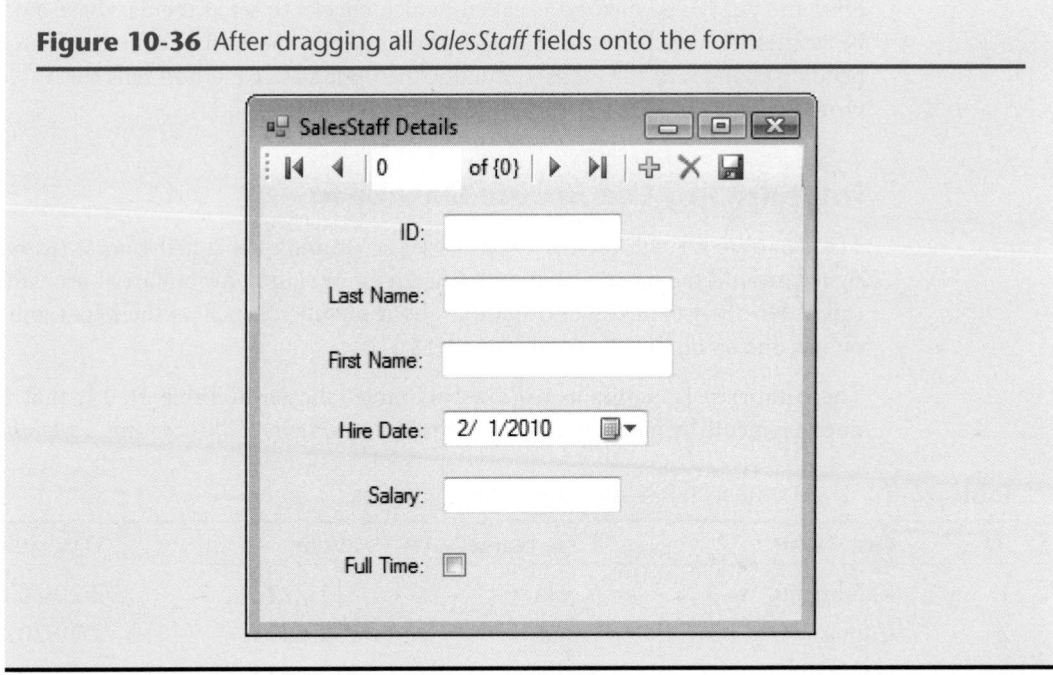

More about The ToolStrip in Data-Bound Forms

Filling the DataSet

You have seen how Visual Studio adds a ToolStrip control with buttons whenever you drag a table from the *Data Source* window onto a form. In fact, a certain amount of code is generated inside the form, which may be of interest to you.

The `Form1_Load` event handler contains comments, followed by a call to the `Fill` method of the SalesStaffTableAdapter object:

```
Private Sub Form1_Load(...) Handles MyBase.Load

    ' TODO: This line of code loads data into the
    ' SalesStaffDataSet.SalesStaff table. You can move,
    ' or remove it, as needed.

    Me.SalesStaffTableAdapter.Fill(Me.SalesStaffDataSet.SalesStaff)

End Sub
```

Earlier, we said that the job of a TableAdapter is to pull data from the database and copy it into the DataSet. In fact, this is exactly what the `Fill` method does, as it copies the data into the SalesStaff table of the SalesStaffDataSet object.

Saving Changes to the Data

The data binding examples we saw earlier also contained a procedure that saves changes made by the user when the *Save* button is clicked in the ToolStrip control:

```
Private Sub SalesStaffBindingNavigatorSaveItem_Click(...)Handles...
    Me.Validate()
    Me.SalesStaffBindingSource.EndEdit()
    Me.TableAdapterManager.UpdateAll(Me.SalesStaffDataSet)
End Sub
```

First, the `Validate` method is called, which checks to see if the database data is ready to be written to the database. Second, the `EndEdit` method is called, which applies any pending changes to the dataset. Finally, the `UpdateAll` method tells the TableAdapter to write the data changes back to the database.

Introducing the *Karate* Database

The database we will use for the next set of examples is called *Karate* (*Karate.mdf*), designed around the membership and scheduling of classes for a martial arts school. A table called *Members* contains information about members, such as their first and last names, phone, and so on. It is listed in Table 10-10.

The database also contains a *Payments* table, shown in Table 10-11, that holds recent dues payments by members. Each row in the *Payments* table contains a *Member_Id* value,

Table 10-10 The *Members* table from the *Karate* database

ID	Last_Name	First_Name	Phone	Date_Joined
1	Kahumanu	Keoki	111-2222	2/20/2002
2	Chong	Anne	232-2323	2/20/2010
3	Hasegawa	Elaine	313-3455	2/20/2004
4	Kahane	Brian	646-9387	5/20/2008
5	Gonzalez	Aldo	123-2345	6/6/2009
6	Kousevitzky	Jascha	414-2345	2/20/2010
7	Taliafea	Moses	545-2323	5/20/2005
8	Concepcion	Rafael	602-3312	5/20/2007
9	Taylor	Winifred	333-2222	2/20/2010

Table 10-11 The *Payments* table from the *Karate* database

ID	Member_Id	Payment_Date	Amount
1	1	10/20/2009	$48.00
2	2	02/20/2010	$80.00
3	6	03/20/2010	$75.00
4	4	12/16/2009	$50.00
5	5	04/11/2009	$65.00
6	3	02/16/2009	$75.00
7	9	03/20/2010	$77.00
8	8	02/27/2010	$44.00
9	6	04/20/2010	$77.00
10	5	01/16/2010	$66.00
11	8	05/11/2010	$77.00
13	6	02/20/2010	$77.00
14	7	07/16/2009	$77.00
15	1	03/11/2010	$44.00
16	3	03/28/2010	$43.00
17	4	03/27/2010	$44.00
19	9	02/20/2010	$44.00
22	2	03/20/2010	$55.00

which identifies the member (from the *Members* table) who made a dues payment. Their relationship is shown by the diagram in Figure 10-37. The line connects the *ID* field in the *Members* table to the *Member_Id* field in the *Payments* table. In tutorials 10-5 and 10-6, you will work with these two tables.

Figure 10-37 Relationship between the *Members* and *Payments* tables

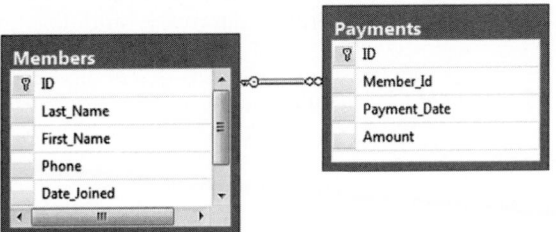

Binding to ListBox and ComboBox Controls

ListBox and ComboBox controls are ideal tools for displaying lists of items and permitting users to select individual items. When working with databases, you need to set the following properties:

- DataSource: The **DataSource property** identifies the table within the dataset that supplies the data.
- DisplayMember: The **DisplayMember property** identifies the column within the table that displays in the list box or combo box.

When you use the mouse to drag a table column from the *Data Sources* window onto a list box or combo box, Visual Studio automatically creates the necessary data components: a dataset, binding source, and table adapter.

Tutorial 10-5 shows you how to display the *Members* table in a list box.

Tutorial 10-5:
Displaying the *Karate Members* table in a ListBox

In this tutorial, you will use a ListBox control to display the last names of members from the *Members* table in the *Karate* database. When the user clicks a member name, the program will display the date when the member joined.

Step 1: Create a new Windows Forms Application project named *Member List*. Save the project immediately.

Step 2: Click *Add New Data Source* in the *Data Sources* window. (If you cannot see the *Data Sources* window, select *Show Data Sources* from the *Data* menu.)

Step 3: Follow the steps in the *Data Source Configuration Wizard* to create a connection to the *Members* table in the *Karate.mdf* database, located in the student sample programs folder named *Chap10*. Name the dataset *MembersDataSet*.

Step 4: Set the form's Text property to *Member List*.

Step 5: Add a ListBox control to the form and name it `lstMembers`. Set the ListBox control's Size.Width property to 125, and its Size.Height property to 134.

Step 6: Add a Label just above the list box and set its Text property to *Member Names*. Widen the form so it appears similar to the one shown in Figure 10-38.

Step 7: Select the list box, and then click the down-arrow next to its DataSource property in the *Properties* window. Expand the *Other Data Sources* group, expand *Project Data Sources*, expand *MembersDataSet*, and select *Members* (shown in Figure 10-39). Notice that Visual Studio immediately adds three components to the form's component tray: a dataset, a binding source, and a table adapter.

Figure 10-38 *Member List* program with list box

Figure 10-39 Setting the list box's DataSource property

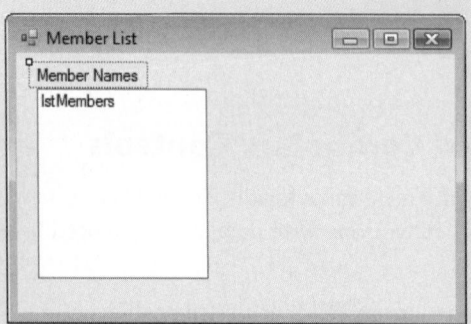

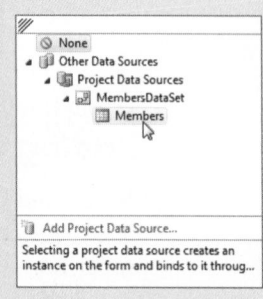

Step 8: Set the list box's DisplayMember property to *Last_Name*.

Step 9: Save and run the application. The list box should contain the last names of members, as shown in Figure 10-40. Close the window and return to Design mode.

Figure 10-40 List box filled, at runtime

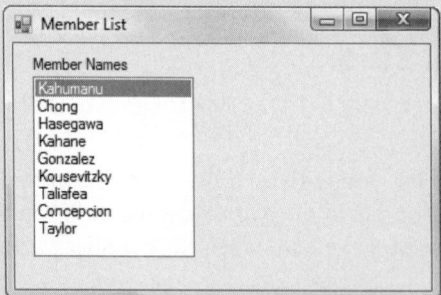

Step 10: Next, you will add a data-bound TextBox control to the form that displays the member's phone number. To do this, expand the *Members* table in the *Data Sources* window, and then use the mouse to drag the *Phone* field from the *Data Sources* window onto the form.

Step 11: Save and run the program. As you click each member's name, notice how the current phone number is displayed. For a sample, see Figure 10-41.

Let's analyze what's happening here. When the user selects a name in the list box, the form's data binding mechanism moves to the dataset row containing the person's name. The *Phone* TextBox control shares the same binding source as the ListBox, so it displays the phone number of the person selected in the list box.

Figure 10-41 Phone number of selected member displays in a TextBox control

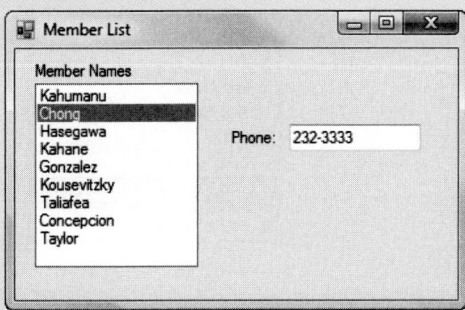

Step 12: Add the remaining fields by dragging the field names from the *Data Sources* window onto the form, as shown in Figure 10-42. Choose the Label control type for the *ID* field. In the figure, a DateTimePicker control was used for the *Date_Joined* field. The DateTimePicker control's Format property was set to *Short*. Reposition the controls and resize the form as necessary. The Label control displaying the *ID* field looks best with its BorderStyle property set to *Fixed3D* and its AutoSize property set to False.

Figure 10-42 Displaying the *Members* table in detail controls

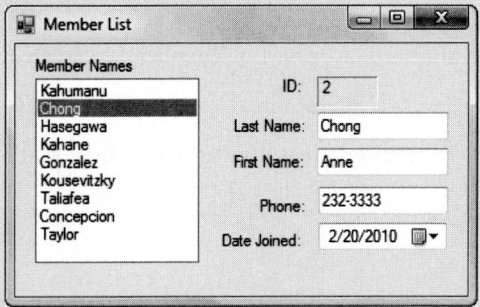

Step 13: Save and rerun the program. Now you have a way to navigate through dataset rows by selecting from a list box!

Step 14: End the program.

Adding Rows to a Database Table

The easiest way for an application to add a row to a database table is to use a TableAdapter. To find one, you have to open a dataset's **Schema Defintion**. When you add a data source to a project, a special file called a **schema definition file** is created. This is a file with a designer window that displays the names and data types of fields in the table. It has a filename extension of *xsd*. In Tutorial 10-5, for example, the *Members* table was used as a data source and the *Solution Explorer* window contained a file named *MembersDataSet.xsd*. To edit a schema definition file, double-click its name in the *Solution Explorer* window. An editor window will open, as shown in Figure 10-43. A DataTable named *Members* was created automatically when this data source was added to the project. Associated with every DataTable is a **TableAdapter**, which in this case is named *MembersTableAdapter*.

Figure 10-43 The MembersDataSet schema definition file, containing the *Members* DataTable and the *MembersTableAdapter*

Suppose you would like the code in your application to add a new row to the *Members* table. You can call the TableAdapter's `Insert` method, passing it the column values for the row being added. Here is an example:

```
MembersTableAdapter.Insert(10, "Hasegawa", "Adrian",
                           "305-999-8888",#5/15/2010#)
```

Identity Columns

A database table can have what is known as an **identity column.** When new rows are added to the table, the identity column is assigned a new unique integer value. That is the case for the *Payments* table in the *Karate* database. The primary key column, named ID, is also an identity column. Its values are automatically generated in sequence when new rows are added to the table. If we were to call the `Insert` method for the *Payments* table, we would omit the ID column value and just pass the Member_Id, Payment_Date, and Amount values:

```
PaymentsTableAdapter.Insert(5, #5/15/2010#, 50D)
```

Tutorial 10-6 shows you how to insert new rows into the *Payments* table of the *Karate* database.

Tutorial 10-6:
Inserting *Karate* member payments

In this tutorial, you will write a program that inserts new rows into the *Payments* table of the *Karate* database.

Step 1: Create a new Windows Forms Application project named *Insert Karate Payments*.

Step 2: In the *Data Sources* window, add a new data source named `PaymentsDataSet`, which uses the *Payments* table from the *Karate.mdf* database. Answer *Yes* when Visual Studio asks if you want the database copied to the project directory.

Step 3: Add three text boxes to the form with appropriate labels. One is named `txtMemberId`, another is named `txtDate`, and the third is named `txtAmount`. Set the form's Text property to *Insert Karate Payments*. Use Figure 10-44 as a guide.

Figure 10-44 The startup form in the *Insert Karate Payments* application

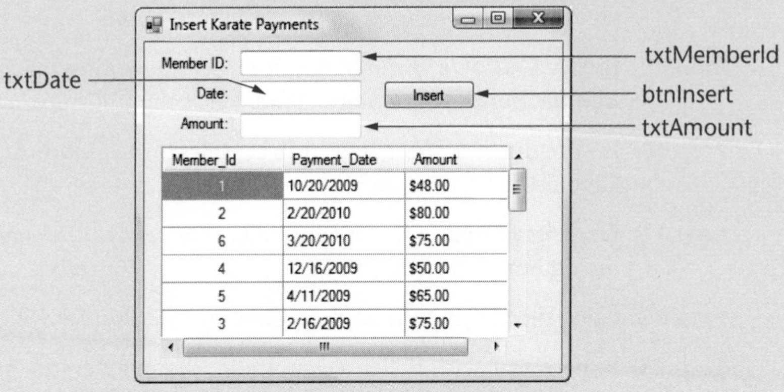

txtDate

txtMemberId

btnInsert

txtAmount

Step 4: Add a Button control to the form, and set its name to `btnInsert`. Set the button's Text property to *Insert*.

Step 5: Add a DataGridView control and set the following properties: Name = *dgvPayments*; BorderStyle = *None*; BackgroundColor = *Control*; ReadOnly = *True*; RowHeadersVisible = *False*. The ReadOnly property prevents the user from making any changes to the grid's data at runtime.

Step 6: Click the grid's smart tag (the arrow in the grid's upper right corner) to display the *DataGridView Tasks* window. Set its data source to the *Payments* table of the `PaymentsDataSet`.

Step 7: Select the grid's Columns property, which opens the *Edit Columns* window and remove the *ID* column. Figure 10-45 shows the Edit Columns window after the ID column was removed.

Figure 10-45 Editing the Columns property of the *dgvPayments* grid

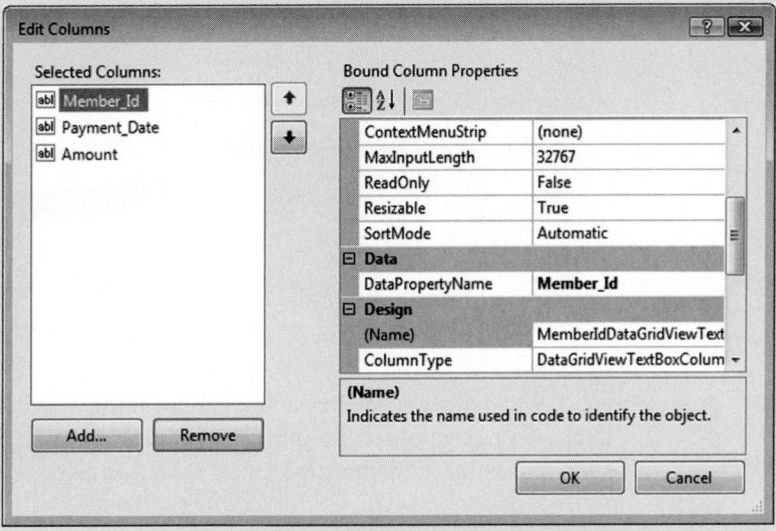

Step 8: Still in the *Edit Columns* window, select the *Member_Id* column, and open the DefaultCellStyle property in the right-hand list box. The *CellStyle Builder* window will appear, as shown in Figure 10-46.

Step 9: In the *CellStyle Builder* window, set the following properties: Alignment = *MiddleCenter*; ForeColor = *Blue*. Click the *OK* button to close the window.

Step 10: In the *Edit Columns* window, select the *Amount* column and open its DefaultCellStyle property.

Step 11: Open its Format property and select *Currency*. Click the *OK* button to close the dialog box.

Step 12: Click the *OK* button to close the *CellStyle Builder* window.

Step 13: Experiment with the three columns, changing colors and formats as you wish. When you finish, click the *OK* button to close the *Edit Columns* window.

Step 14: Save and run the program. You should see a list of payments in the grid. Halt the program.

Figure 10-46 Editing the *Member_Id* column in the *CellStyle Builder* window

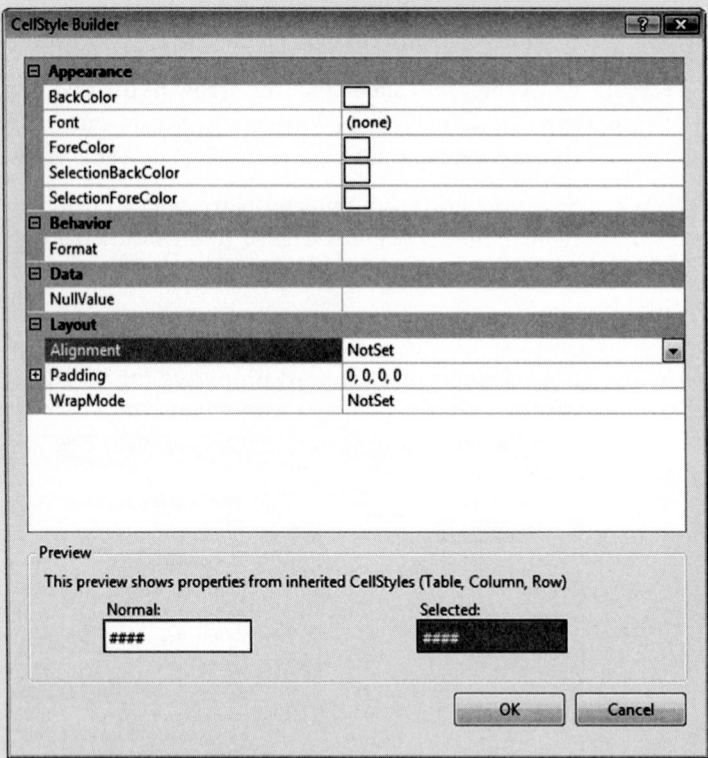

Step 15: Next, you will add code to the Insert button that lets the program save new payments. In Design mode, double-click the *Insert* button. Add the following code, shown in bold, to the button's Click event handler:

```
Private Sub btnInsert_Click(...) Handles btnInsert.Click
    Try
        Me.PaymentsTableAdapter.Insert(CShort(txtMemberID.Text),
                    CDate(txtDate.Text), CDec(txtAmount.Text))
        Me.PaymentsTableAdapter.Fill(PaymentsDataSet.Payments)
    Catch ex As Exception
        MessageBox.Show(ex.Message, "Data Input Error")
    End Try
End Sub
```

The code you added calls the TableAdapter's `Insert` method, passing to the method the values of the three columns we want to add: *Member_Id*, *Date*, and *Amount*. Each must be converted to a type that matches the appropriate dataset column type. Then, the *Fill* method is called so you can see the new payment in the grid.

 TIP: The `Me` object referred to in Step 15 refers to the current Form object. Its use is optional.

Step 16: Add the following lines, marked in bold, to the `Form_Load` event handler. As the comment says, we want the text box to display today's date.

```
Private Sub Form1_Load(...) Handles MyBase.Load
    'TODO: This line of code loads data into the...
    Me.PaymentsTableAdapter.Fill(Me.PaymentsDataSet.Payments)

    ' Set the text box to today's date.
    txtDate.Text = Today().ToString("d")
End Sub
```

Step 17: Save and run the application. Add a new payment, using a *Member_Id* value between 1 and 9. Verify that your payment appears in the grid after clicking the *Insert* button. This payment was saved in the database.

Step 18: Add a payment that uses an invalid date format or a nonnumeric value for the amount. When you click the *Insert* button, observe the error message (generated by the `Try-Catch` statement). An application should always recover gracefully when users enter invalid data.

Step 19: End the application.

Using Loops with DataTables

Techniques you've learned about loops and collections in previous chapters apply easily to database tables. You can iterate over the `Rows` collection of a table using the `For Each` statement. Usually, it's best to create a strongly typed row that matches the type of rows in the table.

The following loop iterates over the `Rows` collection of the *Payments* table of the `PaymentsDataSet` dataset, adding the *Amount* column to a total. The dataset was built from the *Payments* table in the *Karate* database when we added a new data source to the project.

```
Dim row As PaymentsDataSet.PaymentsRow
Dim decTotal As Decimal = 0

For Each row In Me.PaymentsDataSet.Payments.Rows
    decTotal += row.Amount
Next
```

Tutorial 10-7 shows how to add a total to the *Karate* student payments application.

Tutorial 10-7:
Adding a total to the *Karate* student payments

In this tutorial, you will add statements that calculate the total amount of payments made by students in the Karate School.

Step 1: Open the *Insert Karate Payments* project you created in Tutorial 10-6.

Step 2: Add a new button to the form, just below the *Insert* button. (You may have to move the *Insert* button up a little to make room. See Figure 10-47 for an example). Set its properties as follows: Name = btnTotal; Text = *Total Payments*

Step 3: Double-click the *Total Payments* button and insert the following code, shown in bold, in its Click event handler. This code uses a loop to get the payment amount value from each row in the dataset and add the value to a total:

```
Private Sub btnTotal_Click(...) Handles btnTotal.Click
    Dim decTotal As Decimal = 0
    Dim row As PaymentsDataSet.PaymentsRow

    For Each row In Me.PaymentsDataSet.Payments.Rows
      decTotal += row.Amount
    Next

    MessageBox.Show("Total payments are equal to " &
                    decTotal.ToString("c"), "Total")
End Sub
```

Step 4: Save and run the program. Click the *Total Payments* button and observe the results. An example is shown in Figure 10-47.

Step 5: Insert a new payment. Then click the *Total Payments* button, and note that the value of the total payments has increased.

Step 6: End the program.

Figure 10-47 Calculating the total payments

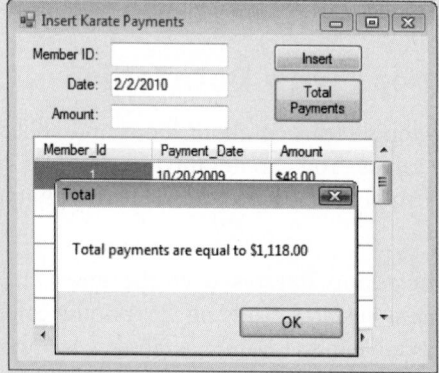

Checkpoint

10.11 Which Visual Studio window displays the list of datasets belonging to a project?

10.12 The _____ _____ *Configuration Wizard* is a tool you can use to create a connection to a database and select a database table.

10.13 If a certain data source exists, how do you bind it to a DataGridView control?

10.14 How do you bind a single data source column to a text box?

10.15 By default, which control binds to a DateTime field in a data source?

10.16 What is the Visual Studio menu command for adding a new data source to the current project?

10.5 Structured Query Language (SQL)

SQL, which stands for *Structured Query Language*, is a standard language for working with database management systems. SQL has been standardized by the American National Standards Institute (ANSI) and adopted by almost every database software vendor as the language of choice for interacting with their Database Management System (DBMS).

SQL consists of a limited set of keywords. You use the keywords to construct statements known as **database queries**. These statements are submitted to the DBMS, and in response, the DBMS carries out operations on its data.

 NOTE: Although SQL is a language, you don't use it to write applications. It is intended only as a standard means of interacting with a DBMS. You still need a general programming language such as Visual Basic to write database-related applications.

SELECT Statement

The SELECT statement retrieves data from a database. You can use it to select rows, columns, and tables. The most basic format for a single table is as follows:

```
SELECT ColumnList
FROM Table
```

The members of `ColumnList` must be table column names separated by commas. The following statement selects the *ID* and *Salary* columns from the *SalesStaff* table:

```
SELECT ID, Salary
FROM SalesStaff
```

In a Visual Basic program, the dataset produced by this query would have just two columns: *ID* and *Salary*. There is no required formatting or capitalization of SQL statements or field names. The following queries are equivalent:

```
SELECT ID, Salary FROM SalesStaff
select ID, Salary from SalesStaff
Select id, salary from salesstaff
```

As a matter of style and readability, you should try to use consistent capitalization.

If field names contain embedded spaces, they must be surrounded by square brackets, as in the following example:

```
SELECT [Last Name], [First Name]
FROM Employees
```

The * character in the column list selects all columns from a table, as shown in the following example:

```
SELECT *
FROM SalesStaff
```

Aliases for Column Names

Column names can be renamed, using the AS keyword. The new column name is called an *alias*, as in the following example that renames the Hire_Date column to

```
Date_Hired:
  SELECT
    Last_Name, Hire_Date AS Date_Hired
  FROM
    SalesStaff
```

Renaming columns is useful for two reasons: First, you might want to hide the real column names from users for security purposes. Second, column headings in reports can be made more user friendly if you substitute your own names for the column names used inside the database.

Creating Alias Columns from Other Columns

A query can create a new column (called an *alias*) from other existing columns. For example, we might want to combine *Last_Name* and *First_Name* from a table named *Members*. We can insert a comma and space between the columns as follows:

```
SELECT Last_Name + ', ' + First_Name AS Full_Name
FROM Members
```

Now the *Full_Name* column can conveniently be inserted into a list box or combo box. In general, when strings occur in queries, they must always be surrounded by apostrophes. The + operator concatenates multiple strings into a single string.

Calculated Columns

You can create new columns, whose contents are calculated from existing column values. Suppose a table named *Payroll* contains columns named employeeId, hoursWorked, and hourlyRate. The following statement creates a new column named payAmount using hoursWorked and hourlyRate:

```
SELECT employeeId,
  hoursWorked * hourlyRate AS payAmount
FROM PayRoll
```

Setting the Row Order with ORDER BY

The SQL SELECT statement has an ORDER BY **clause** that lets you control the display order of the table rows. In other words, you can sort the data on one or more columns. The following is the general form for sorting on a single column:

```
ORDER BY ColumnName [ASC | DESC]
```

ASC indicates ascending order (the default), and DESC indicates descending order. Both are optional, and you can use only one at a time. The following clause sorts the output in ascending order by last name:

```
ORDER BY Last_Name ASC
```

We can do this more simply, as follows:

```
ORDER BY Last_Name
```

The following sorts the output in descending order by salary:

```
ORDER BY Salary DESC
```

You can sort on multiple columns. The following statement sorts in ascending order first by last name; then within each last name, it sorts in ascending order by first name:

```
ORDER BY Last_Name, First_Name
```

The following SELECT statement returns the first name, last name, and date joined, sorting by last name and first name in the *Members* table of the *Karate* database:

```
SELECT
    First_Name, Last_Name, Date_Joined
FROM
    Members
ORDER BY Last_Name, First_Name
```

Selecting Rows with the WHERE Clause

The SQL SELECT statement has an optional **WHERE clause** that you can use to *filter*, or select which rows you want to retrieve from a database table. The simplest form of the **WHERE** clause is as follows:

```
WHERE ColumnName = Value
```

In this format, `ColumnName` must be one of the table columns, and `Value` must be in a format that is consistent with the column type. The following SELECT statement, for example, specifies that *Last_Name* must be equal to *Gomez*:

```
SELECT First_Name, Last_Name, Salary
FROM SalesStaff
WHERE Last_Name = 'Gomez'
```

Because *Last_Name* is a *nvarchar* column, it must be compared to a string literal enclosed in apostrophes. If the person's name contains an apostrophe (such as O'Leary), the apostrophe must be repeated. The following is an example:

```
SELECT First_Name, Last_Name, Salary
FROM SalesStaff
WHERE Last_Name = 'O''Leary'
```

Relational Operators

Table 10-12 lists the operators that can be used in WHERE clauses. The following expression matches last names starting with letters B–Z:

```
WHERE Last_Name >= 'B'
```

The following expression matches non-zero salary values:

```
WHERE Salary <> 0
```

Table 10-12 SQL relational operators

Operator	Meaning
=	equal to
<>	not equal to
<	less than
<=	less than or equal to
>	greater than
>=	greater than or equal to

Numeric and Date Values

Numeric literals are not surrounded by quotation marks. The following expression matches all rows in which *Salary* is greater than $30,000. The use of parentheses is optional.

```
WHERE (Salary > 30000)
```

Date literals must be delimited by apostrophes:

```
WHERE (Hire_Date > '12/31/2010')
```

The following expression matches rows containing hire dates falling between (and including) January 1, 2010 and December 31, 2010:

```
WHERE (Hire_Date BETWEEN '1/1/2010' AND '12/31/2010')
```

The following is a complete SELECT statement using the WHERE clause that selects rows according to *Hire_Date* and sorts by last name:

```
SELECT First_Name, Last_Name, Hire_Date
FROM SalesStaff
WHERE (Hire_Date BETWEEN '1/1/2010' AND '12/31/2010')
ORDER BY Last_Name
```

LIKE Operator

The **LIKE operator** can be used to create partial matches with varchar column values. When combined with LIKE, the underscore character matches a single unknown character. For example, the following expression matches all three-character Account_ID values beginning with X and ending with 4:

```
WHERE Account_ID LIKE 'X_4'
```

The % character matches multiple unknown characters. We call % a **wildcard** symbol. For example, the following matches all last names starting with the letter A:

```
WHERE Last_Name LIKE 'A%'
```

Wildcard symbols can be combined. For example, the following matches all *First_Name* values in the table that have 'dr' in the second and third positions:

```
WHERE First_Name LIKE '_dr%'
```

Compound Expressions (AND, OR, and NOT)

SQL uses the AND, OR, and NOT operators to create compound expressions. In most cases, you should use parentheses to clarify the order of operations. The following expression matches rows in which the person was hired after 1/1/2010 and their salary is greater than $40,000.

```
WHERE (Hire_Date > '1/1/2010') AND (Salary > 40000)
```

The following expression matches rows in which the person was hired either before 2005 or after 2009:

```
WHERE (Hire_Date < '1/1/2005') OR (Hire_Date > '12/31/2009')
```

The following expression matches two types of employees: (1) employees hired after 1/1/2010 whose salaries are greater than $40,000; (2) part-time employees:

```
WHERE (Hire_Date > '1/1/2010') AND (Salary > 40000)
OR (Full_Time = 'False')
```

The following expression matches rows in which the hire date does not fall between 1/1/2005 and 12/31/2009:

```
WHERE (Hire_Date NOT BETWEEN '1/1/2005' AND '12/31/2009')
```

The following expression matches rows in which the last name does not begin with the letter A:

```
WHERE (Last_Name NOT LIKE 'A%')
```

Modifying the Query in a Data Source

To modify (edit) a query used by a data source, open its dataset schema file from the *Solution Explorer* window. Suppose an application contains a dataset named *SalesStaffDataSet*. Then the corresponding dataset schema file would be named *SalesStaffDataSet.xsd*. You can open a schema file in *Solution Explorer* by double-clicking its filename. An example is shown in Figure 10-48. The top line shows the database name. The next several lines list the columns in the dataset, identifying the ID column as the primary key. The *SalesStaffTableAdapter* appears next, followed by a list of its database queries. By default, there is one query named *Fill, GetData()* that fills the dataset when the form loads.

Figure 10-48 *SalesStaffDataSet,* in the *Dataset Designer* window

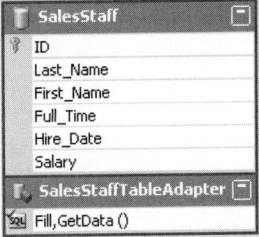

If you right-click the name *SalesStaffTableAdapter* and select *Configure* from the pop-up menu, you can modify the currently selected query using the *TableAdapter Configuration Wizard*, as shown in Figure 10-49. If the query text is simple enough, you can modify it directly in this window. If the query is more complicated, you may want to use the *Query Builder*, which can be launched by clicking the *Query Builder* button. An example is shown in Figure 10-50.

To close the *Query Builder*, click the *OK* button. Then click the *Finish* button to close the *TableAdapter Configuration Wizard*. Finally, you should save the dataset in the *DataSet Designer* window before closing it. Let's take a closer look at the *Query Builder* tool.

Query Builder

Query Builder is a tool provided by Visual Studio for creating and modifying SQL queries. It consists of four sections, called *panes*, as shown in Figure 10-50.

- The **diagram pane** displays all the tables used in the query, with a check mark next to each field that will be used in the dataset.

- The **grid pane** (also known as the **criteria pane**) displays the query in a spreadsheet-like format, which is particularly well suited to choosing a sort order and entering selection criteria.
- The **SQL pane** displays the actual SQL query that corresponds to the tables and fields selected in the diagram and grid panes. Advanced SQL users usually write queries directly into this pane.
- The **results pane** displays the data rows returned by executing the current SQL query. To fill the results pane, right-click in the *Query Builder* window and select *Run* from the *context* menu.

Figure 10-49 Using the *TableAdapter Configuration Wizard*

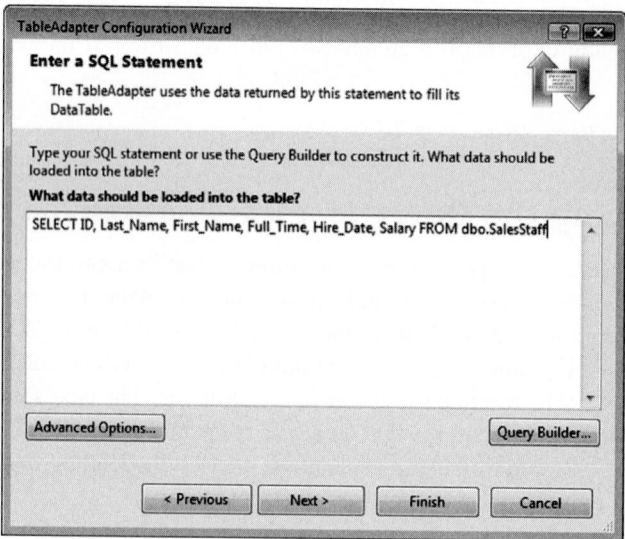

Figure 10-50 *Query Builder* window

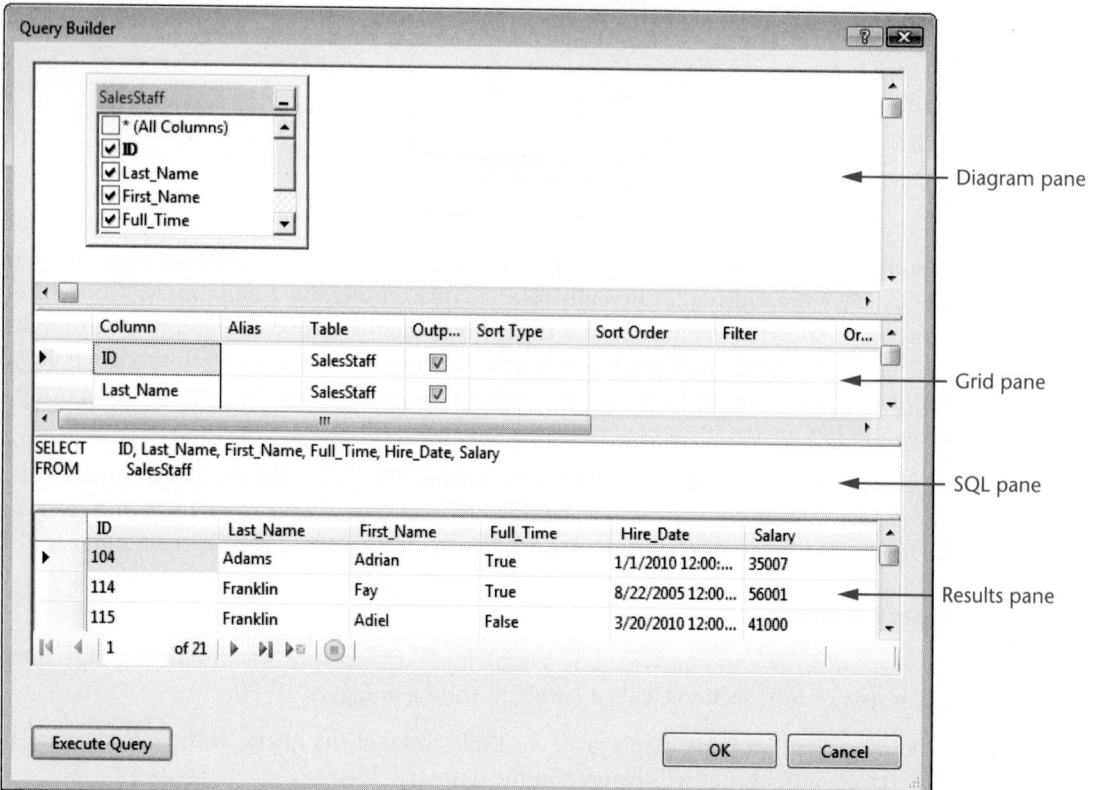

To remove and restore panes, do the following:

- To remove a pane, right-click it and select *Remove Pane* from the pop-up menu.
- To restore a pane that was removed, right-click in the window, select *Show Panes* from the pop-up menu, and select a pane from the list that appears.

To add a new table to the *Query Builder* window, right-click inside the diagram pane and select *Add Table* from the pop-up menu. To close *Query Builder*, click the *OK* button.

Adding a Query to a TableAdapter

If you want to filter (limit the display of) rows in a DataGridView control, the easiest way to do it is to add a new query to the TableAdapter attached to the grid. Suppose *Sales-StaffTableAdapter* is attached to a DataGridView displaying the *SalesStaff* table from the Company database. In the component tray at the bottom of the Form in the Design view, right-click the table adapter icon and select *Add Query* (shown in Figure 10-51). The *Search Criteria Builder* window appears, as shown in Figure 10-52. Let's modify the query so it looks as follows:

```
SELECT ID, Last_Name, First_Name, Full_Time, Hire_Date, Salary
FROM SalesStaff
WHERE Salary < 45000
```

Figure 10-53 shows what the window looks like after adding a WHERE clause to the SELECT statement. Notice that you can give a name to the query, which we called *Salary_query*. When you click the *OK* button, a ToolStrip control is added to the form, with a query button, as shown in Figure 10-54. When we run the program and click the *Salary_query* button on the tool strip, the results are as shown in Figure 10-55. Only rows with salaries less than $45,000 are displayed.

Figure 10-51 Adding a query to a TableAdapter

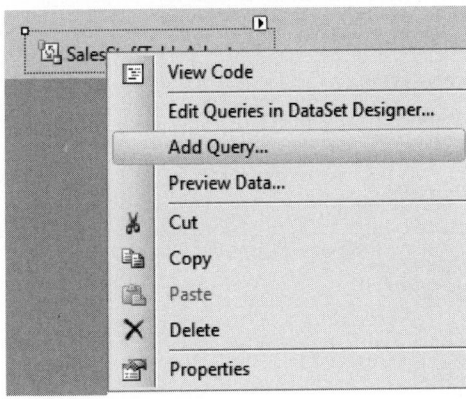

Figure 10-52 *Search Criteria Builder* window

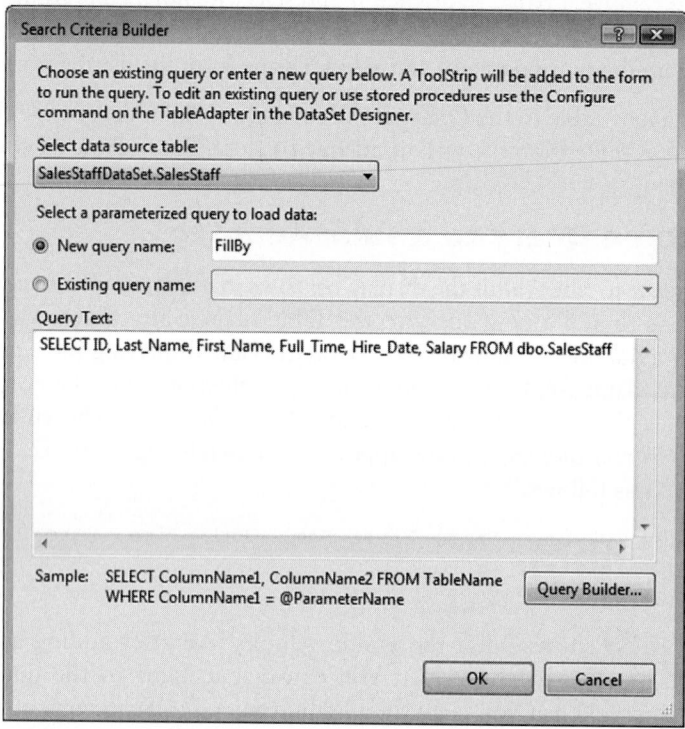

Figure 10-53 Entering a query in the *Search Criteria Builder*

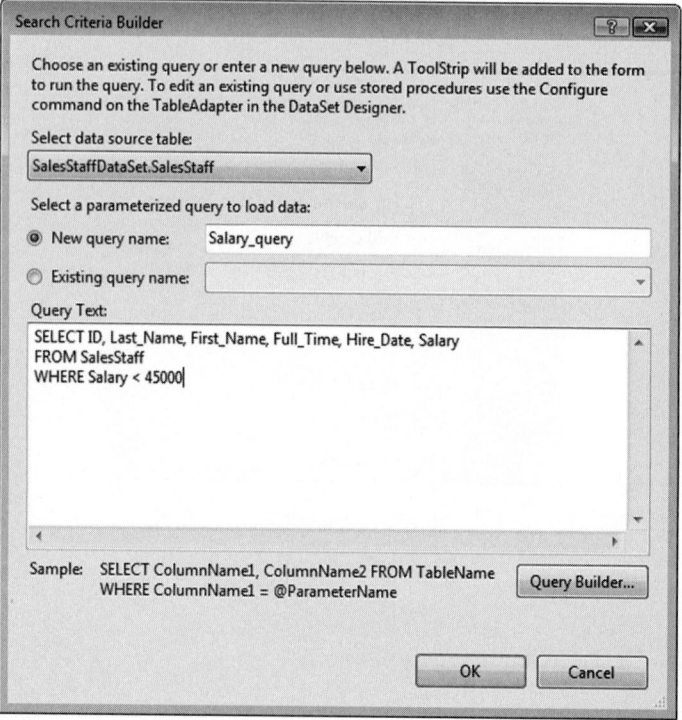

Figure 10-54 Tool strip added to the form, with a query button

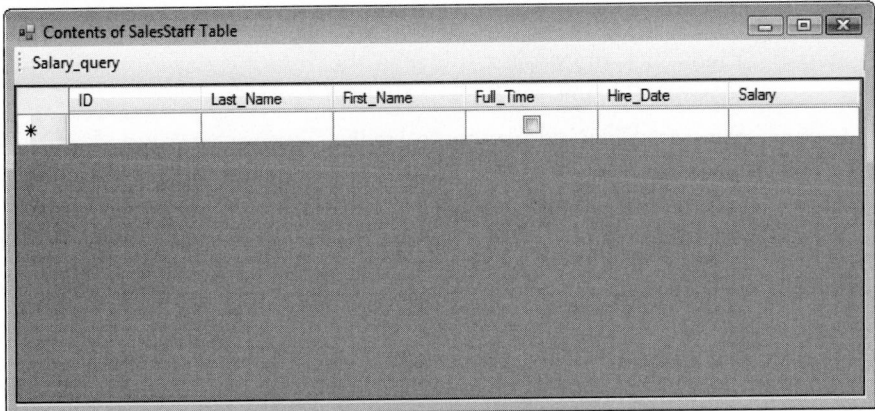

Figure 10-55 Rows filtered by a query named *Salary_query*

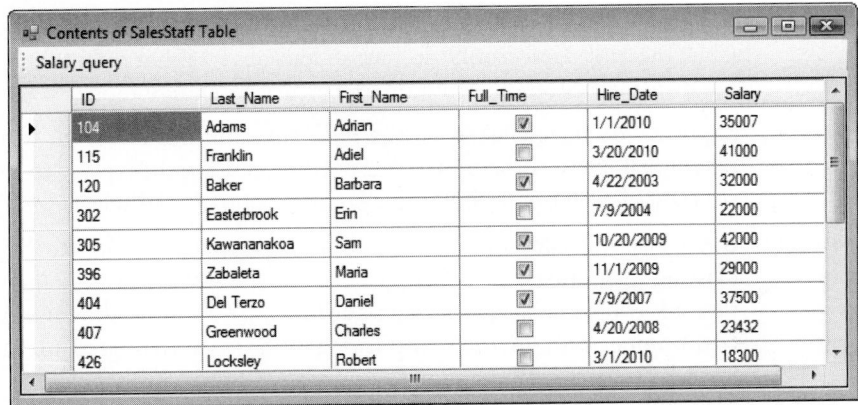

Tutorial 10-8 shows how to filter rows in the *SalesStaff* table.

Tutorial 10-8:
Filtering rows in the *SalesStaff* table

In this tutorial, you will create a query that changes the way *SalesStaff* rows display in a DataGridView control.

Step 1: Make sure Visual Studio is closed. Then, copy the *SalesStaff 1* project folder you created in Tutorial 10-1 to a new folder named *SalesStaff Queries*.

> **TIP:** To copy a folder in Windows Explorer, right-click its name with the mouse and select *Copy* from the pop-up menu; right-click again and select *Paste* from the pop-up menu. The new folder will be named *<name> - Copy*, where *<name>* is the original folder name. Right-click the copied folder and select *Rename* from the pop-up menu. Type the new folder name and press (Enter). (The same procedure works when copying files.)

Step 2: Open the project from the *SalesStaff Queries* folder (the solution file will still be named *SalesStaff 1.sln*).

Step 3: Right-click the project folder in the *Solution Explorer* window, and choose *Rename*. Rename the folder *SalesStaff Queries*.

Step 4: Select the DataGridView control in the *Designer* window and set its Dock property to None. Then, drag the top edge of the DataGridView control downward about three-quarters of an inch. This will leave room for two ToolStrip controls. Set the DataGridView control's Anchor property so that it anchors on all four sides.

Step 5: Right-click the SalesStaffTableAdapter control in the component tray, and select *Add Query* from the pop-up menu.

Step 6: In the *Search Criteria Builder* window, name the query *Full_Time*. Set its query text to the following:

```
SELECT ID, Last_Name, First_Name, Full_Time, Hire_Date, Salary
FROM dbo.SalesStaff
WHERE Full_Time = 'True'
```

Step 7: Click the *OK* button to save the query. Save the project and run the application. Click the *Full_Time* ToolStrip button and observe that only full time employees are displayed. Stop the program and return to *Design* mode.

Step 8: Suppose you have clicked on the *Full_Time* button, but want to return to displaying all rows in the table. You need to add another query to do that. To do so, right-click the SalesStaffTableAdapter control, and select *Add Query*.

Step 9: In the Search *Criteria Builder* window, name the query *All_Rows*, and keep the existing query text. Click *OK* to close the window and create the query. Notice that a second tool strip has been added to the form, as shown in Figure 10-56. If the upper part of the DataGridView has been covered up, adjust its top border position with the mouse.

Figure 10-56 *SalesStaff* table in a DataGridView, with two query buttons

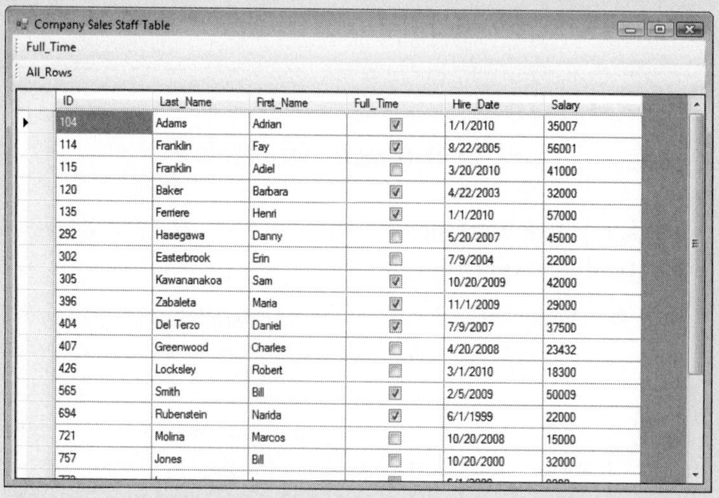

Step 10: Run the program and click both query buttons. The display should alternate between displaying all rows and only rows for full-time employees.

Step 11: End the program and close the project.

This tutorial has shown you an easy way to create queries that select rows from a database table. Ease of use, however, can mean a lack of flexibility. Eventually, it would be a good idea to let the user modify query values at run time. Later in this chapter we will show you how to use query parameters to pass different values to SQL queries.

Checkpoint

10.17 What does the acronym SQL represent, in relation to databases?

10.18 Why do SQL queries work with any database?

10.19 Write an SQL SELECT statement that retrieves the *First_Name* and *Last_Name* columns from a table named *Employees*.

10.20 How do you add a query to a TableAdapter in the component tray of a form?

10.21 Write a WHERE clause that limits the returned data to rows in which the field named Salary is less than or equal to $85,000.

10.22 Write a SELECT statement that retrieves the *pay_rate, employee_id*, and *hours_worked* columns from a table named *Payroll*, and sorts the rows in descending order by *hours_worked*.

10.23 Write a SELECT statement that creates an alias named *Rate_of_Pay* for the existing column named *pay_rate* in the *Payroll* table.

10.24 Write a SELECT statement for the *Payroll* table that creates a new output column named *gross_pay* by multiplying the *pay_rate* column by the *hours_worked* column.

10.25 Write a SELECT statement for the *Payroll* table that returns only rows in which the pay rate is greater than 20,000 and less than or equal to 55,000.

10.26 Write a SELECT statement for the *Payroll* table that returns only rows in which the *employee_id* column begins with the characters *FT*. The remaining characters in the *employee_id* are unimportant.

Focus on Problem Solving: *Karate School Management* Application

Suppose you are a member of the Kyoshi Karate School and Sensei (the teacher) has asked you to create a management application with the following capabilities:

1. Displays a list of all members, and lets the user sort on any column, edit individual rows, and delete rows.
2. Adds new people to the *Members* table.
3. Displays members having similar last names.
4. Displays payments by all members, permitting the user to sort on any column.

Techniques for completing most of the tasks have already been demonstrated earlier in this chapter. Other tasks will require some new skills, which we will explain along the way. Before beginning to code an application, you would normally consult with the customer to clarify some user interface details. Your next step is to determine which types of controls would provide the most effective user interface. To illustrate, we will do that for the current application:

- For Requirement 1, we will use a DataGridView control. We will set options that permit modifying and removing rows. The user will be able to sort by clicking on column headings.
- For Requirement 2, we will create a data input form with TextBox controls and a DateTimePicker control.
- For Requirement 3, the user will type a partial last name into a text box. The application will display a grid containing all members whose last names begin with the name entered by the user.
- For Requirement 4, we will create an SQL query that combines the *Members* and *Payments* tables and displays the results in a DataGridView control.

When possible, we will avoid duplication of effort by using existing datasets and Data-GridView controls.

General Design Guidelines

Each form will have a *File* menu with a *Close window* option. A startup form will display a menu and a program logo. Each major requirement will be carried out on a separate form to allow for future expansion. When the Karate teacher sees how easy the program is to use, he will surely want to add more capabilities.

Before we start to create the application, let's look at the finished version. Doing so will give you a better idea of how the detailed steps fit into the overall picture. In real life, programmers usually create a **prototype** or demonstration copy of their program. The prototype lets you try out different versions of the user interface, requiring some reworking, problem-solving, and discussions with the customer. To save time, we will skip the prototyping stage and move directly to the program implementation.

The startup form, called MainForm, displays a program logo and a menu with three major choices, as shown in Figure 10-57.

Figure 10-57 *Karate School Manager* startup form

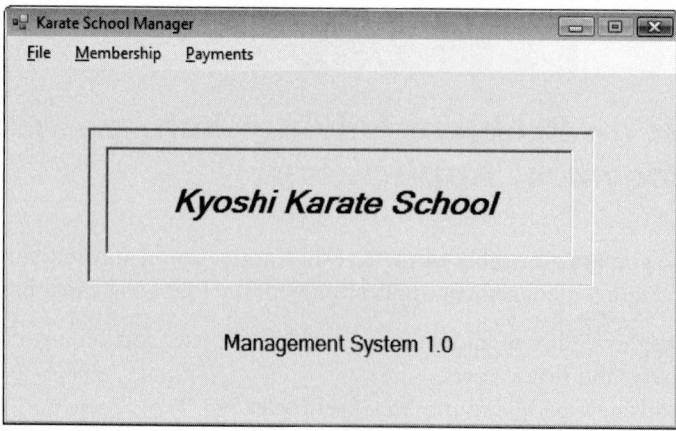

The startup form should be simple, to avoid overwhelming the user with details. The menu makes it clear that our system handles two major types of functions: membership and payments. The menu selections are as follows:

```
File
   Exit
Membership
   List all
   Find member
   Add new member
Payments
   All members
```

Membership Forms

The Karate teacher wants to view a list of all members, so we have provided the *All Members* form, as shown in Figure 10-58. The grid allows users to sort on any column, select and delete rows, and modify individual cells within each row. If the user wants to save changes they've made back into the database, they select *Save changes* from the *File* menu.

The *Find Member by Last Name* form, shown in Figure 10-59, lets the user enter all or part of a member's last name. When the user clicks the *Go* button or presses Enter, a list of matching member rows displays in the grid. The Karate teacher has asked that name searches be case insensitive.

Figure 10-58 *All Members* form

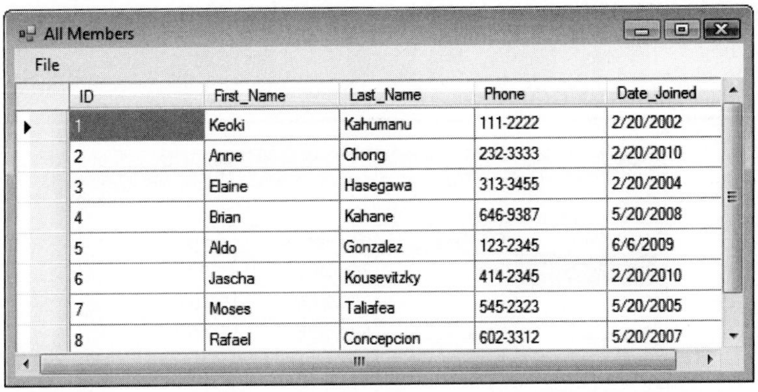

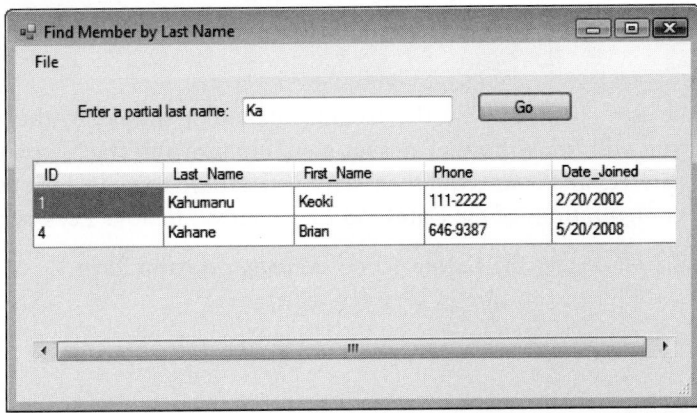

Figure 10-59 *Find Member by Last Name* form

The *Add New Member* form, as shown in Figure 10-60, lets the user add a new person to the *Members* table. After entering the fields and choosing a data from the DateTimePicker control, the user selects *Save and close* from the *File* menu. Or, if the user wants to close the form without saving the data, he or she selects *Close without saving* from the *File* menu.

Figure 10-60 *Add New Member* form

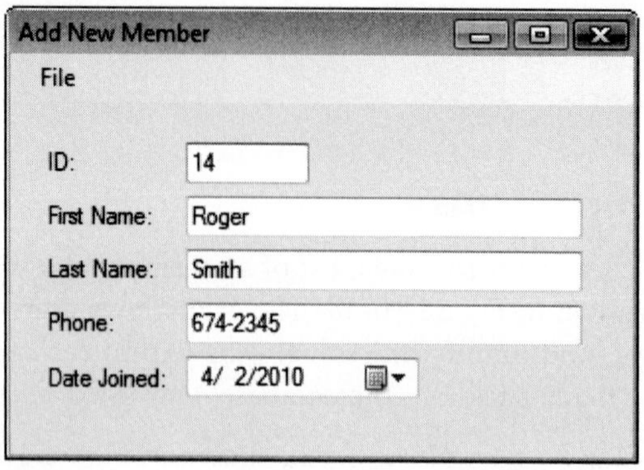

Payment Form

We now turn our attention to the *Payments* subsystem of our application. When the user selects *All members* from the *Payments* menu on the startup form, the *Payments by All Members* form appears, as shown in Figure 10-61. The rows are initially ordered by last name, but the user can sort on any column by clicking on the column header (once for an ascending sort, and a second time for a descending sort).

Figure 10-61 *Payments by All Members* form

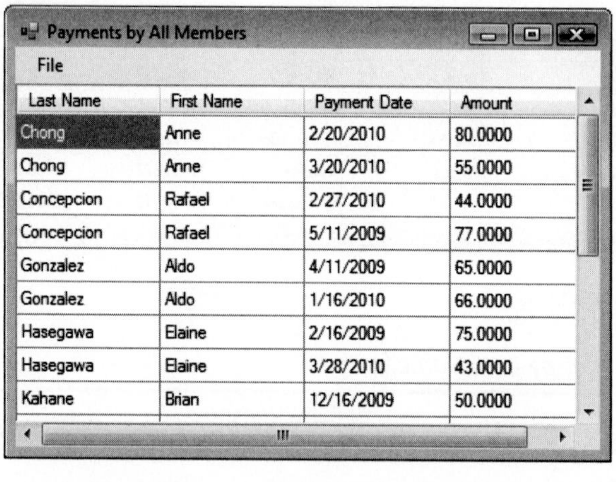

From the user's point of view, the program should be simple. By the time you finish creating it, you will know how to design a simple user interface, open multiple windows, create datasets and connections, search for database rows in various ways, and perform simple configurations of the DataGridView control. Ready? Let's begin.

Tutorial 10-9 creates the *Karate School Manager* startup form.

Tutorial 10-9:
Creating the *Karate School Manager* startup form

In this tutorial, you will create the startup form that first displays when the *Karate School Manager* runs.

Step 1: Create a new Windows Forms application named *Karate School Manager*.

Step 2: Change the name of *Form1.vb* to *MainForm.vb* in the *Solution Explorer* window.

Step 3: Open the form and set its Size.Width property to *530*, and its Size.Height property to *320*. Change its Text property to *Karate School Manager*. Change its StartPosition property to *CenterScreen*. Set its MaximizeBox property to *False*. Set the FormBorderStyle to *FixedSingle*.

Step 4: Insert a Panel control on the form and set its Size.Width and Size.Height properties to *390* and *115*, respectively. Insert another Panel control inside the first one, and set its Size property to *360, 80*. Set the BorderStyle property of both panels to *Fixed3D*. Use Figure 10-57 as a guide to the placement of the panels.

Step 5: Insert a Label control inside the smaller panel and set its Text property to *Kyoshi Karate School*. Set the font to Bold Italic 18 points, so it looks like the text shown in Figure 10-57.

Step 6: Add another Label control near the bottom of the form and set its Text property to *Management System 1.0*. Center the text, and use an 12-point font.

Step 7: Add a MenuStrip control to the form containing the top-level menu names *File*, *Membership*, and *Payments*. In the *File* submenu, insert *Exit*. In the *Membership* submenu, insert three items: *List all*, *Find member*, and *Add new member*. In the *Payments* menu, insert one item: *All members*. Insert the & character in each menu item according to your preference.

Step 8: Rename the *File/Exit* menu item to `mnuFileExit`. Double-click the item and insert the following statement in its event handler:

```
Me.Close()
```

Step 9: Save the project. When you run the application, verify that the form closes when you click the *File/Exit* menu item.

Tutorial 10-10 focuses on adding the Membership subsystem to the application.

Tutorial 10-10:
Adding the *Membership / List all* function to the *Karate School Manager*

In this tutorial, you will enable the part of the *Karate School Manager* application that lists all members.

Step 1: Open the *Karate School Manager* project, if it is not already open. Open the MainForm form in the *Designer* window.

Step 2:   Add a new form to the project named *AllMembersForm.vb*. Resize the form so it looks similar to the one shown in Figure 10-59. Set its Text property to *All Members*.

Step 3:   Open the MainForm form in the *Designer* window. Double-click the *Membership / List all* menu item and insert the following code in its event handler:

```
' Create an instance of AllMembersForm
Dim frmAllMembers As New AllMembersForm

' Display the form.
frmAllMembers.ShowDialog()
```

Step 4:   In the *Data Sources* window, add a new data source that connects to the Members table in the Karate database. As shown in Figure 10-62, name the dataset *AllMembersDataSet*. Respond with *Yes* when asked to copy the database file into the project.

Figure 10-62 Creating the `AllMembersDataSet` dataset in the *Data Source Configuration Wizard*

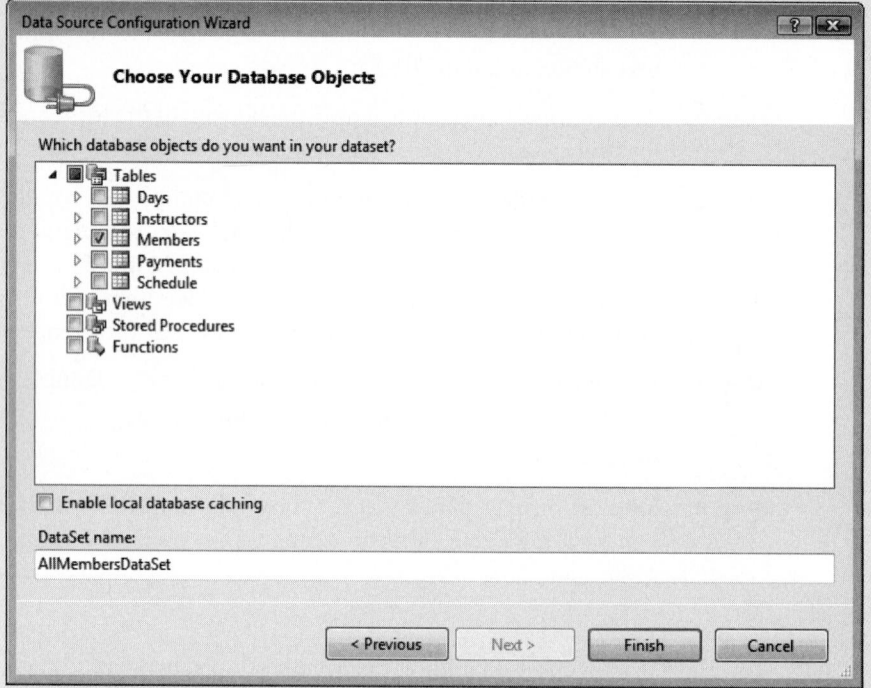

Step 5:   In the AllMembersForm form, place a DataGridView control on the form and name it *dgvMembers*. Set its Dock property to *Fill*. Set its BackgroundColor property to *Control*. Set its BorderStyle property to *None*.

Step 6:   Click the smart tag arrow icon in the upper right corner of *dgvMembers*, showing the *DataGridView Tasks* window, as shown in Figure 10-63. In the *Choose Data Source* drop-down list, select the *Members* table from the `AllMembersDataSet` dataset. Adjust the check boxes in the *Tasks* window so that only *Enable Editing* is checked.

Step 7:   If the grid's columns do not appear as shown earlier in Figure 10-58, click the grid's Columns property. Use the arrows next to the column names list to adjust the column order, as shown in Figure 10-64.

Figure 10-63 Tasks for the *dgrMembers* DataGridView control

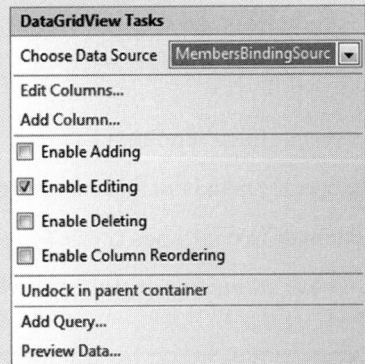

Figure 10-64 Adjusting the column order in the DataGridView control

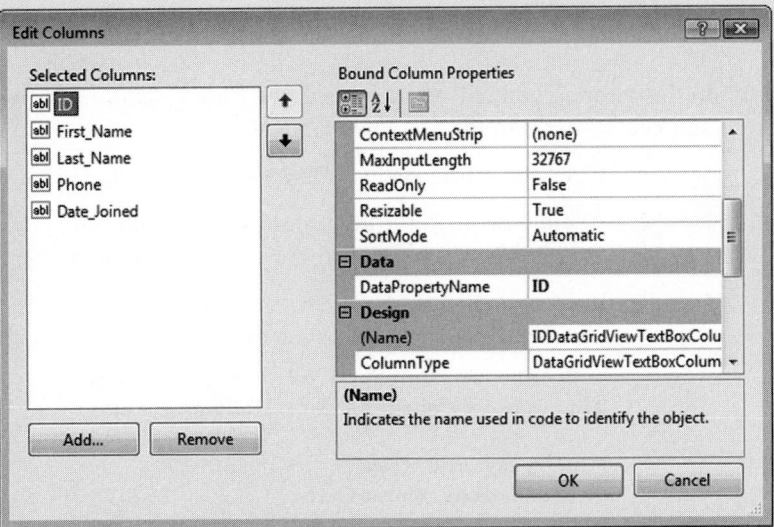

Step 8: Add a *File* menu to the AllMembersForm form, with two submenu items: *Save* and *Close*. In the *Close* menu item's Click handler, insert the `Me.Close()` statement. Insert the following statement in the Click handler for the *Save* menu item:

```
Me.MembersTableAdapter.Update(Me.AllMembersDataSet.Members)
```

Step 9: Save the project and run the application. From the MainForm menu, select *Membership / List all*. You should see a list of members similar to that shown earlier in Figure 10-58. Experiment by modifying one of the grid rows, and selecting *Save* from the *File* menu. Then, close the *All Members* form and reopen it to verify that your changes were saved.

Step 10: End the program and return to *Design* mode.

In Tutorial 10-11, you will add the *Membership / Add new member* function to the *Karate School Manager* application.

Using a Binding Source to Add Table Rows

When you bind a data source to controls on a form, Visual Studio automatically adds a BindingSource component to the form. The name of the binding source is derived from the dataset name. If a dataset is named `MembersDataSet`, for instance, its binding source will be named `MembersBindingSource`.

A binding source's `AddNew` method adds a blank new row to a dataset. For example:

```
MembersBindingSource.AddNew()
```

The `AddNew` method clears the controls on the form that are bound to the dataset so the user can begin to enter data. The addition does not become permanent until the `EndEdit` method is called as follows:

```
MembersBindingSource.EndEdit()
```

Or, to cancel the operation and not add the new row, call the `CancelEdit` method as follows:

```
MembersBindingSource.CancelEdit()
```

In any case, you have complete control over whether the row is added to the dataset.

Tutorial 10-11:
Adding the *Membership / Add new member* function to the *Karate School Manager*

In this tutorial, you will add a form to the *Karate School Manager* program that lets users add new students to the *Members* table.

Step 1: Open the *Karate School Manager* program if it is not already open.

Step 2: Add a new form to the project named AddMemberForm. Set its Text property to *Add New Member*. Set its FormBorderStyle property to *FixedDialog*.

Step 3: In the MainForm form's Design view, double-click the *Membership / Add new member* menu item and insert the following code in its Click event handler:

```
' Create an instance of AddMemberForm
Dim frmAddMember As New AddMemberForm

' Display the form.
frmAddMember.ShowDialog()
```

Step 4: Open the AddMemberForm form in Design view. Then, in the *Data Sources* window, locate the *Members* table under the `AllMembersDataSet` entry. Click next to the *Members* table in the *Data Sources* window and select *Details*. Then drag the table onto the form. This will create a set of data-bound controls. Align the controls as necessary, and move the *First_Name* field above the *Last_Name* field. Use Figure 10-65 as a guide. Set the Format property of the Date-TimePicker control to *Short*. Adjust the form's tab stops as necessary.

Figure 10-65 Adding a new member to the *Members* table

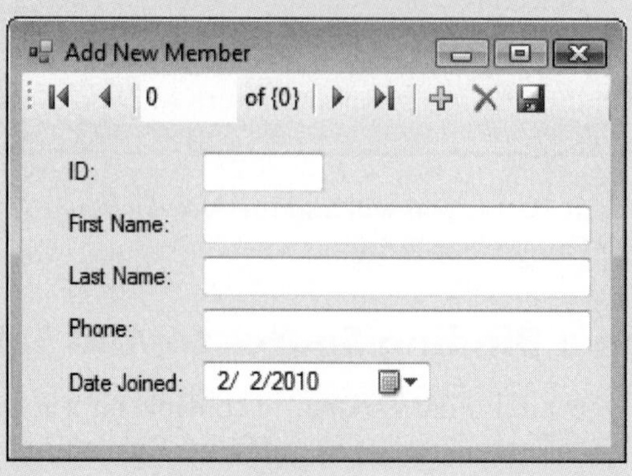

Step 5: Delete the `MembersBindingNavigator` component from the form's component tray. This will cause the ToolStrip (just under the menu) to disappear. You will not need it. Add a MenuStrip control to the form.

Step 6: Add a *File* menu to the MenuStrip control and insert two submenu items: *Save and close*, and *Close without saving*. Double-click the *Save and close* item and insert the following statements in its event handler:

```
Try
   Me.MembersBindingSource.EndEdit()
   Me.MembersTableAdapter.Update(AllMembersDataSet.Members)
   Me.Close()
Catch ex As Exception
   MessageBox.Show(Me, "Error: " & ex.Message, "Save",
      MessageBoxButtons.OK, MessageBoxIcon.Warning)
End Try
```

These statements call `EndEdit`, which saves the new row in the dataset. Then the `Update` method call writes the dataset's modifications back to the database.

Step 7: Replace the current contents of the `AddMemberForm_Load` event handler with the following code:

```
Me.MembersBindingSource.AddNew()
Date_JoinedDateTimePicker.Value = Today()
```

The first line puts the dataset into *add new row* mode. The second line initializes the DateTimePicker control to today's date.

Step 8: Double-click the *Close without saving* menu item and insert the following statements in its handler:

```
Me.MembersBindingSource.CancelEdit()
Me.Close()
```

Step 9: Save the project and run the application. Click the *Membership / Add new member* menu selection, and add a new member. Choose a member ID that did not appear when you listed all members in Tutorial 10-10. Or, if you're not sure, display a list of all members first. After you have added the new member, close the dialog (Save and close). Then select *List all* from the *Membership* menu and look for the member you added. Next, try adding a new member who has the same ID number as an existing member. You should see an error message dialog containing *Error: Violation of PRIMARY KEY contstraint. . .* etc.

Step 10: End the program.

Using Query Parameters

When you write SQL queries that search for selected records in database tables, you usually don't know ahead of time what values the user might want to find. While it is possible to modify an SQL query using program code at runtime, it's not easy because program variables must be concatenated with SQL statements. Instead, the designers of SQL included the ability to pass values to queries at runtime, using what are known as query parameters. A **query parameter** is a special variable (preceded by the @ symbol) that is embedded within an SQL query.

We can show why query parameters are useful. Suppose the user had entered a name in the `txtLastName` control, and you wanted to write a query that would locate all rows in the *Members* table having the same last name. You could write the following statements, but the resulting code is both messy and prone to typing errors:

```
Dim query As String
query = "SELECT ID, Last_Name, First_Name, Phone, Date_Joined "
    & "FROM Members WHERE Last_Name = '" & txtLastName.Text & "'"
```

Instead, we will insert a query parameter named @Last_Name directly into the SELECT statement:

```
SELECT ID, Last_Name, First_Name, Phone, Date_Joined
FROM Members
WHERE Last_Name = @Last_Name
```

When you call the TableAdapter's Fill method, the second argument is assigned to the query's @Last_Name parameter as follows:

```
Me.MembersTableAdapter.Fill(Me.FindMemberDataSet.Members,
                            txtLastName.Text)
```

If a query contains more than one parameter, the additional required query parameter values are passed as arguments when calling the Fill method. We will use a parameterized query (a query containing a parameter) in Tutorial 10-12.

Tutorial 10-12:

Adding the *Membership / Find member* function to the *Karate School Manager*

In this tutorial, you will add a form that lets users search for members by last name. You will use a partial string match, so if the user does not know the exact spelling of the member name, they can view a list of similar names.

Step 1: Open the *Karate School Manager* project.

Step 2: Add a new form to the project named FindMemberForm. Set its Text property to *Find Member by Last Name*. Set the form's size to 470 by 300.

Step 3: In the MainForm form, double-click the *Membership / Find member* menu item and insert the following code in its event handler:

```
' Create an instance of FindMemberForm
Dim frmFindMember As New FindMemberForm

' Display the form.
frmFindMember.ShowDialog()
```

Step 4: Add a MenuStrip control to the FindMemberForm form and create a *File* menu with one selection: *Close*. In this menu item's Click handler, insert the Me.Close() statement.

Step 5: Add a label, a text box named txtLastName, and a button named btnGo to the form. Use Figure 10-59, shown earlier, as a guide.

Step 6: From the *Data* menu, select *Add New Data Source*. When you get to the *Choose Your Data Connection* step in the *Data Source Configuration* wizard, you can use the existing connection string and just click the *Next* button to go to the next step. Create a dataset named FindMemberDataSet, which uses the *Members* table. Figure 10-66 shows the *Data Source Configuration Wizard* window, in which you name the dataset and select the *Members* table.

Figure 10-66 Adding the `FindMemberDataSet` dataset to the application

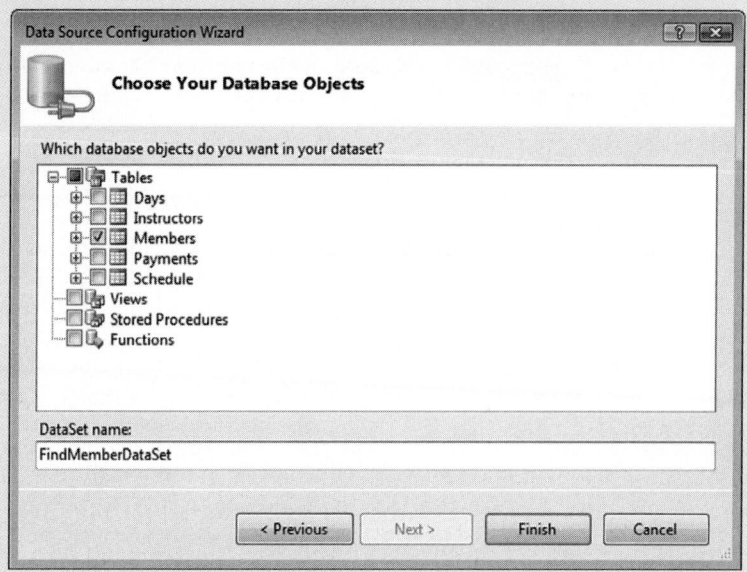

Step 7: Next, you will modify `FindMemberDataSet` by adding a query parameter that lets the program find members by their last names. In the *Solution Explorer* window, double-click to open the *Design* window for *FindMemberDataSet.xsd*. Right-click the entry labeled *Fill, GetData()*, and select *Configure* from the pop-up menu. Change the query text to the following, and click the *Finish* button:

```
SELECT ID, Last_Name, First_Name, Phone, Date_Joined
FROM dbo.Members
WHERE (Last_Name LIKE @Last_Name + '%')
```

Step 8: Back in the FindMemberForm form, place a DataGridView control on the form and name it *dgvMembers*. Set its properties as follows: BackgroundColor = *Control*; BorderStyle = *None*; Anchor = *Top, Bottom, Left, Right*; RowHeadersVisible = *False*. Use Figure 10-59, shown earlier, as a guide.

Step 9: Click the smart tag in the grid's upper right corner, displaying the *DataGridView Tasks* window, as shown in Figure 10-67. Bind the grid to the *Members* table belonging to the `FindMemberDataSet` dataset. Disable adding, editing, and deleting of rows by removing the appropriate check marks.

Figure 10-67 Selecting DataGridView *databinding* options

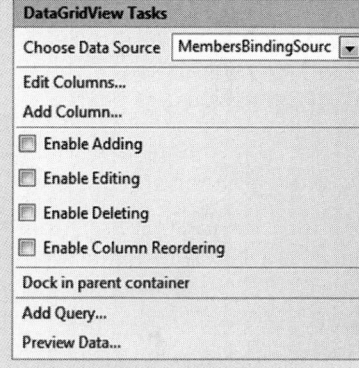

Step 10: Next, you will add a call to the `Fill` method in the event handler for the button that activates the search. Double-click the *Go* button and insert the following code in its event handler:

```
' Perform a wildcard search for last name.
Me.MembersTableAdapter.Fill(Me.FindMemberDataSet.Members,
                            txtLastName.Text)
```

Normally, the `Fill` method has only one parameter, the dataset. But here you pass a second parameter, which is the value to be assigned to the query parameter.

Step 11: In Design view for the FindMemberForm form, select the form with the mouse and set the Form's AcceptButton property to `btnGo`. This will allow the user to press Enter when activating the search.

Step 12: Remove any statements that might be inside the form's Load event handler. (You don't want the grid to fill with data until a member's name has been entered.)

Step 13: Save the project and run the application. From the startup form, click *Membership/Find member* from the menu. When the *Find Member* form appears, enter a partial last name, such as *Ka* and click the *Go* button or press the Enter key. Your output should be similar to that shown in Figure 10-59.

Step 14: Experiment with other partial last names, checking your results against the grid that displays all members.

In Tutorial 10-13, you will add the *Payments / All members* function to the *Karate School Manager*.

Tutorial 10-13:
Adding the *Payments / All members* function to the *Karate School Manager*

In this tutorial, you will create a dataset by joining two tables: *Members* and *Payments*. The dataset will be displayed in a grid.

Step 1: Open the *Karate School Manager* project if it is not already open.

Step 2: Add a new form named AllPaymentsForm to the project. Set its Text property to *Payments by All Members*.

Step 3: In the MainForm form, double-click the *Payments / All members* menu item and insert the following code in its event handler:

```
' Create an instance of AllPaymentsForm
Dim frmPaymentsAll As New AllPaymentsForm

' Display the form.
frmPaymentsAll.ShowDialog()
```

Step 4: Back in the AllPaymentsForm form, add a MenuStrip control and create a *File* menu with one submenu item: *Close*. In its Click event handler, insert the `Me.Close()` statement.

Step 5: Select *Add New Data Source* from the *Data* menu. Add a new data source that uses the existing Karate database connection. Select the Payments table, and name the dataset *AllPaymentsDataSet*. After the data source has been created, double-click the *AllPaymentsDataSet.xsd* file in the *Solution Explorer* window. Now, in the DataSet designer window, right-click the *Fill, GetData()* entry, and choose *Configure* from the pop-up menu.

Step 6: In the *TableAdapter Configuration Wizard* window that says *Enter a SQL Statement*, click the *Query Builder* button.

Step 7: Add the *Members* table to the upper pane of the *Query Builder* by right-clicking inside the upper pane, and selecting *Add Table*. The *Add Table* window will appear. Select the *Members* table and then click *Add*. Click *Close* to close the *Add Table* window. After adding the *Members* table, a line should appear between the two tables, as shown in Figure 10-68. This line, with a diamond in the middle, indicates that the Member_Id column in the Payments table is related to the ID column in the Members table.

Figure 10-68 *Query Builder* window, after adding the *Members* table

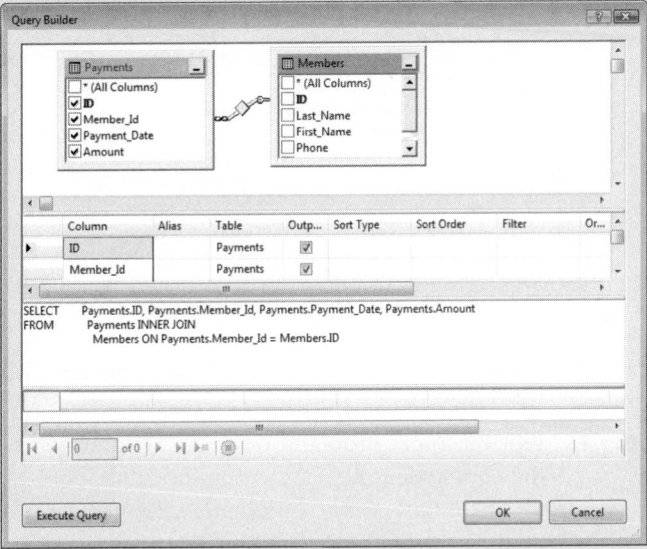

Step 8: Remove all checks from the boxes next to the column names in the upper pane. Then re-check the following fields, in order: *Last_Name*, *First_Name*, *Payment_Date*, and *Amount*.

Step 9: In the *Sort Type* column in the grid pane, select *Ascending* in the *Last_Name* row.

Step 10: Click the *Execute Query* button; a list of names and payments should appear in the bottom pane, as shown in Figure 10-69.

Step 11: Click the *OK* button to close *Query Builder*, and click the *Finish* button to save changes to the dataset. Save your project and close the *Design* window for *AllPaymentsDataSet*.

Step 12: Place a DataGridView control on the AllPaymentsForm form and name it *dgvPayments*. Set its properties as follows: BackgroundColor = *Control*; BorderStyle = *None*; Dock = Fill; RowHeadersVisible = *False*.

Step 13: Open the *DataGridView tasks* window. For the Data Source, choose the *Payments* table of `AllPaymentsDataSet`. Unselect the *Enable Adding*, *Enable Editing*, and *Enable Deleting* check boxes.

Step 14: Save the project and run the application. Display the *Payments by All members* window. Although the payment information appears, the columns are not in the order we would like. Fortunately, it's easy to modify the column ordering in the DataGridView control.

Figure 10-69 Executing a query containing *Payments* and *Members* tables

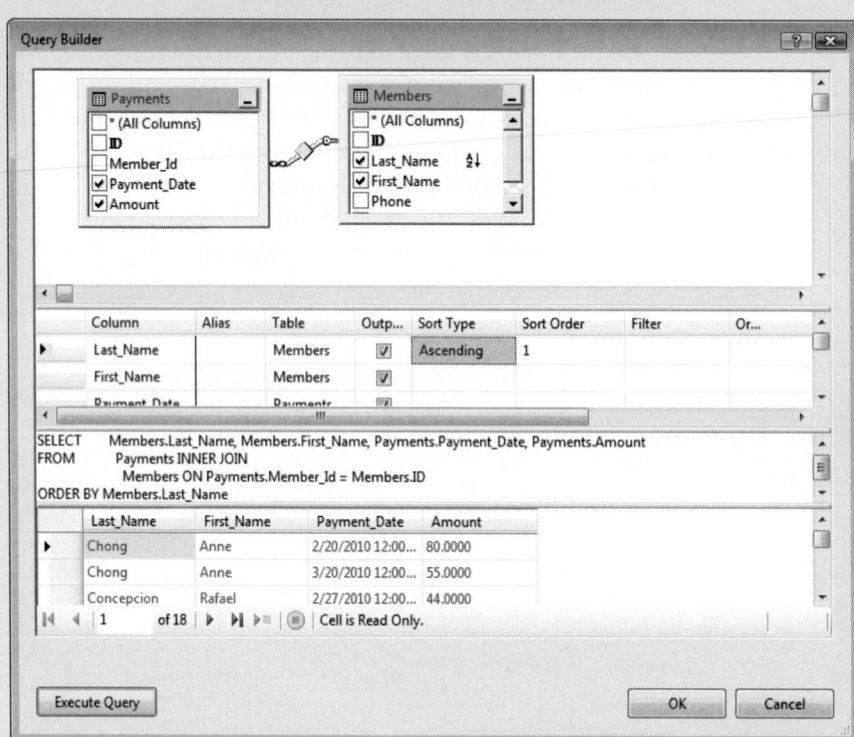

Step 15: Exit the application and return to Design mode. Click the Columns property of the `dgvPayments` grid, causing the Edit Columns dialog to open. Set the column order to: *Last Name*, *First Name*, *Payment Date*, and *Amount*. Use the arrows next to the Selected Columns list to change the column order. Optionally, you can use the HeaderText property of each column to modify its displayed column heading. A sample of the form at runtime is shown in Figure 10-70.

Figure 10-70 *Payments by All Members* form

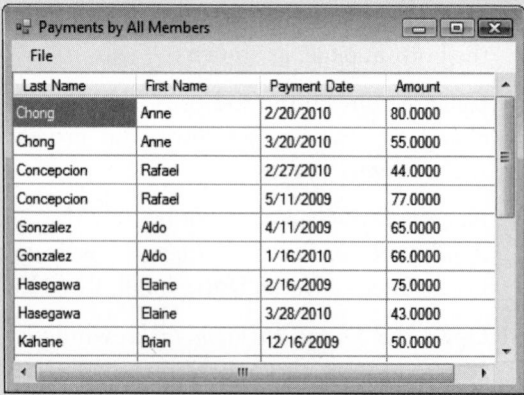

Step 16: Save the project and rerun it.

You've completed this tutorial. You have successfully joined two database tables, using a relation based on the Member_Id table column. You have seen how a dataset can easily join two database tables.

Complete Source Code

Following is a listing of all the source code in the *Karate School Manager* application. Option Strict has been set *On*. Some extraneous comment lines and portions of some procedure headers have been removed.

MainForm.vb:

```
Public Class MainForm
    Private Sub mnuFileExit_Click(...) Handles mnuFileExit.Click
        Me.Close()
    End Sub

    Private Sub ListAllToolStripMenuItem_Click(...) Handles ...
        ' Create an instance of AllMembersForm
        Dim frmAllMembers As New AllMembersForm

        ' Display the form.
        frmAllMembers.ShowDialog()
    End Sub

    Private Sub AddNewMemberToolStripMenuItem_Click(...) Handles ...
        ' Create an instance of AddMemberForm
        Dim frmAddMember As New AddMemberForm

        ' Display the form.
        frmAddMember.ShowDialog()
    End Sub

    Private Sub FindMemberToolStripMenuItem_Click(...) Handles ...
        ' Create an instance of FindMemberForm
        Dim frmFindMember As New FindMemberForm

        ' Display the form.
        frmFindMember.ShowDialog()
    End Sub

    Private Sub AllMembersToolStripMenuItem_Click(...) Handles ...
        ' Create an instance of AllPaymentsForm
        Dim frmPaymentsAll As New AllPaymentsForm

        ' Display the form.
        frmPaymentsAll.ShowDialog()
    End Sub
End Class
```

AllMembersForm.vb:

```
Public Class AllMembersForm

    Private Sub AllMembersForm_Load(...) Handles MyBase.Load
        'TODO: This line of code loads data into the
        'AllMembersDataSet.Members' table. You can move, or remove it,
        'as needed.
        Me.MembersTableAdapter.Fill(Me.AllMembersDataSet.Members)

    End Sub

    Private Sub SaveToolStripMenuItem_Click(...) Handles ...
        Me.MembersTableAdapter.Update(Me.AllMembersDataSet.Members)
    End Sub

    Private Sub CloseToolStripMenuItem_Click(...) Handles ...
        Me.Close()
    End Sub
End Class
```

FindMemberForm.vb:

```vb
Public Class FindMemberForm

    Private Sub CloseToolStripMenuItem_Click(...) Handles ...
        Me.Close()
    End Sub

    Private Sub btnGo_Click(...) Handles btnGo.Click
        ' Perform a wildcard search for last name.
        Me.MembersTableAdapter.Fill(Me.FindMemberDataSet.Members,
                                    txtLastName.Text)
    End Sub
End Class
```

AddMemberForm.vb:

```vb
Public Class AddMemberForm

    Private Sub MembersBindingNavigatorSaveItem_Click(...)
        Me.Validate()
        Me.MembersBindingSource.EndEdit()
        Me.TableAdapterManager.UpdateAll(Me.AllMembersDataSet)
    End Sub

    Private Sub AddMemberForm_Load(...) Handles MyBase.Load
        Me.MembersBindingSource.AddNew()
        Date_JoinedDateTimePicker.Value = Today()
    End Sub

    Private Sub SaveAndCloseToolStripMenuItem_Click(...) Handles ...
        Try
            Me.MembersBindingSource.EndEdit()
            Me.MembersTableAdapter.Update(AllMembersDataSet.Members)
            Me.Close()
        Catch ex As Exception
            MessageBox.Show(Me, "Error: " & ex.Message, "Save",
                            MessageBoxButtons.OK, MessageBoxIcon.Warning)
        End Try
    End Sub

    Private Sub CloseWithoutSavingToolStripMenuItem_Click(...) Handles ...
        Me.MembersBindingSource.CancelEdit()
        Me.Close()
    End Sub
End Class
```

AllPaymentsForm.vb:

```vb
Public Class AllPaymentsForm

    Private Sub CloseToolStripMenuItem_Click(...) Handles ...
        Me.Close()
    End Sub

    Private Sub AllPaymentsForm_Load(...) Handles MyBase.Load
        'TODO: This line of code loads data into the
        'AllPaymentsDataSet.Payments' table. You can move,
        'or remove it, as needed.
        Me.PaymentsTableAdapter.Fill(Me.AllPaymentsDataSet.Payments)
    End Sub
End Class
```

Using the ListBox's ValueMember Property

One of the most useful features of a data-bound ListBox control is its ValueMember property. This property identifies a column from the DataTable that is bound to the control. For example, using the Karate database, we could select member names from a ListBox and then use the ValueMember property to tell the ListBox to return the member's ID number. Let's see how this is done.

First, we create a data source that links to the Members table of the Karate database. We name this dataset *MembersDataSet*, shown in Figure 10-71.

Figure 10-71 MembersDataSet added to the DataSources window

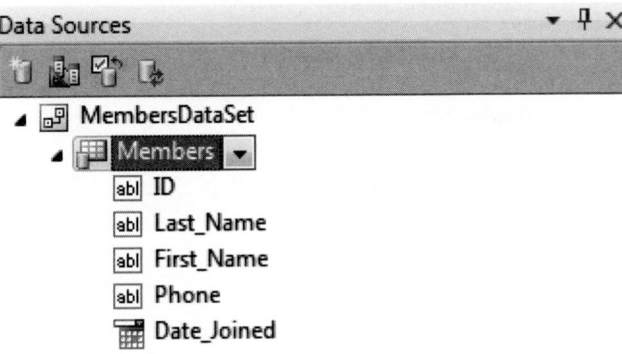

Next, we open the dataset in the *DataSet Designer* window, right-click *MembersTableAdapter*, and select *Configure*, as shown in Figure 10-72.

Figure 10-72 Configuring the query in the MembersTableAdapter

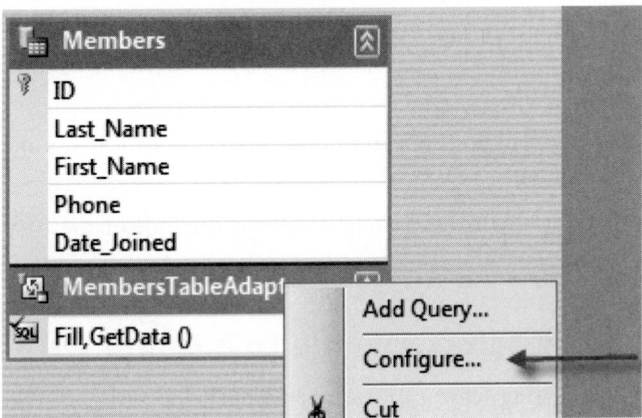

In the *TableAdapter Configuration Wizard*, we change the query by combining the Last_Name and First_Name columns into a single column named Full_Name. The only other column we need is ID:

```
SELECT ID, Last_Name + ', ' + First_Name AS Full_Name
FROM dbo.Members
ORDER BY Last_Name
```

 TIP: The + operator in a SQL query lets you combine the values of two or more columns. When combining columns, you can insert other characters such as commas and spaces.

Next, we add a ListBox to the startup form and bind it to the data source, as shown in Figure 10-73. We set the DataSource property to the Members table of our new dataset. The DisplayMember property is set to Full_Name, so we can see both the first and last names of each person. We also set the ValueMember property to ID, so when the user selects a member name at runtime, we can get the selected member's ID number.

Figure 10-73 Binding the ListBox to the Members table

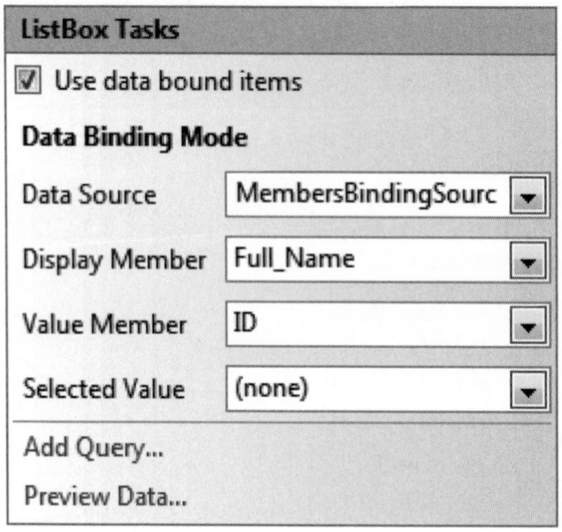

Next, a message box inside the ListBox's SelectedIndexChanged event handler displays the ID of the member selected by the user. The ID is obtained from the SelectedValue property of the ListBox, which is named `lstMembers`:

```
Private Sub lstMembers_SelectedIndexChanged(...) Handles...

    MessageBox.Show("The member's ID is " &
                    lstMembers.SelectedValue.ToString())
End Sub
```

So now when we run and program and select any member, a message box appears, displaying the member's ID.

A project named *ListBox SelectedValue* that does all of these tasks can be found in the student sample programs folder for this chapter.

Passing the SelectedValue to a Query with Parameters

There are interesting ways to use the SelectedValue property of a ListBox. For example, when a member is selected from a ListBox and we know its ID number, we could pass the ID to the input of a parameterized query. Suppose, for example, that we want to create a query that returns payments by a certain member of the Payments table in the Karate database. A SQL query to do this is:

```
SELECT Payment_Date, Amount
FROM Payments
WHERE Member_Id 5 @Member_Id
```

If this query were added to a TableAdapter connected to the Payments table, the TableAdapter's Fill method would have two parameters: the DataTable to be filled, and the `Member_Id` parameter that would be passed to the query.

 **Checkpoint**

10.27 In the *Karate* database, which table contains the names and dates when students joined the school?

10.28 In the AllPaymentsForm form, which two tables are required when filling the grid?

10.29 Which property of a DataGridView control lets you alter the order in which columns appear?

10.30 What special operator is used in the WHERE clause of a query when you want to perform a wildcard comparison?

 ## 10.7 Introduction to LINQ

CONCEPT: LINQ (Language Integrated Query) is a query language that is built into Visual Basic and can be used to query data from many sources other than databases.

In this chapter you've learned about SQL, which allows you to query the data in a database. Visual Studio also provides another querying language named **LINQ** (which stands for Language Integrated Query). Whereas SQL allows you to query the data in a database, LINQ allows you to query many types of data from virtually any source. In this section we will look at how you can use LINQ to query the data in an array. Suppose we have declared the following array of Integers:

```
Dim intNumbers() As Integer = {4, 104, 2, 102, 1, 101, 3, 103}
```

If we want to query this array to get all of the values that are greater than 100, we can write the following statement:

```
Dim queryResults =  From item In intNumbers
                    Where item > 100
                    Select item
```

Let's take a closer look at the statement. First, notice that the statement begins with Dim queryResults. We are declaring an object named queryResults, which will hold the results of the LINQ query. Notice that we have not specified a data type. Visual Basic will automatically determine the data type for the object. On the right side of the = operator is the LINQ query. The = operator will assign the results of the LINQ query to the queryResults object. The LINQ query reads:

```
From item In intNumbers
Where item > 100
Select item
```

The results of this query will be all the items in the intNumbers array that are greater than 100. After the statement executes, we can use a For Each loop to examine the values stored in the queryResults object. For example, the following code segment shows how we can add the values to a list box named lstResults.

```
' Create an array of integers.
Dim intNumbers() As Integer = {4, 104, 2, 102, 1, 101, 3, 103}

' Use LINQ to query the array for all numbers
' that are greater than 100.
```

```
Dim queryResults =  From item In intNumbers
                    Where item > 100
                    Select item

' Add the query results to the list box.
For Each intNum As Integer In queryResults
  lstResults.Items.Add(intNum)
Next
```

After this code executes, the values 104, 102, 101, and 103 will be added to the list box, in that order. If you want the results of the LINQ query to be sorted in ascending order, you can use the Order By operator as shown here:

```
Dim queryResults =  From item In intNumbers
                    Where item > 100
                    Select item
                    Order By item
```

Adding the Descending key word to the Order By operator causes the results of the query to be sorted in descending order. Here is an example:

```
Dim queryResults =  From item In intNumbers
                    Where item > 100
                    Select item
                    Order By item Descending
```

As you can see from these examples, LINQ uses operators such as Where, Select, and Order By, that are similar to SQL operators. Unlike the SQL operators, however, the LINQ operators are built into the Visual Basic language. When you write a LINQ query, you write it directly into your Visual Basic program. As a result, the VB compiler checks the syntax of your query and you know immediately if you've made a mistake. An application named *LINQ Example* can be found in the *Chap10* student sample programs folder.

NOTE: In this section we've looked only at how LINQ can be used to query the data in an array. LINQ can be used to query any data that is stored in memory as an object. This includes not only arrays and databases, but many other types of data collections.

Summary

10.1 Database Management Systems

- A database is a collection of one or more tables, each containing data related to a particular topic. A table is a logical grouping of related information. Each row of a table is also called a record. Table columns are also called fields.
- Each table has a design, which specifies each column's name, data type, and range or size. A database schema is the design of tables, columns, and relationships between tables for the database.
- A primary key column uniquely identifies each row of a table. A primary key will sometimes consist of two or more combined columns.
- When you use Visual Basic to read a database table, you must select variable types that match the type of data in the table.
- Most well-designed databases keep redundant data to a minimum. They use key fields to link data stored in multiple tables. This reduces data entry errors and reduces the likelihood of inconsistenet data.
- A relationship is a link that relies on a common field value in the primary and foreign keys to join rows from two different tables. The most common type of relationship is a one-to-many relation.

10.2 Database Concepts

- A data source is usually a database, but can include text files and other sources of data outside a program.
- A binding source keeps track of the database name, location, username, password, and other connection information.
- A table adapter pulls data from one or more database tables and passes it to your program.
- A dataset is an in-memory copy of data pulled from database tables.
- A TableAdapter object's `Fill` method opens a database connection, reads data from a database into the dataset, and closes the connection.

10.3 DataGridView Control

- The DataGridView control allows you to display a database table in a grid. The grid can be used at runtime to sort and edit the contents of the table.
- Visual Basic uses a technique called data binding to link database tables to controls.
- A data source usually connects to a database, but can also connect to text files, Excel spreadsheets, XML data, and Web services.
- A binding source connects data-bound controls to a dataset.
- A table adapter pulls data from one or more database tables and passes it to your program.
- A dataset is an in-memory copy of the data pulled from database tables.
- The DataGridView's smart tag opens the DataGridView Tasks window. In this window, you can choose a data source, edit the grid columns, and enable operations on data such as adding, editing, and deleting.

10.4 Data-Bound Controls

- Using a data source, you can bind its fields to individual controls such as text boxes, labels, and list boxes.
- Data-bound controls update their contents automatically when you move from one row to the next in a dataset.
- You can bind an existing data source to a DataGridView control by dragging a table from the *Data Sources* window to an open area of a form. Similarly, you can

individually create data-bound controls such as text boxes and labels by dragging individual fields in the *Data Sources* window onto the open area of a form.

- ListBox and ComboBox controls have two important properties that are required when using data binding: the DataSource property identifies the table within the dataset that supplies the data; the DisplayMember property identifies the column to be displayed.

10.5 Structured Query Language (SQL)

- SQL is a universal language for creating, updating, and retrieving data from databases.
- The SQL SELECT statement has an optional ORDER BY clause that lets you control the display order of the table rows.
- Applications often need to filter certain rows when retrieving data from data sources. Filtering, or choosing rows to display in a dataset is done by creating a query. In SQL, the WHERE statement limits the rows retrieved from a database table.
- The TableAdapter Configuration Wizard and Search Criteria Builder can be used to modify queries.

10.6 Focus on Problem Solving: *Karate School Management* Application

- This section shows how to create the *Karate School Management* application, which displays a list of all members; permits the user to sort on any column, edit individual rows, and delete rows; adds new students to the *Members* table; displays members having similar last names; and displays payments by all members.

10.7 Introduction to LINQ

- LINQ, which stands for Language Integrated Query, is a query language that can be used to select, display, and filter data from virtually any source. The LINQ operators are built into .NET, and as a result, LINQ queries appear as statements in Visual Basic programs.

Key Terms

binding source	DisplayMember property
components	field
data binding	foreign key
data source	grid pane
database	identity column
database management system (DBMS)	Language Integrated Query (LINQ)
database query	LIKE operator (SQL)
database schema	one-to-many relationship
data-bound controls	ORDER BY clause (SQL)
DataGridView control	primary key
dataset	prototype
DataSource property	query parameter
DateTimePicker control	relation
design	relational model
diagram pane	results pane

schema definition file
SELECT statement (SQL)
SQL pane
Structured Query Language
   (SQL)

table
table adapter
WHERE clause (SQL)
wildcard
wizard

Review Questions and Exercises

Fill-in-the-Blank

1. A database _____ describes the design of tables, columns, and relationships between tables.

2. A _____ _____ creates a connection to an external data source such as a database.

3. A _____ control displays data directly from a dataset, without any programming required.

4. The _____ control lets the user select a date using the mouse.

5. Another word for a database table row is a _____.

Multiple Choice

1. Which of the following is an in-memory copy of data pulled from one or more database tables?
   a. Table adapter
   b. Table relation
   c. Dataset
   d. Data record

2. Which of the following is not an SQL Server field type?
   a. bit
   b. datetime
   c. largedatetime
   d. float

3. A Visual Basic Double data type corresponds best to which of the following SQL Server column types?
   a. float
   b. currency
   c. integer
   d. real

4. Which of the following is not a property of a ListBox control?
   a. ValueMember
   b. DataSource
   c. DisplayMember
   d. DataMember

5. Which of the following keywords and relational operators is used by SQL when performing wildcard matches?
   a. EQUAL
   b. LIKE
   c. MATCH
   d. =

True or False

Indicate whether the following statements are true or false.

1. T F: A TableAdapter's `Fill` method receives a dataset argument.

2. T F: A one-to-many relationship involves connecting a TableAdapter to a dataset.

3. T F: A primary key can involve only a single column of a database table.

4. T F: A data source field such as *Last_Name* can be bound to a TextBox or Label control.

5. T F: The default type of control bound to DateTime fields is the TextBox.

6. T F: The *Karate School Manager* application joins the *Members* table to the *Payments* table when displaying payments by all members.

7. T F: The *Karate School Manager* application requires you to write special event handling code that makes sorting in a DataGridView possible.

8. T F: When the user makes changes to a dataset, the changes are not permanent unless other measures are taken to write the dataset back to a database.

9. T F: In an SQL Server, query parameter names always begin with the @ sign.

10. T F: Query parameters are passed to datasets as arguments when calling a TableAdapter's `Fill` method.

Short Answer

1. Which property of a ListBox control must be set before a program can use the SelectedValue property at runtime?

2. What type of relationship existed between the *Employees* and *Department* tables in Section 10.1?

3. If the *Employees* table contains a foreign key named *dept_id*, is it likely that the values in this field will be unique?

4. What type of component keeps track of the database name, location, username, password, and other connection information?

5. What happens when you drag a table name from the *Data Sources* window onto an open area of a form?

6. Write a statement that uses a TableAdapter named MembersTableAdapter to add a new row to its dataset. The fields to be inserted are MemberID, last name, first name, phone number, and date joined.

7. Which property of a DataGridView control causes the buttons at the beginning of each row to appear?

What Do You Think?

1. When displaying the contents of the *Payments* table in a DataGridView control, the *ID* column displays by default. What would you do to limit the columns to just *Payment_Date* and *Amount*?

2. Suppose you wanted to add a new row to the *Payments* table in the *Karate School Management* application. How would you determine which *Member_id* value to insert in the row?

Algorithm Workbench

1. Suppose a database table named *Address* contains fields named *City* and *State*. Write an SQL SELECT statement that combines these fields into a new field named *CityState*.

2. Suppose a database table named *Students* contains the fields *FirstName*, *LastName* and *IDNumber*. Write an SQL SELECT statement that retrieves the *IDNumber* field for all records that have a *LastName* equal to "Ford".

3. Write an SQL query that retrieves the *ID*, *Title*, *Artist*, and *Price* from a database table named *Albums*. The query should sort the rows in ascending order by *Artist*.

4. Write an SQL query that uses a query parameter to retrieve a row from the *Albums* table that has a particular *ID* value. Retrieve the *ID*, *Title*, *Artist*, and *Price*.

5. Write an SQL query that retrieves columns from the *Payments* table when the *Payment_Date* is earlier than January 1, 2000.

6. Write a statement that fills a table named *Members* in a dataset named *AllMembersDataSet*. The table adapter is named *MembersTableAdapter*.

7. Write an SQL query that retrieves the *ID*, *Last_Name*, and *First_Name* from the *Members* table. You only want rows having a *Date_Joined* value greater than or equal to the value of a query parameter.

Programming Challenges

VideoNote

The Karate Members Grid Problem

1. **Kayak Browser**

   Create an application named *Kayak Browser* that lets the user select different types of kayaks from a list box. When each ListBox entry is selected by the user, the application must display a description of the kayak type in a Label control. Figure 10-74 shows an example of how the application's form should appear. Use the Kayaks.mdf database supplied with the Student Sample programs.

Figure 10-74 Kayak Browser application

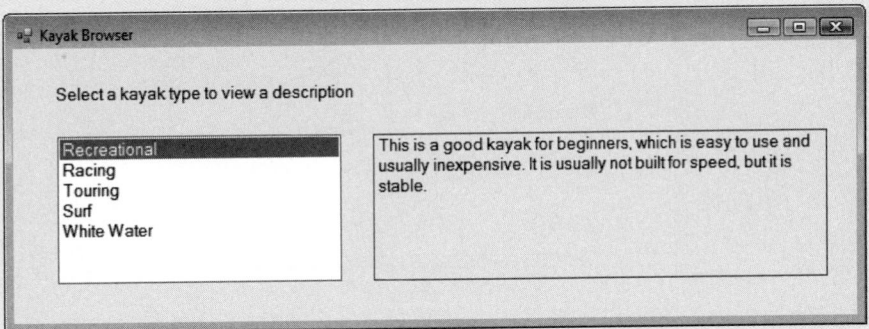

2. **Kayak Rental Prices**

   Create an application named *Kayak Rental Prices* that displays a DataGridView containing kayak types, along with their hourly, daily, and weekly rental rates. Figure 10-75 shows an example of how the application's form should appear. Format all prices with two digits to the right of the decimal point. Use the Kayaks.mdf database supplied with the Student Sample programs. Disable adding, editing, and deleting in the grid, and remove the row headers. Remove the underscore characters from the column headings. *Suggestion:* When you create the new data source, select the KayakTypes table. Then, in the *DataSet Designer* window, modify the *Fill, GetData* entry of the TableAdapter, open the *Query Builder* window, and add the RentalPrices table. This was the approach used in Tutorial 10-13.

Figure 10-75 Kayak Rental Prices application

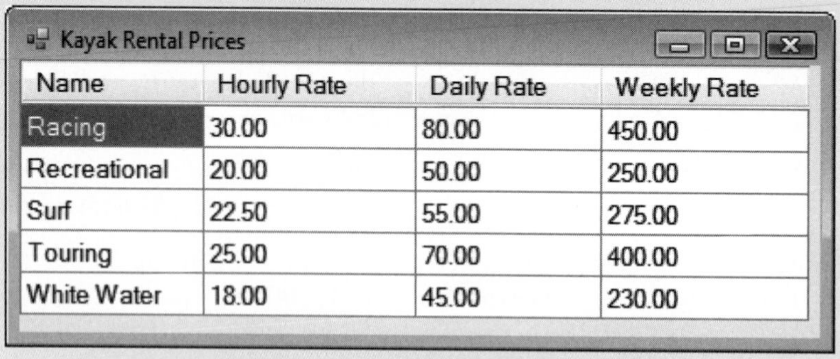

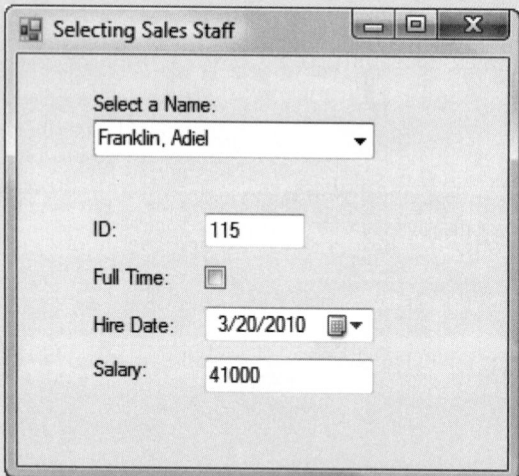

Kayak Rental Prices
Name
Hourly Rate
Daily Rate
Weekly Rate
Racing 30.00 80.00 450.00
Recreational 20.00 50.00 250.00
Surf 22.50 55.00 275.00
Touring 25.00 70.00 400.00
White Water 18.00 45.00 230.00

3. **Selecting Sales Staff**

   Create a program that lets the user select rows from the *SalesStaff* table in the *Company.mdf* database. Fill a ComboBox control with the full names (last, first). Use a parameterized query (a query containing a parameter) to retrieve the matching table row and display it in data-bound controls. An example is shown in Figure 10-76. You may want to use a DateTimePicker control to display the *Hire Date* field.

Figure 10-76 *Selecting Sales Staff*

Selecting Sales Staff
Select a Name:
Franklin, Adiel
ID:
115
Full Time:
Hire Date:
3/20/2010
Salary:
41000

4. **Sales Staff Salaries**

   Using the *SalesStaff* table in the *Company.mdf* database, let the user choose between lists of part-time versus full-time employees. Use radio buttons to make the selection. Display the average salary of the selected group in a label. An example is shown in Figure 10-77. When the program starts, the *Full-time* button is automatically selected.

Figure 10-77 Displaying average salaries of full-time employees

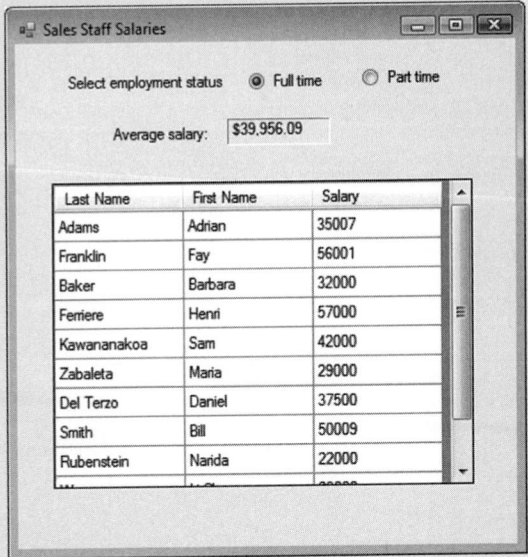

5. Karate Member Dates

Create a program that uses the *Members* table of the *Karate.mdf* database. Let the user select a date from a DateTimePicker control. The program must display the first and last names, the phone numbers, and dates joined of all members who joined before the selected date (see Figure 10-78). Use a parameterized query to retrieve the matching table rows and display them in a DataGridView control.

Figure 10-78 Finding members who joined before a selected date

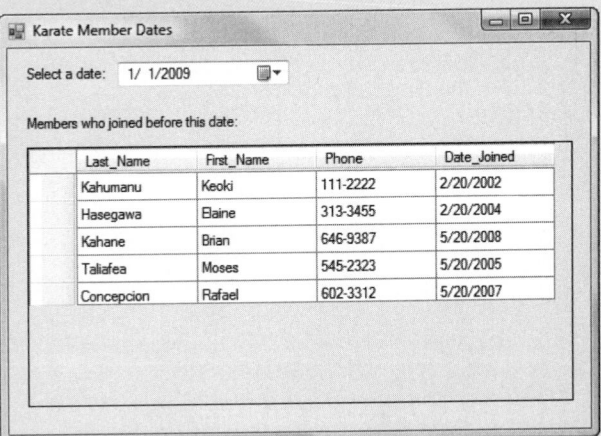

6. Advanced Karate Member Dates

(*Extra challenge project*) Enhance the program you created in Programming Challenge 3 by giving the user a choice between displaying members who have joined before a given date or members who have joined on or after that date. In Figure 10-79, the program shows members who joined before March 1, 2004. In Figure 10-80, a list of members who joined on or after January 1, 2010 is displayed.

You should create two datasets, one for each type of search. After binding the grid to the first dataset, a component named *MembersBindingSource* is created. If you then bind the grid to the second dataset, a second component named *Members-BindingSource1* is created. At runtime, when the user switches between the radio buttons, their event handlers can assign one of the two binding sources to the Data-Source property of the DataGridView control. That would be a good time to call the `Fill` method of the appropriate DataAdapter.

Figure 10-79 Showing members who joined before the chosen date

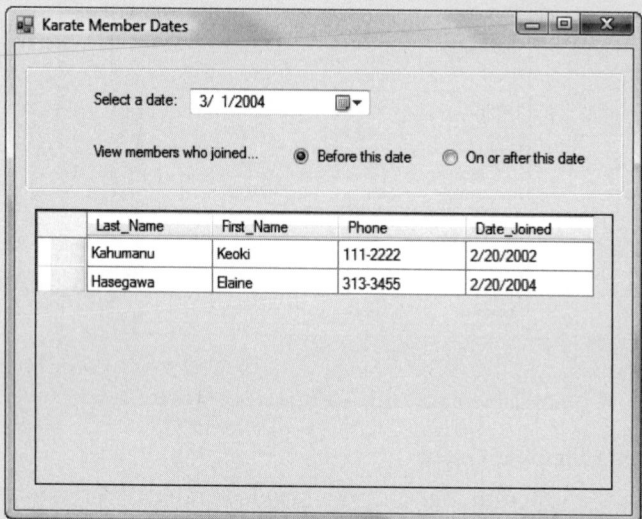

Figure 10-80 Showing *Karate* members who joined on or after the chosen date

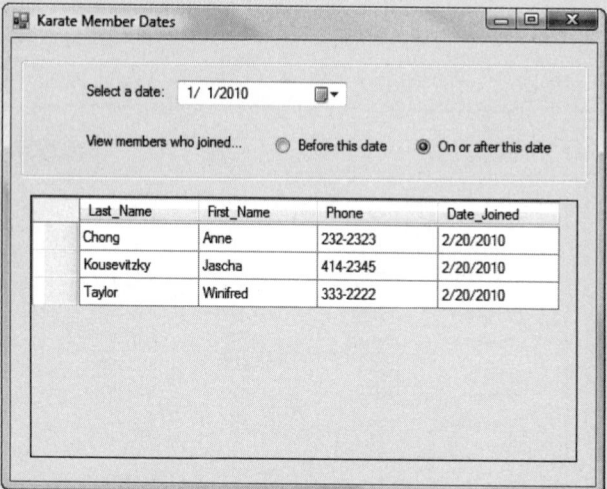

VideoNote

The Karate
Payments by a
Single Member
Problem

7. **Modify Existing Karate School Payments**

Using the Karate School application from Tutorial 10-13 as a starting point, add a new form, shown in Figure 10-81 that lets the user make modifications to the Payments table. The *Details* view works well for modifying the payments, but you also must add a DataGridView to the form that displays member names and ID numbers. This grid helps the user to associate member IDs with member names.

8. **Karate Payments by a Single Member**

Using the Karate School application from Tutorial 10-13 as a starting point, add a new form, shown in Figure 10-82, that lets the user view all payments made by a single member. The ListBox control displays a list of member names. When the user selects a name in the ListBox, the DataGridView control on the same form displays the payment date and amount of all payments made by the selected member.

Figure 10-81 Modifying Existing Karate School Payments

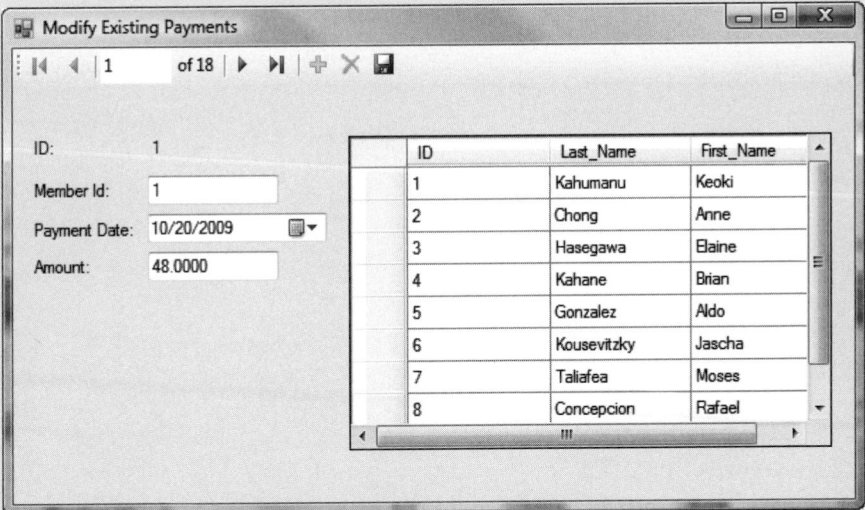

Figure 10-82 Viewing Karate School Payments by One Member

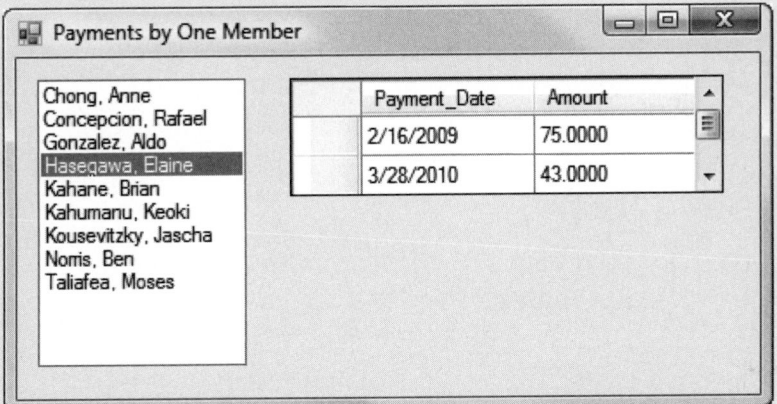

You will need two data sources for this form:

1. The first one selects ID and (Last_Name + ',' + First_Name) from the Members table, ordered by Last_Name.

2. The second data source selects Member_Id, Payment_Date, and Amount from the Payments table listed in ascending order by Payment_Date. You will need to add a query to the TableAdapter of this dataset. The query returns payment rows that match a particular member ID value.

When the user selects a name from the ListBox, your event handler will obtain the SelectedValue property from the ListBox and assign its value to the query parameter for the query that fills the grid. In that way, the grid shows only payments by the selected member. In Design mode, when you bind the ListBox to the data source, be sure to assign ID to the ListBox's ValueMember property.

11 Developing Web Applications

TOPICS

In this chapter, you will learn how to create ASP.NET applications that run under Web Browsers such as Internet Explorer, Chrome, Safari, and Firefox. Most of the time, we think of running browser-based applications on the Internet, but they can be just as effective on networks limited to a single organization. You will use either Visual Studio 2010 or Visual Web Developer 2010 to create Web applications. Except in cases where we must make a distinction between the two programs, we will refer to both as Visual Studio.

11.1 Programming for the Web

CONCEPT: A Web application runs on a Web server and presents its content to the user across a network, in a Web browser.

HyperText Markup Language

When the Web first became popular, HTML was the only available tool for creating pages with text, graphics buttons, and input forms. HTML, which stands for **HyperText Markup Language**, is a standardized language that describes the appearance of pages. It uses special sequences of characters called tags to embed commands inside the text appearing on a Web page. For example, the following line instructs the browser to display "This text is in bold." in bold type.

```
<b>This text is in bold.</b>This text is normal.
```

The `<b>` tag begins the bold font, and the `</b>` tag ends it. There are a large number of markup tags, explained by many excellent books. Special Web design editors such as

Microsoft Expression Web and Adobe Dreamweaver make editing HTML easy without having to memorize HTML tags.

But what about Web programming? Rather than display static content such as pictures and text, many applications require Web pages to be fully functional programs. Companies like Microsoft and Sun Microsystems decided that Web applications should be written using advanced programming languages. Web-based technologies and tools such as Java Server Pages and Microsoft ASP.NET were created. Scripting languages such as JavaScript and PHP have made Web programming much easier.

ASP.NET

The acronym ASP originally stood for **Active Server Pages**. It was the first server-side Web programming technology introduced by Microsoft. **ASP.NET**, the next generation, is called a **platform** because it provides development tools, code libraries, and visual controls for browser-based applications. ASP.NET provides a way to separate ordinary HTML from object-oriented program code. It also provides many powerful controls, which are similar to Windows Forms controls. ASP.NET lets you transfer a lot of your Visual Basic knowledge to Web applications. Visual Studio checks your Web application's code for errors before running it. Visual Basic code can be stored in a separate file from a page's text and HTML, making it easier for you to code and maintain program logic.

Web applications written for ASP.NET consist of the following parts:

- Content: Web forms, HTML code, Web forms controls, images, and other multimedia
- Program logic, in compiled Visual Basic (or C#) code
- Configuration information

How Web Applications Work

Web applications are designed around a **client-server model**, which means that an entity called a **server** produces data consumed by another entity called a *client*. Put another way, clients make requests satisfied by responses from servers.

When you use a Web browser such as Internet Explorer to access a Web site, your browser is the client. A program called a *Web server* runs on the computer hosting the Web site. Web browsers, such as Internet Explorer, Safari, or Netscape, display data encoded in HTML. Web browsers connect to Web sites, causing HTML data to be sent to the client's computer. The browsers interpret, or render the HTML, displaying the fonts, colors, and images from the pages in the browser windows.

Uniform Resource Locator (URL)

A URL (**Uniform Resource Locator**) is the universal way of addressing objects and pages on a network. It always starts with a **protocol**, such as http://, https://, or ftp://. It is followed by a **domain name**, such as microsoft.com, ibm.com, or aw.com. A specially defined domain name for your local computer is called localhost. Then, the URL may end with a specific folder path and/or filename. The following is a complete URL with folder path and filename:

```
http://pearsonhighered.com
```

Displaying a Web Page

What happens when a Web page is displayed by a Web browser? In preparation, a computer must be running a **Web server**. The server waits for connection requests, which occur in two steps:

1. A user running a Web browser connects to the server by opening a network connection and passing a URL to the connection. An example is http://microsoft.com.
2. Using the URL it receives from the user's Web browser, the Web server translates the URL into a physical location within the server computer's file system. The server reads the requested file, now called a **Web page**. The server sends the Web page over the network connection to the user's computer. The user's Web browser renders (interprets) the HTML. Output consists of text, graphics, and sound.

After sending the Web page to the user, the server immediately breaks the connection. It becomes free to handle Web page requests from other users.

After a Web page is displayed, the user may click a **button control** or press ⁅Enter⁆, causing the page contents to be sent back to the Web server. This action, callled a **postback**, occurs when the server processes the page contents and resends the modified page to the browser. The processing might involve updating controls and executing functions in the application's compiled code.

Web Forms

Web applications written in ASP.NET use special Web pages called Web forms. A **Web form**, which can be identified by its *.aspx* filename extension, contains text, **HTML tags**, **HTML controls** (such as buttons and text boxes), and special interactive controls called **Web server controls**. The latter, known also as **ASP.NET Server controls**, are interactive controls such as buttons, list boxes, and text boxes that execute on the server. Although they look like HTML controls, they are more powerful because they have a larger set of properties and they use event handler procedures to carry out actions based on user input. In effect, they behave a lot like Windows Forms controls.

The source code for a Web form is usually stored in a related file called a **code-behind file**, with the filename extension *aspx.vb*. This part of the application is called the **program logic**.

Configuration information can be stored in two files. One file, *Web.config*, contains information about the runtime environment. Another file, *Styles.css*, is a **Cascading Style Sheet (CSS)** file containing HTML styles for customizing the appearance of Web forms.

Web Servers

Web applications must be run using a Web server. You have three choices as follows:

- The **ASP.NET Development Server** is installed automatically with Visual Studio. It is easy to use and requires no special security setup.
- **Internet Information Services (IIS)** is a professional production tool, which is available as an option with various versions of Microsoft Windows. It must be configured carefully to ensure security against hackers.
- A remote Web server is typically available through an Internet Service Provider (ISP) or a corporate Web server. You can copy your application to a remote Web server before running it. You must always have a username and password to publish on a remote server.

HTML Designer

HTML Designer is the tool in Visual Studio that simplifies the design of Web pages and Web forms. The designer generates HTML source code and embeds special codes that identify ASP.NET Web controls. It is possible to create Web forms using a plain text editor, but doing so requires considerable practice. We will use the designer in this book. The designer offers the following views of a Web page:

- *Design* view: You can visually edit Web pages, using the mouse to drag controls and table borders. This view most closely resembles Visual Studio's editor for Windows Forms projects.
- *Source* view: You use this view to directly edit the HTML source code that makes up a Web form.
- *Split* view: This view displays the page's *Design* view and *Source* view in separate panels.

Web Browser Support

Web pages would be easier to create if all end users ran the same Web browser. Unfortunately, browsers have different capabilities and characteristics. To make it easier to adapt to different browsers, the Web server automatically detects the browser type and makes the information available to ASP.NET programs. The programs automatically generate HTML that is appropriate for the user's browser.

> **TIP:** Before publishing your Web applications for end users, test them with browsers other than Internet Explorer (the default). Chrome, Safari, and Firefox are good choices. Chrome can be downloaded from www.google.com/chrome, Safari can be downloaded from www.apple.com/safari, and Firefox can be downloaded from www.mozilla.com.

Types of Controls

When you are designing Web forms, the *Toolbox* window contains Web-related controls placed in the following groups:

- **Standard:** This group contains the most commonly used controls on Web forms. Some are close relatives of Windows forms controls, including Label, Button, ListBox, CheckBox, CheckBoxList, and RadioButton. Others are unique to Web programming, such as the LinkButton and HyperLink controls.
- **Data:** Controls for connecting to data sources; displaying database and XML data in grids and lists.
- **Validation:** Controls for validating user input into controls such as text boxes.
- **Navigation:** Advanced controls for navigating between Web pages.
- **Login:** Controls related to authenticating users when they log into a Web site with usernames and passwords.
- **WebParts:** Controls that let a Web site's users modify the content, appearance, and behavior of Web pages directly from a browser.
- **AJAX Extensions:** Controls that provide rich interface experiences in the user's Web browser.
- **Reporting:** Contains the MicrosoftReportViewer control for displaying Web-based reports.
- **HTML:** Controls found on HTML Web pages, such as buttons, check boxes, radio buttons, lists, and text boxes. They are compatible with standard HTML, have a limited number of properties, and have no associated classes. Most importantly, they do not generate user events such as `Click` or `SelectedIndexChanged`.

 **Checkpoint**

11.1 Describe a Web application in your own words.

11.2 Describe the client-server relationship in a Web application.

11.3 What is a postback?

11.4 Why is ASP.NET called a platform?

11.5 What is meant by *content* in an ASP.NET application?

11.2 Creating ASP.NET Applications

CONCEPT: You can use Visual Studio or Visual Web Developer Express Edition to create Web applications in Visual Basic.

Types of Web Sites

In Visual Studio or Visual Web Developer Express, you select *Open Web Site* from the *File* menu when you want to open an existing Web application. The following types of Web sites are available in the *Open Web Site* dialog box in Figure 11-1: File System, Local IIS, FTP Site, and Remote Site. (You may see a fifth type, *Source Control*, which we do not discuss in this book.) ASP.NET applications are also known as Web sites or **Web applications**.

A **File System Web site** runs directly under the *ASP.NET Development Server* supplied with Visual Studio. The application files can be stored in any disk directory you select, or on a network computer. The server is simple to use and does not leave your computer open to security attacks. This type of Web site is best suited to college laboratory environments and non-administrative users (students). We will use File System Web sites in this chapter.

Figure 11-1 The *Open Web Site* dialog box

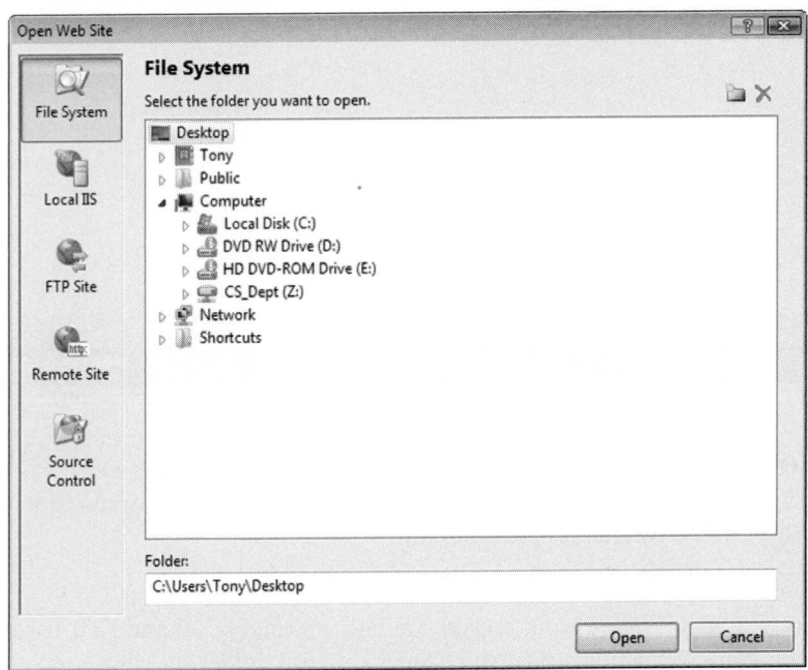

A Local IIS Web site runs under a Windows operating system utility named **Internet Information Services** (IIS). It is a professional-quality Web server with powerful security and configuration features, but requires some expertise to set up and maintain. IIS requires you to have administrative rights on the computer running the server in order to test and debug Web applications.

An **FTP Site** is a web site located on a different machine, usually on the Internet. If you were to sign up for an Internet hosting account, for example, they would assign you some disk storage, a Web address, and a username and password. You would use this information to copy your web site from your local computer to the remote hosting account. FTP stands for *File Transfer Protocol*, a way of copying files from one computer to another that is universally understood by all computer systems.

A **Remote Site** is also a web site located across a network, with a special requirement: It must be configured with Microsoft FrontPage Extensions. Many internet service providers include this option. When FrontPage Extensions are enabled, you can very easily update your remote site directly from Visual Studio.

VideoNote

Creating a
Simple Web
Application

Creating a Web Application

In Visual Studio, you create a new Web application (Web site) by choosing *New Web Site* from the *File* menu. The *New Web Site* dialog box provides a list of possible Web sites, as shown in Figure 11-2. In this chapter, we will always select the *ASP.NET Empty Web Site* item when creating new Web sites.

Figure 11-2 *New Web Site* dialog box

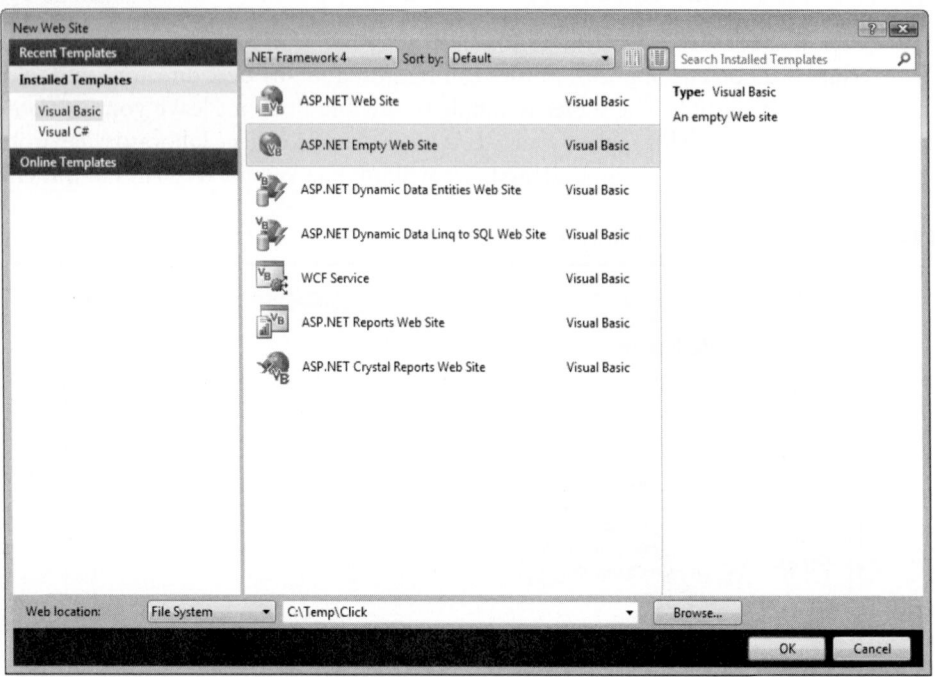

NOTE: If you are using Visual Studio, make sure *.NET Framework 4* is selected in the drop-down list at the top of the *New Web Site* window. This option does not appear in Visual Web Developer Express Edition.

For the Web location, your choices are File System, HTTP, and FTP. If you select File System, your Web application can be located in any folder on your computer or a network drive. If you select HTTP, your Web application will be located on a Web site set up by

Internet Information Services (IIS). If you select FTP, you must already have a Web site set up on a remote computer.

If you create a File System Web site, the edit box just to the right of the location lets you choose the path and folder name for your project. Suppose, for example, you create an application named *Click* in the *C:\Temp* folder. Then a project folder named *C:\Temp\Click* is created automatically.

If, on the other hand, you were to create an HTTP Web site, you would choose a location determined by the Internet Information Services (IIS) Web Server. IIS is beyond the scope of this book.

Application Files

When an empty Web site is created, it contains only one file, named *web.config*. The *web.config* file contains necessary configuration data for the Web site. Figure 11-3 shows the *Solution Explorer* after we have created a sample Web site named *Click*. In the figure you can see entry for the *web.config* file.

Figure 11-3 An empty Web site project

Once we have created an empty Web site, we will add a Web Form file named *Default.aspx* to the project. This is the Web page that will be displayed when we run the Web application. When we add the *Default.aspx* Web form to the project, another file named *Default.aspx.vb* is automatically created. This is called a code-behind file because it will hold all of the Visual Basic code that we will write for event handlers and program logic. Figure 11-4 shows a project in the *Solution Explorer* window with a *Default.aspx* file, a *Default.aspx.vb* file, and a *web.config* file.

Figure 11-4 *Solution Explorer* after adding *Default.aspx*

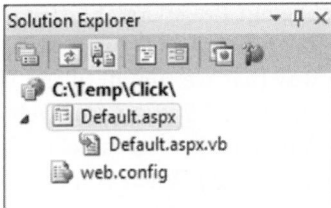

Displaying the Formatting Toolbar

The Visual Studio Formatting toolbar, shown in Figure 11-5, is useful when creating text on a Web page. If you do not see the Formatting toolbar, click *View* on the menu, then select *Toolbars*, and then select *Formatting*.

Figure 11-5 Formatting toolbar

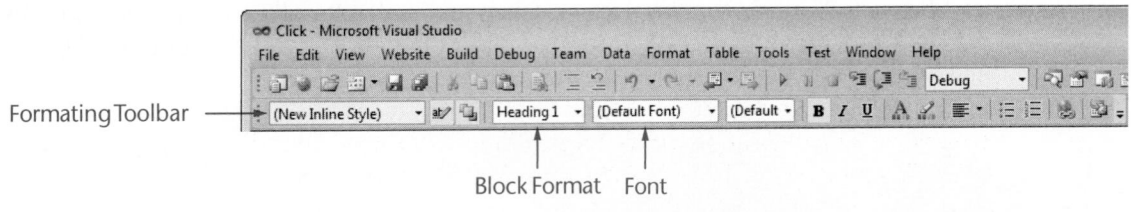

Opening an Existing Web Application Project

To open an existing Web application project, click *File* on the menu, and then click *Open Web Site . . .* This will display the *Open Web Site* window shown previously in Figure 11-1. Simply browse to and select the folder that contains the project, and click *Open.* The Web application project that is stored in that folder will be opened.

Selecting a Web Browser to Run the Application

When you run a Web application in Visual Studio, a default Web browser will be selected for you. It's a good idea, however, to test programs with more than one browser. To see a list of available browsers, right-click your project name in the *Solution Explorer* window and select *Browse With . . .* from the *pop-up* menu. The *Browse With* dialog box shown in Figure 11-6 will appear.

Figure 11-6 Selecting Internet Explorer to run the application

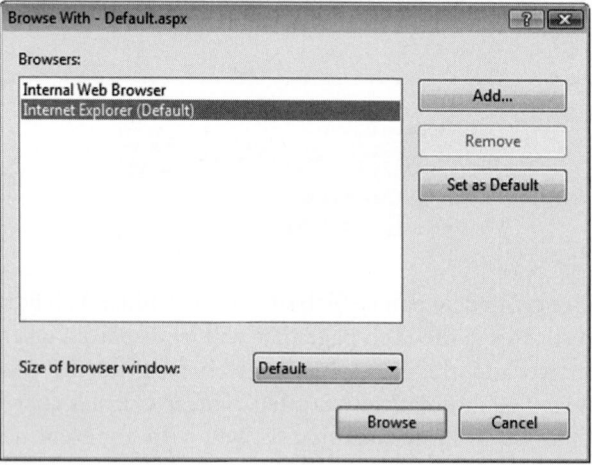

Running a Web Application Project

To run a Web application project you have two choices:

- **Start without debugging:** Press Ctrl+F5 to run the Web application without being able to use debugging tools such as single-stepping, stepping into, stepping over, and so on. This is the way that we run all of the Web application projects in this book.
- **Start with debugging:** Press F5 to run the Web application with the ability to use the debugging tools. (Alternatively you can click *Debug* on the Visual Studio menu, and then select *Start Debugging.*) When you do this, you will see the window shown in Figure 11-7. Before you can use the debugging tools in a Web application, Visual Studio must modify the application's Web.config file. To continue running the Web application with debugging enabled, select *Modify the Web.config file to enable debugging,* then click *OK.* (If you decide at this point that you do not want to use the debugging tools, you can select *Run without debugging* and click *OK.*)

Static Text

Static text is text you type directly onto a form. Web forms behave like documents, similar to Microsoft Word. In Windows forms, labels are needed for all text displayed on forms; but Web forms do not need labels for that type of text. In Figure 11-8, for example, three lines of text were typed directly onto a Web form in *Design* mode.

Figure 11-7 *Debugging Not Enabled* window

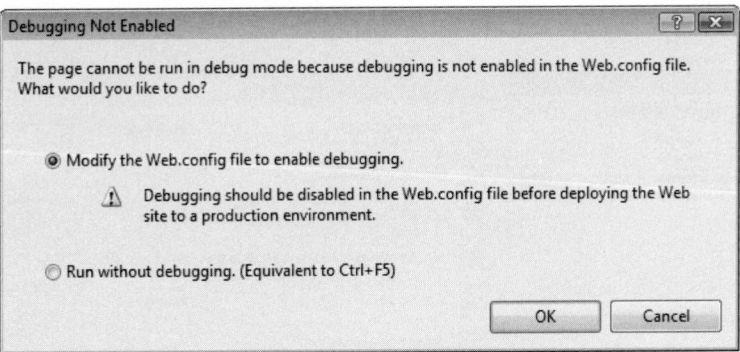

Figure 11-8 Static text typed directly on a form, in *Design* view

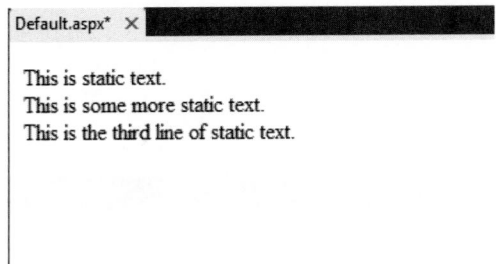

In Tutorial 11-1, you create the *Click* application.

Tutorial 11-1:

Creating the *Click* application

Now you're ready to create your first Web application. Microsoft went to great lengths to make Web development as similar as possible to Windows Forms programming. Your first application will have a short, but elegant name: *Click*.

As a preparation step, decide which directory you will use to save your Web projects. In our examples we will use a directory named *C:\Temp*, but you can choose any name.

Step 1:   Start Visual Studio (or Visual Web Developer Express Edition).

Step 2:   Select *New Web Site* from the *File* menu. Figure 11-9 shows the *New Web Site* window. Make sure *ASP.NET Empty Web Site* is selected. (If you are using Visual Studio, you should also make sure *.NET Framework 4* is selected in the drop-down list at the top of the window.)

At the bottom of the window, enter the path of the folder where you want to save your new Web site, followed by **Click**. (In the example shown in Figure 11-9, we have entered C:\Temp\Click as the location for the Web site. Choose an appropriate location that exists on your system.) Click *OK* to close the dialog box.

Step 3:   Now you will add the *Default.aspx* Web Form file to the project. Click *Website* on the menu, and then select *Add New Item . . .* You will see the *Add New Item* window shown in Figure 11-10. As shown in the figure, make sure *Web Form* is the selected type, and the file is named *Default.aspx*. Also make sure *Place code in separate file* is checked, and *Select master page* is not checked. Click the *Add* button.

Figure 11-9 *New Web Site* dialog box

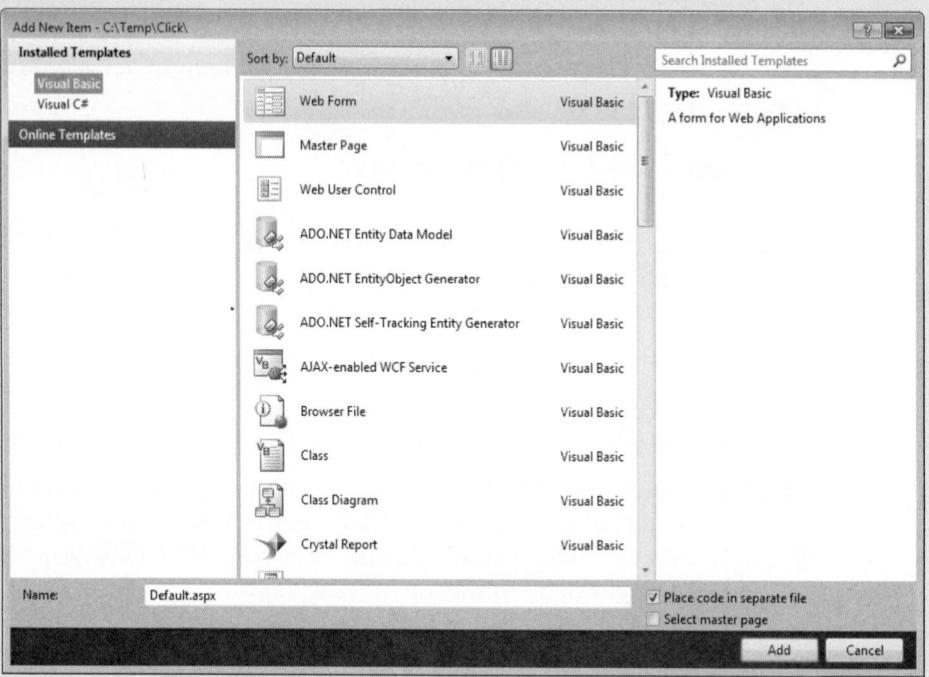

Figure 11-10 *Add New Item* window

Step 4: Figure 11-11 shows Visual Studio with the Default.aspx Web Form open in *Design* view. At the bottom of the *Design* view you should see three tabs named *Design*, *Split*, and *Source*. The *Design* tab is currently selected, indicating that the Web Form is open in *Design* view. If you select the *Split* tab the view will split, showing the form's XHTML code in one window and the form in *Design* view in another. If you select the *Source* tab you will see only the form's XHTML code.

Figure 11-11 After adding the *Default.aspx* Web form

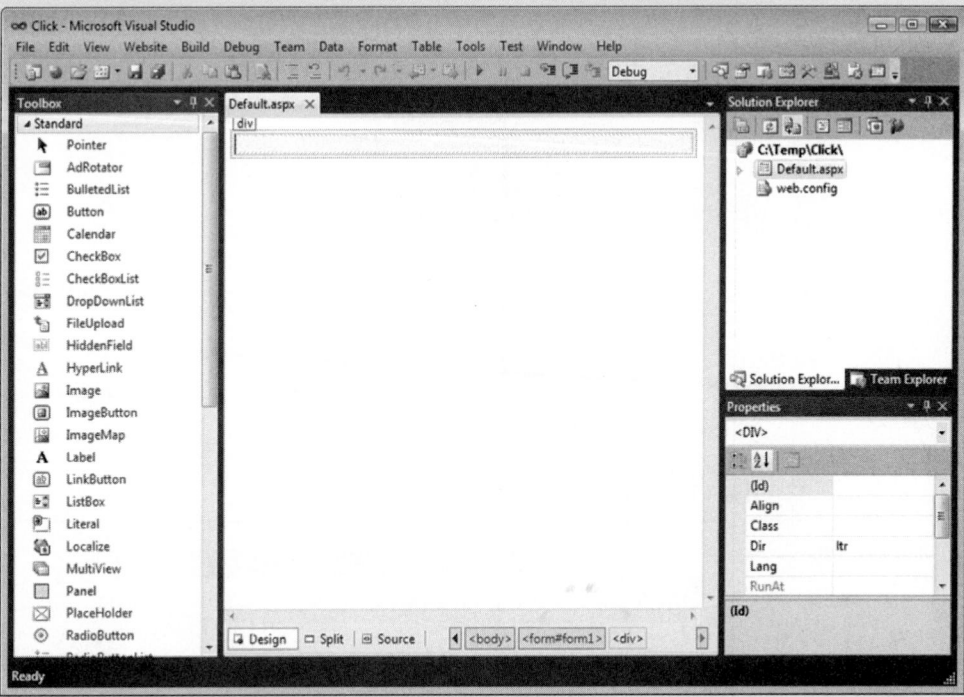

Step 5: Next, you will create a title that displays in the title bar of the Web browser when the application runs. Click inside the Web page in *Design* view, select *DOCUMENT* from the drop-down list that appears in the *Properties* window, and then set the Title property to *Click Application*. Figure 11-12 shows the appearance of the *Properties* window.

Figure 11-12 Properties window for the Document object

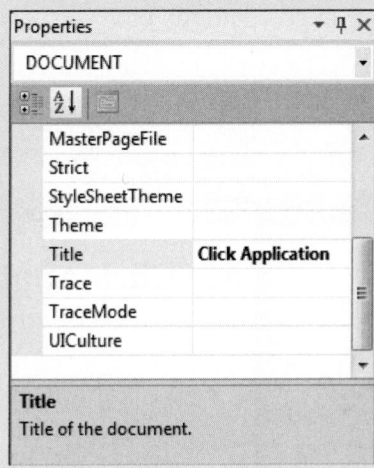

Step 6: Click inside the light blue box that appears on the form in *Design* view. Then, select *Toolbars* from the *View* menu, and then select *Formatting* (if it is not already selected). The formatting toolbar should appear just below the standard toolbar. Look for the *Block Format* drop-down list on the left side of the formatting toolbar (see Figure 11-13). Select *Heading 1 <H1>*. This will cause a small tag labeled *h1* to appear in the upper-left corner of the light blue box on

Figure 11-13 Block format drop-down list, on formatting toolbar

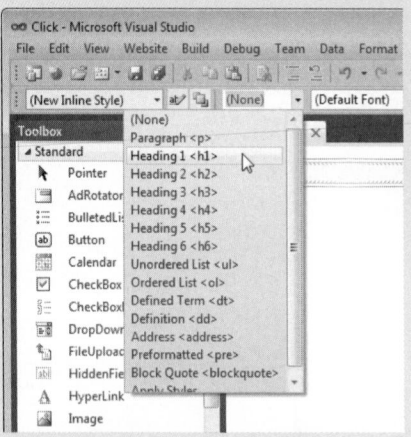

Figure 11-14 *h1* tag displayed

the form, as shown in Figure 11-14. The *Block Format* list contains a list of standard HTML formats that affect the font size, color, and other attributes.

Step 7: Click the mouse inside the blue box labeled *h1* on the Web form and type **My Click Application**. Press ⌷Enter⌷ to move to the next line. Figure 11-15 shows a sample of your work so far.

Figure 11-15 After typing the program heading in *Heading 1* style

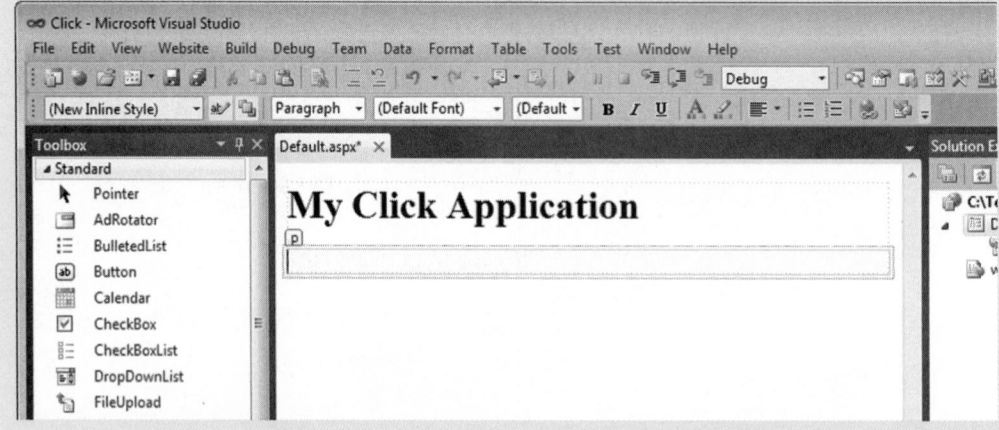

Step 8: Double-click the Button control icon in the *Toolbox* to create a Button control on your form. In the *Properties* window, set its Text property to *Click Here*. Set its ID property to btnClick.

Step 9: Click the mouse just to the right of the button and press ⏎ Enter to move to the next line. Insert a Label control on the next line. Set its ID property to `lblMessage` and erase its Text property. A sample of the form in *Design* mode is shown in Figure 11-16.

Figure 11-16 Design window, after adding Button and Label controls

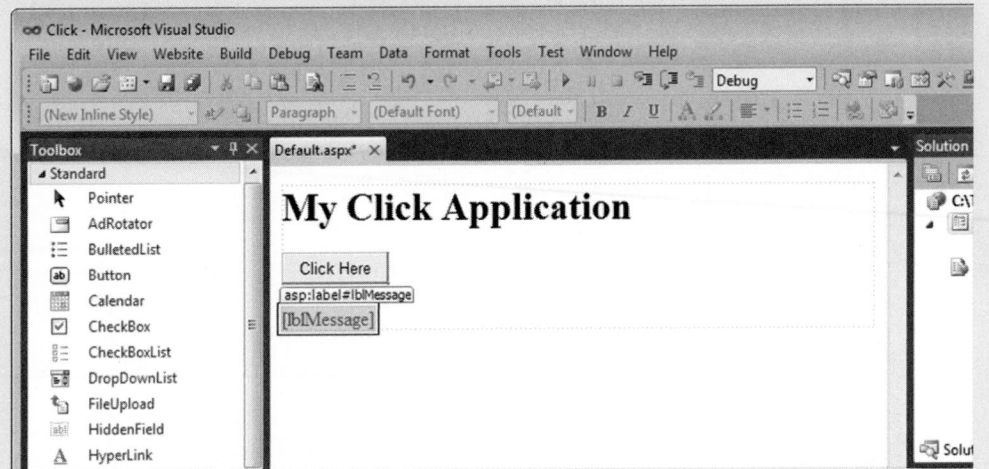

Step 10: Next, you will add code to the button's Click event handler that assigns a string to the label. Double-click the Button control and add the following statement (shown in bold) to its event handler:

```
Protected Sub btnClick_Click(...) Handles btnClick.Click
    lblMessage.Text = "Thank you for clicking the button!"
End Sub
```

You have opened the file named *Default.aspx.vb*, called the code-behind file for this Web form. The Visual Basic code in this file is contained in a class named `_Default` (the same name as the form). It works almost exactly the same as code written for Windows Forms applications.

Step 11: Save the project, and run the application by pressing Ctrl + F5 . When the Web browser opens your application, click the *Click Here* button. A message should appear below the button, as shown in Figure 11-17. Our example uses the Internet Explorer Web browser, but your computer may display a different browser, based on its default settings.

Step 12: Close the browser to end the application.

Let's take a final look at the contents of the Web page, which is in many ways like a text document. In the *Design* view, you can type text directly onto a Web page. Text typed directly on a page is called *static text* because it does not require the use of Label controls. The button on your Web page that says *Click Here* is an ASP.NET server control. The blank Label control named *lblMessage* is also an ASP.NET server control. You may want to try adding more random text, buttons, and labels to the Web page. Experiment with using HTML styles, available in the drop-down list on the left side of the formatting toolbar.

Figure 11-17 After clicking the button in the *Click* application

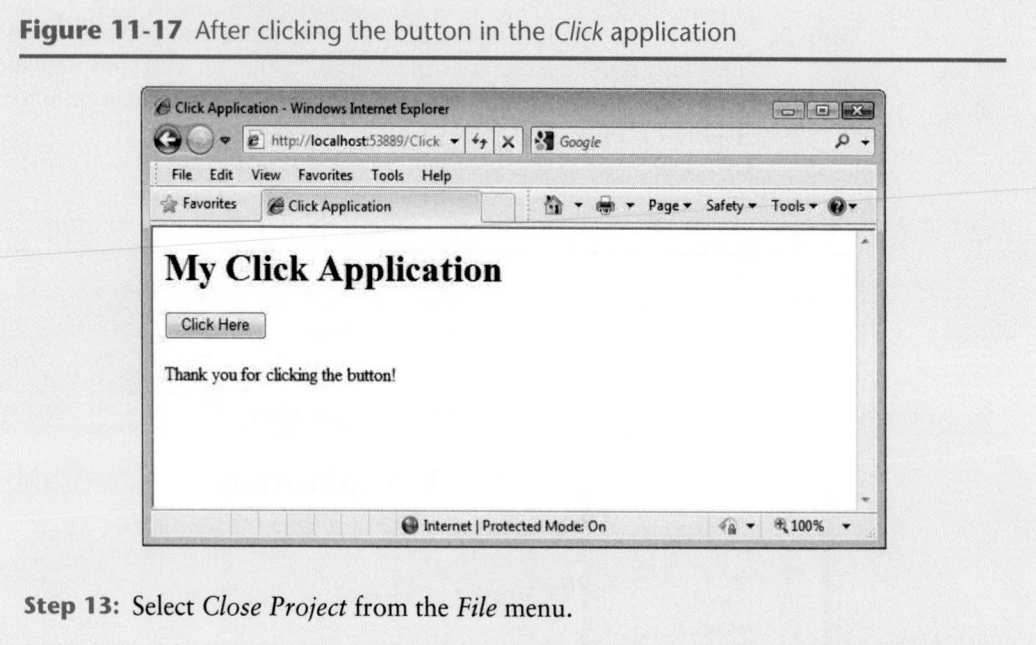

Step 13: Select *Close Project* from the *File* menu.

 **Checkpoint**

11.6 Name three types of Web sites you can create with Visual Studio.

11.7 When you edit a Web page, which tab must you click to switch from the page's *Source* view to *Design* view?

11.8 How do you select from a list of Web browsers when running your Web application?

11.9 What is static text, and is it similar to or different from Label controls in Windows forms?

11.10 In the *Click* application, how did you specify the block format named *Heading 1* for the first line of text in the Web form?

11.11 What happens the first time you run a Web application in Debug mode?

11.3 Web Server Controls

CONCEPT: Web Server controls are similar to controls used in Windows applications. You use Web Server controls to make ASP.NET Web applications interactive.

Web server controls make ASP.NET applications dynamic and interactive. The controls are powerful because each is defined by a class with a rich set of properties, methods, and events. The controls look and feel like Windows Forms controls, making them easy for Visual Basic programmers to learn. We often refer to Web server controls simply as *Web controls*.

The following Web controls are the ones you are likely to use often. Except where noted by an asterisk (*), all have counterparts among the controls used on Windows forms.

- Button
- ImageButton
- LinkButton
- TextBox
- Label
- RadioButton
- RadioButtonList*
- CheckBox

- CheckBoxList*
- ListBox
- DropDownList (similar to ComboBox control)
- Image (similar to PictureBox control)
- Calendar (similar to MonthCalendar control)
- HyperLink*

Web controls have similar properties to their Windows Forms counterparts. Examples of such properties are Text, Enabled, Visible, Font, BorderStyle, ReadOnly, and TabIndex. The following, however, are a few important differences between Web controls and Windows controls:

- The ID property of Web controls is the counterpart to the Name property of Windows controls.
- Web controls have an important new property named AutoPostBack.
- Web controls lose their runtime properties when the user moves away from the current page. Special programming techniques, called *saving state*, are available to overcome this challenge.

How Web Controls Are Processed

Web server controls are unique to ASP.NET. When a user connects to an ASP.NET Web page, a special process takes place, as shown in Figure 11-18. In Step 2, the Web server reads and interprets the Web controls on the page and executes Visual Basic statements in the application's code-behind file. In Step 3, the server creates a modified Web page consisting of standard HTML tags and controls. In Step 4, the modified Web page is sent back to the user and displayed in the Web browser.

Figure 11-18 Connecting to ASP Web pages

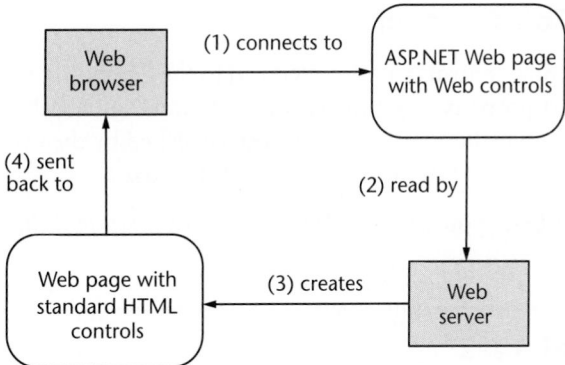

Label Control

The Web **Label control** is almost identical to the Label control on Windows forms. When displaying text, you need to use a Label only if its contents will change at runtime, or if you plan to change its Visible property. Always assign a name to a Label's ID property so you can access it in code. You can create interesting effects by varying the BorderStyle and Border-Width properties, as shown in Figure 11-19.

Figure 11-19 *BorderStyle* and *BorderWidth* samples for the Label control

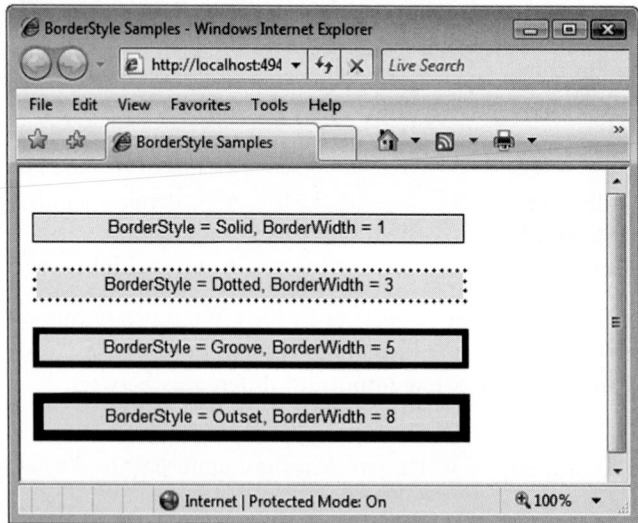

TextBox Control

The **TextBox** Web **control** is similar in many ways to the TextBox control for Windows forms. The Text property holds text input by the user. The MaxLength property lets you limit the number of characters the user is permitted to type. The TextMode property has the following choices:

- SingleLine: permits the user to enter only a single line of input
- MultiLine: permits the user to enter multiple lines of input
- Password: characters typed by the user appear as asterisks

Internet Explorer and other browsers behave differently when using the TextBox control. To be as compatible as possible with all Web browsers, you should use the Columns property to control the width of the text box. If you want the user to enter multiple lines of input, set the Rows property accordingly.

CheckBox Control

The **CheckBox control** is almost identical to the CheckBox in Windows forms applications. Use the Text property to set the visible text, and evaluate the Checked property at runtime to determine whether the control has been checked by the user. The TextAlign property lets you position the text to the left or right of the box.

In Tutorial 11-2, you create a Web sign-up for a *Student Picnic* application.

Tutorial 11-2

Student Picnic application

VideoNote

Tutorial 11-2
Walkthrough

In this tutorial, you will create a Web sign-up form for a computer department picnic. It will have a title, text boxes for a user to enter his or her name, a check box, and a button that displays a confirmation message. Figure 11-20 shows the program's output after the *Confirm* button was clicked.

Figure 11-20 The *Student Picnic* application

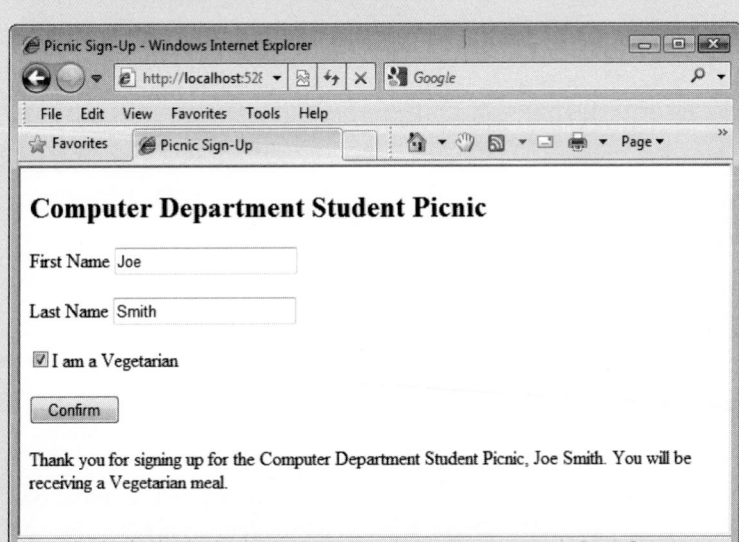

Step 1: Select *New Web Site* from the Visual Studio *File* menu. In the *New Web Site* window select *ASP.NET Empty Web Site* as the type, and set the project folder name to *Picnic*, using the same directory path you used in Tutorial 11–1. (If you are using Visual Studio, make sure *.NET Framework 4* is selected in the drop-down list at the top of the *New Web Site* window.)

Step 2: Add a new Web form named Default.aspx to the project.

Step 3: With Default.aspx open in *Design* view, Select *DOCUMENT* in the *Properties* window and set its Title property to *Picnic Sign-Up*. This text will appear in the browser's title bar when the application runs.

Step 4: Type the heading `Computer Department Student Picnic` directly onto the form (inside the box that appears near the top of the form), and press ⌨Enter. Then select the first line of text with the mouse and set its Block format style to *Heading 2 <H2>*. (The Block format tool is located on the left side of the formatting toolbar.)

Step 5: Type **First Name** and **Last Name** on separate lines, leaving a blank line between them.

Step 6: Insert a single space and a TextBox control at the end of the same line as First Name. Set its ID property to `txtFirst`.

Step 7: Insert a single space and a TextBox control at the end of the same line as Last Name. Set its ID property to `txtLast`. A sample of the form in *Design* view is shown in Figure 11-21.

Step 8: After a blank line, insert a CheckBox control and set its ID property to `chkVegetarian`. Set its Text property to *I am a Vegetarian*.

Step 9: Insert a blank line, then on the next line insert a Button control. Set its ID property to `btnConfirm`, and set its Text property to *Confirm*.

Figure 11-21 Picnic Application Design view, after inserting the TextBox controls

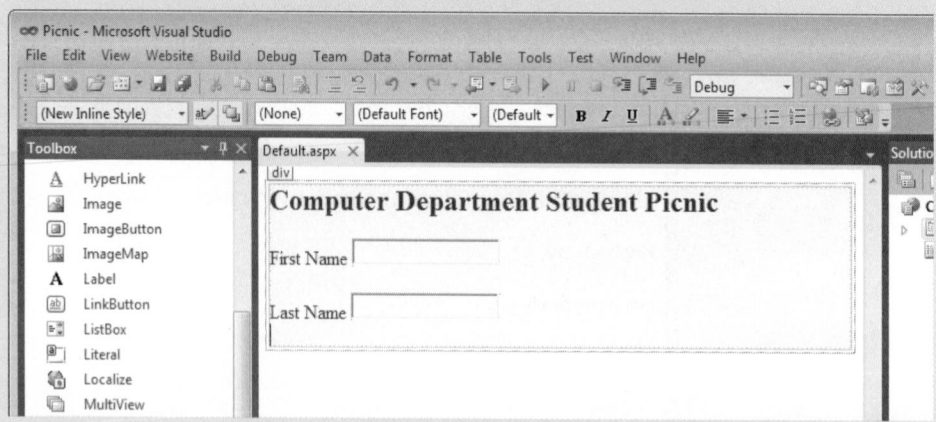

Step 10: Insert a blank line, then on the next line insert a Label control. Set its ID property to `lblMessage`. Clear its Text property. A sample of the form in Design mode is shown in Figure 11-22.

Figure 11-22 Picnic Application, after inserting all controls

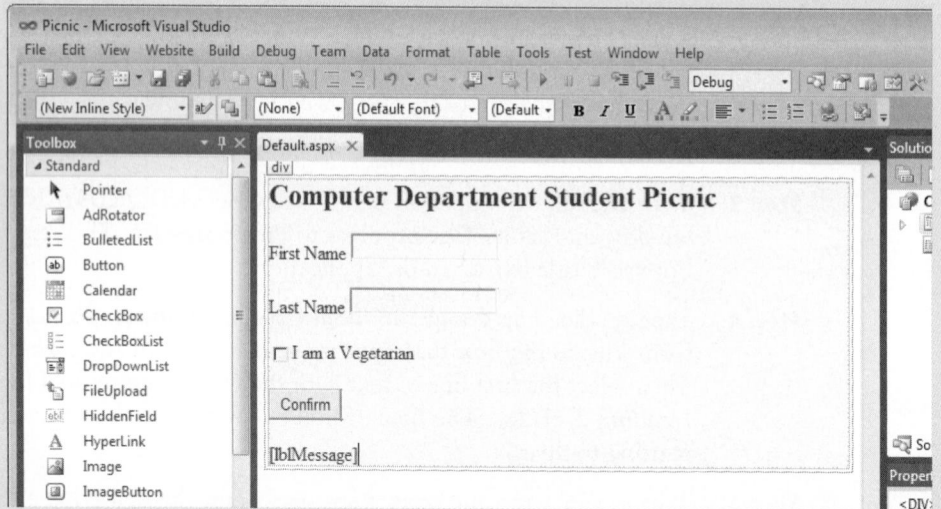

Step 11: Next, you will insert code in the *Confirm* button's Click event handler. Double-click the button and add the following statements, shown in bold:

```
Protected Sub btnConfirm_Click(...) Handles btnConfirm.Click
    lblMessage.Text = "Thank you for signing up for the " &
        "picnic, " & txtFirst.Text & " " & txtLast.Text & "."
    If chkVegetarian.Checked = True Then
        lblMessage.Text &= " You will be receiving a " &
            "Vegetarian meal."
    End If
End Sub
```

Step 12: Save the application and press Ctrl+F5 to run it. Enter a person's name, click the check box, and click the *Submit* button. The output should show the name and an additional comment about the meal because the check box was selected. The application's sample output was shown earlier in Figure 11-20.

Event Handling in Web Forms

Events are fired in a different sequence in Web forms than they are in Windows forms. In a Web form, the Page_Load event occurs when the page is first loaded into the user's browser, and again every time the page is posted back to the server. The Web form shown in Figure 11-23 inserts a message in the list box every time the Page_Load event fires. From the program display, we can see that `Page_Load` fired when the page was first displayed.

Figure 11-23 Loading a Web form

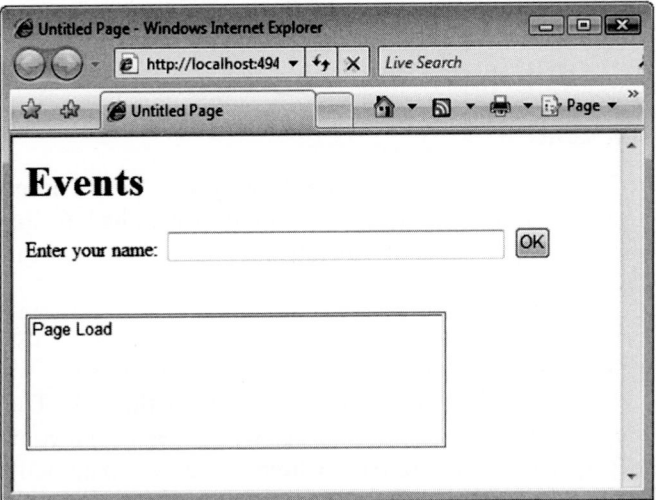

When the user types in a name and clicks the *OK* button, as shown in Figure 11-24, the Page_Load event fires again because a postback event occurs. Next, the TextChanged event handler executes. This unusual event sequence can be unsettling if you expect the TextChanged event to fire immediately, as it does in Windows Forms applications. In particular, you must be careful not to execute any code in the Page_Load event handler that changes the states of controls whose event handlers have not yet had a chance to execute.

Figure 11-24 After entering a name and clicking the *OK* button

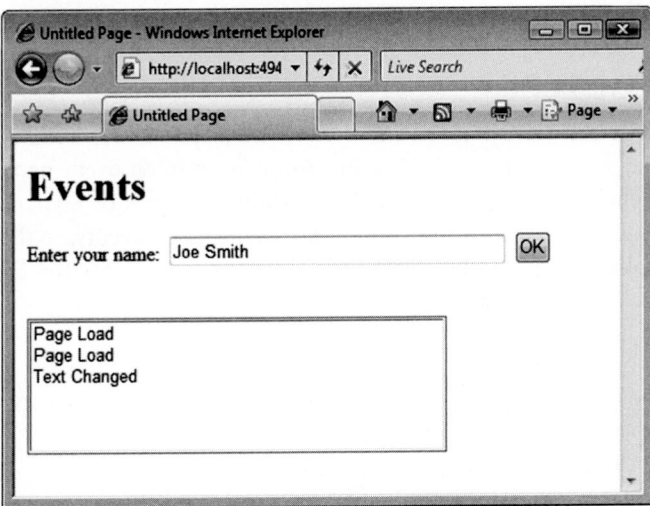

The AutoPostBack Property

When a control's **AutoPostBack property** equals *True*, clicking on the control causes the form to be posted back to the server. You might, for example, want to trigger a database row lookup when the user makes a selection in a list box. The server redisplays the form quickly or slowly, depending on how busy it is at the moment.

AutoPostBack defaults to *False* for the following controls: CheckBox, CheckBoxList, DropDownList, ListBox, ListControl, RadioButton, RadioButtonList, and TextBox. Not all controls have an AutoPostBack property. In particular, the Button, LinkButton, and ImageButton controls automatically post the current page back to the server.

HyperLink, ImageButton, LinkButton, and RadioButtonList

HyperLink Control

The **HyperLink control** provides a simple, easy way to add a link to your page that lets users navigate from the current page to another page. The link appears as underlined text. The HyperLink control does not generate any events, but it has three important properties as follows:

- The Text property contains the text shown to the user at runtime.
- The NavigateURL property contains the location of the Web page you would like the program to display when the user clicks the link. The property editor has a *Browse* button you can use to locate Web pages within your project.
- The Target property controls whether the new page will appear in the current browser window (the default), or in a separate window. To open in a separate browser window, set Target equal to *_blank*.

ImageButton Control

Web pages typically use clickable images as navigation tools. You can create the same effect with the **ImageButton control**. It does not look like or bounce like a typical button—instead, it simply shows an image. When the user hovers the mouse over the image, the mouse cursor changes shape. When the user clicks the image, a Click event is generated.

Assign an image's relative URL (path from the current page to the image file location) to the button's ImageUrl property. Ordinarily, you copy the image file into your project folder. The button generates a Click event when the image is clicked by the user. An example of a relative URL is *Images/photo.gif*, where the file named *photo.gif* is located in the *Images* subdirectory.

LinkButton Control

The **LinkButton control** looks and behaves much like a HyperLink control, with one major difference: it generates a Click event. You can write an event handler that executes when the user clicks the button. Figure 11-25 shows samples of HyperLink, ImageButton, and LinkButton controls. The latter two controls fire Click events, so the labels on the right side of the figure have been filled by the Click event handlers. See the *Button Demo* application in the student sample programs folder for this chapter.

Figure 11-25 Examples of button-type controls

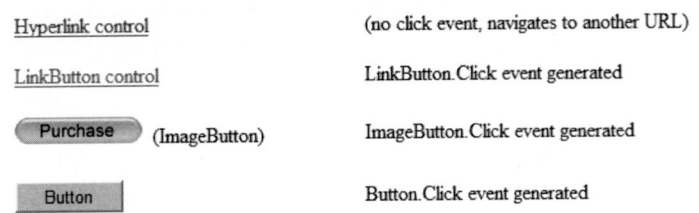

Hyperlink control	(no click event, navigates to another URL)
LinkButton control	LinkButton.Click event generated
Purchase (ImageButton)	ImageButton.Click event generated
Button	Button.Click event generated

RadioButtonList Control

The **RadioButtonList control** displays a group of radio buttons, as shown in Figure 11-26. You can create individual **RadioButton controls**, but the RadioButtonList is easier to use. Similar to a ListBox, it has SelectedIndex, SelectedItem, and SelectedValue properties. You can arrange the buttons horizontally or vertically, using the RepeatDirection property. You can use the BorderStyle, BorderWidth, and BorderColor properties to create a frame around the buttons. It has an Items property containing ListItem objects. You can add items using the ListItem collection editor window, as shown in Figure 11-27.

Figure 11-26 *RadioButtonList* example

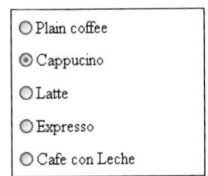

Figure 11-27 *ListItem Collection Editor* window

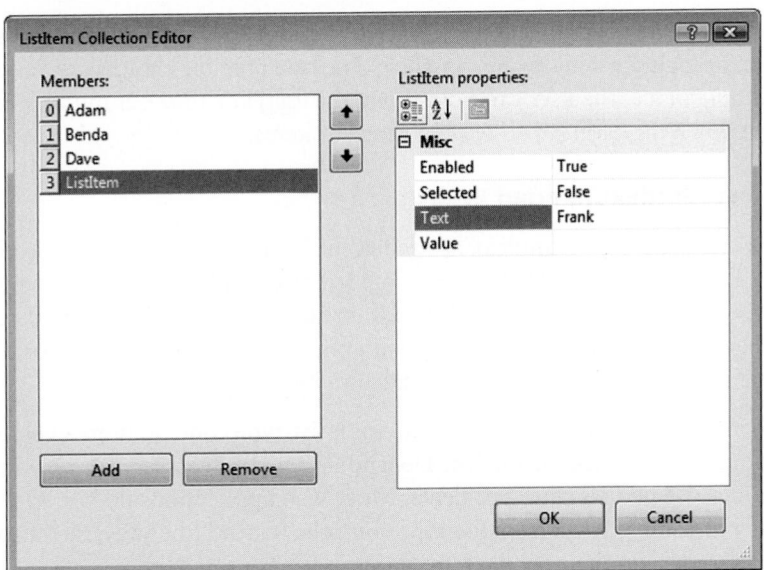

ListBox Control

In many ways, the Web **ListBox control** is similar to the Windows forms ListBox control. It has an Items collection and a SelectedIndexChanged event. You can retrieve the following properties at runtime:

- **SelectedIndex:** returns the index of the selected item
- **SelectedItem:** returns the currently selected item, a ListItem object
- **SelectedValue:** returns the contents of the selected item's Value property

In Figure 11-28, the index of the selected item from a list of sales staff members is displayed in a label below the *OK* button.

Figure 11-28 Displaying the SelectedIndex of a ListBox control

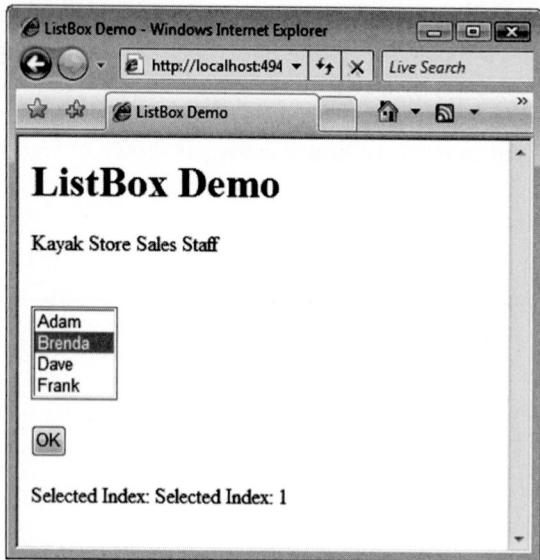

SelectionMode

You can use the SelectionMode property to determine whether users can select only a single item, or multiple items from a ListBox. The two possible choices are *Single* and *Multiple*. In *Multiple* mode, the user can hold down the Ctrl key to select multiple individual items or hold down the Shift key to select a range of items.

SelectedIndexChanged Event

You can use a SelectedIndexChanged event handler to respond to selections by the user in any list-type control. There is one important consideration, however: the AutoPostBack property must be set to *True* if you want the user's selection to be detected immediately. Otherwise, the SelectedIndexChanged event will not fire until the form is posted back to the server by some other control (such as a button).

When you set AutoPostBack to *True* for a list-type control, users experience a short delay each time they click on the list. Depending on the Web server's response time, the delay could cause performance problems. Most Web applications do not post back to the server every time users select from list-type controls. Instead, the sites use button controls to post all selections on the page back to the server at the same time.

CheckBoxList Control

The **CheckBoxList control** looks like a group of check boxes, but works just like a ListBox. It has SelectedIndex, SelectedItem, and SelectedValue properties. It has an Items collection, and each item has a Selected property (*True* or *False*). Figure 11-29 shows two CheckBoxLists, one with no border, and another with a 1-pixel-wide solid border.

Figure 11-29 CheckBoxList control

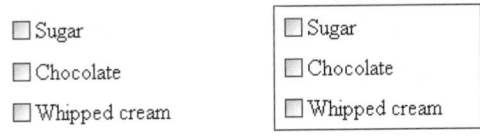

Usually, you will want to iterate over the Items collection to find out which boxes have been checked. The following is a sample:

```
Dim item As ListItem
For Each item In chkAddOns.Items
    If item.Selected Then
        (use the item in some way)
    End If
Next
```

DropDownList Control

The **DropDownList control** lets the user select a single item from a list. There are two noticeable differences between the DropDownList and its Windows Forms counterpart, the ComboBox. First, in a DropDownList, the initial value of SelectedIndex is always 0, causing the first item to display when the form is loaded. Second, users cannot enter an arbitrary string into the DropDownList, as they can in a ComboBox.

Figure 11-30 shows a simple example of a DropDownList when first displayed on a Web form. It contains an initial entry named *(none)* in the first row, located at index position 0.

Figure 11-30 Using the DropDownList control

 **Checkpoint**

11.12 Which Web control is the counterpart to the ComboBox in Windows forms?

11.13 Which Web control displays an image and fires a Click event?

11.14 Which Web control looks like a hyperlink and fires a Click event?

11.15 How can you determine which button in a RadioButtonList control was selected by the user?

11.16 How does setting AutoPostBack to *True* affect a ListBox control?

11.17 Which list-type control automatically initializes its SelectedIndex property to zero?

 **11.4** **Designing Web Forms**

CONCEPT: HTML tables can be used to design a Web application's user interface. HTML tables provide a convenient way to align the elements of a Web form.

Using Tables to Align Text and Controls

An **HTML table** is an essential tool for designing the layout of Web forms. You can use it to align text, graphics, and controls in rows and columns. In Figure 11-31, for example, a table contains five rows and three columns. Static text has been placed in column 1, and text boxes have been placed in column 3. The table cells in column 1 are right justified, and the cells in column 3 are left justified. Column 2 is intentionally left blank so it can be used as a spacer between the first and third columns.

Figure 11-31 Aligning text and text boxes with a table

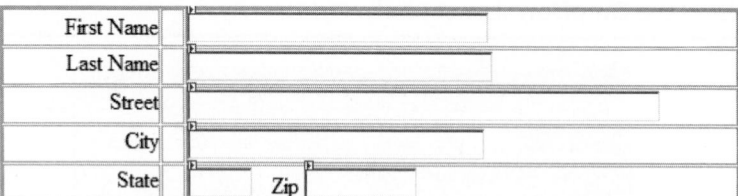

There are two ways to insert a table when the *Design* view of a form is active:

- Select *Insert Table* from the *Table* menu. When you do so, the *Insert Table* dialog box appears, letting you set various table layout options (see Figure 11-32).

Figure 11-32 *Insert Table* dialog box

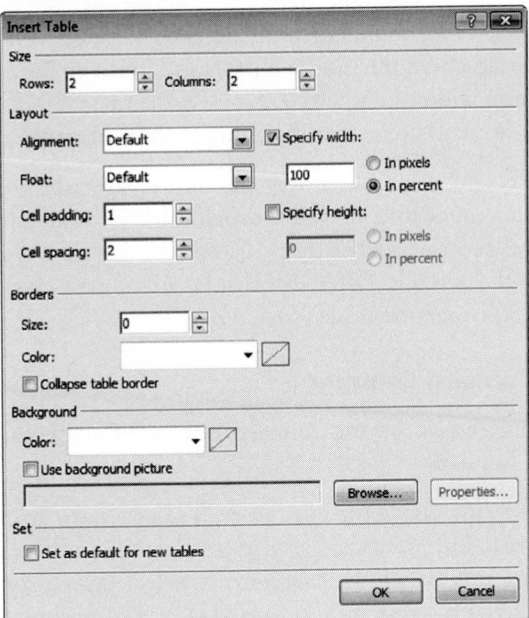

- Select the Table control from the HTML section of the *Toolbox* window. A basic 3 × 3 table is placed on the form, which you can resize by dragging the handles along its right and bottom sides. A sample is shown in Figure 11-33.

Figure 11-33 Empty HTML Table control, in Design view

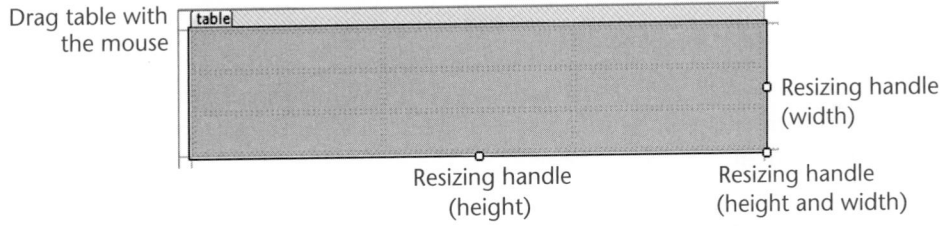

Although the table borders show in Design view, they are invisible at runtime because (by default) the border width equals zero. If you set the Border property to an integer value greater than zero, the table borders appear at runtime. An example is shown in Figure 11-34.

Figure 11-34 Table displayed at runtime with Border = *1* and text in each cell

A	B	C
D	E	F
G	H	I

Adjusting Row Heights and Column Widths

To adjust the width of a column, hover the mouse over the double bar along the column's right border. When the mouse cursor changes to a double vertical bar with arrows pointing left and right, hold down the mouse button and drag the border to its new location. As you do so, the column width (in pixels) displays inside the column. Often, the displayed number gives you a more accurate idea of the column width than the table's visual display.

To adjust the height of a row, hover the mouse over the row's lower border. When the mouse cursor changes to a double horizontal line with arrows pointing up and down, drag the mouse and the border up or down. As you do so, the column height (in pixels) displays inside the column. Often, the displayed number gives you a more accurate idea of the column height than the table's visual display.

Inserting Rows and Columns

The *Table* menu gives you tools to insert new rows and columns, relative to the currently selected cell:

- To insert a row above the current row, select *Insert* from the *Table* menu, and select *Row Above*. Or, press the Ctrl+Alt+↑ keyboard shortcut.
- To insert a row below the current row, select *Insert* from the *Table* menu, and select *Row Below*. Or, press the Ctrl+Alt+↓ keyboard shortcut.
- To insert a column to the left of the current column, select *Insert* from the *Table* menu, and select *Column to the Left*. Or, press the Ctrl+Alt+← keyboard shortcut.
- To insert a column to the right of the current column, select *Insert* from the *Table* menu, and select *Column to the Right*. Or, press the Ctrl+Alt+→ keyboard shortcut.

In each case, the inserted row or column will have the same attributes as the row or column that was selected when you issued the command. Use similar commands in the *Table* menu to delete rows and columns.

Aligning Text Inside Cells

By default, static text typed into table cells is left justified. Each cell's Align property controls the placement of text and graphics in the cell. The possible values are center, left, and right.

Merging Adjacent Cells

Sometimes it is useful to merge, or combine adjacent table cells into a single cell. The cells must be in the same column or row. To do this, drag the mouse over the cells, and select *Merge Cells* from the *Table* menu. Figure 11-35 shows several cells that have been selected by the mouse, prior to being merged.

Figure 11-35 Selecting multiple cells

Final Notes

If the height of a row seems to change when you switch from *Design* mode to Run mode, drag the bottom of the row with the mouse. This causes a specific row height to be encoded in the Style property of each cell in the row.

Start with more columns and rows than you think you need. It's much easier to delete an existing column than to insert a new one without messing up the existing table alignment.

In *Design* mode, avoid pressing [Enter] as the last action while editing a cell. Doing so inserts a paragraph tag which is difficult to remove. A paragraph tag can be removed by editing the HTML directly, and removing the <P> and </P> tags from the cells. In HTML, a table cell is defined by the <TD> and </TD> tags.

If you're an expert, go ahead and edit the HTML in your forms. However, be careful, because it's easy to introduce errors. If Visual Studio is unable to understand your HTML, it will refuse to load some or all of the controls on your Web form.

In Tutorial 11-3, you write a program that allows users to sign up for a *Kayak Tour*.

Tutorial 11-3:
Signing up for a *Kayak Tour*

In this tutorial, you will write a program that lets the user sign up for kayak tours in Key Largo, Florida. You will use DropDownList, CheckBoxList, ListBox, and Button controls. You will use an HTML table to align the text and controls. You will write short event handlers for the buttons. A sample of the program when running is shown in Figure 11-36.

Figure 11-36 Signing up for a *Kayak Tour*

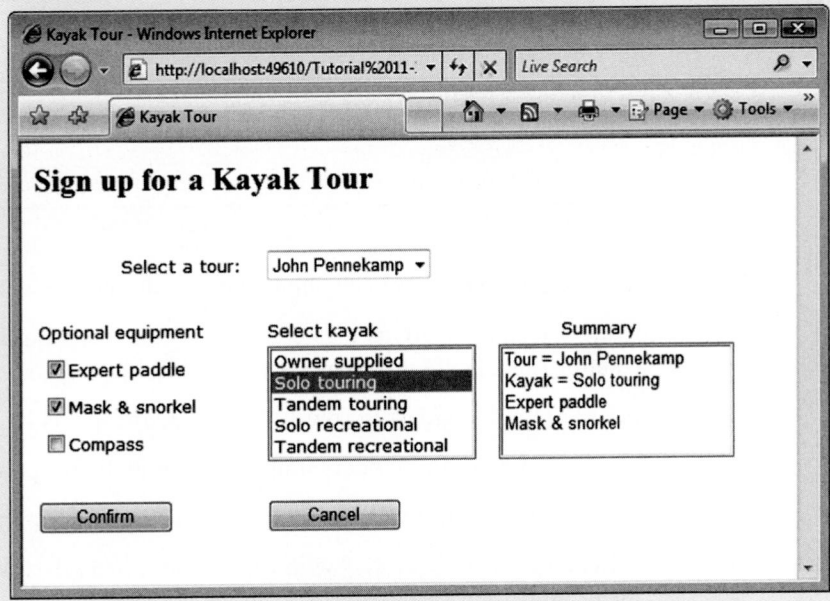

Step 1: Create a new empty Web site named *Kayak Tour*. Add a Web form named Default.aspx to the project. Click the *Design* tab at the bottom of the Default.aspx editor window to make sure you are in *Design* view of the form.

Step 2: Select *DOCUMENT* in the *Properties* window and set its Title property to *Kayak Tour*.

Step 3: Type *Sign up for a Kayak Tour* in the first line of the Web page and set its block format to *Heading 2*. Press Enter at the end of the line.

Step 4: Select *Insert Table* from the *Table* menu and set the size to 6 rows and 5 columns. Click the *OK* button to insert the table.

Step 5: Select the entire table (choose *Select/Table* from the *Table* menu) and modify its Style property. In the *Modify Style* dialog box, shown in Figure 11-37, experiment with various fonts and colors. For our sample, we select Verdana from the font-family dropdown list, and set the font-size attribute to .85 em. Click *OK* to close the *Modify Style* dialog box.

Figure 11-37 Modifying the Style properties for the HTML table

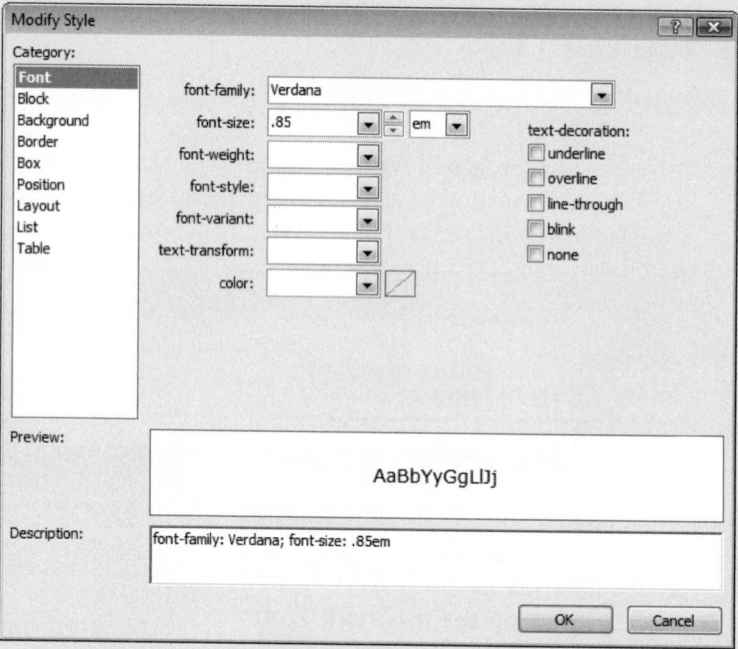

Step 6: Insert static text and set cell alignments, as shown in Figure 11-38.

Step 7: Using the same figure as a reference, insert a CheckBoxList control in row 4, column 1. Set its ID property to `chkEquipment`.

Step 8: Insert a DropDownList in row 1, column 3, and set its ID property to `ddlTour`.

Step 9: Insert a ListBox in row 4, column 3, and set its ID property to `lstKayak`.

Step 10: Insert a ListBox in row 4, column 5, and set its ID property to `lstSummary`.

Step 11: Select all the cells in Row 5 with the mouse. Then select *Modify* from the *Table* menu, and then select *Merge Cells*. This will cause all cells in row 5 to be merged into a single cell.

Figure 11-38 The Web form, in Design mode

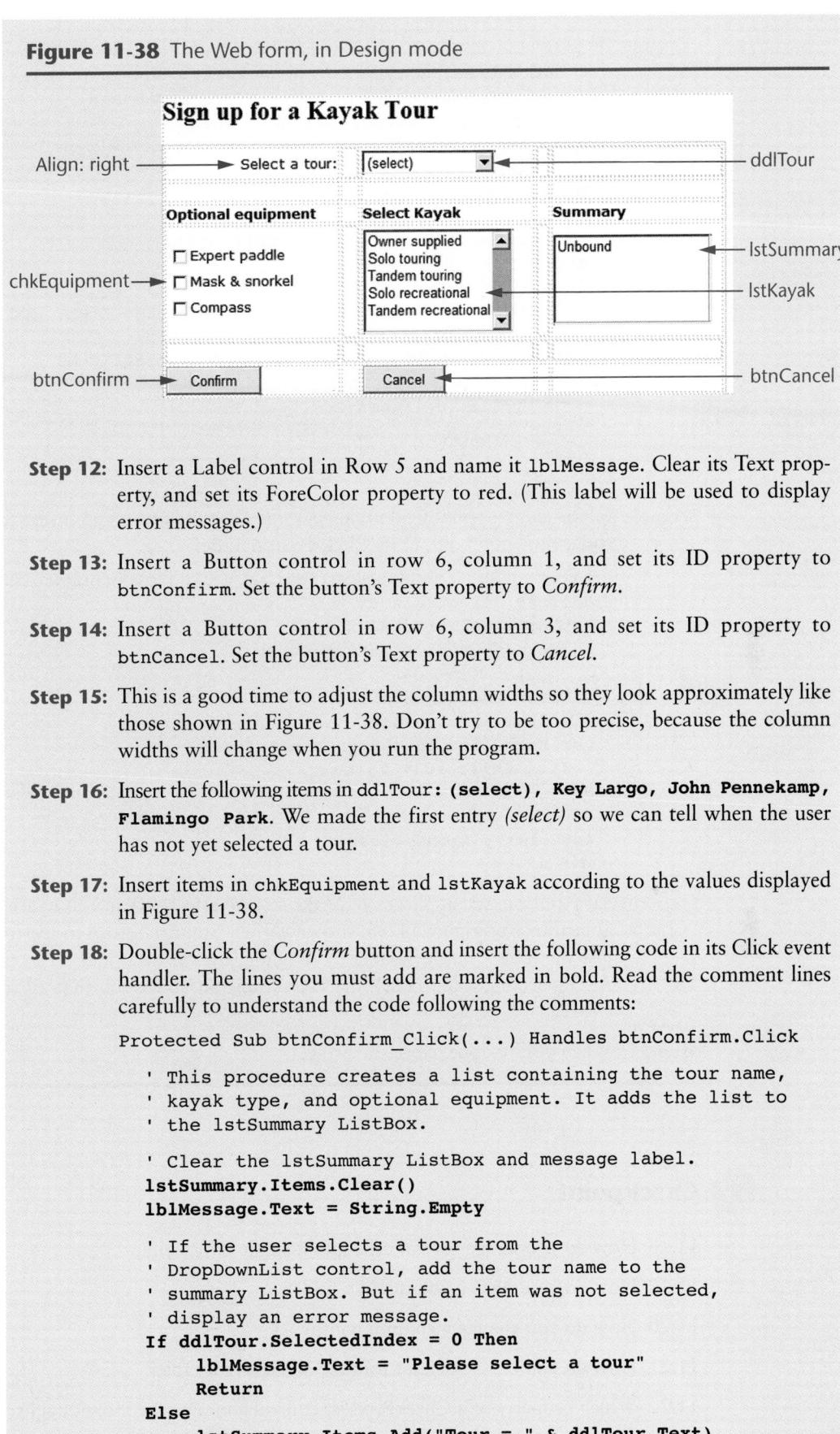

Step 12: Insert a Label control in Row 5 and name it lblMessage. Clear its Text property, and set its ForeColor property to red. (This label will be used to display error messages.)

Step 13: Insert a Button control in row 6, column 1, and set its ID property to btnConfirm. Set the button's Text property to *Confirm*.

Step 14: Insert a Button control in row 6, column 3, and set its ID property to btnCancel. Set the button's Text property to *Cancel*.

Step 15: This is a good time to adjust the column widths so they look approximately like those shown in Figure 11-38. Don't try to be too precise, because the column widths will change when you run the program.

Step 16: Insert the following items in ddlTour: **(select), Key Largo, John Pennekamp, Flamingo Park**. We made the first entry *(select)* so we can tell when the user has not yet selected a tour.

Step 17: Insert items in chkEquipment and lstKayak according to the values displayed in Figure 11-38.

Step 18: Double-click the *Confirm* button and insert the following code in its Click event handler. The lines you must add are marked in bold. Read the comment lines carefully to understand the code following the comments:

```
Protected Sub btnConfirm_Click(...) Handles btnConfirm.Click

    ' This procedure creates a list containing the tour name,
    ' kayak type, and optional equipment. It adds the list to
    ' the lstSummary ListBox.

    ' Clear the lstSummary ListBox and message label.
    lstSummary.Items.Clear()
    lblMessage.Text = String.Empty

    ' If the user selects a tour from the
    ' DropDownList control, add the tour name to the
    ' summary ListBox. But if an item was not selected,
    ' display an error message.
    If ddlTour.SelectedIndex = 0 Then
        lblMessage.Text = "Please select a tour"
        Return
    Else
        lstSummary.Items.Add("Tour = " & ddlTour.Text)
    End If
```

```
' If the user selects a kayak type from the ListBox,
' add the kayak type to the summary. But if a kayak
' was not selected, display an error message.
If lstKayak.SelectedIndex = -1 Then
    lblMessage.Text = "Please select a kayak type"
    Return
Else
    lstSummary.Items.Add("Kayak = " &
        lstKayak.SelectedItem.ToString())
End If
' Loop through the items in the Optional Equipment
' CheckBoxList control. For each selected item, add
' its description to the summary ListBox.
For Each item As ListItem In chkEquipment.Items
    If item.Selected Then
        lstSummary.Items.Add(item.Text)
    End If
Next
End Sub
```

Step 19: In the *Design* window, double-click the *Cancel* button and insert the following code, shown in bold, in its Click event handler:

```
Protected Sub btnCancel_Click(...) Handles btnCancel.Click
    ddlTour.SelectedIndex = 0
    lstKayak.SelectedIndex = -1
    lblMessage.Text = String.Empty

    ' Clear the CheckBoxList
    Dim item As ListItem
    For Each item In chkEquipment.Items
        item.Selected = False
    Next

    lstSummary.Items.Clear()
End Sub
```

Step 20: Save and run the application. Make several selections and compare your form's appearance to Figure 11-36, shown earlier. You can return to *Design* mode, adjust the table column widths by dragging the borders, and rerun the program. After selecting a tour, click the *Cancel* button and verify that all selections are cleared.

Step 21: When you're done, close the project.

Checkpoint

11.18 How do you merge several cells into a single table cell?

11.19 How do you select a column in a table?

11.20 How do you change a column width?

11.21 How do you set the default font for all cells in a table?

11.22 Which property of a CheckBoxList control contains the individual list items?

11.5 Applications with Multiple Web Pages

> **CONCEPT:** A Web application may use multiple Web pages to display data and interact with the user.

Before long, you will want to create Web applications that have multiple pages. You might collect information on one page, and display a summary on another page. Or, you might display supplementary information on a second page, which the user can select at will. First we will talk about how you add a new page to a project, and then we will show how your program can navigate from one page to another.

Adding New Web Forms to a Project

Each Web page in your application is designed using a Web form in Visual Studio. There are two ways to add a new Web form to a project:

- Select *Add New Item* from the *Website* menu
- Right-click the name of the project in the *Solution Explorer* window and select *Add New Item*

The *Add New Item* window displays a wide variety of pages, controls, and other objects that can be added to a project. In Figure 11-39, notice that the *Place code in separate file* option is selected. If you do not select it, your Visual Basic statements (such as event handlers) are embedded in the same file as the Web server controls and HTML. Some programmers prefer it that way, but we do not.

Figure 11-39 Adding a Web form to a project

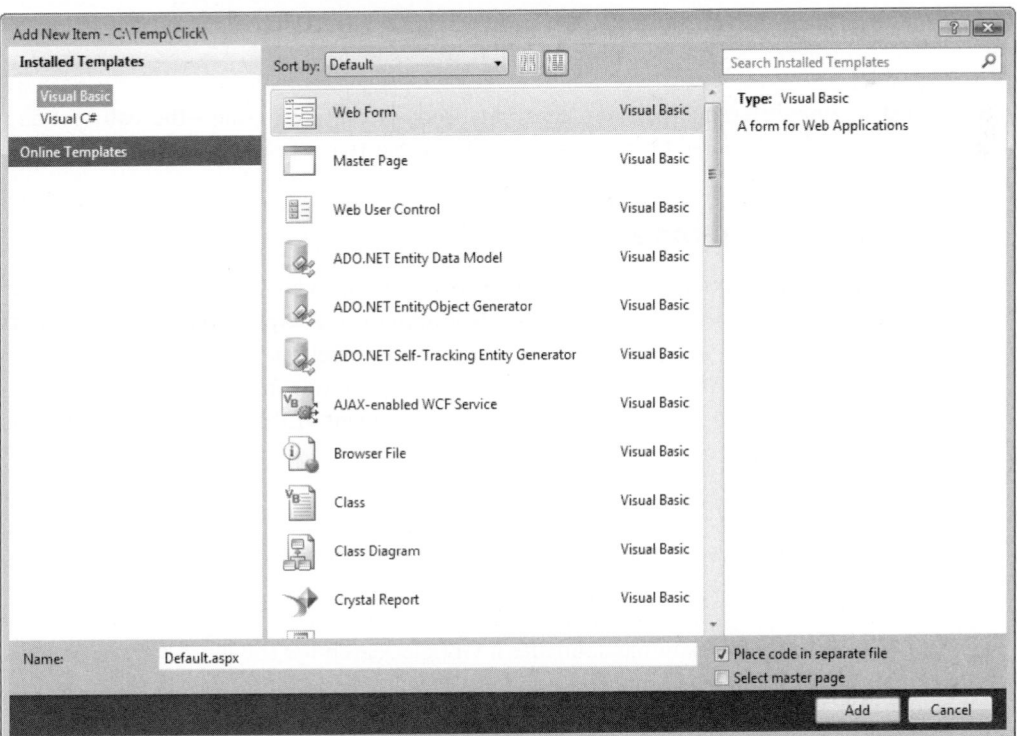

Moving between Pages

There are three common things you can do that will let a program move from a Web page we will call the *source page* to another Web page we will call the *target page*:

- Place the URL of the target page in the NavigateURL property of a HyperLink control. We discussed the HyperLink control in Section 11.3.
- Write code in the Click event handler of a Button, ImageButton, or LinkButton control. In a moment, we will show how to call the `Response.Redirect` method.
- Convert a block of static text to a hyperlink. Select a block of text with the mouse, click the *Convert to Hyperlink* button on the formatting toolbar (as shown in Figure 11-40), and enter the URL of the target page. Optionally, you can click the *Browse* button to locate a file within your project, as shown in Figure 11-41.

Figure 11-40 Converting a block of text to a hyperlink

Figure 11-41 Selecting the target page for the hyperlink

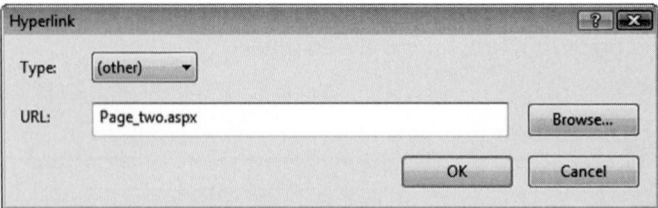

The major difference between these methods is that only one—the call to `Response.Redirect`—is initiated by program code. The other two require the user to click a hyperlink.

Calling `Response.Redirect`

In your program code, you can tell the browser to navigate to another page in your application, or any other page on the Web by calling the **Response.Redirect** method. A **Response** object automatically exists in every Web page. It is an instance of the HttpResponse class. Suppose, for example, a program must transfer to a page named *Page_two.aspx*. We would put the following statement in the Click event handler of a Button, ImageButton, or LinkButton control:

```
Response.Redirect("Page_two.aspx")
```

If the target page is on another Web server, we must supply a fully formed URL as follows:

```
Response.Redirect("http://microsoft.com")
```

The following, for example, launches a Google search for the word *horses*:

```
http://www.google.com/search?q=horses
```

In Tutorial 11-4, you add a description form to the *Kayak Tour* application.

Tutorial 11-4:

Adding a description form to the *Kayak Tour* application

In this tutorial, you will extend the *Kayak Tour* program you created in Tutorial 11–3. You will add a Web form that describes the different kayak tours and use a HyperLink control to navigate to the form.

Step 1: Open the *Kayak_Tour* project folder you created in Tutorial 11–3.

Step 2: Add a new Web form named *Tours.aspx*. Set the form's Title property to *Kayak Tour Descriptions*. Type the text shown in Figure 11-42, shortening it if necessary. We used a Verdana font.

Step 3: In the *Default.aspx* form, add a HyperLink control to the cell in row 1, column 5. Set its Text property to *Tour descriptions*. Set its NavigateURL property to *Tours.aspx*. Set its Target property to *_blank*, which will cause the new form to be displayed in a separate browser window.

Figure 11-42 The *Kayak Tour* description Web form

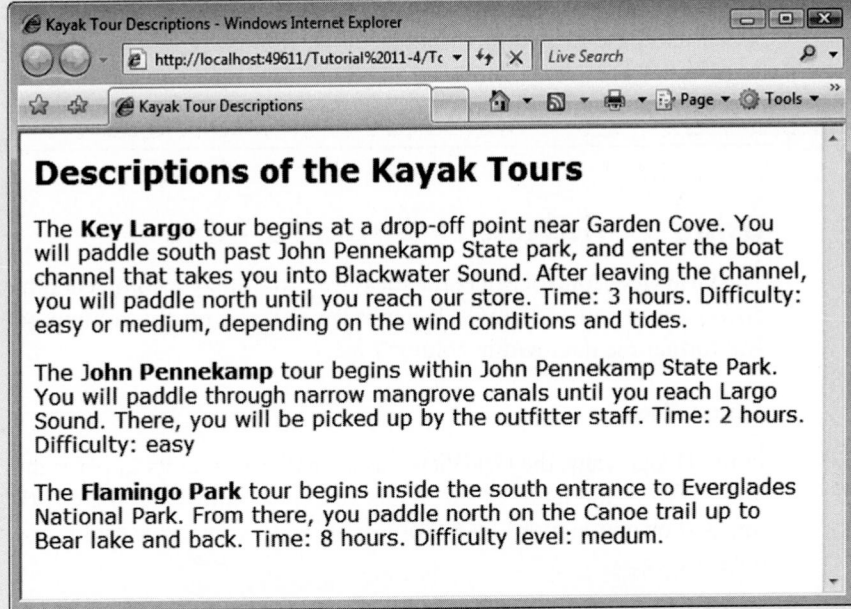

Step 4: Save and run the program. Click the *Tour Descriptions* link, and verify that the *Kayak Tour Descriptions* window opens in a separate browser window. (The user can glance at the descriptions while filling in the *Kayak Tour* form.)

Step 5: Close both browser windows to end the application.

Checkpoint

11.23 Which menu command adds a new Web form to a project?

11.24 How can a HyperLink control be used to navigate between Web pages?

11.25 How do you convert a block of static text to a hyperlink?

11.26 Which method in the Response object navigates to a different Web page?

11.6 Using Databases

CONCEPT: ASP.NET provides several Web controls for displaying and updating a database from a Web application.

You can display and update the contents of database tables very easily in ASP.NET applications. First, we will show how to use the GridView control to display database tables. Then we will show how to use the DetailsView control to display a single row at a time, and how to add a new row to a database table.

Web applications use a specialized type of ASP.NET control for accessing databases, generally called a *DataSource control*. Actually, there are two specific controls, depending on which type of database you're using. One control is named *AccessDataSource*, for MS Access databases. The other is named *SqlDataSource*, for SQL Server databases. We will use the latter. One important characteristic of the DataSource controls is that they directly update the database, with no separate Update method call required.

TIP: In all of our database examples, we will assume that you are connecting to SQL Server database files, rather than a full version of SQL Server. If your college lab uses a database server, please contact your classroom instructor or network administrator for database connection information.

Using a GridView to Display a Table

The **GridView control** offers the ideal way to display a complete table. Similar to the Windows control named DataGridView, it lets you sort on any column, select the column order, and format the data within columns.

Smart Tags

In the Design view, the GridView has a small arrow in its upper right corner called a *smart tag*, as shown in Figure 11-43. When you click on this tag, the *GridView Tasks* menu pops up, as shown in Figure 11-44. You can use it to set various grid properties and connect to a data source.

Figure 11-43 GridView control with smart tag (Design view)

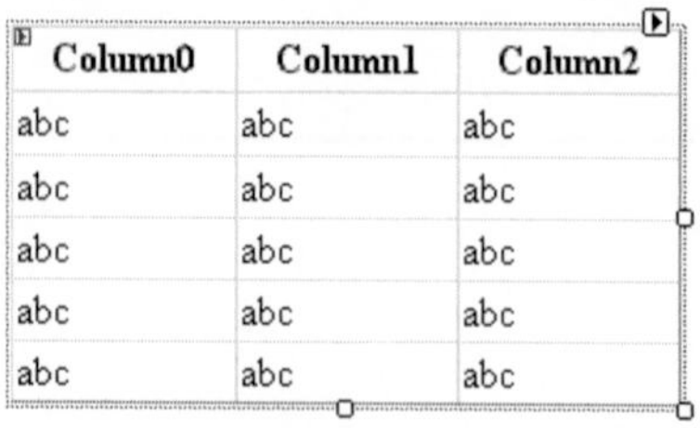

Figure 11-44 The smart tag activates the *GridView Tasks* menu

Column0	Column1	Column2
abc	abc	abc
abc	abc	abc
abc	abc	abc
abc	abc	abc
abc	abc	abc

Column0	Column1	Column2	GridView Tasks
abc	abc	abc	Auto Format...
abc	abc	abc	Choose Data Source: (None)
abc	abc	abc	Edit Columns...
abc	abc	abc	Add New Column...
abc	abc	abc	Edit Templates

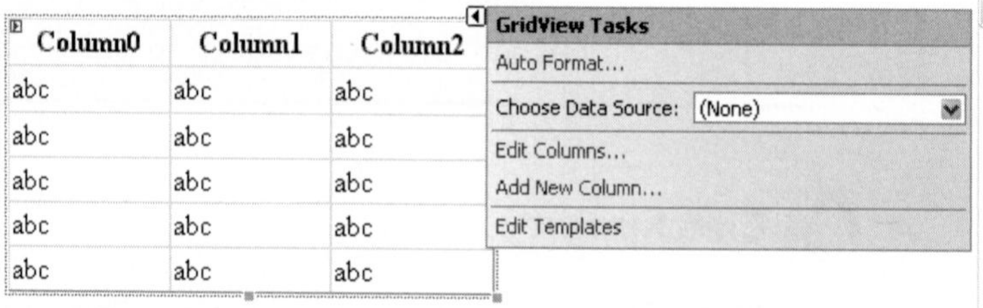

Setting Up a Connection

The general steps required to connect your Web form to a database follow. Don't try to do them yet, because we need to provide a few more details during the upcoming tutorial.

1. Inside the *Solution Explorer* window, add an *App_Data* folder to your project, and then in Windows Explorer, copy the database file to the *App_Data* folder.
2. Add a GridView control to the form, click its smart tag, and select <*New data source . . .*> from the *Choose Data Source* DropDown list.
3. Select the Data Source type, as shown in Figure 11-45.

Figure 11-45 Choosing a *Data Source Type*

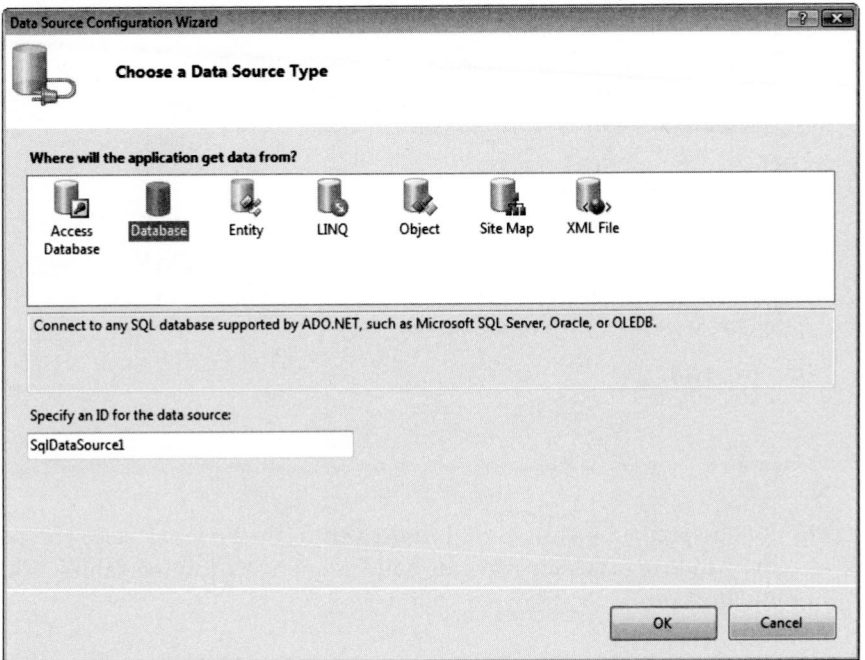

4. Select the database name within the *App_Data* folder, as shown in Figure 11-46.

Figure 11-46 Identifying the *Database* file

5. Configure the SELECT statement for the database query, as shown in Figure 11-47. If your query involves more than one table, select the option that says *Specify a custom SQL statement or stored procedure* and click the *Next* button.

Figure 11-47 Configuring the SELECT statement

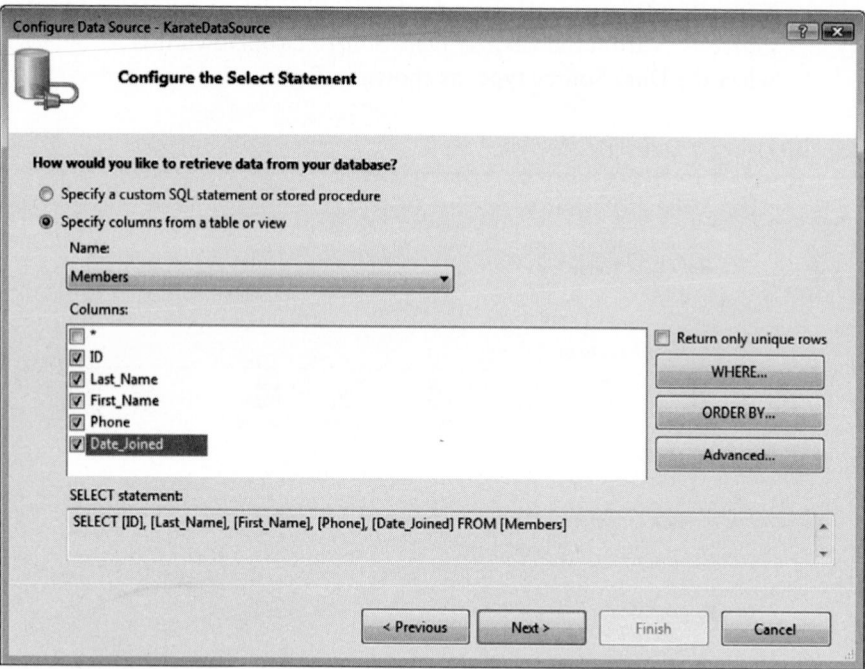

6. If you specified a custom SQL statement in the previous step, Figure 11-48 shows the window in which you can build a query by joining tables. Click the *Query Builder* button.

Figure 11-48 Building a custom SQL statement

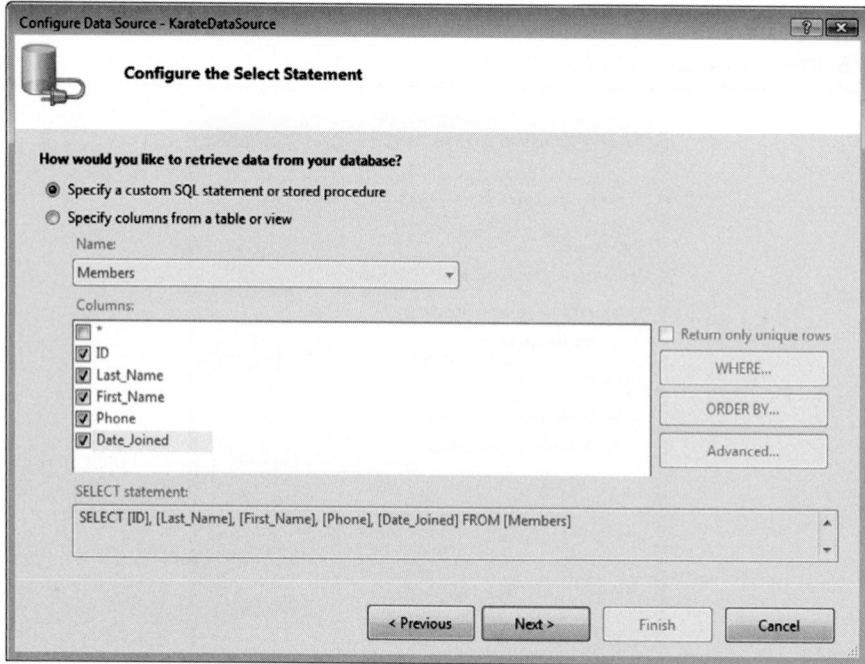

When you're finished, an **SqlDataSource Control** is placed on your Web form.

In Tutorial 11-5, you display the *Karate Members* table in a GridView.

Tutorial 11-5:
Displaying the *Karate Members* table in a GridView

In this tutorial, you will create a connection to the *Karate* database, and display the *Members* table in a GridView control. You will perform some basic configuration of the grid's appearance.

Step 1: Create a new emtpy Web site named *MemberGrid*. Add a new Web form named Default.aspx to the project.

Step 2: Right-click the project name in the *Solution Explorer* window, then click *New Folder* on the pop-up menu. Name the folder *App_Data*.

Step 3: Open a *Windows Explorer* window and copy the *Karate.mdf* file from the student sample programs folder named *Chap11* to your project's *App_Data* folder.

Step 4: In the *Solution Explorer* window, right-click the project name and select *Refresh Folder*. Then expand the entry under *App_Data* and look for the *Karate.mdf* filename, as shown in Figure 11-49.

Figure 11-49 Locating the *Karate.mdf* file under *App_Data* in the *Solution Explorer* window

Step 5: In the *Design* view window of the Default.aspx form, select *DOCUMENT* in the *Properties* window and set its Title property to *Karate Members*.

Step 6: On the first line of the Web page (in *Design* view) type **Members Table, Karate Database**. Set the block style to *Heading 2*, and press `Enter` at the end of the line.

Step 7: Place a GridView control on the form. You can find it in the *Data* section of the *Toolbox* window. Drag its right handle until its Width property equals about 640 pixels. Its Height property should be blank.

Step 8: Click the grid's smart tag, opening the *GridView Tasks* dialog box. Select *<New data source . . .>* from the *Choose Data Source* DropDown list.

Step 9: In the *Data Source Configuration Wizard*, select *Database*, change the ID value to *KarateDataSource*, and click the *OK* button.

Step 10: The next step in the wizard is named *Choose Your Data Connection*. Click the *New Connection* button. When the *Add Connection* window appears, as shown in Figure 11-50, make sure the *Data Source* field is set to *Microsoft SQL Server Database File (SqlClient)*. If some other value appears in the field, change it.

Figure 11-50 Select the *Karate.mdf* database file

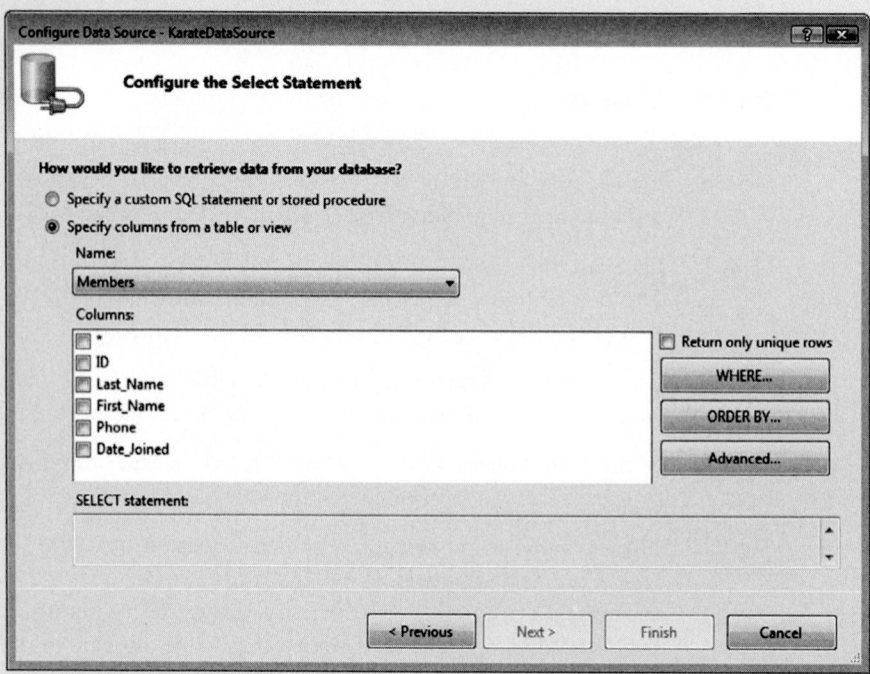

Step 11: For the Database file name entry, click the *Browse* button, select your project's *App_Data* folder, select *Karate.mdf*, and click the *Open* button. Then, click the *OK* button to close the *Add Connection* dialog. When you return to the window that reads *Choose Your Data Connection,* click the *Next* button. When a window appears that reads *Save the Application Connection String to the Application Configuration File,* click the *Next* button.

Step 12: You will be asked to configure the SELECT statement that pulls rows and columns from the database. From the *Name* DropDown list, select the *Members* table, as shown in Figure 11-51.

Figure 11-51 Configuring the SELECT statement

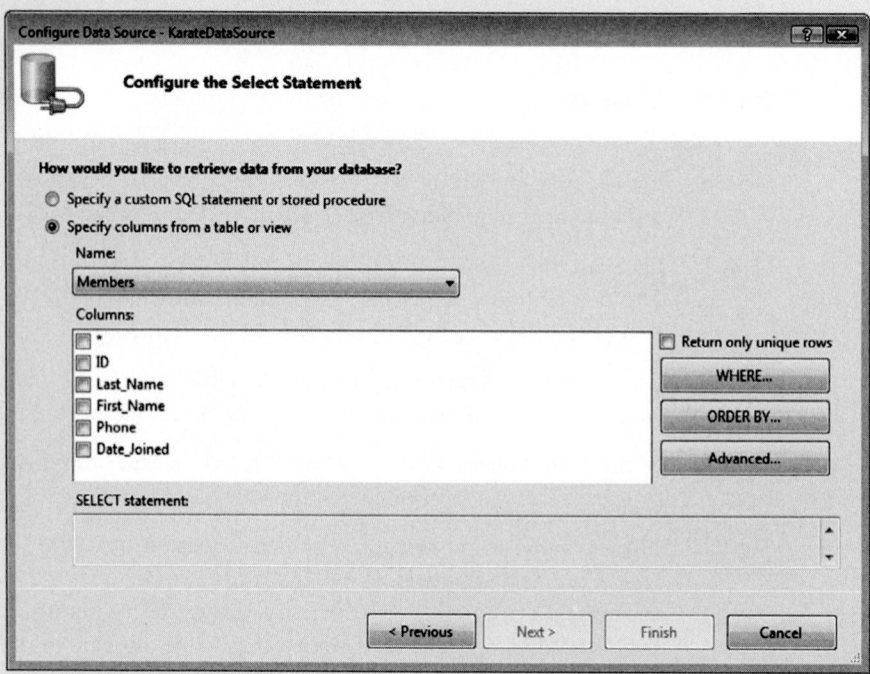

Step 13: Place check marks next to the following columns, in order: *ID*, *Last_Name*, *First_Name*, *Phone*, and *Date_Joined*.

Step 14: Click the *ORDER BY . . .* button. In the dialog box shown in Figure 11-52, sort by the *Last_Name* column. Click *OK* to close the dialog box.

Step 15: Returning to the *Configure the Select Statement* dialog box, click the *Next* button, which takes you to the *Test Query* dialog box. Click the *Test Query* button. If the displayed columns match those shown in Figure 11-53, click the *Finish* button to close the window.

Figure 11-52 Adding the ORDER BY clause

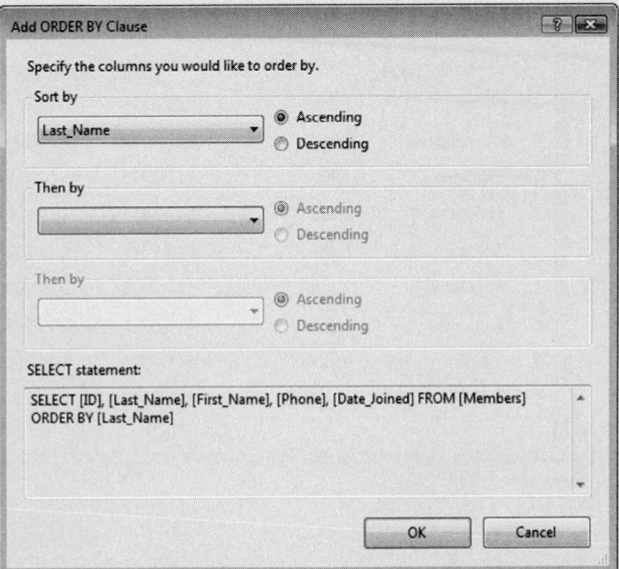

Figure 11-53 Testing the SELECT query

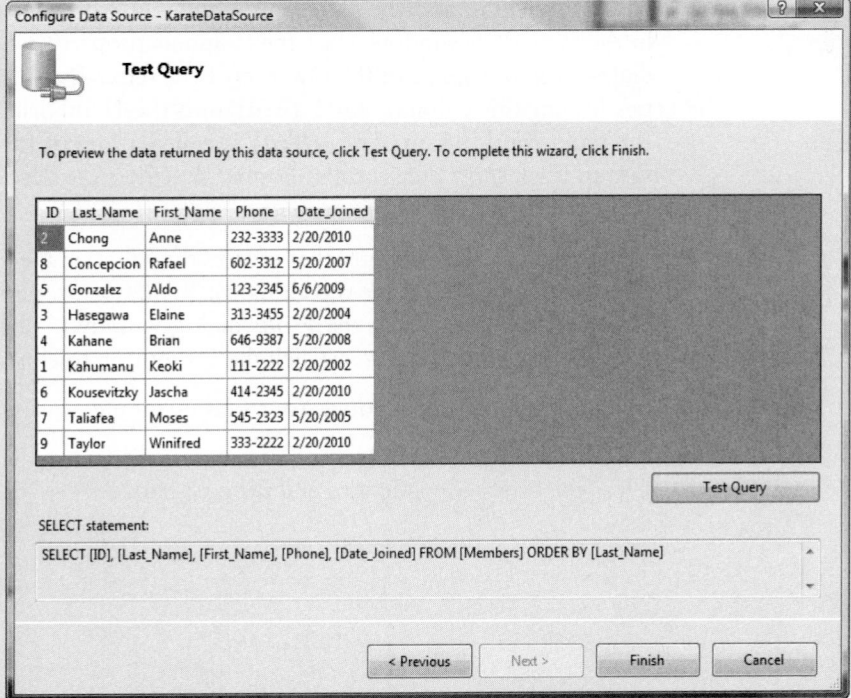

Step 16: Click the *GridView*'s smart tag again and check the *Enable Sorting* check box.

Step 17: Save and run the Web application. You should see the display shown in Figure 11-54, although some of the data in the rows may be different.

Figure 11-54 Running the Web application

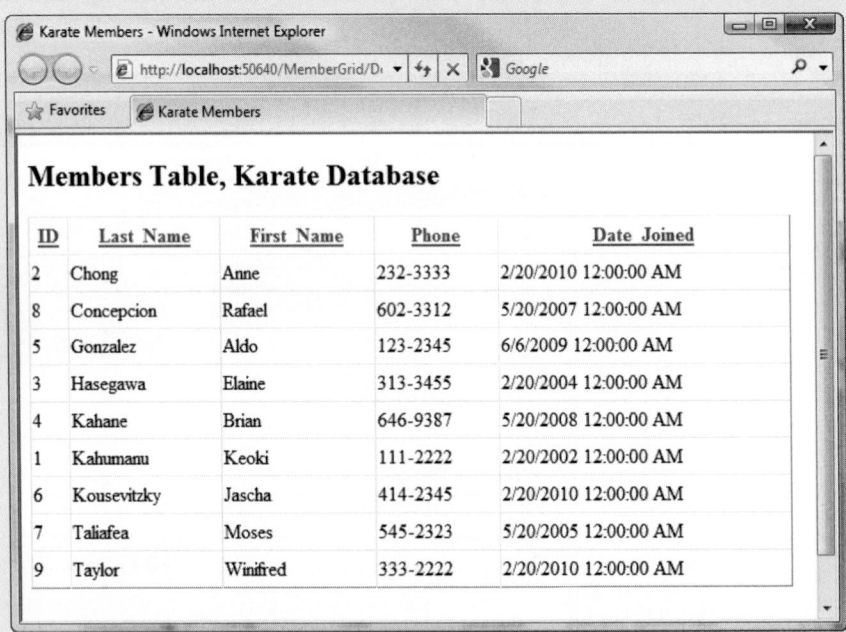

Step 18: Experiment with sorting columns by clicking each of the column headers. If you click the same column twice in a row, it reverses the sort order. Close the browser to end the application.

Step 19: Next, you will format the *Date_Joined* column. Select the grid with the mouse. In the *Properties* window, click the Columns property, which causes the *Fields* dialog box to display. In the lower left box, select *Date_Joined*. In the properties list for this column, enter `{0:d}` into the DataFormatString property, as shown in Figure 11-55. The `{0:d}` is called a *format specifier*. In this case, it says to use a *short date* format. Format specifiers are described in MSDN Help under the topic *Formatting overview*.

Step 20: Next, you will set a property that centers the values in the *Date_Joined* column. Expand the entries under the column's ItemStyle property (last in the list of *BoundField* properties in the *Fields* dialog window). Change the Horizontal-Align subproperty to *Center*. Click the *OK* button to close the dialog box.

Step 21: Save and run the application. Your output should be similar to that shown in Figure 11-56.

Step 22: Close the browser window to end the program.

Figure 11-55 Formatting the *Date_Joined* column

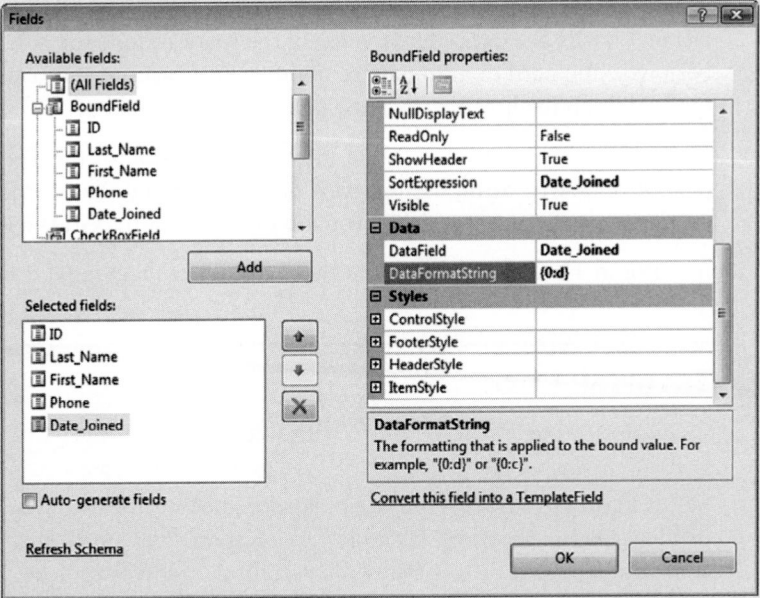

Figure 11-56 After formatting the *Date_Joined* column

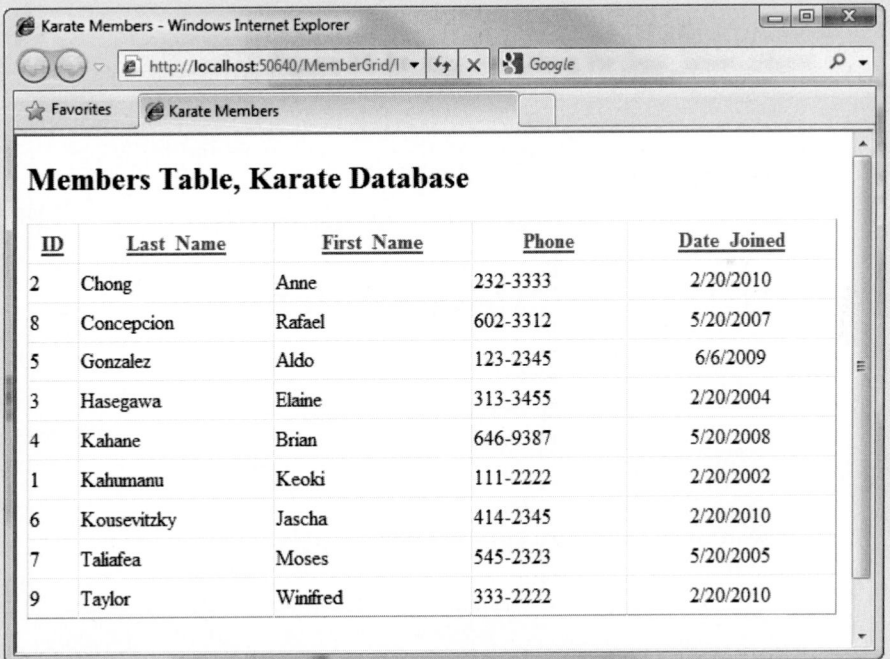

In addition to the formats you modified just now, there are many detailed formatting changes you can make to a GridView control.

Using a DetailsView Control to Modify Table Rows

The **DetailsView control** makes it easy to view, edit, delete, or add rows to a database table. To use it, you must create a data source, as you did in Tutorial 11–5. When you connect the DetailsView to the data source, most of the work is done for you. Microsoft engineers have been working hard to automate as many menial tasks as they can, and database table editing is high on the list of tasks most programmers would prefer *not* to do repeatedly.

The DetailsView control is found in the Data section of the *Toolbox* window. When you place it on a Web form, use its smart tag (upper right-hand corner) to add a database connection and set various options. You did the same for the GridView control in Tutorial 11–5.

In Tutorial 11-6, you will update the *Karate Members* table using a DetailsView control.

Tutorial 11-6:
Updating the *Karate Members* table

In this tutorial, you will write an application that lets the user view, edit, insert, and delete individual rows in the *Members* table in the *Karate* database. You will create an SqlDataSource control and hook it up to a DetailsView control. You will not have to write any program code.

Figure 11-57 shows the finished program right after it starts, with rows sorted by last name. The underlined words *Edit*, *Delete*, and *New* are called *link buttons* (LinkButton controls). They look like HTML links, but function like ordinary button controls.

Figure 11-57 Adding a member at runtime

In Figure 11-58, the user has clicked the *New* button and begun to enter data for a new member. The user will soon click the *Insert (link)* button, which will save the new row in the database.

Figure 11-59 shows the same form after the user has clicked the *Insert* button. The new member (Eric Baker) appears in the detail fields.

If the user tries to add a row having an ID number equal to an existing ID in the table, an error page displays, as shown in Figure 11-60. The user can click the browser's *Back* button, enter a different ID, and try again.

Figure 11-58 About to insert a new member

Figure 11-59 After clicking the *Insert* button

Figure 11-60 Error displayed when the user tries to add a row with a duplicate ID

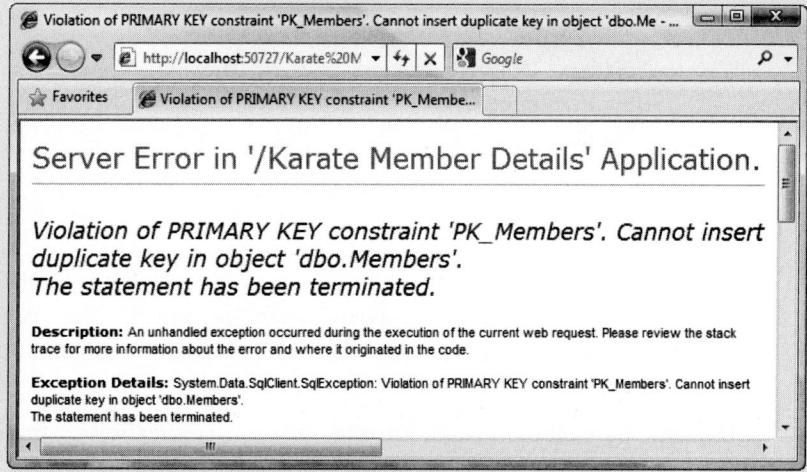

When the user clicks the *Edit* button, he or she can modify any of the member fields, as shown in Figure 11-61. When the user clicks the *Update* button, changes to the record are saved in the database.

Figure 11-61 After clicking the *Edit* button

Now let's build the program.

Step 1: Create a new empty Web site named *Karate Member Details*. Add the following items to the project:
- a Web form named *Default.aspx*
- a folder named *App_Data*

Step 2: Copy the *Karate.mdf* database file into your project's *App_Data* folder.

Step 3: Right-click the project name in the *Solution Explorer* window and select *Refresh Folder*. Verify that *Karate.mdf* appears under the *App_Data* entry.

Step 4: Switch to the Design view of Default.aspx, select *DOCUMENT* in the *Properties* window, and set its Title property to *Members Table Details*.

Step 5: On the first line of the page, insert **Members Table Details**, and give it a *Heading 2* block style. Then, press Enter to go to the next line.

Step 6: Add a DetailsView control to the page, and set its ID property to **dvwAddMember**. Widen it to about 300 pixels. Make sure its Height property is blank.

Step 7: Save the project. Figure 11-62 shows your work so far.

Next, you will add a data source to the project.

Step 8: Select the smart tag in the upper right corner of *dvwAddMember*. From the *Choose Data Source* DropDown list, select *<New data source . . .>*. Select *Database*, and name the data source **MembersDataSource**, as shown in Figure 11-63. Click the *OK* button to continue.

Step 9: As in the previous tutorial, create a connection to the *Karate.mdf* file in the project's *App_Data* folder.

Figure 11-62 Designing the *Karate Member Details* form

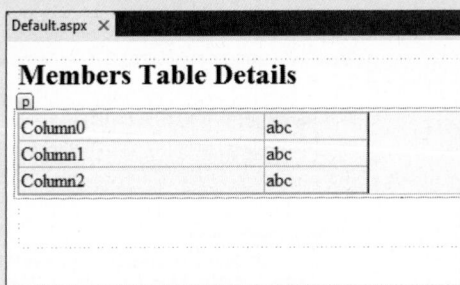

Figure 11-63 Creating the data source

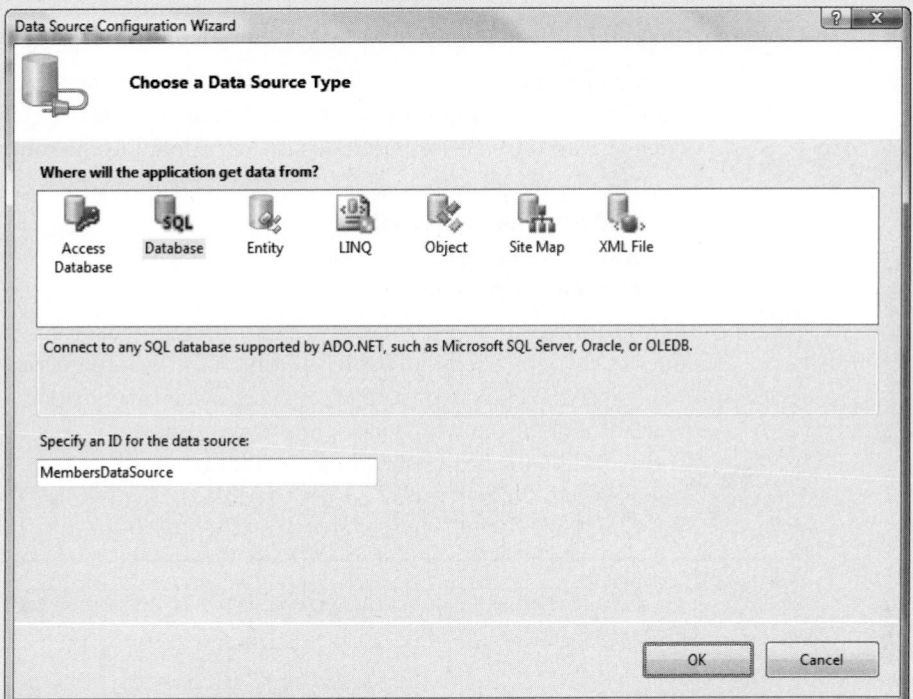

Step 10: When the window entitled *Save the Connection String to the Application Configuration File* appears, click the *Next* button.

Step 11: In the next window, select all columns in the *Members* table, and order the rows by *Last_Name* in ascending order. When you return to the window entitled *Configure the Select Statement*, click the *Advanced* button.

Step 12: In the *Advanced SQL Generation Options* dialog box, select the *Generate INSERT, UPDATE, and DELETE statements* option, as shown in Figure 11-64. Click the *OK* button, and then click the *Next* button.

Step 13: Click the *Finish* button to close the *Configure Data Source* window. Back in the *Smart Tag* menu for `dvwAddMember`, select the check boxes to enable *Inserting*, *Editing*, and *Deleting*.

Figure 11-64 Selecting *Advanced SQL Generation Options*

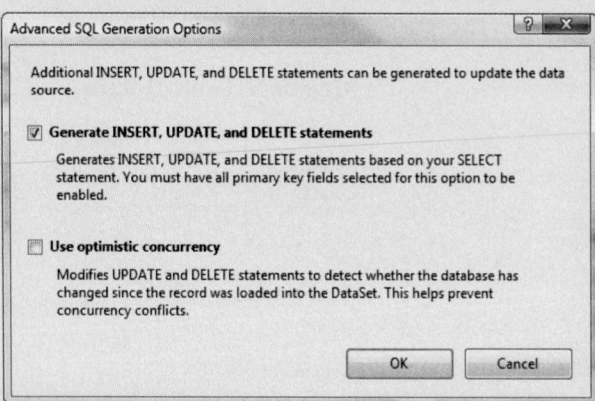

Step 14: Save and run the application. Sample output is shown in Figure 11-65.

Let's pause and reflect on what you have accomplished so far in this tutorial. You have created a connection to the Members database table, and you have created a useful Web form that lets the user do all of the following:

1. Display the Members table
2. Add new rows to the table
3. Modify (Edit) existing rows
4. Delete rows from the table

Behind this useful control, as you can imagine, are the same types of SQL queries that you used in Chapter 10. In fact, the SQL queries are embedded directly into the HTML of your web page. When this tutorial is over, we will take a closer look at the way queries are stored. But, now, let's test the DetailsView control while the browser window is still open.

Figure 11-65 Running the *Karate Member Details* application for the first time

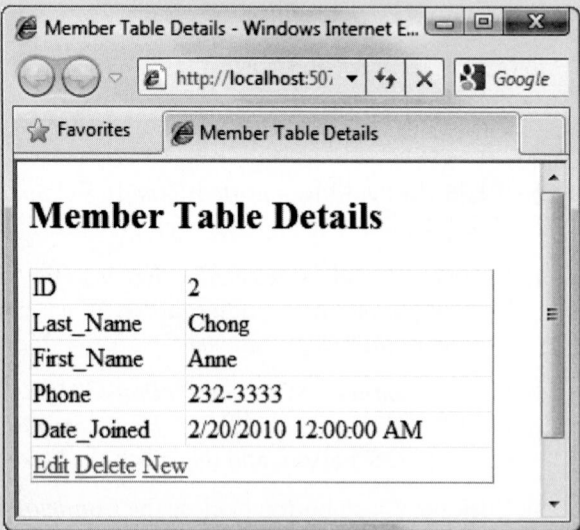

Step 15: Click the *Edit* button, change the values of one of the fields, and click the *Update* button. You should notice that the field value has been changed.

Step 16: Close the browser window and return to Design mode. Let's improve the appearance of the DetailView just a bit. Select it, and set its BorderWidth property

Figure 11-66 *Fields* dialog box for the DetailsView control

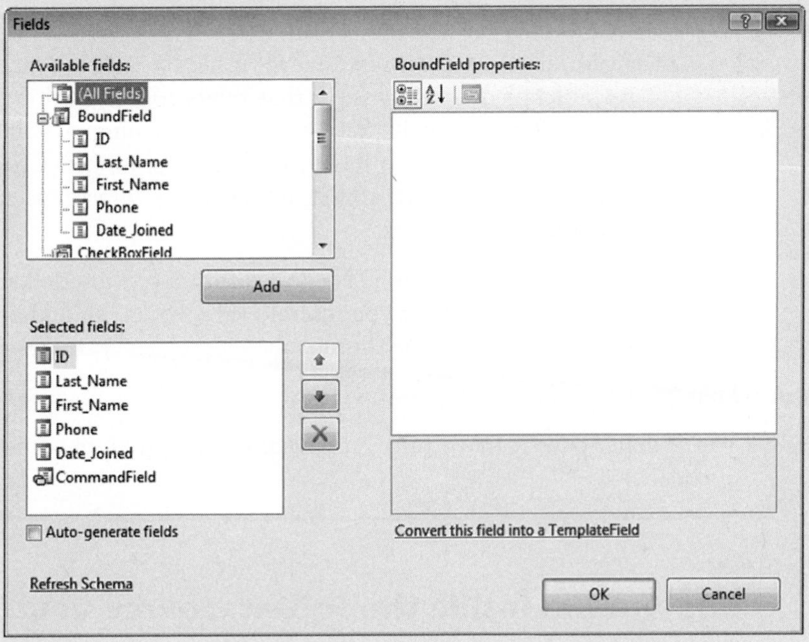

to *0px* (zero pixels wide). Next, select its Fields property, causing the *Fields* dialog box to display (see Figure 11-66).

Step 17: In the *Fields* dialog box, select the *Date_Joined* field in the lower left list box. Then in the right-hand list box, set its DataFormatString property to *{0:d}*. You may recall this is the same short date format specifier we used in the GridView control.

Step 18: Next, you will change the field order slightly. Select the *First_Name* field in the lower left list box, and use the arrow on the right side of the box to move the *First_Name* field above the *Last_Name* field.

Step 19: Click *OK* to close the *Fields* dialog box. Next, find the GridLines property and set it equal to None.

Step 20: Save and run the application. It should now appear as shown in Figure 11-67.

Figure 11-67 After modifying the field display in the DetailsView control

Step 21: Click the *New* button, and notice that all the text boxes become empty. Enter the following data: **14, Eric, Baker, 654–3210, 3/1/2010.** Then click the *Insert* button. The display should now show the record you inserted.

Step 22: Again, try to insert a new record, using the same ID number (14). You should see a detailed error message that refers to a Violation of a primary key constraint. Because the ID field values must be unique, you cannot add two members to the table who have the same ID number. Click the browser's *Back* button, change the ID to **15**, and click the *Insert* button. This time, the insert operation should work.

Step 23: Click the *Delete* button. The last member you inserted should disappear. Then, the previous member you inserted (Eric Baker) should display. Click the Delete button again to delete this member.

Step 24: Close the Web browser window.

You're done. You created a fully functional update program without writing a single line of code.

SQL Queries Inside the SqlDataSource Control

In Tutorial 11–6, you created a simple web application that used the SqlDataSource control to populate a DetailsView control. The user was able to display, modify, insert, and delete rows from the Karate Members table. You might be interested to see how a SqlDataSource is represented in your web form's HTML code. You can click the *Source* tab for the Default.aspx page in the *Karate Member Details* application and then look for the SqlDataSource control named *MembersDataSource*. This is the beginning of the code that defines it:

```
<asp:SqlDataSource ID="MembersDataSource" runat="server"
```

The *asp:SqlDataSource* tag identifies the type of control and assigns it an ID (*MembersDataSource*). The *runat* property indicates that this control executes on the Web server. Next, you will see the name of the connection string that ties this control to the database:

```
ConnectionString="<%$ ConnectionStrings:karateConnectionString %>"
```

Next, you will find the *DeleteCommand* property, which contains an SQL query that deletes rows from the Members table. It uses a query parameter (named *@ID*) to identify exactly which member is to be deleted:

```
DeleteCommand="DELETE FROM [Members] WHERE [ID] = @ID"
```

Next is the *InsertCommand* property, which contains the query used to insert new rows into the Members table. It has a parameter for each column in the table:

```
InsertCommand="INSERT INTO [Members] ([ID], [Last_Name],
[First_Name], [Phone], [Date_Joined]) VALUES (@ID, @Last_Name,
@First_Name, @Phone, @Date_Joined)"
```

Although we do not show them here, the control also contains *SelectCommand* and *UpdateCommand* properties, with their respective queries. With practice, you can edit the properties of ASP.NET controls directly in Source mode. Expert web programmers do just that, because they feel that HTML editing gives them more precise control over a Web form than they could get by using Visual Studio's *Design* mode.

Checkpoint

11.27 Which Web control displays database table rows and columns in a grid-like format?

11.28 In a Web form, what type of object provides a connection to an SQL Server database?

11.29 Which property in a DetailsView control permits you to modify the formatting of a column containing a date?

11.30 Which property in a DetailsView control permits you to modify the order of the columns?

11.31 Which Web control lets you display individual fields in each row from a database, using text boxes?

Summary

11.1 Programming for the Web

- Web applications are designed around a client-server model: an entity called a server produces data consumed by another entity called a client. Web applications must be run using a Web server.
- When the Web first became popular, HTML was the only available encoding method for creating Web pages with text, graphics buttons, and input forms.
- Active Server Pages (ASP) was the first server-side Web programming technology introduced by Microsoft. ASP.NET, the current generation, is called a platform because it provides development tools, code libraries, and visual controls for browser-based applications.
- Web applications written for ASP.NET consist of content, in the form of Web forms, HTML code, Web forms controls, images, and other multimedia; program logic, in compiled Visual Basic (or C#) code; and configuration information.
- Visual Studio simplifies the way Web applications are developed.
- A URL (Uniform Resource Locator) provides a universal way of addressing objects and pages on a network.
- Web applications written in ASP.NET use special Web pages called Web forms. A Web form, which can be identified by its *.aspx* file name extension, contains text, HTML tags, HTML controls (such as buttons and text boxes), and Web server controls.

11.2 Creating ASP.NET Applications

- Using Visual Studio, you can create a Web site in the local File System, Local or remote Web server, or remote FTP site.
- A File System Web site runs directly under the ASP.NET development server supplied with Visual Studio. An HTTP Web site runs under a Windows operating system utility named Internet Information Services (IIS). An FTP Web site references an existing ASP.NET Web site located on a remote computer (network or Web).
- ASP.NET applications are also known as Web sites or Web applications.
- You can start a program in *Debug* mode by selecting *Start Debugging* from the *Debug* menu.

11.3 Web Server Controls

- Web server controls make ASP.NET applications dynamic and interactive. The controls are far more powerful than standard HTML controls because each is defined by a class with a rich set of properties, methods, and events.
- The ID property of Web controls is the counterpart to the Name property of Windows controls. Web controls lose their runtime properties when the user moves away from the current page.
- The Label Web control is almost identical to the Label control on Windows forms. Use a Label only if its contents will change at runtime, or if you plan to change its Visible property.
- The TextBox Web control is similar in many ways to the TextBox control for Windows forms. The Text property holds text input by the user.
- The CheckBox control is almost identical to the CheckBox in Windows forms. Use the Text property to set the visible text and evaluate the Checked property at runtime.
- Events are fired in a different sequence in Web forms than they are in Windows forms. In a Web form, the Page_Load event occurs when the page is first loaded into the user's browser, and again every time the page is posted back to the server.
- When a control's AutoPostBack property equals *True*, clicking on the control causes the form to be posted back to the server.

11.4 Designing Web Forms

- An HTML table is an essential tool for designing the layout of Web forms. Use it to align text, graphics, and controls in rows and columns.
- To insert a table when viewing a form in Design view, select *Insert Table* from the *Table* menu or double-click the HTML Table control from the Toolbox window.
- To adjust the width of a column, hover the mouse over the double bar along the column's right-hand border. To adjust the height of a row, hover the mouse over the row's lower border. After finding the border in this way, hold down the left mouse button and drag the border to change the column or row size.

11.5 Applications with Multiple Web Pages

- Most Web applications have multiple pages. You might collect information on one page, and display a summary on another page. Or, you might display supplementary information on a second page.
- There are two ways to add a new Web page to a project: select *Add New Item* from the *Web site* menu, or right-click in the *Solution Explorer* window and select *Add New Item*.
- To permit your application to navigate from one Web page to another, you can use a HyperLink control, code a call to `Response.Redirect`, or convert a block of static text to a hyperlink.

11.6 Using Databases

- Web applications use a different model for accessing databases than Windows Forms applications. Rather than using a dataset, Web applications often use a DataSource Web server control.
- The GridView control, similar to the Windows control named DataGridView, lets you sort on any column, select the column order, and format the data within columns.
- The DetailsView, like the GridView, connects to a DataSource Web server control.
- Tutorial 11–6 shows how to view, edit, insert, and delete individual rows in the *Members* table of the *Karate* database.

Key Terms

Active Server Pages (ASP)
ASP.NET
ASP.NET Development Server
ASP.NET Server controls
AutoPostBack property
button control
Cascading Style Sheet (CSS)
CheckBox control
CheckBoxList control
client-server model
code-behind file
DataSource control
DetailsView control
domain name
DropDownList control
File System Web site
FTP Site
GridView control

HTML control
HTML Designer
HTML table
HTML tag
HTTP Web site
HyperLink control
HyperText Markup Language (HTML)
ImageButton control
Internet Information Services (IIS)
Label control
LinkButton control
ListBox control
platform
postback
program logic
protocol

RadioButton controls
RadioButtonList control
`Response` object
`Response.Redirect` method
server
static text
TextBox Web control

Uniform Resource Locator (URL)
Web application
Web form
Web page
Web server
Web server control

Review Questions and Exercises

Fill-in-the-Blank

1. Conventional Web pages contain tags based on the _____ Markup Language.

2. ASP stands for Active _____ Pages.

3. URL stands for Uniform _____ Locator.

4. Web server controls are also known as _____ server controls.

5. A powerful Web server used by Web developers is named Internet _____ Services (IIS).

6. The _____ control displays a sequence of check boxes.

7. The _____ control displays a hyperlink and has a property named NavigateURL.

8. When creating a new Web site, the choices of location type are _____, HTTP, and FTP.

9. Debugging configuration information is stored in a file named _____.

10. The _____ property of a Label control can be used to make its border solid, dotted, or dashed.

11. The _____ property of a TextBox control determines whether the box will permit multiple lines of input.

12. When a postback occurs on a Web page, the first event handler to execute is _____.

13. The _____ property of an ImageButton control holds the name of the image file.

Multiple Choice

1. Which of the following is the name of the grid-like control that displays database tables?
   a. DataGrid
   b. DataGridView
   c. GridView
   d. TableGrid

2. Which of the following is the standard file name extension for Web forms?
   a. *.aspx*
   b. *.asp*
   c. *.htm*
   d. *.html*

3. Which of the following is not a control category in the *Toolbox* window?

   a. Navigation
   b. Login
   c. WebParts
   d. FileServer

4. Which of the following Web site types requires running Internet Information Services on the local computer?

   a. File system
   b. Local IIS
   c. FTP
   d. Remote Web

5. Which of the following is not a Web server control described in this chapter?

   a. NavigateButton
   b. RadioButtonList
   c. CheckBoxList
   d. LinkButton

6. Which of the following cannot be assigned to the TextMode property of a TextBox control?

   a. MultiLine
   b. Hidden
   c. Password
   d. SingleLine

7. Which of the following properties is (are) found in both the RadioButtonList and ListBox controls?

   a. SelectedIndex
   b. ImageIndex
   c. RepeatDirection
   d. Items
   e. Two of the above are correct

True or False

Indicate whether the following statements are true or false.

1. T F: ASP.NET applications will only work if the user's Web browser is Internet Explorer Version 5.0 or above.

2. T F: The DropDownList control permits the user to type text directly into the first line.

3. T F: The AutoPostBack property does not affect the ListBox control.

4. T F: The ListBox control fires a SelectedIndexChanged event.

5. T F: To create Web sites on your local computer, you must be running Internet Information Services (IIS).

6. T F: The default value of SelectedIndex for a DropDownList control is zero.

7. T F: The HyperLink control does not generate a Click event.

8. T F: The ImageButton control generates a Click event, and does not look like a button.

9. T F: The `Response.NavigateTo` method lets your code transfer control to a different Web page.

10. T F: To fill a GridView control, you must create a data adapter and a dataset.

11. T F: The DetailsView control does not permit deleting a row from a database table.

12. T F: When adding text to a Web form, you can type static text directly onto the form.

Short Answer

1. What are the three basic parts of an ASP.NET application?

2. Which control has a NavigateURL property?

3. How are Web server controls different from HTML controls?

4. What special requirement do remote Web servers have, as opposed to local Web servers?

5. What are the two ways to view a Web form inside Visual Studio?

6. What command lets you select which Web browser will run your Web application?

7. How do you open an existing Web application?

8. What happens the first time you try to run a Web application in Debug mode?

9. How is the DropDownList control different from the ComboBox control?

10. How are the HyperLink and LinkButton controls different?

11. Which Web control property corresponds to the Name property in Windows controls?

12. When the user selects an item from a ListBox and then posts the page back to the server (called a postback), which method executes first: `Page_Load` or `SelectedIndexChanged`?

13. Which property in a ListBox governs whether or not the user's selection is posted back to the server immediately?

14. Which property of a HyperLink control affects whether the target page will display in a new browser window?

What Do You Think?

1. What advantages does a File System Web site have over an HTTP Web site?

2. Why is the HTML Table control useful when designing Web forms?

3. Why should you to test your application with different Web browsers?

4. Why should debugging be disabled when distributing your Web site to the general public?

5. What disadvantage is there to setting AutoPostBack to *True* for a DropDownList control?

Algorithm Workbench

1. Write a code statement that transfers control to a Web page named *PageTwo.aspx*.

2. Write a statement that checks if the first button in a RadioButtonList control named `radButtons` has been selected by the user.

3. Write a statement that removes all items from a ListBox named `lstSummary`.

4. Write a loop that selects all check boxes in a CheckBoxList control named `chkOptions`.

Programming Challenges

VideoNote

The Stadium
Seating
Problem

1. **Stadium Seating**

    Create an ASP.NET version of the solution program for Programming Challenge 2 in Chapter 3, named *Stadium Seating*.

2. **Room Charge Calculator**

    Implement the *Room Charge Calculator* application from Section 3.10 as a Web application. In place of Group boxes, use Panel Web controls.

3. **Bank Charges**

    Create an ASP.NET version of the solution program for Programming Challenge 6 in Chapter 4, named *Bank Charges*.

4. **Long-Distance Calls**

    Create an ASP.NET version of the solution program for Programming Challenge 10 in Chapter 4, named *Long-Distance Calls*. Create a hyperlink on the startup form that displays a second browser window containing details about the calling rates.

5. **Karate Payments Grid**

    Write an ASP.NET application that displays the first name, last name, payment date, and payment amounts paid by members in the *Karate.mdf* database. Permit the user to display payments, but not to perform any modifications to the data. Sort the rows by last name. Display the Payment Date column in mm/dd/yyyy format, and display the Amount column in Currency format, encoded as {0:c}. For each column except the payment date, left justify the heading by setting the HeaderStyle.HorizonalAlign property to *Left*. Put a blue border around the grid, 1 pixel wide. Use the grid's HeaderStyle property to give the headings white text on a dark blue background. A sample is shown in Figure 11-68.

Figure 11-68 Grid showing *Karate* members names, dates, and payments

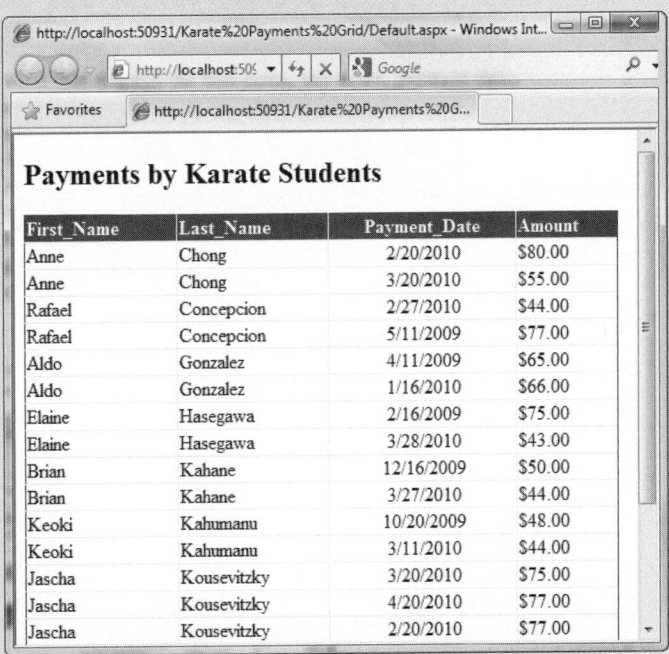

6. **Karate Schedule Details**

The *Schedule* table in the *Karate.mdf* database contains the following columns: *ID*, *Day*, *Time*, and *Instructor_Id*. The *Day* value is an integer between 0 and 6, where 0 indicates Monday and 6 indicates Sunday. Display the table in a DetailsView control, and permit the user to add, remove, and update records. Also, display the same table in a GridView control just below the DetailsView. Center all grid columns, and format the time as {0:t}.

A sample is shown in Figure 11-69.

Figure 11-69 DetailsView and GridView displays of the Karate Schedule table

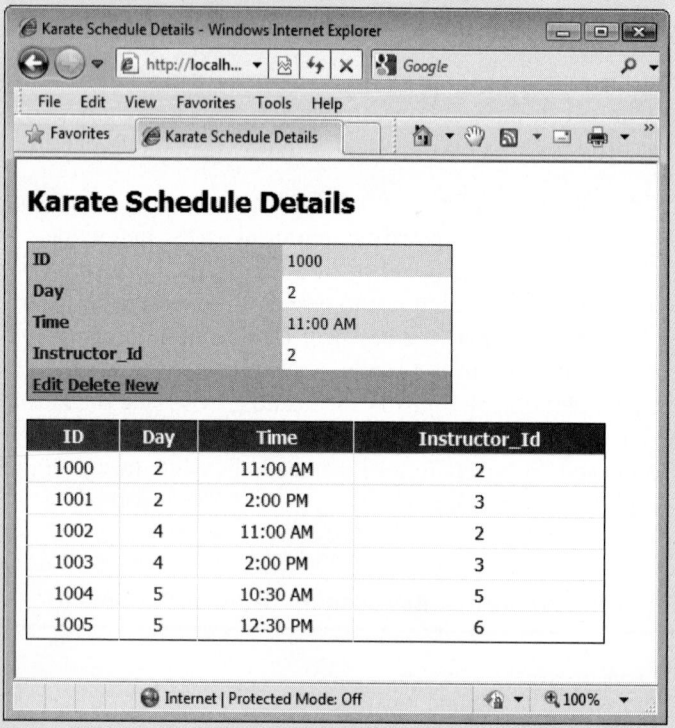

12 Classes, Collections, and Inheritance

TOPICS

This chapter introduces abstract data types and shows you how to create them with classes. The process of analyzing a problem and determining its classes is discussed, and techniques for creating objects, properties, and methods are introduced. Collections, which are structures for holding groups of objects, are also covered. The Object Browser, which allows you to see information about the classes, properties, methods, and events available to your project, is discussed. The chapter concludes by introducing inheritance, a way for new classes to be created from existing ones.

12.1 Classes and Objects

CONCEPT: Classes are program structures that define abstract data types and are used to create objects.

One of the most exciting developments in computer software over the last 30 years has been object-oriented programming. **Object-oriented programming (OOP)** is a way of designing and coding applications such that interchangeable software components can be used to build larger programs. Object-oriented programming languages, such as ALGOL, SmallTalk, and C++ first appeared in the early 1980s. The legacy from these languages has been the gradual development of object-like visual tools for building programs. In Visual Basic, for example, forms, buttons, check boxes, list boxes, and other controls are ideal examples of objects. Object-oriented designs help us produce programs that are well suited to ongoing development and expansion.

Abstract Data Types

An **abstract data type** (ADT) is a data type created by a programmer. ADTs are very important in computer science and especially significant in object-oriented programming. An **abstraction** is a general model of something—a definition that includes only the general characteristics of an object. For example, the term *dog* is an abstraction. It defines a general type of animal. The term captures the essence of what all dogs are without specifying the detailed characteristics of any particular breed of dog or any individual animal. According to *Webster's New Collegiate Dictionary*, a dog is "a highly variable carnivorous domesticated mammal (*Canis familiaris*) probably descended from the common wolf."

In real life, however, there is no such thing as a mere dog. There are specific dogs, each sharing common characteristics such as paws, fur, whiskers, and a carnivorous diet. For example, Travis owns a rottweiler named Bailey, and Shirley owns a poodle named Snuggles. In this analogy, the abstraction (dog), is like a data type and the specific dogs (Bailey and Snuggles) are instances of the type.

Classes

A **class** is a program structure that defines an abstract data type. You create a class, and then create instances of the class. All class instances share common characteristics. For example, Visual Basic controls and forms are classes. In the Visual Studio Toolbox, each icon represents a class. When you select the *Button* tool from the toolbox and place it on a form, as shown in Figure 12-1, you create an instance of the Button class. An instance is also called an **object**.

Figure 12-1 Instances of the Button class

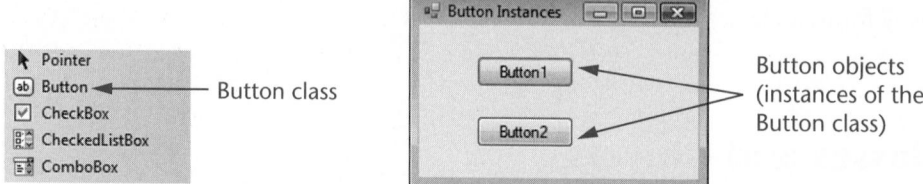

Class Properties, Methods, and Event Procedures

The way a program communicates with each object is determined by the properties and methods defined in the object's class. The Button class, for example, has properties such as Location, Text, and Name. Each Button object contains its own unique set of property values. In the example shown in Figure 12-1, the two buttons have different values in their Location and Text properties.

Methods are shared by all instances of a class. For example, the Button class has a method named Focus, which is the same for all Button objects.

Event handlers are also methods, but they are specific to individual objects. For example, a form with several buttons will almost always have different code written in each button's Click event procedure.

Object-Oriented Design

Object-oriented programming is not just a matter of randomly dropping classes into a program. The challenge is to design classes in such a way that the resulting objects will effectively cooperate and communicate. The primary goal of object-oriented design is to address the needs of the application or problem being solved. A secondary goal is to design classes that can outlive the current application and possibly be useful in future programs.

The first step, after creating the program specifications, is to analyze the application requirements. **Object-oriented analysis**, as it is called, often starts with a detailed specification of the problem to be solved. A term often applied to this process is **finding the classes**. A famous sculptor once said that inside every block of marble is a work of art waiting to be discovered. So, too, in every problem and every application there are classes waiting to be found. It is the designer's job to discover them.

Finding the Classes

Classes are the fundamental building blocks of object-oriented applications. When designing object-oriented programs, first we select classes that reflect physical entities in the application domain. For example, the user of a record-keeping program for a college might describe some of the application's requirements as follows:

> We need to keep a *list of students* that lets us track the courses they have completed. Each student has a *transcript* that contains all information about his or her completed courses. At the end of each semester, we will calculate the grade point average of each *student*. At times, users will search for a particular *course* taken by a student.

Notice the italicized nouns and noun phrases in this description: list of students, transcript, student, and course. These would ordinarily become classes in the program's design.

Looking for Control Structures

Classes can also be discovered in the description of processing done by an application or in the description of control structures. For example, if the application involved scheduling college classes for students, another description from the program specifications might be:

> We also want to schedule classes for students, using the college's master schedule to determine the times and room numbers for each student's class. When the optimal arrangement of classes for each student has been determined, each student's class schedule will be printed and distributed.

In this description, we anticipate a need for a controlling agent that could be implemented as a class. We might call it `Scheduler`, a class that matches each student's schedule with the college's master schedule.

Describing the Classes

The next step, after finding the classes in an application, is to describe the classes in terms of attributes and operations. **Attributes** are characteristics of each object that will be implemented as properties. Attributes describe the properties that all objects of the same class have in common. Classes also have **operations**, which are actions the class objects may perform or messages to which they can respond. Operations are implemented as class methods. Table 12-1 describes some of the important attributes and operations of the record-keeping application that we described earlier.

Table 12-1 Sample attributes and operations

Class	Attributes (properties)	Operations (methods)
Student	LastName, FirstName, IdNumber	Display, Input
StudentList	AllStudents, Count	Add, Remove, FindStudent
Course	Semester, Name, Grade, Credits	Display, Input
Transcript	CourseList, Count	Display, Search, CalculateGPA

The complete set of attributes and operations is often incomplete during the early stages of design because it is difficult to anticipate all the application requirements. As a design develops, the need often arises for additional properties and methods that improve communication between objects. Rather than a weakness, however, this ability to accommodate ongoing modifications is one of the strengths of the object-oriented design process.

Interface and Implementation

The **class interface** is the portion of the class that is visible to the application programmer. The program written to use a class is sometimes called the **client program**, in reference to the client-server relationship between a class and the programs that use it. The class interface provides a way for clients to communicate (send messages) to class objects. In Visual Basic, a class interface is created by declaring public properties, methods, and events.

The **class implementation** is the portion of a class that is hidden from client programs; it is created from private member variables, private properties, and private methods. The hiding of data and procedures inside a class is achieved through a process called **encapsulation**. In this, it might be helpful to visualize the class as a *capsule* around its data and procedures.

 Checkpoint

12.1 Give some examples of objects in Visual Basic.

12.2 A text box tool appears in the toolbox and a Textbox control has been placed on a form. Which represents the `TextBox` class and which is an instance of the `TextBox` class?

12.3 When analyzing a problem, how do we select useful classes?

12.4 What is an attribute of a class? How are attributes implemented?

12.5 What is an operation of a class? How are operations implemented?

12.6 What is a class interface?

12.7 What is the class implementation?

 **12.2 Creating a Class**

CONCEPT: To create a class in Visual Basic, you create a class declaration. The class declaration specifies the member variables, properties, methods, and events that belong to the class.

VideoNote

Creating
a Class

You create a class in Visual Basic by creating a **class declaration**. We will use the following general format when writing class declarations:

```
Public Class ClassName
    MemberDeclarations
End Class
```

ClassName is the name of the class. *MemberDeclarations* are the declarations of all the variables, constants, and methods (procedures) that will belong to the class. Follow these steps to add a class declaration to a Windows application project:

1. Click *Project* on the menu bar, then click *Add Class*. The *Add New Item* dialog box, shown in Figure 12-2, should appear. Make sure that *Class* is selected as the type. Notice that in the figure, the name *Class1.vb* appears in the *Name* text box. In this example, *Class1.vb* is the default name for the file that the class declaration will be stored in, and *Class1* is the default name for the class.

NOTE: The default name may be different, depending on the number of classes already in the project.

Figure 12-2 *Add New Item* dialog box

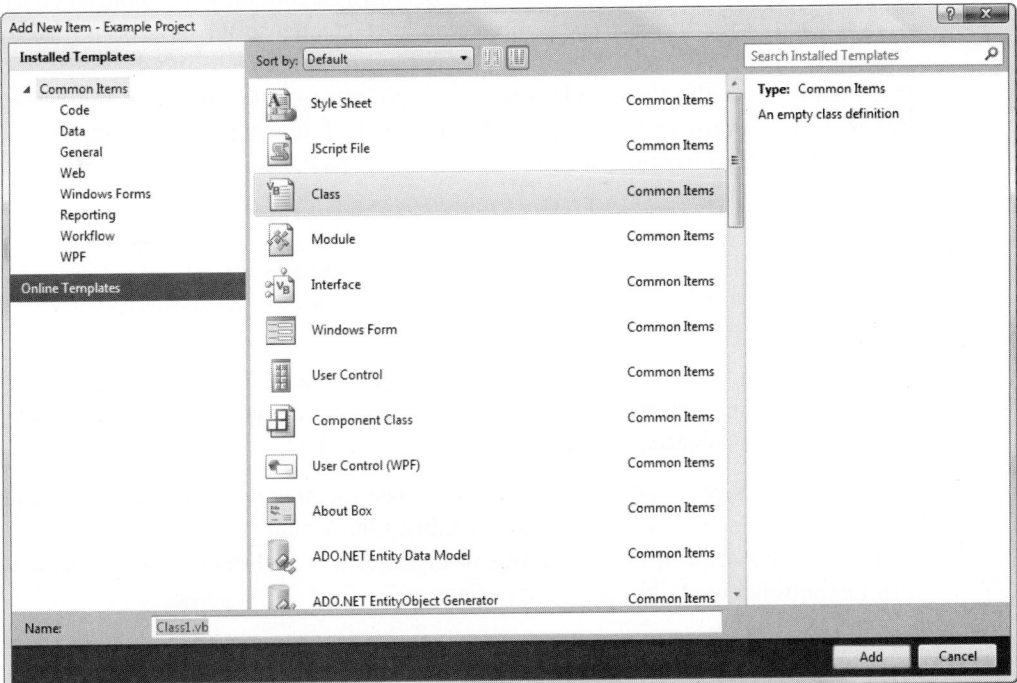

2. Change the default name displayed in the *Name* text box to the name you wish to give the new class file. For example, if you wish to name the new class `Student`, enter *Student.vb* in the *Name* text box.
3. Click the *Add* button.

   A new, empty class declaration will be added to your project. The empty class declaration will be displayed in the *Code* window and an entry for the new class file will

Figure 12-3 *Solution Explorer* window showing two forms and one class

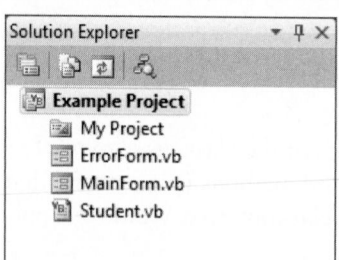

appear in the *Solution Explorer* window. The *Solution Explorer* window in Figure 12-3 shows two forms and one class: ErrorForm, MainForm, and Student.

Member Variables

A **member variable** is a variable that is declared inside a class declaration. The variable is a member of the class. A member variable declaration has the following general format:

```
AccessSpecifer VariableName As DataType
```

AccessSpecifier determines the accessibility of the variable. Variables declared with the Public access specifier may be accessed by statements outside the class, and even outside the same assembly. Roughly speaking, an assembly is a container that holds a collection of classes. Each of the Visual Basic projects you have created so far have been used to create assemblies. Variables declared with the Private access specifier may be accessed only by statements inside the class declaration. *VariableName* is the name of the variable and *DataType* is the variable's data type. For example, the following code declares a class named Student. The class has three member variables: strLastName, strFirstName, and strId.

```
Public Class Student
    Private strLastName As String      ' Holds last name
    Private strFirstName As String     ' Holds first name
    Private strId As String            ' Holds ID number
End Class
```

As with structures, a class declaration does not create an instance of the class. It only establishes a blueprint for the class's organization. To actually work with the class, you must create **class objects**, which are instances of the class.

Another access type is called **Friend access**. A class member with Friend access can be used only by other classes inside the same assembly. One Visual Basic program can use classes from another assembly, but it cannot call methods having Friend access specifiers. It can call methods having Public access specifiers.

Creating an Instance of a Class

Creating an instance of a class is a two-step process: You declare an object variable, and then you create an instance of the class in memory and assign its address to the object variable. Although there are only two steps in the process, there are two different techniques for performing these steps. The first method performs both steps in one line of code, as shown in the following example:

```
Dim freshman As New Student
```

This statement creates an object variable named freshman. The New keyword causes the class instance to be created in memory. The object's address is assigned to freshman.

The second method requires two lines of code, as shown in the following example:

```
Dim freshman As Student
freshman = New Student
```

The `Dim` statement in the first line creates an object variable named `freshman`. By default, the object variable is initialized to the value `Nothing`. The second line uses the `New` keyword to create an instance of the `Student` class and assigns its memory address to the `freshman` variable.

When you create instances of a class, each instance has its own copy of the class's member variables.

Accessing Members

Once you have created a class object, you can work with its `Public` members in code. You access the `Public` members of a class object with the dot (`.`) operator. Suppose the `Student` class was declared as follows:

```
Public Class Student
   Public strLastName As String
   Public strFirstName As String
   Public strId As String
End Class
```

In a Windows form, we might create a button `Click` handler procedure that declares `freshman` as a `Student` object. The following statements store values in the object's public member variables:

```
Private Sub btnOk_Click(...) Handles btnOk.Click
   ' Create an instance of the Student class.
   Dim freshman As New Student

   ' Assign values to the object's members.
   freshman.strFirstName = "Joy"
   freshman.strLastName = "Robinson"
   freshman.strId = "23G794"
End Sub
```

One might think that `strFirstName`, `strLastName`, and `strId` are properties of the `Student` class. But implementing properties as public member variables directly is not a good idea. Doing so allows users of the class to modify the variables directly and prevents the author of the class from including range checking or validating of values assigned to variables. Instead, a much better approach is to implement properties as property procedures.

Property Procedures

A **property procedure** is a function that defines a class property. The general format of a property procedure is as follows:

```
Public Property PropertyName() As DataType
   Get
      Statements
   End Get
   Set(ParameterDeclaration)
      Statements
   End Set
End Property
```

PropertyName is the name of the property procedure, and hence the name of the property that the procedure implements. *DataType* is the type of data (such as Integer, String, or Decimal) that can be assigned to the property. Notice that the procedure has two sections: a Get section and a Set section. The **Get section** holds the code that is executed when the property value is retrieved, and the **Set section** holds the code that is executed when a value is stored in the property.

> **TIP:** Properties are almost always declared with the Public access specifier so they can be accessed from outside their enclosing class module.

> **TIP:** After you type the word Get inside a property procedure, Visual Basic will build a code template for the rest of the procedure.

For example, let's add a property to the Student class that holds the student's test score average. The modified code for the class follows:

```
Public Class Student
    Private strLastName As String        ' Holds last name
    Private strFirstName As String       ' Holds first name
    Private strId As String              ' Holds ID number
    Private dblTestAverage As Double     ' Holds test average

    Public Property TestAverage() As Double
      Get
        Return dblTestAverage
      End Get
      Set(ByVal value As Double)
        dblTestAverage = value
      End Set
    End Property
End Class
```

Notice that a private member variable named dblTestAverage was added to the class to hold the actual value stored in the TestAverage property. We have declared the variable private to prevent code outside the class from storing values directly in it. To store a test average in an object, the property procedure must be used. This allows us to perform validation on the value before it is stored in an object.

Let's look at the Get and Set sections of the property procedure. The Get section does one thing: It only returns the value stored in the dblTestAverage member variable. The code for the Get section follows:

```
Get
   Return dblTestAverage
End Get
```

Here is the code for the Set section:

```
Set(ByVal value As Double)
   dblTestAverage = value
End Set
```

The Set section has a declaration for a parameter named value. When a number is stored in the TestAverage property, the Set section is executed and the number being stored in the property is passed into the value parameter. The procedure then assigns the value parameter to the dblTestAverage member variable.

The following code shows an example of the TestAverage property in use:

```
Dim freshman As New Student
freshman.TestAverage = 82.3
```

The last statement stores the value 82.3 in the TestAverage property. Because a value is being stored in the property, this statement causes the Set section of the TestAverage property procedure to execute. The number 82.3 is passed into the value parameter. The value parameter is then assigned to the object's dblTestAverage member variable.

Any statement that retrieves the value in the TestAverage property causes the property procedure's Get section to execute. For example, the following code assigns the value in the TestAverage property to the variable dblAverage:

```
dblAverage = freshman.TestAverage
```

This statement causes the property's Get section to execute, which returns the value stored in the dblTestAverage member variable. The following code displays the value in the TestAverage property in a message box:

```
MessageBox.Show(freshman.TestAverage.ToString())
```

Creating Property Procedures for the Student Class

Now, let's modify the Student class by implementing the following property procedures: FirstName, LastName, IdNumber, and TestAverage. The code follows:

```
Public Class Student
    Private strLastName As String      ' Holds last name
    Private strFirstName As String     ' Holds first name
    Private strId As String            ' Holds ID number
    Private dblTestAverage As Double   ' Holds test average

    ' LastName property procedure

    Public Property LastName() As String
      Get
        Return strLastName
      End Get
      Set(ByVal value As String)
        strLastName = value
      End Set
    End Property

    ' FirstName property procedure

    Public Property FirstName() As String
      Get
        Return strFirstName
      End Get
      Set(ByVal value As String)
        strFirstName = value
      End Set
    End Property

    ' IdNumber property procedure

    Public Property IdNumber() As String
      Get
        Return strId
      End Get
      Set(ByVal value As String)
        strId = value
      End Set
    End Property
```

```
' TestAverage property procedure

Public Property TestAverage() As Double
   Get
      Return dblTestAverage
   End Get
   Set(ByVal value As Double)
      dblTestAverage = value
   End Set
End Property
End Class
```

Read-Only Properties

Sometimes it is useful to make a property read-only. Client programs can query a **read-only property** to get its value, but cannot modify it. The general format of a read-only property procedure is as follows:

```
Public ReadOnly Property PropertyName() As DataType
   Get
      Statements
   End Get
End Property
```

The first line of a read-only property procedure contains the ReadOnly keyword. Notice that the procedure has no Set section. It is only capable of returning a value. For example, the following code demonstrates a read-only property named Grade that we might add to our Student class:

```
' Grade read-only property procedure

Public ReadOnly Property Grade() As String
   Get
      ' Variable to hold the grade.
      Dim strGrade As String

      ' Determine the grade.
      If dblTestAverage >= 90.0 Then
         strGrade = "A"
      ElseIf dblTestAverage >= 80.0 Then
         strGrade = "B"
      ElseIf dblTestAverage >= 70.0 Then
         strGrade = "C"
      ElseIf dblTestAverage >= 60.0 Then
         strGrade = "D"
      Else
         strGrade = "F"
      End If

      ' Return the grade.
      Return strGrade
   End Get
End Property
```

This property returns one of the following string values, depending on the contents of the dblTestAverage member variable: "A", "B", "C", "D", or "F".

A compiler error occurs if a client program attempts to store a value in a read-only property. For example, the following statement would result in an error:

```
freshman.Grade = "A"                    ' Error
```

Removing Objects and Garbage Collection

It is a good practice to remove objects that are no longer needed, allowing the application to free memory for other purposes. To remove an object, set all the object variables that reference it to `Nothing`. For example, the following statement sets the object variable `freshman` to `Nothing`:

```
freshman = Nothing
```

After this statement executes, the `freshman` variable will no longer reference an object. If the object that it previously referenced is no longer referenced by any other variables, it will be removed from memory by the .NET garbage collector. The **garbage collector** is a utility program that removes objects from memory when they are no longer needed.

> **NOTE:** The garbage collector might not remove an object from memory immediately when the last reference to it has been removed. The system uses an algorithm to determine when it should periodically remove unused objects. As the amount of available memory decreases, the garbage collector removes unreferenced objects more often.

Going Out of Scope

Like all variables, an object variable declared inside a procedure is local to that procedure. If an object is referenced only by a procedure's local object variable, it becomes eligible to be removed from memory by the garbage collector after the procedure ends. This is called **going out of scope**. For example, look at the following procedure:

```
Sub CreateStudent()
   Dim sophomore As Student ' Object variable

   ' Create an instance of the Student class.
   sophomore = New Student()

   ' Assign values to its properties.
   sophomore.FirstName = "Travis"
   sophomore.LastName = "Barnes"
   sophomore.IdNumber = "17H495"
   sophomore.TestAverage = 94.7
End Sub
```

This procedure declares an object variable named sophomore. An instance of the `Student` class is created and referenced by the sophomore variable. When this procedure ends, the object referenced by sophomore is no longer accessible.

An object is not removed from memory if there are still references to it. For example, assume an application has a global module-level variable named `g_studentVar`. Look at the following code:

```
Sub CreateStudent()
   Dim sophomore As Student ' Object variable

   ' Create an instance of the Student class.
   sophomore = New Student()

   ' Assign values to its properties.
   sophomore.FirstName = "Travis"
   sophomore.LastName = "Barnes"
   sophomore.IdNumber = "17H495"
   sophomore.TestAverage = 94.7

   ' Assign the object to a global variable.
   g_studentVar = sophomore
End Sub
```

The last statement in the procedure assigns `g_studentVar` the object referenced by `sophomore`. This means that both `g_studentVar` and `sophomore` reference the same object. When this procedure ends, the object referenced by `sophomore` will not be removed from memory because it is still referenced by the module-level variable `g_studentVar`.

Comparing Object Variables with the `Is` and `IsNot` Operators

Multiple object variables can reference the same object in memory. For example, the following code declares two object variables: `collegeStudent` and `transferStudent`. Both object variables are made to reference the same instance of the `Student` class.

```
Dim collegeStudent As Student
Dim transferStudent As Student
collegeStudent = New Student
transferStudent = collegeStudent
```

After this code executes, both `collegeStudent` and `transferStudent` reference the same object. You cannot use the = operator in an `If` statement to determine whether two object variables reference the same object. Instead, use the **`Is` operator**. For example, the following statement properly determines if `collegeStudent` and `transferStudent` reference the same object:

```
If collegeStudent Is transferStudent Then
   ' Perform some action
End If
```

You can use the **`IsNot` operator** to determine whether two variables do not reference the same object. The following is an example:

```
If collegeStudent IsNot transferStudent Then
   ' Perform some action
End If
```

If you wish to compare an object variable to the special value `Nothing`, use either the `Is` or `IsNot` operator, as shown in the following code:

```
If collegeStudent Is Nothing Then
   ' Perform some action
End If
If transferStudent IsNot Nothing Then
   ' Perform some action
End If
```

Creating an Array of Objects

You can create an array of object variables, and then create an object for each element of the array to reference. The following code declares `mathStudents` as an array of 10 `Student` objects. Then it uses a loop to assign a `Student` to each element of the array.

```
Dim mathStudents(9) As Student
Dim intCount As Integer
For intCount = 0 To 9
   mathStudents(intCount) = New Student
Next
```

You can use another loop to release the memory used by the array, as shown in the following statements:

```
Dim intCount As Integer

For intCount = 0 To 9
  mathStudents(intCount) = Nothing
Next
```

Writing Procedures and Functions That Work with Objects

Procedures and functions can accept object variables as arguments. For example, the following procedure accepts an object variable that references an instance of the Student class as its argument and displays the student's grade.

```
Sub DisplayStudentGrade(ByVal s As Student)
  ' Displays a student's grade.
  MessageBox.Show("The grade for " & s.FirstName &
                  " " & s.LastName & " is " &
                  s.TestGrade.ToString())
End Sub
```

The parameter named s references a Student object. To call the procedure, pass an object variable that references a Student object, as shown in the following code:

```
DisplayStudentGrade(freshman)
```

When this statement executes, the DisplayStudentGrade procedure is called, and the freshman object variable is passed as an argument. Inside the procedure, the parameter variable s will reference the same object that freshman references.

Passing Objects by Value and by Reference

Object variable parameters may be declared either as ByVal or ByRef. Be aware, however, that the ByVal keyword does not prevent a procedure from accessing and modifying the object referenced by the variable that was passed to the procedure. For example, look at the following ClearStudent procedure:

```
Sub ClearStudent(ByVal s As Student)
  s.FirstName = String.Empty
  s.LastName = String.Empty
  s.IdNumber = String.Empty
  s.TestAverage = 0.0
End Sub
```

Let's assume that an object variable referencing a Student object is passed to ClearStudent. The procedure clears the FirstName, LastName, IdNumber, and TestAverage properties of the object referenced by the parameter variable s. For example, look at the following code, which initializes various properties of a Student object and then passes the object to the ClearStudent procedure:

```
freshman.FirstName = "Joy"
freshman.LastName = "Robinson"
freshman.IdNumber = "23G794"
freshman.TestAverage = 82.3

' Clear the properties of the object.
ClearStudent(freshman)
```

After the `ClearStudent` procedure executes, the properties of the object referenced by the `freshman` variable are cleared.

If, inside the body of a procedure, we assign a different object to a `ByVal` parameter variable, the assignment does not affect the object that was passed as an argument into the parameter variable. For example, the following procedure accepts an object as its argument, and then assigns the parameter variable `s` to another object.

```
Sub ResetStudent(ByVal s As Student)
    ' Create an instance of the Student class.
    Dim newStudent As Student

    ' Assign values to the object's properties.
    newStudent.FirstName = "Bill"
    newStudent.LastName = "Owens"
    newStudent.IdNumber = "56K789"
    newStudent.TestAverage = 84.6

    ' Assign the new object to the s parameter.
    s = newStudent
End Sub
```

Suppose we call the procedure, as shown in the following code:

```
freshman.FirstName = "Joy"
freshman.LastName = "Robinson"
freshman.IdNumber = "23G794"
freshman.TestAverage = 82.3
ResetStudent(freshman)
```

After the `ResetStudent` procedure executes, the object referenced by the `freshman` variable still contains the data for Joy Robinson. If the parameter variable `s` was declared `ByRef`, on the other hand, the variable named `freshman` would contain Bill Owens' information after the procedure call.

Returning an Object from a Function

It is also possible to return an object from a function. For example, the following function prompts the user to enter the data for a `Student` object. The object is then returned to the caller.

```
' Get student data and return it as an object.

Function GetStudent() As Student
    ' Create an instance of the Student class.
    Dim s As New Student

    ' Get values for the object's properties.
    s.FirstName = InputBox("Enter the student's first name.")
    s.LastName = InputBox("Enter the student's last name.")
    s.IdNumber = InputBox("Enter the student's ID number.")
    s.TestAverage = CDbl(InputBox("Enter the student's test average."))

    ' Return the object's address.
    Return s
End Function
```

The following code assigns the function's return value to the `freshman` object variable:

```
Dim freshman As Student = GetStudent()
```

Methods

A **method** is a procedure or function that is a member of a class. The method performs some operation on the data stored in the class. For example, suppose we wish to add a `Clear` method to the `Student` class, as shown in the following code. To simplify the code listing, the property procedures have been omitted.

```
Public Class Student
   ' Member variables
   Private strLastName As String      ' Holds last name
   Private strFirstName As String     ' Holds first name
   Private strId As String            ' Holds ID number
   Private dblTestAverage As Double   ' Holds test average

   (...Property procedures omitted...)

   ' Clear method
   Public Sub Clear()
      strFirstName = String.Empty
      strLastName = String.Empty
      strId = String.Empty
      dblTestAverage = 0.0
   End Sub
End Class
```

The `Clear` method clears the private member variables that hold the student's first name, last name, ID number, and test average. The following statement calls the method using the object referenced by `freshman`:

```
freshman.Clear()
```

Constructors

A **constructor** is a method that is automatically called when an instance of the class is created. It is helpful to think of constructors as initialization routines. They are useful for initializing member variables or performing other startup operations. To create a constructor, create a method named `New` inside the class. (Alternatively, you can select *New* from the method name drop-down list and a code template is created for you.) Each time an instance of the class is created, the `New` procedure is executed.

For example, let's add a constructor to the `Student` class that initializes the private member variables. The code follows:

```
Public Class Student
   ' Member variables
   Private strLastName As String      ' Holds last name
   Private strFirstName As String     ' Holds first name
   Private strId As String            ' Holds ID number
   Private dblTestAverage As Double   ' Holds test average

   ' Constructor
   Public Sub New()
      strFirstName = "(unknown)"
      strLastName = "(unknown)"
      strId = "(unknown)"
      dblTestAverage = 0.0
   End Sub

   (The rest of this class is omitted.)

End Class
```

The following statement creates a `Student` object:

```
Dim freshman As New Student
```

When this statement executes, an instance of the `Student` class is created and its constructor is executed. The result is that `freshman.LastName`, `freshman.FirstName`, and `freshman.IdNumber` will hold the string `"(unknown)"` and `freshman.TestAverage` will hold `0.0`.

Finalizers

A **finalizer** is a class method named `Finalize`, which is automatically called just before an instance of the class is removed from memory. If you wish to execute code immediately before an object is removed, create a `Finalize` method in your class. Because the syntax of `Finalize` is unfamilar, it's easier to let Visual Basic create a code template. When you select `Finalize` in the method name drop-down list, the following code template is created:

```
Protected Overrides Sub Finalize()
    MyBase.Finalize()
End Sub
```

Any code you wish to execute should be placed after the `MyBase.Finalize()` statement. The garbage collector uses an algorithm to determine when it should periodically release all unreferenced objects from memory. Therefore, you cannot predict exactly when the `Finalize` method will be executed.

Displaying Messages in the *Output* Window

Before beginning our class-building tutorial, let's discuss a valuable debugging tool: the ***Output* window**. The *Output* window, shown in Figure 12-4, normally appears at the bottom of the Visual Basic environment while an application is running. If you do not see the *Output* window, you can display it by clicking the *View* menu, then *Other Windows*, then *Output*. Alternatively you can press Ctrl+Alt+O. This window displays various messages while an application is being compiled.

Figure 12-4 *Output* window

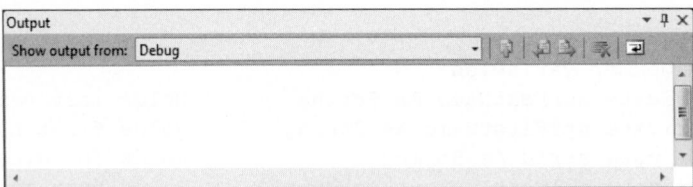

You can display your own messages in the *Output* window with the `Debug.WriteLine` method. The method has the following general format:

```
Debug.WriteLine(Output)
```

Output is an expression whose value is to be displayed in the *Output* window. To enable debug messages, insert the following line in your startup form's `Load` event handler:

```
Debug.Listeners.Add(New ConsoleTraceListener())
```

We will use this method in Tutorial 12-1 to display status messages from a class constructor and finalizer. The constructor will be modified as follows:

```
' Constructor
Public Sub New()
   Debug.WriteLine("Student object being created.")
   strFirstName = String.Empty
   strLastName = String.Empty
   strId = String.Empty
   dblTestAverage = 0.0
End Sub
```

The `Debug.WriteLine` method displays a message in the *Output* window each time a `Student` object is created. We can add a similar statement to the `Finalize` method, as follows:

```
Protected Overrides Sub Finalize()
   MyBase.Finalize()
   Debug.WriteLine("Student object destroyed.")
End Sub
```

Each time a `Student` object is removed from memory, the `Debug.Writeline` method will display a message in the *Output* window.

In Tutorial 12-1, you create the `Student` class we have been using as an example, and use it in an application that saves student data to a file.

Tutorial 12-1:
Creating the *Student Data* application

Step 1:   Create a new Windows Forms Application project named *Student Data*.

Step 2:   Set up the application's form as shown in Figure 12-5.

Step 3:   Perform the following steps to add a new class to the project:
- Click *Project* on the menu bar, and then click *Add Class*.
- In the *Add New Item* dialog box, make sure *Class* is selected in the *Templates* pane. In the *Name* text box, type **Student.vb**.
- Click the *Add* button.

Figure 12-5 *Student Data* form

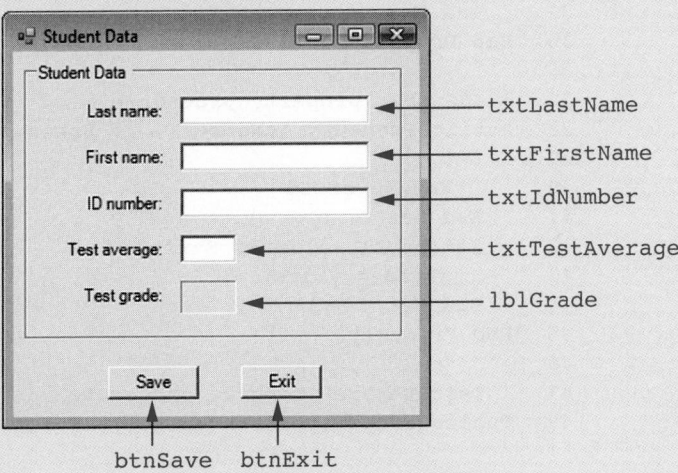

A new class file is created and opened in the *Code* window. The contents of the class appear as follows:

```
Public Class Student


End Class
```

Step 4: Complete the class by entering the following code shown in bold, in lines 2 through 79. (Don't type the line numbers. They are shown only for reference.)

```
 1 Public Class Student
 2   ' Member variables
 3   Private strLastName As String      ' Holds last name
 4   Private strFirstName As String     ' Holds first name
 5   Private strId As String            ' Holds ID number
 6   Private dblTestAverage As Double   ' Holds test average
 7
 8   ' Constructor
 9   Public Sub New()
10     Debug.WriteLine("Student object being created.")
11     strFirstName = "(unknown)"
12     strLastName = "(unknown)"
13     strId = "(unknown)"
14     dblTestAverage = 0.0
15   End Sub
16
17   ' LastName property procedure
18   Public Property LastName() As String
19     Get
20       Return strLastName
21     End Get
22     Set(ByVal value As String)
23       strLastName = value
24     End Set
25   End Property
26
27   ' FirstName property procedure
28   Public Property FirstName() As String
29     Get
30       Return strFirstName
31     End Get
32     Set(ByVal value As String)
33       strFirstName = value
34     End Set
35   End Property
36
37   ' IdNumber property procedure
38   Public Property IdNumber() As String
39     Get
40       Return strId
41     End Get
42     Set(ByVal value As String)
43       strId = value
44     End Set
45   End Property
46
47   ' TestAverage property procedure
48   Public Property TestAverage() As Double
```

```
49        Get
50          Return dblTestAverage
51        End Get
52        Set(ByVal value As Double)
53          dblTestAverage = value
54        End Set
55    End Property
56
57    ' Grade read-only property procedure
58    Public ReadOnly Property Grade() As String
59      Get
60        ' Variable to hold the grade.
61        Dim strGrade As String
62
63        ' Determine the grade.
64        If dblTestAverage >= 90.0 Then
65          strGrade = "A"
66        ElseIf dblTestAverage >= 80.0 Then
67          strGrade = "B"
68        ElseIf dblTestAverage >= 70.0 Then
69          strGrade = "C"
70        ElseIf dblTestAverage >= 60.0 Then
71          strGrade = "D"
72        Else
73          strGrade = "F"
74        End If
75
76        ' Return the grade.
77        Return strGrade
78      End Get
79    End Property
80 End Class
```

Step 5: Now you will add a finalizer to the Student class that displays a message in the *Output* window. In the method name drop-down list, select Finalize. A code template should appear. Complete the template by entering the statement shown in bold in the following code:

```
Protected Overrides Sub Finalize()
  MyBase.Finalize()
  Debug.WriteLine("Student object destroyed.")
End Sub
```

Step 6: Now write the procedures and event handlers for Form1, shown here in bold. Notice the Imports statement in line 1. (Don't type the line numbers. They are shown only for reference.)

```
1 Imports System.IO
2
3 Public Class Form1
4
5    ' The GetData procedure gets data from the text boxes
6    ' and stores it in the object referenced by objStudent.
7    Private Sub GetData(ByVal objStudent As Student)
8      Try
9        ' Assign values from the form to the object properties.
10       objStudent.LastName = txtLastName.Text
11       objStudent.FirstName = txtFirstName.Text
12       objStudent.IdNumber = txtIdNumber.Text
13       objStudent.TestAverage = CDbl(txtTestAverage.Text)
14     Catch ex As Exception
```

```
15            ' Display an error message.
16            MessageBox.Show(ex.Message)
17        End Try
18    End Sub
19
20    Private Sub SaveRecord(ByVal objStudent As Student)
21        Dim writer As StreamWriter
22
23        Try
24            ' Open the file in Append mode.
25            writer = File.AppendText("Students.txt")
26
27            ' Save the Student object's properties.
28            writer.WriteLine(objStudent.IdNumber)
29            writer.WriteLine(objStudent.FirstName)
30            writer.WriteLine(objStudent.LastName)
31            writer.WriteLine(objStudent.TestAverage.ToString())
32            writer.WriteLine(objStudent.Grade)
33
34            ' Close the StreamWriter.
35            writer.Close()
36        Catch ex As Exception
37            ' Display an error message.
38            MessageBox.Show(ex.Message)
39        End Try
40    End Sub
41
42    ' The ClearForm procedure clears the form.
43    Private Sub ClearForm()
44        ' Clear the text boxes.
45        txtFirstName.Clear()
46        txtLastName.Clear()
47        txtIdNumber.Clear()
48        txtTestAverage.Clear()
49        lblGrade.Text = String.Empty
50
51        ' Reset the focus.
52        txtLastName.Focus()
53    End Sub
54
55    Private Sub btnSave_Click(...) Handles btnSave.Click
56        ' Create an instance of the Student class.
57        Dim objStudent As New Student
58
59        ' Get data from the form.
60        GetData(objStudent)
61
62        ' Display the student's grade.
63        lblGrade.Text = objStudent.Grade
64
65        ' Save this student's record.
66        SaveRecord(objStudent)
67
68        ' Confirm that the record was saved.
69        MessageBox.Show("Student record saved.")
70
71        ' Clear the form.
72        ClearForm()
73    End Sub
```

```
74
75    Private Sub btnExit_Click(...) Handles btnExit.Click
76       ' Close the form.
77       Me.Close()
78    End Sub
79
80    Private Sub Form1_Load(...) Handles MyBase.Load
81       ' Enable output to the Output window.
82       Debug.Listeners.Add(New ConsoleTraceListener())
83    End Sub
84 End Class
```

Step 7: Save the project and run the application. On the application's form, enter the following data:

Last name:	**Green**
First name:	**Sara**
ID number:	**27R8974**
Test average:	**92.3**

Click the *Save* button to save the student data to a file. A message box appears indicating that the record was saved. Notice that the message *Student object being created* is displayed in the *Output* window. This message was displayed by the `Student` class constructor. Click the *OK* button on the message box.

Step 8: Click the *Exit* button. If the message *Student object destroyed* has not yet been displayed by the class's `Finalize` method, it will be when you click the *Exit* button.

Checkpoint

12.8   How do you add a class module to a project?

12.9   What two steps must you perform when creating an instance of a class?

12.10 How do you remove an object from memory?

12.11 If an object is created inside a procedure, it is automatically removed from memory when the procedure ends, if no variables declared at the class or module level reference it. What is the name of the process that removes the object?

12.12 What are member variables?

12.13 What is a property procedure?

12.14 What does the `Get` section of a property procedure do?

12.15 What does the `Set` section of a property procedure do?

12.16 What is a constructor? What is the `Finalize` method?

12.3 Collections

> **CONCEPT:** A collection holds a group of items. It automatically expands and shrinks in size to accommodate the items added to it. It allows items to be stored with associated key values, which may then be used in searches.

VideoNote

Collections

A **collection** is similar to an array. It is a single unit that contains several items. You can access the individual items in a collection with an index, which is similar to an array subscript. The difference between an array's subscript and a collection's index is that the latter begins at 1. You might recall that an array's subscripts begin at 0.

Another difference between arrays and collections is that collections automatically expand as items are added and shrink as items are removed. Also, the items stored in a collection do not have to be of the same type.

Visual Basic provides a class named `Collection`. When you create a collection in an application you are creating an instance of the `Collection` class. So, creating a collection is identical to creating any other class object. The following statements declare an object variable named `customers`, and then assign a new `Collection` instance to it:

```
Dim customers As Collection
customers = New Collection
```

You can also create a `Collection` instance and assign it to an object variable in one statement as follows:

```
Dim customers As New Collection
```

Adding Items to a Collection

You add items to a collection with the **Add** method. We will use the following general format:

```
CollectionName.Add(Item [, Key])
```

CollectionName is the name of an object variable that references a collection. The *Item* argument is the object, variable, or value that is to be added to the collection. *Key* is an optional string expression that is associated with the item and can be used to search for it. (*Key* must be unique for each member of a collection.)

Let's define a simple class named `Customer` with two variables and corresponding properties. The properties are abbreviated to save space.

```
Public Class Customer
   Private strName As String
   Private strPhone As String

   Public Property Name As String
      ...
   End Property

   Public Property Phone As String
      ...
   End Property
End Class
```

Suppose we are writing code for a form in our application. At the top of the form, at the class level, we can declare a `Collection` object:

```
Private customers As New Collection
```

Then, in a button's `Click` event handler procedure, we will declare a `Customer` object and assign TextBox values to its properties:

```
Dim myCustomer As New Customer
myCustomer.Name = txtName.Text
myCustomer.Phone = txtPhone.Text
```

Next, we will insert the `Customer` in the `customers` collection:

```
customers.Add(myCustomer)
```

We have not provided a key value, so we probably do not plan to search for customers later on. The collection is simply acting as a convenient container to hold customers.

Suppose, however, that we plan to search for customers at a later time while the application is running. In that case, we can use a different form of the `Add` statement, which allows us to pass a key value as the second argument:

```
customers.Add(myCustomer, myCustomer.Name)
```

This statement adds the `myCustomer` object to the collection, using the `myCustomer.Name` property as a key. Later, we will be able to search the collection for this object by specifying the customer's name.

Handling Exceptions

An `ArgumentException` is thrown if you attempt to add a member with the same `Key` as an existing member. The following code example shows how to handle the exception:

```
Try
   customers.Add(myCustomer, myCustomer.Name)
Catch ex as ArgumentException
   MessageBox.Show(ex.Message)
End Try
```

Accessing Items by their Indexes

You can access an item in a collection by passing an integer to the **Item** method as follows:

```
CollectionName.Item(index)
```

CollectionName is the name of the variable that references the collection, and *index* is the integer index of the item that you want to retrieve. The following statements locate the `Customer` object at index 1 in the collection named customers, assign the object to a `Customer` variable, and then display the customer's name in a message box:

```
Dim cust As Customer = CType(customers.Item(1), Customer)
MessageBox.Show("Customer found: " & cust.Name & ": " &
                cust.Phone)
```

Calling the CType method is necessary because the Item method of a collection returns an Object. We must cast (convert) the Object into a Customer.

Because `Item` is the default method for collections, you can use an abbreviated format such as the following to locate a collection item:

```
Dim cust As Customer = CType(customers(3), Customer)
```

The IndexOutOfRange Exception

An exception of the IndexOutOfRange type occurs if you use an index that does not match the index of any item in a collection. The following code example shows how to handle the exception:

```
Try
    Dim cust As Customer

    ' Get the collection index from user input
    Dim index As Integer = CInt(txtIndex.Text)

    ' Locate the customer in the collection
    cust = CType(customers.Item(index), Customer)

    ' Display the customer information
    MessageBox.Show("Customer found: " & cust.Name & ": " &
                    cust.Phone)

Catch ex As IndexOutOfRangeException
    MessageBox.Show(ex.Message)
End Try
```

The Count Property

Each collection has a Count property that holds the number of items stored in the collection. Suppose an application has a list box named lstNames and a collection named names. The following code uses the Count property as the upper limits of the For Next loop.

```
Dim intX As Integer
For intX = 1 To names.Count
    lstNames.Items.Add(names(intX).ToString())
Next
```

Searching for an Item by Key Value Using the Item Method

You have already seen how the Item method can be used to retrieve an item with a specific index. It can also be used to retrieve an item with a specific key value. When used this way, the general format of the method is as follows:

```
CollectionNameItem(Expression)
```

CollectionName is the name of a collection. Expression can be either a numeric or a string expression. If Expression is a string, the Item method returns the member with the key value that matches the string. If no member exists with an index or key value matching Expression, an exception of the type IndexOutOfRangeException occurs. (If Expression is a numeric expression, it is used as an index value and the Item method returns the member at the specified index location.)

For example, the following code searches the studentCollection collection for an item with the key value 49812:

```
Dim s as Student
s = CType(studentCollection.Item("49812"), Student)
```

After this code executes, if the item is found, the s variable will reference the object returned by the Item method.

The following code uses the `Item` method to retrieve members by index. It retrieves each member from the collection and displays the value of the LastName property in a message box.

```
Dim intIndex As Integer
Dim aStudent As Student

For intIndex = 1 To studentCollection.Count
   aStudent = CType(studentCollection.Item(intIndex), Student)
   MessageBox.Show(aStudent.LastName)
Next
```

Using References versus Copies

When an item in a collection is of a fundamental Visual Basic data type, such as Integer or Single, you retrieve a copy of the member only. For example, suppose the following code is used to add integers to a collection named `numbers`:

```
Dim intInput As Integer
intInput = InputBox("Enter an integer value.")
numbers.Add(intInput)
```

Suppose the following code is used to retrieve the integer stored at index 1 and to change its value. Because `intNum` is only a copy of a value in the collection, the item stored at index 1 is unchanged.

```
Dim intNum As Integer
intNum = CType(numbers(1), Integer)
intNum = 0
```

When an item in a collection is a class object, however, you retrieve a reference to it, not a copy. For example, the following code retrieves the member of the `studentCollection` collection with the key value `49812`, and changes the value of its LastName property to *Griffin*.

```
Dim s as Student
s = CType(studentCollection.Item("49812"), Student)
s.LastName = "Griffin"
```

Because a reference to the member is returned, the LastName property of the object in the collection is modified.

Using the `For Each...Next` Loop with a Collection

You may also use the `For Each...Next` loop to access the individual members of a collection, eliminating the need to compare a counter variable against the collection's Count property. For example, the following code prints the LastName property of each member of the `studentCollection` collection.

```
Dim s As Student
For Each s In studentCollection
   MessageBox.Show(s.LastName)
Next
```

Removing Members

Use the **Remove** method to remove a member from a collection. The general format is:

```
CollectionName.Remove(Expression)
```

CollectionName is the name of a collection. *Expression* can be either a numeric or string expression. If it is a numeric expression, it is used as an index value and the member at the specified index location is removed. If *Expression* is a string, the member with the key value that matches the string is removed. If an index is provided, and it does not match an index of any item in the collection, an exception of the `IndexOutOfRangeException` type occurs. If a key value is provided, and it does not match the key value of any item in the collection, an exception of the `ArgumentException` type occurs.

For example, the following statement removes the member with the key value `"49812"` from the `studentCollection` collection:

```
studentCollection.Remove("49812")
```

The following statement removes the member at index location 7 from the `studentCollection` collection:

```
studentCollection.Remove(7)
```

To avoid throwing an exception, always check the range of the index you pass to the `Remove` method. The following is an example:

```
Dim intIndex As Integer
' (assign value to intIndex...)

If intIndex > 0 and intIndex <= studentCollection.Count Then
  studentCollection.Remove(intIndex)
End If
```

Similarly, make sure a key value exists before using it to remove an item, as shown here:

```
Dim strKeyToRemove As String
' (assign value to strKeyToRemove...)

If studentCollection.Contains(strKeyToRemove) Then
  studentCollection.Remove(strKeyToRemove))
End If
```

Writing Sub Procedures and Functions That Use Collections

Sub procedures and functions can accept collections as arguments, and functions can return collections. Remember that a collection is an instance of a class, so follow the same guidelines for passing any class object as an argument, or returning a class object from a function.

Relating the Items in Parallel Collections

Sometimes it is useful to store related data in two or more parallel collections. For example, assume a company assigns a unique employee number to each employee. An application that calculates gross pay has the following collections:

```
Dim hoursWorked As New Collection     ' To hold hours worked
Dim payRates As New Collection        ' To hold hourly pay rates
```

The `hoursWorked` collection stores the number of hours each employee has worked, and the `payRates` collection stores each employee's hourly pay rate.

When an item is stored in the `hoursWorked` or `payRates` collections, the employee's number is the key. For instance, let's say James Bourne's ID number is 55678. He has worked 40 hours and his pay rate is $12.50. The following statements add his data to the appropriate collection:

```
hoursWorked.Add(40, "55678")
payRates.Add(12.5, "55678")
```

To calculate his gross pay, we retrieve his data from each collection, using his ID number as the key:

```
sngGrossPay = hoursWorked.Item("55678") * payRate.Item("55678")
```

Employee Collection Program Example

The following code expands this idea. In addition to the hoursWorked and payRates collection, this code uses a collection to hold the employee names and a collection to hold the employee ID numbers.

```
Dim empNumbers As New Collection       ' Holds employee numbers
Dim employees As New Collection        ' Holds employee names
Dim hoursWorked As New Collection      ' Holds hours worked
Dim payRates As New Collection         ' Holds hourly pay rates

Dim strEmpNumber As String             ' Employee ID number
Dim strEmpName As String               ' Employee name
Dim decGrossPay, decHours, decRate As Decimal
Dim i As Integer                       ' Loop counter

' Add each employee's number to the empNumbers collection.
empNumbers.Add("55678")
empNumbers.Add("78944")
empNumbers.Add("84417")

' Add the employee names to the employees
' collection, with the employee ID number
' as the key.
employees.Add("James Bourne", "55678")
employees.Add("Jill Davis", "78944")
employees.Add("Kevin Franklin", "84417")

' Add each employee's hourly worked to the
' hoursWorked collection, with the employee
' ID number as the key.
hoursWorked.Add(40, "55678")
hoursWorked.Add(35, "78944")
hoursWorked.Add(20, "84417")

' Add each employee's hours pay rate to the
' payRates collection, with the employee
' ID number as the key.
payRates.Add(12.5, "55678")
payRates.Add(18.75, "78944")
payRates.Add(9.6, "84417")

' Compute and display each employee's
' gross pay.

For intIndex = 1 To employees.Count

    ' Get an employee ID number to use as a key.
    strEmpNumber = empNumbers(intIndex).ToString()

    ' Get this employee's name.
    strEmpName = employees.Item(strEmpNumber).ToString()
```

```
        ' Get the hours worked for this employee.
        decHours = CDec(hoursWorked.Item(strEmpNumber))

        ' Get the pay rate for this employee.
        decRate = CDec(payRates.Item(strEmpNumber))

        ' Calculate this employee's gross pay.
        decGrossPay = decHours * decRate

        ' Display the results for this employee.
        lblResult.Text &= "Gross pay for " & strEmpName & _
            " is " & decGrossPay.ToString("c") & vbCrLf
    Next
```

 Checkpoint

12.17 How do collections differ from arrays?

12.18 How do you add members to a collection?

12.19 How is a key value useful when you are adding an item to a collection?

12.20 How do you search for a specific member of a collection?

12.21 How do you remove a member from a collection?

 **12.4 Focus on Problem Solving: Creating the *Student Collection* Application**

Campus Systems, Inc. is developing software for a university and has hired you as a programmer. Your first assignment is to develop an application that allows the user to select a student's ID number from a list box to view information about the student. The user should also be able to add new student records and delete student records. The application will use the Student class and a collection of Student class objects. A test application with two forms has already been created for you.

In Tutorial 12-2, you examine the existing forms of the *Student Collection* application.

 Tutorial 12-2:

Completing the *Student Collection* application

VideoNote

Tutorial 12-2
Walkthrough

Step 1: Open the *Student Collection* project from the student sample programs folder named *Chap12\Student Collection*.

The project already has two forms, as shown in Figures 12-6 and 12-7. The MainForm form has a list box, lstIdNumbers, which will display a list of student ID numbers. When a student's ID number is selected from the list box, the data for that student will be displayed in the following Label controls: lblLastName, lblFirstName, lblIdNumber, lblTestAverage, and lblGrade. The *Add Student* button causes the AddForm form to be displayed. The *Remove* button removes the student whose ID number is currently selected.

Figure 12-6 MainForm form

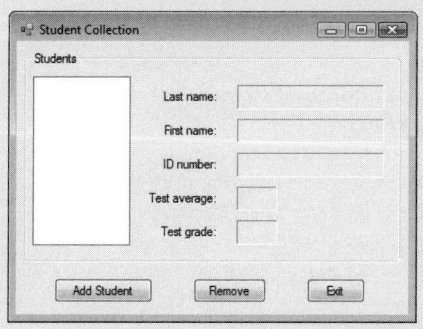

Figure 12-7 AddForm form

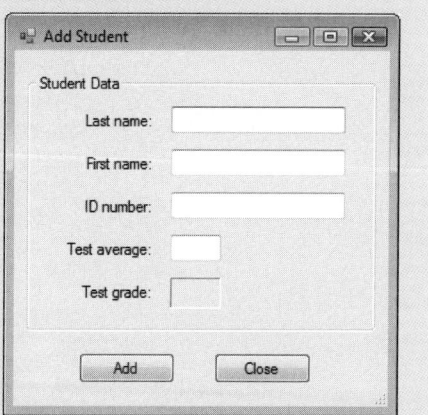

Step 2: Add the `Student` class you created in Tutorial 12-1 to the project. (Click *Project* on the menu bar, and then click *Add Existing Item*. Browse to the folder containing the *Student.vb* file. Select the *Student.vb* file and click the *Add* button.)

Step 3: Add a module to the project. Name the module ***StudentCollectionModule.vb***. Complete the module by entering the following code, shown in bold. (Don't type the line numbers. They are shown only for reference.)

```
 1 Module StudentCollectionModule
 2   ' Create a collection to hold Student objects.
 3   Public studentCollection As New Collection
 4
 5   ' The AddRecord procedure adds the object referenced
 6   ' by s to the collection. It uses the student ID number
 7   ' as the key.
 8
 9   Public Sub AddRecord(ByVal s As Student)
10     Try
11       studentCollection.Add(s, s.IdNumber)
12     Catch ex As Exception
13       MessageBox.Show(ex.Message)
14     End Try
15   End Sub
16 End Module
```

The statement in line 3 creates a collection, referenced by the object variable `studentCollection`. Because it is declared as `Public`, it will be available to all the forms in the project. The `AddRecord` procedure in lines 9 through 15, also declared as `Public`, accepts a `Student` object as an argument, and adds that object to the `studentCollection` collection.

Step 4: Now write the procedures and event handlers for the MainForm form, shown here. (Don't type the line numbers. They are shown only for reference.) Before you begin entering the code, make sure you understand how to create the code template for the `lstIdNumbers_SelectedIndexChanged` event handler in lines 84 through 101. This event handler will execute anytime the user selects an item in the `lstIdNumbers` list box. To create the code template, simply open MainForm in the *Designer* window and double-click the `lstIdNumbers` list box. (The comments that appear in lines 81 through 83 are there only as a reminder of how to create the code template. You do not need to type those comments into your code.)

```
1  Public Class MainForm
2    ' The ClearForm procedure clears the form.
3    Private Sub ClearForm()
4        lblFirstName.Text = String.Empty
5        lblLastName.Text = String.Empty
6        lblIdNumber.Text = String.Empty
7        lblTestAverage.Text = String.Empty
8        lblGrade.Text = String.Empty
9    End Sub
10
11   ' The UpdateListBox procedure updates the
12   ' contents of the list box.
13   Private Sub UpdateListBox()
14       ' Clear the list box.
15       lstIdNumbers.Items.Clear()
16
17       ' Load the ID numbers in the collection
18       ' into the list box.
19       Dim s As Student
20       For Each s In studentCollection
21         lstIdNumbers.Items.Add(s.IdNumber)
22       Next
23
24       ' Select the first item in the list.
25       If lstIdNumbers.Items.Count > 0 Then
26         lstIdNumbers.SelectedIndex = 0
27       Else
28         ClearForm()
29       End If
30   End Sub
31
32   ' The DisplayData procedure displays the data contained
33   ' in the Student object parameter.
34   Private Sub DisplayData(ByVal s As Student)
35       lblLastName.Text = s.LastName
36       lblFirstName.Text = s.FirstName
37       lblIdNumber.Text = s.IdNumber
38       lblTestAverage.Text = s.TestAverage.ToString()
39       lblGrade.Text = s.Grade
40   End Sub
41
42   Private Sub btnAdd_Click(...) Handles btnAdd.Click
43       ' Create an instance of the AddForm form.
44       Dim frmAdd As New AddForm
45
46       ' Display the form.
47       frmAdd.ShowDialog()
48
49       ' Update the contents of the list box.
50       UpdateListBox()
51   End Sub
52
53   Private Sub btnRemove_Click(...) Handles btnRemove.Click
```

```
 54        Dim intIndex As Integer
 55
 56        ' Make sure an item is selected.
 57        If lstIdNumbers.SelectedIndex <> -1 Then
 58           ' Confirm that the user wants to remove the item.
 59           If MessageBox.Show("Are you sure?", "Confirm Deletion",
 60                         MessageBoxButtons.YesNo) =
 61                         Windows.Forms.DialogResult.Yes Then
 62
 63              ' Retrieve the student's data from the collection.
 64              intIndex = lstIdNumbers.SelectedIndex
 65
 66              Try
 67                 ' Remove the selected item from the collection.
 68                 studentCollection.Remove(
 69                    lstIdNumbers.SelectedItem.ToString())
 70
 71                 ' Update the list box.
 72                 UpdateListBox()
 73              Catch ex As Exception
 74                 ' Error message
 75                 MessageBox.Show(ex.Message)
 76              End Try
 77           End If
 78        End If
 79     End Sub
 80
 81     ' Note to the student: To create the code template for the
 82     ' following event handler, double-click the lstIdNumbers
 83     ' list box in the Designer window.
 84     Private Sub lstIdNumbers_SelectedIndexChanged(...) Handles...
 85        Dim objStudent As Student
 86
 87        ' See if an item is selected.
 88        If lstIdNumbers.SelectedIndex <> -1 Then
 89           ' Retrieve the student's data from the collection.
 90           Try
 91              objStudent = CType(studentCollection.Item(
 92                 lstIdNumbers.SelectedItem), Student)
 93
 94              ' Display the student data.
 95              DisplayData(objStudent)
 96           Catch ex As Exception
 97              ' Error message
 98              MessageBox.Show(ex.Message)
 99           End Try
100        End If
101     End Sub
102
103     Private Sub btnExit_Click(...) Handles btnExit.Click
104        ' Close the form.
105        Me.Close()
106     End Sub
107 End Class
```

Step 5: Now write the procedures and event handlers for the AddForm form, shown here. (Don't type the line numbers. They are shown only for reference.)

```
1 Public Class AddForm
2   ' The GetData procedure gets data from the form
3   ' and stores it in the Student object parameter.
4   Private Sub GetData(ByVal s As Student)
5     s.LastName = txtLastName.Text
6     s.FirstName = txtFirstName.Text
7     s.IdNumber = txtIdNumber.Text
8     s.TestAverage = CDbl(txtTestAverage.Text)
9   End Sub
10
11  ' The ClearForm procedure clears the form.
12  Private Sub ClearForm()
13    ' Clear the text boxes.
14    txtFirstName.Text = String.Empty
15    txtLastName.Text = String.Empty
16    txtIdNumber.Text = String.Empty
17    txtTestAverage.Text = String.Empty
18    lblGrade.Text = String.Empty
19
20    ' Reset the focus.
21    txtLastName.Focus()
22  End Sub
23
24  Private Sub btnAdd_Click(...) Handles btnAdd.Click
25    ' Create an instance of the Student class.
26    Dim objStudent As New Student
27
28    ' Get data from the form.
29    GetData(objStudent)
30
31    ' Display the student's grade.
32    lblGrade.Text = objStudent.Grade
33
34    ' Save the student's record.
35    AddRecord(objStudent)
36
37    ' Confirm that the record was saved.
38    MessageBox.Show("Record added.")
39
40    ' Clear the form.
41    ClearForm()
42  End Sub
43
44  Private Sub btnClose_Click(...) Handles btnClose.Click
45    ' Close the form.
46    Me.Close()
47  End Sub
48 End Class
```

Step 6: Save the project and run the application. Click the *Add Student* button and add the following students:

Student 1

Last name: **Green**
First name: **Sara**
ID number: **27R8974**
Test average: **92.3**

Student 2

Last name:	**Robinson**
First name:	**Joy**
ID number:	**89G4561**
Test average:	**97.3**

Student 3

Last name:	**Williams**
First name:	**Jon**
ID number:	**71A4478**
Test average:	**78.6**

Step 7: Close the AddForm form. The main form should now appear as shown in Figure 12-8.

Step 8: Select a student's ID number in the list box. That student's data is displayed in the Label controls.

Step 9: Remove each student by selecting an ID number and then clicking the *Remove* button. Click *Yes* when asked *Are you sure?*

Step 10: Exit the application. Leave the *Student Collection* project loaded for Tutorial 12-3.

Figure 12-8 MainForm with students added

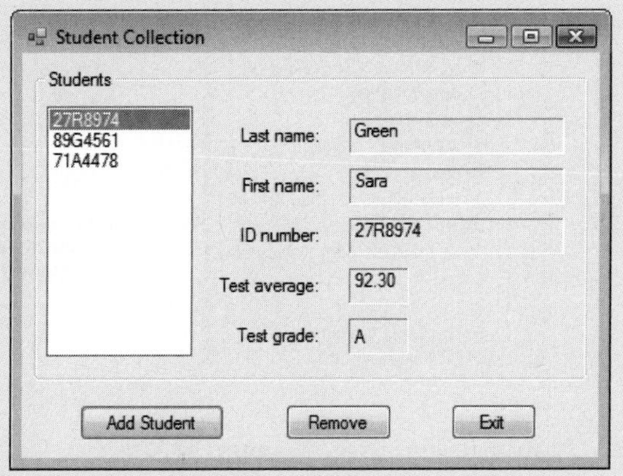

The Object Browser

12.5

CONCEPT: The Object Browser is a dialog box that allows you to browse all classes and components available to your project.

The **Object Browser** is a dialog box that displays information about objects. You can use the Object Browser to examine classes you have created, as well as the namespaces, classes, and other components that Visual Basic makes available to your project. Tutorial 12-3 guides you through the process of using the Object Browser to examine the classes you created in the *Student Collection* project.

Tutorial 12-3:
Using the Object Browser

Step 1: Make sure that you have the *Student Collection* project you created in Tutorial 12-2 opened in Visual Studio.

Step 2: Open the Object Browser by performing one of the following actions:
*   Click *View* on the menu bar, and then click *Object Browser*.
*   Press the F2 key.

The *Object Browser* window appears as shown in Figure 12-9. The left pane is the *objects* pane, and the right pane is the *members* pane. When you select an item in the *objects* pane on the left, information about that item appears in the *members* pane on the right.

Figure 12-9 *Object Browser* window

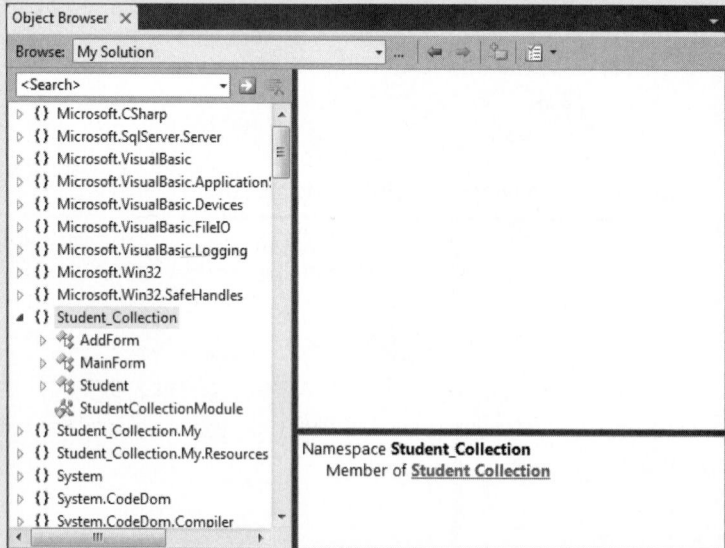

Step 3: Notice in Figure 12-9 that a *{} Student_Collection* entry appears in the objects pane. The braces *{}* indicate that Student_Collection is a namespace. Visual Basic has created a namespace for this project and named it Student_Collection. The contents of the project are stored in this namespace. Click the small arrow at the left of this entry to expand it. Now entries appear for AddForm, Main-Form, Student, and StudentCollection Module.

Step 4: Click the entry for Student. All members of the Student class should be listed in the *members* pane, as shown in Figure 12-10. If you click an entry in the *members* pane, a brief summary of the member is displayed below the pane. If you double-click an entry, the *Code* window appears with the cursor positioned at the selected item's declaration statement.

Step 5: Click some other entries under *{} Student_Collection* in the *object* window, such as MainForm and StudentCollectionModule, to view their members in the *members* window.

Figure 12-10 Members of the Student class displayed in the *members* pane

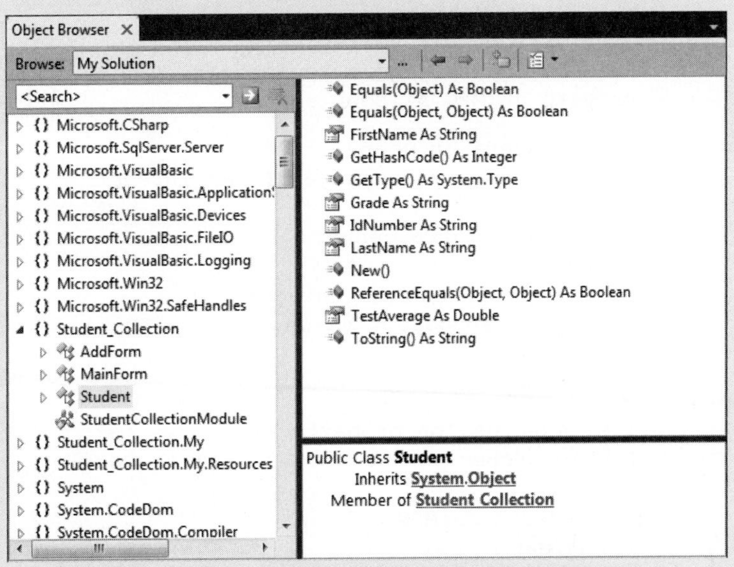

Step 6: Because Visual Basic forms and controls are classes, the Object Browser can be used to examine them as well. You can use this tool to quickly find out what methods and properties a control has. For example, type **TextBox** in the Search box and press ⏎Enter. The results of the search will appear in the left-hand pane. Double-click the entry for *System.Windows.Forms.TextBox*. The TextBox class should appear selected in the *Objects* pane and the members of the TextBox class should appear in the *members* pane.

Step 7: Close the Object Browser and close the project.

12.6 Introduction to Inheritance

CONCEPT: Inheritance allows a new class to be based on an existing class. The new class inherits the accessible member variables, methods, and properties of the class on which it is based.

An important aspect of object-oriented programming is inheritance. **Inheritance** allows you to create new classes that inherit, or derive, characteristics of existing classes. For example, you might start with the Student class we discussed earlier, which has only general information for all types of students. But special types of students might require the creation of classes such as GraduateStudent, ExchangeStudent, StudentEmployee, and so on. These new classes would share all the characteristics of the Student class, and they would each add the new characteristics that make them specialized.

In an inheritance relationship, there is a base class and a derived class. The **base class** is a general-purpose class that other classes may be based on. The **derived class** is based on the base class, and inherits characteristics from it. You can think of the base class as the parent and the derived class as the child.

Let's look at an example. The following Vehicle class has two private variables and two property procedures: Passengers and MilesPerGallon. The Passengers property uses the intPassengers member variable and the MilesPerGallon property uses the sngMPG member variable.

```
Public Class Vehicle
   ' Private member variables
   Private intPassengers As Integer        ' Number of passengers
   Private dblMPG As Double                ' Miles per gallon

   ' Passengers property
   Public Property Passengers() As Integer
     Get
        Return intPassengers
     End Get
     Set(ByVal value As Integer)
        intPassengers = value
     End Set
   End Property

   ' MilesPerGallon property
   Public Property MilesPerGallon() As Double
     Get
        Return dblMPG
     End Get
     Set(ByVal value As Double)
        dblMPG = value
     End Set
   End Property
End Class
```

(The *Vehicle Inheritance* program in the Chapter 12 student sample programs folder contains the code examples shown here.) The Vehicle class holds only general data about a vehicle. By using it as a base class, however, we can create other classes that hold more specialized data about specific types of vehicles. For example, look at the following code for a Truck class:

```
Public Class Truck
   Inherits Vehicle

     ' Private member variables
     Private dblCargoWeight As Double      ' Maximum cargo weight
     Private blnFourWheelDrive As Boolean  ' Four wheel drive

     ' MaxCargoWeight property
     Public Property MaxCargoWeight() As Double
       Get
          Return dblCargoWeight
       End Get
       Set(ByVal value As Single)
          dblCargoWeight = value
       End Set
     End Property

     ' FourWheelDrive property
     Public Property FourWheelDrive() As Boolean
       Get
          Return blnFourWheelDrive
       End Get
       Set(ByVal value As Boolean)
          blnFourWheelDrive = value
       End Set
     End Property
   End Class
```

Notice the second line of this class declaration:

```
Inherits Vehicle
```

This statement indicates that this class is derived from the `Vehicle` class. Because it is derived from the `Vehicle` class, the `Truck` class inherits all the `Vehicle` class member variables, methods, and properties that are not declared as private. In addition to the inherited base class members, the `Truck` class adds two properties of its own: `MaxCargoWeight`, which hold the maximum cargo weight, and FourWheelDrive, which indicates whether the truck uses four-wheel drive.

In the Form1 form, the following statements create an instance of the `Truck` class:

```
Dim pickUp as Truck
pickUp = New Truck
```

And the following statements store values in all of the object's properties:

```
pickUp.Passengers = 2
pickUp.MilesPerGallon = 18.0
pickUp.MaxCargoWeight = 2000.0
pickUp.FourWheelDrive = True
```

Notice that values are stored not only in the MaxCargoWeight and FourWheelDrive properties, but also in the Passengers and MilesPerGallon properties. The `Truck` class inherits the Passengers and MilesPerGallon properties from the `Vehicle` class.

Overriding Properties and Methods

Sometimes a property procedure or method in a base class is not appropriate for a derived class. If this is the case, you can **override** the base class property procedure or method by adding one with the same name to the derived class. When an object of the derived class accesses the property or calls the method, the overridden version in the derived class is executed rather than the version in the base class. For example, the `Vehicle` class has the following property procedure:

```
Public Property Passengers() As Integer
  Get
    Return intPassengers
  End Get
  Set(ByVal value As Integer)
    intPassengers = value
  End Set
End Property
```

The `Set` section of this property procedure stores any value passed to it in the `intPassengers` variable. Suppose that in the `Truck` class we want to restrict the number of passengers to either 1 or 2. We can override the Passengers property procedure by writing another version of it in the `Truck` class.

First, we must add the `Overridable` keyword to the property procedure in the `Vehicle` class, as follows:

```
Public Overridable Property Passengers() As Integer
  Get
    Return intPassengers
  End Get
  Set(ByVal value As Integer)
    intPassengers = value
  End Set
End Property
```

The **Overridable** keyword indicates that the procedure may be overridden in a derived class. If we do not add this keyword to the declaration, a compiler error will occur when we attempt to override the procedure. The general format of a property procedure with the Overridable keyword is as follows:

```
Public Overridable Property PropertyName() As DataType
   Get
      Statements
   End Get
   Set(ParameterDeclaration)
      Statements
   End Set
End Property
```

> **NOTE:** A private property cannot be overridable.

Next, we write the overridden property procedure in the Truck class, as follows:

```
' Passengers property
Public Overrides Property Passengers() As Integer
   Get
      Return MyBase.Passengers
   End Get
   Set(ByVal value As Integer)
      If value >= 1 And value <= 2 Then
         MyBase.Passengers = value
      Else
         MessageBox.Show("Passengers must be 1 or 2.", "Error")
      End If
   End Set
End Property
```

This procedure uses the **Overrides** keyword, indicating that it overrides a procedure in the base class. The general format of a property procedure that overrides a base class property procedure is as follows:

```
Public Overrides Property PropertyName() As DataType
   Get
      Statements
   End Get
   Set(ParameterDeclaration)
      Statements
   End Set
End Property
```

Let's see how the procedure works. The Get section has the following statement:

```
Return MyBase.Passengers
```

The **MyBase** keyword refers to the base class. The expression MyBase.Passengers refers to the base class's Passengers property. This statement returns the same value returned from the base class's Passengers property.

The Set section uses an If statement to validate that value is 1 or 2. If value is 1 or 2, the following statement is executed:

```
MyBase.Passengers = value
```

This statement stores value in the base class's Passenger property. If value is not 1 or 2, an error message is displayed. So, the following code will cause the error message to appear:

```
Dim pickUp As New Truck
pickUp.Passengers = 5
```

The complete code for the modified `Vehicle` and `Truck` classes follows:

```
Public Class Vehicle
    ' Private member variables
    Private intPassengers As Integer       ' Number of passengers
    Private dblMPG As Double               ' Miles per gallon

    ' Passengers property
    Public Overridable Property Passengers() As Integer
        Get
            Return intPassengers
        End Get
        Set(ByVal value As Integer)
            intPassengers = value
        End Set
    End Property

    ' MilesPerGallon property
    Public Property MilesPerGallon() As Double
        Get
            Return dblMPG
        End Get
        Set(ByVal value As Double)
            dblMPG = value
        End Set
    End Property
End Class

Public Class Truck
    Inherits Vehicle

    ' Private member variables
    Private dblCargoWeight As Double        ' Maximum cargo weight
    Private blnFourWheelDrive As Boolean    ' Four wheel drive

    ' MaxCargoWeight property
    Public Property MaxCargoWeight() As Double
        Get
            Return dblCargoWeight
        End Get
        Set(ByVal value As Double)
            dblCargoWeight = value
        End Set
    End Property

    ' FourWheelDrive property
    Public Property FourWheelDrive() As Boolean
        Get
            Return blnFourWheelDrive
        End Get
        Set(ByVal value As Boolean)
            blnFourWheelDrive = value
        End Set
    End Property

    ' Passengers property
    Public Overrides Property Passengers() As Integer
        Get
            Return MyBase.Passengers
        End Get
        Set(ByVal value As Integer)
            If value >= 1 And value <= 2 Then
                MyBase.Passengers = value
```

```
        Else
          MessageBox.Show("Passengers must be 1 or 2.", "Error")
        End If
      End Set
    End Property
End Class
```

Overriding Methods

Class methods may be overridden in the same manner as property procedures. The general format of an overridable base class Sub procedure is as follows:

```
Public Overridable Sub ProcedureName()
   Statements
End Sub
```

The general format of an overridable base class function is as follows:

```
Public Overridable Function FunctionName() As DataType
   Statements
End Function
```

NOTE: A private procedure or function cannot be overridable.

The general format of a Sub procedure that overrides a base class Sub procedure is as follows:

```
AccessSpecifier Overrides Sub ProcedureName()
   Statements
End Sub
```

The general format of a function that overrides a base class function is as follows:

```
AccessSpecifier Overrides Function FunctionName() As DataType
   Statements
End Sub
```

Because a derived class cannot access the private members of its base class, the overridable methods in the base class cannot be declared `Private`. A derived class method that overrides a base class method must keep the same access level (such as `Public`).

Overriding the `ToString` Method

By now you are familiar with the `ToString` method that all Visual Basic data types provide. This method returns a string representation of the data stored in a variable or object.

Every class you create in Visual Basic is automatically derived from a built-in class named `Object`. The **Object class** has a method named `ToString` which returns a fully qualified class name (`System.String`), which includes the namespace named *System*. You can override this method so it returns a string representation of the data stored in an object. For example, we can add the following `ToString` method to the `Vehicle` class:

```
' Overriden ToString method
Public Overrides Function ToString() As String
   ' Return a string representation
   ' of a vehicle.
   Dim str As String

   str = "Passengers: " & intPassengers.ToString() &
         " MPG: " & dblMPG.ToString()
   Return str
End Function
```

Our `ToString` method must be declared `Public` because `ToString` has already been given public visibility in the `Object` class. The `ToString` implementation shown here returns a string showing a vehicle's number of passengers and the miles-per-gallon. When a method is declared with the `Overrides` keyword, it is also implicitly declared as `Overridable`. So, we can override this `ToString` method in the `Truck` class, as follows:

```
Public Overrides Function ToString() As String
   ' Return a string representation
   ' of a truck.
   Dim str As String
   str = MyBase.ToString() & " Max. Cargo: " &
      dblCargoWeight.ToString() & " 4WD: " &
      blnFourWheelDrive.ToString()
   Return str
End Function
```

This method calls `MyBase.ToString`, which is the `Vehicle` class's `ToString` method. To that method's return value, it appends string versions of the `sngCargoWeight` and `blnFourWheelDrive` variables. The resulting string is then returned. The following statements, located in a separate class, create a `Truck` object, assign values to its properties, and call the `ToString` method:

```
Dim bigTruck As New Truck
bigTruck.Passengers = 2
bigTruck.MilesPerGallon = 14.0
bigTruck.MaxCargoWeight = 8000.0
bigTruck.FourWheelDrive = True
MessageBox.Show(bigTruck.ToString())
```

This code will display the following string in a message box:

```
Passengers: 2 MPG: 14.0 Max. Cargo: 8000.0 4WD: True
```

Base Class and Derived Class Constructors

Earlier in this chapter, you learned that a constructor is a special class method named `New`, and the constructor is automatically called when an instance of the class is created. It is possible for both a base class and a derived class to have constructors. For example, look at the following abbreviated versions of the `Vehicle` and `Truck` classes containing constructors:

```
Public Class Vehicle

   Public Sub New()
      MessageBox.Show("This is the base class constructor.")
   End Sub
   ' (other properties and methods...)
End Class

Public Class Truck
      Inherits Vehicle

   Public Sub New()
      MessageBox.Show("This is the derived class constructor.")
   End Sub
   ' (other properties and methods...)
End Class
```

When an instance of the derived class is created, the base class constructor is automatically called first and then the derived class constructor is called. So, creating an instance of the `Truck` class will cause the message *This is the base class constructor* to be displayed, followed by the message *This is the derived class constructor.*

> **NOTE:** The `Overridable` and `Overrrides` keywords are not used with constructors.

Protected Members

In addition to `Private` and `Public`, we will also study the `Protected` access specifier. The **Protected access specifier** may be used in the declaration of a base class member, such as the following:

```
Protected decCost As Decimal
```

This statement declares a protected variable named `decCost`. Protected base class members are like private members, except they may be accessed by methods and property procedures in derived classes. To all other classes, however, protected class members are just like private class members.

In Tutorial 12-4, you complete an application that uses inheritance.

Tutorial 12-4:
Completing an application that uses inheritance

In this tutorial, you will complete an application that keeps records about the number of course hours completed by computer science students. You will create a class named `GeneralStudent`, which will have properties to hold the following data: first name, last name, ID number, math hours completed, communications hours completed, humanities hours completed, elective hours completed, and total hours completed. This class will have a method named `UpdateHours` that will calculate the total hours completed when any of the other hours are changed. In addition, the class will override the `ToString` method.

You will also create a class named `CsStudent`, derived from the `GeneralStudent` class. The `CsStudent` class will have a property to hold the number of computer science hours completed. This class will override the `GeneralStudent` class's `UpdateHours` method to add the number of computer science hours.

Step 1: Open the Computer Science Student project from the Chapter 12 student sample programs folder. The forms have already been built for you. Figure 12-11 shows the MainForm form and Figure 12-12 shows the DisplayForm form.

Figure 12-11 MainForm form

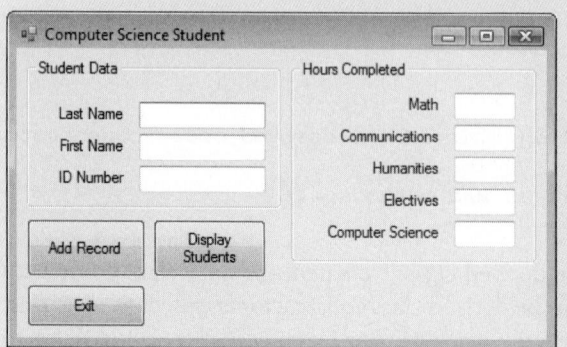

Figure 12-12 DisplayForm form

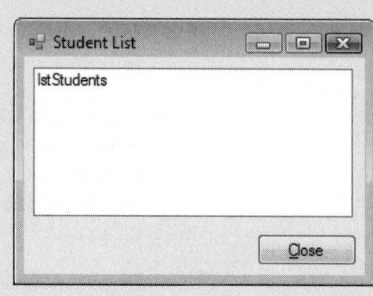

Step 2: Add a new class named GeneralStudent to the project. (Name the class file *GeneralStudent.vb*.) Complete the class by entering the following code, shown in bold. (Don't type the line numbers. They are shown only for reference.)

```
 1 Public Class GeneralStudent
 2   ' Member variables for last name, first name,
 3   ' and ID number
 4   Private strLastName As String
 5   Private strFirstName As String
 6   Private strIdNum As String
 7
 8   ' Member variables for hours completed
 9   Private dblMathHours As Double
10   Private dblCommHours As Double
11   Private dblHumHours As Double
12   Private dblElectHours As Double
13   Protected dblTotalHours As Double
14
15   ' Constructor to initialize member variables
16   Public Sub New()
17     strLastName = "(Unknown)"
18     strFirstName = "(Unknown)"
19     strIdNum = "(Unknown)"
20     dblMathHours = 0.0
21     dblCommHours = 0.0
22     dblHumHours = 0.0
23     dblElectHours = 0.0
24     dblTotalHours = 0.0
25   End Sub
26
27   ' The UpdateHours procedure updates the hours completed.
28   Public Overridable Sub UpdateHours()
29     dblTotalHours = dblMathHours + dblCommHours +
30       dblHumHours + dblElectHours
31   End Sub
32
33   ' Last Name property
34   Public Property LastName() As String
35     Get
36       Return strLastName
37     End Get
38     Set(ByVal value As String)
39       strLastName = value
40     End Set
41   End Property
42
43   ' First name property
44   Public Property FirstName() As String
45     Get
46       Return strFirstName
47     End Get
48     Set(ByVal value As String)
49       strFirstName = value
50     End Set
51   End Property
52
53   ' IdNumber property
54   Public Property IdNumber() As String
55     Get
56       Return strIdNum
57     End Get
```

```
 58       Set(ByVal value As String)
 59         strIdNum = value
 60       End Set
 61    End Property
 62
 63    ' MathHours property
 64    Public Property MathHours() As Double
 65       Get
 66          Return dblMathHours
 67       End Get
 68       Set(ByVal value As Double)
 69          dblMathHours = value
 70          UpdateHours()
 71       End Set
 72    End Property
 73
 74    ' CommunicationsHours property
 75    Public Property CommunicationsHours() As Double
 76       Get
 77          Return dblCommHours
 78       End Get
 79       Set(ByVal value As Double)
 80          dblCommHours = value
 81          UpdateHours()
 82       End Set
 83    End Property
 84
 85    ' HumanitiesHours property
 86    Public Property HumanitiesHours() As Double
 87       Get
 88          Return dblHumHours
 89       End Get
 90       Set(ByVal value As Double)
 91          dblHumHours = value
 92          UpdateHours()
 93       End Set
 94    End Property
 95
 96    ' ElectiveHours property
 97    Public Property ElectiveHours() As Double
 98       Get
 99          Return dblElectHours
100       End Get
101       Set(ByVal value As Double)
102          dblElectHours = value
103          UpdateHours()
104       End Set
105    End Property
106
107    ' HoursCompleted property (read-only)
108    Public ReadOnly Property HoursCompleted() As Double
109       Get
110          Return dblTotalHours
111       End Get
112    End Property
113
114    ' Overridden ToString method
115    Public Overrides Function ToString() As String
116       Dim str As String
117          str = "Name: " & strLastName & ", " &
118             strFirstName & " Completed Hours: " &
```

```
119          dblTotalHours.ToString()
120       Return str
121    End Function
122 End Class
```

Step 3: Add another class named CsStudent to the project. (Name the class file *CsStudent.vb*.) This class will be derived from the GeneralStudent class. Complete the class by entering the following code, shown in bold. (Don't type the line numbers. They are shown only for reference.)

```
1 Public Class CsStudent
2    Inherits GeneralStudent
3
4    ' Member variable for CS hours completed
5    Private dblCompSciHours As Double
6
7    ' Constructor
8    Public Sub New()
9       dblCompSciHours = 0.0
10   End Sub
11
12   ' Overridden UpdateHours method
13   Public Overrides Sub UpdateHours()
14      MyBase.UpdateHours()
15      dblTotalHours += dblCompSciHours
16   End Sub
17
18   ' CompSciHours property
19   Public Property CompSciHours() As Double
20      Get
21         Return dblCompSciHours
22      End Get
23      Set(ByVal value As Double)
24         dblCompSciHours = value
25         UpdateHours()
26      End Set
27   End Property
28 End Class
```

Step 4: Add a module named *CompSciStudentModule.vb* to the project. Complete the module by entering the following code, shown in bold. (Don't type the line numbers. They are shown only for reference.)

```
1 Module CompSciStudentModule
2    ' Collection for computer science students
3    Public csStudentCollection As New Collection
4
5    ' The AddStudent procedure adds a CsStudent object
6    ' to the collection and uses the IdNumber property
7    ' as the key.
8
9    Public Sub AddStudent(ByVal objCsStudent As CsStudent)
10      Try
11         csStudentCollection.Add(objCsStudent,
12                              objCsStudent.IdNumber)
13      Catch ex As Exception
14         MessageBox.Show(ex.Message)
15      End Try
16   End Sub
17 End Module
```

Line 3 creates a public collection named `csStudentCollection`. We will use this collection to hold `CsStudent` objects. The `AddStudent` public procedure in lines 9 through 16 accepts a `CsStudent` object as an argument and adds it to the `csStudentCollection` collection.

Step 5: Now you will write the procedures and event handlers for the MainForm form. Complete the form as follows by entering the code shown in bold. (Don't type the line numbers. They are shown only for reference.)

```
1 Public Class MainForm
2    ' The GetData procedure assigns values from the form
3    ' to a CsStudent object's properties.
4    Private Sub GetData(ByVal objCsStudent As CsStudent)
5      Try
6        ' Get name and ID number
7        objCsStudent.LastName = txtLastName.Text
8        objCsStudent.FirstName = txtFirstName.Text
9        objCsStudent.IdNumber = txtIdNumber.Text
10
11       ' Get hours
12       objCsStudent.MathHours = CDbl(txtMath.Text)
13       objCsStudent.CommunicationsHours = CDbl(txtComm.Text)
14       objCsStudent.HumanitiesHours = CDbl(txtHum.Text)
15       objCsStudent.ElectiveHours = CDbl(txtElect.Text)
16       objCsStudent.CompSciHours = CDbl(txtCompSci.Text)
17     Catch ex As Exception
18       ' Error message
19       MessageBox.Show("Enter valid numeric values for all hours.")
20     End Try
21   End Sub
22
23   ' The ClearForm procedure clears the form.
24   Private Sub ClearForm()
25     ' Clear the text boxes.
26     txtLastName.Clear()
27     txtFirstName.Clear()
28     txtIdNumber.Clear()
29     txtMath.Clear()
30     txtComm.Clear()
31     txtHum.Clear()
32     txtElect.Clear()
33     txtCompSci.Clear()
34
35     ' Set the focus.
36     txtLastName.Focus()
37   End Sub
38
39   Private Sub btnAdd_Click(...) Handles btnAdd.Click
40     ' Create an instance of the CsStudent class.
41     Dim objCsStudent As New CsStudent
42
43     ' Get data from the form.
44     GetData(objCsStudent)
45
46     ' Add the CsStudent object to the collection.
47     AddStudent(objCsStudent)
48
49     ' Clear the form.
50     ClearForm()
51
```

```
52        ' Display a confirmation message.
53        MessageBox.Show("Student record added successfully")
54    End Sub
55
56    Private Sub btnDisplay_Click(...) Handles btnDisplay.Click
57        ' Create an instance of the DisplayForm form.
58        Dim frmDisplay As New DisplayForm
59
60        ' Display the form.
61        frmDisplay.ShowDialog()
62    End Sub
63
64    Private Sub btnExit_Click(...) Handles btnExit.Click
65        ' Close the form.
66        Me.Close()
67    End Sub
68 End Class
```

Step 6: Now you will write the event handlers for the DisplayForm form. Complete the form as follows by entering the code shown in bold. (Don't type the line numbers. They are shown only for reference.)

```
1 Public Class DisplayForm
2
3    Private Sub DisplayForm_Load(...) Handles MyBase.Load
4        ' Declare an object variable that can reference
5        ' a CsStudent object.
6        Dim objCsStudent As CsStudent
7
8        ' Get each object in the collection and add its
9        ' data to the list box.
10       For Each objCsStudent In csStudentCollection
11           lstStudents.Items.Add(objCsStudent.ToString())
12       Next
13   End Sub
14
15   Private Sub btnClose_Click(...) Handles btnClose.Click
16       ' Close the form.
17       Me.Close()
18   End Sub
19 End Class
```

Step 7: Save the project and run the application. On the main form, add data for a fictitious student, and then click the *Add Record* button. Repeat this for at least two more students. Click the *Display Students* button to see a list of the students you have added. Figure 12-13 shows an example.

Figure 12-13 *Student List* displayed

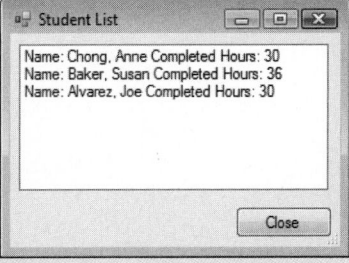

Step 8: Click the *Close* button and end the application.

Checkpoint

12.22 The beginning of a class declaration follows. What is the name of the base class, and what is the name of the derived class?

```
Public Class Fly
    Inherits Insect
```

12.23 What does a derived class inherit from its base class?

12.24 What is overriding, when speaking of class declarations?

12.25 What keyword must you include in the declaration of a property procedure or method in order for it to be overridden in a derived class?

12.26 What keyword must you include in the declaration of a property procedure or method in order for it to override one that exists in the base class?

12.27 When both a base class and its derived class have a constructor, which constructor executes first?

12.28 What is a protected base class member?

Summary

12.1 Classes and Objects

- Object-oriented programming is a way of designing and coding applications that allows interchangeable software components to be used to build larger programs.
- The primary goal of object-oriented design is to address the needs of the application or problem being solved. A secondary goal is to design classes that can outlive the current application and possibly be used in future programs.
- The class interface is the portion that is visible to the application programmer who uses the class. The program written by such a person is also called the client program, in reference to the client-server relationship between a class and the programs that use it.
- The class implementation is the portion of a class that is hidden from client programs; it is created from private member variables, private properties, and private methods.

12.2 Creating a Class

- The steps that must occur when an instance of a class is created are (1) declare an object variable and (2) create an instance of the class in memory and assign its address to the object variable. Each instance of a class has its own unique copy of the class's member variables.
- Members, properties, and methods of a class object are accessed with the dot (.) operator.
- Properties are generally implemented as property procedures. A property procedure is a function that behaves like a property. Property procedures have two sections: Get and Set. The Get section is executed when the value of the property is retrieved. The Set section is executed when a value is stored in the property. A read-only property cannot be set by a client program. It is implemented as a property procedure declared with the ReadOnly keyword, and does not have a Set section.
- To remove an object, set all the object variables that reference it to Nothing; it will be removed from memory by the .NET garbage collector.
- An object variable declared inside a procedure is local to that procedure. If an object is referenced only by a procedure's local object variable, the object is automatically removed from memory by the garbage collector after the procedure ends.
- The Is and IsNot operators compare two object variables to determine if they reference the same object.
- You can create arrays of objects, and you can write Sub procedures and functions that work with arrays of objects.
- A method is a Sub procedure or function that is a member of a class. The method performs some operation on the data stored in the class. You write methods inside the class declaration.
- A constructor is a class method that is automatically called when an instance of the class is created. Constructors are useful for initializing member variables or performing other startup operations. To create a constructor, create a Sub procedure named New in the class.
- A finalizer is a class method named Finalize, which is automatically called just before an instance of the class is removed from memory.
- Use the *Add Existing Item* dialog box to add an existing class to a project.

12.3 Collections

- A collection is a structure that holds a group of items. It automatically expands and shrinks to accommodate the items added to it, and allows items to be stored with an associated key value, which may be used when searching for collection members.

- The Count property indicates the number of items stored in a collection. The Add method stores an item in a collection. The Item method finds and returns an object in a collection. The Remove method is used to remove an item from a collection.

12.4 Focus on Problem Solving: Creating the *Student Collection* Application

- Tutorial 12-2 develops an application that builds a collection of students and allows the user to select a student's ID number from a list box to view information about the student.

12.5 The Object Browser

- The Object Browser displays information about the classes, properties, methods, and events available to a project.

12.6 Introduction to Inheritance

- Inheritance allows you to create new classes that inherit, or derive, characteristics of existing classes. In an inheritance relationship, there is a base class and a derived class. The base class can be thought of as the parent and the derived class as the child.
- Sometimes a property procedure or method in a base class does not work adequately for a derived class. When this happens, you can override the base class property procedure or method by writing one with the same name in the derived class.
- You must use the Overridable keyword in the declaration of a method or property procedure in a base class that is to be overridden. You must use the Overrides keyword in the declaration of a method or property procedure in a derived class that overrides another one in the base class.
- Every class that you create in Visual Basic is automatically derived from a built-in class named Object. The Object class has a method named ToString that returns a fully qualified class name. You can override this method so it returns a string representation of the data stored in a class.
- It is possible for both a base class and a derived class to have constructors. When an instance of the derived class is created, the base class constructor is called before the derived class constructor.
- Protected base class members are like private members, except they may be accessed by methods and property procedures in derived classes. To all other classes, however, protected class members are just like private class members.

Key Terms

abstract data type (ADT)	derived class
abstraction	encapsulation
Add method	finalizer
attributes	finding the classes
base class	Friend access
class	garbage collector
class declaration	Get section
class implementation	going out of scope
class interface	inheritance
class objects	Is operator
client program	IsNot operator
collection	Item method
constructor	member variable

method
MyBase keyword
object
Object Browser
Object class
object-oriented analysis
object-oriented programming
(OOP)
operations

Output window
Overridable keyword
override
Overrides keyword
property procedure
Protected access specifier
read-only property
Remove method
Set section

Review Questions and Exercises

Fill-in-the-Blank

1. A(n) _____ is a data type created by a programmer.

2. A(n) _____ is a program structure that defines an abstract data type.

3. An object is a(n) _____ of a class.

4. The _____ is the portion of a class that is visible to the client program that uses the class.

5. The _____ is the portion of a class that is hidden from client programs.

6. A(n) _____ procedure is a function that behaves like a class property.

7. The _____ section of a Property procedure is executed when a client program retrieves the value of a property.

8. The _____ section of a Property procedure executes when a client program stores a value in a property.

9. A(n) _____ property cannot be set by a client program.

10. A(n) _____ is a procedure or function that is a member of the class.

11. A(n) _____ is a class method that is automatically called when an instance of the class is created.

12. A(n) _____ is a class method that is automatically called just before an instance of the class is removed from memory.

13. You can display messages for debugging purposes in the _____ window.

14. A(n) _____ is a structure that holds a group of items.

15. The _____ window displays information about the classes, properties, methods, and events available to a project.

16. _____ is an object-oriented programming feature that allows you to create new classes that derive characteristics of existing classes.

17. A(n) _____ class is a general-purpose class on which other classes may be based.

18. A(n) _____ class is based on another class, and inherits characteristics from it.

19. You can _____ a base class property procedure or method by writing one with the same name in a derived class.

20. _____ base class members are like private members, except that they may be accessed by methods and property procedures in derived classes.

Multiple Choice

1. Which of the following program structures defines an abstract data type?
    a. Variable
    b. Exception
    c. Class
    d. Class object

2. If the variable `status` is declared inside a class, which of the following describes `status`?
    a. Global variable
    b. Constructor
    c. Finalizer
    d. Member variable

3. An object is automatically released when all references to it are set to which of the following?
    a. `Nothing`
    b. `Empty`
    c. `Clear`
    d. `Done`

4. This section of a property procedure returns the value of the property.
    a. `Value`
    b. `Property`
    c. `Get`
    d. `Set`

5. This section of a property procedure stores a value of the property.
    a. `Value`
    b. `Property`
    c. `Get`
    d. `Set`

6. A class constructor is a procedure by this name.
    a. `New`
    b. `Constructor`
    c. `Finalizer`
    d. `Main`

7. A class finalizer is a procedure by this name.
    a. `New`
    b. `Finalizer`
    c. `Finalize`
    d. `Main`

8. Which section is missing from a read-only property procedure?
    a. `Get`
    b. `Set`
    c. `Store`
    d. `Save`

9. This process runs periodically to free the memory used by all unreferenced objects.
    a. Garbage collector
    b. Memory collector
    c. Housekeeper
    d. RAM dumper

10. You must use this operator to determine whether two object variables reference the same object.

    a. `=`
    b. `<>`
    c. `Is`
    d. `Equal`

11. Which method is used to store an item in a collection?

    a. `Store`
    b. `Insert`
    c. `Add`
    d. `Collect`

12. Which method is used to search for an item in a collection?

    a. `Find`
    b. `Item`
    c. `Search`
    d. `Member`

13. Which method removes an item from a collection?

    a. `Remove`
    b. `Item`
    c. `Delete`
    d. `Erase`

14. Which property indicates the number of items stored in a collection?

    a. Items
    b. Number
    c. Count
    d. Members

15. Which of the following displays information about the classes, properties, methods, and events available to a project?

    a. Object Browser
    b. Object Navigator
    c. Class Browser
    d. Class Resource List

16. In an inheritance relationship, which class is usually a generalized class from which other, more specialized, classes are derived?

    a. Derived
    b. Base
    c. Protected
    d. Public

17. Which type of class member is not visible to derived classes?

    a. Private
    b. Public
    c. Protected
    d. ReadOnly

18. Which keyword indicates that the procedure may be overridden in a derived class?

    a. `Private`
    b. `Overrides`
    c. `Public`
    d. `Overridable`

19. Which keyword indicates that a procedure in a derived class overrides a procedure in the base class?

   a. `Private`
   b. `Overrides`
   c. `Public`
   d. `Overridable`

20. When used in a derived class, which keyword refers to the base class?

   a. `BaseClass`
   b. `Base`
   c. `MyBase`
   d. `Parent`

21. Every class in Visual Basic is derived from a built-in class having which of the following names?

   a. `Object`
   b. `SuperClass`
   c. `Parent`
   d. `System`

22. Class members declared with this access specifier are like private members, except that they may be accessed by methods and property procedures in derived classes.

   a. `Special`
   b. `Secret`
   c. `Public`
   d. `Protected`

True or False

Indicate whether the following statements are true or false.

1. T F: Public properties are part of the class interface.

2. T F: Private member variables are part of the class interface.

3. T F: A class's `New` procedure must be called from a client program.

4. T F: A class method may be either a procedure or a function.

5. T F: A runtime error will occur when you attempt to add a member with the same key to a collection as an existing member.

6. T F: You can use both the `Before` and `After` arguments of a collection's `Add` method at the same time.

7. T F: When retrieving an item from a collection, if the item is of the Integer data type, you can retrieve only a copy of the member.

8. T F: The Object Browser does not display information about the standard Visual Basic controls.

9. T F: If you attempt to retrieve an item from a collection and specify a nonexistent index, a runtime error is generated.

10. T F: A private property or method cannot be overridden.

11. T F: The `ToString` method cannot be overridden.

12. T F: Protected base class members cannot be accessed by derived classes.

Short Answer

1. How is a class interface created in Visual Basic?

2. What is encapsulation?

3. In the statement `Dim newStudent As Student`, which is the class and which is the object variable?

4. How do you create a read-only property?

5. How is an object different from a class?

6. Do the icons in the Visual Studio Toolbox represent classes or objects?

7. How are properties different from methods?

8. What is the difference between retrieving a collection item that is of a fundamental Visual Basic data type and retrieving one that is a class object?

9. What is encapsulation?

10. What happens to an object created inside a procedure when the procedure finishes?

11. Suppose class A has the following members:

    Private member variable x
    Public member variable y
    Public property `Data`
    Protected method `UpdateData`

    Suppose also that class B is derived from class A. Which of class A's members are inherited by class B?

12. When a property procedure or method in a base class is not appropriate for a derived class, what can you do?

13. Suppose class B is derived from class A. Class A's `UpdateData` method has been overridden in class B. How can the `UpdateData` method in class B call the `UpdateData` method in class A?

What Do You Think?

1. Suppose that when developing an application, you create a class named `Bank-Account` and you declare an object variable of the `BankAccount` type named `checking`. Which is the abstract data type, `BankAccount` or `checking`?

2. Look at the following problem description and identify the potential classes.

   We need to keep a list of customers and record our business transactions with them. Each time a customer purchases a product, an order is filled out. Each order shows a list of items kept in our central warehouse.

3. Does each button on the same form have its own copy of the Visible property?

4. In a student record-keeping program, what attributes might be assigned to a college transcript class?

5. Why are member variables usually declared `Private` in classes?

6. At the end of the following example, how many `Student` objects exist?

   ```
   Dim st1 As New Student
   Dim st2 As Student
   st2 = st1
   ```

7. At the end of the following example, how many `Student` objects exist?

```
Dim st1 As New Student
Dim st2 As Student
st2 = st1
st1 = Nothing
```

8. Suppose that an application at an animal hospital uses two classes: `Mammal` and `Dog`. Which do you think is the base class and which is the derived class? Why?

9. Why does it make sense that you cannot use the `Overridable` keyword in a private base class member declaration?

Find the Error

For each of the following questions assume `Customer` is a class. Find the errors.

1. `Dim Customer as New customerData`

2.
```
Dim customerData as Customer
customerData.LastName = "Smith"
```

3.
```
customerData = Nothing
customerData.LastName = "Smith"
```

4.
```
Public Property LastName() As String
   Set
     Return lname
   End Get
   Get(ByVal value As String)
     lname = value
   End Set
End Property
```

5.
```
Dim customerCollection as Collection
customerCollection.Add customerData
```

6. The following code appears in a base class:

```
Private Overridable Function GetData() As Integer
   ' (statements...)
End Sub
```

The following code appears in a derived class:

```
' This function overrides the base class function.
Public Function GetData() As Integer
   ' (statements...)
End Sub
```

Algorithm Workbench

1. Suppose that an application declares an array of objects with the following statement:

```
Dim employees(9) As Employee
```

Write a loop that creates ten instances of the class and assigns them to the elements of the array.

2. Code a `Dim` statement that declares an object variable of the class type `Transcript`. The statement should not create an instance of the class.

3. Code a statement that creates a `Transcript` object and assigns it to the variable from Question 2.

4. Code a statement that removes the reference used by the object variable used in Questions 2 and 3.

5. Code a single statement that declares an object variable and creates a new instance of the Transcript class.

6. Write the property procedures for a property named CustomerNumber that assigns a string value to a member variable named strCustomerNumber.

7. Look at the following code for the Book class:

```
Public Class Book
    ' Private member variables
    Private strTitle As String
    Private strAuthor As String
    Private strPublisher As String
    Private strIsbn As String

    ' Constructor
    Public Sub New()
        strTitle = String.Empty
        strAuthor = String.Empty
        strPublisher = String.Empty
        strIsbn = String.Empty
    End Sub

    ' Title Property
    Public Property Title() As String
        Get
            Return strTitle
        End Get
        Set(ByVal value As String)
            strTitle = value
        End Set
    End Property

    ' Author property
    Public Property Author() As String
        Get
            Return strAuthor
        End Get
        Set(ByVal value As String)
            strAuthor = value
        End Set
    End Property

    ' Publisher property
    Public Property Publisher() As String
        Get
            Return strPublisher
        End Get
        Set(ByVal value As String)
            strPublisher = value
        End Set
    End Property

    ' Isbn property
    Public Property Isbn() As String
        Get
            Return strIsbn
        End Get
        Set(ByVal value As String)
            strIsbn = value
        End Set
    End Property
End Class
```

Design a class named `TextBook` that is derived from the `Book` class. The `TextBook` class should have the following properties:

- Course (string). This property holds the name of the course that the textbook is used for.
- OrderQuantity (integer). This property holds the number of books to order for the course.

The OrderQuantity property cannot be negative, so provide error checking in the property procedure.

Programming Challenges

1. **E-Mail Address Book**

   Write a program that lets the user display and modify an address book containing names, e-mail addresses, and phone numbers. The program should contain a class named `Address`. The `Address` class should contain the following information about one person: name, e-mail address, phone, and comments. The application should also have a collection named `addressList`, which stores a collection of `Address` objects.

   The main window, shown in Figure 12-14 displays the names from the address book in a list box. The user should be able to input new names and addresses, using a form similar to the one shown in Figure 12-15.

Figure 12-14 *E-mail Address Book* form

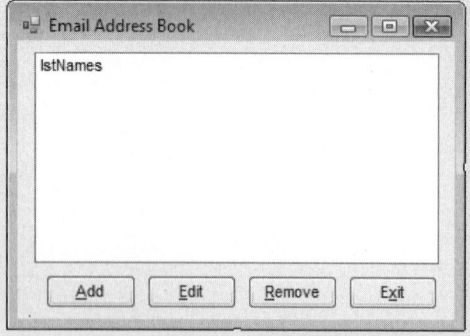

Figure 12-15 *Add New Name* form

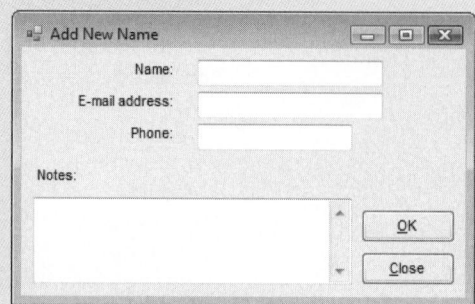

2. **Carpet Price Calculator**

   The Westfield Carpet Company has asked you to write an application that calculates the price of carpeting. To calculate the price of a carpeting, you multiply the area of the floor (width × length) by the price per square foot of carpet. For example, the area of a floor that is 12 feet long and 10 feet wide is 120 feet. To cover that floor with carpet that costs $8 per square foot would cost $960.

   You should create a class named `Rectangle` with the following properties:

   Width: A single
   Length: A single
   Area: A single

   The Area property should be read-only. Provide a method named `CalcArea` that calculates width × length and stores the result in the Area property.

   Next, create a class named `Carpet` with the following properties:

   Color: A string
   Style: A string
   Price: A decimal

The application should have a form similar to the one shown in Figure 12-16. (The carpet price is the price per square foot.) When the *Calculate* button is clicked, the application should copy the data in the text boxes into the appropriate object properties, and then display the area and price.

Figure 12-16 *Carpet Price Calculator* form

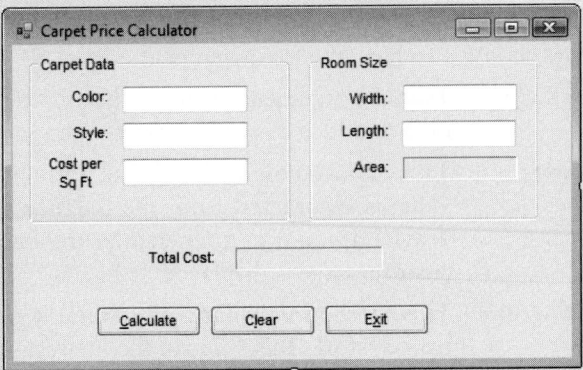

Design Your Own Forms

3. **Saving the Student Collection**

   Modify the student collection application from this chapter so it saves the collection in a file or a database before the program exits. When the program starts up, load the collection from the file or database.

VideoNote

The Motor
Class Problem

4. **Motor Class**

   Create an application that tracks electric motors in a manufacturing plant. The application should have a Motor class with the following properties:

   - MotorId: Five-digit string, such as `"02340"`
   - Description: String
   - RPM: Double, values in the range 10 to 10000
   - Voltage: Double, values in the range 1 to 500
   - Status: String, three characters.

   The Status values are:

   - ON: Motor is online and running.
   - OFF: Motor is online but not running.
   - MNT: Motor is undergoing maintenance and cleaning.
   - NA: Motor is not available.

   The application should be able to store at least 10 Motor class objects in an array. Create an input form in the application that allows users to input new motor records to be added to the array. Create another form that displays all the motors in the array in a list box.

5. **MotorCollection Class**

   Modify the application you created in Programming Challenge 4 so it uses a collection instead of an array to hold the Motor class objects. When the application ends, it should save the contents of the collection to a file or a database. When the application starts up, it should load the data from the file or database into the collection. Be sure to write the appropriate error handlers.

6. **Account Class**

    You are a programmer for the Home Software Company. You have been assigned to develop a class that models the basic workings of a bank account. The class should have the following properties:

    - Balance: Holds the current account balance.
    - IntRate: Holds the interest rate for the period.
    - Interest: Holds the interest earned for the current period.
    - Transactions: Holds the number of transactions for the current period.

    The class should also have the following methods:

    MakeDeposit   Takes an argument, which is the amount of the deposit. This argument is added to the Balance property.

    Withdraw   Takes an argument that is the amount of the withdrawal. This value is subtracted from the Balance property, unless the withdrawal amount is greater than the balance. If this happens, an error message is displayed.

    CalcInterest   This method calculates the amount of interest for the current period, stores this value in the Interest property, and adds it to the Balance property.

    Demonstrate the class in an application that performs the following tasks:

    - Allows deposits to be made to the account.
    - Allows withdrawals to be taken from the account.
    - Calculates interest for the period.
    - Reports the current account balance at any time.
    - Reports the current number of transactions at any time.

7. **Inventory Item Class**

    Create an application that stores inventory records for a retail store. The application should have an Inventory class with the following properties:

    InvNumber: A string used to hold an inventory number. Each item in the inventory should have a unique inventory number.

    Description: A string that holds a brief description of the item.

    Cost: A decimal value that holds the amount that the retail store paid for the item.

    Retail: A decimal value that holds the retail price for the item.

    OnHand: An integer value that holds the number of items on hand. This value cannot be less than 0.

    The application should store Inventory class objects in a collection. Create an input form in the application that allows users to input new inventory items to be added to the collection. The user should also be able to look up items by their inventory number.

8. **Inventory Class Modification**

    Modify the application you created in Programming Challenge 7 so it saves the contents of the collection to a file or a database. When the application starts up, it should load the data from the file or database into the collection. Be sure to use exception handling.

9. **Cash Register**

    Create an application that serves as a simple cash register for a retail store. Use the Inventory class you created in Programming Challenge 7 to store data about the items in the store's inventory. When the application starts up, it should load the entire store's inventory from a file or a database into a collection of Inventory objects.

When a purchase is made, the cashier should select an item from a list box. (If an item's OnHand property is set to zero, the item should not be available in the list box.) The item's description, retail price, and number of units on hand should be displayed on the form when selected. The cashier should enter the quantity being purchased, and the application should display the sales tax and the total of the sale. (The quantity being purchased cannot exceed the number of units on hand.) The quantity being purchased should be subtracted from the item's OnHand property. When the application ends, the contents of the collection should be saved to the file or database.

10. **Person** Class

Begin a new project named *Customer Information*, and design a class named `Person` with the following properties:

- LastName (string)
- FirstName (string)
- Address (string)
- City (string)
- State (string)
- Zip (string)
- Phone (string)

Implement the properties as public property procedures.

Create a form that allows you to assign values to each property of a `Person` object.

11. Derived **Customer** Class

Open the *Customer Information* project you created in Programming Challenge 10. Design a new class named `Customer`, which is derived from the `Person` class. The `Customer` class should have the following properties:

- CustomerNumber (integer)
- MailingList (Boolean)
- Comments (String)

The CustomerNumber property will be used to hold a unique number for each customer. The Mailing List property will be set to *True* if the customer wishes to be on a mailing list, or *False* if the customer does not wish to be on a mailing list. The comments property holds miscellaneous comments about the customer.

Modify the form so that it allows you to store data in each property of a Customer object. To enter the customer comments, use a TextBox control with its Multiline and WordWrap properties set to *True*.

12. Derived **PreferredCustomer** Class

A retail store has a preferred customer plan where customers may earn discounts on all their purchases. The amount of a customer's discount is determined by the amount of the customer's cumulative purchases in the store.

- When a preferred customer spends $500, he or she gets a 5% discount on all future purchases.
- When a preferred customer spends $1000, he or she gets a 6% discount on all future purchases.
- When a preferred customer spends $1500, he or she gets a 7% discount on all future purchases.
- When a preferred customer spends $2000 or more, he or she gets a 10% discount on all future purchases.

Open the *Customer Information* project that you modified in Programming Challenge 11. Design a new class named PreferredCustomer, which is derived from the Customer class. The PreferredCustomer class should have the following properties:

- PurchasesAmount (decimal)
- DiscountLevel (single)

Modify the application's form so it allows you to store data in each property of a PreferredCustomer object. Add the object to a collection, using the customer number as a key. Allow the user to look up a preferred customer by the customer number, edit the customer data, and remove a customer from the collection.

A Advanced User Interface Controls and Techniques

The chapters in this textbook have introduced you to the fundamental Visual Basic controls. There are many more controls available in Visual Basic and this appendix introduces you to several of them. It also discusses some advanced programming techniques, and user interface design guidelines. The examples shown in this appendix can be found in the Student Sample Program Files folder on the Student CD.

Scroll Bars

Scroll bars provide a visual way to adjust a value within a range of values. These types of controls display a slider that may be dragged along a track. Visual Basic provides a horizontal scroll bar control named **HScrollBar**, and a vertical scroll bar control named **VScrollBar**. Figure A-1 shows examples of each of these controls. You can find these controls in the Toolbox, in the *All Windows Forms* group.

Here is a summary of the important properties of each of these controls:

- The Value property is an integer value that is adjusted as the user moves the control's slider. (The default value is 0.)
- The Minimum property is the lower limit of the scrollable range. (The default value is 0.)
- The Maximum property is the upper limit of the scrollable range. (The default value is 100.)
- The LargeChange property is the integer amount by which the Value property changes when the user clicks the scroll bar area that lies to either side of the slider. This is also the amount by which the Value property changes when the user presses the Page Up or Page Down keys on the keyboard while the control has the focus. (The default value is 10.)
- The SmallChange property is the integer amount by which the Value property changes when the user clicks one of the arrows that appear at either end of a scroll bar control. (The default value is 1.)

Figure A-1 Horizontal and vertical scroll bars

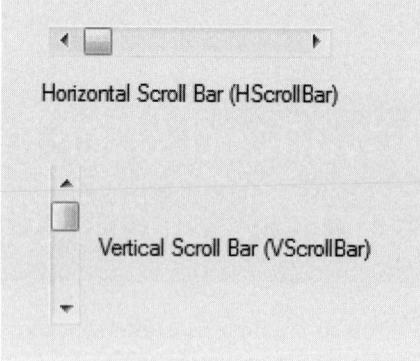

When a horizontal scroll bar's slider is moved toward its left side, the Value property is decreased. When the slider is moved toward the scroll bar's right side, the Value property is increased. When a vertical scroll bar's slider is moved toward its top, the Value property is decreased. When the slider is moved toward the scroll bar's bottom, the Value property is increased.

When the user moves the slider on a scroll bar control, a Scroll event occurs. If you write a Scroll event handler for the control, the event handler will execute any time the slider is moved. To generate a code template for the Scroll event handler, simply double-click the scroll bar control in the *Designer* window.

Figure A-2 shows the form in an example application that demonstrates the HScrollBar control. The HScrollBar control is named `hsbScrollBar` and the label that displays the value is named `lblValue`. The form's code follows. This project can be found on the Student CD. You will also find a similar project that demonstrates the VScrollBar control.

Figure A-2 HScrollBar Demo application form

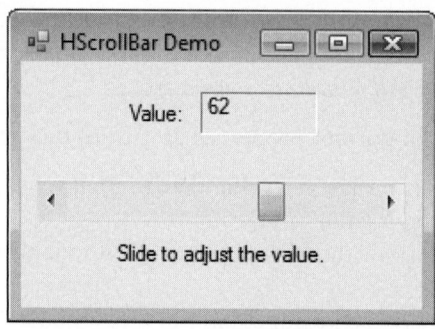

```
Public Class Form1

    Private Sub Form1_Load(...) Handles MyBase.Load
        ' Set the property values for the scroll bar control.
        ' These properties can also be set at Design
        ' time in the Properties window.
        hsbScrollBar.Value = 0
        hsbScrollBar.Minimum = 0
        hsbScrollBar.Maximum = 100
        hsbScrollBar.LargeChange = 10
        hsbScrollBar.SmallChange = 1
```

```
         ' Display the scroll bar's initial value
         ' in the label control.
         lblValue.Text = hsbScrollBar.Value.ToString()
      End Sub

      Private Sub hsbScrollBar_Scroll(...) Handles hsbScrollBar.Scroll
         ' Display the scroll bar value.
         lblValue.Text = hsbScrollBar.Value.ToString()
      End Sub
   End Class
```

Using a TabControl to Organize a Form

A **TabControl** allows you to create a user interface that is made of multiple pages, with each page containing its own set of controls. The TabControl appears as a container on a form, with one or more tabs positioned along its top edge. Each tab represents a different page, known as a **TabPage**. When the user clicks a tab, the control displays that page. You can find the TabControl in the Toolbox, in the *Containers* group.

When you insert a new TabControl, it will contain two TabPage controls named Tab-Page1 and TabPage2. This is shown in Figure A-3. Keep in mind that a TabControl is a container that contains TabPage controls. When you are working with a TabControl in the Designer window, you can select the TabControl (the container) or you can select the individual TabPage controls that it contains. When you work with a TabControl for the first time, you should practice selecting each of the controls in the group so you know at all times which one you are working with.

Figure A-3 a TabControl with two TabPages

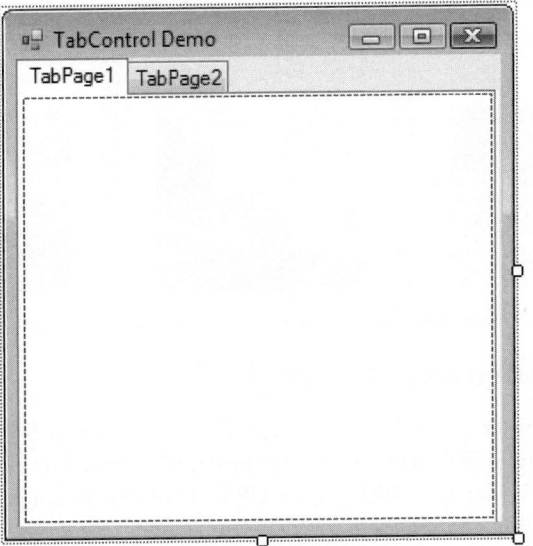

Each of the TabPage controls has its own set of properties that can be changed in the *Properties* window. For example, to change the text that is displayed on a TabPage's tab, you change that TabPage control's Text property.

As previously mentioned, a TabControl contains two TabPage controls when first inserted in a form. To add more TabPages, select the TabControl, and then select its TabPages property. (Click the ellipses button [...] that appears next to the TabPages property window.) This opens the TabPage Collection Editor, shown in Figure A-4. This window allows you to add new TabPages, remove existing TabPages, and edit each TabPage properties.

Figure A-4 *TabPage Collection Editor* window

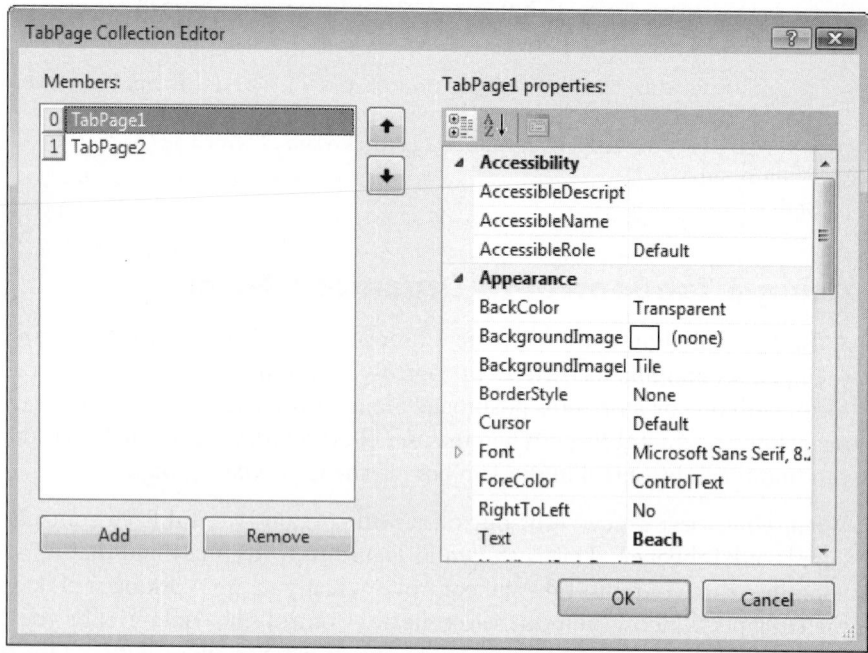

Figure A-5 shows the *TabControl Demo* application that can be found on the Student CD. The application's form has a TabControl with three TabPages. Each TabPage contains a PictureBox control displaying an image. (There is no code in the application.)

Figure A-5 *TabControl Demo* application

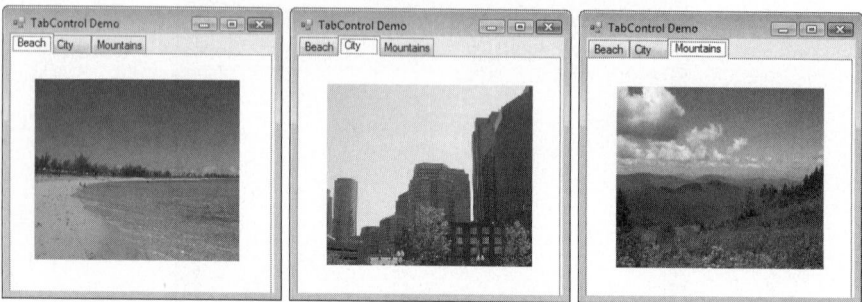

The WebBrowser Control

The **WebBrowser** control (found in the *Common Controls* group in the *Toolbox*) allows you to display a Web page on an application's form. The control has a property named Url that can be set to a Web page's URL (Uniform Resource Locator). At runtime, that Web page will be displayed in the control.

At design time, you can use the Properties window set the Url property. You simply type a valid URL such as http://www.gaddisbooks.com into the property's value box. If you want to set the Url property in code, you must create a Uri object (Uniform Resource Identifier) and assign that object to the property. Here is an example:

```
WebBrowser1.Url = New Uri("http://www.gaddisbooks.com")
```

Alternatively, you can call the control's Navigate method to display a Web page, as shown here:

```
WebBrowser1.Navigate(New Uri("http://www.gaddisbooks.com"))
```

In either of these approaches, an exception will be thrown if an invalid Web address is used.

When a Web page has finished loading, a DocumentCompleted event occurs. If you want to perform some action after a page has loaded, you can write a handler for this event. (Just double-click the WebBrowser control in the Designer window to create a code template for the DocumentCompleted event handler.)

Figure A-6 shows the *WebBrowser Demo* application on the Student CD. The application's form has a WebBrowser control named `WebBrowser1`, a TextBox control named `txtURL`, and a Button control named `btnGo`. When the user clicks the `btnGo` button, the application sets the `WebBrowser1` control's Url property to the address that has been typed into the `txtURL` text box. The application's code follows.

```
Public Class Form1

    Private Sub btnGo_Click(...) Handles btnGo.Click
        Try
            WebBrowser1.Url = New Uri(txtURL.Text)
        Catch ex As Exception
            ' Error message for an invalid Web address.
            MessageBox.Show(ex.Message)
        End Try
    End Sub
End Class
```

Figure A-6 *WebBrowser Demo* application

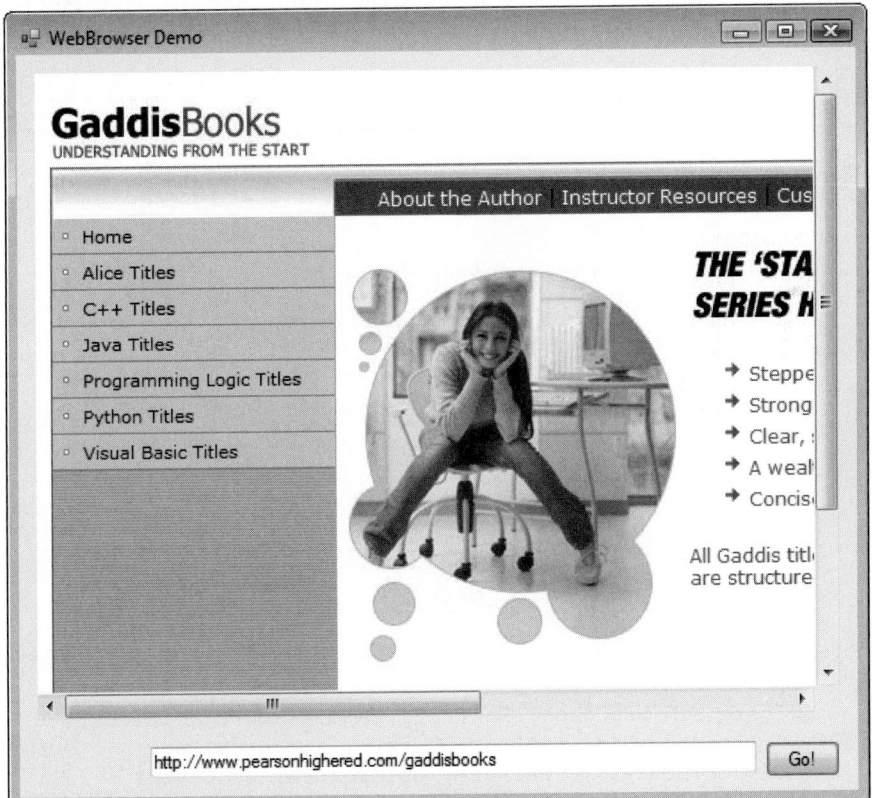

The ErrorProvider Component

The **ErrorProvider** component (found in the *Components* group in the *Toolbox*) allows you to indicate that the user has entered an invalid value by displaying a blinking error icon (🔴) next to a specific control on the application's form. When the user hovers the mouse pointer over the icon, an error message is displayed as a tooltip.

When you insert an ErrorProvider component, it appears in the component tray at the bottom of the Designer window, with a default name such as `ErrorProvider1`. In code, when the user enters an invalid value with a specific control, you call the ErrorProvider component's `SetError` method. Here is the general format for calling the method:

```
ErrorProviderName.SetError(ControlName, ErrorMessage)
```

In the general format, `ErrorProviderName` is the name of the ErrorProvider component, `ControlName` is the name of the control that you want to display the error icon next to, and `ErrorMessage` is the error message to associate with the error. Here is an example:

```
ErrorProvider1.SetError(txtPayRate, "Invalid pay rate")
```

This statement uses the `ErrorProvider1` component to display an error icon next to the `txtPayRate` control. When the user hovers the mouse pointer over the error icon, the message *Invalid pay rate* will be displayed as a tooltip.

The error icon will remain displayed next to the specified control until you call the `SetError` method again, passing the same control name as the first argument, and `String.Empty` as the second argument. Here is an example:

```
ErrorProvider1.SetError(txtPayRate, String.Empty)
```

Figure A-7 shows the *ErrorProvider Demo* application on the Student CD. The user enters a number of hours in the `txtHours` TextBox, a numeric pay rate in the `txtPayRate` TextBox, and then clicks the `btnCalc` button to calculate gross pay. If a nonnumeric value is entered for either the hours or the pay rate, an ErrorProvider component displays an error icon next to the control containing the invalid value. In Figure A-7 the user has entered an invalid value for the pay rate. The application's code follows.

Figure A-7 *ErrorProvider Demo* application

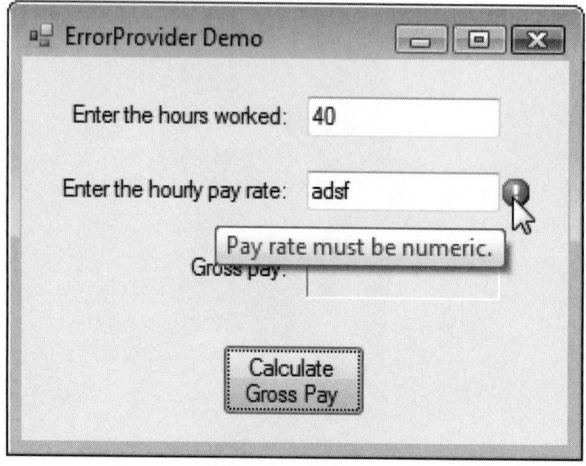

```
Public Class Form1

    Private Sub btnCalc_Click(...) Handles btnCalc.Click
        ' Variables for hours, pay rate, and gross pay
        Dim dblHours, dblPayRate, dblGrossPay As Double

        ' Clear any existing errors.
        ErrorProvider1.SetError(txtHours, String.Empty)
        ErrorProvider1.SetError(txtPayRate, String.Empty)

        ' Get values and calculate gross pay.
        Try
            ' Get the hours worked.
            dblHours = CDbl(txtHours.Text)
```

```
        Try
            ' Get the pay rate.
            dblPayRate = CDbl(txtPayRate.Text)

            ' Calculate the gross pay.
            dblGrossPay = dblHours * dblPayRate

            ' display the gross pay.
            lblGrossPay.Text = dblGrossPay.ToString("c")
        Catch ex As Exception
            ' Invalid pay rate
            ErrorProvider1.SetError(txtPayRate, "Pay rate must be numeric.")
        End Try
    Catch ex As Exception
        ' Invalid hours
        ErrorProvider1.SetError(txtHours, "Hours must be numeric.")
    End Try
  End Sub
End Class
```

Writing Code to Select Text in a TextBox

TextBox controls have two properties, **SelectionStart** and **SelectionLength,** that you can use to make the process of correcting invalid input more convenient for the user. When the user enters an invalid value, you can display an error message and then use these properties to automatically select the invalid input for the user. Then, the user can immediately retype the input without having to use the mouse to select the TextBox.

The SelectionStart and SelectionLength properties can be used in code to automatically select the text in a text box. The SelectionStart property holds the position of the first selected character in the text box. The SelectionLength property holds the number of characters that are selected. For example, look at the following code and assume that txtName is a text box that the user has typed input into:

```
txtName.Focus()
txtName.SelectionStart = 0
txtName.SelectionLength = 5
```

The first statement gives txtName the focus. The second statement establishes that the first character in txtName (which is at position 0), is the first selected character. The next statement establishes that five characters will be selected. Together, the statements cause the first five characters in txtName to be selected.

So, how do you use similar code to select all the text in a TextBox? You use the TextBox's Length property to get the length of the text, and assign that value to the TextBox 's SelectionLength property. Here is an example:

```
txtName.Focus()
txtName.SelectionStart = 0
txtName.SelectionLength = txtName.Text.Length
```

After these statements execute, all of the contents of the txtName TextBox will be selected. When the user types a key, that keystroke will immediately erase all of the selected text.

Figure A-8 shows the *Selected Text Demo* application on the Student CD. This is a modified version of the *ErrorProvider Demo* application previously shown. In this version, after the ErrorProvider displays an error icon, the content of the TextBox containing the invalid input is automatically selected. In the figure, the user has entered an invalid value for the hours. The application's code follows.

Figure A-8 *Selected Text Demo* application

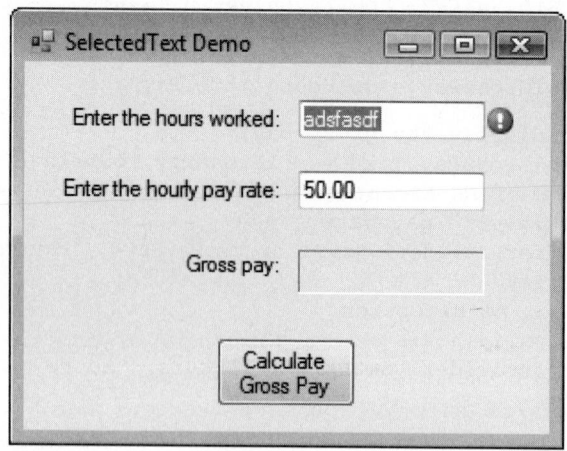

```
Public Class Form1

    Private Sub btnCalc_Click(...) Handles btnCalc.Click
        ' Variables for hours, pay rate, and gross pay
        Dim dblHours, dblPayRate, dblGrossPay As Double

        ' Clear any existing errors.
        ErrorProvider1.SetError(txtHours, String.Empty)
        ErrorProvider1.SetError(txtPayRate, String.Empty)

        ' Get values and calculate gross pay.
        Try
            ' Get the hours worked.
            dblHours = CDbl(txtHours.Text)

            Try
                ' Get the pay rate.
                dblPayRate = CDbl(txtPayRate.Text)

                ' Calculate the gross pay.
                dblGrossPay = dblHours * dblPayRate

                ' display the gross pay.
                lblGrossPay.Text = dblGrossPay.ToString("c")
            Catch ex As Exception
                ' Invalid pay rate
                ErrorProvider1.SetError(txtPayRate, "Pay rate must be numeric.")

                ' Select the invalid input.
                txtPayRate.Focus()
                txtPayRate.SelectionStart = 0
                txtPayRate.SelectionLength = txtPayRate.Text.Length
            End Try
        Catch ex As Exception
            ' Invalid hours
            ErrorProvider1.SetError(txtHours, "Hours must be numeric.")
            ' Select the invalid input.
            txtHours.Focus()
            txtHours.SelectionStart = 0
            txtHours.SelectionLength = txtHours.Text.Length
        End Try
    End Sub
End Class
```

Using Control-Level Validation

You've seen many examples in this book of code using Try-Catch statements to respond to the exceptions that occur when the user has entered invalid data in a TextBox. Visual Basic provides another approach to input validation that can be useful when a form contains many fields that must be validated, or when more complex validation must be applied to user input.

Most controls have a Boolean property named **CausesValidation** that is set to *True* by default. When the focus is shifting from one control to another, if the control that is receiving the focus has its CausesValidation property set to True, then a Validating event will occur for the control that is losing the focus.

Suppose an application has two text box controls: txtFirst and txtSecond. The user has just entered a value into txtFirst and pressed the Tab key, which should shift the focus from txtFirst to txtSecond. But txtSecond's CausesValidation property is set to *True*, so txtFirst's Validating event is triggered before the focus shifts. The txtFirst control has a Validating event handler, which is executed as a result of the Validating event being triggered.

The Validating event handler contains code that checks the value in txtFirst. If the value is invalid, the event handler does the following:

- It displays an error message instructing the user to reenter the data.
- It cancels the event, which prevents the focus from shifting. This lets the user correct the invalid value.

If the value is valid, however, the event handler allows the focus to shift.

The Validating event handler has a parameter named e. This parameter is a special type of object known as a CancelEventArgs object. It has a Boolean property named Cancel that, if set to True, will prevent the focus from shifting after the handler finishes executing. If the e.Cancel property is set to False, however, the focus will continue to shift after the handler finishes executing.

Figure A-9 shows the *Validation Demo* application on the Student CD. The user enters a number of hours in the txtHours TextBox, a numeric pay rate in the txtPayRate TextBox, and then clicks the btnCalc button to calculate gross pay. The CausesValidation property of all the controls on the form is set to True. The txtHours control has a Validating event handler that executes when focus shifts away from txtHours. It makes sure the hours entered is a valid number and within the range of 0 through 40. The txtPayRate control also has a Validating event handler, that executes when focus shifts away from txtPayRate. It makes sure the pay rate is a valid number and is 0 or greater. The application's code follows.

Figure A-9 *Validation Demo* application

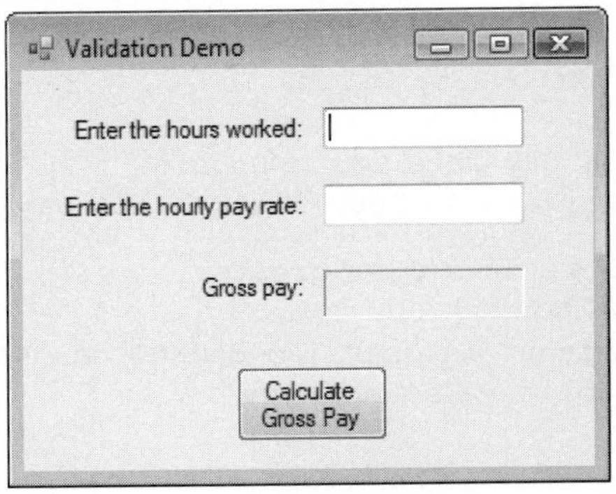

> **NOTE:** The form has a FormClosing event handler that sets e.Cancel to False. This is a necessary workaround in case the user tries to close the form without entering a value into the txtHours TextBox. Without this statement in the FormClosing event handler, the user will not be able to close the form without entering a valid value in txtHours.

```
Public Class Form1

    Private Sub btnCalc_Click(...) Handles btnCalc.Click
        ' Variables for hours, pay rate, and gross pay
        Dim dblHours, dblPayRate, dblGrossPay As Double

        ' Get the hours worked.
        dblHours = CDbl(txtHours.Text)

        ' Get the pay rate.
        dblPayRate = CDbl(txtPayRate.Text)

        ' Calculate the gross pay.
        dblGrossPay = dblHours * dblPayRate

        ' display the gross pay.
        lblGrossPay.Text = dblGrossPay.ToString("c")
    End Sub

    Private Sub txtHours_Validating(...) Handles txtHours.Validating
        Try
            ' Get the hours, as a Double.
            Dim dblHours As Double = CDbl(txtHours.Text)

            ' Make sure it's in the range 0 - 40.
            If dblHours >= 0.0 And dblHours <= 40.0 Then
                ' The input is okay, so do NOT cancel the event.
                e.Cancel = False
            Else
                ' The input is out of range, so display an
                ' error message.
                MessageBox.Show("Hours must be in the range 0 through 40.")
                ' Now cancel the event.
                e.Cancel = True
            End If
        Catch ex As Exception
            ' The input is not a valid number, so display
            ' an error message.
            MessageBox.Show("Hours must be a valid number.")

            ' Cancel the event.
            e.Cancel = True
        End Try
    End Sub

    Private Sub txtPayRate_Validating(...) Handles txtPayRate.Validating
        Try
            ' Get the pay rate, as a Double.
            Dim dblPayRate As Double = CDbl(txtPayRate.Text)

            ' Make sure it's 0 or greater.
            If dblPayRate >= 0.0 Then
                ' The input is okay, so do NOT cancel the event.
                e.Cancel = False
```

```
      Else
        ' The input is out of range, so display an
        ' error message.
        MessageBox.Show("Pay rate must be 0 or greater.")

        ' Now cancel the event.
        e.Cancel = True
      End If
    Catch ex As Exception
      ' The input is not a valid number, so display
      ' an error message.
      MessageBox.Show("Pay rate must be a valid number.")

      ' Cancel the event.
      e.Cancel = True
    End Try
  End Sub

  Private Sub Form1_FormClosing(...) Handles Me.FormClosing
    e.Cancel = False
  End Sub
End Class
```

The DateTimePicker and MonthCalendar Controls

The DateTimePicker and MonthCalendar controls (found in the Toolbox's *Common Controls* group) provide a much simpler and more reliable way for users to enter dates on a form than typing them into a TextBox. Both of these controls display a small scroll-able calendar, showing an entire month, that the user may pick a date from. The selected date is stored, as a Date value, in the control's Value property. Initially, the Value property is set to the current date, and the current date will appear selected in the control's calendar.

When the user selects a date from either of these controls, a ValueChanged event is triggered. If you write a ValueChanged event handler for the control, the event handler will execute any time a date is selected. To generate a code template for the ValueChanged event handler, simply double-click the DateTimePicker or MonthCalendar control in the *Designer* window.

The difference between the two controls is that a DateTimePicker is a drop-down control (showing the calendar only when the user clicks an arrow) and the MonthCalendar always displays the calendar.

Figure A-10 shows the *Date Demo* application on the Student CD. The user selects a date from the DateTimePicker control's drop-down calendar, and then the selected date is displayed in the lblDate label control. The application's code follows.

```
Public Class Form1

  Private Sub DateTimePicker1_ValueChanged(...) Handles
      DateTimePicker1.ValueChanged
    lblDate.Text = DateTimePicker1.Value.ToShortDateString
  End Sub
End Class
```

Figure A-10 The *Date Demo* application

User Interface Design Guidelines

When developing an application, you should carefully plan the design of its user interface. A correctly designed user interface should be simple, self explanatory, and without distracting features. This remainder of this appendix covers several important areas of user interface design.

Adhere to Windows Standards

The users of your application are probably experienced with other Windows applications. They will expect your application to provide the features and exhibit the behavior that is common to all Windows applications. The guidelines provided here cover many of the Windows standards. Additionally, you should carefully study applications such as Microsoft Word and Microsoft Excel to observe their forms, menus, controls, and behavior.

Provide a Menu System

Avoid using too many buttons on a form. If an application provides many commands or operations for the user to choose from, place them in a menu system. Of course, an application that uses a menu system will have some menus and menu commands that are unique to that application. However, there are many menu commands that are common to most, if not all, applications. Windows applications that use a menu system normally have the following standard menus:

- **File menu commands.** *New, Open, Close, Save, Save As, Print,* and *Exit*
- **Edit menu commands.** *Copy, Cut, Paste,* and *Select All.* If an application provides searching capabilities, such as *Find* or *Replace* commands, they are typically found on the *Edit* menu.
- **Help menu commands.** *About*

Color

Use of color should be tailored to your audience. Business applications should use at most one or two colors, preferably subdued. Multimedia applications (such as Windows Media player) tend to be more colorful and use more graphics. In any event, it's a good idea to show your program to potential users and get their feedback. The color combinations that you consider attractive may not be appealing to others. The following are some general color usage guidelines for business applications:

- **Use dark text on a light background.** Combining certain colors for text and background makes the text difficult to read. Use dark colors for the text and light colors for the background. The contrast between dark and light colors makes the text easier to read.
- **Use predefined Windows colors.** Windows uses a predefined set of colors for forms, controls, text, and so on. These colors may be customized by the user. To ensure that your application conforms to a customized color scheme, you should use the predefined system colors. To find the system colors in the *Properties* window, select a color-related property such as *BackColor*. Then click the property's down-arrow button to display a pop-up list of colors. Select the *System* tab to display the system colors.
- **Avoid bright colors.** Bright colors are not recommended in business applications because they can distract the user and make the application appear cluttered and unprofessional. Additionally, users with color-defective vision can have difficulty trying to distinguish between certain colors.

Text

The use of nonstandard or multiple fonts can be distracting and makes your forms difficult to read. The following are some suggestions regarding font usage:

- **Use default fonts.** In most cases, stick with the default font for labels and text boxes. Avoid using italic and underlined styles, as they are less readable than plain fonts.
- **Use standard type sizes.** For ordinary text, Microsoft recommends 8, 9, or 11 point type. For window title bars, Microsoft recommends 10 point type.
- **Limit your exceptions to these rules.** If you insist on changing the font and/or font size, do so sparingly; do not use more than two fonts and two font sizes on a form.

Define a Logical Tab Order

Recall from Chapter 3 that a control's TabIndex property specifies the control's position in the tab order. The user expects the focus to shift logically when the Tab key is pressed. Typically, the control in the upper left corner of the form will be first in the tab order. The control that appears below it or next to it will be next. The tab order will continue in this fashion. If the focus shifts randomly around the form, a user may become confused and frustrated.

Assign Tool Tips

Recall from Chapter 5 that a tool tip is a small box that is displayed when you hold the mouse cursor over a control for a few seconds. The box gives a short description of what the button does. You can define tool tips for a form by creating a ToolTip control.

Provide Keyboard Access

Many users are proficient with the keyboard and can perform operations with it faster than with the mouse. For their convenience, you should develop your applications so they support both mouse and keyboard input. The following are some suggestions:

- **Use keyboard access keys.** Assign keyboard access keys to buttons, option buttons, check boxes, and menu items.
- **Assign a default button.** If a form uses buttons, you should always make the one that is most frequently clicked the default button. Do this by selecting that button as the form's AcceptButton. Recall from Chapter 3 that when a button is selected in a form's AcceptButton property, the button's Click event procedure is triggered when the user presses the Enter key while the form is active.
- **Assign a cancel button.** If a form has a cancel button, you should select it in the form's CancelButton property. Recall from Chapter 3 that when a button is selected in a form's CancelButton property, the button's Click event procedure is triggered when the user presses the Escape key while the form is active.

Group Controls

If a form has several controls, try to simplify the form's layout by grouping related controls inside group boxes. This visually divides the form's surface area into separate sections, making it more intuitive for the user.

Form Location

To center a form when it first appears, set its StartPosition property to *CenterScreen*.

Windows Presentation Foundation (WPF)

Imagine a single application that has the usual set of menus and controls, along with rich text displayed in columns, a 3D bar chart, and live video. Imagine being able to combine all these elements on the same page. This is the type of capability provided to advanced developers using Microsoft's new **Windows Presentation Foundation (WPF)**. In the past, developers with a wide variety of specialties and skills would be required to create such an application. They would have to integrate different toolkits and spend a lot of time testing and debugging. To make matters worse, they might have to completely redo these applications for the Web.

Microsoft created the Windows Presentation Foundation (WPF) technology for a number of reasons: (1) They wanted developers to be able to create applications that could run both on the desktop and the Web. (2) They wanted to make it easy to incorporate advanced 2D and 3D graphics and multimedia into applications without having to manually link together separate tools.

WPF was first introduced in Visual Studio 2008, and has been greatly expanded in Visual Studio 2010. Microsoft has reworked the traditional Windows Forms technology (which we have covered throughout this book) to allow it to incorporate WPF forms within the same applications. In the future, WPF will be Microsoft's new solution for applications that run on both the desktop and the Web.

Visual Studio contains an interactive design surface that provides drag and drop support for WPF layout and controls, a new property editor, and Intellisense support for XAML editing. **Microsoft Expression Blend** is the tool used by designers to create advanced interactive visual elements in applications. Animation, multimedia, and advanced styles are often developed in this way.

XAML

XAML (*eXtensible Application Markup Language*) is used to describe the visual elements in an application. In some ways, it resembles the XHTML markup used in ASP.NET Web applications (see Chapter 11). It can be generated by both Expression Blend and Visual Studio. It can be referenced by coding statements at runtime.

In the past, artistic designers and programmers had great difficulty working together unless they were extensively trained to do so. The designer might create a graphic design for a Web page, and then pass it along to the programer, who would then add the functions needed by the application. But the designer might not know whether their design vision could be implemented by the programmer. Making matters worse, once the programmer started to add code, it was nearly impossible to make any changes or improvements to the visual design.

By creating XAML and WPF, Microsoft allows designers and programmers to work together, each taking advantage of their special skills. The same project can be passed back and forth between the designer and the programmer as it gradually takes shape. Using XAML, the designer can create rich visual interfaces that lend themselves very neatly to coding by a programmer.

Layout and Controls

A WPF application controls its layout through the use of containers called *panels*. Each panel can contain child elements such as controls like buttons and checkboxes, or other panels. There are three types of panels:

- DockPanel—allows child elements to be positioned along the edges of the panel
- Grid—allows child elements to be positioned in predetermined rows and columns, much like one would with a table
- Canvas—allows child elements to be positioned anywhere in the panel.

All of the standard controls are available, such as TextBox, CheckBox, and ComboBox. More advanced controls are also available, including DocumentViewer, MediaElement, and ViewPort3D.

Types of Applications

Standalone WPF

A Standalone WPF application runs like any other Windows application. You do not need to use a Web browser to run it. This type of program runs with the same privileges as the current user, so it can access the computer's hard drive, use network sockets, and so on. It can be installed from a local disk, a network server, or by a method named **ClickOnce**. Using ClickOnce, the user can use a Web browser to connect to a page containing a button that lets them download and install the WPF application on their computer.

There is a clear advantage to creating ClickOnce applications. You can publish the application to a Web server for others to use. Later, when you have made improvements to the program, you can republish the application. This makes it easy for users to get the latest version of your work.

XAML Browser Applications (XBAPs)

A XAML Browser Application (XBAP) runs inside Internet Explorer. It can act as a client for Web applications. It can use most of the capabilities of WPF in a browser application.

An XBAP is silently loaded via ClickOnce, and looks just like a Web page. It is given only a limited amount of trust, so it does not have all the privileges normally given to desktop applications. For example, it cannot create other windows, display dialog boxes, access the full file system of the computer, or execute user interface code created with Windows Forms.

Tutorial 1:
Creating the Kayak Tour Reservations application

In this tutorial, you will begin to create a WPF application named **Kayak Tour Reservations** that lets the user sign up for a kayak tour. By the time you finish this set of tutorials, the user will be able to select the type of kayak they want to use, the tour location, and the tour date.

Step 1: On the File menu, select *New Project*. Select *WPF Application* from the list of application templates. Name the project *KayakTourWPF* and click the OK button.

Step 2: Select *Save All* from the File menu. When the *Save Project* dialog appears, choose a folder location for your project and click the *Save* button.

Step 3: The *MainWindow.xaml* Design window should appear, as shown in Figure 1. You should also see another tab, labeled *MainWindow.xaml.vb*. When you click this tab, you see the code file for the MainWindow, where you will write event handlers.

Figure 1 Design window, immediately after creating a new WPF project

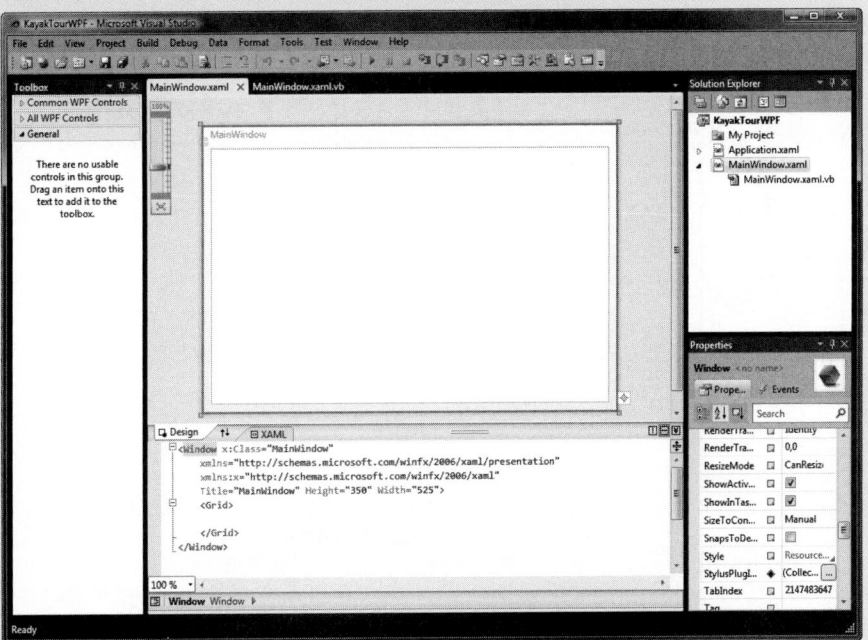

Step 4: Using the mouse, drag the slider in the upper-left corner of the Design window to zoom the form's display in and out, making it appear larger and smaller. This adjustment does not change the actual size of the window object. Look for its Height and Width properties in the Properties window to verify that their values do not change.

Step 5: Using the mouse to drag the corner of the window, expand the window's size to about 380 units high and 600 units wide. Now you can see that Height and Width properties have changed.

Step 6: Set the window's Title property to *Register for a Kayak Tour*.

> The design surface automatically contains a single Grid control. The advantage to using a grid is that you can use the mouse to drag controls from the Toolbox onto the grid and position them anywhere you want. In some applications, you will insert additional rows and columns into the grid, to help you align the different controls.

Step 7: Open the Toolbox window and expand the *Common WPF Controls* group of controls.

Step 8: Drag a Label control from the Toolbox into the middle of the grid, near the top. Set the following properties for the Label: FontSize = 30; Content = *Our Featured Kayak Tours*. Drag the borders of the label with the mouse so that all the text in the label is visible. A sample is shown in Figure 2.

Figure 2 A Label containing the application title

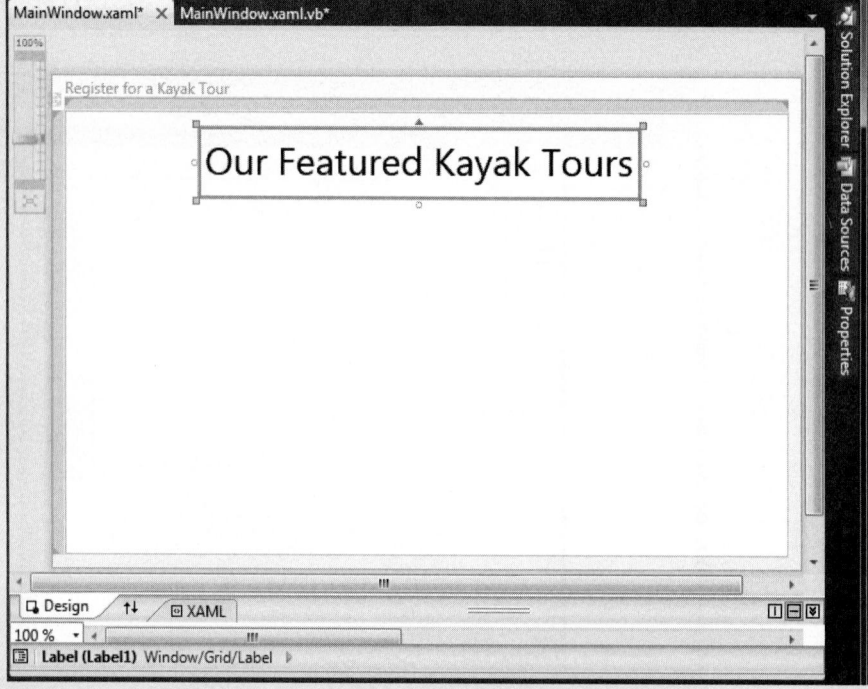

Step 9: Drag a Label control onto the grid near the left side, and set its Content property to *Select a Type of Kayak*.

Step 10: Drag a ListBox control on to the grid, just below the label on the left side. Set its Name property to *lstKayaks*. Select its Items property, and click the *Add* button to add three items, as shown in Figure 3. For each, you need to enter a value into its Content property. The values are:

Solo recreational
Tandem recreational
Solo sea kayak

Click the OK button to close the dialog. Figure 4 shows the design of the form after adding the ListBox.

Figure 3 Adding items to the lstKayak ListBox

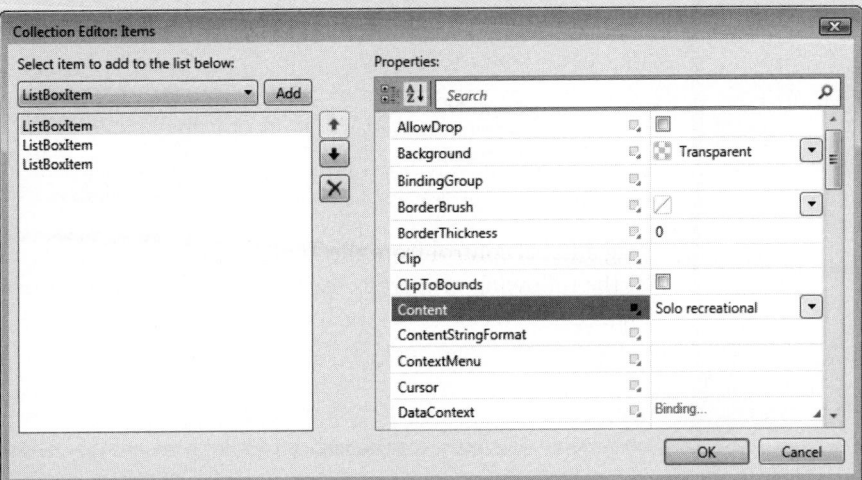

Step 11: Add another label to the right side of the form and set its Content property to *Select a Kayak Tour*.

Step 12: Add a ComboBox control to the right side of the form and name it cboTour. Select its Items property, and add three items. Set the Content properties of the three items to the following:

> *Na Pali Coast tour*
> *Hanalei Bay tour*
> *Wailua River tour*

Step 13: We would also like to let the user select the date of their tour. Just below the ComboBox control, add a DatePicker control. In the following figure, you can see the ComboBox control, with the DatePicker just below it:

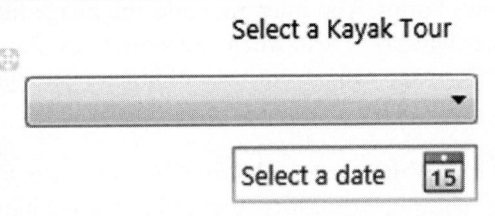

Step 14: Save the project and run the application by selecting *Start Debugging* from the Debug menu. Verify that you can select kayak types from the list box, and you can select tour names from the ComboBox. Click the ShowCalendar control, which causes the month calendar to appear, as shown in Figure 4. When you select a date, the calendar closes and the date appears in the text box.

Step 15: Close the application window and return to Design mode.

Figure 4 Select the DatePicker control, causing a month calendar to drop down

Tutorial 2:
Adding Images to the Kayak Tour Reservations application

Most customers who go on kayak tours for the first time are not familiar with the various types of kayaks that they might be able to use. A well-designed reservation system should, therefore, display a picture of each kayak type to help the user make a selection. In this tutorial you will add three kayak images to the Kayak Tour Reservations application. The pictures will be displayed by a WPF Image control. When the user selects each type of kayak in the ListBox, the appropriate image will display at the bottom of the window.

Adding an image to a WPF application is a little different from the way it's done in Windows Forms. You must first add the image file to the project, using the Solution Explorer window. Then, when you want to display the image in an Image control, you select the image name from a list of images belonging to the project.

Step 1: Copy three image files from the *Appendix B* sample programs folder into your application's directory (the directory containing the file named *MainWindow.xaml*). The image filenames are: *rec_kayak.jpg*, *sea_kayak.jpg*, and *tandem_rec_kayak.jpg*.

Step 2: Right-click the project name in Solution Explorer, select *Add*, and select *Existing Item*. In the *Add Existing Item* dialog window, select *Image Files* in the *file type* dropdown list in the lower corner of the window, as shown here:

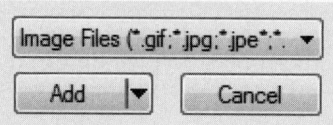

Select the three image files from your project directory, then click the *Add* button. The three filenames should appear in the list of files in your Solution Explorer window.

Step 3: Add three Image controls to the form, positioned near the bottom. Set each Image control's Width property to 168 and Height property to 100. For each, set its Visibility property to *Hidden*.

Step 4: Select the first image control, set its Name property to *imgRecKayak*. Click its Source property, and select the *rec_kayak.jpg* image from the list of images shown in the dialog window.

Step 5: Select the second image control, set its Name property to *imgRecTandem*. Click its Source property, and select the *tandem_rec_kayak.jpg* image from the list of images shown in the dialog window.

Step 6: Select the third image control, set its Name property to *imgSeaKayak*. Click its Source property, and select the *sea_kayak.jpg* image from the list of images shown in the dialog window.

If you were to run the application now, the images would not appear. We made the Image controls hidden, of course! But what we want to happen is for the images to pop out and become visible when the appropriate type of kayak is selected in the ListBox control. How will that happen? We need to write a SelectionChanged event handler for the ListBox.

Step 7: Select click the `lstKayaks` ListBox control with the mouse. At the top of the Properties window, click the events tab (lightning bolt icon) to display all the ListBox event types. Double click the box to the right of the **SelectionChanged** event in the Properties window. You should now see the code window editor for *MainWindow.xaml.vb*, containing the `lstKayaks_SelectionChanged` event handler procedure. Add the following code, listed in bold:

```
Private Sub lstKayaks_SelectionChanged(...)Handles lstKayaks.SelectionChanged

    imgRecKayak.Visibility = Windows.Visibility.Hidden
    imgRecTandem.Visibility = Windows.Visibility.Hidden
    imgSeaKayak.Visibility = Windows.Visibility.Hidden

    If lstKayaks.SelectedIndex = 0 Then
       imgRecKayak.Visibility = Windows.Visibility.Visible
    ElseIf lstKayaks.SelectedIndex = 1 Then
       imgRecTandem.Visibility = Windows.Visibility.Visible
    ElseIf lstKayaks.SelectedIndex = 2 Then
       imgSeaKayak.Visibility = Windows.Visibility.Visible
    End If

End Sub
```

Therefore, depending on the SelectedIndex of the kayak selected in the ListBox, we set one of the Image controls to *Visible*. The other two images remain set to *Hidden*.

Step 8: Save the project and run the application by selecting *Start Debugging* from the Debug menu. Experiment with selecting each of the kayak types from the ListBox. Notice that each time you do so, a different kayak photo appears. See Figure 5 for a sample.

Figure 5 Viewing the kayak photos while running the application

Tutorial 3:
Publishing the *Kayak Tour Reservations* application

If you have access to a Web server, you can easily publish a WPF appplication. From Visual Studio, you identify the web site where the application will be published. When users navigate to the site using a Web browser, they can install your application just by clicking a button. Microsoft's name for this technology is *Click-Once Deployment*.

This tutorial is designed as a demonstration. We will use a website named *http://kipirvine.com* for this demonstration. If you wish to reproduce the steps, you will need to substitute the name of your own web site.

Step 1: We select *Publish KayakTourWPF* from the *Build* menu. The *Publish Wizard* window appears, as shown in Figure 6. We enter the web address of a folder on our web site, and click the *Next* button.

Step 2: Next, shown in Figure 7, the *Publish Wizard* asks which location users will access when they want to install the application. We have selected a folder named *Install* on the same web site.

Figure 6 Selecting a location where the KayakTour application will be published

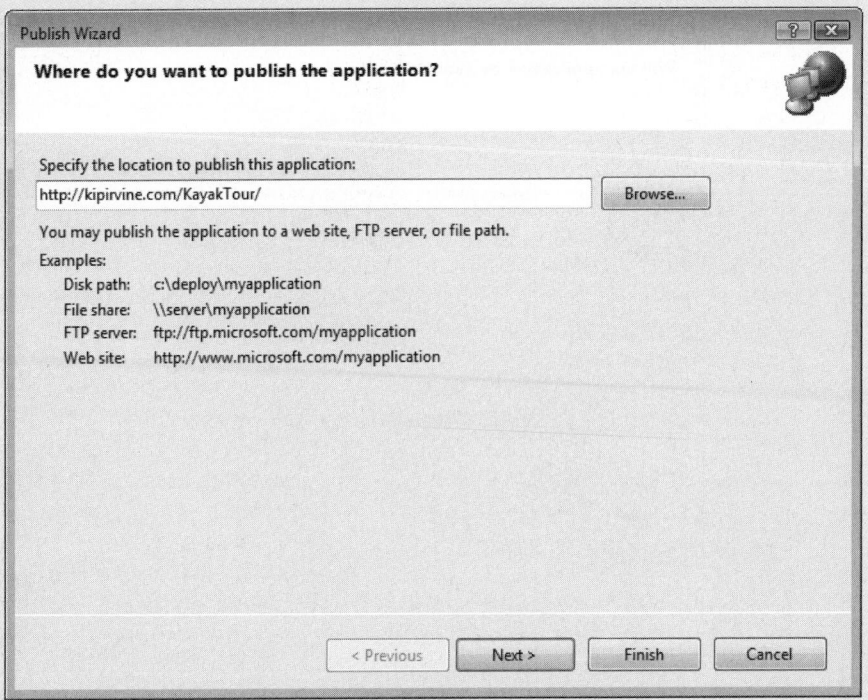

Figure 7 Selecting the Install location

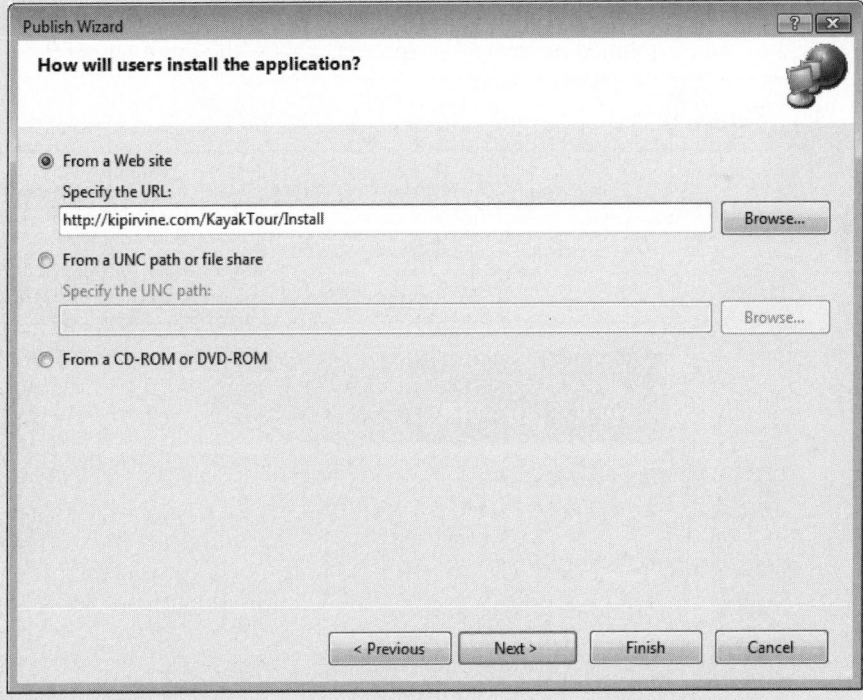

Step 3: The *Publish Wizard* then asks if the application will only be available online (shown in Figure 8), or whether it should be added to the Start menu of the user's computer. We do not wish to install any software on the local computer, so we will select the Web-only option.

Figure 8 Choosing to make the application available only online

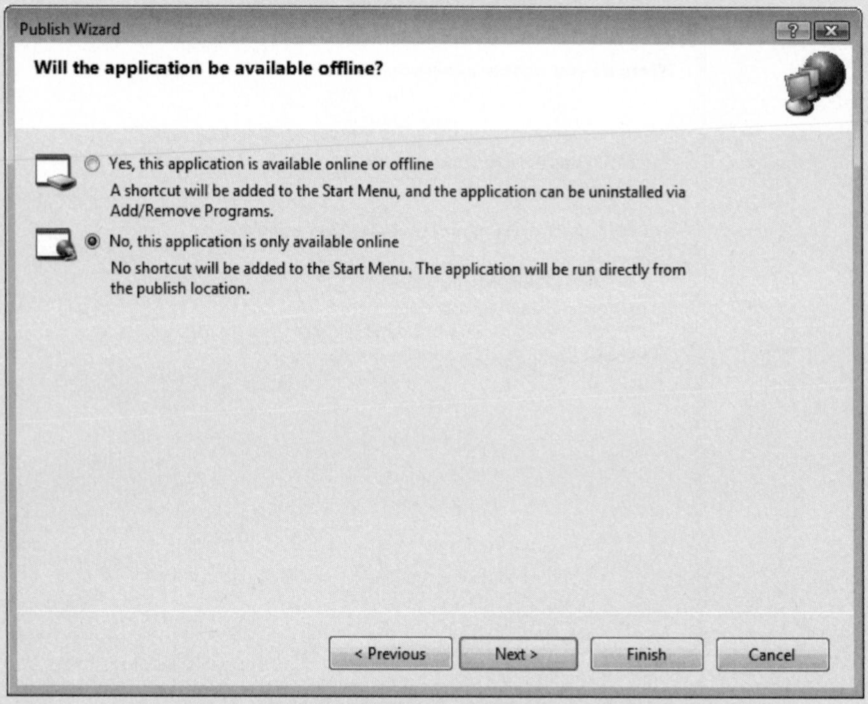

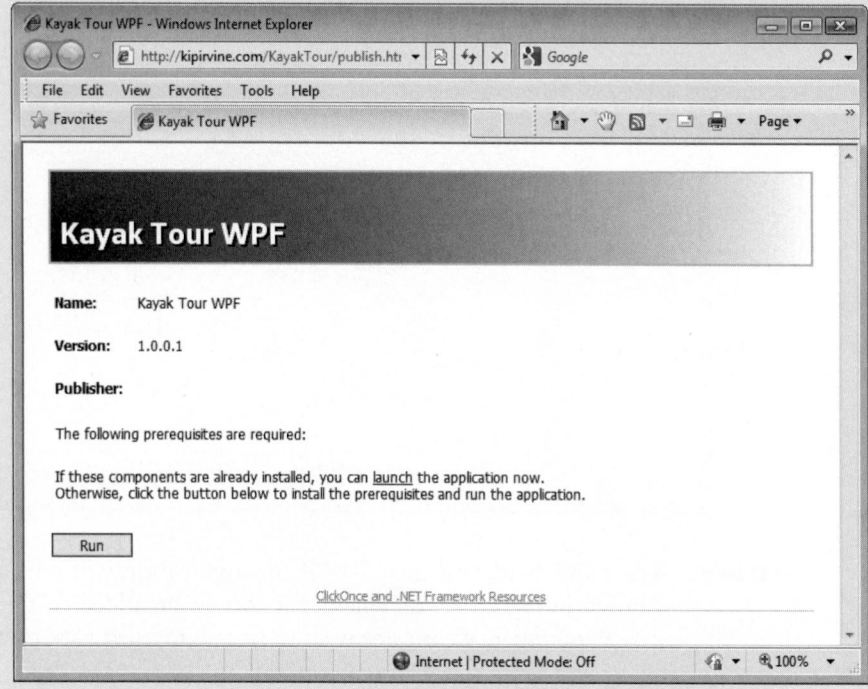

Step 4: Next, Visual Studio opens the web site and asks for user authentication (user-name and password). After a brief pause during which Visual Studio copies the application to the remote web site, the application's published Web page (named *publish.htm*) appears. This is shown in Figure 9.

Figure 9 Displaying the published application Web page (publish.htm)

If the user's local computer were to be missing any required components, they would have to click the *Run* button and wait for the components to be installed directly from Microsoft's web site. In our sample, however, there are no missing components.

Step 5: The user clicks the hyperlink named *launch*. A dialog window shown in Figure 10 appears briefly, while Windows verifies that all required software components exist on the user's computer. Then, the application window appears, as in Figure 11.

Figure 10 Launching the application

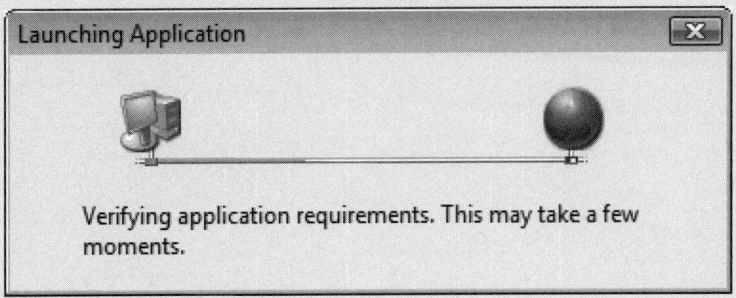

Figure 11 The Kayak Tour application window

Our WPF application does not run in a web browser window. It runs in what might be called a *desktop application* mode, on the local computer. The web browser is only used when launching the application.

You can run the application by browsing directly to its application file. In our Kayak Tour program, the direct execution URL is

http://kipirvine.com/KayakTour/KayakTourWPF.application

APPENDIX C — Converting Mathematical Expressions to Programming Statements

In mathematical expressions, it is not always necessary to use an operator for multiplication. For example, the expression $2xy$ is understood to mean "2 times x times y." Visual Basic, however, requires an operator for any mathematical operation. Table C-1 shows some mathematical expressions that perform multiplication and the equivalent Visual Basic expression.

Table C-1 Math expressions in Visual Basic

Mathematical Expression	Operation	Visual Basic Equivalent
$6b$	6 times b	`6 * b`
$(3)(12)$	3 times 12	`3 * 12`
$4xy$	4 times x times y	`4 * x * y`

When converting mathematical expressions to Visual Basic programming statements, you may have to insert parentheses that do not appear in the mathematical expression. For example, look at the following expression:

$$x = \frac{a + b}{c}$$

To convert this to a Visual Basic statement, $a + b$ will have to be enclosed in parentheses:

```
x = (a + b) / c
```

Table C-2 shows more mathematical expressions and their Visual Basic equivalents.

Table C-2 More math expressions in Visual Basic

Mathematical Expression	Visual Basic Expression
$y = 3\dfrac{x}{2}$	y = x / 2 * 3
$z = 3bc + 4$	z = 3 * b * c + 4
$a = \dfrac{3x+2}{4a-1}$	a = (3 * x + 2) / (4 * a - 1)

D Answers to Checkpoints

Chapter 1

1.1 Central Processing Unit (CPU), main memory, secondary storage, input devices, and output devices

1.2 Main memory holds the sequences of instructions in the programs that are running and the data with which those programs are working. RAM is usually a volatile type of memory that is used only for temporary storage.

1.3 Program instructions and data are stored in main memory while the program is operating. Main memory is volatile and loses its content when power is removed from the computer. Secondary storage holds data for long periods of time—even when there is no power to the computer.

1.4 Operating systems and application software

1.5 A set of well-defined steps for performing a task or solving a problem

1.6 To ease the task of programming; programs may be written in a programming language and then converted to machine language

1.7 An object is an item in a program that contains data and has the ability to perform operations. A control is a specific type of object that usually appears in a program's graphical user interface.

1.8 An application responds to events that occur or actions that take place, such as the clicking of a mouse.

1.9 A property is a piece of data that determines some characteristics of a control.

1.10 The default name is not descriptive; it does not indicate the purpose of the control.

1.11 A Text Box

1.12 TextBox1

1.13 No; the + symbol is an illegal character for control names.

1.14 The program's purpose, information to be input, the processing to take place, and the desired output

1.15 Planning helps the programmer create a good design and avoid errors that may not otherwise be anticipated.

1.16 To imagine what the computer screen looks like when the program is running; it's the first step in creating an application's forms or windows.

1.17 A diagram that graphically depicts a program's flow

1.18 A cross between human language and a programming language

1.19 A mistake that does not prevent an application from executing, but causes it to produce incorrect results; a mistake in a mathematical formula is a common type of runtime error

1.20 To find and correct runtime errors.

1.21 Testing is a part of each design step. Flowcharts should be tested, code should be desk-checked, and the application should be run with test data to verify that it produces the correct output.

1.22 The *Solution Explorer* window shows a file-oriented view of a project. It allows quick navigation among the project files.

1.23 The *Properties* window shows and allows you to change most of the currently selected object's properties and their values.

1.24 The standard toolbar contains buttons that execute frequently used commands.

1.25 The toolbar contains buttons that execute frequently used menu commands. The toolbox provides buttons for placing controls.

1.26 A ToolTip is a small box that is displayed when you hold the mouse cursor over a button on the toolbar or in the toolbox for a few seconds. The box gives a short description of what the button does.

Chapter 2

2.1 The Text property.

2.2 With the form selected, double-click the Label control tool in the toolbox.

2.3 To resize the control's bounding box.

2.4 Select it and press the [Delete] key.

2.5 The image will be resized both horizontally and vertically to fit in the PictureBox control. If the image is resized more in one direction than the other, it will appear stretched.

2.6 Bounding box

2.7 Design mode, run mode, and break mode.

2.8 • Click *File* on the menu bar, and then select *Open Project...* The *Open Project* window will appear. Use the window to locate and select either the solution file (.sln) or the project file (.vbproj) for the project that you wish to open.

- Click *File* on the menu bar, and then select *Recent Projects and Solutions*. If the project is one that you have opened recently, it might be listed here. If it is, select either the solution file (.sln) or the project file (.vbproj) for the project that you wish to open.
- Use the *Start Page* to open the project. To display the *Start Page*, click *View* on the menu bar, then select *Start Page*. Then, either click the *Open Project* link to display the *Open Project* window, or select the name of project in the *Recent Projects* list.

2.9 Alphabetical and categorized. Select alphabetical mode by clicking the *Alphabetical* button. Select categorized mode by clicking the *Categorized* button. When the *Alphabetical* button is clicked, the properties are displayed alphabetically. When the *Categorized* button is clicked, related properties are listed in groups.

2.10 Text is listed under the *Appearance* category. Name is listed under the *Design* category.

2.11 Select it from the list of objects displayed in the object box drop-down list.

2.12 If a control will be accessed in code or will have code associated with it (such as an event handler), assign it a name. Otherwise, keep the control's default name.

2.13 A property that may only have one of two values: *True* or *False*

2.14 `btnShowName_Click()`

2.15 It assigns True to the `lblGreeting` control's Visible property. As a result, the `lblGreeting` control will be visible on the application's form at runtime.

2.16 A comment, or remark, is a note of explanation that documents something in a program.

2.17 `lblSecretAnswer.Visible = False`

2.18 It closes the current form.

2.19 The F7 key

2.20 Custom, Web, and System

2.21 The background color of the Label's text changes.

2.22 The color of the Label's text changes.

2.23 FormBorderStyle

2.24 You cannot move them until they are unlocked.

2.25 Right-click over an empty spot on the form and select *Lock Controls* from the pop-up menu.

2.26 The same way that you locked the controls: Right-click over an empty spot on the form, and select *Lock Controls* from the pop-up menu.

2.27 `lblTemperature.Text = "48 degrees"`

2.28 When AutoSize is set to *False*, you can set the bounding box of a Label control to be larger than the text it holds. When a label's AutoSize property is set to *True*, the label's bounding box automatically resizes to the length of the text in the label's Text property.

2.29 The BorderStyle property can hold one of the following values: *None*, *FixedSingle*, and *Fixed 3D*. When set to *None*, the label has no border. (This is the default value.) When set to *FixedSingle*, the label is outlined with a border that is a single pixel wide. When set to *Fixed3D*, the label has a recessed 3-dimensional appearance.

2.30 `lblName.TextAlign = ContentAlignment.TopRight`
`lblName.TextAlign = ContentAlignment.BottomLeft`
`lblName.TextAlign = ContentAlignment.TopCenter`

2.31 A dialog box is a small window that is typically used to display a message to the user. A message box is an example of a dialog box.

2.32 `MessageBox.Show("Welcome to our hotel!")`

2.33 The statement is missing the dot that should appear between `MessageBox` and `Show`. The statement should read `MessageBox.Show("Invalid password")`

2.34 A help screen that is displayed for the currently selected item when the [F1] key is pressed

2.35 Compile errors and runtime errors

Chapter 3

3.1 Text

3.2 `lblMessage.Text = txtInput.Text`

3.3 Hello Jonathon, how are you?

3.4 Appending one string to another.

3.5 The control is accepting keyboard and/or mouse input from the user.

3.6 `txtLastName.Focus()`

3.7 The order in which controls receive the focus when the user presses the [Tab] key.

3.8 The TabIndex property, which contains a numeric value, determines the position of a control in the tab order. The control that has the lowest TabIndex value (usually 0) on a form is the first in the tab order. The control with the next highest TabIndex (usually 1) will be the next in the tab order. This sequence continues.

3.9 In the order that controls are created

3.10 That control is skipped in the tab order.

3.11 The & character has two effects: It assigns an access key to the button (in this case, the access key is [Alt]+[M] because the & is in front of the *M*) and it causes the *M* to appear underlined on the button.

3.12 An accept button is a form's button that is clicked when the user presses the [Enter] key. A cancel button is a form's button that is clicked when the user presses the [Esc] key. You select accept and cancel buttons with the form's AcceptButton and CancelButton properties.

3.13 A variable is a storage location in the computer's memory; used for holding data while the program is running.

3.14 `Dim intCount As Integer`

3.15 `decInterestRate` is written with the convention used in this book.

3.16 a. `count`   Legal
      b. `rate*Pay`   Illegal; cannot use the * character
      c. `deposit.amount`   Illegal; cannot use a period
      d. `down_payment`   Legal

3.17 a. 0   d. 0
      b. 0.0   e. 12:00:00 AM, January 1 of year 1
      c. False

3.18 `#2/20/2010 5:35:00 PM#`

3.19 Charles Simonyi. He introduced the use of prefixes in variable names, called Hungarian Notation, a popular naming convention often used in Visual Basic and many other programming languages.

3.20 a. 21   d. 18
      b. 2   e. 3.0
      c. 17   f. 36

3.21 a. 1
      b. 2

3.22 `dtmThisTime = TimeOfDay`

3.23 `dtmCurrent = Now`

3.24 Integer division throws away any fractional part of the quotient. The result of integer division is always an integer.

3.25 `dblResult` will be set to `4.7`

3.26 `dblResult` will be set to `7.0`

3.27 `dblResult` will be set to `3.0`

3.28 a. 21
      b. 2
      c. 17
      d. 18

3.29 `dblResult` will be set to `28`

3.30 `dblResult` will be set to `186478.39`

3.31 A named constant is like a variable whose content is read-only, and cannot be changed by a programming statement while the program is running.

3.32 a. 27
      b. 13
      c. 12
      d. 18

3.33 `CDbl` function

3.34 a. 48   (rounds to nearest even integer)
      b. 35   (rounds up)
      c. 2300
      d. ** cannot be converted **

3.35 `dblSalary.ToString("c")`

3.36 a. `"c"`   d. `"p"`
      b. `"e"`   e. `"f"`
      c. `"n"`

3.37 `ToString("c")`

3.38

Number Value	Format String	**ToString** Value
12.3	n4	12.3000
12.348	n1	12.3
1234567.1	n3	1,234,567.100
123456.0	f1	123456.0
123456.0	e3	1.235E+005
.234	p2	23.40%
−1234567.8	c3	($1,234,567.800)

3.39 `datStart.ToString("T")`

3.40 `datBirth.ToString("D")`

3.41 Local variables are not visible to statements outside the procedure in which they are declared. Class-level variables are visible to all of the procedures in a class.

3.42 Class-level variables are declared at the class-level (inside the class, but not in any procedure).

3.43 You can make a form appear more organized by grouping related controls inside group boxes.

3.44 Select the GroupBox with the mouse.

3.45 Copy the control to the clipboard, select the GroupBox with the mouse, and then paste the control from the clipboard into the GroupBox.

3.46 The TabIndex value of the controls inside the GroupBox are relative to the GroupBox control's TabIndex property.

3.47 *Form_*Load

3.48 A compile error (or syntax error), will prevent an application from starting. Examples are misspelled keywords and incorrect use of operators or punctuation. Compiler errors are often reported as soon as you type them. A logic error is a programming mistake that does not prevent an application from starting, but causes the application to produce incorrect results. Examples are incorrect math statements and copying the wrong value to a variable.

3.49 A breakpoint is a line of code that causes a running application to pause execution and enter break mode. While the application is paused, you may perform debugging operations, such as examining variable contents and the values stored in control properties.

3.50 Single-stepping is a useful debugging technique for locating logic errors. In single-stepping, you execute an application's code one line at a time. After each line executes, you can examine variable and property contents. This process allows you to identify the line or lines of code causing the error.

Chapter 4

4.1 a. T e. T
    b. T f. F
    c. F g. T
    d. T

4.2 If the Boolean variable `blnIsInvalid` equals `True`.

4.3 Yes, they both perform the same operation. Only the indentation is different.

4.4 The following statement is preferred because the conditionally executed statement is indented. The indention makes the statement easier to read.
```
If decSales > 10000 Then
   decCommissionRate = 0.15
End If
```

4.5 a. 99
   b. 0
   c. 99

4.6 Three times

4.7 One time by the `If...Then...ElseIf` statement and four times by the set of `If...Then` statements

4.8 | **Logical Expression** | **Result** |
| --- | --- |
| `True And False` | `False` |
| `True And True` | `True` |
| `False And True` | `False` |
| `False And False` | `False` |
| `True Or False` | `True` |
| `True Or True` | `True` |
| `False Or True` | `True` |
| `False Or False` | `False` |
| `True Xor False` | `True` |
| `True Xor True` | `False` |
| `Not True` | `False` |
| `Not False` | `True` |

4.9 a. *False*
   b. *False*
   c. *True*

4.10 f, g, a, b, i, h, e, c, d

4.11 c, a, d, b

4.12 `DialogResult.Abort`

4.13 `MessageBox.Show("William" & ControlChars.CrLf &`
     `"Joseph" & ControlChars.CrLf & "Smith")`

4.14
```
Select Case intQuantity
   Case 0 To 9
      decDiscount = 0.1
   Case 10 To 19
      decDiscount = 0.2
   Case 20 To 29
      decDiscount = 0.3
   Case Is >= 30
      decDiscount = 0.4
   Case Else
      MessageBox.Show("Invalid Data")
End Select
```

4.15 By examining its Checked property. If the property equals `True`, the radio button is selected. If the property equals `False`, the radio button is not selected.

4.16 Only one

4.17 By examining its Checked property. If the property equals `True`, the check box is selected. If the property equals `False`, the check box is not selected.

4.18 Any or all of them

4.19 By pressing the spacebar

Chapter 5

5.1 `strInput = InputBox("Enter a number", "Please Respond", "500")`

5.2 `strInput = InputBox("Enter a number", "Please Respond",`
`                        "500" 100, 300)`

5.3 0

5.4 `Items.Count`

5.5 11

5.6 SelectedItem

5.7 SelectedIndex

5.8 `strSelectedName = lstNames.Items(1).ToString()`

5.9 The loop is an infinite loop because it does not change the value of `intCount`.

5.10 Ten times

5.11 One time

5.12 `intX` is the counter and `intY` is the accumulator.

5.13
```
Dim intCount As Integer = 5

Do While intCount >= 1
  lstOutput.Items.Add(intCount)
  intCount -= 1
Loop
```

5.14
```
Dim intTotal As Integer = 0
Dim intNumber As Integer

Do While intTotal <= 300
  intNumber = CInt(InputBox("Enter a number"))
  intTotal += intNumber
Loop
```

5.15 Posttest

5.16 The loop will execute five times. The message box will display 10.

5.17
```
Dim intCount As Integer

For intCount = 0 To 100 Step 5
  lstOutput.Items.Add(intCount)
Next
```

5.18
```
Dim intCount As Integer
Dim intTotal As Integer
Dim intNum As Integer

intTotal = 0
For intCount = 0 To 7
  intNum = CInt(InputBox("Enter a number"))
  intTotal += intNum
Next
MessageBox.Show("The total is " & intTotal.ToString())
```

5.19 The `For` loop

5.20 The `Do While` loop

5.21 The `Do Until` loop

5.22 1, 1, 2, 2, 1, 2, 3, 1, 2

5.23 600 times

5.24 0

5.25 Items.Count

5.26 SelectedIndex

5.27 A drop-down combo box allows the user to type text into its text area. A drop-down list combo box does not allow the user to type text. The user can only select an item from the list.

5.28 By retrieving the value in the Text property

5.29 A drop-down list combo box

5.30 It returns a random integer value somewhere between 0 and 2,147,483,647.

5.31 It returns a random floating-point number between 0.0 and 1.0 (not including 1.0).

5.32 `Dim rand as New Random`

`intRandomNumber = rand.Next(101)`

5.33 `Dim rand as New Random`

`intRandomNumber = rand.Next(301) + 100`

5.34 When a `Random` object is created in memory, it retrieves the system time from the computer's internal clock, and uses that as the seed value.

5.35 If a `Random` object uses the same seed each time it is created, it will always generate the same series of random numbers.

Chapter 6

6.1 If you enter 10, the following will be displayed:

I saw Elba
Able was I

If you enter 5, the following will be displayed:

Able was I
I saw Elba

6.2 Static local variables retain their value between procedure calls. Regular local variables do not.

6.3
```
Sub TimesTen(ByVal intValue As Integer)
    Dim intResult As Integer
    intResult = intValue * 10
    MessageBox.Show(intResult.ToString())
End Sub
```

6.4 `TimesTen(25)`

6.5
```
Sub PrintTotal(ByVal intNum1 As Integer, ByVal intNum2 As Integer,
               ByVal intNum3 As Integer)
    Dim intTotal As Integer
    intTotal = intNum1 + intNum2 + intNum3
    MessageBox.Show(intTotal.ToString())
End Sub
```

6.6 `PrintTotal(intUnits, intWeight, intCount)`

6.7 `ByVal`

6.8 a. Distance
b. Two
c. sngRate and sngTime; they are both Singles
d. Single

6.9
```
Function Days(ByVal intYears As Integer, ByVal intMonths As Integer,
              ByVal intWeeks As Integer) As Integer
```

6.10 `intNumDays = Days(intY, intM, intW)`

6.11 `Function LightYears(ByVal lngMiles As Long) As Single`

6.12 `sngDistance = LightYears(m)`

6.13
```
Function TimesTwo(intNumber As Integer) As Integer
    Return intNumber * 2
End Function
```

6.14 Step Out; Ctrl + Shift + F8

6.15 Step Into; F8

6.16 Step Over; Shift + F8

Chapter 7

7.1 Make it the startup form in the project's properties.

7.2 `frm`

7.3 To add a new form to a project either: Click the *Add New Item* button on the tool bar, and then select *Windows form*, or select *Add Windows Form* from the *Project* menu. In both cases, the *Add New Item* dialog appears. You can enter a form name and click the *Add* button.

7.4 To exclude a form from a project in Visual Studio: Right-click the form's entry in the *Solution Explorer* window. On the pop-up menu, click *Exclude From Project*.

7.5 A form file contains a form's code. It has the *.vb* extension.

7.6 When a modal form is displayed, no other form in the application can receive the focus until the modal form is closed. Also, when a statement displays a modal form, no other statements in that procedure will execute until the modal form is closed. A modeless form, however, allows the user to switch focus to another form while it is displayed. When a statement uses a method call to display a modeless form, the statements that follow the method call will continue to execute after the modeless form is displayed.

7.7 `frmResults.ShowDialog()`

7.8 `frmResults.Show()`

7.9 In the form's Activated event handler.

7.10 `frmInfo.lblCustomer.Text = "Jim Jones"`

7.11 The `Me` keyword indicates the currently active form. This can be useful when a form needs to call one of its own methods.

7.12 `Public dblAverage As Double`

7.13 It contains procedures, functions, and the declarations of variables and/or constants.

7.14 *.vb*

7.15 (1) Click the *Add New Item* button on the toolbar, or click *Project* on the menu bar, and then click *Add Module*. The *Add New Item* dialog box should appear. (2) Select *Module* as the type of item. (3) Change the default name that is displayed in the *Name* text box to the name you wish to give the new module.

7.16 When you create large application with multiple forms, quite often you will find that the code in several different forms needs to call the same general-purpose functions and/or procedures. These functions and/or procedures can be placed in a module to eliminate the duplication of code that would result if they were written into each form file.

7.17 1. Click *Project* on the menu bar, and then click *Add Existing Item*.
   2. The *Add Existing Item* dialog box appears. Use the dialog box to locate the module file you want to add to the project. When you locate the file, select it and click the *Open* button. The module is now added to the project.

7.18 a. The name of a drop-down menu, which appears on the form's menu bar
   b. A command that appears on a drop-down menu, and may be selected by the user
   c. A menu item that appears dimmed and cannot be selected by the user
   d. A menu item that appears with a check mark to its left
   e. A key or combination of keys that causes a menu command to execute
   f. Another menu that appears when a command on a drop-down menu is selected
   g. A horizontal bar used to separate groups of commands on a menu

7.19 Shortcut keys are different from access keys in that a command's shortcut key may be used at any time the form is active, while a command's access key may only be used while the drop-down menu containing the command is visible.

7.20 `mnu`

7.21 `mnuFileSave, mnuFileSaveAs, mnuFilePrint,` and `mnuFileExit`

7.22 By placing an ampersand (&) before a character in the Text property.

7.23 The item initially appears as a checked menu item, meaning it appears with a check mark displayed next to it.

7.24 By setting its Enabled property to *False*.

7.25 By testing the value of the menu item's Checked property.

7.26 A Click event occurs for the ToolStripMenuItem.

7.27 By right-clicking a control

7.28 By setting the control's ContextMenuStrip property to the name of the ContextMenuStrip control.

Chapter 8

8.1 a. `Dim intEmpNums(99) As Integer`
b. `Dim decPayRate(23) As Decimal`
c. `Dim intMiles() As Integer = { 10, 20, 30, 40, 50 }`
d. `Dim strNames(12) As String`
e. `Dim strDivisions() As String = {"North", "South",`
`"East", "West"}`

8.2 The upper boundary (4) cannot appear inside the parentheses when an initialization list is provided.

8.3 a. 101
b. 3
c. 1

8.4 The runtime system throws an exception if a subscript is outside the range of subscripts for an array.

8.5
```
For intCount = 0 To intMAX_SUBSCRIPT
   MessageBox.Show(intPoints(intCount).ToString())
Next
```

8.6
```
Dim intNumber As Integer
For Each intNumber In intPoints
   MessageBox.Show(intNumber.ToString())
Next
```

8.7 a. 10.00
b. 25.00
c. 32.50
d. 50.00

8.8
```
intTotal = 0              ' Initialize accumulator.
For intCount = 0 To 99
   intTotal += intValues(intCount)
Next
```

8.9
```
intTotal = 0              ' Initialize accumulator.
For intCount= 0 To (points.Length - 1)
   intTotal += intPoints(intCount)
Next
dblAverage = intTotal / points.Length
```

8.10 `Array.Sort(strSerialNumbers)`

8.11 0 18 0
1 4 4
2 27 54
3 52 156
4 100 400

8.12 `ReDim Preserve decSales(49)`

8.13 (Code example)
```
blnFound = False
intCount = 0
Do While Not blnFound And intCount < intValidNumbers.Length
   If intValidNumbers (intCount) = 247 Then
      blnFound = True
      intPosition = intCount
   End If
   intCount+= 1
```

```
      Loop
      'Was 100 found in the array?
      If blnFound Then
        MessageBox.Show("The value was found at position " &
                        intPosition.ToString())
      Else
        MessageBox.Show("The value was not found.")
      End If
```

8.14 `Dim intGrades(29, 9) As Integer`

8.15 24 elements (6 rows by 4 columns)

8.16 `decSales(0, 0) = 56893.12`

8.17 `MessageBox.Show(decSales(5, 3).ToString())`

8.18 `Dim intSettings(2, 4) As Integer`

8.19 Four rows and five columns

8.20 `Dim strMovies(49, 9, 24) As String`

8.21 `If radLifeTimeMember.Checked = True Then`
     `   chkFreePizza.Enabled = True`
     `   chkFreeCola.Enabled = True`
     `End If`

8.22 500

8.23 It allows you to anchor the control to one or more edges of a form. When a control is anchored to a form's edge, the distance between the control's edge and the form's edge will remain constant, even when the user resizes the form.

8.24 It allows you to dock a control. When a control is docked, it is positioned directly against one of the edges of a form. Additionally, the length or width of a docked control is changed to match the length or width of the form's edge.

Chapter 9

9.1 (1) open the file, (2) write data to the file or read data from the file, and (3) close the file

9.2 `StreamWriter, StreamReader`

9.3 `outputFile = System.IO.File.CreateText("Test.txt")`

9.4 `outputFile.WriteLine(intX)`

9.5 `inputFile = System.IO.File.OpenText("Test.txt")`

9.6 `intX = inputFile.ReadLine`

9.7 With the `System.IO.File.Exists` method

9.8 With the `Peek` method; when `Peek` returns -1, the end of the file has been reached

9.9 Most Windows users are accustomed to using a dialog box to browse their disk for a file to open, or for a location to save a file.

9.10 Filter: These list boxes display a filter that specifies the type of files that are visible in the dialog box. You store a string in the Filter property that specifies the filter(s) available in the list boxes.

   InitialDirectory: You store the path of the directory whose contents are to be initially displayed in the dialog box.

Title: The string stored in this property is displayed in the dialog box's title bar.

Filename: The filename selected or entered by the user is stored in this property.

9.11
```
Text files (*.txt)|*.txt|Word files (*.doc)|*.doc|
All files(*.*)
```

9.12 The ColorDialog control's Color property.

9.13 The FontDialog control's Font property.

9.14 By setting the FontDialog control's ShowColor property to *True* before calling the ShowDialog method.

9.15 in the FontDialog control's Color property.

9.16 By calling the control's Print method.

9.17
```
e.Graphics.DrawString("Joe Smith", New Font("MS sans Serif",
     18, FontStyle.Bold), Brushes.Black, 100, 20)
```

9.18 Header, body, and footer.

9.19 The characters in a proportionally spaced font do not occupy the same amount of horizontal space. All the characters in a monospaced font use the same amount of space.

9.20
```
e.Graphics.DrawString(String.Format("{0,12} {1,8} ", a, b),
     New Font("Courier", 12, FontStyle.Regular),
     Brushes.Black, 10, 50)
```

9.21
```
e.Graphics.DrawString(String.Format("{0,-12} {1,8} ", a, b),
     New Font("Courier", 12, FontStyle.Regular),
     Brushes.Black, 10, 50)
```

9.22
```
Structure Movie
    strName As String
    strDirector As String
    strProducer As String
    intYear As Integer
End Structure
```

9.23
```
Dim film As Movie
```

9.24 The following statements assume the variable is named `film`:
```
film.strName = "Wheels of Fury"
film.strDirector = "Arlen McGoo"
film.strProducer = "Vincent Van Dough"
film.intYear = 2010
```

9.25 The following statements assume the variable is named `film`:
```
With film

   .strName = "Wheels of Fury"
   .strDirector = "Arlen McGoo"
   .strProducer = "Vincent Van Dough"
   .intYear = 2010
End With
```

Chapter 10

10.1 A database is a container for one or more tables. A table is a set of rows and columns holding logically related data.

10.2 Employee_ID

10.3   Boolean

10.4   There would be too great a chance for misspellings by the data entry person. Also, the department name could change in the future, making maintenance a problem.

10.5   Individual values of a foreign key column can occur multiple times in a table, whereas a primary key can contain values that occur only once. Also, a foreign key links its table with some other table's primary key.

10.6   Data binding

10.7   TableAdapter

10.8   The database is not affected by changes to a dataset unless a special `Update` method is called.

10.9   DataGridView control

10.10   DataConnection object

10.11   Data Sources window

10.12   DataSource

10.13   Click the DataGridView's smart tag (arrow in the upper right corner), and select the data source. Alternatively, you can select the DataGridView's DataSource property in the Properties window and select the data source from a list.

10.14   Select the column in the *Data Sources* window and drag it onto the form.

10.15   DateTimePicker control

10.16   Select *Add New Data Source* from the *Data* menu.

10.17   Structured Query Language

10.18   SQL queries are written using an industry-standard language

10.19   `SELECT First_Name, Last_Name FROM Employees`

10.20   Right-click the table adapter icon in the form's component tray and select *Add Query*.

10.21   `WHERE Salary <= 85000`

10.22   `SELECT pay_rate, employee_id, hours_worked FROM Payroll`
`    ORDER by hours_worked DESC`

10.23   `SELECT pay_rate AS Rate_of_Pay FROM Payroll`

10.24   `SELECT pay_rate, hours_worked, pay_rate * hours_worked`
`    AS gross_pay FROM Payroll`

10.25   `SELECT * FROM Payroll WHERE pay_rate > 20000`
`    AND pay_rate <= 55000`

10.26   `SELECT * FROM Payroll WHERE employee_id LIKE "FT%"`

10.27   *Members* table

10.28   *Payments* and *Members* tables

10.29   Columns property

10.30   `LIKE`

Chapter 11

11.1 A Web application is a program running on a Web server that interacts with Web browsers. The connection might be across the Internet, or it might be within a company intranet.

11.2 The Web server generates Web pages, which are consumed by clients (end users) running Web browsers. The clients make requests and the server satisfies the requests.

11.3 A postback occurs when the end user clicks a button or activates a control that sends the contents of the Web page back to the Web server.

11.4 ASP.NET is called a platform because it provides development tools, code libraries, and visual controls for browser-based applications.

11.5 Content is comprised of Web forms, HTML code, Web controls, images, and other multimedia.

11.6 File system, HTTP, and FTP

11.7 Click the *Design* tab.

11.8 Right-click the *Solution Explorer* window and select *Browse with* . . . .

11.9 Static text is text typed directly onto a form in *Design* mode. In can be used in place of Labels (the type used in Windows forms) when you do not need to access it at runtime in program code.

11.10 By selecting the text with the mouse, and then selecting *Heading 1* from the *Block format* pull-down list on the left side of the formatting toolbar

11.11 A dialog window explains that a confirmation option must be set in the *Web.config* file. It creates the file and adds it to the *Solution Explorer* window.

11.12 DropDownList

11.13 ImageButton

11.14 LinkButton

11.15 The SelectedIndex property contains an integer that indicates the selected button.

11.16 As soon as the user makes a ListBox selection, the page is posted back to the server.

11.17 DropDownList

11.18 Drag the mouse over the cells and select *Merge Cells* from the *Layout* menu.

11.19 Click the column select button just above the column along the table border.

11.20 Drag the right-hand border of the column with the mouse.

11.21 From the *Layout* menu, choose *Select*, and then choose *Table*. Open the Style property of the table, and modify the font in the *Style Builder* dialog.

11.22 Items collection

11.23 Select *Add New Item* from the Web site menu.

11.24 Assign the new Web page location to the NavigateURL property.

11.25 Select the block with the mouse and click the *HyperLink* button on the formatting toolbar.

11.26 The `Redirect` method

11.27 GridView control

11.28 SqlDataSource object

11.29 DataFormatString property

11.30 Fields property

11.31 DetailsView control

Chapter 12

12.1 Forms, buttons, check boxes, list boxes, and other controls.

12.2 The TextBox tool represents the class and a specific TextBox control on the form is an instance of the class.

12.3 Select classes by finding the physical entities in the application domain.

12.4 Attributes describe the properties that all objects of the same class have in common. They are implemented as properties.

12.5 Operations are actions the class objects may perform or messages to which they can respond. They are implemented as methods.

12.6 A class interface is the portion that is visible to the application programmer who uses the class.

12.7 A class implementation is the portion of a class that is hidden from client programs.

12.8 (1) Click the *Add New Item* button () on the toolbar, or click *Project* on the menu bar, and then click *Add Class*. The *Add New Item* dialog box should appear. Make sure that *Class* is selected in the *Templates* pane. (2) Change the default class name in the Name text box to the name you wish to give the new class file. (3) Click the *Add* button.

12.9 Declare an object variable, and then create an instance of the class in memory and assign its address to the variable.

12.10 An object is removed by setting all variables that reference it to `Nothing`.

12.11 Garbage collection.

12.12 Variables declared in a class module, but outside of any class methods

12.13 A procedure that behaves like a Class property

12.14 It allows a client program to retrieve the value of a property.

12.15 It allows a client program to set the value of a property.

12.16 A constructor is a class method that is executed automatically when an instance of a class is created. A `Finalize` method is called just before the Garbage Collector removes an object from memory.

12.17 Unlike arrays, which have fixed sizes, collection objects automatically expand as items are added to them, and shrink as items are removed from them. Another difference is this: all elements in an array must be of the same type, but members of collections do not have to be of the same type.

12.18 Use the Add method to add members to a collection.

12.19 By adding a key value, you will be more easily able to search for items.

12.20 With the `Item` method

12.21 With the `Remove` method

12.22 `Insect` is the base class and `Fly` is the derived class.

12.23 All of the base class's members (variables, properties, and methods)

12.24 Overriding is replacing a base Class property procedure or method with one of the same name in the derived class.

12.25 `Overridable`

12.26 `Overrides`

12.27 The base class constructor executes first, followed by the derived class constructor.

12.28 Protected base class members are like private members, except they may be accessed by methods and property procedures in derived classes. To all other code, however, protected class members are just like private class members.

About box—a dialog box that usually displays brief information about the application

abstract data type (ADT)—a data type created by a programmer

abstraction—a model that includes only the general characteristics of an object

accept button—a button on a form that is clicked when the user presses the Enter key

access key—a key that is pressed in combination with the Alt key; access keys allow the user to access buttons and menu items using the keyboard; also known as a mnemonic

accumulator—the variable used to keep a running total

Activated event handler—created in response to an Activated event

Activated event—a form event that occurs each time the user switches focus to a form from another form or another application

Active Server Pages (ASP)—Microsoft's technology for creating Web-enabled applications

Add method—used to add items to a collection

algorithm—a set of well-defined steps for performing a task or solving a problem

Alphabetical button—a button on the Properties window that causes properties to be displayed alphabetically

Anchor property—a control property that allows you to anchor the control to one or more edges of a form

And operator—a logical operator that combines two expressions into one; both expressions must be true for the overall expression to be true

AndAlso operator—uses short-circuit evaluation in compound expressions

append—to write new data immediately following existing data in a file

application software—programs that make the computer useful to the user by solving specific problems or performing general operations

argument—a value passed to a procedure or function

array—a group of variables with a single name

array bounds checking—a runtime feature of Visual Basic that does not allow a statement to use a subscript outside the range of subscripts for an array

ascending order—when items are arranged in order, from lowest to highest value

aspect ratio—the image's width to height ratio

ASP.NET—Microsoft's platform for Web applications; an improvement over Active Server Pages

ASP.NET development server—ASP.NET development software that is automatically installed with Visual Studio and Visual Web Developer Express Edition

ASP.NET Server Controls—interactive controls such as buttons, list boxes, and text boxes that execute on the server

assignment operator—the equal sign (=); it copies the value on its right into the item on its left in an assignment statement

assignment statement—a programming statement that uses the assignment operator to copy a value from one object to another

attributes—the data contained in an object; the characteristics of an object that will be implemented as properties

Auto Hide—when this feature is turned on, the window is displayed only as a tab along one of the edges of the Visual Studio window; click the pushpin icon to turn it on or off

AutoPostBack property—used on Web forms to force the page to be sent to the server when the user clicks on the control

AutoSize property—a Label control property that, when set to *True*, causes the label's size to display all the text in the Text property

Autos window—a debugging window that displays the value and data type of the variables that appear in the current statement, the three statements before, and the three statements after the current statement

BackColor property—establishes the background color for text

base class—the class that a derived class is based on

binary files—files whose contents are not stored as plain text, but as binary data; cannot be read by a text editor

binary number—a number that is a sequence of 1s and 0s

binary operator—an operator that works with two operands

binding source—keeps track of a database name, location, username, password, and other connection information

Boolean expression—the expression tested in an `If...Then` statement; can be either *True* or *False*

Boolean property—a value that can be either *True* or *False*

BorderStyle property—a Label control property that determines the type of border, if any, that will appear around the control

bounding box—a transparent rectangular area that defines a control's size on a form

break mode—the mode in which an application has been suspended for debugging purposes

breakpoint—a line of code that causes a running application to pause execution and enter break mode; while the application is paused, you may examine variable contents and the values stored in certain control properties

buffer—a small holding section of memory that data is first written to; when the buffer is filled, all the information stored there is written to the file

button—a rectangular button-shaped control that performs an action when clicked with the mouse

Button control—when clicked by a user on a Web page, causes the page contents to be sent back to the Web server

`ByRef`—keyword used to declare a parameter variable, causing its argument to be passed by reference

by reference—when passing an argument to a procedure, the procedure has access to the original argument and can make changes to it

`ByVal` keyword—indicates that arguments passed into the variable are passed by value

by value—when passing an argument to a procedure, only a portion of the argument is passed to the procedure

`Call` keyword—a keyword that may be optionally used to call a procedure

cancel button—a button on a form that is clicked when the user presses the [Esc] key

Cascading Style Sheet (CSS)—file containing HTML styles that affect the appearance of text and graphics on Web pages

catch block—one or more statements following the Catch clause in a Try-Catch statement; execute only if an exception is thrown from the try block

Catch clause—part of a Try-Catch statement; appears after the last statement in a try block; marks the beginning of a catch block; program execution jumps here if an exception is thrown in the try block

Categorized button—a button on the *Properties* window that causes related properties to be displayed in groups

class declaration—specifies the member variables, properties, methods, and events that belong to the class

central processing unit (CPU)—the part of the computer that fetches instructions, carries out operations commanded by the instructions, and produces some outcome

CheckBox—a box that is checked or unchecked when clicked with the mouse

CheckBox control—allows the user to make yes/no or on/off selections; may appear alone or in groups

CheckBoxList control—looks like a group of check boxes, but works like a list box

CheckedChanged event—occurs when the state of a radio button or check box changes

CheckOnClick property—setting this property to *True* gives a menu item the ability to become checked or unchecked when it is clicked by the user

Checked property—A property of radio buttons and check boxes; it is set to *True* when the control is selected and *False* when the control is deselected. Also a MenuItem object property that may be set to *True* or *False*; when set to *True*, the object becomes a checked menu item.

`Chr` function—an intrinsic function that accepts a character code as an argument and returns the character that corresponds to the code

class—a program structure that defines an abstract data type

class declaration—defines a class and member variables, properties, events, and methods

class implementation—the portion of a class that is hidden from client programs

class interface—the portion of a class that is visible to the application programmer who uses the class

class objects—instances of a class

client—entity that consumes data and makes requests of a server

client program—a program written to use a class; this term is in reference to the client-server relationship between a class and the programs that use it

client-server model—describes interaction between users of a program (the clients) and the server (as in a Web server)

`Close` method—closes a form and releases its visual par from memory

Closed event handler—a form event procedure that executes after a form has closed

Closing event handler—a form event procedure that executes as a form is in the process of closing, but before it has closed

code—the statements that are written in a program; commonly called source code, or simply code

code-behind file—stores the source code for a Web form

code template—code that is automatically inserted into an event handler, consisting of the first and last lines of the procedure; you must add the code that appears between these two lines

code outlining—a Visual Studio tool that lets you expand and collapse sections of code

Code window—a text-editing window in which you write code

collection—an object that is similar to an array; it is a single unit that contains several items and dynamically expands or shrinks in size as items are added or removed

Color dialog box—allows the user to select a color

ColorDialog control—displays a *Color* dialog box

columns—the vertical lists of data in a database table

combined assignment operators—combine an arithmetic operator with an assignment operator

combo box—similar to list boxes; display lists of items to the user

ComboBox—a control that is the combination of a ListBox and a TextBox

comments—notes of explanation that document lines or sections in a method; also known as remarks

Common Gateway Interface (CGI)—typically written in languages such as C or Perl; process information collected by HTML controls

compiler—special software that converts the program into machine language

compile errors—syntax errors, such as misspelled keywords and incorrect use of operators or punctuation; statements containing compile errors are underlined with a jagged blue line

components—special controls in Visual Basic that provide the linking mechanism in a database

compound operators—*see* combined assignment operators

conditionally executed statements—statements that are executed only when certain conditions exist; usually determined by the value of a Boolean expression

connection object—provides the low-level functionality to interact with a data source

connector symbol—a flowcharting symbol used to connect two flowcharts when a flowchart does not fit on a single sheet of paper or must be divided into sections

constructor—a method that is automatically called when an instance of the class is created

Contents button—on the *Dynamic Help* window; displays a table of contents in which related help topics are organized into groups

context menu—a pop-up menu that is displayed when the user right-clicks a form or control

context-sensitive help—a help screen that is displayed when the F1 key is pressed (for the item that is currently selected)

ControlChars.CrLf—a value that can be concatenated with a string to produce multiple line displays

control—a specific type of object that usually appears in a program's graphical user interface

Count property—a collection property that holds the number of items in the collection

counter—a variable that is regularly incremented or decremented each time a loop iterates

database—a collection of tables that hold related data

database management system (DBMS)—software that is specifically designed to store, retrieve, and manipulate large amounts of data in an organized and efficient manner

database schema—the design of tables, columns, and relationships between tables for the database

data binding—a Visual Basic technique that links database tables to controls on a program's forms

data-bound controls—update their contents automatically when you move from one row to the next in a dataset

DataGridView control—bound to DateTime fields

dataset—an in-memory cache of records that is separate from the data source but still allows you to work with the data

data source—usually a database, but can include text files, Excel spreadsheets, XML data, or Web services

DataSource control—visible only at design time; for example, AccessDataSource or SqlDataSource

DataSource property—identifies the table within the dataset that supplies the data

data type—the type of information that the variable can hold

DateTimePicker control—bound to DateTime fields

decision structure—a program structure that allows a program to have more than one path of execution

delimiter—an item that separates other items

derived class—a class that is based on another class

design—in a database table, specifies each column's name, data type, and range or size

Design mode—the mode in which you design and build an application

design time—see Design mode

Designer window—contains the application's forms; where one designs the application's user interface by creating forms and placing controls on them

DetailsView control—makes it easy to view, edit, delete, or add rows to a database table

diagram pane—displays all the tables used in the query, with a check mark next to each field that will be used in the dataset

dialog box—a small window that displays a message to the user; see message box

disk drive—stores information by magnetically encoding it onto a circular disk

DisplayMember property—identifies the column within the table that displays in the list box or combo box

DLLs—dynamic-link library files

docked—describes windows that are attached to each other or to one of the edges of the Visual Studio window

Dock property—a control property that allows you to dock a control against a form's edge

domain name—in a URL, the specific designation, such as microsoft.com

Do Until loop—a looping structure that causes one or more statements to repeat until its test expression is true

Do While loop—a looping structure that causes one or more statements to repeat as long as an expression is true

DropDownList control—permits the user to select a single item from a list

elements—variables stored within an array

empty string—represented by two quotation marks, with no space between them

Enabled property—a control property that, when set to *False*, disables the control; therefore the control cannot receive the focus, cannot respond to events generated by the user, and appears dimmed or grayed out on the form

encapsulation—the hiding of data and procedures inside a class

event-driven—a type of program that responds to events or actions that occur while the program is running

event handler—a type of method that responds to events, such as mouse clicks and key presses at the keyboard

event procedure—*see* event handler

exception—an event or condition that happens unexpectedly and causes the application to halt

exception handler—in most modern programming languages, a simple mechanism for handling exceptions

exception object—contains various data about an exception; created when an exception is thrown; can optionally be assigned a name in the Catch clause of a Try-Catch statement to access properties

execution point—while single-stepping through an application's code, the next line of code that will execute

`Exit Do` statement—stops the execution of a `Do While` or `Do Until` loop

`Exit For` statement—stops the execution of a `For...Next` loop

field—*see* columns

file—a collection of data stored on a computer's disk

`File.AppendText` method—a method that opens a text file for data to be written to it; if the file method already exists, data is appended to its current contents

`File.CreateText` method—a method that opens a text file for data to be written to it; if the file does not exist, it is created

`File.Exists` method—a method that returns `True` if the specified file exists, or `False` if it does not

`File.OpenText` method—a method that opens a text file for reading

Filename property—a property of the OpenFileDialog and SaveFileDialog controls that holds the name of the file selected or entered by the user with the *Open* and *Save As* dialog boxes

File System Web site—runs directly under the ASP.NET development server supplied with Visual Studio and Visual Web Developer

Filter property—a property of the OpenFileDialog and SaveFileDialog controls used to set filters that control what file types are displayed in the *Open* and *Save As* dialog boxes

finalizer—a class method named `Finalize`; automatically called just before an instance of the class is removed from memory

finding the classes—the object-oriented analysis process of discovering the classes within a problem

flag—a Boolean variable that signals when some condition exists in the program

floating—when windows, such as *Project Explorer*, *Properties*, or *Form Layout* are not docked (attached)

flowchart—a diagram that graphically depicts the flow of a method

focus—the control that has the focus is the one that receives the user's keyboard input or mouse clicks

Focus method—gives the focus to a control

Font dialog box—allows the user to select a font, style, and size

Font property—indicates the size and style of a text font

FontDialog control—displays a *Font* dialog box

`For Each` loop—a special loop designed specifically to access values from arrays and array-like structures

foreign key—a column in one table that references a primary key in another table

`For...Next` loop—a loop specifically designed to initialize, test, and increment a counter variable

ForeColor property—establishes the foreground color for text

Form—a window, onto which other controls may be placed

formatting—the way a value is printed or displayed

FormBorderStyle property—a property that configures a form's border; allows or prevents resizing, minimizing, or maximizing a window

FormClosed event handler—used to execute code immediately after a form has closed

FormClosing event handler—used to execute code in response to a form's closing

Friend access—an access type; a class member with Friend access can be used only by other classes inside the same assembly

FTP site—references an existing ASP.NET Web site located on a remote computer (network or Web)

function—a specialized routine that performs a specific operation, and then returns or produces information

function procedure—a collection of statements that performs an operation and returns a value

garbage collector—a process that destroys objects when they are no longer needed

Get section—in a property procedure; allows a client program to retrieve the value of a property

global variable—a module-level or class-level variable that is declared with the Public access specifier

going out of scope—what happens when an object is created inside a procedure, and is automatically removed from memory when the procedure ends

graphical user interface (GUI)—the graphical interface used by modern operating systems

grid pane—(also known as the criteria pane) displays the query in a spreadsheet-like format, which is particularly well suited to choosing a sort order and entering selection criteria

GridView control—displays database tables; allows you to sort on any column, select the column order, and format data within columns

GroupBox—a rectangular border that functions as a container for other controls

GroupBox control—a control that appears as a rectangular border with an optional title that appears in the upper left corner; you group other controls by drawing them inside a GroupBox control

hardware—a computer's physical components

`Hide` method—removes a form or control, but does not remove it from memory

HScrollBar—a horizontal slider bar that, when moved with the mouse, increases or decreases a value

HTML control—controls found on most Web pages (not ASP.NET)

HTML designer—the tool in Visual Studio that simplifies the design of Web pages and Web forms

HTML Table control—an essential tool for designing the layout of Web forms; used to align text, graphics, and controls in rows and columns

HTML tag—used to design the layout of a Web form

HTTP Web site—runs under a Windows operating system utility named Internet Information Services (IIS)

Hungarian notation—system in which a three-letter prefix is used in variable names to identify their data type

HyperLink control—Web forms control that displays underlined text; when the user clicks on the text, the program navigates to a new Web page

Hypertext Markup Language (HTML)—the notation used when creating ordinary Web pages; determines fonts, images, and positioning of elements

identity column—a column in a database table that is assigned a unique integer value when new rows are added to the table

`If...Then`—a statement that can cause other statements to execute under certain conditions

`If...Then...Else`—a statement that will execute one group of statements if a condition is true, or another group of statements if a condition is false

`If...Then...ElseIf`—a statement that is like a chain of `If...Then...ElseIf` statements; they perform their tests, one after the other, until one of them is found to be true

Image property—specifies the image file that is to be displayed by the control

ImageButton control—Web forms control that displays an image on a clickable button

Immediate window—a debugging window used by advanced programmers; allows you to type debugging commands using the keyboard

implicit type conversion—when you assign a value of one data type to a variable of another data type, Visual Basic attempts to convert the value being assigned to the data type of the variable

index—*see* subscript

Index—button a button on the *Dynamic Help* window that displays a searchable alphabetized index of all help topics

IndexOf method—searches for a character or a string within a string

infinite loop—a loop that never stops repeating

inheritance—an object-oriented programming feature that allows you to create classes that are based on other classes

InitialDirectory property—a property of the OpenFileDialog and SaveFileDialog controls used to set the path of the directory initially displayed in *Open* and *Save As* dialog boxes

initialization—specifying an initial value for a variable

input—data the computer collects from the outside world

input box—a Windows dialog box that displays a message to the user; it provides a text box for the user to enter input

input device—a device that collects information and sends it to the computer

input file—file from which a program reads data

input validation—the process of inspecting input values and determining whether they are valid

integer division—a division operation performed with the \ operator in which the result is always an integer; if the result has a fractional part, it is discarded

integrated development environment (IDE)—an application that provides the necessary tools for creating, testing, and debugging software

IntelliSense—a feature of Visual Basic that provides help and some automatic code completion while you are developing an application

Internet Information Services (IIS)—Microsoft professional-level Web server

Interval property—a property of the timer control; the value stored in the Interval property is the number of milliseconds that elapse between timer events

intranet—network within a company, usually protected by a firewall

`IPmt` function—returns the required interest payment for a specific period on a loan

`Is` operator—used to compare two object variables to determine whether they reference the same object

IsNot operator—used to determine whether two variables do not reference the same object

`IsNumeric` function—an intrinsic function that accepts a string as its argument, and returns True if the string contains a number; the function returns False if the string's contents cannot be recognized as a number

`Item` method—a collection method that searches for a specific member of the collection and returns a reference to it

Items property—items that are displayed in a list box or combo box are stored as strings in the Items property

`Items.Add` method—a list box and combo box method that adds an item to the end of the control's Item property

Items.Count property—holds the number of items in a list box or combo box

`Items.Insert` method—a list box and combo box method that adds an item at a specific index of the control's Item property

`Items.Remove` method—a list box and combo box method that removes an item from the control's Item property

`Items.RemoveAt` method—a list box and combo box method that removes an item at a specific index of the control's Item property

iteration—one execution of a loop's conditionally-executed statements

JavaScript—scripting language used on Web pages, usually for client-side programming; runs under the control of the browser, not the Web server

keywords—programming language words that have a special meaning; keywords may only be used for their intended purpose

Label—text that cannot be changed or entered by the user; created with a Label control

Label control—used to create labels to display text on a Web form

Language Integrated Query (LINQ)—a query language that can be used to query many types of data from virtually any source.

leading space—a space that appears at the beginning of a string

`Length` property—a string method that returns the number of characters in the string

lifetime—the time during which the variable exists in memory

`LIKE` operator (SQL)—used to create partial matches with Text column values

LinkButton control—used on Web forms; looks like a hyperlink, but generates a Click event

LINQ—*see* Language Integrated Query

ListBox—a control that appears as a box containing a list of items

ListBox control—displays a list of items and allows the user to select one or more items from the list

Load event procedure—a procedure that is executed each time a form loads into memory

local variables—variables declared inside a procedure

Locals window—a debugging window that displays the current value and the data type of all the variables in the currently running procedure

logic error—a programming mistake that does not prevent an application from running but causes the application to produce incorrect results; see runtime error

logical operators—operators, such as `And` or `Or`, which connect two or more relational expressions into one, or `Not`, which reverse the logic of an expression

loop—one or more programming statements that repeat

machine language instructions—instructions that are stored in memory as a series of 1s and 0s and can only be processed by the CPU

main memory—also known as random-access memory, or RAM; where the computer stores information while programs are running

mathematical expression—an expression that uses multiple operators

`Me` keyword—may be substituted for the name of the currently active form or object

member variable—declared inside a class declaration; the variable is a member of the class

menu designer—allows you to create a custom menu system for any form in an application

MenuStrip control—consists of ToolStripMenuItem objects; used to construct a menu system on a form

menu system—a collection of commands organized in one or more drop-down menus

MenuItem objects—menu names, menu commands, or separator bars on a menu system

message box—a dialog box that displays a message to the user

methods—Procedures or functions that are members of a class; perform some operation on the data stored in the class

method call—statement that causes a method to execute

Microsoft Developer Network (MSDN) library—provides complete documentation for Visual Basic, as well as other programming languages included in Visual Studio

millisecond—1/1000 of a second

mnemonic—a key that you press in combination with the [Alt] key to access a control such as a button quickly; also called an *access key*

mnu—standard prefix for menu controls

modal form—when a modal form displayed, no other form in the application can receive the focus until the modal form is closed; no other statements in the procedure that displayed the modal form will execute until the modal form is closed

modeless form—Allows the user to switch focus to another form while it is displayed; statements that follow the modeless `Show` method call will continue to execute after the modeless form is displayed. Visual Basic will not wait until the modeless form is closed to execute these statements.

module—a Visual Basic file that contains only code; used for general-purpose procedures, functions, and declarations that are available to all forms in a project

modularize—to break an application's code into small, manageable procedures

module-level variable—a variable declared inside a module, but not inside a procedure or function

module scope—the scope of a module-level variable declared with the Dim keyword or the Private access specifier

Multiline property—a TextBox control property that, when set to *True*, allows the text box's text to span multiple lines

`MyBase` keyword—refers to a derived class's base class

Name property—a property that holds the control's name; controls are accessed and manipulated in code by their names

named constant—like a variable whose content is *read-only* and cannot be changed by a programming statement while the program is running

narrowing conversion—if you assign a real number to an integer variable, Visual Basic attempts to perform this conversion, which sometimes results in lost data

nested `If` statement—an If statement in the conditionally executed code of another If statement

nested loop—a loop inside another loop

newline character—an invisible character that separates text by breaking it into another line when displayed on the screen

`Next` method—a `Random` class method that is used to get a random integer number

`NextDouble` method—a `Random` class method that is used to get a random floating-point number between 0.0 and 1.0 (not including 1.0)

`Not` operator—a logical operator that reverses the *truth* of an expression; it makes a true expression false and a false expression true

object—a programming element that contains data and actions

object box—a drop-down list of the objects in the project that appears in the *Properties* window

Object Browser—a dialog box that allows you to browse the many classes and components available to your project

`Object` class—all classes are derived from the built-in `Object` class

object variable—a variable that holds the memory address of an object and allows you to work with the object

object-oriented analysis—during object-oriented design, the process of analyzing application requirements

object-oriented programming (OOP)—a programming technique centered on creating objects; a way of designing and coding applications that has led to using interchangeable software components

one-dimensional array—an array with one subscript

one-to-many relationship—when connecting two database tables indicates multiple occurrences of a foreign key

Open dialog box—gives users the capability of browsing their disks for a file to open, instead of typing a long path and filename

OpenFileDialog control—displays an *Open* dialog box

operand—a piece of data, such as a number, on which operators perform operations

operating system (OS)—a set of programs that manages the computer's hardware devices and controls their processes

operations—actions performed by class objects

operators—perform operations on one or more operands

Option Strict—in Visual Basic, a configuration option that determines whether certain implicit conversions are legal

`ORDER BY` clause (SQL)—lets you control the display order of the table rows

`OrElse` operator—uses short-circuit evaluation in compound expressions

`Or` operator—combines two expressions into one; one or both expressions must be true for the overall expression to be true (it is only necessary for one to be true, and it does not matter which one)

output—data a computer sends to the outside world

output device—a device that formats and presents output information

output file—a file into which a program writes data

Output window—displays various messages while an application is being compiled; you may write your own messages with the `Debug.WriteLine` method

`Overridable` keyword—in a procedure declaration, indicates that the procedure may be overridden in a derived class

override—to override a property or method in a base class means to create one of the same name in a derived class; when an object of the derived class accesses the property or procedure, it accesses the one in the derived class instead of the one in the base class

`Overrides` keyword—in a procedure declaration, indicates that the procedure overrides a procedure in the base class

parallel arrays—two or more arrays that hold related data; the related elements in each array are accessed with a common subscript

parameter—a special variable that receives an argument being passed into a method, procedure, or function

parse—to analyze a string of characters for some purpose

Pascal casing—a style of mixing uppercase and lowercase characters in procedure, method, and class names; the first character in the name and the first character of each subsequent word in the name are capitalized and all other characters are lowercase

`Peek` method—a `StreamReader` method that looks ahead in the file, without moving the current read position, and returns the next character that will be read; returns –1 when it reaches the end of the file

PHP—popular server-side scripting language used for many Web applications; major competitor of ASP.NET

PictureBox—displays a graphic image

PictureBox control—a control that can be used to display a graphic image

platform—Operating system + computer hardware; creates a complete environment under which programs can run. May also mean a virtual machine such as JVM (Java Virtual Machine) or CLR (Common Language Runtime).

`Pmt` function—returns the periodic payment amount for a loan

postback—when a Web page is sent back to the Web server for more processing

posttest loop—evaluates its test-expression after each iteration

`PPmt` function—returns the principal payment for a specific period on a loan

precedence—a ranking system that determines which operator works first in an expression where two operators share an operand

pretest loop—evaluates its test-expression before each iteration

primary key—a field, or the combination of multiple fields, that uniquely identify each row in a database table

`Print` method—a method of the PrintDocument control that triggers a PrintPage event

PrintDocument control—gives an application the ability to print output on a printer

PrintPage event handler—a PrintDocument control event procedure in which you write code that sends printed output to the printer

Private keyword—used to explicitly declare class-level variables private, making the source code more self-documenting

procedure—a set of programming language statements that are executed by the computer

procedure call—a statement that calls, or executes, a procedure

procedure declaration—specifies the name, parameter list, and statements that make up a procedure

program—a sequence of instructions stored in the computer's memory; the instructions enable the computer to solve a problem or perform a task

program code—generally, statements inside methods

program logic—program source code, written in languages such as Visual Basic and C#; in ASP.NET, the program logic is stored in the codebehind file

programmer-defined name—word or name defined by the programmer

programming languages—languages that use words instead of numbers to program the computer

project—a group of files that make up a Visual Basic application

project file—a file ending with the .vbproj extension that contains data describing the Visual Basic project

Prompt—a string displayed, typically on a Form or in an Input Box, requesting the user to enter a value

properties—in Visual Basic, an object's attributes

Properties window—shows and allows you to change most of the currently selected object's properties, and those properties' values

property procedure—a function that is a member of a class, and behaves like a property

Protected access specifier—Protected base class members are like private members, except they may be accessed by methods and property procedures in derived classes. To all other code, however, protected class members are just like private class members.

protocol—in a URL, the designation http://, https://, or ftp://

prototype—a demonstration copy of a program

pseudocode—statements that are a cross between human language and a programming language

pseudo-random—numbers that only seem to be random

Public keyword—used in the declaration of a module level variable or procedure, which makes it available to statements outside the module

query—an SQL statement that retrieves and/or manipulates data in a database

query parameter—when a query contains more than one parameter, these required values are passed as arguments when calling the **Fill** method

RadioButton—a round button that is either selected or deselected when clicked with the mouse

RadioButton control—usually appears in groups and allows the user to select one of several possible options

RadioButtonList control—Web control that displays a grouped list of radio buttons

RadioChecked property—a MenuItem object property that may be set to *True* or *False*; when set to *True* for a checked menu item, the item appears with a radio button instead of a check mark

random-access file—a file whose records may be accessed in any order

random-access memory (RAM)—*see* main memory

Random object—a special type of object that has methods and properties that make generating random numbers fairly easy

Read method—a **StreamReader** method that reads the next character from a file

read position—the position of the next item to be read from a file

ReadLine method—a **StreamReader** method that reads a line of data from a file

read-only property—a property whose value may be read, but may not be set by a client program

ReadToEnd method—a **StreamReader** method that reads and returns the entire contents of a file, beginning at the current read position

record—a complete set of data about a single item, consisting of one or more fields

relation—a link or relationship that relies on a common field value to join rows from two different tables

relational model—in databases; relations exist between tables

relational operator—determines if a specific relationship, such as less than or greater than, exists between two values

remarks—also known as comments; notes of explanation that document lines or sections in a method

Remove method—a collection method that removes a member

repetition structure—*see* loop

report body—the part of a report that contains the report's data, and is often formatted in columns

report footer—an optional part of a report that contains the sum of one or more columns of data

report header—the part of a report that is printed first and usually contains the name of the report, the date and time the report was printed, and other general information about the data in the report

Response object—automatically exits in every Web page; its Redirect method is used to navigate to other Web pages

reserved words—*see* keywords

results pane—displays the data rows returned by executing the current SQL query

Response.Redirect method—transfers control from the current Web form to another Web page or URL on the Internet

returning a value—the term used when a function returns a value as output

Rnd function—generates a single precision random number in the range of 0.0 to 1.0

row—*see* record

Run mode—the runtime mode in which you run and test an application

runtime—*see* run mode

running total—a sum of numbers that accumulates with each iteration of a loop

runtime error—a mistake, such as an incorrect mathematical formula, that does not prevent the application from executing; see runtime errors

runtime errors—mistakes that do not prevent an application from executing, but cause it to produce incorrect results

Save As dialog box—gives users the capability of browsing their disks for a location to save a file to, as well as specifying a file's name

SaveFileDialog control—displays a standard Windows *Save As* dialog box

SaveFileDialog property—displays a *Save As* dialog box

schema definition file—a file with a designer window that displays the names and data types of fields in the table; created when a data source is added to a project

scope—the part of the program where the variable is visible, and may be accessed by programming statements

Search button—a button on the *Dynamic Help* window that allows you to search for help topics using keywords

secondary storage—a device, such as a disk drive, that can hold information for long periods of time

seed value—used in the calculation that returns the next random number in the series; a value from the system timer is used by default; a value can be specified when creating a Random object

`Select Case` statement—a statement in which one of several possible actions is taken, depending on the value of an expression

`SELECT` statement (SQL)—used to find records within a database table

SelectedIndex property—holds the index of the selected item in a list box or combo box

SelectedItem property—holds the currently selected item of a list box or combo box

separator bar—a horizontal bar used to separate groups of commands on a menu

sequence structure—a code structure where the statements are executed in sequence, without branching off in another direction

sequential-access file—a file whose contents must be read from beginning to end

sequential search—an algorithm that uses a loop to search for a value in an array; it examines the elements in the array, one after the other, starting with the first one

server—entity that produces data consumed by a client

`Set` section—in a property procedure; executes when a client program sets the property to a value

short-circuit evaluation—allows you to skirt the `CheckValue` function; it is the default in languages such as C#, C++, and Java

shortcut key—a key or combination of keys that cause a menu command to execute

ShortcutKeys property—a ToolStripMenuItem object property used to select a shortcut key

`ShowDialog` method—displays a modal form and causes it to receive the focus

`Show` method—displays a modeless form and causes it to receive the focus

ShowShortcut property—a ToolStripMenuItem object property; values may be *True* or *False*; when *True*, the menu item's shortcut key (selected with the ShortcutKeys property) is displayed, when *False*, the shortcut key is not displayed

single dimension array—an array with one subscript, whichis useful for storing and working with a single set of data

single-step—a debugging technique where you execute an application's programming statements one at a time; after each statement executes you can examine variable and property contents, which allows you to identify code causing a logic error

SizeMode property—a PictureBox property that determines how the control will position and scale its graphic image

sizing handles—small boxes that appear around a control when it is selected during design mode; used to enlarge or shrink the control

software—programs that run on a computer

Solution—a container for holding Visual Basic projects

Solution Explorer window—allows quick navigation among the files in the application

solution file—a file that ends with the .sln extension and contains data describing a solution

Sorted property—causes the items in the Items property of a list box to be displayed alphabetically

source code—the statements that are written in a program

SQL—*see* Structured Query Language

SQL pane—displays the actual SQL query that corresponds to the tables and fields selected in the diagram and grid panes; advanced SQL users usually write queries directly into this pane

standard toolbar—situated below the menu bar; contains buttons that execute frequently used commands

startup form—the form that is displayed when the project executes

statement—an instruction that you write in a program; can consist of keywords, operators, punctuation, and other allowable programming elements, arranged in the proper sequence to perform an operation

`Static`—keyword used to declare static local variables

static local variables—variables that are not destroyed when a procedure or function returns; they exist for the lifetime of the application, even though their scope is only the procedure or function in which they are declared and they retain their values between procedure calls

static text—ordinary text typed directly onto a Web form in Design mode

Step Into command—a debugging command that allows you to execute a single programming statement (*see* single-step); if the statement contains a call to a procedure or function, the next execution point that will be displayed is the first line of code in that procedure or function

Step Out command—a debugging command executed while the application is in Break mode; it causes the remainder of the current procedure or function to complete execution without single stepping; after the procedure or function has completed, the line following the procedure or function call is highlighted, and single-stepping may resume

Step Over command—a debugging command executed while the application is in Break mode; it causes the currently highlighted line to execute; if the line contains a procedure or function call, however, the procedure or function is executed and there is no opportunity to single-step through its statements; the entire procedure or function is executed, and the next line in the current procedure is highlighted

step value—the value added to the counter variable at the end of each iteration of a `For...Next` loop

`StreamReader` class—a class that provides methods for reading data to sequential files

`StreamReader` object—an instance of the `Streamreader` class; used to read data to sequential files

`StreamWriter` class—a class that provides methods for writing data to sequential files

`StreamWriter` object—an instance of the `StreamWriter` class, used to write data to sequential files

string concatenation—when one string is appended to another

string literal—a group of characters inside quotation marks

structure—a data type created by the programmer that contains one or more variables, which are known as members

`Structure` statement—used to create a structure

Structured Query Language (SQL)—the standard database language for data storage, retrieval, and (SQL) manipulation

`Sub`—a keyword that precedes the name of a procedure

Sub procedure—a collection of statements that performs a specific task and does not return a value; see procedure

subscript—a number that identifies a specific element within an array; also known as an index

`Substring` method—returns a substring, or a string within a string

syntax—rules that must be followed when constructing a method; dictate how keywords, operators, and programmer-defined names may be used

tab order—the order in which controls receive the focus

tab order selection mode—establishes a tab order when you click controls in the desired sequence

TabIndex property—contains a numeric value, which indicates the control's position in the tab order

table—holds data in a database; organized in rows and columns

table adapter—pulls data from one or more database tables and passes it to the program

TabStop property—when set to *True*, causes a control to be skipped in the tab order

TextAlign property—a property that aligns text within a control

text box—a rectangular area on a form in which the user can enter text, or the program can display text

TextBox control—allows you to capture input that the user has typed on the keyboard

text file—contains plain text and may be opened in a text editor

Text property—in Visual Basic, stores the value that becomes the text in a control

TextBox Web control—similar in many ways to the TextBox control for Windows forms; The Text property holds text input by the user

Timer control—allows an application to automatically execute code at regular time intervals

Title property—a property of the OpenFileDialog and SaveFileDialog controls used to set the string displayed in the *Open* and *Save As* dialog box title bars

`ToLower` method—a string method that returns a lowercase version of a string

Toolbar, layout—contains buttons for formatting the layout of controls on a form

Toolbar, standard—contains buttons that execute frequently used commands

Toolbox window—contains buttons, or tools, for Visual Basic controls

ToolStripMenuItem objects—items added to a menu in the menu designer; each item has properties such as Name and Text

ToolTip—a small box that pops up when you hover the mouse over a button on the Toolbar on in the Toolbox; it contains a short description of the button's purpose

ToolTip control—a control that allows you to create ToolTips for the other controls on a form

`ToString` method—a method that returns the string representation of a variable

`ToUpper` method—a string method that returns an uppercase version of a string

trailing space—a space that appears at the end of a string

`Trim` method—returns a copy of the string without leading or trailing spaces

`TrimEnd` method—returns a copy of the string without trailing spaces

`TrimStart` method—returns a copy of the string without leading spaces

truncation—occurs when the fractional part of a number is dropped

try block—one or more statements that follow the Try clause in a Try-Catch statement and can potentially throw an exception

`Try-Catch` statement—a construct used for handling exceptions

twip—1/1440th of an inch; twips are used as a measurement for positioning input boxes on the screen

two-dimensional array—an array of arrays; can be used to hold multiple sets of values type conversion error—a runtime error that is generated when a nonnumeric value that cannot be automatically converted to a numeric value is assigned to a numeric variable or property

type mismatch error—*see* type conversion error

Unicode—A set of numeric codes that represent all the letters of the alphabet (both lowercase and uppercase), the printable digits 0 through 9, punctuation symbols, and special characters. The Unicode system is extensive enough to encompass all the world's alphabets.

unary operator—an operator that requires only a single operand

Uniform Resource Locator (URL)—universal way of addressing objects and pages on a network

user—the person who uses a program

user interface—the part of the program that users interact with

variable—a storage location in the computer's memory, used for holding information while the program is running

variable array—a group of variables with a single name

variable declaration—a statement that causes Visual Basic to create a variable in memory

variable scope—the area of a program in which a variable is visible

VScrollBar—a vertical slider bar that, when moved with the mouse, increases or decreases a value

Visible property—a Boolean property that causes a control to be visible on the form when set to *True*, or hidden when set to *False*

Visual Web Developer Express—Microsoft product that simplifies the way you develop Web applications

VScrollBar control—used to create a vertical scroll bar

Watch window—a debugging window that allows you to add the names of variables that you want to watch; displays only the variables that you have added

Web application—an application that runs on a Web server and presents its content to the user across a network, in a Web browser

Web form—a Web page that contains text, HTML tags, HTML controls, and Web server controls

Web page—information requested by a Web browser; Sent by a Web server; displayed to the user in the form of text, graphics, and sound

Web server—the program running on a host Web site that processes requests from end users running Web browsers

Web server controls—same as Web forms controls—type of interactive controls used on Web forms that must be decoded and processed by a Web server; generate runtime events such as Click, SelectedIndexChanged, and TextChanged

WHERE clause (SQL)—used to filter, or select zero or more rows retrieved from a database table

widening conversion—a conversion in which no data is lost

wildcard—a symbol that matches unknown characters

window—a rectangular area that contains other visual elements such as text, buttons that can be clicked with the mouse, boxes that accept keyboard input, and so forth

With...End With statement—allows you to create a With block; statements inside a With block may perform several operations on the same object without specifying the name of the object each time

wizard—software tool that guides you through the process of linking a control to a database

WordWrap property—a TextBox control property that causes the contents of a multiline text box to word wrap

Write method—a StreamWriter method that writes data to a file

WriteLine method—a StreamWriter method used to write a line of data to a file

Xor operator—Combines two expressions into one. One expression (not both) must be true for the overall expression to be true. If both expressions are true, or both expressions are false, the overall expression is false.

Index